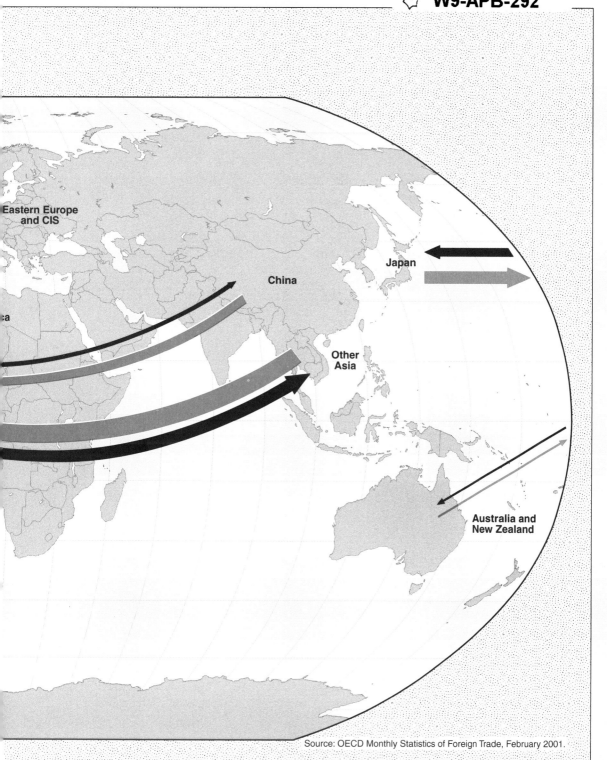

Source: OECD Monthly Statistics of Foreign Trade, February 2001.

Congratulations!

As a student purchasing Krugman and Obstfeld's *International Economics: Theory and Policy*, 6e, you are entitled to a prepaid subscription to premium services on our Companion Web Site at www.aw.com/krugman_obstfeld. Be sure to visit the Web Site for Web applications, review quizzes, and more!

The duration of your subscription is 6 months.

METHING MISSING?

tear-out card is
ng from this book,
you're missing out
important part of
earning package.
e to buy a new
ook, or visit the
anion Web Site at
w.com/krugman_obstfeld
formation on
asing a subscription.

HERE - - - - - - - - - - - - →

To activate your prepaid subscription:

1. Launch your Web browser and go to the Companion Web Site at www.aw.com/krugman_obstfeld.

2. Click on *Register/Log In*.

3. Follow the instructions on the screen to register yourself as a new user. Your pre-assigned Access Code is located below:

   Access Code:

   WSKOIE-KNOWS-PUPPY-DOPED-LOBBY-MOLES

4. During registration, you will choose a personal Login Name and Password for use in logging into the Companion Web Site.

5. Once your personal Login Name and Password are confirmed, you can begin using the Companion Web Site.

This Access Code can be used only once to establish a subscription. This subscription is not transferable.

If you did not purchase a new textbook, this Access Code may not be valid!

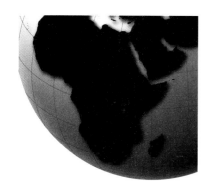

International Economics

Theory and Policy

The Addison-Wesley Series in Economics

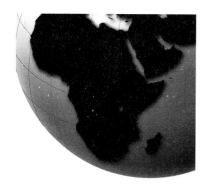

International Economics

Theory and Policy

SIXTH EDITION

Paul R. Krugman
Princeton University

Maurice Obstfeld
University of California, Berkeley

Boston San Francisco New York
London Toronto Sydney Tokyo Singapore Madrid
Mexico City Munich Paris Cape Town Hong Kong Montreal

For Robin and Leslie Ann

Editor-In-Chief: Denise Clinton
Executive Development Manager: Sylvia Mallory
Development Editor: Jane Tufts
Web Development: Melissa Honig
Managing Editor: James Rigney
Production Supervisor: Katherine Watson
Design Manager: Regina Kolenda
Text Design, Electronic Composition, and Project Management:
  Elm Street Publishing Services, Inc.
Cover Designer: Regina Kolenda
Cover Image: © Digital Vision Ltd.
Supplements Editor: Andrea Basso
Marketing Manager: Adrienne D'Ambrosio
Manufacturing Coordinator: Hugh Crawford

Library of Congress Cataloging-in-Publication Data
Krugman, Paul R.
    International economics: theory and policy / Paul R. Krugman,
  Maurice Obstfeld. – 6th ed.
      p.   cm.
    Previously published: Reading, Mass. : Addison-Wesley, © 2000
    Includes bibliographical references and index.
    ISBN 0-201-77037-7
    1. International economic relations. 2. International finance.
I. Obstfeld, Maurice. II. Title.

HF1359.K78 2002
337—dc21
                                                    2002018488

1 2 3 4 5 6 7 8 9 10—CRW—06 05 04 03 02

BRIEF CONTENTS

CONTENTS

Part 3
Exchange Rates and Open-Economy Macroeconomics   293

PREFACE

At the start of the twenty-first century, international aspects of economics remain as important and controversial as ever. In the last decade alone, major currency and financial crises have rocked industrializing countries from East Asia to Latin America; countries in Europe have given up their national currencies in favor of a common currency, the euro; and growing trade and financial linkages between industrial and developing countries have sparked debate and even open protest inspired by claims that economic "globalization" has worsened worldwide ills ranging from poverty to pollution. Although the United States is more self-sufficient than nations with smaller economies, problems of international economic policy have assumed primacy and now occupy a prominent place on newspapers' front pages.

Recent general developments in the world economy raise concerns that have preoccupied international economists for more than two centuries, such as the nature of the international adjustment mechanism and the merits of free trade compared with protection. As always in international economics, however, the interplay of events and ideas has led to new modes of analysis. Three notable examples of recent progress are the asset market approach to exchange rates; new theories of foreign trade based on increasing returns and market structure rather than comparative advantage; and the intertemporal analysis of international capital flows, which has been central both in refining the concept of "external balance" and in examining the determinants of developing country borrowing and default.

The idea of writing this book came out of our experience in teaching international economics to undergraduates and business students since the late 1970s. We perceived two main challenges in teaching. The first was to communicate to students the exciting intellectual advances in this dynamic field. The second was to show how the development of international economic theory has traditionally been shaped by the need to understand the changing world economy and analyze actual problems in international economic policy.

We found that published textbooks did not adequately meet these challenges. Too often, international economics textbooks confront students with a bewildering array of special models and assumptions from which basic lessons are difficult to extract. Because many of these special models are outmoded, students are left puzzled about the real-world relevance of the analysis. As a result, many textbooks often leave a gap between the somewhat antiquated material to be covered in class and the exciting issues that dominate current research and policy debates. That gap has widened dramatically as the importance of international economic problems—and enrollments in international economics courses—have grown.

This book is our attempt to provide an up-to-date and understandable analytical framework for illuminating current events and bringing the excitement of international economics into the classroom. In analyzing both the real and monetary sides of the subject, our approach has been to build up, step by step, a simple, unified framework for communicating the grand traditional insights as well as the newest findings and approaches. To help the student grasp and retain the underlying logic of international economics, we motivate the theoretical development at each stage by pertinent data or policy questions.

The Place of This Book in the Economics Curriculum

Students assimilate international economics most readily when it is presented as a method of analysis vitally linked to events in the world economy, rather than as a body of abstract theorems about abstract models. Our goal has therefore been to stress concepts and their application rather than theoretical formalism. Accordingly, the book does not presuppose an extensive background in economics. Students who have had a course in economic principles will find the book accessible, but students who have taken further courses in microeconomics or macroeconomics will find an abundant supply of new material. Specialized appendices and mathematical postscripts have been included to challenge the most advanced students.

We follow the standard practice of dividing the book into two halves, devoted to trade and to monetary questions. Although the trade and monetary portions of international economics are often treated as unrelated subjects, even within one textbook, similar themes and methods recur in both subfields. One example is the idea of gains from trade, which is important in understanding the effects of free trade in assets as well as free trade in goods. International borrowing and lending provide another example. The process by which countries trade present for future consumption is best understood in terms of comparative advantage (which is why we introduce it in the book's first half), but the resulting insights deepen understanding of the external macroeconomic problems of developing and developed economies alike. We have made it a point to illuminate connections between the trade and monetary areas when they arise.

At the same time, we have made sure that the book's two halves are completely self-contained. Thus, a one-semester course on trade theory can be based on Chapters 2 through 11, and a one-semester course on international monetary economics can be based on Chapters 12 through 22. If you adopt the book for a full-year course covering both subjects, however, you will find a treatment that does not leave students wondering why the principles underlying their work on trade theory have been discarded over the winter break.

Some Distinctive Features of *International Economics: Theory and Policy*

This book covers the most important recent developments in international economics without shortchanging the enduring theoretical and historical insights that have traditionally formed the core of the subject. We have achieved this comprehensiveness by stressing how recent theories have evolved from earlier findings in response to an evolving world economy. Both the real trade portion of the book (Chapters 2 through 11) and the monetary portion (Chapters 12 through 22) are divided into a core of chapters focused on theory, followed by chapters applying the theory to major policy questions, past and current.

In Chapter 1 we describe in some detail how this book addresses the major themes of international economics. Here we emphasize several of the newer topics that previous authors failed to treat in a systematic way.

Asset Market Approach to Exchange Rate Determination

The modern foreign exchange market and the determination of exchange rates by national interest rates and expectations are at the center of our account of open-economy macroeconomics. The main ingredient of the macroeconomic model we develop is the interest parity relation (augmented later by risk premiums). Among the topics we address using the model are exchange rate "overshooting"; behavior of real exchange rates; balance-of-payments crises under fixed exchange rates; and the causes and effects of central bank intervention in the foreign exchange market.

Increasing Returns and Market Structure

After discussing the role of comparative advantage in promoting trade and gains from trade, we move to the frontier of research (in Chapter 6) by explaining how increasing returns and product differentiation affect trade and welfare. The models explored in this discussion capture significant aspects of reality, such as intraindustry trade and shifts in trade patterns due to dynamic scale economies. The models show, too, that mutually beneficial trade need not be based on comparative advantage.

Politics and Theory of Trade Policy

Starting in Chapter 3, we stress the effect of trade on income distribution as the key political factor behind restrictions on free trade. This emphasis makes it clear to students why the prescriptions of the standard welfare analysis of trade policy seldom prevail in practice. Chapter 11 explores the popular notion that governments should adopt activist trade policies aimed at encouraging sectors of the economy seen as crucial. The chapter includes a theoretical discussion of such trade policy based on simple ideas from game theory.

International Macroeconomic Policy Coordination

Our discussion of international monetary experience (Chapters 18, 19, 20, and 22) stresses the theme that different exchange rate systems have led to different *policy coordination* problems for their members. Just as the competitive gold scramble of the interwar years showed how beggar-thy-neighbor policies can be self-defeating, the current float challenges national policymakers to recognize their interdependence and formulate policies cooperatively. Chapter 19 presents a detailed discussion of this very topical problem of the current system.

The World Capital Market and Developing Countries

A broad discussion of the world capital market is given in Chapter 21, which takes up the welfare implications of international portfolio diversification as well as problems of prudential supervision of offshore financial institutions. Chapter 22 is devoted to the long-term growth prospects and to the specific macroeconomic stabilization and liberalization problems of industrializing and newly industrialized countries. The chapter reviews emerging market crises and places in historical perspective the interactions among developing country borrowers, developed country lenders, and official financial institutions such as the International Monetary Fund.

International Factor Movements

In Chapter 7 we emphasize the potential substitutability of international trade and international movements of factors of production. A feature in the chapter is our analysis of international borrowing and lending as *intertemporal trade*, that is, the exchange of present consumption for future consumption. We draw on the results of this analysis in the book's second half to throw light on the macroeconomic implications of the current account.

New to the Sixth Edition

For this sixth edition of *International Economics: Theory and Policy*, we have extensively redesigned several chapters. These changes respond both to users' suggestions and to some important developments on the theoretical and practical sides of international economics. The most far-reaching changes are the following:

Chapter 9, The Political Economy of Trade Policy This chapter now includes the role of special-interest payments in influencing political decisions over trade policy. Coverage of the World Trade Organization is brought up to date.

Chapter 11, Controversies in Trade Policy A new title signals that this chapter expands its coverage beyond its predecessor's focus on strategic trade policy. In addition, Chapter 11 now covers the recent globalization debate—including the effects of trade on income distribution and the environment, as well as the role of international labor standards.

Chapter 12, National Income Accounting and the Balance of Payments The revised Chapter 12 reflects the new balance of payments accounting conventions adopted by the United States and other countries.

Chapter 18, The International Monetary System, 1870–1973 This chapter now pays more attention to the political economy of exchange rate regimes, using as an example the battle over the gold standard that dominated American politics in the late nineteenth century.

Chapter 19, Macroeconomic Policy and Coordination under Floating Exchange Rates We have replaced the detailed two-country model of earlier editions with a brief intuitive discussion of the major results on international policy repercussions. That change allows the instructor to focus more on important policy issues and less on dry technical details.

Chapter 20, Optimum Currency Areas and the European Experience As recently as the mid-1990s, Europe's vision of a single currency looked like a distant and possibly unreachable goal. As of 2002, however, twelve European countries had replaced their national currencies with the euro, and others are poised to follow. Chapter 20 has been revised to cover the first years of experience with the euro.

Chapter 21, The Global Capital Market: Performance and Policy Problems To make room for more topical material elsewhere in the book, we have streamlined this chapter by removing the detailed exposition of Eurocurrency creation contained in earlier editions.

In addition to these structural changes, we have updated the book in other ways to maintain current relevance. Thus we extend our coverage of the welfare effect of newly industrializing countries' exports on more advanced economies (Chapter 5); we update the discussion of Japanese policy toward the semiconductor industry (Chapter 11); we discuss Japan's liquidity trap (Chapter 17) and evidence on the effect of currency unions on trade volume (Chapter 20); and we recount the collapse of Argentina's currency in 2002 (Chapter 22).

Learning Features

This book incorporates a number of special learning features that will maintain students' interest in the presentation and help them master its lessons.

Case Studies
Theoretical discussions are often accompanied by case studies that perform the threefold role of reinforcing material covered earlier, illustrating its applicability in the real world, and providing important historical information.

Special Boxes
Less central topics that nonetheless offer particularly vivid illustrations of points made in the text are treated in boxes. Among these are the political backdrops of Ricardo's and Hume's theories (pp. 59 and 540); the surprising potential importance of NAFTA's effect on California's demand for water (p. 227); the astonishing ability of disputes over banana trade to generate acrimony among countries far too cold to grow any of their own bananas (p. 245); the story of the Bolivian hyperinflation (p. 380); and the 1994 speculative attack on the Mexican peso (p. 506).

Captioned Diagrams
More than 200 diagrams are accompanied by descriptive captions that reinforce the discussion in the text and help the student in reviewing the material.

Summary and Key Terms
Each chapter closes with a summary recapitulating the major points. Key terms and phrases appear in boldface type when they are introduced in the chapter and are listed at the end of each chapter. To further aid student review of the material, key terms are italicized when they appear in the chapter summary.

Problems
Each chapter is followed by problems intended to test and solidify students' comprehension. The problems range from routine computational drills to "big picture" questions suitable for classroom discussion. In many problems we ask students to apply what they have learned to real-world data or policy questions.

Further Reading
For instructors who prefer to supplement the textbook with outside readings, and for students who wish to probe more deeply on their own, each chapter has an annotated bibliography that includes established classics as well as up-to-date examinations of recent issues.

Study Guide, Instructor's Manual, and Web Site

International Economics: Theory and Policy is accompanied by a Study Guide written by Linda S. Goldberg of the Federal Reserve Bank of New York, Michael W. Klein of Tufts University, and Jay C. Shambaugh of Dartmouth College. The Study Guide aids students by providing a review of central concepts from the text, further illustrative examples, and additional practice problems. An Instructor's Manual, also by Linda S. Goldberg, Michael W. Klein, and Jay C. Shambaugh, includes chapter overviews, answers to the end-of-chapter problems, and suggestions for classroom presentation of the book's contents. The Study Guide and Instructor's Manual have been updated to reflect the changes in the sixth edition.

We are also pleased to recommend the companion Web site to accompany *International Economics,* Sixth Edition, at **www.aw.com/krugman_obstfeld**. The site offers students self-check quizzes for each chapter, links to sites of interest, and occasional updates on late-breaking developments. All new to the site for this edition is an animated PowerPoint program of the text's figures and tables, prepared by Iordanis Petsas of the University of Florida under the direction of Professor Elias Dinopoulos. And also featured on the Web site is a brand-new, comprehensive Test Bank for the instructor, prepared by Yochanan Shachmurove of the City College of the City University of New York and the University of Pennsylvania, and Mitchell H. Kellman of the City College of the City University of New York and the Graduate Center of the City University of New York. The Test Bank offers a rich array of multiple-choice and essay questions, plus mathematical and graphical problems, for each textbook chapter.

For those interested in course management, a Course Compass Web site is also available. Contact your Addison-Wesley sales representative for details.

Acknowledgments

Our primary debts are to Jane E. Tufts, the development editor, and to Sylvia Mallory and Denise Clinton, the economics editors in charge of the project. Jane's judgment and skill have been reflected in all six editions of this book; we cannot thank her enough for her contributions. Heather Johnson's efforts as project editor are greatly appreciated. We thank the other editors who helped make the first five editions as good as they were.

We owe a debt of gratitude to Galina Hale, who painstakingly updated data, checked proofs, and critiqued chapters. Annie Wai-Kuen Shun provided sterling assistance. For constructive suggestions we thank Syed M. Ahsan, Daniel Borer, Petra Geraats, Alan M. Taylor, Hans Visser, and Mickey Wu.

We thank the following reviewers for their recommendations and insights:

Michael Arghyrou, *Brunel University, U.K.*
Debajyoti Chakrabarty, *Rutgers University*
Adhip Chaudhuri, *Georgetown University*
Barbara Craig, *Oberlin College*
Robert Driskill, *Vanderbilt University*
Hugh Kelley, *Indiana University*
Michael Kevane, *Santa Clara University*

Shannon Mudd, *Thunderbird American Graduate School of International Management*
Steen Nielsen, *Copenhagen Business School*
Nina Pavcnik, *Dartmouth College*
Iordanis Petsas, *University of Florida*

Very helpful comments on earlier editions were received from the following reviewers:

Jaleel Ahmad, *Concordia University*
Myrvin Anthony, *University of Strathclyde, U.K.*
Richard Ault, *Auburn University*
George H. Borts, *Brown University*
Francisco Carrada-Bravo, *American Graduate School of International Management*
Jay Pil Choi, *Michigan State University*
Brian Copeland, *University of British Columbia*
Ann Davis, *Marist College*
Gopal C. Dorai, *William Paterson University*
Gerald Epstein, *University of Massachusetts at Amherst*
JoAnne Feeney, *University of Colorado, Boulder*
Robert Foster, *American Graduate School of International Management*
Diana Fuguitt, *Eckerd College*
Byron Gangnes, *University of Hawaii at Manoa*
Ranjeeta Ghiara, *California State University, San Marcos*
Neil Gilfedder, *Stanford University*
Patrick Gormely, *Kansas State University*
Bodil Olai Hansen, *Copenhagen Business School*
Henk Jager, *University of Amsterdam*
Arvind Jaggi, *Franklin & Marshall College*
Mark Jelavich, *Northwest Missouri State University*
Patrice Franko Jones, *Colby College*
Philip R. Jones, *University of Bath and University of Bristol, U.K.*
Maureen Kilkenny, *Pennsylvania State University*
Faik Koray, *Louisiana State University*
Corinne Krupp, *Duke University*
Bun Song Lee, *University of Nebraska, Omaha*
Francis A. Lees, *St. Johns University*
Rodney D. Ludema, *The University of Western Ontario*
Marcel Mérette, *Yale University*
Shannon Mitchell, *Virginia Commonwealth University*
Kaz Miyagiwa, *University of Washington*
Ton M. Mulder, *Erasmus University, Rotterdam*
E. Wayne Nafziger, *Kansas State University*
Terutomo Ozawa, *Colorado State University*
Arvind Panagariya, *University of Maryland*

Donald Schilling, *University of Missouri, Columbia*
Ronald M. Schramm, *Columbia University*
Craig Schulman, *University of Arkansas*
Yochanan Shachmurove, *University of Pennsylvania*
Margaret Simpson, *The College of William and Mary*
Robert M. Stern, *University of Michigan*
Rebecca Taylor, *University of Portsmouth, U.K.*
Scott Taylor, *University of British Columbia*
Aileen Thompson, *Carleton University*
Sarah Tinkler, *Weber State University*
Arja H. Turunen-Red, *University of Texas, Austin*
Dick vander Wal, *Free University of Amsterdam*

Although we have not been able to make each and every suggested change, we found reviewers' observations invaluable in revising the book. Obviously, we bear sole responsibility for its remaining shortcomings.

Paul R. Krugman
Maurice Obstfeld

CHAPTER 1

Introduction

You could say that the study of international trade and finance is where the discipiine of economics as we know it began. Historians of economic thought often describe the essay "Of the balance of trade" by the Scottish philosopher David Hume as the first real exposition of an economic model. Hume published his essay in 1758, almost 20 years before his friend Adam Smith published *The Wealth of Nations*. And the debates over British trade policy in the early nineteenth century did much to convert economics from a discursive, informal field to the model-oriented subject it has been ever since.

Yet the study of international economics has never been as important as it is now. At the beginning of the twenty-first century, nations are more closely linked through trade in goods and services, through flows of money, through investment in each other's economies than ever before. And the global economy created by these linkages is a turbulent place: both policymakers and business leaders in every country, including the United States, must now take account of what are sometimes rapidly changing economic fortunes halfway around the world.

A look at some basic trade statistics gives us a sense of the unprecedented importance of international economic relations. Figure 1-1 shows the levels of U.S. exports and imports as shares of gross domestic product from 1959 to 2000. The most obvious feature of the figure is the sharp upward trend in both shares: international trade has roughly tripled in importance compared with the economy as a whole.

Almost as obvious is that while both exports and imports have increased, in the late 1990s imports grew much faster, leading to a large excess of imports over exports. How was the United States able to pay for all those imported goods? The answer is that the money was supplied by large inflows of capital, money invested by foreigners eager to buy a piece of the booming U.S. economy. Inflows of capital on that scale would once have been inconceivable; now they are taken for granted. And so the gap between imports and exports is an indicator of another aspect of growing international linkages, in this case the growing linkages between national capital markets.

If international economic relations have become crucial to the United States, they are even more crucial to other nations. Figure 1-2 shows the shares of imports and exports in GDP for a sample of countries. The United States, by virtue of its size and the diversity of its resources, relies less on international trade than almost any other country.

Figure 1-1 │ Exports and Imports as a Percentage of U.S. National Income

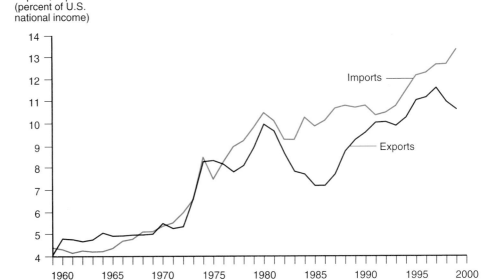

Exports, imports
(percent of U.S.
national income)

From the 1960s to 1980, both exports and imports rose steadily as shares of U.S. income. Since 1980, exports have fluctuated sharply.

Figure 1-2 │ Exports and Imports as Percentages of National Income in 1994

International trade is even more important to most other countries than it is to the United States.

Source: Statistical Abstract of the United States

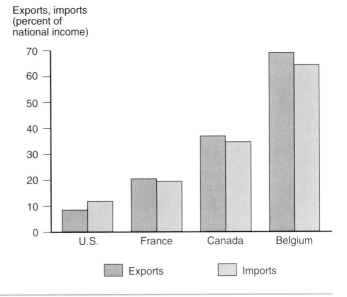

Exports, imports
(percent of
national income)

Consequently, for the rest of the world, international economics is even more important than it is for the United States.

This book introduces the main concepts and methods of international economics and illustrates them with applications drawn from the real world. Much of the book is devoted to old ideas that are still as valid as ever: the nineteenth-century trade theory of David Ricardo and even the eighteenth-century monetary analysis of David Hume remain highly relevant to the twenty-first-century world economy. At the same time, we have made a special effort to bring the analysis up to date. The global economy of the 1990s threw up many new challenges, from the backlash against globalization to an unprecedented series of financial crises. Economists were able to apply existing analyses to some of these challenges, but they were also forced to rethink some important concepts. Furthermore, new approaches have emerged to old questions, such as the impacts of changes in monetary and fiscal policy. We have attempted to convey the key ideas that have emerged in recent research while stressing the continuing usefulness of old ideas.

What Is International Economics About?

International economics uses the same fundamental methods of analysis as other branches of economics, because the motives and behavior of individuals are the same in international trade as they are in domestic transactions. Gourmet food shops in Florida sell coffee beans from both Mexico and Hawaii; the sequence of events that brought those beans to the shop is not very different, and the imported beans traveled a much shorter distance! Yet international economics involves new and different concerns, because international trade and investment occur between independent nations. The United States and Mexico are sovereign states; Florida and Hawaii are not. Mexico's coffee shipments to Florida could be disrupted if the U.S. government imposed a quota that limits imports; Mexican coffee could suddenly become cheaper to U.S. buyers if the peso were to fall in value against the dollar. Neither of those events can happen in commerce within the United States because the Constitution forbids restraints on interstate trade and all U.S. states use the same currency.

The subject matter of international economics, then, consists of issues raised by the special problems of economic interaction between sovereign states. Seven themes recur throughout the study of international economics: the gains from trade, the pattern of trade, protectionism, the balance of payments, exchange rate determination, international policy coordination, and the international capital market.

The Gains From Trade

Everybody knows that some international trade is beneficial—nobody thinks that Norway should grow its own oranges. Many people are skeptical, however, about the benefits of trading for goods that a country could produce for itself. Shouldn't Americans buy American goods whenever possible, to help create jobs in the United States?

Probably the most important single insight in all of international economics is that there are *gains from trade*—that is, when countries sell goods and services to each other, this exchange is almost always to their mutual benefit. The range of circumstances under which international trade is beneficial is much wider than most people imagine. It is a common misconception that trade is harmful if there are large disparities between countries in productivity or wages. On one side, businessmen in less technologically advanced countries, such as India, often worry that opening their economies to international trade will lead to disaster because their industries won't be able to compete. On the other side, people in technologically advanced nations where workers earn high wages often fear that trading with less advanced, lower-wage countries will drag their standard of living down—one presidential candidate memorably warned of a "giant sucking sound" if the United States were to conclude a free-trade agreement with Mexico.

Yet the first model of trade in this book (Chapter 2) demonstrates that two countries can trade to their mutual benefit even when one of them is more efficient than the other at producing everything, and when producers in the less efficient country can compete only by paying lower wages. We'll also see that trade provides benefits by allowing countries to export goods whose production makes relatively heavy use of resources that are locally abundant while importing goods whose production makes heavy use of resources that are locally scarce (Chapter 4). International trade also allows countries to specialize in producing narrower ranges of goods, giving them greater efficiencies of large-scale production.

Nor are the benefits of international trade limited to trade in tangible goods. International migration and international borrowing and lending are also forms of mutually beneficial trade—the first a trade of labor for goods and services, the second a trade of current goods for the promise of future goods (Chapter 7). Finally, international exchanges of risky assets such as stocks and bonds can benefit all countries by allowing each country to diversify its wealth and reduce the variability of its income (Chapter 21). These invisible forms of trade yield gains as real as the trade that puts fresh fruit from Latin America in Toronto markets in February.

While nations generally gain from international trade, however, it is quite possible that international trade may hurt particular groups *within* nations—in other words, that international trade will have strong effects on the distribution of income. The effects of trade on income distribution have long been a concern of international trade theorists, who have pointed out that:

> International trade can adversely affect the owners of resources that are "specific" to industries that compete with imports, that is, cannot find alternative employment in other industries (Chapter 3).
>
> Trade can also alter the distribution of income between broad groups, such as workers and the owners of capital (Chapter 4).

These concerns have moved from the classroom into the center of real-world policy debate, as it has become increasingly clear that the real wages of less-skilled workers in the United States have been declining even though the country as a whole is continuing to grow richer. Many commentators attribute this development to growing international trade, especially the rapidly growing exports of manufactured goods from low-wage countries. Assessing this claim has become an important task for international economists and is a major theme of both Chapters 4 and 5.

The Pattern of Trade

Economists cannot discuss the effects of international trade or recommend changes in government policies toward trade with any confidence unless they know their theory is good enough to explain the international trade that is actually observed. Thus attempts to explain the pattern of international trade—who sells what to whom—have been a major preoccupation of international economists.

Some aspects of the pattern of trade are easy to understand. Climate and resources clearly explain why Brazil exports coffee and Saudi Arabia exports oil. Much of the pattern of trade is more subtle, however. Why does Japan export automobiles, while the United States exports aircraft? In the early nineteenth century English economist David Ricardo offered an explanation of trade in terms of international differences in labor productivity, an explanation that remains a powerful insight (Chapter 2). In the twentieth century, however, alternative explanations have also been proposed. One of the most influential, but still controversial, links trade patterns to an interaction between the relative supplies of national resources such as capital, labor, and land on one side and the relative use of these factors in the production of different goods on the other. We present this theory in Chapter 4. Recent efforts to test the implications of this theory, however, appear to show that it is less valid than many had previously thought. More recently still, some international economists have proposed theories that suggest a substantial random component in the pattern of international trade, theories that are developed in Chapter 6.

How Much Trade?

If the idea of gains from trade is the most important theoretical concept in international economics, the seemingly eternal debate over how much trade to allow is its most important policy theme. Since the emergence of modern nation-states in the sixteenth century, governments have worried about the effect of international competition on the prosperity of domestic industries and have tried either to shield industries from foreign competition by placing limits on imports or to help them in world competition by subsidizing exports. The single most consistent mission of international economics has been to analyze the effects of these so-called protectionist policies—and usually, though not always, to criticize protectionism and show the advantages of freer international trade.

The debate over how much trade to allow took a new direction in the 1990s. Since World War II the advanced democracies, led by the United States, have pursued a broad policy of removing barriers to international trade; this policy reflected the view that free trade was a force not only for prosperity but also for promoting world peace. In the first half of the 1990s several major free-trade agreements were negotiated. The most notable were the North American Free Trade Agreement (NAFTA) between the United States, Canada, and Mexico, approved in 1993, and the so-called Uruguay Round agreement establishing the World Trade Organization in 1994.

Since then, however, an international political movement opposing "globalization" has gained many adherents. The movement achieved notoriety in 1999, when demonstrators representing a mix of traditional protectionists and new ideologies disrupted a major international trade meeting in Seattle. If nothing else, the anti-globalization movement has forced advocates of free trade to seek new ways to explain their views.

As befits both the historical importance and the current relevance of the protectionist issue, roughly a quarter of this book is devoted to this subject. Over the years, international economists have developed a simple yet powerful analytical framework for determining the effects of government policies that affect international trade. This framework not only predicts the effects of trade policies, it also allows cost-benefit analysis and defines criteria for determining when government intervention is good for the economy. We present this framework in Chapters 8 and 9 and use it to discuss a number of policy issues in those chapters and in the following two.

In the real world, however, governments do not necessarily do what the cost-benefit analysis of economists tells them they should. This does not mean that analysis is useless. Economic analysis can help make sense of the politics of international trade policy, by showing who benefits and who loses from such government actions as quotas on imports and subsidies to exports. The key insight of this analysis is that conflicts of interest *within* nations are usually more important in determining trade policy than conflicts of interest *between* nations. Chapters 3 and 4 show that trade usually has very strong effects on income distribution within countries, while Chapters 9, 10, and 11 reveal that the relative power of different interest groups within countries, rather than some measure of overall national interest, is often the main determining factor in government policies toward international trade.

Balance of Payments

In 1998 both China and South Korea ran large trade surpluses of about $40 billion each. In China's case the trade surplus was not out of the ordinary—the country had been running large surpluses for several years, prompting complaints from other countries, including the United States, that China was not playing by the rules. So is it good to run a trade surplus, and bad to run a trade deficit? Not according to the South Koreans: their trade surplus was forced on them by an economic and financial crisis, and they bitterly resented the necessity of running that surplus.

This comparison highlights the fact that a country's *balance of payments* must be placed in the context of an economic analysis to understand what it means. It emerges in a variety of specific contexts: in discussing international capital movements (Chapter 7), in relating international transactions to national income accounting (Chapter 12), and in discussing virtually every aspect of international monetary policy (Chapters 16 through 22). Like the problem of protectionism, the balance of payments has become a central issue for the United States because the nation has run huge trade deficits in every year since 1982.

Exchange Rate Determination

The euro, a new common currency for most of the nations of western Europe, was introduced on January 1, 1999. On that day the euro was worth about $1.17. Almost immediately, however, the euro began to slide, and in early 2002 it was worth only about $0.85. This slide was a major embarrassment to European politicians, though many economists argued that the sliding euro had actually been beneficial to the European economy—and that the strong dollar had become a problem for the United States.

A key difference between international economics and other areas of economics is that countries usually have their own currencies. And as the example of the euro-dollar exchange rate illustrates, the relative values of currencies can change over time, sometimes drastically.

The study of exchange rate determination is a relatively new part of international economics, for historical reasons. For most of the twentieth century, exchange rates have been fixed by government action rather than determined in the marketplace. Before World War I the values of the world's major currencies were fixed in terms of gold, while for a generation after World War II the values of most currencies were fixed in terms of the U.S. dollar. The analysis of international monetary systems that fix exchange rates remains an important subject. Chapters 17 and 18 are devoted to the working of fixed-rate systems, Chapter 19 to the debate over which system, fixed or floating rates, is better, and Chapter 20 to the economics of currency areas such as the European monetary union. For the time being, however, some of the world's most important exchange rates fluctuate minute by minute and the role of changing exchange rates remains at the center of the international economics story. Chapters 13 through 16 focus on the modern theory of floating exchange rates.

International Policy Coordination

The international economy comprises sovereign nations, each free to choose its own economic policies. Unfortunately, in an integrated world economy one country's economic policies usually affect other countries as well. For example, when Germany's Bundesbank raised interest rates in 1990—a step it took to control the possible inflationary impact of the reunification of West and East Germany—it helped precipitate a recession in the rest of Western Europe. Differences in goals between countries often lead to conflicts of interest. Even when countries have similar goals, they may suffer losses if they fail to coordinate their policies. A fundamental problem in international economics is how to produce an acceptable degree of harmony among the international trade and monetary policies of different countries without a world government that tells countries what to do.

For the last 45 years international trade policies have been governed by an international treaty known as the General Agreement on Tariffs and Trade (GATT), and massive international negotiations involving dozens of countries at a time have been held. We discuss the rationale for this system in Chapter 9 and look at whether the current rules of the game for international trade in the world economy can or should survive.

While cooperation on international trade policies is a well-established tradition, coordination of international macroeconomic policies is a newer and more uncertain topic. Only in the last few years have economists formulated at all precisely the case for macroeconomic policy coordination. Nonetheless, attempts at international macroeconomic coordination are occurring with growing frequency in the real world. Both the theory of international macroeconomic coordination and the developing experience are reviewed in Chapters 18 and 19.

The International Capital Market

During the 1970s, banks in advanced countries lent large sums to firms and governments in poorer nations, especially in Latin America. In 1982, however, this era of easy credit came to a sudden end when Mexico, then a number of other countries, found themselves unable to pay the money they owed. The resulting "debt crisis" persisted until 1990. In the 1990s investors once again became willing to put hundreds of billions of dollars into "emerging markets," both in Latin America and in the rapidly growing economies of Asia. All too soon, however, this investment boom too came to grief; Mexico experienced another financial crisis at the end of 1994, and much of Asia was caught up in a massive crisis beginning in the summer of 1997. This roller coaster history contains many lessons, the most undisputed of which is the growing importance of the international capital market.

In any sophisticated economy there is an extensive capital market: a set of arrangements by which individuals and firms exchange money now for promises to pay in the future. The growing importance of international trade since the 1960s has been accompanied by a growth in the *international* capital market, which links the capital markets of individual countries. Thus in the 1970s oil-rich Middle Eastern nations placed their oil revenues in banks in London or New York, and these banks in turn lent money to governments and corporations in Asia and Latin America. During the 1980s Japan converted much of the money it earned from its booming exports into investments in the United States, including the establishment of a growing number of U.S. subsidiaries of Japanese corporations.

International capital markets differ in important ways from domestic capital markets. They must cope with special regulations that many countries impose on foreign investment; they also sometimes offer opportunities to evade regulations placed on domestic markets. Since the 1960s, huge international capital markets have arisen, most notably the remarkable London Eurodollar market, in which billions of dollars are exchanged each day without ever touching the United States.

Some special risks are associated with international capital markets. One risk is that of currency fluctuations: If the euro falls against the dollar, U.S. investors who bought euro bonds suffer a capital loss—as the many investors who had assumed that Europe's new currency would be strong discovered to their horror. Another risk is that of national default: A nation may simply refuse to pay its debts (perhaps because it cannot), and there may be no effective way for its creditors to bring it to court.

The growing importance of international capital markets and their new problems demand greater attention than ever before. This book devotes two chapters to issues arising from international capital markets: one on the functioning of global asset markets (Chapter 21) and one on foreign borrowing by developing countries (Chapter 22).

International Economics: Trade and Money

The economics of the international economy can be divided into two broad subfields: the study of *international trade* and the study of *international money*. International trade analysis focuses primarily on the *real* transactions in the international economy, that is, on those transactions that involve a physical movement of goods or a tangible commitment of economic resources. International monetary analysis focuses on the *monetary* side of the international economy, that is, on financial transactions such as foreign purchases of U.S. dollars. An example of an international trade issue is the conflict between the United States and Europe over Europe's subsidized exports of agricultural products; an example of an international monetary issue is the dispute over whether the foreign exchange value of the dollar should be allowed to float freely or be stabilized by government action.

In the real world there is no simple dividing line between trade and monetary issues. Most international trade involves monetary transactions, while, as the examples in this chapter already suggest, many monetary events have important consequences for trade. Nonetheless, the distinction between international trade and international money is useful. The first half of this book covers international trade issues. Part One (Chapters 2 through 7) develops the analytical theory of international trade, and Part Two (Chapters 8 through 11) applies trade theory to the analysis of government policies toward trade. The second half of the book is devoted to international monetary issues. Part Three (Chapters 12 through 17) develops international monetary theory, and Part Four (Chapters 18 through 22) applies this analysis to international monetary policy.

PART I   International Trade Theory

CHAPTER 2

Labor Productivity and Comparative Advantage: The Ricardian Model

Countries engage in international trade for two basic reasons, each of which contributes to their gain from trade. First, countries trade because they are different from each other. Nations, like individuals, can benefit from their differences by reaching an arrangement in which each does the things it does relatively well. Second, countries trade to achieve economies of scale in production. That is, if each country produces only a limited range of goods, it can produce each of these goods at a larger scale and hence more efficiently than if it tried to produce everything. In the real world, patterns of international trade reflect the interaction of both these motives. As a first step toward understanding the causes and effects of trade, however, it is useful to look at simplified models in which only one of these motives is present.

The next four chapters develop tools to help us to understand how differences between countries give rise to trade between them and why this trade is mutually beneficial. The essential concept in this analysis is that of comparative advantage.

Although comparative advantage is a simple concept, experience shows that it is a surprisingly hard concept for many people to understand (or accept). Indeed, Paul Samuelson—the Nobel laureate economist who did much to develop the models of international trade discussed in Chapters 3 and 4—has described comparative advantage as the best example he knows of an economic principle that is undeniably true yet not obvious to intelligent people.

In this chapter we begin with a general introduction to the concept of comparative advantage, then proceed to develop a specific model of how comparative advantage determines the pattern of international trade.

The Concept of Comparative Advantage

On Valentine's Day, 1996, which happened to fall less than a week before the crucial February 20 primary in New Hampshire, Republican presidential candidate Patrick Buchanan stopped at a nursery to buy a dozen roses for his wife. He took the occasion to make a speech denouncing the growing imports of flowers into the United States, which he claimed were putting American flower growers out of business. And it is indeed true that a growing share of the market for winter roses in the United States is being supplied by imports flown in from South America. But is that a bad thing?

The case of winter roses offers an excellent example of the reasons why international trade can be beneficial. Consider first how hard it is to supply American sweethearts with fresh roses in February. The flowers must be grown in heated greenhouses, at great expense in terms of energy, capital investment, and other scarce resources. Those resources could have been used to produce other goods. Inevitably, there is a trade-off. In order to produce winter roses, the U.S. economy must produce less of other things, such as computers. Economists use the term **opportunity cost** to describe such trade-offs: The opportunity cost of roses in terms of computers is the number of computers that could have been produced with the resources used to produce a given number of roses.

Suppose, for example, that the United States currently grows 10 million roses for sale on Valentine's Day, and that the resources used to grow those roses could have produced 100,000 computers instead. Then the opportunity cost of those 10 million roses is 100,000 computers. (Conversely, if the computers were produced instead, the opportunity cost of those 100,000 computers would be 10 million roses.)

Those 10 million Valentine's Day roses could instead have been grown in South America. It seems extremely likely that the opportunity cost of those roses in terms of computers would be less than it would be in the United States. For one thing, it is a lot easier to grow February roses in the Southern Hemisphere, where it is summer in February rather than winter. Furthermore, South American workers are less efficient than their U.S. counterparts at making sophisticated goods such as computers, which means that a given amount of resources used in computer production yields fewer computers in South America than in the United States. So the trade-off in South America might be something like 10 million winter roses for only 30,000 computers.

This difference in opportunity costs offers the possibility of a mutually beneficial rearrangement of world production. Let the United States stop growing winter roses and devote the resources this frees up to producing computers; meanwhile, let South America grow those roses instead, shifting the necessary resources out of its computer industry. The resulting changes in production would look like Table 2-1.

Look what has happened: The world is producing just as many roses as before, but it is now producing more computers. So this rearrangement of production, with the United States concentrating on computers and South America concentrating on roses, increases the size of the world's economic pie. Because the world as a whole is producing more, it is possible in principle to raise everyone's standard of living.

The reason that international trade produces this increase in world output is that it allows each country to specialize in producing the good in which it has a comparative advantage.

Table 2-1 | Hypothetical Changes in Production

	Million Roses	**Thousand Computers**
United States	−10	+100
South America	+10	−30
Total	0	+70

A country has a **comparative advantage** in producing a good if the opportunity cost of producing that good in terms of other goods is lower in that country than it is in other countries.

In this example, South America has a comparative advantage in winter roses and the United States has a comparative advantage in computers. The standard of living can be increased in both places if South America produces roses for the U.S. market, while the United States produces computers for the South American market. We therefore have an essential insight about comparative advantage and international trade: *Trade between two countries can benefit both countries if each country exports the goods in which it has a comparative advantage.*

This is a statement about possibilities, not about what will actually happen. In the real world, there is no central authority deciding which country should produce roses and which should produce computers. Nor is there anyone handing out roses and computers to consumers in both places. Instead, international production and trade is determined in the marketplace where supply and demand rule. Is there any reason to suppose that the potential for mutual gains from trade will be realized? Will the United States and South America actually end up producing the goods in which each has a comparative advantage? Will the trade between them actually make both countries better off?

To answer these questions, we must be much more explicit in our analysis. In this chapter we will develop a model of international trade originally developed by the British economist David Ricardo, who introduced the concept of comparative advantage in the early nineteenth century.[1] This approach, in which international trade is solely due to international differences in the productivity of labor, is known as the **Ricardian model**.

A One-Factor Economy

To introduce the role of comparative advantage in determining the pattern of international trade, we begin by imagining that we are dealing with an economy—which we call Home—that has only one factor of production. (In later chapters we extend the analysis to models in which there are several factors.) We imagine that only two goods, wine and cheese, are produced. The technology of Home's economy can be summarized by labor productivity in each industry, expressed in terms of the **unit labor requirement**, the number of hours of labor required to produce a pound of cheese or a gallon of wine. For example, it might require 1 hour of labor to produce a pound of cheese, 2 hours to produce a gallon of wine. For future reference, we define a_{LW} and a_{LC} as the unit labor requirements in wine and cheese production, respectively. The economy's total resources are defined as L, the total labor supply.

Production Possibilities

Because any economy has limited resources, there are limits on what it can produce, and there are always trade-offs; to produce more of one good the economy must sacrifice some production of another good. These trade-offs are illustrated graphically by a **production**

---

[1]The classic reference is David Ricardo, *The Principles of Political Economy and Taxation,* first published in 1817.

Figure 2-1 | Home's Production Possibility Frontier

The line *PF* shows the maximum amount of cheese Home can produce given any production of wine, and vice versa.

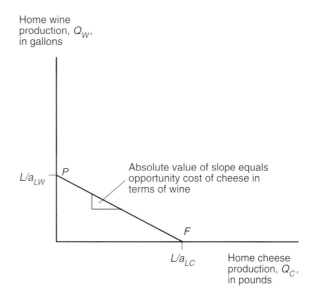

Home wine production, Q_W, in gallons

L/a_{LW} P

Absolute value of slope equals opportunity cost of cheese in terms of wine

F

L/a_{LC} Home cheese production, Q_C, in pounds

possibility frontier (line *PF* in Figure 2-1), which shows the maximum amount of wine that can be produced once the decision has been made to produce any given amount of cheese, and vice versa.

When there is only one factor of production the production possibility frontier of an economy is simply a straight line. We can derive this line as follows: If Q_W is the economy's production of wine and Q_C its production of cheese, then the labor used in producing wine will be $a_{LW}Q_W$, the labor used in producing cheese $a_{LC}Q_C$. The production possibility frontier is determined by the limits on the economy's resources—in this case, labor. Because the economy's total labor supply is L, the limits on production are defined by the inequality

$$a_{LC}Q_C + a_{LW}Q_W \leq L. \qquad (2\text{-}1)$$

When the production possibility frontier is a straight line, the *opportunity cost* of a pound of cheese in terms of wine is constant. As we saw in the previous section, this opportunity cost is defined as the number of gallons of wine the economy would have to give up in order to produce an extra pound of cheese. In this case, to produce another pound would require a_{LC} person-hours. Each of these person-hours could in turn have been used to produce $1/a_{LW}$ gallons of wine. Thus the opportunity cost of cheese in terms of wine is a_{LC}/a_{LW}. For example, if it takes one person-hour to make a pound of cheese and two hours to produce a gallon of wine, the opportunity cost of cheese in terms of wine is one-half. As Figure 2-1 shows, this opportunity cost is equal to the absolute value of the slope of the production possibility frontier.

Relative Prices and Supply

The production possibility frontier illustrates the different mixes of goods the economy *can* produce. To determine what the economy will actually produce, however, we need to look at prices. Specifically, we need to know the relative price of the economy's two goods, that is, the price of one good in terms of the other.

In a competitive economy, supply decisions are determined by the attempts of individuals to maximize their earnings. In our simplified economy, since labor is the only factor of production, the supply of cheese and wine will be determined by the movement of labor to whichever sector pays the higher wage.

Let P_C and P_W be the prices of cheese and wine, respectively. It takes a_{LC} person-hours to produce a pound of cheese; since there are no profits in our one-factor model, the hourly wage in the cheese sector will equal the value of what a worker can produce in an hour, P_C/a_{LC}. Since it takes a_{LW} person-hours to produce a gallon of wine, the hourly wage rate in the wine sector will be P_W/a_{LW}. Wages in the cheese sector will be higher if $P_C/P_W > a_{LC}/a_{LW}$; wages in the wine sector will be higher if $P_C/P_W < a_{LC}/a_{LW}$. Because everyone will want to work in whichever industry offers the higher wage, the economy will specialize in the production of cheese if $P_C/P_W > a_{LC}/a_{LW}$; it will specialize in the production of wine if $P_C/P_W < a_{LC}/a_{LW}$. Only when P_C/P_W is equal to a_{LC}/a_{LW} will both goods be produced.

What is the significance of the number a_{LC}/a_{LW}? We saw in the previous section that it is the opportunity cost of cheese in terms of wine. We have therefore just derived a crucial proposition about the relationship between prices and production: *The economy will specialize in the production of cheese if the relative price of cheese exceeds its opportunity cost; it will specialize in the production of wine if the relative price of cheese is less than its opportunity cost.*

In the absence of international trade, Home would have to produce both goods for itself. But it will produce both goods only if the relative price of cheese is just equal to its opportunity cost. Since opportunity cost equals the ratio of unit labor requirements in cheese and wine, we can summarize the determination of prices in the absence of international trade with a simple labor theory of value: *In the absence of international trade, the relative prices of goods are equal to their relative unit labor requirements.*

Trade in a One-Factor World

To describe the pattern and effects of trade between two countries when each country has only one factor of production is simple. Yet the implications of this analysis can be surprising. Indeed to those who have not thought about international trade many of these implications seem to conflict with common sense. Even this simplest of trade models can offer some important guidance on real-world issues, such as what constitutes fair international competition and fair international exchange.

Before we get to these issues, however, let us get the model stated. Suppose that there are two countries. One of them we again call Home and the other we call Foreign. Each of these countries has one factor of production (labor) and can produce two goods, wine and cheese. As before, we denote Home's labor force by L and Home's unit labor requirements in wine and cheese production by a_{LW} and a_{LC}, respectively. For Foreign we will use a convenient notation throughout this book: When we refer to some aspect of Foreign, we will use the same symbol that we use for Home, but with an asterisk. Thus Foreign's labor force will be denoted by L^*; Foreign's unit labor requirements in wine and cheese will be denoted by a_{LW}^* and a_{LC}^*, respectively, and so on.

In general the unit labor requirements can follow any pattern. For example, Home could be less productive than Foreign in wine but more productive in cheese, or vice versa. For the moment, we make only one arbitrary assumption: that

$$a_{LC}/a_{LW} < a_{LC}^*/a_{LW}^* \tag{2-2}$$

or, equivalently, that

$$a_{LC}/a_{LC}^* < a_{LW}/a_{LW}^* \tag{2-3}$$

In words, we are assuming that the ratio of the labor required to produce a pound of cheese to that required to produce a gallon of wine is lower in Home than it is in Foreign. More briefly still, we are saying that Home's relative productivity in cheese is higher than it is in wine.

But remember that the ratio of unit labor requirements is equal to the opportunity cost of cheese in terms of wine; and remember also that we defined comparative advantage precisely in terms of such opportunity costs. So the assumption about relative productivities embodied in equations (2-2) and (2-3) amounts to saying that *Home has a comparative advantage in cheese.*

One point should be noted immediately: The condition under which Home has this comparative advantage involves all four unit labor requirements, not just two. You might think that to determine who will produce cheese, all you need to do is compare the two countries' unit labor requirements in cheese production, a_{LC} and a_{LC}^*. If $a_{LC} < a_{LC}^*$, Home labor is more efficient than Foreign in producing cheese. When one country can produce a unit of a good with less labor than another country, we say that the first country has an **absolute advantage** in producing that good. In our example, Home has an absolute advantage in producing cheese.

What we will see in a moment, however, is that we cannot determine the pattern of trade from absolute advantage alone. One of the most important sources of error in discussing international trade is to confuse comparative advantage with absolute advantage.

Given the labor forces and the unit labor requirements in the two countries, we can draw the production possibility frontier for each country. We have already done this for Home, by drawing *PF* in Figure 2-1. The production possibility frontier for Foreign is shown as *PF** in Figure 2-2. Since the slope of the production possibility frontier equals the opportunity cost of cheese in terms of wine, Foreign's frontier is steeper than Home's.

In the absence of trade the relative prices of cheese and wine in each country would be determined by the relative unit labor requirements. Thus in Home the relative price of cheese would be a_{LC}/a_{LW}; in Foreign it would be a_{LC}^*/a_{LW}^*.

Once we allow for the possibility of international trade, however, prices will no longer be determined purely by domestic considerations. If the relative price of cheese is higher in Foreign than in Home, it will be profitable to ship cheese from Home to Foreign and to ship

COMPARATIVE ADVANTAGE
IN PRACTICE: THE CASE OF BABE RUTH

Everyone knows that Babe Ruth was the greatest slugger in the history of baseball. Only true fans of the sport know, however, that Ruth also was one of the greatest *pitchers* of all time. Because Ruth stopped pitching after 1918 and played outfield during all the time he set his famous batting records, most people don't realize that he even could pitch. What explains Ruth's lopsided reputation as a batter? The answer is provided by the principle of comparative advantage.

As a player with the Boston Red Sox early in his career, Ruth certainly had an *absolute* advantage in pitching. According to historian Geoffrey C. Ward and filmmaker Ken Burns:

In the Red Sox's greatest years, he was their greatest player, the best left-handed pitcher in the American League, winning 89 games in six seasons. In 1916 he got his first chance to pitch in the World Series and made the most of it. After giving up a run in the first, he drove in the tying run himself, after which he held the Brooklyn Dodgers scoreless for eleven innings until his teammates could score the winning run. . . . In the 1918 series, he would show that he could still handle them, stretching his series record to 29-2/3

scoreless innings, a mark that stood for forty-three years.*

The Babe's World Series pitching record was broken by New York Yankee Whitey Ford in the same year, 1961, that his teammate Roger Maris shattered Ruth's 1927 record of 60 home runs in a single season.

Although Ruth had an absolute advantage in pitching, his skill as a batter relative to his teammates' abilities was even greater: his *comparative* advantage was at the plate. As a pitcher, however, Ruth had to rest his arm between appearances and therefore could not bat in every game. To exploit Ruth's comparative advantage, the Red Sox moved him to center field in 1919 so that he could bat more frequently.

The payoff to having Ruth specialize in batting was huge. In 1919 he hit 29 home runs, "more than any player had ever hit in a single season," according to Ward and Burns. The Yankees kept Ruth in the outfield (and at the plate) after they acquired him in 1920. They knew a good thing when they saw it. That year, Ruth hit 54 home runs, set a slugging record (bases divided by at bats) that remains untouched to this day, and turned the Yankees into baseball's most renowned franchise.

*See Ward and Burns, *Baseball: An Illustrated History* (New York: Knopf, 1994), p. 155. Ruth's career preceded the designated hitter rule, so American League pitchers, like National League pitchers today, took their turns at bat.

wine from Foreign to Home. This cannot go on indefinitely, however. Eventually Home will export enough cheese and Foreign enough wine to equalize the relative price. But what determines the level at which that price settles?

Determining the Relative Price after Trade

Prices of internationally traded goods, like other prices, are determined by supply and demand. In discussing comparative advantage, however, we must apply supply-and-demand analysis carefully. In some contexts, such as some of the trade policy analysis in Chapters 8 through 11, it is acceptable to focus only on supply and demand in a single market. In assessing the effects of U.S. import quotas on sugar, for example, it is reasonable to use **partial equilibrium analysis**, that is, to study a single market, the sugar market. When

Figure 2-2 | Foreign's Production Possibility Frontier

Because Foreign's relative unit labor requirement in cheese is higher than Home's (it needs to give up many more units of wine to produce one more unit of cheese), its production possibility frontier is steeper.

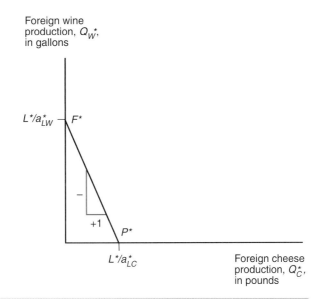

we study comparative advantage, however, it is crucial to keep track of the relationships between markets (in our example the markets for wine and cheese). Since Home exports cheese only in return for imports of wine, and Foreign exports wine in return for cheese, it can be misleading to look at the cheese and wine markets in isolation. What is needed is **general equilibrium analysis**, which takes account of the linkages between the two markets.

One useful way to keep track of two markets at once is to focus not just on the quantities of cheese and wine supplied and demanded but also on the *relative* supply and demand, that is, on the number of pounds of cheese supplied or demanded divided by the number of gallons of wine supplied or demanded.

Figure 2-3 shows world supply and demand for cheese relative to wine as functions of the price of cheese relative to that of wine. The **relative demand curve** is indicated by *RD;* the **relative supply curve** is indicated by *RS*. World general equilibrium requires that relative supply equal relative demand, and thus the world relative price is determined by the intersection of *RD* and *RS*.

The striking feature of Figure 2-3 is the funny shape of the relative supply curve *RS:* a "step" with flat sections linked by a vertical section. Once we understand the derivation of the *RS* curve, we will be almost home-free in understanding the whole model.

First, as drawn, the *RS* curve shows that there is no supply of cheese if the world price drops below a_{LC}/a_{LW}. To see why, recall that we showed that Home will specialize in the production of wine whenever $P_C/P_W < a_{LC}/a_{LW}$. Similarly, Foreign will specialize in wine production whenever $P_C/P_W < a^*_{LC}/a^*_{LW}$. At the start of our discussion of equation (2-2) we made the assumption that $a_{LC}/a_{LW} < a^*_{LC}/a^*_{LW}$. So at relative prices of cheese below a_{LC}/a_{LW}, there will be no world cheese production.

Figure 2-3 | World Relative Supply and Demand

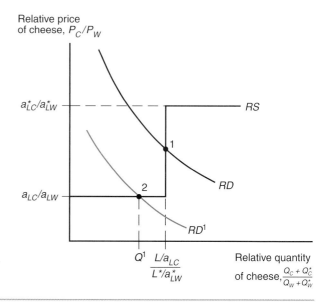

The *RD* and *RD*^{1} curves show that the demand for cheese relative to wine is a decreasing function of the price of cheese relative to that of wine, while the *RS* curve shows that the supply of cheese relative to wine is an increasing function of the same relative price.

Next, when the relative price of cheese, P_C/P_W, is exactly a_{LC}/a_{LW}, we know that workers in Home can earn exactly the same amount making either cheese or wine. So Home will be willing to supply any relative amount of the two goods, producing a flat section to the supply curve.

We have already seen that if P_C/P_W is above a_{LC}/a_{LW}, Home will specialize in the production of cheese. As long as $P_C/P_W < a^*_{LC}/a^*_{LW}$, however, Foreign will continue to specialize in producing wine. When Home specializes in cheese production, it produces L/a_{LC} pounds. Similarly, when Foreign specializes in wine it produces L^*/a^*_{LW} gallons. So for any relative price of cheese between a_{LC}/a_{LW} and a^*_{LC}/a^*_{LW} the relative supply of cheese is

$$(L/a_{LC})/(L^*/a^*_{LW}). \qquad (2\text{-}4)$$

At $P_C/P_W = a^*_{LC}/a^*_{LW}$, we know that Foreign workers are indifferent between producing cheese and wine. Thus here we again have a flat section of the supply curve.

Finally, for $P_C/P_W > a^*_{LC}/a^*_{LW}$, both Home and Foreign will specialize in cheese production. There will be no wine production, so that the relative supply of cheese will become infinite.

The relative demand curve *RD* does not require such exhaustive analysis. The downward slope of *RD* reflects substitution effects. As the relative price of cheese rises, consumers will tend to purchase less cheese and more wine, so the relative demand for cheese falls.

The equilibrium relative price of cheese is determined by the intersection of the relative supply and relative demand curves. Figure 2-3 shows a relative demand curve *RD* that intersects the *RS* curve at point 1, where the relative price of cheese is between the two countries' pretrade prices. In this case each country specializes in the production of the good in which it has a comparative advantage: Home produces only cheese, Foreign only wine.

This is not, however, the only possible outcome. If the relevant *RD* curve were *RD'*, for example, relative supply and relative demand would intersect on one of the horizontal sections of *RS*. At point 2 the world relative price of cheese after trade is a_{LC}/a_{LW}, the same as the opportunity cost of cheese in terms of wine in Home.

What is the significance of this outcome? If the relative price of cheese is equal to its opportunity cost in Home, the Home economy need not specialize in producing either cheese or wine. In fact, at point 2 Home must be producing both some wine and some cheese; we can infer this from the fact that the relative supply of cheese (point *Q'* on horizontal axis) is less than it would be if Home were in fact completely specialized. Since P_C/P_W is below the opportunity cost of cheese in terms of wine in Foreign, however, Foreign does specialize completely in producing wine. It therefore remains true that if a country does specialize, it will do so in the good in which it has a comparative advantage.

Let us for the moment leave aside the possibility that one of the two countries does not completely specialize. Except in this case, the normal result of trade is that the price of a traded good (e.g., cheese) relative to that of another good (wine) ends up somewhere in between its pretrade levels in the two countries.

The effect of this convergence in relative prices is that each country specializes in the production of that good in which it has the relatively lower unit labor requirement. The rise in the relative price of cheese in Home will lead Home to specialize in the production of cheese, producing at point *F* in Figure 2-4a. The fall in the relative price of cheese in Foreign will lead Foreign to specialize in the production of wine, producing at point *F** in Figure 2-4b.

The Gains From Trade

We have now seen that countries whose relative labor productivities differ across industries will specialize in the production of different goods. We next show that both countries derive **gains from trade** from this specialization. This mutual gain can be demonstrated in two alternative ways.

The first way to show that specialization and trade are beneficial is to think of trade as an indirect method of production. Home could produce wine directly, but trade with Foreign allows it to "produce" wine by producing cheese and then trading the cheese for wine. This indirect method of "producing" a gallon of wine is a more efficient method than direct production. Consider two alternative ways of using an hour of labor. On one side, Home could use the hour directly to produce $1/a_{LW}$ gallons of wine. Alternatively, Home could use the hour to produce $1/a_{LC}$ pounds of cheese. This cheese could then be traded for wine, with each pound trading for P_C/P_W gallons, so our original hour of labor yields $(1/a_{LC})$ (P_C/P_W) gallons of wine. This will be more wine than the hour could have produced directly as long as

$$(1/a_{LC})(P_C/P_W) > 1/a_{LW}, \tag{2-5}$$

or

$$P_C/P_W > a_{LC}/a_{LW}.$$

But we just saw that in international equilibrium, if neither country produces both goods, we must have $P_C/P_W > a_{LC}/a_{LW}$. This shows that Home can "produce" wine more efficiently by making cheese and trading it than by producing wine directly for itself. Similarly,

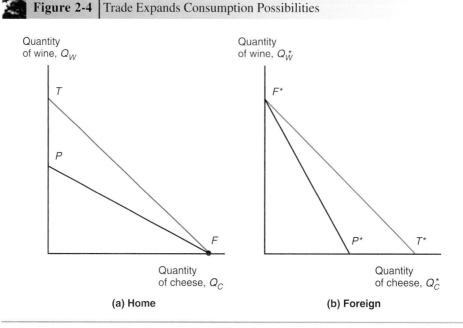

Figure 2-4 | Trade Expands Consumption Possibilities

International trade allows Home and Foreign to consume anywhere within the colored lines, which lie outside the countries' production possibility frontiers.

Foreign can "produce" cheese more efficiently by making wine and trading it. This is one way of seeing that both countries gain.

Another way to see the mutual gains from trade is to examine how trade affects each country's possibilities for consumption. In the absence of trade, consumption possibilities are the same as production possibilities (the solid lines *PF* and *P*F** in Figure 2-4). Once trade is allowed, however, each economy can consume a different mix of cheese and wine from the mix it produces. Home's consumption possibilities are indicated by the colored line *TF* in Figure 2-4a, while Foreign's consumption possibilities are indicated by *T*F** in Figure 2-4b. In each case trade has enlarged the range of choice, and therefore it must make residents of each country better off.

A Numerical Example

In this section, we use a numerical example to solidify our understanding of two crucial points:

> When two countries specialize in producing the goods in which they have a comparative advantage, both countries gain from trade.
>
> *Comparative* advantage must not be confused with *absolute* advantage; it is comparative, not absolute, advantage that determines who will and should produce a good.

Suppose, then, that Home and Foreign have the unit labor requirements illustrated in Table 2-2.

Table 2-2	Unit Labor Requirements	
	Cheese	**Wine**
Home	$a_{LC} = 1$ hour per pound	$a_{LW} = 2$ hours per gallon
Foreign	$a_{LC}^* = 6$ hours per pound	$a_{LW}^* = 3$ hours per gallon

A striking feature of this table is that Home has lower unit labor requirements, that is, has higher labor productivity, in both industries. Let us leave this observation for a moment, however, and focus on the pattern of trade.

The first thing we need to do is determine the relative price of cheese P_C/P_W. While the actual relative price depends on demand, we know that it must lie between the opportunity cost of cheese in the two countries. In Home, we have $a_{LC} = 1$, $a_{LW} = 2$; so the opportunity cost of cheese in terms of wine in Home is $a_{LC}/a_{LW} = 1/2$. In Foreign, $a_{LC}^* = 6$, $a_{LW}^* = 3$; so the opportunity cost of cheese is 2. In world equilibrium, the relative price of cheese must lie between these values. In our example we assume that in world equilibrium a pound of cheese trades for a gallon of wine on world markets so that $P_C/P_W = 1$.

If a pound of cheese sells for the same price as a gallon of wine, both countries will specialize. It takes only half as many person-hours in Home to produce a pound of cheese as it takes to produce a gallon of wine (1 versus 2); so Home workers can earn more by producing cheese, and Home will specialize in cheese production. Conversely, it takes twice as many Foreign person-hours to produce a pound of cheese as it takes to produce a gallon of wine (6 versus 3), so Foreign workers can earn more by producing wine, and Foreign will specialize in wine production.

Let us confirm that this pattern of specialization produces gains from trade. First, we want to show that Home can "produce" wine more efficiently by making cheese and trading it for wine than by direct production. In direct production, an hour of Home labor produces only ½ gallon of wine. The same hour could be used to produce 1 pound of cheese, which can then be traded for 1 gallon of wine. Clearly, Home does gain from trade. Similarly, Foreign could use 1 hour of labor to produce ⅙ pound of cheese; if, however, it uses the hour to produce ⅓ gallon of wine it could then trade the ⅓ gallon of wine for ⅓ pound of cheese. This is twice as much as the ⅙ pound of cheese it gets using the hour to produce the cheese directly. In this example, each country can use labor twice as efficiently to trade for what it needs instead of producing its imports for itself.

Relative Wages

Political discussions of international trade often focus on comparisons of wage rates in different countries. For example, opponents of trade between the United States and Mexico often emphasize the point that workers in Mexico are paid only about $2 per hour, compared with more than $15 per hour for the typical worker in the United States. Our discussion of international trade up to this point has not explicitly compared wages in the two countries, but it is possible in the context of this numerical example to determine how the wage rates in the two countries compare.

In this example, once the countries have specialized, all Home workers are employed producing cheese. Since it takes 1 hour of labor to produce 1 pound of cheese, workers in

THE LOSSES FROM NON-TRADE

Our discussion of the gains from trade was considered a "thought experiment" in which we compared two situations: one in which countries do not trade at all, another in which they have free trade. It's a hypothetical case that helps us to understand the principles of international economics, but it doesn't have much to do with actual events. After all, countries don't suddenly go from no trade to free trade or vice versa. Or do they?

As the economic historian Douglas Irwin* has pointed out, in the early history of the United States the country actually did carry out something very close to the thought experiment of moving from free trade to no trade. The historical context was as follows: at the time Britain and France were engaged in a massive military struggle, the Napoleonic Wars. Both countries endeavored to bring economic pressures to bear: France tried to keep European countries from trading with Britain, while Britain imposed a blockade on France. The young United States was neutral in the conflict but suffered considerably. In particular, the British navy often seized U.S. merchant ships, and on occasion forcibly recruited their crews into its service.

In an effort to pressure Britain into ceasing these practices, President Thomas Jefferson declared a complete ban on overseas shipping. This embargo would deprive both the United States and Britain of the gains from trade, but Jefferson hoped that Britain would be hurt more and would agree to stop its depredations.

Irwin presents evidence suggesting that the embargo was quite effective: although some smuggling took place, trade between the United States and the rest of the world was drastically reduced. In effect, the United States gave up international trade for a while.

The costs were substantial. Although quite a lot of guesswork is involved, Irwin suggests that real income in the United States may have fallen by about 8 percent as a result of the embargo. When you bear in mind that in the early nineteenth century only a fraction of output could be traded—transport costs were still too high, for example, to allow large-scale shipments of commodities like wheat across the Atlantic—that's a pretty substantial sum.

Unfortunately for Jefferson's plan, Britain did not seem to feel equal pain and showed no inclination to give in to U.S. demands. Fourteen months after the embargo was imposed, it was repealed. Britain continued its practices of seizing American cargoes and sailors; three years later the two countries went to war.

*Douglas Irwin, "The Welfare Cost of Autarky: Evidence from the Jeffersonian Trade Embargo, 1807–1809," National Bureau of Economic Research Working Paper no. 8692, Dec. 2001.

Home earn the value of 1 pound of cheese per hour of their labor. Similarly, Foreign workers produce only wine; since it takes 3 hours for them to produce each gallon, they earn the value of $\frac{1}{3}$ of a gallon of wine per hour.

To convert these numbers into dollar figures, we need to know the prices of cheese and wine. Suppose that a pound of cheese and a gallon of wine both sell for $12; then Home workers will earn $12 per hour, while Foreign workers will earn $4 per hour. The **relative wage** of a country's workers is the amount they are paid per hour, compared with the amount workers in another country are paid per hour. The relative wage of Home workers will therefore be 3.

Clearly, this relative wage does not depend on whether the price of a pound of cheese is $12 or $20, as long as a gallon of wine sells for the same price. As long as the relative price of cheese—the price of a pound of cheese divided by the price of a gallon of wine—is 1, the wage of Home workers will be three times that of Foreign workers.

Notice that this wage rate lies between the ratios of the two countries' productivities in the two industries. Home is six times as productive as Foreign in cheese, but only one-and-a-half times as productive in wine, and it ends up with a wage rate three times as high as Foreign's. It is precisely because the relative wage is between the relative productivities that each country ends up with a *cost* advantage in one good. Because of its lower wage rate, Foreign has a cost advantage in wine, even though it has lower productivity. Home has a cost advantage in cheese, despite its higher wage rate, because the higher wage is more than offset by its higher productivity.

We have now developed the simplest of all models of international trade. Even though the Ricardian one-factor model is far too simple to be a complete analysis of either the causes or the effects of international trade, a focus on relative labor productivities can be a very useful tool for thinking about international trade. In particular, the simple one-factor model is a good way to deal with several common misconceptions about the meaning of comparative advantage and the nature of the gains from free trade. These misconceptions appear so frequently in public debate about international economic policy, and even in statements by those who regard themselves as experts, that in the next section we take time out to discuss some of the most common misunderstandings about comparative advantage in light of our model.

Misconceptions About Comparative Advantage

There is no shortage of muddled ideas in economics. Politicians, business leaders, and even economists frequently make statements that do not stand up to careful economic analysis. For some reason this seems to be especially true in international economics. Open the business section of any Sunday newspaper or weekly news magazine and you will probably find at least one article that makes foolish statements about international trade. Three misconceptions in particular have proved highly persistent, and our simple model of comparative advantage can be used to see why they are incorrect.

Productivity and Competitiveness

Myth 1: Free trade is beneficial only if your country is strong enough to stand up to foreign competition. This argument seems extremely plausible to many people. For example, a well-known historian recently criticized the case for free trade by asserting that it may fail to hold in reality: "What if there is nothing you can produce more cheaply or efficiently than anywhere else, except by constantly cutting labor costs?" he worried.[2]

The problem with this commentator's view is that he failed to understand the essential point of Ricardo's model, that gains from trade depend on *comparative* rather than *absolute* advantage. He is concerned that your country may turn out not to have anything it produces more efficiently than anyone else—that is, that you may not have an absolute advantage in anything. Yet why is that such a terrible thing? In our simple numerical example of trade, Home has lower unit labor requirements and hence higher productivity in both the cheese and wine sectors. Yet, as we saw, both countries gain from trade.

---

[2] Paul Kennedy, "The Threat of Modernization." *New Perspectives Quarterly* (Winter 1995), pp. 31–33.

It is always tempting to suppose that the ability to export a good depends on your country having an absolute advantage in productivity. But an absolute productivity advantage over other countries in producing a good is neither a necessary nor a sufficient condition for having a *comparative* advantage in that good. In our one-factor model the reason why absolute productivity advantage in an industry is neither necessary nor sufficient to yield competitive advantage is clear: *The competitive advantage of an industry depends not only on its productivity relative to the foreign industry, but also on the domestic wage rate relative to the foreign wage rate.* A country's wage rate, in turn, depends on relative productivity in its other industries. In our numerical example, Foreign is less efficient than Home in the manufacture of wine, but at even a greater relative productivity disadvantage in cheese. Because of its overall lower productivity, Foreign must pay lower wages than Home, sufficiently lower that it ends up with lower costs in wine production. Similarly, in the real world, Portugal has low productivity in producing, say, clothing as compared with the United States, but because Portugal's productivity disadvantage is even greater in other industries it pays low enough wages to have a comparative advantage in clothing all the same.

But isn't a competitive advantage based on low wages somehow unfair? Many people think so; their beliefs are summarized by our second misconception.

The Pauper Labor Argument

Myth 2: Foreign competition is unfair and hurts other countries when it is based on low wages. This argument, sometimes referred to as the **pauper labor argument**, is a particular favorite of labor unions seeking protection from foreign competition. People who adhere to this belief argue that industries should not have to cope with foreign industries that are less efficient but pay lower wages. This view is widespread and has acquired considerable political influence. In 1993 Ross Perot, a self-made billionaire and former presidential candidate, warned that free trade between the United States and Mexico, with its much lower wages, would lead to a "giant sucking sound" as U.S. industry moved south. In the same year Sir James Goldsmith, another self-made billionaire who was an influential member of the European Parliament, offered similar if less picturesquely expressed views in his book *The Trap,* which became a best-seller in France.

Again, our simple example reveals the fallacy of this argument. In the example, Home is more productive than Foreign in both industries, and Foreign's lower cost of wine production is entirely due to its much lower wage rate. Foreign's lower wage rate is, however, irrelevant to the question of whether Home gains from trade. Whether the lower cost of wine produced in Foreign is due to high productivity or low wages does not matter. All that matters to Home is that it is cheaper *in terms of its own labor* for Home to produce cheese and trade it for wine than to produce wine for itself.

This is fine for Home, but what about Foreign? Isn't there something wrong with basing one's exports on low wages? Certainly it is not an attractive position to be in, but the idea that trade is good only if you receive high wages is our final fallacy.

Exploitation

Myth 3: Trade exploits a country and makes it worse off if its workers receive much lower wages than workers in other nations. This argument is often expressed in emotional terms. For example, one columnist contrasted the $2 million income of the chief executive officer of the clothing chain The Gap with the $0.56 per hour paid to the Central

DO WAGES REFLECT PRODUCTIVITY?

In the numerical example that we use to puncture common misconceptions about comparative advantage, we assume that the relative wage of the two countries reflects their relative productivity—specifically, that the ratio of Home to Foreign wages is in a range that gives each country a cost advantage in one of the two goods. This is a necessary implication of our theoretical model. But many people are unconvinced by that model. In particular, rapid increases in productivity in "emerging" economies like China have worried some Western observers, who argue that these countries will continue to pay low wages even as their productivity increases—putting high-wage countries at a cost disadvantage—and dismiss the contrary predictions of orthodox economists as unrealistic theoretical speculation. Leaving aside the logic of this position, what is the evidence?

As it happens, growth in the "newly industrializing economies" of Asia provides a clear test. The so-called Asian tigers—South Korea, Taiwan, Hong Kong, and Singapore—began a rapid process of development in the 1960s and achieved much higher rates of productivity growth than Western nations through the last few decades of the twentieth century. For example, output per worker in South Korea was only 20 percent of the U.S. level in 1975; it had risen to more than half the U.S. level by 1998.

Did wages stay low during this productivity surge, or did wages in the newly industrializing economies rise along with their productivity? The answer, illustrated in Table 2-3, is that wages rose. The first two columns show compensation (wages plus benefits) as a percent of the U.S. level in 1975 and 1999; clearly there was a dramatic convergence of wages toward the U.S. level.

Did Asian relative wages rise more or less than their relative productivity? The U.S. Bureau of Labor Statistics has calculated rates of change in unit labor costs for South Korea and Taiwan, though not for the other Asian economies. If wage growth lagged behind productivity, unit labor costs would fall compared with the United States; if wage growth exceeded productivity, relative unit labor costs would rise. In fact, as the third column of the table shows, South Korea's unit labor costs lagged slightly behind those in the United States, while Taiwan's grew more rapidly.

In short, the evidence strongly supports the view, based on economic models, that productivity increases are reflected in wage increases.

Table 2-3 | Changes in Wages and Unit Labor Costs

	Compensation per Hour, 1975 (US = 100)	Compensation per Hour, 2000 (US = 100)	Annual Rate of Increase in Unit Labor Costs, 1979–2000
United States	100	100	1.1
South Korea	5	41	0.7
Taiwan	6	30	3.6
Hong Kong	12	28	NA
Singapore	13	37	NA

Source: Bureau of Labor Statistics (foreign labor statistics home page, www.bls.gov/fls/home.htm)

American workers who produce some of its merchandise.[3] It can seem hard-hearted to try to justify the terrifyingly low wages paid to many of the world's workers.

If one is asking about the desirability of free trade, however, the point is not to ask whether low-wage workers deserve to be paid more but to ask whether they and their country are worse off exporting goods based on low wages than they would be if they refused to enter into such demeaning trade. And in asking this question one must also ask, *what is the alternative?*

Abstract though it is, our numerical example makes the point that one cannot declare that a low wage represents exploitation unless one knows what the alternative is. In that example, Foreign workers are paid much less than Home workers, and one could easily imagine a columnist writing angrily about their exploitation. Yet if Foreign refused to let itself be "exploited" by refusing to trade with Home (or by insisting on much higher wages in its export sector, which would have the same effect), real wages would be even lower: The purchasing power of a worker's hourly wage would fall from ⅓ to ⅙ pound of cheese.

The columnist who pointed out the contrast in incomes between the executive at The Gap and the workers who make its clothes was angry at the poverty of Central American workers. But to deny them the opportunity to export and trade might well be to condemn them to even deeper poverty.

Comparative Advantage with Many Goods

In our discussion so far we have relied on a model in which only two goods are produced and consumed. This simplified analysis allows us to capture many essential points about comparative advantage and trade and, as we saw in the last section, gives us a surprising amount of mileage as a tool for discussing policy issues. To move closer to reality, however, it is necessary to understand how comparative advantage functions in a model with a larger number of goods.

Setting Up the Model

Again, imagine a world of two countries, Home and Foreign. As before, each country has only one factor of production, labor. Each of these countries will now, however, be assumed to consume and to be able to produce a large number of goods—say, N different goods altogether. We assign each of the goods a number from 1 to N.

The technology of each country can be described by its unit labor requirement for each good, that is, the number of hours of labor it takes to produce one unit of each. We label Home's unit labor requirement for a particular good as a_{Li}, where i is the number we have assigned to that good. If cheese is now good number 7, a_{L7} will mean the unit labor requirement in cheese production. Following our usual rule, we label the corresponding Foreign unit labor requirements a_{Li}^*.

To analyze trade, we next pull one more trick. For any good we can calculate a_{Li}/a_{Li}^*, the ratio of Home's unit labor requirement to Foreign's. The trick is to relabel the goods so that

[3]Bob Herbert, "Sweatshop Beneficiaries: How to Get Rich on 56 Cents an Hour," *New York Times* (July 24, 1995), p. A13.

the lower the number, the lower this ratio. That is, we reshuffle the order in which we number goods in such a way that

$$a_{L1}/a_{L1}^* < a_{L2}/a_{L2}^* < a_{L3}/a_{L3}^* < \ldots < a_{LN}/a_{LN}^*. \tag{2-6}$$

Relative Wages and Specialization

We are now prepared to look at the pattern of trade. This pattern depends on only one thing: the ratio of Home to Foreign wages. Once we know this ratio, we can determine who produces what.

Let w be the wage rate per hour in Home and w^* be the wage rate in Foreign. The ratio of wage rates is then w/w^*. The rule for allocating world production, then, is simply this: Goods will always be produced where it is cheapest to make them. The cost of making some good, say good i, is the unit labor requirement times the wage rate. To produce good i in Home will cost wa_{Li}. To produce the same good in Foreign will cost $w^*a^*_{Li}$. It will be cheaper to produce the good in Home if

$$wa_{Li} < w^*a^*_{Li},$$

which can be rearranged to yield

$$a^*_{Li}/a_{Li} > w/w^*.$$

On the other hand, it will be cheaper to produce the good in Foreign if

$$wa_{Li} > w^*a^*_{Li},$$

which can be rearranged to yield

$$a^*_{Li}/a_{Li} < w/w^*.$$

Thus we can restate the allocation rule: Any good for which $a^*_{Li}/a_{Li} > w/w^*$ will be produced in Home, while any good for which $a^*_{Li}/a_{Li} < w/w^*$ will be produced in Foreign.

We have already lined up the goods in increasing order of a_{Li}/a^*_{Li} (equation (2-6)). This criterion for specialization tells us that what happens is a "cut" in that lineup, determined by the ratio of the two countries' wage rates, w/w^*. All the goods to the left of the cut end up being produced in Home; all the goods to the right end up being produced in Foreign. (It is possible, as we will see in a moment, that the ratio of wage rates is exactly equal to the ratio of unit labor requirements for one good. In that case this borderline good may be produced in both countries.)

Table 2-4 offers a numerical example in which Home and Foreign both consume and are able to produce *five* goods: apples, bananas, caviar, dates, and enchiladas.

The first two columns of this table are self-explanatory. The third column is the ratio of the Foreign unit labor requirement to the Home unit labor requirement for each good—or, stated differently, the relative Home productivity advantage in each good. We have labeled the goods in order of Home productivity advantage, with the Home advantage greatest for apples and least for enchiladas.

Table 2-4 | Home and Foreign Unit Labor Requirements

Good	Home Unit Labor Requirement (a_{Li})	Foreign Unit Labor Requirement (a^*_{Li})	Relative Home Productivity Advantage (a^*_{Li}/a_{Li})
Apples	1	10	10
Bananas	5	40	8
Caviar	3	12	4
Dates	6	12	2
Enchiladas	12	9	0.75

Which country produces which goods depends on the ratio of Home and Foreign wage rates. Home will have a cost advantage in any good for which its relative productivity is higher than its relative wage, and Foreign will have the advantage in the others. If, for example, the Home wage rate is five times that of Foreign (a ratio of Home wage to Foreign wage of five to one), apples and bananas will be produced in Home and caviar, dates, and enchiladas in Foreign. If the Home wage rate is only three times that of Foreign, Home will produce apples, bananas, and caviar, while Foreign will produce only dates and enchiladas.

Is such a pattern of specialization beneficial to both countries? We can see that it is by using the same method we used earlier: comparing the labor cost of producing a good directly in a country with that of indirectly "producing" it by producing another good and trading for the desired good. If the Home wage rate is three times the Foreign wage (put another way, Foreign's wage rate is one-third that of Home), Home will import dates and enchiladas. A unit of dates requires 12 units of Foreign labor to produce, but its cost in terms of Home labor, given the three-to-one wage ratio, is only 4 person-hours ($12 \div 3$). This cost of 4 person-hours is less than the 6 person-hours it would take to produce the unit of dates in Home. For enchiladas, Foreign actually has higher productivity along with lower wages; it will cost Home only 3 person-hours to acquire a unit of enchiladas through trade, compared with the 12 person-hours it would take to produce it domestically. A similar calculation will show that Foreign also gains; for each of the goods Foreign imports it turns out to be cheaper in terms of domestic labor to trade for the good rather than produce the good domestically. For example, it would take 10 hours of Foreign labor to produce a unit of apples; even with a wage rate only one-third that of Home workers, it will require only 3 hours of labor to earn enough to buy that unit of apples from Home.

In making these calculations, however, we have simply assumed that the relative wage rate is 3. How does this relative wage rate actually get determined?

Determining the Relative Wage in the Multigood Model

In the two-good model we determined relative wages by first calculating Home wages in terms of cheese and Foreign wages in terms of wine, then using the price of cheese relative to that of wine to deduce the ratio of the two countries' wage rates. We could do this because we knew that Home would produce cheese and Foreign wine. In the many-good case, who produces what can be determined only after we know the relative wage rate, so this procedure is unworkable. To determine relative wages in a multigood economy we must look behind the relative demand for goods to the implied relative demand for labor. This is not a direct demand on the part of consumers; rather, it is a **derived demand** that results from the demand for goods produced with each country's labor.

The relative derived demand for Home labor will fall when the ratio of Home to Foreign wages rises, for two reasons. First, as Home labor becomes more expensive relative to Foreign labor, goods produced in Home also become relatively more expensive, and world demand for these goods falls. Second, as Home wages rise, fewer goods will be produced in Home and more in Foreign, further reducing the demand for Home labor.

We can illustrate these two effects using our numerical example. Suppose we start with the following situation: The Home wage is initially 3.5 times the Foreign wage. At that level, Home would produce apples, bananas, and caviar while Foreign would produce dates and enchiladas. If the relative Home wage were to increase from 3.5 to just under 4, say 3.99, the pattern of specialization would not change, but as the goods produced in Home became relatively more expensive, the relative demand for these goods would decline and the relative demand for Home labor would decline with it.

Suppose now that the relative wage were to increase slightly from 3.99 to 4.01. This small further increase in the relative Home wage would bring about a shift in the pattern of specialization. Because it is now cheaper to produce caviar in Foreign than in Home, the production of caviar shifts from Home to Foreign. What does this imply for the relative demand for Home labor? Clearly it implies that as the relative wage rises from a little less than 4 to a little more than 4 there is an abrupt drop-off in the relative demand, as Home production of caviar falls to zero and Foreign acquires a new industry. If the relative wage continues to rise, relative demand for Home labor will gradually decline, then drop off abruptly at a relative wage of 8, at which wage production of bananas shifts to Foreign.

We can illustrate the determination of relative wages with a diagram like Figure 2-5. Unlike Figure 2-3, this diagram does not have relative quantities of goods or relative prices of goods on its axes. Instead it shows the relative quantity of labor and the relative wage rate. The world demand for Home labor relative to its demand for Foreign labor is shown by the curve *RD*. The world supply of Home labor relative to Foreign labor is shown by the line *RS*.

The relative supply of labor is determined by the relative size of Home and Foreign labor forces. Assuming that the number of person-hours available does not vary with the wage, the relative wage has no effect on relative labor supply and *RS* is a vertical line.

Our discussion of the relative demand for labor explains the "stepped" shape of *RD*. Whenever we increase the wage rate of Home workers relative to Foreign workers, the relative demand for goods produced in Home will decline and the demand for Home labor will decline with it. In addition, the relative demand for Home labor will drop off abruptly whenever an increase in the relative Home wage makes a good cheaper to produce in Foreign. So the curve alternates between smoothly downward sloping sections where the pattern of specialization does not change and "flats" where the relative demand shifts abruptly because of shifts in the pattern of specialization. As shown in the figure, these "flats" correspond to relative wages that equal the ratio of Home to Foreign productivity for each of the five goods.

The equilibrium relative wage is determined by the intersection of *RD* and *RS*. As drawn, the equilibrium relative wage is 3. At this wage, Home produces apples, bananas, and caviar while Foreign produces dates and enchiladas. The outcome depends on the relative size of the countries (which determines the position of *RS*) and the relative demand for the goods (which determines the shape and position of *RD*).

Figure 2-5 | Determination of Relative Wages

In a many-good Ricardian model, relative wages are determined by the intersection of the derived relative demand curve for labor *RD* with the relative supply *RS*.

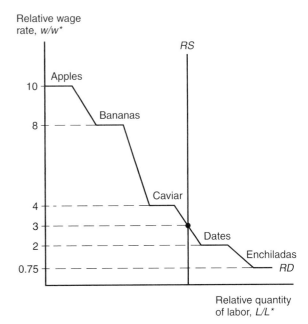

If the intersection of *RD* and *RS* happens to lie on one of the flats, both countries produce the good to which the flat applies.

Adding Transport Costs and Nontraded Goods

We now extend our model another step closer to reality by considering the effects of transport costs. Transportation costs do not change the fundamental principles of comparative advantage or the gains from trade. Because transport costs pose obstacles to the movement of goods and services, however, they have important implications for the way a trading world economy is affected by a variety of factors such as foreign aid, international investment, and balance of payments problems. While we will not deal with the effects of these factors yet, the multigood one-factor model is a good place to introduce the effects of transport costs.

First, notice that the world economy described by the model of the last section is marked by very extreme international specialization. At most there is one good that both countries produce; all other goods are produced either in Home or in Foreign, not in both.

There are three main reasons why specialization in the real international economy is not this extreme:

1. The existence of more than one factor of production reduces the tendency toward specialization (as we see in the next two chapters).

2. Countries sometimes protect industries from foreign competition (discussed at length in Chapters 8 through 11).
3. It is costly to transport goods and services, and in some cases the cost of transportation is enough to lead countries into self-sufficiency in certain sectors.

In the multigood example of the last section we found that at a relative Home wage of 3, Home could produce apples, bananas, and caviar more cheaply than Foreign, while Foreign could produce dates and enchiladas more cheaply than Home. *In the absence of transport costs,* then, Home will export the first three goods and import the last two.

Now suppose there is a cost to transporting goods, and that this transport cost is a uniform fraction of production cost, say 100 percent. This transportation cost will discourage trade. Consider, for example, dates. One unit of this good requires 6 hours of Home labor or 12 hours of Foreign labor to produce. At a relative wage of 3, 12 hours of Foreign labor cost only as much as 4 hours of Home labor; so in the absence of transport costs Home imports dates. With a 100 percent transport cost, however, importing dates would cost the equivalent of 8 hours of Home labor, so Home will produce the good for itself instead.

A similar cost comparison shows that Foreign will find it cheaper to produce its own caviar than import it. A unit of caviar requires 3 hours of Home labor to produce. Even at a relative Home wage of 3, which makes this the equivalent of 9 hours of Foreign labor, this is cheaper than the 12 hours Foreign would need to produce caviar for itself. In the absence of transport costs, then, Foreign would find it cheaper to import caviar than to make it domestically. With a 100 percent cost of transportation, however, imported caviar would cost the equivalent of 18 hours of Foreign labor and would therefore be produced locally instead.

The result of introducing transport costs in this example, then, is that while Home still exports apples and bananas and imports enchiladas, caviar and dates become **nontraded goods**, which each country produces for itself.

In this example we have assumed that transport costs are the same fraction of production cost in all sectors. In practice there is a wide range of transportation costs. In some cases transportation is virtually impossible: Services such as haircuts and auto repair cannot be traded internationally (except where there is a metropolitan area that straddles a border, like Detroit, Michigan-Windsor, Ontario). There is also little international trade in goods with high weight-to-value ratios, like cement. (It is simply not worth the transport cost of importing cement, even if it can be produced much more cheaply abroad). Many goods end up being nontraded either because of the absence of strong national cost advantages or because of high transportation costs.

The important point is that nations spend a large share of their income on nontraded goods. This observation is of surprising importance in our later discussion of international transfers of income (Chapter 5) and in international monetary economics.

Empirical Evidence on the Ricardian Model

The Ricardian model of international trade is an extremely useful tool for thinking about the reasons why trade may happen and about the effects of international trade on national welfare. But is the model a good fit to the real world? Does the Ricardian model make accurate predictions about actual international trade flows?

The answer is a heavily qualified yes. Clearly there are a number of ways in which the Ricardian model makes misleading predictions. First, as mentioned in our discussion of nontraded goods, the simple Ricardian model predicts an extreme degree of specialization that we do not observe in the real world. Second, the Ricardian model assumes away effects of international trade on the distribution of income *within* countries, and thus predicts that countries as a whole will always gain from trade; in practice, international trade has strong effects on income distribution, which is the focus of Chapter 3. Third, the Ricardian model allows no role for differences in resources among countries as a cause of trade, thus missing an important aspect of the trading system (the focus of Chapter 4). Finally, the Ricardian model neglects the possible role of economies of scale as a cause of trade, which leaves it unable to explain the large trade flows between apparently similar nations—an issue discussed in Chapter 6.

In spite of these failings, however, the basic prediction of the Ricardian model—that countries should tend to export those goods in which their productivity is relatively high—has been strongly confirmed by a number of studies over the years.

Several classic tests of the Ricardian model were performed using data from the early post–World War II period comparing British with American productivity and trade.[4] This was an unusually illuminating comparison. British labor productivity was less than American in almost every sector. Thus America had an absolute advantage in everything. Nonetheless, the amount of British overall exports was about as large as American at the time. Clearly then, there must have been some sectors in which Britain had a comparative advantage in spite of its lower absolute productivity. The Ricardian model would predict that these would be the sectors in which America's productivity advantage was smallest.

Figure 2-6 illustrates the evidence in favor of the Ricardian model, using data presented in a paper by the Hungarian economist Bela Balassa in 1963. The figure compares the ratio of U.S. to British exports in 1951 with the ratio of U.S. to British labor productivity for 26 manufacturing industries. The productivity ratio is measured on the horizontal axis, the export ratio on the vertical axis. Both axes are given a logarithmic scale; this is not of any basic importance, but turns out to produce a clearer picture.

Ricardian theory would lead us broadly to expect that the higher the relative productivity in the U.S. industry, the more likely U.S. rather than U.K. firms would export in that industry. And that is what Figure 2-6 shows. In fact, the scatterplot lies quite close to an upward-sloping line, also shown in the figure. Bearing in mind that the data used for this comparison are, like all economic data, subject to substantial measurement errors, the fit is remarkably close.

As expected, the evidence in Figure 2-6 confirms the basic insight that trade depends on *comparative,* not *absolute* advantage. At the time to which the data refer, U.S. industry had much higher labor productivity than British industry—on average about twice as high. The commonly held misconception that a country can be competitive only if it can match other countries' productivity, which we discussed earlier in this chapter, would have led one

---

[4]The pioneering study by G. D. A. MacDougall is listed in Further Reading at the end of the chapter. A well-known follow-up study, on which we draw here, was Bela Balassa, "An Empirical Demonstration of Classical Comparative Cost Theory," *Review of Economics and Statistics* 4, August 1963, pp. 231–238; we use Balassa's numbers as an illustration.

Figure 2-6 | Productivity and Exports

A comparative study showed that U.S. exports were high relative to British exports in industries in which the United States had high relative labor productivity. Each dot represents a different industry.

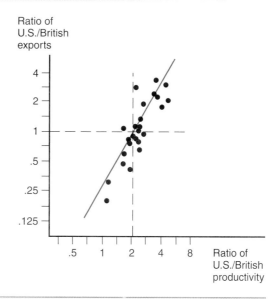

to predict a U.S. export advantage across the board. The Ricardian model tells us, however, that having high productivity in an industry compared with foreigners is not enough to ensure that a country will export that industry's products; the relative productivity must be high compared with relative productivity in other sectors. As it happens, U.S. productivity exceeded British in all 26 sectors (indicated by dots) shown in Figure 2-6, by margins ranging from 11 to 366 percent. In 12 of the sectors, however, Britain actually had larger exports than the United States. A glance at the figure shows that in general, U.S. exports were larger than U.K. exports only in industries where the U.S. productivity advantage was somewhat more than two to one.

More recent evidence on the Ricardian model has been less clear-cut. In part, this is because the growth of world trade and the resulting specialization of national economies means that we do not get a chance to see what countries do badly! In the world economy of the 1990s, countries often do not produce goods for which they are at a comparative disadvantage, so there is no way to measure their productivity in those sectors. For example, most countries do not produce airplanes, so there are no data on what their unit labor requirements would be if they did. Nonetheless, there are several pieces of evidence suggesting that differences in labor productivity continue to play an important role in determining world trade patterns.

Perhaps the most important point is that there continue to be both large differences in labor productivity between countries and considerable variation in those productivity differences across industries. For example, one study found that the average productivity of labor in Japanese manufacturing in 1990 was 20 percent lower than labor productivity in the United States. But in the automobile and auto parts industries Japanese productivity was 16 to 24 percent *higher* than American productivity.[5] It is not hard to believe that this disparity explained much of Japan's ability to export millions of automobiles to the United States.

In the case of automobiles, one might argue that the pattern of trade simply reflected absolute advantage: Japan had the highest productivity and was also the world's largest exporter. The principle of *comparative* advantage may be illustrated by the case of world trade in clothing. By any measure, advanced countries like the United States have higher labor productivity in the manufacture of clothing than newly industrializing countries like Mexico or China. But because the technology of clothing manufacture is relatively simple, the productivity advantage of advanced nations in the clothing industry is less than their advantage in many other industries. For example, in 1992 the average U.S. manufacturing worker was probably about five times as productive as the average Mexican worker; but in the clothing industry the productivity advantage was only about 50 percent. The result is that clothing is a major export from low-wage to high-wage nations.

In sum, while few economists believe that the Ricardian model is a fully adequate description of the causes and consequences of world trade, its two principal implications—that productivity differences play an important role in international trade and that it is comparative rather than absolute advantage that matters—do seem to be supported by the evidence.

Summary

1. We examined the *Ricardian model,* the simplest model that shows how differences between countries give rise to trade and gains from trade. In this model labor is the only factor of production and countries differ only in the productivity of labor in different industries.

2. In the Ricardian model, countries will export goods that their labor produces relatively efficiently and import goods that their labor produces relatively inefficiently. In other words, a country's production pattern is determined by *comparative advantage.*

3. That trade benefits a country can be shown in either of two ways. First, we can think of trade as an indirect method of production. Instead of producing a good for itself, a country can produce another good and trade it for the desired good. The simple model shows that whenever a good is imported it must be true that this indirect "production" requires less labor than direct production. Second, we can show that trade enlarges a country's consumption possibilities, implying *gains from trade.*

4. The distribution of the gains from trade depends on the relative prices of the goods countries produce. To determine these relative prices it is necessary to look at the *relative world supply and demand* for goods. The relative price implies a *relative wage rate* as well.

---

[5]McKinsey Global Institute, *Manufacturing Productivity,* Washington, D.C., 1993.

5. The proposition that trade is beneficial is unqualified. That is, there is no requirement that a country be "competitive" or that the trade be "fair." In particular, we can show that three commonly held beliefs about trade are wrong. First, a country gains from trade even if it has lower productivity than its trading partner in all industries. Second, trade is beneficial even if foreign industries are competitive only because of low wages. Third, trade is beneficial even if a country's exports embody more labor than its imports.

6. Extending the one-factor, two-good model to a world of many commodities does not alter these conclusions. The only difference is that it becomes necessary to focus directly on the relative demand for labor to determine relative wages rather than to work via relative demand for goods. Also, a many-commodity model can be used to illustrate the important point that transportation costs can give rise to a situation in which some nontraded goods exist.

7. While some of the predictions of the Ricardian model are clearly unrealistic, its basic prediction—that countries will tend to export goods in which they have relatively high productivity—has been confirmed by a number of studies.

Key Terms

absolute advantage, p. 15
comparative advantage, p. 12
derived demand, p. 29
gains from trade, p. 19
general equilibrium analysis, p. 17
nontraded goods, p. 31
opportunity cost, p. 11
partial equilibrium analysis, p. 16

pauper labor argument, p. 24
production possibility frontier, p. 12, 13
relative demand curve, p. 17
relative supply curve, p. 17
relative wage, p. 22
Ricardian model, p. 12
unit labor requirement, p. 12

Problems

1. Home has 1200 units of labor available. It can produce two goods, apples and bananas. The unit labor requirement in apple production is 3, while in banana production it is 2.
   a. Graph Home's production possibility frontier.
   b. What is the opportunity cost of apples in terms of bananas?
   c. In the absence of trade, what would the price of apples in terms of bananas be? Why?

2. Home is as described in problem 1. There is now also another country, Foreign, with a labor force of 800. Foreign's unit labor requirement in apple production is 5, while in banana production it is 1.
   a. Graph Foreign's production possibility frontier.
   b. Construct the world relative supply curve.

3. Now suppose world relative demand takes the following form: Demand for apples/ demand for bananas = price of bananas/price of apples
   a. Graph the relative demand curve along with the relative supply curve.

    b. What is the equilibrium relative price of apples?

    c. Describe the pattern of trade.

    d. Show that both Home and Foreign gain from trade.

4. Suppose that instead of 1200 workers, Home had 2400. Find the equilibrium relative price. What can you say about the efficiency of world production and the division of the gains from trade between Home and Foreign in this case?

5. Suppose that Home has 2400 workers, but they are only half as productive in both industries as we have been assuming. Construct the world relative supply curve and determine the equilibrium relative price. How do the gains from trade compare with those in the case described in problem 4?

6. "Korean workers earn only $2.50 an hour; if we allow Korea to export as much as it likes to the United States, our workers will be forced down to the same level. You can't import a $5 shirt without importing the $2.50 wage that goes with it." Discuss.

7. Japanese labor productivity is roughly the same as that of the United States in the manufacturing sector (higher in some industries, lower in others), while the United States is still considerably more productive in the service sector. But most services are nontraded. Some analysts have argued that this poses a problem for the United States, because our comparative advantage lies in things we cannot sell on world markets. What is wrong with this argument?

8. Anyone who has visited Japan knows it is an incredibly expensive place; although Japanese workers earn about the same as their U.S. counterparts, the purchasing power of their incomes is about one-third less. Extend your discussion from question 7 to explain this observation. (Hint: Think about wages and the implied prices of nontraded goods.)

9. How does the fact that many goods are nontraded affect the extent of possible gains from trade?

10. We have focused on the case of trade involving only two countries. Suppose that there are many countries capable of producing two goods, and that each country has only one factor of production, labor. What could we say about the pattern of production and trade in this case? (Hint: Try constructing the world relative supply curve.)

Further Reading

Donald Davis. "Intraindustry Trade: A Heckscher-Ohlin-Ricardo Approach." *Journal of International Economics* 39 (November 1995), pp. 201–226. A recent revival of the Ricardian approach to explain trade between countries with similar resources.

Rudiger Dornbusch, Stanley Fischer, and Paul Samuelson. "Comparative Advantage, Trade and Payments in a Ricardian Model with a Continuum of Goods." *American Economic Review* 67 (December 1977), pp. 823–839. More recent theoretical modeling in the Ricardian mode, developing the idea of simplifying the many-good Ricardian model by assuming that the number of goods is so large as to form a smooth continuum.

Giovanni Dosi, Keith Pavitt, and Luc Soete. *The Economics of Technical Change and International Trade.* Brighton: Wheatsheaf, 1988. An empirical examination that suggests that international trade in manufactured goods is largely driven by differences in national technological competences.

G. D. A. MacDougall. "British and American Exports: A Study Suggested by the Theory of Comparative Costs." *Economic Journal* 61 (December 1951), pp. 697–724; 62 (September 1952), pp. 487–521. In this famous study, MacDougall used comparative data on U.S. and U.K. productivity to test the predictions of the Ricardian model.

John Stuart Mill. *Principles of Political Economy.* London: Longmans, Green, 1917. Mill's 1848 treatise extended Ricardo's work into a full-fledged model of international trade.

David Ricardo. *The Principles of Political Economy and Taxation.* Homewood, IL: Irwin, 1963. The basic source for the Ricardian model is Ricardo himself in this book, first published in 1817.

CHAPTER 3

Specific Factors and Income Distribution

As we saw in Chapter 2, international trade can be mutually beneficial to the nations engaged in it. Yet throughout history, governments have protected sectors of the economy from import competition. For example, despite its commitment in principle to free trade, the United States limits imports of textiles, sugar, and other commodities. If trade is such a good thing for the economy, why is there opposition to its effects? To understand the politics of trade, it is necessary to look at the effects of trade, not just on a country as a whole but on the distribution of income within that country.

The Ricardian model of international trade developed in Chapter 2 illustrates the potential benefits from trade. In that model trade leads to international specialization, with each country shifting its labor force from industries in which that labor is relatively ineffi-cient to industries in which it is relatively more efficient. Because labor is the only factor of production in the model, and it is assumed to be able to move freely from one industry to another, there is no possibility that individuals will be hurt by trade. The Ricardian model thus suggests not only that all countries gain from trade, but that every *individual* is made better off as a result of international trade, because trade does not affect the distribution of income. In the real world, however, trade has substantial effects on the income distrib-ution within each trading nation, so that in practice the benefits of trade are often distrib-uted very unevenly.

There are two main reasons why international trade has strong effects on the distribu-tion of income. First, resources cannot move immediately or costlessly from one industry to another. Second, industries differ in the factors of production they demand: A shift in the mix of goods that a country produces will ordinarily reduce the demand for some factors of production, while raising the demand for others. For both of these reasons, international trade is not as unambiguously beneficial as it appeared to be in Chapter 2. While trade may benefit a nation as a whole, it often hurts significant groups within the country, at least in the short run.

Consider the effects of Japan's rice policy. Japan allows very little rice to be imported, even though the scarcity of land means that rice is much more expensive to produce in Japan than in other countries (including the United States). There is little question that Japan as a whole would have a higher standard of living if free imports of rice were allowed. Japanese rice farmers, however, would be hurt by free trade. While the farmers displaced by imports could probably find jobs in manufacturing or services in Japan's full employment economy, they would find changing employment costly and inconvenient. Furthermore, the value of the land that the farmers own would fall along with the price of rice. Not surprisingly, Japanese rice farmers are vehemently opposed to free trade in rice, and their organized political opposition has counted for more than the potential gains from trade for the nation as a whole.

A realistic analysis of trade must go beyond the Ricardian model to models in which trade can affect income distribution. This chapter concentrates on a particular model, known as the specific factors model, that brings income distribution into the story in a particularly clear way. ⬮

The Specific Factors Model

The **specific factors model** was developed by Paul Samuelson and Ronald Jones.[1] Like the simple Ricardian model, it assumes an economy that produces two goods and that can allocate its labor supply between the two sectors. Unlike the Ricardian model, however, the specific factors model allows for the existence of factors of production besides labor. Whereas labor is a **mobile factor** that can move between sectors, these other factors are assumed to be **specific**. That is, they can be used only in the production of particular goods.

Assumptions of the Model

Imagine an economy that can produce two goods, manufactures and food. Instead of one factor of production, however, the country has *three:* labor (L), capital (K), and land (T for *terrain*). Manufactures are produced using capital and labor (but not land), while food is produced using land and labor (but not capital). Labor is therefore a *mobile* factor that can be used in either sector, while land and capital are both *specific* factors that can be used only in the production of one good.

How much of each good does the economy produce? The economy's output of manufactures depends on how much capital and labor are used in that sector. This relationship is summarized by a **production function** that tells us the quantity of manufactures that can be produced given any input of capital and labor. The production function for manufactures can be summarized algebraically as

$$Q_M = Q_M(K, L_M), \qquad (3\text{-}1)$$

where Q_M is the economy's output of manufactures, K is the economy's capital stock, and L_M is the labor force employed in manufactures. Similarly, for food we can write the production function

$$Q_F = Q_F(T, L_F), \qquad (3\text{-}2)$$

[1]Paul Samuelson, "Ohlin Was Right," *Swedish Journal of Economics* 73 (1971), pp. 365–384: and Ronald W. Jones, "A Three-Factor Model in Theory, Trade, and History," in Jagdish Bhagwati et al., eds., *Trade, Balance of Payments, and Growth* (Amsterdam: North-Holland, 1971), pp. 3–21.

WHAT IS A SPECIFIC FACTOR?

In the model developed in this chapter, we assume that there are two factors of production, land and capital, which are permanently tied to particular sectors of the economy. In advanced economies, however, agricultural land receives only a small part of national income. When economists apply the specific factors model to economies like that of the United States or France, they typically think of factor specificity not as a permanent condition but as a matter of time. For example, the vats used to brew beer and the stamping presses used to build auto bodies cannot be substituted for each other, and so these different kinds of equipment are industry-specific. Given time, however, it is possible to redirect investment from auto factories to breweries or vice versa, and so in a long-term sense both vats and stamping presses can be considered to be two manifestations of a single, mobile factor called capital.

In practice, then, the distinction between specific and mobile factors is not a sharp line. It is a question of the speed of adjustment, with factors more specific the longer it takes to redeploy them between industries. So how specific are the factors of production in the real economy?

Workers who have fairly general skills, as opposed to highly specific training, seem to be quite mobile, if not quite as mobile as labor in the model. One useful clue comes from the time it takes labor to move between geographic locations. One influential study finds that when a U.S. state hits economic difficulties, workers quickly begin leaving for other states; within six years the unemployment rate falls back to the national average.* This compares with a lifetime of 15 or 20 years for a typical specialized machine, and perhaps 50 years for a shopping mall or office building. So labor is certainly a less specific factor than most kinds of capital. On the other hand, highly trained workers are pretty much stuck with their craft: A brain surgeon might have made a pretty good violinist, but she cannot switch careers in mid-life.

*Olivier Blanchard and Lawrence Katz, "Regional Evolutions," *Brookings Papers on Economic Activity,* 1991.

---

where Q_F is the economy's output of food, T is the economy's supply of land, and L_F is the labor force devoted to food production. For the economy as a whole, the labor employed must equal the total labor supply L:

$$L_M + L_F = L. \tag{3-3}$$

Production Possibilities

The specific factors model assumes that each of the specific factors capital and land can be used in only one sector, manufactures and food, respectively. Only labor can be used in either sector. Thus to analyze the economy's production possibilities, we need only to ask how the economy's mix of output changes as labor is shifted from one sector to the other. This can be done graphically, first by representing the production functions (3-1) and (3-2), then by putting them together to derive the production possibility frontier.

Figure 3-1 illustrates the relationship between labor input and output of manufactures. The larger the input of labor, for a given capital supply, the larger will be output. In Figure 3-1, the slope of $Q_M(K, L_M)$ represents the **marginal product of labor**, that is, the addition to output generated by adding one more person-hour. However, if labor input is

Figure 3-1 | The Production Function for Manufactures

The more labor that is employed in the production of manufactures, the larger the output. As a result of diminishing returns, however, each successive person-hour increases output by less than the previous one; this is shown by the fact that the curve relating labor input to output gets flatter at higher levels of employment.

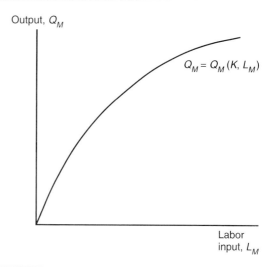

Output, Q_M

$Q_M = Q_M(K, L_M)$

Labor input, L_M

increased without increasing capital as well, there will normally be **diminishing returns**: Because adding a worker means that each worker has less capital to work with, each successive increment of labor will add less to production than the last. Diminishing returns are reflected in the shape of the production function: $Q_M(K,L_M)$ gets flatter as we move to the right, indicating that the marginal product of labor declines as more labor is used. Figure 3-2 shows the same information a different way. In this figure we directly plot the marginal product of labor as a function of the labor employed. (In the appendix to this chapter we show that the area under the marginal product curve represents the total output of manufactures.)

A similar pair of diagrams can represent the production function for food. These diagrams can then be combined to derive the production possibility frontier for the economy, as illustrated in Figure 3-3. As we saw in Chapter 2, the **production possibility frontier** shows what the economy is capable of producing; in this case it shows how much food it can produce for any given output of manufactures and vice versa.

Figure 3-3 is a four-quadrant diagram. In the lower right quadrant we show the production function for manufactures illustrated in Figure 3-1. This time, however, we turn the figure on its side: A movement downward along the vertical axis represents an increase in the labor input to the manufactures sector, while a movement to the right along the horizontal axis represents an increase in the output of manufactures. In the upper left quadrant we show the corresponding production function for food; this part of the figure is also flipped around, so that a movement to the left along the horizontal axis indicates an increase in labor input to the food sector, while an upward movement along the vertical axis indicates an increase in food output.

The lower left quadrant represents the economy's allocation of labor. Both quantities are measured in the reverse of the usual direction. A downward movement along the vertical axis indicates an increase in the labor employed in manufactures; a leftward movement

Figure 3-2 | The Marginal Product of Labor

The marginal product of labor in the manufactures sector, equal to the slope of the production function shown in Figure 3-1, is lower the more labor the sector employs.

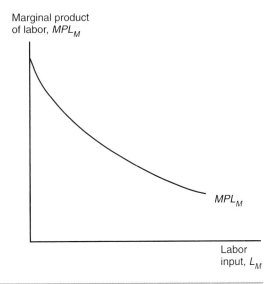

along the horizontal axis indicates an increase in labor employed in food. Since an increase in employment in one sector must mean that less labor is available for the other, the possible allocations are indicated by a downward sloping line. This line, labeled AA, slopes downward at a 45-degree angle, that is, it has a slope of -1. To see why this line represents the possible labor allocations, notice that if all labor were employed in food production, L_F would equal L, while L_M would equal 0. If one were then to move labor gradually into the manufacturing sector, each person-hour moved would increase L_M by one unit while reducing L_F by one unit, tracing a line with a slope of -1, until all the entire labor supply L was employed in manufactures. Any particular allocation of labor between the two sectors can then be represented by a point on AA, such as point 2.

We can now see how to determine production given any particular allocation of labor between the two sectors. Suppose that the allocation of labor were represented by point 2 in the lower left quadrant, that is, with L_M^2 hours in manufacturing and L_F^2 hours in food. Then we can use the production function for each sector to determine output: Q_M^2 units are produced in manufacturing, Q_F^2 in food. Using these coordinates Q_M^2, Q_F^2, point 2′ in the upper right quadrant of Figure 3-3 shows the resulting output of manufactures and food.

To trace the whole production possibility frontier, we simply imagine repeating this exercise for many alternative allocations of labor. We might start with most of the labor allocated to food production, as at point 1 in the lower left quadrant, then gradually increase the amount of labor used in manufactures until very few workers are employed in food, as at point 3; the corresponding points in the upper right quadrant will trace out the curve running from 1′ to 3′. Thus PP in the upper right quadrant shows the economy's production possibilities for given supplies of land, labor, and capital.

In the Ricardian model, where labor is the only factor of production, the production possibility frontier is a straight line because the opportunity cost of manufactures in terms of

Figure 3-3 | The Production Possibility Frontier in the Specific Factors Model

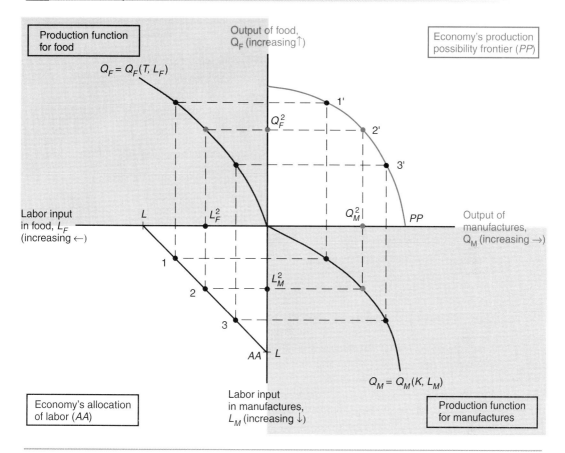

Production of manufactures and food is determined by the allocation of labor. In the lower left quadrant, the allocation of labor between sectors can be illustrated by a point on the line AA, which represents all combinations of labor input to manufactures and food that sum up to the total labor supply L. Corresponding to any particular point on AA, such as point 2, is a labor input to manufactures (L_M^2) and a labor input to food (L_F^2). The curves in the lower-right and upper-left quadrants represent the production functions for manufactures and food, respectively; these allow determination of output (Q_M^2, Q_F^2) given labor input. Then in the upper-right quadrant the curve PP shows how the output of the two goods varies as the allocation of labor is shifted from food to manufactures, with the output points $1', 2', 3'$ corresponding to the labor allocations $1, 2, 3$. Because of diminishing returns, PP is a bowed-out curve instead of a straight line.

food is constant. In the specific factors model, however, the addition of other factors of production changes the shape of the production possibility frontier PP to a curve. The curvature of PP reflects diminishing returns to labor in each sector; these diminishing returns are the crucial difference between the specific factors and the Ricardian models.

Notice that when tracing PP we shift labor from the food to the manufacturing sector. If we shift one person-hour of labor from food to manufactures, however, this extra input will increase output in that sector by the marginal product of labor in manufactures, MPL_M. To increase manufactures output by one unit, then, we must increase labor input by $1/MPL_M$ hours. Meanwhile, each unit of labor input shifted out of food production will lower output in that sector by the marginal product of labor in food, MPL_F. To increase output of manufactures by one unit, then, the economy must reduce output of food by MPL_F/MPL_M units. The slope of PP, which measures the opportunity cost of manufactures in terms of food—that is, the number of units of food output that must be sacrificed to increase manufactures output by one unit—is therefore

$$\text{Slope of production possibilities curve} = -MPL_F/MPL_M.$$

We can now see why PP has the bowed shape it does. As we move from $1'$ to $3'$, L_M rises and L_F falls. We saw in Figure 3-2, however, that as L_M rises, the marginal product of labor in manufactures falls; correspondingly, as L_F falls, the marginal product of labor in food rises. So PP gets steeper as we move down it to the right.

We have now shown how output is determined, given the allocation of labor. The next step is to ask how a market economy determines the allocation of labor.

Prices, Wages, and Labor Allocation

How much labor will be employed in each sector? To answer this we need to look at supply and demand in the labor market. The demand for labor in each sector depends on the price of output and the wage rate. In turn, the wage rate depends on the combined demand for labor by food and manufactures. Given the prices of manufactures and food together with the wage rate, we can determine each sector's employment and output.

First, let us focus on the demand for labor. In each sector, profit-maximizing employers will demand labor up to the point where the value produced by an additional person-hour equals the cost of employing that hour. In the manufacturing sector, for example, the value of an additional person-hour is the marginal product of labor in manufacturing multiplied by the price of one unit of manufactures: $MPL_M \times P_M$. If w is the wage rate of labor, employers will therefore hire workers up to the point where

$$MPL_M \times P_M = w. \tag{3-4}$$

But the marginal product of labor in manufacturing, already illustrated in Figure 3-2, slopes downward because of diminishing returns. So for any given price of manufactures P_M, the value of that marginal product, $MPL_M \times P_M$, will also slope down. We can therefore think of equation (3-4) as defining the demand curve for labor in manufactures: If the wage rate falls, other things equal, employers in the manufacturing sector will want to hire more workers.

Similarly, the value of an additional person-hour in food is $MPL_F \times P_F$. The demand curve for labor in the food sector may therefore be written

$$MPL_F \times P_F = w. \tag{3-5}$$

Figure 3-4 | The Allocation of Labor

Labor is allocated so that the value of its marginal product ($P \times MPL$) is the same in manufactures and food. In equilibrium, the wage rate is equal to the value of labor's marginal product.

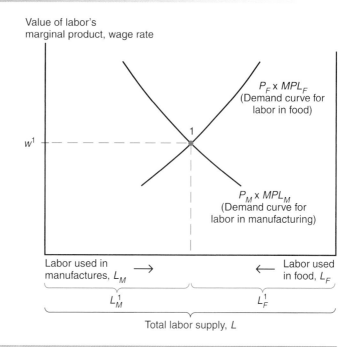

Value of labor's marginal product, wage rate

$P_F \times MPL_F$
(Demand curve for labor in food)

$P_M \times MPL_M$
(Demand curve for labor in manufacturing)

w^1

1

Labor used in manufactures, L_M $\rightarrow$

$\leftarrow$ Labor used in food, L_F

L_M^1

L_F^1

Total labor supply, L

The wage rate w must be the same in both sectors, because of the assumption that labor is freely mobile between sectors. That is, because labor is a mobile factor, it will move from the low-wage sector to the high-wage sector until wages are equalized. The wage rate, in turn, is determined by the requirement that total labor demand (total employment) equal total labor supply:

$$L_M + L_F = L. \tag{3-6}$$

By representing these three equations in a diagram (Figure 3-4), we can see how the wage rate and employment in each sector are determined given the prices of food and manufactures. Along the horizontal axis of Figure 3-4 we show the total labor supply L. Measuring from the left of the diagram, we show the value of the marginal product of labor in manufactures, which is simply the MPL_M curve from Figure 3-2 multiplied by P_M. This is the demand curve for labor in the manufacturing sector. Measuring from the right, we show the value of the marginal product of labor in food, which is the demand for labor in food. The equilibrium wage rate and allocation of labor between the two sectors is represented by point 1. At the wage rate w^1 the sum of labor demanded by manufactures (L_M^1) and food (L_F^1) just equals the total labor supply L.

There is a useful relationship between relative prices and output that emerges clearly from this analysis of labor allocation; this relationship applies to more general situations than that described by the specific factors model. Equations (3-4) and (3-5) imply that

Figure 3-5 | Production in the Specific Factors Model

The economy produces at the point on its production possibility frontier (*PP*) where the slope of that frontier equals minus the relative price of manufactures.

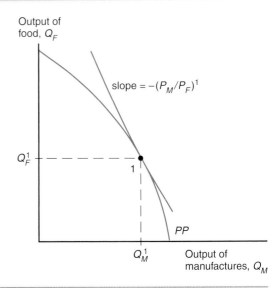

$$MPL_M \times P_M = MPL_F \times P_F = w$$

or, rearranging, that

$$-MPL_F/MPL_M = -P_M/P_F. \tag{3-7}$$

The left side of equation (3-7) is the slope of the production possibility frontier at the actual production point; the right side is minus the relative price of manufactures. This result tells us that *at the production point the production possibility frontier must be tangent to a line whose slope is minus the price of manufactures divided by that of food.* The result is illustrated in Figure 3-5: If the relative price of manufactures is $(P_M/P_F)^1$ the economy produces at point 1.

What happens to the allocation of labor and the distribution of income when the prices of food and manufactures change? Notice that any price change can be broken into two parts: an equal proportional change in both P_M and P_F, and a change in only one price. For example, suppose that the price of manufactures rises 17 percent and the price of food rises 10 percent. We can analyze the effects of this by first asking what happens if manufactures and food prices both rise by 10 percent, then by finding out what happens if manufactures prices rise by 7 percent. This allows us to separate the effect of changes in the overall price level from the effect of changes in relative prices.

An Equal Proportional Change in Prices.   Figure 3-6 shows the effect of an equal proportional increase in P_M and P_F. P_M rises from P_M^1 to P_M^2; P_F rises from P_F^1 to P_F^2. If both goods' prices increase by 10 percent, the labor demand curves will both shift up by 10 percent as well. As you can see from the diagram, these shifts lead to a 10 percent increase in

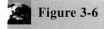 **Figure 3-6** | An Equal Proportional Increase in the Prices of Manufactures and Food

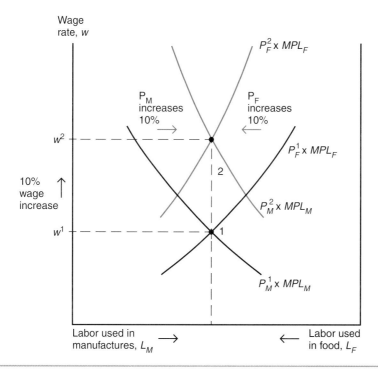

The labor demand curves in manufactures and food both shift up in proportion to the rise in P_M from P_M^1 to P_M^2 and the rise in P_F from P_F^1 to P_F^2. The wage rate rises in the same proportion, from w^1 to w^2, but the allocation of labor between the two sectors does not change.

the wage rate from w^1 (point 1) to w^2 (point 2). The allocation of labor between the sectors and the outputs of the two goods do not change.

In fact, when P_M and P_F change in the same proportion, no real changes occur. The wage rate rises in the same proportion as the prices, so *real* wage rates, the ratios of the wage rate to the prices of goods, are unaffected. With the same amount of labor employed in each sector, receiving the same real wage rate, the real incomes of capital owners and landowners also remain the same. So everyone is in exactly the same position as before. This illustrates a general principle: Changes in the overall price level have no real effects, that is, do not change any physical quantities in the economy. Only changes in relative prices—which in this case means the price of manufactures relative to food, P_M/P_F—affect welfare or the allocation of resources.

A Change in Relative Prices.   Consider the effect of a price change that *does* affect relative prices. Figure 3-7 shows the effect of a change in the price of only one good, in this case a 7 percent rise in P_M from P_M^1 and P_M^2. The increase in P_M shifts the manufacturing labor demand curve in the same proportion as the price increase and shifts the equilibrium

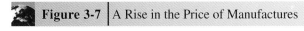

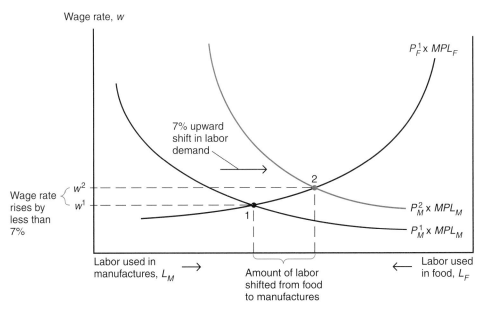

The manufacturing labor demand curve rises in proportion to the 7 percent increase in P_M, but the wage rate rises less than proportionately. Output of manufactures rises; output of food falls.

from point 1 to point 2. Notice two important facts about the results of this shift. First, although the wage rate rises, it rises by *less* than the increase in the price of manufactures. This can be seen by comparing Figures 3-6 and 3-7. In Figure 3-6, which represents the results of a 10 percent increase in both P_M and P_F, we saw that w increased by 10 percent as well. If only P_M increases, w clearly rises by less—say 5 percent.

Second, when only P_M rises, in contrast to the case of a simultaneous rise in P_M and P_F, labor shifts from the food sector to the manufacturing sector and the output of manufactures rises while that of food falls. (This is why w does not rise as much as P_M: Because manufacturing employment rises, the marginal product of labor in that sector falls.)

The effect of a rise in the relative price of manufactures can also be seen directly by looking at the production possibility curve. In Figure 3-8, we show the effects of the same rise in the price of manufactures, which raises the *relative* price of manufactures from $(P_M/P_F)^1$ to $(P_M/P_F)^2$. The production point, which is always located where the slope of PP equals minus the relative price, shifts from 1 to 2. Food output falls and manufactures output rises as a result of the rise in the relative price of manufactures.

Since higher relative prices of manufactures lead to higher output of manufactures relative to that of food, we can draw a relative supply curve showing Q_M/Q_F as a function of P_M/P_F. This relative supply curve is shown as RS in Figure 3-9. As we showed in Chapter 2, we can also draw a relative demand curve, which is illustrated by the downward-sloping

Figure 3-8 | The Response of Output to a Change in the Relative Price of Manufactures

The economy always produces at the point on its production possibility frontier (*PP*) where the slope of *PP* equals minus the relative price of manufactures. Thus an increase in P_M/P_F causes production to move down and to the right along the production possibilities frontier corresponding to higher output of manufactures and lower output of food.

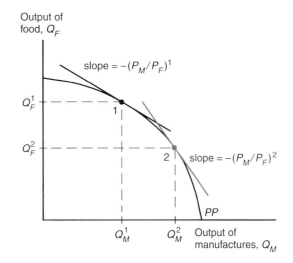

line *RD*. The equilibrium relative price $(P_M/P_F)^1$ and output $(Q_M/Q_F)^1$ are determined by the intersection of *RS* and *RD*.

Relative Prices and the Distribution of Income

So far we have examined the following aspects of the specific factors model: (1) the determination of production possibilities given an economy's resources and technology and (2) the determination of resource allocation, production, and relative prices in a market economy. Before turning to the effects of international trade we must consider the effect of changes in relative prices on the distribution of income.

Look again at Figure 3-7, which shows the effect of a rise in the price of manufactures. We have already noted that the demand curve for labor in the manufacturing sector will shift upward in proportion to the rise in P_M, so that if P_M rises by 10 percent, the curve defined by $P_M \times MPL_M$ also rises by 10 percent. We have also seen that unless the price of food also rises by at least 10 percent, w will rise by *less* than P_M. Thus if manufacturing prices rise by 10 percent, we would expect the wage rate to rise by only, say, 5 percent.

Let's look at what this outcome implies for the incomes of three groups: workers, owners of capital, and owners of land. Workers find that their wage rate has risen, but less than in proportion to the rise in P_M. Thus their real wage in terms of manufactures, w/P_M, falls, while their real wage in terms of food, w/P_F, rises. Given this information, we cannot say whether workers are better or worse off; this depends on the relative importance of manufactures and food in workers' consumption, a question that we will not pursue further.

Owners of capital, however, are definitely better off. The real wage rate in terms of manufactures has fallen, so that the profits of capital owners in terms of what they produce rises.

Figure 3-9 | Determination of Relative Prices

In the specific factors model a higher relative price of manufactures will lead to an increase in the output of manufactures relative to that of food. Thus the relative supply curve *RS* is upward sloping. Equilibrium relative quantities and prices are determined by the intersection of *RS* with the relative demand curve *RD*.

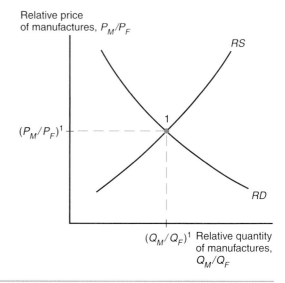

That is, the income of capital owners will rise more than proportionately with the rise in P_M. Since P_M in turn has risen relative to P_F, the income of capitalists has clearly gone up in terms of both goods.

Conversely, landowners are definitely worse off. They lose for two reasons: The real wage in terms of food rises, squeezing their income, and the rise in manufactures prices reduces the purchasing power of any given income.

International Trade in the Specific Factors Model

Now that we know how the specific factors model works for a single economy, we can turn to an analysis of international trade. Imagine that two countries, Japan and America, trade with each other; let's examine the effects of this trade on their welfare.

For trade to take place, the two countries must differ in the relative price of manufactures that would prevail in the absence of trade. In Figure 3-9 we saw how P_M/P_F is determined in a single economy in the absence of trade. Japan and America could have different relative prices of manufactures either because they differ in their relative demand or because they differ in their relative supply. We will assume away demand differences: that is, we assume that at any given P_M/P_F, relative demand is the same in the two countries. If both countries face the same relative price of manufactures, they will consume food and manufactures in the same proportions. Thus both countries will have the same relative demand curve. We will therefore focus on differences in relative supply as the source of international trade.

Why might relative supply differ? The countries could have different technologies, as in the Ricardian model. Now that our model has more than one factor of production,

Figure 3-10 | Changing the Capital Stock

An increase in the capital stock raises the marginal product of labor in manufactures for any given level of employment. This raises the demand for labor in the manufacturing sector, which drives up the overall wage rate. Because labor is pulled out of the food sector, output of manufactures rises, while output of food falls.

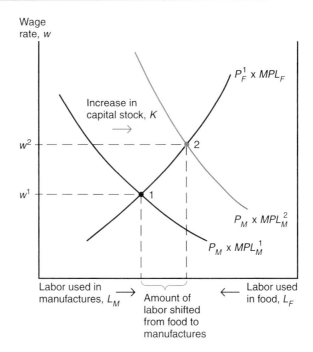

however, the countries could also differ in their resources. It is worth examining how differences in resources can affect relative supply.

Resources and Relative Supply

The basic relationship between resources and relative supply is straightforward: A country with a lot of capital and not much land will tend to produce a high ratio of manufactures to food at any given prices, while a country with a lot of land and not much capital will do the reverse. Consider what would happen if one of the countries experienced an increase in the supply of some resource. Suppose, for example, that Japan were to increase its capital stock. The effects of such an increase are shown in Figure 3-10.

Other things equal, an increase in the quantity of capital would raise the marginal productivity of labor in the manufacturing sector. Thus the demand curve for labor in manufacturing would shift to the right, from $P_M \times MPL_M^1$ to $P_M \times MPL_M^2$. At any given prices of manufactures and food, this increase in demand for manufacturing labor would shift the equilibrium from point 1 to point 2. More workers would be drawn into the manufacturing sector out of the food sector. Manufacturing output would rise, for two reasons: There would be more workers in the sector and they would have more capital to work with. Food output would fall because of reduced labor input. So at any given relative price of manufactures, the relative output of manufactures would rise. We therefore conclude that an increase in the supply of capital would shift the relative supply curve to the right.

Figure 3-11 | Trade and Relative Prices

In the figure, Japan is assumed to have more capital per worker than America, while America has more land per worker than Japan. As a result, Japan's relative supply curve lies to the right of America's. When the two economies trade, the *world* relative supply curve RS_{WORLD} lies between the two national curves, and the equilibrium world relative price of manufactures—determined by the intersection of RS_{WORLD} with the relative demand curve RD_{WORLD}—lies between the levels of P_M/P_F that would have prevailed in the two countries in the absence of trade.

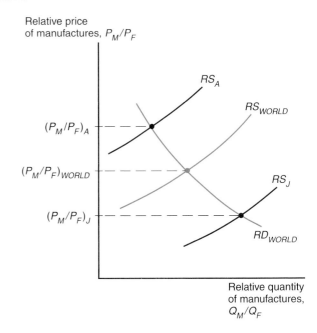

Correspondingly, an increase in the supply of land would increase food output and reduce manufacturing output; the relative supply curve would shift left.

What about the effect of an increase in the labor force? This is a less clear-cut case. To induce employers to hire the additional workers, the wage rate must fall. This will lead to increased employment and output of *both* manufactures and food; the effect on relative output is ambiguous.

Suppose, however, that America and Japan have the same labor force, but that Japan has a larger supply of capital than America, while America has a larger supply of land than Japan. Then the situation will look like that in Figure 3-11. Japan's relative supply curve RS_J lies to the right of America's curve RS_A, because Japan's abundance of capital and scarcity of land leads it to produce a large quantity of manufactures and relatively little food at any given relative price of manufactures, whereas the reverse is true for America.

Trade and Relative Prices

In this model, as always, international trade leads to a convergence of relative prices, illustrated in Figure 3-11. Since relative demand is the same in Japan and America, RD_{WORLD} is both each country's relative demand curve and the world relative demand curve when the two countries trade. RS_J and RS_A represent the relative supply curves of Japan and America, respectively. Japan is assumed to be relatively well-endowed with capital and poorly endowed with land, while America is the reverse, so RS_J lies to the right of RS_A. The pretrade relative price of manufactures in Japan, $(P_M/P_F)_J$, is lower than the pretrade relative price in America, $(P_M/P_F)_A$.

When the two countries open trade, they create an integrated world economy whose production of manufactures and food is the sum of the national outputs of the two goods. The world relative supply of manufactures (RS_{WORLD}) lies between the relative supplies in the two countries. The world relative price of manufactures, $(P_M/P_F)_{WORLD}$, therefore lies between the national pretrade prices. Trade has increased the relative price of manufactures in Japan and has lowered it in America.

The Pattern of Trade

If trade occurs initially because of differences in relative prices of manufactures, how does the convergence of P_M/P_F translate into a pattern of international trade? To answer this question, we need to state some basic relationships among prices, production, and consumption.

In a country that cannot trade, the output of a good must equal its consumption. If D_M is consumption of manufactures and D_F consumption of food, then in a closed economy $D_M = Q_M$ and $D_F = Q_F$. International trade makes it possible for the mix of manufactures and food consumed to differ from the mix produced. While the amounts of each good that a country consumes and produces may differ, however, a country cannot spend more than it earns: The *value* of consumption must be equal to the value of production. That is,

$$P_M \times D_M + P_F \times D_F = P_M \times Q_M + P_F \times Q_F. \tag{3-8}$$

Equation (3-8) can be rearranged to yield the following:

$$D_F - Q_F = (P_M/P_F) \times (Q_M - D_M). \tag{3-9}$$

$D_F - Q_F$ is the economy's food *imports,* the amount by which its consumption of food exceeds its production. The right-hand side of the equation is the product of the relative price of manufactures and the amount by which production of manufactures exceeds consumption, that is, the economy's *exports* of manufactures. The equation, then, states that imports of food equal exports of manufactures times the relative price of manufactures. While it does not tell us how much the economy will import or export, the equation does show that the amount the economy can afford to import is limited, or constrained, by the amount it exports. Equation (3-9) is therefore known as a **budget constraint**.[2]

Figure 3-12 illustrates two important features of the budget constraint for a trading economy. First, the slope of the budget constraint is minus P_M/P_F, the relative price of manufactures. The reason is that consuming one less unit of manufactures saves the economy P_M; this is enough to purchase P_M/P_F extra units of food. Second, the budget constraint is tangent to the production possibility frontier at the point that represents the economy's

---

[2]The constraint that the value of consumption equals that of production (or, equivalently, that imports equal exports in value) may not hold when countries can borrow from other countries or lend to them. For now we assume that these possibilities are not available and that the budget constraint (equation (3-9)) therefore holds. International borrowing and lending are examined in Chapter 7, which shows that an economy's consumption *over time* is still constrained by the necessity of paying its debts to foreign lenders.

Figure 3-12 │ The Budget Constraint for a Trading Economy

Point 1 represents the economy's production. The economy's consumption must lie along a line that passes through point 1 and has a slope equal to minus the relative price of manufactures.

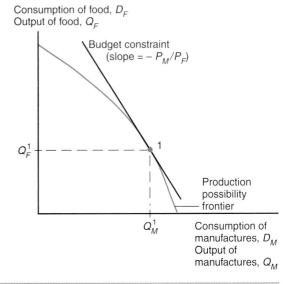

choice of production given the relative price of manufactures, shown in the figure as point 1. That is, the economy can always afford to consume what it produces.

We can now use the budget constraints of Japan and America to construct a picture of the trading equilibrium. In Figure 3-13, we show the outputs, budget constraints, and consumption choices of Japan and America at equilibrium prices. In Japan, the rise in the relative price of manufactures leads to a rise in the consumption of food relative to manufactures and a fall in the relative output of food. Japan produces Q_F^J of food but consumes D_F^J; it therefore becomes a manufactures exporter and a food importer. In America, the post-trade fall in the relative price of manufactures leads to a rise in the consumption of manufactures relative to food and a fall in the relative output of manufactures; America therefore becomes a manufactures importer and a food exporter. In equilibrium Japan's exports of manufacturers must exactly equal America's imports and Japan's imports of food exactly equal America's exports. The qualities are shown by the equality of the two colored triangles in Figure 3-13.

Income Distribution and the Gains From Trade

We have seen how production possibilities are determined by resources and technology; how the choice of what to produce is determined by the relative price of manufactures; how changes in the relative price of manufactures affect the real incomes of different factors of production; and how trade affects both relative prices and the economy's budget constraint. Now we can ask the crucial question: Who gains and who loses from international trade?

Figure 3-13 | Trading Equilibrium

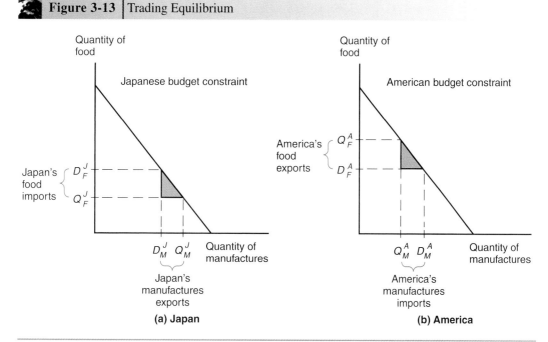

Japan's imports of food are exactly equal to America's exports, and America's imports of manufactures are exactly equal to Japan's exports.

We begin by asking how the welfare of particular groups is affected, and then how trade affects the welfare of the country as a whole.

To assess the effects of trade on particular groups, the key point is that international trade shifts the relative price of manufactures and food. Consider first what happens in Japan. We are assuming that in the absence of trade Japan would have had a lower relative price of manufactures than the rest of the world. If this is the case, trade, which leads to a convergence of relative prices, will mean a rise in P_M/P_F. In Japan, then (as we saw in the previous section), the result of a rise in P_M/P_F is that owners of capital are better off, workers experience an ambiguous shift in their position, and landowners are worse off.

In America, the effect of trade on relative prices is just the reverse: The relative price of manufactures falls. So in America landowners are better off and capital owners worse off, and the effect on workers is once again ambiguous.

The general outcome, then, is simple: *Trade benefits the factor that is specific to the export sector of each country but hurts the factor specific to the import-competing sectors, with ambiguous effects on mobile factors.*

Do the gains from trade outweigh the losses? One way you might try to answer this question would be to sum up the gains of the winners and the losses of the losers and compare them. The problem with this procedure is that we are comparing welfare, an inherently subjective thing. Suppose that capitalists are dull people who get hardly any satisfaction

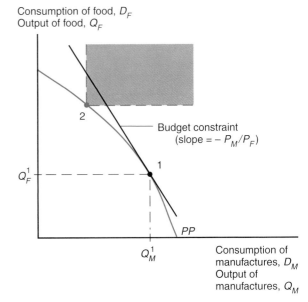

Figure 3-14 | Trade Expands the Economy's Consumption Possibilities

Before trade, economy's production and consumption were at point 2 on its production possibilities frontier (*PP*). After trade, the economy can consume at any point on its budget constraint. The portion of the budget constraint in the colored region consists of feasible post-trade consumption choices with consumption of both goods higher than at the pretrade point 2.

out of increased consumption, while landowners are bons vivants who get immense pleasure out of it. Then one might well imagine that trade reduces the total amount of pleasure in Japan. But the reverse could equally be true. More to the point, it is outside the province of what we normally think of as economic analysis to try to figure out how much enjoyment individuals get out of their lives.

A better way to assess the overall gains from trade is to ask a different question: Could those who gain from trade compensate those who lose, and still be better off themselves? If so, then trade is *potentially* a source of gain to everyone.

To illustrate that trade is a source of potential gain for everyone, we proceed in three steps:

1. First, we notice that in the absence of trade the economy would have to produce what it consumed, and vice versa. Thus the *consumption* of the economy in the absence of trade would have to be a point on the *production* possibility frontier. In Figure 3-14, a typical pretrade consumption point is shown as point 2.

2. Next, we notice that it is possible for a trading economy to consume more of *both* goods than it would have in the absence of trade. The budget constraint in Figure 3-14 represents all the possible combinations of food and manufactures that the country could consume given the world relative price of manufactures. Part of that budget constraint— the part in the colored region—represents situations in which the economy consumes more of both manufactures and food than it could in the absence of trade. Notice that this result does not depend on the assumption that pretrade production and consumption was at point 2; unless pretrade production was at point 1, so that trade has no effect on production at all, there is always a part of the budget constraint that allows consumption of more of both goods.

3. Finally, observe that if the economy as a whole consumes more of both goods, then it is possible in principle to give each *individual* more of both goods. This would make everyone better off. This shows, then, that it is possible to ensure that everyone is better off as a result of trade. Of course, everyone might be still better off if they had less of one good and more of the other, but this only reinforces the conclusion that everyone can potentially gain from trade.

The fundamental reason why trade potentially benefits a country is that it *expands the economy's choices.* This expansion of choice means that it is always possible to redistribute income in such a way that everyone gains from trade.[3]

That everyone *could* gain from trade unfortunately does not mean that everyone actually does. In the real world, the presence of losers as well as winners from trade is one of the most important reasons why trade is not free.

The Political Economy of Trade: A Preliminary View

Trade often produces losers as well as winners. This insight is crucial to understanding the considerations that actually determine trade policy in the modern world economy. Trade policy is examined in detail in Chapters 8 through 11; it is possible, however, to take a preliminary view at this point.

There are two ways to look at trade policy (or any government policy): (1) Given its objectives, what *should* the government do? What is its *optimal* trade policy? (2) What are governments likely to do in practice? The income distribution effects of trade are important to the first way of looking at the issue and are crucial to the second.

Optimal Trade Policy

Suppose a government wants to maximize the welfare of its population. If everyone were exactly the same in tastes and in income there would be a straightforward solution: The government would choose policies that make the representative individual as well off as possible. In this homogeneous economy, free international trade would clearly serve the government's objective.

When people are not exactly alike, however, the government's problem is less well-defined. The government must somehow weigh one person's gain against another person's loss. If, for example, the Japanese government is relatively more concerned about hurting landowners than about helping capitalists, then international trade, which in our analysis benefited capital owners and hurt landowners in Japan, might be a bad thing from the Japanese government's point of view.

---

[3]The argument that trade is beneficial because it enlarges an economy's choices is much more general than this picture. For a thorough discussion see Paul Samuelson, "The Gains from International Trade Once Again," *Economic Journal* 72 (1962), pp. 820–829.

There are many reasons why one group might matter more than another, but one of the most compelling reasons is that some groups need special treatment because they are already relatively poor. There is widespread sympathy in the United States for restrictions on imports of garments and shoes, even though the restrictions raise consumer prices, because workers in these industries are already poorly paid. The gains that affluent consumers would realize if more imports were allowed do not matter as much to the U.S. public as the losses low-paid shoe and garment workers would suffer.

Does this mean that trade should be allowed only if it doesn't hurt lower-income people? Few international economists would agree. In spite of the real importance of income distribution, most economists remain strongly in favor of more or less free trade. There are three main reasons why economists do *not* generally stress the income distribution effects of trade:

1. Income distribution effects are not specific to international trade. Every change in a nation's economy, including technological progress, shifting consumer preferences, exhaustion of old resources and discovery of new ones, and so on, affects income distribution. If every change in the economy were allowed only after it had been examined for its distributional effects, economic progress could easily end up snarled in red tape.

2. It is always better to allow trade and compensate those who are hurt by it than to prohibit the trade. (This applies to other forms of economic change as well.) All modern industrial countries provide some sort of "safety net" of income support programs (such as unemployment benefits and subsidized retraining and relocation programs) that can cushion the losses of groups hurt by trade. Economists would argue that if this cushion is felt to be inadequate, more support rather than less trade is the right answer.

3. Those who stand to lose from increased trade are typically better organized than those who stand to gain. This imbalance creates a bias in the political process that requires a counterweight. It is the traditional role of economists to strongly support free trade, pointing to the overall gains; those who are hurt usually have little trouble making their complaints heard.

Most economists, then, while acknowledging the effects of international trade on income distribution, believe that it is more important to stress the potential gains from trade than the possible losses to some groups in a country. Economists do not, however, often have the deciding voice in economic policy, especially when conflicting interests are at stake. Any realistic understanding of how trade policy is determined must look at the actual motivations of policy.

Income Distribution and Trade Politics

It is easy to see why groups that lose from trade lobby their governments to restrict trade and protect their incomes. You might expect that those who gain from trade would lobby as strongly as those who lose from it, but this is rarely the case. In the United States and in most countries, those who want trade limited are more effective politically than those who want it extended. Typically, those who gain from trade in any particular product are a much less concentrated, informed, and organized group than those who lose.

A good example of this contrast between the two sides is the U.S. sugar industry. The United States has limited imports of sugar for many years; at the time of writing the price of

SPECIFIC FACTORS AND THE BEGINNINGS OF TRADE THEORY

The modern theory of international trade began with the demonstration by David Ricardo, writing in 1817, that trade is mutually beneficial to countries. We studied Ricardo's model in Chapter 2. Ricardo used his model to argue for free trade, in particular for an end to the tariffs that restricted England's imports of food. Yet almost surely the British economy of 1817 was better described by a specific factors model than by the one-factor model Ricardo presented.

To understand the situation, recall that from the beginning of the French Revolution in 1789 until the defeat of Napoleon at Waterloo in 1815, Britain was almost continuously at war with France. This war interfered with Britain's trade: Privateers (pirates licensed by foreign governments) raided shipping and the French attempted to impose a blockade on British goods. Since Britain was an exporter of manufactures and an importer of agricultural products, this limitation of trade raised the relative price of food in Britain. The profits of manufacturers suffered, but landowners actually prospered during the long war.

After the war, food prices in Britain fell. To avoid the consequences, the politically influen-tial landowners were able to get legislation, the so-called Corn Laws, that imposed fees to discourage importation of grain. It was against these Corn Laws that Ricardo was arguing.

Ricardo knew that repeal of the Corn Laws would make capitalists better off but landowners worse off. From his point of view this was all to the good; a London businessman himself, he preferred hard-working capitalists to idle landed aristocrats. But he chose to present his argument in the form of a model that assumed away issues of internal income distribution.

Why did he do this? Almost surely the answer is political: While Ricardo was in reality to some extent representing the interest of a single group, he emphasized the gains to the nation as a whole. This was a clever and thoroughly modern strategy, one that pioneered the use of economic theory as a political instrument. Then as now, politics and intellectual progress are not incompatible: The Corn Laws were repealed more than a century and a half ago, yet Ricardo's model of trade remains one of the great insights in economics.

sugar in the U.S. market was about twice its price in the world market. Most estimates put the cost of U.S. consumers of this import limitation at about $2 billion a year—that is, about $8 a year for every man, woman, and child. The gains to producers are much smaller, probably less than half as large.

If producers and consumers were equally able to get their interests represented, this policy would never have been enacted. In absolute terms, however, each consumer suffers very little. Eight dollars a year is not much; furthermore, most of the cost is hidden, because most sugar is consumed as an ingredient in other foods rather than purchased directly. Thus most consumers are unaware that the import quota even exists, let alone that it reduces their standard of living. Even if they were aware, $8 is not a large enough sum to provoke people into organizing protests and writing letters to their congressional representatives.

The sugar producers' situation is quite different. The average sugar producer gains thousands of dollars a year from the import quota. Furthermore, sugar producers are organized into trade associations and cooperatives that actively pursue their members' political interests. So the complaints of sugar producers about the effects of imports are loudly and effectively expressed.

As we will see in Chapters 8 through 11, the politics of import restriction in the sugar industry are an extreme example of a kind of political process that is common in international trade. That world trade in general became steadily freer from 1945 to 1980 depended, as we will see in Chapter 9, on a special set of circumstances that controlled what is probably an inherent political bias against international trade.

Summary

1. International trade often has strong effects on the distribution of income within countries, so that it often produces losers as well as winners. Income distribution effects arise for two reasons: Factors of production cannot move instantaneously and costlessly from one industry to another, and changes in an economy's output mix have differential effects on the demand for different factors of production.
2. A useful model of income distribution effects of international trade is the *specific factors model,* which allows for a distinction between general-purpose factors that can move between sectors and factors that are specific to particular uses. In this model, differences in resources can cause countries to have different relative supply curves, and thus cause international trade.
3. In the specific factors model, factors specific to export sectors in each country gain from trade, while factors specific to import-competing sectors lose. Mobile factors that can work in either sector may either gain or lose.
4. Trade nonetheless produces overall gains in the limited sense that those who gain could in principle compensate those who lose while still remaining better off than before.
5. Most economists do not regard the effects of international trade on income distribution as a good reason to limit this trade. In its distributional effects, trade is no different from many other forms of economic change, which are not normally regulated. Furthermore, economists would prefer to address the problem of income distribution directly, rather than by interfering with trade flows.
6. Nonetheless, in the actual politics of trade policy income distribution is of crucial importance. This is true in particular because those who lose from trade are usually a much more informed, cohesive, and organized group than those who gain.

Key Terms

budget constraint, p. 53

diminishing returns, p. 41

marginal product of labor, p. 40

mobile factor, p. 39

production function, p. 39

production possibility frontier, p. 41

specific factor, p. 39

specific factors model, p. 39

Problems

1. In 1986, the price of oil on world markets dropped sharply. Since the United States is an oil-importing country, this was widely regarded as good for the U.S. economy. Yet in Texas and Louisiana 1986 was a year of economic decline. Why?

2. An economy can produce good 1 using labor and capital and good 2 using labor and land. The total supply of labor is 100 units. Given the supply of capital, the outputs of the two goods depends on labor input as follows:

Labor Input to Good 1	Output of Good 1	Labor Input to Good 2	Output of Good 2
0	0.0	0	0.0
10	25.1	10	39.8
20	38.1	20	52.5
30	48.6	30	61.8
40	57.7	40	69.3
50	66.0	50	75.8
60	73.6	60	81.5
70	80.7	70	86.7
80	87.4	80	91.4
90	93.9	90	95.9
100	100	100	100

a. Graph the production functions for good 1 and good 2.
b. Graph the production possibility frontier. Why is it curved?

3. The marginal product of labor curves corresponding to the production functions in problem 2 are as follows:

Workers Employed	MPL in Sector 1	MPL in Sector 2
10	1.51	1.59
20	1.14	1.05
30	0.97	0.82
40	0.87	0.69
50	0.79	0.61
60	0.74	0.54
70	0.69	0.50
80	0.66	0.46
90	0.63	0.43
100	0.60	0.40

a. Suppose that the price of good 2 relative to that of good 1 is 2. Determine graphically the wage rate and the allocation of labor between the two sectors.
b. Using the graph drawn for problem 2, determine the output of each sector. Then confirm graphically that the slope of the production possibility frontier at that point equals the relative price.
c. Suppose that the relative price of good 2 falls to 1. Repeat (a) and (b).
d. Calculate the effects of the price change on the income of the specific factors in sectors 1 and 2.

4. In the text we examined the impacts of increases in the supply of capital and land. But what if the mobile factor, labor, increases in supply?

a. Analyze the qualitative effects of an increase in the supply of labor in the specific factors model, holding the prices of both goods constant.

b. Graph the effect on the equilibrium for the numerical example in problems 2 and 3, given a relative price of 1, when the labor force expands from 100 to 140.

Further Reading

Avinash Dixit and Victor Norman. *Theory of International Trade.* Cambridge: Cambridge University Press, 1980. The problem of establishing gains from trade when some people may be made worse off has been the subject of a long debate. Dixit and Norman show it is always possible in principle for a country's government to use taxes and subsidies to redistribute income in such a way that everyone is better off with free trade than with no trade.

Michael Mussa. "Tariffs and the Distribution of Income: The Importance of Factor Specificity, Substitutability, and Intensity in the Short and Long Run." *Journal of Political Economy* 82 (1974), pp. 1191–1204. An extension of the specific factors model that relates it to the factor proportions model of Chapter 4.

J. Peter Neary. "Short-Run Capital Specificity and the Pure Theory of International Trade." *Economic Journal* 88 (1978), pp. 488–510. A further treatment of the specific factors model that stresses how differing assumptions about mobility of factors between sectors affect the model's conclusions.

Mancur Olson. *The Logic of Collective Action.* Cambridge: Harvard University Press, 1965. A highly influential book that argues the proposition that in practice government policies favor small, concentrated groups over large ones.

David Ricardo. *The Principles of Political Economy and Taxation.* Homewood, IL: Irwin, 1963. While Ricardo's *Principles* emphasizes the national gains from trade at one point, elsewhere in his book the conflict of interest between landowners and capitalists is a central issue.

APPENDIX TO CHAPTER 3

Further Details on Specific Factors

The specific factors model developed in this chapter is such a convenient tool of analysis that we take the time here to spell out some of its details more fully. We give a fuller treatment of two related issues: (1) the relationship between marginal and total product within each sector; (2) the income distribution effects of relative price changes.

Marginal and Total Product

In the text we illustrated the production function in manufacturing two different ways. In Figure 3-1 we showed total output as a function of labor input, holding capital constant. We then observed that the slope of that curve is the marginal product of labor and illustrated that marginal product in Figure 3-2. We now want to demonstrate that the total output is measured by the area under the marginal product curve. (Students who are familiar with calculus will find this obvious: Marginal product is the derivative of total, so total is the integral of marginal. Even for these students, however, an intuitive approach can be helpful.)

In Figure 3A-1 we show once again the marginal product curve in manufacturing. Suppose that we employ L_M person-hours. How can we show the total output of manufactures? Let's approximate this using the marginal product curve. First, let's ask what would happen if we used slightly fewer person-hours, say dL_M fewer. Then output would be less. The fall in output would be approximately

$$dL_M \times MPL_M,$$

that is, the reduction in the work force times the marginal product of labor at the initial level of employment. This reduction in output is represented by the area of the colored rectangle in Figure 3A-1. Now subtract another few person-hours; the output loss will be another rectangle. This time the rectangle will be taller, because the marginal product of labor rises as the quantity of labor falls. If we continue this process until all the labor is gone, our approximation of the total output loss will be the sum of all the rectangles shown in the figure. When no labor is employed, however, output will fall to zero. So we can approximate the total output of the manufacturing sector by the sum of the areas of all the rectangles under the marginal product curve.

This is, however, only an approximation, because we used the marginal product of only the first person-hour in each batch of labor removed. We can get a better approximation if we take smaller groups—the smaller the better. As the groups of labor removed get infinitesimally small, however, the rectangles get thinner and thinner, and we approximate ever more closely the total area under the marginal product curve. In the end, then, we find that the total output of manufactures produced with labor L_M is equal to the area under the marginal product of labor curve MPL_M up to L_M.

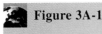

Figure 3A-1 | Showing that Output Is Equal to the Area Under the Marginal Product Curve

By approximating the marginal product curve with a series of thin rectangles, one can show that the total output of manufactures is equal to the area under the curve.

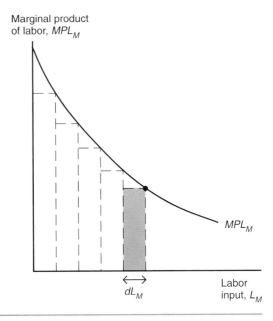

Relative Prices and the Distribution of Income

Figure 3A-2 uses the result we just found to show the distribution of income within the manufacturing sector for a given real wage. We know that employers will hire labor up to the point where the real wage in terms of manufactures, w/P_M, equals the marginal product. We can immediately read off the graph the total output to manufactures as the area under the marginal product curve. We can also read off the graph the part of manufacturing output that is paid out as wages, which is equal to the real wage times employment, and thus to the area of the rectangle shown. The part of the output that is kept by owners of capital, then, is the remainder. We can determine the distribution of food production between labor and landowners in the same way.

Suppose the relative price of manufactures now rises. We saw in Figure 3-7 that a rise in P_M/P_F lowers the real wage in terms of manufactures while raising it in terms of food. The effects of this on the income of capitalists and landowners can be seen in Figures 3A-3 and 3A-4. In the manufactures sector, the real wage is shown as falling from $(w/P_M)^1$ to $(w/P_M)^2$; as a result capitalists receive increased income. In the food sector, the real wage rises from $(w/P_F)^1$ to $(w/P_F)^2$, and landowners receive less income.

This effect on incomes is reinforced by the change in P_M/P_F itself. Owners of capital receive more income *in terms of manufactures;* their purchasing power is further increased by the rise in the price of manufactures relative to food. Landowners receive less income *in terms of food;* they are made still worse off because of the rise in the relative price of manufactures.

Figure 3A-2 The Distribution of Income Within the Manufacturing Sector

Labor income is equal to the real wage times employment. The rest of output accrues as income to the owners of capital.

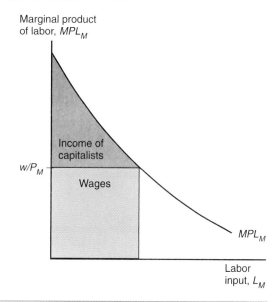

Figure 3A-3 A Rise in P_M Benefits the Owners of Capital

The real wage in terms of manufactures falls, leading to a rise in the income of capital owners.

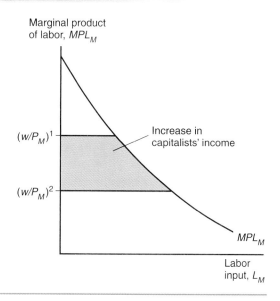

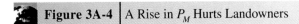

Figure 3A-4 | A Rise in P_M Hurts Landowners

The real wage in terms of food rises,
reducing the income of land.

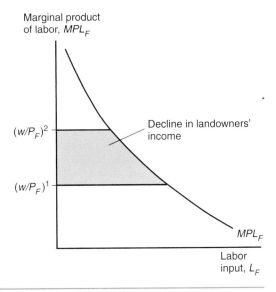

Marginal product
of labor, MPL_F

$(w/P_F)^2$

$(w/P_F)^1$

Decline in landowners'
income

MPL_F

Labor
input, L_F

CHAPTER 4

Resources and Trade: The Heckscher-Ohlin Model

If labor were the only factor of production, as the Ricardian model assumes, comparative advantage could arise only because of international differences in labor productivity. In the real world, however, while trade is partly explained by differences in labor productivity, it also reflects differences in countries' *resources*. Canada exports forest products to the United States not because its lumberjacks are more productive relative to their U.S. counterparts than other Canadians but because sparsely populated Canada has more forested land per capita than the United States. A realistic view of trade must allow for the importance not just of labor, but of other factors of production such as land, capital, and mineral resources.

To explain the role of resource differences in trade, this chapter examines a model in which resource differences are the *only* source of trade. This model shows that comparative advantage is influenced by the interaction between nations' resources (the relative **abundance** of factors of production) and the technology of production (which influences the relative **intensity** with which different factors of production are used in the production of different goods). The same idea was present in the specific factors model of Chapter 3, but the model we study in this chapter puts the interaction between abundance and intensity in sharper relief.

That international trade is largely driven by differences in countries' resources is one of the most influential theories in international economics. Developed by two Swedish economists, Eli Heckscher and Bertil Ohlin (Ohlin received the Nobel Prize in economics in 1977), the theory is often referred to as the **Heckscher-Ohlin theory**. Because the theory emphasizes the interplay between the proportions in which different factors of production are available in different countries and the proportions in which they are used in producing different goods, it is also referred to as the **factor-proportions theory**.

To develop the factor-proportions theory we begin by describing an economy that does not trade, then ask what happens when two such economies trade with each other. Since the factor-proportions theory is both an important theory and a controversial one, the chapter concludes with a discussion of the empirical evidence for and against the theory.

A Model of a Two-Factor Economy

The simplest factor-proportions model is in many ways very similar to the specific factors model developed in Chapter 3. As in that model, it is assumed that each economy is able to produce two goods and that production of each good requires the use of two factors of production. In this case, however, we no longer assume that one of the factors used in each industry is specific to that industry. Instead, the *same* two factors are used in both sectors. This leads to a somewhat more difficult model, but also to some important new insights.

Assumptions of the Model

The economy we are analyzing can produce two goods: cloth (measured in yards) and food (measured in calories). Production of these goods requires two inputs that are in limited supply: labor, which we measure in hours, and land, which we measure in acres. Let us define the following expressions:

a_{TC} = acres of land used to produce one yard of cloth
a_{LC} = hours of labor used to produce one yard of cloth
a_{TF} = acres of land used to produce one calorie of food
a_{LF} = hours of labor used to produce one calorie of food
L = economy's supply of labor
T = economy's supply of land

Notice that we speak in these definitions of the quantity of land or labor *used* to produce a given amount of food or cloth, rather than the amount *required* to produce that amount. The reason for this change from the Ricardian model is that in a two-factor economy there may be some room for choice in the use of inputs. A farmer, for example, may be able to grow more food per acre if he or she is willing to use more labor input to prepare the soil, weed, and so on. Thus the farmer may be able to choose to use less land and more labor per unit of output. In each sector, then, producers will face not fixed input requirements (as in the Ricardian model) but trade-offs like the one illustrated by curve *II* in Figure 4-1, which shows alternative input combinations that can be used to produce one calorie of food.

What input choice will producers actually make? It depends on the relative cost of land and labor. If land rents are high and wages low, farmers will choose to produce using relatively little land and a lot of labor; if rents are low and wages high, they will save on labor and use a lot of land. If w is the wage rate per hour of labor and r the cost of one acre of land, then the input choice will depend on the ratio of these two **factor prices**, w/r.[1] The relationship between factor prices and the ratio of land to labor use in production of food is shown in Figure 4-2 as the curve *FF*.

There is a corresponding relationship between w/r and the land-labor ratio in cloth production. This relationship is shown in Figure 4-2 as the curve *CC*. As drawn, *CC* lies to the left of *FF* indicating that at any given factor prices production of food will always use a higher ratio of land to labor than production of cloth. When this is true, we say that production of food is *land-intensive,* while production of cloth is *labor-intensive.* Notice

---

[1]The optimal choice of the land-labor ratio is explored at greater length in the appendix to this chapter.

Figure 4-1 | Input Possibilities in Food Production

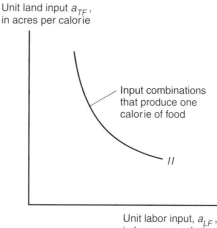

A farmer can produce a calorie of food with less land if he or she uses more labor, and vice versa.

Unit land input a_{TF}, in acres per calorie

Input combinations that produce one calorie of food

II

Unit labor input, a_{LF}, in hours per calorie

that the definition of intensity depends on the ratio of land to labor used in production, not the ratio of land or labor to output. Thus a good cannot be both land- and labor-intensive.

Factor Prices and Goods Prices

Suppose for a moment that the economy produces both cloth and food. (This need not be the case if the economy engages in international trade, because it might specialize completely in producing one good or the other; but let us temporarily ignore this possibility.) Then competition among producers in each sector will ensure that the price of each good equals its cost of production. The cost of producing a good depends on factor prices: If the rental rate on land is higher, then other things equal the price of any good whose production involves land input will also have to be higher.

The importance of a particular factor price to the cost of producing a good depends, however, on how much of that factor the good's production involves. If cloth production makes use of very little land, then a rise in the price of land will not have much effect on the price of cloth; whereas if food production uses a great deal of land, a rise in land prices will have a large effect on its price. We can therefore conclude that there is a one-to-one relationship between the ratio of the wage rate to the rental rate, w/r, and the ratio of the price of cloth to that of food, P_C/P_F. This relationship is illustrated by the upward-sloping curve SS in Figure 4-3.[2]

It is possible to put Figures 4-2 and 4-3 together. In Figure 4-4, the left panel is Figure 4-3 (of the SS curve) turned on its side, while the right panel reproduces Figure 4-2.

---

[2] The relationship between goods prices and factor prices was clarified in a classic paper by Wolfgang Stolper and Paul Samuelson, "Protection and Real Wages," *Review of Economic Studies* 9 (1941), pp. 58–73, and is therefore known as the *Stolper-Samuelson effect*.

Figure 4-2 | Factor Prices and Input Choices

In each sector, the ratio of land to labor used in production depends on the cost of labor relative to the cost of land, w/r. The curve FF shows the land-labor ratio choices in food production, the curve CC the corresponding choices in cloth production. At any given wage-rental ratio, food production uses a higher land-labor ratio; when this is the case, we say that food production is *land-intensive* and that cloth production is *labor-intensive*.

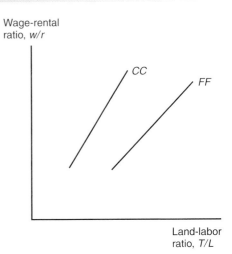

Figure 4-3 | Factor Prices and Goods Prices

Because cloth production is labor-intensive while food production is land-intensive, there is a one-to-one relationship between the factor price ratio w/r and the relative price of cloth P_C/P_F; the higher the relative cost of labor, the higher must be the relative price of the labor-intensive good. The relationship is illustrated by the curve SS.

By putting these two diagrams together, we see what may seem at first to be a surprising linkage of the prices of goods to the ratio of land to labor used in the production of each good. Suppose that the relative price of cloth is $(P_C/P_F)^1$ (left panel of Figure 4-4); if the economy produces both goods, the ratio of the wage rate to the rental rate on land must equal $(w/r)^1$. This ratio then implies that the ratios of land to labor employed in the production of cloth and food must be $(T_C/L_C)^1$ and $(T_F/L_F)^1$, respectively (right panel). If the relative price of cloth were to rise to the level indicated by $(P_C/P_F)^2$, the ratio of the wage rate

Figure 4-4 From Goods Prices to Input Choices

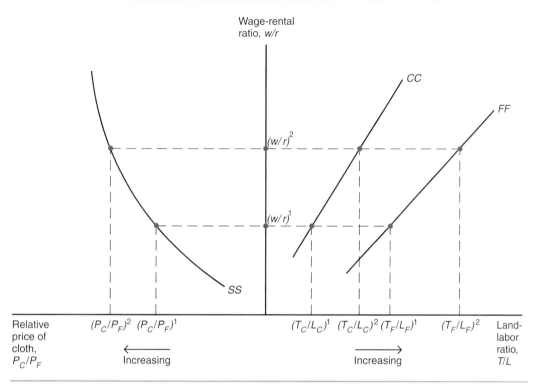

Given the relative price of cloth $(P_C/P_F)^1$, the ratio of the wage rate to the rental rate on land must equal $(w/r)^1$. This wage-rental ratio then implies that the ratios of land to labor employed in the production of cloth and food must be $(T_C/L_C)^1$ and $(T_F/L_F)^1$. If the relative price of cloth rises to $(P_C/P_F)^2$, the wage-rental ratio must rise to $(w/r)^2$. This will cause the land-labor ratio used in the production of both goods to rise.

to the rental rate on land would rise to $(w/r)^2$. Because land is now relatively cheaper the ratios of land to labor employed in the production of cloth and food would therefore rise to $(T_C/L_C)^2$ and $(T_F/L_F)^2$.

We can learn one more important lesson from this diagram. The left panel already tells us that an increase in the price of cloth relative to that of food will raise the income of workers relative to that of landowners. But it is possible to make a stronger statement: Such a change in relative prices will unambiguously raise the purchasing power of workers and lower the purchasing power of landowners, by raising real wages and lowering real rents in terms of *both* goods.

How do we know this? When P_C/P_F increases, the ratio of land to labor rises in both cloth and food production. But as we saw in Chapter 3, in a competitive economy factors of production are paid their marginal product—the real wage of workers in terms of cloth is equal to the marginal productivity of labor in cloth production, and so on. When the ratio of land to labor rises in producing either good, the marginal product of labor in terms of that good increases—so workers find their real wage higher in terms of both goods. On the other hand, the marginal product of land falls in both industries, so landowners find their real income lower in terms of both goods.

In this model, then, as in the specific factors model, changes in relative prices have strong effects on income distribution. Not only does a change in goods prices change the distribution of income; it always changes it so much that owners of one factor of production gain while owners of the other are made worse off.

Resources and Output

We can now complete the description of a two-factor economy by describing the relationship between goods prices, factor supplies, and output.

Suppose that we take the relative price of cloth as given. We know from Figure 4-4 that this determines the wage-rental ratio w/r, and thus the ratio of land to labor used in the production of both cloth and food. But the economy must fully employ its supplies of labor and land. It is this last condition that determines the allocation of resources between the two industries and, therefore, the economy's output.

A convenient way to analyze the allocation of resources in a two-factor economy is to use a "box diagram" like Figure 4-5. The width of the box represents the economy's total supply of labor; the height of the box its total supply of land. The allocation of resources between two industries can be represented by a single point within the box, such as point 1. We measure the use of labor and land in the cloth sector as the horizontal and vertical distances of such a point from O_C; thus at point 1 $O_C L_C$ is the labor used in cloth production and $O_C T_C$ is the land used in cloth production. We measure inputs into the food sector starting from the opposite corner: $O_F L_F$ is the labor, $O_F T_F$ the land used in food production.

How can we determine the location of this resource allocation point? From Figure 4-4 we know that given goods prices, we can determine the ratio of land to labor in cloth production, T_C/L_C. Draw a straight line from O_C whose slope equals that land-labor ratio, such as the line $O_C C$; point 1 must lie on this line. Similarly, the known land-labor ratio in food production determines the slope of another line, $O_F F$; point 1 must also lie on *this* line. ($O_F F$ is steeper than $O_C C$, because, as we saw earlier, the ratio of land to labor is higher in food than in cloth production.) Thus the economy's resource allocation is identified by the point at which the two lines representing land-labor ratios cross—here, at point 1.[3]

Given the prices of cloth and food and the supplies of land and labor, then, it is possible to determine how much of each resource the economy devotes to the production of each good; and thus also to determine the economy's output of each good. The next question is how these outputs change when the economy's resources change.

The initially surprising answer is shown in Figure 4-6, which shows what happens when the economy's supply of land is increased, holding both goods prices and the labor supply fixed. With the increased supply of land the box is taller. This means that inputs into food production can no longer be measured from O_F (now labeled O_F^1), but must be measured

---

[3]Some readers may notice that $O_C C$ and $O_F F$ need not intersect inside the box. What happens then? The answer is that in that case the economy specializes in producing only one good, and uses all its land and labor to produce that good. Remember that the relationship between goods prices and factor prices shown in Figures 4-3 and 4-4 depends on the assumption that the economy is producing both goods.

Figure 4-5 The Allocation of Resources

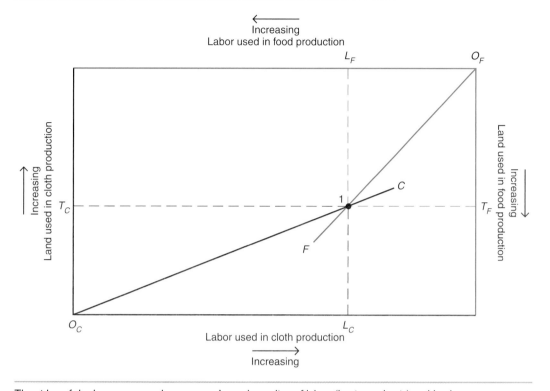

The sides of the box measure the economy's total supplies of labor (horizontal axis) and land (vertical axis). Inputs into cloth production are measured from the lower-left corner; inputs into food production from the upper-right corner. Given the land-labor ratio in cloth production, T_C/L_C, the cloth industry's employment of resources must lie on the line O_CC, which is a line drawn from the origin with the slope T_C/L_C. Similarly, the food industry's employment of resources must lie on the line O_FF. The allocation of resources can therefore be read off from point 1, where these lines intersect.

from the corner of the new, enlarged box, O_F^2, and the original line $O_F^1F^1$ must be replaced with $O_F^2F^2$. The resource allocation point must therefore move from 1 to 2.

What is surprising about this result? Notice that the quantities of labor and land used in cloth production actually *fall*, from L_C^1 and T_C^1 to L_C^2 and T_C^2. Thus an increase in the economy's supply of land will, holding prices constant, lead to a fall in the output of the labor-intensive good. What happens to the land and labor no longer used in cloth production? It is now used in the food sector, whose output must have risen more than proportionately to the increase in land supply; for example, if land supply were to rise by 10 percent, food output might rise by 15 or 20 percent.

The best way to think about this result is in terms of how resources affect the economy's production possibilities. In Figure 4-7 the curve TT^1 represents the economy's production

Figure 4-6 | An Increase in the Supply of Land

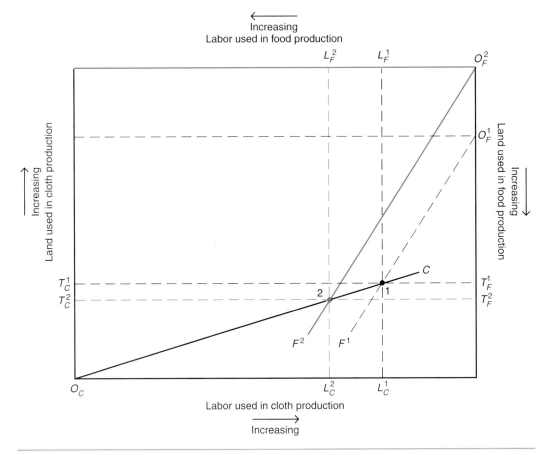

An increased land supply makes the box representing the economy's resources taller; resources allocated to food production must now be measured from O_F^2. If goods prices remain unchanged, and thus factor prices and land-labor ratios remain the same, resources allocation moves from point 1 to point 2, with more land and more labor devoted to food production. The output of clothing falls, while output of food rises more than proportionately to the increase in land supply.

possibilities before the increase in land supply. Output is at point 1, where the slope of the production possibility frontier equals minus the relative price of cloth, $-P_C/P_F$, and the economy produces Q_C^1 and Q_F^1 of cloth and food. The curve TT^2 shows the production possibility frontier after an increase in land supply. The production possibility frontier shifts out to TT_2, that is, the economy could produce more of both cloth and food than before. The outward shift of the frontier is, however, much larger in the direction of food than of clothing, that is, there is a **biased expansion of production possibilities** which occurs when the production possibility frontier shifts out much more in one direction than in the other. In this case, the expansion is so strongly biased toward food production that at unchanged relative

Figure 4-7 Resources and Production Possibilities

An increase in the supply of land shifts the economy's production possibility frontier outward from TT^1 to TT^2, but does so disproportionately in the direction of food production. The result is that at an unchanged relative price of cloth (indicated by the slope $-P_C/P_F$), cloth production actually declines from Q_C^1 to Q_C^2.

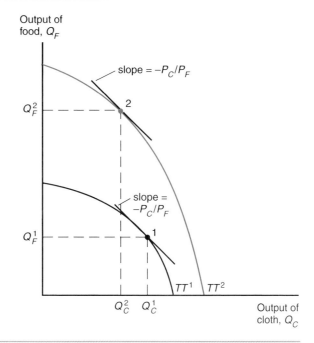

prices production moves from point 1 to point 2, which involves an actual fall in cloth output from Q_C^1 to Q_C^2 and a large increase in food output from Q_F^1 to Q_F^2.

The biased effect of increases in resources on production possibilities is the key to understanding how differences in resources give rise to international trade.[4] An increase in the supply of land expands production possibilities disproportionately in the direction of food production, while an increase in the supply of labor expands them disproportionately in the direction of cloth production. Thus an economy with a high ratio of land to labor will be relatively better at producing food than an economy with a low ratio of land to labor. *Generally, an economy will tend to be relatively effective at producing goods that are intensive in the factors with which the country is relatively well-endowed.*

Effects of International Trade Between Two-Factor Economies

Having outlined the production structure of a two-factor economy, we can now look at what happens when two such economies, Home and Foreign, trade. As always, Home and Foreign are similar along many dimensions. They have the same tastes and therefore have

---

[4]The biased effect of resource changes on production was pointed out in a paper by the Polish economist T. M. Rybczynski, "Factor Endowments and Relative Commodity Prices," *Economica* 22 (1955), pp. 336–341. It is therefore known as the *Rybczynski effect*.

identical relative demands for food and cloth when faced with the same relative price of the two goods. They also have the same technology: A given amount of land and labor yields the same output of either cloth or food in the two countries. The only difference between the countries is in their resources: Home has a higher ratio of labor to land than Foreign does.

Relative Prices and the Pattern of Trade

Since Home has a higher ratio of labor to land than Foreign, Home is *labor-abundant* and Foreign is *land-abundant.* Note that abundance is defined in terms of a ratio and not in absolute quantities. If America has 80 million workers and 200 million acres (a labor-to-land ratio of one-to-two-and-a-half), while Britain has 20 million workers and 20 million acres (a labor-to-land ratio of one-to-one) we consider Britain to be labor-abundant even though it has less total labor than America. "Abundance" is always defined in relative terms, by comparing the ratio of labor to land in the two countries, so that no country is abundant in everything.

Since cloth is the labor-intensive good, Home's production possibility frontier relative to Foreign's is shifted out more in the direction of cloth than in the direction of food. Thus, other things equal, Home tends to produce a higher ratio of cloth to food.

Because trade leads to a convergence of relative prices, one of the other things that will be equal is the price of cloth relative to food. Because the countries differ in their factor abundances, however, for any given ratio of the price of cloth to that of food Home will produce a higher ratio of cloth to food than Foreign will: Home will have a larger *relative supply* of cloth. Home's relative supply curve, then, lies to the right of Foreign's.

The relative supply schedules of Home (*RS*) and Foreign (*RS**) are illustrated in Figure 4-8. The relative demand curve, which we have assumed to be the same for both countries, is shown as *RD*. If there were no international trade, the equilibrium for Home would be at point 1, the equilibrium for Foreign at point 3. That is, in the absence of trade the relative price of cloth would be lower in Home than in Foreign.

When Home and Foreign trade with each other, their relative prices converge. The relative price of cloth rises in Home and declines in Foreign, and a new world relative price of cloth is established at a point somewhere between the pretrade relative prices, say at point 2. In Home, the rise in the relative price of cloth leads to a rise in the production of cloth and a decline in relative consumption, so Home becomes an exporter of cloth and an importer of food. Conversely, the decline in the relative price of cloth in Foreign leads it to become an importer of cloth and an exporter of food.

To sum up what we have learned about the pattern of trade: Home has a higher ratio of labor to land than Foreign; that is, Home is abundant in labor and Foreign is abundant in land. Cloth production uses a higher ratio of labor to land in its production than food; that is, cloth is labor-intensive and food is land-intensive. Home, the labor-abundant country, exports cloth, the labor-intensive good; Foreign, the land-abundant country, exports food, the land-intensive good. The general statement of the result is: *Countries tend to export goods whose production is intensive in factors with which they are abundantly endowed.*

Trade and the Distribution of Income

Trade produces a convergence of relative prices. Changes in relative prices, in turn, have strong effects on the relative earnings of labor and land. A rise in the price of cloth raises the

Figure 4-8 | Trade Leads to a Convergence of Relative Prices

In the absence of trade, Home's equilibrium would be at point 1, where domestic relative supply *RS* intersects the relative demand curve *RD*. Similarly, Foreign's equilibrium would be at point 3. Trade leads to a world relative price that lies between the pretrade prices, e.g., at point 2.

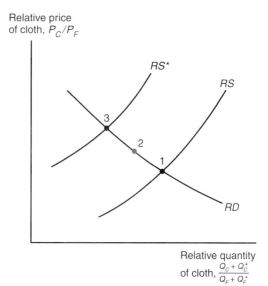

Relative price of cloth, P_C/P_F

Relative quantity of cloth, $\dfrac{Q_C + Q_C^*}{Q_F + Q_F^*}$

purchasing power of labor in terms of both goods while lowering the purchasing power of land in terms of both goods. A rise in the price of food has the reverse effect. Thus international trade has a powerful effect on income distribution. In Home, where the relative price of cloth rises, people who get their income from labor gain from trade but those who derive their income from land are made worse off. In Foreign, where the relative price of cloth falls, the opposite happens: Laborers are made worse off and landowners are made better off.

The resource of which a country has a relatively large supply (labor in Home, land in Foreign) is the **abundant factor** in that country, and the resource of which it has a relatively small supply (land in Home, labor in Foreign) is the **scarce factor**. The general conclusion about the income distribution effects of international trade is: *Owners of a country's abundant factors gain from trade, but owners of a country's scarce factors lose.*

This conclusion is similar to the one reached in our analysis of the case of specific factors. There we found that factors of production that are "stuck" in an import-competing industry lose from the opening of trade. Here we find that factors of production that are used intensively by the import-competing industry are hurt by the opening of trade. As a practical matter, however, there is an important difference between these two views. The specificity of factors to particular industries is often only a temporary problem: Garment makers cannot become computer manufacturers overnight, but given time the U.S. economy can shift its manufacturing employment from declining sectors to expanding ones. Thus income distribution effects that arise because labor and other factors of production are immobile represent a temporary, transitional problem (which is not to say that such effects are not painful to those who lose). In contrast, effects of trade on the distribution of income among land, labor, and capital are more or less permanent.

We will see shortly that the trade pattern of the United States suggests that compared with the rest of the world the United States is abundantly endowed with highly skilled labor and that low-skilled labor is correspondingly scarce. This means that international trade tends to make low-skilled workers in the United States worse off—not just temporarily, but on a sustained basis. The negative effect of trade on low-skilled workers poses a persistent political problem. Industries that use low-skilled labor intensively, such as apparel and shoes, consistently demand protection from foreign competition, and their demands attract considerable sympathy because low-skilled workers are relatively badly off to begin with.

The distinction between income distribution effects due to immobility and those due to differences in factor intensity also reveals that there is frequently a conflict between short-term and long-term interests in trade. Consider a highly skilled U.S. worker who is employed in an industry that is intensive in low-skilled labor. Her short-term interest is to restrict international trade, because she cannot instantly shift jobs. Over the long term, however, she would be better off with free trade, which will raise the income of skilled workers generally.

Factor Price Equalization

In the absence of trade, labor would earn less in Home than in Foreign, and land would earn more. Without trade, labor-abundant Home would have a lower relative price of cloth than land-abundant Foreign, and the difference in relative prices of *goods* implies an even larger difference in the relative prices of *factors.*

When Home and Foreign trade, the relative prices of goods converge. This convergence, in turn, causes convergence of the relative prices of land and labor. Thus there is clearly a tendency toward **equalization of factor prices**. How far does this tendency go?

The surprising answer is that in the model the tendency goes all the way. International trade leads to complete equalization of factor prices. Although Home has a higher ratio of labor to land than Foreign, once they trade with each other the wage rate and the rent on land are the same in both countries. To see this, refer back to Figure 4-3, which shows that given the prices of cloth and food we can determine the wage rate and the rental rate without reference to the supplies of land and labor. If Home and Foreign face the same relative prices of cloth and food, they will also have the same factor prices.

To understand how this equalization occurs, we have to realize that when Home and Foreign trade with each other more is happening than a simple exchange of goods. In an indirect way the two countries are in effect trading factors of production. Home lets Foreign have the use of some of its abundant labor, not by selling the labor directly but by trading goods produced with a high ratio of labor to land for goods produced with a low labor-land ratio. The goods that Home sells require more labor to produce than the goods it receives in return; that is, more labor is *embodied* in Home's exports than in its imports. Thus Home exports its labor, embodied in its labor-intensive exports. Conversely, Foreign's exports embody more land than its imports, thus Foreign is indirectly exporting its land. When viewed this way, it is not surprising that trade leads to equalization of the two countries' factor prices.

Although this view of trade is simple and appealing, there is a major problem: In the real world factor prices are *not* equalized. For example, there is an extremely wide range of

Table 4-1	Comparative International Wage Rates (United States = 100)

Country	Hourly compensation of production workers, 2000
United States	100
Germany	121
Japan	111
Spain	55
South Korea	41
Portugal	24
Mexico	12
Sri Lanka*	2

*1969

Source: Bureau of Labor Statistics, *Foreign Labor Statistics Home Page.*

wage rates across countries (Table 4-1). While some of these differences may reflect differences in the quality of labor, they are too wide to be explained away on this basis alone.

To understand why the model doesn't give us an accurate prediction, we need to look at its assumptions. Three assumptions crucial to the prediction of factor price equalization are in reality certainly untrue. These are the assumptions that (1) both countries produce both goods; (2) technologies are the same; and (3) trade actually equalizes the prices of goods in the two countries.

1. To derive the wage and rental rates from the prices of cloth and food in Figure 4-3, we assumed that the country produced both goods. This need not, however, be the case. A country with a very high ratio of labor to land might produce only cloth, while a country with a very high ratio of land to labor might produce only food. This implies that factor price equalization occurs only if the countries involved are sufficiently similar in their relative factor endowments. (A more thorough discussion of this point is given in the appendix to this chapter.) Thus, factor prices need not be equalized between countries with radically different ratios of capital to labor or of skilled to unskilled labor.

2. The proposition that trade equalizes factor prices will not hold if countries have different technologies of production. For example, a country with superior technology might have both a higher wage rate and a higher rental rate than a country with an inferior technology. As described later in this chapter, recent work suggests that it is essential to allow for such differences in technology to reconcile the factor proportions model with actual data on world trade.

3. Finally, the proposition of complete factor price equalization depends on complete convergence of the prices of goods. In the real world, prices of goods are not fully equalized by international trade. This lack of convergence is due to both natural barriers (such as transportation costs) and barriers to trade such as tariffs, import quotas, and other restrictions.

CASE STUDY

North-South Trade and Income Inequality

Between the late 1970s and the early 1990s there was a sharp increase in the inequality of wages in the United States. For example, while the real wage of male workers at the 90th percentile (i.e., those earning more than the bottom 90 percent but less than the top 10 percent) rose 15 percent between 1970 and 1989, that of workers at the 10th percentile fell by 25 percent over the same period. The growing inequality of wages in the United States has arguably worsened the country's social problems: Falling wages at the bottom have made it more difficult for families to climb out of poverty, while the contrast between stagnating incomes for many families and rapidly rising incomes at the top may have contributed to a general social and political malaise.

Why has wage inequality increased? Many observers attribute the change to the growth of world trade and in particular to the growing exports of manufactured goods from newly industrializing economies (NIEs), such as South Korea and China. Until the 1970s trade between advanced industrial nations and less-developed economies—often referred to as "North-South" trade because most advanced nations are still in the temperate zone of the Northern Hemisphere—consisted overwhelmingly of an exchange of Northern manufactures for Southern raw materials and agricultural goods, such as oil and coffee. From 1970 onward, however, former raw material exporters increasingly began to sell manufactured goods to high-wage countries like the United States. As Table 4-2 shows, between the early 1970s and the mid 1990s, developing countries dramatically changed the kinds of goods they exported, moving away from their traditional reliance on agricultural and mineral products to a focus on manufactured goods. While NIEs also provided a rapidly growing market for exports from the high-wage nations, the exports of the newly industrializing economies obviously differed greatly in factor intensity from their imports. Overwhelmingly, NIE exports to advanced nations consisted of clothing, shoes, and other relatively unsophisticated products whose production is intensive in unskilled labor, while advanced-country exports to the NIEs consisted of capital- or skill-intensive goods such as chemicals and aircraft.

To many observers the conclusion seemed straightforward: What was happening was a move toward factor price equalization. Trade between advanced countries that are abundant in capital and skill and NIEs with their abundant supply of unskilled labor was raising the wages of highly skilled workers and lowering the wages of less-skilled workers in the skill- and capital-abundant countries, just as the factor proportions model predicts.

Table 4-2 | Composition of Developing-Country Exports (Percent of Total)

	Agricultural Products	Mining Products	Manufactured Goods
1973	30	47.5	22
1995	14	22.5	62.5

Source: World Trade Organization

This is an argument with much more than purely academic significance. If one regards the growing inequality of income in advanced nations as a serious problem, as many people do, and if one also believes that growing world trade is the main cause of that problem, it becomes difficult to maintain the traditional support of economists for free trade. (As we pointed out in Chapter 3, in principle taxes and government payments can offset the effect of trade on income distribution, but one may argue that this is unlikely to happen in practice.) Some influential commentators have argued that advanced nations will have to restrict their trade with low-wage countries if they want to remain basically middle-class societies.

While some economists believe that growing trade with low-wage countries has been the main cause of growing inequality of income in the United States, however, most empirical workers believed at the time of writing that international trade has been at most a contributing factor to that growth, and that the main causes lie elsewhere.[5] This skepticism rested on four main observations.

First, although advanced countries were exporting capital-intensive goods and importing labor-intensive goods, as of the early 1990s there had been virtually no change in the distribution of income between capital and labor; the share of compensation (wages plus benefits) in U.S. national income was the same (73 percent) in 1993 as it had been in 1973. So at most the trade story could apply to a shift in the distribution of income between skilled and unskilled workers, rather than between workers and capital.

Second, the factor proportions model says that international trade affects the income distribution via a change in relative goods prices. So if international trade was the main driving force behind growing income inequality, there ought to be clear evidence of a rise in the price of skill-intensive products compared with those of unskilled-labor-intensive goods. Studies of international price data, however, failed to find clear evidence of such a change in relative prices.

Third, the model predicts that relative factor prices should converge: If wages of skilled workers are rising and those of unskilled workers falling in the skill-abundant country, the reverse should be happening in the labor-abundant country. While data on wages and income distribution in the NIEs are poor, casual observation suggested that in many countries, notably in China, the reverse was true: Income inequality was increasing at least as rapidly in the NIEs as in the advanced countries, and skilled workers were doing very well.

Fourth, although trade between advanced countries and NIEs has grown rapidly, it still constitutes only a small percentage of total spending in the advanced nations. As a result, estimates of the "factor content" of this trade—the skilled labor exported, in effect, by advanced countries embodied in skill-intensive exports, and the unskilled labor, in effect, imported in labor-intensive exports—are still only a small fraction of the total supplies of skilled and unskilled labor. This suggests that these trade flows cannot have had a very large impact on income distribution.

What, then, *is* responsible for the growing gap between skilled and unskilled workers in the United States? The view of the majority is that the villain is not trade but technology, which has devalued less-skilled work. The view that trade is in fact the main explanation still has a number of adherents, however.

---

[5]Among the important entries in the discussion of the impact of trade on income distribution have been Robert Lawrence and Matthew Slaughter, "Trade and U.S. Wages: Giant Sucking Sound or Small Hiccup?" *Brookings Papers on Economic Activity* 1:1993; Jeffrey Sachs and Howard Shatz, "Trade and Jobs in U.S. Manufacturing," *Brookings Papers on Economic Activity* 1:1994; and Adrian Wood, *North-South Trade, Employment, and Income Inequality,* Oxford: Clarendon, 1994. For a survey of this debate and related issues, see Robert Lawrence, *Single World, Divided Nations: Globalization and OECD Labor Markets,* Paris: OECD, 1995.

Empirical Evidence on the Heckscher-Ohlin Model

Since the factor-proportions theory of trade is one of the most influential ideas in international economics, it has been the subject of extensive empirical testing.

Testing the Heckscher-Ohlin Model

Tests on U.S. Data.   Until recently, and to some extent even now, the United States has been a special case among countries. The United States was until a few years ago much wealthier than other countries, and U.S. workers visibly worked with more capital per person than their counterparts in other countries. Even now, although some Western European countries and Japan have caught up, the United States continues to be high on the scale of countries as ranked by capital-labor ratios.

One would expect, then, that the United States would be an exporter of capital-intensive goods and an importer of labor-intensive goods. Surprisingly, however, this was not the case in the 25 years after World War II. In a famous study published in 1953, the economist Wassily Leontief (winner of the Nobel Prize in 1973) found that U.S. exports were less capital-intensive than U.S. imports.[6] This result is known as the **Leontief paradox**. It is the single biggest piece of evidence against the factor-proportions theory.

Table 4-3 illustrates the Leontief paradox as well as other information about U.S. trade patterns. We compare the factors of production used to produce $1 million worth of 1962 U.S. exports with those used to produce the same value of 1962 U.S. imports. As the first two lines in the table show, Leontief's paradox was still present in that year: U.S. exports were produced with a lower ratio of capital to labor than U.S. imports. As the rest of the table shows, however, other comparisons of imports and exports are more in line with what one might expect. The U.S. exported products that were more *skilled* labor-intensive than its imports as measured by average years of education. We also tended to export products that were "technology-intensive," requiring more scientists and engineers per unit of sales. These observations are consistent with the position of the United States as a high-skill country, with a comparative advantage in sophisticated products.

Why, then, do we observe the Leontief paradox? No one is quite sure. A plausible explanation, however, might be the following: The United States has a special advantage in producing new products or goods made with innovative technologies such as aircraft and sophisticated computer chips. Such products may well be *less* capital-intensive than products whose technology has had time to mature and become suitable for mass production techniques. Thus the United States may be exporting goods that heavily use skilled labor and innovative entrepreneurship, while importing heavy manufactures (such as automobiles) that use large amounts of capital.[7]

---

[6] See Leontief, "Domestic Production and Foreign Trade: The American Capital Position Re-Examined," *Proceedings of the American Philosophical Society* 97 (1953), pp. 331–349.

[7] Recent studies point to the disappearance of the Leontief paradox by the early 1970s. For example, see Robert M. Stern and Keith E. Maskus, "Determinants of the Structure of U.S. Foreign Trade, 1958–76," *Journal of International Economics* 11 (May 1981), pp. 207–224. These studies show, however, the continuing importance of *human* capital in explaining U.S. exports.

Table 4-3 | Factor Content of U.S. Exports and Imports for 1962

	Imports	**Exports**
Capital per million dollars	$2,132,000	$1,876,000
Labor (person-years) per million dollars	119	131
Capital-labor ratio (dollars per worker)	$17,916	$14,321
Average years of education per worker	9.9	10.1
Proportion of engineers and scientists in work force	0.0189	0.0255

Source: Robert Baldwin, "Determinants of the Commodity Structure of U.S. Trade," *American Economic Review* 61 (March 1971), pp. 126–145.

Tests on Global Data.   More recently, economists have attempted to test the Heckscher-Ohlin model using data for a large number of countries. An important study by Harry P. Bowen, Edward E. Leamer, and Leo Sveikauskas[8] was based on the idea, described earlier, that trading goods is actually an indirect way of trading factors of production. Thus if we were to calculate the factors of production embodied in a country's exports and imports, we should find that a country is a net exporter of the factors of production with which it is relatively abundantly endowed, a net importer of those with which it is relatively poorly endowed.

Table 4-4 shows one of the key tests of Bowen et al. For a sample of 27 countries and 12 factors of production, the authors calculated the ratio of each country's endowment of each factor to the world supply. They then compared these ratios with each country's share of world income. If the factor-proportions theory was right, a country would always export factors for which the factor share exceeded the income share, import factors for which it was less. In fact, for two-thirds of the factors of production, trade ran in the predicted direction less than 70 percent of the time. This result confirms the Leontief paradox on a broader level: Trade often does not run in the direction that the Heckscher-Ohlin theory predicts.

Tests on North-South Trade.   Although the overall pattern of international trade does not seem to be very well accounted for by a pure Heckscher-Ohlin model, North-South trade in manufactures seems to fit the theory much better (as our case study on North-South trade and income distribution already suggested). Consider, for example, Table 4-5, which shows some elements of the trade between the United States and South Korea.

Clearly the goods that the United States exports to South Korea are very different from those it imports in return! And it is also clear that the U.S. exports tend to be sophisticated, skill-intensive products like scientific instruments, while South Korean exports are still largely simple products like shoes. One would therefore expect that the predictions of the Heckscher-Ohlin model might look considerably better when applied to North-South trade than they do for overall international trade. And this turns out to be true in most studies.[9]

---

[8] See Bowen, Leamer, and Sveikauskas, "Multicountry, Multifactor Tests of the Factor Abundance Theory," *American Economic Review* 77 (December 1987), pp. 791–809.

[9] See Adrian Wood, "Give Heckscher and Ohlin a Chance!" *Weltwirtschaftliches Archiv* 130 (January 1994), pp. 20–49.

Table 4-4	Testing the Heckscher-Ohlin Model

Factor of Production	Predictive Success*
Capital	0.52
Labor	0.67
Professional workers	0.78
Managerial workers	0.22
Clerical workers	0.59
Sales workers	0.67
Service workers	0.67
Agricultural workers	0.63
Production workers	0.70
Arable land	0.70
Pasture land	0.52
Forest	0.70

*Fraction of countries for which net exports of factor runs in predicted direction.

Source: Harry P. Bowen, Edward E. Leamer, and Leo Sveikauskas, "Multicountry, Multifactor Tests of the Factor Abundance Theory," *American Economic Review* 77 (December 1987), pp. 791–809.

Table 4-5	Trade Between the United States and South Korea, 1992 (million dollars)

Type of Product	U.S. Exports to South Korea	U.S. Imports from South Korea
Chemicals, plastics, pharmaceuticals	1340	105
Power-generating equipment	705	93
Professional and scientific instruments	512	96
Transport equipment other than road vehicles (mainly aircraft)	1531	78
Clothing and shoes	11	4203

Source: Statistical Abstract of the United States, 1994.

These findings do not, however, contradict the observation that overall the Heckscher-Ohlin model does not seem to work very well, because North-South trade in manufactures accounts for only about 10 percent of total world trade.

The Case of the Missing Trade.   In an influential recent paper, Daniel Trefler[10] points out a previously overlooked empirical problem with the Heckscher-Ohlin model. He notes that if one thinks about trade in goods as an indirect way of trading factors of

[10] Daniel Trefler, "The case of the missing trade and other mysteries," *American Economic Review,* 85 (December 1995), pp. 1029–1046.

production, this predicts not only the direction but the volume of that trade. Factor trade in general turns out to be much smaller than the Heckscher-Ohlin model predicts.

A large part of the reason for this disparity comes from a false prediction of large-scale trade in labor between rich and poor nations. Consider the United States, on one side, and China on the other. The United States has about 25 percent of world income but only about 5 percent of the world's workers; so a simple factor-proportions story would suggest that U.S. imports of labor embodied in trade should be huge, something like four times as large as the nation's own labor force. In fact, calculations of the factor content of U.S. trade show only small net imports of labor. Conversely, China has less than 3 percent of world income but approximately 15 percent of the world's workers; it therefore "should" export most of its labor via trade—but it does not.

Many trade economists now believe that this puzzle can be resolved only by dropping the Heckscher-Ohlin assumption that technologies are the same across countries. The way this resolution works is roughly as follows: if workers in the United States are much more efficient than those in China, then the "effective" labor supply in the United States is much larger compared with that of China than the raw data suggest—and hence the expected volume of trade between labor-abundant China and labor-scarce America is correspondingly less. As we pointed out earlier, technological differences across countries are also one likely explanation for the dramatic failure of factor-price equalization to hold, as documented in Table 4-1.

If one makes the working assumption that technological differences between countries take a simple multiplicative form—that is, that a given set of inputs produces only δ times as much in China as it does in the United States, where δ is some number less than 1—it is possible to use data on factor trade to estimate the relative efficiency of production in different countries. Table 4-6 shows Trefler's estimates for a sample of countries; they suggest that technological differences are in fact very large.

But in any case, once we conclude that technology varies across countries, why should we assume that it is the same across all industries? Why not suppose instead that different countries have specific areas of expertise: the British are good at software, the Italians at furniture, the Americans at action movies, and so on? In that case the pattern of international trade might be determined as much by these differing technological capacities as by factor endowments.

Implications of the Tests

The mixed results of tests of the factor-proportions theory place international economists in a difficult position. We saw in Chapter 2 that empirical evidence broadly supports the Ricardian model's prediction that countries will export goods in which their labor is especially productive. Most international economists, however, regard the Ricardian model as too limited to serve as their basic model of international trade. By contrast, the Heckscher-Ohlin model has long occupied a central place in trade theory, because it allows a simultaneous treatment of issues of income distribution and the pattern of trade. So the model that predicts trade best is too limiting for other purposes, while there is by now strong evidence against the pure Heckscher-Ohlin model.

While the Heckscher-Ohlin model has been less successful at explaining the actual patterns of international trade than one might hope, it remains vital for understanding the *effects* of trade, especially its effects on the distribution of income. Indeed, the growth of

Table 4-6	Estimated Technological Efficiency, 1983 (United States = 1)

Country	
Bangladesh	0.03
Thailand	0.17
Hong Kong	0.40
Japan	0.70
West Germany	0.78

Source: Trefler, *American Economic Review,* (December 1995), p. 1037.

North-South trade in manufactures—a trade in which the factor intensity of the North's imports is very different from that of its exports—has brought the factor proportions approach into the center of practical debates over international trade policy.

Summary

1. To understand the role of resources in trade we develop a model in which two goods are produced using two factors of production. The two goods differ in their *factor intensity,* that is, at any given wage-rental ratio, production of one of the goods will use a higher ratio of land to labor than production of the other.
2. As long as a country produces both goods, there is a one-to-one relationship between the relative prices of *goods* and the relative prices of *factors* used to produce the goods. A rise in the relative price of the labor-intensive good will shift the distribution of income in favor of labor, and will do so very strongly: The real wage of labor will rise in terms of both goods, while the real income of landowners will fall in terms of both goods.
3. An increase in the supply of one factor of production expands production possibilities, but in a strongly *biased* way: At unchanged relative goods prices, the output of the good intensive in that factor rises while the output of the other good actually falls.
4. A country that has a large supply of one resource relative to its supply of other resources is *abundant* in that resource. A country will tend to produce relatively more of goods that use its abundant resources intensively. The result is the basic Heckscher-Ohlin theory of trade: Countries tend to export goods that are intensive in the factors with which they are abundantly supplied.
5. Because changes in relative prices of goods have very strong effects on the relative earnings of resources, and because trade changes relative prices, international trade has strong income distribution effects. The owners of a country's abundant factors gain from trade, but the owners of scarce factors lose.
6. In an idealized model international trade would actually lead to equalization of the prices of factors such as labor and capital between countries. In reality, complete *factor price equalization* is not observed because of wide differences in resources, barriers to trade, and international differences in technology.

7. Empirical evidence is mixed on the Heckscher-Ohlin model, but most researchers do not believe that differences in resources alone can explain the pattern of world trade or world factor prices. Instead, it seems to be necessary to allow for substantial international differences in technology. Nonetheless, the Heckscher-Ohlin model is extremely useful, especially as a way to analyze the effects of trade on income distribution.

Key Terms

abundant factor, p. 77

biased expansion of production
  possibilities, p. 74

equalization of factor prices, p. 78

factor abundance, p. 67

factor intensity, p. 67

factor prices, p. 68

factor-proportions theory, p. 67

Heckscher-Ohlin theory, p. 67

Leontief paradox, p. 82

scarce factor, p. 77

Problems

1. In the United States where land is cheap, the ratio of land to labor used in cattle raising is higher than that of land used in wheat growing. But in more crowded countries, where land is expensive and labor is cheap, it is common to raise cows by using less land and more labor than Americans use to grow wheat. Can we still say that raising cattle is land intensive compared with farming wheat? Why or why not?

2. Suppose that at current factor prices cloth is produced using 20 hours of labor for each acre of land, and food is produced using only 5 hours of labor per acre of land.
   a. Suppose that the economy's total resources are 600 hours of labor and 60 acres of land. Using a diagram determine the allocation of resources.
   b. Now suppose that the labor supply increases first to 800, then 1000, then 1200 hours. Using a diagram like Figure 4-6, trace out the changing allocation of resources.
   c. What would happen if the labor supply were to increase even further?

3. "The world's poorest countries cannot find anything to export. There is no resource that is abundant—certainly not capital nor land, and in small poor nations not even labor is abundant." Discuss.

4. The U.S. labor movement—which mostly represents blue-collar workers rather than professionals and highly educated workers—has traditionally favored limits on imports from less-affluent countries. Is this a shortsighted policy or a rational one in view of the interests of union members? How does the answer depend on the model of trade?

5. There is substantial inequality of wage levels between regions within the United States. For example, wages of manufacturing workers in equivalent jobs are about 20 percent lower in the Southeast than they are in the Far West. Which of the explanations of failure of factor price equalization might account for this? How is this case different from the divergence of wages between the United States and Mexico (which is geographically closer to both the U.S. Southeast and the Far West than the Southeast and Far West are to each other)?

6. Explain why the Leontief paradox and the more recent Bowen, Leamer, and Svei-kauskas results reported in the text contradict the factor-proportions theory.
7. In the discussion of empirical results on the Heckscher-Ohlin model, we noted that recent work suggests that the efficiency of factors of production seems to differ internationally. Explain how this would affect the concept of factor price equalization.

Further Reading

Alan Deardorff. "Testing Trade Theories and Predicting Trade Flows," in Ronald W. Jones and Peter B. Kenen, eds. *Handbook of International Economics.* Vol. 1. Amsterdam: North-Holland, 1984. A survey of empirical evidence on trade theories, especially the factor-proportions theory.

Ronald W. Jones. "Factor Proportions and the Heckscher-Ohlin Theorem." *Review of Economic Studies* 24 (1956), pp. 1–10. Extends Samuelson's 1948–1949 analysis (cited below), which focuses primarily on the relationship between trade and income distribution, into an overall model of international trade.

Ronald W. Jones. "The Structure of Simple General Equilibrium Models." *Journal of Political Economy* 73 (1965), pp. 557–572. A restatement of the Heckscher-Ohlin-Samuelson model in terms of elegant algebra.

Ronald W. Jones and J. Peter Neary. "The Positive Theory of International Trade," in Ronald W. Jones and Peter B. Kenen, eds. *Handbook of International Economics.* Vol. 1. Amsterdam: North-Holland, 1984. An up-to-date survey of many trade theories, including the factor-proportions theory.

Bertil Ohlin. *Interregional and International Trade.* Cambridge: Harvard University Press, 1933. The original Ohlin book presenting the factor-proportions view of trade remains interesting—its complex and rich view of trade contrasts with the more rigorous and simplified mathematical models that followed.

Robert Reich. *The Work of Nations.* New York: Basic Books, 1991. An influential tract that argues that the increasing integration of the United States in the world economy is widening the gap between skilled and unskilled workers.

Paul Samuelson. "International Trade and the Equalisation of Factor Prices." *Economic Journal* 58 (1948), pp. 163–184, and "International Factor Price Equalisation Once Again." *Economic Journal* 59 (1949), pp. 181–196. The most influential formalizer of Ohlin's ideas is Paul Samuelson (again!), whose two *Economic Journal* papers on the subject are classics.

APPENDIX TO CHAPTER 4

Factor Prices, Goods Prices, and Input Choices

In the main body of this chapter we made two assertions that were true but not carefully derived. First was the assertion, embodied in Figure 4-2, that the ratio of land to labor employed in each industry depended on the wage-rental ratio w/r. Second was the assertion, embodied in Figure 4-3, that there is a one-to-one relationship between relative goods prices P_C/P_F and the wage-rental ratio. This appendix briefly demonstrates both propositions.

Choice of Technique

Figure 4A-1 illustrates again the trade-off between labor and land input in producing one unit of food—the *unit isoquant* for food production shown in curve *II*. It also, however, illustrates a number of *isocost lines:* combinations of land and labor input that cost the same amount.

An isocost line may be constructed as follows: The cost of purchasing a given amount of labor L is wL; the cost of renting a given amount of land T is rT. So if one is able to produce a unit of food using a_{LF} units of labor and a_{TF} units of land, the total cost of producing that unit, K, is

$$K = wa_{LF} + ra_{TF}.$$

A line showing all combinations of a_{LF} and a_{TF} with the same cost has the equation

$$a_{TF} = \frac{K}{r} - (w/r)a_{LF}.$$

That is, it is a straight line with a slope of $-w/r$.

The figure shows a family of such lines, each corresponding to a different level of costs; lines further from the origin indicate higher total costs. A producer will choose the lowest possible cost given the technological trade-off outlined by curve *II*. Here, this occurs at point 1, where *II* is *tangent* to the isocost line and the slope of *II* equals $-w/r$. (If these results seem reminiscent of the proposition in Figure 3-5, that the economy produces at a point on the production possibility frontier whose slope equals minus P_C/P_F, you are right: The same principle is involved.)

Now compare the choice of land-labor ratio for two different factor price ratios. In Figure 4A-2 we show input choice given a low relative price of labor, $(w/r)^1$, and a high relative price of labor, $(w/r)^2$. In the former case the input choice is at 1: in the latter case at 2. That is, the higher relative price of labor leads to the choice of a higher land-labor ratio, as assumed in Figure 4-2.

Figure 4A-1 | Choosing the Optimal Land-Labor Ratio

To minimize costs, a producer must get to the lowest possible isocost line; this means choosing the point on the unit isoquant (the curve II) where the slope is equal to minus the wage-rental ratio w/r.

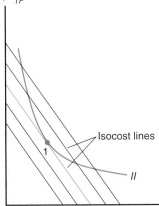

Units of land used to produce one calorie of food, a_{TF}

Isocost lines

II

Units of labor used to produce one calorie of food, a_{LF}

Figure 4A-2 | Changing the Wage-Rental Ratio

A rise in w/r shifts the lowest-cost input choice from point 1 to point 2, that is, it leads to the choice of a higher land-labor ratio.

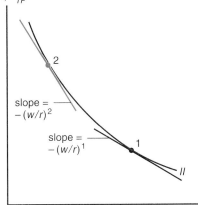

Units of land used to produce one calorie of food, a_{TF}

$\text{slope} = -(w/r)^2$

$\text{slope} = -(w/r)^1$

II

Units of labor used to produce one calorie of food, a_{LF}

Figure 4A-3 | Determining the Wage-Rental Ratio

The two isoquants *CC* and *FF* show the inputs necessary to produce *one dollar's worth* of cloth and food, respectively. Since price must equal the cost of production, the inputs into each good must also cost one dollar; this means that the wage-rental ratio must equal minus the slope of a line tangent to both isoquants.

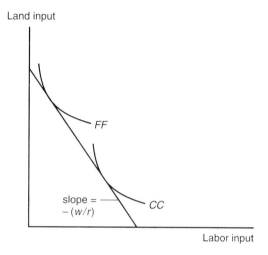

Land input

FF

slope = $-(w/r)$

CC

Labor input

Goods Prices and Factor Prices

We now turn to the relationship between goods prices and factor prices. There are several equivalent ways of approaching this problem; here we follow the analysis introduced by Abba Lerner in the 1930s.

Figure 4A-3 shows land and labor inputs into both cloth and food production. In previous figures we have shown the inputs required to produce one unit of a good. In this figure, however, we show the inputs required to produce *one dollar's worth* of each good. (Actually, any dollar amount will do, as long as it is the same for both goods.) Thus the isoquant for cloth, *CC*, shows the possible input combinations for producing $1/P_C$ units of cloth; the isoquant for food, *FF*, shows the possible combinations for producing $1/P_F$ units of food. Notice that as drawn, food production is land-intensive: For any given w/r, food production will always use a higher land-labor ratio than cloth production.

If the economy produces both goods, then it must be the case that the cost of producing one dollar's worth of each good is, in fact, one dollar. In particular, the cost of producing one dollar's worth of both goods must be the same. This outcome is only possible, however, if the minimum-cost point of production for both goods lie on the *same* isocost line. Thus the wage-rental ratio w/r must be the slope of the line shown, which is just tangent to both isoquants.

Finally, now, consider the effects of a rise in the price of cloth on the wage-rental ratio. If the price of cloth rises, it is necessary to produce fewer yards of cloth in order to have one dollar's worth. Thus the isoquant corresponding to a dollar's worth of cloth shift inward. In Figure 4A-4, the original isoquant is shown as CC^1, the new isoquant as CC^2.

Once again we must draw a line that is just tangent to both isoquants; the slope of that line is minus the wage-rental ratio. It is immediately apparent from the increased steepness of the isocost line (slope $= -(w/r)^2$) that the new w/r is higher than the previous one: A higher relative price of cloth implies a higher wage-rental ratio.

Figure 4A-4 | A Rise in the Price of Cloth

If the price of cloth rises, a smaller output is now worth one dollar; so CC^1 is replaced by CC^2. The implied wage-rental ratio must therefore rise from $(w/r)^1$ to $(w/r)^2$.

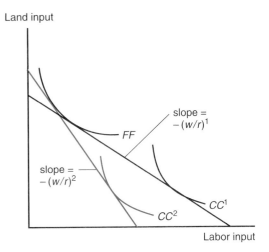

C H A P T E R   5

The Standard
Trade Model

Previous chapters developed three different models of international trade, each of which makes different assumptions about the determinants of production possibilities. To bring out important points, each of these models leaves out aspects of reality that the others stress. These models are:

- *The Ricardian model.* Production possibilities are determined by the allocation of a single resource, labor, between sectors. This model conveys the essential idea of comparative advantage but does not allow us to talk about the distribution of income.
- *The specific factors model.* While labor can move freely between sectors, there are other factors specific to particular industries. This model is ideal for understanding income distribution but awkward for discussing the pattern of trade.
- *The Heckscher-Ohlin model.* Multiple factors of production can move between sectors. This is a harder model to work with than the first two but conveys a deeper understanding of how resources may drive trade patterns.

When we analyze real problems, we want to base our insights on a mixture of the models. For example, in the 1990s one of the central changes in world trade was the rapid growth in exports from newly industrializing economies. These countries experienced rapid productivity growth; to discuss the implications of this productivity growth we may want to apply the Ricardian model of Chapter 2. The changing pattern of trade has differential effects on different groups in the United States; to understand the effects of increased Pacific trade for U.S. income distribution, we may want to apply the specific factors model of Chapter 3. Finally, over time the resources of the newly industrializing nations have changed, as they accumulate capital and their labor grows more educated, while unskilled labor becomes scarcer. To understand the implications of this shift, we may wish to turn to the Heckscher-Ohlin model of Chapter 4.

In spite of the differences in their details, our models share a number of features:

1. The productive capacity of an economy can be summarized by its production possibility frontier, and differences in these frontiers give rise to trade.
2. Production possibilities determine a country's relative supply schedule.

3. World equilibrium is determined by world relative demand and a *world* relative supply schedule that lies between the national relative supply schedules.

Because of these common features, the models we have studied may be viewed as special cases of a more general model of a trading world economy. There are many important issues in international economics whose analysis can be conducted in terms of this general model, with only the details depending on which special model you choose. These issues include the effects of shifts in world supply resulting from economic growth; shifts in world demand resulting from foreign aid, war reparations, and other international transfers of income; and simultaneous shifts in supply and demand resulting from tariffs and export subsidies.

This chapter stresses those insights from international trade theory that are not strongly dependent on the details of the economy's supply side. We develop a standard model of a trading world economy of which the models of Chapters 2, 3, and 4 can be regarded as special cases and use this model to ask how a variety of changes in underlying parameters affect the world economy.   ●

A Standard Model of a Trading Economy

The **standard trade model** is built on four key relationships: (1) the relationship between the production possibility frontier and the relative supply curve; (2) the relationship between relative prices and relative demand; (3) the determination of world equilibrium by world relative supply and world relative demand; and (4) the effect of the **terms of trade**—the price of a country's exports divided by the price of its imports—on a nation's welfare.

Production Possibilities and Relative Supply

For the purposes of our standard model we assume that each country produces two goods, food (F) and cloth (C), and that each country's production possibility frontier is a smooth curve like that illustrated by TT in Figure 5-1.[1]

The point on its production possibility frontier at which an economy actually produces depends on the price of cloth relative to food, P_C/P_F. It is a basic proposition of microeconomics that a market economy that is not distorted by monopoly or other market failures is efficient in production, that is, maximizes the value of output at given market prices, $P_C Q_C + P_F Q_F$.

We can indicate the market value of output by drawing a number of **isovalue lines**—that is, lines along which the value of output is constant. Each of these lines is defined by an equation of the form $P_C Q_C + P_F Q_F = V$, or by rearranging, $Q_F = V/P_F - (P_C/P_F)Q_C$, where V is the value of output. The higher V is, the farther out an isovalue line lies; thus isovalue lines farther from the origin correspond to higher values of output. The slope of an isovalue line is minus the relative price of cloth. The economy will produce the highest value of

---

[1]We have seen that when there is only one factor of production, as in Chapter 2, the production possibility frontier is a straight line. For most models, however, it will be a smooth curve, and the Ricardian result can be viewed as an extreme case.

Figure 5-1 | Relative Prices Determine the Economy's Output

An economy whose production possibility frontier is *TT* will produce at *Q*, which is on the highest possible isovalue line.

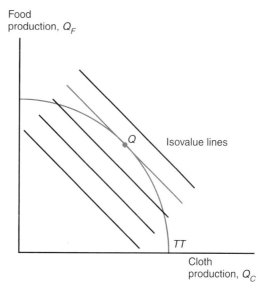

Food
production, Q_F

Q

Isovalue lines

TT

Cloth
production, Q_C

output it can, which can be achieved by producing at point *Q*, where *TT* is just tangent to an isovalue line.[2]

Now suppose that P_C/P_F were to rise. Then the isovalue lines would be steeper than before. In Figure 5-2 the highest isovalue line the economy could reach before the change in P_C/P_F is shown as VV^1; the highest line after the price change is VV^2, the point at which the economy produces shifts from Q^1 to Q^2. Thus, as we might expect, a rise in the relative price of cloth leads the economy to produce more cloth and less food. The relative supply of cloth will therefore rise when the relative price of cloth rises.

Relative Prices and Demand

Figure 5-3 shows the relationship among production, consumption, and trade in the standard model. As we pointed out in Chapter 3, the value of an economy's consumption equals the value of its production:

$$P_C Q_C + P_F Q_F = P_C D_C + P_F D_F = V,$$

where D_C and D_F are the consumption of cloth and food, respectively. The equation above says that production and consumption must lie on the same isovalue line.

---

[2]In our analysis of the specific factors model in Chapter 3 we showed explicitly that the economy always produces at a point on its production possibility curve where the slope of that curve equals the ratio of the two goods prices—that is, where the price line is tangent to the production possibility curve. Students may want to refer back to p. 46 in Chapter 3 to refresh their intuition.

Figure 5-2 | How an Increase in the Relative Price of Cloth Affects Relative Supply

The isovalue lines become steeper when the relative price of cloth rises from $(P_C/P_F)^1$ to $(P_C/P_F)^2$ (shown by the rotation from VV^1 to VV^2). As a result, the economy produces more cloth and less food and the equilibrium output shifts from Q^1 to Q^2.

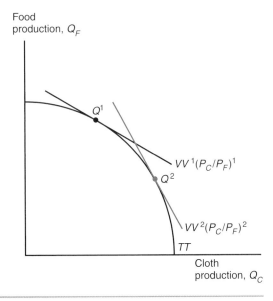

The economy's choice of a point on the isovalue line depends on the tastes of its consumers. For our standard model, we make the useful simplifying assumption that the economy's consumption decisions may be represented as if they were based on the tastes of a single representative individual.[3]

The tastes of an individual can be represented graphically by a series of **indifference curves**. An indifference curve traces a set of combinations of cloth (C) and food (F) consumption that leave the individual equally well off. Indifference curves have three properties:

1. They are downward sloping: If an individual is offered less F, then to be made equally well off she must be given more C.
2. The farther up and to the right an indifference curve lies, the higher the level of welfare to which it corresponds: An individual will prefer more of both goods to less.
3. Each indifference curve gets flatter as we move to the right: The more C and the less F an individual consumes, the more valuable a unit of F is at the margin compared with a unit of C, so more C will have to be provided to compensate for any further reduction in F.

[3]There are several sets of circumstances that can justify this assumption. One is that all individuals have the same tastes and the same share of all resources. Another is that the government redistributes income so as to maximize its view of overall social welfare. Essentially, the assumption requires that effects of changing income distribution on demand not be too important.

Figure 5-3 | Production, Consumption, and Trade in the Standard Model

The economy produces at point Q, where the production possibility frontier is tangent to the highest possible isovalue line. It consumes at point D, where that isovalue line is tangent to the highest possible indifference curve. The economy produces more cloth than it consumes and therefore exports cloth; correspondingly, it consumes more food than it produces and therefore imports food.

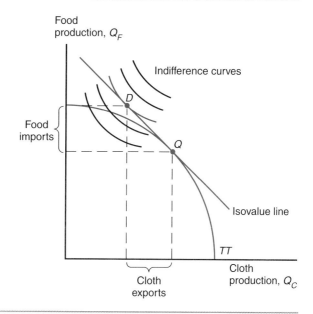

In Figure 5-3 we show a set of indifference curves for the economy that have these three properties. The economy will choose to consume at the point on the isovalue line that yields the highest possible welfare. This point is where the isovalue line is tangent to the highest reachable indifference curve, shown here as point D. Notice that at this point the economy exports cloth (the quantity of cloth produced exceeds the quantity of cloth consumed) and imports food. (If this is not obvious, refer back to our discussion of the pattern of trade in Chapter 3.)

Now consider what happens when P_C/P_F is increased. In Figure 5-4 we show the effects. First, the economy produces more C and less F, shifting production from Q^1 to Q^2. This shifts the isovalue line on which consumption must lie, from VV^1 to VV^2. The economy's consumption choice therefore also shifts, from D^1 to D^2.

The move from D^1 to D^2 reflects two effects of the rise in P_C/P_F. First, the economy has moved to a higher indifference curve: It is better off. The reason is that this economy is an exporter of cloth. When the relative price of cloth rises, the economy can afford to import more food for any given volume of exports. Thus the higher relative price of its export good represents an advantage. Second, the change in relative prices leads to a shift along the indifference curve, toward food and away from cloth.

These two effects are familiar from basic economic theory. The rise in welfare is an *income effect;* the shift in consumption at any given level of welfare is a *substitution effect.* The income effect tends to increase consumption of both goods, while the substitution effect acts to make the economy consume less C and more F.

Figure 5-4 | Effects of a Rise in the Relative Price of Cloth

The slope of the isovalue lines is equal to minus the relative price of cloth P_C/P_F, so when that relative price rises all isovalue lines become steeper. In particular, the maximum-value line rotates from VV^1 to VV^2. Production shifts from Q^1 to Q^2; consumption shifts from D^1 to D^2.

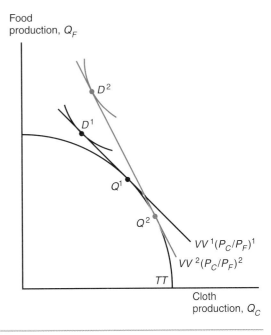

It is possible in principle that the income effect will be so strong that when P_C/P_F rises, consumption of both goods actually rises. Normally, however, the ratio of C consumption to F consumption will fall, that is, *relative* demand for C will decline. This is the case shown in the figure.

The Welfare Effect of Changes in the Terms of Trade

When P_C/P_F increases, a country that initially exports cloth is made better off, as illustrated by the movement from D^1 to D^2 in Figure 5-4. Conversely, if P_C/P_F were to decline, the country would be made worse off; for example, consumption might move back from D^2 to D^1.

If the country were initially an exporter of food instead of cloth, the direction of this effect would of course be reversed. An increase in P_C/P_F would mean a fall in P_F/P_C, and the country would be worse off; a fall in P_C/P_F would make it better off.

We cover all cases by defining the terms of trade as the price of the good a country initially exports divided by the price of the good it initially imports. The general statement, then, is that *a rise in the terms of trade increases a country's welfare, while a decline in the terms of trade reduces its welfare.*

Determining Relative Prices

Let's now suppose that the world economy consists of two countries, once again named Home (which exports cloth) and Foreign (which exports food). Home's terms of trade are

Figure 5-5 | World Relative Supply and Demand

The higher P_C/P_F is, the larger the world supply of cloth relative to food (*RS*) and the lower the world demand for cloth relative to food (*RD*). Equilibrium relative price (here, $(P_C/P_F)^1$) is determined by the intersection of the world relative supply and demand curves.

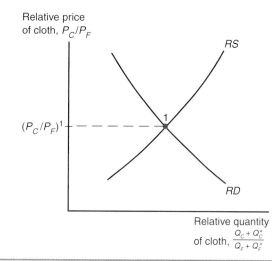

measured by P_C/P_F, while Foreign's are measured by P_F/P_C. Q_C and Q_F are the quantities of cloth and food produced by Home: Q_C^* and Q_F^* are the quantities produced by Foreign.

To determine P_C/P_F we find the intersection of world relative supply of cloth and world relative demand. The world relative supply curve (*RS* in Figure 5-5) is upward sloping because an increase in P_C/P_F leads both countries to produce more cloth and less food. The world relative demand curve (*RD*) is downward sloping because an increase in P_C/P_F leads both countries to shift their consumption mix away from cloth toward food. The intersection of the curves (point 1) determines the equilibrium relative price $(P_C/P_F)^1$.

Now that we know how relative supply, relative demand, the terms of trade, and welfare are determined in the standard model, we can use it to understand a number of important issues in international economics.

Economic Growth: A Shift of the *RS* Curve

The effects of economic growth in a trading world economy are a perennial source of concern and controversy. The debate revolves around two questions. First, is economic growth in other countries good or bad for our nation? Second, is growth in a country more or less valuable when that nation is part of a closely integrated world economy?

In assessing the effects of growth in other countries, commonsense arguments can be made on either side. On one side, economic growth in the rest of the world may be good for our economy because it means larger markets for our exports. On the other side, growth in other countries may mean increased competition for our exporters.

Similar ambiguities seem present when we look at the effects of growth at home. On one hand, growth in an economy's production capacity should be more valuable when that country can sell some of its increased production to the world market. On the other hand, the benefits of growth may be passed on to foreigners in the form of lower prices for the country's exports rather than retained at home.

The standard model of trade developed in the last section provides a framework that can cut through these seeming contradictions and clarify the effects of economic growth in a trading world.

Growth and the Production Possibility Frontier

Economic growth means an outward shift of a country's production possibility frontier. This growth can result either from increases in a country's resources or from improvements in the efficiency with which these resources are used.

The international trade effects of growth result from the fact that such growth typically has a *bias*. **Biased growth** takes place when the production possibility frontier shifts out more in one direction than in the other. Figure 5-6a illustrates growth biased toward cloth, and Figure 5-6b shows growth biased toward food. In each case the production possibility frontier shifts from TT^1 to TT^2.

Growth may be biased for two main reasons:

1. The Ricardian model of Chapter 2 shows that technological progress in one sector of the economy will expand the economy's production possibilities more in the direction of that sector's output than in the direction of the other sector's output.

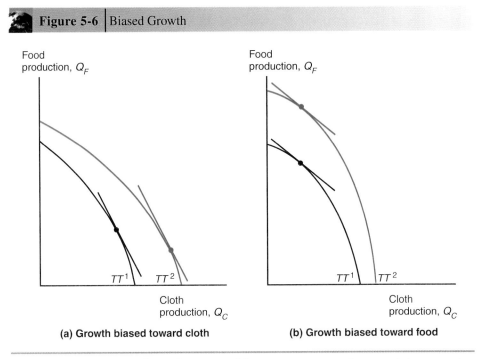

Figure 5-6 | Biased Growth

Food production, Q_F

Food production, Q_F

TT^1 TT^2

TT^1 TT^2

Cloth production, Q_C

Cloth production, Q_C

(a) Growth biased toward cloth

(b) Growth biased toward food

Growth is biased when it shifts production possibilities out more toward one good than toward another. In both cases shown the production possibility frontier shifts out from TT^1 to TT^2. In case (a) this shift is biased toward cloth, in case (b) toward food.

2. The specific factors model of Chapter 3 and the factor proportions model of Chapter 4 both showed that an increase in a country's supply of a factor of production—say, an increase in the capital stock resulting from saving and investment—will produce biased expansion of production possibilities. The bias will be in the direction of either the good to which the factor is specific or the good whose production is intensive in the factor whose supply has increased. Thus the same considerations that give rise to international trade will also lead to biased growth in a trading economy.

The biases of growth in Figure 5-6a and 5-6b are strong. In each case the economy is able to produce more of both goods, but at an unchanged relative price of cloth the output of food actually falls in Figure 5-6a, while the output of cloth actually falls in Figure 5-6b. Although growth is not always as strongly biased as it is in these examples, even growth that is more mildly biased toward cloth will lead, *for any given relative price of cloth,* to a rise in the output of cloth *relative* to that of food. The reverse is true for growth biased toward food.

Relative Supply and the Terms of Trade

Suppose now that Home experiences growth strongly biased toward cloth, so that its output of cloth rises at any given relative price of cloth, while its output of food declines. Then for the world as a whole the output of cloth relative to food will rise at any given price and the world relative supply curve will shift to the right from RS^1 to RS^2 (Figure 5-7a). This shift results in a decrease in the relative price of cloth from $(P_C/P_F)^1$ to $(P_C/P_F)^2$, a worsening of Home's terms of trade and an improvement in Foreign's terms of trade.

Notice that the important consideration here is not which economy grows but the bias of the growth. If Foreign had experienced growth biased toward cloth, the effect on the relative supply curve and thus on the terms of trade would have been the same. On the other hand, either Home or Foreign growth biased toward food (Figure 5-7b) leads to a *leftward* shift of the RS curve (RS^1 to RS^2) and thus to a rise in the relative price of cloth from $(P_C/P_F)^1$ to $(P_C/P_F)^2$. This increase is an improvement in Home's terms of trade, a worsening of Foreign's.

Growth that disproportionately expands a country's production possibilities in the direction of the good it exports (cloth in Home, food in Foreign) is **export-biased growth**. Similarly, growth biased toward the good a country imports is **import-biased growth**. Our analysis leads to the following general principle: *Export-biased growth tends to worsen a growing country's terms of trade, to the benefit of the rest of the world; import-biased growth tends to improve a growing country's terms of trade at the rest of the world's expense.*

International Effects of Growth

Using this principle, we are now in a position to resolve our questions about the international effects of growth. Is growth in the rest of the world good or bad for our country? Does the fact that our country is part of a trading world economy increase or decrease the benefits of growth? In each case the answer depends on the *bias* of the growth. Export-biased growth in the rest of the world is good for us, improving our terms of trade, while import-biased growth abroad worsens our terms of trade. Export-biased growth in our own

Figure 5-7 | Growth and Relative Supply

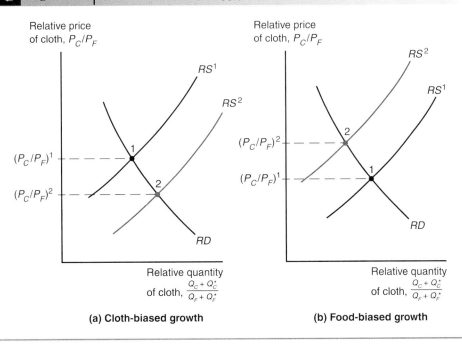

(a) Cloth-biased growth   **(b) Food-biased growth**

Growth biased toward cloth shifts the RS curve to the right (a), while growth biased toward food shifts it to the left (b).

country worsens our terms of trade, reducing the direct benefits of growth, while import-biased growth leads to an improvement of our terms of trade, a secondary benefit.

During the 1950s, many economists from poorer countries believed that their nations, which primarily exported raw materials, were likely to experience steadily declining terms of trade over time. They believed that growth in the industrial world would be marked by an increasing development of synthetic substitutes for raw materials, while growth in the poorer nations would take the form of a further extension of their capacity to produce what they were already exporting rather than a move toward industrialization. That is, the growth in the industrial world would be import biased, while that in the less developed world would be export biased.

Some analysts suggested that growth in the poorer nations would actually be self-defeating. They argued that export-biased growth by poor nations would worsen their terms of trade so much that they would be worse off than if they had not grown at all. This situation is known to economists as the case of **immiserizing growth**.

In a famous paper published in 1958, the economist Jagdish Bhagwati of Columbia University showed that such perverse effects of growth can in fact arise within a rigorously specified economic model.[4] The conditions under which immiserizing growth can occur

---

[4]"Immiserizing Growth: A Geometrical Note," *Review of Economic Studies* 25 (June 1958), pp. 201–205.

are, however, extreme: Strongly export-biased growth must be combined with very steep *RS* and *RD* curves, so that the change in the terms of trade is large enough to offset the initial favorable effects of an increase in a country's productive capacity. Most economists now regard the concept of immiserizing growth as more a theoretical point than a real-world issue.

While growth at home normally raises our own welfare even in a trading world, however, this is by no means true of growth abroad. Import-biased growth is not an unlikely possibility, and whenever the rest of the world experiences such growth, it worsens our terms of trade. Indeed, as we point out below, it is possible that the United States has suffered some loss of real income because of foreign growth over the postwar period.

CASE STUDY

Has the Growth of Newly Industrializing Countries Hurt Advanced Nations?

In the early 1990s, many observers began warning that the growth of newly industrializing economies poses a threat to the prosperity of advanced nations. In the case study in Chapter 4 on North-South trade we addressed one way in which that growth might prove a problem: It might aggravate the growing gap in incomes between high-skilled and low-skilled workers in advanced nations. Some alarmists, however, believed that the threat was still broader—that the overall real income of advanced nations, as opposed to its distribution, had been or would be reduced by the appearance of new competitors. For example, a 1993 report released by the European Commission (the administrative arm of the European Union), in listing reasons for Europe's economic difficulties, emphasized the fact that "other countries are becoming industrialized and competing with us—even on our own markets—at cost levels which we simply cannot match." Another report by an influential private organization went even further, arguing that the rising productivity of low-wage countries would put immense pressure on high-wage nations, to such an extent that "the raison d'etre of many countries is at stake."[5]

Are these concerns justified? At first look it may seem obvious that the growth of formidable new competitors threatens a country's standard of living. As we have just seen, however, the effect of growth abroad on income at home is by no means necessarily, or even presumptively, negative. The effect of one country's growth on another country's real income depends on the bias of that growth; only if it is biased toward the other country's exports will it reduce its real income via worsened terms of trade.

It is difficult to determine the direction of bias in the growth of newly industrializing economies. It is easy, however, to check directly whether the terms of trade of advanced countries have in fact deteriorated sufficiently to be a major drag on their real incomes. Table 5-1, from the International Monetary Fund, shows average annual percentage changes in the terms of trade for three groups of countries over two decades (the numbers for 1993–2002 are partly a

---

[5]Commission of the European Communities, *Growth, Competitiveness, Employment,* Brussels 1993; World Economic Forum, *World Competitiveness Report 1994.*

Table 5-1 | Average Annual Percent Changes in Terms of Trade

	1983–1992	1993–2002
Advanced countries	1.1	0.1
Oil-exporting developing countries	−7.5	2.0
Non-oil-exporting developing countries	−0.6	−0.2

Source: International Monetary Fund, *World Economic Outlook*, May 2001.

projection but seem to have come out about right). The first group is the advanced countries; the second consists of developing countries that export oil; the third, which includes almost all of the newly industrializing countries of Asia, comprises developing countries that do not export oil.

If the claim that competition from newly industrializing economies hurts advanced countries were true, we should see large negative numbers for the terms of trade of advanced countries. In the Mathematical Postscript to this chapter we show that the percentage real income effect of a change in the terms of trade is approximately equal to the percent change in the terms of trade, multiplied by the share of imports in income. Since advanced countries on average spend about 20 percent of their income on imports, a 1 percent decline in the terms of trade would reduce real income by only about 0.2 percent. So the terms of trade would have to decline by several percent per year to be a noticeable drag on economic growth.

What we actually see is that the terms of trade of advanced countries *improved* between 1983 and 1992 and showed little change thereafter. The main reason for the improvement was a decline in the price of oil; that's why the terms of trade of oil-exporting countries showed a sharp decline.

The lesson from these numbers is that any adverse impact of competition from developing countries on advanced countries was too small to be visible in the data—and therefore too small to matter.

International Transfers of Income: Shifting the *RD* Curve

We now turn from terms of trade changes originating on the supply side of the world economy to changes that originate on the demand side.

Relative world demand for goods may shift for many reasons. Tastes may change: With rising concern over cholesterol, demand for fish has risen relative to the demand for red meat. Technology may also change demand: Whale oil fueled lamps at one time but was supplanted by kerosene, later by gas, and finally by electricity. In international economics, however, perhaps the most important and controversial issue is the shift in world relative demand that can result from international **transfers of income**.

In the past, transfers of income between nations often occurred in the aftermath of wars. Germany demanded a payment from France after the latter's defeat in the Franco-Prussian war of 1871; after World War I the victorious Allies demanded large reparations payments from Germany (mostly never paid). After World War II, the United States provided aid to defeated Japan and Germany as well as to its wartime allies to help them rebuild. Since the 1950s, advanced countries have provided aid to poorer nations, although the sums have made a major contribution to the income of only a few of the very poorest countries.

International loans are not strictly speaking transfers of income, since the current transfer of spending power that a loan implies comes with an obligation to repay later. In the short run, however, the economic effects of a sum of money given outright to a nation and the same sum lent to that nation are similar. Thus an analysis of international income transfers is also useful in understanding the effects of international loans.

The Transfer Problem

The issue of how international transfers affect the terms of trade was raised in a famous debate between two great economists, Bertil Ohlin (one of the originators of the factor-proportions theory of trade) and John Maynard Keynes. The subject of the debate was the reparations payments demanded of Germany after World War I, and the question was how much of a burden these payments represented to the German economy.[6]

Keynes, who made a forceful case that the vengeful terms of the Allies (the "Carthaginian peace") were too harsh, argued that the monetary sums being demanded were an understatement of the true burden on Germany. He pointed out that to pay money to other countries Germany would have to export more and import less. To do this, he argued, Germany would have to make its exports cheaper relative to its imports. The resulting worsening of Germany's terms of trade would add an excess burden to the direct burden of the payment.

Ohlin questioned whether Keynes was right in assuming that Germany's terms of trade would worsen. He counterargued that when Germany raised taxes to finance its reparations, its demand for foreign goods would automatically decrease. At the same time, the reparation payment would be distributed in other countries in the form of reduced taxes or increased government spending, and some of the resulting increased foreign demand would be for German exports. Thus Germany might be able to reduce imports and increase exports without having its terms of trade worsen.

In the particular case in dispute the debate turned out to be beside the point: In the end, Germany paid very little of its reparations. The issue of the terms of trade effects of a transfer, however, arises in a surprisingly wide variety of contexts in international economics.

Effects of a Transfer on the Terms of Trade

If Home makes a transfer of some of its income to Foreign, Home's income is reduced, and it must reduce its expenditure. Correspondingly, Foreign increases its expenditure. This shift in the national division of world spending may lead to a shift in world relative demand and thus affect the terms of trade.

The shift in the *RD* curve (if it occurs) is the only effect of a transfer of income. The *RS* curve does not shift. As long as only income is being transferred, and not physical resources like capital equipment, the production of cloth and food for any given relative price will not change in either country. Thus the transfer problem is a purely demand-side issue.

---

[6]See Keynes, "The German Transfer Problem" and Ohlin, "The German Transfer Problem: A Discussion," both in *Economic Journal* 39 (1929), pp. 1–7 and pp. 172–182, respectively.

The *RD* curve does not necessarily shift when world income is redistributed, however (this was Ohlin's point). If Foreign allocates its extra income between cloth and food in the same proportions that Home reduces its spending, then *world* spending on cloth and food will not change. The *RD* curve will not shift, and there will be no terms of trade effect.

If the two countries do not allocate their change in spending in the same proportions, however, there will be a terms of trade effect; the direction of the effect will depend on the difference in Home and Foreign spending patterns. Suppose that Home allocates a higher proportion of a marginal shift in expenditure to cloth than Foreign does. That is, Home has a higher **marginal propensity to spend** on cloth than Foreign. (Correspondingly, Home in this case must have a lower marginal propensity to spend on food.) Then at any given relative price Home's transfer payment to Foreign reduces demand for cloth and increases demand for food. In this case the *RD* curve shifts to the left, from RD^1 to RD^2 (Figure 5-8) and equilibrium shifts from point 1 to point 2. This shift lowers the relative price of cloth from $(P_C/P_F)^1$ to $(P_C/P_F)^2$, worsening Home's terms of trade (because it exports cloth) while improving Foreign's. This is the case that Keynes described: The indirect effect of an international transfer on terms of trade reinforces its original effect on the incomes of the two countries.

There is, however, another possibility. If Home has a *lower* marginal propensity to spend on cloth, a transfer by Home to Foreign shifts the *RD* curve right, and improves Home's terms of trade at Foreign's expense. This effect offsets both the negative effect on Home's income and the positive effect on Foreign's income.

In general, then, *a transfer worsens the donor's terms of trade if the donor has a higher marginal propensity to spend on its export good than the recipient.* If the donor has a *lower* marginal propensity to spend on its export, its terms of trade will actually improve.

Figure 5-8 | Effects of a Transfer on the Terms of Trade

If Home has a higher marginal propensity to spend on cloth than Foreign, a transfer of income by Home to Foreign shifts the *RD* curve left from RD^1 to RD^2, reducing the equilibrium relative price of cloth.

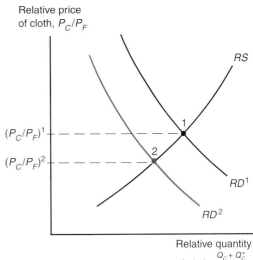

A paradoxical possibility is implied by this analysis. A transfer payment—say foreign aid—could conceivably improve the donor's terms of trade so much that it leaves the donor better off and the recipient worse off. In this case it is definitely better to give than to receive! Some theoretical work has shown that this paradox, like the case of immiserizing growth, is possible in a rigorously specified model. The conditions are, however, even more stringent than those for immiserizing growth, and this possibility is almost surely purely theoretical.[7]

This analysis shows that the terms of trade effects of reparations and foreign aid can go either way. Thus Ohlin was right about the general principle. Many would still argue, however, that Keynes was right in suggesting that there is a presumption that transfers cause terms of trade effects that reinforce their effects on the incomes of donors and recipients.

Presumptions about the Terms of Trade Effects of Transfers

A transfer will worsen the donor's terms of trade if the donor has a higher marginal propensity to spend on its export good than the recipient. If differences in marginal propensities to spend were simply a matter of differences in taste, there would be no presumption either way: Which good a country exports depends for the most part on differences in technology or resources, which need have nothing to do with tastes. When we look at actual spending patterns, however, each country seems to have a relative preference for its own goods. The United States, for example, produces only about 25 percent of the value of output of the world's market economies, so that total sales of U.S. goods are 25 percent of world sales. If spending patterns were the same everywhere, the United States would spend only 25 percent of its income on U.S. products. In fact, imports are only 11 percent of national income; that is, the United States spends 89 percent of its income domestically. On the other hand, the rest of the world spends less than 3 percent of its income on U.S. products. This difference in spending patterns certainly suggests that if the United States were to transfer some of its income to foreigners, the relative demand for U.S. goods would fall and the U.S. terms of trade would decline, just as Keynes argued.

The United States spends so much of its income at home because of barriers to trade, both natural and artificial. Transportation costs, tariffs (taxes on imports), and import quotas (government regulations that limit the quantity of imports) cause residents of each country to buy a variety of goods and services at home rather than import them from abroad. As we noted in Chapter 2, the effect of such barriers to trade is to create a set of nontraded goods. Even if every country divides its income among different goods in the same proportions, local purchase of nontraded goods will ensure that spending has a national bias.

Consider the following example. Suppose that there are not two but *three* goods: cloth, food, and haircuts. Only Home produces cloth; only Foreign produces food. Haircuts, however, are a nontraded good that each country produces for itself. Each country spends one-third of its income on each good. Even though these countries have the same tastes, each of them spends two-thirds of its income domestically and only one-third on imports.

---

[7]For examples of how an immiserizing transfer might occur, see Graciela Chichilnisky, "Basic Goods, the Effects of Commodity Transfers and the International Economic Order," *Journal of Development Economics* 7 (1980), pp. 505–519; and Jagdish Bhagwati, Richard Brecher, and Tatsuo Hatta, "The Generalized Theory of Transfers and Welfare," *American Economic Review* 73 (1983), pp. 606–618.

Nontraded goods can give rise to what looks like a national preference for all goods produced domestically. But to analyze the effects of a transfer on the terms of trade we need to know what happens to the supply and demand for *exports*. Here the crucial point is that a country's nontraded goods compete with exports for resources. A transfer of income from the United States to the rest of the world lowers the demand for nontraded goods in the United States, releasing resources that can be used to produce U.S. exports. As a result, the supply of U.S. exports rises. At the same time, the transfer of income from the United States to the rest of the world increases the rest of the world's demand for nontraded goods because some of that income is spent on haircuts and other nontradables. The increase in the demand for nontraded goods in the rest of the world draws foreign resources away from exports and reduces the supply of foreign exports (which are U.S. imports). The result is that a transfer by the United States to other countries may lower the price of U.S. exports relative to foreign, worsening U.S. terms of trade.

Demand shifts also cause resources to move between the nontraded and import-competing sectors. As a practical matter, however, most international economists believe that the effect of barriers to trade *is* to validate the presumption that an international transfer of income worsens the donor's terms of trade. Thus, Keynes was right in practice.

CASE STUDY

The Transfer Problem and the Asian Crisis

In 1997 to 1998, several Asian nations—including Thailand, Indonesia, Malaysia, and South Korea—experienced a sudden reversal of international capital flows. During the preceding few years, these nations, as the favorites of international investors, had attracted large inflows of money, allowing them to import considerably more than they exported. But confidence in these economies collapsed in 1997; foreign banks that had been lending heavily to Asian companies now demanded that the loans be repaid, stock market investors began selling off their holdings, and many domestic residents also began shifting funds overseas.

We discuss the causes of this crisis, and the disputes that have raged over its management, in Chapter 22. For now we simply note that whatever the reasons investors first blew hot, then cold, on Asian economies, in effect these economies went quickly from receiving large *inward* transfers to making large *outward* transfers. If Keynes's presumption about the effects of transfers were right, this reversal of fortune should have produced a noticeable deterioration of Asian terms of trade, exacerbating what was already a severe economic blow.

In fact, some observers worried that with so many countries in crisis at the same time and all trying to export more simultaneously, their terms of trade would drastically deteriorate, making the crisis that much worse.

As it turned out, however, the terms of trade of developing countries in Asia did not worsen nearly as much as feared. Export prices fell sharply: in 1998 developing countries in Asia exported the same volume of goods as they had in 1997, but the dollar value of their exports dropped 8 percent. However, import prices also fell.

What seems to have saved Asia from a severe transfer problem was that other things were happening at the same time. Oil prices fell sharply, benefitting all the crisis countries except Indonesia. Japan, the leading exporter to the region, also saw its export prices fall as the yen plunged against the U.S. dollar. So there probably was a transfer problem for Asia, but its effects were masked by other forces.

Tariffs and Export Subsidies: Simultaneous Shifts in *RS* and *RD*

Import tariffs (taxes levied on imports) and **export subsidies** (payments given to domestic producers who sell a good abroad) are not usually put in place to affect a country's terms of trade. These government interventions in trade usually take place for income distribution, for the promotion of industries thought to be crucial to the economy, or for balance of payments (these motivations are examined in Chapters 9, 10, and 11). Whatever the motive for tariffs and subsidies, however, they *do* have terms of trade effects that can be understood by using the standard trade model.

The distinctive feature of tariffs and export subsidies is that they create a difference between prices at which goods are traded on the world market and their prices within a country. The direct effect of a tariff is to make imported goods more expensive inside a country than they are outside. An export subsidy gives producers an incentive to export. It will therefore be more profitable to sell abroad than at home unless the price at home is higher, so such a subsidy raises the price of exported goods inside a country.

The price changes caused by tariffs and subsidies change both relative supply and relative demand. The result is a shift in the terms of trade of the country imposing the policy change and in the terms of trade of the rest of the world.

Relative Demand and Supply Effects of a Tariff

Tariffs and subsidies drive a wedge between the prices at which goods are traded internationally (**external prices**) and the prices at which they are traded within a country (**internal prices**). This means that we have to be careful in defining the terms of trade. The terms of trade are intended to measure the ratio at which countries exchange goods; for example, how many units of food can Home import for each unit of cloth that it exports? The terms of trade therefore correspond to external, not internal, prices. When analyzing the effects of a tariff or export subsidy, we want to know how it affects relative supply and demand *as a function of external prices.*

If Home imposes a 20 percent tariff on the value of food imports, the internal price of food relative to cloth faced by Home producers and consumers will be 20 percent higher than the external relative price of food on the world market. Equivalently, the internal relative price of cloth on which Home residents base their decisions will be lower than the relative price on the external market.

At any given world relative price of cloth, then, Home producers will face a lower relative cloth price and therefore will produce less cloth and more food. At the same time,

Figure 5-9 | Effects of a Tariff on the Terms of Trade

An import tariff imposed by Home both reduces the relative supply of cloth (from RS^1 to RS^2) and increases the relative demand (from RD^1 to RD^2). As a result, the relative price of cloth must rise.

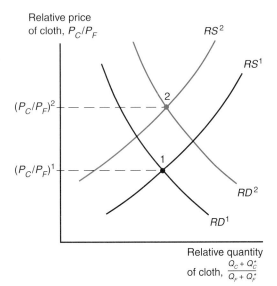

Home consumers will shift their consumption toward cloth and away from food. From the point of view of the world as a whole, the relative supply of cloth will fall (from RS^1 to RS^2 in Figure 5-9) while the relative demand for cloth will rise (from RD^1 to RD^2). Clearly, the world relative price of cloth rises from $(P_C/P_F)^1$ to $(P_C/P_F)^2$, and thus Home's terms of trade improve at Foreign's expense.

The extent of this terms of trade effect depends on how large the country imposing the tariff is relative to the rest of the world—if the country is only a small part of the world, it cannot have much effect on world relative supply and demand and therefore cannot have much effect on relative prices. If the United States, a very large country, were to impose a 20 percent tariff, some estimates suggest that the U.S. terms of trade might rise by 15 percent. That is, the price of U.S. imports relative to exports might fall by 15 percent on the world market, while the relative price of imports would rise only 5 percent inside the United States. On the other hand, if Luxembourg or Paraguay were to impose a 20 percent tariff, the terms of trade effect would probably be too small to measure.

Effects of an Export Subsidy

Tariffs and export subsidies are often treated as similar policies, since they both seem to support domestic producers, but they have opposite effects on the terms of trade. Suppose that Home offers a 20 percent subsidy on the value of any cloth exported. For any given world prices this subsidy will raise Home's internal price of cloth relative to food by 20 percent. The rise in the relative price of cloth will lead Home producers to produce more cloth and less food, while leading Home consumers to substitute food for cloth. As illustrated in Figure 5-10, the subsidy will increase the world relative supply of cloth (from RS^1 to RS^2) and decrease the world relative demand for cloth (from RD^1 to RD^2), shifting equi-

Figure 5-10 | Effects of a Subsidy on the Terms of Trade

An export subsidy's effect are the reverse of those of a tariff. Relative supply of cloth rises, while relative demand falls. Home's terms of trade decline as the relative price of cloth falls from $(P_C/P_F)^1$ to $(P_C/P_F)^2$.

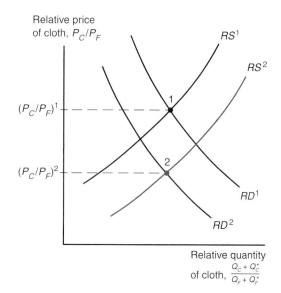

Relative price of cloth, P_C/P_F

RS^1

RS^2

$(P_C/P_F)^1$

$(P_C/P_F)^2$

RD^1

RD^2

Relative quantity of cloth, $\dfrac{Q_C + Q_C^*}{Q_F + Q_F^*}$

librium from point 1 to point 2. A Home export subsidy worsens Home's terms of trade and improves Foreign's.

Implications of Terms of Trade Effects: Who Gains and Who Loses?

The question of who gains and who loses from tariffs and export subsidies has two dimensions. First is the issue of the *international* distribution of income: second is the issue of the distribution of income *within* each of the countries.

The International Distribution of Income.   If Home imposes a tariff, it improves its terms of trade at Foreign's expense. Thus tariffs hurt the rest of the world.

The effect on Home's welfare is not quite as clear-cut. The terms of trade improvement benefits Home; however, a tariff also imposes costs by distorting production and consumption incentives within Home's economy (see Chapter 8). The terms of trade gains will outweigh the losses from distortion only as long as the tariff is not too large: We will see later how to define an optimum tariff that maximizes net benefit. (For small countries that cannot have much impact on their terms of trade, the optimum tariff is near zero.)

The effects of an export subsidy are quite clear. Foreign's terms of trade improve at Home's expense, leaving it clearly better off. At the same time, Home loses from terms of trade deterioration *and* from the distorting effects of its policy.

This analysis seems to show that export subsidies never make sense. In fact, it is difficult to come up with any situation in which export subsidies would serve the national interest. The use of export subsidies as a policy tool usually has more to do with the peculiarities of trade politics than with economic logic.

Are foreign tariffs always bad for a country and foreign export subsidies always benefi-cial? Not necessarily. Our model is of a two-country world, where the other country exports the good we import and vice versa. In the real world of many countries, a foreign govern-ment may subsidize the export of a good that competes with U.S. exports; this foreign sub-sidy will obviously hurt the U.S. terms of trade. A good example of this effect is European subsidies to agricultural exports (see Chapter 8). Alternatively, a country may impose a tariff on something the United States also imports, lowering its price and benefiting the United States. We thus need to qualify our conclusions from a two-country analysis: Sub-sidies to exports of things *the United States imports* help us, while tariffs *against U.S. exports* hurt us.

The view that subsidized foreign sales to the United States are good for us is not a pop-ular one. When foreign governments are charged with subsidizing sales in the United States, the popular and political reaction is that this is unfair competition. Thus when a Commerce Department study determined that European governments were subsidizing exports of steel to the United States, our government demanded that they raise their prices. The standard model tells us that when foreign governments subsidize exports to the United States, the appropriate response from a national point of view should be to send them a note of thanks!

Of course this never happens, largely because of the effects of foreign subsidies on income distribution within the United States. If Europe subsidizes exports of steel to the United States, most U.S. residents gain from cheaper steel, but steelworkers, the owners of steel company stock, and industrial workers in general may not be so cheerful.

The Distribution of Income Within Countries.   Foreign tariffs or subsidies change the relative prices of goods. Such changes have strong effects on income distribution because of factor immobility and differences in the factor intensity of different industries.

At first glance, the direction of the effect of tariffs and export subsidies on relative prices, and therefore on income distribution, may seem obvious. A tariff has the direct effect of raising the internal relative price of the imported good, while an export subsidy has the direct effect of raising the internal relative price of the exported good. We have just seen, however, that tariffs and export subsidies have an indirect effect on a country's terms of trade. The terms of trade effect suggests a paradoxical possibility. A tariff might improve a country's terms of trade so much—that is, raise the relative price of its export good so much on world markets—that even after the tariff rate is added, the internal relative price of the import good *falls*. Similarly, an export subsidy might worsen the terms of trade so much that the internal relative price of the export good falls in spite of the subsidy. If these paradoxi-cal results occur, the income distribution effects of trade policies will be just the opposite of what is expected.

The possibility that tariffs and export subsidies might have perverse effects on internal prices in a country was pointed out and demonstrated by the University of Chicago econo-mist Lloyd Metzler and is known as the **Metzler paradox**.[8] This paradox has roughly the same status as immiserizing growth and a transfer that makes the recipient worse off; that is,

---

[8]See Metzler, "Tariffs, the Terms of Trade, and the Distribution of National Income," *Journal of Political Econo-my* 57 (February 1949), pp. 1–29.

it is possible in theory but will happen only under extreme conditions and is not likely in practice.

Leaving aside the possibility of a Metzler paradox, then, a tariff will help the import-competing sector at home while hurting the exporting sector; an export subsidy will do the reverse. These shifts in the distribution of income *within* countries are often more obvious and more important to the formation of policy than the shifts in the distribution of income *between* countries that result from changes in the terms of trade.

Summary

1. The standard trade model derives a world relative supply curve from production possibilities and a world relative demand curve from preferences. The price of exports relative to imports, a country's terms of trade, is determined by the intersection of the world relative supply and demand curves. Other things equal, a rise in a country's terms of trade increases its welfare. Conversely, a decline in a country's terms of trade will leave the country worse off.

2. Economic growth means an outward shift in a country's production possibility frontier. Such growth is usually biased; that is, the production possibility frontier shifts out more in the direction of some goods than in the direction of others. The immediate effect of biased growth is to lead, other things equal, to an increase in the world relative supply of the goods toward which the growth is biased. This shift in the world relative supply curve in turn leads to a change in the growing country's terms of trade, which can go in either direction. If the growing country's terms of trade improve, this improvement reinforces the initial growth at home but hurts the rest of the world. If the growing country's terms of trade worsen, this decline offsets some of the favorable effects of growth at home but benefits the rest of the world.

3. The direction of the terms of trade effects depends on the nature of the growth. Growth that is export-biased (growth that expands the ability of an economy to produce the goods it was initially exporting more than it expands the ability to produce goods that compete with imports) worsens the terms of trade. Conversely, growth that is import-biased, disproportionately increasing the ability to produce import-competing goods, improves a country's terms of trade. It is possible for import-biased growth abroad to hurt a country.

4. International transfers of income, such as war reparations and foreign aid, may affect a country's terms of trade by shifting the world relative demand curve. If the country receiving a transfer spends a higher proportion of an increase in income on its export good than the giver, a transfer raises world relative demand for the recipient's export good and thus improves its terms of trade. This improvement reinforces the initial transfer and provides an indirect benefit in addition to the direct income transfer. On the other hand, if the recipient has a lower propensity to spend on its export at the margin than the donor, a transfer worsens the recipient's terms of trade, offsetting at least part of the transfer's effect.

5. In practice, most countries spend a much higher share of their income on domestically produced goods than foreigners do. This is not necessarily due to differences in

taste but rather to barriers to trade, natural and artificial, which cause many goods to be nontraded. If nontraded goods compete with exports for resources, transfers will usually raise the recipient's terms of trade. The evidence suggests that this is, in fact, the case.

6. Import tariffs and export subsidies affect both relative supply and demand. A tariff raises relative supply of a country's import good while lowering relative demand. A tariff unambiguously improves the country's terms of trade at the rest of the world's expense. An export subsidy has the reverse effect, increasing the relative supply and reducing the relative demand for the country's export good, and thus worsening the terms of trade.

7. The terms of trade effects of an export subsidy hurt the subsidizing country and benefit the rest of the world, while those of a tariff do the reverse. This suggests that export subsidies do not make sense from a national point of view and that foreign export subsidies should be welcomed rather than countered. Both tariffs and subsidies, however, have strong effects on the distribution of income within countries, and these effects often weigh more heavily on policy than the terms of trade concerns.

Key Terms

biased growth, p. 100
export-biased growth, p. 101
export subsidy, p. 109
external price, p. 109
immiserizing growth, p. 102
import-biased growth, p. 101
import tariff, p. 109
indifference curves, p. 96

internal price, p. 109
isovalue lines, p. 94
marginal propensity to spend, p. 106
Metzler paradox, p. 112
standard trade model, p. 94
terms of trade, p. 94
transfers of income, p. 104

Problems

1. In some economies relative supply may be unresponsive to changes in prices. For example, if factors of production were completely immobile between sectors, the production possibility frontier would be right-angled, and output of the two goods would not depend on their relative prices. Is it still true in this case that a rise in the terms of trade increases welfare? Analyze graphically.

2. The counterpart to immobile factors on the supply side would be lack of substitution on the demand side. Imagine an economy where consumers always buy goods in rigid proportions—for example, one yard of cloth for every pound of food—regardless of the prices of the two goods. Show that an improvement in the terms of trade benefits this economy, as well.

3. Japan primarily exports manufactured goods, while importing raw materials such as food and oil. Analyze the impact on Japan's terms of trade of the following events:

   a. A war in the Middle East disrupts oil supply.

   b. Korea develops the ability to produce automobiles that it can sell in Canada and the United States.

   c. U.S. engineers develop a fusion reactor that replaces fossil fuel electricity plants.

   d. A harvest failure in Russia.

   e. A reduction in Japan's tariffs on imported beef and citrus fruit.

4. Countries A and B have two factors of production, capital and labor, with which they produce two goods, X and Y. Technology is the same in the two countries. X is capital intensive; A is capital abundant.

   Analyze the effects on the terms of trade and the welfare of the two countries of the following:

   a. An increase in A's capital stock.

   b. An increase in A's labor supply.

   c. An increase in B's capital stock.

   d. An increase in B's labor supply.

5. It is just as likely that economic growth will worsen a country's terms of trade as that it will improve them. Why, then, do most economists regard immiserizing growth, where growth actually hurts the growing country, as unlikely in practice?

6. In practice much foreign aid is "tied"; that is, it comes with restrictions that require that the recipient spend the aid on goods from the donor country. For example, France might provide money for an irrigation project in Africa, on the condition that the pumps, pipelines, and construction equipment be purchased from France rather than from Japan. How does such tying of aid affect the transfer problem analysis? Does tying of aid make sense from the donor's point of view? Can you think of a scenario in which tied aid actually makes the recipient worse off?

7. During 1989 a wave of political change swept over Eastern Europe, raising prospects not only of democracy but also of a shift from centrally planned to market economies. One consequence might be a shift in how Western Europe uses its money: Nations, especially Germany, that during the 1980s were lending heavily to the United States might start to lend to nearby Eastern European nations instead.

   Using the analysis of the transfer problem, how do you think this should affect the prices of Western European goods relative to those from the United States and Japan? (Hint: how would the likely use of a dollar of financial resources differ in, say East Germany, from its use in the United States?)

8. Suppose that one country subsidizes its exports and the other country imposes a "countervailing" tariff that offsets its effect, so that in the end relative prices in the second country are unchanged. What happens to the terms of trade? What about welfare in the two countries?

   Suppose, on the other hand, that the second country retaliates with an export subsidy of its own. Contrast the result.

Further Reading

Rudiger Dornbusch, Stanley Fischer, and Paul Samuelson. "Comparative Advantage, Trade, and Payments in a Ricardian Model with a Continuum of Goods." *American Economic Review* (1977). This paper, cited in Chapter 2, also gives a clear exposition of the role of nontraded goods in establishing the presumption that a transfer improves the recipient's terms of trade.

J. R. Hicks. "The Long Run Dollar Problem." *Oxford Economic Papers* 2 (1953), pp. 117–135. The modern analysis of growth and trade has its origins in the fears of Europeans, in the early years after World War II, that the United States had an economic lead that could not be overtaken (this sounds dated today, but many of the same arguments have now resurfaced about Japan). The paper by Hicks is the most famous exposition.

Harry G. Johnson. "Economic Expansion and International Trade." *Manchester School of Social and Economic Studies* 23 (1955), pp. 95–112. The paper that laid out the crucial distinction between export- and import-biased growth.

Paul Krugman. "Does Third World Growth Hurt First World Prosperity?" *Harvard Business Review* (July–August 1994), pp. 113–121. An analysis that attempts to explain why growth in developing countries need not hurt advanced countries in principle and probably does not do so in practice.

Paul Samuelson. "The Transfer Problem and Transport Costs." *Economic Journal* 62 (1952), pp. 278–304 (Part I) and 64 (1954), pp. 264–289 (Part II). The transfer problem, like so many issues in international economics, was given its basic formal analysis by Paul Samuelson.

John Whalley. *Trade Liberalization Among Major World Trading Areas.* Cambridge: MIT Press, 1985. The impact of tariffs on the international economy has been the subject of extensive study. Most impressive are the huge "computable general equilibrium" models, numerical models based on actual data that allow computation of the effects of changes in tariffs and other trade policies. Whalley's book presents one of the most carefully constructed of these.

APPENDIX TO CHAPTER 5

Representing International Equilibrium with Offer Curves

For most purposes, analyzing international equilibrium in terms of relative supply and demand is the simplest and most useful technique. In some circumstances, however, it is useful to analyze trade in a diagram that shows directly what each country ships to the other. A diagram that does this is the *offer curve* diagram.

Deriving a Country's Offer Curve

In Figure 5-3 we showed how to determine a country's production and consumption given the relative price P_C/P_F. Trade is the difference between production and consumption. In an offer curve diagram we show directly the trade flows that correspond to any given relative price. On one axis of Figure 5A-1 we show the country's exports $(Q_C - D_C)$, on the other its imports $(D_F - Q_F)$. Point T in Figure 5A-1 corresponds to the situation shown in Figure 5-3 (production at Q, consumption at D). Since

$$(D_F - Q_F) = (Q_C - D_C) \times (P_C/P_F), \tag{5A-1}$$

the slope of the line from the origin of Figure 5A-1 to T is equal to P_C/P_F. T is Home's offer at the assumed relative price: At that price, Home residents are willing to trade $(Q_C - D_C)$ units of cloth for $(D_F - Q_F)$ units of food.

 Figure 5A-1 | Home's Desired Trade at a Given Relative Price

At the relative price corresponding to the slope of the line from the origin, Home makes the offer to trade $Q_C - D_C$ units of cloth for $D_F - Q_F$ units of food.

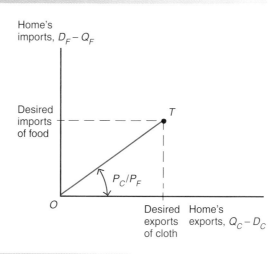

Figure 5A-2 | Home's Offer Curve

The offer curve is generated by tracing out how Home's offer varies as the relative price of cloth is changed.

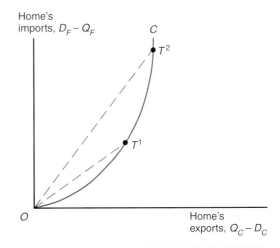

By calculating Home's offer at different relative prices, we trace out Home's offer curve (Figure 5A-2). We saw in Figure 5-4 that as P_C/P_F rises, Q_C rises, Q_F falls, D_F rises, and D_C may rise or fall. Desired $(Q_C - D_C)$ and $(D_F - Q_F)$, however, both normally rise if income effects are not too strong. In Figure 5A-2, T^1 is the offer corresponding to Q^1, D^1 in Figure 5-4; T^2 the offer corresponding to Q^2, D^2. By finding Home's offer at many prices we trace out the Home offer curve OC.

Foreign's offer curve OF may be traced out in the same way (Figure 5A-3). On the vertical axis we plot $(Q_F^* - D_F^*)$, Foreign's desired exports of food, while on the horizontal axis we plot $(D_C^* - Q_C^*)$, desired imports of cloth. The lower P_C/P_F is, the more food Foreign will want to export and the more cloth it will want to import.

International Equilibrium

In equilibrium it must be true that $(Q_C - D_C) = (D_C^* - Q_C^*)$, and also that $(D_F - Q_F) = (Q_F^* - D_F^*)$. That is, world supply and demand must be equal for both cloth and food. Given these equivalences, we can plot the Home and Foreign offer curves on the same diagram (Figure 5A-4). Equilibrium is at the point where the Home and Foreign offer curves cross. At the equilibrium point E the relative price of cloth is equal to the slope of OE. Home's exports of cloth, which equal Foreign's imports, are OX. Foreign's exports of food, which equal Home's imports, are OY.

This representation of international equilibrium helps us see that equilibrium is in fact *general* equilibrium, in which supply and demand are equalized in both markets at the same time.

Figure 5A-3 Foreign's Offer Curve

Foreign's offer curve shows how that country's desired imports of cloth and exports of food vary with the relative price.

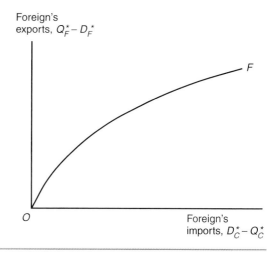

Figure 5A-4 Offer Curve Equilibrium

World equilibrium is where the Home and Foreign offer curves intersect.

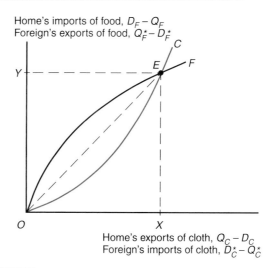

C H A P T E R   6

Economies of Scale, Imperfect Competition, and International Trade

In Chapter 2 we pointed out that there are two reasons why countries specialize and trade. First, countries differ either in their resources or in technology and specialize in the things they do relatively well; second, economies of scale (or increasing returns) make it advantageous for each country to specialize in the production of only a limited range of goods and services. The past four chapters considered models in which all trade is based on comparative advantage; that is, differences between countries are the only reason for trade. This chapter introduces the role of economies of scale.

The analysis of trade based on economies of scale presents certain problems that we have so far avoided. Up to now we have assumed that markets are perfectly competitive, so that all monopoly profits are always competed away. When there are increasing returns, however, large firms usually have an advantage over small, so that markets tend to be dominated by one firm (monopoly) or, more often, by a few firms (oligopoly). When increasing returns enter the trade picture, then, markets usually become imperfectly competitive.

This chapter begins with an overview of the concept of economies of scale and the economics of imperfect competition. We then turn to two models of international trade in which economies of scale and imperfect competition play a crucial role: the monopolistic competition model and the dumping model. The rest of the chapter addresses the role of a different kind of increasing returns, external economies, in determining trade patterns. ●

Economies of Scale and International Trade: An Overview

The models of comparative advantage already presented were based on the assumption of constant returns to scale. That is, we assumed that if inputs to an industry were doubled, industry output would double as well. In practice, however, many industries are characterized by economies of scale (also referred to as increasing returns), so that production is more efficient the larger the scale at which it takes place. Where there are economies of scale, doubling the inputs to an industry will more than double the industry's production.

A simple example can help convey the significance of economies of scale for international trade. Table 6-1 shows the relationship between input and output of a hypothetical

Table 6-1	Relationship of Input to Output for a Hypothetical Industry	
Output	**Total Labor Input**	**Average Labor Input**
5	10	2
10	15	1.5
15	20	1.333333
20	25	1.25
25	30	1.2
30	35	1.166667

industry. Widgets are produced using only one input, labor; the table shows how the amount of labor required depends on the number of widgets produced. To produce 10 widgets, for example, requires 15 hours of labor, while to produce 25 widgets requires 30 hours. The presence of economies of scale may be seen from the fact that doubling the input of labor from 15 to 30 more than doubles the industry's output—in fact, output increases by a factor of 2.5. Equivalently, the existence of economies of scale may be seen by looking at the average amount of labor used to produce each unit of output: If output is only 5 widgets the average labor input per widget is 2 hours, while if output is 25 units the average labor input falls to 1.2 hours.

We can use this example to see why economies of scale provide an incentive for international trade. Imagine a world consisting of two countries, America and Britain, both of whom have the same technology for producing widgets, and suppose that initially each country produces 10 widgets. According to the table this requires 15 hours of labor in each country, so in the world as a whole 30 hours of labor produce 20 widgets. But now suppose that we concentrate world production of widgets in one country, say America, and let America employ 30 hours of labor in the widget industry. In a single country these 30 hours of labor can produce 25 widgets. So by concentrating production of widgets in America, the world economy can use the same amount of labor to produce 25 percent more widgets.

But where does America find the extra labor to produce widgets, and what happens to the labor that was employed in the British widget industry? To get the labor to expand its production of some goods, America must decrease or abandon the production of others; these goods will then be produced in Britain instead, using the labor formerly employed in the industries whose production has expanded in America. Imagine that there are many goods subject to economies of scale in production, and give them numbers: 1, 2, 3, ... To take advantage of economies of scale, each of the countries must concentrate on producing only a limited number of goods. Thus, for example, America might produce goods 1, 3, 5, and so on while Britain produces 2, 4, 6, and so on. If each country produces only some of the goods, then each good can be produced at a larger scale than would be the case if each country tried to produce everything, and the world economy can therefore produce more of each good.

How does international trade enter the story? Consumers in each country will still want to consume a variety of goods. Suppose that industry 1 ends up in America and industry 2 in Britain; then American consumers of good 2 will have to buy goods imported from

Britain, while British consumers of good 1 will have to import it from America. International trade plays a crucial role: It makes it possible for each country to produce a restricted range of goods and to take advantage of economies of scale without sacrificing variety in consumption. Indeed, as we will see below, international trade typically leads to an increase in the variety of goods available.

Our example, then, suggests how mutually beneficial trade can arise as a result of economies of scale. Each country specializes in producing a limited range of products, which enables it to produce these goods more efficiently than if it tried to produce everything for itself; these specialized economies then trade with each other to be able to consume the full range of goods.

Unfortunately, to go from this suggestive story to an explicit model of trade based on economies of scale is not that simple. The reason is that economies of scale typically lead to a market structure other than that of perfect competition, and it is necessary to be careful about analyzing this market structure.

Economies of Scale and Market Structure

In the example in Table 6-1, we represented economies of scale by assuming that the labor input per unit of production is smaller the more units produced. We did not say how this production increase was achieved—whether existing firms simply produced more, or whether there was instead an increase in the number of firms. To analyze the effects of economies of scale on market structure, however, one must be clear about what kind of production increase is necessary to reduce average cost. **External economies of scale** occur when the cost per unit depends on the size of the industry but not necessarily on the size of any one firm. **Internal economies of scale** occur when the cost per unit depends on the size of an individual firm but not necessarily on that of the industry.

The distinction between external and internal economies can be illustrated with a hypothetical example. Imagine an industry that initially consists of ten firms, each producing 100 widgets, for a total industry production of 1000 widgets. Now consider two cases. First, suppose the industry were to double in size, so that it now consists of 20 firms, each one still producing 100 widgets. It is possible that the costs of each firm will fall as a result of the increased size of the industry; for example, a bigger industry may allow more efficient provision of specialized services or machinery. If this is the case, the industry exhibits external economies of scale. That is, the efficiency of firms is increased by having a larger industry, even though each firm is the same size as before.

Second, suppose the industry's output were held constant at 1000 widgets, but that the number of firms is cut in half so that each of the remaining five firms produces 200 widgets. If the costs of production fall in this case, then there are internal economies of scale: A firm is more efficient if its output is larger.

External and internal economies of scale have different implications for the structure of industries. An industry where economies of scale are purely external (that is, where there are no advantages to large firms) will typically consist of many small firms and be perfectly competitive. Internal economies of scale, by contrast, give large firms a cost advantage over small and lead to an imperfectly competitive market structure.

Both external and internal economies of scale are important causes of international trade. Because they have different implications for market structure, however, it is difficult to discuss both types of scale economy–based trade in the same model. We will therefore deal with them one at a time.

We begin with a model based on internal economies of scale. As we have just argued, however, internal economies of scale lead to a breakdown of perfect competition. This outcome forces us to take time out to review the economics of imperfect competition before we can turn to the analysis of the role of internal economies of scale in international trade.

The Theory of Imperfect Competition

In a perfectly competitive market—a market in which there are many buyers and sellers, none of whom represents a large part of the market—firms are *price takers*. That is, sellers of products believe that they can sell as much as they like at the current price and cannot influence the price they receive for their product. For example, a wheat farmer can sell as much wheat as she likes without worrying that if she tries to sell more wheat she will depress the market price. The reason she need not worry about the effect of her sales on prices is that any individual wheat grower represents only a tiny fraction of the world market.

When only a few firms produce a good, however, matters are different. To take perhaps the most dramatic example, the aircraft manufacturing giant Boeing shares the market for large jet aircraft with only one major rival, the European firm Airbus. Boeing therefore knows that if it produces more aircraft it will have a significant effect on the total supply of planes in the world and will therefore significantly drive down the price of airplanes. Or to put it the other way around, Boeing knows that if it wants to sell more airplanes, it can do so only by significantly reducing its price. In **imperfect competition**, then, firms are aware that they can influence the prices of their products and that they can sell more only by reducing their price. Imperfect competition is characteristic both of industries in which there are only a few major producers and of industries in which each producer's product is seen by consumers as strongly differentiated from those of rival firms. Under these circumstances each firm views itself as a *price setter*, choosing the price of its product, rather than a price taker.

When firms are not price takers, it is necessary to develop additional tools to describe how prices and outputs are determined. The simplest imperfectly competitive market structure to examine is that of a **pure monopoly**, a market in which a firm faces no competition; the tools we develop can then be used to examine more complex market structures.

Monopoly: A Brief Review

Figure 6-1 shows the position of a single, monopolistic firm. The firm faces a downward-sloping demand curve, shown in the figure as D. The downward slope of D indicates that the firm can sell more units of output only if the price of the output falls. As you may recall from basic microeconomics, a **marginal revenue** curve corresponds to the demand curve. Marginal revenue is the extra or marginal revenue the firm gains from selling an

Figure 6-1 | Monopolistic Pricing and Production Decisions

A monopolistic firm chooses an output at which marginal revenue, the increase in revenue from selling an additional unit, equals marginal cost, the cost of producing an additional unit. This profit-maximizing output is shown as Q_M; the price at which this output is demanded is P_M. The marginal revenue curve MR lies below the demand curve D, because, for a monopoly, marginal revenue is always less than the price. The monopoly's profits are equal to the area of the shaded rectangle, the difference between price and average cost times Q_M.

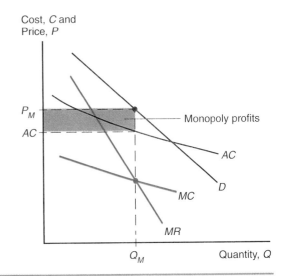

additional unit. Marginal revenue for a monopolist is always less than the price because to sell an additional unit the firm must lower the price of *all* units (not just the marginal one). Thus for a monopolist the marginal revenue curve, *MR*, always lies below the demand curve.

Marginal Revenue and Price.   For our analysis of the monopolistic competition model later in this section it is important to determine the relationship between the price the monopolist receives per unit and marginal revenue. Marginal revenue is always less than the price—but how much less? The relationship between marginal revenue and price depends on two things. First, it depends on how much output the firm is already selling: A firm that is not selling very many units will not lose much by cutting the price it receives on those units. Second, the gap between price and marginal revenue depends on the slope of the demand curve, which tells us how much the monopolist has to cut his price to sell one more unit of output. If the curve is very flat, then the monopolist can sell an additional unit with only a small price cut and will therefore not have to lower the price on units he would have sold otherwise by very much, so marginal revenue will be close to the price per unit. On the other hand, if the demand curve is very steep, selling an additional unit will require a large price cut, implying marginal revenue much less than price.

We can be more specific about the relationship between price and marginal revenue if we assume that the demand curve the firm faces is a straight line. When this is so, the dependence of the monopolist's total sales on the price it charges can be represented by an equation of the form

$$Q = A - B \times P,   \tag{6-1}$$

where Q is the number of units the firm sells, P the price it charges per unit, and A and B are constants. We show in the appendix to this chapter that in this case marginal revenue is

$$\text{Marginal revenue} = MR = P - Q/B, \tag{6-2}$$

implying

$$P - MR = Q/B.$$

Equation (6-2) reveals that the gap between price and marginal revenue depends on the initial sales Q of the firm and the slope parameter B of its demand curve. If sales quantity, Q, is higher, marginal revenue is lower, because the decrease in price required to sell a greater quantity costs the firm more. The greater is B, that is, the more sales fall for any given increase in price and the closer marginal revenue is to the price of the good. Equation (6-2) is crucial for our analysis of the monopolistic competition model of trade (pp. 132–150).

Average and Marginal Costs.   Returning to Figure 6-1, AC represents the firm's **average cost** of production, that is, its total cost divided by its output. The downward slope reflects our assumption that there are economies of scale, so that the larger the firm's output is the lower are its costs per unit. MC represents the firm's **marginal cost** (the amount it costs the firm to produce one extra unit). We know from basic economics that when average costs are a decreasing function of output, marginal cost is always less than average cost. Thus MC lies below AC.

Equation (6-2) related price and marginal revenue. There is a corresponding formula relating average and marginal cost. Suppose the costs of a firm, C, take the form

$$C = F + c \times Q, \tag{6-3}$$

where F is a fixed cost that is independent of the firm's output, c is the firm's marginal cost, and Q is once again the firm's output. (This is called a linear cost function.) *The fixed cost in a linear cost function gives rise to economies of scale, because the larger the firm's output, the less is the fixed cost per unit.* Specifically, the firm's average cost (total cost divided by output) is

$$\text{Average cost} = AC = C/Q = F/Q + c. \tag{6-4}$$

This average cost declines as Q increases because the fixed cost is spread over a larger output.

If, for example, $F = 5$ and $c = 1$ the average cost of producing 10 units is $5/10 + 1 = 1.5$ and the average cost of producing 25 units is $5/25 + 1 = 1.2$. These numbers may look familiar, because they were used to construct Table 6-1. The relationship between output, average costs, and marginal costs given in Table 6-1 is shown graphically in Figure 6-2. Average cost approaches infinity at zero output and approaches marginal cost at very large output.

The profit-maximizing output of a monopolist is that at which marginal revenue (the revenue gained from selling an extra unit) equals marginal cost (the cost of producing an

Figure 6-2 | Average Versus Marginal Cost

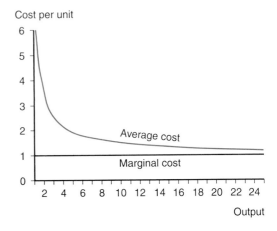

This figure illustrates the average and marginal costs corresponding to the total cost function $C = 5 + x$. Marginal cost is always 1; average cost declines as output rises.

extra unit), that is, at the intersection of the *MC* and *MR* curves. In Figure 6-1 we can see that the price at which the profit-maximizing output Q_M is demanded is P_M, which is greater than average cost. When $P > AC$, the monopolist is earning some monopoly profits.[1]

Monopolistic Competition

Monopoly profits rarely go uncontested. A firm making high profits normally attracts competitors. Thus situations of pure monopoly are rare in practice. Instead, the usual market structure in industries characterized by internal economies of scale is one of **oligopoly**: several firms, each of them large enough to affect prices, but none with an uncontested monopoly.

The general analysis of oligopoly is a complex and controversial subject because in oligopolies the pricing policies of firms are *interdependent*. Each firm in an oligopoly will, in setting its price, consider not only the responses of consumers but also the expected responses of competitors. These responses, however, depend in turn on the competitors' expectations about the firm's behavior—and we are therefore in a complex game in which firms are trying to second-guess each others' strategies. We will briefly discuss the general problems of modeling oligopoly below. However, there is a special case of oligopoly, known as monopolistic competition, which is relatively easy to analyze. Since 1980 monopolistic competition models have been widely applied to international trade.

In **monopolistic competition** models two key assumptions are made to get around the problem of interdependence. First, each firm is assumed to be able to *differentiate its*

---

[1]The economic definition of *profits* is not the same as that used in conventional accounting, where any revenue over and above labor and material costs is called a profit. A firm that earns a rate of return on its capital less than what that capital could have earned in other industries is not making profits; from an economic point of view the normal rate of return on capital represents part of the firm's costs, and only returns over and above that normal rate of return represent profits.

product from that of its rivals. That is, because they want to buy this firm's particular product, the firm's customers will not rush to buy other firms' products because of a slight price difference. Product differentiation assures that each firm has a monopoly in its particular product within an industry and is therefore somewhat insulated from competition. Second, each firm is assumed to take the prices charged by its rivals as given—that is, it ignores the impact of its own price on the prices of other firms. As a result, the monopolistic competition model assumes that even though each firm is in reality facing competition from other firms, it behaves as if it were a monopolist—hence the model's name.

Are there any monopolistically competitive industries in the real world? Some industries may be reasonable approximations. For example, the automobile industry in Europe, where a number of major producers (Ford, General Motors, Volkswagen, Renault, Peugeot, Fiat, Volvo—and more recently Nissan) offer substantially different yet nonetheless competing automobiles, may be fairly well described by monopolistically competitive assumptions. The main appeal of the monopolistic competition model is not, however, its realism, but its simplicity. As we will see in the next section of this chapter, the monopolistic competition model gives us a very clear view of how economies of scale can give rise to mutually beneficial trade.

Before we can examine trade, however, we need to develop a basic model of monopolistic competition. Let us therefore imagine an industry consisting of a number of firms. These firms produce differentiated products, that is, goods that are not exactly the same but that are substitutes for one another. Each firm is therefore a monopolist in the sense that it is the only firm producing its particular good, but the demand for its good depends on the number of other similar products available and on the prices of other firms in the industry.

Assumptions of the Model.   We begin by describing the demand facing a typical monopolistically competitive firm. In general, we would expect a firm to sell more the larger the total demand for its industry's product and the higher the prices charged by its rivals. On the other hand, we expect the firm to sell less the greater the number of firms in the industry and the higher its own price. A particular equation for the demand facing a firm that has these properties is[2]

$$Q = S \times [1/n - b \times (P - \bar{P})], \tag{6-5}$$

where Q is the firm's sales, S is the total sales of the industry, n the number of firms in the industry, b a constant term representing the responsiveness of a firm's sales to its price, P the price charged by the firm itself, and $\bar{P}$ the average price charged by its competitors. Equation (6-5) may be given the following intuitive justification: If all firms charge the same price, each will have a market share $1/n$. A firm charging more than the average of other firms will have a smaller market share, a firm charging less a larger share.[3]

It is helpful to assume that total industry sales S are unaffected by the average price $\bar{P}$ charged by firms in the industry. That is, we assume that firms can gain customers only at

---

[2]Equation (6-5) can be derived from a model in which consumers have different preferences and firms produce varieties tailored to particular segments of the market. See Stephen Salop, "Monopolistic Competition with Outside Goods," *Bell Journal of Economics* 10 (1979), pp. 141–156 for a development of this approach.

[3]Equation (6-5) may be rewritten as $Q = S/n - S \times b \times (P - \bar{P})$. If $P = \bar{P}$, this reduces to $Q = S/n$. If $P > \bar{P}$, $Q < S/n$, while if $P < \bar{P}$, $Q > S/n$.

each others' expense. This is an unrealistic assumption, but it simplifies the analysis and helps focus on the competition among firms. In particular, it means that S is a measure of the size of the market and that if all firms charge the same price, each sells S/n units.

Next we turn to the costs of a typical firm. Here we simply assume that total and average costs of a typical firm are described by equations (6-3) and (6-4).

Market Equilibrium. To model the behavior of this monopolistically competitive industry, we will assume that all firms in this industry are *symmetric,* that is, the demand function and cost function are identical for all firms (even though they are producing and selling somewhat differentiated products). When the individual firms are symmetric, the state of the industry can be described without enumerating the features of all firms in detail: All we really need to know to describe the industry is how many firms there are and what price the typical firm charges. To analyze the industry, for example to assess the effects of international trade, we need to determine the number of firms n and the average price they charge $\bar{P}$. Once we have a method for determining n and $\bar{P}$, we can ask how they are affected by international trade.

Our method for determining n and $\bar{P}$ involves three steps. (1) First, we derive a relationship between the number of firms and the *average cost* of a typical firm. We show that this relationship is upward sloping; that is, the more firms there are, the lower the output of each firm, and thus the higher its cost per unit of output. (2) We next show the relationship between the number of firms and the price each firm charges, which must equal $\bar{P}$ in equilibrium. We show that this relationship is downward sloping: the more firms there are, the more intense is competition among firms, and as a result the lower the prices they charge. (3) Finally, we argue that when the price exceeds average cost additional firms will enter the industry, while when the price is less than average cost firms will exit. So in the long run the number of firms is determined by the intersection of the curve that relates average cost to n and the curve that relates price to n.

1. *The number of firms and average cost.* As a first step toward determining n and $\bar{P}$, we ask how the average cost of a typical firm depends on the number of firms in the industry. Since all firms are symmetric in this model, in equilibrium they will all charge the same price. But when all firms charge the same price, so that $P = \bar{P}$, equation (6-5) tells us that $Q = S/n$; that is, each firm's output Q, is a $1/n$ share of the total industry sales S. But we saw in equation (6-4) that average cost depends inversely on a firm's output. We therefore conclude that average cost depends on the size of the market and the number of firms in the industry:

$$AC = F/Q + c = n \times F/S + c. \qquad (6\text{-}6)$$

Equation (6-6) tells us that other things equal, *the more firms there are in the industry the higher is average cost.* The reason is that the more firms there are, the less each firm produces. For example, imagine an industry with total sales of 1 million widgets annually. If there are five firms in the industry, each will sell 200,000 annually. If there are ten firms, each will sell only 100,000, and therefore each firm will have higher average cost. The upward-sloping relationship between n and average cost is shown as CC in Figure 6-3.

Figure 6-3 | Equilibrium in a Monopolistically Competitive Market

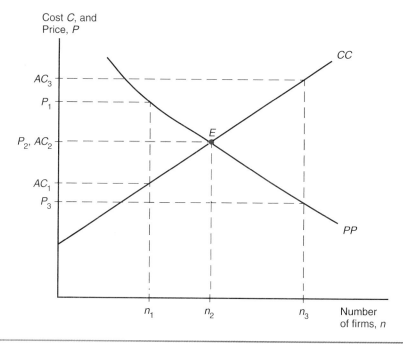

The number of firms in a monopolistically competitive market, and the prices they charge, are determined by two relationships. On one side, the more firms there are, the more intensely they compete, and hence the lower is the industry price. This relationship is represented by *PP*. On the other side, the more firms there are, the less each firm sells and therefore the higher is its average cost. This relationship is represented by *CC*. If price exceeds average cost (if the *PP* curve is above the *CC* curve), the industry will be making profits and additional firms will enter the industry; if price is less than average cost, the industry will be incurring losses and firms will leave the industry. The equilibrium price and number of firms occurs when price equals average cost, at the intersection of *PP* and *CC*.

2. *The number of firms and the price.* Meanwhile, the price the typical firm charges also depends on the number of firms in the industry. In general, we would expect that the more firms there are, the more intense will be the competition among them, and hence the lower the price. This turns out to be true in this model, but proving it takes a moment. The basic trick is to show that each firm faces a straight-line demand curve of the form we showed in equation (6-1), and then to use equation (6-2) to determine prices.

First recall that in the monopolistic competition model firms are assumed to take each others' prices as given; that is, each firm ignores the possibility that if it changes its price other firms will also change theirs. If each firm treats $\bar{P}$ as given, we can rewrite the demand curve (6-5) in the form

$$Q = (S/n + S \times b \times \bar{P}) - S \times b \times P, \tag{6-7}$$

where b is the parameter in equation (6-5) that measured the sensitivity of each firm's market share to the price it charges. Now this is in the same form as (6-1), with $S/n + S \times b \times \bar{P}$ in place of the constant term A and $S \times b$ in place of the slope coefficient B. If we plug these values back into the formula for marginal revenue (6-2), we have a marginal revenue for a typical firm of

$$MR = P - Q/(S \times b). \tag{6-8}$$

Profit-maximizing firms will set marginal revenue equal to their marginal cost c, so that

$$MR = P - Q/(S \times b) = c,$$

which can be rearranged to give the following equation for the price charged by a typical firm:

$$P = c + Q/(S \times b). \tag{6-9}$$

We have already noted, however, that if all firms charge the same price, each will sell an amount $Q = S/n$. Plugging this back into (6-9) gives us a relationship between the number of firms and the price each firm charges:

$$P = c + 1/(b \times n). \tag{6-10}$$

Equation (6-10) says algebraically that *the more firms there are in the industry, the lower the price each firm will charge*. Equation (6-10) is shown in Figure 6-3 as the downward-sloping curve *PP*.

3. *The equilibrium number of firms.* Let us now ask what Figure 6-3 means. We have summarized an industry by two curves. The downward-sloping curve *PP* shows that the more firms there are in the industry, the lower the price each firm will charge. This makes sense: The more firms there are, the more competition each firm faces. The upward-sloping curve *CC* tells us that the more firms there are in the industry, the higher the average cost of each firm. This also makes sense: If the number of firms increases, each firm will sell less, so firms will not be able to move as far down their average cost curve.

The two schedules intersect at point E, corresponding to the number of firms n_2. The significance of n_2 is that it is the *zero-profit* number of firms in the industry. When there are n_2 firms in the industry, their profit-maximizing price is P_2, which is exactly equal to their average cost AC_2.

What we will now argue is that in the long run the number of firms in the industry tends to move toward n_2, so that point E describes the industry's long-run equilibrium.

To see why, suppose that n were less than n_2, say n_1. Then the price charged by firms would be P_1, while their average cost would be only AC_1. Thus firms would be making monopoly profits. Conversely, suppose that n were greater than n_2, say n_3. Then firms would charge only the price P_3, while their average cost would be AC_3. Firms would be suffering losses.

Over time, firms will enter an industry that is profitable, exit one in which they lose money. The number of firms will rise over time if it is less than n_2, fall if it is greater. This means that n_2 is the equilibrium number of firms in the industry and P_2 the equilibrium price.[4]

We have now developed a model of a monopolistically competitive industry in which we can determine the equilibrium number of firms and the average price that firms charge. We can use this model to derive some important conclusions about the role of economies of scale in international trade. But before we do, we should take a moment to note some limitations of the monopolistic competition model.

Limitations of the Monopolistic Competition Model

The monopolistic competition model captures certain key elements of markets where there are economies of scale and thus imperfect competition. However, few industries are well described by monopolistic competition. Instead, the most common market structure is one of small-group oligopoly, where only a few firms are actively engaged in competition. In this situation the key assumption of the monopolistic competition model, which is that each firm will behave as if it were a true monopolist, is likely to break down. Instead, firms will be aware that their actions influence the actions of other firms and will take this interdependence into account.

Two kinds of behavior arise in the general oligopoly setting that are excluded by assumption from the monopolistic competition model. The first is *collusive* behavior. Each firm may keep its price higher than the apparent profit-maximizing level as part of an understanding that other firms will do the same; since each firm's profits are higher if its competitors charge high prices, such an understanding can raise the profits of all the firms (at the expense of consumers). Collusive price-setting behavior may be managed through explicit agreements (illegal in the United States) or through tacit coordination strategies, such as allowing one firm to act as a price leader for the industry.

Firms may also engage in *strategic* behavior; that is, they may do things that seem to lower profits, but that affect the behavior of competitors in a desirable way. For example a firm may build extra capacity not to use it but to deter potential rivals from entering its industry.

These possibilities for both collusive and strategic behavior make the analysis of oligopoly a complex matter. There is no one generally accepted model of oligopoly behavior, which makes modeling trade in monopolistic industries problematic.

The monopolistic competition approach to trade is attractive because it avoids these complexities. Even though it may leave out some features of the real world, the monopolistic competition model is widely accepted as a way to provide at least a first cut at the role of economies of scale in international trade.

---

[4]This analysis slips past a slight problem: The number of firms in an industry must, of course be a whole number like 5 or 8. What if n_2 turns out to equal 6.37? The answer is that there will be 6 firms in the industry, all making small monopoly profits, but not challenged by new entrants because everyone knows that a seven-firm industry would lose money. In most examples of monopolistic competition, this whole-number or "integer constraint" problem turns out not to be very important, and we ignore it here.

Monopolistic Competition and Trade

Underlying the application of the monopolistic competition model to trade is the idea that trade increases market size. In industries where there are economies of scale, both the variety of goods that a country can produce and the scale of its production are constrained by the size of the market. By trading with each other, and therefore forming an integrated world market that is bigger than any individual national market, nations are able to loosen these constraints. Each country can specialize in producing a narrower range of products than it would in the absence of trade; yet by buying goods that it does not make from other countries, each nation can simultaneously increase the variety of goods available to its consumers. As a result, trade offers an opportunity for mutual gain even when countries do not differ in their resources or technology.

Suppose, for example, that there are two countries, each with an annual market for 1 million automobiles. By trading with each other, these countries can create a combined market of 2 million autos. In this combined market, more varieties of automobiles can be produced, at lower average costs, than in either market alone.

The monopolistic competition model can be used to show how trade improves the trade-off between scale and variety that individual nations face. We will begin by showing how a larger market leads, in the monopolistic competition model, to both a lower average price and the availability of a greater variety of goods. Applying this result to international trade, we observe that trade creates a world market larger than any of the national markets that comprise it. Integrating markets through international trade therefore has the same effects as growth of a market within a single country.

The Effects of Increased Market Size

The number of firms in a monopolistically competitive industry and the prices they charge are affected by the size of the market. In larger markets there usually will be both more firms and more sales per firm; consumers in a large market will be offered both lower prices and a greater variety of products than consumers in small markets.

To see this in the context of our model, look again at the CC curve in Figure 6-3, which showed that average costs per firm are higher the more firms there are in the industry. The definition of the CC curve is given by equation (6-6):

$$AC = F/Q + c = n \times F/S + c.$$

Examining this equation, we see that an increase in total sales S will reduce average costs for any given number of firms n. The reason is that if the market grows while the number of firms is held constant, sales per firm will increase and the average cost of each firm will therefore decline. Thus if we compare two markets, one with higher S than the other, the CC curve in the larger market will be below that in the smaller one.

Meanwhile, the PP curve in Figure 6-3, which relates the price charged by firms to the number of firms, does not shift. The definition of that curve is given in equation (6-10):

$$P = c + 1/(b \times n).$$

The size of the market does not enter into this equation, so an increase in S does not shift the PP curve.

Figure 6-4 | Effects of a Larger Market

An increase in the size of the market allows each firm, other things equal, to produce more and thus have lower average cost. This is represented by a downward shift from CC_1 to CC_2. The result is a simultaneous increase in the number of firms (and hence in the variety of goods available) and fall in the price of each.

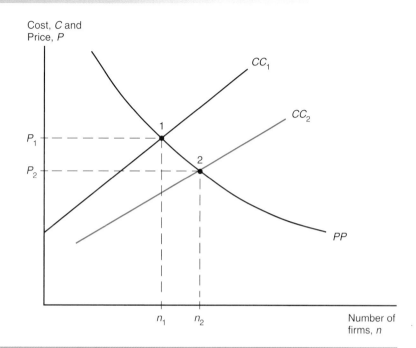

Figure 6-4 uses this information to show the effect of an increase in the size of the market on long-run equilibrium. Initially, equilibrium is at point 1, with a price P_1 and a number of firms n_1. An increase in the size of the market, measured by industry sales S, shifts the CC curve down from CC_1 to CC_2, while it has no effect on the PP curve. The new equilibrium is at point 2: The number of firms increases from n_1 to n_2, while the price falls from P_1 to P_2.

Clearly, consumers would prefer to be part of a large market rather than a small one. At point 2, a greater variety of products is available at a lower price than at point 1.

Gains from an Integrated Market: A Numerical Example

International trade can create a larger market. We can illustrate the effects of trade on prices, scale, and the variety of goods available with a specific numerical example.

Imagine that automobiles are produced by a monopolistically competitive industry. The demand curve facing any given producer of automobiles is described by equation (6-5), with $b = 1/30,000$ (this value has no particular significance; it was chosen to make the example come out neatly). Thus the demand facing any one producer is given by

$$Q = S \times [1/n - (1/30,000) \times (P - \bar{P})],$$

where Q is the number of automobiles sold per firm, S the total sales of the industry, n the number of firms, P the price that a firm charges, and $\bar{P}$ the average price of other firms. We also assume that the cost function for producing automobiles is described by equation (6-3), with a fixed cost $F = \$750,000,000$ and a marginal cost $c = \$5000$ per automobile (again these values are chosen to give nice results). The total cost is

$$C = 750,000,000 + (5000 \times Q).$$

The average cost curve is therefore

$$AC = (750,000,000/Q) + 5000.$$

Now suppose there are two countries, Home and Foreign. Home has annual sales of 900,000 automobiles; Foreign has annual sales of 1.6 million. The two countries are assumed, for the moment, to have the same costs of production.

Figure 6-5a shows the *PP* and *CC* curves for the Home auto industry. We find that in the absence of trade, Home would have six automobile firms, selling at a price of $10,000 each. (It is also possible to solve for *n* and *P* algebraically, as shown in the Mathematical Postscript to this chapter.) To confirm that this is the long-run equilibrium, we need to show both that the pricing equation (6-10) is satisfied and that the price equals average cost.

Substituting the actual values of the marginal cost *c*, the demand parameter *b*, and the number of Home firms *n* into equation (6-10), we find

$$P = \$10,000 = c + 1/(b \times n) = \$5000 + 1/[(1/30,000) \times 6] = \$5000 + \$5000,$$

so the condition for profit maximization—that marginal revenue equal marginal cost—is satisfied. Each firm sells 900,000 units/6 firms = 150,000 units/firm. Its average cost is therefore

$$AC = (\$750,000,000/150,000) + \$5000 = \$10,000.$$

Since the average cost of $10,000 per unit is the same as the price, all monopoly profits have been competed away. Thus six firms, selling at a price of $10,000, with each firm producing 150,000 cars, is the long-run equilibrium in the Home market.

What about Foreign? By drawing the *PP* and *CC* curves (panel (b) in Figure 6-5) we find that when the market is for 1.6 million automobiles, the curves intersect at $n = 8$, $P = 8750$. That is, in the absence of trade Foreign's market would support eight firms, each producing 200,000 automobiles, and selling them at a price of $8750. We can again confirm that this solution satisfies the equilibrium conditions:

$$P = \$8750 = c + 1/(b \times n) = \$5000 + 1/[(1/30,000) \times 8] = \$5000 + \$3750,$$

and

$$AC = (\$750,000,000/200,000) + \$5000 = \$8750.$$

Now suppose it is possible for Home and Foreign to trade automobiles costlessly with one another. This creates a new, integrated market (panel (c) in Figure 6-5) with total sales of 2.5 million. By drawing the *PP* and *CC* curves one more time, we find that this integrated

Figure 6-5 Equilibrium in the Automobile Market

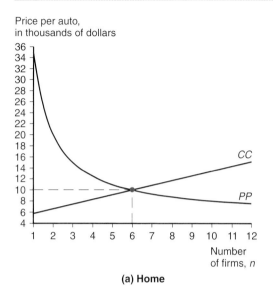

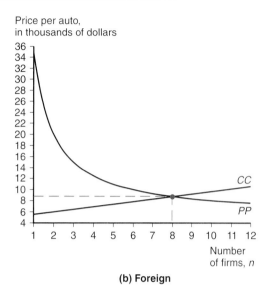

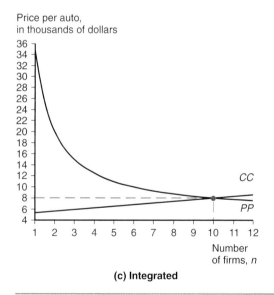

(a) The Home market: With a market size of 900,000 automobiles, Home's equilibrium, determined by the intersection of the *PP* and *CC* curves, occurs with six firms and an industry price of $10,000 per auto. (b) The Foreign market: With a market size of 1.6 million automobiles, Foreign's equilibrium occurs with eight firms and an industry price of $8750 per car. (c) The combined market: Integrating the two markets creates a market for 2.5 million autos. This market supports ten firms, and the price of an auto is only $8000.

market will support ten firms, each producing 250,000 cars and selling them at a price of $8000. The conditions for profit maximization and zero profits are again satisfied:

$$P = \$8000 = c + 1/(b \times n) = \$5000 + 1/[(1/30,000) \times 10] = \$5000 + \$3000,$$

and

$$AC = (\$750,000,000/250,000) + \$5000 = \$8000.$$

We summarize the results of creating an integrated market in Table 6-2. The table compares each market alone with the integrated market. The integrated market supports more firms, each producing at a larger scale and selling at a lower price than either national market did on its own.

Clearly everyone is better off as a result of integration. In the larger market, consumers have a wider range of choice, yet each firm produces more and is therefore able to offer its product at a lower price.

To realize these gains from integration, the countries must engage in international trade. To achieve economies of scale, each firm must concentrate its production in one country—either Home or Foreign. Yet it must sell its output to customers in both markets. So each product will be produced in only one country and exported to the other.

Economies of Scale and Comparative Advantage

Our example of a monopolistically competitive industry says little about the pattern of trade that results from economies of scale. The model assumes that the cost of production is the same in both countries and that trade is costless. These assumptions mean that although we know that the integrated market will support ten firms, we cannot say where they will be located. For example, four firms might be in Home and six in Foreign—but it is equally possible, as far as this example goes, that all ten will be in Foreign (or in Home).

To say more than that the market will support ten firms, it is necessary to go behind the partial equilibrium framework that we have considered so far and think about how economies of scale interact with comparative advantage to determine the pattern of international trade.

Let us therefore now imagine a world economy consisting, as usual, of our two countries Home and Foreign. Each of these countries has two factors of production, capital and

Table 6-2 | Hypothetical Example of Gains from Market Integration

	Home Market, before Trade	Foreign Market, before Trade	Integrated Market, after Trade
Total sales of autos	900,000	1,600,000	2,500,000
Number of firms	6	8	10
Sales per firm	150,000	200,000	250,000
Average cost	10,000	8,750	8,000
Price	10,000	8,750	8,000

labor. We assume that Home has a higher overall capital-labor ratio than Foreign, that is, that Home is the capital-abundant country. Let's also imagine that there are two industries, manufactures and food, with manufactures the more capital-intensive industry.

The difference between this model and the factor proportions model of Chapter 4 is that we now suppose that manufactures is not a perfectly competitive industry producing a homogeneous product. Instead, it is a monopolistically competitive industry in which a number of firms all produce differentiated products. *Because of economies of scale, neither country is able to produce the full range of manufactured products by itself; thus, although both countries may produce some manufactures, they will be producing different things.* The monopolistically competitive nature of the manufactures industry makes an important difference to the trade pattern, a difference that can best be seen by looking at what would happen if manufactures were *not* a monopolistically competitive sector.

If manufactures were *not* a differentiated product sector, we know from Chapter 4 what the trade pattern would look like. Because Home is capital-abundant and manufactures capital-intensive, Home would have a larger relative supply of manufactures and would therefore export manufactures and import food. Schematically, we can represent this trade pattern with a diagram like Figure 6-6. The length of the arrows indicates the value of trade in each direction; the figure shows that Home would export manufactures equal in value to the food it imports.

If we assume that manufactures is a monopolistically competitive sector (each firm's products are differentiated from other firms'), Home will still be a *net* exporter of manufactures and an importer of food. However, Foreign firms in the manufactures sector will produce products different from those that Home firms produce. Because some Home consumers will prefer Foreign varieties, Home, although running a trade surplus in manufactures, will import as well as export within the manufacturing industry. With manufactures monopolistically competitive, then, the pattern of trade will look like Figure 6-7.

We can think of world trade in a monopolistic competition model as consisting of two parts. There will be two-way trade *within* the manufacturing sector. This exchange of manufactures for manufactures is called **intraindustry trade**. The remainder of trade is an exchange of manufactures for food called **interindustry trade**.

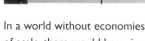 **Figure 6-6** | Trade in a World Without Increasing Returns

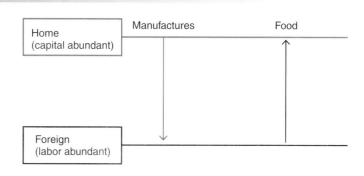

In a world without economies of scale, there would be a simple exchange of manufactures for food.

Figure 6-7 | Trade with Increasing Returns and Monopolistic Competition

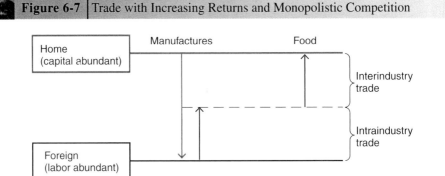

If manufactures is a monopolistically competitive industry, Home and Foreign will produce differentiated products. As a result, even if Home is a net exporter of manufactured goods, it will import as well as export manufactures, giving rise to intraindustry trade.

Notice these four points about this pattern of trade:

1. *Interindustry* (manufactures for food) trade reflects comparative advantage. The pattern of interindustry trade is that Home, the capital-abundant country, is a net exporter of capital-intensive manufactures and a net importer of labor-intensive food. So comparative advantage continues to be a major part of the trade story.

2. *Intraindustry* trade (manufactures for manufactures) does *not* reflect comparative advantage. Even if the countries had the same overall capital-labor ratio, their firms would continue to produce differentiated products and the demand of consumers for products made abroad would continue to generate intraindustry trade. It is economies of scale that keep each country from producing the full range of products for itself; thus economies of scale can be an independent source of international trade.

3. The pattern of intraindustry trade itself is unpredictable. We have not said anything about which country produces which goods within the manufactures sector because there is nothing in the model to tell us. All we know is that the countries will produce different products. Since history and accident determine the details of the trade pattern, an unpredictable component of the trade pattern is an inevitable feature of a world where economies of scale are important. Notice, however, that the unpredictability is not total. While the precise pattern of intraindustry trade within the manufactures sector is arbitrary, the pattern of interindustry trade between manufactures and food is determined by underlying differences between countries.

4. The relative importance of intraindustry and interindustry trade depends on how similar countries are. If Home and Foreign are similar in their capital-labor ratios, then there will be little interindustry trade, and intraindustry trade, based ultimately on economies of scale, will be dominant. On the other hand, if the capital-labor ratios are very different, so that, for example, Foreign specializes completely in food production, there will be no intraindustry trade based on economies of scale. All trade will be based on comparative advantage.

The Significance of Intraindustry Trade

About one-fourth of world trade consists of intraindustry trade, that is, two-way exchanges of goods within standard industrial classifications. Intraindustry trade plays a particularly large role in the trade in manufactured goods among advanced industrial nations, which accounts for most of world trade. Over time, the industrial countries have become increasingly similar in their levels of technology and in the availability of capital and skilled labor. Since the major trading nations have become similar in technology and resources, there is often no clear comparative advantage within an industry, and much of international trade therefore takes the form of two-way exchanges within industries—probably driven in large part by economies of scale—rather than interindustry specialization driven by comparative advantage.

Table 6-3 shows measures of the importance of intraindustry trade for a number of U.S. manufacturing industries in 1993. The measure shown is intraindustry trade/total trade.[5] The measure ranges from 0.99 for inorganic chemicals—an industry in which U.S. exports and imports are nearly equal—to 0.00 for footwear, an industry in which the United States has large imports but virtually no exports. The measure would be zero for an industry in which the United States was only an exporter or only an importer, not both; it would be one in an industry for which U.S. exports exactly equaled U.S. imports.

Table 6-3 shows that in many industries a large part of trade is intraindustry (closer to one) rather than interindustry (closer to zero). The industries are ranked by the relative importance of intraindustry trade, those with higher intraindustry trade first. Industries with high levels of intraindustry trade tend to be sophisticated manufactured goods, such as chemicals, pharmaceuticals, and power-generating equipment. These goods are exported principally by advanced nations and are probably subject to important economies of scale in production. At the other end of the scale, the industries with very little intraindustry trade are typically labor-intensive products, such as footwear and apparel. These are goods that the United States imports primarily from less developed countries, where comparative advantage is clear-cut and is the primary determinant of U.S. trade with these countries.[6]

---

[5] To be more precise, the standard formula for calculating the importance of intraindustry trade within a given industry is

$$I = 1 - \frac{|\text{exports} - \text{imports}|}{\text{exports} + \text{imports}}$$

where the expression |exports − imports| means "absolute value of the trade balance": if exports are $100 million more than imports, the numerator of the fraction is 100, but if exports are $100 million *less* than imports, it is also 100. In comparative-advantage models of international trade, we expect a country either to export a good or to import it, not both; in that case I would always equal zero. On the other hand, if a country's exports and imports within an industry are equal, we find $I = 1$.

[6] The growing trade between low-wage and high-wage nations sometimes produces trade that is classified as intraindustry even though it is really driven by comparative advantage. Suppose, for example, a U.S. company produces some sophisticated computer chips in California, ships them to Asia where they are assembled into a computer, and then ships that computer back home. Both the exported components and the imported computer are likely to be classified as being "computers and related devices," so that the transactions will be counted as intraindustry trade. Nonetheless, what is really going on is that the United States is exporting skill-intensive products (chips) and importing a labor-intensive service (computer assembly). Such "pseudo-intraindustry" trade is particularly common in trade between the United States and Mexico.

Table 6-3	Indexes of Intraindustry Trade for U.S. Industries, 1993
Inorganic chemicals	0.99
Power-generating machinery	0.97
Electrical machinery	0.96
Organic chemicals	0.91
Medical and pharmaceutical	0.86
Office machinery	0.81
Telecommunications equipment	0.69
Road vehicles	0.65
Iron and steel	0.43
Clothing and apparel	0.27
Footwear	0.00

Why Intraindustry Trade Matters

Table 6-3 shows that a sizeable part of international trade is intraindustry trade rather than the interindustry trade we studied in Chapters 2 through 5. But does the importance of intraindustry trade change any of our conclusions?

First, intraindustry trade produces extra gains from international trade, over and above those from comparative advantage, because intraindustry trade allows countries to benefit from larger markets. As we have seen, by engaging in intraindustry trade a country can simultaneously reduce the number of products it produces *and* increase the variety of goods available to domestic consumers. By producing fewer varieties, a country can produce each at larger scale, with higher productivity and lower costs. At the same time, consumers benefit from the increased range of choice. In our numerical example of the gains from integrating a market, Home consumers found that intraindustry trade expanded their range of choice from six automobile models to ten even as it reduced the price of autos from $10,000 to $8000. As the case study of the North American auto industry indicates (p. 141), the advantages of creating an integrated industry in two countries can be substantial in reality as well.

In our earlier analysis of the distribution of gains from trade (Chapters 3 and 4), we were pessimistic about the prospects that everyone will benefit from trade, even though international trade could potentially raise everyone's income. In the models discussed earlier, trade had all its effects through changes in relative prices, which in turn have very strong effects on the distribution of income.

Suppose, however, that intraindustry trade is the dominant source of gains from trade. This will happen (1) when countries are similar in their relative factor supplies, so that there is not much interindustry trade, and (2) when scale economies and product differentiation are important, so that the gains from larger scale and increased choice are large. In these circumstances the income distribution effects of trade will be small and there will be substantial extra gains from intraindustry trade. The result may well be that despite the effects of trade on income distribution, everyone gains from trade.

When will this be most likely to happen? Intraindustry trade tends to be prevalent between countries that are similar in their capital-labor ratios, skill levels, and so on. Thus, intraindustry trade will be dominant between countries at a similar level of economic development. Gains from this trade will be large when economies of scale are strong and products are highly differentiated. This is more characteristic of sophisticated manufactured goods than of raw materials or more traditional sectors (such as textiles or footwear). Trade without serious income distribution effects, then, is most likely to happen in manufactures trade between advanced industrial countries.

This conclusion is borne out by postwar experience, particularly in Western Europe. In 1957 the major countries of continental Europe established a free trade area in manufactured goods, the Common Market, or European Economic Community (EEC). (The United Kingdom entered the EEC later, in 1973.) The result was a rapid growth of trade. Trade within the EEC grew twice as fast as world trade as a whole during the 1960s. One might have expected this rapid growth in trade to produce substantial dislocations and political problems. The growth in trade, however, was almost entirely intraindustry rather than interindustry; drastic economic dislocation did not occur. Instead of, say, workers in France's electrical machinery industry being hurt while those in Germany's gained, workers in both sectors gained from the increased efficiency of the integrated European industry. The result was that the growth in trade within Europe presented far fewer social and political problems than anyone anticipated.

There is both a good and a bad side to this favorable view of intraindustry trade. The good side is that under some circumstances trade is relatively easy to live with and therefore relatively easy to support politically. The bad side is that trade between very different countries or where scale economies and product differentiation are not important remains politically problematic. In fact, the progressive liberalization of trade that characterized the 30-year period from 1950 to 1980 was primarily concentrated on trade in manufactures among the advanced nations, as we will see in Chapter 9. If progress on other kinds of trade is important, the past record does not give us much encouragement.

CASE STUDY

Intraindustry Trade in Action: The North American Auto Pact of 1964

An unusually clear-cut example of the role of economies of scale in generating beneficial international trade is provided by the growth in automotive trade between the United States and Canada during the second half of the 1960s. While the case does not fit our model exactly, it does show that the basic concepts we have developed are useful in the real world.

Before 1965, tariff protection by Canada and the United States produced a Canadian auto industry that was largely self-sufficient, neither importing nor exporting much. The Canadian industry was controlled by the same firms as the U.S. industry—a departure from our model, since we have not yet examined the role of multinational firms—but these firms found it cheaper to have largely separate production systems than to pay the tariffs. Thus the Canadian industry was in effect a miniature version of the U.S. industry, at about one-tenth the scale.

The Canadian subsidiaries of U.S. firms found that small scale was a substantial disadvantage. This was partly because Canadian plants had to be smaller than their U.S. counterparts. Perhaps more important, U.S. plants could often be "dedicated"—that is, devoted to producing a single model or component—while Canadian plants had to produce several different things, requiring the plants to shut down periodically to change over from producing one item to producing another, to hold larger inventories, to use less specialized machinery, and so on. The Canadian auto industry had a labor productivity about 30 percent lower than that of the United States.

In an effort to remove these problems, the United States and Canada agreed in 1964 to establish a free trade area in automobiles (subject to certain restrictions). This allowed the auto companies to reorganize their production. Canadian subsidiaries of the auto firms sharply cut the number of products made in Canada. For example, General Motors cut in half the number of models assembled in Canada. The overall level of Canadian production and employment was, however, maintained. This was achieved by importing from the United States products no longer made in Canada and exporting the products Canada continued to make. In 1962, Canada exported $16 million worth of automotive products to the United States while importing $519 million worth. By 1968 the numbers were $2.4 and $2.9 billion, respectively. In other words, both exports and imports increased sharply: intraindustry trade in action.

The gains seem to have been substantial. By the early 1970s the Canadian industry was comparable to the U.S. industry in productivity.

Dumping

The monopolistic competition model helps us understand how increasing returns promote international trade. As we noted earlier, however, this model assumes away many of the issues that can arise when firms are imperfectly competitive. Although it recognizes that imperfect competition is a necessary consequence of economies of scale, the monopolistic competition analysis does not focus on the possible consequences of imperfect competition itself for international trade.

In reality, imperfect competition has some important consequences for international trade. The most striking of these is that firms do not necessarily charge the same price for goods that are exported and those that are sold to domestic buyers.

The Economics of Dumping

In imperfectly competitive markets, firms sometimes charge one price for a good when that good is exported and a different price for the same good when it is sold domestically. In general, the practice of charging different customers different prices is called **price discrimination**. The most common form of price discrimination in international trade is **dumping**, a pricing practice in which a firm charges a lower price for exported goods than it does for the same goods sold domestically. Dumping is a controversial issue in trade policy, where it is widely regarded as an "unfair" practice and is subject to special rules and penalties. We will discuss the policy dispute surrounding dumping in Chapter 9. For now, we present some basic economic analysis of the dumping phenomenon.

Dumping can occur only if two conditions are met. First, the industry must be imperfectly competitive, so that firms set prices rather than taking market prices as given. Second, markets must be *segmented,* so that domestic residents cannot easily purchase goods intended for export. Given these conditions, a monopolistic firm may find that it is profitable to engage in dumping.

An example may help to show how dumping can be a profit-maximizing strategy. Imagine a firm that currently sells 1000 units of a good at home and 100 units abroad. Currently selling the good at $20 per unit domestically, it gets only $15 per unit on export sales. One might imagine that the firm would conclude that additional domestic sales are much more profitable than additional exports.

Suppose, however, that to expand sales by one unit, in either market, would require reducing the price by $0.01. Reducing the domestic price by a penny, then, would increase sales by one unit—directly adding $19.99 in revenue, but reducing the receipts on the 1000 units that would have sold at the $20 price by $10. So the marginal revenue from the extra unit sold is only $9.99. On the other hand, reducing the price charged to foreign customers and thereby expanding exports by one unit would directly increase revenue by only $14.99. The indirect cost of reduced receipts on the 100 units that would have been sold at the original price, however, would be only $1, so that marginal revenue on export sales would be $13.99. It would therefore be more profitable in this case to expand exports rather than domestic sales, even though the price received on exports is lower.

This example could be reversed, with the incentive being to charge less on domestic than foreign sales. However, price discrimination in favor of exports is more common. Since international markets are imperfectly integrated due to both transportation costs and protectionist trade barriers, domestic firms usually have a larger share of home markets than they do of foreign markets. This in turn usually means that their foreign sales are more affected by their pricing than their domestic sales. A firm with a 20 percent market share need not cut its price as much to double its sales as a firm with an 80 percent share. So firms typically see themselves as having less monopoly power, and a greater incentive to keep their prices low, on exports than on domestic sales.

Figure 6-8 offers a diagrammatic example of dumping. It shows an industry in which there is a single monopolistic domestic firm. The firm sells in two markets: a domestic market, where it faces the demand curve D_{DOM}, and an export market. In the export market we take the assumption that sales are highly responsive to the price the firm charges to an extreme, assuming the firm can sell as much as it wants at the price P_{FOR}. The horizontal line P_{FOR} is thus the demand curve for sales in the foreign market. We assume the markets are segmented, so that the firm can charge a higher price for domestically sold goods than it does for exports. MC is the marginal cost curve for total output, which can be sold on either market.

To maximize profits, the firm must set marginal revenue equal to marginal cost in *each* market. Marginal revenue on domestic sales is defined by the curve MR_{DOM}, which lies below D_{DOM}. Export sales take place at a constant price P_{FOR}, so the marginal revenue for an additional unit exported is just P_{FOR}. To set marginal cost equal to marginal revenue in both markets it is necessary to produce the quantity $Q_{MONOPOLY}$, to sell Q_{DOM} on the domestic market, and to export $Q_{MONOPOLY} - Q_{DOM}$.[7] The cost of producing an additional unit in this

---

[7]It might seem that the monopolist should set domestic sales at the level where MC and MR_{DOM} intersect. But remember that the monopolist is producing a total output $Q_{MONOPOLY}$: this means that the cost of producing one more unit is equal to P_{FOR}, whether that unit is destined for the foreign or domestic market. And it is the actual cost of producing one more unit that must be set equal to marginal revenue. The intersection of MC and MR_{DOM} is where the firm would produce *if it did not have the option of exporting*—but that is irrelevant.

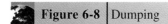

Figure 6-8 | Dumping

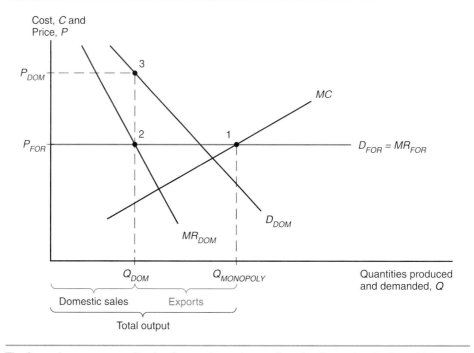

The figure shows a monopolist that faces a demand curve D_{DOM} for domestic sales, but which can also sell as much as it likes at the export price P_{FOR}. Since an additional unit can always be sold at P_{FOR}, the firm increases output until the marginal cost equals P_{FOR}; this profit-maximizing output is shown as $Q_{MONOPOLY}$. Since the firm's marginal cost at $Q_{MONOPOLY}$ is P_{FOR}, it sells output on the domestic market up to the point where marginal revenue equals P_{FOR}, this profit-maximizing level of domestic sales is shown as Q_{DOM}. The rest of its output, $Q_{MONOPOLY} - Q_{DOM}$, is exported.

The price at which domestic consumers demand Q_{DOM} is P_{DOM}. Since $P_{DOM} > P_{FOR}$, the firm sells exports at a lower price than it charges domestic consumers.

case is equal to P_{FOR}, the marginal revenue from exports, which in turn is equal to the marginal revenue for domestic sales.

The quantity Q_{DOM} will be demanded domestically at a price of P_{DOM}, which is above the export price P_{FOR}. Thus the firm is indeed dumping, selling more cheaply abroad than at home.

In both our numerical example and Figure 6-8, the reason the firm chooses to dump is the difference in the responsiveness of sales to price in the export and domestic markets. In Figure 6-8 we assume the firm can increase exports without cutting its price, so marginal revenue and price coincide on the export market. Domestically, by contrast, increased sales do lower the price. This is an extreme example of the general condition for price discrimination presented in microeconomics courses: Firms will price-discriminate when sales are more price-responsive in one market than in another.[8] (In this case we have assumed export demand is infinitely price-responsive.)

Dumping is widely regarded as an unfair practice in international trade. There is no good economic justification for regarding dumping as particularly harmful, but U.S. trade law prohibits foreign firms from dumping in our market and automatically imposes tariffs when such dumping is discovered.

The situation shown in Figure 6-8 is simply an extreme version of a wider class of situations in which firms have an incentive to sell exports for a lower price than the price they charge domestic customers.

CASE STUDY

Antidumping as Protectionism

In the United States and a number of other countries, dumping is regarded as an unfair competitive practice. Firms that claim to have been injured by foreign firms who dump their products in the domestic market at low prices can appeal, through a quasi-judicial procedure, to the Commerce Department for relief. If their complaint is ruled valid an "antidumping duty" is imposed, equal to the calculated difference between the actual and "fair" price of imports. In practice, the Commerce Department accepts the great majority of complaints by U.S. firms about unfair foreign pricing. The determination that this unfair pricing has actually caused injury, however, is in the hands of a different agency, the International Trade Commission, which rejects about half of its cases.

Economists have never been very happy with the idea of singling dumping out as a prohibited practice. For one thing, price discrimination between markets may be a perfectly legitimate business strategy—like the discounts that airlines offer to students, senior citizens, and travelers who are willing to stay over a weekend. Also, the legal definition of dumping deviates substantially from the economic definition. Since it is often difficult to prove that foreign firms charge higher prices to domestic than export customers, the United States and other nations instead often try to calculate a supposed fair price based on estimates of foreign production costs. This "fair price" rule can interfere with perfectly normal business practices: A firm may well be willing to sell a product for a loss while it is lowering its costs through experience or breaking into a new market.

In spite of almost universal negative assessments from economists, however, formal complaints about dumping have been filed with growing frequency since about 1970. As of April 2001, the United States had anti-dumping duties or "countervailing" duties (which are supposed to offset foreign subsidies) on 265 items from 40 different countries. Among the 38 items from China subject to duties were cased pencils, cotton shop towels, paper clips, paintbrushes, sparklers, and freshwater crawfish tailmeat. Is this just cynical abuse of the law, or does it reflect a real increase in the importance of dumping? The answer may be a little of both.

---

[8]The formal condition for price discrimination is that firms will charge lower prices in markets in which they face a higher *elasticity* of demand, where the elasticity is the percentage decrease in sales that results from a 1 percent increase in price. Firms will dump if they perceive a higher elasticity on export sales than on domestic sales.

Why may dumping have increased? Because of the uneven pace at which countries have opened up their markets. Since 1970 trade liberalization and deregulation have opened up international competition in a number of previously sheltered industries. For example, it used to be taken for granted that telephone companies would buy their equipment from domestic manufacturers. With the breakup of AT&T in the United States and the privatization of phone companies in other countries, this is no longer the case everywhere. But in Japan and several European countries the old rules still apply. It is not surprising that the manufacturers of telephone equipment in these countries would continue to charge high prices at home while offering lower prices to customers in the United States—or at least that they would be accused of doing so.

Reciprocal Dumping

The analysis of dumping suggests that price discrimination can actually give rise to international trade. Suppose there are two monopolies, each producing the same good, one in Home and one in Foreign. To simplify the analysis, assume that these two firms have the same marginal cost. Suppose also that there are some costs of transportation between the two markets, so that if the firms charge the same price there will be no trade. In the absence of trade, each firm's monopoly would be uncontested.

If we introduce the possibility of dumping, however, trade may emerge. Each firm will limit the quantity it sells in its home market, recognizing that if it tries to sell more it will drive down the price on its existing domestic sales. If a firm can sell a little bit in the other market, however, it will add to its profits even if the price is lower than in the domestic market, because the negative effect on the price of existing sales will fall on the other firm, not on itself. So each firm has an incentive to "raid" the other market, selling a few units at a price that (net of transportation costs) is lower than the home market price but still above marginal cost.

If both firms do this, however, the result will be the emergence of trade even though there was (by assumption) no initial difference in the price of the good in the two markets, and even though there are some transportation costs. Even more peculiarly, there will be two-way trade in the same product. For example, a cement plant in country A might be shipping cement to country B while a cement plant in B is doing the reverse. The situation in which dumping leads to two-way trade in the same product is known as **reciprocal dumping**.[9]

This may seem like a strange case, and it is admittedly probably rare in international trade for exactly identical goods to be shipped in both directions at once. However, the reciprocal dumping effect probably tends to increase the volume of trade in goods that are not quite identical.

Is such peculiar and seemingly pointless trade socially desirable? The answer is ambiguous. It is obviously wasteful to ship the same good, or close substitutes, back and forth when transportation is costly. However, notice that the emergence of reciprocal dumping in our story

---

[9]The possibility of reciprocal dumping was first noted by James Brander, "Intraindustry Trade in Identical Commodities," *Journal of International Economics* 11 (1981), pp. 1–14.

eliminates what were initially pure monopolies, leading to some competition. The increased competition represents a benefit that may offset the waste of resources in transportation. The net effect of such peculiar trade on a nation's economic welfare is therefore uncertain.

The Theory of External Economies

In the monopolistic competition model of trade it is presumed that the economies of scale that give rise to international trade occur at the level of the individual firm. That is, the larger any particular firm's output of a product, the lower its average cost. The inevitable result of such economies of scale at the level of the firm is imperfect competition, which in turn allows such practices as dumping.

As we pointed out early in this chapter, however, not all scale economies apply at the level of the individual firm. For a variety of reasons, it is often the case that concentrating production of an industry in one or a few locations reduces the industry's costs, even if the individual firms in the industry remain small. When economies of scale apply at the level of the industry rather than at the level of the individual firm, they are called *external economies*. The analysis of external economies goes back more than a century to the British economist Alfred Marshall, who was struck by the phenomenon of "industrial districts"— geographical concentrations of industry that could not be easily explained by natural resources. In Marshall's time the most famous examples included such concentrations of industry as the cluster of cutlery manufacturers in Sheffield and the cluster of hosiery firms in Northampton. Modern examples of industries where there seem to be powerful external economies include the semiconductor industry, concentrated in California's famous Silicon Valley; the investment banking industry, concentrated in New York; and the entertainment industry, concentrated in Hollywood.

Marshall argued that there were three main reasons why a cluster of firms may be more efficient than an individual firm in isolation: the ability of a cluster to support **specialized suppliers**; the way that a geographically concentrated industry allows **labor market pooling**; and the way that a geographically concentrated industry helps foster **knowledge spillovers**. These same factors continue to be valid today.

Specialized Suppliers

In many industries, the production of goods and services—and to an even greater extent, the development of new products—requires the use of specialized equipment or support services; yet an individual company does not provide a large enough market for these services to keep the suppliers in business. A localized industrial cluster can solve this problem by bringing together many firms that collectively provide a large enough market to support a wide range of specialized suppliers. This phenomenon has been extensively documented in Silicon Valley: A 1994 study recounts how, as the local industry grew, "engineers left established semiconductor companies to start firms that manufactured capital goods such as diffusion ovens, step-and-repeat cameras, and testers, and materials and components such as photomasks, testing jigs, and specialized chemicals. . . . This independent equipment sector promoted the continuing formation of semiconductor firms by freeing individual producers from the expense of developing capital equipment internally and by spreading the costs of development. It also reinforced the tendency toward industrial localization, as most of these specialized inputs were not available elsewhere in the country."[10]

As the quote suggests, the availability of this dense network of specialized suppliers has given high-technology firms in Silicon Valley some considerable advantages over firms elsewhere. Key inputs are cheaper and more easily available because there are many firms competing to provide them, and firms can concentrate on what they do best, contracting out other aspects of their business. For example, some Silicon Valley firms that specialize in providing highly sophisticated computer chips for particular customers have chosen to become "fabless," that is, they do not have any factories in which chips can be fabricated. Instead, they concentrate on designing the chips, then hire another firm actually to fabricate them.

A company that tried to enter the industry in another location—for example, in a country that did not have a comparable industrial cluster—would be at an immediate disadvantage because it would lack easy access to Silicon Valley's suppliers and would either have to provide them for itself or be faced with the task of trying to deal with Silicon Valley–based suppliers at long distance.

Labor Market Pooling

A second source of external economies is the way that a cluster of firms can create a pooled market for workers with highly specialized skills. Such a pooled market is to the advantage of both the producers and the workers as the producers are less likely to suffer from labor shortages, while the workers are less likely to become unemployed.

The point can best be made with a simplified example. Imagine that there are two companies that both use the same kind of specialized labor, say, two film studios that make use of experts in computer animation. Both employers are, however, uncertain about how many workers they will want to hire: If demand for its product is high, both companies will want to hire 150 workers, but if it is low, they will only want to hire 50. Suppose also that there are 200 workers with this special skill. Now compare two situations: one with both firms and all 200 workers in the same city, the other with the firms and 100 workers in two different cities. It is straightforward to show that both the workers and their employers are better off if everyone is in the same place.

First, consider the situation from the point of view of the companies. If they are in different locations, whenever one of the companies is doing well it will be confronted with a labor shortage; it will want to hire 150 workers, but only 100 will be available. If the firms are near each other, however, it is at least possible that one will be doing well when the other is doing badly, so that both firms may be able to hire as many workers as they want. So by locating near each other, the companies increase the likelihood that they will be able to take advantage of business opportunities.

From the workers' point of view, having the industry concentrated in one location is also an advantage. If the industry is divided between two cities, then whenever one of the firms has a low demand for workers the result will be unemployment; the firm will be willing to hire only 50 of the 100 workers who live nearby. But if the industry is concentrated in a single city, low labor demand from one firm will at least sometimes be offset by high demand from the other. As a result, workers will have a lower risk of unemployment.

---

[10]See the book listed in Further Reading by Saxenian, p. 40.

Again, these advantages have been documented for Silicon Valley, where it is common both for companies to expand rapidly and for workers to change employers. The same study of Silicon Valley that was quoted previously notes that the concentration of firms in a single location makes it easy to switch employers, quoting one engineer as saying that "it wasn't that big a catastrophe to quit your job on Friday and have another job on Monday. . . . You didn't even necessarily have to tell your wife. You just drove off in another direction on Monday morning."[11] This flexibility makes Silicon Valley an attractive location both for highly skilled workers and for the companies that employ them.

Knowledge Spillovers

It is by now a cliché that in the modern economy knowledge is at least as important an input as factors of production like labor, capital, and raw materials. This is especially true in highly innovative industries, where being only a few months behind the cutting edge in production techniques or product design can put a company at a major disadvantage.

But where does the specialized knowledge that is crucial to success in innovative industries come from? Companies can acquire technology through their own research and development efforts. They can also try to learn from competitors by studying their products and, in some cases, taking them apart to "reverse engineer" their design and manufacture. An important source of technical know-how, however, is the informal exchange of information and ideas that takes place at a personal level. And this kind of informal diffusion of knowledge often seems to take place most effectively when an industry is concentrated in a fairly small area, so that employees of different companies mix socially and talk freely about technical issues.

Marshall described this process memorably when he wrote that in a district with many firms in the same industry, "The mysteries of the trade become no mystery, but are as it were in the air. . . . Good work is rightly appreciated, inventions and improvements in machinery, in processes and the general organization of the business have their merits promptly discussed: if one man starts a new idea, it is taken up by others and combined with suggestions of their own; and thus it becomes the source of further new ideas."[12]

A journalist described how these knowledge spillovers worked during the rise of Silicon Valley (and also gave an excellent sense of the amount of specialized knowledge involved in the industry) as follows: "Every year there was some place, the Wagon Wheel, Chez Yvonne, Rickey's, the Roundhouse, where members of this esoteric fraternity, the young men and women of the semiconductor industry, would head after work to have a drink and gossip and trade war stories about phase jitters, phantom circuits, bubble memories, pulse trains, bounceless contacts, burst modes, leapfrog tests, p-n junctions, sleeping sickness modes, slow-death episodes, RAMs, NAKs, MOSes, PCMs, PROMs, PROM blowers, PROM blasters, and teramagnitudes. . . ."[13] This kind of informal information flow means that it is easier for companies in the Silicon Valley area to stay near the technological frontier than it is for companies elsewhere; indeed, many multinational firms have established research centers and even factories in Silicon Valley simply in order to keep up with the latest technology.

---

[11]Saxenian, p. 35.

[12]Alfred Marshall, *Principles of Economics,* London: MacMillan, 1920.

[13]Tom Wolfe, quoted in Saxenian, p. 33.

External Economies and Increasing Returns

A geographically concentrated industry is able to support specialized suppliers, provide a pooled labor market, and facilitate knowledge spillovers in a way that a geographically dispersed industry cannot. But a country cannot have a large concentration of firms in an industry unless it possesses a large industry. Thus the theory of external economies indicates that when these external economies are important, a country with a large industry will, other things being equal, be more efficient in that industry than a country with a small industry. Or to put it differently, external economies can give rise to increasing returns to scale *at the level of the national industry*.

While the details of external economies in practice are often quite subtle and complex (as the example of Silicon Valley shows), it can be useful to abstract from the details and represent external economies simply by assuming that an industry's costs are lower, the larger the industry. If we ignore possible imperfections in competition, this means that the industry will have a **forward-falling supply curve**: The larger the industry's output, the lower the price at which firms are willing to sell their output.

External Economies and International Trade

External economies, like economies of scale that are internal to firms, play an important role in international trade, but they may be quite different in their effects. In particular, external economies can cause countries to get "locked in" to undesirable patterns of specialization and can even lead to losses from international trade.

External Economies and the Pattern of Trade

When there are external economies of scale, a country that has large production in some industry will tend, other things equal, to have low costs of producing that good. This gives rise to an obvious circularity, since a country that can produce a good cheaply will also therefore tend to produce a lot of that good. Strong external economies tend to confirm existing patterns of interindustry trade, whatever their original sources: Countries that start out as large producers in certain industries, for whatever reason, tend to remain large producers. They may do so even if some other country could potentially produce the goods more cheaply.

Figure 6-9 illustrates this point. We show the cost of producing a watch as a function of the number of watches produced annually. Two countries are shown: "Switzerland" and "Thailand." The Swiss cost of producing a watch is shown as AC_{SWISS}; the Thai cost as AC_{THAI}. D represents the world demand for watches, which we assume can be satisfied either by Switzerland or by Thailand.

Suppose that the economies of scale in watch production are entirely external to firms, and that since there are no economies of scale at the level of the firm the watch industry in each country consists of many small perfectly competitive firms. Competition therefore drives the price of watches down to its average cost.

We assume that the Thai cost curve lies below the Swiss curve, say because Thai wages are lower than Swiss. This means that at any given level of production, Thailand could manufacture watches more cheaply than Switzerland. One might hope that this would always imply that Thailand will in fact supply the world market. Unfortunately, this need not be the case. Suppose that Switzerland, for historical reasons, establishes its watch

Figure 6-9 | External Economies and Specialization

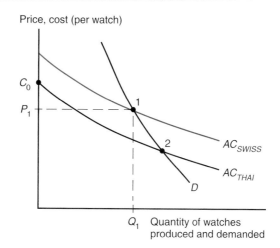

The average cost curve for Thailand, AC_{THAI}, lies below the average cost curve for Switzerland, AC_{SWISS}. Thus Thailand could potentially supply the world market more cheaply than Switzerland. If the Swiss industry gets established first, however, it may be able to sell watches at the price P_1, which is below the cost C_0 that an individual Thai firm would face if it began production on its own. So a pattern of specialization established by historical accident may persist even when new producers could potentially have lower costs.

industry first. Then initially world watch equilibrium will be established at point 1 in Figure 6-9, with Swiss production of Q_1 units per year and a price of P_1. Now introduce the possibility of Thai production. If Thailand could take over the world market, the equilibrium would move to point 2. However, if there is no initial Thai production ($Q = 0$), any individual Thai firm considering manufacture of watches will face a cost of production of C_0. As we have drawn it, this cost is above the price at which the established Swiss industry can produce watches. So although the Thai industry could potentially make watches more cheaply than Switzerland, Switzerland's head start enables it to hold onto the industry.

As this example shows, external economies potentially give a strong role to historical accident in determining who produces what, and may allow established patterns of specialization to persist even when they run counter to comparative advantage.

Trade and Welfare with External Economies

Trade based on external economies has more ambiguous effects on national welfare than either trade based on comparative advantage or trade based on economies of scale at the level of the firm. There may be gains to the world economy from concentrating production in particular industries to realize external economies. On the other hand, there is no guarantee that the right country will produce a good subject to external economies, and it is possible that trade based on external economies may actually leave a country worse off than it would have been in the absence of trade.

An example of how a country can actually be worse off with trade than without is shown in Figure 6-10. In this example, as before, we imagine that Thailand and Switzerland could both manufacture watches, that Thailand could make them more cheaply, but that Switzerland has gotten there first. D_{WORLD} is the world demand for watches, and, given that Switzerland produces the watches, the equilibrium is at point 1. However, we now add to the figure the Thai demand for watches, D_{THAI}. If no trade in watches were allowed and

Figure 6-10 | External Economies and Losses from Trade

When there are external economies, trade can potentially leave a country worse off than it would be in the absence of trade. In this example, Thailand imports watches from Switzerland, which is able to supply the world market (D_{WORLD}) at a price (P_1) low enough to block entry by Thai producers who must initially produce the watches at cost C_0. Yet if Thailand were to block all trade in watches, it would be able to supply its domestic market (D_{THAI}) at the lower price P_2.

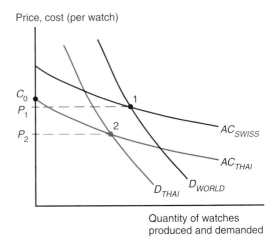

Thailand were forced to be self-sufficient, then the Thai equilibrium would be at point 2. Because of its lower average cost curve, the price of Thai-made watches at point 2, P_2, is actually lower than the price of Swiss-made watches at point 1, P_1.

We have shown a situation in which the price of a good that Thailand imports would actually be lower if there were no trade and the country were forced to produce the good for itself. Clearly in this situation trade leaves the country worse off than it would be in the absence of trade.

There is an incentive in this case for Thailand to protect its potential watch industry from foreign competition. Before concluding that this justifies protectionism, however, we should note that in practice identifying cases like that in Figure 6-10 is far from easy. Indeed, as we will emphasize in Chapters 10 and 11, the difficulty of identifying external economies in practice is one of the main arguments against activist government policies toward trade.

It is also worth pointing out that while external economies can sometimes lead to disadvantageous patterns of specialization and trade, it is still to the benefit of the *world* economy to take advantage of the gains from concentrating industries. Canada might be better off if Silicon Valley were near Toronto instead of San Francisco; Germany might be better off if the City (London's financial district, which, along with Wall Street, dominates world financial markets) could be moved to Frankfurt. The world as a whole is, however, more efficient and thus richer because international trade allows nations to specialize in different industries and thus reap the gains from external economies as well as the gains from comparative advantage.

Dynamic Increasing Returns

Some of the most important external economies probably arise from the accumulation of knowledge. When an individual firm improves its products or production techniques through experience, other firms are likely to imitate the firm and benefit from its knowl-

TINSELTOWN ECONOMICS

What is America's most important export sector? The answer depends to some extent on definitions; some people will tell you that it is agriculture, others that it is aircraft. By any measure, however, one of the biggest exporters in the United States is the entertainment sector, which earned more than $8 billion in overseas sales in 1994. American-made movies and television programs are shown almost everywhere on earth. The overseas market has also become crucial to Hollywood's finances: Action movies, in particular, often earn more outside the United States than they do at home.

Why is the United States the world's dominant exporter of entertainment? There are important advantages arising from the sheer size of the American market. A film aimed primarily at the French or Italian markets, which are far smaller than that of the United States, cannot justify the huge budgets of many American films. Thus films from these countries are typically dramas or comedies whose appeal fails to survive dubbing or subtitles. Meanwhile, American films can transcend the language barrier with lavish productions and spectacular special effects.

But an important part of the American dominance in the industry also comes from the external economies created by the immense concentration of entertainment firms in Hollywood. Hollywood clearly generates two of Marshall's types of external economies: specialized suppliers and labor market pooling. While the final product is provided by movie studios and television networks, these in turn draw on a complex web of independent producers, casting and talent agencies, legal firms, special effects experts, and so on. And the need for labor market pooling is obvious to anyone who has watched the credits at the end of a movie: Each production requires a huge but temporary army that includes not just cameramen and makeup artists but musicians, stunt men and women, and mysterious occupations like gaffers and grips (and—oh yes—actors and actresses). Whether it also generates the third kind of external economies—knowledge spillovers—is less certain. After all, as the author Nathaniel West once remarked, the key to understanding the movie business is to realize that "nobody knows anything." Still, if there is any knowledge to spill over, surely it does so better in the intense social environment of Hollywood than it could anywhere else.

An indication of the force of Hollywood's external economies has been its persistent ability to draw talent from outside the United States. From Garbo and von Sternberg to Arnold Schwarzenegger and Paul Verhoeven, "American" films have often been made by ambitious foreigners who moved to Hollywood—and in the end reached a larger audience even in their original nations than they could have if they had remained at home.

Is Hollywood unique? No, similar forces have led to the emergence of several other entertainment complexes. In India, whose film market has been protected from American domination partly by government policy and partly by cultural differences, a movie-making cluster known as "Bollywood" has emerged in Bombay. A substantial film industry catering to Chinese speakers has emerged in Hong Kong. And a specialty industry producing Spanish-language television programs for all of Latin America, focusing on so-called *telenovelas,* long-running soap operas, has emerged in Caracas, Venezuela. This last entertainment complex has discovered some unexpected export markets: Television viewers in Russia, it turns out, identify more readily with the characters in Latin American soaps than with those in U.S. productions.

edge. This spillover of knowledge gives rise to a situation in which the production costs of individual firms fall as the industry as a whole accumulates experience.

Notice that external economies arising from the accumulation of knowledge differ somewhat from the external economies considered so far, in which industry costs depend on current output. In this alternative situation industry costs depend on experience, usually

Figure 6-11 | The Learning Curve

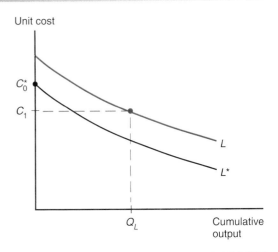

The learning curve shows that unit cost is lower the greater the cumulative output of a country's industry to date. A country that has extensive experience in an industry (L) may have lower unit cost than another country with little or no experience, even if the second country's learning curve (L^*) is lower, for example, because of lower wages.

Unit cost

C_0^*

C_1

L

L^*

Q_L

Cumulative
output

measured by the cumulative output of the industry to date. For example, the cost of producing a ton of steel might depend negatively on the total number of tons of steel produced by a country since the industry began. This kind of relationship is often summarized by a **learning curve** that relates unit cost to cumulative output. Such learning curves are illustrated in Figure 6-11. They are downward sloping because of the effect of the experience gained through production on costs. When costs fall with cumulative production over time, rather than with the current rate of production, this is referred to as a case of **dynamic increasing returns**.

Like ordinary external economies, dynamic external economies can lock in an initial advantage or head start in an industry. In Figure 6-11, the learning curve L is that of a country that pioneered an industry, while L^* is that of another country that has lower input costs—say, lower wages—but less production experience. Provided that the first country has a sufficiently large head start, the potentially lower costs of the second country may not allow it to enter the market. For example, suppose the first country has a cumulative output of Q_L units, giving it a unit cost of C_1, while the second country has never produced the good. Then the second country will have an initial start-up cost C_0^* that is higher than the current unit cost, C_1, of the established industry.

Dynamic scale economies, like external economies at a point in time, potentially justify protectionism. Suppose that a country could have low enough costs to produce a good for export if it had more production experience, but that given the current lack of experience the good cannot be produced competitively. Such a country might increase its long-term welfare either by encouraging the production of the good by a subsidy or by protecting it from foreign competition until the industry could stand on its own feet. The argument for temporary protection of industries to enable them to gain experience is known as the **infant industry argument** and has played an important role in debates over the role of trade policy in economic development. We will discuss the infant industry argument at greater length in Chapter 10, but for now we simply note that situations like that illustrated in Figure 6-11 are just as hard to identify in practice in those involving nondynamic increasing returns.

Summary

1. Trade need not be the result of comparative advantage. Instead, it can result from increasing returns or economies of scale, that is, from a tendency of unit costs to be lower with larger output. Economies of scale give countries an incentive to specialize and trade even in the absence of differences between countries in their resources or technology. Economies of scale can be internal (depending on the size of the firm) or external (depending on the size of the industry).

2. Economies of scale normally lead to a breakdown of perfect competition, so that trade in the presence of economies of scale must be analyzed using models of imperfect competition. Two important models of this kind are the monopolistic competition model and the dumping model. A third model, that of external economies, is consistent with perfect competition.

3. In monopolistic competition, an industry contains a number of firms producing differentiated products. These firms act as individual monopolists, but additional firms enter a profitable industry until monopoly profits are competed away. Equilibrium is affected by the size of the market: A large market will support a larger number of firms, each producing at larger scale and thus lower average cost, than a small market.

4. International trade allows creation of an integrated market that is larger than any one country's market, and thus makes it possible simultaneously to offer consumers a greater variety of products and lower prices.

5. In the monopolistic competition model, trade may be divided into two kinds. Two-way trade in differentiated products within an industry is called intraindustry trade; trade that exchanges the products of one industry for the products of another is called interindustry trade. Intraindustry trade reflects economies of scale; interindustry trade reflects comparative advantage. Intraindustry trade does not generate the same strong effects on income distribution as interindustry trade.

6. Dumping occurs when a monopolistic firm charges a lower price on exports than it charges domestically. It is a profit-maximizing strategy when export sales are more price-responsive than domestic sales, and when firms can effectively segment markets, that is, prevent domestic customers from buying goods intended for export markets. Reciprocal dumping occurs when two monopolistic firms dump into each others' home markets; such reciprocal dumping can be a cause of international trade.

7. External economies are economies of scale that occur at the level of the industry instead of the firm. They give an important role to history and accident in determining the pattern of international trade. When external economies are important, a country starting with a large industry may retain that advantage even if another country could potentially produce the same goods more cheaply. When external economies are important, countries can conceivably lose from trade.

Key Terms

Problems

1. For each of the following examples, explain whether this is a case of external or internal economies of scale:
   a. Most musical wind instruments in the United States are produced by more than a dozen factories in Elkhart, Indiana.
   b. All Hondas sold in the United States are either imported or produced in Marysville, Ohio.
   c. All airframes for Airbus, Europe's only producer of large aircraft, are assembled in Toulouse, France.
   d. Hartford, Connecticut, is the insurance capital of the northeastern United States.

2. In perfect competition, firms set price equal to marginal cost. Why isn't this possible when there are internal economies of scale?

3. It is often argued that the existence of increasing returns is a source of conflict between countries, since each country is better off if it can increase its production in those industries characterized by economies of scale. Evaluate this view in terms of both the monopolistic competition and the external economy models.

4. Suppose the two countries we considered in the numerical example on pages 133–136 were to integrate their automobile market with a third country with an annual market for 3.75 million automobiles. Find the number of firms, the output per firm, and the price per automobile in the new integrated market after trade.

5. Evaluate the relative importance of economies of scale and comparative advantage in causing the following:
   a. Most of the world's aluminum is smelted in Norway or Canada.
   b. Half of the world's large jet aircraft are assembled in Seattle.
   c. Most semiconductors are manufactured in either the United States or Japan.
   d. Most Scotch whiskey comes from Scotland.
   e. Much of the world's best wine comes from France.

6. There are some shops in Japan that sell *Japanese* goods imported back from the United States at a discount over the prices charged by other Japanese shops. How is this possible?

7. Consider a situation similar to that in Figure 6-9, in which two countries that can produce a good are subject to forward-falling supply curves. In this case, however,

suppose that the two countries have the same costs, so that their supply curves are identical.

    a. What would you expect to be the pattern of international specialization and trade? What would determine who produces the good?

    b. What are the *benefits* of international trade in this case? Do they accrue only to the country that gets the industry?

8. It is fairly common for an industrial cluster to break up and for production to move to locations with lower wages when the technology of the industry is no longer rapidly improving—when it is no longer essential to have the absolutely most modern machinery, when the need for highly skilled workers has declined, and when being at the cutting edge of innovation conveys only a small advantage. Explain this tendency of industrial clusters to break up in terms of the theory of external economies.

Further Reading

Frank Graham. "Some Aspects of Protection Further Considered." *Quarterly Journal of Economics* 37 (1923), pp. 199–227. An early warning that international trade may be harmful in the presence of external economies of scale.

Elhanan Helpman and Paul Krugman. *Market Structure and Foreign Trade.* Cambridge: MIT Press, 1985. A technical presentation of monopolistic competition and other models of trade with economies of scale.

Henryk Kierzkowski, ed. *Monopolistic Competition in International Trade.* Oxford: Clarendon Press, 1984. A collection of papers representing many of the leading researchers in imperfect competition and international trade.

Staffan Burenstam Linder. *An Essay on Trade and Transformation.* New York: John Wiley and Sons, 1961. An early and influential statement of the view that trade in manufactures among advanced countries mainly reflects forces other than comparative advantage.

Michael Porter. *The Competitive Advantage of Nations.* New York: Free Press, 1990. A best-selling book that explains national export success as the result of self-reinforcing industrial clusters, that is, external economies.

Annalee Saxenian. *Regional Advantage.* Cambridge: Harvard University Press, 1994. A fascinating comparison of two high-technology industrial districts, California's Silicon Valley and Boston's Route 128.

APPENDIX TO CHAPTER 6

Determining Marginal Revenue

In our exposition of monopoly and monopolistic competition, we found it useful to have an algebraic statement of the marginal revenue faced by a firm given the demand curve it faced. Specifically, we asserted that if a firm faces the demand curve

$$Q = A - B \times P, \tag{6A-1}$$

its marginal revenue is

$$MR = P - (1/B) \times Q. \tag{6A-2}$$

In this appendix we demonstrate why this is true.

Notice first that the demand curve can be rearranged to state the price as a function of the firm's sales rather than the other way around. By rearranging (6A-1) we get

$$P = (A/B) - (1/B) \times Q. \tag{6A-3}$$

The revenue of a firm is simply the price it receives per unit multiplied by the number of units it sells. Letting R denote the firm's revenue, we have

$$R = P \times Q = [(A/B) - (1/B) \times Q] \times Q. \tag{6A-4}$$

Let us next ask how the revenue of a firm changes if it changes its sales. Suppose that the firm decides to increase its sales by a small amount dX, so that the new level of sales is $Q = Q + dQ$. Then the firm's revenue after the increase in sales, R', will be

$$R' = P' \times Q' = [(A/B) - (1/B) \times (Q + dQ)] \times (Q + dQ)$$
$$= [(A/B) - (1/B) \times Q] \times Q + [(A/B) - (1/B) \times Q] \times dQ$$
$$- (1/B) \times Q \times dQ - (1/B) \times (dQ)^2. \tag{6A-5}$$

Equation (6A-5) can be simplified by substitution in from (6A-1) and (6A-4) to get

$$R' = R + P \times dQ - (1/B) \times Q \times dQ - (1/B) \times (dQ)^2. \tag{6A-6}$$

When the change in sales dQ is small, however, its square $(dQ)^2$ is very small (e.g., the square of 1 is 1, but the square of 1/10 is 1/100). So for a small change in Q, the last term in (6A-6) can be ignored. This gives us the result that the *change* in revenue from a small change in sales is

$$R' - R = [P - (1/B) \times Q] \times dQ. \tag{6A-7}$$

So the increase in revenue *per unit of additional sales*—which is the definition of marginal revenue—is

$$MR = (R' - R)/dQ = P - (1/B) \times Q,$$

which is just what we asserted in equation (6A-2).

CHAPTER 7

International Factor Movements

Up to this point we have concerned ourselves entirely with international *trade*. That is, we have focused on the causes and effects of international exchanges of goods and services. Movement of goods and services is not, however, the only form of international integration. This chapter is concerned with another form of integration, international movements of factors of production, or **factor movements**. Factor movements include labor migration, the transfer of capital via international borrowing and lending, and the subtle international linkages involved in the formation of multinational corporations.

The principles of international factor movement do not differ in their essentials from those underlying international trade in goods. Both international borrowing and lending and international labor migration can be thought of as analogous in their causes and effects to the movement of goods analyzed in Chapters 2 through 5. The role of the multinational corporation may be understood by extending some of the concepts developed in Chapter 6. So when we turn from trade in goods and services to factor movements we do not make a radical shift in emphasis.

Although there is a fundamental economic similarity between trade and factor movements, however, there are major differences in the political context. A labor-abundant country may under some circumstances import capital-intensive goods; under other circumstances it may acquire capital by borrowing abroad. A capital-abundant country may import labor-intensive goods or begin employing migrant workers. A country that is too small to support firms of efficient size may import goods where large firms have an advantage or allow those goods to be produced locally by subsidiaries of foreign firms. In each case the alternative strategies may be similar in their purely economic consequences but radically different in their political acceptability.

On the whole, international factor movement tends to raise even more political difficulties than international trade. Thus factor movements are subject to more restriction than trade in goods. Immigration restrictions are nearly universal. Until the 1980s several European countries, such as France, maintained controls on capital movements even though they had virtually free trade in goods with their neighbors. Investment by foreign-based multinational corporations is regarded with suspicion and tightly regulated through much of the world. The result is that factor movements are probably less important in practice than trade in goods, which is why we took an analysis of trade in the absence of factor movements as our starting point. Nonetheless, factor movements are very important, and it is valuable to spend a chapter on their analysis.

This chapter is in three parts. We begin with a simple model of international labor mobility. We then proceed to an analysis of international borrowing and lending, in which we show that this lending can be interpreted as trade *over time:* The lending country gives up resources now to receive repayment in the future, while the borrower does the reverse. Finally, the last section of the chapter analyzes multinational corporations. ●

International Labor Mobility

We begin our discussion with an analysis of the effects of labor mobility. In the modern world, restrictions on the flow of labor are legion—just about every country imposes restrictions on immigration. Thus labor mobility is less prevalent in practice than capital mobility. It remains important, however; it is also simpler in some ways to analyze than capital movement, for reasons that will become apparent later in the chapter.

A One-Good Model Without Factor Mobility

As in the analysis of trade, the best way to understand factor mobility is to begin with a world that is not economically integrated, then examine what happens when international transactions are allowed. Let's assume that we have, as usual, a two-country world consisting of Home and Foreign, each with two factors of production, land and labor. We assume for the moment, however, that this world is even simpler than the one we examined in Chapter 4, in that the two countries produce only *one* good, which we will simply refer to as "output." Thus there is no scope for ordinary trade, the exchange of different goods, in this world. The only way for these economies to become integrated with each other is via movement of either land or labor. Land almost by definition cannot move, so this is a model of integration via international labor mobility.

Before we introduce factor movements, however, let us analyze the determinants of the level of output in each country. Land (T) and labor (L) are the only scarce resources. Thus the output of each country will depend, other things equal, on the quantity of these factors available. The relationship between the supplies of factors on one side and the output of the economy on the other is referred to as the economy's production function, which we denote by $Q(T, L)$.

We have already encountered the idea of a production function in Chapter 3. As we noted there, a useful way to look at the production function is to ask how output depends on the supply of one factor of production, holding the quantity of the other factor fixed. This is done in Figure 7-1, which shows how a country's output varies as its employment of labor is varied, holding fixed the supply of land; the figure is the same as Figure 3-1. The slope of the production function measures the increase in output that would be gained by using a little more labor and is thus referred to as the *marginal product of labor.* As the curve is drawn in Figure 7-1, the marginal product of labor is assumed to fall as the ratio of labor to land rises. This is the normal case: As a country seeks to employ more labor on a given amount of land, it must move to increasingly labor-intensive techniques of production, and this will normally become increasingly difficult the further the substitution of labor for land goes.

Figure 7-1 | An Economy's Production Function

This production function, $Q(T, L)$, shows how output varies with changes in the amount of labor employed, holding the amount of land, T, fixed. The larger the supply of labor, the larger is output; however, the marginal product of labor declines as more workers are employed.

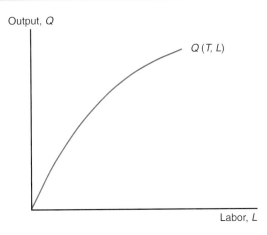

Figure 7-2, corresponding to Figure 3-2, contains the same information as Figure 7-1 but plots it in a different way. We now show directly how the marginal product of labor depends on the quantity of labor employed. We also indicate that the real wage earned by each unit of labor is equal to labor's marginal product. This will be true as long as the economy is perfectly competitive, which we assume to be the case.

What about the income earned by land? As we showed in the appendix to Chapter 3, the total output of the economy can be measured by the area under the marginal product curve. Of that total output, wages earned by workers equal the real wage rate times the employment of labor, and hence equal the indicated area on the figure. The remainder, also shown, equals rents earned by landowners.

Assume that Home and Foreign have the same technology but different overall land-labor ratios. If Home is the labor-abundant country, workers in Home will earn less than those in Foreign, while land in Home earns more than in Foreign. This obviously creates an incentive for factors of production to move. Home workers would like to move to Foreign; Foreign landowners would also like to move their land to Home, but we are supposing that this is impossible. Our next step is to allow workers to move and see what happens.

International Labor Movement

Now suppose that workers are able to move between our two countries. Workers will move from Home to Foreign. This movement will reduce the Home labor force and thus raise the real wage in Home, while increasing the labor force and reducing the real wage in Foreign. If there are no obstacles to labor movement, this process will continue until the marginal product of labor is the same in the two countries.

Figure 7-3 illustrates the causes and effects of international labor mobility. The horizontal axis represents the total world labor force. The workers employed in Home are measured from the left, the workers employed in Foreign from the right. The left vertical axis shows the marginal product of labor in Home; the right vertical axis shows the marginal product of labor in Foreign. Initially we assume that there are OL^1 workers in Home, L^1O^*

Figure 7-2 | The Marginal Product of Labor

The marginal product of labor declines with employment. The area under the marginal product curve equals total output. Given the level of employment, the marginal product determines the real wage; thus the total payment to labor (the real wage times the number of employees) is shown by the rectangle in the figure. The rest of output consists of land rents.

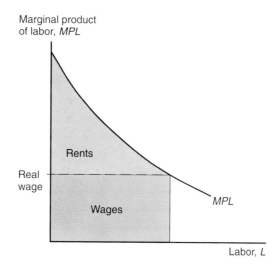

workers in Foreign. Given this allocation, the real wage rate would be lower in Home (point C) than in Foreign (point B). If workers can move freely to whichever country offers the higher real wage, they will move from Home to Foreign until the real wage rates are equalized. The eventual distribution of the world's labor force will be one with OL^2 workers in Home, L^2O^* workers in Foreign (point A).

Three points should be noted about this redistribution of the world's labor force.

1. It leads to a convergence of real wage rates. Real wages rise in Home, fall in Foreign.
2. It increases the world's output as a whole. Foreign's output rises by the area under its marginal product curve from L^1 to L^2, while Home's falls by the corresponding area under its marginal product curve. We see from the figure that Foreign's gain is larger than Home's loss, by an amount equal to the colored area ABC in the figure.
3. Despite this gain, some people are hurt by the change. Those who would originally have worked in Home receive higher real wages, but those who would originally have worked in Foreign receive lower real wages. Landowners in Foreign benefit from the larger labor supply, but landowners in Home are made worse off. As in the case of the gains from international trade, then, international labor mobility, while allowing everyone to be made better off in principle, leaves some groups worse off in practice.

Extending the Analysis

We have just seen that a very simple model tells us quite a lot about both why international factor movements occur and what effects they have. Labor mobility in our simple model, like trade in the model of Chapter 4, is driven by international differences in resources; also like trade, it is beneficial in the sense that it increases world production yet is associated with strong income distribution effects that make those gains problematic.

Figure 7-3 | Causes and Effects of International Labor Mobility

Initially OL^1 workers are employed in Home, while L^1O^* workers are employed in Foreign. Labor migrates from Home to Foreign until OL^2 workers are employed in Home, L^2O^* in Foreign, and wages are equalized.

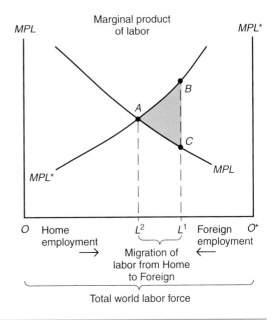

Let us consider briefly how the analysis is modified when we add some of the complications we have assumed away.

We need to remove the assumption that the two countries produce only one good. Suppose, then, that the countries produce two goods, one more labor intensive than the other. We already know from our discussion of the factor proportions model in Chapter 4 that in this case trade offers an alternative to factor mobility. Home can in a sense export labor and import land by exporting the labor-intensive good and importing the land-intensive good. It is possible in principle for such trade to lead to a complete equalization of factor prices without any need for factor mobility. If this happened, it would of course remove any incentive for labor to move from Home to Foreign.

In practice, while trade is indeed a substitute for international factor movement, it is not a perfect substitute. The reasons are those already summarized in Chapter 4. Complete factor price equalization is not observed in the real world because countries are sometimes too different in their resources to remain unspecialized; there are barriers to trade, both natural and artificial; and there are differences in technology as well as resources between countries.

We might wonder on the other side whether factor movements do not remove the incentive for international trade. Again the answer is that while in a simple model movement of factors of production can make international trade in goods unnecessary, in practice there are substantial barriers to free movement of labor, capital, and other potentially mobile resources. And some resources cannot be brought together—Canadian forests and Caribbean sunshine cannot migrate.

Extending the simple model of factor mobility, then, does not change its fundamental message. The main point is that trade in factors is, in purely economic terms, very much like trade in goods; it occurs for much the same reasons and produces similar results.

CASE STUDY

Wage Convergence in the Age of Mass Migration

Although there are substantial movements of people between countries in the modern world, the truly heroic age of labor mobility—when immigration was a major source of population growth in some countries, while emigration caused population in other countries to decline—was in the late nineteenth and early twentieth centuries. In a global economy newly integrated by railroads, steamships, and telegraph cables, and not yet subject to many legal restrictions on migration, tens of millions of people moved long distances in search of a better life. Chinese moved to Southeast Asia and California; Indians to Africa and the Caribbean; a substantial number of Japanese moved to Brazil. Above all, people from the periphery of Europe—from Scandinavia, Ireland, Italy, and Eastern Europe—moved to places where land was abundant and wages were high: the United States, but also Canada, Argentina, and Australia.

Did this process cause the kind of real wage convergence that our model predicts? Indeed it did. The accompanying table shows real wages in 1870, and the change in these wages up to the eve of World War I, for four major "destination" countries and for four important "origin" countries. As the table shows, at the beginning of the period real wages were much higher in the destination than the origin countries. Over the next four decades real wages rose in all countries, but (except for a surprisingly large increase in Canada) they increased much more rapidly in the origin than the destination countries, suggesting that migration actually did move the world toward (although not by any means all the way to) wage equalization.

As documented in the case study on the U.S. economy, legal restrictions put an end to the age of mass migration after World War I. For that and other reasons (notably a decline in world trade, and the direct effects of two world wars), convergence in real wages came to a halt and even reversed itself for several decades, only to resume in the postwar years.

	Real wage, 1870 (U.S. = 100)	Percentage increase in real wage, 1870–1913
Destination countries		
Argentina	53	51
Australia	110	1
Canada	86	121
United States	100	47
Origin countries		
Ireland	43	84
Italy	23	112
Norway	24	193
Sweden	24	250

Source: Jeffrey G. Williamson, "The Evolution of Global Labor Markets since 1830: Background Evidence and Hypotheses," *Explorations in Economic History* 32 (1995), pp. 141–196.

CASE STUDY

Immigration and the U.S. Economy

During the twentieth century, the United States has experienced two great waves of immigration. The first, which began in the late nineteenth century, was brought to an end by restrictive legislation introduced in 1924. A new surge of immigration began in the mid-1960s, spurred in part by a major revision of the law in 1965. There is also a rising number of illegal immigrants; the U.S. government estimates their number at 200,000 to 300,000 per year.

In the period between the two great waves of immigration, immigrants probably had little effect on the U.S. economy, for two reasons. First, they were not very numerous. Second, the immigration laws allocated visas based on the 1920 ethnic composition of the U.S. population; as a result, immigrants came mainly from Canada and Europe, and so their educational level was fairly similar to that of the people already here. After 1965, however, immigrants came primarily from Latin America and Asia, where workers, on average, were substantially less educated than the average American worker.

The accompanying table illustrates this effect by showing the ratio of immigrants to native-born workers by education level in the years 1980 and 1990. As you can see from the table, the ratio of immigrants to native-born rose in all categories, but by far the largest increase occurred among workers who had not completed high school. Thus immigration, other things being the same, tended to make less-educated workers more abundant and highly educated workers scarcer. This suggests that immigration may have played a role in the widening wage gap between less and more educated workers over the same period.

However, this cannot have been the whole story. Despite the effects of immigration, the fraction of U.S. workers without a high school education dropped over the decade, while the fraction with a college education rose. So overall, educated workers became more abundant, yet their relative wage still increased—probably as a result of technological changes that placed an increasing premium on education.

	Immigrants as % of native-born workers, 1980	Immigrants as % of native-born workers, 1990	Change, 1980–1990
High-school dropouts	12.2	26.2	14.0
High school	4.4	6.1	1.7
Some college	5.8	6.9	1.1
College	7.5	9.7	2.2

Source: George Borjas, Richard Freeman, and Lawrence Katz, "Searching for the effect of immigration on the labor market," *American Economic Review*, May 1996.

International Borrowing and Lending

International movements of capital are a prominent feature of the international economic landscape. It is tempting to analyze these movements in a way parallel to our analysis of labor mobility and this is sometimes a useful exercise. There are some important differences, however. When we speak of international labor mobility, it is clear that workers are physically moving from one country to another. International capital movements are not so simple. When we speak of capital flows from the United States to Mexico, we do not mean that U.S. machines are literally being unbolted and shipped south. We are instead talking of a *financial* transaction. A U.S. bank lends to a Mexican firm, or U.S. residents buy stock in Mexico, or a U.S. firm invests through its Mexican subsidiary. We focus for now on the first type of transaction, in which U.S. residents make loans to Mexicans—that is, the U.S. residents grant Mexicans the right to spend more than they earn today in return for a promise to repay in the future.

The analysis of financial aspects of the international economy is the subject of the second half of this book. It is important to realize, however, that financial transactions do not exist simply on paper. They have real consequences. International borrowing and lending, in particular, can be interpreted as a kind of international trade. The trade is not of one good for another at a point in time but of goods today for goods in the future. This kind of trade is known as **intertemporal trade**; we will have much more to say about it later in this text, but for present purposes a simple model will be sufficient to make our point.[1]

Intertemporal Production Possibilities and Trade

Even in the absence of international capital movements, any economy faces a trade-off between consumption now and consumption in the future. Economies usually do not consume all of their current output; some of their output takes the form of investment in machines, buildings, and other forms of productive capital. The more investment an economy undertakes now, the more it will be able to produce and consume in the future. To invest more, however, an economy must release resources by consuming less (unless there are unemployed resources, a possibility we temporarily disregard). Thus there is a trade-off between current and future consumption.

Let's imagine an economy that consumes only one good and will exist for only two periods, which we will call present and future. Then there will be a trade-off between present and future production of the consumption good, which we can summarize by drawing an **intertemporal production possibility frontier**. Such a frontier is illustrated in Figure 7-4. It looks just like the production possibility frontiers we have been drawing between two goods at a point in time.

The shape of the intertemporal production possibility frontier will differ among countries. Some countries will have production possibilities that are biased toward present output, while others are biased toward future output. We will ask what real differences these biases correspond to in a moment, but first let's simply suppose that there are two

---

[1]The appendix to this chapter contains a more detailed examination of the model developed in this section.

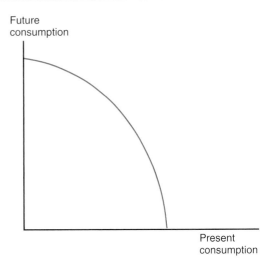

Figure 7-4 | The Intertemporal Production Possibility Frontier

A country can trade current consumption for future consumption in the same way that it can produce more of one good by producing less of another.

countries, Home and Foreign, with different intertemporal production possibilities. Home's possibilities are biased toward current consumption, while Foreign's are biased toward future consumption.

Reasoning by analogy, we already know what to expect. In the absence of international borrowing and lending, we would expect the relative price of future consumption to be higher in Home than in Foreign, and thus if we open the possibility of trade over time, we would expect Home to export present consumption and import future consumption.

This may, however, seem a little puzzling. What is the relative price of future consumption, and how does one trade over time?

The Real Interest Rate

How does a country trade over time? Like an individual, a country can trade over time by borrowing or lending. Consider what happens when an individual borrows: She is initially able to spend more than her income or, in other words, to consume more than her production. Later, however, she must repay the loan with interest, and therefore in the future she consumes *less* than she produces. By borrowing, then, she has in effect traded future consumption for current consumption. The same is true of a borrowing country.

Clearly the price of future consumption in terms of present consumption has something to do with the interest rate. As we will see in the second half of this book, in the real world the interpretation of interest rates is complicated by the possibility of changes in the overall price level. For now, we bypass that problem by supposing that loan contracts are specified in "real" terms: When a country borrows, it gets the right to purchase some quantity of consumption at present in return for repayment of some larger quantity in the future. Specifically, the quantity of repayment in future will be $(1 + r)$ times the quantity borrowed in present, where r is the **real interest rate** on borrowing. Since the trade-off is one unit of consumption in present for $(1 + r)$ units in future, the relative price of future consumption is $1/(1 + r)$.

The parallel with our standard trade model is now complete. If borrowing and lending are allowed, the relative price of future consumption, and thus the world real interest rate, will be determined by the world relative supply and demand for future consumption. Home, whose intertemporal production possibilities are biased toward present consumption, will export present consumption and import future consumption. That is, Home will lend to Foreign in the first period and receive repayment in the second.

Intertemporal Comparative Advantage

We have assumed that Home's intertemporal production possibilities are biased toward present production. But what does this mean? The sources of intertemporal comparative advantage are somewhat different from those that give rise to ordinary trade.

A country that has a comparative advantage in future production of consumption goods is one that in the absence of international borrowing and lending would have a low relative price of future consumption, that is, a high real interest rate. This high real interest rate corresponds to a high return on investment, that is, a high return to diverting resources from current production of consumption goods to production of capital goods, construction, and other activities that enhance the economy's future ability to produce. So countries that borrow in the international market will be those where highly productive investment opportunities are available relative to current productive capacity, while countries that lend will be those where such opportunities are not available domestically.

The pattern of international borrowing and lending in the 1970s illustrates the point. Table 22-3 compares the international lending of three groups of countries: industrial countries, non-oil developing countries, and major oil exporters. From 1974 to 1981, the oil exporters lent $395 billion, the less-developed countries borrowed $315 billion, and the (much larger) industrial countries borrowed a smaller amount, $265 billion. In the light of our model, this is not surprising. During the 1970s, as a result of a spectacular increase in oil prices, oil exporters like Saudi Arabia found themselves with very high current income. They did not, however, find any comparable increase in their domestic investment opportunities. That is, they had a comparative advantage in current consumption. With small populations, limited resources other than oil, and little expertise in industrial or other production, their natural reaction was to invest much of their increased earnings abroad. By contrast, rapidly developing countries such as Brazil and South Korea expected to have much higher incomes in the future and saw highly productive investment opportunities in their growing industrial sectors; they had a comparative advantage in future income. Thus in this time frame (1974 to 1981) the oil exporters also exported current consumption by lending their money, in part, to less-developed countries.

Direct Foreign Investment and Multinational Firms

In the last section we focused on international borrowing and lending. This is a relatively simple transaction, in that the borrower makes no demands on the lender other than that of repayment. An important part of international capital movement, however, takes a different form, that of **direct foreign investment**. By direct foreign investment we mean international

DOES CAPITAL MOVEMENT TO DEVELOPING COUNTRIES HURT WORKERS IN HIGH-WAGE COUNTRIES?

We have turned repeatedly in this textbook to concerns created by the rapid economic growth of newly industrializing economies (NIEs), mainly in Asia. In Chapter 4 we discussed the concern that trade with the NIEs might, via the Stolper-Samuelson effect, reduce the real wages of less-skilled workers in advanced nations and saw that it had some justification. In Chapter 5 we turned to the possibility that growth in the NIEs might, by worsening the terms of trade of advanced nations, lower their overall real income but saw that this was unlikely. In the 1990s there was growing worry among some commentators that the export of capital to the NIEs would have a severe impact on the wages of workers in advanced countries.

The logic of this view is as follows: If high-wage countries finance investment on low-wage countries, this will mean less savings available to build up the capital stock at home. Because each worker at home will have less capital to work with than she otherwise would, her marginal product—and hence her wage rate—will be lower than it would have been in the absence of the capital movement. Overall real income, including the returns from capital invested abroad, may be higher for the home country than it would otherwise have been, but more than all the gains will go to capital, with labor actually worse off.

While this adverse effect is possible in principle, how important is it likely to be in practice? Some influential people have issued stark warnings. For example, Klaus Schwab, the head of Switzerland's influential World Economic Forum, warned that the world faced a "massive redeployment of

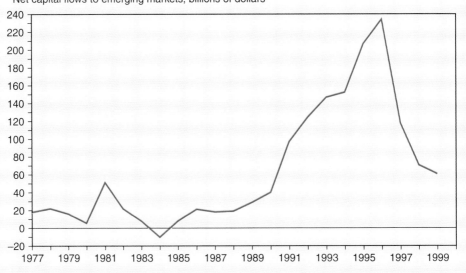

Capital Flows to Developing Countries

Net capital flows to emerging markets, billions of dollars

Flows of capital to low-wage countries. Large capital flows to "non-oil" developing countries (less-developed countries other than major oil exporters) began in the 1970s, then collapsed during the debt crisis of the 1980s. They resumed again after about 1990.

Source: International Monetary Fund, *International Financial Statistics Yearbook,* 1997.

assets" that would end the ability of workers in advanced countries to earn high wages.* Similiar views have been expressed by many journalists.

Economists, however, have been generally unimpressed by this argument. They point out that over the longer term capital movements to developing countries have been quite limited. The accompanying figure shows net capital movements to "emerging market" economies between 1977 and 1999. Such capital movements came to a virtual halt during the debt crisis of the 1980s, discussed in Chapter 22. They resumed in the 1990s, only to drop off sharply with the Asian financial crisis of 1997. The movement in 1996, $233 billion, sounds large; but the economies of advanced nations are almost inconceivably large, and even this represented only about 7 percent of their total investment.

*Klaus Schwab and Claude Smadja, "Power and Policy: The New Economic World Order," *Harvard Business Review* 72, no. 6 (November–December 1994), pp. 40–47.

capital flows in which a firm in one country creates or expands a subsidiary in another. The distinctive feature of direct foreign investment is that it involves not only a transfer of resources but also the acquisition of *control*. That is, the subsidiary does not simply have a financial obligation to the parent company; it is part of the same organizational structure.

When is a corporation multinational? In U.S. statistics, a U.S. company is considered foreign-controlled, and therefore a subsidiary of a foreign-based multinational, if 10 percent or more of the stock is held by a foreign company; the idea is that 10 percent is enough to convey effective control. A U.S.-based company is considered multinational if it has a controlling share of companies abroad.

Alert readers will notice that these definitions make it possible for a company to be considered both a U.S. subsidiary of a foreign company and a U.S. multinational. And this sometimes happens: from 1981 until 1995 the chemical company DuPont was officially foreign-controlled (because the Canadian company Seagram owned a large block of its stock) but was also considered an American multinational. In practice, such strange cases are rare: usually multinational companies have a clear national home base.

Multinational firms are often a vehicle for international borrowing and lending. Parent companies often provide their foreign subsidiaries with capital, in the expectation of eventual repayment. To the extent that multinational firms provide financing to their foreign subsidiaries, direct foreign investment is an alternative way of accomplishing the same things as international lending. This still leaves open the question, however, of why direct investment rather than some other way of transferring funds is chosen. In any case, the existence of multinational firms does not necessarily reflect a net capital flow from one country to another. Multinationals sometimes raise money for the expansion of their subsidiaries in the country where the subsidiary operates rather than in their home country. Furthermore, there is a good deal of two-way foreign direct investment among industrial countries, U.S. firms expanding their European subsidiaries at the same time that European firms expand their U.S. subsidiaries, for example.

The point is that while multinational firms sometimes act as a vehicle for international capital flows, it is probably a mistake to view direct foreign investment as primarily an alternative way for countries to borrow and lend. Instead, the main point of direct foreign investment is to allow the formation of multinational organizations. That is, the extension of control is the essential purpose.

But why do firms seek to extend control? Economists do not have as fully developed a theory of multinational enterprise as they do of many other issues in international economics. There is some theory on the subject, however, which we now review.

The Theory of Multinational Enterprise

The basic necessary elements of a theory of multinational firms can best be seen by looking at an example. Consider the European operations of American auto manufacturers. Ford and General Motors, for example, sell many cars in Europe, but nearly all those cars are manufactured in plants in Germany, Britain, and Spain. This arrangement is familiar, but we should realize that there are two obvious alternatives. On one side, instead of producing in Europe the U.S. firms could produce in the United States and export to the European market. On the other side, the whole market could be served by European producers such as Volkswagen and Renault. Why, then, do we see this particular arrangement, in which the *same* firms produce in *different* countries?

The modern theory of multinational enterprise starts by distinguishing between the two questions of which this larger question is composed. First, why is a good produced in two (or more) different countries rather than one? This is known as the question of **location**. Second, why is production in different locations done by the same firm rather than by separate firms? This is known, for reasons that will become apparent in a moment, as the question of **internalization**. We need a theory of location to explain why Europe does not import its automobiles from the United States; we need a theory of internalization to explain why Europe's auto industry is not independently controlled.

The theory of location is not a difficult one in principle. It is, in fact, just the theory of trade that we developed in Chapters 2 through 6. The location of production is often determined by resources. Aluminum mining must be located where the bauxite is, aluminum smelting near cheap electricity. Minicomputer manufacturers locate their skill-intensive design facilities in Massachusetts or northern California and their labor-intensive assembly plants in Ireland or Singapore. Alternatively, transport costs and other barriers to trade may determine location. American firms produce locally for the European market partly to reduce transport costs; since the models that sell well in Europe are often quite different from those that sell well in the United States, it makes sense to have separate production facilities and to put them on different continents. As these examples reveal, the factors that determine a multinational corporation's decisions about where to produce are probably not much different from those that determine the pattern of trade in general.

The theory of internalization is another matter. Why not have independent auto companies in Europe? We may note first that there are always important transactions between a multinational's operations in different countries. The output of one subsidiary is often an input into the production of another. Or technology developed in one country may be used in others. Or management may usefully coordinate the activities of plants in several countries. These transactions are what tie the multinational firm together, and the firm presumably exists to facilitate these transactions. But international transactions need not be carried out inside a firm. Components can be sold in an open market, and technology can be licensed to other firms. Multinationals exist because it turns out to be more profitable to carry out these transactions within a firm rather than between firms. This is why the motive for multinationals is referred to as "internalization."

We have defined a concept, but we have not yet explained what gives rise to internalization. Why are some transactions more profitably conducted within a firm rather than between firms? Here there are a variety of theories, none as well-grounded either in theory or in evidence as our theories of location. We may note two influential views, however, about why activities in different countries may usefully be integrated in a single firm.

The first view stresses the advantages of internalization for **technology transfer**. Technology, broadly defined as any kind of economically useful knowledge, can sometimes be sold or licensed. There are important difficulties in doing this, however. Often the technology involved in, say, running a factory has never been written down; it is embodied in the knowledge of a group of individuals and cannot be packaged and sold. Also, it is difficult for a prospective buyer to know how much knowledge is worth—if the buyer knew as much as the seller, there would be no need to buy! Finally, property rights in knowledge are often hard to establish. If a European firm licenses technology to a U.S. firm, other U.S. firms may legally imitate that technology. All these problems may be reduced if a firm, instead of selling technology, sets about capturing the returns from the technology in other countries by setting up foreign subsidiaries.

The second view stresses the advantages of internalization for **vertical integration**. If one firm (the "upstream" firm) produces a good that is used as an input for another firm (the "downstream" firm), a number of problems can result. For one thing, if each has a monopoly position, they may get into a conflict as the downstream firm tries to hold the price down while the upstream firm tries to raise it. There may be problems of coordination if demand or supply is uncertain. Finally, a fluctuating price may impose excessive risk on one or the other party. If the upstream and downstream firms are combined into a single "vertically integrated" firm, these problems may be avoided or at least reduced.

It should be clear that these views are by no means as rigorously worked out as the analysis of trade carried out elsewhere in this book. The economic theory of organizations—which is what we are talking about when we try to develop a theory of multinational corporations—is still in its infancy. This is particularly unfortunate because in practice multinationals are a subject of heated controversy—praised by some for generating economic growth, accused by others of creating poverty.

Multinational Firms in Practice

Multinational firms play an important part in world trade and investment. For example, about half of U.S. imports are transactions between "related parties." By this we mean that the buyer and the seller are to a significant extent owned and presumably controlled by the same firm. Thus half of U.S. imports can be regarded as transactions between branches of multinational firms. At the same time, 24 percent of U.S. assets abroad consists of the value of foreign subsidiaries of U.S. firms. So U.S. international trade and investment, while not dominated by multinational firms, are to an important extent conducted by such firms.

Multinational firms may, of course, be either domestic or foreign-owned. Foreign-owned multinational firms play an important role in most economies and an increasingly important role in the United States. Table 7-l compares the role of foreign-owned firms in the manufacturing sectors of three major economies. (Bear in mind that foreigners typically own a much larger share of manufacturing than of the economy as a whole.) The table is illuminating, especially for Americans who are not used to the idea of working for foreign-owned

Table 7-1	France, United Kingdom, and United States: Shares of Foreign-Owned Firms in Manufacturing Sales, Value Added, and Employment, 1985 and 1990 (percentages)

	Sales		Value added		Employment	
Country	1985	1990	1985	1990	1985	1990
France	26.7	28.4	25.3	27.1	21.1	23.7
United Kingdom	20.3	24.1	18.7	21.1	14.0	14.9
United States	8.0	16.4	8.3	13.4	8.0	10.8

Source: U.S. Department of Commerce, *Foreign Direct Investment in the United States: An Update* (1994).

companies and sometimes get nervous about the implications of rising foreign ownership. The first thing the table tells us is that while large-scale foreign ownership may be novel here, it is old hat elsewhere: France is a country proud of its cultural independence, but as long ago as 1985 more than a fifth of French manufacturing workers were employed by foreign firms. The table also confirms, however, that the United States did experience a sharp increase in foreign ownership during the 1980s; for example, the share of foreign-owned firms in sales doubled between 1985 and 1990. This increase made the United States more similar to other countries, where substantial foreign ownership has long been a fact of life.

Although comparable statistics do not exist, it turns out that the real exception among major economies is Japan, which has very little foreign ownership. This is not because of overt legal restrictions: On paper, foreigners are free to open plants in Japan and buy Japanese companies, with only a few exceptions. But cultural obstacles, such as the unwillingness of many Japanese to work for foreign companies, and perhaps also red-tape barriers thrown up by bureaucrats have prevented large-scale operation of foreign-based multinationals.

The important question, however, is what difference multinationals make. With only a limited understanding of why multinationals exist, this is a hard question to answer. Nonetheless, the existing theory suggests some preliminary answers.

Notice first that much of what multinationals do could be done without multinationals, although perhaps not as easily. Two examples are the shift of labor-intensive production from industrial countries to labor-abundant nations and capital flows from capital-abundant countries to capital-scarce countries. Multinational firms are sometimes the agents of these changes and are therefore either praised or condemned for their actions (depending on the commentator's point of view). But these shifts reflect the "location" aspect of our theory of multinationals, which is really no different from ordinary trade theory. If multinationals were not there, the same things would still happen, though perhaps not to the same extent. This observation leads international economists to attribute less significance to multinational enterprise than most lay observers.

Notice, too, that in a broad sense what multinational corporations do by creating organizations that extend across national boundaries is similar to the effects of trade and simple factor mobility; that is, it is a form of international economic integration. By analogy with the other forms of international integration we have studied, we would expect multinational enterprise to produce overall gains but to produce income distribution effects that leave some people worse off. These income distribution effects are probably mostly effects *within* rather than *between* countries.

To sum up, multinational corporations probably are not as important a factor in the world economy as their visibility would suggest; their role is neither more nor less likely to be beneficial than other international linkages. This does not, however, prevent them from being cast in the role of villains or (more rarely) heroes, as we will see in our discussion of trade and development in Chapter 10.

CASE STUDY

Foreign Direct Investment in the United States

Until the 1980s, the United States was almost always regarded as a "home" country for multi-national companies rather than as a "host" for foreign-based multinationals. Indeed, when the French author Jean-Jacques Servan-Schreiber wrote a best-seller warning of the growing power of multinationals, his book—published in 1968—was titled *The American Challenge.*

This perspective changed in the middle of the 1980s. Figure 7-5 shows U.S. inflows of foreign direct investment—that is, capital either used to acquire control of a U.S. company or invested in a company that foreigners already controlled—as a percentage of GDP. In the second half of the 1980s these flows, which had previously averaged less than 0.5 percent of GDP, surged. Japanese companies began building automobile plants in the United States, and European companies began buying U.S. banks and insurance companies. Foreign direct investment then slumped in the early 1990s, before beginning an astonishing rise in the late 1990s.

What was behind these fluctuations? Rather paradoxically, the boom in direct investment in the late 1980s and the even bigger boom in the late 1990s happened for nearly opposite reasons.

Much foreign direct investment in the 1980s was driven by a perception of U.S. weakness. At the time, Japanese manufacturing companies, especially in the auto industry, had pulled ahead of their U.S. competitors in productivity and technology. The lower prices and superior quality of Japanese products allowed them to take a rapidly growing share of the U.S. market; in order to serve that market better, the Japanese began to open plants in the United States.

Also, in the late 1980s the U.S. dollar was quite weak against both the Japanese yen and European currencies such as the German mark. This made assets in the United States appear cheap and encouraged foreign companies to move in.

Perhaps because of the perception that foreigners were taking advantage of U.S. weakness, the surge in foreign direct investment in the 1980s provoked a political backlash. The height of this backlash probably came in 1992, when Michael Crichton published the best-seller *Rising Sun,* a novel about the evil machinations of a Japanese company operating in the United States. The novel, which was made into a movie starring Sean Connery the next year, came with a long postscript warning about the dangers that Japanese companies posed to the United States.

As you can see from Figure 7-5, however, foreign direct investment in the United States was slumping even as *Rising Sun* hit the bookstores. And public concern faded along with the investment itself.

Figure 7-5 | Foreign Direct Investment in the United States

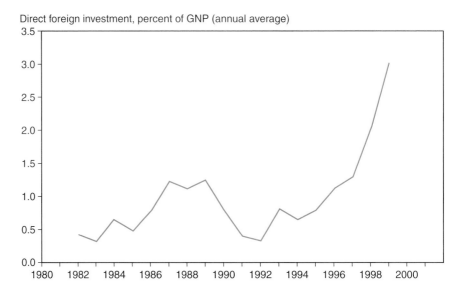

Direct foreign investment, percent of GNP (annual average)

Foreign direct investment flows into the United States surged in 1986–1989 and again after 1992, rapidly raising the share of U.S. production controlled by foreign firms.
Source: U.S. Commerce Dept.

When foreign direct investment surged again, in the late 1990s, the situation was very different: now the wave of investment was driven by perceptions of U.S. strength rather than weakness. The United States was experiencing a remarkable economic boom; meanwhile, European growth was modest, and Japan languished in the middle of a decade of economic stagnation. Given the revived economic dominance of the United States, nearly every large company on the planet felt that it had to have a stake in the U.S. economy. And so companies flocked to the United States, mainly by acquiring control of existing U.S. companies. Whether this was a good idea is another question: the troubled acquisition of Chrysler by the German company Daimler-Benz, discussed on p. 177, became a celebrated example of how investing in America could go wrong.

The political reception for foreign investors in the 1990s was utterly different from that given to the previous wave. It's not clear to what extent Americans were even aware of the wave of money pouring in; Michael Crichton gave up on economics and went back to writing about dinosaurs. To the extent that the inflow of direct investment was noticed, it was perceived as a tribute to U.S. strength, not as a threat.

At the time of writing, the inflow of foreign direct investment was still in progress, even though the U.S. boom officially came to an end in 2001.

TAKEN FOR A RIDE?

In November 1998 Germany's Daimler-Benz corporation, the makers of the Mercedes-Benz, acquired control of America's Chrysler corporation for $40 billion—about $13 billion more than the market value of Chrysler's stock at the time. The new, merged company was named DaimlerChrysler.

For the deal to make business sense, the combined company had to be worth more than the two companies were worth separately. In fact, given the premium that Daimler-Benz paid to acquire Chrysler, the merger in effect had to create at least $13 billion in value. Where would this gain come from?

The answer, according to executives in both companies, was that there would be "synergy" between the two companies—that the whole would be more than the sum of the parts because each company would supply something the other lacked. Skeptical analysts were not convinced. They pointed out that although both companies were in the automobile business, they occupied almost completely different market niches: Daimler-Benz had built its reputation on classy luxury sedans, while Chrysler was much more down-

market: its signature vehicles were minivans and SUVs. So it was unclear whether there would be much gain in terms of either marketing or production efficiencies. In that case, where would the extra value come from?

It soon became clear that far from generating synergies, the deal had at least initially created new problems, particularly at Chrysler. Put simply, the cultural differences between the two companies—partly a matter of national style, partly a matter of the personalities involved—created a great deal of misunderstanding and bad feelings. The initial deal was supposedly a merger of equals, but it soon became clear that the German company was the senior partner; many Chrysler executives left within a year after the merger. Partly as a result of these departures, Chrysler's product development and marketing lagged; within two years after the deal, Chrysler had gone from large profits to large losses. These developments were reflected in a plunge in the new company's stock price: two years after the merger, far from being worth more than the sum of the two companies before the deal, DaimlerChrysler was worth less than *either* company alone.

Summary

1. International factor movements can sometimes substitute for trade, so it is not surprising that international migration of labor is similar in its causes and effects to international trade based on differences in resources. Labor moves from countries where it is abundant to countries where it is scarce. This movement raises total world output, but it also generates strong income distribution effects, so that some groups are hurt.

2. International borrowing and lending can be viewed as a kind of international trade, but one that involves trade of present consumption for future consumption rather than trade of one good for another. The relative price at which this intertemporal trade takes place is one plus the real rate of interest.

3. Multinational firms, while they often serve as vehicles for international borrowing and lending, primarily exist as ways of extending control over activities taking place in two or more different countries. The theory of multinational firms is not as well

developed as other parts of international economics. A basic framework can be presented that stresses two crucial elements that explain the existence of a multinational: a location motive that leads the activities of the firm to be in different countries, and an internalization motive that leads these activities to be integrated in a single firm.

4. The location motives of multinationals are the same as those behind all international trade. The internalization motives are less well understood; current theory points to two main motives: the need for a way to transfer technology and the advantages in some cases of vertical integration.

Key Terms

direct foreign investment, p. 169
factor movements, p. 160
intertemporal production possibility
  frontier, p. 167
intertemporal trade, p. 167

location and internalization motives
  of multinationals, p. 172
real interest rate, p. 168
technology transfer, p. 173
vertical integration, p. 173

Problems

1. In Home and Foreign there are two factors of production, land and labor, used to produce only one good. The land supply in each country and the technology of production are exactly the same. The marginal product of labor in each country depends on employment as follows:

Number of Workers Employed	Marginal Product of Last Worker
1	20
2	19
3	18
4	17
5	16
6	15
7	14
8	13
9	12
10	11
11	10

Initially, there are 11 workers employed in Home, but only 3 workers in Foreign.
    Find the effect of free movement of labor from Home to Foreign on employment, production, real wages, and the income of landowners in each country.

2. Suppose that a labor-abundant country and a land-abundant country both produce labor- and land-intensive goods with the same technology. Drawing on the analysis in Chapter 4, first analyze the conditions under which trade between the two countries eliminates the incentive for labor to migrate. Then, using the analysis in Chapter 5, show that a tariff by one country will create an incentive for labor migration.

3. Explain the analogy between international borrowing and lending and ordinary international trade.

4. Which of the following countries would you expect to have intertemporal production possibilities biased toward current consumption goods, and which biased toward future consumption goods?

   a. A country, like Argentina or Canada in the last century, that has only recently been opened for large-scale settlement and is receiving large inflows of immigrants.

   b. A country, like the United Kingdom in the late nineteenth century or the United States today, that leads the world technologically but is seeing that lead eroded as other countries catch up.

   c. A country that has discovered large oil reserves that can be exploited with little new investment (like Saudi Arabia).

   d. A country that has discovered large oil reserves that can be exploited only with massive investment (like Norway, whose oil lies under the North Sea).

   e. A country like South Korea that has discovered the knack of producing industrial goods and is rapidly gaining on advanced countries.

5. Which of the following are direct foreign investments, and which are not?

   a. A Saudi businessman buys $10 million of IBM stock.

   b. The same businessman buys a New York apartment building.

   c. A French company merges with an American company; stockholders in the U.S. company exchange their stock for shares in the French firm.

   d. An Italian firm builds a plant in Russia and manages the plant as a contractor to the Russian government.

6. The Karma Computer Company has decided to open a Brazilian subsidiary. Brazilian import restrictions have prevented the firm from selling into that market, while the firm has been unwilling to sell or lease its patents to Brazilian firms because it fears this will eventually hurt its technological advantage in the U.S. market. Analyze Karma's decision in terms of the theory of multinational enterprise.

Further Reading

Richard A. Brecher and Robert C. Feenstra. "International Trade and Capital Mobility Between Diversified Economies." *Journal of International Economics* 14 (May 1983), pp. 321–339. A synthesis of the theories of trade and international factor movements.

Richard E. Caves. *Multinational Enterprises and Economic Analysis.* Cambridge: Harvard University Press, 1982. A view of multinational firms' activities.

Wilfred J. Ethier. "The Multinational Firm." *Quarterly Journal of Economics* 101 (November 1986), pp. 805–833. Models the internalization motive of multinationals.

Irving Fisher. *The Theory of Interest.* New York: Macmillan, 1930. The "intertemporal" approach described in this chapter owes its origin to Fisher.

Edward M. Graham and Paul R. Krugman. *Foreign Direct Investment in the United States.* Washington, D.C.: Institute for International Economics, 1989. A survey of the surge of foreign investment in the United States, with an emphasis on policy issues.

Charles P. Kindleberger. *American Business Abroad.* New Haven: Yale University Press, 1969. A good discussion of the nature and effects of multinational firms, written at a time when such firms were primarily United States–based.

Charles P. Kindleberger. *Europe's Postwar Growth: The Role of Labor Supply.* Cambridge: Harvard University Press, 1967. A good account of the role of labor migration during its height in Europe.

G. D. A. MacDougall. "The Benefits and Costs of Private Investment from Abroad: A Theoretical Approach." *Economic Record* 36 (1960), pp. 13–35. A clear analysis of the costs and benefits of factor movement.

Robert A. Mundell. "International Trade and Factor Mobility." *American Economic Review* 47 (1957), pp. 321–335. The paper that first laid out the argument that trade and factor movement can substitute for each other.

Jeffrey Sachs. "The Current Account and Macroeconomic Adjustment in the 1970s." *Brookings Papers on Economic Activity,* 1981. A study of international capital flows that takes the approach of viewing such flows as intertemporal trade.

APPENDIX TO CHAPTER 7

More on Intertemporal Trade

This appendix contains a more detailed examination of the two-period intertemporal trade model described in the chapter. The concepts used are the same as those used in Chapter 5 to analyze international exchanges of different consumption goods at a *single* point in time. In the present setting, however, the trade model explains international patterns of investment and borrowing and the determination of the *intertemporal* terms of trade (that is, the real interest rate).

First consider Home, whose intertemporal production possibility frontier is shown in Figure 7A-1. Recall that the quantities of present and future consumption goods produced at Home depend on the amount of present consumption goods invested to produce future goods. As currently available resources are diverted from present consumption to investment, production of present consumption, Q_P, falls and production of future consumption, Q_F, rises. Increased investment therefore shifts the economy up and to the left along the intertemporal production possibility frontier.

The chapter showed that the price of future consumption in terms of present consumption is $1/(1 + r)$, where r is the real interest rate. Measured in terms of present consumption, the value of the economy's total production over the two periods of its existence is therefore

$$V = Q_P + Q_F/(1 + r).$$

 Figure 7A-1 | Determining Home's Intertemporal Production Pattern

At a world real interest rate of r, Home's investment level maximizes the value of production over the two periods that the economy exists.

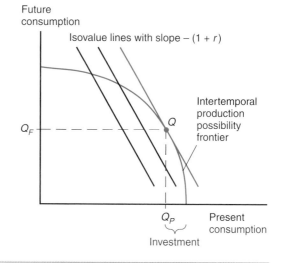

Figure 7A-1 shows the isovalue lines corresponding to the relative price $1/(1 + r)$ for different values of V. These are straight lines with slope $-(1 + r)$ (because future consumption is on the vertical axis). As in the standard trade model, firms' decisions lead to a production pattern that maximizes the value of production at market prices, $Q_P + Q_F/(1 + r)$. Production therefore occurs at point Q. The economy invests the amount shown, leaving Q_P available for present consumption and producing an amount Q_F of future consumption when the first-period investment pays off.

Notice that at point Q, the extra future consumption that would result from investing an additional unit of present consumption just equals $(1 + r)$. It would be inefficient to push investment beyond point Q because the economy could do better by lending additional present consumption to foreigners instead. Figure 7A-1 implies that a rise in the world real interest rate r, which steepens the isovalue lines, causes investment to fall.

Figure 7A-2 shows how Home's consumption pattern is determined for a given world interest rate. Let D_P and D_F represent the demands for present and future consumption goods, respectively. Since production is at point Q, the economy's consumption possibilities over the two periods are limited by the *intertemporal budget constraint:*

$$D_P + D_F/(1 + r) = Q_P + Q_F/(1 + r)$$

This constraint states that the value of Home's consumption over the two periods (measured in terms of present consumption) equals the value of consumption goods produced in the two periods (also measured in present consumption units). Put another way, production and consumption must lie on the same isovalue line.

Figure 7A-2 | Determining Home's Intertemporal Consumption Pattern

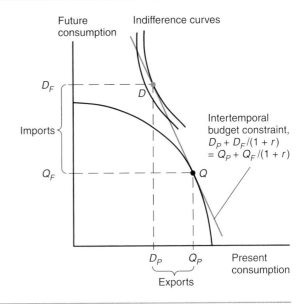

Home's consumption places it on the highest indifference curve touching its intertemporal budget constraint. The economy exports $Q_P - D_P$ units of present consumption and imports $D_F - Q_F = (1 + r) \times (Q_P - D_P)$ units of future consumption.

Point *D*, where Home's budget constraint touches the highest attainable indifference curve, shows the present and future consumption levels chosen by the economy. Home's demand for present consumption, D_P, is smaller than its production of present consumption, Q_P, so it exports (that is, lends) $Q_P - D_P$ units of present consumption to Foreigners. Correspondingly, Home imports $D_F - Q_F$ units of future consumption from abroad when its first-period loans are repaid to it with interest. The intertemporal budget constraint implies that $D_F - Q_F = (1 + r) \times (Q_P - D_P)$, so that trade is *intertemporally* balanced.

Figure 7A-3 shows how investment and consumption are determined in Foreign. Foreign is assumed to have a comparative advantage in producing *future* consumption goods. The diagram shows that at a real interest rate of *r*, Foreign borrows consumption goods in the first period and repays this loan using consumption goods produced in the second period. Because of its relatively rich domestic investment opportunities and its relative preference for present consumption, Foreign is an importer of present consumption and an exporter of future consumption.

As in Chapter 5 (appendix), international equilibrium can be portrayed by an offer curve diagram. Recall that a country's offer curve is the result of plotting its desired exports against its desired imports. Now, however, the exchanges plotted involve present and future consumption. Figure 7A-4 shows that the equilibrium real interest rate is determined by the intersection of the Home and Foreign offer curves *OP* and *OF* at point *E*. The ray *OE* has slope $(1 + r^1)$, where r^1 is the equilibrium world interest rate. At point *E*, Home's desired export of present consumption equals Foreign's desired import of present consumption. Put another way, at point *E*, Home's desired first-period lending equals Foreign's desired first-period borrowing. Supply and demand are therefore equal in both periods.

Figure 7A-3 | Determining Foreign's Intertemporal Production and Consumption Patterns

Foreign produces at point Q^* and consumes at point D^*, importing $D_P^* - Q_P^*$ units of present consumption and exporting $Q_F^* - D_F^* = (1 + r) \times (D_P^* - Q_P^*)$ units of future consumption.

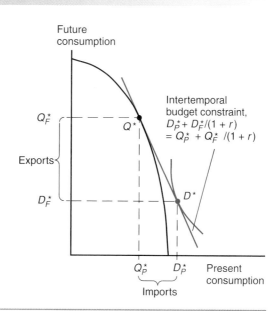

Figure 7A-4 | International Intertemporal Equilibrium
                 | in Terms of Offer Curves

Equilibrium is at point E (with interest rate r^1) because desired Home exports of present consumption equal desired Foreign imports and desired Foreign exports of future consumption equal desired Home imports.

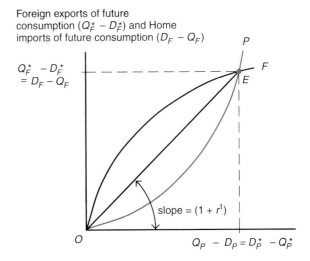

Foreign exports of future consumption ($Q_F^* - D_F^*$) and Home imports of future consumption ($D_F - Q_F$)

$Q_F^* - D_F^*$
$= D_F - Q_F$

slope $= (1 + r^1)$

O

$Q_P - D_P = D_P^* - Q_P^*$

Home exports of present consumption ($Q_P - D_P$) and Foreign imports of future consumption ($D_P^* - Q_P^*$)

PART 2　International Trade Policy

CHAPTER 8

The Instruments of Trade Policy

Previous chapters have answered the question, "Why do nations trade?" by *describing* the causes and effects of international trade and the functioning of a trading world economy. While this question is interesting in itself, its answer is much more interesting if it helps answer the question, "What should a nation's trade policy be?" Should the United States use a tariff or an import quota to protect its automobile industry against competition from Japan and South Korea? Who will benefit and who will lose from an import quota? Will the benefits outweigh the costs?

This chapter examines the policies that governments adopt toward international trade, policies that involve a number of different actions. These actions include taxes on some international transactions, subsidies for other transactions, legal limits on the value or volume of particular imports, and many other measures. The chapter provides a framework for understanding the effects of the most important instruments of trade policy.

Basic Tariff Analysis

A tariff, the simplest of trade policies, is a tax levied when a good is imported. **Specific tariffs** are levied as a fixed charge for each unit of goods imported (for example, $3 per barrel of oil). **Ad valorem tariffs** are taxes that are levied as a fraction of the value of the imported goods (for example, a 25 percent U.S. tariff on imported trucks). In either case the effect of the tariff is to raise the cost of shipping goods to a country.

Tariffs are the oldest form of trade policy and have traditionally been used as a source of government income. Until the introduction of the income tax, for instance, the U.S. government raised most of its revenue from tariffs. Their true purpose, however, has usually been not only to provide revenue but to protect particular domestic sectors. In the early nineteenth century the United Kingdom used tariffs (the famous Corn Laws) to protect its agriculture from import competition. In the late nineteenth century both Germany and the United States protected their new industrial sectors by imposing tariffs on imports of manufactured goods. The importance of tariffs has declined in modern times, because modern governments usually prefer to protect domestic industries through a variety of **nontariff barriers**, such as **import quotas** (limitations on the quantity of imports) and **export restraints** (limitations on the quantity of exports—usually imposed by the exporting country at the importing country's request). Nonetheless, an understanding of the effects of a tariff remains a vital basis for understanding other trade policies.

In developing the theory of trade in Chapters 2 through 7 we adopted a *general equilibrium* perspective. That is, we were keenly aware that events in one part of the economy have repercussions elsewhere. However, in many (though not all) cases trade policies toward one sector can be reasonably well understood without going into detail about the repercussions of that policy in the rest of the economy. For the most part, then, trade policy can be examined in a *partial equilibrium* framework. When the effects on the economy as a whole become crucial, we will refer back to general equilibrium analysis.

Supply, Demand, and Trade in a Single Industry

Let's suppose there are two countries, Home and Foreign, both of which consume and produce wheat, which can be costlessly transported between the countries. In each country wheat is a simple competitive industry in which the supply and demand curves are functions of the market price. Normally Home supply and demand will depend on the price in terms of Home currency, and Foreign supply and demand will depend on the price in terms of Foreign currency, but we assume that the exchange rate between the currencies is not affected by whatever trade policy is undertaken in this market. Thus we quote prices in both markets in terms of Home currency.

Trade will arise in such a market if prices are different in the absence of trade. Suppose that in the absence of trade the price of wheat is higher in Home than it is in Foreign. Now allow foreign trade. Since the price of wheat in Home exceeds the price in Foreign, shippers begin to move wheat from Foreign to Home. The export of wheat raises its price in Foreign and lowers its price in Home until the difference in prices has been eliminated.

To determine the world price and the quantity traded, it is helpful to define two new curves: the Home **import demand curve** and the Foreign **export supply curve**, which are derived from the underlying domestic supply and demand curves. Home import demand is the excess of what Home consumers demand over what Home producers supply; Foreign export supply is the excess of what Foreign producers supply over what Foreign consumers demand.

Figure 8-1 shows how the Home import demand curve is derived. At the price P^1 Home consumers demand D^1, while Home producers supply only S^1, so Home import demand is $D^1 - S^1$. If we raise the price to P^2, Home consumers demand only D^2, while Home producers raise the amount they supply to S^2, so import demand falls to $D^2 - S^2$. These price-quantity combinations are plotted as points 1 and 2 in the right-hand panel of Figure 8-1. The import demand curve MD is downward sloping because as price increases, the quantity of imports demanded declines. At P_A, Home supply and demand are equal in the absence of trade, so the Home import demand curve intercepts the price axis at P_A (import demand = zero at P_A).

Figure 8-2 shows how the Foreign export supply curve XS is derived. At P^1 Foreign producers supply S^{*1}, while Foreign consumers demand only D^{*1}, so the amount of the total supply available for export is $S^{*1} - D^{*1}$. At P^2 Foreign producers raise the quantity they supply to S^{*2} and Foreign consumers lower the amount they demand to D^{*2}, so the quantity of the total supply available to export rises to $S^{*2} - D^{*2}$. Because the supply of goods available for export rises as the price rises, the Foreign export supply curve is upward

Figure 8-1 | Deriving Home's Import Demand Curve

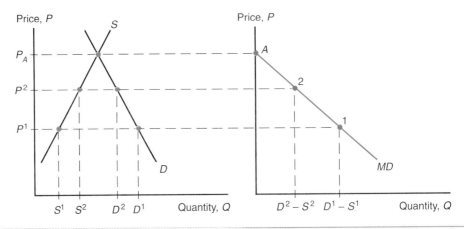

As the price of the good increases, Home consumers demand less, while Home producers supply more, so that the demand for imports declines.

Figure 8-2 | Deriving Foreign's Export Supply Curve

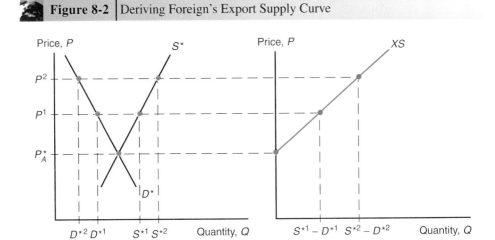

As the price of the good rises, Foreign producers supply more while Foreign consumers demand less, so that the supply available for export rises.

sloping. At P_A^*, supply and demand would be equal in the absence of trade, so the Foreign export supply curve intercepts the price axis at P_A^* (export supply = zero at P_A^*).

World equilibrium occurs when Home import demand equals Foreign export supply (Figure 8-3). At the price P_W, where the two curves cross, world supply equals world demand. At the equilibrium point 1 in Figure 8-3,

Figure 8-3 | World Equilibrium

The equilibrium world price is where Home import demand (MD curve) equals Foreign export supply (XS curve).

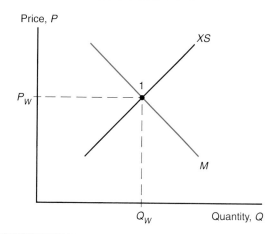

Home demand − Home supply = Foreign supply − Foreign demand.

By adding and subtracting from both sides, this equation can be rearranged to say that

Home demand + Foreign demand = Home supply + Foreign supply

or, in other words,

World demand = World supply.

Effects of a Tariff

From the point of view of someone shipping goods, a tariff is just like a cost of transportation. If Home imposes a tax of $2 on every bushel of wheat imported, shippers will be unwilling to move the wheat unless the price difference between the two markets is at least $2.

Figure 8-4 illustrates the effects of a specific tariff of t per unit of wheat (shown as t in the figure). In the absence of a tariff, the price of wheat would be equalized at P_W, in both Home and Foreign as seen at point 1 in the middle panel, which illustrates the world market. With the tariff in place, however, shippers are not willing to move wheat from Foreign to Home unless the Home price exceeds the Foreign price by at least t. If no wheat is being shipped, however, there will be an excess demand for wheat in Home and an excess supply in Foreign. Thus the price in Home will rise and that in Foreign will fall until the price difference is t.

Introducing a tariff, then, drives a wedge between the prices in the two markets. The tariff raises the price in Home to P_T and lowers the price in Foreign to $P_T^* = P_T - t$. In Home producers supply more at the higher price, while consumers demand less, so that fewer imports are demanded (as you can see in the move from point 1 to point 2 on the MD

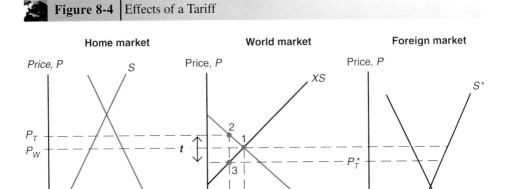

Figure 8-4 | Effects of a Tariff

A tariff raises the price in Home while lowering the price in Foreign. The volume traded declines.

curve). In Foreign the lower price leads to reduced supply and increased demand, and thus a smaller export supply (as seen in the move from point 1 to point 3 on the XS curve). Thus the volume of wheat traded declines from Q_W, the free trade volume, to Q_T, the volume with a tariff. At the trade volume Q_T, Home import demand equals Foreign export supply when $P_T - P_T^* = t$.

The increase in the price in Home, from P_W to P_T, is less than the amount of the tariff, because part of the tariff is reflected in a decline in Foreign's export price and thus is not passed on to Home consumers. This is the normal result of a tariff and of any trade policy that limits imports. The size of this effect on the exporters' price, however, is often in practice very small. When a small country imposes a tariff, its share of the world market for the goods it imports is usually minor to begin with, so that its import reduction has very little effect on the world (foreign export) price.

The effects of a tariff in the "small country" case where a country cannot affect foreign export prices are illustrated in Figure 8-5. In this case a tariff raises the price of the imported good in the country imposing the tariff by the full amount of the tariff, from P_W to $P_W + t$. Production of the imported good rises from S^1 to S^2, while consumption of the good falls from D^1 to D^2. As a result of the tariff, then, imports fall in the country imposing the tariff.

Measuring the Amount of Protection

A tariff on an imported good raises the price received by domestic producers of that good. This effect is often the tariff's principal objective—to *protect* domestic producers from the low prices that would result from import competition. In analyzing trade policy in practice, it is important to ask how much protection a tariff or other trade policy actually provides. The answer is usually expressed as a percentage of the price that would prevail under free

Figure 8-5 | A Tariff in a Small Country

When a country is small, a tariff it imposes cannot lower the foreign price of the good it imports. As a result, the price of the import rises from P_W to $P_W + t$ and the quantity of imports demanded falls from $D^1 - S^1$ to $D^2 - S^2$.

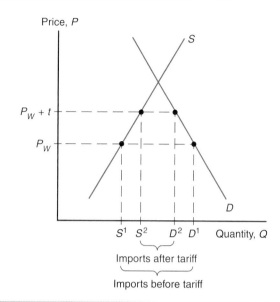

trade. An import quota on sugar could, for example, raise the price received by U.S. sugar producers by 45 percent.

Measuring protection would seem to be straightforward in the case of a tariff: If the tariff is an ad valorem tax proportional to the value of the imports, the tariff rate itself should measure the amount of protection; if the tariff is specific, dividing the tariff by the price net of the tariff gives us the ad valorem equivalent.

There are two problems in trying to calculate the rate of protection this simply. First, if the small country assumption is not a good approximation, part of the effect of a tariff will be to lower foreign export prices rather than to raise domestic prices. This effect of trade policies on foreign export prices is sometimes significant.[1]

The second problem is that tariffs may have very different effects on different stages of production of a good. A simple example illustrates this point.

Suppose that an automobile sells on the world market for $8000 and that the parts out of which that automobile is made sell for $6000. Let's compare two countries: one that wants to develop an auto assembly industry and one that already has an assembly industry and wants to develop a parts industry.

To encourage a domestic auto industry, the first country places a 25 percent tariff on imported autos, allowing domestic assemblers to charge $10,000 instead of $8000. In this case it would be wrong to say that the assemblers receive only 25 percent protection.

---

[1]In theory (though rarely in practice) a tariff could actually lower the price received by domestic producers (the Metzler paradox discussed in Chapter 5).

Before the tariff, domestic assembly would take place only if it could be done for $2000 (the difference between the $8000 price of a completed automobile and the $6000 cost of parts) or less; now it will take place even if it costs as much as $4000 (the difference between the $10,000 price and the cost of parts). That is, the 25 percent tariff rate provides assemblers with an **effective rate of protection** of 100 percent.

Now suppose the second country, to encourage domestic production of parts, imposes a 10 percent tariff on imported parts, raising the cost of parts to domestic assemblers from $6000 to $6600. Even though there is no change in the tariff on assembled automobiles, this policy makes it less advantageous to assemble domestically. Before the tariff it would have been worth assembling a car locally if it could be done for $2000 ($8000 − $6000); after the tariff local assembly takes place only if it can be done for $1400 ($8000 − $6600). The tariff on parts, then, while providing positive protection to parts manufacturers, provides negative effective protection to assembly at the rate of −30 percent (−600/2000).

Reasoning similar to that seen in this example has led economists to make elaborate calculations to measure the degree of effective protection actually provided to particular industries by tariffs and other trade policies. Trade policies aimed at promoting economic development, for example (Chapter 10), often lead to rates of effective protection much higher than the tariff rates themselves.[2]

Costs and Benefits of a Tariff

A tariff raises the price of a good in the importing country and lowers it in the exporting country. As a result of these price changes, consumers lose in the importing country and gain in the exporting country. Producers gain in the importing country and lose in the exporting country. In addition, the government imposing the tariff gains revenue. To compare these costs and benefits, it is necessary to quantify them. The method for measuring costs and benefits of a tariff depends on two concepts common to much microeconomic analysis: consumer and producer surplus.

Consumer and Producer Surplus

Consumer surplus measures the amount a consumer gains from a purchase by the difference between the price he actually pays and the price he would have been willing to pay. If, for example, a consumer would have been willing to pay $8 for a bushel of wheat but the price is only $3, the consumer surplus gained by the purchase is $5.

Consumer surplus can be derived from the market demand curve (Figure 8-6). For example, suppose the maximum price at which consumers will buy 10 units of a good is $10.

---

[2]The effective rate of protection for a sector is formally defined as $(V_T − V_W)/V_W$, where V_W is value added in the sector at world prices and V_T value added in the presence of trade policies. In terms of our example, let P_A be the world price of an assembled automobile, P_C the world price of its components, t_A the ad valorem tariff rate on imported autos, and t_C the ad valorem tariff rate on components. You can check that if the tariffs don't affect world prices, they provide assemblers with an effective protection rate of

$$\frac{V_T − V_W}{V_W} = t_A + P_C\left(\frac{t_A − t_C}{P_A − P_C}\right).$$

Figure 8-6 | Deriving Consumer Surplus from the Demand Curve

Consumer surplus on each unit sold is the difference between the actual price and what consumers would have been willing to pay.

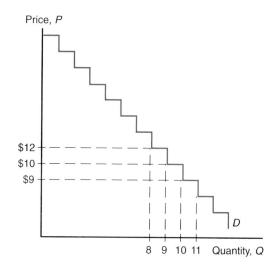

Then the tenth unit of the good purchased must be worth $10 to consumers. If it were worth less, they would not purchase it; if it were worth more, they would have been willing to purchase it even if the price were higher. Now suppose that to get consumers to buy 11 units the price must be cut to $9. Then the eleventh unit must be worth only $9 to consumers.

Suppose that the price is $9. Then consumers are just willing to purchase the eleventh unit of the good and thus receive no consumer surplus from their purchase of that unit. They would have been willing to pay $10 for the tenth unit, however, and thus receive $1 in consumer surplus from that unit. They would have been willing to pay $12 for the ninth unit; if so, they receive $3 of consumer surplus on that unit, and so on.

Generalizing from this example, if P is the price of a good and Q the quantity demanded at that price, then consumer surplus is calculated by subtracting P times Q from the area under the demand curve up to Q (Figure 8-7). If the price is P^1, the quantity demanded is Q^1 and the consumer surplus is measured by the area labeled a. If the price falls to P^2, the quantity demanded rises to Q^2 and consumer surplus rises to equal a plus the additional area b.

Producer surplus is an analogous concept. A producer willing to sell a good for $2 but receiving a price of $5 gains a producer surplus of $3. The same procedure used to derive consumer surplus from the demand curve can be used to derive producer surplus from the supply curve. If P is the price and Q the quantity supplied at that price, then producer surplus is P times Q minus the area under the supply curve up to Q (Figure 8-8). If the price is P^1, the quantity supplied will be Q^1, and producer surplus is measured by the area c. If the price rises to P^2, the quantity supplied rises to Q^2, and producer surplus rises to equal c plus the additional area d.

Some of the difficulties related to the concepts of consumer and producer surplus are technical issues of calculation that we can safely disregard. More important is the question of

Figure 8-7 | Geometry of Consumer Surplus

Consumer surplus is equal to the area under the demand curve and above the price.

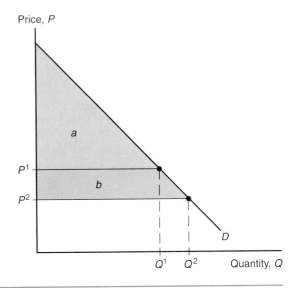

Figure 8-8 | Geometry of Producer Surplus

Producer surplus is equal to the area above the supply curve and below the price.

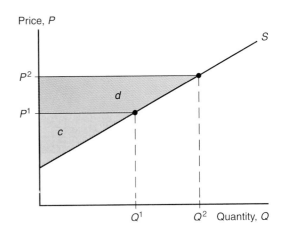

whether the direct gains to producers and consumers in a given market accurately measure the *social* gains. Additional benefits and costs not captured by consumer and producer surplus are at the core of the case for trade policy activism discussed in Chapter 9. For now, however, we will focus on costs and benefits as measured by consumer and producer surplus.

Figure 8-9 | Costs and Benefits of a Tariff for the Importing Country

The costs and benefits to different groups can be represented as sums of the five areas $a, b, c, d,$ and e.

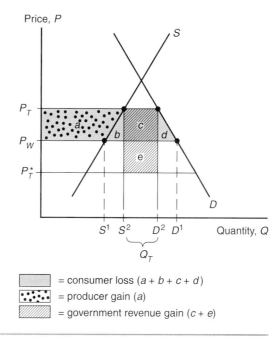

◻◻◻ = consumer loss $(a + b + c + d)$
∴∴∴ = producer gain (a)
▨▨▨ = government revenue gain $(c + e)$

Measuring the Costs and Benefits

Figure 8-9 illustrates the costs and benefits of a tariff for the importing country.

The tariff raises the domestic price from P_W to P_T but lowers the foreign export price from P_W to P_T^* (refer back to Figure 8-4). Domestic production rises from S^1 to S^2, while domestic consumption falls from D^1 to D^2. The costs and benefits to different groups can be expressed as sums of the areas of five regions, labeled a, b, c, d, e.

Consider first the gain to domestic producers. They receive a higher price and therefore have higher producer surplus. As we saw in Figure 8-8, producer surplus is equal to the area below the price but above the supply curve. Before the tariff, producer surplus was equal to the area below P_W but above the supply curve; with the price rising to P_T, this surplus rises by the area labeled a. That is, producers gain from the tariff.

Domestic consumers also face a higher price, which makes them worse off. As we saw in Figure 8-7, consumer surplus is equal to the area above the price but below the demand curve. Since the price consumers face rises from P_W to P_T, the consumer surplus falls by the area indicated by $a + b + c + d$. So consumers are hurt by the tariff.

There is a third player here as well: the government. The government gains by collecting tariff revenue. This is equal to the tariff rate t times the volume of imports $Q_T = D^2 - S^2$. Since $t = P_T - P_T^*$, the government's revenue is equal to the sum of the two areas c and e.

Since these gains and losses accrue to different people, the overall cost-benefit evaluation of a tariff depends on how much we value a dollar's worth of benefit to each group. If, for example, the producer gain accrues mostly to wealthy owners of resources, while the consumers are poorer than average, the tariff will be viewed differently than if the good is a luxury bought by the affluent but produced by low-wage workers. Further ambiguity is introduced by the role of the government: Will it use its revenue to finance vitally needed public services or waste it on $1000 toilet seats? Despite these problems, it is common for analysts of trade policy to attempt to compute the net effect of a tariff on national welfare by assuming that at the margin a dollar's worth of gain or loss to each group is of the same social worth.

Let's look, then, at the net effect of a tariff on welfare. The net cost of a tariff is

$$\text{Consumer loss} - \text{producer gain} - \text{government revenue,} \tag{8-1}$$

or, replacing these concepts by the areas in Figure 8-9,

$$(a + b + c + d) - a - (c + e) = b + d - e. \tag{8-2}$$

That is, there are two "triangles" whose area measures loss to the nation as a whole and a "rectangle" whose area measures an offsetting gain. A useful way to interpret these gains and losses is the following: The loss triangles represent the **efficiency loss** that arises because a tariff distorts incentives to consume and produce, while the rectangle represents the **terms of trade gain** that arise because a tariff lowers foreign export prices.

The gain depends on the ability of the tariff-imposing country to drive down foreign export prices. If the country cannot affect world prices (the "small country" case illustrated in Figure 8-5), region *e,* which represents the terms of trade gain, disappears, and it is clear that the tariff reduces welfare. It distorts the incentives of both producers and consumers by inducing them to act as if imports were more expensive than they actually are. The cost of an additional unit of consumption to the economy is the price of an additional unit of imports, yet because the tariff raises the domestic price above the world price, consumers reduce their consumption to the point where that marginal unit yields them welfare equal to the tariff-inclusive domestic price. The value of an additional unit of production to the economy is the price of the unit of imports it saves, yet domestic producers expand production to the point where the marginal cost is equal to the tariff-inclusive price. Thus the economy produces at home additional units of the good that it could purchase more cheaply abroad.

The net welfare effects of a tariff, then, are summarized in Figure 8-10. The negative effects consist of the two triangles *b* and *d*. The first triangle is a **production distortion loss**, resulting from the fact that the tariff leads domestic producers to produce too much of this good. The second triangle is a domestic **consumption distortion loss**, resulting from the fact that a tariff leads consumers to consume too little of the good. Against these losses must be set the terms of trade gain measured by the rectangle *e,* which results from the decline in the foreign export price caused by a tariff. In the important case of a small country that cannot significantly affect foreign prices, this last effect drops out, so that the costs of a tariff unambiguously exceed its benefits.

Other Instruments of Trade Policy

Tariffs are the simplest trade policies, but in the modern world most government intervention in international trade takes other forms, such as export subsidies, import quotas,

Figure 8-10 Net Welfare Effects of a Tariff

The colored triangles represent efficiency losses, while the rectangle represents a terms of trade gain.

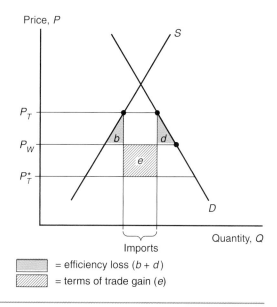

= efficiency loss ($b + d$)

= terms of trade gain (e)

voluntary export restraints, and local content requirements. Fortunately, once we understand tariffs it is not too difficult to understand these other trade instruments.

Export Subsidies: Theory

An **export subsidy** is a payment to a firm or individual that ships a good abroad. Like a tariff, an export subsidy can be either specific (a fixed sum per unit) or ad valorem (a proportion of the value exported). When the government offers an export subsidy, shippers will export the good up to the point where the domestic price exceeds the foreign price by the amount of the subsidy.

The effects of an export subsidy on prices are exactly the reverse of those of a tariff (Figure 8-11). The price in the exporting country rises from P_W to P_S, but because the price in the importing country falls from P_W to P_S^*, the price rise is less than the subsidy. In the exporting country, consumers are hurt, producers gain, and the government loses because it must expend money on the subsidy. The consumer loss is the area $a + b$; the producer gain is the area $a + b + c$; the government subsidy (the amount of exports times the amount of the subsidy) is the area $b + c + d + e + f + g$. The net welfare loss is therefore the sum of the areas $b + d + e + f + g$. Of these, b and d represent consumption and production distortion losses of the same kind that a tariff produces. In addition, and in contrast to a tariff, the export subsidy *worsens* the terms of trade by lowering the price of the export in the foreign market from P_W to P_S^*. This leads to the additional terms of trade loss $e + f + g$, equal to $P_W - P_S^*$ times the quantity exported with the subsidy. So an export subsidy unambiguously leads to costs that exceed its benefits.

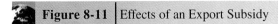

Figure 8-11 | Effects of an Export Subsidy

An export subsidy raises prices in the exporting country while lowering them in the importing country.

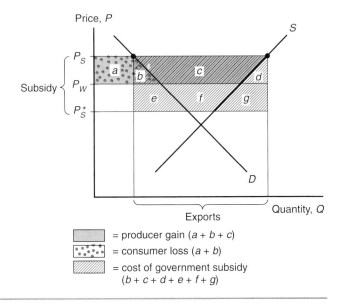

= producer gain ($a + b + c$)

= consumer loss ($a + b$)

= cost of government subsidy ($b + c + d + e + f + g$)

CASE STUDY

Europe's Common Agricultural Policy

Since 1957, six Western European nations—Germany, France, Italy, Belgium, the Netherlands, and Luxembourg—have been members of the European Economic Community; they were later joined by the United Kingdom, Ireland, Denmark, Greece, and, most recently, Spain and Portugal. Now called the European Union (EU), its two biggest effects are on trade policy. First, the members of the European Union have removed all tariffs with respect to each other, creating a customs union (discussed in the next chapter). Second, the agricultural policy of the European Union has developed into a massive export subsidy program.

The European Union's Common Agricultural Policy (CAP) began not as an export subsidy, but as an effort to guarantee high prices to European farmers by having the European Union buy agricultural products whenever the prices fell below specified support levels. To prevent this policy from drawing in large quantities of imports, it was initially backed by tariffs that offset the difference between European and world agricultural prices.

Since the 1970s, however, the support prices set by the European Union have turned out to be so high that Europe, which would under free trade be an importer of most agricultural products, was producing more than consumers were willing to buy. The result was that the European Union found itself obliged to buy and store huge quantities of food. At the end of 1985, Euro-

Figure 8-12 | Europe's Common Agricultural Program

Agricultural prices are fixed not only above world market levels but above the price that would clear the European market. An export subsidy is used to dispose of the resulting surplus.

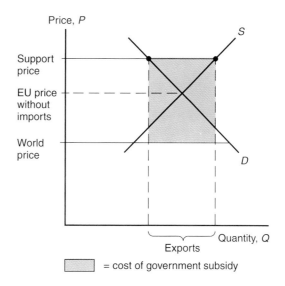

pean nations had stored 780,000 tons of beef, 1.2 million tons of butter, and 12 million tons of wheat. To avoid unlimited growth in these stockpiles, the European Union turned to a policy of subsidizing exports to dispose of surplus production.

Figure 8-12 shows how the CAP works. It is, of course, exactly like the export subsidy shown in Figure 8-11, except that Europe would actually be an importer under free trade. The support price is set not only above the world price that would prevail in its absence but also above the price that would equate demand and supply even without imports. To export the resulting surplus, an export subsidy is paid that offsets the difference between European and world prices. The subsidized exports themselves tend to depress the world price, increasing the required subsidy. Cost-benefit analysis would clearly show that the combined costs to European consumers and taxpayers exceed the benefits to producers.

Despite the considerable net costs of the CAP to European consumers and taxpayers, the political strength of farmers in the EU has been so strong that the program has faced little effective internal challenge. The main pressure against the CAP has come from the United States and other food-exporting nations, who complain that Europe's export subsidies drive down the price of their own exports. During the Uruguay round of trade negotiations (discussed in Chapter 9) the United States initially demanded a complete end to European subsidies by the year 2000. These demands were eventually scaled back considerably, but even so the opposition of European farmers to any cuts nearly caused the negotiations to collapse. In the end the EU agreed to cut subsidies by about a third over six years.

Import Quotas: Theory

An import quota is a direct restriction on the quantity of some good that may be imported. The restriction is usually enforced by issuing licenses to some group of individuals or firms. For example, the United States has a quota on imports of foreign cheese. The only firms allowed to import cheese are certain trading companies, each of which is allocated the right to import a maximum number of pounds of cheese each year; the size of each firm's quota is based on the amount of cheese it imported in the past. In some important cases, notably sugar and apparel, the right to sell in the United States is given directly to the governments of exporting countries.

It is important to avoid the misconception that import quotas somehow limit imports without raising domestic prices. *An import quota always raises the domestic price of the imported good.* When imports are limited, the immediate result is that at the initial price the demand for the good exceeds domestic supply plus imports. This causes the price to be bid up until the market clears. In the end, an import quota will raise domestic prices by the same amount as a tariff that limits imports to the same level (except in the case of domestic monopoly, when the quota raises prices more than this; see the second appendix to this chapter).

The difference between a quota and a tariff is that with a quota the government receives no revenue. When a quota instead of a tariff is used to restrict imports, the sum of money that would have appeared as government revenue with a tariff is collected by whomever receives the import licenses. License holders are able to buy imports and resell them at a higher price in the domestic market. The profits received by the holders of import licenses are known as **quota rents**. In assessing the costs and benefits of an import quota, it is crucial to determine who gets the rents. When the rights to sell in the domestic market are assigned to governments of exporting countries, as is often the case, the transfer of rents abroad makes the costs of a quota substantially higher than the equivalent tariff.

CASE STUDY

An Import Quota in Practice: U.S. Sugar

The U.S. sugar problem is similar in its origins to the European agricultural problem: A domestic price guarantee by the federal government has led to U.S. prices above world market levels. Unlike the European Union, however, the domestic supply in the United States does not exceed domestic demand. Thus the United States has been able to keep domestic prices at the target level with an import quota on sugar.

A special feature of the import quota is that the rights to sell sugar in the United States are allocated to foreign governments, who then allocate these rights to their own residents. As a result, rents generated by the sugar quota accrue to foreigners.

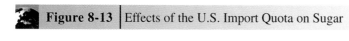

Figure 8-13 | Effects of the U.S. Import Quota on Sugar

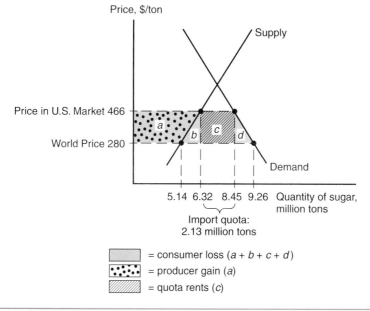

The sugar import quota holds imports to about half the level that would occur under free trade. The result is that the price of sugar is $466 per ton, versus the $280 price on world markets. This produces a gain for U.S. sugar producers, but a much larger loss for U.S. consumers. There is no offsetting gain in revenue because the quota rents are collected by foreign governments.

Figure 8-13 shows an estimate of the effects of the sugar quota in 1990.[3] The quota restricted imports to approximately 2.13 million tons; as a result, the price of sugar in the United States was a bit more than 40 percent above that in the outside world. The figure is drawn on the assumption that the United States is "small" in the world sugar market, that is, that removing the quota would not have a significant effect on the price. According to this estimate, free trade would roughly double sugar imports, to 4.12 million tons.

The welfare effects of the import quota are indicated by the areas *a, b, c,* and *d.* Consumers from the United States lose the surplus $a + b + c + d$, with a total value of $1.646 billion. Part of this consumer loss represents a transfer to U.S. sugar producers, who gain the producer surplus *a:* $1.066 billion. Part of the loss represents the production distortion *b* ($0.109 billion) and the consumption distortion *d* ($0.076 billion). The rents to the foreign governments that receive import rights are summarized by area *c*, equal to $0.395 billion.

---

[3]The estimates are based on data in Hufbauer and Elliott (1994), cited in Further Reading. This presentation simplifies slightly from their model, which assumes that consumers would be willing to pay somewhat more for U.S. sugar even under free trade.

The net loss to the United States is the distortions ($b + d$) plus the quota rents (c), a total of $580 million per year. Notice that most of this net loss comes from the fact that foreigners get the import rights!

The sugar quota illustrates in an extreme way the tendency of protection to provide benefits to a small group of producers, each of whom receives a large benefit, at the expense of a large number of consumers, each of whom bears only a small cost. In this case, the yearly consumer loss amounts to only about $6 per capita, or perhaps $25 for a typical family. Not surprisingly, the average American voter is unaware that the sugar quota exists, and so there is little effective opposition.

From the point of view of the sugar producers, however, the quota is a life-or-death issue. The U.S. sugar industry employs only about 12,000 workers, so the producer gains from the quota represent an implicit subsidy of about $90,000 per employee. It should be no surprise that sugar producers are very effectively mobilized in defense of their protection.

Opponents of protection often try to frame their criticism not in terms of consumer and producer surplus but in terms of the cost to consumers of every job "saved" by an import restriction. Economists who have studied the sugar industry believe that even with free trade, most of the U.S. industry would survive; only 2000 or 3000 workers would be displaced. Thus the consumer cost per job saved is more than $500,000.

Voluntary Export Restraints

A variant on the import quota is the **voluntary export restraint (VER)**, also known as a voluntary restraint agreement (VRA). (Welcome to the bureaucratic world of trade policy, where everything has a three-letter symbol.) A VER is a quota on trade imposed from the exporting country's side instead of the importer's. The most famous example is the limitation on auto exports to the United States enforced by Japan after 1981.

Voluntary export restraints are generally imposed at the request of the importer and are agreed to by the exporter to forestall other trade restrictions. As we will see in Chapter 9, certain political and legal advantages have made VERs preferred instruments of trade policy in recent years. From an economic point of view, however, a voluntary export restraint is exactly like an import quota where the licenses are assigned to foreign governments and is therefore very costly to the importing country.

A VER is always more costly to the importing country than a tariff that limits imports by the same amount. The difference is that what would have been revenue under a tariff becomes rents earned by foreigners under the VER, so that the VER clearly produces a loss for the importing country.

A study of the effects of the three major U.S. voluntary export restraints—in textiles and apparel, steel, and automobiles—found that about two-thirds of the cost to consumers of these restraints is accounted for by the rents earned by foreigners.[4] In other words, the bulk

---

[4]See David G. Tarr, *A General Equilibrium Analysis of the Welfare and Employment Effects of U.S. Quotas in Textiles, Autos, and Steel* (Washington, D.C.: Federal Trade Commission, 1989).

of the cost represents a transfer of income rather than a loss of efficiency. This calculation also emphasizes the point that from a national point of view, VERs are much more costly than tariffs. Given this, the widespread preference of governments for VERs over other trade policy measures requires some careful analysis.

Some voluntary export agreements cover more than one country. The most famous multilateral agreement is the Multi-Fiber Arrangement, an agreement that limits textile exports from 22 countries. Such multilateral voluntary restraint agreements are known by yet another three-letter abbreviation as OMAs, for orderly marketing agreements.

CASE STUDY

A Voluntary Export Restraint in Practice: Japanese Autos

For much of the 1960s and 1970s the U.S. auto industry was largely insulated from import competition by the difference in the kinds of cars bought by U.S. and foreign consumers. U.S. buyers, living in a large country with low gasoline taxes, preferred much larger cars than Europeans and Japanese, and, by and large, foreign firms have chosen not to challenge the United States in the large-car market.

In 1979, however, sharp oil price increases and temporary gasoline shortages caused the U.S. market to shift abruptly toward smaller cars. Japanese producers, whose costs had been falling relative to their U.S. competitors in any case, moved in to fill the new demand. As the Japanese market share soared and U.S. output fell, strong political forces in the United States demanded protection for the U.S. industry. Rather than act unilaterally and risk creating a trade war, the U.S. government asked the Japanese government to limit its exports. The Japanese, fearing unilateral U.S. protectionist measures if they did not do so, agreed to limit their sales. The first agreement, in 1981, limited Japanese exports to the United States to 1.68 million automobiles. A revision raised that total to 1.85 million in 1984 to 1985. In 1985, the agreement was allowed to lapse.

The effects of this voluntary export restraint were complicated by several factors. First, Japanese and U.S. cars were clearly not perfect substitutes. Second, the Japanese industry to some extent responded to the quota by upgrading its quality, selling larger autos with more features. Third, the auto industry is clearly not perfectly competitive. Nonetheless, the basic results were what the discussion of voluntary export restraints earlier would have predicted: The price of Japanese cars in the United States rose, with the rent captured by Japanese firms. The U.S. government estimates the total costs to the United States at $3.2 billion in 1984, primarily in transfers to Japan rather than efficiency losses.

Local Content Requirements

A **local content requirement** is a regulation that requires that some specified fraction of a final good be produced domestically. In some cases this fraction is specified in physical units, like the U.S. oil import quota in the 1960s. In other cases the requirement is stated in

AMERICAN BUSES, MADE IN HUNGARY

In 1995, sleek new buses began rolling on the streets of Miami and Baltimore. Probably very few riders were aware that these buses were made in, of all places, Hungary.

Why Hungary? Well, before the fall of communism in Eastern Europe Hungary had in fact manufactured buses for export to other Eastern bloc nations. These buses were, however, poorly designed and badly made; few people thought the industry could start exporting to Western countries any time soon.

What changed the situation was the realization by some clever Hungarian investors that there is a loophole in a little-known but important U.S. law, the Buy American Act, originally passed in 1933. This law in effect imposes local content requirements on a significant range of products.

The Buy American Act affects *procurement:* purchases by government agencies, including state and local governments. It requires that American firms be given preference in all such purchases. A bid by a foreign company can only be accepted if it is a specified percentage below the lowest bid by a domestic firm. In the case of buses and other transportation equipment, the foreign bid must be at least 25 percent below the domestic bid, effectively shutting out foreign producers in most cases. Nor can an American company simply act as a sales agent for foreigners: While "American" products can contain some foreign parts, 51 percent of the materials must be domestic.

What the Hungarians realized was that they could set up an operation that just barely met this criterion. They set up two operations: One in Hungary, producing the shells of buses (the bodies, without anything else), and an assembly operation in Georgia. American axles and tires were shipped to Hungary, where they were put onto the bus shells; these were then shipped back to the United States, where American-made engines and transmissions were installed. The whole product was slightly more than 51 percent American, and thus these were legally "American" buses which city transit authorities were allowed to buy. The advantage of the whole scheme was the opportunity to use inexpensive Hungarian labor: Although Hungarian workers take about 1500 hours to assemble a bus compared with less than 900 hours in the United States, their $4 per hour wage rate made all the transshipment worthwhile.

value terms, by requiring that some minimum share of the price of a good represent domestic value added. Local content laws have been widely used by developing countries trying to shift their manufacturing base from assembly back into intermediate goods. In the United States, a local content bill for automobiles was proposed in 1982 but was never acted on.

From the point of view of the domestic producers of parts, a local content regulation provides protection in the same way an import quota does. From the point of view of the firms that must buy locally, however, the effects are somewhat different. Local content does not place a strict limit on imports. It allows firms to import more, provided that they also buy more domestically. This means that the effective price of inputs to the firm is an average of the price of imported and domestically produced inputs.

Consider, for example, the earlier automobile example in which the cost of imported parts is $6000. Suppose that to purchase the same parts domestically would cost $10,000 but that assembly firms are required to use 50 percent domestic parts. Then they will face an average cost of parts of $8000 (0.5 × $6000 + 0.5 × $10,000), which will be reflected in the final price of the car.

The important point is that a local content requirement does not produce either government revenue or quota rents. Instead, the difference between the prices of imports and domestic goods in effect gets averaged in the final price and is passed on to consumers.

An interesting innovation in local content regulations has been to allow firms to satisfy their local content requirement by exporting instead of using parts domestically. This has become important in several cases: For example, U.S. auto firms operating in Mexico have chosen to export some components from Mexico to the United States, even though those components could be produced in the United States more cheaply, because this allows them to use less Mexican content in producing cars in Mexico for Mexico's market.

Other Trade Policy Instruments

There are many other ways in which governments influence trade. We list some of them briefly.

1. *Export credit subsidies.* This is like an export subsidy except that it takes the form of a subsidized loan to the buyer. The United States, like most countries, has a government institution, the Export-Import Bank, that is devoted to providing at least slightly subsidized loans to aid exports.

2. *National procurement.* Purchases by the government or strongly regulated firms can be directed toward domestically produced goods even when these goods are more expensive than imports. The classic example is the European telecommunications industry. The nations of the European Union in principle have free trade with each other. The main purchasers of telecommunications equipment, however, are phone companies—and in Europe these companies have until recently all been government-owned. These government-owned telephone companies buy from domestic suppliers even when the suppliers charge higher prices than suppliers in other countries. The result is that there is very little trade in telecommunications equipment within Europe.

3. *Red-tape barriers.* Sometimes a government wants to restrict imports without doing so formally. Fortunately or unfortunately, it is easy to twist normal health, safety, and customs procedures so as to place substantial obstacles in the way of trade. The classic example is the French decree in 1982 that all Japanese videocassette recorders must pass through the tiny customs house at Poitiers—effectively limiting the actual imports to a handful.

The Effects of Trade Policy: A Summary

The effects of the major instruments of trade policy can be usefully summarized by Table 8-1, which compares the effect of four major kinds of trade policy on the welfare of consumers, producers, the government, and the nation as a whole.

This table does not look like an advertisement for interventionist trade policy. All four trade policies benefit producers and hurt consumers. The effects of the policies on economic welfare are at best ambiguous; two of the policies definitely hurt the nation as a whole, while tariffs and import quotas are potentially beneficial only for large countries that can drive down world prices.

Why, then, do governments so often act to limit imports or promote exports? We turn to this question in Chapter 9.

Table 8-1 | Effects of Alternative Trade Policies

	Tariff	Export subsidy	Import quota	Voluntary export restraint
Producer surplus	Increases	Increases	Increases	Increases
Consumer surplus	Falls	Falls	Falls	Falls
Government revenue	Increases	Falls (government spending rises)	No change (rents to license holders)	No change (rents to foreigners)
Overall national welfare	Ambiguous (falls for small country)	Falls	Ambiguous (falls for small country)	Falls

Summary

1. In contrast to our earlier analysis, which stressed the general equilibrium interaction of markets, for analysis of trade policy it is usually sufficient to use a partial equilibrium approach.

2. A tariff drives a wedge between foreign and domestic prices, raising the domestic price but by less than the tariff rate. An important and relevant special case, however, is that of a "small" country that cannot have any substantial influence on foreign prices. In the small country case a tariff is fully reflected in domestic prices.

3. The costs and benefits of a tariff or other trade policy may be measured using the concepts of consumer surplus and producer surplus. Using these concepts, we can show that the domestic producers of a good gain, because a tariff raises the price they receive; the domestic consumers lose, for the same reason. There is also a gain in government revenue.

4. If we add together the gains and losses from a tariff, we find that the net effect on national welfare can be separated into two parts. There is an efficiency loss, which results from the distortion in the incentives facing domestic producers and consumers. On the other hand, there is a terms of trade gain, reflecting the tendency of a tariff to drive down foreign export prices. In the case of a small country that cannot affect foreign prices, the second effect is zero, so that there is an unambiguous loss.

5. The analysis of a tariff can be readily adapted to other trade policy measures, such as export subsidies, import quotas, and voluntary export restraints. An export subsidy causes efficiency losses similar to a tariff but compounds these losses by causing a deterioration of the terms of trade. Import quotas and voluntary export restraints differ from tariffs in that the government gets no revenue. Instead, what would have been government revenue accrues as rents to the recipients of import licenses in the case of a quota and to foreigners in the case of a voluntary export restraint.

Key Terms

Problems

1. Home's demand curve for wheat is

$$D = 100 - 20P.$$

   Its supply curve is

$$S = 20 + 20P.$$

   Derive and graph Home's *import* demand schedule. What would the price of wheat be in the absence of trade?

2. Now add Foreign, which has a demand curve

$$D^* = 80 - 20P,$$

   and a supply curve

$$S^* = 40 + 20P.$$

   a. Derive and graph Foreign's *export* supply curve and find the price of wheat that would prevail in Foreign in the absence of trade.
   b. Now allow Foreign and Home to trade with each other, at zero transportation cost. Find and graph the equilibrium under free trade. What is the world price? What is the volume of trade?

3. Home imposes a specific tariff of 0.5 on wheat imports.
   a. Determine and graph the effects of the tariff on the following: (1) the price of wheat in each country; (2) the quantity of wheat supplied and demanded in each country; (3) the volume of trade.
   b. Determine the effect of the tariff on the welfare of each of the following groups: (1) Home import-competing producers; (2) Home consumers; (3) the Home government.
   c. Show graphically and calculate the terms of trade gain, the efficiency loss, and the total effect on welfare of the tariff.

4. Suppose that Foreign had been a much larger country, with domestic demand

$$D^* = 800 - 200P, S^* = 400 + 200P.$$

(Notice that this implies that the Foreign price of wheat in the absence of trade would have been the same as in problem 2.)

Recalculate the free trade equilibrium and the effects of a 0.5 specific tariff by Home. Relate the difference in results to the discussion of the "small country" case in the text.

5. The aircraft industry in Europe receives aid from several governments, according to some estimates equal to 20 percent of the purchase price of each aircraft. For example, an airplane that sells for $50 million may have cost $60 million to produce, with the difference made up by European governments. At the same time, approximately half the purchase price of a "European" aircraft represents the cost of components purchased from other countries (including the United States). If these estimates are correct, what is the *effective* rate of protection received by European aircraft producers?

6. Return to the example of problem 2. Starting from free trade, assume that Foreign offers exporters a subsidy of 0.5 per unit. Calculate the effects on the price in each country and on welfare, both of individual groups and of the economy as a whole, in both countries.

7. The nation of Acirema is "small," unable to affect world prices. It imports peanuts at the price of $10 per bag. The demand curve is

$$D = 400 - 10P.$$

The supply curve is

$$S = 50 + 5P.$$

Determine the free trade equilibrium. Then calculate and graph the following effects of an import quota that limits imports to 50 bags.
a. The increase in the domestic price
b. The quota rents
c. The consumption distortion loss
d. The production distortion loss

Further Reading

Jagdish Bhagwati. "On the Equivalence of Tariffs and Quotas," in Robert E. Baldwin et al., eds. *Trade, Growth, and the Balance of Payments*. Chicago: Rand McNally, 1965. The classic comparison of tariffs and quotas under monopoly.

W. M. Corden. *The Theory of Protection*. Oxford: Clarendon Press, 1971. A general survey of the effects of tariffs, quotas, and other trade policies.

Robert W. Crandall. *Regulating the Automobile*. Washington, D.C.: Brookings Institution, 1986. Contains an analysis of the most famous of all voluntary export restraints.

Gary Clyde Hufbauer and Kimberly Ann Elliot. *Measuring the Costs of Protection in the United States.* Washington D.C.: Institute for International Economics, 1994. An up-to-date assessment of U.S. trade policies in 21 different sectors.

Kala Krishna. "Trade Restrictions as Facilitating Practices." *Journal of International Economics* 26 (May 1989). pp. 251–270. A pioneering analysis of the effects of import quotas when both foreign and domestic producers have monopoly power, showing that the usual result is an increase in the profits of both groups—at consumers' expense.

D. Rousslang and A. Suomela. "Calculating the Consumer and Net Welfare Costs of Import Relief." U.S. International Trade Commission Staff Research Study 15. Washington, D.C.: International Trade Commission, 1985. An exposition of the framework used in this chapter, with a description of how the framework is applied in practice to real industries.

APPENDIX I TO CHAPTER 8

Tariff Analysis in General Equilibrium

The text of this chapter takes a partial equilibrium approach to the analysis of trade policy. That is, it focuses on the effects of tariffs, quotas, and other policies in a single market without explicitly considering the consequences for other markets. This partial equilibrium approach usually is adequate, and it is much simpler than a full general equilibrium treatment that takes cross-market effects into account. Nonetheless, it is sometimes important to do the general equilibrium analysis. In Chapter 5 we presented a brief discussion of the effects of tariffs in general equilibrium. This appendix presents a more detailed analysis.

The analysis proceeds in two stages. First, we analyze the effects of a tariff in a small country, one that cannot affect its terms of trade; then we analyze the case of a large country.

A Tariff in a Small Country

Imagine a country that produces and consumes two goods, manufactures and food. The country is small, unable to affect its terms of trade; we will assume that it exports manufactures and imports food. Thus the country sells its manufactures to the world market at a given world price P_M^* and buys food at a given world price P_F^*.

Figure 8AI-1 illustrates the position of this country in the absence of a tariff. The economy produces at the point on its production possibility frontier that is tangent to a line with slope $-P_M^*/P_F^*$, indicated by Q^1. This line also defines the economy's budget constraint, that is, all the consumption points it can afford. The economy chooses the point on the budget constraint that is tangent to the highest possible indifference curve; this point is shown as D^1.

Now suppose the government imposes an ad valorem tariff at a rate t. Then the price of food facing both consumers and domestic producers rises to $P_F^*(1 + t)$, and the relative price line therefore gets flatter, with a slope $-P_M^*/P_F^*(1 + t)$.

The effect of this fall in the relative price of manufactures on production is straightforward: Output of manufactures falls, while output of food rises. In Figure 8AI-2, this shift in production is shown by the movement of the production point from Q^1, shown in Figure 8AI-1, to Q^2.

The effect on consumption is more complicated; the tariff generates revenue, which must be spent somehow. In general, the precise effect of a tariff depends on exactly how the government spends the tariff revenue. Consider the case in which the government returns any tariff revenue to consumers. In this case the budget constraint of consumers is *not* the line with slope $-P_M^*/P_F^*(1 + t)$ that passes through the production point Q^2; consumers can spend more than this, because in addition to the income they generate by producing goods they receive the tariff revenue collected by the government.

How do we find the true budget constraint? Notice that trade must still be balanced at world prices. That is,

$$P_M^* \times (Q_M - D_M) = P_F^* \times (D_F - Q_F)$$

Figure 8AI-1 | Free Trade Equilibrium for a Small Country

The country produces at the point on its production frontier that is tangent to a line whose slope equals relative prices, and consumes at the point on the budget line tangent to the highest possible indifference curve.

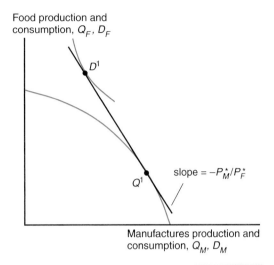

where Q refers to output and D to consumption of manufactures and food, respectively. The left-hand side of this expression therefore represents the value of exports at world prices, while the right-hand side represents the value of imports. This expression may be rearranged to show that the value of consumption equals the value of production at world prices:

$$P^*_M \times Q_M + P^*_F \times Q_F = P^*_M \times D_M + P^*_F \times D_F.$$

This defines a budget constraint that passes through the production point Q^2, with a slope of $-P^*_M/P^*_F$. The consumption point must lie on this new budget constraint.

Consumers will not, however, choose the point on the new budget constraint at which this constraint is tangent to an indifference curve. Instead, the tariff causes them to consume less food and more manufactures. In Figure 8AI-2 the consumption point after the tariff is shown as D^2: It lies on the new budget constraint, but on an indifference curve that is tangent to a line with slope $-P^*_M/P^*_F(1 + t)$. This line lies above the line with the same slope that passes through the production point Q^2; the difference is the tariff revenue redistributed to consumers.

By examining Figure 8AI-2 and comparing it with Figure 8AI-1, we can see three important points:

1. Welfare is less with a tariff than under free trade. That is, D^2 lies on a lower indifference curve than D^1.
2. The reduction in welfare comes from two effects. (a) The economy no longer produces at a point that maximizes the value of income at world prices. The budget constraint that passes through Q^2 lies inside the constraint passing through Q^1. (b) Consumers do not choose the welfare-maximizing point on the budget constraint; they do

Figure 8AI-2 │ A Tariff in a Small Country

The country produces less of its export good and more of its imported good. Consumption is also distorted. The result is a reduction in both welfare and the volume of the country's trade.

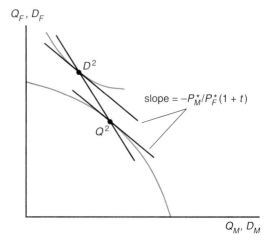

not move up to an indifference curve that is tangent to the economy's true budget constraint. Both (a) and (b) result from the fact that domestic consumers and producers face prices that are different from world prices. The loss in welfare due to inefficient production (a) is the general equilibrium counterpart of the production distortion loss we described in the partial equilibrium approach in this chapter, and the loss in welfare due to inefficient consumption (b) is the counterpart of the consumption distortion loss.

3. Trade is reduced by the tariff. Exports and imports are both less after the tariff is imposed than before.

These are the effects of a tariff imposed by a small country. We next turn to the effects of a tariff imposed by a large country.

A Tariff in a Large Country

To address the large country case, we use the offer curve technique developed in the appendix to Chapter 5. We consider two countries: Home, which exports manufactures and imports food, and its trading partner Foreign. In Figure 8AI-3, Foreign's offer curve is represented by OF. Home's offer curve in the absence of a tariff is represented by OM^1. The free trade equilibrium is determined by the intersection of OF and OM^1, at point 1, with a relative price of manufactures on the world market $(P_M^*/P_F^*)^1$.

Now suppose that Home imposes a tariff. We first ask, how would its trade change if there were no change in its terms of trade? We already know the answer from the small country analysis: For a given world price, a tariff reduces both exports and imports. Thus if the world relative price of manufactures remained at $(P_M^*/P_F^*)^1$, Home's offer would shift in from point 1 to point 2. More generally, if Home imposes a tariff its overall offer curve will shrink in to a curve like OM^2, passing through point 2.

Figure 8AI-3 | Effect of a Tariff on the Terms of Trade

The tariff causes the country to trade less at any *given* terms of trade; thus its offer curve shifts in. This implies, however, that the terms of trade must improve. The gain from improved terms of trade may offset the losses from the distortion of production and consumption, which reduces welfare at any given terms of trade.

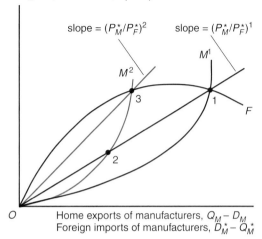

Home imports of food, $D_F - Q_F$
Foreign exports of food, $Q_F^* - D_F^*$

slope = $(P_M^*/P_F^*)^2$ slope = $(P_M^*/P_F^*)^1$

M^2 M^1

3   1

2   F

O Home exports of manufacturers, $Q_M - D_M$
Foreign imports of manufacturers, $D_M^* - Q_M^*$

But this shift in Home's offer curve will change the equilibrium terms of trade. In Figure 8AI-3, the new equilibrium is at point 3, with a relative price of manufactures $(P_M^*/P_F^*)^2 > (P_M^*/P_F^*)^1$. That is, the tariff improves Home's terms of trade.

The effects of the tariff on Home's welfare are ambiguous. On one side, if the terms of trade did not improve, we have just seen from the small country analysis that the tariff would reduce welfare. On the other side, the improvement in Home's terms of trade tends to increase welfare. So the welfare effect can go either way, just as in the partial equilibrium analysis.

APPENDIX II TO CHAPTER 8

Tariffs and Import Quotas in the Presence of Monopoly

The trade policy analysis in this chapter assumed that markets are perfectly competitive, so that all firms take prices as given. As we argued in Chapter 6, however, many markets for internationally traded goods are imperfectly competitive. The effects of international trade policies can be affected by the nature of the competition in a market.

When we analyze the effects of trade policy in imperfectly competitive markets, a new consideration appears: International trade limits monopoly power, and policies that limit trade may therefore increase monopoly power. Even if a firm is the only producer of a good in a country, it will have little ability to raise prices if there are many foreign suppliers and free trade. If imports are limited by a quota, however, the same firm will be free to raise prices without fear of competition.

The link between trade policy and monopoly power may be understood by examining a model in which a country imports a good and its import-competing production is controlled by only *one* firm. The country is small on world markets, so that the price of the import is unaffected by its trade policy. For this model, we examine and compare the effects of free trade, a tariff, and an import quota.

The Model with Free Trade

Figure 8AII-1 shows free trade in a market where a domestic monopolist faces competition from imports. D is the domestic demand curve: demand for the product by domestic residents. P_W is the world price of the good; imports are available in unlimited quantities at that price. The domestic industry is assumed to consist of only a single firm, whose marginal cost curve is MC.

If there were no trade in this market, the domestic firm would behave as an ordinary profit-maximizing monopolist. Corresponding to D is a marginal revenue curve MR, and the firm would choose the monopoly profit-maximizing level of output Q_M and price P_M.

With free trade, however, this monopoly behavior is not possible. If the firm tried to charge P_M, or indeed any price above P_W, nobody would buy its product, because cheaper imports would be available. Thus international trade puts a lid on the monopolist's price at P_W.

Given this limit on its price, the best the monopolist can do is produce up to the point where marginal cost is equal to the world price, at Q_f. At the price P_W, domestic consumers will demand D_f units of the good, so imports will be $D_f - Q_f$. This outcome, however, is exactly what would have happened if the domestic industry had been perfectly competitive. With free trade, then, the fact that the domestic industry is a monopoly does not make any difference to the outcome.

Figure 8AII-1 | A Monopolist Under Free Trade

The threat of import competition forces the monopolist to behave like a perfectly competitive industry.

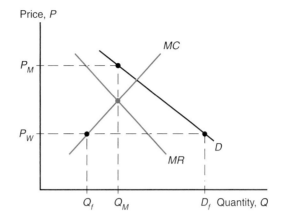

 Figure 8AII-2 | A Monopolist Protected by a Tariff

The tariff allows the monopolist to raise its price, but the price is still limited by the threat of imports.

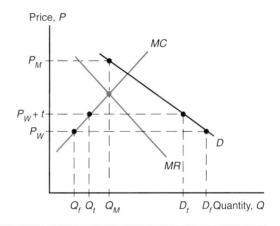

The Model with a Tariff

The effect of a tariff is to raise the maximum price the domestic industry can charge. If a specific tariff t is charged on imports, the domestic industry can now charge $P_W + t$ (Figure 8AII-2). The industry still is not free to raise its price all the way to the monopoly price, however, because consumers will still turn to imports if the price rises above the world price plus the tariff. Thus the best the monopolist can do is to set price equal to marginal cost, at Q_t. The tariff raises the domestic price as well as the output of the domestic industry,

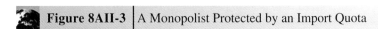

Figure 8AII-3 | A Monopolist Protected by an Import Quota

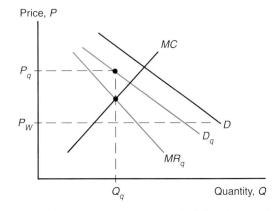

The monopolist is now free to raise prices, knowing that the domestic price of imports will rise too.

while demand falls to D_t and thus imports fall. However, the domestic industry still produces the same quantity as if it were perfectly competitive.[1]

The Model with an Import Quota

Suppose the government imposes a limit on imports, restricting their quantity to a fixed level $\bar{Q}$. Then the monopolist knows that when it charges a price above P_W, it will not lose all its sales. Instead, it will sell whatever domestic demand is at that price, minus the allowed imports $\bar{Q}$. Thus the demand facing the monopolist will be domestic demand less allowed imports. We define the postquota demand curve as D_q; it is parallel to the domestic demand curve D but shifted $\bar{Q}$ units to the left (Figure 8AII-3).

Corresponding to D_q is a new marginal revenue curve MR_q. The firm protected by an import quota maximizes profit by setting marginal cost equal to this new marginal revenue, producing Q_q and charging the price P_q. (The license to import one unit of the good will therefore yield a rent of $P_q - P_W$.)

Comparing a Tariff and a Quota

We now ask how the effects of a tariff and a quota compare. To do this, we compare a tariff and a quota that lead to *the same level of imports* (Figure 8AII-4). The tariff level t leads to a level of imports $\bar{Q}$; we therefore ask what would happen if instead of a tariff the government simply limited imports to $\bar{Q}$.

We see from the figure that the results are not the same. The tariff leads to domestic production of Q_t and a domestic price of $P_W + t$. The quota leads to a lower level of domestic

---

[1] There is one case in which a tariff will have different effects on a monopolistic industry than on a perfectly competitive one. This is the case where a tariff is so high that imports are completely eliminated (a prohibitive tariff). For a competitive industry, once imports have been eliminated, any further increase in the tariff has no effect. A monopolist, however, will be forced to limit its price by the *threat* of imports even if actual imports are zero. Thus an increase in a prohibitive tariff will allow a monopolist to raise its price closer to the profit-maximizing price P_M.

Figure 8AII-4 | Comparing a Tariff and a Quota

A quota leads to lower domestic output and a higher price than a tariff that yields the same level of imports.

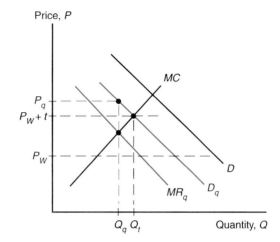

production, Q_q, and a higher price, P_q. When protected by a tariff the monopolistic domestic industry behaves as if it were perfectly competitive; when protected by a quota it clearly does not.

The reason for this difference is that an import quota creates more monopoly power than a tariff. When monopolistic industries are protected by tariffs, domestic firms know that if they raise their prices too high they will still be undercut by imports. An import quota, on the other hand, provides absolute protection: No matter how high the domestic price, imports cannot exceed the quota level.

This comparison seems to say that if governments are concerned about domestic monopoly power, they should prefer tariffs to quotas as instruments of trade policy. In fact, however, protection has increasingly drifted away from tariffs toward nontariff barriers, including import quotas. To explain this, we need to look at considerations other than economic efficiency that motivate governments.

CHAPTER 9

The Political Economy
of Trade Policy

I n 1981 the United States asked Japan to limit its exports of autos to the United
States. This raised the prices of imported cars and forced U.S. consumers to buy domestic autos they clearly did not like as much. While Japan was willing to accommodate the
U.S. government on this point, it was unwilling to do so on another—a request that Japan
eliminate import quotas on beef and citrus products—quotas that forced Japanese consumers to buy incredibly expensive domestic products instead of cheap imports from the
United States. The governments of both countries were thus determined to pursue policies that, according to the cost-benefit analysis developed in Chapter 8, produced more
costs than benefits. Clearly, government policies reflect objectives that go beyond simple
measures of cost and benefit.

In this chapter we examine some of the reasons governments either should not or, at
any rate, do not base their policy on economists' cost-benefit calculations. The examination
of the forces motivating trade policy in practice continues in Chapters 10 and 11, which
discuss the characteristic trade policy issues facing developing and advanced countries,
respectively.

The first step toward understanding actual trade policies is to ask what reasons there
are for governments *not* to interfere with trade—that is, what is the case for free trade?
With this question answered, arguments for intervention can be examined as challenges to
the assumptions underlying the case for free trade.

The Case for Free Trade

Few countries have anything approaching completely free trade. The city of Hong Kong,
which is legally part of China but maintains a separate economic policy, may be the only
modern economy with no tariffs or import quotas. Nonetheless, since the time of Adam
Smith economists have advocated free trade as an ideal toward which trade policy should
strive. The reasons for this advocacy are not quite as simple as the idea itself. At one level,
theoretical models suggest that free trade will avoid the efficiency losses associated with
protection. Many economists believe that free trade produces additional gains beyond the
elimination of production and consumption distortions. Finally, even among economists

who believe free trade is a less than perfect policy, many believe free trade is usually better than any other policy a government is likely to follow.

Free Trade and Efficiency

The **efficiency case for free trade** is simply the reverse of the cost-benefit analysis of a tariff. Figure 9-1 shows the basic point once again for the case of a small country that cannot influence foreign export prices. A tariff causes a net loss to the economy measured by the area of the two triangles; it does so by distorting the economic incentives of both producers and consumers. Conversely, a move to free trade eliminates these distortions and increases national welfare.

A number of efforts have been made to add the total costs of distortions due to tariffs and import quotas in particular economies. Table 9-1 presents some representative estimates. It is noteworthy that the costs of protection to the United States are measured as quite small relative to national income. This situation reflects two facts: (1) the United States is relatively less dependent on trade than other countries, and (2) with some major exceptions, U.S. trade is fairly free. By contrast, some smaller countries that impose very restrictive tariffs and quotas are estimated to lose as much as 10 percent of their potential national income to distortions caused by their trade policies.

Additional Gains From Free Trade[1]

There is a widespread belief among economists that calculations of the kind reported in Table 9-1, even though they report substantial gains from free trade in some cases, do not represent the whole story. In small countries in general and developing countries in particular, many economists would argue that there are important gains from free trade not accounted for in conventional cost-benefit analysis.

One kind of additional gain involves economies of scale. Protected markets not only fragment production internationally, but by reducing competition and raising profits, they also lead too many firms to enter the protected industry. With a proliferation of firms in narrow domestic markets, the scale of production of each firm becomes inefficient. A good example of how protection leads to inefficient scale is the case of the Argentine automobile industry, which emerged because of import restrictions. An efficient scale assembly plant should make from 80,000 to 200,000 automobiles per year, yet in 1964 the Argentine industry, which produced only 166,000 cars, had no less than 13 firms! Some economists argue that the need to deter excessive entry and the resulting inefficient scale of production is a reason for free trade that goes beyond the standard cost-benefit calculations.

Another argument for free trade is that by providing entrepreneurs with an incentive to seek new ways to export or compete with imports, free trade offers more opportunities for learning and innovation than are provided by a system of "managed" trade, where the government largely dictates the pattern of imports and exports. Chapter 10 discusses the

---

[1]The additional gains from free trade that are discussed here are sometimes referred to as "dynamic" gains, because increased competition and innovation may need more time to take effect than the elimination of production and consumption distortions.

Figure 9-1 | The Efficiency Case for Free Trade

A trade restriction, such as a tariff, leads to production and consumption distortions.

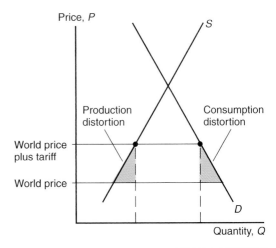

experiences of less-developed countries that discovered unexpected export opportunities when they shifted from systems of import quotas and tariffs to more open trade policies.

These additional arguments for free trade are for the most part not quantified. In 1985, however, Canadian economists Richard Harris and David Cox attempted to quantify the gains for Canada of free trade with the United States, taking into account the gains from a more efficient scale of production within Canada. They estimated that Canada's real income would rise by 8.6 percent—an increase about three times as large as the one typically estimated by economists who do not take into account the gains from economies of scale.[2]

Table 9-1 | Estimated Cost of Protection, as a Percentage of National Income

Brazil (1966)	9.5
Turkey (1978)	5.4
Philippines (1978)	5.4
United States (1983)	0.26

Sources: Brazil: Bela Balassa, *The Structure of Protection in Developing Countries* (Baltimore: The Johns Hopkins Press, 1971); Turkey and Philippines, World Bank, *The World Development Report 1987* (Washington: World Bank, 1987); United States: David G. Tarr and Morris E. Morkre, *Aggregate Costs to the United States of Tariffs and Quotas on Imports* (Washington D.C.: Federal Trade Commission, 1984).

---

[2]See Harris and Cox, *Trade, Industrial Policy, and Canadian Manufacturing* (Toronto: Ontario Economic Council, 1984); and, by the same authors, "Trade Liberalization and Industrial Organization: Some Estimates for Canada," *Journal of Political Economy* 93 (February 1985), pp. 115–145.

If the additional gains from free trade are as large as some economists believe, the costs of distorting trade with tariffs, quotas, export subsidies, and so on are correspondingly larger than the conventional cost-benefit analysis measures.

Political Argument for Free Trade

A **political argument for free trade** reflects the fact that a political commitment to free trade may be a good idea in practice even though there may be better policies in principle. Economists often argue that trade policies in practice are dominated by special-interest politics rather than consideration of national costs and benefits. Economists can sometimes show that in theory a selective set of tariffs and export subsidies could increase national welfare, but in reality any government agency attempting to pursue a sophisticated program of intervention in trade would probably be captured by interest groups and converted into a device for redistributing income to politically influential sectors. If this argument is correct, it may be better to advocate free trade without exceptions, even though on purely economic grounds free trade may not always be the best conceivable policy.

The three arguments outlined in the previous section probably represent the standard view of most international economists, at least in the United States:

1. The conventionally measured costs of deviating from free trade are large.
2. There are other benefits from free trade that add to the costs of protectionist policies.
3. Any attempt to pursue sophisticated deviations from free trade will be subverted by the political process.

Nonetheless, there are intellectually respectable arguments for deviating from free trade, and these arguments deserve a fair hearing.

CASE STUDY

The Gains from 1992

In 1987 the nations of the European Community (now known as the European Union) agreed on what formally was called the Single European Act, with the intention to create a truly unified European market. Because the act was supposed to go into effect within five years, the measures it embodied came to be known generally as "1992."

The unusual thing about 1992 was that the European Community was already a customs union, that is, there were no tariffs or import quotas on intra-European trade. So what was left to liberalize? The advocates of 1992 argued that there were still substantial barriers to international trade within Europe. Some of these barriers involved the costs of crossing borders; for example, the mere fact that trucks carrying goods between France and Germany had to stop for legal formalities often meant long waits that were costly in time and fuel. Similar costs were imposed on business travelers, who might fly from London to Paris in an hour, then spend another hour waiting to clear immigration and customs. Differences in regulations also had the effect of limiting the integration of markets. For example, because health regulations on food differed among the European nations, one could not simply fill a truck with British goods and take them to France, or vice versa.

Eliminating these subtle obstacles to trade was a very difficult political process. Suppose France is going to allow goods from Germany to enter the country without any checks. What is to prevent the French people from being supplied with manufactured goods that do not meet French safety standards, foods that do not meet French health standards, or medicines that have not been approved by French doctors? The only way that countries can have truly open borders is if they are able to agree on common standards, so that a good that meets French requirements is acceptable in Germany and vice versa. The main task of the 1992 negotiations was therefore one of harmonization of regulations in hundreds of areas, negotiations that were often acrimonious because of differences in national cultures.

The most emotional examples involved food. All advanced countries regulate things such as artificial coloring, to ensure that consumers are not unknowingly fed chemicals that are carcinogens or otherwise harmful. The initially proposed regulations on artificial coloring would, however, have destroyed the appearance of several traditional British foods: pink bangers (breakfast sausages) would have become white, golden kippers gray, and mushy peas a drab rather than a brilliant green. Continental consumers did not mind; indeed they could not understand how the British could eat such things in the first place. But in Britain the issue became tied up with fear over the loss of national identity, and loosening the proposed regulations became a top priority for the government. Britain succeeded in getting the necessary exemptions. On the other hand, Germany was forced to accept imports of beer that did not meet its centuries-old purity laws, and Italy to accept pasta made from—horrors!—the wrong kind of wheat.

But why engage in all this difficult negotiating? What were the potential gains from 1992? Attempts to estimate the direct gains have always suggested that they are fairly modest. Costs associated with crossing borders amount to no more than a few percent of the value of the goods shipped; removing these costs could add at best a fraction of a percent to the real income of Europe as a whole. Yet economists at the European Commission (the administrative arm of the European Community) argued that the true gains would be much larger.

Their reasoning relied to a large extent on the view that the unification of the European market would lead to greater competition among firms and to a more efficient scale of production. Much was made of the comparison with the United States, a country whose purchasing power and population are similar to those of the European Union, but which is a borderless, fully integrated market. Commission economists pointed out that in a number of industries Europe seemed to have markets that were segmented: Instead of treating the whole continent as a single market, firms seemed to have carved it into local zones served by relatively small-scale national producers. They argued that with all barriers to trade removed, there would be a consolidation of these producers, with substantial gains in productivity. These putative gains raised the overall estimated benefits from 1992 to several percent of the initial income of European nations. The Commission economists argued further that there would be indirect benefits, because the improved efficiency of the European economy would improve the trade-off between inflation and unemployment. At the end of a series of calculations, the Commission estimated a gain from 1992 of 7 percent of European income.[3]

---

[3]See *The Economics of 1992* (Brussels: Commission of the European Communities, 1988).

While nobody involved in this discussion regarded 7 percent as a particularly reliable number, many economists shared the conviction of the Commission that the gains would be large. There were, however, skeptics, who suggested that the segmentation of markets had more to do with culture than trade policy. For example, Italian consumers wanted washing machines that were quite different from those preferred in Germany. Italians tend to buy relatively few clothes, but those they buy are stylish and expensive, so they prefer slow, gentle washing machines that conserve their clothing investment.

A decade after 1992, it was clear that both the supporters and the skeptics had a valid point. In some cases there have been notable consolidations of industry. For example, Hoover closed its vacuum cleaner plant in France and concentrated all its production in an efficient plant in Britain. In some cases old market segmentations have clearly broken down, and sometimes in surprising ways, like the emergence of British sliced bread as a popular item in France. But in other cases markets have shown little sign of merging. The Germans have shown little taste for imported beer, and the Italians none for pasta made with soft wheat.

National Welfare Arguments Against Free Trade

Most tariffs, import quotas, and other trade policy measures are undertaken primarily to protect the income of particular interest groups. Politicians often claim, however, that the policies are being undertaken in the interest of the nation as a whole, and sometimes they are even telling the truth. Although economists often argue that deviations from free trade reduce national welfare, there are, in fact, some theoretical grounds for believing that activist trade policies can sometimes increase the welfare of the nation as a whole.

The Terms of Trade Argument for a Tariff

One argument for deviating from free trade comes directly out of cost-benefit analysis: For a large country that is able to affect the prices of foreign exporters, a tariff lowers the price of imports and thus generates a terms of trade benefit. This benefit must be set against the costs of the tariff, which arise because the tariff distorts production and consumption incentives. It is possible, however, that in some cases the terms of trade benefits of a tariff outweigh its costs, so there is a **terms of trade argument for a tariff**.

The appendix to this chapter shows that for a sufficiently small tariff the terms of trade benefits must outweigh the costs. Thus at small tariff rates a large country's welfare is higher than with free trade (Figure 9-2). As the tariff rate is increased, however, the costs eventually begin to grow more rapidly than the benefits and the curve relating national welfare to the tariff rate turns down. A tariff rate that completely prohibits trade (t_p in Figure 9-2) leaves the country worse off than with free trade; further increases in the tariff rate beyond t_p have no effect, so the curve flattens out.

At point 1 on the curve in Figure 9-2, corresponding to the tariff rate t_o, national welfare is maximized. The tariff rate t_o that maximizes national welfare is the **optimum tariff**. (By convention the phrase *optimum tariff* is usually used to refer to the tariff justified by a terms

Figure 9-2 | The Optimum Tariff

For a large country, there is an optimum tariff t_o at which the marginal gain from improved terms of trade just equals the marginal efficiency loss from production and consumption distortion.

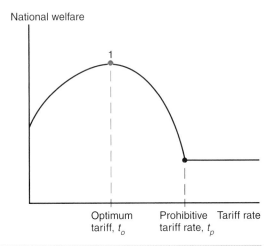

of trade argument rather than to the best tariff given all possible considerations.) The optimum tariff rate is always positive but less than the prohibitive rate (t_p) that would eliminate all imports.

What policy would the terms of trade argument dictate for *export* sectors? Since an export subsidy *worsens* the terms of trade, and therefore unambiguously reduces national welfare, the optimal policy in export sectors must be a negative subsidy, that is, a *tax* on exports that raises the price of exports to foreigners. Like the optimum tariff, the optimum export tax is always positive but less than the prohibitive tax that would eliminate exports completely.

The policy of Saudi Arabia and other oil exporters has been to tax their exports of oil, raising the price to the rest of the world. Although oil prices fell in the mid-1980s, it is hard to argue that Saudi Arabia would have been better off under free trade.

The terms of trade argument against free trade has some important limitations, however. Most small countries have very little ability to affect the world prices of either their imports or other exports, so that the terms of trade argument is of little practical importance. For big countries like the United States, the problem is that the terms of trade argument amounts to an argument for using national monopoly power to extract gains at other countries' expense. The United States could surely do this to some extent, but such a predatory policy would probably bring retaliation from other large countries. A cycle of retaliatory trade moves would, in turn, undermine the attempts at international trade policy coordination described later in this chapter.

The terms of trade argument against free trade, then, is intellectually impeccable but of doubtful usefulness. In practice, it is emphasized more by economists as a theoretical proposition than it is used by governments as a justification for trade policy.

The Domestic Market Failure Argument Against Free Trade

Leaving aside the issue of the terms of trade, the basic theoretical case for free trade rested on cost-benefit analysis using the concepts of consumer and producer surplus. Many economists have made a case against free trade based on the counterargument that these concepts, producer surplus in particular, do not properly measure costs and benefits.

Why might producer surplus not properly measure the benefits of producing a good? We consider a variety of reasons in the next two chapters: These include the possibility that the labor used in a sector would otherwise be unemployed or underemployed, the existence of defects in the capital or labor markets that prevent resources from being transferred as rapidly as they should be to sectors that yield high returns, and the possibility of technological spillovers from industries that are new or particularly innovative. These can all be classified under the general heading of **domestic market failures**. That is, each of these examples is one in which some market in the country is not doing its job right—the labor market is not clearing, the capital market is not allocating resources efficiently, and so on.

Suppose, for example, that the production of some good yields experience that will improve the technology of the economy as a whole but that the firms in the sector cannot appropriate this benefit and therefore do not take it into account in deciding how much to produce. Then there is a **marginal social benefit** to additional production that is not captured by the producer surplus measure. This marginal social benefit can serve as a justification for tariffs or other trade policies.

Figure 9-3 illustrates the domestic market failure argument against free trade. Figure 9-3a shows the conventional cost-benefit analysis of a tariff for a small country (which rules out terms of trade effects). Figure 9-3b shows the marginal benefit from production that is not taken account of by the producer surplus measure. The figure shows the effects of a tariff that raises the domestic price from P_W to $P_W + t$. Production rises from S^1 to S^2, with a resulting production distortion indicated by the area labeled a. Consumption falls from D^1 to D^2, with a resulting consumption distortion indicated by the area b. If we considered only consumer and producer surplus, we would find that the costs of the tariff exceed its benefits. Figure 9-3b shows, however, that this calculation overlooks an additional benefit that may make the tariff preferable to free trade. The increase in production yields a social benefit that may be measured by the area under the marginal social benefit curve from S^1 to S^2, indicated by c. In fact, by an argument similar to that in the terms of trade case, we can show that if the tariff is small enough the area c must always exceed the area $a + b$ and that there is some welfare-maximizing tariff that yields a level of social welfare higher than that of free trade.

The domestic market failure argument against free trade is a particular case of a more general concept known in economics as the **theory of the second best**. This theory states that a hands-off policy is desirable in any one market only if all other markets are working properly. If they are not, a government intervention that appears to distort incentives in one market may actually increase welfare by offsetting the consequences of market failures elsewhere. For example, if the labor market is malfunctioning and fails to deliver full employment, a policy of subsidizing labor-intensive industries, which would be undesirable in a full-employment economy, might turn out to be a good idea. It would be better to fix the labor market, for example, by making wages more flexible, but if for some reason this cannot be done, intervening in other markets may be a "second-best" way of alleviating the problem.

When economists apply the theory of the second best to trade policy, they argue that imperfections in the *internal* functioning of an economy may justify interfering in its external economic relations. This argument accepts that international trade is not the source of the problem but suggests nonetheless that trade policy can provide at least a partial solution.

Figure 9-3 | The Domestic Market Failure Argument for a Tariff

If production of a good yields extra social benefits (measured in panel (b) by area c) not captured as producer surplus (area b in panel (a)), a tariff can increase welfare.

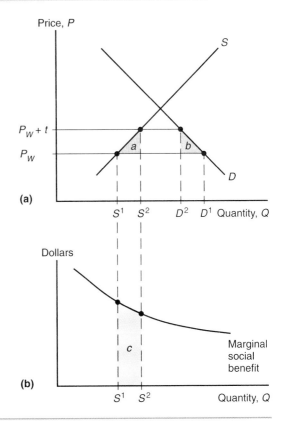

How Convincing Is the Market Failure Argument?

When they were first proposed, market failure arguments for protection seemed to undermine much of the case for free trade. After all, who would want to argue that the real economies we live in are free from market failures? In poorer nations, in particular, market imperfections seem to be legion. For example, unemployment and massive differences between rural and urban wage rates are present in many less-developed countries (Chapter 10). The evidence that markets work badly is less glaring in advanced countries, but it is easy to develop hypotheses suggesting major market failures there as well—for example, the inability of innovative firms to reap the full rewards of their innovations. How can we defend free trade given the likelihood that there are interventions that could raise national welfare?

There are two lines of defense for free trade: The first argues that domestic market failures should be corrected by domestic policies aimed directly at the problems' sources; the second argues that economists cannot diagnose market failure well enough to prescribe policy.

The point that domestic market failure calls for domestic policy changes, not international trade policies, can be made by cost-benefit analysis, modified to account for any

MARKET FAILURES CUT BOTH WAYS: THE CASE OF CALIFORNIA

Critics of free trade sometimes seem to argue that market failures create a general presumption in favor of protection. In fact, the domestic market failure argument cuts both ways. It is just as likely that an industry will have hidden marginal social costs as that it will have hidden marginal social benefits, and thus it is just as possible that a tariff or import quota will produce extra costs over and above the conventional measures as that it will turn out to be beneficial.

An interesting case in which domestic market failure reinforces the case for free trade was noticed by some economists studying the likely effects of free trade between the United States and Mexico.

One of the important effects of the North American Free Trade Agreement (NAFTA) is that it opens the U.S. market to increased imports of fruits and vegetables from Mexico. These increased imports surely lead to some reduction in U.S. production, especially in southern California.

The interesting point that these economists noticed is that southern California's agriculture is overwhelmingly dependent on irrigation and that, for complex political and historical reasons, the farmers get their water at extremely subsidized prices. Southern California is an arid region; its water must be brought in from all over the western United States at a heavy cost in terms of the building and maintenance of dams, aqueducts, and so on. There are also significant if hard-to-measure costs in terms of environmental impact. And when California experiences a drought, as it sometimes

does, it must impose water rationing, at considerable economic cost. Yet farmers pay very low prices for their water, only about one-seventh of the price paid by urban consumers, and (in the view of many economists) an even smaller fraction of the true economic cost.

What the economists studying NAFTA realized was that the increased importing of fruits and vegetables, causing southern California agriculture to contract, would free up water from a use in which it had a very low marginal social product precisely because it has been made available at such a low price. Potential benefits are that urban consumers would be less likely to face water shortages; governments would not need to invest as much in dams and aqueducts; and the burden on the environment would decrease. These indirect benefits of fruit and vegetable imports might be surprisingly large: The study estimated an annual benefit to the United States of more than $100 million.

The "first-best" answer to the problem of water use in California would, of course, be to induce conservation of water by requiring that everyone who uses it pay a price corresponding to its true marginal social cost. But the provision of cheap water for irrigation, like the import quota on sugar discussed in Chapter 8, is a classic example of a policy that provides large benefits to a few people, imposes much larger but diffuse costs on a large number of people, and yet seems to be politically untouchable.

---

unmeasured marginal social benefits. Figure 9-3 showed that a tariff might raise welfare, despite the production and consumption distortion it causes, because it leads to additional production that yields social benefits. If the same production increase were achieved via a production subsidy rather than a tariff, however, the price to consumers would not increase and the consumption loss b would be avoided. In other words, by targeting directly the particular activity we want to encourage, a production subsidy would avoid some of the side costs associated with a tariff.

This example illustrates a general principle when dealing with market failures: It is always preferable to deal with market failures as directly as possible, because indirect policy responses lead to unintended distortions of incentives elsewhere in the economy. Thus, trade policies justified by domestic market failure are never the most efficient response; they are always "second-best" rather than "first-best" policies.

This insight has important implications for trade policymakers: Any proposed trade policy should always be compared with a purely domestic policy aimed at correcting the same problem. If the domestic policy appears too costly or has undesirable side effects, the trade policy is almost surely even less desirable—even though the costs are less apparent.

In the United States, for example, an import quota on automobiles has been supported on the grounds that it is necessary to save the jobs of autoworkers. The advocates of an import quota argue that U.S. labor markets are too inflexible for autoworkers to remain employed either by cutting their wages or by finding jobs in other sectors. Now consider a purely domestic policy aimed at the same problem: a subsidy to firms that employ autoworkers. Such a policy would encounter massive political opposition. For one thing, to preserve current levels of employment without protection would require large subsidy payments, which would either increase the federal government budget deficit or require a tax increase. Furthermore, autoworkers are among the highest-paid workers in the manufacturing sector; the general public would surely object to subsidizing them. It is hard to believe an employment subsidy for autoworkers could pass Congress. Yet an import quota *would be even more expensive,* because while bringing about the same increase in employment, it would also distort consumer choice. The only difference is that the costs would be less visible, taking the form of higher automobile prices rather than direct government outlays.

Critics of the domestic market failure justification for protection argue that this case is typical: Most deviations from free trade are adopted not because their benefits exceed their costs but because the public fails to understand their true costs. Comparing the costs of trade policy with alternative domestic policies is a useful way to focus attention on how large these costs are.

The second defense of free trade is that because market failures are typically hard to identify precisely, it is difficult to be sure about the appropriate policy response. For example, suppose there is urban unemployment in a less-developed country; what is the appropriate policy? One hypothesis (examined more closely in Chapter 10) says that a tariff to protect urban industrial sectors will draw the unemployed into productive work and thus generate social benefits that more than compensate for its costs. Another hypothesis says, however, that this policy will encourage so much migration to urban areas that unemployment will, in fact, increase. It is difficult to say which of these hypotheses is right. While economic theory says much about the working of markets that function properly, it provides much less guidance on those that don't; there are many ways in which markets can malfunction, and the choice of a second-best policy depends on the details of the market failure.

The difficulty of ascertaining the right second-best trade policy to follow reinforces the political argument for free trade mentioned earlier. If trade policy experts are highly uncertain about how policy should deviate from free trade and disagree among themselves, it is all too easy for trade policy to ignore national welfare altogether and become dominated by special-interest politics. If the market failures are not too bad to start with, a commitment to free trade might in the end be a better policy than opening the Pandora's box of a more flexible approach.

This is, however, a judgment about politics rather than economics. We need to realize that economic theory does *not* provide a dogmatic defense of free trade, something that it is often accused of doing.

Income Distribution and Trade Policy

The discussion so far has focused on national welfare arguments for and against tariff policy. It is appropriate to start there, both because a distinction between national welfare and the welfare of particular groups helps to clarify the issues and because the advocates of trade policies usually claim they will benefit the nation as a whole. When looking at the actual politics of trade policy, however, it becomes necessary to deal with the reality that there is no such thing as national welfare; there are only the desires of individuals, which get more or less imperfectly reflected in the objectives of government.

How do the preferences of individuals get added up to produce the trade policy we actually see? There is no single, generally accepted answer, but there has been a growing body of economic analysis that explores models in which governments are assumed to be trying to maximize political success rather than an abstract measure of national welfare.

Electoral Competition

Political scientists have long used a simple model of competition among political parties to show how the preferences of voters might be reflected in actual policies.[4] The model runs as follows: Suppose that there are two competing parties, each of which is willing to promise whatever will enable it to win the next election. Suppose that policy can be described along a single dimension, say, the level of the tariff rate. And finally, suppose that voters differ in the policies they prefer. For example, imagine that a country exports skill-intensive goods and imports labor-intensive goods. Then voters with high skill levels will favor low tariff rates, but voters with low skills will be better off if the country imposes a high tariff (because of the Stolper-Samuelson effect discussed in Chapter 4). We can therefore think of lining up all the voters in the order of the tariff rate they prefer, with the voters who favor the lowest rate on the left and those who favor the highest rate on the right.

What policies will the two parties then promise to follow? The answer is that they will try to find the middle ground—specifically, both will tend to converge on the tariff rate preferred by the **median voter**, the voter who is exactly halfway up the lineup. To see why, consider Figure 9-4. In the figure, voters are lined up by their preferred tariff rate, which is shown by the hypothetical upward-sloping curve; t_M is the median voter's preferred rate. Now suppose that one of the parties has proposed the tariff rate t_A, which is considerably above that preferred by the median voter. Then the other party could propose the slightly lower rate t_B, and its program would be preferred by almost all voters who wanted a lower tariff, that is, by a majority. In other words, it would always be in the political interest of a party to undercut any tariff proposal that is higher than what the median voter wants.

But similar reasoning shows that self-interested politicians will always want to promise a higher tariff if their opponents propose one that is lower than the tariff the median voter prefers. So both parties end up proposing a tariff close to the one the median voter wants.

Political scientists have modified this simple model in a number of ways. For example, some analysts stress the importance of party activists to getting out the vote; since these activists are often ideologically motivated, the need for their support may prevent parties from being quite as cynical, or adopting platforms quite as indistinguishable, as this model

---

[4]See Anthony Downs, *An Economic Theory of Democracy* (Washington: Brookings, 1957).

Figure 9-4 │ Political Competition

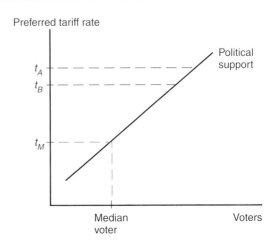

Voters are lined up in order of the tariff rate they prefer. If one party proposes a high tariff of t_A, the other party can win over most of the voters by offering a somewhat lower tariff, t_B. This political competition drives both parties to propose tariffs close to t_M, the tariff preferred by the median voter.

suggests. Nonetheless, the median voter model of electoral competition has been very helpful as a way of thinking about how political decisions get made in the real world, where the effects of policy on income distribution may be more important than their effects on efficiency.

One area in which the median voter model does not seem to work very well, however, is trade policy! In fact, it makes an almost precisely wrong prediction. According to this model, a policy should be chosen on the basis of how many voters it pleases. A policy that inflicts large losses on a few people but benefits a large number of people should be a political winner; a policy that inflicts widespread losses but helps a small group should be a loser. In fact, however, protectionist policies are more likely to fit the latter than the former description. Recall the example of the U.S. sugar import quota, discussed in Chapter 8: According to the estimates presented there, the quota imposed a loss of more than $1.6 billion on U.S. consumers—that is, on tens of millions of voters—while providing a gain of only about half that much to a few thousand sugar industry workers and businesspersons. How can such a thing happen politically?

Collective Action

In a now famous book, the economist Mancur Olson pointed out that political activity on behalf of a group is a public good; that is, the benefits of such activity accrue to all members of the group, not just the individual who performs the activity.[5] Suppose a consumer writes a letter to his congressperson demanding a lower tariff rate on his favorite imported good, and this letter helps change the congressperson's vote, so that the lower tariff is approved. Then all consumers who buy the good benefit from lower prices, even if they did not bother to write letters.

---

[5]Mancur Olson, *The Logic of Collective Action* (Cambridge: Harvard University Press, 1965).

This public good character of politics means that policies that impose large losses in total, but small losses on any individual, may not face any effective opposition. Again take the example of the sugar import quota. This policy imposes a cost on a typical American family of approximately $25 per year. Should a consumer lobby his or her Congressperson to remove the quota? From the point of view of individual self-interest, surely not. Since one letter has only a marginal effect on the policy, the individual payoff from such a letter is probably literally not worth the paper it is written on, let alone the postage stamp. (Indeed, it is surely not worth even learning of the quota's existence unless you are interested in such things for their own sake.) And yet if a million voters were to write demanding an end to the quota, it would surely be repealed, bringing benefits to consumers far exceeding the cost of sending the letters. In Olson's phrase, there is a problem of **collective action**: While it is in the interests of the group as a whole to press for favorable policies, it is not in any individual's interest to do so.

The problem of collective action can best be overcome when a group is small (so that each individual reaps a significant share of the benefits of favorable policies) and/or well-organized (so that members of the group can be mobilized to act in their collective interest). The reason that a policy like the sugar quota can happen is that the sugar producers form a relatively small, well-organized group that is well aware of the size of the implicit subsidy members receive; while sugar consumers are a huge population that does not even perceive itself as an interest group. The problem of collective action, then, can explain why policies that not only seem to produce more costs than benefits but that also seem to hurt far more voters than they help can nonetheless be adopted.

Modeling the Political Process

While the logic of collective action has long been invoked by economists to explain seemingly irrational trade policies, it is somewhat vague on the way in which organized interest groups actually go about influencing policy. A growing body of recent analysis tries to fill this gap with simplified models of the political process.[6]

The starting point of this analysis is an obvious point: While politicians may win elections partly because they advocate popular policies, a successful campaign also requires money for advertising, polling, and so on. It may therefore be in the interest of a politician to adopt positions that are against the interest of the typical voter if he or she is offered a sufficiently large financial contribution to do so; the extra money may be worth more votes than those lost by taking the unpopular position.

Recent models of the political economy of trade policy therefore envision a sort of auction, in which interest groups "buy" policies by offering contributions contingent on the policies followed by the government. Politicians will not ignore overall welfare, but they will be willing to trade off some reduction in the welfare of voters in return for a larger campaign fund. As a result, well-organized groups—that is, groups that have been able to overcome the problem of collective action—will be able to get policies that favor their interests at the expense of the public as a whole.

---

[6]See, in particular, Gene Grossman and Elhanan Helpman, "Protection for Sale," *American Economic Review* (September 1994), pp. 833–850.

Who Gets Protected?

As a practical matter, which industries actually get protected from import competition? Many developing countries traditionally have protected a wide range of manufacturing, in a policy known as import-substituting industrialization. We discuss this policy and the reasons why it has become considerably less popular in recent years in Chapter 10. The range of protectionism in advanced countries is much narrower; indeed, much protectionism is concentrated in just two sectors, agriculture and clothing.

Agriculture.   There are not many farmers in modern economies—in the United States, agriculture employs only about 2 percent of the work force. Farmers are, however, usually a well-organized and politically effective group, which has been able in many cases to achieve very high rates of effective protection. We discussed Europe's Common Agricultural Policy in Chapter 8; the export subsidies in that program mean that a number of agricultural products sell at two or three times world prices. In Japan, the government has traditionally banned imports of rice, thus driving up internal prices of the country's staple food to more than five times as high as the world price. This ban was slightly relaxed in the face of bad harvests in the mid-1990s, but in late 1998—over the protests of other nations, including the United States—Japan imposed a 1000-percent tariff on rice imports.

The United States is by and large a food exporter, which means that tariffs or import quotas cannot raise prices. (Sugar is an exception.) While farmers have received considerable subsidy from the federal government, the government's reluctance to pay money out directly (as opposed to imposing more or less hidden costs on consumers) has limited the size of these subsidies. As a result of the government's reluctance, much of the protection in the United States is concentrated on the other major protected sector: the clothing industry.

Clothing.   The clothing industry consists of two parts: textiles (spinning and weaving of cloth) and apparel (assembly of that cloth into clothing). Both industries, but especially the apparel industry, have been heavily protected both through tariffs and through import quotas; they are currently subject to the Multi-Fiber Arrangement, which sets both export and import quotas for a large number of countries.

Apparel production has two key features. It is labor-intensive: A worker needs relatively little capital, in some cases no more than a sewing machine, and can do the job without extensive formal education. And the technology is relatively simple: There is no great difficulty in transferring the technology even to very poor countries. As a result, the apparel industry is one in which low-wage nations have a strong comparative advantage and high-wage countries have a strong comparative disadvantage. It is also traditionally a well-organized sector in advanced countries; for example, many American apparel workers have long been represented by the International Ladies' Garment Worker's Union.

Table 9-2 gives an indication of the dominant role of the clothing industry in modern U.S. protection; it also suggests how hard it is to rationalize actual policies in terms of any economic logic. As the table suggests, apparel and textiles together accounted for more than three-fourths of the consumer costs of protection in 1990, and more than five-sixths of the overall welfare costs. What is peculiar is that because clothing imports are limited by the Multi-Fiber Agreement—which assigns import licenses to exporting countries—most of the welfare cost comes not from distortion of production and consumption but from the transfer of quota rents to foreigners.

POLITICIANS FOR SALE: EVIDENCE FROM THE 1990S

As we explained in the text, it's hard to make sense of actual trade policy if you assume that governments are genuinely trying to maximize national welfare. On the other hand, actual trade policy does make sense if you assume that special-interest groups can buy influence. But is there any direct evidence that politicians really are for sale?

Votes by the U.S. Congress on some crucial trade issues in the 1990s offer useful test cases. The reason is that U.S. campaign finance laws require politicians to reveal the amounts and sources of campaign contributions; this disclosure allows economists and political scientists to look for any relationship between those contributions and actual votes.

A 1998 study by Robert Baldwin and Christopher Magee* focuses on two crucial votes: the 1993 vote on the North American Free Trade Agreement (generally known as NAFTA, and described at greater length below), and the 1994 vote ratifying the latest agreement under the General Agreement on Tariffs and Trade (generally known as GATT, also described below). Both votes were bitterly fought, largely along business-versus-labor lines— that is, business groups were strongly in favor; labor unions were strongly against. In both cases the free-trade position backed by business won; in the NAFTA vote the outcome was in doubt until the last minute, and the margin of victory—34 votes in the House of Representatives—was not very large.

Baldwin and Magee estimate an econometric model of congressional votes that controls for such factors as the economic characteristics of members' districts and that also includes business and labor contributions to the congressional representative. They find a strong impact of money on the voting pattern. One way to assess this impact is to run a series of "counterfactuals": how different would the overall vote have been if there had been no business contributions, no labor contributions, or no contributions at all?

The table on the following page summarizes the results. The first line shows how many representatives voted in favor of each bill; bear in mind that passage required at least 214 votes. The second line shows the number of votes predicted by Baldwin and Magee's equations: their model gets it right in the case of NAFTA and overpredicts by a few votes in the case of GATT. The third line shows how many votes each bill would have received, according to the model, in the absence of labor contributions; the next line shows how many would have voted in favor in the absence of business contributions. The last line shows how many would have voted in favor if both business and labor contributions had been absent.

If these estimates are correct, contributions had big impacts on the vote totals. In the case of NAFTA, labor contributions induced 62 representatives who would otherwise have supported the

---

Table 9-2 | Effects of Protection in the United States ($ billion)

Effect	Apparel	Textiles	All Industries
Consumer cost	21.16	3.27	32.32
Producer gain	9.90	1.75	15.78
Tariff revenue	3.55	0.63	5.86
Quota rent	5.41	0.71	7.12
Producer and consumer distortion	2.30	0.18	3.55
Overall welfare loss	7.71	0.89	10.42

Source: Gary Hufbauer and Kimberly Elliott, *Measuring the Costs of Protection in the United States.* Washington: Institute for International Economics, 1994, pp. 8–9.

	Vote for NAFTA	Vote for GATT
Actual	229	283
Predicted by model	229	290
Without labor contributions	291	346
Without business contributions	195	257
Without any contributions	256	323

bill to vote against; business contributions moved 34 representatives the other way. If there had been no business contributions, according to this estimate, NAFTA would have received only 195 votes—not enough for passage.

On the other hand, given that both sides were making contributions, their effects tended to cancel out. Baldwin and Magee's estimates suggest that in the absence of contributions from either labor or business, both NAFTA and the GATT would have passed anyway.

It's probably wrong to emphasize the fact that in these particular cases contributions from the two sides did not change the final outcome. The really important result is that politicians are, indeed, for sale—which means that theories of trade policy that emphasize special interests are on the right track.

---

*Robert E. Baldwin and Christopher S. Magee, "Is trade policy for sale? Congressional voting on recent trade bills," National Bureau of Economic Research Working Paper no. 6376.

International Negotiations and Trade Policy

Our discussion of the politics of trade policy has not been very encouraging. We have argued that it is difficult to devise trade policies that raise national welfare and that trade policy is often dominated by interest group politics. "Horror stories" of trade policies that produce costs that greatly exceed any conceivable benefits abound; it is easy to be highly cynical about the practical side of trade theory.

Yet, in fact, from the mid-1930s until about 1980 the United States and other advanced countries gradually removed tariffs and some other barriers to trade, and by so doing aided a rapid increase in international integration. Figure 9-5 shows the average U.S. tariff rate on dutiable imports from 1920 to 1993; after rising sharply in the early 1930s, the rate has steadily declined.[7] Most economists believe this progressive trade liberalization was highly

---

[7]Measures of changes in the average rate of protection can be problematic, because the composition of imports changes—partly because of tariff rates themselves. Imagine, for example, a country that imposes a tariff on some goods that is so high that it shuts off all imports of these goods. Then the average tariff rate on goods actually imported will be zero! To try to correct for this, the measure we use in Figure 9-5 shows the rate only on "dutiable" imports; that is, it excludes imports that for some reason were exempt from tariff. At their peak, U.S. tariff rates were so high that goods subject to tariffs accounted for only one-third of imports; by 1975 that share had risen to two-thirds. As a result, the average tariff rate on all goods fell much less than the rate on dutiable goods. The numbers shown in Figure 9-5, however, give a more accurate picture of the major liberalization of trade actually experienced by the United States.

Figure 9-5 | The U.S. Tariff Rate

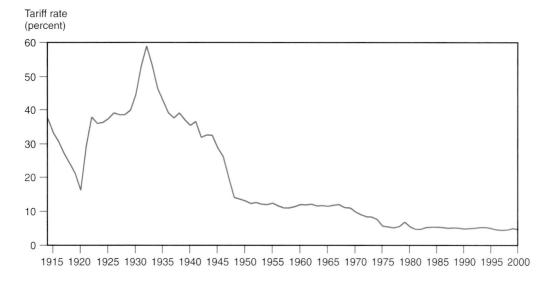

Tariff rate
(percent)

After rising sharply at the beginning of the 1930s, the average tariff rate of the United States has steadily declined.

beneficial. Given what we have said about the politics of trade policy, however, how was this removal of tariffs politically possible?

At least part of the answer is that the great postwar liberalization of trade was achieved through **international negotiation**. That is, governments agreed to engage in mutual tariff reduction. These agreements linked reduced protection for each country's import-competing industries to reduced protection by other countries against that country's export industries. Such a linkage, as we will now argue, helps to offset some of the political difficulties that would otherwise prevent countries from adopting good trade policies.

The Advantages of Negotiation

There are at least two reasons why it is easier to lower tariffs as part of a mutual agreement than to do so as a unilateral policy. First, a mutual agreement helps mobilize support for freer trade. Second, negotiated agreements on trade can help governments avoid getting caught in destructive trade wars.

The effect of international negotiations on support for freer trade is straightforward. We have noted that import-competing producers are usually better informed and organized than consumers. International negotiations can bring in domestic exporters as a counterweight. The United States and Japan, for example, could reach an agreement in which the United States refrains from imposing import quotas to protect some of its manufacturers from Japanese competition in return for removal of Japanese barriers to U.S. exports of agricultural or high-technology products to Japan. U.S. consumers might not be effective politically in opposing such import quotas on foreign goods, even though these quotas may be costly to them, but exporters who want access to foreign markets may, through their lobbying for mutual elimination of import quotas, protect consumer interests.

International negotiation can also help to avoid a **trade war**. The concept of a trade war can best be illustrated with a stylized example.

Imagine that there are only two countries in the world, the United States and Japan, and that these countries have only two policy choices, free trade or protection. Suppose that these are unusually clear-headed governments that can assign definite numerical values to their satisfaction with any particular policy outcome (Table 9-3).

The particular values of the payoffs given in the table represent two assumptions. First we assume that each country's government would choose protection if it could take the other country's policy as given. That is, whichever policy Japan chooses, the U.S. government is better off with protection. This assumption is by no means necessarily true; many economists would argue that free trade is the best policy for the nation, regardless of what other governments do. Governments, however, must act not only in the public interest but in their own political interest. For the reasons discussed in the previous section, governments often find it politically difficult to avoid giving protection to some industries.

The second assumption built into Table 9-3 is that even though each government acting individually would be better off with protection, they would both be better off if both chose free trade. That is, the U.S. government has more to gain from an opening of Japanese markets than it has to lose from opening its own markets, and the same is true for Japan. We can justify this assumption simply by appealing to the gains from trade.

To those who have studied game theory, this situation is known as a **Prisoner's dilemma**. Each government, making the best decision for itself, will choose to protect. These choices lead to the outcome in the lower right box of the table. Yet both governments are better off if neither protects: The upper left box of the table yields a payoff that is higher for both countries. By acting unilaterally in what appear to be their best interests, the governments fail to achieve the best outcome possible. If the countries act unilaterally to protect, there is a trade war that leaves both worse off. Trade wars are not as serious as shooting wars, but avoiding them is similar to the problem of avoiding armed conflict or arms races.

Obviously, Japan and the United States need to establish an agreement (such as a treaty) to refrain from protection. Each government will be better off if it limits its own freedom of action, provided the other country limits its freedom of action as well. A treaty can make everyone better off.

This is a highly simplified example. In the real world there are both many countries and many gradations of trade policy between free trade and complete protection against imports.

Table 9-3 | The Problem of Trade Warfare

U.S. \ Japan	Free trade	Protection
Free trade	10 / 10	20 / −10
Protection	−10 / 20	−5 / −5

Nonetheless, the example suggests both that there is a need to coordinate trade policies through international agreements and that such agreements can actually make a difference. Indeed, the current system of international trade is built around a series of international agreements.

International Trade Agreements: A Brief History

Internationally coordinated tariff reduction as a trade policy dates back to the 1930s. In 1930, the United States passed a remarkably irresponsible tariff law, the Smoot-Hawley Act. Under this act, tariff rates rose steeply and U.S. trade fell sharply; some economists argue that the Smoot-Hawley Act helped deepen the Great Depression. Within a few years after the act's passage, the U.S. administration concluded that tariffs needed to be reduced, but this posed serious problems of political coalition building. Any tariff reduction would be opposed by those members of Congress whose districts contained firms producing competing goods, while the benefits would be so widely diffused that few in Congress could be mobilized on the other side. To reduce tariff rates, tariff reduction needed to be linked to some concrete benefits for exporters. The initial solution to this political problem was bilateral tariff negotiations. The United States would approach some country that was a major exporter of some good—say, a sugar exporter—and offer to lower tariffs on sugar if that country would lower its tariffs on some U.S. exports. The attractiveness of the deal to U.S. exporters would help counter the political weight of the sugar interest. In the foreign country, the attractiveness of the deal to foreign sugar exporters would balance the political influence of import-competing interests. Such bilateral negotiations helped reduce the average duty on U.S. imports from 59 percent in 1932 to 25 percent shortly after World War II.

Bilateral negotiations, however, do not take full advantage of international coordination. For one thing, benefits from a bilateral negotiation may "spill over" to countries that have not made any concessions. For example, if the United States reduces tariffs on coffee as a result of a deal with Brazil, Colombia will also gain from a higher world coffee price. Furthermore, some advantageous deals may inherently involve more than two countries: The United States sells more to Europe, Europe sells more to Saudi Arabia, Saudi Arabia sells more to Japan, and Japan sells more to the United States. Thus the next step in international trade liberalization was to proceed to multilateral negotiations involving a number of countries.

Multilateral negotiations began soon after the end of World War II. Originally diplomats from the victorious Allies imagined that such negotiations would take place under the auspices of a proposed body called the International Trade Organization, paralleling the International Monetary Fund and the World Bank (described in the second half of this book). In 1947, unwilling to wait until the ITO was in place, a group of 23 countries began trade negotiations under a provisional set of rules that became known as the **General Agreement on Tariffs and Trade**, or **GATT**. As it turned out, the ITO was never established because it ran into severe political opposition, especially in the United States. So the provisional agreement ended up governing world trade for the next 48 years.

Officially, the GATT was an agreement, not an organization—the countries participating in the agreement were officially designated as "contracting parties," not members. In practice the GATT did maintain a permanent "secretariat" in Geneva, which everyone referred to as "the GATT." In 1995 the **World Trade Organization**, or **WTO**, was established, finally creating the formal organization envisaged 50 years earlier. However, the GATT rules remain in force, and the basic logic of the system remains the same.

One way to think about the GATT-WTO approach to trade is to use a mechanical analogy: it's like a device designed to push a heavy object, the world economy, gradually up a slope—the path to free trade. To get there requires both "levers" to push the object in the right direction, as well as "ratchets" to prevent backsliding.

The principal ratchet in the system is the process of **binding**. When a tariff rate is "bound," the country imposing the tariff agrees not to raise the rate in the future. At present, almost all tariff rates in developed countries are bound, as are about three-quarters of the rates in developing countries. There is some wiggle room in bound tariffs: a country can raise a tariff if it gets the agreement of other countries, which usually means providing compensation by reducing other tariffs. In practice, binding has been highly effective, with very little backsliding in tariffs over the past half-century.

In addition to binding tariffs, the GATT-WTO system generally tries to prevent non-tariff interventions in trade. Export subsidies are not allowed, with one big exception: back at the GATT's inception the United States insisted on a loophole for agricultural exports, which has since been exploited on a large scale by the European Union.

As we pointed out earlier in this chapter, most of the actual cost of protection in the United States comes from import quotas. The GATT-WTO system in effect "grandfathers" existing import quotas, though there has been an ongoing and often successful effort to remove such quotas or convert them to tariffs. New import quotas are generally forbidden except as temporary measures to deal with "market disruption," an undefined phrase usually interpreted to mean surges of imports that threaten to put a domestic sector suddenly out of business.

The lever used to make forward progress is the somewhat stylized process known as a **trade round**, in which a large group of countries get together to negotiate a set of tariff reductions and other measures to liberalize trade. Eight trade rounds have occurred since 1947, the last of which—the "Uruguay Round," completed in 1994—established the WTO. In 1999 an attempt to start a new round in Seattle failed; we discuss the causes of that failure and the events that surrounded it in Chapter 11. Two years later, as this book went to press, a meeting at the Persian Gulf city of Doha formally began a ninth round.

The first five trade rounds under the GATT took the form of "parallel" bilateral negotiations, where each country negotiates pair-wise with a number of countries at once. For example, if Germany were to offer a tariff reduction that would benefit both France and Italy, it could ask both of them for reciprocal concessions. The ability to make more extensive deals, together with the worldwide economic recovery from the war, helped to permit substantial tariff reductions.

The sixth multilateral trade agreement, known as the Kennedy Round, was completed in 1967. This agreement involved an across-the-board 50 percent reduction in tariffs by the major industrial countries, except for specified industries whose tariffs were left unchanged. The negotiations were over which industries to exempt rather than over the size of the cut for industries not given special treatment. Overall, the Kennedy Round reduced average tariffs by about 35 percent.

The so-called Tokyo Round of trade negotiations (completed in 1979) reduced tariffs by a formula more complex than that of the Kennedy Round. In addition, new codes were established in an effort to control the proliferation of nontariff barriers, such as voluntary export restraints and orderly marketing agreements. Finally, in 1994 an eighth round of negotiations, the so-called Uruguay Round, was completed. The provisions of that round were approved by the U.S. Congress after acrimonious debate; we describe the results of these negotiations below.

The Uruguay Round

Major international trade negotiations invariably open with a ceremony in one exotic locale and conclude with a ceremonial signing in another. The eighth round of global trade negotiations carried out under the GATT began in 1986, with a meeting at the coastal resort of Punta del Este, Uruguay (hence the name Uruguay Round). The participants then repaired to Geneva, where they engaged in seven years of offers and counteroffers, threats and counterthreats, and, above all, tens of thousands of hours of meetings so boring that even the most experienced diplomat had difficulty staying awake. The round was scheduled for completion by 1990 but ran into serious political difficulties. In late 1993 the negotiators finally produced a basic document consisting of 400 pages of agreements, together with supplementary documents detailing the specific commitments of member nations with regard to particular markets and products—about 22,000 pages in all. The agreement was signed in Marrakesh, Morocco, in April 1994, and ratified by the major nations—after bitter political controversy in some cases, including the United States—by the end of that year.

As the length of the document suggests, the end results of the Uruguay Round are not that easy to summarize. The most important results may, however, be grouped under two headings, trade liberalization and administrative reforms.

Trade Liberalization

The Uruguay Round, like previous GATT negotiations, cut tariff rates around the world. The numbers can sound impressive: The average tariff imposed by advanced countries will fall almost 40 percent as a result of the round. However, tariff rates were already quite low. In fact, the average tariff rate will fall only from 6.3 to 3.9 percent, enough to produce only a small increase in world trade.

More important than this overall tariff reduction are the moves to liberalize trade in two important sectors, agriculture and clothing.

World trade in agricultural products has been highly distorted. Japan is notorious for import restrictions that lead to internal prices of rice, beef, and other foods several times as high as world market prices; Europe's massive export subsidies under the Common Agricultural Program were described in Chapter 8. At the beginning of the Uruguay Round the United States had an ambitious goal: free trade in agricultural products by the year 2000. The actual achievement was far more modest but still significant. The agreement required agricultural exporters to reduce the value of subsidies by 36 percent, and the volume of subsidized exports by 21 percent, over a six-year period. Countries that protect their farmers with import quotas, like Japan, were required to replace quotas with tariffs, which may not be increased in the future.

World trade in textiles and clothing has also been highly distorted by the Multi-Fiber Arrangement also described in Chapter 8. The Uruguay Round will phase out the MFA over a ten-year period, eliminating all quantitative restrictions on trade in textiles and clothing. (Some high tariffs will, however, remain in place.) This is a fairly dramatic liberalization— remember that most estimates suggest that protection of clothing imposes a larger cost on

U.S. consumers than all other protectionist measures combined. It is worth noting, however, that the formula to be used in phasing out the MFA is heavily "backloaded": Much of the liberalization will be postponed until late in the transition period, that is, around 2003 or 2004. Some trade experts are worried about the credibility of such long-range commitments, wondering whether a treaty signed in 1994 can really force politicians to take a politically difficult action ten years later.

A final important trade action under the Uruguay Round is a new set of rules concerning government procurement, purchases made not by private firms or consumers, but by government agencies. Such procurement has long provided protected markets for many kinds of goods, from construction equipment to vehicles. (Recall the box on Hungarian buses in Chapter 8.) The Uruguay Round set new rules that should open up a wide range of government contracts to imported products.

From the GATT to the WTO

Much of the publicity surrounding the Uruguay Round, and much of the controversy swirling around the world trading system since then, has focused on the round's creation of a new institution, the World Trade Organization. In 1995 this organization replaced the ad hoc secretariat that administered the GATT. As we'll see in Chapter 11, the WTO has become the organization that opponents of globalization love to hate; it has been accused by both the left and the right of acting as a sort of world government, undermining national sovereignty.

How different is the WTO from the GATT? From a legal point of view, the GATT was a provisional agreement, while the WTO is a full-fledged international organization; however, the actual bureaucracy remains small (a staff of 500). An updated version of the original GATT text has been incorporated into the WTO rules. The GATT, however, applied only to trade in goods; world trade in services—that is, intangible things like insurance, consulting, and banking—was not subject to any agreed-upon set of rules. As a result, many countries applied regulations that openly or de facto discriminated against foreign suppliers. The GATT's neglect of trade in services became an increasingly glaring omission, because modern economies have increasingly focused on the production of services rather than physical goods. So the WTO agreement included rules on trade in services (the General Agreement on Trade in Services, or GATS). In practice, these rules have not yet had much impact on trade in services; their main purpose is to serve as the basis for negotiating future trade rounds.

In addition to a broad shift from producing goods to producing services, advanced countries have also experienced a shift from depending on physical capital to depending on "intellectual property," protected by patents and copyrights. (Thirty years ago General Motors was the quintessential modern corporation; now it's Microsoft.) Thus defining the international application of international property rights has also become a major preoccupation. The WTO tries to take on this issue with its Agreement on Trade-Related Aspects of Intellectual Property (TRIPS). The application of TRIPS in the pharmaceutical industry has become a subject of heated debate.

The most important new aspect of the WTO, however, is generally acknowledged to be its "dispute settlement" procedure. The basic problem arises when one country accuses another of violating the rules of the trading system. Suppose, for example, that Canada accuses the United States of unfairly limiting timber imports—and the United States denies the charge. What happens next?

Before the WTO, there were international tribunals in which Canada could press its case, but such proceedings tended to drag on for years, even decades. And even when a ruling had been issued, there was no way to enforce it. This did not mean that the GATT's rules had no force: neither the United States nor other countries wanted to acquire a reputation as scoff-laws, so they made considerable efforts to keep their actions "GATT-legal." But gray-area cases tended to go unresolved.

The WTO contains a much more formal and effective procedure. Panels of experts are selected to hear cases, normally reaching a final conclusion in less than a year; even with appeals the procedure is not supposed to take more than 15 months.

Suppose that the WTO concludes that a nation has, in fact, been violating the rules—and the country nonetheless refuses to change its policy. Then what? The WTO itself has no enforcement powers. What it can do is grant the country that filed the complaint the right to retaliate. To use our Canada-U.S. example, the government of Canada might be given the right to impose restrictions on U.S. exports, without itself being considered in violation of WTO rules. In the case of the banana dispute described in the box on p. 245, a WTO ruling found the European Union in violation; when Europe remained recalcitrant, the United States temporarily imposed tariffs on such items as designer handbags.

The hope and expectation is that few disputes will get this far. In many cases the threat to bring a dispute before the WTO should lead to a settlement; in the great majority of other cases countries accept the WTO ruling and change their policies.

The box on p. 242 describes an example of the WTO dispute settlement procedure at work: the U.S.-Venezuela dispute over imported gasoline. As the box explains, this case has also become a prime example for those who accuse the WTO of undermining national sovereignty.

Benefits and Costs

The economic impact of the Uruguay Round is difficult to estimate. If nothing else, think about the logistics: To do an estimate, one must translate an immense document from one impenetrable jargon (legalese) into another (economese), assign numbers to the translation, then feed the whole thing into a computer model of the world economy. The matter is made worse by the fact that as described above, much of the important action is "backloaded," so that we will not really see some of the important provisions of the round work in practice until nearly a decade after its signing.

The most widely cited estimates are those of the GATT itself and of the Organization for Economic Cooperation and Development, another international organization (this one consisting only of rich countries, and based in Paris). Both estimates suggest a gain to the world economy as a whole of more than $200 billion annually once the agreement is fully in force; this would raise world real income by about 1 percent. As always, there are dissenting estimates on both sides. Some economists claim that the estimated gains are exaggerated, particularly because they assume that exports and imports will respond strongly to the new liberalizing moves. A probably larger minority of critics argues that these estimates are considerably too low, for the "dynamic" reasons discussed earlier in this chapter.

In any case, it is clear that the usual logic of trade liberalization will apply: The costs of the Uruguay Round will be felt by concentrated, often well-organized groups, while much of the benefit will accrue to broad, diffuse populations. The progress on agriculture will

SETTLING A DISPUTE—AND CREATING ONE

The very first application of the WTO's new dispute settlement procedure has also been one of the most controversial. To WTO supporters, it illustrates the new system's effectiveness. To opponents, it shows that the organization stands in the way of important social goals such as protecting the environment.

The case arose out of new U.S. air pollution standards. These standards set rules for the chemical composition of gasoline sold in the United States. A uniform standard would clearly have been legal under WTO rules. However, the new standards included some loopholes: refineries in the United States, or those selling 75 percent or more of their output in the United States, were given "baselines" that depended on their 1990 pollutant levels. This provision generally set a less strict standard than was set for imported gasoline, and thus in effect introduced a preference for gasoline from domestic refineries.

Venezuela, which ships considerable quantities of gasoline to the United States, brought a complaint against the new pollution rules early in 1995. Venezuela argued that the rules violated the principle of "national treatment," which says that imported goods should be subject to the same regulations as domestic goods (so that regulations are not used as an indirect form of protectionism). A year later the panel appointed by the WTO ruled in Venezuela's favor; the United States appealed, but the appeal was rejected. The United States and Venezuela then negotiated a revised set of rules.

At one level, this outcome was a demonstration of the WTO doing exactly what it was supposed to do. The United States introduced measures that pretty clearly violated the letter of its trade agreements; when a smaller, less influential country appealed against those measures, it got fairly quick results.

On the other hand, environmentalists were understandably upset: the WTO ruling in effect blocked a measure that would have made the air cleaner. Furthermore, there was little question that the clean-air rules were promulgated in good faith—that is, they were really intended to reduce air pollution, not to exclude exports.

Defenders of the WTO point out that the United States clearly could have written a rule that did not discriminate against imports; the fact that it did not was a political concession to the refining industry, which *did* in effect constitute a sort of protectionism. The most you can say is that the WTO's rules made it more difficult for U.S. environmentalists to strike a political deal with industry.

In the mythology of the anti-globalization movement, which we discuss in Chapter 11, the WTO's intervention against clean-air standards has taken on iconic status: the case is seen as a prime example of how the organization deprives nations of their sovereignty, preventing them from following socially and environmentally responsible policies. The reality of the case, however, is nowhere near that clear-cut: if the United States had imposed a "clean" clean-air rule that did not discriminate among sources, the WTO would have had no complaints.

directly hurt the small but influential populations of farmers in Europe, Japan, and other countries where agricultural prices are far above world levels. These losses should be much more than offset by gains to consumers and taxpayers in those countries, but because these benefits will be very widely spread they may be little noticed. Similarly, the liberalization of trade in textiles and clothing will produce some concentrated pain for workers and companies in those industries, offset by considerably larger but far less visible consumer gains.

Given these strong distributional impacts of the Uruguay Round, it is actually remarkable that an agreement was reached at all. Indeed, after the failure to achieve anything close to agreement by the 1990 target, many commentators began to pronounce the whole trade negotiation process to be dead. That in the end agreement was achieved, if on a more modest scale than originally hoped, may be attributed to an interlocking set of political calculations. In the United States, the gains to agricultural exporters and the prospective gains to service exporters if the GATS opens the door to substantial liberalization helped offset the complaints of the clothing industry. Many developing countries supported the round because of the new opportunities it would offer to their own textile and clothing exports. Also, some of the "concessions" negotiated under the agreement were an excuse to make policy changes that would eventually have happened anyway. For example, the sheer expense of Europe's Common Agricultural Program in a time of budget deficits made it ripe for cutting in any case.

An important factor in the final success of the round, however, was fear of what would happen if it failed. By 1993, protectionist currents were evidently running strong in the United States and elsewhere. Trade negotiators in countries that might otherwise have refused to go along with the agreement—such as France, Japan, or South Korea, in all of which powerful farm lobbies angrily opposed trade liberalization—therefore feared that failure to agree would be dangerous. That is, they feared that a failed round would not mean mere lack of progress but substantial backsliding on the progress made toward free trade over the previous four decades.

Preferential Trading Agreements

The international trade agreements that we have described so far all involved a "nondiscriminatory" reduction in tariff rates. For example, when the United States agrees with Germany to lower its tariff on imported machinery, the new tariff rate applies to machinery from any nation rather than just imports from Germany. Such nondiscrimination is normal in most tariffs. Indeed, the United States grants many countries a status known formally as that of "most favored nation" (MFN), a guarantee that their exporters will pay tariffs no higher than that of the nation that pays the lowest. All countries granted MFN status pay the same rates. Tariff reductions under GATT always—with one important exception—are made on an MFN basis.

There are some important cases, however, in which nations establish **preferential trading agreements** under which the tariffs they apply to each others' products are lower than the rates on the same goods coming from other countries. The GATT in general prohibits such agreements but makes a rather strange exception: It is against the rules for country A to have lower tariffs on imports from country B than on those from country C, but it is acceptable if countries B and C agree to have zero tariffs on each others' products. That is, the GATT forbids preferential trading agreements in general, as a violation of the MFN principle, but allows them if they lead to free trade between the agreeing countries.[8]

In general, two or more countries agreeing to establish free trade can do so in one of two ways. They can establish a **free trade area**, in which each country's goods can be shipped

---

[8]The logic here seems to be legal rather than economic. Nations are allowed to have free trade within their boundaries: Nobody insists that California wine pay the same tariff as French wine when it is shipped to New York. That is, the MFN principle does not apply within political units. But what is a political unit? The GATT sidesteps that potentially thorny question by allowing any group of economies to do what countries do, and establish free trade within some defined boundary.

FREE TRADE AREA VERSUS CUSTOMS UNION

The difference between a free trade area and a customs union is, in brief, that the first is politically straightforward but an administrative headache, while the second is just the opposite.

Consider first the case of a customs union. Once such a union is established, tariff administration is relatively easy: Goods must pay tariffs when they cross the border of the union, but from then on can be shipped freely between countries. A cargo that is unloaded at Marseilles or Rotterdam must pay duties there, but will not face any additional charges if it then goes by truck to Munich. To make this simple system work, however, the countries must agree on tariff rates: The duty must be the same whether the cargo is unloaded at Marseilles, Rotterdam, or for that matter Hamburg, because otherwise importers would choose the point of entry that minimized their fees. So a customs union requires that Germany, France, the Netherlands, and all the other countries agree to charge the same tariffs. This is not easily done: Countries are, in effect, ceding part of their sovereignty to a supranational entity, the European Union.

This has been possible in Europe for a variety of reasons, including the belief that economic unity would help cement the post-war political alliance between European democracies. (One of the founders of the European Union once joked that it should erect a statue of Joseph Stalin, without whose menace the Union might never have been created.) But elsewhere these conditions are lacking. The three nations that formed NAFTA would find it very difficult to cede control over tariffs to any supranational body; if nothing else, it would be hard to devise any arrangement that would give due weight to U.S. interests without effectively allowing the United States to dictate

trade policy to Canada and Mexico. NAFTA, therefore, while it permits Mexican goods to enter the United States without tariffs and vice versa, does not require that Mexico and the United States adopt a common external tariff on goods they import from other countries.

This, however, raises a different problem. Under NAFTA, a shirt made by Mexican workers can be brought into the United States freely. But suppose that the United States wants to maintain high tariffs on shirts imported from other countries, while Mexico does not impose similar tariffs. What is to prevent someone from shipping a shirt from, say, Bangladesh to Mexico, then putting it on a truck bound for Chicago?

The answer is that even though the United States and Mexico may have free trade, goods shipped from Mexico to the United States must still pass through a customs inspection. And they can enter the United States without duty only if they have documents proving that they are in fact Mexican goods, not trans-shipped imports from third countries.

But what is a Mexican shirt? If a shirt comes from Bangladesh, but Mexicans sew on the buttons, does that make it Mexican? Probably not. But if everything except the buttons were made in Mexico, it probably should be considered Mexican. The point is that administering a free trade area that is not a customs union requires not only that the countries continue to check goods at the border, but that they specify an elaborate set of "rules of origin" that determine whether a good is eligible to cross the border without paying a tariff.

As a result, free trade agreements like NAFTA impose a large burden of paperwork, which may be a significant obstacle to trade even when such trade is in principle free.

to the other without tariffs, but in which the countries set tariffs against the outside world independently. Or they can establish a **customs union**, in which the countries must agree on tariff rates. The North American Free Trade Agreement, which establishes free trade among Canada, the United States, and Mexico, creates a free trade area: There is no requirement in the agreement that, for example, Canada and Mexico have the same tariff rate on textiles from China. The European Union, on the other hand, is a full customs union. All of the

DO TRADE PREFERENCES HAVE APPEAL?

Over the last few years the European Union has slipped repeatedly into bunches of trouble over the question of trade preferences for bananas.

Most of the world's banana exports come from several small Central American nations—the original "banana republics." Several European nations have, however, traditionally bought their bananas instead from their past or present West Indian colonies in the Caribbean. To protect the island producers, France and the United Kingdom impose import quotas against the "dollar bananas" of Central America, which are typically about 40 percent cheaper than the West Indian product. Germany, however, which has never had West Indian colonies, allowed free entry to dollar bananas.

With the integration of European markets after 1992, the existing banana regime became impossible to maintain, because it was easy to import the cheaper dollar bananas into Germany and then ship them elsewhere in Europe. To prevent this outcome, the European Commission announced plans in 1993 to impose a new common European import quota against dollar bananas. Germany angrily protested the move and even denied its legality: The Germans pointed out that the Treaty of Rome, which established the European Community, contains an explicit guarantee (the "banana protocol") that Germany would be able to import bananas freely.

Why did the Germans go ape about bananas? During the years of communist rule in East Germany, bananas were a rare luxury. The sudden availability of inexpensive bananas after the fall of the Berlin Wall made them a symbol of freedom. So the German government was very unwilling to introduce a policy that would sharply increase banana prices.

In the end the Germans grudgingly went along with a new, unified system of European trade preferences on bananas. But that did not end the controversy: In 1995 the United States entered the fray, claiming that by monkeying around with the existing system of preferences the Europeans were hurting the interests not only of Central American nations but those of a powerful U.S. corporation, the Chiquita Banana Company, whose CEO has donated large sums to both Democratic and Republican politicians.

In 1997 the World Trade Organization found that Europe's banana import regime violated international trade rules. Europe then imposed a somewhat revised regime; but this halfhearted attempt to resolve the banana split proved fruitless. The dispute with the United States escalated, with the United States eventually retaliating by imposing high tariffs on a variety of European goods, including designer handbags and pecorino cheese.

Finally, in 2001 Europe and the United States agreed on a plan to phase out the banana import quotas over time. The plan created much distress and alarm in Caribbean nations, which feared dire consequences from their loss of privileged access to the European market.

---

countries must agree to charge the same tariff rate on each imported good. Each system has both advantages and disadvantages; these are discussed in the accompanying box.

Subject to the qualifications mentioned earlier in this chapter, tariff reduction is a good thing that raises economic efficiency. At first it might seem that preferential tariff reductions are also good, if not as good as reducing tariffs all around. After all, isn't half a loaf better than none?

Perhaps surprisingly, this conclusion is too optimistic. It is possible for a country to make itself worse off by joining a customs union. The reason may be illustrated by a hypothetical example, using Britain, France, and the United States. The United States is a low-cost producer of wheat ($4 per bushel), France a medium-cost producer ($6 per bushel), and Britain a high-cost producer ($8 per bushel). Both Britain and France maintain tariffs against all wheat imports. If Britain forms a customs union with France, the tariff against French, but not U.S., wheat will be abolished. Is this good or bad for Britain? To answer this, consider two cases.

First, suppose that Britain's initial tariff was high enough to exclude wheat imports from either France or the United States. For example, with a tariff of $5 per bushel it would cost $9 to import U.S. wheat and $11 to import French wheat, so British consumers would buy $8 British wheat instead. When the tariff on French wheat is eliminated, imports from France will replace British production. From Britain's point of view this is a gain, because it costs $8 to produce a bushel of wheat domestically, while Britain needs to produce only $6 worth of export goods to pay for a bushel of French wheat.

On the other hand, suppose the tariff was lower, for example, $3 per bushel, so that before joining the customs union Britain bought its wheat from the United States (at a cost to consumers of $7 per bushel) rather than producing its own wheat. When the customs union is formed, consumers will buy French wheat at $6 rather than U.S. wheat at $7. So imports of wheat from the United States will cease. However, U.S. wheat is really cheaper than French wheat; the $3 tax that British consumers must pay on U.S. wheat returns to Britain in the form of government revenue and is therefore not a net cost to the British economy. Britain will have to devote more resources to exports to pay for its wheat imports and will be worse off rather than better off.

This possibility of a loss is another example of the theory of the second best. Think of Britain as initially having two policies that distort incentives: a tariff against U.S. wheat and a tariff against French wheat. Although the tariff against French wheat may seem to distort incentives, it may help to offset the distortion of incentives resulting from the tariff against the United States, by encouraging consumption of the cheaper U.S. wheat. Thus, removing the tariff on French wheat can actually reduce welfare.

Returning to our two cases, notice that Britain gains if the formation of a customs union leads to new trade—French wheat replacing domestic production—while it loses if the trade within the customs union simply replaces trade with countries outside the union. In the analysis of preferential trading arrangements, the first case is referred to as **trade creation**, while the second is **trade diversion**. Whether a customs union is desirable or undesirable depends on whether it largely leads to trade creation or trade diversion.

CASE STUDY

Trade Diversion in South America

In 1991 four South American nations, Argentina, Brazil, Paraguay, and Uruguay, formed a free-trade area known as Mercosur. The pact had an immediate and dramatic effect on trade: within four years the value of trade among the nations tripled. Leaders in the region proudly claimed Mercosur as a major success, part of a broader package of economic reform.

But while Mercosur clearly was successful in increasing intraregional trade, the theory of preferential trading areas tells us that this need not be a good thing: if the new trade came at the expense of trade that would otherwise have taken place with the rest of the world—if the pact diverted trade instead of creating it—it could actually have reduced welfare. And sure enough, in 1996 a study prepared by the World Bank's chief trade economist concluded that despite Mercosur's success in increasing regional trade—or rather, because that success came at the expense of other trade—the net effects on the economies involved were probably negative.

In essence, the report argued that as a result of Mercosur, consumers in the member countries were being induced to buy expensively produced manufactured goods from their neighbors rather than cheaper but heavily tariffed goods from other countries. In particular, because of Mercosur, Brazil's highly protected and somewhat inefficient auto industry had in effect acquired a captive market in Argentina, displacing imports from elsewhere, just like our text example in which French wheat displaces American wheat in the British market. "These findings," concluded the initial draft of the report, "appear to constitute the most convincing, and disturbing, evidence produced thus far concerning the potential adverse effects of regional trade arrangements."

But that is not what the final, published report said. The initial draft was leaked to the press and generated a firestorm of protest from Mercosur governments, Brazil in particular. Under pressure, the World Bank first delayed publication, then eventually released a version that included a number of caveats. Still, even in its published version the report made a fairly strong case that Mercosur, if not entirely counterproductive, nonetheless has produced a considerable amount of trade diversion.

Summary

1. Although few countries practice free trade, most economists continue to hold up free trade as a desirable policy. This advocacy rests on three lines of argument. First is a formal case for the efficiency gains from free trade that is simply the cost-benefit analysis of trade policy read in reverse. Second, many economists believe that free trade produces additional gains that go beyond this formal analysis. Finally, given the difficulty of translating complex economic analysis into real policies, even those who do not see free trade as the best imaginable policy see it as a useful rule of thumb.

2. There is an intellectually respectable case for deviating from free trade. One argument that is clearly valid in principle is that countries can improve their *terms of trade* through optimal tariffs and export taxes. This argument is not too important in practice, however. Small countries cannot have much influence on their import or export prices, so they cannot use tariffs or other policies to raise their terms of trade. Large countries, on the other hand, *can* influence their terms of trade, but in imposing tariffs they run the risk of disrupting trade agreements and provoking retaliation.

3. The other argument for deviating from free trade rests on *domestic market failures*. If some domestic market, such as the labor market, fails to function properly, deviating from free trade can sometimes help reduce the consequences of this malfunctioning. The *theory of the second best* states that if one market fails to work properly it is no longer optimal for the government to abstain from intervention in other markets. A

tariff may raise welfare if there is a *marginal social benefit* to production of a good that is not captured by producer surplus measures.

4. Although market failures are probably common, the domestic market failure argument should not be applied too freely. First, it is an argument for domestic policies rather than trade policies; tariffs are always an inferior, "second-best" way to offset domestic market failure, which is always best treated at its source. Furthermore, market failure is difficult to analyze well enough to be sure of the appropriate policy recommendation.

5. In practice, trade policy is dominated by considerations of income distribution. No single way of modeling the politics of trade policy exists, but several useful ideas have been proposed. Political scientists often argue that policies are determined by competition among political parties that try to attract as many votes as possible. In the simplest case, this leads to the adoption of policies that serve the interests of the *median voter.* While useful for thinking about many issues, however, this approach seems to yield unrealistic predictions for trade policies, which typically favor the interest of small, concentrated groups over the general public. Economists and political scientists generally explain this by appealing to the problem of *collective action.* Because individuals may have little incentive to act politically on behalf of groups to which they belong, those groups which are well organized—typically small groups with a lot at stake—are often able to get policies that serve their interests at the expense of the majority.

6. If trade policy were made on a purely domestic basis, progress toward freer trade would be very difficult to achieve. In fact, however, industrial countries have achieved substantial reductions in tariffs through a process of *international negotiation.* International negotiation helps the cause of tariff reduction in two ways: It helps broaden the constituency for freer trade by giving exporters a direct stake, and it helps governments avoid the mutually disadvantageous *trade wars* that internationally uncoordinated policies could bring.

7. Although some progress was made in the 1930s toward trade liberalization via bilateral agreements, since World War II international coordination has taken place primarily via multilateral agreements under the auspices of the *General Agreement on Tariffs and Trade.* The GATT, which comprises both a bureaucracy and a set of rules of conduct, is the central institution of the international trading system. The most recent worldwide GATT agreement also sets up a new organization, the World Trade Organization (WTO), to monitor and enforce the agreement.

8. In addition to the overall reductions in tariffs that have taken place through multilateral negotiation, some groups of countries have negotiated *preferential trading agreements* under which they lower tariffs with respect to each other but not the rest of the world. Two kinds of preferential trading agreements are allowed under the GATT: *customs unions,* in which the members of the agreement set up common external tariffs, and *free trade areas,* in which they do not charge tariffs on each others' products but set their own tariff rates against the outside world. Either kind of agreement has ambiguous effects on economic welfare. If joining such an agreement leads to replacement of high-cost domestic production by imports from other members of the agreement—the case of *trade creation*—a country gains. But if joining leads to the replacement of low-cost imports from outside the zone with higher-cost goods from member nations—the case of *trade diversion*—a country loses.

Key Terms

Problems

1. "For a small country like the Philippines, a move to free trade would have huge advantages. It would let consumers and producers make their choices based on the real costs of goods, not artificial prices determined by government policy; it would allow escape from the confines of a narrow domestic market; it would open new horizons for entrepreneurship; and, most important, it would help to clean up domestic politics." Separate out and identify the arguments for free trade in this statement.

2. Which of the following are potentially valid arguments for tariffs or export subsidies, and which are not (explain your answers)?

   a. "The more oil the United States imports, the higher the price of oil will go in the next world shortage."

   b. "The growing exports of off-season fruit from Chile, which now accounts for 80 percent of the U.S. supply of such produce as winter grapes, are contributing to sharply falling prices of these former luxury goods."

   c. "U.S. farm exports don't just mean higher incomes for farmers—they mean higher income for everyone who sells goods and services to the U.S. farm sector."

   d. "Semiconductors are the crude oil to technology; if we don't produce our own chips, the flow of information that is crucial to every industry that uses microelectronics will be impaired."

   e. "The real price of timber has fallen 40 percent, and thousands of timber workers have been forced to look for other jobs."

3. A small country can import a good at a world price of 10 per unit. The domestic supply curve of the good is

$$S = 50 + 5P.$$

The demand curve is

$$D = 400 - 10P.$$

In addition, each unit of production yields a marginal social benefit of 10.

    a. Calculate the total effect on welfare of a tariff of 5 per unit levied on imports.

    b. Calculate the total effect of a production subsidy of 5 per unit.

    c. Why does the production subsidy produce a greater gain in welfare than the tariff?

    d. What would the *optimal* production subsidy be?

4. Suppose that demand and supply are exactly as described in problem 3 but there is no marginal social benefit to production. However, for political reasons the government counts a dollar's worth of gain to producers as being worth $2 of either consumer gain or government revenue. Calculate the effects *on the government's objective* of a tariff of 5 per unit.

5. "There is no point in the United States complaining about trade policies in Japan and Europe. Each country has a right to do whatever is in its own best interest. Instead of complaining about foreign trade policies, the United States should let other countries go their own way, and give up our own prejudices about free trade and follow suit." Discuss both the economics and the political economy of this viewpoint.

6. Which of the following actions would be legal under GATT, and which would not?

    a. A U.S. tariff of 20 percent against any country that exports more than twice as much to the United States as it imports in return.

    b. A subsidy to U.S. wheat exports, aimed at recapturing some of the markets lost to the European Union.

    c. A U.S. tariff on Canadian lumber exports, not matched by equivalent reductions on other tariffs.

    d. A Canadian tax on lumber *exports,* agreed to at the demand of the United States to placate U.S. lumber producers.

    e. A program of subsidized research and development in areas related to high-technology goods such as electronics and semiconductors.

    f. Special government assistance for workers who lose their jobs because of import competition.

7. As a result of political and economic liberalization in Eastern Europe, there has been widespread speculation that Eastern European nations such as Poland and Hungary may join the European Union. Discuss the potential economic *costs* of such an expansion of the European Union, from the point of view of (1) Western Europe; (2) Eastern Europe; and (3) other nations.

Further Reading

Robert E. Baldwin. *The Political Economy of U.S. Import Policy.* Cambridge: MIT Press, 1985. A basic reference on how and why trade policies are made in the United States.

Robert E. Baldwin. "Trade Policies in Developed Countries," in Ronald W. Jones and Peter B. Kenen, eds. *Handbook of International Economics.* Vol. 1. Amsterdam: North-Holland, 1984. A comprehensive survey of theory and evidence on a broad range of trade-related policies.

Jagdish Bhagwati, ed. *Import Competition and Response.* Chicago: University of Chicago Press, 1982. Analytical papers on the economic and political issues raised when imports compete with domestic production.

Jagdish Bhagwati. *Protectionism.* Cambridge: MIT Press, 1988. A cogent summary of the arguments for and against protectionism, ending with a set of proposals for strengthening free trade.

W. Max Corden. *Trade Policy and Economic Welfare.* Oxford: Clarendon Press, 1974. A careful survey of economic arguments for and against protection.

Harry Flam. "Product Markets and 1992: Full Integration, Large Gains?" *The Journal of Economic Perspectives* (Fall 1992), pp. 7–30. A careful review of the possible economic effects of "1992," the effort to integrate European markets. Notable for the way it tries to test the common belief that there will be large "dynamic" gains from removing trade barriers, even though the measured costs of those barriers appear small.

John H. Jackson. *The World Trading System.* Cambridge: MIT Press, 1989. A comprehensive view of the legal framework of international trade, with emphasis on the role of the GATT.

Dominick Salvatore, ed. *The New Protectionist Threat to World Welfare.* Amsterdam: North-Holland, 1987. A collection of essays on the causes and consequences of increasing protectionist pressure in the 1980s.

Jeffrey Schott. *The Uruguay Round: An Assessment.* Washington, D.C.: Institute for International Economics, 1994. A mercifully brief and readable survey of the issues and accomplishments of the most recent GATT round, together with a survey of much of the relevant research.

Robert M. Stern, ed. *U.S. Trade Policies in a Changing World Economy.* Cambridge: MIT Press, 1987. More essays on current trade policy issues.

APPENDIX TO CHAPTER 9

Proving that the Optimum Tariff Is Positive

A tariff always improves the terms of trade of a large country but at the same time distorts production and consumption. This appendix shows that for a sufficiently small tariff the terms of trade gain is always larger than the distortion loss. Thus there is always an optimal tariff that is positive.

To make the point, we focus on the case where all demand and supply curves are *linear,* that is, are straight lines.

Demand and Supply

We assume that Home, the importing country, has a demand curve whose equation is

$$D = a - b\tilde{P},\tag{9A-1}$$

where $\tilde{P}$ is the internal price of the good, and a supply curve whose equation is

$$Q = e + f\tilde{P}.\tag{9A-2}$$

Home's import demand is equal to the difference between domestic demand and supply,

$$D - Q = (a - e) - (b + f)\tilde{P}.\tag{9A-3}$$

Foreign's export supply is also a straight line,

$$(Q^* - D^*) = g + hP_W,\tag{9A-4}$$

where P_W is the world price. The internal price in Home will exceed the world price by the tariff,

$$\tilde{P} = P_W + t.\tag{9A-5}$$

The Tariff and Prices

A tariff drives a wedge between internal and world prices, driving the internal Home price up and the world price down (Figure 9A-1).

In world equilibrium, Home import demand equals Foreign export supply:

$$(a - e) - (b + f) \times (P_W + t) = g + hP_W.\tag{9A-6}$$

Figure 9A-1 | Effects of a Tariff on Prices

In a linear model we can calculate the exact effect of a tariff on prices.

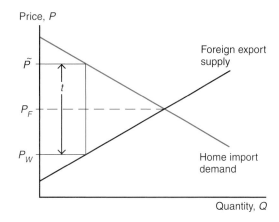

Let P_F be the world price that would prevail if there were no tariff. Then a tariff t will raise the internal price to

$$\tilde{P} = P_F + th/(b + f + h), \qquad (9A\text{-}7)$$

while lowering the world price to

$$P_W = P_F - t(b + f)/(b + f + h). \qquad (9A\text{-}8)$$

(For a small country, foreign supply is highly elastic, that is, h is very large. So for a small country a tariff will have little effect on the world price while raising the domestic price almost one-for-one.)

The Tariff and Domestic Welfare

We now use what we have learned to derive the effects of a tariff on Home's welfare (Figure 9A-2). Q^1 and D^1 represent the free trade levels of consumption and production. With a tariff the internal price rises, with the result that Q rises to Q^2 and D falls to D^2, where

$$Q^2 = Q^1 + tfh/(b + f + h) \qquad (9A\text{-}9)$$

and

$$D^2 = D^1 - tbh/(b + f + h). \qquad (9A\text{-}10)$$

The gain from a lower world price is the area of the rectangle in Figure 9A-2, the fall in the price multiplied by the level of imports after the tariff:

Figure 9A-2 | Welfare Effects of a Tariff

The net benefit of a tariff is equal to the area of the colored rectangle minus the area of the two shaded triangles.

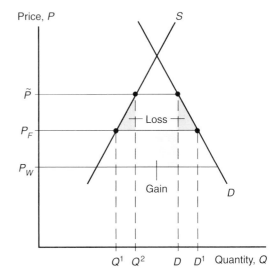

$$\text{Gain} = (D^2 - Q^2) \times t(b + f)/(b + f + h)$$

$$= t \times (D^1 - Q^1) \times (b + f)/(b + f + h) - (t)^2 \times h(b + f)^2/(b + f + h)^2. \quad \text{(9A-11)}$$

The loss from distorted consumption is the sum of the areas of the two triangles in Figure 9A-2:

$$\text{Loss} = (1/2) \times (Q^2 - Q^1) \times (\tilde{P} - P_F) + (1/2) \times (D^1 - D^2) \times (\tilde{P} - P_F)$$

$$= (t)^2 \times (b + f) \times (h)^2/2(b + f + h)^2. \quad \text{(9A-12)}$$

The net effect on welfare, therefore, is

$$\text{Gain} - \text{loss} = t \times U - (t)^2 \times V, \quad \text{(9A-13)}$$

where U and V are complicated expressions that are, however, independent of the level of the tariff and positive. That is, the net effect is the sum of a positive number times the tariff rate and a negative number times the *square* of the tariff rate.

We can now see that when the tariff is small enough, the net effect must be positive. The reason is that when we make a number smaller the square of that number gets smaller faster than the number itself. Suppose that a tariff of 20 percent turns out to produce a net loss. Then try a tariff of 10 percent. The positive term in that tariff's effect will be only half as large as with a 20 percent tariff, but the negative part will be only one-quarter as large. If the net effect is still negative, try a 5 percent tariff; this will again reduce the negative effect twice as much as the positive effect. At some sufficiently low tariff, the negative effect will have to be outweighed by the positive effect.

CHAPTER 10

Trade Policy in Developing Countries

So far we have analyzed the instruments of trade policy and its objectives without specifying the context—that is, without saying much about the country undertaking these policies. Each country has its own distinctive history and issues, but in discussing economic policy one obvious difference between countries is in their income levels. As Table 10-1 suggests, nations differ greatly in their per capita incomes. At one end of the spectrum are the developed or advanced nations, a club whose members include Western Europe, several countries largely settled by Europeans (including the United States), and Japan; these countries have per capita incomes that in many cases exceed $20,000 per year. Most of the world's population, however, live in nations that are substantially poorer. The income range among these **developing countries**[1] is itself very wide. Some of these countries, such as Singapore, are in fact on the verge of being "graduated" to advanced country status, both in terms of official statistics and in the way they think about themselves. Others, such as Bangladesh, remain desperately poor. Nonetheless, for virtually all developing countries the attempt to close the income gap with more advanced nations has been a central concern of economic policy.

Why are some countries so much poorer than others? Why have some countries that were poor a generation ago succeeded in making dramatic progress, while others have not? These are deeply disputed questions, and to try to answer them—or even to describe at length the answers that economists have proposed over the years—would take us outside the scope of this book. What we can say, however, is that changing views about economic development have had a major role in determining trade policy.

For about 30 years after World War II trade policies in many developing countries were strongly influenced by the belief that the key to economic development was creation of a strong manufacturing sector, and that the best way to create that manufacturing sector was by protecting domestic manufacturers from international competition. The first part of this chapter describes the rationale for this strategy of import-substituting industrialization, as

---

[1]*Developing country* is a term used by international organizations that has now become standard, even though some "developing" countries have had declining living standards for a decade or more. A more descriptive but less polite term is *less-developed countries* (LDCs).

Table 10-1	Gross Domestic Product Per Capita, 1999 (dollars)
United States	33,900
Japan	23,400
Germany	22,700
Singapore	27,800
South Korea	13,300
Mexico	8,500
China	3,800
India	1,800

Source: CIA, *World Factbook,* 2000.

well as the critiques of that strategy that became increasingly common after about 1970, and the emergence in the late 1980s of a new conventional wisdom that stressed the virtues of free trade.

While the main concern of economic policy in developing countries has been the low overall level of income, it is also the case that many developing countries are characterized by large differences in income *between* regions and sectors. This problem of economic dualism gives rise to some special policy issues and is the subject of the second part of this chapter.

Finally, while economists have debated the reasons for persistent large income gaps between nations, since the mid-1960s a widening group of East Asian nations has astonished the world by achieving spectacular rates of economic growth. The third part of this chapter is devoted to the interpretation of this "East Asian miracle," and its (much disputed) implications for international trade policy.

Import-Substituting Industrialization

From World War II until the 1970s many developing countries attempted to accelerate their development by limiting imports of manufactured goods to foster a manufacturing sector serving the domestic market. This strategy became popular for a number of reasons, but theoretical economic arguments for import substitution played an important role in its rise. Probably the most important of these arguments was the *infant industry argument,* which we mentioned in Chapter 6.

The Infant Industry Argument

According to the infant industry argument, developing countries have a *potential* comparative advantage in manufacturing, but new manufacturing industries in developing countries cannot initially compete with well-established manufacturing in developed countries. To allow manufacturing to get a toehold, governments should temporarily support new industries, until they have grown strong enough to meet international competition. Thus it makes sense, according to this argument, to use tariffs or import quotas as temporary measures to get industrialization started. It is a historical fact that the world's three largest market economies all began their industrialization behind trade barriers: The United States and Germany had high tariff rates on manufacturing in the nineteenth century, while Japan had extensive import controls until the 1970s.

Problems with the Infant Industry Argument. The infant industry argument seems highly plausible, and in fact it has been persuasive to many governments. Yet economists have pointed out many pitfalls in the argument, suggesting that it must be used cautiously.

First, it is not always good to try to move today into the industries that will have a comparative advantage in the future. Suppose that a country that is currently labor abundant is in the process of accumulating capital: When it accumulates enough capital, it will have a comparative advantage in capital-intensive industries. That does not mean it should try to develop these industries immediately. In the 1980s, for example, South Korea became an exporter of automobiles; it would probably not have been a good idea for South Korea to have tried to develop its auto industry in the 1960s, when capital and skilled labor were still very scarce.

Second, protecting manufacturing does no good unless the protection itself helps make industry competitive. Pakistan and India have protected their manufacturing sectors for decades and have recently begun to develop significant exports of manufactured goods. The goods they export, however, are light manufactures like textiles, not the heavy manufactures that they protected; a good case can be made that they would have developed their manufactured exports even if they had never protected manufacturing. Some economists have warned of the case of the "pseudoinfant industry," where industry is initially protected, then becomes competitive for reasons that have nothing to do with the protection. In this case infant industry protection ends up looking like a success but may actually have been a net cost to the economy.

More generally, the fact that it is costly and time-consuming to build up an industry is not an argument for government intervention unless there is some domestic market failure. If an industry is supposed to be able to earn high enough returns for capital, labor, and other factors of production to be worth developing, then why don't private investors develop the industry without government help? Sometimes it is argued that private investors take into account only the current returns in an industry and fail to take account of the future prospects, but this is not consistent with market behavior. In advanced countries at least, investors often back projects whose returns are uncertain and lie far in the future. (Consider, for example, the U.S. biotechnology industry, which attracted hundreds of millions of dollars of capital years before it made even a single commercial sale.)

Market Failure Justifications for Infant Industry Protection. To justify the infant industry argument, it is necessary to go beyond the plausible but questionable view that industries always need to be sheltered when they are new. Whether infant industry protection is justified depends on an analysis of the kind we discussed in Chapter 9. That is, the argument for protecting an industry in its early growth must be related to some particular set of market failures that prevent private markets from developing the industry as rapidly as they should. Sophisticated proponents of the infant industry argument have identified two market failures as reasons why infant industry protection may be a good idea: **imperfect capital markets** and the problem of **appropriability**.

The *imperfect capital markets justification* for infant industry protection is as follows. If a developing country does not have a set of financial institutions (such as efficient stock markets and banks) that would allow savings from traditional sectors (such as agriculture) to be used to finance investment in new sectors (such as manufacturing), then growth of new industries will be restricted by the ability of firms in these industries to earn current profits. Thus low initial profits will be an obstacle to investment even if the long-term returns on this investment are high. The first-best policy is to create a better capital market, but protection of new industries, which would raise profits and thus allow more rapid growth, can be justified as a second-best policy option.

The *appropriability argument* for infant industry protection can take many forms, but all have in common the idea that firms in a new industry generate social benefits for which they are not compensated. For example, the firms that first enter an industry may have to incur "start-up" costs of adapting technology to local circumstances or of opening new markets. If other firms are able to follow their lead without incurring these start-up costs, the pioneers will be prevented from reaping any returns from these outlays. Thus, pioneering firms may, in addition to producing physical output, create intangible benefits (such as knowledge or new markets) in which they are unable to establish property rights. In some cases the social benefits from creation of a new industry will exceed its costs, yet because of the problem of appropriability no private entrepreneurs will be willing to enter. The first-best answer is to compensate firms for their intangible contributions. When this is not possible, however, there is a second-best case for encouraging entry into a new industry by using tariffs or other trade policies.

Both the imperfect capital markets argument and the appropriability case for infant industry protection are clearly special cases of the *market failures* justification for interfering with free trade. The difference is that in this case the arguments apply specifically to new industries rather than to any industry. The general problems with the market failure approach remain, however. In practice it is difficult to evaluate which industries really warrant special treatment, and there are risks that a policy intended to promote development will end up being captured by special interests. There are many stories of infant industries that have never grown up and remain dependent on protection.

Promoting Manufacturing Through Protection

Although there are doubts about the infant industry argument, many developing countries have seen this argument as a compelling reason to provide special support for the development of manufacturing industries. In principle such support could be provided in a variety of ways. For example, countries could provide subsidies to manufacturing production in general, or they could focus their efforts on subsidies for the export of some manufactured goods in which they believe they can develop a comparative advantage. In most developing countries, however, the basic strategy for industrialization has been to develop industries oriented toward the domestic market by using trade restrictions such as tariffs and quotas to encourage the replacement of imported manufactures by domestic products. The strategy of encouraging domestic industry by limiting imports of manufactured goods is known as the strategy of **import-substituting industrialization**.

One might ask why a choice needs to be made. Why not encourage both import substitution and exports? The answer goes back to the general equilibrium analysis of tariffs in Chapter 5: A tariff that reduces imports also necessarily reduces exports. By protecting import-substituting industries, countries draw resources away from actual or potential export sectors. So a country's choice to seek to substitute for imports is also a choice to discourage export growth.

The reasons why import substitution rather than export growth has usually been chosen as an industrialization strategy are a mixture of economics and politics. First, until the 1970s many developing countries were skeptical about the possibility of exporting manufactured goods (although this skepticism also calls into question the infant industry argument for manufacturing protection). They believed that industrialization was necessarily based on a substitution of domestic industry for imports rather than on a growth of manufactured exports. Second, in many cases import-substituting industrialization policies dovetailed naturally with existing political biases. We have already noted the case of Latin American nations that were compelled to develop substitutes for imports during the 1930s because of the Great Depression and during the first half of the 1940s because of the wartime disruption of trade (Chapter 9). In these countries import substitution directly benefited powerful, established interest groups, while export promotion had no natural constituency.

It is also worth pointing out that some advocates of a policy of import substitution believed that the world economy was rigged against new entrants, that the advantages of established industrial nations were simply too great to be overcome by newly industrializing economies. Extreme proponents of this view called for a general policy of delinking developing countries from advanced nations; but even among milder advocates of protectionist development strategies the view that the international economic system systematically works against the interests of developing countries remained common until the 1980s.

The 1950s and 1960s saw the high tide of import-substituting industrialization. Developing countries typically began by protecting final stages of industry, such as food processing and automobile assembly. In the larger developing countries, domestic products almost completely replaced imported consumer goods (although the manufacturing was often carried out by foreign multinational firms). Once the possibilities for replacing consumer goods imports had been exhausted, these countries turned to protection of intermediate goods, such as automobile bodies, steel, and petrochemicals.

In most developing economies, the import-substitution drive stopped short of its logical limit: Sophisticated manufactured goods such as computers, precision machine tools, and so on continued to be imported. Nonetheless, the larger countries pursuing import-substituting industrialization reduced their imports to remarkably low levels. Usually, the smaller a country's economic size (as measured, for example, by the value of its total output) the larger will be the share of imports and exports in national income. Yet as Table 10-2 shows, India, with a domestic market less than 5 percent that of the United States, exported a smaller fraction of its output than the United States did in 1999. Brazil is the most extreme case: In 1990, exports were only 7 percent of output, a share less than that of the United States and far less than that of large industrial countries such as Germany.

As a strategy for encouraging growth of manufacturing, import-substituting industrialization has clearly worked. Latin American economies now generate almost as large a share of their output from manufacturing as advanced nations. (India generates less, but only because its poorer population continues to spend a high proportion of its income on food.) For these countries, however, the encouragement of manufacturing was not a goal in itself; it was a means to the end goal of economic development. Has import-substituting industrialization promoted economic development? Here serious doubts have appeared.

Table 10-2	Exports as a Percentage of National Income, 1999
Brazil	8
India	11
United States	12
Japan	11
Germany	27
South Korea	42
Hong Kong	132
Singapore	202

Source: World Bank, *World Development Report*. Washington, D.C.: World Bank, 2001.

Although many economists approved of import-substitution measures in the 1950s and early 1960s, since the 1960s import-substituting industrialization has come under increasingly harsh criticism. Indeed, much of the focus of economic analysts and of policymakers has shifted from trying to encourage import substitution to trying to correct the damage done by bad import-substitution policies.

CASE STUDY

The End of Import Substitution in Chile

Chile was one of the first countries to abandon the strategy of import-substituting industrialization. Until the early 1970s Chile, a relatively affluent developing country with an unusually strong democratic tradition, had followed policies similar to those of other Latin American nations. A manufacturing base was developed behind elaborate import restrictions, while the country's exports continued to consist largely of traditional products, particularly copper. In the early 1970s, however, the election of an avowedly communist government led to political turmoil and finally to a seizure of power by the country's military, which brutally and bloodily suppressed its opponents.

The new government brought with it what was at the time an unusual faith in free market policies. Import restrictions were removed, replaced with low tariff rates. Whether because of these policies or in spite of them (a drastic fall in world copper prices contributed to Chile's woes), the economy passed through a very difficult period in the mid-1970s. A recovery in the late 1970s and early 1980s was followed by a second severe slump, as Chile was caught up in the world debt crisis (see Chapter 22).

By the second half of the 1980s, however, Chilean economic performance was beginning to look quite impressive. New exports, including off-season fruits shipped to Northern Hemisphere markets in winter, increasingly high-quality wine, and manufactured goods such as furniture, had weaned the country from its previous dependence on copper. The Chilean economy began growing faster than it ever had before, outpacing other Latin American nations and nearly matching the performance of Asian countries. As a result, free-trade policies—originally very unpopular, and identified with the harsh rule of the Chilean military—began to command wide political support.

In 1990 the military withdrew from Chilean politics, although it remains at the time of writing a sort of state within the state, unwilling to take orders from civilian politicians. By this time, however, the economic policies of the past 17 years were widely credited with leading the way to Chilean prosperity. As a result, the thrust of economic policy under the freely elected government remained unchanged. And Chile's economic success story continued: In 1990–1994 the economy achieved a growth rate of 6.9 percent, far higher than that of the rest of Latin America.

Results of Favoring Manufacturing: Problems of Import-Substituting Industrialization

The attack on import-substituting industrialization starts from the fact that many countries that have pursued import substitution have not shown any signs of catching up with the advanced countries. In some cases, the development of a domestic manufacturing base seems to have led to a stagnation of per capita income instead of an economic takeoff. This is true of India, which, after 20 years of ambitious economic plans between the early 1950s and the early 1970s, found itself with per capita income only a few percent higher than before. It is also true of Argentina, once considered a wealthy country, whose economy grew at a snail's pace until it freed up trade at the end of the 1980s. Other countries, such as Mexico, have achieved economic growth but have not narrowed the gap between themselves and advanced countries. Only a few developing countries really seem to have moved dramatically upward on the income scale—and these countries either have never pursued import substitution or have moved sharply away from it.

Why didn't import-substituting industrialization work the way it was supposed to? The most important reason seems to be that the infant industry argument was not as universally valid as many people assumed. A period of protection will not create a competitive manufacturing sector if there are fundamental reasons why a country lacks a comparative advantage in manufacturing. Experience has shown that the reasons for failure to develop often run deeper than a simple lack of experience with manufacturing. Poor countries lack skilled labor, entrepreneurs, and managerial competence and have problems of social organization that make it difficult to maintain reliable supplies of everything from spare parts to electricity. These problems may not be beyond the reach of economic policy, but they cannot be solved by *trade* policy: An import quota can allow an inefficient manufacturing sector to survive, but it cannot directly make that sector more efficient. The infant industry argument is that, given the temporary shelter of tariffs or quotas, the manufacturing industries of less-developed nations will learn to be efficient. In practice, this is not always, or even usually, true.

With import substitution failing to deliver the promised benefits, attention has turned to the costs of the policies used to promote industry. On this issue, a growing body of evidence shows that the protectionist policies of many less-developed countries have badly distorted incentives. Part of the problem has been that many countries have used excessively complex

Table 10-3	Effective Protection of Manufacturing in Some Developing Countries (percent)
Mexico (1960)	26
Philippines (1965)	61
Brazil (1966)	113
Chile (1961)	182
Pakistan (1963)	271

Source: Bela Balassa. *The Structure of Protection In Developing Countries.* Baltimore: Johns Hopkins Press, 1971.

methods to promote their infant industries. That is, they have used elaborate and often overlapping import quotas, exchange controls, and domestic content rules instead of simple tariffs. It is often difficult to determine how much protection an administrative regulation is actually providing, and studies show that the degree of protection is often both higher and more variable across industries than the government intended. As Table 10-3 shows, some industries in Latin America and South Asia have been protected by regulations that are the equivalent of tariff rates of 200 percent or more. These high rates of effective protection have allowed industries to exist even when their cost of production is three or four times the price of the imports they replace. Even the most enthusiastic advocates of market failure arguments for protection find rates of effective protection that high difficult to defend.

A further cost that has received considerable attention is the tendency of import restrictions to promote production at an inefficiently small scale. The domestic markets of even the largest developing countries are only a small fraction of the size of that of the United States or the European Union. Often, the whole domestic market is not large enough to allow an efficient-scale production facility. Yet when this small market is protected, say, by an import quota, if only a single firm were to enter the market it could earn monopoly profits. The competition for these profits typically leads several firms to enter a market that does not really even have room enough for one, and production is carried out at highly inefficient scale. The answer for small countries to the problem of scale is, as noted in Chapter 6, to specialize in the production and export of a limited range of products and to import other goods. Import-substituting industrialization eliminates this option by focusing industrial production on the domestic market.

Those who criticize import-substituting industrialization also argue that it has aggravated other problems, such as income inequality and unemployment (discussed later in this chapter under Problems of the Dual Economy).

By the late 1980s, the critique of import-substituting industrialization had been widely accepted, not only by economists but by international organizations like the World Bank and even by policymakers in the developing countries themselves. Statistical evidence appeared to suggest that developing countries that followed relatively free trade policies had on average grown more rapidly than those that followed protectionist policies (although this statistical evidence has been challenged by some economists).[2] This intellectual sea change

---

[2]See Sebastian Edwards, "Openness, Trade Liberalization, and Growth in Developing Countries," *Journal of Economic Literature* (September 1993) for a survey of this evidence.

led to a considerable shift in actual policies, as many developing countries removed import quotas and lowered tariff rates.

Problems of the Dual Economy

While the trade policy of less-developed countries is partly a response to their relative backwardness as compared with advanced nations, it is also a response to uneven development *within* the country. Often a relatively modern, capital-intensive, high-wage industrial sector exists in the same country as a very poor traditional agricultural sector. The division of a single economy into two sectors that appear to be at very different levels of development is referred to as **economic dualism**, and an economy that looks like this is referred to as a **dual economy**.

Why does dualism have anything to do with trade policy? One answer is that dualism is probably a sign of markets working poorly: In an efficient economy, for example, workers would not earn hugely different wages in different sectors. Whenever markets are working badly, there may be a market failure case for deviating from free trade. The presence of economic dualism is often used to justify tariffs that protect the apparently more efficient manufacturing sector.

A second reason for linking dualism to trade policy is that trade policy may itself have a great deal to do with dualism. As import-substituting industrialization has come under attack, some economists have argued that import-substitution policies have actually helped to create the dual economy or at least aggravate some of its symptoms.

The Symptoms of Dualism

There is no precise definition of a dual economy, but in general a dual economy is one in which there is a "modern" sector (typically producing manufactured goods that are protected from import competition) that contrasts sharply with the rest of the economy in a number of ways:

1. The value of output per worker is much higher in the modern sector than in the rest of the economy. In most developing countries, the goods produced by a worker in the manufacturing sector carry a price several times that of the goods produced by an agricultural worker. Sometimes this difference runs as high as 15 to 1.

2. Accompanying the high value of output per worker is a higher wage rate. Industrial workers may earn ten times what agricultural laborers make (although their wages still seem low in comparison with North America, Western Europe, or Japan).

3. Although wages are high in the manufacturing sector, however, returns on capital are not necessarily higher. In fact, it often seems to be the case that capital earns *lower* returns in the industrial sector.

4. The high value of output per worker in the modern sector is at least partly due to a higher capital intensity of production. Manufacturing in less-developed countries typically has much higher capital intensity than agriculture (this is *not* true of advanced countries, where agriculture is quite capital-intensive). In the developing world, agricultural workers often work with primitive tools, while industrial facilities are not much different from those in advanced nations.

5. Many less-developed countries have a persistent unemployment problem. Especially in urban areas, there are large numbers of people either without jobs or with only occasional, extremely low-wage employment. These urban unemployed coexist with the relatively well-paid urban industrial workers.

CASE STUDY

Economic Dualism In India

The economy of India presents a classic case of dualism. Although it contains huge cities, India remains overwhelmingly rural, with two-thirds of the labor force still employed in agriculture. However, those agricultural workers produce less than one-fourth of the value of India's GDP. Much of the reason for this asymmetry is that over the past 50 years the government has consistently favored industry over agriculture, through both protectionism and subsidies.

If industry is favored over agriculture, why aren't more people employed in industry? The answer is that public policies have also led to a large wage differential between industrial and agricultural workers. There are minimum wage laws on the books for both industry and agriculture; but these laws go almost entirely unenforced in the countryside, and apply mainly to companies with 100 workers or more. Unions also have considerable power in large enterprises, thanks to labor laws designed to protect workers' rights. And much Indian industry is owned by the government, which typically pays higher wages than the private sector.

Economists believe that this wage differential, which encourages capital-intensive production, is a large part of the reason why employment in manufacturing has grown more slowly than total employment, despite the policies favoring industry. This slow growth means that the original hope of Indian economic planners—that growing industry would pull many people off the land—has not materialized.

In the 1990s India embarked on economic reforms that produced some deregulation of the industrial sector. The very existence of such strong dualism meant, however, that workers in the industrial sector were very wary about any moves to change the system.

Dual Labor Markets and Trade Policy

The symptoms of dualism are present in many countries and are clear signs of an economy that is not working well, especially in its labor markets. The trade policy implications of these symptoms have been a subject of great dispute among students of economic development.

In the 1950s many economists argued that wage differences between manufacturing and agriculture provided another justification, beyond the infant industry argument, for encouraging manufacturing at agriculture's expense. This argument, known as the **wage differentials argument**, can be stated in market failure terms. Suppose that, for some reason, an equivalent worker would receive a higher wage in manufacturing than he would in agriculture. Whenever a manufacturing firm decides to hire an additional worker, then, it generates a marginal social benefit for which it receives no reward, because a worker gains a wage increase when he

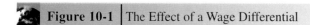

Figure 10-1 | The Effect of a Wage Differential

If manufactures must pay a higher wage than food, the economy will employ too few workers in manufactures and too many in food, resulting in an output shortfall equal to the area of triangle *ABC*.

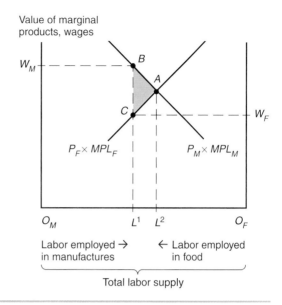

moves from agriculture to manufacturing. This is in contrast to what would happen without a wage difference, where the marginal worker would be indifferent between manufacturing and agricultural employment and there would be no marginal social benefit of hiring a worker other than the profits earned by the hiring firm.

The effects of a wage differential on the economy's allocation of labor can be illustrated using the *specific factors model* presented in Chapter 3. Assume that an economy produces only two goods, manufactures and food. Manufactures are produced using labor and capital; food is produced using labor and land. Then the allocation of resources can be represented with a diagram like Figure 10-1. The vertical axis represents wage rates and marginal products; the horizontal axis represents employment. Employment in manufactures is measured from the left origin O_M, while employment in food is measured from the right origin O_F. MPL_M is the marginal product of labor in manufactures, MPL_F the marginal product in food; P_M is the price of manufactures, P_F the price of food. Thus the two curves in the figure represent the *value* of the marginal product of an additional worker in each sector.

When there is a wage differential, workers in manufactures must be paid a higher wage than workers in food; in the figure the manufactures wage is assumed to be W_M, the food wage W_F. Employers in each sector will hire workers up to the point where the value of a worker's marginal product equals his wage; thus employment in manufactures is $O_M L^1$ (point *B*), employment in food is $L^1 O_F$ (point *C*).

Suppose the economy were now able to shift one worker from food to manufactures. Manufactures output would rise; food output would fall. The value of the additional manufactures output, however, would be the wage rate in manufactures, W_M, while the value of the reduction in food output would be the lower wage rate in food, W_F. The total value of the economy's output, then, would rise by $W_M - W_F$. The fact that the value of output can be increased by shifting labor from food to manufactures shows that the economy is allocating too little labor to manufactures. An efficient economy would set the marginal product of labor equal in both sectors, which would be achieved if $O_M L^2$ workers were employed in manufactures, $L^2 O_F$ in food (point A). (The increase in output achieved by moving to this efficient allocation of labor would be equal to the colored area ABC in the figure.)

If there is a wage differential, then, markets will misallocate labor; firms in the industrial sector will hire too few workers. A government policy that induces them to hire more can raise national welfare.

As usual, trade policy is not the first-best policy to expand manufacturing employment. Ideally, government policy should target employment directly, either by eliminating the wage differential or by subsidizing firms to hire more workers. A subsidy to manufacturing production is not as good, because it encourages capital as well as labor to move into manufacturing[3]—and capital does not receive an especially high return in manufacturing. A tariff or import quota is still worse, because it also distorts demand. Nonetheless, as a second-best alternative (or more strictly third-best), a tariff on manufactures could be justified by the wage differentials argument.

In the 1950s and 1960s this seemed to be a fairly convincing argument. In a famous paper published in 1970, however, the economists John Harris and Michael Todaro offered a devastating reinterpretation of the labor markets of less-developed countries.[4] They pointed out a link between rural-urban migration and unemployment that undermines the case for favoring manufacturing employment, even though manufacturing does offer higher wages.

Harris and Todaro began from the observation that countries with highly dualistic economies also seem to have a great deal of urban unemployment. Although one might suppose that this unemployment strengthens the case for creating more urban jobs in manufacturing, Harris and Todaro pointed out that despite this unemployment, migration from rural to urban areas continues. They concluded that rural workers were willing to come to the cities and take the risk of being unemployed in return for the chance of getting high-paying industrial jobs. The chance of getting a job depends, of course, on how many jobs are available.

According to the Harris-Todaro model, an increase in the number of manufacturing jobs will lead to a rural-urban migration so large that urban unemployment actually rises. When an additional worker is hired by the manufacturing sector, two or three more workers may leave agriculture to swell the ranks of the urban unemployed. Although the lucky worker gains, his wage gain will be largely (maybe even completely) offset by the wage losses of the newly unemployed. The supposed social benefit of additional manufacturing employment is therefore lost.

Like the infant industry argument, the wage differentials argument for protection is now in disfavor with economists. This is partly because of arguments like that of Harris and

---

[3]This cannot be seen in the specific factors model, because that model assumes that capital cannot be used in the agricultural sector. In the factor proportions model, however, the superiority of a wage subsidy to a production subsidy can be demonstrated. See Harry G. Johnson. "Optimal Trade Intervention in the Presence of Domestic Distortions," in Robert E. Baldwin et al., *Trade, Growth, and the Balance of Payments*. Chicago: Rand McNally, 1965, pp. 3–34.

[4]John R. Harris and Michael P. Todaro. "Migration, Unemployment, and Development: A Two-Sector Analysis," *American Economic Review* 60 (1970), pp. 126–142.

Todaro and partly because of the general backlash against import-substitution policies. In fact, trade policies adopted as a response to economic dualism are now often accused of actually making that dualism worse.

Trade Policy as a Cause of Economic Dualism

Trade policy has been accused both of widening the wage differential between manufacturing and agriculture and of fostering excessive capital intensity.

The reasons for huge wage differentials between agriculture and industry are not well understood. Some economists believe these differentials are a natural market response. Firms, so the argument goes, offer high wages to ensure low turnover and high work effort in countries not used to the discipline of industrial work. Other economists argue, however, that the wage differentials also reflect the monopoly power of unions whose industries are sheltered by import quotas from foreign competition. With freer trade, they argue, industrial wages would be lower and agricultural wages higher. If so, dualism—and unemployment— may be worsened by import restrictions, especially those undertaken in the name of import substitution.

The excessive capital intensity of manufacturing is partly due to relatively high wages, which give firms an incentive to substitute capital for labor. To the extent that trade restrictions are responsible for these high wages, they are to blame. Also, in some countries a controlled banking system in effect provides subsidized credit to industrial firms, making capital-labor substitution cheap. The most direct channel, however, has been through selective import control. In many cases, imports of capital goods enter without tariff or other restriction, and sometimes with de facto import subsidies. This policy further encourages the use of capital-intensive techniques.

Export-Oriented Industrialization: The East Asian Miracle

As pointed out previously, in the 1950s and 1960s it was widely believed that developing countries could create industrial bases only by substituting domestic manufactured goods for imports. From the mid-1960s onward, however, it became increasingly apparent that there was another possible path to industrialization: via *exports* of manufactured goods, primarily to advanced nations. Moreover, the countries that developed in this manner—a group that the World Bank now refers to as the **high performance Asian economies (HPAEs)**[5]—achieved spectacular economic growth, in some cases at more than 10 percent per year. The economies of the HPAEs were severely affected by the financial crisis that began in 1997; nonetheless, their achievements up to that point were remarkable.

While the achievement of the HPAEs is not in doubt, and while there is also no question that their success refutes the previous conventional wisdom that industrial development must take place via import substitution, there remain major controversies about the implications of

---

[5]For an extremely useful survey of the growth of the HPAEs, see World Bank, *The East Asian Miracle: Economic Growth and Public Policy.* Oxford: Oxford University Press, 1993.

the "East Asian miracle." In particular, different observers place very different interpretations on the role of government policies, including trade policy, in fostering economic growth. To some observers the success of Asian economies demonstrates the virtues of relatively free trade and a hands-off government policy; to others it demonstrates the effectiveness of sophisticated government intervention; and there are some economists who believe that trade and industrial policy made little difference either way.

The Facts of Asian Growth

The World Bank's definition of HPAEs contains three groups of countries, whose "miracles" began at different times. First is Japan, which began rapid economic growth soon after World War II and now has per capita income comparable to the United States and Western Europe; we will leave the discussion of Japanese experience to Chapter 11, which presents trade and industrial policy in advanced countries. In the 1960s rapid economic growth began in four smaller Asian economies, often known as the four "tigers": Hong Kong, Taiwan, South Korea, and Singapore.[6] Finally, in the late 1970s and the 1980s rapid growth began in Malaysia, Thailand, Indonesia, and, most spectacularly, in China.

Each group achieved very high growth rates. Real gross domestic product in the "tiger" economies grew at an average of 8–9 percent from the mid-1960s until the 1997 Asian crisis, compared with 2–3 percent in the United States and Western Europe. Recent growth rates in the other Asian economies have been comparable, and China has reported growth rates of more than 10 percent (although there are some questions about the accuracy of Chinese statistics).

In addition to their very high growth rates, the HPAEs have another distinguishing feature: They are very open to international trade, and have become more so over time. In fact, the rapidly growing Asian economies are much more export oriented than other developing countries, particularly in Latin America and South Asia. Table 10-2 shows exports as a share of gross domestic product for several of the HPAEs; the numbers are remarkably high, in the case of both Singapore and Hong Kong exceeding 100 percent of GDP. How is it possible for a country's exports to exceed its total output? Gross domestic product represents the value *added* by an economy, not the total sales. For example, when a clothing factory in Hong Kong assembles cloth woven elsewhere into a suit, the addition to GDP is only the difference between the cost of the cloth and the value of the suit, not the whole price of the suit. But if the suit is exported, its full price counts as part of the export total. Because modern manufacturing often consists of adding a relatively small amount of value to imported inputs, exports can easily exceed total national output.

The undisputed facts, then, are that a group of Asian economies achieved high rates of economic growth and did so via a process that involves rapid growth of exports rather than substitution of domestic production for imports. But what does their experience say about economic policy?

---

[6]The political status of two of the tigers is confusing. Hong Kong was a British colony during its takeoff, but reverted to Chinese control in 1997. The treaty returning Hong Kong to China states that the city will retain its social and economic institutions, i.e., remain a free-market economy, but many observers are skeptical. Taiwan is a de facto independent nation claimed by China, which has avoided explicitly claiming independence to avoid provoking its powerful neighbor. The World Bank tiptoes around the issue by referring pedantically to "Taiwan, China."

Trade Policy in the HPAEs

Some economists have tried to tell a simple story that attributes the success of East Asian economies to an "outward-oriented" trade policy. In this view, the high ratios of exports and imports to GDP in Asian nations are the consequences of trade policies that, while they might not correspond precisely to free trade, nonetheless leave trade much freer than in developing countries that have tried to develop through import substitution. And high growth rates are the payoff to this relatively open trade regime.

Unfortunately, the evidence for this story is not as strong as its advocates would like. In the first place, it is unclear to what extent the high trade ratios in the HPAEs can really be attributed to free trade policies. With the exception of Hong Kong, the HPAEs have in fact not had anything very close to free trade: All of them continue to have fairly substantial tariffs, import quotas, export subsidies, and other policies that manage their trade. Are the HPAEs following policies that are closer to free trade than those of other developing countries? Probably, although the complexity of the trade policies followed by developing countries in general makes comparisons difficult.[7] Table 10-4 shows data assembled by the World Bank, comparing average rates of protection (tariffs plus the tariff equivalent of import quotas) for several groups of developing countries: The data do suggest that the HPAEs have been less protectionist than other, less successful developing countries, although they have by no means followed a policy of complete free trade.

While trade policy has thus contributed to the openness of the HPAEs, however, most economists who have studied these economies believe that their high trade ratios are as much an effect as a cause of their economic success. For example, both the exports and the imports of Thailand soared in the 1990s. Why? Because the country became a favorite production site for multinational companies. These companies directly generated most of the new exports, and their imports of raw material also accounted for much of the surge in imports; the rest is accounted for by the rising income of the Thai population. So Thailand had large imports and exports because it was doing well, not the other way around.

This conclusion means that while there is a *correlation* between rapid growth in exports and rapid overall economic growth, the correlation does not necessarily demonstrate that free trade policies have been the main reason for the high growth. Instead, most economists who have studied the issue now believe that while the relatively low rates of protection in the HPAEs helped them to grow, they are only a partial explanation of the "miracle."

Table 10-4	Average Rates of Protection, 1985 (percent)
High-performance Asian economies	24
Other Asia	42
South America	46
Sub-Saharan Africa	34

Source: World Bank, *The East Asian Miracle: Economic Growth and Public Policy.* Oxford: Oxford University Press, 1993, p. 300.

---

[7]See World Bank, *The East Asian Miracle,* Chapter 6 for some attempts at international comparisons of protection.

CHINA'S BOOM

Although China, with 1.2 billion citizens, is by far the world's most populous country, until recently it played little role in the world economy. From 1949 to 1978 the country's communist regime largely sealed the country off from international trade. In any case, political factors stunted the economy's growth. Not only was private enterprise forbidden, but individual success of any kind was suspect; for example, during the so-called Cultural Revolution from 1966 to 1972 many managers, civil servants, teachers, and so on were forced from their jobs and sent to hard labor in the countryside.

In 1978, however, Chinese policy took a surprising turn. Declaring that "to grow rich is glorious," the Communist party opened the doors both to internal private enterprise and to external trade. The results were astonishing. Since 1978 the Chinese economy has reported growth rates averaging nearly 10 percent per year. By some estimates China has already become the world's second-largest economy after the United States. Although China is still far poorer than Japan, the second-biggest advanced country, it has ten times the population, and may well have more than one-tenth of Japan's per capita income.

How has China achieved this growth? Recent research is beginning to offer a provisional set of answers. Part of the explanation of Chinese growth is that it never happened, that is, that some of the growth is a statistical illusion. There is evidence that Chinese statistics understate inflation and overstate real growth; the actual growth rates have been at least 2 percentage points below the official numbers. But this still leaves a very impressive growth of 7 percent or more per year.

A second piece of the explanation is that China has had a very high savings rate (about 30 percent of GDP) and thus has rapidly increased its capital stock. This is consistent with the experience of other HPAEs, which have grown rapidly in large part simply through rapid accumulation of inputs.

Finally, researchers believe that China can be seen as an economy in the process of correcting a very serious problem of dualism. China's pre-1978 policies discouraged workers from moving to urban industrial jobs, and at the same time prevented the agricultural sector from shedding unproductive labor. As a result, the marginal product of workers in the farm sector was very low compared with that in the cities. With the liberalization of the economy, there has been a massive shift of workers out of agriculture. This has had little effect on farm output, because the farm sector had large amounts of surplus labor in any case, but has helped make the spectacular expansion of manufacturing possible.

Can China continue to grow this fast? Probably not: The farm sector is starting to run out of surplus labor, and the high investment rates will probably start to run into diminishing returns. There are also some potentially serious problems looming on the horizon, notably the continuing inefficiency of a large state-owned sector and massive corruption among government officials. Nonetheless, to the surprise of many observers, China weathered the 1997–1998 Asian financial crisis quite well. Indeed, at the beginning of the new millennium China continued to grow much faster than its neighbors.

And one should always remember that given China's huge population it does not need to be as productive as the current advanced nations to become one of the world's most important economies. Indeed, it is sobering to realize that China need only achieve one-fifth of America's per capita income to become the world's largest economy.

Industrial Policy in the HPAEs

Some commentators believe that the success of the HPAEs, far from demonstrating the effectiveness of free trade policies, actually represents a payoff to sophisticated interventionism.[8] It is in fact the case that several of the highly successful economies have pursued policies that favor particular industries over others; such *industrial policies* included not only tariffs, import restrictions, and export subsidies, but also more complex policies such as low-interest loans and government support for research and development.

The assessment of industrial policies is, in general, quite difficult; we will discuss this issue at some length in Chapter 11. Here, we just need to note that most economists studying this issue have been skeptical about the importance of such policies, for at least three reasons.

First, HPAEs have followed a wide variety of policies, ranging from detailed government direction of the economy in Singapore to virtual laissez-faire in Hong Kong. South Korea deliberately promoted the formation of very large industrial firms; Taiwan's economy remains dominated by small, family-run companies. Yet all of these economies have achieved similarly high growth rates.

Second, despite considerable publicity given to industrial policies, the actual impact on industrial structure may not have been large. The World Bank, in its study of the Asian miracle, found surprisingly little evidence that countries with explicit industrial policies have moved into the targeted industries any faster than those which have not.

Finally, there have been some notable failures of industrial policy even in otherwise highly successful economies. For example, from 1973 to 1979 South Korea followed a policy of promoting "heavy and chemical" industries, chemicals, steel, automobiles, and so on. This policy proved extremely costly, and was eventually judged to be premature and was abandoned.

While it is probably fair to say that the mainstream position is that industrial policy was not a key driving force behind Asian success, this is by no means a settled debate, and the attempt to assess the impact of industrial policies remains a major area of research.

Other Factors in Growth

In the last few years several researchers have suggested that the whole focus on trade and industrial policy in Asian growth may have been misplaced. After all, international trade and trade policy are only part of the story for any economy, even one with a high ratio of exports to national income. Other aspects of the economy may well have been more important determinants of success.

And in fact, the fast-growing Asian economies are distinctive in ways other than their high trade shares. Almost all of these economies, it turns out, have very high savings rates, which means that they are able to finance very high rates of investment. Almost all of them have also made great strides in public education. Several recent estimates suggest that the combination of high investment rates and rapidly improving educational levels explains a large

---

[8]For the most part, commentators who believe that rapid growth in the HPAEs is due to aggressive government intervention are not trained economists; indeed, the whole debate over the sources of Asian growth is tied up with a broader and quite acrimonious debate over the usefulness of economic theory in general. For an influential example both of the claim that Asian growth was fostered by interventionist policies, and of hostility to economists, see James Fallows, *Looking at the Sun: The Rise of the New East Asian Economic and Political System.* New York: Pantheon, 1994.

fraction, perhaps almost all, of the rapid growth in East Asia.[9] If this is true, the whole focus on trade and industrial policy is largely misplaced. Perhaps one can argue that the Asian economies have had trade policy that is good in the sense that it has *permitted* rapid growth, but it is greatly overstating the importance of that policy to say that it *caused* growth.

Like almost everything that concerns Asian growth, this interpretation is highly controversial. Nonetheless, it has helped shake the certainties of all sides in the ongoing debate.

One thing is, however, certain about the East Asian experience. Whatever else one may say about it, it definitely refutes some assumptions about economic development that used to be widely accepted. First, the presumption that industrialization and development must be based on an inward-looking strategy of import substitution is clearly false. On the contrary, the success stories of development have all involved an outward-looking industrialization based on exports of manufactured goods. Second, the pessimistic view that the world market is rigged against new entrants, preventing poor countries from becoming rich, has turned out to be spectacularly wrong: Never in human history have so many people seen their standard of living rise so rapidly.

Summary

1. Trade policy in less-developed countries can be analyzed using the same analytical tools used to discuss advanced countries. The particular issues characteristic of *developing countries* are, however, different. In particular, trade policy in developing countries is concerned with two objectives: promoting industrialization and coping with the uneven development of the domestic economy.

2. Government policy to promote industrialization has often been justified by the infant industry argument, which says that new industries need a temporary period of protection from competition from established competitors in other countries. The infant industry argument is valid only if it can be cast as a market failure argument for intervention. Two usual justifications are the existence of *imperfect capital markets* and the problem of *appropriability* of knowledge generated by pioneering firms.

3. Using the infant industry argument as justification, many less-developed countries have pursued policies of *import-substituting industrialization* in which domestic industries are created under the protection of tariffs or import quotas. Although these policies have succeeded in promoting manufacturing, by and large they have not delivered the expected gains in economic growth and living standards. Many economists are now harshly critical of the results of import substitution, arguing that it has fostered high-cost, inefficient production.

4. Most developing countries are characterized by economic *dualism:* A high-wage, capital-intensive industrial sector coexists with a low-wage traditional sector. Dual economies also often have a serious problem of urban unemployment.

---

[9]For a summary of this research and its implications, see P. Krugman, "The Myth of Asia's Miracle." *Foreign Affairs* (November 1994).

5. The difference in wages between the modern and traditional sectors has sometimes been used as a case for tariff protection of the industrial sector. This is the *wage differentials* case for protection. This view no longer receives much credence among economists, however. More recent analyses suggest that protection will lead to more rural-urban migration, which worsens the urban unemployment problem and may worsen the symptoms of dualism.

6. The view that economic development must take place via import substitution—and the pessimism about economic development that spread as import substituting industrialization seemed to fail—have been confounded by the rapid economic growth of a number of Asian economies. These high performance Asian economies (HPAEs) have industrialized not via import substitution but via exports of manufactured goods. They are characterized both by very high ratios of trade to national income and by extremely high growth rates. The reasons for the success of the HPAEs are highly disputed. Some observers point to the fact that, while they do not practice free trade, they do have lower rates of protection than other developing countries. Others assign a key role to the interventionist *industrial policies* pursued by some of the HPAEs. Recent research suggests, however, that the roots of success may lie largely in domestic causes, especially high savings rates and rapid improvements in education.

Key Terms

appropriability, p. 257

developing countries, p. 255

dual economy, p. 263

economic dualism, p. 263

high performance Asian economies
  (HPAEs), p. 267

imperfect capital markets, p. 257

import-substituting industrialization, p. 258

wage differentials argument, p. 264

Problems

1. "Japan's experience makes the infant industry case for protection better than any theory. In the early 1950s Japan was a poor nation that survived by exporting textiles and toys. The Japanese government protected what at first were inefficient, high-cost steel and automobile industries, and those industries came to dominate world markets." Discuss critically.

2. A country currently imports automobiles at $8000 each. Its government believes domestic producers could manufacture autos for only $6000 given time but that there would be an initial shakedown period during which autos would cost $10,000 to produce domestically.

   a. Suppose that each firm that tries to produce autos must go through the shakedown period of high costs on its own. Under what circumstances would the existence of the initial high costs justify infant industry protection?

   b. Now suppose, on the contrary, that once one firm has borne the costs of learning to produce autos at $6000 each, other firms can imitate it and do the same. Explain how this can prevent development of a domestic industry, and how infant industry protection can help.

3. Why might import-substituting industrialization be more successful in large developing countries such as Brazil than in smaller nations such as Ghana?

4. The very small economy of Cantabrigia has a total labor force of 20 workers. These workers can produce two goods, manufactures and food. In production of manufactures, the *marginal* product of labor depends on employment as follows:

Number of workers	Marginal product of last worker
1	20
2	18
3	16
4	14
5	12
6	11
7	10
8	9
9	8
10	7

In the food sector the marginal product of labor is independent of employment, and is 9. The world price of a unit of manufactures is $10, so is the world price of a unit of food.

a. Suppose there were no distortion in the labor market; find the wage rate, the allocation of labor between manufactures and food, and the output of each good.

b. Now suppose that for some reason the minimum wage in the manufactures sector is $150. Full employment, however, is maintained. Find the output of the economy in this case. How large is the cost of the distortion?

c. Finally, suppose that workers migrate from the country to the city until the wage of city workers multiplied by the probability of being employed equals the rural wage. Find the level of output and unemployment.

5. Suppose a country has the Harris-Todaro problem. That is, for some reason urban wages are much higher than rural, leading to inefficiently low manufacturing production, but at the same time there is high urban unemployment because rural workers migrate to the cities in search of high-wage jobs. What policy or combination of policies would you advocate to solve this problem?

6. "Import quotas on capital-intensive industrial goods and subsidies for the import of capital equipment were meant to create manufacturing jobs in many developing countries. Unfortunately, they have probably helped create the urban unemployment problem." Explain this remark.

Further Reading

Jagdish N. Bhagwati, ed. *The New International Economic Order.* Cambridge: MIT Press, 1977. The North-South debate reached its height in the late 1970s, with widespread demands for a "new international economic order" that would redistribute income from rich to poor nations. This volume gives a good overview of the debate.

Jagdish N. Bhagwati and T. N. Srinivasan. "Trade Policy and Development," in Rudiger Dorn-busch and Jacob A. Frenkel, eds. *International Economic Policy: Theory and Evidence*. Balti-more: Johns Hopkins University Press, 1979, pp. 1–35. Reviews research findings on the links between trade policy and economic development.

W. Max Corden. *Trade Policy and Economic Welfare*. Oxford: Clarendon Press, 1974. A clear ana-lytical discussion of the role of trade policy in economic development.

Anne O. Krueger. "Trade Policies in Developing Countries," in Ronald W. Jones and Peter B. Kenen, eds. *Handbook of International Economics*, Vol. 1. Amsterdam: North-Holland, 1984. An analytical survey of developing country trade issues.

W. Arthur Lewis. *The Theory of Economic Development*. Homewood, IL: Irwin, 1955. A good example of the upbeat view taken of trade policies for economic development during the import-substitution high tide of the 1950s and 1960s.

I. M. D. Little. *Economic Development*. New York: Basic Books, 1982. An entertaining discussion of the not always scientific process by which ideas about trade policy for developing countries have come into and out of vogue.

I. M. D. Little, Tibor Scitovsky, and Maurice Scott. *Industry and Trade in Some Developing Countries*. New York: Oxford University Press, 1970. A key work in the emergence of a more downbeat view of import substitution in the 1970s and 1980s.

Dani Rodrik. "Imperfect Competition, Scale Economies and Trade Policy in Developing Coun-tries," in Robert E. Baldwin, ed. *Trade Policy Issues and Empirical Analysis*. Chicago: Uni-versity of Chicago Press, 1988. Looks at commercial policy in developing countries from the perspective of trade models with imperfect competition.

World Bank. *The East Asian Miracle: Economic Growth and Public Policy*. Oxford: Oxford Uni-versity Press, 1993. An extremely useful survey of the growth of the HPAEs.

World Bank. *World Development Report 1991: The Challenge of Development*. Washington, D.C.: World Bank, 1991. A comprehensive survey of evidence on development policy.

Alwyn Young. "A Tale of Two Cities: Factor Accumulation and Technical Change in Hong Kong and Singapore," in O. J. Blanchard and S. Fischer, eds. *NBER Macroeconomics Annual 1992*. A fascinating comparison of the process of growth in two rapidly growing city-states.

Alwyn Young. "The Tyranny of Numbers: Confronting the Statistical Realities of the East Asian Growth Experience," *Quarterly Journal of Economics* 101 (August 1994), pp. 641–680. Makes the case that the spectacular growth of the HPAEs can be explained in terms of the rapid growth in measurable inputs.

CHAPTER 11

Controversies
in Trade Policy

As we have seen, the theory of international trade policy, like the theory of international trade itself, has a long intellectual tradition. Experienced international economists tend to have a cynical attitude toward people who come along with "new" issues in trade—the general feeling tends to be that most supposedly new concerns are simply old fallacies in new bottles.

Every once in a while, however, truly new issues do emerge. This chapter describes two controversies over international trade that arose in the 1980s and 1990s, each raising issues that previously had not been seriously analyzed by international economists.

First, in the 1980s a new set of sophisticated arguments for government intervention in trade emerged in advanced countries. These arguments focused on the "high-technology" industries that came to prominence as a result of the rise of the silicon chip. While some of the arguments were closely related to the market failure analysis in Chapter 9, the new theory of **strategic trade policy** was based on different ideas, and created a considerable stir.

Second, in the 1990s a heated dispute arose over the effects of growing international trade on workers in developing countries—and whether trade agreements should include standards for wage rates and labor conditions. This dispute often widened into a broader debate about the effects of globalization; it was a debate played out not just in academic journals but also, in some cases, in the streets.

Sophisticated Arguments for Activist Trade Policy

Nothing in the analytical framework developed in Chapters 8 and 9 rules out the desirability of government intervention in trade. That framework *does* show that activist government policy needs a specific kind of justification; namely, it must offset some preexisting domestic market failure. The problem with many arguments for activist trade policy is precisely that they do not link the case for government intervention to any particular failure of the assumptions on which the case for laissez-faire rests.

The problem with market failure arguments for intervention is how to know a market failure when you see one. Economists studying industrial countries have identified two kinds of market failure that seem to be present and relevant to the trade policies of advanced countries. One of these is the inability of firms in high-technology industries to capture the benefits of that part of their contribution to knowledge that spills over to other firms. The other is the presence of monopoly profits in highly concentrated oligopolistic industries.

Technology and Externalities

The discussion of the infant industry argument in Chapter 10 noted that there is a potential market failure arising from difficulties of appropriating knowledge. If firms in an industry generate knowledge that other firms can also use without paying for it, the industry is in effect producing some extra output—the marginal social benefit of the knowledge—that is not reflected in the incentives of firms. Where such **externalities** (benefits that accrue to parties other than the firms that produce them) can be shown to be important, there is a good case for subsidizing the industry.

At an abstract level this argument is the same for the infant industries of less-developed countries as it is for the established industries of the advanced countries. In advanced countries, however, the argument has a special edge because in those countries there are important high-technology industries in which the generation of knowledge is in many ways the central aspect of the enterprise. In high-technology industries, firms devote a great deal of their resources to improving technology, either by explicit spending on research and development or by being willing to take initial losses on new products and processes to gain experience. Such activities take place in nearly all industries, of course, so that there is no sharp line between high-tech and the rest of the economy. There are clear differences in degree, however, and it makes sense to talk of a high-technology sector in which investment in knowledge is the key part of the business.

The point for activist trade policy is that while firms can appropriate some of the benefits of their own investment in knowledge (otherwise they would not be investing!), they usually cannot appropriate them fully. Some of the benefits accrue to other firms that can imitate the ideas and techniques of the leaders. In electronics, for example, it is not uncommon for firms to "reverse engineer" their rivals' designs, taking their products apart to figure out how they work and how they were made. Because patent laws provide only weak protection for innovators, there is a reasonable presumption that under laissez-faire high-technology firms do not receive as strong an incentive to innovate as they should.

The Case for Government Support of High-Technology Industries.   Should the U.S. government subsidize high-technology industries? While there is a pretty good case for such a subsidy, we need to exercise some caution. Two questions in particular arise: first, the ability of government policy to target the right thing; second, the quantitative importance of the argument.

Although high-technology industries probably produce extra social benefits because of the knowledge they generate, much of what goes on even in a high-technology industry has nothing to do with generating knowledge. There is no reason to subsidize the employment of capital or nontechnical workers in high-technology industries; on the other hand, innovation and technological spillovers happen to some extent even in industries that are mostly not at all high-tech. A general principle is that trade and industrial policy should be targeted specifically on the activity in which the market failure occurs. Thus policy should seek to subsidize the generation of knowledge that firms cannot appropriate. A general subsidy for a set of industries in which this kind of knowledge generation is believed to go on is a pretty blunt instrument for the purpose.

Perhaps, instead, government should subsidize research and development wherever it occurs. The problem here is one of definition. How do we know when a firm is engaged in creating knowledge? A loose definition could lend itself to abuse: Who is to say whether paper clips and company cars were really supporting the development of knowledge or were placed in the research department's budget to inflate the subsidy? A strict definition, on the other hand, would risk favoring large, bureaucratic forms of research where the allocation of funds can be strictly documented over the smaller, informal organizations that are widely believed to be the key to the most original thinking.

The United States *does* in effect subsidize research and development (R&D), at least as compared with other kinds of investment. Research and development can be claimed by firms as a current expense and thus counts as an immediate deduction against the corporate profit tax. By contrast, investment in plant and equipment cannot be claimed as an immediate expense and can be written off only through gradual depreciation. This effective favorable treatment for knowledge is an accident of tax history rather than an explicit policy, but we should note it before concluding that the United States spends too little on R&D or that the high-technology sector needs further encouragement. To reach such a conclusion we would need to know how much subsidy is justified.

How Important Are Externalities?   The question of the appropriate level of subsidy for high technology depends on the answer to a difficult empirical problem: How important, quantitatively, is the technological spillover argument for targeting high-technology industries? Is the optimal subsidy 10, 20, or 100 percent? The honest answer is that no one has a good idea. It is in the nature of externalities, benefits that do not carry a market price, that they are hard to measure.

Further, even if the externalities generated by high-technology industries could be shown to be large, there may be only a limited incentive for any one country to support these industries. The reason is that many of the benefits of knowledge created in one country may in fact accrue to firms in other countries. Thus if, say, a Belgian firm develops a new technique for making steel, most of the firms that can imitate this technique will be in other European countries, the United States, and Japan rather than in Belgium. A world government might find it worthwhile to subsidize this innovation; the Belgian government might not. Such problems of appropriability at the level of the *nation* (as opposed to the firm) are less severe but still important even for a nation as large as the United States.

Despite the criticism, the technological spillover argument is probably the best case one can make intellectually for an active industrial policy. In contrast to many simplistic criteria for choosing "desirable" industries, which can be strongly rejected, the case for or against targeting "knowledge-intensive" industries is a judgment call.

Imperfect Competition and Strategic Trade Policy

During the 1980s a new argument for industrial targeting received substantial theoretical attention. Originally proposed by the economists Barbara Spencer and James Brander of the University of British Columbia, this argument locates the market failure that justifies government intervention in the lack of perfect competition. In some industries, they point out, there are only a few firms in effective competition. Because of the small number of firms, the assumptions of perfect competition do not apply. In particular, there will typically be **excess returns**; that is, firms will make profits above what equally risky investments elsewhere in the economy can earn. There will be an international competition over who gets these profits.

Spencer and Brander noticed that, in this case, it is possible in principle for a government to alter the rules of the game to shift these excess returns from foreign to domestic firms. In the simplest case, a subsidy to domestic firms, by deterring investment and production by foreign competitors, can raise the profits of domestic firms by more than the amount of the subsidy. Setting aside the effects on consumers—for example, when the firms are selling only in foreign markets—this capture of profits from foreign competitors would mean the subsidy raises national income at other countries' expense.

The Brander-Spencer Analysis: An Example. The **Brander-Spencer analysis** can be illustrated with a simple example in which there are only two firms competing, each from a different country. Bearing in mind that any resemblance to actual events may be coincidental, let's call the firms Boeing and Airbus, and the countries the United States and Europe. Suppose there is a new product, 150-seat aircraft, that both firms are capable of making. For simplicity, assume each firm can make only a yes/no decision: either to produce 150-seat aircraft or not.

Table 11-1 illustrates how the profits earned by the two firms might depend on their decisions. (The setup is similar to the one we used to examine the interaction of different countries' trade policies in Chapter 9.) Each row corresponds to a particular decision by Boeing, each column to a decision by Airbus. In each box are two entries: The entry on the lower left represents the profits of Boeing, while that on the upper right represents the profits of Airbus.

As set up, the table reflects the following assumption: Either firm alone could earn profits making 150-seat aircraft, but if both firms try to produce them, both will make losses. Which firm will actually get the profits? This depends on who gets there first. Suppose Boeing is able to get a small head start and commits itself to produce 150-seat aircraft before Airbus can get going. Airbus will find that it has no incentive to enter. The outcome will be in the upper right of the table, with Boeing earning profits.

Now comes the Brander-Spencer point: The European government can reverse this situation. Suppose the European government commits itself to pay its firm a subsidy of 25 if it enters. The result will be to change the table of payoffs to that represented in Table 11-2. It is now profitable for Airbus to produce 150-seat aircraft whatever Boeing does.

Table 11-1 | Two-Firm Competition

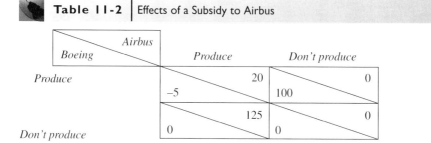

Table 11-2 | Effects of a Subsidy to Airbus

Boeing \ Airbus	Produce		Don't produce	
Produce		20		0
	−5		100	
Don't produce		125		0
	0		0	

Let's work through the implications of this shift. Boeing now knows that whatever it does, it will have to compete with Airbus and will therefore lose money if it chooses to produce. So now it is Boeing that will be deterred from entering. In effect, the government subsidy has removed the advantage of a head start that we assumed was Boeing's and has conferred it on Airbus instead.

The end result is that the equilibrium shifts from the upper right of Table 11-1 to the lower left of Table 11-2. Airbus ends up with profits of 125 instead of 0, profits that arise because of a government subsidy of only 25. That is, the subsidy raises profits by more than the amount of the subsidy itself, because of its deterrent effect on foreign competition. The subsidy has this effect because it creates an advantage for Airbus comparable with the *strategic* advantage it would have had if it, not Boeing, had had a head start in the industry.

Problems with the Brander-Spencer Analysis.   This hypothetical example might seem to indicate that this strategic trade policy argument provides a compelling case for government activism. A subsidy by the European government sharply raises profits of a European firm at the expense of its foreign rivals. Leaving aside the interest of consumers, this seems clearly to raise European welfare (and reduce U.S. welfare). Shouldn't the U.S. government put this argument into practice?

In fact, this strategic justification for trade policy, while it has attracted much interest, has also received much criticism. Critics argue that to make practical use of the theory would require more information than is likely to be available, that such policies would risk foreign retaliation, and that in any case the domestic politics of trade and industrial policy would prevent use of such subtle analytical tools.

The problem of insufficient information has two aspects. The first is that even when looking at an industry in isolation, it may be difficult to fill in the entries in a table like Table 11-1 with any confidence. And if the government gets it wrong, a subsidy policy may turn out to be a costly misjudgment. To see this, suppose that instead of Table 11-1 the reality is represented by the seemingly similar payoffs in Table 11-3. The numbers are not much different, but the difference is crucial. In Table 11-3, Boeing is assumed to have some underlying advantage—maybe a better technology—so that even if Airbus enters, Boeing will still find it profitable to produce. Airbus, however, cannot produce profitably if Boeing enters.

In the absence of a subsidy, the outcome in Table 11-3 will be in the upper right corner; Boeing produces and Airbus does not. Now suppose that, as in the previous case, the European government provides a subsidy of 25, which is sufficient to induce Airbus to produce. The new table of payoffs is illustrated as Table 11-4. The result is that both firms

Table 11-3 | Two-Firm Competition: An Alternative Case

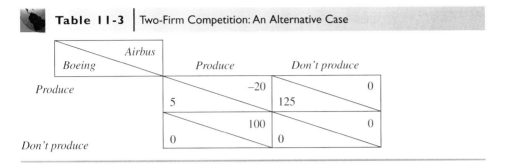

Boeing \ Airbus	Produce	Don't produce
Produce	Airbus −20 / Boeing 5	Airbus 0 / Boeing 125
Don't produce	Airbus 100 / Boeing 0	Airbus 0 / Boeing 0

Table 11-4 | Effects of a Subsidy to Airbus

Boeing \ Airbus	Produce	Don't produce
Produce	Airbus 5 / Boeing 5	Airbus 0 / Boeing 125
Don't produce	Airbus 125 / Boeing 0	Airbus 0 / Boeing 0

produce: The outcome is in the upper left. In this case Airbus, which receives a subsidy of 25, earns profits of only 5. That is, we have reversed the result above, in which a subsidy raised profits by more than the amount of the subsidy. The reason for the difference in outcome is that this time the subsidy has failed to act as a deterrent to Boeing.

Initially the two cases look very similar, yet in one case a subsidy looks like a good idea, while in the other it looks like a terrible idea. It seems the desirability of strategic trade policies depends on an exact reading of the situation. This leads some economists to ask whether we are ever likely to have enough information to use the theory effectively.

The information requirement is complicated by the fact that we cannot consider industries in isolation. If one industry is subsidized, it will draw resources from other industries and lead to increases in their costs. Thus, even a policy that succeeds in giving U.S. firms a strategic advantage in one industry will tend to cause strategic disadvantage elsewhere. To ask whether the policy is justified, the U.S. government needs to weigh these offsetting effects. Even if the government has a precise understanding of one industry, this is not enough; it needs an equally precise understanding of those industries with which that industry competes for resources.

If a proposed strategic trade policy can overcome these criticisms, it still faces the problem of foreign retaliation, essentially the same problem faced when considering the use of a tariff to improve the terms of trade (Chapter 9). Strategic policies are **beggar-thy-neighbor policies** that increase our welfare at other countries' expense. These policies therefore risk a trade war that leaves everyone worse off. Few economists would advocate that the United States be the initiator of such policies. Instead, the most that is usually argued for is that the United States itself be prepared to retaliate when other countries appear to be using strategic policies aggressively.

Finally, can theories like this ever be used in a political context? We discussed this issue in Chapter 9, where the reasons for skepticism were placed in the context of a political skeptic's case for free trade.

CASE STUDY

When the Chips Were Up

During the years when arguments about the effectiveness of strategic trade policy were at their height, advocates of a more interventionist trade policy on the part of the United States often claimed that Japan had prospered by deliberately promoting key industries. By the early 1990s, one example in particular—that of semiconductor chips—had become Exhibit A in the case that promoting key industries "works." Indeed, when author James Fallows published a series of articles in 1994 attacking free-trade ideology and alleging the superiority of Japanese-style interventionism, he began with a piece titled "The parable of the chips." By the end of the 1990s, however, the example of semiconductors had come to seem an object lesson in the pitfalls of activist trade policy.

A semiconductor chip is a small piece of silicon on which complex circuits have been etched. The industry began in the United States in 1971 when the U.S. firm Intel introduced the first microprocessor, the brains of a computer on a chip. Since then the industry has experienced rapid yet peculiarly predictable technological change: roughly every 18 months the number of circuits that can be etched on a chip doubles, a rule known as Moore's Law. This progress underlies much of the information technology revolution of the last three decades.

Japan broke into the semiconductor market in the late 1970s. The industry was definitely targeted by the Japanese government, which supported a research effort that helped build domestic technological capacity. The sums involved in this subsidy, however, were fairly small. The main component of Japan's activist trade policy, according to U.S. critics, was tacit protectionism. Although Japan had few formal tariffs or other barriers to imports, U.S. firms found that once Japan was able to manufacture a given type of semiconductor chip, few U.S. products were sold there. Critics alleged that there was a tacit understanding by Japanese firms in such industries as consumer electronics, in which Japan was already a leading producer, that they should buy domestic semiconductors, even if the price was higher or the quality lower than for competing U.S. products. Was this assertion true? The facts of the case are in dispute to this day.

Observers also alleged that the protected Japanese market—if that was what it was—indirectly promoted Japan's ability to export semiconductors. The argument went like this: Semiconductor production is characterized by a steep learning curve (recall the discussion of dynamic scale economies in Chapter 6). Guaranteed a large domestic market, Japanese semiconductor producers were certain that they would be able to work their way down the learning curve, which meant that they were willing to invest in new plants that could also produce for export.

It remains unclear to what extent these policies led to Japan's success in taking a large share of the semiconductor market. Some features of the Japanese industrial system may have given the country a "natural" comparative advantage in semiconductor production, where quality control is a crucial concern. During the 1970s and 1980s Japanese factories developed a new approach to manufacturing based on, among other things, setting acceptable levels of defects much lower than those that had been standard in the United States.

In any case, by the mid 1980s Japan had surpassed the United States in sales of one type of semiconductor, which was widely regarded as crucial to industry success: random access memories, or RAMs. The argument that RAM production was the key to dominating the whole semiconductor industry rested on the belief that it would yield both strong technological externalities and excess returns. RAMs were the largest-volume form of semiconductors; industry experts asserted that the know-how acquired in RAM production was essential to a nation's ability to keep up with advancing technology in other semiconductors, such as microprocessors. So it was widely predicted that Japan's dominance in RAMs would soon translate into dominance in the production of semiconductors generally—and that this supremacy, in turn, would give Japan an advantage in the production of many other goods that used semiconductors.

It was also widely believed that although the manufacture of RAMs had not been a highly profitable business before 1990, it would eventually become an industry characterized by excess returns. The reason was that the number of firms producing RAMs had steadily fallen: in each successive generation of chips, some producers had exited the sector, with no new entrants. Eventually, many observers thought, there would be only two or three highly profitable RAM producers left.

During the decade of the 1990s, however, both justifications for targeting RAMs—technological externalities and excess returns—apparently failed to materialize. On one side, Japan's lead in RAMs ultimately did not translate into an advantage in other types of semiconductor: for example, American firms retained a secure lead in microprocessors. On the other side, instead of continuing to shrink, the number of RAM producers began to rise again, with the main new entrants from South Korea and other newly industrializing economies. By the end of the 1990s, RAM production was regarded as a "commodity" business: many people could make RAMs, and there was nothing especially strategic about the sector.

The important lesson seemed to be how hard it is to select industries to promote. The semiconductor industry appeared, on its face, to have all the attributes of a sector suitable for activist trade policy. But in the end it yielded neither strong externalities nor excess returns.

Globalization and Low-Wage Labor

It's a good bet that most of the clothing you are wearing as you read this came from a developing country far poorer than the United States. The rise of manufactured exports from developing countries is one of the major shifts in the world economy over the last generation; even a desperately poor nation like Bangladesh, with a per capita GDP less than 5 percent than that of the United States, now relies more on exports of manufactured goods than on exports of traditional agricultural or mineral products. (A government official in a developing country remarked to one of the authors, "We are not a banana republic—we are a pajama republic.")

It should come as no surprise that the workers who produce manufactured goods for export in developing countries are paid very little by advanced-country standards—often less than $1 per hour, sometimes less than $0.50. After all, the workers have few good alternatives in such generally poor economies. Nor should it come as any surprise that the conditions of work are also very bad in many cases.

Should low wages and poor working conditions be a cause for concern? Many people think so. In the 1990s the anti-globalization movement attracted many adherents in advanced countries, especially on college campuses. Outrage over wages and working conditions in developing-country export industries was a large part of the movement's appeal, although other concerns (discussed below) were also part of the story.

It's fair to say that most economists have viewed the anti-globalization movement as at best misguided. The standard analysis of comparative advantage suggests that trade is mutually beneficial to the countries that engage in it; it suggests, furthermore, that when labor-abundant countries export labor-intensive manufactured goods like clothing, not only should their national income rise but the distribution of income should shift in favor of labor. But is the anti-globalization movement entirely off base?

The Anti-Globalization Movement

Before 1995 most complaints about international trade by citizens of advanced countries targeted its effects on people who were also citizens of advanced countries. In the United States most critics of free trade in the 1980s focused on the alleged threat of competition from Japan; in the early 1990s there was substantial concern in both the United States and Europe over the effects of imports from low-wage countries on the wages of less-skilled workers at home.

In the second half of the 1990s, however, a rapidly growing movement—drawing considerable support from college students—began stressing the alleged harm that world trade was doing to workers in the developing countries. Activists pointed to the low wages and working conditions in Third World factories producing for Western markets. A crystallizing event was the discovery in 1996 that clothes sold in Wal-Mart, and endorsed by television personality Kathie Lee Gifford, were produced by very poorly paid workers in Honduras.

The anti-globalization movement grabbed world headlines in November 1999, when a major meeting of the World Trade Organization took place in Seattle. The purpose of the meeting was to start another trade round, following on the Uruguay Round described in Chapter 9. Thousands of activists converged on Seattle, motivated by the belief that the WTO was riding roughshod over national independence and imposing free-trade ideas that hurt workers. Despite ample warnings, the police were ill prepared, and the demonstrations brought considerable disruption to the meetings. In any case, negotiations were not going well: nations had failed to agree on an agenda in advance, and it soon became clear that there was not sufficient agreement on the direction of a new trade round to get one started.

In the end the meeting was regarded as a failure. Most experts on trade policy believe that the meeting would have failed even in the absence of the demonstrations, but the anti-globalization movement achieved at least the appearance of disrupting an important international conference.

Over the next two years, large demonstrations also rocked meetings of the International Monetary Fund and World Bank in Washington, as well as a summit meeting of major economic powers in Genoa; at the latter event Italian police killed one activist.

In a relatively short period of time, in other words, the anti-globalization movement became a highly visible presence. But what was the movement's goal—and was it right?

Trade and Wages Revisited

One strand of the opposition to globalization is familiar from the analysis in Chapter 2. Activists pointed to the very low wages earned by many workers in developing-country export industries. These critics argued that the low wages (and the associated poor working conditions) showed that, contrary to the claims of free-trade advocates, globalization was not helping workers in developing countries.

For example, some activists pointed to the example of Mexico's *maquiladoras,* factories near the U.S. border that had expanded rapidly, roughly doubling in employment, in the five years following the signing of the North American Free Trade Agreement. Wages in those factories were in some cases below $5 per day, and conditions were appalling by U.S. standards. Opponents of the free trade agreement argued that by making it easier for employers to replace high-wage workers in the United States with lower-paid workers in Mexico, the agreement had hurt labor on both sides of the border.

The standard economist's answer to this argument goes back to our analysis in Chapter 2 of misconceptions about comparative advantage. We saw that it is a common misconception that trade must involve the exploitation of workers if they earn much lower wages than their counterparts in a richer country.

Table 11-5 repeats that analysis briefly. In this case we assume that there are two countries, the United States and Mexico, and two industries, high-tech and low-tech. We also assume that labor is the only factor of production, and that U.S. labor is more productive than Mexican labor in all industries. Specifically, it takes only one hour of U.S. labor to produce a unit of output in either industry; it takes two hours of Mexican labor to produce a unit of low-tech output, and eight hours to produce a unit of high-tech output. The upper part of the table shows the real wages of workers in each country in terms of each good in the absence of trade: the real wage in each case is simply the quantity of each good that a worker could produce in one hour.

Table 11-5 | Real Wages

(A) Before trade

	High-tech goods/hour	Low-tech goods/hour
United States	1	1
Mexico	1/8	1/2

(B) After trade

	High-tech goods/hour	Low-tech goods/hour
United States	1	2
Mexico	1/4	1/2

Now suppose that trade is opened. In the equilibrium after trade, the relative wage rates of U.S. and Mexican workers would be somewhere between the relative productivity of workers in the two industries—for example, U.S. wages might be four times Mexican wages. Thus it would be cheaper to produce low-tech goods in Mexico and high-tech goods in the United States.

A critic of globalization might look at this trading equilibrium and conclude that trade works against the interest of workers. First of all, in low-tech industries highly paid jobs in the United States are replaced with lower-paid jobs in Mexico. Moreover, you could make a plausible case that the Mexican workers are underpaid: although they are half as productive in low-tech manufacturing as the U.S. workers they replace, their wage rate is only $\frac{1}{4}$ (not $\frac{1}{2}$) that of U.S. workers.

But as shown in the lower half of Table 11-5, in this example the purchasing power of wages has actually increased in both countries. U.S. workers, all of whom are now employed in high-tech, can purchase more low-tech goods than before: two units per hour of work versus one. Mexican workers, all of whom are now employed in low-tech, find that they can purchase more high-tech goods with an hour's labor than before: $\frac{1}{4}$ instead of $\frac{1}{8}$. Because of trade, the price of each country's imported good in terms of that country's wage rate has fallen.

The point of this example is not to reproduce the real situation in any exact way; it is to show that the evidence usually cited as proof that globalization hurts workers in developing countries is exactly what you would expect to see even if the world were well described by a model that says that trade actually benefits workers in both advanced and developing countries.

One might argue that this model is misleading because it assumes that labor is the only factor of production. It is true that if one turns from the Ricardian model to the factor proportions model discussed in Chapter 4, it becomes possible that trade hurts workers in the labor-scarce, high-wage country—that is, the United States in this example. But this does not help the claim that trade hurts workers in developing countries. On the contrary, the case for believing that trade is beneficial to workers in the low-wage country actually becomes stronger: Standard economic analysis says that while workers in a capital-abundant nation like the United States might be hurt by trade with a labor-abundant country like Mexico, the workers in the labor-abundant country should benefit from a shift in the distribution of income in their favor.

In the specific case of the *maquiladoras,* economists argue that while wages in the *maquiladoras* are very low compared with wages in the United States, that is inevitable because of the lack of other opportunities in Mexico, which has far lower overall productivity. And it follows that while wages and working conditions in the *maquiladoras* may appear terrible, they represent an improvement over the alternatives available in Mexico. Indeed, the rapid rise of employment in those factories indicated that workers preferred the jobs they could find there to the alternatives. (Many of the new workers in the *maquiladoras* are in fact peasants from remote and desperately poor areas of Mexico. One could say that they have moved from intense but invisible poverty to less severe but conspicuous poverty, simultaneously achieving an improvement in their lives and becoming a source of guilt for U.S. residents unaware of their former plight.)

The standard economist's argument, in other words, is that despite the low wages earned by workers in developing countries, those workers are better off than they would be if globalization had not taken place. Some activists do not accept this argument—they maintain that increased trade makes workers in both advanced and developing countries worse off. It is hard, however, to find a clear statement of the channels through which this is supposed to happen. Perhaps the most popular argument is that capital is mobile internationally, while labor is not; and that this mobility gives capitalists a bargaining advantage. As we saw in Chapter 7, however, international factor mobility is similar in its effects to international trade.

Labor Standards and Trade Negotiations

Free-trade proponents and anti-globalization activists may debate the big questions such as, is globalization good for workers or not? Narrower practical policy issues are at stake, however: whether and to what extent international trade agreements should also contain provisions aimed at improving wages and working conditions in poor countries.

The most modest proposals have come from economists who argue for a system that monitors wages and working conditions and makes the results of this monitoring available to consumers. Their argument is a version of the market failure analysis in Chapter 9. Suppose, they suggest, that consumers in advanced countries feel better about buying manufactured goods that they know were produced by decently paid workers. Then a system that allows these consumers to know, without expending large efforts on information gathering, whether the workers were indeed decently paid offers an opportunity for mutual gain. (Kimberly Ann Elliott, cited in the Further Reading list at the end of the chapter, quotes a teenager: "Look, I don't have time to be some kind of major political activist every time I go to the mall. Just tell me what kinds of shoes are okay to buy, okay?") Because consumers can choose to buy only "certified" goods, they are better off because they feel better about their purchases. Meanwhile, workers in the certified factories gain a better standard of living than they otherwise would have had.

Proponents of such a system admit that it would not have a large impact on the standard of living in developing countries. The main reason is that it would affect only the wages of workers in export factories, who are a small minority of the work force even in highly export-oriented economies. But they argue that it would do some good and little harm.

A stronger step would be including formal labor standards—that is, conditions that export industries are supposed to meet—as part of trade agreements. Such standards have considerable political support in advanced countries; indeed, President Bill Clinton spoke in favor of such standards at the disastrous Seattle meeting described above.

The economic argument in favor of labor standards in trade agreements is similar to the argument in favor of a minimum wage rate for domestic workers: While economic theory suggests that the minimum wage reduces the number of low-skill jobs available, some (though by no means all!) reasonable economists argue that such effects are small and are outweighed by the effect of the minimum wage in raising the income of the workers who remain employed.

Labor standards in trade are, however, strongly opposed by most developing countries, which believe that they would inevitably be used as a protectionist tool: politicians in advanced countries would set standards at levels that developing countries cannot meet, in effect pricing their goods out of world markets. A particular concern—in fact it was one of the concerns that led to the collapse of the talks in Seattle—is that labor standards will be used as the basis for private lawsuits against foreign companies, similar to the way anti-dumping legislation has been used by private companies to harass foreign competitors.

Environmental and Cultural Issues

Complaints against globalization go beyond labor issues. Many critics argue that globalization is bad for the environment. It is unmistakably true that environmental standards in developing-country export industries are much lower than in advanced-country industries. It is also true that in a number of cases, substantial environmental damage has been and is being done in order to provide goods to advanced-country markets. A notable example is the heavy logging of Southeast Asian forests to produce forest products for sale to Japanese and Western markets.

On the other hand, there are at least as many cases of environmental damage that has occurred in the name of "inward-looking" policies by countries reluctant to integrate with the global economy. A notable example is the destruction of many square miles of rain forest in Brazil, the consequence partly of a domestic policy that subsidizes development in the interior. This policy has nothing to do with exports, and in fact began during the years when Brazil was attempting to pursue inward-looking development.

As in the case of labor standards, there is debate over whether trade agreements should include environmental standards. On one side, proponents argue that such agreements can lead to at least modest improvements in the environment, benefitting all concerned. On the other side, opponents insist that attaching environmental standards to trade agreements will in effect shut down potential export industries in poor countries, which cannot afford to maintain anything like Western standards. (The case of the Indian shipbreaking industry, described in the Case Study on p. 289, illustrates both sides of the debate.)

An even trickier issue involves the effect of globalization on local and national cultures. It is unmistakably true that the growing integration of markets has led to a homogenization of cultures around the world. People around the world increasingly tend to wear the same clothing, eat the same food, listen to the same music, and watch the same films and TV shows.

Much but not all of this homogenization is also Americanization. For example, McDonald's is now found almost everywhere; but so is sushi. Hollywood action films dominate the global box office; but the stylized fight scenes in Hollywood blockbusters like *The Matrix* are based on the conventions of Hong Kong martial arts films.

It is hard to deny that something is lost as a result of this cultural homogenization. One can therefore make a market failure argument on behalf of policies that attempt to preserve national cultural differences, for example by limiting the number of American films that can be shown in theaters, or the fraction of TV time that can be taken up with programming from overseas.

As soon as one advances this argument, however, it becomes clear that there is another principle involved: the right of individuals in free societies to entertain themselves as they like. How would you feel if someone denied you the right to listen to the Rolling Stones or watch Jackie Chan movies, on the grounds that American cultural independence must be safeguarded?

The WTO and National Independence

One recurrent theme in the anti-globalization movement is that the drive for free trade and free flow of capital has undermined national sovereignty. In the extreme versions of this complaint, the World Trade Organization is characterized as a supranational power, able to prevent national governments from pursuing policies in their own interests. How much substance is there to this charge?

The short answer is that the WTO does not look anything like a world government; its authority is basically limited to that of requiring countries to live up to their international trade agreements. However, the small grain of truth in the view of the WTO as a supranational authority is that its mandate allows it to monitor not only the traditional instruments of trade policy—tariffs, export subsidies, and quantitative restrictions—but also domestic policies that are de facto trade policies. And since the line between legitimate domestic policies and de facto protectionism is fuzzy, there have been cases in which the WTO seems to some observers to be interfering in domestic policy.

On p. 242 we described a celebrated example, which illustrates the ambiguity of the issue. As we saw, the United States amended its Clean Air Act to require imported gasoline to be no more polluting than the average of gasoline supplied by domestic refineries. The WTO ruled that this requirement was a violation of existing trade agreements. To critics of the WTO, this ruling exemplified how the institution could frustrate an attempt by a democratically elected government to improve the environment.

As defenders of the WTO pointed out, however, the ruling was based on the fact that the United States was applying a different standard to imports and to domestic production. After all, some U.S. refineries supply gasoline that is more polluting than the average, yet are allowed to remain in operation. So the rule in effect prevented the sale of polluting gasoline from Venezuela in U.S. markets, but permitted the sale of equally polluting gasoline if it came from a domestic refinery. If the new rule had applied the same standards to domestic and foreign gasoline, it would have been acceptable to the WTO.

CASE STUDY

The Shipbreakers of Alang

In the late 1990s a controversy erupted over India's "shipbreaking" industry—an industry that disassembles worn-out ships to recover their scrap metal and other valuable components. The dispute illustrated in particularly stark form the dilemmas and moral ambiguities of the debate over globalization.

One way to look at shipbreaking is to say that it is a form of recycling. Instead of leaving a ship to rust, a shipbreaking firm extracts and reuses its components. Ultimately this salvaging means that less iron ore must be mined, less oil extracted, and so on; so one might expect shipbreaking to be good for the environment. The task itself, however, can be environmentally hazardous: everything from the residual oil in a ship's tanks to the plastic in its chairs and interior fittings, if not handled carefully, can be toxic to the local environment. Shipbreaking can also be a very dangerous activity, because large pieces of metal must be cut up, oil fumes remaining in the tanks and engine can be explosive, and so on.

At sufficient expense and with enough specialized equipment, workers in advanced countries can break up ships cleanly and without too much risk to themselves. However, the expense of such capital-intensive shipbreaking is prohibitive: it costs more than the value of the recovered materials.

But developing countries, India in particular, have discovered that shipbreaking need not be a capital-intensive industry. At Alang, on the west coast of India, is a six-mile stretch of beach.

Old ships are brought to that beach and run aground. Then men equipped with little more than blowtorches swarm over the ships, cut them into pieces, and cart the pieces away.

Although the small companies that do the work try to extract as much from the ships as they can, inevitably a considerable amount of waste material pollutes the beach and its surroundings. And although the foremen are experienced and knowledgeable, many accidents occur; there are enough willing workers that it does not pay to take expensive precautions.

In 1998 the shipbreaking industry of Alang became a target of activist groups around the world, with the environmental organization Greenpeace taking the leading role in the protests. Greenpeace focused mainly on the pollution involved; other groups targeted the hazardous working conditions. A common theme of the protests was that advanced countries should clean up their own messes, not send them to poor countries.

But others pointed out that the shipbreaking industry of Alang was in many ways exactly what a country like India needed. Local entrepreneurs had found a labor-intensive way to do something that was capital-intensive in advanced countries, thereby making the best use of their nation's most abundant resource. In so doing they had created a new industry, one that directly or indirectly supported perhaps a million people and provided India with overseas earnings it desperately needed. The workers of Alang earned very low wages and endured terrible working conditions by Western standards, but by Indian standards they were relatively well paid. And beyond economics, there was something heroic about the industry: the shipbreakers were proud of what they did, of their skill and courage.

So was the shipbreaking industry of Alang something to be condemned or praised? In their efforts to shut it down, were activists helping India, or were they depriving desperately poor people of much-needed opportunities in order to satisfy their own fastidiousness?

Summary

1. Some new arguments for government intervention in trade emerged in the 1980s and 1990s. In the 1980s the new theory of *strategic trade policy* offered reasons why countries might gain from promoting particular industries. In the 1990s a new critique of globalization emerged, focused on the effects of globalization on workers in developing countries.

2. Activist trade policy arguments rest on two ideas. One is the argument that governments should promote industries that yield *technological externalities.* The other, which represents a greater departure from standard market-failure arguments, is the *Brander-Spencer analysis,* which suggests that strategic intervention can enable nations to capture *excess returns.* These arguments are theoretically persuasive; however, many economists worry that they are too subtle and require too much information to be useful in practice.

3. With the rise of manufactured exports from developing countries, a new movement opposed to globalization has emerged. The central concern of this movement is with the low wages paid to export workers, although there are other themes as well. The response of most economists is that developing-country workers may earn low

wages by Western standards, but that trade allows them to earn more than they otherwise would.

4. An examination of cases suggests how difficult the discussion of globalization really is, especially when one tries to view it as a moral issue; it is all too easy for people to do harm when they are trying to do good. The causes most favored by activists, like labor standards, are feared by developing countries, which believe they will be used as protectionist devices.

5. Even more difficult problems arise over such issues as cultural homogenization and environmental standards.

Key Terms

beggar-thy-neighbor policies, p. 281
Brander-Spencer analysis, p. 279
excess returns, p. 279

externalities, p. 277
strategic trade policy, p. 276

Problems

1. Suppose the U.S. government were able to determine which industries will grow most rapidly over the next 20 years. Why doesn't this automatically mean that the nation should have a policy of supporting these industries' growth?

2. The U.S. Commerce Department has urged that the United States provide special support for its high-technology industries. It argues that these industries have the prospect of rapid future growth, provide inputs to many other industries, and generate technology that benefits the whole economy. Furthermore, some U.S. high-technology industries such as aircraft and microelectronics face challenges by government-supported foreign competitors. Which of these arguments might be valid reasons for the United States to have a policy targeting these industries?

3. If the United States had its way, it would demand that Japan spend more money on basic research in science and less on applied research into industrial applications. Explain why in terms of the analysis of appropriability.

4. Tables 11-1 and 11-2 presented a situation in which European governments were able to use a subsidy to achieve a strategic advantage, while Tables 11-3 and 11-4 presented a situation in which it could not. What is the crucial distinction between these two cases? That is, what is the general rule for determining when a subsidy can work?

5. "The new strategic trade policy argument demonstrates the wisdom of policies like that of South Korea, which subsidizes its exports across the board. The subsidy gives each industry the strategic advantage it needs to establish itself in world competition." Discuss.

6. Does the U.S. military budget help or hurt the strategic position of U.S. high-technology industries? Make the case for either point of view.

7. Suppose that the European Commission asked you to develop a brief on behalf of subsidizing European software development—bearing in mind that the software industry is currently dominated by U.S. firms, notably Microsoft. What arguments would you use? What are the weaknesses in those arguments?

8. France, in addition to its occasional stabs at strategic trade policy, pursues an active nationalist *cultural* policy, promoting French art, music, fashion, cuisine, and so on.

This may be primarily a matter of attempting to preserve a national identity in an increasingly homogeneous world, but some French officials also defend this policy on economic grounds. In what sense could some features of such a policy be defended as a kind of strategic trade policy?

Further Reading

James A. Brander and Barbara J. Spencer. "Export Subsidies and International Market Share Rivalry." *Journal of International Economics* 16 (1985), pp. 83–100. A basic reference on the potential role of subsidies as a tool of strategic trade policy.

Kimberly Ann Elliott. *Can Labor Standards Improve Under Globalization?* Washington: Institute for International Economics, 2001. A survey of the issues by an economist sympathetic to the cause of the activists.

Edward M. Graham. *Fighting the Wrong Enemy: Antiglobalization Activists and Multinational Corporations.* Washington: Institute for International Economics, 2001. A survey of the issues by an economist less sympathetic to the activists.

Elhanan Helpman and Paul Krugman. *Trade Policy and Market Structure.* Cambridge: MIT Press, 1989. A survey and synthesis of the literature on strategic trade policy and related topics.

William Langewiesche. "The Shipbreakers," *The Atlantic Monthly,* August 2000. A fascinating description of the shipbreaking industry of Alang and the dispute it has generated.

Laura d'Andrea Tyson. *Who's Bashing Whom? Trade Conflict in High-Technology Industries.* Washington: Institute for International Economics, 1992. A sophisticated, cautious defense of strategic trade policy. Soon after this book's publication Tyson was named as President Bill Clinton's chief economic adviser.

PART 3

Exchange Rates and Open-Economy Macroeconomics

CHAPTER 12

National Income Accounting and the Balance of Payments

Over the decade from 1991 to 2000, Japan's national product grew at an annual average rate of only 1.5 percent, while that of the United States grew by nearly 3.5 percent per year. At the same time, Japan's unemployment rate rose, reaching nearly 5 percent and overtaking that of the United States for the first time in fifty years. In 2001, however, the U.S. economy entered a recession and the entire world economy slowed. Can economic analysis help us to understand both the interdependencies among national economies as well as the reasons why their fortunes often differ?

Previous chapters have been concerned primarily with the problem of making the best use of the world's scarce productive resources at a single point in time. The branch of economics called **microeconomics** studies this problem from the perspective of individual firms and consumers. Microeconomics works "from the bottom up" to show how individual economic actors, by pursuing their own interests, collectively determine how resources are used. In our study of international microeconomics we have learned how individual production and consumption decisions produce patterns of international trade and specialization. We have seen that while free trade usually encourages efficient resource use, government intervention or market failures can cause waste even when all factors of production are fully employed.

With this chapter we shift our focus and ask: How can economic policy ensure that factors of production *are* fully employed? And what determines how an economy's capacity to produce goods and services changes over time? To answer these questions we must understand **macroeconomics**, the branch of economics that studies how economies' overall levels of employment, production, and growth are determined. Like microeconomics, macroeconomics is concerned with the effective use of scarce resources. But while microeconomics focuses on the economic decisions of individuals, macroeconomics analyzes the behavior of the economy as a whole. In our study of international macroeconomics, we will learn how the interactions of national economies influence the worldwide pattern of macroeconomic activity.

Macroeconomic analysis emphasizes four aspects of economic life that we have usually kept in the background until now to simplify our discussion of international economics:

    1. *Unemployment.* We know that in the real world workers may be unemployed and factories may be idle. Macroeconomics studies the factors that cause unemployment and the steps governments can take to prevent it. A main concern of international macroeconomics is the problem of ensuring full employment in economies open to international trade.

2. *Saving.* In earlier chapters we usually assumed that every country consumes an amount exactly equal to its income—no more and no less. In reality, though, households can put aside part of their income to provide for the future, or they can borrow temporarily to spend more than they earn. A country's saving or borrowing behavior affects domestic employment and future levels of national wealth. From the standpoint of the international economy as a whole, the world saving rate determines how quickly the world stock of productive capital can grow.

3. *Trade imbalances.* As we saw in earlier chapters, the value of a country's imports equals the value of its exports when spending equals income. This state of balanced trade is seldom attained by actual economies, however. Trade imbalances play a large role in the following chapters because they redistribute wealth among countries and are a main channel through which one country's macroeconomic policies affect its trading partners. It should be no surprise, therefore, that trade imbalances, particularly when they are large and persistent, quickly can become a source of international discord.

4. *Money and the price level.* The trade theory you have studied so far is a barter theory, one in which goods are exchanged directly for other goods on the basis of their relative prices. In practice it is more convenient to use money, a widely acceptable medium of exchange, in transactions, and to quote prices in terms of money. Because money changes hands in virtually every transaction that takes place in a modern economy, fluctuations in the supply of money or the demand for it can affect both output and employment. International macroeconomics takes into account that every country uses a currency and that a monetary change in one country (for example, a change in money supply) can have effects that spill across its borders to other countries. Stability in money price levels is an important goal of international macroeconomic policy.

This chapter takes the first step in our study of international macroeconomics by explaining the accounting concepts economists use to describe a country's level of production and its international transactions. To get a complete picture of the macroeconomic linkages among economies that engage in international trade, we have to master two related and essential tools. The first of these tools, **national income accounting**, records all the expenditures that contribute to a country's income and output. The second tool, **balance of payments accounting**, helps us keep track of both changes in a country's indebtedness to foreigners and the fortunes of its export- and import-competing industries. The balance of payments accounts also show the connection between foreign transactions and national money supplies.

The National Income Accounts

Of central concern to macroeconomic analysis is a country's **gross national product (GNP)**, the value of all final goods and services produced by its factors of production and sold on the market in a given time period. GNP, which is the basic measure of a country's output studied by macroeconomists, is calculated by adding up the market value of all expenditures on final output. GNP therefore includes the value of goods like bread sold in a supermarket and textbooks sold in a bookstore, as well as the value of services provided by supermarket checkers and baggers and by university professors. Because output cannot be produced without the aid of factor inputs, the expenditures that make up GNP are closely linked to the employment of labor, capital, and other factors of production.

To distinguish among the different types of expenditure that make up a country's GNP, government economists and statisticians who compile national income accounts divide GNP among the four possible uses for which a country's output is purchased: *consumption* (the amount consumed by private domestic residents), *investment* (the amount put aside by private firms to build new plant and equipment for future production), *government purchases* (the amount used by the government), and the *current account balance* (the amount of net exports of goods and services to foreigners). The term *national income accounts,* rather than *national output accounts,* is used to describe this fourfold classification because a country's income in fact equals its output. Thus, the national income accounts can be thought of as classifying each transaction that contributes to national income according to the type of expenditure that gives rise to it. Figure 12-1 shows how U.S. GNP was divided among its four components in 2000.[1]

Why is it useful to divide GNP into consumption, investment, government purchases, and the current account? One major reason is that we cannot hope to understand the cause of a particular recession or boom without knowing how the main categories of spending have changed. And without such an understanding, we cannot recommend a sound policy response. In addition, the national income accounts provide information essential for studying why some countries are rich—that is, have a high level of GNP relative to population size— while some are poor.

National Product and National Income

Our first task in understanding how economists analyze GNP is to explain in greater detail why the GNP a country generates over some time period must equal its **national income**, the income earned in that period by its factors of production.

The reason for this equality is that every dollar used to purchase goods or services automatically ends up in somebody's pocket. A visit to the doctor provides a simple example of how an increase in national output raises national income by the same amount. The $75 you pay the doctor represents the market value of the services he or she provides for you, so your visit raises GNP by $75. But the $75 you pay the doctor also raises his or her income. So national income rises by $75.

The principle that output and income are the same also applies to goods, even goods that are produced with the help of many factors of production. Consider the example of an economics textbook. When you purchase a new book from the publisher, the value of your purchase enters GNP. But your payment enters the income of the productive factors that have cooperated in producing the book, because the publisher must pay for their services with the proceeds of sales. First, there are the authors, editors, artists, and typesetters who provide

---

[1]Our definition of the current account is not strictly accurate when a country is a net donor or recipient of foreign gifts. This possibility, along with some others, also complicates our identification of GNP with national income. We describe later in this chapter how the definitions of national income and the current account must be changed in such cases.

Figure 12-1 | U.S. GNP and Its Components

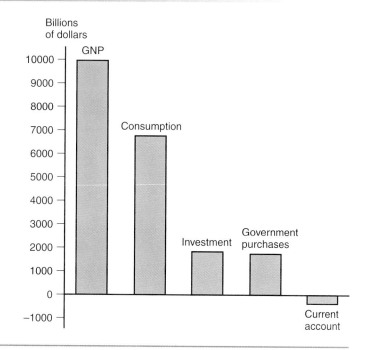

America's $9.9 trillion 2000 gross national product can be broken down into the four components shown.

Source: *Economic Indicators,* U.S. Government Printing Office, April 2001.

the labor inputs necessary for the book's production. Second, there are the publishing company's shareholders, who receive dividends for having financed acquisition of the capital used in production. Finally, there are the suppliers of paper and ink, who provide the intermediate materials used in producing the book.

The paper and ink purchased by the publishing house to produce the book are *not* counted separately in GNP because their contribution to the value of national output is already included in the book's price. It is to avoid such double counting that we allow only the sale of *final* goods and services to enter into the definition of GNP. Sales of intermediate goods, such as paper and ink purchased by a publisher, are not counted. Notice also that the sale of a used textbook does not enter GNP. Our definition counts only final goods and services that are *produced* and a used textbook does not qualify: It was counted in GNP at the time it was first sold. Equivalently, the sale of a used textbook does not generate income for any factor of production.

Capital Depreciation, International Transfers, and Indirect Business Taxes

Because we have defined GNP and national income so that they are necessarily equal, their equality is really an identity. Some adjustments to the definition of GNP must be made, however, before the identification of GNP and national income is entirely correct in practice.

1. GNP does not take into account the economic loss due to the tendency of machinery and structures to wear out as they are used. This loss, called *depreciation,* reduces the income of capital owners. To calculate national income over a given period, we must therefore subtract from GNP the depreciation of capital over the period. GNP less depreciation is called *net national product* (NNP).

2. A country's income may include gifts from residents of foreign countries, called *unilateral transfers.* Examples of unilateral transfers of income are pension payments to retired citizens living abroad, reparation payments, and foreign aid such as relief funds donated to drought-stricken nations. For the United States in 2000, the balance of such payments amounted to around $53.2 billion, representing a 0.53 percent of GNP net transfer to foreigners. Net unilateral transfers are part of a country's income but are not part of its product, and they must be added to NNP in calculations of national income.

3. National income depends on the prices producers *receive* for their goods, GNP on the prices purchasers *pay.* These two sets of prices need not, however, be identical. For example, sales taxes make buyers pay more than sellers receive, leading GNP to over-estimate national income. The amount of this tax wedge, called *indirect business taxes,* must therefore be subtracted from GNP in calculating true national income.

National income equals GNP *less* depreciation, *plus* net unilateral transfers, *less* indirect business taxes. The difference between GNP and national income is by no means an insignificant amount, but macroeconomics has little to say about it, and it is of little importance for macroeconomic analysis. Therefore, for the purposes of this text we usually use the terms *GNP* and *national income* interchangeably, emphasizing the distinction between the two only when it is essential.

Gross Domestic Product

Most countries other than the United States have long reported **gross domestic product (GDP)** rather than GNP as their primary measure of national economic activity. In 1991 the United States began to follow this practice as well. GDP is supposed to measure the volume of production within a country's borders. GNP equals GDP *plus* net receipts of factor income from the rest of the world. These net receipts are primarily the income domestic residents earn on wealth they hold in other countries less the payments domestic residents make to foreign owners of wealth located at home.

GDP does not correct, as GNP does, for the portion of countries' production carried out using services provided by foreign-owned capital. Consider an example. The earnings of a Spanish factory with British owners are counted in Spain's GDP but are part of Britain's GNP. The services British capital provides in Spain are a service export from Britain, therefore they are added to British GDP in calculating British GNP. At the same time, to figure Spain's GNP we must subtract from its GDP the corresponding service import from Britain.

As a practical matter, movements in GDP and GNP usually do not differ greatly. We will focus on GNP in this book, however, because GNP tracks national income more closely than GDP, and national welfare depends more directly on national income than on domestic product.

National Income Accounting for an Open Economy

In this section we extend to the case of an open economy the closed-economy national income accounting framework you may have seen in earlier economics courses. We begin with a discussion of the national income accounts because they highlight the key role of international trade in open-economy macroeconomic theory. Since a closed economy's residents cannot purchase foreign output or sell their own to foreigners, all of national income must be generated by domestic consumption, investment, or government purchases. In an economy open to international trade, however, the closed-economy version of national income accounting must be modified because some domestic output is exported to foreigners while some domestic income is spent on imported foreign products.

The main lesson of this section concerns the relation among national saving, investment, and trade imbalances. We will see that in open economies, saving and investment are not necessarily equal as they are in a closed economy. This is because countries can save by exporting more than they import, and they can *dissave*—that is, reduce their wealth—by exporting less than they import.

Consumption

The portion of GNP purchased by the private sector to fulfill current wants is called **consumption**. Purchases of movie tickets, food, dental work, and washing machines all fall into this category. Consumption expenditure is the largest component of GNP in most economies. In the United States, for example, the fraction of GNP devoted to consumption has fluctuated in a range of about 62 to 69 percent since the Korean War.

Investment

The part of output used by private firms to produce future output is called **investment**. Investment spending may be viewed as the portion of GNP used to increase the nation's stock of capital. Steel and bricks used to build a factory are part of investment spending, as are services provided by a technician who helps build business computers. Firms' purchases of inventories are also counted in investment spending because carrying inventories is just another way for firms to transfer output from current use to future use. Investment is usually more variable than consumption. In the United States, (gross) investment has fluctuated between 12 and 19 percent of GNP in recent years. While we often use the word *investment* to describe individual households' purchases of stocks, bonds, or real estate, you should be careful not to confuse this everyday meaning of the word with the economic definition of investment as a component of GNP. When you buy a share of Microsoft stock, you are buying neither a good nor a service, so your purchase does not show up in GNP.

Government Purchases

Any goods and services purchased by federal, state, or local governments are classified as **government purchases** in the national income accounts. Included in government purchases are federal military spending, government support of cancer research, and government funds spent on highway repair and education. Government transfer payments like social security and unemployment benefits do not require the recipient to give the government any goods or services in return. Thus, transfer payments are not included in government purchases.

Government purchases currently take up about 18 percent of U.S. GNP, and this share has not changed much since the late 1950s. (The corresponding figure for 1959, for example, was around 20 percent.) In 1929, however, government purchases accounted for only 8.5 percent of U.S. GNP.

The National Income Identity for an Open Economy

In a closed economy any final good or service that is not purchased by households or the government must be used by firms to produce new plant, equipment, and inventories. If consumption goods are not sold immediately to consumers or the government, firms (perhaps reluctantly) add them to existing inventories, thus increasing investment.

This information leads to a fundamental identity for closed economies. Let Y stand for GNP, C for consumption, I for investment, and G for government purchases. Since all of a closed economy's output must be consumed, invested, or bought by the government, we can write

$$Y = C + I + G.$$

We derived the national income identity for a closed economy by assuming that all output was consumed or invested by the country's citizens or purchased by its government. When foreign trade is possible, however, some output is purchased by foreigners while some domestic spending goes to purchase goods and services produced abroad. The GNP identity for open economies shows how the national income a country earns by selling its goods and services is divided between sales to domestic residents and sales to foreign residents.

Since residents of an open economy may spend some of their income on imports, that is, goods and services purchased from abroad, only the portion of their spending that is not devoted to imports is part of domestic GNP. The value of imports, denoted by IM, must be subtracted from total domestic spending, $C + I + G$, to find the portion of domestic spending that generates domestic national income. Imports from abroad add to foreign countries' GNPs but do not add directly to domestic GNP.

Similarly, the goods and services sold to foreigners make up a country's exports. Exports, denoted by EX, are the amount foreign residents' purchases add to the national income of the domestic economy.

The national income of an open economy is therefore the sum of domestic and foreign expenditure on the goods and services produced by domestic factors of production. Thus, the national income identity for an open economy is

$$Y = C + I + G + EX - IM. \qquad (12\text{-}1)$$

An Imaginary Open Economy

To make identity (12-1) concrete, let's consider an imaginary closed economy, Agraria, whose only output is wheat. Each citizen of Agraria is a consumer of wheat, but each is also a farmer and therefore can be viewed as a firm. Farmers invest by putting aside a portion of

| **Table 12-1** | National Income Accounts for Agraria, an Open Economy (bushels of wheat) |

GNP (total output)	=	Consumption	+	Investment	+	Government purchases	+	Exports	−	Imports
100	=	75[a]	+	25	+	10	+	10	−	20[b]

[a]55 bushels of wheat + (0.5 bushel per gallon) × (40 gallons of milk).
[b]0.5 bushel per gallon × 40 gallons of milk.

each year's crop as seed for the following year's planting. There is also a government that appropriates part of the crop to feed the Agrarian army. Agraria's total annual crop is 100 bushels of wheat. Agraria can import milk from the rest of the world in exchange for exports of wheat. We cannot draw up the Agrarian national income accounts without knowing the price of milk in terms of wheat because all the components in the GNP identity (12-1) must be measured in the same units. If we assume the price of milk is 0.5 bushel of wheat per gallon, and that at this price Agrarians want to consume 40 gallons of milk, then Agraria's imports are equal in value to 20 bushels of wheat.

In Table 12-1 we see that Agraria's total output is 100 bushels of wheat. Consumption is divided between wheat and milk, with 55 bushels of wheat and 40 gallons of milk (equal in value to 20 bushels of wheat) consumed over the year. The value of consumption in terms of wheat is 55 + (0.5 × 40) = 55 + 20 = 75.

The 100 bushels of wheat produced by Agraria are used as follows: 55 are consumed by domestic residents, 25 are invested, 10 are purchased by the government, and 10 are exported abroad. National income ($Y = 100$) equals domestic spending ($C + I + G = 110$) plus exports ($EX = 10$) less imports ($IM = 20$).

The Current Account and Foreign Indebtedness

In reality a country's foreign trade is exactly balanced only rarely. The difference between exports of goods and services and imports of goods and services is known as the **current account balance** (or current account). If we denote the current account by *CA*, we can express this definition in symbols as

$$CA = EX - IM.$$

When a country's imports exceed its exports, we say the country has a *current account deficit*. A country has a *current account surplus* when its exports exceed its imports.[2]

---

[2]In addition to net exports of goods and services, the current account balance includes net unilateral transfers of income, which we discussed briefly above. Following our earlier assumption, we continue to ignore such transfers for now to simplify the discussion. We will see how transfers of current income enter the current account later in this chapter when we analyze the U.S. balance of payments in detail.

The GNP identity, equation (12-1), shows one reason why the current account is important in international macroeconomics. Since the right-hand side of (12-1) is total expenditure on domestic output, changes in the current account can be associated with changes in output and, thus, employment.

The current account is also important because it measures the size and direction of international borrowing. When a country imports more than it exports, it is buying more from foreigners than it sells to them and must somehow finance this current account deficit. How does it pay for additional imports once it has spent its export earnings? Since the country as a whole can import more than it exports only if it can borrow the difference from foreigners, a country with a current account deficit must be increasing its net foreign debts by the amount of the deficit.[3]

Similarly, a country with a current account surplus is earning more from its exports than it spends on imports. This country finances the current account deficit of its trading partners by lending to them. The foreign wealth of a surplus country rises because foreigners pay for any imports not covered by their exports by issuing IOUs that they will eventually have to redeem. The preceding reasoning shows that *a country's current account balance equals the change in its net foreign wealth.*

We have defined the current account as the difference between exports and imports. Equation (12-1) says that the current account is also equal to the difference between national income and domestic residents' spending $C + I + G$:

$$Y - (C + I + G) = CA.$$

It is only by borrowing abroad that a country can have a current account deficit and use more output than it is currently producing. If it uses less than its output, it has a current account surplus and is lending the surplus to foreigners.[4] International borrowing and lending were identified with *intertemporal trade* in Chapter 7. A country with a current account deficit is importing present consumption and exporting future consumption. A country with a current account surplus is exporting present consumption and importing future consumption.

As an example, consider again the imaginary economy of Agraria described in Table 12-1. The total value of its consumption, investment, and government purchases, at 110 bushels of wheat, is greater than its output of 100 bushels. This inequality would be impossible in a closed economy; it is possible in this open economy because Agraria now imports 40 gallons of milk, worth 20 bushels of wheat, but exports only 10 bushels of wheat. The current account deficit of 10 bushels is the value of Agraria's borrowing from foreigners, which the country will have to repay in the future.

---

[3]Alternatively, a country could finance a current account deficit by using previously accumulated foreign wealth to pay for imports. This country would be running down its net foreign wealth, which is the same as running up its net foreign debts.

   Our discussion here is ignoring the possibility that a country receives *gifts* of foreign assets (or gives such gifts), as when one country agrees to forgive another's debts. As we will discuss below, such asset transfers (unlike transfers of current income) are not part of the current account, but they nonetheless do affect net foreign wealth. They are recorded in the *capital account* of the balance of payments.

[4]The sum $C + I + G$ is often called domestic *absorption* in the literature on international macroeconomics. Using this terminology, we can describe the current account surplus as the difference between income and absorption.

Figure 12-2 | The U.S. Current Account and Net Foreign Wealth Position, 1977–2000

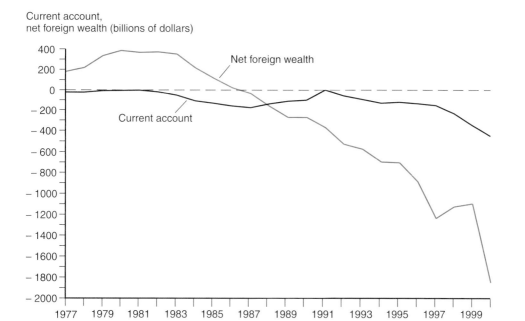

A string of current account deficits in the 1980s reduced America's net foreign wealth until, by the decade's end, the country had accumulated a substantial net foreign debt.

Source: U.S. Government Printing Office, *Economic Indicators,* March 1998, April 2001.

Figure 12-2 gives a vivid illustration of how a string of current account deficits can add up to a large foreign debt. The figure plots the U.S. current account balance since the late 1970s along with a measure of the nation's stock of net foreign wealth. As you can see, the United States had accumulated substantial foreign wealth by the early 1980s, when a sustained current account deficit of proportions unprecedented in the twentieth century opened up. In 1987 the country became a net debtor to foreigners for the first time since World War I.

As the Case Study on p. 316 shows, it is surprisingly hard to measure accurately a country's net foreign wealth. Some economic analysts therefore question the data in Figure 12-2 and disagree over when the United States became a debtor country and how large its foreign debt really is. But there is no question that a large decrease in U.S. foreign assets did occur over the 1980s.

Saving and the Current Account

Simple as it is, the GNP identity has many illuminating implications. To explain the most important of these implications, we define the concept of **national saving**, that is, the portion of output, *Y,* that is not devoted to household consumption, *C,* or government purchases,

G.[5] *In a closed economy, national saving always equals investment.* This tells us that the economy as a whole can increase its wealth only by accumulating new capital.

Let S stand for national saving. Our definition of S tells us that

$$S = Y - C - G.$$

Since the closed-economy GNP identity, $Y = C + I + G$, may also be written as $I = Y - C - G$, then

$$S = I,$$

and national saving must equal investment in a closed economy. While in a closed economy saving and investment must always be equal, in an open economy they can differ. Remembering that national saving, S, equals $Y - C - G$ and that $CA = EX - IM$, we can rewrite the GNP identity (12-1) as

$$S = I + CA.$$

The equation highlights an important difference between open and closed economies: *An open economy can save either by building up its capital stock or by acquiring foreign wealth, but a closed economy can save only by building up its capital stock.*

Unlike a closed economy, an open economy with profitable investment opportunities does not have to increase its saving in order to exploit them. The preceding expression shows that it is possible simultaneously to raise investment and foreign borrowing without changing saving. For example, if New Zealand decides to build a new hydroelectric plant, it can import the materials it needs from the United States and borrow American funds to pay for them. This transaction raises New Zealand's domestic investment because the imported materials contribute to expanding the country's capital stock. The transaction also raises New Zealand's current account deficit by an amount equal to the increase in investment. New Zealand's saving does not have to change, even though investment rises. For this to be possible, however, U.S. residents must be willing to save more so that the resources needed to build the plant are freed for New Zealand's use. The result is another example of intertemporal trade, in which New Zealand imports present consumption (when it borrows from the United States) and exports future consumption (when it pays off the loan).

Because one country's savings can be borrowed by a second country to increase the second country's stock of capital, a country's current account surplus is often referred to as its *net foreign investment.* Of course, when one country lends to another to finance investment, part of the income generated by the investment in future years must be used to pay back the lender. Domestic investment and foreign investment are two different ways in which a country can use current savings to increase its future income.

---

[5]The U.S. national income accounts assume that government purchases are not used to enlarge the nation's capital stock. We follow this convention here by subtracting *all* government purchases from output to calculate national saving. Most other countries' national accounts distinguish between government consumption and government investment (for example, investment by publicly owned enterprises) and include the latter as part of national saving. Often, however, government investment figures include purchases of military equipment.

Private and Government Saving

So far our discussion of saving has not stressed the distinction between saving decisions made by the private sector and saving decisions made by the government. Unlike private saving decisions, however, government saving decisions are often made with an eye toward their effect on output and employment. The national income identity can help us to analyze the channels through which government saving decisions influence macroeconomic conditions. To use the national income identity in this way, we first have to divide national saving into its private and government components.

Private saving is defined as the part of disposable income that is saved rather than consumed. Disposable income is national income, Y, less the net taxes collected from households and firms by the government, T.[6] Private saving, denoted S^p, can therefore be expressed as

$$S^p = Y - T - C.$$

Government saving is defined similarly to private saving. The government's "income" is its net tax revenue, T, while its "consumption" is government purchases, G. If we let S^g stand for government saving, then

$$S^g = T - G.$$

The two types of saving we have defined, private and government, add up to national saving. To see why, recall the definition of national saving, S, as $Y - C - G$. Then

$$S = Y - C - G = (Y - T - C) + (T - G) = S^p + S^g.$$

We can use the definitions of private and government saving to rewrite the national income identity in a form that is useful for analyzing the effects of government saving decisions on open economies. Because $S = S^p + S^g = I + CA$,

$$S^p = I + CA - S^g = I + CA - (T - G) = I + CA + (G - T). \qquad \text{(12-2)}$$

Equation (12-2) relates private saving to domestic investment, the current account surplus, and government saving. To interpret equation (12-2), we define the **government budget deficit** as $G - T$, that is, as government saving preceded by a minus sign. The government budget deficit measures the extent to which the government is borrowing to finance its expenditures. Equation (12-2) then states that a country's private saving can take three forms: investment in domestic capital (I), purchases of wealth from foreigners (CA), and purchases of the domestic government's newly issued debt ($G - T$).[7] The usefulness of equation (12-2) is illustrated by the following Case Study.

---

[6]Net taxes are taxes less government transfer payments. The term *government* refers to the federal, state, and local governments considered as a single unit.

[7]In a closed economy the current account is always zero, so equation (12-2) is simply $S^p = I + (G - T)$.

CASE STUDY

Government Deficit Reduction May Not Increase the Current Account Surplus

The linkage among the current account balance, investment, and private and government saving given by equation (12-2) is very useful for thinking about the results of economic policies and events. Our predictions about such outcomes cannot possibly be correct unless the current account, investment, and saving rates adjust in a way that is consistent with (12-2). Because that equation is an *identity,* however, and is not based on any theory of economic behavior, we cannot forecast the results of policies without some model of the economy. Equation (12-2) is an identity because it must be included in any valid economic model; but there are any number of models consistent with (12-2).

A good example of how hard it can be to forecast policies' effects comes from thinking about the effects of government deficits on the current account. During the administration of President Ronald Reagan in the early 1980s, the United States slashed taxes and raised some government expenditures, generating both a big government deficit and a sharply increased current account deficit. Those events gave rise to the argument that the government and current account deficits were "twin deficits," both generated primarily by the Reagan policies. If you rewrite identity (12-2) in the form

$$CA = S^p - I - (G - T),$$

you can see how that outcome could have occurred. If the government deficit rises ($G - T$ goes up) and private saving and investment don't change much, the current account surplus must fall by roughly the same amount as the increase in the fiscal deficit. In the United States between 1981 and 1985, the government deficit increased by a bit over 2 percent of GNP, while $S^p - I$ fell by about a half a percent of GNP, so the current account fell from approximate balance to about -3 percent of GNP. (The variables in (12-2) are expressed as percentages of GNP for easy comparison.) Thus, the twin deficits prediction is not too far off the mark.

The twin deficits theory story can lead us seriously astray, however, when changes in government deficits lead to bigger changes in private saving and investment behavior. A good example of these effects comes from European countries' efforts to cut their government budget deficits prior to the launch of their new common currency, the euro, in January 1999. As we will discuss in Chapter 20, the European Union (EU) had agreed that no member country with a large government deficit would be allowed to adopt the new currency along with the initial wave of euro zone members. As 1999 approached, therefore, EU governments made frantic efforts to cut government spending and raise taxes.

Under the "twin deficits" theory, we would have expected the EU's current account surplus to increase sharply as a result of the fiscal change. As the table below shows, however, nothing of the sort actually happened. For the EU as a whole, government deficits fell by about 4.5 percent of output, yet the current account surplus remained about the same.

The table reveals the main reason the current account didn't change much: a sharp fall in the private saving rate, which declined by about 4 percent of output, almost as much as the increase

European Union (percentage of GNP)				
Year	CA	S^p	I	G − T
1995	0.6	25.9	19.9	−5.4
1996	1.0	24.6	19.3	−4.3
1997	1.5	23.4	19.4	−2.5
1998	1.0	22.6	20.0	−1.6
1999	0.2	21.8	20.8	−0.8

Source: Organization for Economic Cooperation and Development, *OECD Economic Outlook 68* (December 2000), Annex Tables 27, 30, and 52 (with investment calculated as the residual).

in government saving. (Investment rose slightly at the same time.) In this case, the behavior of private savers just about neutralized governments' efforts to raise national saving!

It is difficult to know why this offset occurred, but there are a number of possible explanations. One is based on an economic theory known as the "Ricardian equivalence" of taxes and government deficits. (The theory is named after the same David Ricardo who discovered the theory of comparative advantage—recall Chapter 2—although he himself did not believe in Ricardian equivalence.) Ricardian equivalence argues that when the government cuts taxes and raises its deficit, consumers anticipate that they will face higher taxes later to pay off the resulting government debt. In anticipation, they raise their own (private) saving to offset the fall in government saving. Conversely, governments that *lower* their deficits (thereby increasing government saving) will induce the private sector to *lower* its own saving. Qualitatively, this is the kind of behavior we see in Europe in the late 1990s.

Economists' statistical studies suggest, however, that Ricardian equivalence doesn't hold exactly in practice. Most economists would attribute no more than half the decline in European private saving to Ricardian effects. What explains the rest of the decline? The values of European financial assets were generally rising in the late 1990s, a development fueled in part by optimism over the beneficial economic effects of the planned common currency. It is likely that increased household wealth was a second factor lowering the private saving rate in Europe.

Because private saving, investment, the current account, and the government deficit are jointly determined variables, we can never fully determine the cause of a current account change using identity (12-2) alone. Nonetheless, the identity provides an essential framework for thinking about the current account and can furnish useful clues.

The Balance of Payments Accounts

In the previous section, we examined the components of the national income accounts: consumption, investment, government purchases, and the current account (the measure of a country's net foreign investment or, equivalently, of the difference between its exports and imports). In addition to national income accounts, government economists and statisticians also keep balance of payments accounts, a detailed record of the composition of the current account balance and of the many transactions that finance it. Balance of payments figures are of great interest to the general public, as indicated by the attention that various news media pay to them. But press reports sometimes confuse different measures of international payments flows. Should we be alarmed or cheered by a *Wall Street Journal* headline proclaiming "U.S. Chalks Up Record Balance of Payments Deficit"? A thorough understanding of balance of payments accounting will help us evaluate the implications of a country's international transactions.

A country's balance of payments accounts keep track of both its payments to and its receipts from foreigners. Any transaction resulting in a payment to foreigners is entered in the balance of payments accounts as a *debit* and is given a negative ($-$) sign. Any transaction resulting in a receipt from foreigners is entered as a *credit* and is given a positive ($+$) sign.

Three types of international transaction are recorded in the balance of payments:

   1. Transactions that involve the export or import of goods or services and therefore enter directly into the current account. When a French consumer imports American blue jeans, for example, the transaction enters the U.S. balance of payments accounts as a credit on current account.

   2. Transactions that involve the purchase or sale of financial assets. An **asset** is any one of the forms in which wealth can be held, such as money, stocks, factories, or government debt. The **financial account** of the balance of payments records all international purchases or sales of financial assets. When an American company buys a French factory, the transaction enters the U.S. balance of payments as a debit in the financial account. It may seem strange to give a negative sign to a purchase of assets and a positive sign to a sale of assets. It will seem less so if you think in terms of the U.S. "importing" (purchasing) assets and the U.S. "exporting" (selling) assets and give the transaction the same sign you would give to an import ($-$) or export ($+$) transaction recorded in the current account. The difference between a country's exports and imports of assets is called its financial account balance, or financial account for short.

   3. Certain other activities resulting in transfers of wealth between countries are recorded in the **capital account**. These international asset movements—which are generally very small for the United States—differ from those recorded in the financial account. For the most part they result from nonmarket activities, or represent the acquisition or disposal of nonproduced, nonfinancial, and possibly intangible assets (such as copyrights and trademarks). For example, if the United States government forgives $1 billion in debt owed to it by the government of Pakistan, U.S. wealth declines by $1 billion and a $1 billion debit is recorded in the U.S. capital account. As another example, if a Swede immigrates to the United States and brings with him title to $100,000 in Swedish assets, the result would be a $100,000 credit in the U.S. capital account.[8]

---

[8]Until July 1999 the United States classified all transactions either as current account or capital account transactions, including in the (old) capital account the items that are now reported in the financial account and including, in the current account, items that are now placed in the capital account. Thus, the hypothetical example of debt forgiveness to Pakistan would have been considered a current transfer payment to Pakistan under the old accounting rules, and recorded as a $1 billion debit in the current account. The motivation for the changed accounting format was to separate such nonmarket international asset transfers, which "mainly represent changes in ownership of existing assets, which affect nations' balance sheets, from current transfers, which affect nations' income and product in the current period." See Christopher L. Bach, "U.S. International Transactions, Revised Estimates for 1982–98," *Survey of Current Business* (July 1999), p. 61.

You will find the complexities of the balance of payments accounts less confusing if you keep in mind the following simple rule of double-entry bookkeeping: *Every international transaction automatically enters the balance of payments twice, once as a credit and once as a debit.* This principle of balance of payments accounting holds true because every transaction has two sides: If you buy something from a foreigner you must pay him in some way, and the foreigner must then somehow spend or store your payment.

Examples of Paired Transactions

Some examples will show how the principle of double-entry bookkeeping operates in practice.

Imagine you buy a typewriter from the Italian company Olivetti and pay for your purchase with a $1000 check. Your payment to buy a good (the typewriter) from a foreign resident enters the U.S. current account with a negative sign. But where is the offsetting balance of payments credit? Olivetti's U.S. salesperson must do something with your check—let's say he deposits it in Olivetti's account at Citibank in New York. In this case, Olivetti has purchased, and Citibank has sold, a U.S. asset—a bank deposit worth $1000—and the transaction shows up as a $1000 credit in the U.S. financial account. The transaction creates the following two offsetting bookkeeping entries in the U.S. balance of payments:

	Credit	Debit
Typewriter purchase (Current account, U.S. good import)		−$1000
Sale of bank deposit by Citibank (Financial account, U.S. asset export)	+$1000	

As another example, suppose that during your travels in France you pay $200 for a fine dinner at the Restaurant de l'Escargot d'Or. Lacking cash, you place the charge on your Visa credit card. Your payment, which is a tourist expenditure, would be counted as a service import for the United States, and therefore as a current account debit. Where is the offsetting credit? Your signature on the Visa slip entitles the restaurant to receive $200 (actually, its local currency equivalent) from First Card, the company that issued your Visa card. It is therefore an asset, a claim on a future payment from First Card. So when you pay for your meal abroad with your credit card, you are selling an asset to France and generating a $200 credit in the U.S. financial account. The pattern of offsetting debits and credits in this case is

	Credit	Debit
Meal purchase (Current account, U.S. service import)		−$200
Sale of claim on First Card (Financial account, U.S. asset export)	+$200	

Imagine next that your Uncle Sid from Los Angeles buys a newly issued share of stock in the United Kingdom oil giant British Petroleum (BP). He places his order with his stockbroker, Go-for-Broke, Inc., paying $95 with a check drawn on his Go-for-Broke money market account. BP, in turn, deposits the $95 dollars Sid has paid in its own U.S. bank account at Second Bank of Chicago. Uncle Sid's acquisition of the stock creates a $95 debit in the U.S. financial account (he has purchased an asset from a foreign resident, BP), while BP's $95 deposit at its Chicago bank is the offsetting financial-account credit (BP has expanded its U.S. asset holdings). The mirror-image effects on the U.S. balance of payments therefore both appear in the financial account:

	Credit	**Debit**
Uncle Sid's purchase of a share of BP		
(Financial account, U.S. asset import)		−$95
BP's deposit of Uncle Sid's payment at Second Bank		
of Chicago (Financial account, U.S. asset export)	+$95	

Finally, let's consider how the United States balance of payments accounts are affected when U.S. banks forgive (that is, announce that they will simply forget about) $5000 in debt owed to them by the government of the imaginary country of Bygonia. In this case, the United States makes a $5000 capital transfer to Bygonia, which appears as a −$5000 entry in the capital account. The associated credit is in the financial account, in the form of a $5000 reduction in U.S. assets held abroad (a net asset "export," and therefore a positive balance of payments entry):

	Credit	**Debit**
U.S. banks' debt forgiveness		
(Capital account, U.S. transfer payment)		−$5000
Reduction in banks' claims on Bygonia		
(Financial account, U.S. asset export)	+$5000	

These examples show that many different circumstances can affect the way a transaction generates its offsetting balance of payments entry. We can never be sure where the flip side of a particular transaction will show up, but we can be sure it will show up somewhere.

The Fundamental Balance of Payments Identity

Because any international transaction automatically gives rise to two offsetting entries in the balance of payments, the current account balance, the financial account balance, and the capital account balance automatically add up to zero:

$$\text{Current account} + \text{financial account} + \text{capital account} = 0. \qquad (12\text{-}3)$$

This identity can also be understood by recalling the relation linking the current account to international lending and borrowing. Because the sum of the current and capital accounts is the total change in a country's net foreign assets, that sum necessarily equals the difference between a country's imports of assets from foreigners and its exports of assets to them, that is, the capital account balance preceded by a minus sign.

We now turn to a more detailed description of the balance of payments accounts, using as an example the U.S. accounts for 2000. Table 12-2 reproduces the record of America's international transactions in that year.

The Current Account, Once Again

As you have learned, the current account balance measures a country's net exports of goods and services. Table 12-2 shows that U.S. exports were $1,414.9 billion in 2000 while U.S. imports were $1,797.1 billion. Because imports give rise to payments to foreigners, they enter the accounts with a negative sign, as shown.

Table 12-2 | U.S. Balance of Payments Accounts for 2000
(billions of dollars)

	Credits	Debits
Current Account		
(1) Exports	+1,414.9	
Of which:		
Merchandise	+773.3	
Services	+296.2	
Income receipts	+345.4	
(2) Imports		−1,797.1
Of which:		
Merchandise		−1,222.8
Services		−215.2
Income payments		−359.1
(3) Net unilateral current transfers		−53.2
Balance on current account		−435.4
[(1) + (2) + (3)]		
Capital Account		
(4)	+0.7	
Financial Account		
(5) U.S. assets held abroad		−553.3
(increase −)		
Of which:		
Official reserve assets		−0.3
Other assets		−553.0
(6) Foreign assets held in U.S.	+952.4	
(increase +)		
Of which:		
Official reserve assets	+35.9	
Other assets	+916.5	
Balance on financial account	+399.1	
[(5) + (6)]		
Statistical discrepancy	+35.6	
[sum of (1) through (6) with sign reversed]		

Source: U.S. Department of Commerce, *Survey of Current Business,* April 2001. Totals may differ from sums because of rounding.

The balance of payments accounts divide exports and imports into three finer categories. The first is *merchandise* trade, that is, exports or imports of goods. The second category, *services,* includes items such as payments for legal assistance, tourists' expenditures, and shipping fees. The final category, *income,* is made up mostly of international interest and dividend payments and the earnings of domestically owned firms operating abroad. If you own a share of a German firm's stock and receive a dividend payment of $5, that payment shows up in the accounts as a U.S. investment income receipt of $5. Wages that workers earn abroad can also enter the income account.

We include income on foreign investments in the current account because that income really is compensation for the *services* provided by foreign investments. This idea, as we saw earlier, is behind the distinction between GNP and GDP. When a U.S. corporation builds a plant in Canada, for instance, the productive services the plant generates are viewed as a service export from the United States to Canada equal in value to the profits the plant yields for its American owner. To be consistent, we must be sure to include these profits in American GNP and not in Canadian GNP. Remember, the definition of GNP refers to goods and services generated by a country's factors of production, but it does *not* specify that those factors must work within the borders of the country that owns them.

Before calculating the current account, we must include one additional type of international transaction that we have largely ignored until now. In discussing the relation between GNP and national income, we defined unilateral transfers between countries as international gifts, that is, payments that do not correspond to the purchase of any good, service, or asset. Net unilateral transfers are considered part of the current account as well as a part of national income, and the identity $Y = C + I + G + CA$ holds exactly if Y is interpreted as GNP *plus* net transfers. In 2000, the U.S. balance of unilateral transfers was $-\$53.2$ billion.

The table shows a 2000 current account balance of $\$1,414.9$ billion $- \$1,797.1$ billion $- \$53.2$ billion $= -\$435.4$ billion, a deficit. The negative sign means that current payments exceeded current receipts and that U.S. residents used more output than they produced. Since these current account transactions were paid for in some way, we know that this negative $\$435.4$ billion entry must be offset by positive $\$435.4$ billion entries in the other two accounts of the balance of payments.

The Capital Account

The capital account entry in Table 12-2 shows that in 2000, the United States received capital asset transfers of roughly $700 million, or only $0.7 billion. These receipts by the United States are a balance of payments credit that enter with a positive sign. After we add them to the payments deficit implied by the current account, we find that the United States' need to cover its excess payments to foreigners is reduced very slightly, from $435.4 billion to $435.4 billion $- \$0.7$ billion $= \$434.7$ billion. Because overall U.S. foreign receipts must equal foreign payments every year, that $-\$434.7$ billion entry in the U.S. balance of payments must be matched by a $+\$434.7$ billion entry in the remaining balance of payments account, the financial account.

The Financial Account

Just as the current account is the difference between sales of goods and services to foreigners and purchases of goods and services from them, the financial account measures the difference between sales of assets to foreigners and purchases of assets located abroad. When the United States borrows $1 from foreigners, it is selling them an asset—a promise that they will be repaid $1, with interest, in the future. Such a transaction enters the financial account with a positive sign because the loan is itself a payment to the United States, or a **financial inflow** (also sometimes called a **capital inflow**). When the United States lends abroad, however, a payment is made to foreigners and the capital account is debited. This transaction involves the purchase of an asset from foreigners and is called a **financial outflow** (or, alternatively, a **capital outflow**).

To cover its 2000 current plus capital account deficit of $434.7 billion, the United States required a net financial inflow of $434.7 billion. In other words, its net borrowing or sales of assets to foreigners should have amounted to $434.7 billion. We can look again at Table 12-2 to see exactly how this net financial inflow came about.

The table records separately increases in U.S. holdings of assets located abroad (which are financial outflows and enter with a negative sign) and increases in foreign holdings of assets located in the United States (which are financial inflows and enter with a positive sign).

According to Table 12-2, U.S. owned assets held abroad increased by $553.3 billion in 2000, contributing a −$553.3 billion entry to the U.S. balance of payments. Foreign owned assets held in the United States rose by $952.4 billion in the year, and these purchases are shown with a positive sign. We calculate the balance on financial account as $553.3 billion − $952.4 billion = $399.1 billion, a surplus.

The Statistical Discrepancy

We come out with a financial account surplus of $399.1 billion rather than the larger $434.7 billion financial account surplus we expected. If every balance of payments credit automatically generates an equal counterpart debit, and vice versa, how is this difference possible? The reason is that information about the offsetting debit and credit items associated with a given transaction may be collected from different sources. For example, the import debit that a shipment of VCRs from Japan generates may come from a U.S. customs inspector's report and the corresponding financial account credit from a report by the U.S. bank in which the check paying for the VCRs is deposited. Because data from different sources may differ in coverage, accuracy, and timing, the balance of payments accounts seldom balance in practice as they must in theory. Account keepers force the two sides to balance by adding to the accounts a statistical discrepancy. For 2000 unrecorded (or misrecorded) international transactions generated a balancing credit of +$35.6 billion.

We have no way of knowing exactly how to allocate this discrepancy among the current, capital, and financial accounts. (If we did, it wouldn't be a discrepancy!) The financial account is the most likely culprit, since it is notoriously difficult to keep track of the complicated financial trades between residents of different countries. But we cannot conclude that net financial inflows were $35.6 billion higher than recorded, because the current account is also highly suspect. Balance of payments accountants consider merchandise trade data relatively reliable, but data on services are not. Service transactions such as sales of financial advice and computer programming assistance may escape detection. Accurate measurement of international interest and dividend receipts is particularly difficult. (See the box on page 314.)

Official Reserve Transactions

Although there are many types of capital account transaction, one type is important enough to merit separate discussion. This type of transaction involves the purchase or sale of official reserve assets by central banks.

An economy's **central bank** is the institution responsible for managing the supply of money. In the United States, the central bank is the Federal Reserve System. **Official international reserves** are foreign assets held by central banks as a cushion against

THE MYSTERY OF THE MISSING SURPLUS

Because the world as a whole is a closed economy, world saving must equal world investment and world spending must equal world output. Individual countries can run current account surpluses or deficits to invest or borrow abroad. Because one country's lending is another country's borrowing, however, the sum of all these individual current account imbalances necessarily equals zero.

Or does it? National current account data show that the world as a whole is running a substantial current account *deficit* that increased sharply in the early 1980s and has remained high. Below are figures for the sum total of all countries' current account balances between 1980 and 1994.

The global discrepancies in the table are far greater in magnitude than most reported national current accounts. Since positive and negative errors cancel out in the summation leading to the global figures, discrepancies of this size raise the worrisome possibility that the national current account statistics on which policymakers base decisions are seriously inaccurate.

What explains the theoretically impossible deficit shown by total world current account numbers? Your first reaction may be to blame the problem on the statistical discrepancies that bedevil the

national income and balance of payment accounts of individual countries. An additional complication is introduced by timing factors. Goods that leave one country's ports near the end of an accounting year, for example, may not reach their destination in time to be recorded in the recipient's import statistics for the same year.

A general appeal to accounting anomalies such as these does not explain, however, why the world as a whole should appear to be persistently in deficit (rather than in surplus) or why that deficit should have tripled in the early 1980s. A more plausible hypothesis links the missing surplus to one specific cause of accounting discrepancies at the national level, the systematic misreporting of international interest income flows. Interest payments earned abroad are often not reported to government authorities in the recipient's home country. In many cases such interest payments are credited directly to a foreign bank account and do not even cross national borders. There is thus a consistent tendency to observe a negative global balance of international interest flows.

World interest rates rose sharply after 1980, and the size of the world interest payment discrepancy increased with them. The interest payment

national economic misfortune. At one time official reserves consisted largely of gold, but today central banks' reserves include substantial foreign financial assets, particularly U.S. dollar assets such as Treasury bills. The Federal Reserve itself holds only a small level of official reserve assets other than gold; its own holdings of dollar assets are not considered international reserves.

Central banks often buy or sell international reserves in private asset markets to affect macroeconomic conditions in their economies. Official transactions of this type are called **official foreign exchange intervention**. One reason why foreign exchange intervention can alter macroeconomic conditions is that it is a way for the central bank to inject money into the economy or withdraw it from circulation. We will have much more to say later about the causes and consequences of foreign exchange intervention.

Government agencies other than central banks may hold foreign reserves and intervene officially in exchange markets. The U.S. Treasury, for example, operates an Exchange Stabilization Fund that sometimes plays an active role in market trading. Because the operations of such agencies usually have no noticeable impact on the money supply, however, we will simplify our discussion by speaking (when this is not too misleading) as if the central bank alone holds foreign reserves and intervenes.

hypothesis therefore offers a potential explanation for the increase in the global deficit. The downturn in world interest rates after the mid-1980s provides partial confirmation of the hypothesis, since the world current account deficit did drop as interest rates fell. Subsequent data are no less consistent with a key role for interest payments. Interest rates in most of the main industrial countries rose after 1987, and this helped to more than double the world payments gap. The dramatic size of this effect, involving discrepancies even larger than the previous 1982 peak, is explained by the much greater volume of gross international assets and liabilities that existed by the late 1980s. The generalized easing of world interest rates after 1990, a

process that accelerated in 1993 as Europe joined in (see Chapter 20), is clearly associated with yet another fall in the world current account deficit.

Other measurement problems are probably also at work, as an International Monetary Fund (IMF) study of the current account discrepancy concluded (see Further Reading). The IMF found that while interest payments explain a good part of the discrepancy, several additional factors are involved. For example, much of the world's merchant shipping fleet is registered in countries that do not report maritime freight earnings to the IMF. These unrecorded earnings make up a significant portion of the missing world surplus.

 Measured World Current Account Balance, 1980–1994 (Billions of U.S. dollars)

1980	1981	1982	1983	1984	1985	1986	1987	1988	1989	1990	1991	1992	1993	1994
−38.5	−68.3	−100.2	−61.2	−73.4	−80.8	−76.7	−62.3	−78.9	−96.2	−126.0	−118.2	−99.0	−59.7	−50.3

Source: International Monetary Fund, *World Economic Outlook,* 1989–1994, Table A26, October 1997, October 2000, Table A27.

When a central bank purchases or sells a foreign asset, the transaction appears in its country's financial account just as if the same transaction had been carried out by a private citizen. A transaction in which the central bank of Germany (called the Bundesbank) acquires dollar assets might occur as follows. A U.S. auto dealer imports a Volkswagen from Germany and pays the auto company with a check for $15,000. Volkswagen does not want to invest the money in dollar assets, but it so happens that the Bundesbank is willing to give Volkswagen German money in exchange for the $15,000 check. The Bundesbank's international reserves rise by $15,000 as a result of the deal. Because the Bundesbank's dollar reserves are part of total German assets held in the United States, the latter rise by $15,000. This transaction therefore results in a positive $15,000 entry in the U.S. financial account, the other side of the −$15,000 entry in the U.S. current account due to the purchase of the car.[9]

Table 12-2 shows the size and direction of official reserve transactions involving the United States in 2000. United States official reserve assets—that is, international reserves held by the Federal Reserve—*rose* by $0.3 billion (recall that a negative sign here means an increase in U.S. owned assets held abroad, that is, an "import" of assets from foreigners).

---

[9] To test your understanding, see if you can explain why the same sequence of actions causes a $15,000 improvement in Germany's current account but a $15,000 worsening of its financial account.

Foreign central banks purchased $35.9 billion to add to their reserves. The net increase in foreign official reserve claims on the United States *less* the net increase in U.S. official reserves is the *balance of official reserve transactions,* which stood at $35.9 billion − $0.3 billion = $35.6 billion in 2000.

You can think of this $35.6 billion balance as measuring the degree to which monetary authorities in the United States and abroad joined with other lenders to cover the U.S. current account deficit. In the example above, the Bundesbank, by acquiring a $15,000 U.S. bank deposit, indirectly finances an American import of a $15,000 German car. The bookkeeping offset to the balance of official reserve transactions is called the **official settlements balance** or (in less formal usage) the **balance of payments**. This balance is the sum of the current account balance, the capital account balance, the nonreserve portion of the financial account balance, and the statistical discrepancy, and it indicates the payments gap that official reserve transactions need to cover. Thus the U.S. balance of payments in 2000 was −$35.6 billion, that is, the balance of official reserve transactions with its sign reversed.

Table 12-3 reorganizes the major categories in Table 12-2 to emphasize the role of official reserve transactions in bridging the gap between the current (plus capital) account deficit and the *nonreserve* portion of the financial account surplus. The balance of payments played an important historical role as a measure of disequilibrium in international payments, and for many countries it still plays this role. A negative balance of payments (a deficit) may signal a crisis, for it means that a country is running down its international reserve assets or incurring debts to foreign monetary authorities. If a country faces the risk of being suddenly cut off from foreign loans, it will want to maintain a "war chest" of international reserves as a precaution.

Like any summary measure, however, the balance of payments must be interpreted with caution. To return to our running example, the German Bundesbank's decision to expand its U.S. bank deposit holdings by $15,000 swells the measured U.S. balance of payments deficit by the same amount. Suppose the Bundesbank instead places its $15,000 with Barclays Bank in London, which in turn deposits the money with Bankers Trust in New York. Nonreserve U.S. financial inflows rise by $15,000 in this case, and the U.S. balance of payments deficit does not rise. But this "improvement" in the balance of payments is of little economic importance: It makes no difference to the United States whether it borrows the Bundesbank's money directly or through a London bank.

CASE STUDY

Is the United States the World's Biggest Debtor?

The Bureau of Economic Analysis (BEA) of the U.S. Department of Commerce oversees the vast data collection operation behind the U.S. national income and product accounts and balance of payments statistics. In addition, the BEA reports annual estimates of the "international investment position of the United States"—the country's net foreign wealth. These estimates showed that at the end of 1999 the United States had a *negative* net foreign wealth position far greater than that of any other single country.

Table 12-3 | Calculating the U.S. Official Settlements Balance for 2000 (billions of dollars)

	Credits	Debits
Current Account		
(1) Exports	+1,414.9	
(2) Imports		−1,797.1
(3) Net unilateral transfers		−53.2
(4) Balance on current account [(1) + (2) + (3)]		−435.4
Capital Account		
(5)	+0.7	
Nonreserve financial account		
(6) U.S. assets held abroad (excluding U.S. official reserves) (increase −)		−553.0
(7) Foreign assets held in U.S. (excluding foreign official reserves) (increase +)	+916.5	
(8) Balance on nonreserve financial account [(6) + (7)]	+363.5	
(9) Statistical discrepancy	+35.6	
(10) Official settlements balance [(4) + (5) + (8) + (9)]		−35.6
Official reserve transactions		
(11) U.S. official reserve assets held abroad (increase −)		−0.3
Of which:		
Gold		0.0
Special Drawing Rights		−0.7
Reserve position in the International Monetary Fund	+2.3	
Foreign currencies		−1.9
(12) Foreign official reserve assets held in U.S. (increase +)	+35.9	
Of which:		
U.S. government securities	+29.5	
Other U.S. government liabilities		−2.5
Liabilities reported by U.S. banks not included elsewhere	+5.8	
Other	+3.1	
(13) Balance of official reserve transactions [(11) + (12)]	+35.6	

Source: U.S. Department of Commerce, *Survey of Current Business*, April 2001. Totals may differ from sums because of rounding.

We saw earlier that the current account balance measures the flow of new net claims on foreign wealth that a country acquires by exporting more goods and services than it imports. This flow is not, however, the only factor that causes a country's net foreign wealth to change. In addition, changes in the market price of wealth previously acquired can alter a country's net foreign wealth. When Japan's stock market lost three quarters of its value over the 1990s, for example, American and European owners of Japanese shares saw the value of their claims on Japan plummet, and Japan's net *foreign* wealth increased as a result. The BEA must adjust the value of existing claims for such capital gains and losses before arriving at its estimate of U.S. net foreign wealth.

The BEA now reports two estimates of U.S. net foreign wealth that differ in their treatment of foreign direct investments (see Chapter 7). Until 1991 foreign direct investments were valued at their historical, that is, original, purchase prices. Now the BEA uses two different methods to place current values on foreign direct investments: the *current cost* method, which values direct investments at the cost of buying them today, and the *market value* method, which is meant to measure the price at which the investments could be sold. These methods can lead to different valuations, because the cost of replacing a particular direct investment and the price it would command if sold on the market may be hard to measure. (The net foreign wealth data graphed in Figure 12-2 are current cost estimates.)

Table 12-4 reproduces the BEA's account of how it made its valuation adjustments to find the U.S. net foreign position at the end of 1999. Starting with its estimate of 1998 net foreign wealth (−$1,111.8 billion at current cost or −$1,407.7 billion at market value), the BEA (column a) subtracted the amount of the 1999 U.S. net financial inflow of $323.4 billion—the sum of lines 5 and 6 in the 1999 version of Table 12-2. (Do you remember why a financial *inflow* to the United States results in a *reduction* in U.S. net foreign assets?) Then the BEA adjusted the values of previously held assets for various changes in their dollar prices (columns b, c, and d). As a result of these valuation changes, U.S. net foreign wealth *fell* by an amount different from the $323.4 billion in new net financial inflows from abroad. Based on the current cost method for valuing direct investments, the BEA's 1999 estimate of U.S. net foreign wealth was −$1,082.5 billion. On a market value basis, the BEA places 1999 net foreign wealth lower, at −$1,473.7 billion.

This debt is larger than the total foreign debt owed by all the Western Hemisphere's developing countries, which was $764.5 billion in 1999. To put these figures in perspective, however, it is important to realize that the U.S. net foreign debt (at current cost) amounted to less than 12 percent of its GDP, while that of Argentina, Brazil, Mexico, Venezuela, and the other Western Hemisphere debtors was 43 percent of their collective GDP! Thus, the U.S. external debt represents a much lower income drain than that of its southern neighbors.

The United States certainly is the world's biggest debtor. There is no reason to be alarmed, however, because the U.S. GNP is also the world's largest and the United States is not in danger of being unable to repay its foreign debts. Remember also that foreign borrowing may not always be a bad idea: A country that borrows abroad to undertake profitable domestic investments can pay back its creditors and still have money left over (Chapter 7). Unfortunately for the United States, most of its foreign borrowing over the 1980s financed government budget deficits rather than investment, as we saw in the last Case Study. Future generations of U.S. citizens therefore will face a real burden in repaying the resulting foreign debt.

Table 12-4 International Investment Position of the United States at Year End, 1998 and 1999 (millions of dollars)

Line	Type of investment	Position, 1998	Changes in position in 1999 (decrease (–))					Position, 1999 P
				Attributable to:				
			Financial flows	Valuation adjustments			Total	
				Price changes	Exchange rate changes [1]	Other changes [2]		
			(a)	(b)	(c)	(d)	(a+b+c+d)	
	Net international investment position of the United States:							
1	With direct investment positions at current cost (line 3 less line 24)	–1,111,813	–323,377	344,215	–60,235	68,702	29,305	–1,082,508
2	With direct investment positions at market value (line 4 less line 25)	–1,407,670	–323,377	301,897	–57,364	12,829	–66,015	–1,473,685
	U.S.-owned assets abroad:							
3	With direct investment positions at current cost (lines 5+10+15)	5,079,056	430,187	455,115	–71,115	–4,215	809,972	5,889,028
4	With direct investment positions at market value (lines 5+10+16)	6,045,544	430,187	755,413	–63,035	5,264	1,127,829	7,173,373
5	U.S. official reserve assets	146,006	–8,747	642	–1,500	17	–9,588	136,418
6	Gold	75,291	....	[3] 642	....	[4] 17	659	75,950
7	Special drawing rights	10,603	–10		–257		–267	10,336
8	Reserve position in the International Monetary Fund	24,111	–5,484		–677		–6,161	17,950
9	Foreign currencies	36,001	–3,253		–566		–3,819	32,182
10	U.S. Government assets, other than official reserve assets	86,768	–2,751		7	202	–2,542	84,226
11	U.S. credits and other long-term assets [5]	84,850	–3,384		–11	202	–3,193	81,657
12	Repayable in dollars	84,528	–3,363			202	–3,161	81,367
13	Other [6]	322	–21		–11		–32	290
14	U.S. foreign currency holdings and U.S. short-term assets	1,918	633		18		651	2,569
	U.S. private assets:							
15	With direct investment at current cost (lines 17+19+22+23)	4,846,282	441,685	454,473	–69,622	–4,434	822,102	5,668,384
16	With direct investment at market value (lines 18+19+22+23)	5,812,770	441,685	754,771	–61,542	5,045	1,139,959	6,952,729
	Direct investment abroad:							
17	At current cost	1,207,059	150,901	5,475	–17,646	–14,602	124,128	1,331,187
18	At market value	2,173,547	150,901	305,773	–9,566	–5,123	441,985	2,615,532
19	Foreign securities	2,052,929	128,594	448,998	–47,135		530,457	2,583,386
20	Bonds	576,745	14,193	–31,341	–2,849		–19,997	556,748
21	Corporate stocks	1,476,184	114,401	480,339	–44,286		550,454	2,026,638
22	U.S. claims on unaffiliated foreigners reported by U.S. nonbanking concerns	565,466	92,328		–8,037	–6,010	78,281	643,747
23	U.S. claims reported by U.S. banks, not included elsewhere	1,020,828	69,862		3,196	16,178	89,236	1,110,064
	Foreign-owned assets in the United States:							
24	With direct investment at current cost (lines 26+33)	6,190,869	753,564	110,900	–10,880	–72,917	780,667	6,971,536
25	With direct investment at market value (lines 26+34)	7,453,214	753,564	453,516	–5,671	–7,565	1,193,844	8,647,058
26	Foreign official assets in the United States	837,701	42,864	–11,231			31,633	869,334
27	U.S. Government securities	620,285	32,527	–23,905			8,622	628,907
28	U.S. Treasury securities	589,023	12,177	–22,975			–10,798	578,225
29	Other	31,262	20,350	–930			19,420	50,682
30	Other U.S. Government liabilities [7]	18,000	–3,255				–3,255	14,745
31	U.S. liabilities reported by U.S. banks, not included elsewhere	125,883	12,692				12,692	138,575
32	Other foreign official assets	73,533	900	12,674			13,574	87,107
	Other foreign assets:							
33	With direct investment at current cost (lines 35+37+38+41+42+43)	5,353,168	710,700	122,131	–10,880	–72,917	749,034	6,102,202
34	With direct investment at market value (lines 36+37+38+41+42+43)	6,615,513	710,700	464,747	–5,671	–7,565	1,162,211	7,777,724
	Direct investment in the United States:							
35	At current cost	928,645	275,533	1,766	–5,209	–75,521	196,569	1,125,214
36	At market value	2,190,990	275,533	344,382		–10,169	609,746	2,800,736
37	U.S. Treasury securities	729,738	–20,464	–48,552			–69,016	660,722
38	U.S. securities other than U.S. Treasury securities	2,012,431	331,523	168,917	–3,549		496,891	2,509,322
39	Corporate and other bonds	902,155	232,814	–67,690	–3,549		161,575	1,063,730
40	Corporate stocks	1,110,276	98,709	236,607			335,316	1,445,592
41	U.S. currency	228,250	22,407				22,407	250,657
42	U.S. liabilities to unaffiliated foreigners reported by U.S. nonbanking concerns	437,973	34,298		–1,050	2,604	35,852	473,825
43	U.S. liabilities reported by U.S. banks, not included elsewhere	1,016,131	67,403		–1,072		66,331	1,082,462

P Preliminary.
r Revised.
1. Represents gains or losses on foreign-currency-denominated assets due to their revaluation at current exchange rates.
2. Includes changes in coverage, statistical discrepancies, and other adjustments to the value of assets.
3. Reflects changes in the value of the official gold stock due to fluctuations in the market price of gold.
4. Reflects changes in gold stock from U.S. Treasury sales of gold medallions and commemorative and bullion coins; also reflects replenishment through open market purchases. These demonetizations/monetizations are not included in international transactions financial flows.

5. Also includes paid-in capital subscriptions to international financial institutions and outstanding amounts of miscellaneous claims that have been settled through international agreements to be payable to the U.S. Government over periods in excess of 1 year. Excludes World War I debts that are not being serviced.
6. Includes indebtedness that the borrower may contractually, or at its option, repay with its currency, with a third country's currency, or by delivery of materials or transfer of services.
7. Primarily U.S. Government liabilities associated with military sales contracts and other transactions arranged with or through foreign official agencies.

NOTE.—The data in this table are from table 1 in "International Investment Position of the United States at Yearend 1999" in the July 2000 issue of the SURVEY OF CURRENT BUSINESS.

Source: U.S. Department of Commerce, Bureau of Economic Analysis, *Survey of Current Business,* April 2001, p. D-57.

Summary

1. International *macroeconomics* is concerned with the full employment of scarce economic resources and price level stability throughout the world economy. Because they reflect national expenditure patterns and their international repercussions, the *national income accounts* and the *balance of payments accounts* are essential tools for studying the macroeconomics of open, interdependent economies.

2. A country's *gross national product (GNP)* is equal to the income received by its factors of production. The national income accounts divide national income according to the types of spending that generate it: *consumption, investment, government purchases,* and the *current account balance. Gross domestic product (GDP),* equal to GNP less net receipts of factor income from abroad, measures the output produced within a country's territorial borders.

3. In an economy closed to international trade, GNP must be consumed, invested, or purchased by the government. By using current output to build plant, equipment, and inventories, investment transforms present output into future output. For a closed economy, investment is the only way to save in the aggregate, so the sum of the saving carried out by the private and public sectors, *national saving,* must equal investment.

4. In an open economy, GNP equals the sum of consumption, investment, government purchases, and net exports of goods and services. Trade does not have to be balanced if the economy can borrow from and lend to the rest of the world. The difference between the economy's exports and imports, the current account balance, equals the difference between the economy's output and its total use of goods and services.

5. The current account also equals the country's net lending to foreigners. Unlike a closed economy, an open economy can save by domestic *and* foreign investment. National saving therefore equals domestic investment plus the current account balance.

6. Balance of payments accounts provide a detailed picture of the composition and financing of the current account. All transactions between a country and the rest of the world are recorded in its balance of payments accounts. The accounts are based on the convention that any transaction resulting in a payment to foreigners is entered with a minus sign while any transaction resulting in a receipt from foreigners is entered with a plus sign.

7. Transactions involving goods and services appear in the current account of the balance of payments, while international sales or purchases of *assets* appear in the *financial account.* The *capital account* records asset transfers and tends to be small for the United States. Any current account deficit must be matched by an equal surplus in the other two accounts of the balance of payments, and any current account surplus by a deficit somewhere else. This feature of the accounts reflects the fact that discrepancies between export earnings and import expenditures must be matched by a promise to repay the difference, usually with interest, in the future.

8. International asset transactions carried out by *central banks* are included in the financial account. Any central bank transaction in private markets for foreign currency assets is called *official foreign exchange intervention.* One reason intervention is important is that central banks use it as a way of altering the amount of money in cir-

culation. A country has a deficit in its *balance of payments* when it is running down its *official international reserves* or borrowing from foreign central banks; it has a surplus in the opposite case.

Key Terms

asset, p. 308
balance of payments accounting, p. 295
capital account, p. 308
capital inflow, p. 312
capital outflow, p. 313
central bank, p. 313
consumption, p. 299
current account balance, p. 301
financial account, p. 308
financial inflow, p. 312
financial outflow, p. 313
government budget deficit, p. 305
government purchases, p. 299

gross domestic product (GDP), p. 298
gross national product (GNP), p. 295
investment, p. 299
macroeconomics, p. 294
microeconomics, p. 294
national income, p. 296
national income accounting, p. 295
national saving, p. 303
official foreign exchange intervention, p. 314
official international reserves, p. 313
official settlements balance (or balance
  of payments), p. 316
private saving, p. 305

Problems

1. We stated in this chapter that GNP accounts avoid double counting by including only the value of *final* goods and services sold on the market. Should the measure of imports used in the GNP accounts therefore be defined to include only imports of final goods and services from abroad? What about exports?

2. Equation (12-2) tells us that to reduce a current account deficit, a country must increase its private saving, reduce domestic investment, or cut its government budget deficit. In the 1980s, many people recommended restrictions on imports from Japan (and other countries) to reduce the American current account deficit. How would higher U.S. barriers to imports affect its private saving, domestic investment, and government deficit? Do you agree that import restrictions would necessarily reduce a U.S. current account deficit?

3. Explain how each of the following transactions generates two entries—a credit and a debit—in the American balance of payments accounts, and describe how each entry would be classified:

   a. An American buys a share of German stock, paying by writing a check on an account with a Swiss bank.

   b. An American buys a share of German stock, paying the seller with a check on an American bank.

   c. The French government carries out an official foreign exchange intervention in which it uses dollars held in an American bank to buy French currency from its citizens.

   d. A tourist from Detroit buys a meal at an expensive restaurant in Lyons, France, paying with a traveler's check.

    e. A California winegrower contributes a case of cabernet sauvignon for a London wine tasting.

    f. A U.S.-owned factory in Britain uses local earnings to buy additional machinery.

4. A New Yorker travels to New Jersey to buy a $100 telephone answering machine. The New Jersey company that sells the machine then deposits the $100 check in its account at a New York bank. How would these transactions show up in the balance of payments accounts of New York and New Jersey? What if the New Yorker pays cash for the machine?

5. The nation of Pecunia had a current account deficit of $1 billion and a nonreserve financial account surplus of $500 million in 2002.

    a. What was the balance of payments of Pecunia in that year? What happened to the country's net foreign assets?

    b. Assume that foreign central banks neither buy nor sell Pecunian assets. How did the Pecunian central bank's foreign reserves change in 2002? How would this official intervention show up in the balance of payments accounts of Pecunia?

    c. How would your answer to (b) change if you learned that foreign central banks had purchased $600 million of Pecunian assets in 2002? How would these official purchases enter foreign balance of payments accounts?

    d. Draw up the Pecunian balance of payments accounts for 2002 under the assumption that the event described in (c) occurred in that year.

6. Can you think of reasons why a government might be concerned about a large current account deficit or surplus? Why might a government be concerned about its official settlements balance (that is, its balance of payments)?

7. Do data on the U.S. official settlements balance give an accurate picture of the extent to which foreign central banks buy and sell dollars in currency markets?

8. Is it possible for a country to have a current account deficit at the same time it has a surplus in its balance of payments? Explain your answer, using hypothetical figures for the current and nonreserve financial accounts. Be sure to discuss the possible implications for official international reserve flows.

Further Reading

Peter Hooper and J. David Richardson, eds. *International Economic Transactions.* Chicago: University of Chicago Press, 1991. Useful papers on international economic measurement.

David H. Howard. "Implications of the U.S. Current Account Deficit." *Journal of Economic Perspectives 3* (Fall 1989), pp. 153–165. Examines how U.S. current account deficits may affect American welfare and net foreign wealth.

International Monetary Fund. *Final Report of the Working Party on the Statistical Discrepancy in World Current Account Balances.* Washington, D.C.: International Monetary Fund, September 1987. Discusses the statistical discrepancy in the world current account balance, its implications for policy analysis, and recommendations for more accurate measurement.

International Monetary Fund. *Balance of Payments Manual,* 5th edition. Washington, D.C.: International Monetary Fund, 1993. Authoritative treatment of balance of payments accounting.

Robert E. Lipsey. "Changing Patterns of International Investment in and by the United States," in Martin S. Feldstein, ed. *The United States in the World Economy.* Chicago: University of Chicago Press, 1988, pp. 475–545. Historical perspective on capital flows to and from the United States.

Rita M. Maldonado. "Recording and Classifying Transactions in the Balance of Payments." *International Journal of Accounting* 15 (Fall 1979), pp. 105–133. Provides detailed examples of how various international transactions enter the balance of payments accounts.

James E. Meade. *The Balance of Payments,* Chapters 1–3. London: Oxford University Press, 1952. A classic analytical discussion of balance of payments concepts.

Lois Stekler. "Adequacy of International Transactions and Position Data for Policy Coordination," in William H. Branson, Jacob A. Frenkel, and Morris Goldstein, eds. *International Policy Coordination and Exchange Rate Fluctuations.* Chicago: University of Chicago Press, 1990, pp. 347–371. A critical look at the interpretation of official data on current accounts and external indebtedness.

Robert M. Stern, Charles F. Schwartz, Robert Triffin, Edward M. Bernstein, and Walther Lederer. *The Presentation of the Balance of Payments: A Symposium,* Princeton Essays in International Finance 123. International Finance Section, Department of Economics, Princeton University, August 1977. A discussion of changes in the presentation of the U.S. balance of payments accounts.

U.S. Bureau of the Budget, Review Committee for Balance of Payments Statistics. *The Balance of Payments Statistics of the United States: A Review and Appraisal.* Washington, D.C.: Government Printing Office, 1965. A major official reappraisal of U.S. balance of payments accounting procedures. Chapter 9 focuses on conceptual difficulties in defining surpluses and deficits in the balance of payments.

CHAPTER 13

Exchange Rates and the Foreign Exchange Market: An Asset Approach

In the year 2000 Americans flocked to Paris to enjoy French cuisine while shopping for designer clothing and other specialties. When measured in terms of dollars, prices in France had actually fallen enough that an American shopper's savings could offset the cost of the airplane ride from home. What economic forces made French goods appear so cheap to residents of the United States? One major factor was a sharp fall in the dollar price of France's currency, a development that made French lodging, dining, and merchandise cheaper for Americans.

The price of one currency in terms of another is called an **exchange rate**. At 4 P.M. New York time on October 24, 2001, you would have needed 1.1935 dollars to buy one unit of the European currency, the euro, so the dollar's exchange rate against the euro was $0.8935 per euro. Because of their strong influence on the current account and other macroeconomic variables, exchange rates are among the most important prices in an open economy.

Because an exchange rate, as the price of one country's money in terms of another's, is also an asset price, the principles governing the behavior of other asset prices also govern the behavior of exchange rates. As you will recall from Chapter 12, the defining characteristic of an asset is that it is a form of wealth, a way of transferring purchasing power from the present into the future. The price that an asset commands today is therefore directly related to the purchasing power over goods and services that buyers expect it to yield in the future. Similarly, today's dollar/euro exchange rate is closely tied to people's expectations about the *future* level of that rate. Just as the price of Microsoft stock rises immediately upon favorable news about Microsoft's future prospects, so do exchange rates respond immediately to any news concerning future currency values.

Our general goals in this chapter are to understand the role of exchange rates in international trade and how exchange rates are determined. To begin, we first learn how exchange rates allow us to compare the prices of different countries' goods and services. Next we describe the international asset market in which currencies are traded and show how equilibrium exchange rates are determined in that market. A final section underlines our asset market approach by showing how today's exchange rate responds to changes in the expected future values of exchange rates.

Exchange Rates and International Transactions

Each country has a currency in which the prices of goods and services are quoted—the dollar in the United States, the euro in Germany, the pound sterling in Britain, the yen in Japan, and the peso in Mexico, to name just a few. Exchange rates play a central role in international trade because they allow us to compare the prices of goods and services produced in different countries. A consumer deciding which of two American cars to buy must compare their dollar prices, for example, $39,000 (for a Lincoln Continental) or $19,000 (for a Ford Taurus). But how is the same consumer to compare either of these prices with the 3,000,000 yen (¥3,000,000) it costs to import a Subaru from Japan? To make this comparison, he or she must know the relative price of dollars and yen.

The relative prices of currencies are reported daily in newspapers' financial sections. Table 13-1 shows the dollar exchange rates for currencies traded in New York at 4 P.M. on October 24, 2001, as reported in the *Wall Street Journal*. Notice that an exchange rate can be quoted in two ways: as the price of the foreign currency in terms of dollars (for example, $0.008139 per yen) or as the price of dollars in terms of the foreign currency (for example, ¥122.87 per dollar). The first of these exchange rate quotations (dollars per foreign currency unit) is said to be in *direct* (or "American") terms, the second (foreign currency units per dollar) in *indirect* (or "European") terms.

Households and firms use exchange rates to translate foreign prices into domestic currency terms. Once the money prices of domestic goods and imports have been expressed in terms of the same currency, households and firms can compute the *relative* prices that affect intentional trade flows.

Domestic and Foreign Prices

If we know the exchange rate between two countries' currencies, we can compute the price of one country's exports in terms of the other country's money. For example, how many dollars would it cost to buy an Edinburgh Woolen Mill sweater costing 50 British pounds (£50)? The answer is found by multiplying the price of the sweater in pounds, 50, by the price of a pound in terms of dollars—the dollar's exchange rate against the pound. At an exchange rate of $1.50 per pound (expressed in American terms), the dollar price of the sweater is

$$(1.50 \ \$/£) \times (£50) = \$75.$$

A change in the dollar/pound exchange rate would alter the sweater's dollar price. At an exchange rate of $1.25 per pound, the sweater would cost only

$$(1.25 \ \$/£) \times (£50) = \$62.50,$$

assuming its price in terms of pounds remained the same. At an exchange rate of $1.75 per pound, the sweater's dollar price would be higher, equal to

$$(1.75 \ \$/£) \times (£50) = \$87.50.$$

Table 13-1 | Exchange Rate Quotations

CURRENCY TRADING

EXCHANGE RATES

Wednesday, October 24, 2001

The New York foreign exchange mid-range rates below apply to trading among banks in amounts of $1 million and more, as quoted at 4 p.m. Eastern time by Reuters and other sources. Retail transactions provide fewer units of foreign currency per dollar. Rates for the 12 Euro currency countries are derived from the latest dollar-euro rate using the exchange ratios set 1/1/99.

Country	U.S. $ EQUIV. Wed	U.S. $ EQUIV. Tue	CURRENCY PER U.S. $ Wed	CURRENCY PER U.S. $ Tue
Argentina (Peso)	1.0001	1.0001	.9999	.9999
Australia (Dollar)	.5083	.5075	1.9675	1.9704
Austria (Schilling)	.06493	.06473	15.400	15.450
Bahrain (Dinar)	2.6525	2.6525	.3770	.3770
Belgium (Franc)	.0221	.0221	45.1482	45.2927
Brazil (Real)	.3626	.3663	2.7580	2.7300
Britain (Pound)	1.4290	1.4259	.6998	.7013
1-month forward	1.4266	1.4233	.7010	.7026
3-months forward	1.4219	1.4187	.7033	.7049
6-months forward	1.4155	1.4120	.7065	.7082
Canada (Dollar)	.6354	.6363	1.5739	1.5717
1-month forward	.6351	.6360	1.5745	1.5723
3-months forward	.6348	.6357	1.5754	1.5731
6-months forward	.6345	.6353	1.5760	1.5741
Chile (Peso)	.001408	.001408	710.15	710.35
China (Renminbi)	.1208	.1208	8.2767	8.2768
Colombia (Peso)	.0004309	.0004312	2320.50	2319.00
Czech. Rep. (Koruna)				
Commercial rate	.02682	.02679	37.291	37.326
Denmark (Krone)	.1202	.1198	8.3226	8.3495
Ecuador (US Dollar)-e	1.0000	1.0000	1.0000	1.0000
Finland (Markka)	.1503	.1498	6.6544	6.6757
France (Franc)	.1362	.1358	7.3414	7.3649
1-month forward	.1361	.1356	7.3495	7.3735
3-months forward	.1358	.1353	7.3654	7.3886
6-months forward	.1354	.1350	7.3838	7.4074
Germany (Mark)	.4568	.4554	2.1890	2.1960
1-month forward	.4563	.4549	2.1914	2.1985
3-months forward	.4554	.4539	2.1961	2.2030
6-months forward	.4542	.4528	2.2016	2.2086
Greece (Drachma)	.002622	.002614	381.37	382.59
Hong Kong (Dollar)	.1282	.1282	7.8000	7.7998
Hungary (Forint)	.003538	.003550	282.69	281.71
India (Rupee)	.02082	.02084	48.030	47.980
Indonesia (Rupiah)	.0000978	.0000983	10230	10170
Ireland (Punt)	1.1346	1.1308	.8814	.8843
Israel (Shekel)	.2319	.2327	4.3130	4.2980
Italy (Lira)	.0004615	.0004600	2167.06	2174.00

Country	U.S. $ EQUIV. Wed	U.S. $ EQUIV. Tue	CURRENCY PER U.S. $ Wed	CURRENCY PER U.S. $ Tue
Japan (Yen)	.008139	.008151	122.87	122.68
1-month forward	.008155	.008168	122.62	122.42
3-months forward	.008186	.008198	122.16	121.98
6-months forward	.008229	.008242	121.53	121.33
Jordan (Dinar)	1.4104	1.4104	.7090	.7090
Kuwait (Dinar)	3.2658	3.2658	.3062	.3062
Lebanon (Pound)	.0006634	.0006614	1507.50	1512.00
Malaysia (Ringgit)-b	.2632	.2632	3.8000	3.8000
Malta (Lira)	2.2212	2.2163	.4502	.4512
Mexico (Peso)				
Floating rate	.1083	.1084	9.2300	9.2250
Netherlands (Guilder)	.4054	.4042	2.4664	2.4743
New Zealand (Dollar)	.4184	.4181	2.3901	2.3918
Norway (Krone)	.1123	.1120	8.9071	8.9311
Pakistan (Rupee)	.01623	.01626	61.500	61.500
Peru (new Sol)	.2897	.2897	3.4515	3.4520
Philippines (Peso)	.01927	.01925	51.900	51.950
Poland (Zloty)-d	.2429	.2432	4.1175	4.1125
Portugal (Escudo)	.004457	.004443	224.38	225.10
Russia (Ruble)-a	.03381	.03382	29.576	29.564
Saudi Arabia (Riyal)	.2666	.2666	3.7512	3.7510
Singapore (Dollar)	.5472	.5477	1.8275	1.8258
Slovak Rep. (Koruna)	.02048	.02046	48.824	48.869
South Africa (Rand)	.1067	.1059	9.3716	9.4400
South Korea (Won)	.0007731	.0007683	1293.50	1301.50
Spain (Peseta)	.005370	.005353	186.22	186.81
Sweden (Krona)	.0943	.0940	10.6050	10.6382
Switzerland (Franc)	.6033	.6024	1.6575	1.6600
1-month forward	.6034	.6025	1.6573	1.6598
3-months forward	.6035	.6026	1.6571	1.6596
6-months forward	.6038	.6030	1.6561	1.6585
Taiwan (Dollar)	.02896	.02896	34.530	34.530
Thailand (Baht)	.02233	.02233	44.790	44.775
Turkey (Lira)-f	.00000062	.00000062	1615000	1610000
United Arab (Dirham)	.2723	.2723	3.6730	3.6730
Uruguay (New Peso)				
Financial	.07177	.07194	13.933	13.900
Venezuela (Bolivar)	.001346	.001346	742.76	742.75
SDR	1.2687	1.2663	.7882	.7897
Euro	.8935	.8907	1.1192	1.1227

Special Drawing Rights (SDR) are based on exchange rates for the U.S., German, British, French, and Japanese currencies. Source: International Monetary Fund.

a-Russian Central Bank rate. b-Government rate. d-Floating rate; trading band suspended on 4/11/00. e-Adopted U.S. dollar as of 9/11/00. f-Floating rate, eff. Feb. 22.

Changes in exchange rates are described as depreciations or appreciations. A **depreciation** of the pound against the dollar is a fall in the dollar price of pounds, for example, a change in the exchange rate from $1.50 per pound to $1.25 per pound. The preceding example shows that *all else equal, a depreciation of a country's currency makes its goods cheaper for foreigners.* A rise in the pound's price in terms of dollars—for example, from $1.50 per pound to $1.75 per pound—is an **appreciation** of the pound against the dollar. *All else equal, an appreciation of a country's currency makes its goods more expensive for foreigners.*

The exchange rate changes discussed in the example simultaneously alter the prices Britons pay for American goods. At an exchange rate of $1.50 per pound, the pound price of a pair of American designer jeans costing $45 is ($45)/(1.50 $/£) = £30. A change in the exchange rate from $1.50 per pound to $1.25 per pound, while a depreciation of the pound against the dollar, is also a rise in the pound price of dollars, an *appreciation* of the dollar against the pound. This appreciation of the dollar makes the American jeans more expensive for Britons by raising their pound price to

$$(\$45)/(1.25 \ \$/£) = £36.$$

The change in the exchange rate from $1.50 per pound to $1.75 per pound—an appreciation of the pound against the dollar but a depreciation of the dollar against the pound—lowers the pound price of the jeans to

$$(\$45)/(1.75\ \$/\pounds) = \pounds25.71.$$

As you can see, descriptions of exchange rate changes as depreciations or appreciations can be bewildering, because when one currency depreciates against another, the second currency must simultaneously appreciate against the first. To avoid confusion in discussing exchange rates, we must always keep track of which of the two currencies we are examining has depreciated or appreciated against the other.

If we remember that a depreciation of the dollar against the pound is at the same time an appreciation of the pound against the dollar, we reach the following conclusion: *When a country's currency depreciates, foreigners find that its exports are cheaper and domestic residents find that imports from abroad are more expensive. An appreciation has opposite effects: Foreigners pay more for the country's products and domestic consumers pay less for foreign products.*

Exchange Rates and Relative Prices

Import and export demands, like the demands for all goods and services, are influenced by *relative* prices, such as the price of sweaters in terms of designer jeans. We have just seen how exchange rates allow individuals to compare domestic and foreign money prices by expressing them in a common currency unit. Carrying this analysis one step further, we can see that exchange rates also allow individuals to compute the relative prices of goods and services whose money prices are quoted in different currencies.

An American trying to decide how much to spend on American jeans and how much to spend on British sweaters must translate their prices into a common currency to compute the price of sweaters in terms of jeans. As we have seen, an exchange rate of $1.50 per pound means that an American pays $75 for a sweater priced at £50 in Britain. Because the price of a pair of American jeans is $45, the price of sweaters in terms of jeans is ($75 per sweater)/($45 per pair of jeans) = 1.67 pairs of jeans per sweater. Naturally, a Briton faces the same relative price of (£50 per sweater)/(£30 per pair of jeans) = 1.67 pairs of jeans per sweater.

Table 13-2 shows the relative prices implied by exchange rates of $1.25 per pound, $1.50 per pound, and $1.75 per pound, on the assumption that the dollar price of jeans and the pound price of sweaters are unaffected by the exchange rate changes. To test your understanding, try to calculate these relative prices for yourself and confirm that the outcome of the calculation is the same for a Briton and for an American.

The table shows that if the goods' money prices do not change, an appreciation of the dollar against the pound makes sweaters cheaper in terms of jeans (each pair of jeans buys more sweaters) while a depreciation of the dollar against the pound makes sweaters more expensive in terms of jeans (each pair of jeans buys fewer sweaters). The computations illustrate a general principle: *All else equal, an appreciation of a country's currency raises the relative price of its exports and lowers the relative price of its imports. Conversely, a depreciation lowers the relative price of a country's exports and raises the relative price of its imports.*

Table 13-2	$/£ Exchange Rates and the Relative Price of American Designer Jeans and British Sweaters		
Exchange rate ($/£)	1.25	1.50	1.75
Relative price (pairs of jeans/sweater)	1.39	1.67	1.94

Note: The above calculations assume unchanged money prices of $45 per pair of jeans and £50 per sweater.

The Foreign Exchange Market

Just as other prices in the economy are determined by the interaction of buyers and sellers, exchange rates are determined by the interaction of the households, firms, and financial institutions that buy and sell foreign currencies to make international payments. The market in which international currency trades take place is called the **foreign exchange market**.

The Actors

The major participants in the foreign exchange market are commercial banks, corporations that engage in international trade, nonbank financial institutions such as asset-management firms and insurance companies, and central banks. Individuals may also participate in the foreign exchange market—for example, the tourist who buys foreign currency at a hotel's front desk—but such cash transactions are an insignificant fraction of total foreign exchange trading.

We now describe the major actors in the market and their roles.

   1. *Commercial banks.* Commercial banks are at the center of the foreign exchange market because almost every sizable international transaction involves the debiting and crediting of accounts at commercial banks in various financial centers. Thus, the vast majority of foreign exchange transactions involve the exchange of *bank deposits* denominated in different currencies.

   Let's look at an example. Suppose Exxon Corporation wishes to pay €160,000 to a German supplier. First, Exxon gets an exchange rate quotation from its own commercial bank, the Third National Bank. Then it instructs Third National to debit Exxon's dollar account and pay €160,000 into the supplier's account at a German bank. If the exchange rate quoted to Exxon by Third National is $1.2 per euro, $192,000 (= $1.2 per euro × €160,000) is debited from Exxon's account. The final result of the transaction is the exchange of a $192,000 deposit at Third National Bank (now owned by the German bank that supplied the euros) for the €160,000 deposit used by Third National to pay Exxon's German supplier.

   As the example shows, banks routinely enter the foreign exchange market to meet the needs of their customers—primarily corporations. In addition, a bank will also quote to other banks exchange rates at which it is willing to buy currencies from them and sell currencies to them. Foreign currency trading among banks—called **interbank trading**—accounts for most of the activity in the foreign exchange market. In fact, the exchange rates listed in Table 13-1 are interbank rates, the rates banks charge to each other. No amount less than $1 million is traded at those rates. The rates available to cor-

A TALE OF TWO DOLLARS

Back in 1976, the United States dollar and the Canadian dollar traded roughly at par, that is, at a one-to-one exchange rate. In the following decades, however, Canada's dollar has steadily depreciated against its American cousin. By early 2002, a Canadian dollar was worth only about 65 United States cents.*

The tendency of the Canadian currency to depreciate accelerated in the late 1990s as the world prices of many of Canada's natural resource exports slumped. Canadian manufacturing exporters were cheered by their ability to sell goods more easily abroad, while importers grimaced at the higher prices they had to pay. Nowhere were the effects more striking than at Niagara Falls, where thousands cross the U.S.-Canada border, going in both directions, every day. Canadians accustomed to going to the U.S. side for a weekend dinner found it harder to afford the meal. At the same time, Americans could suddenly find bargains on the Canadian side.

Canadian one-dollar coins carry on their backs the picture of a loon, the web-footed, fish-eating bird often seen and heard on Canada's lakes. Canada's dollar therefore is widely known as the "loonie." One group of Canadian birds avoiding the loonie in the late 1990s was the Toronto Blue Jays. Because the American League baseball team plays most of its games south of the Canadian border and participates in a United States–based market for players, 80 percent of its expenses (including players' salaries) are set in U.S. dollars. On the other hand, 80 percent of its revenues (including ballpark receipts) are paid in Canadian dollars. A sudden and sharp depreciation of the loonie thus would cause big losses for the team by raising its expenses relative to its receipts. To protect itself from the vagaries of the exchange rate, the team tries to predict its need for U.S. dollars ahead of time so that it can sell loonies and purchase the American currency in advance to lock in the exchange rate. Errors in the currency market can be more costly to the Blue Jays than errors on the field.[†]

---

*See "Showing in Canada: The Mystery of the Falling Dollar." *New York Times,* Wednesday, January 9, 2002, p. W1.

[†]See "Don't Cry Over Diving Loonies: Canadian Dollar Plummets to a Collective Ho-Hum." *New York Times,* Tuesday, June 23, 1998, p. C1.

---

porate customers, called "retail" rates, are usually less favorable than the "wholesale" interbank rates. The difference between the retail and wholesale rates is the bank's compensation for doing the business.

Because their international operations are so extensive, large commercial banks are well-suited to bring buyers and sellers of currencies together. A multinational corporation wishing to convert $100,000 into Swedish kronor might find it difficult and costly to locate other corporations wishing to sell the right amount of kronor. By serving many customers simultaneously through a single large purchase of kronor, a bank can economize on these search costs.

2. *Corporations.* Corporations with operations in several countries frequently make or receive payments in currencies other than that of the country in which they are headquartered. To pay workers at a plant in Mexico, for example, IBM may need Mexican pesos. If IBM has only dollars earned by selling computers in the United States, it can acquire the pesos it needs by buying them with its dollars in the foreign exchange market.

3. *Nonbank financial institutions.* Over the years, deregulation of financial markets in the United States, Japan, and other countries has encouraged nonbank financial institutions to offer their customers a broader range of services, many of them indistinguishable from those offered by banks. Among these have been services involving foreign exchange transactions. Institutional investors, such as pension funds, often trade foreign currencies.

4. *Central banks.* In the previous chapter we learned that central banks sometimes intervene in foreign exchange markets. While the volume of central bank transactions is typically not large, the impact of these transactions may be great. The reason for this impact is that participants in the foreign exchange market watch central bank actions closely for clues about future macroeconomic policies that may affect exchange rates. Government agencies other than central banks may also trade in the foreign exchange market, but central banks are the most regular official participants.

Characteristics of the Market

Foreign exchange trading takes place in many financial centers, with the largest volume of trade occurring in such major cities as London (the largest market), New York, Tokyo, Frankfurt, and Singapore. The worldwide volume of foreign exchange trading is enormous, and it has ballooned in recent years. In April 1989 the average total value of global foreign exchange trading was close to $600 billion *per day,* of which $184 billion were traded daily in London, $115 billion in the United States, and $111 billion in Tokyo. Only twelve years later, in April 2001, the daily global value of foreign exchange trading had jumped to around $1.2 trillion, of which $504 billion were traded daily in London, $254 billion in New York, and $147 billion in Tokyo.[1]

Direct telephone, fax, and Internet links among the major foreign exchange trading centers make each a part of a single world market on which the sun never sets. Economic news released at any time of the day is immediately transmitted around the world and may set off a flurry of activity by market participants. Even after trading in New York has finished, New York–based banks and corporations with affiliates in other time zones can remain active in the market. Foreign exchange traders may deal from their homes when a late-night communication alerts them to important developments in a financial center on another continent.

The integration of financial centers implies that there can be no significant difference between the dollar/euro exchange rate quoted in New York at 9 A.M. and the dollar/euro exchange rate quoted in London at the same time (which corresponds to 2 P.M. London time). If the euro were selling for $1.1 in New York and $1.2 in London, profits could be made through **arbitrage**, the process of buying a currency cheap and selling it dear. At the prices listed above, a trader could, for instance, purchase €1 million in New York for $1.1 million and immediately sell the euros in London for $1.2 million, making a pure profit of

---

[1] April 1989 figures come from surveys carried out simultaneously by the Federal Reserve Bank of New York, the Bank of England, the Bank of Japan, the Bank of Canada, and monetary authorities from France, Italy, the Netherlands, Singapore, Hong Kong, and Australia. The April 2001 survey was carried out by 48 central banks. Revised figures for 1989–2001 are reported in "Central Bank Survey of Foreign Exchange and Derivatives Market Activity in April 2001: Preliminary Global Data," Press Release, Bank for International Settlements, Basle, Switzerland, October 9, 2001. Daily U.S. foreign currency trading in 1980 averaged only around $18 billion.

$100,000. If all traders tried to cash in on the opportunity, however, their demand for euros in New York would drive up the dollar price of euros there, and their supply of euros in London would drive down the dollar price of euros there. Very quickly, the difference between the New York and London exchange rates would disappear. Since foreign exchange traders carefully watch their computer screens for arbitrage opportunities, the few that arise are small and very short-lived.

While a foreign exchange transaction can involve any two currencies, most transactions between banks (around 90 percent in 2001) involve exchanges of foreign currencies for U.S. dollars. This is true even when a bank's goal is to sell one nondollar currency and buy another! A bank wishing to sell Swiss francs and buy Israeli shekels, for example, will usually sell its francs for dollars and then use the dollars to buy shekels. While this procedure may appear roundabout, it is actually cheaper for the bank than the alternative of trying to find a holder of shekels who wishes to buy Swiss francs. The advantage of trading through the dollar is a result of the United States' importance in the world economy. Because the volume of international transactions involving dollars is so great, it is not hard to find parties willing to trade dollars against Swiss francs or shekels. In contrast, relatively few transactions require direct exchanges of Swiss francs for shekels.[2]

Because of its pivotal role in so many foreign exchange deals, the dollar is sometimes called a **vehicle currency**. A vehicle currency is one that is widely used to denominate international contracts made by parties who do not reside in the country that issues the vehicle currency. It has been suggested that the euro, which was introduced at the start of 1999, will evolve into a vehicle currency on a par with the dollar. By April 2001, however, only about 38 percent of foreign exchange trades involved euros. The pound sterling, once second only to the dollar as a key international currency, has declined in importance.[3]

Spot Rates and Forward Rates

The foreign exchange transactions we have been discussing take place on the spot: two parties agree to an exchange of bank deposits and execute the deal immediately. Exchange rates governing such "on-the-spot" trading are called **spot exchange rates**, and the deal is called a spot transaction.

The term *spot* is a bit misleading because even spot exchanges usually become effective only two days after a deal is struck. The delay occurs because in most cases it takes two days for payment instructions (such as checks) to be cleared through the banking system.[4] Suppose Apple Computer has pounds in an account at the National Westminster Bank in

---

[2]The Swiss franc/shekel exchange rate can be calculated from the dollar/franc and dollar/shekel exchange rates as the dollar/shekel rate divided by the dollar/franc rate. If the dollar/franc rate is $0.80 per franc and the dollar/shekel rate is $0.20 per shekel, then the Swiss franc/shekel rate is (0.20 $/shekel)/(0.80 $/franc) = 0.25 Swiss francs/shekel. Exchange rates between nondollar currencies are called "cross rates" by foreign exchange traders.

[3]For more detailed discussion of vehicle currencies, see Richard Portes and Hélène Rey, "The Emergence of the Euro as an International Currency," *Economic Policy* 26 (April 1998), pp. 307–343. Data on currency shares come from Bank for International Settlements, *op. cit.,* footnote 1.

[4]A major exception involves trades of U.S. dollars for Canadian dollars in New York. These are executed with a one-day lag. Currently international banks are working on ways to reduce these settlement lags through a system called Continuous Linked Settlement that is due to be introduced soon.

London but sells them to the Bank of America in San Francisco, which has offered Apple a more favorable spot exchange rate for pounds than the bank where it has its dollar account, Wells Fargo. On Monday, June 20, Apple pays the pounds to Bank of America with a pound check drawn on National Westminster, while Bank of America, to pay Apple, wires dollars into Apple's account at Wells Fargo. Normally, Apple cannot use the dollars it has bought, nor can Bank of America use its pounds, until Wednesday, June 22, two business days later. In the jargon of the foreign exchange market, the *value date* for a spot transaction—the date on which the parties actually receive the funds they have purchased—occurs two business days after the deal is made.

Foreign exchange deals sometimes specify a value date farther away than two days—30 days, 90 days, 180 days, or even several years. The exchange rates quoted in such transactions are called **forward exchange rates**. In a 30-day forward transaction, for example, two parties may agree on April 1 to a spot exchange of £100,000 for $155,000 on May 1. The 30-day forward exchange rate is therefore $1.55 per pound, and it is generally different from the spot rate and from the forward rates applied to different value dates. When you agree to sell pounds for dollars on a future date at a forward rate agreed on today, you have "sold pounds forward" and "bought dollars forward."

Table 13-1 reports forward exchange rates for the most heavily traded foreign currencies. (The forward quotations, when available, are listed below the corresponding spot quotations.) Forward and spot exchange rates, while not necessarily equal, do move closely together, as illustrated for dollar/pound rates in Figure 13-1. The appendix to this chapter, which discusses how forward exchange rates are determined, explains this close relationship between movements in spot and forward rates.

An example shows why parties may wish to engage in forward exchange transactions. Suppose an American who imports radios from Japan knows that in 30 days he must pay yen to a Japanese supplier for a shipment arriving then. The importer can sell each radio for $100 and must pay his supplier ¥9,000 per radio; so his profit depends on the dollar/yen exchange rate. At the current spot exchange rate of $0.0105 per yen, the importer would pay ($0.0105 per yen) × (¥9,000 per radio) = $94.50 per radio and would therefore make $5.50 on each radio imported. But the importer will not have the funds to pay the supplier until the radios arrive and are sold. If over the next 30 days the dollar unexpectedly depreciates to $0.0115 per yen, the importer will have to pay ($0.0115 per yen) × (¥9,000 per radio) = $103.50 per radio and so will take a $3.50 *loss* on each.

To avoid this risk, the importer can make a 30-day forward exchange deal with his bank. If the bank agrees to sell yen to the importer in 30 days at a rate of $0.0107, the importer is assured of paying exactly ($0.0107 per yen) × (¥9,000 per radio) = $96.30 per radio to the supplier. By buying yen and selling dollars forward, the importer is guaranteed a profit of $3.70 per radio and is insured against the possibility that a sudden exchange rate change will turn a profitable importing deal into a loss.

From now on, when we mention an exchange rate without specifying whether it is a spot rate or a forward rate, we will always be referring to the spot rate.

Foreign Exchange Swaps

A foreign exchange *swap* is a spot sale of a currency combined with a forward repurchase of the currency. For example, a multinational company has just received $1 million from sales and knows it will have to pay those dollars to a California supplier in three months.

Figure 13-1 | Dollar/Pound Spot and Forward Exchange Rates, 1981–2001

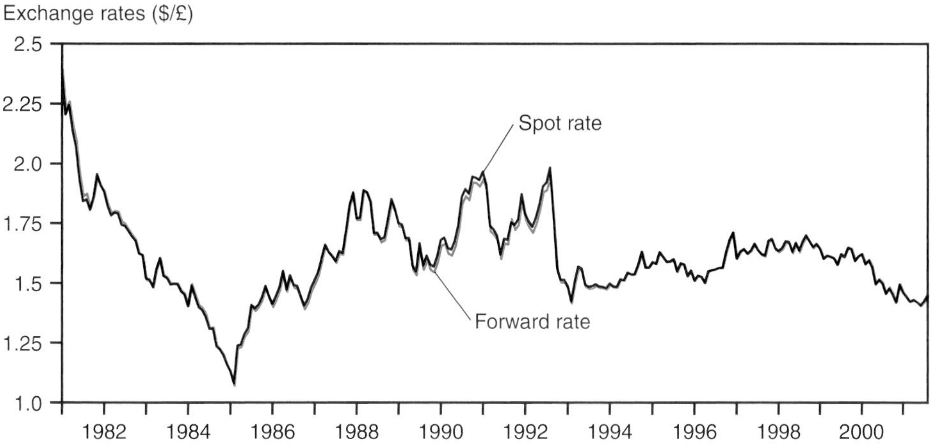

Exchange rates ($/£)

Spot rate

Forward rate

Spot and forward exchange rates tend to move in a highly correlated fashion.

Source: *Datastream.* Rates shown are 90-day forward exchange rates and spot exchange rates, at end of month.

The company's asset-management department would meanwhile like to invest the $1 million in Swiss francs. A three-month swap of dollars into Swiss francs may result in lower brokers' fees than the two separate transactions of selling dollars for spot Swiss francs and selling the Swiss francs for dollars on the forward market. Swaps make up a significant proportion of all foreign exchange trading.

Futures and Options

Several other financial instruments traded in the foreign exchange market, like forward contracts, involve future exchanges of currencies. The timing and terms of the exchanges can differ, however, from those specified in forward contracts, giving traders additional flexibility in avoiding foreign exchange risk. Only 20 years ago, some of these instruments were not traded on organized exchanges.

When you buy a *futures contract,* you buy a promise that a specified amount of foreign currency will be delivered on a specified date in the future. A forward contract between you and some other private party is an alternative way to ensure that you receive the same amount of foreign currency on the date in question. But while you have no choice about fulfilling your end of a forward deal, you can sell your futures contract on an organized futures exchange, realizing a profit or loss right away. Such a sale might appear advantageous, for example, if your views about the future spot exchange rate were to change.

A *foreign exchange option* gives its owner the right to buy or sell a specified amount of foreign currency at a specified price at any time up to a specified expiration date. The other party to the deal, the option's seller, is required to sell or buy the foreign currency at the discretion of the option's owner, who is under no obligation to exercise his right.

Imagine that you are uncertain about when in the next month a foreign currency payment will arrive. To avoid the risk of a loss, you may wish to buy a *put option* giving you the right to sell the foreign currency at a known exchange rate at any time during the month. If instead you expect to make a payment abroad sometime in the month, a *call option,* which gives you the right to buy foreign currency to make the payment at a known price, might be attractive. Options can be written on many underlying assets (including foreign exchange futures), and, like futures, they are freely bought and sold.

The Demand for Foreign Currency Assets

We have now seen how banks, corporations, and other institutions trade foreign currency bank deposits in a worldwide foreign exchange market that operates 24 hours a day. To understand how exchange rates are determined by the foreign exchange market, we first must ask how the major actors' demands for different types of foreign currency deposits are determined.

The demand for a foreign currency bank deposit is influenced by the same considerations that influence the demand for any other asset. Chief among these considerations is our view of what the deposit will be worth in the future. A foreign currency deposit's future value depends in turn on two factors: the interest rate it offers and the expected change in the currency's exchange rate against other currencies.

Assets and Asset Returns

As you will recall, people can hold wealth in many forms—stocks, bonds, cash, real estate, rare wines, diamonds, and so on. The object of acquiring wealth—of saving—is to transfer purchasing power into the future. We may do this to provide for our retirement years, for our heirs, or simply because we earn more than we need to spend in a particular year and prefer to save the balance for a rainy day.

Defining Asset Returns.   Because the object of saving is to provide for future consumption, we judge the desirability of an asset largely on the basis of its **rate of return**, that is, the percentage increase in value it offers over some time period. For example, suppose that at the beginning of 2003 you pay $100 for a share of stock issued by Financial Soothsayers, Inc. If the stock pays you a dividend of $1 at the beginning of 2004, and if the stock's price rises from $100 to $109 per share over the year, then you have earned a rate of return of 10 percent on the stock over 2003—that is, your initial $100 investment has grown in value to $110, the sum of the $1 dividend and the $109 you could get by selling your share. Had Financial Soothsayers stock still paid out its $1 dividend but dropped in price to $89 per share, your $100 investment would be worth only $90 by year's end, giving a rate of return of *negative* 10 percent.

You often cannot know with certainty the return that an asset will actually pay after you buy it. Both the dividend paid by a share of stock and the share's resale price, for example, may be hard to predict. Your decision therefore must be based on an *expected* rate of return. To calculate an expected rate of return over some time period, you make your best forecast of the asset's total value at the period's end. The percentage difference between that expected future value and the price you pay for the asset today equals the asset's expected rate of return over the time period.

When we measure an asset's rate of return, we compare how an investment in the asset changes in total value between two dates. In the previous example, we compared how the value of an investment in Financial Soothsayers stock changed between 2003 ($100) and 2004 ($110) to conclude that the rate of return on the stock was 10 percent per year. We call this a *dollar* rate of return because the two values we compare are expressed in terms of dollars. It is also possible, however, to compute different rates of return by expressing the two values in terms of a foreign currency or a commodity such as gold.

The Real Rate of Return.   The expected rate of return that savers consider in deciding which assets to hold is the expected **real rate of return**, that is, the rate of return computed by measuring asset values in terms of some broad representative basket of products that savers regularly purchase. It is the expected real return that matters because the ultimate goal of saving is future consumption, and only the *real* return measures the goods and services a saver can buy in the future in return for giving up some consumption (that is, saving) today.

To continue our example, suppose the dollar value of an investment in Financial Soothsayers stock increases by 10 percent between 2003 and 2004 but that the dollar prices of all goods and services *also* increase by 10 percent. Then in terms of output—that is, in *real* terms—the investment would be worth no more in 2003 than in 2004. With a real rate of return of zero, Financial Soothsayers stock would not be a very desirable asset.

Although savers care about expected real rates of return, rates of return expressed in terms of a currency can still be used to *compare* real returns on *different* assets. Even if all dollar prices rise by 10 percent between 2003 and 2004, a rare bottle of wine whose dollar price rises by 25 percent is still a better investment than a bond whose dollar value rises by 20 percent. The real rate of return offered by the wine is 15 percent (= 25 percent − 10 percent) while that offered by the bond is only 10 percent (= 20 percent − 10 percent). Notice that the difference between the dollar returns of the two assets (25 percent − 20 percent) must equal the difference between their real returns (15 percent − 10 percent). The reason for this equality is that, given the two assets' dollar returns, a change in the rate at which the dollar prices of goods are rising changes both assets' real returns by the same amount.

The distinction between real rates of return and dollar rates of return illustrates an important concept in studying how savers evaluate different assets: The returns on two assets cannot be compared unless they are measured in the *same* units. For example, it makes no sense to compare directly the real return on the bottle of wine (15 percent in our example) with the dollar return on the bond (20 percent) or to compare the dollar return on old paintings with the euro return on gold. Only after the returns are expressed in terms of a common unit of measure—for example, all in terms of dollars—can we tell which asset offers the highest expected real rate of return.

Risk and Liquidity

All else equal, individuals prefer to hold those assets offering the highest expected real rate of return. Our later discussions of particular assets will show, however, that "all else" often is not equal. Some assets may be valued by savers for attributes other than the expected real rate of return they offer. Savers care about two main characteristics of an asset other than its return: its **risk**, the variability it contributes to savers' wealth, and its **liquidity**, the ease with which the asset can be sold or exchanged for goods.

1. *Risk.* An asset's real return is usually unpredictable and may turn out to be quite different from what savers expect when they purchase the asset. In our last example, savers found the expected real rate of return on an investment in bonds (10 percent) by subtracting from the expected rate of increase in the investment's dollar value (20 percent) the expected rate of increase in dollar prices (10 percent). But if expectations are wrong and the bonds' dollar value stays constant instead of rising by 20 percent, the saver ends up with a real return of *negative* 10 percent (= 0 percent − 10 percent). Savers dislike uncertainty and are reluctant to hold assets that make their wealth highly variable. An asset with a high expected rate of return may appear undesirable to savers if its realized rate of return fluctuates widely.

2. *Liquidity.* Assets also differ according to the cost and speed at which savers can dispose of them. A house, for example, is not very liquid because its sale usually requires time and the services of brokers, inspectors, and lawyers. In contrast, cash is the most liquid of assets: It is always acceptable at face value as payment for goods or other assets. Savers prefer to hold some liquid assets as a precaution against unexpected expenses that might force them to sell less liquid assets at a loss. They will therefore consider an asset's liquidity as well as its expected return and risk in deciding how much of it to hold.

Interest Rates

As in other asset markets, participants in the foreign exchange market base their demands for deposits of different currencies on a comparison of these assets' expected rates of return. To compare returns on different deposits, market participants need two pieces of information. First, they need to know how the money values of the deposits will change. Second, they need to know how exchange rates will change so that they can translate rates of return measured in different currencies into comparable terms.

The first piece of information needed to compute the rate of return on a deposit of a particular currency is the currency's **interest rate**, the amount of that currency an individual can earn by lending a unit of the currency for a year. At a dollar interest rate of 0.10 (quoted as 10 percent per year), the lender of $1 receives $1.10 at the end of the year, $1 of which is principal and 10 cents of which is interest. Looked at from the other side of the transaction the interest rate on dollars is also the amount that must be paid to borrow $1 for a year. When you buy a U.S. Treasury bill, you earn the interest rate on dollars because you are lending dollars to the U.S. government.

Interest rates play an important role in the foreign exchange market because the large deposits traded there pay interest, each at a rate reflecting its currency of denomination. For example, when the interest rate on dollars is 10 percent per year, a $100,000 deposit is worth $110,000 after a year; when the interest rate on euros is 5 percent per year, a €100,000 deposit is worth €105,000 after a year. Deposits pay interest because they are really loans from the depositor to the bank. When a corporation or a financial institution deposits a currency in a bank, it is lending that currency to the bank rather than using it for some current expenditure. In other words, the depositor is acquiring an asset denominated in the currency it deposits.

The dollar interest rate is simply the dollar rate of return on dollar deposits. You "buy" the deposit by lending a bank $100,000, and when you are paid back with 10 percent interest at the end of the year your asset is worth $110,000. This gives a rate of return of $(110{,}000 - 100{,}000)/100{,}000 = 0.10$, or 10 percent per year. Similarly, a foreign currency's interest rate

Figure 13-2 | Interest Rates on Dollar and Deutschemark Deposits, 1975–1998

Interest rates (percent per year)

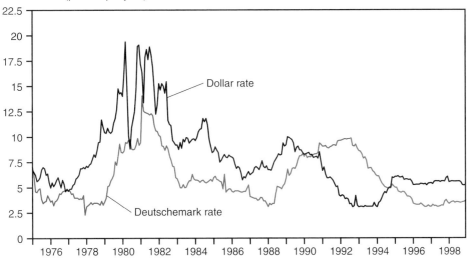

Since dollar and DM interest rates are not measured in comparable terms, they can move quite differently over time.

Source: Datastream. Three-month interest rates are shown.

measures the foreign currency return on deposits of that currency. Figure 13-2 shows the monthly behavior of interest rates on the dollar and the deutschemark (Germany's currency before 1999, which has been replaced by the euro) from 1975 to 1998.[5] These interest rates are not measured in comparable terms, so there is no reason for them to be close to each other or to move in similar ways over time.[6]

Exchange Rates and Asset Returns

The interest rates offered by a dollar and a euro deposit tell us how their dollar and euro values will change over a year. The other piece of information we need to compare the rates of return offered by dollar and euro deposits is the expected change in the dollar/euro exchange rate over the year. To see which deposit, euro or dollar, offers a higher expected rate of return, you must ask the question: If I use dollars to buy a euro deposit, how many

---

[5] Table 13-1 reports the dollar exchange rates of the deutschemark, the French franc, the Italian lira, and other currencies that were replaced by the euro on January 1, 1999. Countries in the euro zone are Austria, Belgium, Finland, France, Germany, Greece, Ireland, Italy, Luxembourg, the Netherlands, Portugal, and Spain. Their currencies, referred to as "legacy currencies," were phased out early in 2002. See Chapter 20 for details.

[6] Chapter 7 presented *real* interest rates, which are simply real rates of return on loans, that is, interest rates expressed in terms of a consumption basket. Interest rates expressed in terms of currencies are called *nominal* interest rates. The connection between real and nominal interest rates is discussed in detail in Chapter 15.

dollars will I get back after a year? When you answer this question, you are calculating the *dollar* rate of return on a euro deposit because you are comparing its *dollar* price today with its *dollar* value a year from today.

To see how to approach this type of calculation, let's look at the following situation: Suppose that today's exchange rate (quoted in American terms) is $1.10 per euro, but that you expect the rate to be $1.165 per euro in a year (perhaps because you expect unfavorable developments in the U.S. economy). Suppose also that the dollar interest rate is 10 percent per year while the euro interest rate is 5 percent per year. This means a deposit of $1.00 pays $1.10 after a year while a deposit of €1 pays €1.05 after a year. Which of these deposits offers the higher return?

The answer can be found in five steps.

Step 1. Use today's dollar/euro exchange rate to figure out the dollar price of a euro deposit of, say, €1. If the exchange rate today is $1.10 per euro, the dollar price of a €1 deposit is just $1.10.

Step 2. Use the euro interest rate to find the amount of euro you will have a year from now if you purchase a €1 deposit today. You know that the interest rate on euro deposits is 5 percent per year. So at the end of a year, your €1 deposit will be worth €1.05.

Step 3. Use the exchange rate you expect to prevail a year from today to calculate the expected dollar value of the euro amount determined in Step 2. Since you expect the dollar to depreciate against the euro over the coming year so that the exchange rate 12 months from today is $1.165 per euro, then you expect the dollar value of your euro deposit after a year to be $1.165 per euro × €1.05 = $1.223.

Step 4. Now that you know the dollar price of a €1 deposit today ($1.10) and can forecast its value in a year ($1.223), you can calculate the expected *dollar* rate of return on a euro deposit as (1.223 − 1.10)/1.10 = 0.11, or 11 percent per year.

Step 5. Since the dollar rate of return on dollar deposits (the dollar interest rate) is only 10 percent per year, you expect to do better by holding your wealth in the form of euro deposits. Despite the fact that the dollar interest rate exceeds the euro interest rate by 5 percent per year, the euro's expected appreciation against the dollar gives euro holders a prospective capital gain that is large enough to make euro deposits the higher-yield asset.

A Simple Rule

There is a simple rule that shortens this calculation. First, define the **rate of depreciation** of the dollar against the euro as the percentage increase in the dollar/euro exchange rate over a year. In the last example, the dollar's expected depreciation rate is (1.165 − 1.10)/1.10 = 0.059, or roughly 6 percent per year. Once you have calculated the rate of depreciation of the dollar against the euro, our rule is this: *The dollar rate of return on euro deposits is approximately the euro interest rate plus the rate of depreciation of the dollar against the euro.* In other words, to translate the euro return on euro deposits into dollar terms, you need to add the rate at which the euro's dollar price rises over a year to the euro interest rate.

In our example, the sum of the euro interest rate (5 percent) and the expected depreciation rate of the dollar (roughly 6 percent) is about 11 percent, which is what we found to be the expected dollar return on euro deposits in our first calculation.

We summarize our discussion by introducing some notation:

$R_{\unicode{8364}}$ = today's interest rate on one-year euro deposits,
$E_{\$/\unicode{8364}}$ = today's dollar/euro exchange rate (number of dollars per euro),
$E_{\$/\unicode{8364}}^{e}$ = dollar/euro exchange rate (number of dollars per euro) expected to prevail a year
  from today.

(The superscript ^{e} attached to this last exchange rate indicates that it is a forecast of the future exchange rate based on what people know today.)

Using these symbols, we write the expected rate of return on a euro deposit, measured in terms of dollars, as the sum of (1) the euro interest rate and (2) the expected rate of dollar depreciation against the euro:

$$R_{\unicode{8364}} + (E_{\$/\unicode{8364}}^{e} - E_{\$/\unicode{8364}})/E_{\$/\unicode{8364}}.$$

This expected return is what must be compared with the interest rate on one-year dollar deposits, $R_{\$}$, in deciding whether dollar or euro deposits offer the higher expected rate of return.[7] The expected rate of return difference between dollar and euro deposits is therefore equal to $R_{\$}$ less the above expression,

$$R_{\$} - [R_{\unicode{8364}} + (E_{\$/\unicode{8364}}^{e} - E_{\$/\unicode{8364}})/E_{\$/\unicode{8364}}] = R_{\$} - R_{\unicode{8364}} - (E_{\$/\unicode{8364}}^{e} - E_{\$/\unicode{8364}})/E_{\$/\unicode{8364}}. \qquad (13\text{-}1)$$

When the difference above is positive, dollar deposits yield the higher expected rate of return; when it is negative, euro deposits yield the higher expected rate of return.

Table 13-3 carries out some illustrative comparisons. In case 1, the interest difference in favor of dollar deposits is 4 percent per year ($R_{\$} - R_{\unicode{8364}} = 0.10 - 0.06 = 0.04$), and no change in the exchange rate is expected [$(E_{\$/\unicode{8364}}^{e} - E_{\$/\unicode{8364}})/E_{\$/\unicode{8364}} = 0.00$]. This means that the expected annual real rate of return on dollar deposits is 4 percent higher than that on euro, so that, other things equal, you would prefer to hold your wealth as dollar rather than euro deposits.

In case 2 the interest difference is the same (4 percent), but it is just offset by an expected depreciation rate of the dollar of 4 percent. The two assets therefore have the same expected rate of return.

---

[7] If you compute the expected dollar return on euro deposits using the exact five-step method we described before introducing the simple rule, you'll find that it actually equals

$$(1 + R_{\unicode{8364}})(E_{\$/\unicode{8364}}^{e}/E_{\$/\unicode{8364}}) - 1.$$

This exact formula can be rewritten, however, as

$$R_{\unicode{8364}} + (E_{\$/\unicode{8364}}^{e} - E_{\$/\unicode{8364}})/E_{\$/\unicode{8364}} + R_{\unicode{8364}} \times (E_{\$/\unicode{8364}}^{e} - E_{\$/\unicode{8364}})/E_{\$/\unicode{8364}}.$$

The expression above is very close to the formula derived from the simple rule when, as is usually the case, the product $R_{\unicode{8364}} \times (E_{\$/\unicode{8364}}^{e} - E_{\$/\unicode{8364}})/E_{\$/\unicode{8364}}$ is a small number.

Table 13-3 | Comparing Dollar Rates of Return on Dollar and Euro Deposits

Case	Dollar Interest Rate $R_\$$	Euro Interest Rate R_ϵ	Expected Rate of Dollar Depreciation against Euro $\dfrac{E^e_{\$/\epsilon} - E_{\$/\epsilon}}{E_{\$/\epsilon}}$	Rate of Return Difference between Dollar and Euro Deposits $R_\$ - R_\epsilon - \dfrac{(E^e_{\$/\epsilon} - E_{\$/\epsilon})}{E_{\$/\epsilon}}$
1	0.10	0.06	0.00	0.04
2	0.10	0.06	0.04	0.00
3	0.10	0.06	0.08	−0.04
4	0.10	0.12	−0.04	0.02

Case 3 is similar to the one discussed earlier: A 4 percent interest difference in favor of dollar deposits is more than offset by an 8 percent expected depreciation of the dollar, so euro deposits are preferred by market participants.

In case 4, there is a 2 percent interest difference in favor of euro deposits, but the dollar is expected to *appreciate* against the euro by 4 percent over the year. The expected rate of return on dollar deposits is therefore 2 percent per year higher than that on euro.

So far we have been translating all returns into dollar terms. But the rate of return differentials we calculated would have been the same had we chosen to express returns in terms of euro or in terms of some third currency. Suppose, for example, we wanted to measure the return on dollar deposits in terms of euro. Following our simple rule, we would add to the dollar interest rate $R_\$$ the expected rate of depreciation of the euro against the dollar. But the expected rate of depreciation of the euro against the dollar is approximately the expected **rate of appreciation** of the dollar against the euro, that is, the expected rate of depreciation of the dollar against the euro with a minus sign in front of it. This means that in terms of euro, the return on a dollar deposit is

$$R_\$ - (E^e_{\$/\epsilon} - E_{\$/\epsilon})/E_{\$/\epsilon}.$$

The difference between the expression above and R_ϵ is identical to equation (13-1). Thus, it makes no difference to our comparison whether we measure returns in terms of dollars or euros, as long as we measure in terms of a single currency.

Return, Risk, and Liquidity in the Foreign Exchange Market

We observed earlier that a saver deciding which assets to hold may care about assets' riskiness and liquidity in addition to their expected real rates of return. Similarly, the demand for foreign currency assets depends not only on returns but on risk and liquidity. Even if the expected dollar return on euro deposits is higher than that on dollar deposits, for example, people may be reluctant to hold euro deposits if the payoff to holding them varies erratically.

There is no consensus among economists about the importance of risk in the foreign exchange market. Even the definition of "foreign exchange risk" is a topic of debate. For now we will avoid the complex questions involved by assuming that the real returns on all deposits have equal riskiness, regardless of the currency of denomination. In other words, we are assuming that risk differences do not influence the demand for foreign currency assets. We discuss the role of foreign exchange risk in greater detail, however, in Chapters 17 and 21.[8]

Some market participants may be influenced by liquidity factors in deciding which currencies to hold. Most of these participants are firms and individuals involved in international trade. An American importer of French goods, for example, may find it convenient to hold French francs for routine payments even if the expected rate of return on francs is lower than that on dollars. Because payments connected with international trade make up a very small fraction of total foreign exchange transactions, we ignore the liquidity motive for holding foreign currencies.

We are therefore assuming for now that participants in the foreign exchange market base their demands for foreign currency assets exclusively on a comparison of those assets' expected rates of return. The main reason for making this assumption is that it simplifies our analysis of how exchange rates are determined in the foreign exchange market. In addition, the risk and liquidity motives for holding foreign currencies appear to be of secondary importance for many of the international macroeconomic issues discussed in the next few chapters.

Equilibrium in the Foreign Exchange Market

We now use what we have learned about the demand for foreign currency assets to describe how exchange rates are determined. We will show that the exchange rate at which the market settles is the one that makes market participants content to hold existing supplies of deposits of all currencies. When market participants willingly hold the existing supplies of deposits of all currencies, we say that the foreign exchange market is in equilibrium.

The description of exchange rate determination given in this section is only a first step: A full explanation of the exchange rate's current level can be given only after we examine how participants in the foreign exchange market form their expectations about exchange rates they expect to prevail in the future. The next two chapters look at the factors that influence expectations of future exchange rates. For now, however, we will take expected future exchange rates as given.

Interest Parity: The Basic Equilibrium Condition

The foreign exchange market is in equilibrium when deposits of all currencies offer the same expected rate of return. The condition that the expected returns on deposits of any two currencies are equal when measured in the same currency is called the **interest parity**

---

[8] In discussing spot and forward foreign exchange transactions, some textbooks make a distinction between foreign exchange "speculators"—market participants who allegedly care only about expected returns—and "hedgers"— market participants whose concern is to avoid risk. We depart from this textbook tradition because it can mislead the unwary: While the speculative and hedging motives are both potentially important in exchange rate determination, the same person can be both a speculator and a hedger if she cares about both return and risk. Our tentative assumption that risk is unimportant in determining the demand for foreign currency assets means, in terms of the traditional language, that the speculative motive for holding foreign currencies is far more important than the hedging motive.

condition. It implies that potential holders of foreign currency deposits view them all as equally desirable assets.

Let's see why the foreign exchange market is in equilibrium only when the interest parity condition holds. Suppose the dollar interest rate is 10 percent and the euro interest rate is 6 percent, but that the dollar is expected to depreciate against the euro at an 8 percent rate over a year. (This is case 3 in Table 13-3.) In the circumstances described, the rate of return on euro deposits would be 4 percent per year higher than that on dollar deposits. We assumed at the end of the last section that individuals always prefer to hold deposits of currencies offering the highest expected return. This means that if the expected return on euro deposits is 4 percent greater than that on dollar deposits, no one will be willing to continue holding dollar deposits, and holders of dollar deposits will be trying to sell them for euro deposits. There will therefore be an excess supply of dollar deposits and an excess demand for euro deposits in the foreign exchange market.

As a contrasting example, suppose that dollar deposits again offer a 10 percent interest rate but euro deposits offer a 12 percent rate and the dollar is expected to *appreciate* against the euro by 4 percent over the coming year. (This is case 4 in Table 13-3.) Now the return on dollar deposits is 2 percent higher. In this case no one would demand euro deposits, so they would be in excess supply and dollar deposits would be in excess demand.

When, however, the dollar interest rate is 10 percent, the euro interest rate is 6 percent, and the dollar's expected depreciation rate against the euro is 4 percent, dollar and euro deposits offer the same rate of return and participants in the foreign exchange market are willing to hold either. (This is case 2 in Table 13-3.)

Only when all expected rates of return are equal—that is, when the interest parity condition holds—is there no excess supply of some type of deposit and no excess demand for another. The foreign exchange market is in equilibrium when no type of deposit is in excess demand or excess supply. We can therefore say that the foreign exchange market is in equilibrium when the interest parity condition holds.

To represent interest parity between dollar and euro deposits symbolically, we use expression (13-1), which shows the difference between the two assets' expected rates of return measured in dollars. The expected rates of return are equal when

$$R_\$ = R_\mathbb{C} + (E^e_{\$/\mathbb{C}} - E_{\$/\mathbb{C}})/E_{\$/\mathbb{C}}. \tag{13-2}$$

You probably suspect that when dollar deposits offer a higher return than euro deposits, the dollar will appreciate against the euro as investors all try to shift their funds into dollars. Conversely, the dollar should depreciate against the euro when it is euro deposits that initially offer the higher return. This intuition is exactly correct. To understand the mechanism at work, however, we must take a careful look at how exchange rate changes like these help to maintain equilibrium in the foreign exchange market.

How Changes in the Current Exchange Rate Affect Expected Returns

As a first step in understanding how the foreign exchange market finds its equilibrium, we examine how changes in today's exchange rate affect the expected return on a foreign currency deposit when interest rates and expectations about the future exchange rate do not change. Our analysis will show that, other things equal, depreciation of a country's currency today *lowers* the expected domestic currency return on foreign currency deposits. Conversely, appreciation of the domestic currency today, all else equal, *raises* the domestic currency return expected of foreign currency deposits.

It is easiest to see why these relationships hold by looking at an example: How does a change in today's dollar/euro exchange rate, all else held constant, change the expected return, measured in terms of dollars, on euro deposits? Suppose that today's dollar/euro rate is $1.00 per euro and the exchange rate you expect for this day next year is $1.05 per euro. Then the expected rate of dollar depreciation against the euro is $(1.05 - 1.00)/1.00 = 0.05$, or 5 percent per year. This means that when you buy a euro deposit, you not only earn the interest R_{ϵ} but also get a 5 percent "bonus" in terms of dollars. Now suppose that today's exchange rate suddenly jumps up to $1.03 per euro (a depreciation of the dollar and an appreciation of the euro) but the expected future rate is *still* $1.05 per euro. What has happened to the "bonus" you expected to get from the euro's increase in value in terms of dollars? The expected rate of dollar depreciation is now only $(1.05 - 1.03)/1.03 = 0.019$, or 1.9 percent instead of 5 percent. Since R_{ϵ} has not changed, the dollar return on euro deposits, which is the sum of R_{ϵ} and the expected rate of dollar depreciation, has *fallen* by 3.1 percentage points per year (5 percent $-$ 1.9 percent).

In Table 13-4 we work out the dollar return on euro deposits for various levels of today's dollar/euro exchange rate $E_{S/\epsilon}$, always assuming the expected *future* exchange rate remains fixed at $1.05 per euro and the euro interest rate is 5 percent per year. As you can see, a rise in today's dollar/euro exchange rate (a depreciation of the dollar against the euro) always *lowers* the expected dollar return on euro deposits (as in our example), while a fall in today's dollar/euro rate (an appreciation of the dollar against the euro) always *raises* this return.

It may run counter to your intuition that a depreciation of the dollar against the euro makes euro deposits less attractive relative to dollar deposits (by lowering the expected dollar return on euro deposits) while an appreciation of the dollar makes euro deposits more attractive. This result will seem less surprising if you remember we have assumed that the expected future dollar/euro rate and interest rates do not change. A dollar depreciation today, for example, means the dollar now needs to depreciate by a *smaller* amount to reach any given expected future level. If the expected future dollar/euro exchange rate does not

Table 13-4 | Today's Dollar/Euro Exchange Rate and the Expected Dollar Return on Euro Deposits When $E^{e}_{S/\epsilon} = \$1.05$ per Euro

Today's Dollar/Euro Exchange Rate $E_{S/\epsilon}$	Interest Rate on Euro Deposits R_{ϵ}	Expected Dollar Depreciation Rate against Euro $\dfrac{1.05 - E_{S/\epsilon}}{E_{S/\epsilon}}$	Expected Dollar Return on Euro Deposits $R_{\epsilon} + \dfrac{1.05 - E_{S/\epsilon}}{E_{S/\epsilon}}$
1.07	0.05	-0.019	0.031
1.05	0.05	0.00	0.05
1.03	0.05	0.019	0.069
1.02	0.05	0.029	0.079
1.00	0.05	0.05	0.10

change when the dollar depreciates today, the dollar's expected future depreciation against the euro therefore falls, or, alternatively, the dollar's expected future appreciation rises. Since interest rates also are unchanged, today's dollar depreciation thus makes euro deposits less attractive compared with dollar deposits.

Put another way, a current dollar depreciation that affects neither exchange rate expectations nor interest rates leaves the expected future dollar payoff of a euro deposit the same but raises the deposit's current dollar cost. This change naturally makes euro deposits less attractive relative to dollars.

It may also run counter to your intuition that *today's* exchange rate can change while the exchange rate expected for the *future* does not. We will indeed study cases later in this book when both of these rates do change at once. We nonetheless hold the expected future exchange rate constant in the present discussion because that is the clearest way to illustrate the effect of today's exchange rate on expected returns. If it helps, you can imagine we are looking at the impact of a *temporary* change so brief that it has no effect on the exchange rate expected for next year.

Figure 13-3 shows the calculations in Table 13-4 in a graphic form that will be helpful in our analysis of exchange rate determination. The vertical axis in the figure measures today's dollar/euro exchange rate and the horizontal axis measures the expected dollar return on euro deposits. For *fixed* values of the expected future dollar/euro exchange rate and the euro interest rate, the relation between today's dollar/euro exchange rate and the expected dollar return on euro deposits defines a downward-sloping schedule.

The Equilibrium Exchange Rate

Now that we understand why the interest parity condition must hold if the foreign exchange market is in equilibrium and how today's exchange rate affects the expected return on foreign currency deposits, we can see how equilibrium exchange rates are determined. Our main conclusion will be that exchange rates always adjust to maintain interest parity. We continue to assume that the dollar interest rate $R_\$$, the euro interest rate R_ϵ, and the expected future dollar/euro exchange rate $E_{\$/\epsilon}^e$, are all *given*.

Figure 13-4 illustrates how the equilibrium dollar/euro exchange rate is determined under this assumption. The vertical schedule in the graph indicates the given level of $R_\$$, the return on dollar deposits measured in terms of dollars. The downward-sloping schedule shows how the expected return on euro deposits measured in terms of dollars depends on the current dollar/euro exchange rate. This second schedule is derived in the same way as the one shown in Figure 13-3.

The equilibrium dollar/euro rate is the one indicated by the intersection of the two schedules at point 1, $E_{\$/\epsilon}^1$. At this exchange rate, the returns on dollar and euro deposits are equal, so that the interest parity condition (13-2),

$$R_\$ = R_\epsilon + (E_{\$/\epsilon}^e - E_{\$/\epsilon}^1)/E_{\$/\epsilon}^1,$$

is satisfied.

Let's see why the exchange rate will tend to settle at point 1 in Figure 13-4 if it is initially at a point such as 2 or 3. Suppose first that we are at point 2, with the exchange rate equal to $E_{\$/\epsilon}^2$. The downward-sloping schedule measuring the expected dollar return on euro deposits

Figure 13-3 The Relation Between the Current Dollar/Euro Exchange Rate and the Expected Dollar Return on Euro Deposits

Given $E_{\$/\euro}^e = 1.05$ and $R_\euro = 0.05$, an appreciation of the dollar against the euro raises the expected return on euro deposits, measured in terms of dollars.

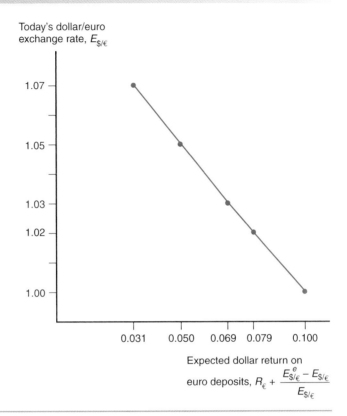

tells us that at the exchange rate $E_{\$/\euro}^2$, the rate of return on euro deposits is less than the rate of return on dollar deposits, $R_\$$. In this situation anyone holding euro deposits wishes to sell them for the more lucrative dollar deposits: The foreign exchange market is out of equilibrium because participants are *unwilling* to hold euro deposits.

How does the exchange rate adjust? The unhappy owners of euro deposits attempt to sell them for dollar deposits, but because the return on dollar deposits is higher than that on euro deposits at the exchange rate $E_{\$/\euro}^2$, no holder of a dollar deposit is willing to sell it for euro at that rate. As euro holders try to entice dollar holders to trade by offering them a better price for dollars, the dollar/euro exchange rate falls toward $E_{\$/\euro}^1$; that is, euros become cheaper in terms of dollars. Once the exchange rate reaches $E_{\$/\euro}^1$, euro and dollar deposits offer equal returns and holders of euro deposits no longer have an incentive to try to sell them for dollars. The foreign exchange market is therefore in equilibrium. In falling from $E_{\$/\euro}^2$ to $E_{\$/\euro}^1$, the exchange rate equalizes the expected returns on the types of deposit by increasing the rate at which the dollar is expected to depreciate in the future, thereby making euro deposits more attractive.

Figure 13-4 | Determination of the Equilibrium Dollar/Euro Exchange Rate

Equilibrium in the foreign exchange market is at point 1, where the expected dollar returns on dollar and euro deposits are equal.

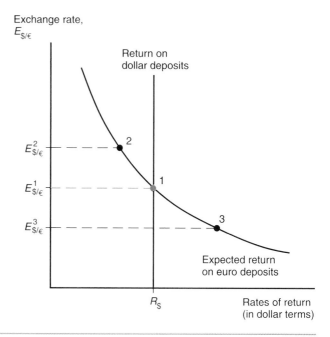

The same process works in reverse if we are initially at point 3 with an exchange rate of $E^3_{\$/\euro}$. At point 3, the return on euro deposits exceeds that on dollar deposits, so there is now an excess supply of the latter. As unwilling holders of dollar deposits bid for the more attractive euro deposits, the price of euros in terms of dollars tends to rise; that is, the dollar tends to depreciate against the euro. When the exchange rate has moved to $E^1_{\$/\euro}$, rates of return are equalized across currencies and the market is in equilibrium. The depreciation of the dollar from $E^3_{\$/\euro}$ to $E^1_{\$/\euro}$ makes euro deposits less attractive relative to dollar deposits by reducing the rate at which the dollar is expected to depreciate in the future.[9]

Interest Rates, Expectations, and Equilibrium

Having seen how exchange rates are determined by interest parity, we now take a look at how current exchange rates are affected by changes in interest rates and in expectations about the future, the two factors we held constant in our previous discussions. We will see

---

[9]We could have developed our diagram from the perspective of Europe, with the euro/dollar exchange rate $E_{\euro/\$}(= 1/E_{\$/\euro})$ on the vertical axis, a schedule vertical at $R_\euro$ to indicate the euro return on euro deposits, and a downward-sloping schedule showing how the euro return on dollar deposits varies with $E_{\euro/\$}$. An exercise at the end of the chapter asks you to show that this alternative way of looking at equilibrium in the foreign exchange market gives the same answers as the method used in the text.

that the exchange rate (which is the relative price of two assets) responds to factors that alter the expected rates of return on those two assets.

The Effect of Changing Interest Rates on the Current Exchange Rate

We often read in the newspaper that the dollar is strong because U.S. interest rates are high or that it is falling because U.S. interest rates are falling. Can these statements be explained using our analysis of the foreign exchange market?

To answer this question we again turn to a diagram. Figure 13-5 shows a rise in the interest rate on dollars, from $R_\$^1$ to $R_\$^2$, as a rightward shift of the vertical dollar deposits schedule. At the initial exchange rate $E_{\$/\euro}^1$, the expected return on dollar deposits is now higher than that on euro deposits by an amount equal to the distance between points 1 and 1'. As we have seen, this difference causes the dollar to appreciate to $E_{\$/\euro}^2$ (point 2). Because there has been no change in the euro interest rate or in the expected future exchange rate, the dollar's appreciation today raises the expected dollar return on euro deposits by increasing the rate at which the dollar is expected to depreciate in the future.

Figure 13-6 shows the effect of a rise in the euro interest rate $R_\euro$. This change causes the downward-sloping schedule (which measures the expected dollar return on euro deposits) to shift rightward. (To see why, ask yourself how a rise in the euro interest rate alters the dollar return on euro deposits, given the current exchange rate and the expected future rate.)

At the initial exchange rate $E_{\$/\euro}^1$, the expected depreciation rate of the dollar is the same as before the rise in $R_\euro$, so the expected return on euro deposits now exceeds that on dollar deposits. The dollar/euro exchange rate rises (from $E_{\$/\euro}^1$ to $E_{\$/\euro}^2$) to eliminate the excess supply of dollar assets at point 1. As before, the dollar's depreciation against the euro eliminates the excess supply of dollar assets by lowering the expected dollar rate of return on euro deposits. A rise in European interest rates therefore leads to a depreciation of the dollar against the euro or, looked at from the European perspective, an appreciation of the euro against the dollar.

Our discussion shows that, all else equal, *an increase in the interest paid on deposits of a currency causes that currency to appreciate against foreign currencies.*

Before we conclude that the newspaper account of the effect of interest rates on exchange rates is correct, we must remember that our assumption of a *constant* expected future exchange rate often is unrealistic. In many cases a change in interest rates will be accompanied by a change in the expected future exchange rate. This change in the expected future exchange rate will depend, in turn, on the economic causes of the interest rate change. We compare different possible relationships between interest rates and expected future exchange rates in Chapter 15. Keep in mind for now that in the real world, we cannot predict how a given interest rate change will alter exchange rates unless we know *why* the interest rate is changing.

The Effect of Changing Expectations on the Current Exchange Rate

Figure 13-6 may also be used to study the effect on today's exchange rate of a rise in the expected future dollar/euro exchange rate, $E_{\$/\euro}^e$.

Given today's exchange rate, a rise in the expected future price of euros in terms of dollars raises the dollar's expected depreciation rate. For example, if today's exchange rate is

Figure 13-5 | Effect of a Rise in the Dollar Interest Rate

A rise in the interest rate offered by dollar deposits from $R_\$^1$ to $R_\$^2$ causes the dollar to appreciate from $E_{\$/€}^1$ (point 1) to $E_{\$/€}^2$ (point 2).

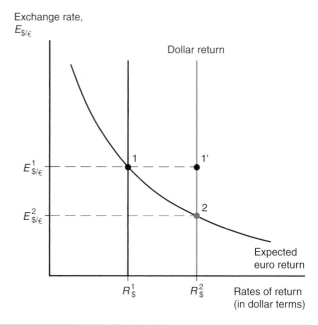

 Figure 13-6 | Effect of a Rise in the Euro Interest Rate

A rise in the interest rate paid by euro deposits causes the dollar to depreciate from $E_{\$/€}^1$ (point 1) to $E_{\$/€}^2$ (point 2). (This figure also describes the effect of a rise in the expected future $/€ exchange rate.)

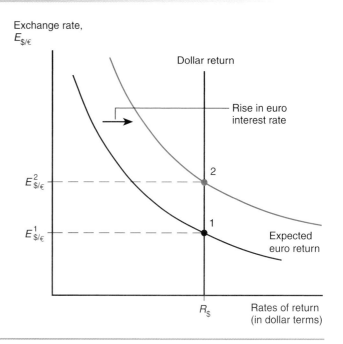

THE PERILS OF FORECASTING EXCHANGE RATES

If exchange rates are asset prices that respond immediately to changes in expectations and interest rates, they should have properties similar to those of other asset prices, for example, stock prices. Like stock prices, exchange rates should respond strongly to "news," that is, to unexpected economic and political events; and, like stock prices, they therefore should be very hard to forecast.

Despite the notorious difficulty of forecasting stock prices, there is no shortage of newsletters and television programs devoted to stock-market prediction. Similarly, numerous firms sell exchange-rate forecasts to individual investors, international corporations, and others with financial interests in the foreign-exchange market. In a well-known study, Richard M. Levich of New York University surveyed the track record of a dozen exchange-rate forecasting companies in making near-term guesses as to future rates.*

The results were depressing for would-be exchange-rate oracles but encouraging for the asset approach to exchange rates. Levich found little evidence over his sample period that professional forecasters do systematically better than an individual who, for example, uses the three-month forward exchange rate as her forecast of the spot rate that will materialize in three months.† This finding does not mean that forward rates are accurate predictors; on the contrary, the evidence suggests that forward rates usually contain little information useful in predicting future spot rates (as we shall see in Chapter 21). What Levich's results do show is that inherently unpredictable "news" plays such a dominant role in determining exchange rates that exchange-rate movements, like movements in stock prices, are almost completely impossible to forecast over horizons of a year or less.

The theory we developed in this chapter suggests that exchange rates should not be completely impossible to forecast. According to the interest parity condition, interest-rate differentials should give an indication of how much currency depreciation to expect. In practice, however, *unexpected* or surprise currency movements are much greater than interest-rate differences and swamp the predictable movements in exchange rates. Forecasts based on economic models seem to be most successful when used for long-run predictions, that is, predictions of exchange rates years ahead. For example, a country with sustained increases in its price level is likely eventually to experience currency depreciation, although the precise timing of the depreciation may be impossible to predict. In the next few chapters we will develop an open-economy model that links exchange rate movements to changes in countries' price levels and other macroeconomic variables.

---

*See "Evaluating the Performance of the Forecasters," in Donald R. Lessard, ed., *International Financial Management: Theory and Application,* 2nd ed. New York: John Wiley & Sons, 1985, pp. 218–233. For updated discussions of forecasting exchange rates see Christian Dunis and Michael Feeny, eds., *Exchange Rate Forecasting,* Chicago, Probus Publishing Co., 1989; and the book by Levich in this chapter's Further Reading.

†This chapter's appendix suggests one reason for thinking that forward exchange rates might be related to expected future spot rates.

$1.00 per euro and the rate expected to prevail in a year is $1.05 per euro, the expected depreciation rate of the dollar against the euro is (1.05 − 1.00)/1.00 = 0.05; if the expected future exchange rate now rises to $1.06 per euro, the expected depreciation rate also rises, to (1.06 − 1.00)/1.00 = 0.06.

Because a rise in the expected depreciation rate of the dollar raises the expected dollar return on euro deposits, the downward-sloping schedule shifts to the right, as in Figure 13-6.

At the initial exchange rate $E^1_{\$/\epsilon}$ there is now an excess supply of dollar deposits: euro deposits offer a higher expected rate of return (measured in dollar terms) than do dollar deposits. The dollar therefore depreciates against the euro until equilibrium is reached at point 2.

We conclude that, all else equal, *a rise in the expected future exchange rate causes a rise in the current exchange rate. Similarly, a fall in the expected future exchange rate causes a fall in the current exchange rate.*

Summary

1. An *exchange rate* is the price of one country's currency in terms of another country's currency. Exchange rates play a role in spending decisions because they enable us to translate different countries' prices into comparable terms. All else equal, a *depreciation* of a country's currency against foreign currencies (a rise in the home currency prices of foreign currencies) makes its exports cheaper and its imports more expensive. An *appreciation* of its currency (a fall in the home currency prices of foreign currencies) makes its exports more expensive and its imports cheaper.

2. Exchange rates are determined in the *foreign exchange market.* The major participants in that market are commercial banks, international corporations, nonbank financial institutions, and national central banks. Commercial banks play a pivotal role in the market because they facilitate the exchanges of interest-bearing bank deposits that make up the bulk of foreign exchange trading. Even though foreign exchange trading takes place in many financial centers around the world, modern telecommunication technology links those centers together into a single market that is open 24 hours a day. An important category of foreign exchange trading is *forward* trading, in which parties agree to exchange currencies on some future date at a prenegotiated exchange rate. In contrast, *spot* trades are (for practical purposes) settled immediately.

3. Because the exchange rate is the relative price of two assets, it is most appropriately thought of as being an asset price itself. The basic principle of asset pricing is that an asset's current value depends on its expected future purchasing power. In evaluating an asset, savers look at the expected *rate of return* it offers, that is, the rate at which the value of an investment in the asset is expected to rise over time. It is possible to measure an asset's expected rate of return in different ways, each depending on the units in which the asset's value is measured. Savers care about an asset's expected *real rate of return,* the rate at which its value expressed in terms of a representative output basket is expected to rise.

4. When relative asset returns are relevant, as in the foreign exchange market, it is appropriate to compare expected changes in assets' currency values, provided those values are expressed in the same currency. If *risk* and *liquidity* factors do not strongly influence the demands for foreign currency assets, participants in the foreign exchange market always prefer to hold those assets yielding the highest expected rate of return.

5. The returns on deposits traded in the foreign exchange market depend on *interest rates* and expected exchange rate changes. To compare the expected rates of return offered by dollar and euro deposits, for example, the return on euro deposits must be expressed in dollar terms by adding to the euro interest rate the expected *rate of*

depreciation of the dollar against the euro (or *rate of appreciation* of the euro against the dollar) over the deposit's holding period.

6. Equilibrium in the foreign exchange market requires *interest parity;* that is, deposits of all currencies must offer the same expected rate of return when returns are measured in comparable terms.

7. For given interest rates and a given expectation of the future exchange rate, the interest parity condition tells us the current equilibrium exchange rate. When the expected dollar return on euro deposits exceeds that on dollar deposits, for example, the dollar immediately depreciates against the euro. Other things equal, a dollar depreciation today reduces the expected dollar return on euro deposits by reducing the depreciation rate of the dollar against the euro expected for the future. Similarly, when the expected return on euro deposits is below that on dollar deposits, the dollar must immediately appreciate against the euro. Other things equal, a current appreciation of the dollar makes euro deposits more attractive by increasing the dollar's expected future depreciation against the European currency.

8. All else equal, a rise in dollar interest rates causes the dollar to appreciate against the euro while a rise in euro interest rates causes the dollar to depreciate against the euro. Today's exchange rate is also altered by changes in its expected future level. If there is a rise in the expected future level of the dollar/euro rate, for example, then at unchanged interest rates today's dollar/euro exchange rate will also rise.

Key Terms

appreciation, p. 326
arbitrage, p. 330
depreciation, p. 326
exchange rate, p. 324
foreign exchange market, p. 328
forward exchange rate, p. 332
interbank trading, p. 328
interest parity condition, p. 341
interest rate, p. 336

liquidity, p. 335
rate of appreciation, p. 340
rate of depreciation, p. 338
rate of return, p. 334
real rate of return, p. 335
risk, p. 335
spot exchange rate, p. 331
vehicle currency, p. 331

Problems

1. In Munich a bratwurst costs 2 euros; a hot dog costs $1 at Boston's Fenway Park. At an exchange rate of $1.50/per euro, what is the price of a bratwurst in terms of hot dogs? All else equal, how does this relative price change if the dollar appreciates to $1.25 per euro? Compared with the initial situation, has a hot dog become more or less expensive relative to a bratwurst?

2. A U.S. dollar costs 7.5 Norwegian kroner, but the same dollar can be purchased for 1.25 Swiss francs. What is the Norwegian krone/Swiss franc exchange rate?

3. Calculate the dollar rates of return on the following assets:
   a. A painting whose price rises from $200,000 to $250,000 in a year.
   b. A bottle of a rare Burgundy, Domaine de la Romanée-Conti 1978, whose price rises from $180 to $216 between 1999 and 2000.

    c. A £10,000 deposit in a London bank in a year when the interest rate on pounds is 10 percent and the $/£ exchange rate moves from $1.50 per pound to $1.38 per pound.

4. What would be the real rates of return on the assets in the preceding question if the price changes described were accompanied by a simultaneous 10 percent increase in all dollar prices?

5. Suppose the dollar interest rate and the pound sterling interest rate are the same, 5 percent per year. What is the relation between the current equilibrium $/£ exchange rate and its expected future level? Suppose the expected future $/£ exchange rate, $1.52 per pound, remains constant as Britain's interest rate rises to 10 percent per year. If the U.S. interest rate also remains constant, what is the new equilibrium $/£ exchange rate?

6. Traders in asset markets suddenly learn that the interest rate on dollars will decline in the near future. Use the diagrammatic analysis of the chapter to determine the effect on the *current* dollar/euro exchange rate, assuming current interest rates on dollar and euro deposits do not change.

7. We noted that we could have developed our diagrammatic analysis of foreign exchange market equilibrium from the perspective of Europe, with the euro/dollar exchange rate $E_{€/\$}$ ($= 1/E_{\$/€}$) on the vertical axis, a schedule vertical at $R_€$ to indicate the euro return on euro deposits, and a downward-sloping schedule showing how the euro return on dollar deposits varies with $E_{€/\$}$. Derive this alternative picture of equilibrium and use it to examine the effect of changes in interest rates and the expected future exchange rate. Do your answers agree with those we found earlier?

8. The following report appeared in the *New York Times* on August 7, 1989 ("Dollar's Strength a Surprise," p. D1):

> But now the sentiment is that the economy is heading for a "soft landing," with the economy slowing significantly and inflation subsiding, but without a recession.
>
> This outlook is good for the dollar for two reasons. A soft landing is not as disruptive as a recession, so the foreign investments that support the dollar are more likely to continue.
>
> Also, a soft landing would not force the Federal Reserve to push interest rates sharply lower to stimulate growth. Falling interest rates can put downward pressure on the dollar because they make investments in dollar-denominated securities less attractive to foreigners, prompting the selling of dollars. In addition, the optimism sparked by the expectation of a soft landing can even offset some of the pressure on the dollar from lower interest rates.

    a. Show how you would interpret the third paragraph of this report using this chapter's model of exchange rate determination.

    b. What additional factors in exchange rate determination might help you explain the second paragraph?

9. Suppose the dollar exchange rates of the euro and the yen are equally variable. The euro, however, tends to depreciate unexpectedly against the dollar when the return on the rest of your wealth is unexpectedly high, while the yen tends to appreciate unexpectedly in the same circumstances. As a U.S. resident, which currency, the euro or the yen, would you consider riskier?

10. Does any of the discussion in this chapter lead you to believe that dollar deposits may have liquidity characteristics different from those of other currency deposits? If so, how would the differences affect the interest differential between, say, dollar and Mexican pesos deposits? Do you have any guesses about how the liquidity of euro and yen deposits may be changing over time?

11. In October 1979, the U.S. central bank (the Federal Reserve System) announced it would play a less active role in limiting fluctuations in dollar interest rates. After this new policy was put into effect, the dollar's exchange rates against foreign currencies became more volatile. Does our analysis of the foreign exchange market suggest any connection between these two events?

12. Imagine that everyone in the world pays a tax of τ percent on interest earnings and on any capital gains due to exchange rate changes. How would such a tax alter the analysis of the interest parity condition? How does the answer change if the tax applies to interest earnings but *not* to capital gains, which are untaxed?

13. Suppose the one-year forward $/€ exchange rate is $1.26 per euro and the spot exchange rate is $1.2 per euro. What is the forward premium on euro (the forward discount on dollars)? What is the difference between the interest rate on one-year dollar deposits and that on one-year euro deposits (assuming no political risk)?

Further Reading

J. Orlin Grabbe. *International Financial Markets,* 3rd edition. Englewood Cliffs: Prentice-Hall, 1996. Chapters 4–7 are especially pertinent to topics discussed in this chapter.

Philipp Hartmann. *Currency Competition and Foreign Exchange Markets: The Dollar, the Yen and the Euro.* Cambridge: Cambridge University Press, 1999. Theoretical and empirical micro-oriented study of the role of international currencies in world trade and asset markets.

John Maynard Keynes. *A Tract on Monetary Reform,* Chapter 3. London: MacMillan, 1923. Classic analysis of the forward exchange market and covered interest parity.

Paul R. Krugman. "The International Role of the Dollar: Theory and Prospect," in John F. O. Bilson and Richard C. Marston, eds. *Exchange Rate Theory and Practice.* Chicago: University of Chicago Press, 1984, pp. 261–278. Theoretical and empirical analysis of the dollar's position as an "international money."

Richard M. Levich. *International Financial Markets: Prices and Policies.* Boston: Irwin McGraw-Hill, 1998. Chapters 3–8 of this comprehensive text focus on the foreign exchange market.

Lyons, Richard K. *The Microstructure Approach to Exchange Rates.* Cambridge: MIT Press, 2001. Advanced treatise on the fine structure of markets for foreign exchange.

Ronald I. McKinnon. *Money in International Exchange: The Convertible Currency System.* New York: Oxford University Press, 1979. Theoretical and institutional analysis of the place of the foreign exchange market in international monetary relations.

Michael Mussa. "Empirical Regularities in the Behavior of Exchange Rates and Theories of the Foreign Exchange Market," in Karl Brunner and Allan H. Meltzer, eds. *Policies for Employment, Prices and Exchange Rates,* Carnegie-Rochester Conference Series on Public Policy 11. Amsterdam: North-Holland, 1979, pp. 9–57. Examines the empirical basis of the asset price approach to exchange rate determination.

Julian Walmsley. *The Foreign Exchange and Money Markets Guide.* New York: John Wiley and Sons, 1992. A basic text on the terminology and institutions of the foreign exchange market.

APPENDIX TO CHAPTER 13

Forward Exchange Rates and Covered Interest Parity

This appendix explains how forward exchange rates are determined. Under the assumption that the interest parity condition always holds, a forward exchange rate equals the spot exchange rate expected to prevail on the forward contract's value date.

As the first step in the discussion, we point out the close connection among the forward exchange rate between two currencies, their spot exchange rate, and the interest rates on deposits denominated in those currencies. The connection is described by the *covered interest parity* condition, which is similar to the (noncovered) interest parity condition defining foreign exchange market equilibrium but involves the forward exchange rate rather than the expected future spot exchange rate.

To be concrete, we again consider dollar and euro deposits. Suppose you want to buy a euro deposit with dollars but would like to be *certain* about the number of dollars it will be worth at the end of a year. You can avoid exchange rate risk by buying a euro deposit and, at the same time, selling the proceeds of your investment forward. When you buy a euro deposit with dollars and at the same time sell the principal and interest forward for dollars, we say you have "covered" yourself, that is, avoided the possibility of an unexpected depreciation of the euro.

The covered interest parity condition states that the rates of return on dollar deposits and "covered" foreign deposits must be the same. An example will clarify the meaning of the condition and illustrate why it must always hold. Let $F_{\$/€}$ stand for the one-year forward price of euros in terms of dollars, and suppose $F_{\$/€} = \$1.113$ per euro. Assume that at the same time, the spot exchange rate $E_{\$/€} = \$1.05$ per euro, $R_\$ = 0.10$, and $R_€ = 0.04$. The (dollar) rate of return on a dollar deposit is clearly 0.10, or 10 percent per year. What is the rate of return on a covered euro deposit?

We answer this question as in the chapter. A €1 deposit costs \$1.05 today, and it is worth €1.04 after a year. If you sell €1.04 forward today at the forward exchange rate of \$1.113 per euro, the dollar value of your investment at the end of a year is (\$1.113 per euro) $\times$ (€ 1.04) = 1.158. The rate of return on a covered purchase of a euro deposit is therefore $(1.158 - 1.05)/1.05 = 0.103$. This 10.3 percent per year rate of return exceeds the 10 percent offered by dollar deposits, so covered interest parity does not hold. In this situation, no one would be willing to hold dollar deposits; everyone would prefer covered euro deposits.

More formally, we can express the covered return on euro deposit as

$$\frac{F_{\$/€}(1 + R_€) - E_{\$/€}}{E_{\$/€}},$$

which is approximately equal to

$$R_€ + \frac{F_{\$/€} - E_{\$/€}}{E_{\$/€}}$$

when the product $R_€ \times (F_{\$/€} - E_{\$/€})/E_{\$/€}$ is a small number. The covered interest parity condition can therefore be written

$$R_\$ = R_€ + (F_{\$/€} - E_{\$/€})/E_{\$/€}.$$

The quantity

$$(F_{\$/€} - E_{\$/€})/E_{\$/€}$$

is called the *forward premium* on euros against dollars. (It is also called the *forward discount* on dollars against euros.) Using this terminology, we can state the covered interest parity condition as follows: *The interest rate on dollar deposits equals the interest rate on euro deposits plus the forward premium on euros against dollars (the forward discount on dollars against euros).*

There is strong empirical evidence that the covered interest parity condition holds for different foreign currency deposits issued within a single financial center. Indeed, currency traders often set the forward exchange rates they quote by looking at current interest rates and spot exchange rates and using the covered interest parity formula.[10] Deviations from covered interest parity can occur, however, if the deposits being compared are located in different countries. These deviations occur when asset holders fear that governments may impose regulations which prevent the free movement of foreign funds across national borders. Our derivation of the covered interest parity condition implicitly assumed there was no political risk of this kind.[11]

By comparing the (noncovered) interest parity condition,

$$R_\$ = R_€ + (E^e_{\$/€} - E_{\$/€})/E_{\$/€},$$

with the *covered* interest parity condition, you will find that both conditions can be true at the same time only if the one-year forward $/€ rate quoted today equals the spot exchange rate people expect to materialize a year from today:

$$F_{\$/€} = E^e_{\$/€}.$$

This makes intuitive sense. When two parties agree to trade foreign exchange on a date in the future, the exchange rate they agree on is the spot rate they expect to prevail on that date. The important difference between covered and noncovered transactions should be kept in

---

[10]Empirical evidence supporting the covered interest parity condition is provided by Frank McCormick in "Covered Interest Arbitrage: Unexploited Profits? Comment," *Journal of Political Economy* 87 (April 1979), pp. 411–417, and by Kevin Clinton in "Transactions Costs and Covered Interest Arbitrage: Theory and Evidence," *Journal of Political Economy* 96 (April 1988), pp. 358–370.

[11]For a more detailed discussion of the role of political risk in the forward exchange market, see Robert Z. Aliber, "The Interest Parity Theorem: A Reinterpretation," *Journal of Political Economy* 81 (November/December 1973), pp. 1451–1459. Of course, actual restrictions on cross-border money movements can also cause covered interest parity deviations.

mind, however. Covered transactions do not involve exchange rate risk, noncovered transactions do.[12]

The theory of covered interest parity helps explain the close correlation between movements in spot and forward exchange rates shown in Figure 13-1, a correlation typical of all major currencies. The unexpected economic events that affect expected asset returns often have a relatively small effect on international interest rate differences between deposits with short maturities (for example, three months). To maintain covered interest parity, therefore, spot and forward rates for the corresponding maturities must change roughly in proportion to each other.

We conclude this appendix with one further application of the covered interest parity condition. To illustrate the role of forward exchange rates, the chapter used the example of an American importer of Japanese radios anxious about the $/¥ exchange rate he would face in 30 days when the time came to pay his supplier. In the example, the importer solved his problem by selling forward for yen enough dollars to cover the cost of the radios. But he could have solved his problem in a different, more complicated way. He could have (1) borrowed dollars from his bank; (2) sold those dollars immediately for yen at the spot exchange rate and placed the yen in a 30-day yen bank deposit; (3) then, after 30 days, used the proceeds of the maturing yen deposit to pay his Japanese supplier; and (4) used the realized proceeds of his U.S. radio sales, less his profits, to repay his original dollar loan.

Which course of action—the forward purchase of yen or the sequence of four transactions described in the preceding paragraph—is more profitable for the importer? We leave it to you, as an exercise, to show that the two strategies yield the same profit when the covered interest parity condition holds.

---

[12]We indicated in the text that the (noncovered) interest parity condition, while a useful simplification, may not always hold exactly if the riskiness of currencies influences demands in the foreign exchange market. Therefore, the forward rate may differ from the expected future spot rate by a risk factor even if *covered* interest parity holds true. As noted earlier, the role of risk in exchange rate determination is discussed more fully in Chapters 17 and 21.

CHAPTER 14

Money, Interest Rates, and Exchange Rates

C hapter 13 showed how the exchange rate between currencies depends on two factors, the interest that can be earned on deposits of those currencies and the expected future exchange rate. To understand fully the determination of exchange rates, however, we have to learn how interest rates themselves are determined and how expectations of future exchange rates are formed. In the next three chapters we examine these topics by building an economic model that links exchange rates, interest rates, and other important macroeconomic variables such as the inflation rate and output.

The first step in building the model is to explain the effects of a country's money supply and of the demand for its money on its interest rate and exchange rate. Because exchange rates are the relative prices of national monies, factors that affect a country's money supply or demand are among the most powerful determinants of its currency's exchange rate against foreign currencies. It is therefore natural to begin a deeper study of exchange rate determination with a discussion of money supply and money demand.

Monetary developments influence the exchange rate *both* by changing interest rates *and* by changing people's expectations about future exchange rates. Expectations about future exchange rates are closely connected with expectations about the future money prices of countries' products; these price movements, in turn, depend on changes in money supply and demand. In examining monetary influences on the exchange rate, we therefore look at how monetary factors influence output prices along with interest rates. Expectations of future exchange rates depend on many factors other than money, however, and these non-monetary factors are taken up in the next chapter.

Once the theories and determinants of money supply and demand are laid out, we use them to examine how equilibrium interest rates are determined by the equality of money supply and money demand. Then we combine our model of interest rate determination with the interest parity condition to study the effects of monetary shifts on the exchange rate, given the prices of goods and services, the level of output, and market expectations about the future. Finally, we take a first look at the long-term effects of monetary changes on output prices and expected future exchange rates.

Money Defined: A Brief Review

We are so accustomed to using money that we seldom notice the roles it plays in almost all of our everyday transactions. As with many other modern conveniences, we take money for granted until something goes wrong with it! In fact, the easiest way to appreciate the importance of money is to imagine what economic life would be like without it.

In this section we do just that. Our purpose in carrying out this "thought experiment" is to distinguish money from other assets and to describe the characteristics of money that lead people to hold it. These characteristics are central to an analysis of the demand for money.

Money as a Medium of Exchange

The most important function of money is to serve as a *medium of exchange,* a generally accepted means of payment. To see why a medium of exchange is necessary, imagine how time-consuming it would be for people to purchase goods and services in a world where the only type of trade possible was barter trade—the trade of goods or services for other goods or services.

Money eliminates the enormous search costs connected with a barter system because it is universally acceptable. It eliminates these search costs by enabling an individual to sell the goods and services she produces to people other than the producers of the goods and services she wishes to consume. A complex modern economy would cease functioning without some standardized and convenient means of payment.

Money as a Unit of Account

Money's second important role is as a *unit of account,* that is, as a widely recognized measure of value. It is in this role that we encountered money in Chapter 13: Prices of goods, services, and assets are typically expressed in terms of money. Exchange rates allow us to translate different countries' money prices into comparable terms.

The convention of quoting prices in money terms simplifies economic calculations by making it easy to compare the prices of different commodities. The international price comparisons in Chapter 13, which used exchange rates to compare the prices of different countries' outputs, are similar to the calculations you would have to do many times each day if different commodities' prices were not expressed in terms of a standardized unit of account. If the calculations in Chapter 13 gave you a headache, imagine what it would be like to have to calculate the relative prices of each good and service you consume in terms of several other goods and services. This thought experiment should give you a keener appreciation of using money as a unit of account.

Money as a Store of Value

Because money can be used to transfer purchasing power from the present into the future, it is also an asset, or a *store of value.* This attribute is essential for any medium of exchange because no one would be willing to accept it in payment if its value in terms of goods and services evaporated immediately.

Money's usefulness as a medium of exchange, however, automatically makes it the most *liquid* of all assets. As you will recall from the last chapter, an asset is said to be liquid when it can be transformed into goods and services rapidly and without high transaction costs, such as brokers' fees. Since money is readily acceptable as a means of payment, money sets the standard against which the liquidity of other assets is judged.

What Is Money?

Currency and bank deposits on which checks may be written certainly qualify as money. These are widely accepted means of payment that can be transferred between owners at low cost. Households and firms hold currency and checking deposits as a convenient way of financing routine transactions as they arise. Assets such as real estate do not qualify as money because, unlike currency and checking deposits, they lack the essential property of liquidity.

When we speak of the **money supply** in this book, we are referring to the monetary aggregate the Federal Reserve calls M1, that is, the total amount of currency and checking deposits held by households and firms. In the United States at the end of 2000, the total money supply amounted to $1.115 trillion, equal to 11.2 percent of that year's GNP.[1]

The large deposits traded by participants in the foreign exchange market are not considered part of the money supply. These deposits are less liquid than money and are not used to finance routine transactions.

How the Money Supply Is Determined

An economy's money supply is controlled by its central bank. The central bank directly regulates the amount of currency in existence and also has indirect control over the amount of checking deposits issued by private banks. The procedures through which the central bank controls the money supply are complex, and we assume for now that the central bank simply sets the size of the money supply at the level it desires. We go into the money supply process in more detail, however, in Chapters 17 and 21.

The Demand for Money by Individuals

Having discussed the functions of money and the definition of the money supply, we now examine the factors that determine the amount of money an individual desires to hold. The determinants of individual money demand can be derived from the theory of asset demand discussed in the last chapter.

We saw in the last chapter that individuals base their demand for an asset on three characteristics:

1. The expected return the asset offers compared with the returns offered by other assets.
2. The riskiness of the asset's expected return.
3. The asset's liquidity.

---

[1]A broader Federal Reserve measure of money supply, M2, includes time deposits, but these are less liquid than the assets included in M1 because the funds in them typically cannot be withdrawn early without penalty. An even broader measure, known as M3, is also tracked by the Fed. A decision on where to draw the line between money and near-money must be somewhat arbitrary and therefore controversial. For further discussion of this question, see Frederic S. Mishkin, *The Economics of Money, Banking and Financial Markets,* 6th ed., Chapter 3. Boston: Addison Wesley, 2001.

While liquidity plays no important role in determining the relative demands for assets traded in the foreign exchange market, households and firms hold money *only* because of its liquidity. To understand how the economy's households and firms decide the amount of money they wish to hold, we must look more closely at how the three considerations listed above influence money demand.

Expected Return

Currency pays no interest. Checking deposits often do pay some interest, but they offer a rate of return that usually fails to keep pace with the higher return offered by less liquid forms of wealth. When you hold money, you therefore sacrifice the higher interest rate you could earn by holding your wealth in a government bond, a large time deposit, or some other relatively illiquid asset. It is this last rate of interest we have in mind when we refer to "the" interest rate. Since the interest paid on currency is zero while that paid on "checkable" deposits tends to be relatively constant, the difference in rates of return between money in general and less-liquid alternative assets is reflected by the market interest rate: The higher the interest rate, the more you sacrifice by holding wealth in the form of money.[2]

Suppose, for example, that the interest rate you could earn from a U.S. Treasury bill is 10 percent per year. If you use $10,000 of your wealth to buy a Treasury bill, you will be paid $11,000 by Uncle Sam at the end of a year, but if you choose instead to keep the $10,000 as cash in a safe-deposit box, you give up the $1000 interest you could have earned by buying the Treasury bill. You thus sacrifice a 10 percent rate of return by holding your $10,000 as money.

The theory of asset demand developed in the last chapter shows how changes in the rate of interest affect the demand for money. The theory states that, other things equal, people prefer assets offering higher expected returns. Because an increase in the interest rate is a rise in the rate of return on less liquid assets relative to the rate of return on money, individuals will want to hold more of their wealth in nonmoney assets that pay the market interest rate and less of their wealth in the form of money if the interest rate rises. We conclude that *all else equal, a rise in the interest rate causes the demand for money to fall.*

We can also describe the influence of the interest rate on money demand in terms of the economic concept of *opportunity cost*—the amount you sacrifice by taking one course of action rather than another. The interest rate measures the opportunity cost of holding money rather than interest-bearing bonds. A rise in the interest rate therefore raises the cost of holding money and causes money demand to fall.

Risk

Risk is not an important factor in money demand. It is risky to hold money because an unexpected increase in the prices of goods and services could reduce the value of your

---

[2]Many of the illiquid assets that individuals can choose from do not pay their returns in the form of interest. Stocks, for example, pay returns in the form of dividends and capital gains. The family summer house on Cape Cod pays a return in the form of capital gains and the pleasure of vacations at the beach. The assumption behind our analysis of money demand is that once allowance is made for risk, all assets other than money offer an expected rate of return (measured in terms of money) equal to the interest rate. This assumption allows us to use the interest rate to summarize the return an individual forgoes by holding money rather than an illiquid asset.

money in terms of the commodities you consume. Since interest-paying assets such as government bonds have face values fixed in terms of money, however, the same unexpected increase in prices would reduce the real value of those assets by the same percentage. Because any change in the riskiness of money causes an equal change in the riskiness of bonds, changes in the risk of holding money need not cause individuals to reduce their demand for money and increase their demand for interest-paying assets.

Liquidity

The main benefit of holding money comes from its liquidity. Households and firms hold money because it is the easiest way of financing their everyday purchases. Some large purchases can be financed through the sale of a substantial illiquid asset. An art collector, for example, could sell one of her Picassos to buy a house. To finance a continuing stream of smaller expenditures at various times and for various amounts, however, households and firms have to hold some money.

An individual's need for liquidity rises when the average daily value of his transactions rises. A student who takes the bus every day, for example, does not need to hold as much cash as a business executive who takes taxis during rush hour. We conclude that *a rise in the average value of transactions carried out by a household or firm causes its demand for money to rise.*

Aggregate Money Demand

Our discussion of how individual households and firms determine their demands for money can now be applied to derive the determinants of **aggregate money demand**, the total demand for money by all households and firms in the economy. Aggregate money demand is just the sum of all the economy's individual money demands.

Three main factors determine aggregate money demand:

1. *The interest rate.* A rise in the interest rate causes each individual in the economy to reduce her demand for money. All else equal, aggregate money demand therefore falls when the interest rate rises.

2. *The price level.* The economy's **price level** is the price of a broad reference basket of goods and services in terms of currency. If the price level rises, individual households and firms must spend more money than before to purchase their usual weekly baskets of goods and services. To maintain the same level of liquidity as before the price level increase, they will therefore have to hold more money.

3. *Real national income.* When real national income (GNP) rises, more goods and services are being sold in the economy. This increase in the real value of transactions raises the demand for money, given the price level.

If P is the price level, R is the interest rate, and Y is real GNP, the aggregate demand for money, M^d, can be expressed as

$$M^d = P \times L(R, Y), \qquad (14\text{-}1)$$

where the value of $L(R, Y)$ falls when R rises, and rises when Y rises.[3] To see why we have specified that aggregate money demand is *proportional* to the price level, imagine that all prices doubled but the interest rate and everyone's *real* incomes remained unchanged. The money value of each individual's average daily transactions would then simply double, as would the amount of money each wished to hold.

We usually write the aggregate money demand relation (14-1) in the equivalent form

$$M^d/P = L(R, Y), \tag{14-2}$$

and call $L(R, Y)$ aggregate *real* money demand. This way of expressing money demand shows that the aggregate demand for liquidity, $L(R, Y)$, is not a demand for a certain number of currency units but is instead a demand to hold a certain amount of purchasing power in liquid form. The ratio M^d/P—that is, desired money holdings measured in terms of a typical reference basket of commodities—equals the amount of purchasing power people would like to hold in liquid form. For example, if people wished to hold $1000 in cash at a price level of $100 per commodity basket, their real money holdings would be equivalent to $1000/($100 per basket) = 10 baskets. If the price level doubled (to $200 per basket), the purchasing power of their $1000 in cash would be halved, since it would now be worth only 5 baskets.

Figure 14-1 shows how aggregate real money demand is affected by the interest rate for a fixed level of real income, Y. The aggregate real money demand schedule $L(R, Y)$ slopes downward because a fall in the interest rate raises the desired real money holdings of each household and firm in the economy.

For a given level of real GNP, changes in interest rates cause movements *along* the $L(R, Y)$ schedule. Changes in real GNP, however, cause the schedule itself to shift. Figure 14-2 shows how a rise in real GNP from Y^1 to Y^2 affects the position of the aggregate real money demand schedule. Because a rise in real GNP raises aggregate real money demand for a given interest rate, the schedule $L(R, Y^2)$ lies to the right of $L(R, Y^1)$ when Y^2 is greater than Y^1.

The Equilibrium Interest Rate: The Interaction of Money Supply and Demand

As you might expect from other economics courses you've taken, the money market is in equilibrium when the money supply set by the central bank equals aggregate money demand. In this section we see how the interest rate is determined by money market equilibrium, given the price level and output, both of which are temporarily assumed to be unaffected by monetary changes.

Equilibrium in the Money Market

If M^s is the money supply, the condition for equilibrium in the money market is

$$M^s = M^d. \tag{14-3}$$

---

[3]Naturally, $L(R, Y)$ rises when R falls, and falls when Y falls.

Figure 14-1 Aggregate Real Money Demand and the Interest Rate

The downward-sloping real money demand schedule shows that for a given real income level, Y, real money demand rises as the interest rate falls.

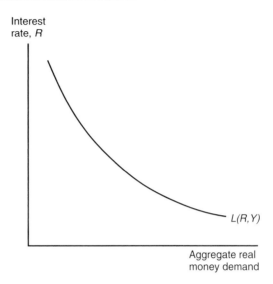

 Figure 14-2 Effect on the Aggregate Real Money Demand Schedule of a Rise in Real Income

An increase in real income from Y^1 to Y^2 raises the demand for real money balances at every level of the interest rate and causes the whole demand schedule to shift upward.

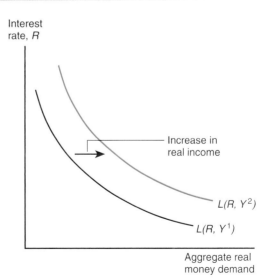

Figure 14-3 | Determination of the Equilibrium Interest Rate

With P and Y given and a real money supply of M^s/P, money market equilibrium is at point 1. At this point aggregate real money demand and the real money supply are equal and the equilibrium interest rate is R^1.

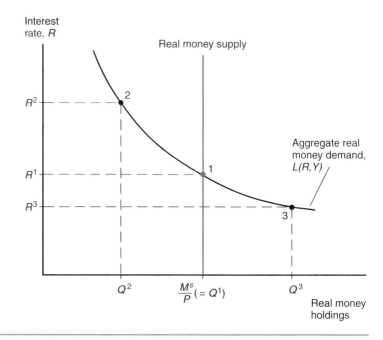

After dividing both sides of this equality by the price level, we can express the money market equilibrium condition in terms of aggregate real money demand as

$$M^s/P = L(R, Y). \qquad (14\text{-}4)$$

Given the price level, P, and output, Y, the equilibrium interest rate is the one at which aggregate real money demand equals the real money supply.

In Figure 14-3, the aggregate real money demand schedule intersects the real money supply schedule at point 1 to give an equilibrium interest rate of R^1. The money supply schedule is vertical at M^s/P because M^s is set by the central bank while P is taken as given.

Let's see why the interest rate tends to settle at its equilibrium level by considering what happens if the market is initially at point 2, with an interest rate, R^2, that is above R^1.

At point 2 the demand for real money holdings falls short of the supply by $Q^1 - Q^2$, so there is an excess supply of money. If individuals are holding more money than they desire given the interest rate of R^2, they will attempt to reduce their liquidity by using some money to purchase interest-bearing assets. In other words, individuals will attempt to get rid of their excess money by lending it to others. Since there is an aggregate excess supply of money at R^2, however, not everyone can succeed in doing this: there are more people who would like to lend money to reduce their liquidity than there are people who would like to borrow it to increase theirs. Those who cannot unload their extra money try to tempt potential borrowers by lowering the interest rate they charge for loans below R^2. The downward pressure on the interest rate continues until the rate reaches R^1. At this interest rate, anyone wishing to lend money can do so because the aggregate excess supply of money has disappeared; that is, supply once again equals demand. Once the market reaches point 1, there is therefore no further tendency for the interest rate to drop.[4]

Similarly, if the interest rate is initially at a level R^3 below R^1, it will tend to rise. As Figure 14-3 shows, there is excess demand for money equal to $Q^3 - Q^1$ at point 3. Individuals therefore attempt to sell interest-bearing assets such as bonds to increase their money holdings (that is, they sell bonds for cash). At point 3, however, not everyone can succeed in selling enough interest-bearing assets to satisfy his or her demand for money. Thus, people bid for money by offering to borrow at progressively higher interest rates and push the interest rate upward toward R^1. Only when the market has reached point 1 and the excess demand for money has been eliminated does the interest rate stop rising.

We can summarize our findings as follows: *The market always moves toward an interest rate at which the real money supply equals aggregate real money demand. If there is initially an excess supply of money, the interest rate falls, and if there is initially an excess demand, it rises.*

Interest Rates and the Money Supply

The effect of increasing the money supply at a given price level is illustrated in Figure 14-4. Initially the money market is in equilibrium at point 1, with a money supply M^1 and an interest rate R^1. Since we are holding P constant, a rise in the money supply to M^2 increases the real money supply from M^1/P to M^2/P. With a real money supply of M^2/P, point 2 is the new equilibrium and R^2 is the new, lower interest rate that induces people to hold the increased available real money supply.

The process through which the interest rate falls is by now familiar. After M^s is increased by the central bank, there is initially an excess real supply of money at the old equilibrium interest rate, R^1, which previously balanced the market. Since people are holding more money than they desire, they use their surplus funds to bid for assets that pay interest. The economy as a whole cannot reduce its money holdings, so interest rates are driven down as unwilling money holders compete to lend their excess cash balances. At point 2 in Figure 14-4, the interest rate has fallen sufficiently to induce an increase in real money demand equal to the increase in the real money supply.

By running the above policy experiment in reverse, we can see how a reduction of the money supply forces interest rates upward. A fall in M^s causes an excess demand for money at the interest rate that previously balanced supply and demand. People attempt to sell interest-bearing assets—that is, to borrow—to rebuild their depleted real money holdings. Since they cannot all be successful when there is excess money demand, the interest rate is pushed upward until everyone is content to hold the smaller real money stock.

We conclude that *an increase in the money supply lowers the interest rate, while a fall in the money supply raises the interest rate, given the price level and output.*

---

[4]Another way to view this process is as follows: We saw in the last chapter that an asset's rate of return falls when its current price rises relative to its future value. When there is an excess supply of money, the current money prices of illiquid assets that pay interest will be bid up as individuals attempt to reduce their money holdings. This rise in current asset prices lowers the rate of return on nonmoney assets, and since this rate of return is equal to the interest rate (after adjustment for risk), the interest rate also must fall.

Figure 14-4 | Effect of an Increase in the Money Supply on the Interest Rate

For a given price level, P, and real income level, Y, an increase in the money supply from M^1 to M^2 reduces the interest rate from R^1 (point 1) to R^2 (point 2).

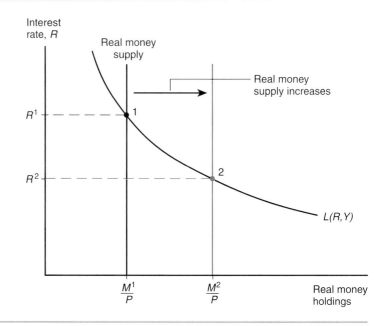

Output and the Interest Rate

Figure 14-5 shows the effect on the interest rate of a rise in the level of output from Y^1 to Y^2, given the money supply and the price level. As we saw earlier, an increase in output causes the entire aggregate real money demand schedule to shift to the right, moving the equilibrium away from point 1. At the old equilibrium interest rate, R^1, there is an excess demand for money equal to $Q^2 - Q^1$ (point 1'). Since the real money supply is given, the interest rate is bid up until it reaches the higher new equilibrium level R^2 (point 2). A fall in output has opposite effects, causing the aggregate real money demand schedule to shift to the left and therefore causing the equilibrium interest rate to fall.

We conclude that *an increase in real output raises the interest rate, while a fall in real output lowers the interest rate, given the price level and the money supply.*

The Money Supply and the Exchange Rate in the Short Run

In Chapter 13 we learned about the interest parity condition, which predicts how interest rate movements influence the exchange rate, given expectations about the exchange rate's future level. Now that we know how shifts in a country's money supply affect the interest rate on nonmoney assets denominated in its currency, we can see how monetary changes affect the exchange rate. We will discover that an increase in a country's money supply causes its currency to depreciate in the foreign exchange market, while a reduction in the money supply causes its currency to appreciate.

Figure 14-5 Effect on the Interest Rate of a Rise in Real Income

Given the real money supply, $M^s/P\ (= Q^1)$, a rise in real income from Y^1 to Y^2 raises the interest rate from R^1 (point 1) to R^2 (point 2).

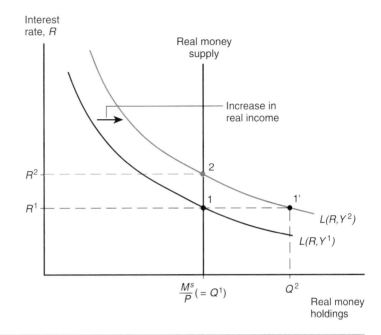

In this section we continue to take the price level (along with real output) as given, and for that reason we label the analysis of this section **short run**. The **long run** analysis of an economic event allows for the complete adjustment of the price level (which may take a long time) and for full employment of all factors of production. Later in this chapter we examine the long-run effects of money supply changes on the price level, the exchange rate, and other macroeconomic variables. Our long-run analysis will show how the money supply influences exchange rate expectations, which we also continue to take as given for now.

Linking Money, the Interest Rate, and the Exchange Rate

To analyze the relation between money and the exchange rate in the short run in Figure 14-6, we combine two diagrams that we have already studied separately. Let's assume once again that we are looking at the dollar/euro exchange rate, that is, the price of euros in terms of dollars.

The first diagram (introduced as Figure 13-4) shows equilibrium in the foreign exchange market and how it is determined given interest rates and expectations about future exchange rates. This diagram appears as the top part of Figure 14-6. The dollar interest rate, $R^1_{\$}$, which is determined in the money market, defines the vertical schedule.

As you will remember from Chapter 13, the downward-sloping expected euro return schedule shows the expected return on euro deposits, measured in dollars. The schedule slopes downward because of the effect of current exchange rate changes on expectations of future depreciation: A strengthening of the dollar today (a fall in $E_{\$/€}$) relative to its *given*

Figure 14-6 | Simultaneous Equilibrium in the U.S. Money Market and the Foreign-Exchange Market

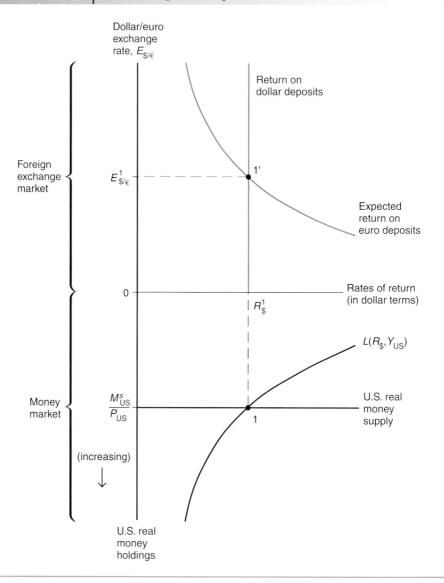

Both asset markets are in equilibrium at the interest rate $R_\$^1$ and exchange rate $E_{\$/€}^1$; at these values money supply equals money demand (point 1) and the interest parity condition holds (point 1').

expected future level makes euro deposits more attractive by leading people to anticipate a sharper dollar depreciation in the future.

At the intersection of the two schedules (point 1′), the expected rates of return on dollar and euro deposits are equal, and therefore interest parity holds. $E^1_{\$/€}$ is the equilibrium exchange rate.

The second diagram we need to examine the relation between money and the exchange rate was introduced as Figure 14-3. This figure shows how a country's equilibrium interest is determined in its money market and it appears as the bottom part of Figure 14-6. For convenience, however, the figure has been rotated clockwise by 90 degrees so that dollar interest rates are measured from 0 on the horizontal axis and the U.S. real money supply is measured from 0 on the descending vertical axis. Money market equilibrium is shown at point 1, where the dollar interest rate $R^1_\$$ induces people to demand real balances equal to the U.S. real money supply, M^s_{US}/P_{US}.

Figure 14-6 emphasizes the link between the U.S. money market (bottom) and the foreign exchange market (top)—the U.S. money market determines the dollar interest rate, which in turn affects the exchange rate that maintains interest parity. (Of course, there is a similar link between the European money market and the foreign exchange market that operates through changes in the euro interest rate.)

Figure 14-7 illustrates these linkages. The U.S. and European central banks, the Federal Reserve System and the European System of Central Banks (ESCB), determine the U.S. and European money supplies, M^s_{US} and M^s_E. Given the price levels and national incomes of the two countries, equilibrium in national money markets leads to the dollar and euro interest rates $R_\$$ and $R_€$. These interest rates feed into the foreign exchange market where, given expectations about the future dollar/euro exchange rate, the current rate $E_{\$/€}$ is determined by the interest parity condition.

U.S. Money Supply and the Dollar/Euro Exchange Rate

We now use our model of asset market linkages (the links between the money and foreign exchange markets) to ask how the dollar/euro exchange rate changes when the Federal Reserve changes the U.S. money supply M^s_{US}. The effects of this change are summarized in Figure 14-8.

At the initial money supply M^1_{US}, the money market is in equilibrium at point 1 with an interest rate $R^1_\$$. Given the euro interest rate and the expected future exchange rate, a dollar interest rate of $R^1_\$$ implies that foreign exchange market equilibrium occurs at point 1′, with an exchange rate equal to $E^1_{\$/€}$.

What happens when the Federal Reserve raises the U.S. money supply from M^1_{US} to M^2_{US}? This increase sets in train the following sequence of events: (1) At the initial interest rate $R^1_\$$ there is an excess supply of money in the U.S. money market, so the dollar interest rate falls to $R^2_\$$ as the money market reaches its new equilibrium position (point 2). (2) Given the initial exchange rate $E^1_{\$/€}$ and the new, lower interest rate on dollars, $R^2_\$$, the expected return on euro deposits is greater than that on dollar deposits. Holders of dollar deposits therefore try to sell them for euro deposits, which are momentarily more attractive. (3) The dollar depreciates to $E^2_{\$/€}$, as holders of dollar deposits bid for euro deposits. The foreign exchange market is once again in equilibrium at point 2′ because the exchange rate's move to $E^2_{\$/€}$ causes a fall in the dollar's expected future depreciation rate sufficient to offset the fall in the dollar interest rate.

Figure 14-7 | Money-Market/Exchange Rate Linkages

Monetary policy actions by the Fed affect the U.S. interest rate, changing the dollar/euro exchange rate that clears the foreign exchange market. The ESCB can affect the exchange rate by changing the European money supply and interest rate.

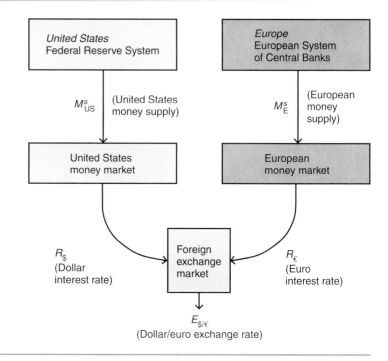

We conclude that *an increase in a country's money supply causes its currency to depreciate in the foreign exchange market.* By running Figure 14-8 in reverse, you can see that *a reduction in a country's money supply causes its currency to appreciate in the foreign exchange market.*

Europe's Money Supply and the Dollar/Euro Exchange Rate

The conclusions we have reached also apply when the ESCB changes Europe's money supply. An increase in M_E^s causes a depreciation of the euro (that is, an appreciation of the dollar, or a fall in $E_{\$/€}$), while a reduction in M_E^s causes an appreciation of the euro (that is, a depreciation of the dollar, or a rise in $E_{\$/€}$).

The mechanism at work, which runs from the European interest rate to the exchange rate, is the same as the one we just analyzed. It is good exercise to verify these assertions by drawing figures similar to Figures 14-6 and 14-8 that illustrate the linkage between the European money market and the foreign exchange market.

Here we use a different approach to show how changes in Europe's money supply affect the dollar/euro exchange rate. In Chapter 13 we learned that a fall in the euro interest rate, $R_€$, shifts the downward-sloping schedule in the upper part of Figure 14-6 to the left. The reason is that for any level of the exchange rate, a fall in $R_€$ lowers the expected rate of return on euro deposits. Since a rise in the European money supply M_E^S lowers $R_€$, we can

Figure 14-8 | Effect on the Dollar/Euro Exchange Rate and Dollar Interest Rate of an Increase in the U.S. Money Supply

Given P_{US} and Y_{US}, when the money supply rises from M_{US}^1 to M_{US}^2, the dollar interest rate declines (as money-market equilibrium is reestablished at point 2) and the dollar depreciates against the euro (as foreign exchange market equilibrium is reestablished at point 2').

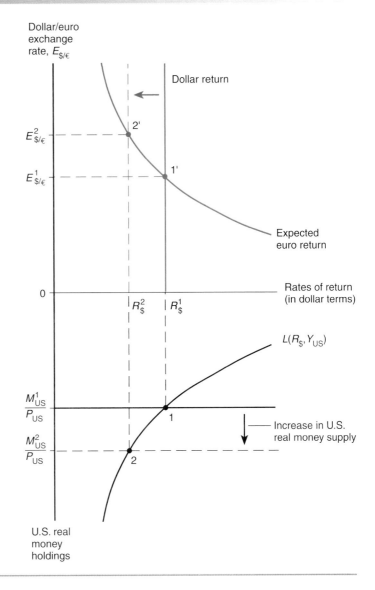

see the effect on the exchange rate by shifting the expected euro return schedule in the top part of Figure 14-6 to the left.

The result of an increase in the European money supply is shown in Figure 14-9. Initially the U.S. money market is in equilibrium at point 1 and the foreign exchange market is in equilibrium at point 1', with an exchange rate $E_{\$/€}^1$. An increase in Europe's money supply

Figure 14-9 | Effect of an Increase in the European Money Supply on the Dollar/Euro Exchange Rate

By lowering the dollar return on euro deposits (shown as a leftward shift in the expected euro return curve), an increase in Europe's money supply causes the dollar to appreciate against the euro. Equilibrium in the foreign exchange market shifts from point l' to point 2', but equilibrium in the U.S. money market remains at point I.

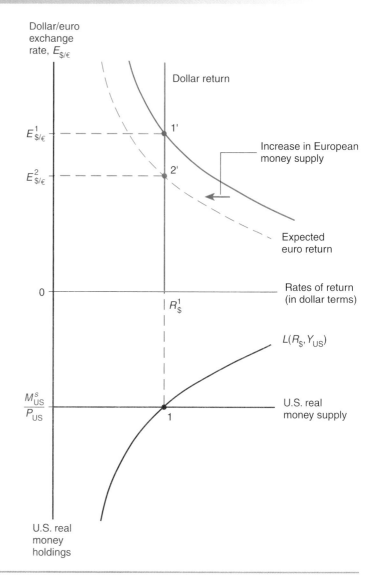

lowers R_ϵ and therefore shifts to the left the schedule linking the expected return on euro deposits to the exchange rate. Foreign exchange market equilibrium is restored at point 2', with an exchange rate of $E^2_{\$/\epsilon}$. We see that the increase in European money causes the euro to depreciate against the dollar (that is, causes a fall in the dollar price of euros). Similarly, a fall in Europe's money supply would cause the euro to appreciate against the dollar ($E_{\$/\epsilon}$

would rise). The change in the European money supply does not disturb the U.S. money market equilibrium, which remains at point 1.[5]

Money, the Price Level, and the Exchange Rate in the Long Run

Our short-run analysis of the link between countries' money markets and the foreign exchange market rested on the simplifying assumption that price levels and exchange rate expectations were given. To extend our understanding of how money supply and money demand affect exchange rates, we must examine how monetary factors affect a country's price level in the long run.

An economy's **long-run equilibrium** is the position it would eventually reach if no new economic shocks occurred during the adjustment to full employment. You can think of long-run equilibrium as the equilibrium that would be maintained after all wages and prices had had enough time to adjust to their market-clearing levels. An equivalent way of thinking of it is as the equilibrium that would occur if prices were perfectly flexible and always adjusted immediately to preserve full employment.

In studying how monetary changes work themselves out over the long run, we will examine how such changes shift the economy's long-run equilibrium. Our main tool is once again the theory of aggregate money demand.

Money and Money Prices

If the price level and output are fixed in the short run, the condition (14-4) of money market equilibrium,

$$M^s/P = L(R, Y),$$

determines the domestic interest rate, R. The money market always moves to equilibrium, however, even if we drop our "short-run" assumption and think of periods over which P and Y, as well as R, can vary. The above equilibrium condition can therefore be rearranged to give

$$P = M^s/L(R, Y), \tag{14-5}$$

which shows how the price level depends on the interest rate, real output, and the domestic money supply.

The *long-run equilibrium price level* is just the value of P that satisfies condition (14-5) when the interest rate and output are at their long-run levels, that is, at levels consistent with full employment. When the money market is in equilibrium and all factors of production are fully employed, the price level will remain steady if the money supply, the aggregate money demand function, and the long-run values of R and Y remain steady.

---

[5]The U.S. money market equilibrium remains at point 1 because the price adjustments that equilibrate the European money market and the foreign exchange market after the increase in Europe's money supply do not change either the money supply or money demand in the United States, given Y_{US} and P_{US}.

One of the most important predictions of the above equation for P concerns the relationship between a country's price level and its money supply, M^s: *All else equal, an increase in a country's money supply causes a proportional increase in its price level.* If, for example, the money supply doubles (to $2M^s$) but output and the interest rate do not change, the price level must also double (to $2P$) to maintain equilibrium in the money market.

The economic reasoning behind this very precise prediction follows from our observation above that the demand for money is a demand for *real* money holdings: Real money demand is not altered by an increase in M^s that leaves R and Y (and thus aggregate real money demand $L(R, Y)$) unchanged. If aggregate real money demand does not change, however, the money market will remain in equilibrium only if the real money supply also stays the same. To keep the real money supply M^s/P constant, P must rise in proportion to M^s.

The Long-Run Effects of Money Supply Changes

Our theory of how the money supply affects the price level *given* the interest rate and output is not yet a theory of how money supply changes affect the price level in the long run. To develop such a theory, we still have to determine the long-run effects of a money supply change on the interest rate and output. This is easier than you might think. As we now argue, *a change in the supply of money has no effect on the long-run values of the interest rate or real output.*[6]

The best way to understand the long-run effects of money supply on the interest rate and output is to think first about a *currency reform,* in which a country's government redefines the national currency unit. For example, the government of France reformed its currency on January 1, 1960, simply by issuing "new" French francs, each equal to 100 "old" French francs. The effect of this reform was to lower the number of currency units in circulation, and all franc prices, to ¹/₁₀₀ of their old franc values. But the redefinition of the monetary unit had no effect on real output, the interest rate, or the relative prices of goods: All that occurred was a one-shot change in all values measured in francs. A decision to measure distance in half-miles rather than miles would have as little effect on real economic variables as the French government's decision to chop two zeros off the end of every magnitude measured in terms of money.

An increase in the supply of a country's currency has the same effect in the long run as a currency reform. A doubling of the money supply, for example, has the same long-run effect as a currency reform in which each unit of currency is replaced by two units of "new" currency. If the economy is initially fully employed, every money price in the economy eventually doubles, but real GNP, the interest rate, and all relative prices return to their long-run or full-employment levels.

Why is a money supply change just like a currency reform in its effects on the economy's long-run equilibrium? The full-employment output level is determined by the economy's endowments of labor and capital, so in the long run real output does not depend on the

---

[6]The preceding statement refers only to changes in the *level* of the nominal money supply and not, for example, to changes in the *rate* at which the money supply is growing over time. The proposition that a one-time change in the level of the money supply has no effects on the long-run values of real economic variables is often called the *long-run neutrality of money.* In contrast, changes in the money supply growth rate need not be neutral in the long run. At the very least, a sustained change in the monetary growth rate will eventually affect equilibrium real money balances by raising the money interest rate (as discussed in the next chapter).

money supply. Similarly, the interest rate is independent of the money supply in the long run. If the money supply and all prices double permanently, there is no reason why people previously willing to exchange $1 today for $1.10 a year from now should not be willing afterward to exchange $2 today for $2.20 a year from now, so the interest rate will remain at 10 percent per annum. Relative prices also remain the same if all money prices double, since relative prices are just ratios of money prices. Thus, money supply changes do not change the long-run allocation of resources. Only the absolute level of money prices changes.[7]

When studying the effect of an increase in the money supply over long time periods, we are therefore justified in assuming that the long-run values of R and Y will not be changed by a change in the supply of money. Thus, we can draw the following conclusion from equation (14-5): *A permanent increase in the money supply causes a proportional increase in the price level's long-run value. In particular, if the economy is initially at full employment, a permanent increase in the money supply eventually will be followed by a proportional increase in the price level.*

Empirical Evidence on Money Supplies and Price Levels

In looking at actual data on money and prices, we should not expect to see an exact proportional relationship over long periods, partly because output, the interest rate, and the aggregate real money demand function can shift for reasons that have nothing to do with the supply of money. Output changes as a result of capital accumulation and technological advance, for example, and money demand behavior may change as a result of demographic trends or financial innovations such as electronic cash-transfer facilities. In addition, actual economies are rarely in positions of long-run equilibrium. Nonetheless, we should expect the data to show a clear-cut positive association between money supplies and price levels. If real-world data did not provide strong evidence that money supplies and price levels move together in the long run, the usefulness of the theory of money demand we have developed would be in severe doubt.

Evidence on the money supply/price level linkage for the world's seven largest industrial countries is shown in Figure 14-10. The horizontal axis measures percentage increases in money supplies between 1973 and 1997, the vertical axis percentage increases in price levels. As you can see, there is a strong positive relation between money supply and price level for this group of countries. A country plotted close to the 45-degree line would be one in which money supplies and price levels increased more or less in proportion over 1973–1997. In several cases, however, the observations stray far away from the 45-degree line along which increases in money and prices are proportional. Germany's price level, for example, rose by a much smaller percentage than its money supply, as indicated by that country's position far below the 45-degree line.

---

[7]To understand more fully why a one-time change in the money supply does not change the long-run level of the interest rate, it may be useful to think of interest rates measured in terms of money as defining relative prices of currency units available on different dates. If the dollar interest rate is R percent per annum, giving up $1 today buys you $(1 + R)$ next year. Thus, $1/(1 + R)$ is the relative price of future dollars in terms of current dollars, and this relative price would not change if the real value of the monetary units were scaled up or down by the same factor on all dates.

> **Figure 14-10** | Monetary Growth and Price-Level Change
> in the Seven Main Industrial Countries, 1973–1997

In a cross-section of countries, long-term changes in money supplies and price levels show a clear positive correlation. (The diagonal line indicates exactly proportional changes in money supplies and price levels.)

Source: OECD, *Main Economic Indicators*, and IMF, *International Financial Statistics*.

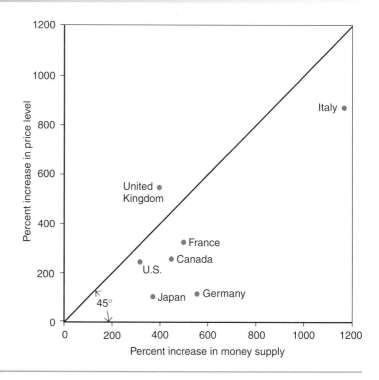

As we observed above, we should expect these discrepancies because the theory of money demand predicts exactly proportional increases in money and price levels only when no other factors affecting the money market (such as real income per capita) change at the same time. These other factors, however, have not remained constant in the countries shown. Countries closer to the 45-degree line in Figure 14-10 are those in which the effects on money market equilibrium of factors other than money supply roughly offset each other. The main lesson to be drawn from Figure 14-10 is that the data confirm the strong long-run link between national money supplies and national price levels predicted by economic theory.

Money and the Exchange Rate in the Long Run

The domestic currency price of foreign currency is one of the many prices in the economy that rise in the long run after a permanent increase in the money supply. If you think again about the effects of a currency reform, you will see how the exchange rate moves in the long run. Suppose, for example, that the U.S. government replaced every pair of "old" dollars with one "new" dollar. Then if the dollar/euro exchange rate had been 1.20 *old* dollars per euro before the reform, it would change to 0.60 *new* dollars per euro immediately after the

INFLATION AND MONEY-SUPPLY GROWTH IN LATIN AMERICA

The wide swings in Latin American rates of inflation in recent years make the region an ideal case study in the relationship between money supplies and price levels. Inflation had been high and variable in Latin America for more than a decade (a situation we discuss in Chapter 22) when efforts at macroeconomic reform began to bring inflation lower by the mid-1990s.

On the basis of our theories, we would expect to find such sharp swings in inflation rates accompanied by swings in growth rates of money supplies. This expectation is confirmed by the figure below, which plots annual average growth rates of the money supply against annual inflation rates: On average, years with higher money growth also tend to be years with higher inflation.

Average Money Growth and Inflation in Western Hemisphere Developing Countries, by Year, 1987–2000

Even year by year, there is a strong positive relation between average Latin American money-supply growth and inflation. (Both axes have logarithmic scales.)

Source: IMF, *World Economic Outlook*, May 1995, October 1997, May 2001. Regional aggregates are weighted by shares of dollar GDP in total regional dollar GDP.

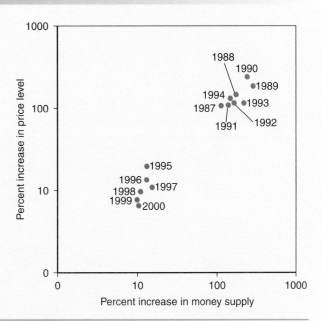

reform. In much the same way, a halving of the U.S. money supply would eventually lead the dollar to appreciate from an exchange rate of 1.20 dollars/euro to one of 0.60 dollars/euro. Since the dollar prices of all U.S. goods and services would also decrease by half, this 50 percent appreciation of the dollar leaves the *relative* prices of all U.S. and foreign goods and services unchanged.

We conclude that, all else equal, *a permanent increase in a country's money supply causes a proportional long-run depreciation of its currency against foreign currencies.*

Similarly, a permanent decrease in a country's money supply causes a proportional long-run appreciation of its currency against foreign currencies.

Inflation and Exchange Rate Dynamics

In this section we tie together our short-run and long-run findings about the effects of monetary changes by examining the process through which the price level adjusts to its long-run position. An economy experiences **inflation** when its price level is rising and **deflation** when its price level is falling. Our examination of inflation will give us a deeper understanding of how the exchange rate adjusts to monetary disturbances in the economy.

Short-Run Price Rigidity versus Long-Run Price Flexibility

Our analysis of the short-run effects of monetary changes assumed that a country's price level, unlike its exchange rate, does not jump immediately. This assumption cannot be exactly correct, because many commodities, such as agricultural products, are traded in markets where prices adjust sharply every day as supply or demand conditions shift. In addition, exchange rate changes themselves may affect the prices of some tradable goods and services that enter into the commodity basket defining the price level.

Many prices in the economy, however, are written into long-term contracts and cannot be changed immediately when changes in the money supply occur. The most important prices of this type are workers' wages, which are negotiated only periodically in many industries. Wages do not enter indices of the price level directly, but they make up a large fraction of the cost of producing goods and services. Since output prices depend heavily on production costs, the behavior of the overall price level is influenced by the sluggishness of wage movements. The short-run "stickiness" of price levels is illustrated by Figure 14-11, which compares data on month-to-month percentage changes in the dollar/deutschemark (DM) exchange rate, $E_{\$/DM}$, with data on month-to-month percentage changes in the ratio of money price levels in the United States and Germany, P_{US}/P_G. (Recall that Germany had its own currency, the DM, until 1999, and that the DM remained as a "legacy currency," fixed against the euro, until 2002.) As you can see, the exchange rate is much more variable than relative price levels, a fact consistent with the view that price levels are relatively rigid in the short run. The pattern shown in the figure applies to all of the main industrial countries in recent years. In light of this and other evidence, we will therefore continue to assume that the price level is given in the short run and does not take significant jumps in response to policy changes.

This assumption would not be reasonable, however, for all countries at all times. In extremely inflationary conditions, such as those seen in the 1980s in some Latin American countries, long-term contracts specifying domestic money payments may go out of use. Automatic price level indexation of wage payments may also be widespread under highly inflationary conditions. Such developments make the price level much less rigid than it would be under moderate inflation, and large price level jumps become possible. (See the boxes on Latin American inflation, page 377, and Bolivia, page 380).

Our analysis assuming short-run price rigidity is therefore most applicable to countries with histories of relative price level stability, such as the United States. Even in the cases of

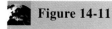

Figure 14-11 | Month-to-Month Variability of the Dollar/DM Exchange Rate and of the U.S./German Price-Level Ratio, 1974–2001

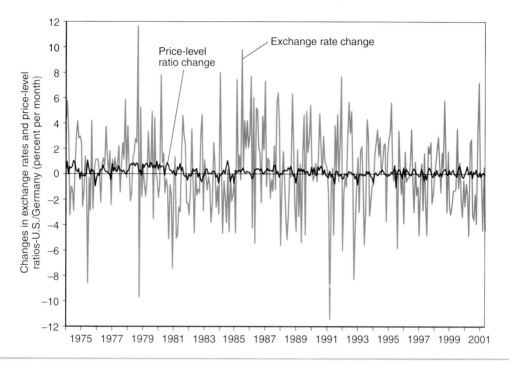

The much greater month-to-month variability of the exchange rate suggests that price levels are relatively sticky in the short run.

Source: OECD, *Main Economic Indicators.*

low-inflation countries, there is a lively academic debate over the possibility that seemingly sticky wages and prices are in reality quite flexible.[8]

Although the price levels appear to display short-run stickiness in many countries, a change in the money supply creates immediate demand and cost pressures that eventually lead to *future* increases in the price level. These pressures come from three main sources:

1. *Excess demand for output and labor.* An increase in the money supply has an expansionary effect on the economy, raising the total demand for final goods and services. To meet this demand, producers of goods and services must employ workers overtime and make new hires. Even if wages are given in the short run, the additional

---

[8]For a discussion of this debate, and empirical evidence that U.S. aggregate prices and wages show significant rigidity, see the book by Hall and Taylor listed in Further Reading. Other summaries of U.S. evidence are given by Mark A. Wynne, "Sticky Prices: What Is the Evidence?" *Federal Reserve Bank of Dallas Economic Review* (First Quarter 1995), pp. 1–12; and John B. Taylor, "Staggered Price and Wage Setting in Macroeconomics," in John B. Taylor and Michael Woodford, eds., *Handbook of Macroeconomics* (Amsterdam: North-Holland, 1999).

MONEY SUPPLY GROWTH AND HYPERINFLATION IN BOLIVIA

In 1984 and 1985 the small Latin American country of Bolivia experienced *hyperinflation*—an explosive and seemingly uncontrollable inflation in which money loses value rapidly and may even go out of use.* During hyperinflations the magnitudes of monetary changes are so enormous that the "long-run" effects of money on the price level can occur very quickly. These episodes therefore provide laboratory conditions well-suited for testing long-run theories about the effects of money supplies on prices.

On the next page we show data on Bolivia's money supply and price level during the hyperinflation. An official exchange rate between the Bolivian peso and the U.S. dollar was controlled by the Bolivian government during this period, so we list instead values for an exchange rate that better reflected market forces, the price of dollars in terms of pesos on the La Paz black market.

The data show a clear tendency for the money supply, price level, and exchange rate to move in step, as the theory in the text would predict. Moreover, the trends in the price level and exchange rate are of the same order of magnitude: The price level rose by 22,908 percent between April 1984 and July 1985 and the peso price of dollars rose by 24,662 percent over the same period. These percentage changes actually are greater than the corresponding percentage increase in the money supply (which is "only" 17,433 percent), but the difference is to be expected. Exploding inflation causes real money demand to fall over time, and this additional monetary change makes money prices rise even more quickly than the money supply itself rises.

We chose July 1985 as the endpoint for the comparison because the Bolivian government introduced a dramatic stabilization plan near the end of August 1985. You can see in the data how the money supply and, more dramatically, the price level and exchange rate all began to level out in the two months after August.

---

*In a classic paper, Columbia University economist Phillip Cagan drew the line between inflation and hyperinflation at an inflation rate of 50 percent per month (which, through the power of compounding, comes out to 12,875 percent per year). See "The Monetary Dynamics of Hyperinflation," in Milton Friedman, ed., *Studies in the Quantity Theory of Money.* Chicago: University of Chicago Press, 1956, pp. 25–117.

---

demand for labor allows workers to ask for higher wages in the next round of wage negotiations. Producers are willing to pay these higher wages, for they know that in a booming economy it will not be hard to pass higher wage costs on to consumers through higher product prices.

2. *Inflationary expectations.* If everyone expects the price level to rise in the future, their expectation will increase the pace of inflation today. Workers bargaining over wage contracts will insist on higher money wages to counteract the effect on their *real* wages of the anticipated general increase in prices. Producers, once again, will give in to these wage demands if they expect product prices to rise and cover the additional wage costs.

3. *Raw materials prices.* Many raw materials used in the production of final goods, for example, petroleum products and metals, are sold in markets where prices adjust sharply even in the short run. By causing the prices of such materials to jump upward, a money supply increase raises production costs in materials-using industries. Eventually, producers in those industries will raise product prices to cover their higher costs.

Macroeconomic Data for Bolivia, April 1984–October 1985

Month	Money Supply (Billions of Pesos)	Price Level (Relative to 1982 Average = 1)	Exchange Rate (Pesos per Dollar)
1984			
April	270	21.1	3,576
May	330	31.1	3,512
June	440	32.3	3,342
July	599	34.0	3,570
August	718	39.1	7,038
September	889	53.7	13,685
October	1,194	85.5	15,205
November	1,495	112.4	18,469
December	3,296	180.9	24,515
1985			
January	4,630	305.3	73,016
February	6,455	863.3	141,101
March	9,089	1,078.6	128,137
April	12,885	1,205.7	167,428
May	21,309	1,635.7	272,375
June	27,778	2,919.1	481,756
July	47,341	4,854.6	885,476
August	74,306	8,081.0	1,182,300
September	103,272	12,647.6	1,087,440
October	132,550	12,411.8	1,120,210

Source: Juan-Antonio Morales, "Inflation Stabilization in Bolivia," in Michael Bruno et al., eds., *Inflation Stabilization: The Experience of Israel, Argentina, Brazil, Bolivia, and Mexico.* Cambridge: MIT Press, 1988, Table 7A-1. Money supply is M1.

Permanent Money Supply Changes and the Exchange Rate

We now apply our analysis of inflation to study the adjustment of the dollar/euro exchange rate following a *permanent* increase in the U.S. money supply. Figure 14-12 shows both the short-run (Figure 14-12a) and long-run (Figure 14-12b) effects of this disturbance. We assume the economy starts with all variables at their long-run levels and that output remains constant as the economy adjusts to the money supply change.

Figure 14-12a assumes the U.S. price level is initially given at P_{US}^1. An increase in the nominal money supply from M_{US}^1 to M_{US}^2 therefore raises the real money supply from M_{US}^1/P_{US}^1 to M_{US}^2/P_{US}^1 in the short run, lowering the interest rate from $R_\$^1$ (point 1) to $R_\$^2$ (point 2). So far our analysis follows exactly as it did earlier in this chapter.

The first change in our analysis comes when we ask how the American money supply change (shown in the bottom part of panel (a)) affects the foreign exchange market (shown

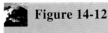

Figure 14-12 | Short-Run and Long-Run Effects of an Increase in the U.S. Money Supply (Given Real Output, Y)

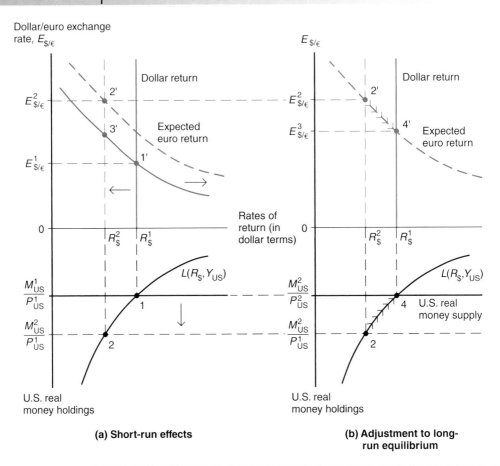

(a) Short-run effects

(b) Adjustment to long-run equilibrium

(a) Short-run adjustment of the asset markets. (b) How the interest rate, price level, and exchange rate move over time as the economy approaches its long-run equilibrium.

in the top part of panel (a)). As before, the fall in the U.S. interest rate is shown as a leftward shift in the vertical schedule giving the dollar return on dollar deposits. This is no longer the whole story, however, for the money supply increase now affects *exchange rate expectations*. Because the U.S. money supply change is permanent, people expect a long-run increase in all dollar prices, including the exchange rate, which is the dollar price of euros. As you will recall from Chapter 13, a rise in the expected future dollar/euro exchange rate (a future dollar depreciation) raises the expected dollar return on euro deposits; it thus shifts the downward-sloping schedule in the top part of Figure 14-12a to the right. The dollar depreciates against the euro, moving from an exchange rate of $E^1_{\$/€}$ (point 1′) to $E^2_{\$/€}$ (point 2′). Notice that the dollar depreciation is *greater* than it would be if the expected future dollar/euro exchange rate stayed fixed (as it might if the money supply increase were temporary rather than permanent). If the expectation $E^e_{\$/\euro}$ did not change, the new short-run equilibrium would be at point 3′ rather than at point 2′.

Figure 14-12b shows how the interest rate and exchange rate behave as the price level rises during the economy's adjustment to its long-run equilibrium. The price level begins to rise from the initially given level P^1_{US}, eventually reaching P^2_{US}. Because the long-run increase in the price level must be proportional to the increase in the money supply, the final *real* money supply, M^2_{US}/P^2_{US}, is shown equal to the initial real money supply, M^1_{US}/P^1_{US}. Since output is given and the real money supply has returned to its original level, the equilibrium interest rate must again equal $R^1_\$$ in the long run (point 4). The interest rate therefore rises from $R^2_\$$ (point 2) to $R^1_\$$ (point 4) as the price level rises from P^1_{US} to P^2_{US}.

The rising U.S. interest rate has exchange rate effects that can also be seen in Figure 14-12b: The dollar *appreciates* against the euro in the process of adjustment. If exchange rate expectations do not change further during the adjustment process, the foreign exchange market moves to its long-run position along the downward-sloping schedule defining the dollar return on euro deposits. The market's path is just the path traced out by the vertical dollar interest rate schedule as it moves rightward because of the price level's gradual rise. In the long run (point 4′) the equilibrium exchange rate, $E^3_{\$/\euro}$, is higher than at the original equilibrium, point 1′. Like the price level, the dollar/euro exchange rate has risen in proportion to the increase in the money supply.

Figure 14-13 shows time paths like the ones just described for the U.S. money supply, the dollar interest rate, the U.S. price level, and the dollar/euro exchange rate. The figure is drawn so that the long-run increases in the price level (Figure 14-13c) and exchange rate (Figure 14-13d) are proportional to the increase in the money supply (Figure 14-13a).

Exchange Rate Overshooting

In its initial depreciation after a money supply rise, the exchange rate jumps from $E^1_{\$/\euro}$ up to $E^2_{\$/\euro}$, a depreciation greater than its *long-run* depreciation from $E^1_{\$/\euro}$ to $E^3_{\$/\euro}$ (see Figure 14-13d). The exchange rate is said to overshoot when its immediate response to a disturbance is greater than its long-run response. **Exchange rate overshooting** is an important phenomenon because it helps explain why exchange rates move so sharply from day to day.

The economic explanation of overshooting comes from the interest parity condition. The explanation is easiest to grasp if we assume that before the money supply increase first occurs, no change in the dollar/euro exchange rate is expected, so that $R^1_\$$ equals $R_\euro$, the given interest rate on euro deposits. A permanent increase in the U.S. money supply doesn't affect $R_\euro$, so it causes $R^1_\$$ to fall below $R_\euro$ and remain below that interest rate (Figure 14-13b) until the U.S. price level has completed the long-run adjustment to P^2_{US} shown in Figure 14-13c. For the foreign exchange market to be in equilibrium during this adjustment process, however, the interest difference in favor of euro deposits must be offset by an expected *appreciation* of the dollar against the euro, that is, by an expected fall in $E_{\$/\euro}$. Only if the dollar/euro exchange rate overshoots $E^3_{\$/\euro}$ initially will market participants expect a subsequent appreciation of the dollar against the euro.

Overshooting is a direct consequence of the short-run rigidity of the price level. In a hypothetical world where the price level could adjust immediately to its new long-run level after a money supply increase, the dollar interest rate would not fall because prices *would* adjust immediately and prevent the real money supply from rising. Thus, there

Figure 14-13 Time Paths of U.S. Economic Variables After a Permanent Increase in the U.S. Money Supply

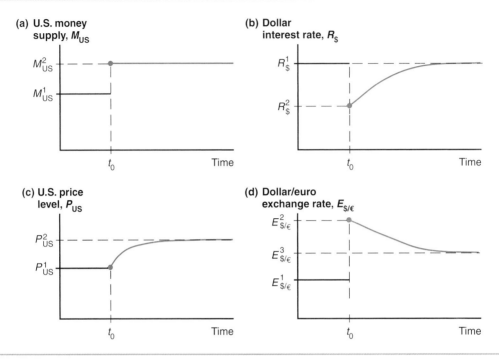

After the money supply increases at t_0 in panel (a), the interest rate (in panel (b)), price level (in panel (c)), and exchange rate (in panel (d)) move as shown toward their long-run levels. As indicated in panel (d) by the initial jump from $E^1_{\$/\epsilon}$ to $E^2_{\$/\epsilon}$, the exchange rate overshoots in the short run before settling down to its long-run level, $E^3_{\$/\epsilon}$.

would be no need for overshooting to maintain equilibrium in the foreign exchange market. The exchange rate would maintain equilibrium simply by jumping to its new long-run level right away.

Summary

1. Money is held because of its liquidity. When considered in real terms, *aggregate money demand* is not a demand for a certain number of currency units but is instead a demand for a certain amount of purchasing power. Aggregate real money demand depends negatively on the opportunity cost of holding money (measured by the domestic interest rate) and positively on the volume of transactions in the economy (measured by real GNP).

2. The money market is in equilibrium when the real *money supply* equals aggregate real money demand. With the *price level* and real output given, a rise in the money supply lowers the interest rate and a fall in the money supply raises the interest rate. A rise in real output raises the interest rate, given the price level, while a fall in real output has the opposite effect.

3. By lowering the domestic interest rate, an increase in the money supply causes the domestic currency to depreciate in the foreign exchange market (even when expectations of future exchange rates do not change). Similarly, a fall in the domestic money supply causes the domestic currency to appreciate against foreign currencies.

4. The assumption that the price level is given in the *short run* is a good approximation to reality in countries with moderate inflation, but it is a misleading assumption over the *long run*. Permanent changes in the money supply push the *long-run equilibrium* price level proportionally in the same direction but do not influence the long-run values of output, the interest rate, or any relative prices. One important money price whose long-run equilibrium level rises in proportion to a permanent money supply increase is the exchange rate, the domestic currency price of foreign currency.

5. An increase in the money supply can cause the exchange rate to overshoot its long-run level in the short run. If output is given, a permanent money supply increase, for example, causes a more-than-proportional short-run depreciation of the currency, followed by an appreciation of the currency to its long-run exchange rate. *Exchange rate overshooting,* which heightens the volatility of exchange rates, is a direct result of sluggish short-run price level adjustment and the interest parity condition.

Key Terms

aggregate money demand, p. 361
deflation, p. 378
exchange rate overshooting, p. 383
inflation, p. 378
long run, p. 367

long-run equilibrium, p. 373
money supply, p. 359
price level, p. 361
short run, p. 367

Problems

1. Suppose there is a reduction in aggregate real money demand, that is, a negative shift in the aggregate real money demand function. Trace the short-run and long-run effects on the exchange rate, interest rate, and price level.

2. How would you expect a fall in a country's population to alter its aggregate money demand function? Would it matter if the fall in population were due to a fall in the number of households or to a fall in the average size of a household?

3. The *velocity* of money, V, is defined as the ratio of real GNP to real money holdings, $V = Y/(M/P)$ in this chapter's notation. Use equation (14-4) to derive an expression for velocity and explain how velocity varies with changes in R and in Y. (Hint: The effect of output changes on V depends on the elasticity of aggregate money demand with respect to real output, which economists believe to be less than unity.) What is the relationship between velocity and the exchange rate?

4. What is the short-run effect on the exchange rate of an increase in domestic real GNP, given expectations about future exchange rates?

5. Does our discussion of money's usefulness as a medium of exchange and unit of account suggest reasons why some currencies become vehicle currencies for foreign exchange transactions? (The concept of a vehicle currency was discussed in Chapter 13.)

6. If a currency reform has no effects on the economy's real variables, why do governments typically institute currency reforms in connection with broader programs aimed at halting runaway inflation? (There are many instances other than the French case mentioned in the text. Recent examples include Israel's switch from the pound to the shekel, Argentina's switches from the peso to the austral and back to the peso, and Brazil's switches from the cruzeiro to the cruzado, from the cruzado to the cruzeiro, from the cruzeiro to the cruzeiro real, and from the cruzeiro real to the real, the current currency, which was introduced in 1994.)

7. Imagine that the central bank of an economy with unemployment doubles its money supply. In the long run, full employment is restored and output returns to its full employment level. On the (admittedly unlikely) assumption that the interest rate before the money supply increase equals the long-run interest rate, is the long-run increase in the price level more than proportional or less than proportional to the money supply change? What if (as is more likely) the interest rate was initially below its long-run level?

8. Between 1984 and 1985, the money supply in the United States increased to $641.0 billion from $570.3 billion, while that of Brazil increased to 106.1 billion cruzados from 24.4 billion. Over the same period, the U.S. consumer price index rose to 100 from a level of 96.6, while the corresponding index for Brazil rose to 100 from a level of only 31. Calculate the 1984–1985 rates of money supply growth and inflation for the United States and Brazil, respectively. Assuming that other factors affecting the money markets did not change too dramatically, how do these numbers match up with the predictions of this chapter's model? How would you explain the apparently different responses of U.S. compared with Brazilian prices?

9. Continuing with the preceding question, note that the monetary value of output in 1985 was $4010 billion in the United States, 1418 billion cruzados in Brazil. Refer back to question 3 and calculate velocity for the two countries in 1985. Why do you think velocity was so much higher in Brazil?

10. In our discussion of short-run exchange rate overshooting, we assumed that real output was given. Assume instead that an increase in the money supply raises real output in the short run (an assumption that will be justified in Chapter 16). How does this affect the extent to which the exchange rate overshoots when the money supply first increases? Is it likely that the exchange rate *under*shoots? (Hint: In Figure 14-l2a, allow the aggregate real money demand schedule to shift in response to the increase in output.)

Further Reading

Ben S. Bernanke, Thomas Laubach, Frederic S. Mishkin, and Adam S. Posen. *Inflation Targeting: Lessons from the International Experience.* Princeton, NJ: Princeton University Press, 1999. Discusses recent monetary policy experience and the consequences for inflation and other macroeconomic variables.

Rudiger Dornbusch. "Expectations and Exchange Rate Dynamics." *Journal of Political Economy* 84 (December 1976), pp. 1161–1176. A theoretical analysis of exchange rate overshooting.

Jacob A. Frenkel and Michael L. Mussa. "The Efficiency of Foreign Exchange Markets and Measures of Turbulence." *American Economic Review* 70 (May 1980) pp. 374–381. Contrasts the behavior of national price levels with that of exchange rates and other asset prices.

Robert E. Hall and John B. Taylor. *Macroeconomics: Theory, Performance, and Policy,* 5th edition. New York: Norton, 1997. Chapters 15 and 16 contain a detailed discussion of short-run price rigidity and longer-run price adjustment in closed economies.

Richard M. Levich. *"Overshooting" in the Foreign Exchange Market.* Occasional Paper 5. New York: Group of Thirty, 1981. An examination of the theory and evidence on exchange rate overshooting.

CHAPTER 15

Price Levels and the Exchange Rate in the Long Run

At the end of 1970 you could have bought 358 Japanese yen with a single American dollar; by Christmas 1980 a dollar was worth only 203 yen. Despite a temporary comeback during the 1980s, the dollar's price in yen slumped to around 120 in the summer of 2001. Many investors found these price changes difficult to predict, and as a result fortunes were lost—and made—in the foreign exchange market. What economic forces lie behind such dramatic long-term movements in exchange rates?

We have seen that exchange rates are determined by interest rates and expectations about the future, which are, in turn, influenced by conditions in national money markets. To understand fully long-term exchange rate movements, however, we have to extend our model in two directions. First, we must complete our account of the linkages among monetary policies, inflation, interest rates, and exchange rates. Second, we must examine factors other than money supplies and demands—for example, demand shifts in markets for goods and services—that also can have sustained effects on exchange rates.

The model of long-run exchange rate behavior that we develop in this chapter provides the framework that actors in asset markets use to forecast future exchange rates. Because the expectations of these agents influence exchange rates immediately, however, predictions about *long-run* movements in exchange rates are important *even in the short run*. We therefore will draw heavily on this chapter's conclusions when we begin our study of *short-run* interactions between exchange rates and output in Chapter 16.

In the long run, national price levels play a key role in determining both interest rates and the relative prices at which countries' products are traded. A theory of how national price levels interact with exchange rates is thus central to understanding why exchange rates can change dramatically over periods of several years. We begin our analysis by discussing the theory of **purchasing power parity** (**PPP**), which explains movements in the exchange rate between two countries' currencies by changes in the countries' price levels. Next, we examine reasons why PPP may fail to give accurate long-run predictions and show how the theory must sometimes be modified to account for supply or demand shifts in countries' output markets. Finally, we look at what our extended PPP theory predicts about how changes in money and output markets affect exchange and interest rates. ●

The Law of One Price

To understand the market forces that might give rise to the results predicted by the purchasing power parity theory, we discuss first a related but distinct proposition known as the **law of one price**. The law of one price states that in competitive markets free of transportation costs and official barriers to trade (such as tariffs), identical goods sold in different countries must sell for the same price when their prices are expressed in terms of the same currency. For example, if the dollar/pound exchange rate is $1.50 per pound, a sweater that sells for $45 in New York must sell for £30 in London. The dollar price of the sweater when sold in London is then ($1.50 per pound) × (£30 per sweater) = $45 per sweater, the same as its price in New York.

Let's continue with this example to see why the law of one price must hold when trade is free and there are no transport costs or other trade barriers. If the dollar/pound exchange rate were $1.45 per pound, you could buy a sweater in London by converting $43.50 (= $1.45 per pound × £30) into £30 in the foreign exchange market. Thus, the dollar price of a sweater in London would be only $43.50. If the same sweater were selling for $45 in New York, U.S. importers and British exporters would have an incentive to buy sweaters in London and ship them to New York, pushing the London price up and the New York price down until prices were equal in the two locations. Similarly, at an exchange rate of $1.55 per pound, the dollar price of sweaters in London would be $46.50 (= $1.55 per pound × £30), $1.50 more than in New York. Sweaters would be shipped from west to east until a single price prevailed in the two markets.

The law of one price is a restatement, in terms of currencies, of a principle that was important in the trade theory portion of this book: When trade is open and costless, identical goods must trade at the same relative prices regardless of where they are sold. We remind you of that principle here because it provides one link between the domestic prices of goods and exchange rates. We can state the law of one price formally as follows: Let P^i_{US} be the dollar price of good i when sold in the U.S., P^i_E the corresponding euro price in Europe. Then the law of one price implies that the dollar price of good i is the same wherever it is sold,

$$P^i_{US} = (E_{\$/\epsilon}) \times (P^i_E).$$

Equivalently, the dollar/euro exchange rate is the ratio of good i's U.S. and European money prices,

$$E_{\$/\epsilon} = P^i_{US}/P^i_E.$$

Purchasing Power Parity

The theory of purchasing power parity states that the exchange rate between two countries' currencies equals the ratio of the countries' price levels. Recall from Chapter 14 that the domestic purchasing power of a country's currency is reflected in the country's price level, the money price of a reference basket of goods and services. The PPP theory therefore predicts that a fall in a currency's domestic purchasing power (as indicated by an increase in the domestic price level) will be associated with a proportional currency depreciation in the foreign exchange market. Symmetrically, PPP predicts that an increase in the currency's domestic purchasing power will be associated with a proportional currency appreciation.

The basic idea of PPP was put forth in the writings of nineteenth-century British economists, among them David Ricardo (the originator of the theory of comparative advantage). Gustav Cassel, a Swedish economist writing in the early twentieth century, popularized PPP by making it the centerpiece of a theory of exchange rates. While there has been much controversy about the general validity of PPP, the theory does highlight important factors behind exchange rate movements.

To express the PPP theory in symbols, let P_{US} be the dollar price of a reference commodity basket sold in the United States and P_E the euro price of the same basket in Europe. (Assume for now that a single basket accurately measures money's purchasing power in both countries.) Then PPP predicts a dollar/euro exchange rate of

$$E_{\$/€} = P_{US}/P_{E}. \tag{15-1}$$

If, for example, the reference commodity basket costs \$200 in the United States and €160 in Europe, PPP predicts a dollar/euro exchange rate of \$1.25 per euro (= \$200 per basket/€160 per basket). If the U.S. price level were to triple (to \$600 per basket), so would the dollar price of a euro. PPP would imply an exchange rate of \$3.75 per euro (= \$600 per basket/€160 per basket).

By rearranging equation (15-1) to read

$$P_{US} = (E_{\$/€}) \times (P_{E}),$$

we get an alternative interpretation of PPP. The left side of this equation is the dollar price of the reference commodity basket in the United States; the right side is the dollar price of the reference basket when purchased in Europe (that is, its euro price multiplied by the dollar price of a euro). These two prices are the same if PPP holds. *PPP thus asserts that all countries' price levels are equal when measured in terms of the same currency.*

Equivalently, the right side of the last equation measures the purchasing power of a dollar when exchanged for euros and spent in Europe. PPP therefore holds when, at going exchange rates, every currency's domestic purchasing power is always the same as its foreign purchasing power.

The Relationship Between PPP and the Law of One Price

Superficially, the statement of PPP given by equation (15-1) looks like the law of one price, which says that $E_{\$/€} = P_{US}^i/P_E^i$ for any commodity i. There is a difference between PPP and the law of one price, however: The law of one price applies to individual commodities (such as commodity i), while PPP applies to the general price level, which is a composite of the prices of all the commodities that enter into the reference basket.

If the law of one price holds true for every commodity, of course, PPP must hold automatically as long as the reference baskets used to reckon different countries' price levels are the same. Proponents of the PPP theory argue, however, that its validity (in particular, its validity as a long-run theory) does not require the law of one price to hold exactly.

Even when the law of one price fails to hold for each individual commodity, the argument goes, prices and exchange rates should not stray too far from the relation predicted by PPP. When goods and services become temporarily more expensive in one country than in others, the demands for its currency and its products fall, pushing the exchange rate and domestic prices back in line with PPP. The opposite situation of relatively cheap domestic products leads, analogously, to currency appreciation and price level inflation. PPP thus asserts that even when the law of one price is not literally true, the economic forces behind it will help eventually to equalize a currency's purchasing power in all countries.

Absolute PPP and Relative PPP

The statement that exchange rates equal relative price levels (equation (15-1)) is sometimes referred to as *absolute* PPP. Absolute PPP implies a proposition known as **relative PPP**, which states that the percentage change in the exchange rate between two currencies over any period equals the difference between the percentage changes in national price levels. Relative PPP thus translates absolute PPP from a statement about price and exchange rate *levels* into one about price and exchange rate *changes*. It asserts that prices and exchange rates change in a way that preserves the ratio of each currency's domestic and foreign purchasing powers.

If the U.S. price level rises by 10 percent over a year while Europe's rises by only 5 percent, for example, relative PPP predicts a 5 percent depreciation of the dollar against the euro. The dollar's 5 percent depreciation against the euro just cancels the 5 percent by which U.S. inflation exceeds European, leaving the relative domestic and foreign purchasing powers of both currencies unchanged.

More formally, relative PPP between the United States and Europe would be written as

$$(E_{\$/\euro,t} - E_{\$/\euro,t-1})/E_{\$/\euro,t-1} = \pi_{US,t} - \pi_{E,t} \tag{15-2}$$

where π_t denotes an inflation rate (that is, $\pi_t = (P_t - P_{t-1})/P_{t-1}$, the percentage change in a price level between dates t and $t-1$).[1] Unlike absolute PPP, relative PPP can be defined only with respect to the time interval over which price levels and the exchange rate change.

---

[1] To be precise, equation (15-1) implies a good approximation to equation (15-2) when rates of change are not too large. The *exact* relationship is

$$E_{\$/\euro,t}/E_{\$/\euro,t-1} = (P_{US,t}/P_{US,t-1})/(P_{E,t}/P_{E,t-1}).$$

After subtracting 1 from both sides, we write the preceding exact equation as

$$(E_{\$/\euro,t} - E_{\$/\euro,t-1})/E_{\$/\euro,t-1} = (\pi_{US,t} + 1)(P_{E,t-1}/P_{E,t}) - (P_{E,t}/P_{E,t}).$$

$$= (\pi_{US,t} - \pi_{E,t})/(1 + \pi_{E,t})$$

$$= (\pi_{US,t} - \pi_{E,t}) - \pi_{E,t}(\pi_{US,t} - \pi_{E,t})/(1 + \pi_{E,t}).$$

But if $\pi_{US,t}$ and $\pi_{E,t}$ are small, the term $-\pi_{E,t}(\pi_{US,t} - \pi_{E,t})/(1 + \pi_{E,t})$ in the last equality is negligibly small, implying a very good approximation to (15-2).

In practice, national governments do not take pains to compute the price level indexes they publish using an internationally standardized basket of commodities. Absolute PPP makes no sense. however, unless the two baskets whose prices are compared in equation (15-1) are the same. (There is no reason to expect *different* commodity baskets to sell for the same price!) The notion of relative PPP therefore comes in handy when we have to rely on government price level statistics to evaluate PPP. It makes logical sense to compare percentage exchange rate changes to inflation differences, as above, even when countries base their price *level* estimates on product baskets that differ in coverage and composition.

Relative PPP is important also because it may be valid even when absolute PPP is not. Provided the factors causing deviations from absolute PPP are more or less stable over time, percentage *changes* in relative price levels can still approximate percentage *changes* in exchange rates.

A Long-Run Exchange Rate Model Based on PPP

When combined with the framework of money demand and supply we developed in Chapter 14, the theory of PPP leads to a useful theory of how exchange rates and monetary factors interact in the long run. Because factors that do not influence money supply or money demand play no explicit role in this theory, it is known as the **monetary approach to the exchange rate**. The monetary approach is this chapter's first step in developing a general long-run theory of exchange rates.

We think of the monetary approach as a *long-run* and not a short-run theory because it does not allow for the price rigidities that seem important in explaining short-run macroeconomic developments, in particular departures from full employment. Instead, the monetary approach proceeds as if prices can adjust right away to maintain full employment as well as PPP. Here, as in the previous chapter, when we refer to a variable's "long-run" value we mean the variable's equilibrium value in a hypothetical world of perfectly flexible output and factor market prices.

There is actually considerable controversy among macroeconomists about the sources of apparent price level stickiness, with some maintaining that prices and wages only appear rigid and in reality adjust immediately to clear markets. To an economist of the aforementioned school, this chapter's models would describe the short-run behavior of an economy in which the speed of price level adjustment is so high that no significant unemployment ever occurs.

The Fundamental Equation of the Monetary Approach

To develop the monetary approach's predictions for the dollar/euro exchange rate, we will assume that in the long run the foreign exchange market sets that rate so that PPP holds (see equation 15-1):

$$E_{\$/\epsilon} = P_{US}/P_E.$$

In other words, we assume the above equation would hold in a world where there were no market rigidities to prevent the exchange rate and other prices from adjusting immediately to levels consistent with full employment.

In the previous chapter, equation (14-5) showed how we can explain domestic price levels in terms of domestic money demands and supplies. In the United States,

$$P_{US} = M_{US}^s / L(R_\$, Y_{US}), \qquad (15\text{-}3)$$

while in Europe,

$$P_E = M_E^s / L(R_\epsilon, Y_E). \qquad (15\text{-}4)$$

As before, we have used the symbol M^s to stand for a country's money supply and $L(R, Y)$ to stand for its aggregate real money demand, which decreases when the interest rate rises and increases when real output rises.[2]

Equations (15-3) and (15-4) show how the monetary approach to the exchange rate comes by its name. According to the statement of PPP in equation (15-1), the dollar price of a euro is simply the dollar price of U.S. output divided by the euro price of European output. These two price levels, in turn, are determined completely by the supply and demand for each currency area's money: The United States' price level is the U.S. money supply divided by U.S. real money demand, as shown in (15-3), and Europe's price level similarly is the European money supply divided by European real money demand, as shown in (15-4). The monetary approach therefore makes the general prediction that *the exchange rate, which is the relative price of American and European money, is fully determined in the long run by the relative supplies of those monies and the relative real demands for them.* Shifts in interest rates and output levels affect the exchange rate only through their influences on money demand.

In addition, the monetary approach makes a number of specific predictions about the long-run effects on the exchange rate of changes in money supplies, interest rates, and output levels:

1. *Money supplies.* Other things equal, a permanent rise in the U.S. money supply M_{US}^s causes a proportional increase in the long-run U.S. price level P_{US}, as equation (15-3) shows. Because under PPP, $E_{\$/\epsilon} = P_{US}/P_E$, however, $E_{\$/\epsilon}$ also rises in the long run in proportion to the increase in the U.S. money supply. (For example, if M_{US}^s rises by 10 percent, P_{US} and $E_{\$/\epsilon}$ both eventually rise by 10 percent as well.) Thus, an increase in the U.S. money supply causes a proportional long-run *depreciation* of the dollar against the euro. Conversely, equation (15-4) shows that a permanent increase in the European money supply causes a proportional increase in the long-run European price level. Under PPP, this price level rise implies a proportional long-run *appreciation* of the dollar against the euro (which is the same as a proportional depreciation of the euro against the dollar).

2. *Interest rates.* A rise in the interest rate $R_\$$ on dollar-denominated assets lowers real U.S. money demand $L(R_\$, Y_{US})$. By (15-3) the long-run U.S. price level rises, and under PPP the dollar must depreciate against the euro in proportion to this U.S. price level increase. A rise in the interest rate R_ϵ on euro-denominated assets has the reverse long-run exchange rate effect. Because real European money demand $L(R_\epsilon, Y_E)$ falls, Europe's

---

[2] To simplify the notation, we assume identical money demand functions for the United States and Europe.

price level rises, by (15-4). Under PPP, the dollar must appreciate against the euro in proportion to Europe's price level increase.

3. *Output levels.* A rise in U.S. output raises real U.S. money demand $L(R_\$, Y_{US})$, leading by (15-3) to a fall in the long-run U.S. price level. According to PPP, there is an appreciation of the dollar against the euro. Symmetrically, a rise in European output raises $L(R_\epsilon, Y_E)$ and, by (15-4), causes a fall in Europe's long-run price level. PPP predicts that this development will make the dollar depreciate against the euro.

To understand these predictions, remember that the monetary approach, like any long-run theory, essentially assumes that price levels adjust as quickly as exchange rates do—that is, right away. For example, a rise in real U.S. output raises the transactions demand for real U.S. money balances. According to the monetary approach, the U.S. price level drops *immediately* to bring about a market-clearing increase in the supply of real balances. PPP implies that this instantaneous American price deflation is accompanied by an instantaneous dollar appreciation on the foreign exchanges.

The monetary approach leads to a result familiar from Chapter 14, that the long-run foreign exchange value of a country's currency moves in proportion to its money supply (prediction 1 above). The theory also raises what seems to be a paradox (prediction 2). In our previous examples, we always found that a currency *appreciates* when the interest rate it offers rises relative to foreign interest rates. How is it that we have now arrived at precisely the opposite conclusion—that a rise in a country's interest rate *depreciates* its currency by lowering the real demand for its money?

At the end of Chapter 13 we warned that no account of how a change in interest rates affects the exchange rate is complete until we specify *exactly why interest rates have changed.* This point explains the apparent contradiction in our findings about interest and exchange rates. To resolve the puzzle, however, we must first examine more closely how monetary policies and interest rates are connected in the long run.

Ongoing Inflation, Interest Parity, and PPP

In the last chapter we saw that a permanent increase in the *level* of a country's money supply ultimately results in a proportional rise in its price level but has no effect on the long-run values of the interest rate or real output. The conceptual experiment of a one-time, stepwise money supply change is useful for thinking about the long-run effects of money, but it is not too realistic as a description of actual monetary policies. More often, the monetary authorities choose a *growth rate* for the money supply, say, 5 or 10 or 50 percent per year, and then allow money to grow gradually, through small but frequent increases. What are the long-run effects of a policy that allows the money supply to grow smoothly forever at a positive rate?

The reasoning in Chapter 14 suggests that continuing money supply growth will require a continuing rise in the price level—a situation of *ongoing* inflation. As firms and workers catch on to the fact that the money supply is growing steadily at, say, a 10 percent annual rate, they will adjust by raising prices and wages by the same 10 percent every year, thus keeping their real incomes constant. Full-employment output depends on supplies of productive factors, but it is safe to assume that factor supplies, and thus output, are unaffected over the long run by different choices of a constant growth rate for the money supply. *Other things equal, money supply growth at a constant rate eventually results in ongoing price level inflation at the same rate, but changes in this long-run inflation rate do not affect the full-employment output level or the long-run relative prices of goods and services.*

The interest rate, however, is definitely not independent of the money supply growth rate in the long run. While the long-run interest rate does not depend on the absolute *level* of the money supply, continuing *growth* in the money supply eventually will affect the interest rate. The easiest way to see how a permanent increase in inflation affects the long-run interest rate is by combining PPP with the interest rate parity condition on which our previous analysis of exchange rate determination was built.

As in the preceding two chapters, the condition of interest parity between dollar and euro assets is

$$R_\$ = R_€ + (E^e_{\$/€} - E_{\$/€})/E_{\$/€}$$

(recall equation (13-2), page 342). Now let's ask how this parity condition, which must hold in the long run as well as in the short run, fits with the other parity condition we are assuming in our long-run model, purchasing power parity. According to relative PPP, the percentage change in the dollar/euro exchange rate over the next year, say, will equal the difference between the inflation rates of the United States and Europe over that year (see equation (15-2)). Since people understand this relationship, however, it must also be true that they *expect* the percentage exchange rate change to equal the U.S.-Europe inflation difference. The interest parity condition written above now tells us the following: *If people expect relative PPP to hold, the difference between the interest rates offered by dollar and euro deposits will equal the difference between the inflation rates expected, over the relevant horizon, in the United States and in Europe.*

Some additional notation is helpful in deriving this result more formally. If P^e is the price level expected in a country for a year from today, the expected inflation rate in that country, π^e, is the expected percentage increase in the price level over the coming year,

$$\pi^e = (P^e - P)/P.$$

If relative PPP holds, however, market participants will also expect it to hold, which means that we can replace the actual depreciation and inflation rates in equation (15-2) with the values the market expects to materialize:

$$(E^e_{\$/€} - E_{\$/€})/E_{\$/€} = \pi^e_{US} - \pi^e_{E}.$$

By combining this "expected" version of relative PPP with the interest parity condition

$$R_\$ = R_€ + (E^e_{\$/€} - E_{\$/€})/E_{\$/€}$$

and rearranging, we arrive at a formula that expresses the international interest rate difference as the difference between expected national inflation rates:

$$R_\$ - R_€ = \pi^e_{US} - \pi^e_{E}. \tag{15-5}$$

If, as PPP predicts, currency depreciation is expected to offset the international inflation difference (so that the expected dollar depreciation rate is $\pi^e_{US} - \pi^e_{E}$), the interest rate difference must equal the expected inflation difference.

The Fisher Effect

Equation (15-5) gives us the long-run relationship between ongoing inflation and interest rates that we need to explain the monetary approach's predictions about how interest rates affect exchange rates. The equation tells us that *all else equal, a rise in a country's expected inflation rate will eventually cause an equal rise in the interest rate that deposits of its currency offer. Similarly, a fall in the expected inflation rate will eventually cause a fall in the interest rate.*

This long-run relationship between inflation and interest rates is called the **Fisher effect**. The Fisher effect implies, for example, that if U.S. inflation were to rise permanently from a constant level of 5 percent per year to a constant level of 10 percent per year, dollar interest rates would eventually catch up with the higher inflation, rising by 5 percentage points per year from their initial level. These changes would leave the *real rate of return* on dollar assets, measured in terms of U.S. goods and services, unchanged. The Fisher effect is therefore another example of the general idea that in the long run, purely monetary developments should have no effect on an economy's relative prices.[3]

The Fisher effect is behind the seemingly paradoxical monetary approach prediction that a currency depreciates in the foreign exchange market when its interest rate rises relative to foreign currency interest rates. In the long-run equilibrium assumed by the monetary approach, a rise in the difference between home and foreign interest rates occurs only when expected home inflation rises relative to expected foreign inflation. This is certainly not the case in the short run, when the domestic price level is sticky. In the short run, as we saw in Chapter 14, the interest rate can rise when the domestic money supply *falls* because the sticky domestic price level leads to an excess demand for real money balances at the initial interest rate. Under the flexible-price monetary approach, however, the price level would fall right away and thus make the interest rate change unnecessary.

We can better understand how interest rates and exchange rates interact under the monetary approach by thinking through an example. Our example illustrates why the monetary approach associates sustained interest rate hikes with current as well as future currency depreciation, sustained interest rate slumps with appreciation.

Imagine that at time t_0 the Federal Reserve unexpectedly increases the growth rate of the U.S. money supply from π to the higher level $\pi + \Delta\pi$. Figure 15-1 illustrates how this change affects the dollar/euro exchange rate $E_{\$/€}$, as well as other U.S. variables, under the assumptions of the monetary approach. To simplify the graphs we assume that in Europe the inflation rate remains constant at zero.

Figure 15-1a shows the sudden acceleration of U.S. money supply growth at time t_0. (We have scaled the vertical axes of the graphs so that constant slopes represent constant proportional growth rates of variables.) The policy change generates expectations of more rapid currency depreciation in the future: Under PPP the dollar will now depreciate at rate $\pi + \Delta\pi$ rather than at the lower rate π. Interest parity therefore requires the dollar interest rate to rise, as shown in Figure 15-1b, from its initial level $R_\$^1$ to a new level that reflects the extra expected dollar depreciation, $R_\$^2 = R_\$^1 + \Delta\pi$ (see equation (15-5)). Notice that this

---

[3] The effect is named after Irving Fisher, one of the great American economists of the early twentieth century. The effect is discussed at length in his book, *The Theory of Interest* (New York: Macmillan, 1930). Fisher, incidentally, gave an early account of the interest parity condition on which our theory of foreign exchange market equilibrium is based.

Figure 15-1 Long-Run Time Paths of U.S. Economic Variables after a Permanent Increase in the Growth Rate of the U.S. Money Supply

(a) U.S. money supply, M_{US}

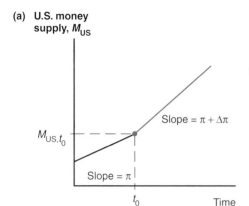

(b) Dollar interest rate, $R_\$$

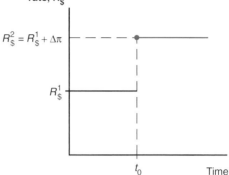

(c) U.S. price level, P_{US}

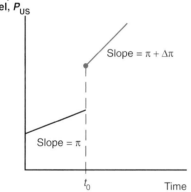

(d) Dollar/euro exchange rate, $E_{\$/€}$

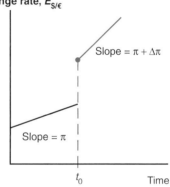

After the money supply growth rate increases at time t_0 in panel (a), the interest rate (in panel (b)), price level (in panel (c)), and exchange rate (in panel (d)) move to new long-run equilibrium paths. (The money supply, price level, and exchange rate are all measured on a *natural logarithmic* scale, which makes variables that change at constant proportional rates appear as straight lines when they are graphed against time. The slope of the line equals the variable's proportional growth rate.)

adjustment leaves the euro interest rate unchanged; but since Europe's money supply and output haven't changed, the original euro interest rate will still maintain equilibrium in Europe's money market.

You can see from Figure 15-1a that the *level* of the money supply does not actually jump upward at t_0—only the *future growth rate* changes. Since there is no immediate increase in the money supply, but there is an interest rate rise that reduces money demand, there would be an excess supply of real U.S. money balances at the price level prevailing just prior to t_0. In the face of this potential excess supply the U.S. price level does jump at t_0 (see Figure 15-1c), reducing the real money supply so that it again equals real money demand (see equation (15-3)). Along with the upward jump in P_{US} at t_0, Figure 15-1d shows the simultaneous proportional upward jump in $E_{\$/\epsilon}$ implied by PPP.

How can we visualize the reaction of the foreign exchange market at time t_0? The dollar interest rate rises in our example not because of a change in current levels of money supply or demand, but solely because people expect more rapid future money supply growth and dollar depreciation. As investors respond by moving into foreign deposits, which momentarily offer higher expected returns, the dollar depreciates sharply in the foreign exchange market, moving to a new trend line along which depreciation is more rapid than it was up to time t_0.[4]

Notice how different assumptions about the speed of price level adjustment lead to contrasting predictions about how exchange and interest rates interact. In the example of a fall in the money supply under sticky prices, an interest rate rise is needed to preserve money market equilibrium, given that the price level cannot do so by dropping immediately in response to the money supply reduction. In that sticky price case, an interest rate rise is associated with lower expected inflation and a long-run currency appreciation, so the currency appreciates immediately. In our monetary-approach example of a rise in money supply growth, however, an interest rate increase is associated with higher expected inflation and a currency that will be weaker on all future dates. An immediate currency *depreciation* is the result.[5]

These contrasting results of interest rate changes underlie our earlier warning that an explanation of exchange rates based on interest rates must carefully account for the factors that cause interest rates to move. These factors can simultaneously affect expected future exchange rates and can therefore have a decisive impact on the foreign exchange market's response to the interest rate change. The appendix to this chapter shows in detail how expectations change in the case we analyzed.

Figure 15-2 bears out the main long-run prediction of the Fisher effect. The figure plots inflation rates and interest rates for three countries that have had somewhat different inflationary experiences since 1970: Switzerland, the United States, and Italy. In each country interest rates tend to rise after inflation rises as prices adjust and as people learn to expect higher inflation in the future; reductions in inflation eventually lower interest rates for the same reason. Moreover, the average level of interest rates is lowest in Switzerland, which has the lowest average inflation rate, and highest in Italy, which has the highest average inflation rate.

The Fisher effect can be broadly correct even when PPP is not, so we can't take the evidence in Figure 15-2 as confirmation of the monetary approach. We now look at evidence bearing more directly on the validity of PPP itself.

---

[4]In the general case in which Europe's inflation rate π_E is not zero, the dollar, rather than depreciating against the euro at rate π before t_0 and at rate $\pi + \Delta\pi$ afterward, depreciates at rate $\pi - \pi_E$ until t_0 and at rate $\pi + \Delta\pi - \pi_E$ thereafter.

[5]National money supplies typically trend upward over time, as in Figure 15-1a. Such trends lead to corresponding upward trends in price levels; if two countries' price level trends differ, PPP implies a trend in their exchange rate as well. From now on, when we refer to a change in the money supply, price level, or exchange rate, we will mean by this a change in the variable *relative to its previously expected trend rate of increase.* When instead we want to consider changes in trends themselves, we will say so explicitly.

Figure 15-2 | Inflation and Interest Rates in Switzerland, the United States, and Italy, 1970–2000

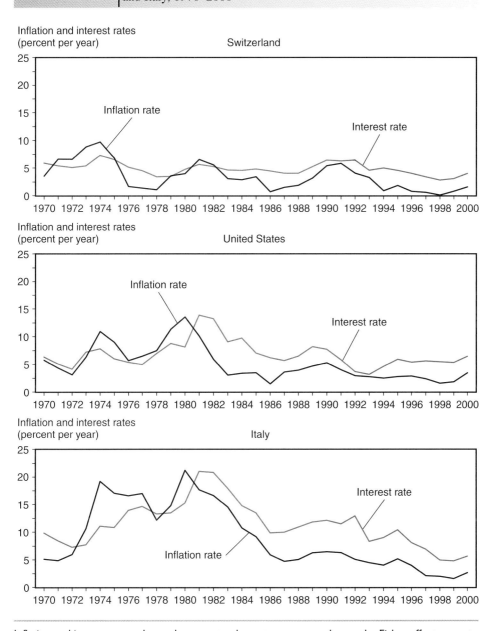

Inflation and interest rates show a long-run tendency to move together, as the Fisher effect suggests.

Source: OECD, *Main Economic Indicators*. Inflation rates are year-to-year percentage changes in consumer price indexes.

Empirical Evidence on PPP and the Law of One Price

How well does the PPP theory explain actual data on exchange rates and national price levels? A brief answer is that all versions of the PPP theory do badly in explaining the facts. In particular, changes in national price levels often tell us little or nothing about exchange rate movements.

Do not conclude from this evidence, however, that the effort you've put into learning about PPP has been wasted. As we'll see later in this chapter, PPP is a key building block of exchange rate models more realistic than the monetary approach. Indeed, the empirical failures of PPP give us important clues about how more realistic models should be set up.

To test *absolute* PPP, economic researchers compare the international prices of a broad reference basket of commodities, making careful adjustments for intercountry quality differences among supposedly identical goods. These comparisons typically conclude that absolute PPP is way off the mark: The prices of identical commodity baskets, when converted to a single currency, differ substantially across countries. Even the law of one price does not fare well in some recent studies of price data broken down by commodity type. Manufactured goods that are very similar to each other have sold at widely different prices in various markets since the early 1970s. Because the argument leading to absolute PPP builds on the law of one price, it is not surprising that PPP does not stand up well to the data.[6]

Relative PPP is sometimes a reasonable approximation to the data, but it, too, usually performs poorly. Figure 15-3 illustrates relative PPP's weakness by plotting both the dollar/deutschemark (DM) exchange rate, $E_{\$/DM}$, and the ratio of the U.S. and German price levels, P_{US}/P_G, through 2000. Price levels are measured by indexes reported by the U.S. and German governments.[7] Relative PPP predicts that $E_{\$/DM}$ and P_{US}/P_G should move proportionally, and, as you can see in the figure, this was more or less so through 1970. But PPP broke down completely after 1970, with the dollar depreciating sharply between 1970 and 1973 even though U.S. prices *fell* slightly relative to German prices over those years. From 1973 through 1979, PPP is somewhat more successful: As U.S. prices rose relative to German prices, the dollar (in all but one of these years) depreciated against the DM. But the magnitude of the dollar's depreciation between 1973 and 1979 was far greater than relative PPP would predict.

---

[6] Some of the negative evidence on absolute PPP is discussed in the Case Study to follow. Regarding the law of one price, see, for example, Peter Isard, "How Far Can We Push the Law of One Price?" *American Economic Review* 67 (December 1977), pp. 942–948; Irving B. Kravis and Robert E. Lipsey, "Price Behavior in the Light of Balance of Payments Theories," *Journal of International Economics* 8 (May 1978), pp. 193–246; and the paper by Goldberg and Knetter in Further Reading.

[7] The price level measures in Figure 15-3 are index numbers, not dollar amounts. For example, the U.S. consumer price index (CPI) was 100 in the base year 1967 and 298.4 in 1983, so the dollar price of a reference commodity basket of typical U.S. consumption purchases nearly tripled between 1967 and 1983. Base years for the U.S. and German price indexes were chosen so that their 1964 ratio would equal the 1964 exchange rate, but this imposed equality does *not* mean that absolute PPP held in 1964. Although Figure 15-3 uses CPIs, other price indexes lead to similar pictures. Recall, once again, that the deutschemark remained in existence through early 2002 even though it was fixed against the euro.

Figure 15-3 | The Dollar/DM Exchange Rate and Relative U.S./German Price Levels, 1964–2000

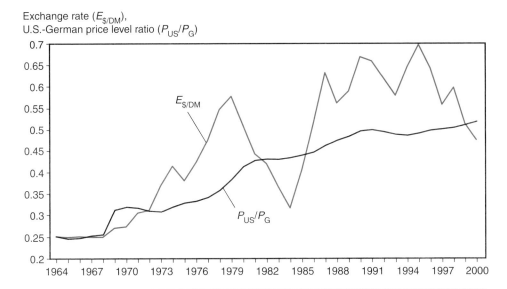

The graph shows that relative PPP did not explain the dollar/DM exchange rate after 1970.

Source: OECD, *Main Economic Indicators*. Exchange rates and price levels are end-of-year data.

A dramatic violation of relative PPP occurs in the years after 1979. In those years the dollar first sustained a massive appreciation against the DM even though the U.S. price level continued to rise relative to that of Germany; subsequently the dollar depreciated by far more than PPP would predict. Relative PPP does hold approximately over the period 1964–1985 taken as a whole: Over those two decades, the percentage rise in the dollar/DM exchange rate is close to the percentage increase in the U.S. price level relative to the German price level. In view of the wide departures from relative PPP over long subperiods of the 1964–1985 span and after 1985, however, PPP appears to be of limited use even as a long-run explanation of exchange rate movements.

Studies of other currencies largely confirm the results in Figure 15-3. Relative PPP has not held up well since the early 1970s, but in the 1960s it was a more reliable guide to the relationship among exchange rates and national price levels.[8] As you will learn later in this

---

[8] See, for example, Hans Genberg, "Purchasing Power Parity Under Fixed and Flexible Exchange Rates," *Journal of International Economics* 8 (May 1978), pp. 247–276; Jacob A. Frenkel, "The Collapse of Purchasing Power Parities During the 1970s," *European Economic Review* 16 (1981), pp. 145–165; and Robert E. Cumby and Maurice Obstfeld, "International Interest Rate and Price Level Linkages Under Flexible Exchange Rates: A Review of Recent Evidence," in John F. O. Bilson and Richard C. Marston, eds., *Exchange Rate Theory and Practice* (Chicago: University of Chicago Press, 1984), pp. 121–151.

SOME MEATY EVIDENCE ON THE LAW OF ONE PRICE

In the summer of 1986 the *Economist* magazine conducted an extensive survey on the prices of Big Mac hamburgers at McDonald's restaurants throughout the world. This apparently whimsical undertaking was not the result of an outbreak of editorial giddiness. The magazine wanted to poke fun at economists who confidently declare exchange rates to be "overvalued" or "undervalued" on the basis of PPP comparisons. Since Big Macs are "sold in 41 countries, with only the most trivial changes of recipe," the magazine argued, a comparison of hamburger prices should serve as a "medium-rare guide to whether currencies are trading at the right exchange rates."* Since 1986 the *Economist* has periodically updated its calculations.

One way of interpreting the *Economist* survey is as a test of the law of one price. Viewed in this way, the results of the initial test were quite startling. The dollar prices of Big Macs turned out to be wildly different in different countries. The price of a Big Mac in New York was 50 percent higher than in Australia and 64 percent higher than in Hong Kong. In contrast, a Parisian Big Mac cost 54 percent more than its New York counterpart; a Tokyo Big Mac cost 50 percent more. Only in Britain and Ireland were the dollar prices of the burgers close to New York levels.

How can this dramatic violation of the law of one price be explained? As the *Economist* noted, transport costs and government regulations are part of the explanation. Product differentiation is probably an important additional factor. Because relatively few close substitutes for Big Macs are available in some countries, product differentiation may give McDonald's some power to tailor prices to the local market. Finally, remember that the price of a Big Mac must cover not only the cost of ground meat and buns, but also the wages of serving people, rent, electricity, and so on. The prices of these nonfood inputs can differ sharply in different countries.

What about the long run? Subsequent Big Mac surveys have shown no universal tendency toward a narrowing of the 1986 price differentials. The April 1989 survey showed the Big Mac selling for only 12 percent more in Paris than in Manhattan but selling for 153 percent more in Manhattan than in Hong Kong.† Significantly, the magazine also reported price differences among the four American cities of Atlanta, Chicago, New York, and San Francisco that were in many cases larger than the international disparities! This suggests that of the possible factors causing the law of one price to break down in this case, direct government restraint of international trade is not the most important.

We have reproduced the table that summarized the *Economist's* April 2001 survey report. Column 1 reports local-currency prices for Big Macs. Column 2 calculates local *dollar* prices by dividing column 1 by column 4, the local-currency price of a U.S. dollar. Column 3 is the local price of a Big Mac (from column 1) divided by its average dollar price in the four U.S. cities mentioned above, $2.54. This "implied PPP" is the exchange rate—quoted in indirect terms, as foreign currency units per dollar—that would prevail if the law of one price governed hamburger prices.

The last column gives the percentage by which the hamburger PPP rate in column 3 exceeds the actual price of a U.S. dollar in column 4. (It is often said that a currency is "overvalued" when its exchange rate makes domestic goods look expensive relative to similar goods sold abroad and "undervalued" in the opposite case.) Thus, the reported 15 percent overvaluation of the Danish krone relative to the dollar means that the dollar price of a Copenhagen Big Mac was 1.15 times the price of a Big Mac in the United States. Similarly, the Swiss price was nearly one and a half times the U.S. price.

Notice that in April 2001 the world's cheapest Big Macs were sold in the Philippines. This fact reflected not only low labor costs, but currency depreciation over the previous months, partly in response to a political crisis.

---

*"On the Hamburger Standard," *Economist,* September 6–12, 1986.
†"The Hamburger Standard," *Economist,* April 15, 1989.

The hamburger standard

	Big Mac prices		Implied PPP* of the dollar	Actual $ exchange rate 17/04/01	Under (−)/ over (+) valuation against the dollar, %
	in local currency	in dollars			
United States†	**$2.54**	**2.54**	—	—	—
Argentina	Peso2.50	2.50	0.98	1.00	−2
Australia	A$3.00	1.52	1.18	1.98	−40
Brazil	Real3.60	1.64	1.42	2.19	−35
Britain	£1.99	2.85	1.28‡	1.43‡	12
Canada	C$3.33	2.14	1.31	1.56	−16
Chile	Peso1260	2.10	496	601	−17
China	Yuan9.90	1.20	3.90	8.28	−53
Czech Rep	Koruna56.00	1.43	22.0	39.0	−44
Denmark	DKr24.75	2.93	9.74	8.46	15
Euro area	€2.57	2.27	0.99§	0.88§	−11
France	FFr18.5	2.49	7.28	7.44	−2
Germany	DM5.10	2.30	2.01	2.22	−9
Italy	Lire4300	1.96	1693	2195	−23
Spain	Pta395	2.09	156	189	−18
Hong Kong	HK$10.70	1.37	4.21	7.80	−46
Hungary	Forint399	1.32	157	303	−48
Indonesia	Rupiah14700	1.35	5787	10855	−47
Japan	¥294	2.38	116	124	−6
Malaysia	M$4.52	1.19	1.78	3.80	−53
Mexico	Peso21.9	2.36	8.62	9.29	−7
New Zealand	NZ$3.60	1.46	1.42	2.47	−43
Philippines	Peso59.00	1.17	23.2	50.3	−54
Poland	Zloty5.90	1.46	2.32	4.03	−42
Russia	Rouble35.00	1.21	13.8	28.9	−52
Singapore	S$3.30	1.82	1.30	1.81	−28
South Africa	Rand9.70	1.19	3.82	8.13	−53
South Korea	Won3000	2.27	1181	1325	−11
Sweden	SKr24.0	2.33	9.45	10.28	−8
Switzerland	SFr6.30	3.65	2.48	1.73	44
Taiwan	NT$70.0	2.13	27.6	32.9	−16
Thailand	Baht55.0	1.21	21.7	45.5	−52

*Purchasing-power parity; local price divided by price in United States
†Average of New York, Chicago, San Francisco and Atlanta
‡Dollars per pound   §Dollars per euro
Source: McDonald's; *The Economist*

Source: "Big Mac Currencies," *The Economist,* April 21, 2001, p. 74. Copyright 2001 The Economist, Ltd. Distributed by The New York Times Special Features.

book, between the end of World War II in 1945 and the early 1970s exchange rates were fixed within narrow internationally agreed margins through the intervention of central banks in the foreign exchange market. During the first half of the 1920s, when many exchange rates were market-determined as in the 1970s and after, important deviations from relative PPP also occurred.[9]

Explaining the Problems with PPP

What explains the negative empirical results described in the previous section? There are several immediate problems with our rationale for the PPP theory of exchange rates, which was based on the law of one price:

1. Contrary to the assumption of the law of one price, transport costs and restrictions on trade certainly do exist. These trade barriers may be high enough to prevent some goods and services from being traded between countries.

2. Monopolistic or oligopolistic practices in goods markets may interact with transport costs and other trade barriers to weaken further the link between the prices of similar goods sold in different countries.

3. Because the inflation data reported in different countries are based on different commodity baskets, there is no reason for exchange rate changes to offset official measures of inflation differences, even when there are no barriers to trade and all products are tradable.

Trade Barriers and Nontradables

Transport costs and governmental trade restrictions make it expensive to move goods between markets located in different countries and therefore weaken the law of one price mechanism underlying PPP. Suppose once again that the same sweater sells for $45 in New York and for £30 in London, but that it costs $2 to ship a sweater between the two cities. At an exchange rate of $1.45 per pound, the dollar price of a London sweater is ($1.45 per pound) $\times$ (£30) = $43.50, but an American importer would have to pay $43.50 + $2 = $45.50 to purchase the sweater in London and get it to New York. At an exchange rate of $1.45 per pound, it therefore would not pay to ship sweaters from London to New York, even though their dollar price would be higher in the latter location. Similarly, at an exchange rate of $1.55 per pound, an American exporter would lose money by shipping sweaters from New York to London even though the New York price of $45 would then be below the dollar price of the sweater in London, $46.50.

The lesson of this example is that transport costs sever the close link between exchange rates and goods prices implied by the law of one price. The greater the transport costs, the greater the range over which the exchange rate can move, given goods prices in different

---

[9]See Paul R. Krugman, "Purchasing Power Parity and Exchange Rates: Another Look at the Evidence," *Journal of International Economics* 8 (August 1978), pp. 397–407; and Paul De Grauwe, Marc Janssens, and Hilde Leliaert, *Real-Exchange-Rate Variability from 1920 to 1926 and 1973 to 1982,* Princeton Studies in International Finance 56 (International Finance Section, Department of Economics, Princeton University, September 1985).

countries. Official trade restrictions such as tariffs have a similar effect, because a fee paid to the customs inspector affects the importer's profit in the same way as an equivalent shipping fee. Either type of trade impediment weakens the basis of PPP by allowing the purchasing power of a given currency to differ more widely from country to country. For example, in the presence of trade impediments, a dollar need not go as far in Tokyo as in Chicago—and it doesn't, as anyone who has been to Tokyo has found out.

As you will recall from Chapter 2, transport costs may be so large relative to the cost of producing some goods and services that they can never be traded internationally at a profit. Such goods and services are called *nontradables*. The time-honored classroom example of a nontradable is the haircut. A Frenchman desiring an American haircut would have to transport himself to the United States or transport an American barber to France; in either case, the cost of transport is so large relative to the price of the service being purchased that (tourists excepted) French haircuts are consumed only by residents of France while American haircuts are consumed only by residents of the United States.

The existence in all countries of nontraded goods and services whose prices are not linked internationally allows systematic deviations even from relative PPP. Because the price of a nontradable is determined entirely by its *domestic* supply and demand curves, shifts in those curves may cause the domestic price of a broad commodity basket to change relative to the foreign price of the same basket. Other things equal, a rise in the price of a country's nontradables will raise its price level relative to foreign price levels (measuring all countries' price levels in terms of a single currency). Looked at another way, the purchasing power of any given currency will fall in countries where the prices of nontradables rise.

Each country's price level includes a wide variety of nontradables, including (along with haircuts) routine medical treatment, aerobic dance instruction, and housing, among others. Broadly speaking, we can identify traded goods with manufactured products, raw materials, and agricultural products. Nontradables are primarily services and the output of the construction industry. There are naturally exceptions to this rule. For example, financial services provided by banks and brokerage houses often can be traded internationally. In addition, trade restrictions, if sufficiently severe, can cause goods that would normally be traded to become nontraded. Thus, in most countries some manufactures are nontraded.

We can get a very rough idea of the importance of nontradables in the American economy by looking at the contribution of the service and construction industries to U.S. GNP. In 2000, the output of these industries accounted for about 53 percent of U.S. GNP.

Numbers like these are likely to understate the importance of nontradables in determining national price levels. Even the prices of tradable products usually include costs of nontraded distribution and marketing services that bring goods from producers to consumers. (See "Some Meaty Evidence on the Law of One Price," pages 402–403.) Nontradables help explain the wide departures from relative PPP illustrated by Figure 15-3.

Departures from Free Competition

When trade barriers and imperfectly competitive market structures occur together, linkages between national price levels are weakened further. An extreme case occurs when a single firm sells a commodity for different prices in different markets. (Recall the analysis of dumping in Chapter 6.)

HONG KONG'S SURPRISINGLY HIGH INFLATION

If purchasing power parity holds true, countries whose currencies are linked by an unchanging exchange rate should experience equal rates of price level inflation. Hong Kong's experience since the early 1980s provides a glaring counter example: Despite an exchange rate that has been fixed at HK$7.73 per U.S. dollar since October 1983, Hong Kong's inflation rate has on average been three times that of the United States. The figure on the next page shows how the two countries' price levels have moved since 1983.

This high inflation is surprising because Hong Kong has erected essentially no barriers to international trade, and thus is one of the world's most open economies. If the forces of international arbitrage work anywhere to keep international price levels in line, it should be in Hong Kong.

Until the early 1970s Hong Kong's currency was pegged to the pound sterling, and for that period, PPP is borne out. Over the period 1965–1972, for example, Hong Kong's average inflation rate was 5.7 percent per year while Britain's was 5.9 percent.*

What has been going on since the early 1980s? The one-word answer is: China. In 1978 China began a drive to liberate its economy from the worst distortions of central planning while maintaining the Communist party's political monopoly.

From an economic viewpoint the reforms have been a success, triggering rapid output growth and transforming China into a major player in world export markets.†

These developments have had a major impact on Hong Kong's economy. As part of its economic strategy, China established special free-enterprise zones on the south China coast not far from Hong Kong. The zones became magnets for investment, most of it from Hong Kong, and the investments' success has enriched many Hong Kong residents. Their growing spending on Hong Kong-produced services and other nontradables has pushed up the prices of those goods, contributing to high inflation in the overall price index despite much more moderate inflation in the prices of tradable goods.

A second, related cause of Hong Kong's inflation has been steep increases in rents and in the price of land. Land has always been scarce in Hong Kong, whose population of 6 million is crammed into less than 400 square miles, much of that unsuited to construction. But the city's growing wealth, coupled with a growing world business demand for office space close to the Chinese market, made real estate prices soar. Purchases by corrupt and wealthy Chinese officials added fur-

---

*See Gavin Peebles, *Hong Kong's Economy* (Hong Kong: Oxford University Press. 1988).

†For an account, see Alan Gelb, Gary Jefferson, and Inderjit Singh, "Can Communist Economies Transform Incrementally? The Experience of China," *NBER Macroeconomics Annual 1993,* pp. 87–133.

When a firm sells the same product for different prices in different markets, we say that it is practicing **pricing to market**. Pricing to market may reflects different demand conditions in different countries. For example, countries where demand is more price-inelastic will tend to be charged higher markups over a monopolistic seller's production cost. Empirical studies of firm-level export data have yielded strong evidence of pervasive pricing to market in manufacturing trade.[10]

---

[10]For a detailed review of the evidence, see the paper by Goldberg and Knetter in this chapter's Further Reading. Theoretical contributions on pricing to market include Rudiger Dornbusch, "Exchange Rates and Prices," *American Economic Review* 77 (March 1987), pp. 93–106; and Paul R. Krugman, "Pricing to Market When the Exchange Rate Changes," in Sven W. Arndt and J. David Richardson, eds., *Real-Financial Linkages among Open Economies* (Cambridge, MA: MIT Press, 1987).

ther momentum to property prices (as well as to general inflation). Through the late 1990s, Hong Kong's rents rose to be among the highest anywhere—a development that raised the rental component of the consumer price index, as well as the prices of all nontradables that use office space as a factor of production. Hong Kong's inflation moderated after 1997 when its economy slowed as a result of the Asian financial crises that we will discuss in Chapter 22.

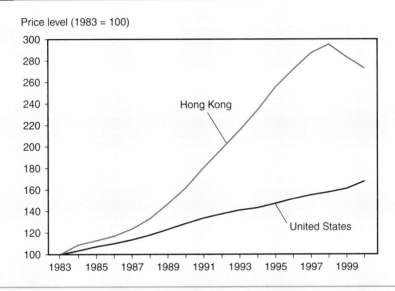

Price Indexes for the United States and Hong Kong, 1983–2000

Hong Kong's price level has risen much more rapidly than that of the United States, despite a fixed exchange rate and no trade barriers.

Source: U.S. Department of Commerce, and Government Secretariat, Hong Kong, *Economic Prospects,* various issues. Hong Kong index is composite CPI.

In the early 1990s, for example, a Nissan automobile built at the Japanese company's Sunderland plant in northeast England could be bought from a dealer near the plant for £16,215. The same model sold in Japan for only £13,375—despite the cost to Nissan of shipping the car 10,600 miles from Sunderland to Tokyo.[11] Such discriminatory pricing to market would be difficult to enforce if it were not costly for drivers to buy autos in Japan and ship them to England. Similarly, if consumers viewed Volkswagens and Fiats as good substitutes for the Nissan, competition among producers would keep the U.K. price of the Japanese cars from getting wildly out of line with production costs. The combination of product differentiation and segmented markets, however, leads to large violations of the law

---

[11]"Why Buyers in Tokyo Spend $5,000 Less for UK-Built Nissan," *Financial Times* (October 5, 1992), p. 16.

of one price and absolute PPP. Shifts in market structure and demand over time can invalidate relative PPP.

International Differences in Price Level Measurement

Government measures of the price level differ from country to country. One reason for these differences is that people living in different countries spend their income in different ways. The average Norwegian consumes more reindeer than her American counterpart, the average Japanese more sushi, and the average Indian more lentils. In constructing a reference commodity basket to measure purchasing power, it is therefore likely that the Norwegian government will put a relatively high weight on reindeer, the Japanese government a high weight on sushi, and the Indian government a high weight on lentils.

Because relative PPP makes predictions about price *changes* rather than price *levels*, it is a sensible concept regardless of the baskets used to define price levels in the countries being compared. If all U.S. prices increase by 10 percent and the dollar depreciates against foreign currencies by 10 percent, relative PPP will be satisfied (assuming there are no changes abroad) for any domestic and foreign choices of price level indexes.

Change in the relative prices of basket components, however, can cause relative PPP to fail tests that are based on official price indexes. For example, a rise in the relative price of fish would raise the dollar price of a Japanese government reference commodity basket relative to that of a U.S. government basket, simply because fish takes up a larger share of the Japanese basket. Relative price changes could lead to PPP violations like those shown in Figure 15-3 even if trade were free and costless.

PPP in the Short Run and in the Long Run

The factors we have examined so far in explaining the PPP theory's poor empirical performance can cause national price levels to diverge even in the long run, after all prices have had time to adjust to their market-clearing levels. As we discussed in Chapter 14, however, many prices in the economy are sticky and take time to adjust fully. Departures from PPP may therefore be even greater in the short run than in the long run.

An abrupt depreciation of the dollar against foreign currencies, for example, makes farm equipment in the United States cheaper relative to similar equipment produced abroad. As farmers throughout the world shift their demand for tractors and reapers to U.S. producers, the price of American farm equipment tends to rise to reduce the divergence from the law of one price caused by the dollar's depreciation. It takes time for this process of price increase to be complete, however, and prices for U.S. and foreign farm equipment may differ considerably while markets adjust to the exchange rate change.

You might suspect that short-run price stickiness and exchange rate volatility help explain a phenomenon we noted in discussing Figure 15-3, that violations of relative PPP have been much more flagrant over periods when exchange rates have floated. Empirical research supports this interpretation of the data. Figure 14-11, which we used to illustrate the stickiness of goods prices compared with exchange rates, is quite typical of floating-rate episodes. In a careful study covering many countries and historical episodes, economist Michael Mussa compared the extent of short-run deviations from PPP under fixed and floating exchange rates. He found that floating exchange rates systematically lead to much larger and more frequent short-run deviations from relative PPP.[12] The box on pp. 412–413 provides an especially vivid illustration of how price stickiness can generate violations of the law of one price even for absolutely identical goods.

Recent research suggests that short-run deviations from PPP such as those due to volatile exchange rates die away over time, with only half the effect of a temporary departure from PPP remaining after four years.[13] Even when these temporary PPP deviations are removed from the data, however, it still appears that the cumulative effect of certain long-run trends causes predictable departures from PPP for many countries. The Case Study entitled "Why Price Levels Are Lower in Poorer Countries" discusses one of the major mechanisms behind such trends.

CASE STUDY

Why Price Levels Are Lower in Poorer Countries

Research on international price level differences has uncovered a striking empirical regularity: When expressed in terms of a single currency, countries' price levels are positively related to the level of real income per capita. In other words, a dollar, when converted to local currency at the market exchange rate, generally goes much farther in a poor country than in a rich one. Figure 15-4 illustrates the relation between price levels and income, with each dot representing a different country.

The previous section's discussion of the role of nontraded goods in the determination of national price levels suggests that international variations in the prices of nontradables may contribute to price level discrepancies between rich and poor nations. The available data indeed show that nontradables tend to be more expensive (relative to tradables) in richer countries.

One reason for the lower relative price of nontradables in poor countries was suggested by Bela Balassa and by Paul Samuelson.[14] The Balassa-Samuelson theory assumes that the labor forces of poor countries are less productive than those of rich countries in the tradables sector

---

[12]See Mussa, "Nominal Exchange Rate Regimes and the Behavior of Real Exchange Rates: Evidence and Implications," in Karl Brunner and Allan H. Meltzer, eds., *Real Business Cycles, Real Exchange Rates and Actual Policies,* Carnegie-Rochester Conference Series on Public Policy 25 (Amsterdam: North-Holland, 1986), pp. 117–214. Charles Engel of the University of Wisconsin has found that under a floating exchange rate, international price differences for the *same* good can be more variable than the relative price of *different* goods within a single country. See Engel, "Real Exchange Rates and Relative Prices: An Empirical Investigation," *Journal of Monetary Economics* 32 (August 1993), pp. 35–50.

[13]See, for example, Jeffrey A. Frankel and Andrew K. Rose, "A Panel Project on Purchasing Power Parity: Mean Reversion Within and Between Countries," *Journal of International Economics* 40 (February 1996), pp. 209–224. The statistical validity of these results is challenged by Paul G. J. O'Connell in "The Overvaluation of Purchasing Power Parity," *Journal of International Economics* 44 (February 1998), pp. 1–19.

[14]See Balassa, "The Purchasing Power Parity Doctrine: A Reappraisal," *Journal of Political Economy* 72 (December 1964), pp. 584–596, and Samuelson, "Theoretical Notes on Trade Problems," *Review of Economics and Statistics* 46 (May 1964), pp. 145–154. The Balassa-Samuelson theory was foreshadowed by some observations of Ricardo. See Jacob Viner, *Studies in the Theory of International Trade* (New York: Harper & Brothers, 1937), p. 315.

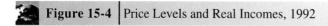

Figure 15-4 | Price Levels and Real Incomes, 1992

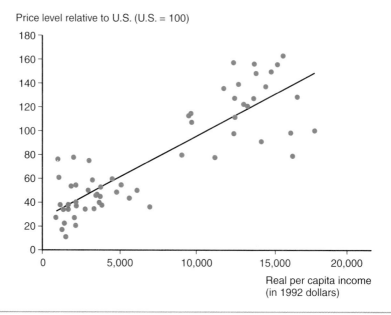

Countries' price levels tend to rise as their real incomes rise. Each dot represents a country. The straight line indicates a statistician's best prediction of a country's price level relative to the United States based on knowing its real per capita income.

but that international productivity differences in nontradables are negligible. If the prices of traded goods are roughly equal in all countries, however, lower labor productivity in the tradables industries of poor countries implies lower wages than abroad, lower production costs in nontradables, and therefore a lower price of nontradables. Rich countries with higher labor productivity in the tradables sector will tend to have higher nontradables prices and higher price levels. Productivity statistics give some empirical support to the Balassa-Samuelson differential productivity postulate. And it is plausible that international productivity differences are sharper in traded than in nontraded goods. Whether a country is rich or poor, a barber can give only so many haircuts in a week, but there may be significant scope for productivity differences across countries in the manufacture of traded goods like personal computers.

An alternative theory that attempts to explain the lower price levels of poor countries was put forth by Jagdish Bhagwati and by Irving Kravis of the University of Pennsylvania and Robert Lipsey of the City University of New York.[15] The Bhagwati-Kravis-Lipsey view relies on differences in endowments of capital and labor rather than productivity differences, but it also predicts that the relative price of nontradables increases as real per capita income increases. Rich countries

---

[15] See Kravis and Lipsey, *Toward an Explanation of National Price Levels,* Princeton Studies in International Finance 52 (International Finance Section, Department of Economics, Princeton University, November 1983); and Bhagwati, "Why Are Services Cheaper in the Poor Countries?" *Economic Journal* 94 (June 1984), pp. 279–280.

have high capital-labor ratios, while poor countries have more labor relative to capital. Because rich countries have higher capital-labor ratios, the marginal productivity of labor is greater in rich countries than in poor countries, and the former will therefore have a higher wage level than the latter.[16] Nontradables, which consist largely of services, are naturally labor-intensive relative to tradables. Because labor is cheaper in poor countries and is used intensively in producing non-tradables, nontradables also will be cheaper there than in the rich, high-wage countries. Once again, this international difference in the relative price of nontradables suggests that overall price levels, when measured in a single currency, should be higher in rich countries than in poor.

Beyond Purchasing Power Parity: A General Model of Long-Run Exchange Rates

Why devote so much discussion to the purchasing power parity theory when it is fraught with exceptions and apparently contradicted by the data? We examined the implications of PPP so closely because its basic idea of relating long-run exchange rates to long-run national price levels is a very useful starting point. The monetary approach presented above, which assumed PPP, is too simple to give accurate predictions about the real world, but we can generalize it by taking account of some of the reasons why PPP predicts badly in practice. In this section we develop a generalized model of long-run exchange rate determination that, while more complicated than the monetary approach, is better at explaining how exchange rates really behave.

Our generalized model provides another reason why PPP is a useful concept, for the model shows that in those important situations where monetary changes are the dominant cause of economic fluctuations, the predictions of the simple monetary approach *are* accurate over the long run.

The long-run analysis below continues to ignore short-run complications caused by sticky prices. An understanding of how exchange rates behave in the long run is, as mentioned earlier, a prerequisite for the more complicated short-run analysis that we undertake in the next chapter.

The Real Exchange Rate

As the first step in extending the PPP theory, we define the concept of a **real exchange rate**. The real exchange rate between two countries' currencies is a broad summary measure of the prices of one country's goods and services relative to the other's. It is natural to introduce the real exchange rate concept at this point because the major prediction of PPP is that real exchange rates never change, at least not permanently. To extend our model so that it describes the world more accurately, we need to examine systematically the forces that can cause dramatic and permanent changes in real exchange rates.

---

[16]This argument assumes that factor endowment differences between rich and poor countries are sufficiently great that factor-price equalization cannot hold.

STICKY PRICES AND THE LAW OF ONE PRICE: EVIDENCE FROM SCANDINAVIAN DUTY-FREE SHOPS

Sticky nominal prices and wages are central to macroeconomic theories, but just why might it be difficult for money prices to change from day to day as market conditions change? One reason is based on the idea of "menu costs." Menu costs could arise from several factors, such as the actual costs of printing new price lists and catalogs. In addition, firms may perceive a different type of menu cost due to their cutsomers' imperfect information about competitors' prices. When a firm raises its price, some customers will shop around elsewhere and find it convenient to remain with a competing seller even if all sellers have raised their prices. In the presence of these various types of menu cost, sellers will often hold price constant after a change in market conditions until they are certain the change is permanent enough to make incurring the costs of price change worthwhile.*

If there were truly no barriers between two markets with goods priced in different currencies, sticky prices would be unable to survive in the face of an exchange rate change. All buyers would simply flock to the market where a good had become cheapest. But when some trade impediments exist, deviations from the law of one price do not induce unlimited arbitrage, so it is feasible for sellers to hold prices constant despite exchange rate changes. In the real world, trade barriers appear to be significant, widespread, and often subtle in nature.

Apparently, arbitrage between two markets may be limited even when the physical distance between them is zero, as a surprising study of pricing behavior in Scandinanvian duty-free outlets shows. Swedish economists Marcus Asplund and Richard Friberg studied pricing behavior in the duty-free stores of two Scandinavian ferry lines and the airline SAS, all of whose catalogs quote the prices of each good in several currencies for the convenience of customers from different countries.† Since it is costly to print the catalogs, they are reissued only from time to time with revised prices. In the interim, however, fluctuations in exchange rates induce multiple, changing prices for the *same* good. For example, on the Birka Line of ferries between Sweden and Finland, prices

---

*It is when economic conditions are very volatile that prices seem to become most flexible. For example, restaurant menus will typically price their catch of the day at "market" so that the price charged (and the fish offered) can reflect the high variability in fishing outcomes.

†"The Law of One Price in Scandinavian Duty-Free Stores," *American Economic Review* 91 (September 2001), pp. 1072–1083.

As we will see, real exchange rates are important not only for quantifying deviations from PPP but also for analyzing macroeconomic demand and supply conditions in open economies. When we wish to differentiate a real exchange rate, which is the relative price of two output baskets, from a relative price of two currencies, we will refer to the latter as a **nominal exchange rate**. But when there is no risk of confusion we will continue to use the shorter term *exchange rate* to cover nominal exchange rates.

Real exchange rates are defined, however, in terms of nominal exchange rates and price levels. So before we can give a more precise definition of real exchange rates, we need to clarify the price level measure we will be using. Let P_{US}, as usual, be the price level in the United States, and P_E the price level in Europe. Since we will not be assuming absolute PPP (as we did in our discussion of the monetary approach), we no longer assume the price level can be measured by the same basket of commodities in the United States as in Europe. Because we will soon want to link our analysis to monetary factors, we require instead that

were listed in both Finnish markka and Swedish kronor between 1975 and 1998, implying that a relative depreciation of the markka would make it cheaper to buy cigarettes or vodka by paying markka rather than kronor.

Despite such price discrepancies, Birka Line was always able to do business in both currencies—passengers did not rush to buy at the lowest price. Swedish passengers, who held relatively large quantities of their own national currency, tended to buy at the kronor prices, whereas Finnish customers tended to buy at markka prices. Often, Birka Line would take advantage of publishing a new catalog to reduce deviations from the law of one price. The average deviation from the law of one price in the month just before such a price adjustment was 7.21 percent, but only 2.22 percent in the month of a price adjustment. One big impediment to taking advantage of the arbitrage opportunities was the cost of changing currencies at the onboard foreign exchange booth—roughly 7.5 percent. That transaction cost, given different passengers' currency preference at the time of embarkation, acted as an effective trade barrier.‡

Surprisingly, Birka Line did not completely eliminate law-of-one-price deviations when it changed catalog prices. Instead, Birka Line practiced a kind of pricing to market on its ferries. Usually, exporters who price to market discriminate between different consumers based on their different locations, but Birka was able to discriminate based on different nationality and currency preference, even with all potential consumers located on the same ferry boat.

The idea that currency preference, exchange costs, and calculation costs create fixed transaction cost bands within which price differentials can persist receives further support from Asplund and Friberg's data on SAS in-flight duty-free catalogs. SAS also practiced pricing to market, but with smaller planned deviations from the law of one price for more expensive items (for example, the $138 Mont Blanc pen). For a given percentage price discrepancy, the gains to purchasing at the lowest price are greater the more expensive the item. The finding that SAS had more latitude for pricing to market with low-cost items is therefore consistent with the presence of fixed barriers to arbitrage.

---

‡Customers could pay in the currency of their choice not only with cash, but also with credit cards, which involve much lower foreign exchange conversion fees but convert at an exchange rate prevailing a few days after the purchase of the goods. Asplund and Friberg hypothesize that for such small purchases, uncertainty and the costs of calculating relative prices (in addition to the credit-card exchange fees) might have been a sufficient deterrent to transacting in a relatively unfamiliar currency.

---

each country's price index give a good representation of the purchases that motivate its residents to demand its money supply.

No measure of the price level does this perfectly, but we must settle on some definition before the real exchange rate can be defined formally. To be concrete, you can think of P_{US} as the dollar price of an unchanging basket containing the typical weekly purchases of U.S. households and firms; P_E, similarly, is based on an unchanging basket reflecting the typical weekly purchases of European households and firms. The point to remember is that *the United States price level will place a relatively heavy weight on commodities produced and consumed in America, the European price level a relatively heavy weight on commodities produced and consumed in Europe.*[17]

---

[17]A similar presumption was made in our discussion of the transfer problem in Chapter 5. As we observed in that chapter, nontradables are one important factor behind the relative preference for home products.

Having described the reference commodity baskets used to measure price levels, we can now formally define the *real dollar/euro exchange rate,* denoted $q_{\$/€}$, as the dollar price of the European basket relative to that of the American. We can express the real exchange rate as the dollar value of Europe's price level divided by the U.S. price level or, in symbols, as

$$q_{\$/€} = (E_{\$/€} \times P_E)/P_{US}. \tag{15-6}$$

A numerical example will clarify the concept of the real exchange rate. Imagine that the European reference commodity basket costs €100 (so that P_E = €100 per European basket), that the U.S. basket costs $120 (so that P_{US} = $120 per U.S. basket), and that the nominal exchange rate is $E_{\$/€}$ = $1.20 per euro. The real dollar/euro exchange rate would then be

$$q_{\$/€} = \frac{(\$1.20 \text{ per euro}) \times (€100 \text{ per European basket})}{(\$120 \text{ per U.S. basket})}$$

$$= (\$120 \text{ per European basket})/(\$120 \text{ per U.S. basket})$$

$$= 1 \text{ U.S. basket per European basket.}$$

A rise in the real dollar/euro exchange rate $q_{\$/€}$, (which we call a **real depreciation** of the dollar against the euro) can be thought of in several equivalent ways. Most obviously, (15-6) shows this change to be a fall in the purchasing power of a dollar within Europe's borders relative to its purchasing power within the United States. This change in relative purchasing power occurs because the dollar prices of European goods ($E_{\$/€} \times P_E$) rise relative to those of U.S. goods (P_{US}).

In terms of our numerical example, a 10 percent nominal dollar depreciation, to $E_{\$/€}$ = $1.32 per euro, causes $q_{\$/€}$ to rise to 1.1 U.S. baskets per European basket, a *real* dollar depreciation of 10 percent against the euro. (The same change in $q_{\$/€}$ could result from a 10 percent rise in P_E or a 10 percent fall in P_{US}.) The real depreciation means that the dollar's purchasing power over European goods and services falls by 10 percent relative to its purchasing power over U.S. goods and services.

Alternatively, even though many of the items entering national price levels are nontraded, it is useful to think of the real exchange rate $q_{\$/€}$ as the relative price of European products in general in terms of American products, that is, the price at which hypothetical trades of American for European commodity baskets would occur if trades at domestic prices were possible. The dollar is considered to *depreciate* in real terms against the euro when $q_{\$/€}$ rises because the hypothetical purchasing power of America's products in general over Europe's declines. America's goods and services become cheaper relative to Europe's.

A **real appreciation** of the dollar against the euro is a fall in $q_{\$/€}$. This fall indicates a decrease in the relative price of products purchased in Europe, or a rise in the dollar's European purchasing power compared with that in the United States.[18]

---

[18]Since $E_{€/\$} = 1/E_{\$/€}$, so that $q_{\$/€} = P_E/(E_{€/\$} \times P_{US}) = 1/q_{€/\$}$, a real depreciation of the dollar against the euro is the same as a real appreciation of the euro against the dollar (that is, a rise in the purchasing power of the euro within the United States relative to its purchasing power within Europe, or a fall in the relative price of American products in terms of European products).

Our convention for describing real depreciations and appreciations of the dollar against the euro is the same one we use for nominal exchange rates (that is, $E_{\$/\epsilon}$ up is a dollar depreciation, $E_{\$/\epsilon}$ down an appreciation). Equation (15-6) shows that at *unchanged* output prices, nominal depreciation (appreciation) implies real depreciation (appreciation). Our discussion of real exchange rate changes thus includes, as a special case, an observation we made in Chapter 13: With the domestic money prices of goods held constant, a nominal dollar depreciation makes U.S. goods cheaper compared with foreign goods, while a nominal dollar appreciation makes them more expensive.

Equation (15-6) makes it easy to see why the real exchange rate can never change when relative PPP holds. Under relative PPP, a 10 percent rise in $E_{\$/\epsilon}$, for instance, would always be exactly offset by a 10 percent fall in the price level ratio P_E/P_{US}, leaving $q_{\$/\epsilon}$ unchanged.

Demand, Supply, and the Long-Run Real Exchange Rate

It should come as no surprise that in a world where PPP does not hold, the long-run values of real exchange rates, just like other relative prices that clear markets, depend on demand and supply conditions. Since a real exchange rate tracks changes in the relative price of two countries' expenditure baskets, however, conditions in *both* countries matter. Changes in countries' output markets can be complex, and we do not want to digress into an exhaustive (and exhausting) catalogue of the possibilities. We focus instead on two specific cases that are both easy to grasp and important in practice for explaining why the long-run values of real exchange rates can change.

1. *A change in world relative demand for American products.* Imagine that total world spending on American goods and services rises relative to total world spending on European goods and services. Such a change could rise from several sources, for example, a shift in private U.S. demand away from European goods and toward American goods; a similar shift in private foreign demand toward American goods; or an increase in U.S. government demand falling primarily on U.S. output. Any increase in relative world demand for U.S. products causes an excess demand for them at the previous real exchange rate. To restore equilibrium, the relative price of American output in terms of European will therefore have to rise: The relative prices of U.S. nontradables will rise and the prices of tradables produced in the United States, and consumed intensively there, will rise relative to the prices of tradables made in Europe. These changes all work to reduce $q_{\$/\epsilon}$, the relative price of Europe's reference expenditure basket in terms of the United States'. We conclude that *an increase in world relative demand for U.S. output causes a long-run real appreciation of the dollar against the euro (a fall in $q_{\$/\epsilon}$). Similarly, a fall in world relative demand for U.S. output causes a long-run real depreciation of the dollar against the euro (a rise in $q_{\$/\epsilon}$).*

2. *A change in relative output supply.* Suppose that the productive efficiency of U.S. labor and capital rises. Since Americans spend part of their increased income on foreign goods, the supplies of all types of U.S. goods and services increase relative to the demand for them, the result being an excess relative supply of American output at the previous real exchange rate. A fall in the relative price of American products—both nontradables and tradables—shifts demand toward them and eliminates the excess supply. This price change is a real depreciation of the dollar against the euro, that is, an increase in $q_{\$/\epsilon}$. *A relative expansion of U.S. output causes a long-run real depreciation of the* *dollar against the euro ($q_{\$/€}$ rises). A relative expansion of European output causes a long-run real appreciation of the dollar against the euro ($q_{\$/€}$ falls).*[19]

Nominal and Real Exchange Rates in Long-Run Equilibrium

We now pull together what we have learned in this chapter and the last one to show how long-run nominal exchange rates are determined. One central conclusion is that changes in national money supplies and demands give rise to the proportional long-run movements in nominal exchange rates and international price level ratios predicted by the relative purchasing power parity theory. Demand and supply shifts in national output markets, however, cause nominal exchange rate movements that do not conform to PPP.

Recall our definition of the real dollar/euro exchange rate as

$$q_{\$/€} = (E_{\$/€} \times P_E)/P_{US}.$$

(See equation (15-6).) If we now solve this equation for the nominal exchange rate, we get an equation that gives us the nominal dollar/euro exchange rate as the real dollar/euro exchange rate times the U.S.-Europe price level ratio:

$$E_{\$/€} = q_{\$/€} \times (P_{US}/P_E). \tag{15-7}$$

Formally speaking, the only difference between (15-7) and equation (15-1), on which we based our exposition of the monetary approach to the exchange rate, is that (15-7) accounts for possible deviations from PPP by adding the *real* exchange rate as an additional determinant of the nominal exchange rate. *The equation implies that for a given real dollar/euro exchange rate, changes in money demand or supply in Europe or the United States affect the long-run nominal dollar/euro exchange rate as in the monetary approach. Changes in the long-run real exchange rate, however, also affect the long-run nominal exchange rate.* The long-run theory of exchange rate determination implied by equation (15-7) thus includes the valid elements of the monetary approach, but in addition it corrects the monetary approach by allowing for nonmonetary factors that can cause sustained deviations from purchasing power parity.

Assuming that all variables start out at their long-run levels, we can now understand the most important determinants of long-run swings in nominal exchange rates:

> **1.** *A shift in relative money supply levels.* Consider an increase in the level of the U.S. money supply. As you will remember from Chapter 14, a permanent one-time increase in a country's money supply has no effect on the long-run levels of output, the interest rate, or any relative price (including the real exchange rate). Thus, (15-3) implies once again

---

[19]Our discussion of the Balassa-Samuelson effect in the Case Study on page 409 would lead you to expect that a productivity increase concentrated in the U.S. tradables sector might cause the dollar to appreciate in real terms against the euro, rather than depreciate. In the last paragraph, however, we have in mind a balanced productivity increase which benefits the traded and nontraded sectors in equal proportion. It causes a real dollar depreciation by causing a drop in the prices of nontraded goods and in those of traded goods that are more important in America's consumer price index than in Europe's.

that P_{US} rises in proportion to M_{US}, while (15-7) shows that the U.S. price level is the sole variable changing in the long run along with the nominal exchange rate $E_{\$/€}$. Because the real exchange rate $q_{\$/€}$ does not change, the nominal exchange rate change is consistent with relative PPP: The only long-run effect of the U.S. money supply increase is to raise all dollar prices, including the dollar price of the euro, in proportion to the increase in the money supply. It should be no surprise that this result is the same as the one we found using the monetary approach, since that approach is designed to account for the long-run effects of monetary changes.

2. *A shift in relative money supply growth rates.* A permanent increase in the *growth rate* of the U.S. money supply raises the long-run U.S. inflation rate and, through the Fisher effect, raises the dollar interest rate relative to the euro interest rate. Because relative U.S. real money demand therefore declines, equation (15-3) implies that P_{US} rises (as shown in Figure 15-1). Because the change bringing this outcome about is purely monetary, however, it is neutral in its long-run effects; specifically, it does not alter the long-run *real* dollar/euro exchange rate. According to (15-7), then, $E_{\$/€}$ rises in proportion to the increase in P_{US} (a depreciation of the dollar against the euro). Once again, a purely monetary change brings about a long-run nominal exchange rate shift in line with relative PPP, just as the monetary approach predicted.

3. *A change in relative output demand.* This type of change is *not* covered by the monetary approach, so now the more general perspective we've developed, in which the real exchange rate can change, is essential. Since a change in relative output demand does not affect long-run national price levels—these depend solely on the factors appearing in equations (15-3) and (15-4)—the long-run nominal exchange rate in (15-7) will change only insofar as the real exchange rate changes. Consider an increase in world relative demand for U.S. products. Earlier in this section we saw that a rise in demand for U.S. products causes a long-run real appreciation of the dollar against the euro (a fall in $q_{\$/€}$); this change is simply a rise in the relative price of U.S. output. Given that long-run national price levels are unchanged, however, (15-7) tells us that a long-run *nominal* appreciation of the dollar against the euro (a fall in $E_{\$/€}$) must also occur. This prediction highlights the important fact that even though exchange rates are nominal prices, they respond to nonmonetary as well as monetary events, even over long horizons.

4. *A change in relative output supply.* As we saw earlier in this section, an increase in relative U.S. output supply causes the dollar to depreciate in real terms against the euro, lowering the relative price of U.S. output. This rise in $q_{\$/€}$ is not, however, the only change in equation (15-7) implied by a relative rise in U.S. output. In addition, the U.S. output increase raises the transactions demand for real U.S. money balances, raising aggregate U.S. real money demand and, by (15-3), pushing the long-run U.S. price level down. Referring back to equation (15-7), you will see that since $q_{\$/€}$ rises while P_{US} falls, the output and money market effects of a change in output supply work in opposite directions, so that the net effect on $E_{\$/€}$ is *ambiguous*. Our analysis of an output-supply change illustrates that even when a disturbance originates in a single market (in this case, the output market), its influence on exchange rates may depend on repercussion effects that are channeled through other markets.

We conclude that when all disturbances are monetary in nature, exchange rates obey relative PPP in the long run. In the long run, a monetary disturbance affects only the general

Table 15-1	Effects of Money Market and Output Market Changes on the Long-Run Nominal Dollar/Euro Exchange Rate, $E_{\$/€}$

Change	Effect on the long-run nominal dollar/euro exchange rate, $E_{\$/€}$
Money market	
1. Increase in U.S. money supply level	Proportional increase (nominal depreciation of $)
2. Increase in European money supply level	Proportional decrease (nominal depreciation of euro)
3. Increase in U.S. money supply growth rate	Increase (nominal depreciation of $)
4. Increase in European money supply growth rate	Decrease (nominal depreciation of euro)
Output market	
1. Increase in demand for U.S. output	Decrease (nominal appreciation of $)
2. Increase in demand for European output	Increase (nominal appreciation of euro)
3. Output supply increase in the United States	Ambiguous
4. Output supply increase in Europe	Ambiguous

purchasing power of a currency, and this change in purchasing power changes equally the currency's value in terms of domestic and foreign goods. When disturbances occur in output markets, the exchange rate is unlikely to obey relative PPP, even in the long run.[20] Table 15-1 summarizes these conclusions regarding the effects of monetary and output market changes on long-run nominal exchange rates.

In the chapters that follow, we will appeal to this section's general long-run exchange rate model even when we are discussing *short-run* macroeconomic events. Long-run factors are important for the short run because of the central role expectations about the future play in the day-to-day determination of exchange rates. The long-run exchange rate model of this section will provide the anchor for market expectations, that is, the framework market participants use to forecast future exchange rates on the basis of information at hand today.

---

[20]These conclusions help explain why empirical applications of completely monetary theories of nominal exchange rates have been more successful in data where the most prominent changes are monetary in nature. For an econometric application of a monetary approach to the German hyperinflation of the 1920s, see Jacob A. Frenkel, "A Monetary Approach to the Exchange Rate: Doctrinal Aspects and Empirical Evidence," in Jan Herin, Assar Lindbeck, and Johan Myhrman, eds., *Flexible Exchange Rates and Stabilization Policy* (Boulder, CO: Westview Press, 1977), pp. 68–92. The monetary approach's failure to explain data from the 1970s is documented in Rudiger Dornbusch, "Exchange Rate Economics: Where Do We Stand?" *Brookings Papers on Economic Activity* 1:1980, pp. 143–185.

CASE STUDY

Why Has the Yen Kept Rising?

Between 1950 and 1971 the Japanese yen was fixed to the U.S. dollar at a nominal exchange rate that could vary by at most ± 1 percent from ¥360 per dollar. Since the early 1970s, when the dollar/yen exchange rate was allowed to *float* or change in response to market forces, the cumulative appreciation of the yen against the dollar has been enormous. In the spring of 1999 the dollar's price hovered near the 120 yen mark: In about 25 years, the dollar had lost two-thirds of its foreign exchange value against the yen!

This development cannot be explained by the simplest PPP theory because there has been no corresponding rise in the U.S. commodity price level relative to Japan's. Can the extended theory of long-run nominal exchange rates we've developed throw light on the dollar's continuing depreciation against the yen?

A crucial first clue comes from looking at the behavior of the dollar's *real* exchange rate against the yen, $q_{\$/¥}$. Figure 15-5 shows that the price of Japanese goods in terms of U.S. goods has followed a steep upward trend since at least 1950. Let's take this trend of real yen appreciation as a given for the moment, and consider its implications for the *nominal* dollar/yen exchange rate, $E_{\$/¥}$. We will then return to the factors causing the upward trend in $q_{\$/¥}$.

Even though $E_{\$/¥}$ was fixed (approximately) at $1/(360 ¥/\$) = 0.2778$ cents per yen, the real exchange rate $q_{\$/¥}$ was able to rise even over the 1950–1971 period because Japan had higher inflation than the United States did. Between 1950 and 1960 Japanese inflation averaged 5.3 percent per year while U.S. inflation averaged only 2.6 percent. Average U.S. inflation was higher than before during the 1960–1971 period, at 3.4 percent per year, but Japan's 5.5 percent average annual inflation rate for the same period still remained considerably above it. With P_J rising more rapidly than P_{US}, the trend rise in $q_{\$/¥} = (E_{\$/¥} \times P_J)/P_{US}$ shown in Figure 15-5 could continue even with $E_{\$/¥}$ fixed.

Things changed with the coming of floating exchange rates in the early 1970s. After suffering through some very high inflation in 1973 and 1974, Japan's leaders began to show a preference for lower inflation than in the United States. Between 1979 and 1993, for example, American inflation averaged 4.7 percent per year while Japanese inflation averaged only 2.3 percent. Looking again at the definition $q_{\$/¥} = (E_{\$/¥} \times P_J)/P_{US}$, we can see that the only way for $q_{\$/¥}$ to keep rising while P_J rises more slowly than P_{US} is for $E_{\$/¥}$ to rise even more sharply. And a steep progressive rise in the dollar price of yen is exactly what we have observed.

Which brings us to the question we put aside earlier: Why *has* $q_{\$/¥}$ been rising, that is, what explains the yen's continuing *real* appreciation against the dollar over the past 50 years? The answer is suggested by our analysis of the Balassa-Samuelson effect in the Case Study on page 409. Japan has had extremely high rates of productivity growth in its traded goods, but the productivity of factors employed in nontraded goods such as services has grown much more slowly. Growing traded goods productivity has tended to raise wages throughout the economy, but since productivity lags in nontradables, producers in that sector can afford to pay higher wages only by raising their products' prices. Thus, the relative price of nontraded goods in terms

Figure 15-5 | The Real Dollar/Yen Exchange Rate, 1950–2000

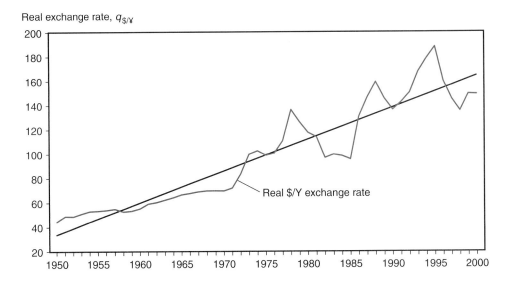

The U.S. dollar has steadily depreciated in real terms against Japan's yen. (The straight line indicates the average trend over time in the real exchange rate.)

Source: Penn World Table, Mark 5.6, as described by Robert Summers and Alan Heston, "The Penn World Table (Mark 5); An Expanded Set of International Comparisons, 1950–1988." *Quarterly Journal of Economics* 106 (May 1991), pp. 327–368. Data for 1993–2000 from International Monetary Fund, *International Financial Statistics Yearbook 1997, 2001.*

of traded goods has risen over time in Japan, and it has done so more quickly than in the United States, where the gap between productivity growth in tradables and nontradables is lower. This effect could, in theory, cause the price of a representative Japanese consumer basket in terms of U.S. baskets, $q_{\$/\yen}$, to rise over time.

Do the data support this explanation? We argued in the last section that a balanced or across-the-board increase in Japanese productivity, one that benefits production in nontradables and tradables alike, would cause a real yen *depreciation*. But balanced productivity growth is not what Japan has experienced, and growth concentrated in traded goods has different implications for real exchange rates than balanced output growth. In a careful study of industry-level data, University of Pennsylvania economist Richard C. Marston found that labor productivity growth in U.S. tradables exceeded that in U.S. nontradables by 13.2 percent over the 1973–1983 period. In Japan, however, productivity growth in tradables outstripped that in nontradables by a massive 73.2 percent. These trends seem to have continued after 1983. A 1993 study commissioned by the management consulting firm McKinsey & Co. found that by 1990, Japanese workers were substantially more productive than their U.S. counterparts in several key manufacturing industries, including autos, auto parts, steel, and consumer electronics. In contrast, Japanese workers appeared less productive than American workers in nontraded goods.[21]

Our earlier reasoning implies that the price of nontradables in terms of tradables should have risen in both countries but that the increase should have been much greater in Japan. This reasoning fits the facts quite well: Marston found that over 1973–1983, the relative price of nontradables rose by 12.4 percent in the United States but by 56.9 percent in Japan. The prices of Japanese-produced tradables did fall sharply relative to those of U.S. tradables, as the last section's theory predicts, but not by nearly enough to offset the real exchange rate effect of Japan's skyrocketing nontradables prices. Japan's more rapidly rising prices for nontraded goods, then, provide the basic reason why $q_{\$/¥}$ has steadily increased.

Figure 15-6 shows that the effect of unbalanced productivity growth on the price of nontradables held up for a cross-section of industrial countries over 1970–1985. The greater the gap between factor productivity growth in tradables and nontradables, the greater the rise in the relative price of nontraded goods, on average. As you can also see from the figure, Japan leads the industrial countries in the rate of increase of its nontradables' prices, and, aside from Norway, leads in the gap between traded and nontraded productivity gains.[22] It is this pattern of productivity change, coupled with Japanese inflation lower than America's, that has kept the yen rising against the dollar over most of the postwar period.

International Interest Rate Differences and the Real Exchange Rate

Earlier in this chapter we saw that relative PPP, when combined with interest parity, implies that international interest rate differences equal differences in countries' expected inflation rates. Because relative PPP does not hold true in general, however, the relation between international interest rate differences and national inflation rates is likely to be more complex in practice than that simple formula suggests. Despite this complexity, economic policymakers who hope to influence exchange rates, as well as private individuals who wish to forecast them, cannot succeed without understanding the factors that cause countries' interest rates to differ.

In this section we therefore extend our earlier discussion of the Fisher effect to include real exchange rate movements. We do this by showing that in general, interest rate differences

---

[21] See Richard C. Marston, "Real Exchange Rates and Productivity Growth in the United States and Japan," in Sven W. Arndt and J. David Richardson, *Real-Financial Linkages Among Open Economies* (Cambridge, MA: MIT Press, 1987), pp. 71–96, and McKinsey Global Institute, *Manufacturing Productivity* (Washington, D.C.: McKinsey & Co., 1993).

[22] Figure 15-6 is taken from José De Gregorio, Alberto Giovannini, and Holger C. Wolf, "International Evidence on Tradables and Nontradables Inflation," *European Economic Review* 38 (June 1994), pp. 1225–1244. For further evidence see Patrick K. Asea and Enrique G. Mendoza, "The Balassa-Samuelson Model: A General-Equilibrium Appraisal," *Review of International Economics* 2 (October 1994), pp. 244–267.

Figure 15-6 | Sectoral Productivity Growth Differences and the Change in the Relative Price of Nontraded Goods, 1970–1985

A higher traded–nontraded productivity growth difference is associated with a higher rate of increase in the relative price of nontradables.

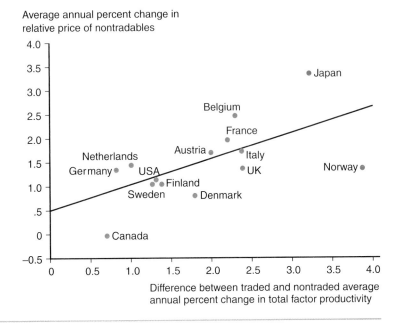

Difference between traded and nontraded average annual percent change in total factor productivity

between countries depend not only on differences in expected inflation, as the monetary approach asserts, but also on expected changes in the real exchange rate.

We begin by recalling that the change in $q_{\$/€}$, the real dollar/euro exchange rate, is the *deviation* from relative PPP; that is, the change in $q_{\$/€}$ is the percentage change in the nominal dollar/euro exchange rate less the international difference in inflation rates between the United States and Europe. We thus arrive at the corresponding relationship between the *expected* change in the real exchange rate, the *expected* change in the nominal rate, and *expected* inflation.

$$(q^e_{\$/€} - q_{\$/€})/q_{\$/€} = [(E^e_{\$/€} - E_{\$/€})/E_{\$/€}] - (\pi^e_{US} - \pi^e_{E}), \qquad (15\text{-}8)$$

where $q^e_{\$/€}$ (as per our usual notation) is the real exchange rate expected for a year from today. Now return to the interest parity condition between dollar and euro deposits,

$$R_{\$} - R_{€} = (E^e_{\$/€} - E_{\$/€})/E_{\$/€}.$$

An easy rearrangement of (15-8) shows that the expected rate of change in the *nominal* dollar/euro exchange rate is just the expected rate of change in the *real* dollar/euro exchange rate *plus* the U.S.-Europe expected inflation difference. Combining (15-8) with the above interest parity condition, we thus are led to the following breakdown of the international interest gap:

$$R_\$ - R_\epsilon = [(q^e_{\$/\epsilon} - q_{\$/\epsilon})/q_{\$/\epsilon}] + (\pi^e_{US} - \pi^e_E). \tag{15-9}$$

Notice that when the market expects relative PPP to prevail, $q^e_{\$/\epsilon} = q_{\$/\epsilon}$ and the first term on the right side of this equation drops out. In this special case, (15-9) reduces to the simpler (15-5), which we derived by assuming relative PPP.

In general, however, the dollar-euro interest difference is the sum of *two* components: (1) the expected rate of real dollar depreciation against the euro and (2) the expected inflation difference between the United States and Europe. For example, if U.S. inflation will be 5 percent per year forever and European inflation zero, the long-run interest difference between dollar and euro deposits need not be the 5 percent that PPP (and interest parity) would suggest. If, in addition, everyone knows that output demand and supply trends will make the dollar decline against the euro in real terms at a rate of 1 percent per year, the international interest spread will actually be 6 percent.

Real Interest Parity

Economics makes an important distinction between **nominal interest rates**, which are rates of return measured in monetary terms, and **real interest rates**, which are rates of return measured in *real* terms, that is, in terms of a country's output. Because real rates of return often are uncertain, we usually will refer to *expected* real interest rates. The interest rates we discussed in connection with the interest parity condition and the determinants of money demand were nominal rates, for example, the dollar return on dollar deposits. But for many other purposes, economists need to analyze behavior in terms of real rates of return. No one who is thinking of investing money, for example, could make a decision knowing only that the nominal interest rate is 15 percent. The investment would be quite attractive at zero inflation, but disastrously unattractive if inflation were bounding along at 100 percent per year![23]

We conclude this chapter by showing that when the nominal interest parity condition equates nominal interest rate differences between currencies to expected changes in *nominal* exchange rates, a *real* interest parity condition equates expected real interest rate differences to expected changes in *real* exchange rates. Only when relative PPP is expected to hold (meaning no real exchange rate change is anticipated) are expected real interest rates in all countries identical.

The expected real interest rate, denoted r^e, is defined as the nominal interest rate, R, less the expected inflation rate, π^e:

$$r^e = R - \pi^e.$$

In other words, the expected real interest rate in a country is just the real rate of return a domestic resident expects to earn on a loan of its currency. The definition of the expected real interest rate clarifies the generality of the forces behind the Fisher effect: Any increase

---

[23]We could get away with examining nominal return *differences* in the foreign exchange market because (as Chapter 13 showed) nominal return differences equal real return differences for any given investor. In the context of the money market, the *nominal* interest rate is the *real* rate of return you sacrifice by holding interest-barren currency.

in the expected inflation rate that does not alter the expected real interest rate must be reflected, one for one, in the nominal interest rate.

A useful consequence of the preceding definition is a formula for the difference in expected real interest rates between two currency areas such as the United States and Europe:

$$r_{US}^e - r_E^e = (R_\$ - \pi_{US}^e) - (R_\text{€} - \pi_E^e).$$

If we rearrange equation (15-9) and combine it with the equation above, we get the desired *real interest parity condition:*

$$r_{US}^e - r_E^e = (q_{\$/\text{€}}^e - q_{\$/\text{€}})/q_{\$/\text{€}}. \qquad \text{(15-10)}$$

Equation (15-10) looks much like the nominal interest parity condition from which it is derived, but it explains differences in expected *real* interest rates between the United States and Europe by expected movements in the dollar/euro *real* exchange rate.

Expected real interest rates are the same in different countries when relative PPP is expected to hold (in which case (15-10) implies that $r_{US}^e = r_E^e$). More generally, however, expected real interest rates in different countries need not be equal, even in the long run, if continuing change in output markets is expected.[24] Suppose, for example, that productivity in the South Korean tradables sector is expected to rise during the next two decades while productivity stagnates in South Korean nontradables and in all U.S. industries. If the Balassa-Samuelson hypothesis is valid, people should expect the U.S. dollar to depreciate in real terms against South Korea's currency, the won, as the prices of South Korea's nontradables trend upward. Equation (15-10) thus implies that the expected real interest rate should be higher in the United States than in South Korea.

Do such real interest differences imply unnoticed profit opportunities for international investors? Not necessarily. A cross-border real interest difference does imply that residents of two countries perceive different real rates of return on wealth. Nominal interest parity tells us, however, that any *given* investor expects the same real return on domestic and foreign currency assets. Two investors residing in different countries need not calculate this single real rate of return in the same way if relative PPP does not link the prices of their consumption baskets, but there is no way either can profit from their disagreement by shifting funds between currencies.

Summary

1. The *purchasing power parity* theory, in its absolute form, asserts that the exchange rate between countries' currencies equals the ratio of their price levels, as measured

---

[24]The two-period analysis of international borrowing and lending in Chapter 7 assumed that all countries face a single worldwide real interest rate. Relative PPP must hold in that analysis, however, because there is only one consumption good in each period.

by the money prices of a reference commodity basket. An equivalent statement of PPP is that the purchasing power of any currency is the same in any country. Absolute PPP implies a second version of the PPP theory, *relative PPP*, which predicts that percentage changes in exchange rates equal differences in national inflation rates.

2. A building block of the PPP theory is the *law of one price,* which states that under free competition and in the absence of trade impediments, a good must sell for a single price regardless of where in the world it is sold. Proponents of the PPP theory often argue, however, that its validity does not require the law of one price to hold for every commodity.

3. The *monetary approach to the exchange rate* uses PPP to explain long-term exchange rate behavior exclusively in terms of money supply and demand. In that theory long-run international interest differentials result from different national rates of ongoing inflation, as the *Fisher effect* predicts. Sustained international differences in monetary growth rates are, in turn, behind different long-term rates of continuing inflation. The monetary approach thus finds that a rise in a country's interest rate will be associated with a depreciation of its currency. Relative PPP implies that international interest differences, which equal the expected percentage change in the exchange rate, also equal the international expected inflation gap.

4. The empirical support for PPP and the law of one price is weak in recent data. The failure of these propositions in the real world is related to trade barriers and departures from free competition, factors that can result in *pricing to market* by exporters. In addition, different definitions of price levels in different countries bedevil attempts to test PPP using the price indexes governments publish. For some products, including many services, international transport costs are so steep that these products become nontradable.

5. Deviations from relative PPP can be viewed as changes in a country's *real exchange rate,* the price of a typical foreign expenditure basket in terms of the typical domestic expenditure basket. All else equal, a country's currency undergoes a long-run *real appreciation* against foreign currencies when the world relative demand for its output rises. In this case the country's real exchange rate, as just defined, falls. The home currency undergoes a long-run *real depreciation* against foreign currencies when home output expands relative to foreign output. In this case the real exchange rate rises.

6. The long-run determination of *nominal exchange rates* can be analyzed by combining two theories: the theory of the long-run *real* exchange rate and the theory of how domestic monetary factors determine long-run price levels. A stepwise increase in a country's money stock ultimately leads to a proportional increase in its price level and a proportional fall in its currency's foreign exchange value, just as relative PPP predicts. Changes in monetary growth rates also have long-run effects consistent with PPP. Supply or demand changes in output markets, however, cause exchange rate movements that do not conform to PPP.

7. The interest parity condition equates international differences in *nominal interest rates* to the expected percentage change in the nominal exchange rate. If interest parity holds in this sense, a real interest parity condition equates international differences in expected *real interest rates* to the expected change in the real exchange rate. Real interest parity also implies that international differences in nominal interest

rates equal the difference in expected inflation *plus* the expected percentage change in the real exchange rate.

Key Terms

Fisher effect, p. 396
law of one price, p. 389
monetary approach to the
   exchange rate, p. 392
nominal exchange rate, p. 412
nominal interest rate, p. 423
pricing to market, p. 406

purchasing power parity (PPP), p. 388
real appreciation, p. 414
real depreciation, p. 414
real exchange rate, p. 411
real interest rate, p. 423
relative PPP, p. 391

Problems

1. Suppose Russia's inflation rate is 100 percent over one year but the inflation rate in Switzerland is only 5 percent. According to relative PPP, what should happen over the year to the Swiss franc's exchange rate against the Russian ruble?

2. Discuss why it is often asserted that exporters suffer when their home currencies appreciate in real terms against foreign currencies and prosper when their home currencies depreciate in real terms.

3. Other things equal, how would you expect the following shifts to affect a currency's real exchange rate against foreign currencies?
   a. The overall level of spending doesn't change, but domestic residents decide to spend more of their income on nontraded products and less on tradables.
   b. Foreign residents shift their demand away from their own goods and toward the home country's exports.

4. Large-scale wars typically bring a suspension of international trading and financial activities. Exchange rates lose much of their relevance under these conditions, but once the war is over governments wishing to fix exchange rates face the problem of deciding what the new rates should be. The PPP theory has often been applied to this problem of postwar exchange rate realignment. Imagine that you are a British Chancellor of the Exchequer and World War I has just ended. Explain how you would figure out the dollar/pound exchange rate implied by PPP. When might it be a bad idea to use the PPP theory in this way?

5. In the late 1970s Britain seemed to have struck it rich. Having developed its North Sea oil-producing fields in earlier years, Britain suddenly found its real income higher as a result of a dramatic increase in world oil prices in 1979–1980. In the early 1980s, however, oil prices receded as the world economy slid into a deep recession and world oil demand faltered.

   On the following page, we show index numbers for the average real exchange rate of the pound against several foreign currencies. (Such average index numbers are called real *effective* exchange rates.) A rise in one of these numbers indicates a real *appreciation* of the pound, that is, an increase in Britain's price level relative to the average price level abroad measured in pounds. A fall is a real depreciation.

Real Effective Exchange Rate of the Pound Sterling, 1976–1984 (1980 = 100)

1976	1977	1978	1979	1980	1981	1982	1983	1984
68.3	66.5	72.2	81.4	100.0	102.8	100.0	92.5	89.8

Source: International Monetary Fund, *International Financial Statistics.* The real exchange rate measures are based on indexes of net output prices called value-added deflators.

Use the clues we have given about the British economy to explain the rise and fall of the pound's real effective exchange rate between 1978 and 1984. Pay particular attention to the role of nontradables.

6. Every week the Federal Reserve announces how quickly the money supply grew in the week ending ten days previously. (There is a ten-day delay because it takes that long to assemble data on bank deposits.) Economists have noticed that when the announced increase in the money supply is greater than expected, nominal interest rates *rise* just after the announcement; they *fall* when the market learns the money supply grew more slowly than expected. Two competing explanations of this phenomenon are (1) unexpectedly high money growth raises expected inflation and thus raises nominal interest rates through the Fisher effect; and (2) unexpectedly high money growth leads the market to expect future Fed action to reduce the money supply, causing a decrease in the amount of deposits supplied to the public by banks but no increase in expected inflation. How would you use data from the foreign exchange market to decide between these two hypotheses? (For an answer, see the paper by Engel and Frankel in Further Reading.)

7. Explain how permanent shifts in national real money-demand functions affect real and nominal exchange rates in the long run.

8. In Chapter 5 we discussed the effect of transfers between countries, such as the indemnity imposed on Germany after World War I. Use the theory developed in this chapter to discuss the mechanisms through which a permanent transfer from Poland to the Czech Republic would affect the real zloty/koruna exchange rate in the long run.

9. Continuing with the preceding problem, discuss how the transfer would affect the long-run *nominal* exchange rate between the two currencies.

10. A country imposes a tariff on imports from abroad. How does its action change the long-run real exchange rate between home and foreign currency? How is the long-run nominal exchange rate affected?

11. Imagine that two identical countries have restricted imports to identical levels, but one has done so using tariffs while the other has done so using quotas. After these policies are in place, both countries experience identical, balanced expansions of domestic spending. Where should the demand expansion cause a greater real currency appreciation, in the tariff-using country or in the quota-using country?

12. Explain how the nominal dollar/euro exchange rate would be affected (all else equal) by permanent changes in the expected rate of real depreciation of the dollar against the euro.

13. Can you suggest an event that would cause a country's nominal interest rate to rise and its currency to appreciate simultaneously, in a world of perfectly flexible prices?

14. Suppose that the expected real interest rate in the United States is 9 percent per year while that in Europe is 3 percent per year. What do you expect to happen to the real dollar/euro exchange rate over the next year?

15. In the short run of a model with sticky prices, a reduction in the money supply raises the nominal interest rate and appreciates the currency (see Chapter 14). What happens to the expected real interest rate? Explain why the subsequent path of the real exchange rate satisfies the real interest parity condition.

16. Discuss the following statement: "When a change in a country's nominal interest rate is caused by a rise in the expected real interest rate, the domestic currency appreciates. When the change is caused by a rise in expected inflation, the currency depreciates."

17. The difference between the nominal interest rate and the actual inflation rate is often called the ex post real interest rate (as opposed to the ex ante, or expected real interest rate). Figure 15-2 shows that between 1976 and 1980, the ex post real interest rate in Switzerland was usually positive while that in the United States was usually negative. Assume that people were able to forecast inflation accurately in both countries during these years. What would you guess about the dollar's strength against the Swiss franc in the foreign exchange market between 1976 and 1980? What do you think happened to the dollar/Swiss franc exchange rate in 1981–1982? Check your answer by looking up the history of the exchange rate. (See, for example. the International Monetary Fund's publication, *International Financial Statistics.)*

Further Reading

Gustav Cassel. *Post-War Monetary Stabilization.* New York: Columbia University Press, 1928. Applies the purchasing power parity theory of exchange rates in analyzing the monetary problems that followed World War I.

Devereux, Michael B. "Real Exchange Rates and Macroeconomics: Evidence and Theory." *Canadian Journal of Economics* 30 (November 1997), pp. 773–808. Reviews recent thinking on the determinants and effects of real exchange rates.

Rudiger Dornbusch. "Purchasing Power Parity," in *The New Palgrave Dictionary of Money & Finance,* Vol. 3. New York: Stockton Press, 1992, pp. 236–244. Examines the role of the purchasing power parity theory in international macroeconomics.

Rudiger Dornbusch. "The Theory of Flexible Exchange Rate Regimes and Macroeconomic Policy," in Jan Herin, Assar Lindbeck, and Johan Myhrman, eds. *Flexible Exchange Rates and Stabilization Policy.* Boulder, CO: Westview Press, 1977, pp. 123–143. Develops a long-run model of exchange rates incorporating traded and nontraded goods and services.

Charles Engel and Jeffrey Frankel. "Why Money Announcements Move Interest Rates: An Answer from the Foreign Exchange Market," in *Sixth West Coast Academic/Federal Reserve Economic Research Seminar* (Economic Review Conference Supplement). San Francisco: Federal Reserve Bank of San Francisco, 1983, pp. 1–26. Studies the link between Fed money announcements, interest rates, and the exchange rate.

Pinelopi Koujianou Goldberg and Michael M. Knetter. "Goods Prices and Exchange Rates: What Have We Learned?" *Journal of Economic Literature* 35 (September 1997), pp. 1243–1272. Excellent survey of micro-level evidence on the law of one price, exchange-rate pass-through, and pricing to market.

Lawrence E. Hinkle and Peter J. Montiel, eds. *Exchange Rate Misalignment: Concepts and Measurement for Developing Countries.* Oxford: Oxford University Press, 1999. Theory and empirical estimation of long-run equilibrium real exchange rates.

Irving B. Kravis. "Comparative Studies of National Incomes and Prices." *Journal of Economic Literature* 22 (March 1984), pp. 1–39. An account of the findings of a United Nations–sponsored research project that compared the real incomes and price levels of more than 100 countries.

Ronald I. McKinnon and Kenichi Ohno. *Dollar and Yen: Resolving Economic Conflict between the United States and Japan.* Cambridge, MA: MIT Press, 1997. Focuses on U.S.-Japan trade conflict as a causal force behind the yen's secular appreciation.

Robin Marris. "Comparing the Incomes of Nations: A Critique of the International Comparison Project." *Journal of Economic Literature* 22 (March 1984), pp. 40–57. A critical appraisal of the research described in the reading by Kravis.

Lloyd A. Metzler. "Exchange Rates and the International Monetary Fund," in *International Monetary Policies.* Postwar Economic Studies 7. Washington, D.C.: Board of Governors of the Federal Reserve System, 1947, pp. 1–45. The author applies purchasing power parity with skill and skepticism to evaluate the fixed exchange rates established by the International Monetary Fund after World War II.

Frederic S. Mishkin. *The Economics of Money, Banking and Financial Markets,* 6th edition. Boston: Addison Wesley, 2001. Chapter 5 discusses inflation and the Fisher effect.

Kenneth Rogoff. "The Purchasing Power Parity Puzzle." *Journal of Economic Literature* 34 (June 1996), pp. 647–668. Up-to-date critical survey of theory and empirical work.

Alan C. Stockman. "The Equilibrium Approach to Exchange Rates." *Federal Reserve Bank of Richmond Economic Review* 73 (March/April 1987), pp. 12–30. Theory and evidence on an equilibrium exchange rate model similar to the long-run model of this chapter.

John Williamson, ed. *Estimating Equilibrium Exchange Rates.* Washington, D.C.: Institute for International Economics, 1994. More essays on alternative approaches to calculating long-run real exchange rates in practice.

APPENDIX TO CHAPTER 15

The Fisher Effect, the Interest Rate, and the Exchange Rate under the Flexible-Price Monetary Approach

The monetary approach to exchange rates, which assumes that the prices of goods are perfectly flexible, implies that a country's currency depreciates when its nominal interest rates rise because of higher expected future inflation. This appendix supplies a detailed analysis of that important result.

Consider again the dollar/euro exchange rate, and imagine that the Federal Reserve raises the future rate of U.S. money-supply growth by the amount $\Delta\pi$. Figure 15A-1 provides a diagram that will help us keep track of how various markets respond to that change.

The lower right quadrant in the figure is our usual depiction of equilibrium in the U.S. money market. It shows that before the increase in U.S. money-supply growth, the nominal interest rate on dollars equals $R_\$^1$ (point 1). The Fisher effect tells us that a rise $\Delta\pi$ in the future rate of U.S. money-supply growth, all else equal, will raise the nominal interest rate on dollars to $R_\$^2 = R_\$^1 + \Delta\pi$ (point 2).

As the diagram shows, the rise in the nominal dollar interest rate reduces money demand and therefore requires an equilibrating fall in the real money supply. But the nominal money stock is unchanged in the short run because it is only the *future* rate of U.S. money-supply growth that has risen. What happens? Given the unchanged nominal money supply M_{US}^1, an upward jump in the U.S. price level, from P_{US}^1 to P_{US}^2, brings about the needed reduction in American real money holdings. The assumed flexibility of prices allows this jump to occur even in the short run.

To see the exchange rate response, we turn to the lower left quadrant. The monetary approach assumes purchasing power parity, implying that as P_{US} rises (while the European price level remains constant, which we assume), the dollar/euro exchange rate $E_{\$/€}$ must rise (a depreciation of the dollar). The lower left quadrant of Figure 15A-1 graphs the implied relationship between U.S. real money holdings, M_{US}/P_{US}, and the exchange rate, $E_{\$/€}$, given an unchanged *nominal* money supply in the United States and an unchanged European price level. Using PPP, we can write the equation graphed there (which is a downward-sloping *hyperbola*) as:

$$E_{\$/€} = P_{US}/P_E = \frac{(M_{US}/P_E)}{(M_{US}/P_{US})}.$$

This equation shows that the fall in the U.S. real money supply, from M_{US}^1/P_{US}^1 to M_{US}^1/P_{US}^2, is associated with a dollar depreciation in which the dollar/euro nominal exchange rate rises from $E_{\$/€}^1$ to $E_{\$/€}^2$.

The 45-degree line in the upper left quadrant of Figure 15A-1 allows you to translate the exchange-rate change given by the lower left quadrant to the vertical axis of the upper right

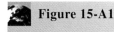

Figure 15-A1 | How a Rise in U.S. Monetary Growth Affects Dollar Interest Rates and the Dollar/Euro Exchange Rate When Goods Prices are Flexible

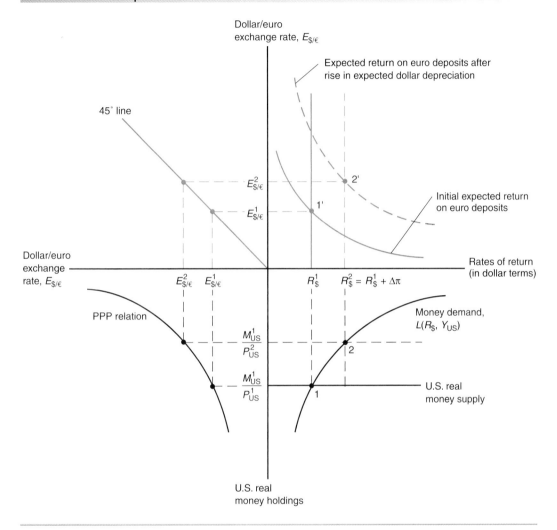

When goods prices are perfectly flexible, the money market equilibrium diagram (southeast quadrant) shows two effects of an increase, $\Delta\pi$, in the future rate of U.S. money-supply growth. The change (i) raises the dollar interest rate from $R^1_\$$ to $R^2_\$ = R^1_\$ + \Delta\pi$, in line with the Fisher effect, and (ii) causes the U.S. price level to jump from P^1_{US} to P^2_{US}. Money-market equilibrium therefore moves from point 1 to point 2. (Because M^1_{US} doesn't change immediately, the real U.S. money supply falls to M^1_{US}/P^2_{US}, bringing the real money supply into line with reduced money demand.) The PPP relationship in the southwest quadrant shows that the price level jump from P^1_{US} to P^2_{US} requires a depreciation of the dollar against the euro (the dollar/euro exchange rate moves up, from $E^1_{\$/€}$ to $E^2_{\$/€}$). In the foreign exchange market diagram (northeast quadrant), this dollar depreciation is shown as the move from point 1′ to point 2′. The dollar depreciates despite a rise in $R_\$$ because heightened expectations of future dollar depreciation against the euro cause an outward shift of the locus measuring the expected dollar return on euro deposits.

quadrant's diagram. The upper right quadrant contains our usual portrayal of equilibrium in the foreign exchange market.

There you can see that the dollar's depreciation against the euro is associated with a move in the foreign exchange market's equilibrium from point 1′ to point 2′. The picture shows why the dollar depreciates, despite the rise in $R_\$$. The reason is an outward shift in the downward-sloping schedule giving the expected dollar rate of return on euro deposits. Why does that schedule shift outward? Higher expected future monetary growth implies faster expected depreciation of the dollar against the euro, and therefore a rise in the attractiveness of euro deposits. It is that change in expectations that leads simultaneously to a rise in the nominal interest rate on dollars and to a depreciation of the dollar in the foreign exchange market.

To summarize, we cannot predict how a rise in the dollar interest rate will affect the dollar's exchange rate without knowing *why* the nominal interest rate has risen. In a flexible-price model in which the home nominal interest rate rises because of higher expected future money-supply growth, the home currency will depreciate, not appreciate, thanks to expectations of more rapid future depreciation.

C H A P T E R   1 6

Output and the
Exchange Rate
in the Short Run

In September 1992 Britain allowed the pound sterling to depreciate in the foreign exchange market. The country's net exports surged as a result, and Britain was lifted out of a recession without a rise in inflation. Ten years later, Argentina let its currency depreciate amidst economic chaos and continuing recession. What explains these sharply contrasting experiences? This chapter will help us to understand the complicated factors that cause output, exchange rates, and inflation to change by completing the macroeconomic model built in the last two chapters.

Chapters 14 and 15 presented the connections among exchange rates, interest rates, and price levels but always assumed that output levels were determined outside of the model. Those chapters give us only a partial picture of how macroeconomic changes affect an open economy because events that change exchange rates, interest rates, and price levels may also affect output. Now we complete the picture by examining how output and the exchange rate are determined in the short run.

Our discussion combines what we have learned about asset markets and the long-run behavior of exchange rates with a new element, a theory of how the output market adjusts to demand changes when product prices in the economy are themselves slow to adjust. As we learned in Chapter 14, institutional factors like long-term nominal contracts can give rise to "sticky" or slowly adjusting output market prices. By putting a short-run model of the output market together with our models of the foreign exchange and money markets (the asset markets), we build a model that explains the short-run behavior of all the important macroeconomic variables in an open economy. The long-run exchange rate model of the preceding chapter provides the framework that participants in the asset markets use to form their expectations about future exchange rates.

Because output changes may push the economy away from full employment, the links among output and other macroeconomic variables such as the merchandise trade balance and the current account are of great concern to economic policymakers. In the last part of this chapter we use our short-run model to examine how macroeconomic policy tools affect output and the current account, and how those tools can be used to maintain full employment. ●

Determinants of Aggregate Demand in an Open Economy

To analyze how output is determined in the short run when product prices are sticky, we introduce the concept of **aggregate demand** for a country's output. Aggregate demand is the amount of a country's goods and services demanded by households and firms throughout the world. Just as the output of an individual good or service depends in part on the demand for it, a country's overall short-run output level depends on the aggregate demand for its products. The economy is at full employment in the long run (by definition) because wages and the price level eventually adjust to ensure full employment. In the long run, domestic output therefore depends only on the available domestic supplies of factors of production such as labor and capital. As we will see, however, these productive factors can be over- or underemployed in the short run as a result of shifts in aggregate demand that have not yet had their full long-run effects on prices.

In Chapter 12 we learned that an economy's output is the sum of four types of expenditure that generate national income: consumption, investment, government purchases, and the current account. Correspondingly, aggregate demand for an open economy's output is the sum of consumption demand (C), investment demand (I), government demand (G), and net export demand, that is, the current account (CA). Each of these components of aggregate demand depends on various factors. In this section we examine the factors that determine consumption demand and the current account. We discuss government demand later in this chapter when we examine the effects of fiscal policy; for now we assume that G is given. To avoid complicating our model, we also assume that investment demand is given. The determinants of investment demand are incorporated into the model in Appendix I to this chapter.

Determinants of Consumption Demand

In this chapter we view the amount a country's residents wish to consume as depending on disposable income, Y^d (that is, national income less taxes, $Y - T$).[1] (C, Y, and T are all measured in terms of domestic output units.) With this assumption, a country's desired consumption level can be written as a function of disposable income:

$$C = C(Y^d).$$

Because each consumer naturally demands more goods and services as his or her real income rises, we expect consumption to increase as disposable income increases at the aggregate level, too. Thus, consumption demand and disposable income are positively related. When disposable income rises, however, consumption demand generally rises by *less* because part of the income increase is saved.

---

[1] A more complete model would allow other factors, such as real wealth and the real interest rate, to affect consumption plans. This chapter's Appendix II links the formulation here to the microeconomic theory of the consumer, which was the basis of the discussion in the appendix to Chapter 7.

Determinants of the Current Account

The current account balance, viewed as the demand for a country's exports less that country's own demand for imports, is determined by two main factors: the domestic currency's real exchange rate against foreign currency (that is, the price of a typical foreign expenditure basket in terms of domestic expenditure baskets) and domestic disposable income. (In reality, a country's current account depends on many other factors, such as the level of foreign expenditure, but for now we regard these other factors as being held constant.)[2]

We express a country's current account balance as a function of its currency's real exchange rate, $q = EP^*/P$, and of domestic disposable income, Y^d:

$$CA = CA(EP^*/P, Y^d).$$

As a reminder of the last chapter's discussion, note that the domestic currency prices of representative foreign and domestic expenditure baskets are, respectively, EP^* and P, where E (the nominal exchange rate) is the price of foreign currency in terms of domestic, P^* is the foreign price level, and P is the home price level. The *real* exchange rate q, defined as the price of the foreign basket in terms of the domestic one, is therefore EP^*/P. If, for example, the representative basket of European goods and services costs €40 (P^*), the representative U.S. basket costs $50 ($P$), and the dollar/euro exchange rate is $1.10 per euro ($E$), then the price of the European basket in terms of U.S. baskets is

$$EP^*/P = \frac{(1.10\ \$/€) \times (40\ €/\text{European basket})}{(50\ \$/\text{U.S. basket})}$$

$$= 0.88\ \text{U.S. basket/European basket}.$$

Real exchange rate changes affect the current account because they reflect changes in the prices of domestic goods and services relative to foreign. Disposable income affects the current account through its effect on total spending by domestic consumers. To understand how these real exchange rate and disposable income effects work, it is helpful to look separately at the demand for a country's exports, EX, and the demand for imports by the country's residents, IM. As we saw in Chapter 12 the current account is related to exports and imports by the identity

$$CA = EX - IM$$

when CA, EX, and IM all are measured in terms of domestic output.

---

[2] In Chapter 19 we study a two-country framework that takes account of how events in the domestic economy affect foreign output and how these changes in foreign output, in turn, feed back to the domestic economy. As the previous footnote observed, we are ignoring a number of factors (such as wealth and interest rates) that affect consumption along with disposable income. Since some part of any consumption change goes into imports, these omitted determinants of consumption also help to determine the current account. Following the convention of Chapter 12, we are also ignoring unilateral transfers in analyzing the current account balance.

How Real Exchange Rate Changes Affect the Current Account

You will recall that a representative domestic expenditure basket includes some imported products but places a relatively heavier weight on goods and services produced domestically. At the same time, the representative foreign basket is skewed toward goods and services produced in the foreign country. Thus a rise in the price of the foreign basket in terms of domestic baskets, say, will be associated with a rise in the relative price of foreign output in general relative to domestic.[3]

To determine how such a change in the relative price of national outputs affects the current account, other things equal, we must ask how it affects both EX and IM. If EP^*/P rises, for example, foreign products have become more expensive relative to domestic products: Each unit of domestic output now purchases fewer units of foreign output. Foreign consumers will respond to this price shift by demanding more of our exports. This response by foreigners will therefore raise EX and will tend to improve the domestic country's current account.

The effect of the same real exchange rate increase on IM is more complicated. Domestic consumers respond to the price shift by purchasing fewer units of the more expensive foreign products. Their response does not imply, however, that IM must fall. IM denotes the value of imports *measured in terms of domestic output,* and not the volume of foreign products imported: Because a rise in EP^*/P tends to raise the value of each unit of imports in terms of domestic output units, imports measured in domestic output units may rise as a result of a rise in EP^*/P even if imports decline when measured in foreign output units. IM can therefore rise or fall when EP^*/P rises, so the effect of a real exchange rate change on the current account CA is ambiguous.

Whether the current account improves or worsens depends on which effect of a real exchange rate change is dominant, the *volume effect* of consumer spending shifts on export and import quantities or the *value effect,* which changes the domestic output worth of a given volume of foreign imports. We assume for now that the volume effect of a real exchange rate change always outweighs the value effect, so that, other things equal, a real depreciation of the currency improves the current account and a real appreciation of the currency worsens the current account.[4]

While we have couched our discussion of real exchange rates and the current account in terms of consumers' responses, *producers'* responses are just as important and work in much the same way. When a country's currency depreciates in real terms, foreign firms will find that the country can supply intermediate production inputs more cheaply. These effects have become stronger as a result of the increasing tendency for multinational firms to locate different stages of their production processes in a variety countries. For example, the German auto manufacturer BMW can shift production from Germany to its Spartanburg, South Carolina plant if a dollar depreciation lowers the relative cost of producing in the

---

[3]The real exchange rate is being used here essentially as a convenient summary measure of the relative prices of domestic against foreign products. A more exact (but much more complicated) analysis would work explicitly with separate demand and supply functions for each country's nontradables and tradables but would lead to conclusions very much like those we reach below.

[4]This assumption requires that import and export demands be relatively *elastic* with respect to the real exchange rate. Appendix III to this chapter describes a precise condition, called the Marshall-Lerner condition, under which the assumption in the text will be valid. The appendix also examines empirical evidence on the time horizon over which the Marshall-Lerner condition holds.

United States. The production shift represents an increase in world demand for U.S. labor and output.

How Disposable Income Changes Affect the Current Account

The second factor influencing the current account is domestic disposable income. Since a rise in Y^d causes domestic consumers to increase their spending on *all* goods, including imports from abroad, an increase in disposable income worsens the current account, other things equal. (An increase in Y^d has no effect on export demand because we are holding foreign income constant and not allowing Y^d to affect it.)

Table 16-1 summarizes our discussion of how real exchange rate and disposable income changes influence the domestic current account.

The Equation of Aggregate Demand

We now combine the four components of aggregate demand to get an expression for total aggregate demand, denoted D:

$$D = C(Y - T) + I + G + CA(EP^*/P, Y - T),$$

where we have written disposable income Y^d as output, Y, less taxes, T. This equation shows that aggregate demand for home output can be written as a function of the real exchange rate, disposable income, investment demand, and government spending:

$$D = D(EP^*/P, Y - T, I, G).$$

We now want to see how aggregate demand depends on the real exchange rate and domestic GNP given the level of taxes, T, investment demand, I, and government purchases, G.

The Real Exchange Rate and Aggregate Demand

A rise in EP^*/P makes domestic goods and services cheaper relative to foreign goods and services and shifts both domestic and foreign spending from foreign goods to domestic goods. As a result, CA rises (as assumed in the previous section) and aggregate demand D therefore goes up. *A real depreciation of the home currency raises aggregate demand for home output, other things equal; a real appreciation lowers aggregate demand for home output.*

Table 16-1 | Factors Determining the Current Account

Change	Effect on current account, CA
Real exchange rate, $EP^*/P\uparrow$	$CA\uparrow$
Real exchange rate, $EP^*/P\downarrow$	$CA\downarrow$
Disposable income, $Y^d\uparrow$	$CA\downarrow$
Disposable income, $Y^d\downarrow$	$CA\uparrow$

Real Income and Aggregate Demand

The effect of domestic real income on aggregate demand is slightly more complicated. If taxes are fixed at a given level, a rise in Y represents an equal rise in disposable income Y^d. While this rise in Y^d raises consumption, it worsens the current account by raising home spending on foreign imports. The first of these effects raises aggregate demand, but the second lowers it. Since the increase in consumption is divided between higher spending on home products and higher spending on foreign imports, however, the first effect (the effect of disposable income on total consumption) is greater than the second (the effect of disposable income on import spending alone). Therefore, *a rise in domestic real income raises aggregate demand for home output, other things equal, and a fall in domestic real income lowers aggregate demand for home output.*

Figure 16-1 shows the relation between aggregate demand and real income Y for fixed values of the real exchange rate, taxes, investment demand, and government spending. As Y rises, consumption rises by a fraction of the increase in income. Part of this increase in consumption, moreover, goes into import spending. The effect of an increase in Y on the aggregate demand for home output is therefore smaller than the accompanying rise in consumption demand, which is smaller, in turn, than the increase in Y. We show this in Figure 16-1 by drawing the aggregate demand schedule with a slope less than 1. (The schedule intersects the vertical axis above the origin because investment, government, and foreign demand would make aggregate demand greater than zero, even in the hypothetical case of zero domestic output.)

How Output Is Determined In the Short Run

Having discussed the factors that influence the demand for an open economy's output, we now study how output is determined in the short run. We show in this section that the output market is in equilibrium when real output, Y, equals the aggregate demand for domestic output:

$$Y = D(EP^*/P,\ Y - T, I, G). \tag{16-1}$$

The equality of aggregate supply and demand therefore determines the short-run equilibrium output level.[5]

Our analysis of real output determination applies to the short run because we assume that the money prices of goods and services are *temporarily fixed.* As we will see later in the chapter, the short-run real output changes that occur when prices are temporarily fixed eventually cause price level changes that move the economy to its long-run equilibrium. In

---

[5] Superficially, equation (16-1), which may be written as $Y = C(Y^d) + I + G + CA(EP^*/P, Y^d)$, looks like the GNP identity we discussed in Chapter 12, $Y = C + I + G + CA$. How do the two equations differ? They differ in that (16-1) is an equilibrium condition, not an identity. As you will recall from Chapter 12, the investment quantity I appearing in the GNP identity includes *undesired* or involuntary inventory accumulation by firms, so that the GNP identity always holds as a matter of definition. The investment demand appearing in equation (16-1), however, is *desired* or planned investment. Thus, the GNP identity always holds but equation (16-1) holds only if firms are not unwillingly building up or drawing down inventories of goods.

Figure 16-1 | Aggregate Demand as a Function of Output

Aggregate demand is a function of the real exchange rate (EP^*/P), disposable income $(Y - T)$, investment demand (I), and government spending (G). If all other factors remain unchanged, a rise in output (real income), Y, increases aggregate demand. Because the increase in aggregate demand is less than the increase in output, the slope of the aggregate demand function is less than 1 (as indicated by its position within the 45-degree angle).

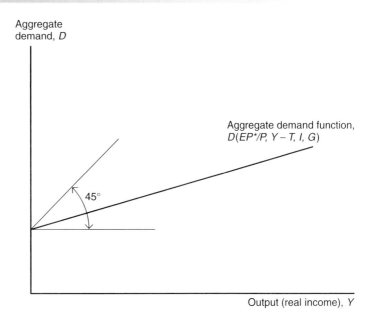

long-run equilibrium, factors of production are fully employed, the level of real output is completely determined by factor supplies, and the real exchange rate has adjusted to equate long-run real output to aggregate demand.[6]

The determination of national output in the short run is illustrated in Figure 16-2, where we again graph aggregate demand as a function of output for fixed levels of the real exchange rate, taxes, investment demand, and government spending. The intersection (at point 1) of the aggregate demand schedule and a 45-degree line drawn from the origin (the equation $D = Y$) gives us the unique output level Y^1 at which aggregate demand equals output.

Let's use Figure 16-2 to see why output tends to settle at Y^1 in the short run. At an output level of Y^2, aggregate demand (point 2) is higher than output. Firms therefore increase their production to meet this excess demand. (If they did not, they would have to meet the excess demand out of inventories, reducing investment below the desired level I.) Thus, output expands until national income reaches Y^1.

At point 3 there is an excess supply of domestic output and firms find themselves involuntarily accumulating inventories (involuntarily raising their investment spending above its desired level). As inventories start to build up, firms cut back on production; only when output has fallen to Y^1 will firms be content with their level of production. Once again, output settles at point 1, the point at which output exactly equals aggregate demand.

---

[6] Thus, equation (16-1) also holds in long-run equilibrium, but the equation determines the long-run real exchange rate when Y is at its long-run value.

Figure 16-2 | The Determination of Output in the Short Run

In the short run output settles at Y^1 (point 1), where aggregate demand, D^1, equals aggregate output, Y^1.

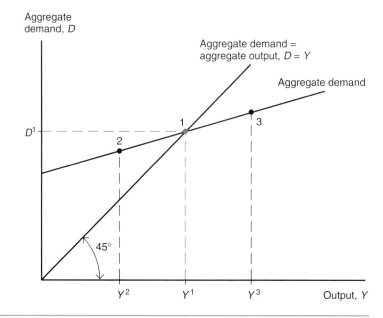

In this short-run equilibrium, consumers, firms, the government, and foreign buyers of domestic products are all able to realize their desired expenditures with no output left over.

Output Market Equilibrium in the Short Run: The *DD* Schedule

Now that we understand how output is determined for a given real exchange rate EP^*/P, let's look at how the exchange rate and output are simultaneously determined in the short run. To understand this process, we need two elements. The first element, developed in this section, is the relationship between output and the exchange rate (the *DD* schedule) that must hold when the output market is in equilibrium. The second element, developed in the next section, is the relationship between output and the exchange rate that must hold when the home money market and the foreign exchange market (the asset markets) are in equilibrium. As we will see, both elements are necessary because the economy as a whole is in equilibrium only when both the output market and the asset markets are in equilibrium.

Output, the Exchange Rate, and Output Market Equilibrium

Figure 16-3 illustrates the relationship between the exchange rate and output implied by output market equilibrium. Specifically, the figure illustrates the effect of a depreciation of the domestic currency against foreign currency (that is, a rise in E from E^1 to E^2) for fixed values of the domestic price level, P, and the foreign price level, P^*. With fixed price levels

Figure 16-3 Output Effect of a Currency Depreciation with Fixed Output Prices

A rise in the exchange rate from E^1 to E^2 (a currency depreciation) raises aggregate demand to *aggregate demand* (E^2) and output to Y^2, all else equal.

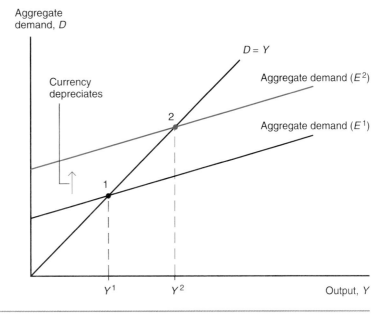

at home and abroad, the rise in the nominal exchange rate makes foreign goods and services more expensive relative to domestic goods and services. This relative price change shifts the aggregate demand schedule upward.

The fall in the relative price of domestic output shifts the aggregate demand schedule upward because at each level of domestic output, the demand for domestic products is now higher. Output expands from Y^1 to Y^2 as firms find themselves faced with excess demand at initial production levels.

Although we have considered the effect of a change in E with P and P^* held fixed, it is straightforward to analyze the effects of changes in P or P^* on output. *Any rise in the real exchange rate EP^*/P (whether due to a rise in E, a rise in P^*, or a fall in P) will cause an upward shift in the aggregate demand function and an expansion of output, all else equal.* (A rise in P^*, for example, has effects qualitatively identical to those of a rise in E.) *Similarly, any fall in EP^*/P, regardless of its cause (a fall in E, a fall in P^*, or a rise in P), will cause output to contract, all else equal.* (A rise in P, with E and P^* held fixed, for example, makes domestic products more expensive relative to foreign products, reduces aggregate demand for domestic output, and causes output to fall.)

Deriving the DD Schedule

If we assume P and P^* are fixed in the short run, a depreciation of the domestic currency (a rise in E) is associated with a rise in domestic output, Y, while an appreciation (a fall in E) is associated with a fall in Y. This association provides us with one of the two relationships between E and Y needed to describe the short-run macroeconomic behavior of an open

Figure 16-4 | Deriving the *DD* Schedule

The *DD* schedule (shown in the lower panel) slopes upward because a rise in the exchange rate from E^1 to E^2, all else equal, causes output to rise from Y^1 to Y^2.

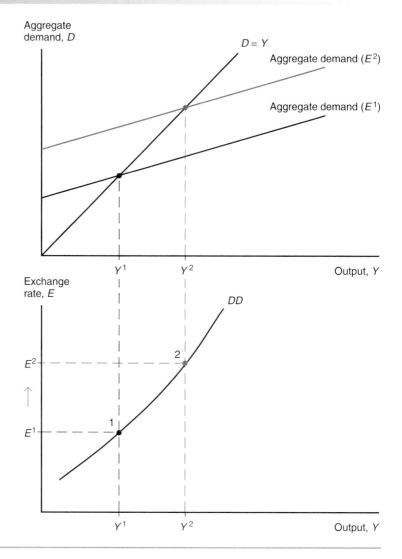

economy. We summarize this relationship by the **DD schedule**, which shows all combinations of output and the exchange rate for which the output market is in short-run equilibrium (aggregate demand = aggregate output).

Figure 16-4 shows how to derive the *DD* schedule, which relates *E* and *Y* when *P* and *P** are fixed. The upper part of the figure reproduces the result of Figure 16-3 (a depreciation of the domestic currency shifts the aggregate demand function upward, causing output to rise). The *DD* schedule in the lower part graphs the resulting relationship between the exchange rate and output (given that *P* and *P** are held constant). Point 1 on the *DD* schedule gives the output level Y^1 at which aggregate demand equals aggregate supply when the exchange rate is E^1. A depreciation of the currency to E^2 leads to the higher output level Y^2 according to the figure's upper part, and this information allows us to locate point 2 on DD.

Factors that Shift the *DD* Schedule

A number of factors affect the position of the DD schedule: the levels of government demand, taxes, and investment; the domestic and foreign price levels; variations in domestic consumption behavior; and the foreign demand for home output. To understand the effects of shifts in each of these factors, we must study how the DD schedule shifts when it changes. In the following discussions we assume that all other factors remain fixed.

1. *A change in G.* Figure 16-5 shows the effect on DD of a rise in government purchases from G^1 to G^2, given a fixed exchange rate of E^0. As shown in the upper part of the figure, the exchange rate E^0 leads to an equilibrium output level Y^1 at the initial level of government demand; so point 1 is one point on DD^1.

An increase in G causes the aggregate demand schedule in the upper part of the figure to shift upward. Everything else remaining unchanged, output increases from Y^1 to Y^2. Point 2 in the bottom part shows the higher level of output Y^2 at which aggregate demand and supply are now equal, *given an unchanged exchange rate of E^0.* Point 2 is on a new DD curve, DD^2.

For any given exchange rate, the level of output equating aggregate demand and supply is higher after the increase in G. This implies that *an increase in G causes DD to shift to the right, as shown in Figure 16-5. Similarly, a decrease in G causes DD to shift to the left.*

The method and reasoning we have just used to study how an increase in G shifts the DD curve can be applied to all the cases that follow. Here we summarize the results. To test your understanding use diagrams similar to Figure 16-5 to illustrate how the economic factors listed below change the curves.

2. *A change in T.* Taxes, *T*, affect aggregate demand by changing disposable income, and thus consumption, for any level of *Y*. It follows that an increase in taxes causes the aggregate demand function of Figure 16-1 to shift *downward* given the exchange rate *E*. Since this effect is the opposite of that of an increase in *G*, an increase in *T* must cause the DD schedule to shift leftward. Similarly, a fall in *T* causes a rightward shift of DD.

3. *A change in I.* An increase in investment demand has the same effect as an increase in *G:* The aggregate demand schedule shifts upward and DD shifts to the right. A fall in investment demand shifts DD to the left.

4. *A change in P.* Given *E* and P^*, an increase in *P* makes domestic output more expensive relative to foreign output and lowers net export demand. The DD schedule shifts to the left as aggregate demand falls. A fall in *P* makes domestic goods cheaper and causes a rightward shift of DD.

5. *A change in P^*.* Given *E* and *P*, a rise in P^* makes foreign goods and services relatively more expensive. Aggregate demand for domestic output therefore rises and DD shifts to the right. Similarly, a fall in P^* causes DD to shift to the left.

6. *A change in the consumption function.* Suppose residents of the home economy suddenly decide they want to consume more and save less at each level of disposable income. If the increase in consumption spending is not devoted entirely to imports from abroad, aggregate demand for domestic output rises and the aggregate demand schedule shifts upward for any given exchange rate *E*. This implies a shift to the right of the DD

Figure 16-5 | Government Demand and the Position of the *DD* Schedule

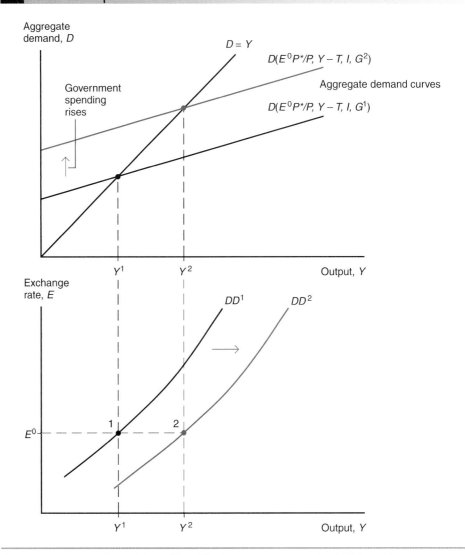

A rise in government demand from G^1 to G^2 raises output at every level of the exchange rate. The change therefore shifts *DD* to the right.

schedule. An autonomous fall in consumption (if it is not entirely due to a fall in import demand) shifts *DD* to the left.

7. *A demand shift between foreign and domestic goods.* Suppose there is no change in the domestic consumption function but domestic and foreign residents suddenly decide to devote more of their spending to goods and services produced in the home country. If home disposable income and the real exchange rate remain the same, this shift in demand *improves* the current account by raising exports and lowering imports.

The aggregate demand schedule shifts upward and *DD* therefore shifts to the right. The same reasoning shows that a shift in world demand away from domestic products and toward foreign products causes *DD* to shift to the left.

You may have noticed that a simple rule allows you to predict the effect on *DD* of any of the disturbances we have discussed: *Any disturbance that raises aggregate demand for domestic output shifts the DD schedule to the right; any disturbance that lowers aggregate demand for domestic output shifts the DD schedule to the left.*

Asset Market Equilibrium in the Short Run: The *AA* Schedule

We have now derived the first element in our account of short-run exchange rate and income determination, the relation between the exchange rate and output that is consistent with the equality of aggregate demand and supply. That relation is summarized by the *DD* schedule, which shows all exchange rate and output levels at which the output market is in short-run equilibrium. As we noted at the beginning of the preceding section, however, equilibrium in the economy as a whole requires equilibrium in the asset markets as well as in the output market, and there is no reason in general why points on the *DD* schedule should lead to asset market equilibrium.

To complete the story of short-run equilibrium, we therefore introduce a second element to ensure that the exchange rate and output level consistent with output market equilibrium are also consistent with asset market equilibrium. The schedule of exchange rate and output combinations that are consistent with equilibrium in the domestic money market and the foreign exchange market is called the *AA* **schedule**.

Output, the Exchange Rate, and Asset Market Equilibrium

In Chapter 13 we studied the interest parity condition, which states that the foreign exchange market is in equilibrium only when the expected rates of return on domestic and foreign currency deposits are equal. In Chapter 14 we learned how the interest rates that enter the interest parity relationship are determined by the equality of real money supply and real money demand in national money markets. Now we combine these asset market equilibrium conditions to see how the exchange rate and output must be related when all asset markets simultaneously clear. Because the focus for now is on the domestic economy, the foreign interest rate is taken as given.

For a given expected future exchange rate, E^e, the interest parity condition describing foreign exchange market equilibrium is equation (13-2),

$$R = R^* + (E^e - E)/E,$$

where R is the interest rate on domestic currency deposits and R^* is the interest rate on foreign currency deposits. In Chapter 14 we saw that the domestic interest rate satisfying the interest parity condition must also equate the real domestic money supply (M^s/P) to aggregate real money demand (see equation (14-4)):

$$M^s/P = L(R, Y).$$

You will recall that aggregate real money demand $L(R, Y)$ rises when the interest rate falls because a fall in R makes interest-bearing nonmoney assets less attractive to hold. (Conversely, a rise in the interest rate lowers real money demand.) A rise in real output, Y, increases real money demand by raising the volume of monetary transactions people must carry out (and a fall in real output reduces real money demand by reducing transactions needs).

We now use the diagrammatic tools developed in Chapter 14 to study the changes in the exchange rate that must accompany output changes so that asset markets remain in equilibrium. Figure 16-6 shows the equilibrium domestic interest rate and exchange rate associated with the output level Y^1 for a given nominal money supply, M^s, a given domestic price level, P, a given foreign interest rate, R^*, and a given value of the expected future exchange rate, E^e. In the lower part of the figure, we see that with real output at Y^1 and the real money supply at M^s/P, the interest rate R^1 clears the home money market (point 1) while the exchange rate E^1 clears the foreign exchange market (point 1'). The exchange rate E^1 clears the foreign exchange market because it equates the expected rate of return on foreign deposits, measured in terms of domestic currency, to R^1.

A rise in output from Y^1 to Y^2 raises aggregate real money demand from $L(R, Y^1)$ to $L(R, Y^2)$, shifting out the entire money demand schedule in the lower part of Figure 16-6. This shift, in turn, raises the equilibrium domestic interest rate to R^2 (point 2). With E^e and R^* fixed, the domestic currency must appreciate from E^1 to E^2 to bring the foreign exchange market back into equilibrium at point 2'. The domestic currency appreciates by just enough that the increase in the rate at which it is expected to *depreciate* in the future offsets the increased interest rate advantage of home currency deposits. *For asset markets to remain in equilibrium, a rise in domestic output must be accompanied by an appreciation of the domestic currency, all else equal, and a fall in domestic output must be accompanied by a depreciation.*

Deriving the AA Schedule

While the *DD* schedule plots exchange rates and output levels at which the output market is in equilibrium, the *AA* schedule relates exchange rates and output levels that keep the money and foreign exchange markets in equilibrium. Figure 16-7 shows the *AA* schedule. From Figure 16-6 we see that for any output level, Y, there is a unique exchange rate, E, satisfying the interest parity condition (given the real money supply, the foreign interest rate, and the expected future exchange rate). Our previous reasoning tells us that other things equal, a rise in Y^1 to Y^2 will produce an appreciation of the domestic currency, that is, a fall in the exchange rate from E^1 to E^2. The *AA* schedule therefore has a negative slope, as shown.

Factors that Shift the AA Schedule

Five factors cause the *AA* schedule to shift: changes in the domestic money supply, M^s; changes in the domestic price level, P; changes in the expected future exchange rate, E^e; changes in the foreign interest rate, R^*; and shifts in the aggregate real money demand schedule.

1. *A change in M^s.* For a fixed level of output, an increase in M^s causes the domestic currency to depreciate in the foreign exchange market, all else equal (that is, E rises).

Figure 16-6 Output and the Exchange Rate in Asset Market Equilibrium

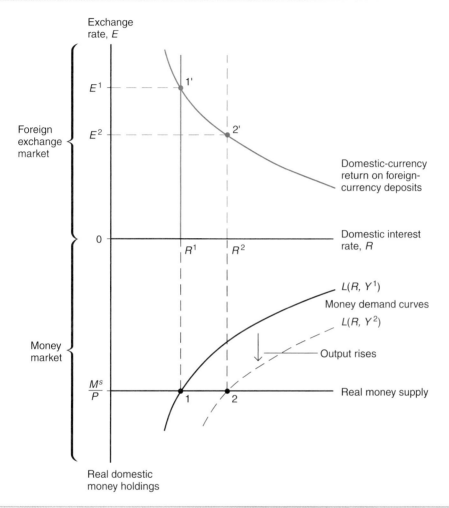

For the asset (foreign exchange and money) markets to remain in equilibrium, a rise in output must be accompanied by an appreciation of the currency, all else equal.

Since for each level of output the exchange rate E is higher after the rise in M^s, the rise in M^s causes AA to shift *upward*. Similarly, a fall in M^s causes AA to shift *downward*.

2. *A change in P.* An increase in P reduces the *real* money supply and drives the interest rate upward. Other things (including Y) equal, this rise in the interest rate causes E to fall. The effect of a rise in P is therefore a downward shift of AA. A fall in P results in an upward shift of AA.

3. *A change in E^e.* Suppose participants in the foreign exchange market suddenly revise their expectations about the exchange rate's future value so that E^e rises. Such a

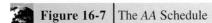

Figure 16-7 | The *AA* Schedule

The asset market equilibrium schedule *AA* slopes downward because a rise in output from Y^1 to Y^2, all else equal, causes a rise in the home interest rate and a domestic currency appreciation from E^1 to E^2.

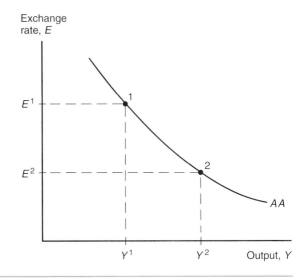

change shifts the curve in the top part of Figure 16-6 (which measures the expected domestic currency return on foreign currency deposits) to the right. The rise in E^e therefore causes the domestic currency to depreciate, other things equal. Because the exchange rate producing equilibrium in the foreign exchange market is higher after a rise in E^e, given output, *AA* shifts upward when a rise in the expected future exchange rate occurs. It shifts downward when the expected future exchange rate falls.

4. *A change in R^*.* A rise in R^* raises the expected return on foreign currency deposits and therefore shifts the downward-sloping schedule at the top of Figure 16-6 to the right. Given output, the domestic currency must depreciate to restore interest parity. A rise in R^* therefore has the same effect on *AA* as a rise in E^e: It causes an upward shift. A fall in R^* results in a downward shift of *AA*.

5. *A change in real money demand.* Suppose domestic residents decide they would prefer to hold lower real money balances at each output level and interest rate. (Such a change in asset-holding preferences is a *reduction in money demand*.) A reduction in money demand implies an inward shift of the aggregate real money demand function $L(R, Y)$ for any fixed level of Y, and it thus results in a lower interest rate and a rise in E. A reduction in money demand therefore has the same effect as an increase in the money supply, in that it shifts *AA* upward. The opposite disturbance of an increase in money demand would shift *AA* downward.

Short-Run Equilibrium for an Open Economy: Putting the *DD* and *AA* Schedules Together

By assuming that output prices are temporarily fixed, we have derived two separate schedules of exchange rate and output levels: the *DD* schedule, along which the output market is in equi-

Figure 16-8 Short-Run Equilibrium: The Intersection of *DD* and *AA*

The short-run equilibrium of the economy occurs at point 1, where the output market (whose equilibrium points are summarized by the *DD* curve) and asset market (whose equilibrium points are summarized by the *AA* curve) simultaneously clear.

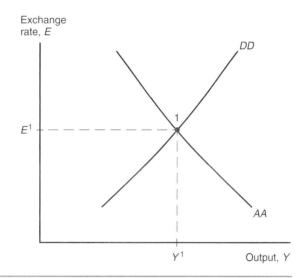

library, and the *AA* schedule, along which the asset markets are in equilibrium. A short-run equilibrium for the economy as a whole must lie on *both* schedules because such a point must bring about equilibrium simultaneously in the output and asset markets. We can therefore find the economy's short-run equilibrium by finding the intersection of the *DD* and *AA* schedules. Once again, it is the assumption that output prices are temporarily fixed that makes this intersection a *short-run* equilibrium. The analysis in this section continues to assume that the foreign interest rate R^* and the expected future exchange rate E^e also are fixed.

Figure 16-8 combines the *DD* and *AA* schedules to locate short-run equilibrium. The intersection of *DD* and *AA* at point 1 is the only combination of exchange rate and output consistent with both the equality of aggregate demand and aggregate supply *and* asset market equilibrium. The short-run equilibrium levels of the exchange rate and output are therefore E^1 and Y^1.

To convince yourself that the economy will indeed settle at point 1, imagine that the economy is instead at a position like point 2 in Figure 16-9. At point 2, which lies above *AA* and *DD*, both the output and asset markets are out of equilibrium. Because *E* is so high relative to *AA,* the rate at which *E* is expected to fall in the future is also high relative to the rate that would maintain interest parity. The high expected future appreciation rate of the domestic currency implies that the expected domestic currency return on foreign deposits is below that on domestic deposits, so there is an excess demand for the domestic currency in the foreign exchange market. The high level of *E* at point 2 also makes domestic goods cheap for foreign buyers (given the goods' domestic-currency prices), causing an excess demand for output at that point.

The excess demand for domestic currency leads to an immediate fall in the exchange rate from E^2 to E^3. This appreciation equalizes the expected returns on domestic and foreign deposits and places the economy at point 3 on the asset market equilibrium curve *AA*. But

Figure 16-9 | How the Economy Reaches Its Short-Run Equilibrium

Because asset markets adjust very quickly, the exchange rate jumps immediately from point 2 to point 3 on *AA*. The economy then moves to point 1 along *AA* as output rises to meet aggregate demand.

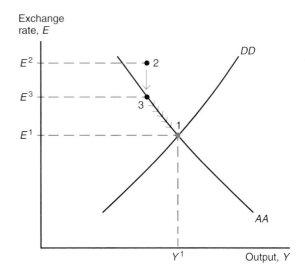

since point 3 is above the *DD* schedule, there is still excess demand for domestic output. As firms raise production to avoid depleting their inventories, the economy travels along *AA* to point 1, where aggregate demand and supply are equal. Because asset prices can jump immediately while changes in production plans take some time, the asset markets remain in continual equilibrium even while output is changing.

The exchange rate falls as the economy approaches point 1 along *AA* because rising national output causes money demand to rise, pushing the interest rate steadily upward. (The currency must appreciate steadily to lower the expected rate of future domestic currency appreciation and maintain interest parity.) Once the economy has reached point 1 on *DD*, aggregate demand equals output and producers no longer face involuntary inventory depletion. The economy therefore settles at point 1, the only point at which the output *and* asset markets clear.

Temporary Changes in Monetary and Fiscal Policy

Now that we have seen how the economy's short-run equilibrium is determined, we can study how shifts in government macroeconomic policies affect output and the exchange rate. Our interest in the effects of macroeconomic policies stems from their usefulness in counteracting economic disturbances that cause fluctuations in output, employment, and inflation. In this section we learn how government policies can be used to maintain full employment in open economies.

We concentrate on two types of government policy, **monetary policy**, which works through changes in the money supply, and **fiscal policy**, which works through changes in government spending or taxes.[7] To avoid the complications that would be introduced by ongoing inflation, however, we do not look at situations in which the money supply grows over time. Thus, the only type of monetary policies we will study explicitly are one-shot increases or decreases in money supplies.[8]

In this section we examine *temporary* policy shifts, shifts that the public expects to be reversed in the near future. The expected future exchange rate, E^e, is now assumed to equal the long-run exchange rate discussed in Chapter 15, that is, the exchange rate that prevails once full employment is reached and domestic prices have adjusted fully to past disturbances in the output and asset markets. In line with this interpretation, a temporary policy change does *not* affect the long-run expected exchange rate, E^e.

We assume throughout that events in the economy we are studying do not influence the foreign interest rate, R^*, or price level, P^*, and that the domestic price level, P, is fixed in the short run.

Monetary Policy

The short-run effect of a temporary increase in the domestic money supply is shown in Figure 16-10. An increased money supply shifts AA^1 upward to AA^2 but does not affect the position of DD. The upward shift of the asset market equilibrium schedule moves the economy from point 1, with exchange rate E^1 and output Y^1, to point 2, with exchange rate E^2 and output Y^2. An increase in the money supply causes a depreciation of the domestic currency, an expansion of output, and therefore an increase in employment.

We can understand the economic forces causing these results by recalling our earlier discussions of asset market equilibrium and output determination. At the initial output level Y^1 and given the fixed price level, an increase in money supply must push down the home interest rate, R. We have been assuming the monetary change is temporary and does not affect the expected future exchange rate, E^e, so to preserve interest parity in the face of a decline in R (given that the foreign interest rate, R^*, does not change), the exchange rate must depreciate immediately to create the expectation that the home currency will appreciate in the future at a faster rate than was expected before R fell. The immediate depreciation of the domestic currency, however, makes home products cheaper relative to foreign products. There is therefore an increase in aggregate demand, which must be matched by an increase in output.

Fiscal Policy

As we saw earlier, expansionary fiscal policy can take the form of an increase in government spending, a cut in taxes, or some combination of the two that raises aggregate demand. A temporary fiscal expansion (which does not affect the expected future exchange rate) therefore shifts the DD schedule to the right but does not move AA.

---

[7] Other policies, such as commercial policies (tariffs, quotas, etc.), have macroeconomic side effects. Such policies, however, are not used routinely for purposes of macroeconomic stabilization, so we do not discuss them in this chapter. (A problem at the end of this chapter does ask you to think about the macroeconomic effects of a tariff.)

[8] You can extend the results below to a setting with ongoing inflation by thinking of the exchange rate and price level changes we describe as departures from time paths along which E and P trend upward at constant rates.

Figure 16-10 | Effects of a Temporary Increase in the Money Supply

By shifting AA^1 upward, a temporary increase in the money supply causes a currency depreciation and a rise in output.

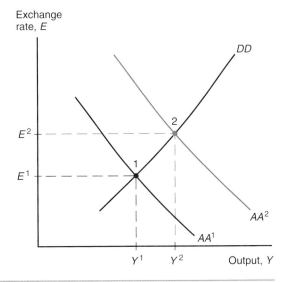

Figure 16-11 shows how expansionary fiscal policy affects the economy in the short run. Initially the economy is at point 1, with an exchange rate E^1 and output Y^1. Suppose the government decides to spend $5 billion to develop a new space shuttle. This one-time increase in government purchases moves the economy to point 2, causing the currency to appreciate to E^2 and output to expand to Y^2. The economy would respond in a similar way to a temporary cut in taxes.

What economic forces produce the movement from point 1 to point 2? The increase in output caused by the increase in government spending raises the transactions demand for real money holdings. Given the fixed price level, this increase in money demand pushes the interest rate, R, upward. Because the expected future exchange rate, E^e, and the foreign interest rate, R^*, have not changed, the domestic currency must appreciate to create the expectation of a subsequent depreciation just large enough to offset the higher international interest rate difference in favor of domestic currency deposits.

Policies to Maintain Full Employment

The analysis of this section can be applied to the problem of maintaining full employment in open economies. Because temporary monetary expansion and temporary fiscal expansion both raise output and employment, they can be used to counteract the effects of temporary disturbances that lead to recession. Similarly, disturbances that lead to overemployment can be offset through contractionary macroeconomic policies.

Figure 16-12 illustrates this use of macroeconomic policy. Suppose the economy's initial equilibrium is at point 1, where output equals its full-employment level, denoted Y^f. Suddenly there is a temporary shift in consumer tastes away from domestic products. As we saw earlier in this chapter, such a shift is a decrease in aggregate demand for domestic

Figure 16-11 | Effects of a Temporary Fiscal Expansion

By shifting DD^1 to the right, a temporary fiscal expansion causes a currency appreciation and a rise in output.

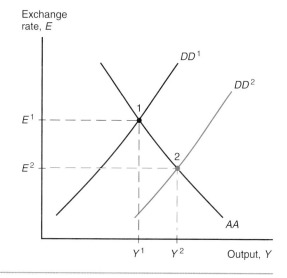

Figure 16-12 | Maintaining Full Employment After a Temporary Fall in World Demand for Domestic Products

A temporary fall in world demand shifts DD^1 to DD^2 reducing output from Y^f to Y^2 and causing the currency to depreciate from E^1 to E^2 (point 2). Temporary fiscal expansion can restore full employment (point 1) by shifting the DD schedule back to its original position. Temporary monetary expansion can restore full employment (point 3) by shifting AA^1 to AA^2. The two policies differ in their exchange rate effects: The fiscal policy restores the currency to its previous value (E^1); the monetary policy causes the currency to depreciate further to E^3.

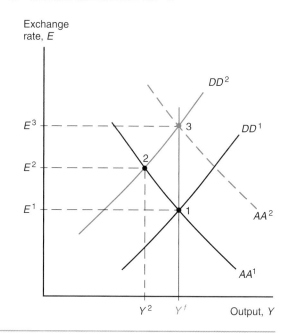

Figure 16-13 | Policies to Maintain Full Employment After a Money-Demand Increase

After a temporary money-demand increase (shown by the shift from AA^1 to AA^2) either an increase in the money supply or temporary fiscal ease can be used to maintain full employment. The two policies have different exchange rate effects: The monetary policy restores the exchange rate back to E^1, the fiscal policy leads to greater appreciation (E^3).

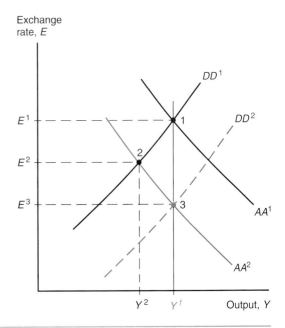

goods, and it causes the curve DD^1 to shift leftward, to DD^2. At point 2, the new short-run equilibrium, the currency has depreciated to E^2 and output, at Y^2, is below its full-employment level and the economy is in a recession. Because the shift in preferences is assumed to be temporary, it does not affect E^e, so there is no change in the position of AA^1.

To restore full employment, the government may use monetary or fiscal policy, or both. A temporary fiscal expansion shifts DD^2 back to its original position, restoring full employment and returning the exchange rate to E^1. A temporary money supply increase shifts the asset market equilibrium curve to AA^2 and places the economy at point 3, a move that restores full employment but causes the home currency to depreciate even further.

Another possible cause of recession is a temporary increase in the demand for money, illustrated in Figure 16-13. An increase in money demand pushes up the domestic interest rate and appreciates the currency, thereby making domestic goods more expensive and causing output to contract. Figure 16-13 shows this asset market disturbance as the downward shift of AA^1 to AA^2, which moves the economy from its initial full-employment equilibrium at point 1 to point 2.

Expansionary macroeconomic policies can again restore full employment. A temporary money supply increase shifts the AA curve back to AA^1 and moves the economy back to its initial position at point 1. This temporary increase in money supply completely offsets the increase in money demand by giving domestic residents the additional money they desire to hold. Temporary fiscal expansion shifts DD^1 to DD^2 and restores full employment at point 3. But the move to point 3 involves an even greater appreciation of the currency.

Inflation Bias and Other Problems of Policy Formulation

The apparent ease with which full employment is maintained in our model is misleading, and you should not come away from our discussion of policy with the idea that it is easy to keep the macroeconomy on a steady course. Here are just a few of the many problems that can arise:

1. Sticky nominal prices not only give governments the power to raise output when it is abnormally low, but also may tempt them to create a politically useful economic boom, say, just before a close election. This temptation causes problems when workers and firms anticipate it in advance, for they will raise wage demands and prices in the expectation of expansionary policies. The government will then find itself in the position of having to use expansionary policy tools merely to prevent the recession that higher domestic prices otherwise would cause! As a result, macroeconomic policy will display an **inflation bias**, leading to high inflation but no average gain in output. The inflation bias problem has led to a search for institutions, for example, central banks that operate independently of the government in power, that might convince market actors that government policies will not be used in a short-sighted way, at the expense of long-term price stability. Many central banks throughout the world now seek to reach announced target levels of (low) inflation. Chapters 20 and 22 will discuss some of these efforts.[9]

2. In practice it is sometimes hard to be sure whether a disturbance to the economy originates in the output or asset markets. Yet a government concerned about the exchange rate effect of its policy response needs to know this before it can choose between monetary and fiscal policy.

3. Real-world policy choices are frequently determined by bureaucratic necessities rather than by detailed consideration of whether shocks to the economy are real (that is, they originate in the output market) or monetary. Shifts in fiscal policy often can be made only after lengthy legislative deliberation, while monetary policy, in contrast, is usually exercised by the central bank. To avoid procedural delays, governments are likely to respond to disturbances by changing monetary policy even when a shift in fiscal policy would be more appropriate.

4. Another problem with fiscal policy is its impact on the government budget. A tax cut or spending increase may lead to a government budget deficit that must sooner or later be closed by a fiscal reversal. Unfortunately, there is no guarantee that the government will have the political will to synchronize these actions with the state of the business cycle. The state of the electoral cycle may be more important, as we have seen.

5. Policies that appear to act swiftly in our simple model operate in reality with lags of varying length. At the same time, the difficulty of evaluating the size and persistence

---

[9] For a clear and detailed discussion of the inflation bias problem, see Chapter 15 in Andrew B. Abel and Ben S. Bernanke, *Macroeconomics,* 3rd ed. (Reading, MA: Addison-Wesley, 1998). The inflation bias problem can arise even when the government's policies are not politically motivated, as Abel and Bernanke explain. The basic idea is that when factors like minimum wage laws keep output inefficiently low by lowering employment, monetary expansion that raises employment may move the economy toward a more efficient use of its total resources. The government might wish to reach a better resource allocation purely on the grounds that such a change potentially benefits everyone in the economy.

of a given shock makes it hard to know precisely how much monetary or fiscal medicine to administer. These uncertainties force policymakers to base their actions on forecasts and hunches that may turn out to be quite wide of the mark.

Permanent Shifts in Monetary and Fiscal Policy

A permanent policy shift affects not only the current value of the government's policy instrument (the money supply, government spending, or taxes) but also the *long-run* exchange rate. This in turn affects expectations about future exchange rates. Because these changes in expectations have a major influence on the exchange rate prevailing in the short run, the effects of permanent policy shifts differ from those of temporary shifts. In this section we look at the effects of permanent changes in monetary and fiscal policy, in both the short and long run.[10]

To make it easier to grasp the long-run effects of policies, we assume that the economy is initially at a long-run equilibrium position and that the policy changes we examine are the only economic changes that occur (our usual "other things equal" clause). These assumptions mean that the economy starts out at full employment with the exchange rate at its long-run level and with no change in the exchange rate expected. In particular, we know that the domestic interest rate must initially equal the foreign rate, R^*.

A Permanent Increase in the Money Supply

Figure 16-14 shows the short-run effects of a permanent increase in the money supply on an economy initially at its full-employment output level Y^f (point 1). As we saw earlier, even a temporary increase in M^s causes the asset market equilibrium schedule to shift upward from AA^1 to AA^2. Because the increase in M^s is now permanent, however, it also affects the exchange rate expected for the future, E^e. Chapter 14 showed how a permanent increase in the money supply affects the long-run exchange rate: A permanent increase in M^s must ultimately lead to a proportional rise in E. Therefore, the rise in M^s causes E^e, the expected future exchange rate, to rise proportionally.

Because a rise in E^e accompanies a *permanent* increase in the money supply, the upward shift of AA^1 to AA^2 is greater than that caused by an equal, but transitory, increase. At point 2, the economy's new short-run equilibrium, Y and E are both higher than they would be were the change in the money supply temporary. (Point 3 shows the equilibrium that might result from a temporary increase in M^s.)

Adjustment to a Permanent Increase in the Money Supply

The increase in the money supply shown in Figure 16-14 is not reversed by the central bank, so it is natural to ask how the economy is affected *over time*. At the short-run equilibrium, shown as point 2 in Figure 16-14, output is above its full-employment level and labor and machines are working overtime. Upward pressure on the price level develops as workers

---

[10]You may be wondering whether a permanent change in fiscal policy is always possible. For example, if a government starts with a balanced budget, doesn't a fiscal expansion lead to a deficit, and thus require an eventual fiscal contraction? Problem 3 at the end of this chapter suggests an answer.

Figure 16-14 | Short-Run Effects of a Permanent Increase in the Money Supply

A permanent increase in the money supply, which shifts AA^1 to AA^2 and moves the economy from point 1 to point 2, has stronger effects on the exchange rate and output than an equal temporary increase, which moves the economy only to point 3.

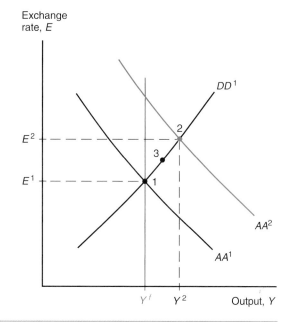

demand higher wages and producers raise prices to cover their increasing production costs. Chapter 14 showed that while an increase in the money supply must eventually cause all money prices to rise in proportion, it has no lasting effect on output, relative prices, or interest rates. Over time, the inflationary pressure that follows a permanent money supply expansion pushes the price level to its new long-run value and returns the economy to full employment.

Figure 16-15 will help you visualize the adjustment back to full employment. Whenever output is greater than its full-employment level Y^f and productive factors are working overtime, the price level P is rising to keep up with rising production costs. Although the DD and AA schedules are drawn for a constant price level P, we have seen how increases in P cause them to shift. A rise in P makes domestic goods more expensive relative to foreign goods, discouraging exports and encouraging imports. A rising domestic price level therefore causes DD^1 to shift to the left over time. Because a rising price level steadily reduces the real money supply over time, AA^2 also travels to the left as prices rise.

The DD and AA schedules stop shifting only when they intersect at the full-employment output level Y^f; as long as output differs from Y^f, the price level will change and the two schedules will continue to shift. The schedules' final positions are shown in Figure 16-15 as DD^2 and AA^3. At point 3, their intersection, the exchange rate, E, and the price level, P, have risen in proportion to the increase in the money supply, as required by the long-run neutrality of money. (AA^2 does not shift all the way back to its original position because E^e is permanently higher after a permanent increase in the money supply: It too has risen by the same percentage as M^s.)

Figure 16-15 | Long-Run Adjustment to a Permanent Increase in the Money Supply

After a permanent money-supply increase, a steadily increasing price level shifts the DD and AA schedules to the left until a new long-run equilibrium (point 3) is reached.

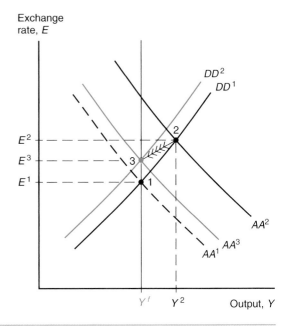

Notice that along the adjustment path between the initial short-run equilibrium (point 2) and the long-run equilibrium (point 3), the domestic currency actually appreciates (from E^2 to E^3) following its initial sharp depreciation (from E^1 to E^2). This exchange rate behavior is an example of the *overshooting* phenomenon discussed in Chapter 14, in which the exchange rate's initial response to some change is greater than its long-run response.[11]

We can draw on our conclusions to describe the proper policy response to a permanent monetary disturbance. A permanent increase in money demand, for example, can be offset with a permanent increase in the money supply of equal magnitude. Such a policy maintains full employment, but because the price level would fall in the absence of the policy, the policy will not have inflationary consequences. Instead, monetary expansion can move the economy straight to its long-run, full-employment position. Keep in mind, however, that it is hard in practice to diagnose the origin or persistence of a particular shock to the economy.

A Permanent Fiscal Expansion

A permanent fiscal expansion not only has an immediate impact in the output market but also affects the asset markets through its impact on long-run exchange rate expectations.

---

[11]While the exchange rate initially overshoots in the case shown in Figure 16-15, overshooting does not have to occur in all circumstances.

Figure 16-16 | Effects of a Permanent Fiscal Expansion
Changing the Capital Stock

Because a permanent fiscal expansion changes exchange-rate expectations, it shifts AA^1 leftward as it shifts DD^1 to the right. The effect on output (point 2) is nil if the economy starts in long-run equilibrium. A comparable *temporary* fiscal expansion, in contrast, would leave the economy at point 3.

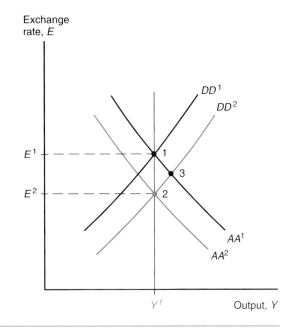

Figure 16-16 shows the short-run effects of a government decision to spend an extra $5 bil-lion a year on its space travel program forever. As before, the direct effect of this rise in G on aggregate demand causes DD^1 to shift right to DD^2. But because the increase in gov-ernment demand for domestic goods and services is permanent in this case, it causes a long-run appreciation of the currency, as we saw in Chapter 15. The resulting fall in E^e pushes the asset market equilibrium schedule AA^1 downward to AA^2. Point 2, where the new schedules DD^2 and AA^2 intersect, is the economy's short-run equilibrium, and at that point the currency has appreciated to E^2 from its initial level while output is unchanged at Y^f.

The important result illustrated in Figure 16-16 is that when a fiscal expansion is permanent, the additional currency appreciation caused by the shift in exchange rate expec-tations reduces the policy's expansionary effect on output. Without this additional expectations effect due to the permanence of the fiscal change, equilibrium would initially be at point 3, with higher output and a smaller appreciation. The greater the downward shift of the asset market equilibrium schedule, the greater the appreciation of the currency. This appreciation "crowds out" aggregate demand for domestic products by making them more expensive rela-tive to foreign products.

Figure 16-16 is drawn to show a case in which fiscal expansion, contrary to what you might have guessed, has no net effect on output. This case is not, however, a special one; in fact, it is inevitable under the assumptions we have made. The argument that establishes this point requires five steps; by taking the time to understand it you will solidify your under-standing of the ground we have covered so far:

1. As a first step, convince yourself (perhaps by reviewing Chapter 14) that because the fiscal expansion does not affect the money supply, M^s, or the long-run values of the domestic interest rate (which equals the foreign interest rate) and output (Y^f), it can have no impact on the long-run price level.

2. Next, recall our assumption that the economy starts out in long-run equilibrium with the domestic interest rate, R, just equal to the foreign rate, R^*, and output equal to Y^f. Observe also that the fiscal expansion leaves the real money supply, M^s/P, unchanged in the short run (neither the numerator nor the denominator changes).

3. Now imagine, contrary to what Figure 16-16 shows, that output *did* rise above Y^f. Because M^s/P doesn't change in the short run (step 2), the domestic interest rate, R, would have to rise above its initial level of R^* to keep the money market in equilibrium. Since the foreign interest rate remains at R^*, however, a rise in Y to any level above Y^f implies an expected *depreciation* of the domestic currency (by interest parity).

4. Notice that there is something wrong with this conclusion: We already know (from step 1) that the long-run price level is not affected by the fiscal expansion, so people can expect a nominal domestic currency depreciation just after the policy change only if the currency depreciates in *real* terms as the economy returns to long-run equilibrium. Such a real depreciation, by making domestic products relatively cheap, would only worsen the initial situation of overemployment that we have imagined to exist, and thus would prevent output from ever actually returning to Y^f.

5. Finally, conclude that the apparent contradiction is resolved only if output does *not* rise at all after the fiscal policy move. The only logical possibility is that the currency appreciates right away to its new long-run value. This appreciation crowds out just enough net export demand to leave output at the full-employment level despite the higher level of G.

Notice that this exchange rate change, which allows the output market to clear at full employment, leaves the asset markets in equilibrium as well. Since the exchange rate has jumped to its new long-run value, R remains at R^*. With output also at Y^f, however, the long-run money market equilibrium condition $M^s/P = L(R^*, Y^f)$ still holds, as it did before the fiscal action. So our story hangs together: The currency appreciation that a permanent fiscal expansion provokes immediately brings the asset markets as well as the output market to positions of long-run equilibrium.

We conclude that *if the economy starts at long-run equilibrium, a permanent change in fiscal policy has no net effect on output. Instead, it causes an immediate and permanent exchange rate jump that offsets exactly the fiscal policy's direct effect on aggregate demand.*

The box on p. 461 gives a recent example of how exchange rate expectations driven by fiscal policy can affect the economy.

Macroeconomic Policies and the Current Account

Policymakers are often concerned about the level of the current account. As we will discuss more fully in Chapter 18, an excessive imbalance in the current account—either a surplus or a deficit—may have undesirable long-run effects on national welfare. Large external imbalances may also generate political pressures for government restrictions on trade. It is

THE DOLLAR EXCHANGE RATE AND THE U.S. ECONOMIC SLOWDOWN OF 2000–2001

The prolonged U.S. economic expansion of the 1990s ended in the autumn of 2000 as U.S. industrial output began a steep decline. The Federal Reserve, which had been raising interest rates as a brake on inflation, abruptly changed course. Between January and November 2001, the Fed lowered its target rate of interest (the "federal funds" rate, which is the rate at which banks make overnight loans to each other) from 6.5 to 2 percent.

With aggregate demand for U.S. goods falling and interest rates falling at the same time, a depreciation of the dollar would seem to be a foregone conclusion. Yet that is not what happened. As the figure on p. 462 shows, the dollar, which had been appreciating prior to the slowdown, did indeed fall after the initial interest rate cuts, but then returned to its upward trend early in 2001. (In the figure, we have defined the average dollar exchange rate against a group of major currencies so that an increase is an appreciation.) The unexpected strengthening of the dollar weakened the demand for U.S products further at a time when manufacturing output was contracting sharply.

In terms of our model, the dollar's appreciation could only be explained by a simultaneous, and significant, expected future appreciation of the dollar. At least two factors pointed in that direc-

tion. First, George W. Bush had narrowly won the presidential election of 2000 on a platform promising a substantial tax cut. The expectation of future fiscal expansion therefore was one factor propelling the dollar's rise. Second, the United States had been the world's most dynamic economy in the 1990s, and with the U.S. economy in trouble, prospects elsewhere looked at least as bleak. As one chief investment officer told the *New York Times,* "Foreigners know that if the United States is in trouble, then their own economies will be in worse trouble, because the U.S. is the global engine of growth. Holding dollars is the safest place to be."*

The dollar was falling again by August 2001 but the September 11 terrorist attacks on New York and Washington caused an appreciation despite another interest rate cut by the Fed. The two factors influencing expectations of future exchange rates were basically the same as those operating at the start of President Bush's administration nine months earlier. The military and security response to the attack was sure to involve a large fiscal expansion. In addition, markets realized that even though it was the United States that had been attacked, major industrial economies abroad were even more vulnerable to disruption.

*See "A Strong Dollar Clouds Prospects for Quick Rebound," *New York Times,* July 8, 2001, p. 1.

---

therefore important to know how monetary and fiscal policies aimed at domestic objectives affect the current account.

Figure 16-17 shows how the *DD-AA* model can be extended to illustrate the effects of macroeconomic policies on the current account. In addition to the *DD* and *AA* curves, the figure contains a new curve, labeled *XX,* which shows combinations of the exchange rate and output at which the current account balance would be equal to some desired level, say $CA(EP^*/P, Y - T) = X$. The curve slopes upward because, other things equal, a rise in output encourages spending on imports and thus worsens the current account if it is not accompanied by a currency depreciation. Since the actual level of *CA* can differ from *X,* the economy's short-run equilibrium does *not* have to be on the *XX* curve.

The central feature of Figure 16-17 is that *XX* is *flatter* than *DD.* The reason is seen by asking how the current account changes as we move up along the *DD* curve from point 1,

U.S. Macroeconomic Data, February 2000–November 2001

Industrial production, average exchange rate
(indexes, February 2000 = 100)

Interest rate
(Federal Reserve target rate)

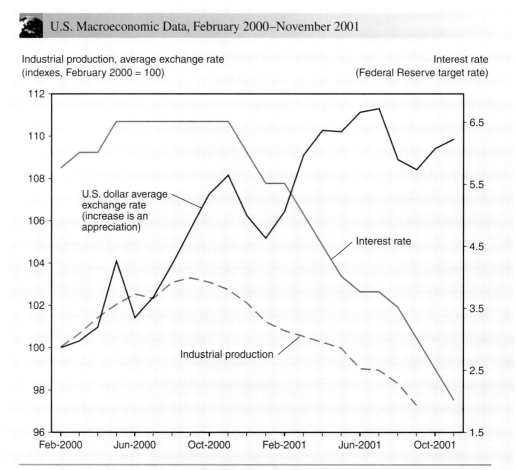

As U.S. output began a sharp decline in the autumn of 2000, the Federal Reserve lowered interest rates aggressively but the dollar continued to appreciate.

where all three curves intersect (so that, initially, $CA = X$). As we increase Y in moving up along DD, the *domestic* demand for domestic output rises by less than the rise in output itself (since some income is saved and some spending falls on imports). Along DD, however, *total aggregate demand has to equal supply.* To prevent an excess supply of home output, E therefore must rise sharply enough along DD to make export demand rise faster than imports. In other words, net foreign demand—the current account—must rise sufficiently along DD as output rises to take up the slack left by domestic saving. Thus to the right of point 1, DD is above the XX curve, where $CA > X$; similar reasoning shows that to the left of point 1 DD lies below the XX curve (where $CA < X$).

The current account effects of macroeconomic policies can now be examined. As shown earlier, an increase in the money supply, for example, shifts the economy to a position like point 2, expanding output and depreciating the currency. Since point 2 lies above XX, the

Figure 16-17 | How Macroeconomic Policies Affect the Current Account

Along the curve XX, the current account is constant at the level $CA = X$. Monetary expansion moves the economy to point 2 and thus raises the current account balance. Temporary fiscal expansion moves the economy to point 3 while permanent fiscal expansion moves it to point 4; in either case the current account balance falls.

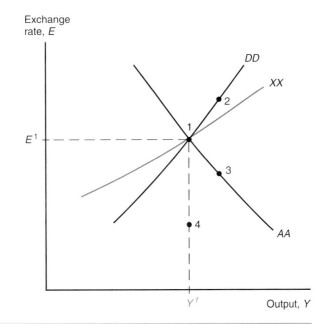

current account has improved as a result of the policy action. *Monetary expansion causes the current account balance to increase in the short run.*

Consider next a temporary fiscal expansion. This action shifts *DD* to the right and moves the economy to point 3 in the figure. Because the currency appreciates and income rises, there is a deterioration in the current account. A permanent fiscal expansion has the additional effect of shifting *AA* leftward, producing an equilibrium at point 4. Like point 3, point 4 is below *XX*, so once again the current account worsens. *Expansionary fiscal policy reduces the current account balance.*

Gradual Trade Flow Adjustment and Current Account Dynamics

An important assumption underlying the *DD-AA* model is that other things equal, a real depreciation of the home currency immediately improves the current account while a real appreciation causes the current account immediately to worsen. In reality, however, the behavior underlying trade flows may be far more complex than we have so far suggested, involving dynamic elements—on the supply as well as the demand side—that lead the current account to adjust only gradually to exchange rate changes. In this section we discuss some dynamic factors that seem important in explaining actual patterns of current account adjustment and indicate how their presence might modify the predictions of our model.

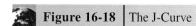

Figure 16-18 | The J-Curve

The J-curve describes the time lag with which a real currency depreciation improves the current account.

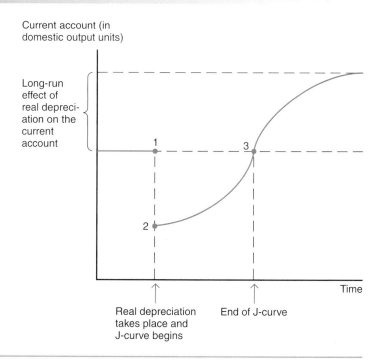

The J-Curve

It is sometimes observed that a country's current account *worsens* immediately after a real currency depreciation and begins to improve only some months later, contrary to the assumption we made in deriving the *DD* curve. If the current account initially worsens after a depreciation, its time path, shown in Figure 16-18, has an initial segment reminiscent of a J and therefore is called the **J-curve**.

The current account, measured in domestic output, can deteriorate sharply right after a real currency depreciation (the move from point 1 to point 2 in the figure) because most import and export orders are placed several months in advance. In the first few months after the depreciation, export and import volumes therefore may reflect buying decisions that were made on the basis of the old real exchange rate: The primary effect of the depreciation is to raise the value of the precontracted level of imports in terms of domestic products. Because exports measured in domestic output do not change while imports measured in domestic output rise, there is an initial fall in the current account, as shown.

Even after the old export and import contracts have been fulfilled, it still takes time for new shipments to adjust fully to the relative price change. On the production side, producers of exports may have to install additional plants and equipment and hire new workers. To the extent that imports consist of intermediate materials used in domestic manufacturing, import adjustment will also occur gradually as importers switch to new production techniques that economize on intermediate inputs. There are lags on the consumption side as well. To expand significantly foreign consumption of domestic exports, for example, it may be necessary to build new retailing outlets abroad, a time-consuming process.

The result of these lags in adjustment is the gradually improving current account shown in Figure 16-18 as the move from point 2 to point 3. Only after point 3 does the current account exceed its predepreciation level. Eventually, the increase in the current account tapers off as the adjustment to the real depreciation is completed.

Empirical evidence indicates for most industrial countries a J-curve lasting more than six months but less than a year. Thus, point 3 in the figure is typically reached within a year of the real depreciation and the current account continues to improve afterward.[12]

The existence of a significant J-curve effect forces us to modify some of our earlier conclusions, at least for the short run of a year or less. Monetary expansion, for example, can depress output initially by depreciating the home currency. In this case, it may take some time before an increase in the money supply results in an improved current account and therefore in higher aggregate demand.

If expansionary monetary policy actually depresses output in the short run, the domestic interest rate will need to fall farther than it normally would to clear the home money market. Correspondingly, the exchange rate will overshoot more sharply to create the larger expected domestic currency appreciation required for foreign exchange market equilibrium. By introducing an additional source of overshooting, J-curve effects amplify the volatility of exchange rates.

Exchange Rate Pass-Through and Inflation

Our discussion of how the current account is determined in the *DD-AA* model has assumed that nominal exchange rate changes cause proportional changes in real exchange rates in the short run. Because the *DD-AA* model assumes that the nominal output prices P and P^* cannot suddenly jump, movements in the real exchange rate, $q = EP^*/P$, correspond perfectly in the short run to movements in the nominal rate, E. In reality, however, even the short-run correspondence between nominal and real exchange rate movements, while quite close, is less than perfect. To understand fully how *nominal* exchange rate movements affect the current account in the short run, we need to examine more closely the linkage between the nominal exchange rate and the prices of exports and imports.

The domestic currency price of foreign output is the product of the exchange rate and the foreign currency price, or EP^*. We have assumed until now that when E rises, for example, P^* remains fixed so that the domestic currency price of goods imported from abroad rises in proportion. The percentage by which import prices rise when the home currency depreciates by one percent is known as the degree of **pass-through** from the exchange rate to import prices. In the version of the *DD-AA* model we studied above, the degree of pass-through is 1; any exchange rate change is passed through completely to import prices.

Contrary to this assumption, however, exchange rate pass-through can be incomplete. One possible reason for incomplete pass-through is international market segmentation, which allows imperfectly competitive firms to price to market by charging different prices for the same product in different countries (recall Chapter 15). A large foreign firm supplying automobiles to the United States may be so worried about losing market share that

---

[12]See the discussion of Table 16AIII-1 in Appendix III.

it does not immediately raise its U S. prices by 10 percent when the dollar depreciates by 10 percent, despite the fact that its revenue from American sales, measured in its own currency, will decline. Similarly, the firm may hesitate to lower its U.S. prices by 10 percent after a dollar appreciation of that size because it can thereby earn higher profits without investing resources immediately in expanding its shipments to the United States. In either case the firm may wait to find out if the currency movement reflects a definite trend before making price and production commitments that are costly to undo. In practice, many U.S. import prices tend to rise by only around half of a typical dollar depreciation over the following year.

We thus see that while a permanent nominal exchange rate change may be fully reflected in import prices in the long run, the degree of pass-through may be far less than 1 in the short run. Incomplete pass-through will have complicated effects, however, on the timing of current account adjustment. On the one hand, the short-run J-curve effect of a nominal currency change will be dampened by a low responsiveness of import prices to the exchange rate. On the other hand, incomplete pass-through implies that currency movements have less-than-proportional effects on the relative prices determining trade volumes. The failure of relative prices to adjust quickly will in turn be accompanied by a slow adjustment of trade volumes.

Notice also how the link between nominal and real exchange rates may be further weakened by *domestic* price responses. In highly inflationary economies, for example, it is difficult to alter the real exchange rate EP^*/P simply by changing the nominal rate E, because the resulting increase in aggregate demand quickly sparks domestic inflation, which in turn raises P. To the extent that a country's export prices rise when its currency depreciates, any favorable effect on its competitive position in world markets will be dissipated. Such price increases, however, like partial pass-through, may weaken the J-curve.

Summary

1. The *aggregate demand* for an open economy's output consists of four components, corresponding to the four components of GNP: consumption demand, investment demand, government demand, and the current account (net export demand). An important determinant of the current account is the real exchange rate, the ratio of the foreign price level (measured in domestic currency) to the domestic price level.

2. Output is determined in the short run by the equality of aggregate demand and aggregate supply. When aggregate demand is greater than output, firms increase production to avoid unintended inventory depletion. When aggregate demand is less than output, firms cut back production to avoid unintended accumulation of inventories.

3. The economy's short-run equilibrium occurs at the exchange rate and output level where—given the price level, the expected future exchange rate, and foreign economic conditions—aggregate demand equals aggregate supply and the asset markets are in equilibrium. In a diagram with the exchange rate and real output on its axes, the short-run equilibrium can be visualized as the intersection of an upward-sloping *DD* schedule, along which the output market clears, and a downward-sloping *AA* schedule, along which the asset markets clear.

4. A temporary increase in the money supply, which does not alter the long-run expected exchange rate, causes a depreciation of the currency and a rise in output. Temporary fiscal expansion also results in a rise in output, but it causes the currency to appreciate. *Monetary policy* and *fiscal policy* can be used by the government to offset the effects of disturbances to output and employment.

5. Permanent shifts in the money supply, which do alter the long-run expected exchange rate, cause sharper exchange rate movements and therefore have stronger short-run effects on output than transitory shifts. If the economy is at full employment, a permanent increase in the money supply leads to a rising price level that ultimately reverses the effect on the real exchange rate of the nominal exchange rate's initial depreciation. In the long run, output returns to its initial level and all money prices rise in proportion to the increase in the money supply.

6. Because permanent fiscal expansion changes the long-run expected exchange rate, it causes a sharper currency appreciation than an equal temporary expansion. If the economy starts out in long-run equilibrium, the additional appreciation makes domestic goods and services so expensive that the resulting "crowding out" of net export demand nullifies the policy's effect on output and employment. In this case, a permanent fiscal expansion has no expansionary effect at all.

7. A major practical problem is to ensure that the government's ability to stimulate the economy does not tempt it to gear policy to short-term political goals, thus creating an *inflation bias*. Other problems include the difficulty in identifying the sources or durations of economic changes and time lags in implementing policies.

8. If exports and imports adjust gradually to real exchange rate changes, the current account may follow a *J-curve* pattern after a real currency depreciation, first worsening and then improving. If such a J-curve exists, currency depreciation may have a contractionary initial effect on output, and exchange rate overshooting will be amplified. Limited exchange rate *pass-through,* along with domestic price increases, may reduce the effect of a nominal exchange rate change on the real exchange rate.

Key Terms

AA schedule, p. 445
aggregate demand, p. 434
DD schedule, p. 442
fiscal policy, p. 450

inflation bias, p. 455
J-curve, p. 464
monetary policy, p. 450
pass-through, p. 465

Problems

1. How does the *DD* schedule shift if there is a decline in investment demand?

2. Suppose the government imposes a tariff on all imports. Use the *DD-AA* model to analyze the effects this measure would have on the economy. Analyze both temporary and permanent tariffs.

3. Imagine that Congress passes a constitutional amendment requiring the U.S. government to maintain a balanced budget at all times. Thus, if the government wishes to change government spending, it must change taxes by the same amount, that is, $\Delta G = \Delta T$ always. Does the constitutional amendment imply that the government

can no longer use fiscal policy to affect employment and output? (Hint: Analyze a "balanced-budget" increase in government spending, one that is accompanied by an equal tax hike.)

4. Suppose there is a permanent fall in private aggregate demand for a country's output (a downward shift of the entire aggregate demand schedule). What is the effect on output? What government policy response would you recommend?

5. How does a permanent cut in taxes affect the current account? What about a permanent increase in government spending? Reread the first Case Study in Chapter 12 and see if your answer accurately reflects the U.S. experience in the early 1980s.

6. If a government initially has a balanced budget but then cuts taxes, it is running a deficit that it must somehow finance. Suppose people think the government will finance its deficit by printing the extra money it now needs to cover its expenditures. Would you still expect the tax cut to cause a currency appreciation?

7. You observe that a country's currency depreciates but its current account worsens at the same time. What data might you look at to decide whether you are witnessing a J-curve effect? What other macroeconomic change might bring about a currency depreciation coupled with a deterioration of the current account, even if there is no J-curve?

8. A new government is elected and announces that once it is inaugurated, it will increase the money supply. Use the *DD-AA* model to study the economy's response to this announcement.

9. Many economists put part of the blame for the persistent U.S. current account deficit of the late 1980s on the apparently small size of the relative price change between U.S. imports and exports. The first Case Study in Chapter 12, however, linked the slow current account adjustment to private and government saving behavior. Try to give a unified account of the current account data, reconciling both price and expenditure effects.

10. How would you draw the *DD-AA* diagram when the current account's response to exchange rate changes follows a J-curve? Use this modified diagram to examine the effects of temporary and permanent changes in monetary and fiscal policy.

11. What does the Marshall-Lerner condition look like if the country whose real exchange rate changes does *not* start out with a current account of zero? (The Marshall-Lerner condition is derived in Appendix III under the "standard" assumption of an initially balanced current account.)

12. Our model takes the price level P as given in the short run, but in reality the currency appreciation caused by a permanent fiscal expansion might cause P to fall a bit by lowering some import prices. If P can fall slightly as a result of a permanent fiscal expansion, is it still true that there are no output effects? (As above, assume an initial long-run equilibrium.)

13. Suppose that interest parity does not hold exactly, but that the true relationship is $R = R* + (E^e - E)/E + \rho$ where ρ is a term measuring the differential riskiness of domestic versus foreign deposits. Suppose a permanent rise in domestic government spending, by creating the prospect of future government deficits, also raises ρ, that is, makes domestic currency deposits more risky. Evaluate the policy's output effects in this situation.

14. If an economy does *not* start out at full employment, is it still true that a permanent change in fiscal policy has no current effect on output?

15. See if you can retrace the steps in the five-step argument on page 460 to show that a permanent fiscal expansion cannot cause output to *fall*.

Further Reading

Victor Argy and Michael G. Porter. "The Forward Exchange Market and the Effects of Domestic and External Disturbances Under Alternative Exchange Rate Systems." *International Monetary Fund Staff Papers* 19 (November 1972), pp. 503–532. Advanced analysis of a macroeconomic model similar to the one in this chapter.

Victor Argy and Joanne K. Salop. "Price and Output Effects of Monetary and Fiscal Policies under Flexible Exchange Rates." *International Monetary Fund Staff Papers* 26 (June 1979), pp. 224–256. The effects of macroeconomic policies under alternative institutional assumptions about wage indexation and the wage-price adjustment process in general.

C. Fred Bergsten. *International Adjustment and Financing: The Lessons of 1985–1991.* Washington, D.C.: Institute for International Economics, 1991. Analysis and debate on the behavior of industrial-economy current accounts.

Ralph C. Bryant et al., eds. *Empirical Macroeconomics for Interdependent Economies.* Washington, D.C.: Brookings Institution, 1988. This study compares what 12 leading econometric models predict about the domestic and foreign effects of individual countries' macroeconomic policies.

Rudiger Dornbusch. "Exchange Rate Expectations and Monetary Policy." *Journal of International Economics* 6 (August 1976), pp. 231–244. A formal examination of monetary policy and the exchange rate in a model with a J-curve.

Rudiger Dornbusch and Paul Krugman. "Flexible Exchange Rates in the Short Run." *Brookings Papers on Economic Activity* 3:1976, pp. 537–575. Theory and evidence on short-run macroeconomic adjustment under floating exchange rates.

Peter Hooper and Jaime Marquez. "Exchange Rates, Prices, and External Adjustment in the United States and Japan." in Peter B. Kenen, ed. *Understanding Interdependence: The Macroeconomics of the Open Economy.* Princeton: Princeton University Press, 1995. Surveys empirical work on the macroeconomic determinants of trade balances.

Robert A. Mundell. *International Economics,* Chapter 17. New York: Macmillan, 1968. A classic account of macroeconomic policy effects under floating exchange rates.

Subramanian Rangan and Robert Z. Lawrence. *A Prism on Globalization.* Washington, D.C.: Brookings Institution, 1999. An examination of multinational firms' responses to exchange rate movements.

APPENDIX 1 TO CHAPTER 16

The *IS-LM* Model and the *DD-AA* Model

In this appendix we examine the relationship between the *DD-AA* model of the chapter and another model frequently used to answer questions in international macroeconomics, the *IS-LM* model. The *IS-LM* model generalizes the *DD-AA* model by allowing the real domestic interest rate to affect aggregate demand.

The diagram usually used to analyze the *IS-LM* model has the nominal interest rate and output, rather than the nominal exchange rate and output, on its axes. Like the *DD-AA* diagram, the *IS-LM* diagram determines the short-run equilibrium of the economy as the intersection of two individual market equilibrium curves, called *IS* and *LM*. The *IS* curve is the schedule of nominal interest rates and output levels at which the output and foreign exchange markets are in equilibrium, while the *LM* curve shows points at which the money market is in equilibrium.[13]

The *IS-LM* model assumes that investment, and some forms of consumer purchases (such as purchases of autos and other durable goods), are negatively related to the expected real interest rate. When the expected real interest rate is low, firms find it profitable to borrow and undertake investment plans. (The appendix to Chapter 7 presented a model of this link between investment and the real interest rate.) A low expected real interest rate also makes it more profitable to carry inventories rather than alternative assets. For both these reasons, we would expect investment to rise when the expected real interest rate falls. Similarly, because consumers find borrowing cheap and saving unattractive when the real interest rate is low, interest-responsive consumer purchases also rise when the real interest rate falls. As the next appendix shows, however, theoretical arguments as well as the evidence suggest the consumption response to the interest rate is weaker than the investment response.

In the *IS-LM* model, aggregate demand is therefore written as a function of the real exchange rate, disposable income, *and* the real interest rate,

$$D(EP^*/P, Y - T, R - \pi^e) = C(Y - T, R - \pi^e) + I(R - \pi^e) + G + CA(EP^*/P, Y - T, R - \pi^e),$$

where π^e is the expected inflation rate and $R - \pi^e$ therefore the expected real interest rate. The model assumes that P, P^*, G, T, R^*, and E^e are all given. (To simplify the notation, we've left G out of the aggregate demand function D.)

---

[13]In a closed-economy context, the original exposition of the *IS-LM* model is in J. R. Hicks, "Mr. Keynes and the 'Classics': A Suggested Interpretation," *Econometrica* 5 (April 1937), pp. 147–159. Hicks's article still makes enjoyable and instructive reading today. The name *IS* comes from the fact that in a closed economy (but not necessarily in an open economy!) the output market is in equilibrium when investment (*I*) and saving (*S*) are equal. Along the *LM* schedule, real money demand (*L*) equals the real money supply (M^s/P in our notation). The open-economy version of the model, with the expectations assumption $E = E^e$ mode for simplicity, is called the *Mundell-Fleming model*. Columbia University economist Robert Mundell won a Nobel Prize in 1999 for his work on the model.

To find the *IS* curve of R and Y combinations such that aggregate demand equals output,

$$Y = D(EP^*/P, Y - T, R - \pi^e),$$

we must first write this output market equilibrium condition so that it does not depend on E.

We solve for E using the interest parity condition, $R = R^* + (E^e - E)/E$. If we solve this equation for E, the result is

$$E = E^e/(1 + R - R^*).$$

Substitution of this expression into the aggregate demand function shows that we can express the condition for output market equilibrium as

$$Y = D[E^eP^*/P(1 + R - R^*), Y - T, R - \pi^e].$$

To get a complete picture of how output changes affect goods market equilibrium, we must remember that the inflation rate in the economy depends positively on the gap between actual output, Y, and full employment output, Y^f. We therefore write π^e as an increasing function of that gap:

$$\pi^e = \pi^e(Y - Y^f).$$

Under this assumption on expectations, the goods market is in equilibrium when

$$Y = D[E^eP^*/P(1 + R - R^*), Y - T, R - \pi^e(Y - Y^f)].$$

This condition shows that a fall in the nominal interest rate R raises aggregate demand through two channels: (1) Given the expected future exchange rate, a fall in R causes a domestic currency depreciation that improves the current account. (2) Given expected inflation, a fall in R directly encourages consumption and investment spending that falls only partly on imports. Only the second of these channels—the effect of the interest rate on spending—would be present in a closed-economy *IS-LM* model.

The *IS* curve is found by asking how output must respond to such a fall in the interest rate to maintain output market equilibrium. Since a fall in R raises aggregate demand, the output market will remain in equilibrium after R falls only if Y rises. The *IS* curve therefore slopes downward, as shown in Figure 16AI-1. Even though the *IS* and *DD* curves both reflect output market equilibrium, *IS* slopes downward while *DD* slopes upward. The reason for this difference is that the interest rate and the exchange rate are inversely related by the interest parity condition, given the expected future exchange rate.[14]

The slope of the *LM* (or money market equilibrium) curve is much easier to derive. Money market equilibrium holds when $M^s/P = L(R, Y)$. Because a rise in the interest rate

---

[14]In concluding that *IS* has a negative slope, we have argued that a rise in output reduces the excess demand for output caused by a fall in R. This reduction in excess demand occurs because while consumption demand rises with a rise in output, it rises by less. Notice, however, that a rise in output also raises expected inflation and thus stimulates demand. So it is conceivable that a fall in output, not a rise, eliminates excess demand in the output market. We assume this perverse possibility (which would give an upward sloping *IS* curve) does not arise.

Figure 16AI-1 | Short-Run Equilibrium in the *IS-LM* Model

Equilibrium is at point 1, where the output and asset markets simultaneously clear.

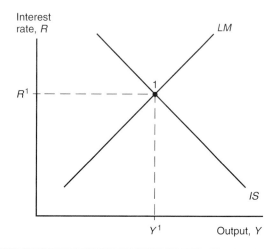

reduces money demand, it results in an excess supply of money for a given output level. To maintain equilibrium in the money market after R rises, Y must therefore rise also (because a rise in output stimulates the transactions demand for money). The *LM* curve thus has a positive slope, as shown in Figure 16AI-1. The intersection of the *IS* and *LM* curves at point 1 determines the short-run equilibrium values of output, Y^1, and the nominal interest rate, R^1. The equilibrium interest rate, in turn, determines a short-run equilibrium exchange rate through the interest parity condition.

The *IS-LM* model can be used to analyze the effects of monetary and fiscal policies. A temporary increase in the money supply, for example, shifts *LM* to the right, lowering the interest rate and expanding output. A *permanent* increase in the money supply, however, shifts *LM* to the right but also shifts *IS* to the right, since in an open economy that schedule depends on E^e, which now rises. The right-hand side of Figure 16AI-2 shows these shifts. At the new short-run equilibrium following a permanent increase in the money supply (point 2), output and the interest rate are higher than at the short-run equilibrium (point 3) following an equal temporary increase. The nominal interest rate can even be higher at point 2 than at point 1. This possibility provides another example of how the Fisher expected inflation effect of Chapter 15 can push the nominal interest rate upward after a monetary expansion.

The left-hand side of Figure 16AI-2 shows how the monetary changes affect the exchange rate. This is our usual picture of equilibrium in the foreign exchange market, but it has been rotated counterclockwise so that a movement to the left along the horizontal axis is an increase in E (a depreciation of the home currency). The interest rate R^2 following a permanent increase in the money supply implies foreign exchange market equilibrium at point 2', since the accompanying rise in E^e shifts the curve that measures the expected domestic currency return on foreign deposits. That curve does not shift if the money supply increase is temporary, so the equilibrium interest rate R^3 that results in this case leads to foreign exchange equilibrium at point 3'.

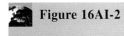

Figure 16AI-2 | Effects of Permanent and Temporary Increases in the Money Supply in the *IS-LM* Model

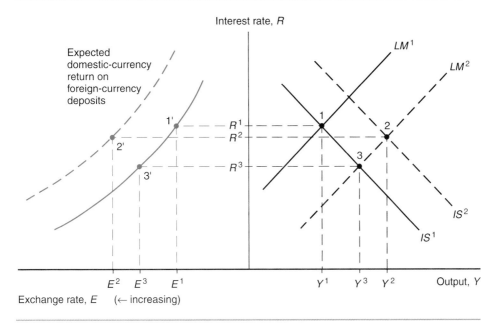

A temporary increase in the money supply shifts the *LM* curve alone to the right, but a permanent increase shifts both the *IS* and *LM* curves in that direction.

Fiscal policy is analyzed in Figure 16AI-3, which assumes a long-run equilibrium starting point. A temporary increase in government spending, for example, shifts IS^1 to the right but has no effect on *LM*. The new short-run equilibrium at point 2 shows a rise in output and a rise in the nominal interest rate, while the foreign exchange market equilibrium at point 2′ indicates a temporary currency appreciation. A permanent increase in government spending causes a fall in the long-run equilibrium exchange rate and thus a fall in E^e. The *IS* curve therefore does not shift out as much as in the case of a temporary policy. In fact, it does not shift at all: As in the *DD-AA* model, *a permanent fiscal expansion has no effect on output or the home interest rate.* The reason why permanent fiscal policy moves are weaker than transitory ones can be seen in the figure's left-hand side (point 3′). The accompanying change in exchange rate expectations generates a sharper currency appreciation and thus, through the response of net exports, a complete "crowding out" effect on aggregate demand.[15]

---

[15]One way the *IS-LM* model differs from the *DD-AA* model is that in the former, monetary expansion can cause a deterioration of the current account (even when there are no J-curve effects) by lowering the real interest rate and thus encouraging domestic spending. We leave it to the interested student to derive the *IS-LM* version of this chapter's *XX* curve.

Figure 16AI-3 | Effects of Permanent and Temporary Fiscal Expansions in the *IS-LM* Model

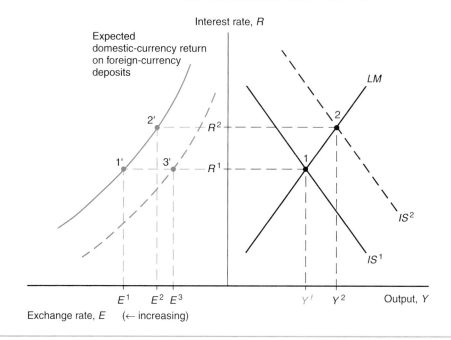

Temporary fiscal expansion has a positive effect on output while permanent fiscal expansion has none.

APPENDIX II TO CHAPTER 16

Intertemporal Trade and Consumption Demand

We assume in the chapter that private consumption demand is a function of disposable income, $C = C(Y^d)$, with the property that when Y^d rises, consumption rises by less (so that saving, $Y - C(Y^d)$, goes up too). This appendix interprets this assumption in the context of the intertemporal model of consumption behavior discussed in the appendix to Chapter 7.

The discussion in Chapter 7 assumed that consumers' welfare depends on present consumption demand D_P and future consumption demand D_F. If present income is Q_P and future income is Q_F, consumers can use borrowing or saving to allocate their consumption over time in any way consistent with the *intertemporal budget constraint*

$$D_P + D_F/(1 + r) = Q_P + Q_F/(1 + r),$$

where r is the real rate of interest.

Figure 16AII-1 reminds you of how consumption and saving were determined in Chapter 7. If present and future output are initially described by the point labeled 1 in the figure, consumers' wishes to pick the highest utility indifference curve consistent with their budget constraints leads to consumption at point 1 as well.

We have assumed zero saving at point 1 to show most clearly the effect of a rise in current output, which we turn to next. Suppose present output rises while future output doesn't, moving the income endowment to point $2'$, which lies horizontally to the right of point 1. You can see that the consumer will wish to spread the increase in consumption this allows her over her *entire* lifetime. She can do this by saving some of the present income rise, $Q_P^2 - Q_P^1$, and moving up to the left along her budget line from her endowment point $2'$ to point 2.

If we now reinterpret the notation so that present output, Q_P, corresponds to disposable income, Y^d, and present consumption demand corresponds to $C(Y^d)$, we see that while consumption certainly depends on factors other than current disposable income—notably, future income and the real interest rate—its behavior does imply that a rise in lifetime income that is concentrated in the present will indeed lead to a rise in current consumption that is less than the rise in current income. Since the output changes we have been considering in this chapter are all temporary changes that result from the short-run stickiness of domestic money prices, the consumption behavior we simply assumed in the chapter does capture the feature of intertemporal consumption behavior essential for the *DD-AA* model to work.

We could also use Figure 16AII-1 to look at the consumption effects of the real interest rate, which we introduced in Appendix I. If the economy is initially at point 1, a fall in the real interest rate r causes the budget line to rotate counterclockwise about point 1, causing a rise in present consumption. If initially the economy had been saving a positive amount, however, as at point 2, this effect would be ambiguous, a reflection of the contrary pulls of

Figure 16AII-1 | Change in Output and Saving

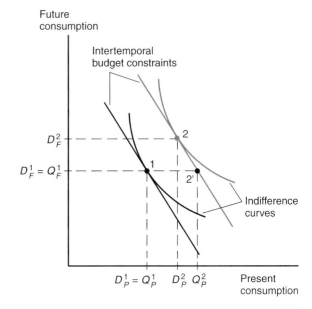

A one-period increase in output raises saving.

the income and substitution effects we introduced in Chapter 5. Empirical evidence indicates that the positive effect of a lower real interest rate on consumption probably is weak.

Use of the preceding framework to analyze the intertemporal aspects of fiscal policy would lead us too far afield, although this is one of the most fascinating topics in macroeconomics. We refer readers instead to any good intermediate macroeconomics text.[16]

---

[16]For example, see Abel and Bernanke, *Macroeconomics*, Chapter 16.

APPENDIX III TO CHAPTER 16

The Marshall-Lerner Condition and Empirical Estimates of Trade Elasticities

The chapter assumed that a real depreciation of a country's currency improves its current account. As we noted, however, the validity of this assumption depends on the response of export and import volumes to real exchange rate changes. In this appendix we derive a condition on those responses for the assumption in the text to be valid. The condition, called the *Marshall-Lerner condition,* states that, all else equal, a real depreciation improves the current account if export and import volumes are sufficiently elastic with respect to the real exchange rate. (The condition is named after two of the economists who discovered it, Alfred Marshall and Abba Lerner.) After deriving the Marshall-Lerner condition, we look at empirical estimates of trade elasticities and analyze their implications for actual current account responses to real exchange rate changes.

To start, write the current account, measured in domestic output units, as the difference between exports and imports of goods and services similarly measured:

$$CA(EP^*/P, Y^d) = EX(EP^*/P) - IM(EP^*/P, Y^d).$$

Above, export demand is written as a function of EP^*/P alone because foreign income is being held constant.

Let q denote the real exchange rate EP^*/P and let EX^* denote domestic imports measured in terms of *foreign,* rather than domestic, output. The notation EX^* is used because domestic imports from abroad, measured in foreign output, equal the volume of foreign exports to the home country. If we identify q with the price of foreign products in terms of domestic products, then IM and EX^* are related by

$$IM = q \times EX^*,$$

that is, imports measured in domestic output = (domestic output units/foreign output unit) $\times$ (imports measured in foreign output units).[17]

---

[17]As we warned earlier in the chapter, the identification of the real exchange rate with relative output prices is not quite exact since, as we defined it, the real exchange rate is the relative price of expenditure baskets. For most practical purposes, however, the discrepancy is not qualitatively important. A more serious problem with our analysis is that national outputs consist in part of nontradables, and the real exchange rate covers their prices as well as those of tradables. To avoid the additional complexity that would result from a more detailed treatment of the composition of national outputs, we assume in deriving the Marshall-Lerner condition that the real exchange rate can be approximately identified with the relative price of imports in terms of exports.

The current account can therefore be expressed as

$$CA(q, Y^d) = EX(q) - q \times EX^*(q, Y^d).$$

Now let EX_q stand for the effect of a rise in q (a real depreciation) on export demand and let EX_q^* stand for the effect of a rise in q on import volume. Thus,

$$EX_q = \Delta EX/\Delta q, \ EX_q^* = \Delta EX^*/\Delta q.$$

As we saw in the chapter, EX_q is positive (a real depreciation makes home products relatively cheaper and stimulates exports) while EX_q^* is negative (a relative cheapening of home products reduces domestic import demand). Using these definitions, we can now ask how a rise in q affects the current account, all else equal.

If superscript ^{1} indicates the initial value of a variable while superscript ^{2} indicates its value after q has changed by $\Delta q = q^2 - q^1$, then the change in the current account caused by a real exchange rate change Δq is

$$\Delta CA = CA^2 - CA^1 = (EX^2 - q^2 \times EX^{*2}) - (EX^1 - q^1 \times EX^{*1})$$

$$= \Delta EX - (q^2 \times \Delta EX^*) - (\Delta q \times EX^{*1}).$$

Dividing through by Δq gives the current account's response to a change in q,

$$\Delta CA/\Delta q = EX_q - (q^2 \times EX_q^*) - EX^{*1}.$$

This equation summarizes the two current account effects of a real depreciation discussed in the text, the *volume* effect and the *value* effect. The terms involving EX_q and EX_q^* represent the volume effect, the effect of the change in q on the number of output units exported and imported. These terms are always positive because $EX_q > 0$ and $EX_q^* < 0$. The last term above, EX^{*1}, represents the value effect, and it is preceded by a minus sign. This last term tells us that a rise in q worsens the current account to the extent that it raises the domestic output value of the initial volume of imports.

We are interested in knowing when the right-hand side of the equation above is positive, so that a real depreciation causes the current account balance to increase. To answer this question, we first define the *elasticity of export demand* with respect to q,

$$\eta = (q^1/EX^1)EX_q,$$

and the *elasticity of import demand* with respect to q,

$$\eta^* = -(q^1/EX^{*1})EX_q^*.$$

(The definition of η^* involves a minus sign because $EX_q^* < 0$ and we are defining trade elasticities as positive numbers.) Returning to our equation for $\Delta CA/\Delta q$, we multiply its right-hand side by (q^1/EX^1) to express it in terms of trade elasticities. Then if the current account is initially zero (that is, $EX^1 = q^1 \times EX^{*1}$), this last step shows that $\Delta CA/\Delta q$ is positive when

$$\eta + (q^2/q^1)\eta^* - 1 > 0.$$

If the change in q is assumed to be small, so that $q^2 \approx q^1$, the condition for an increase in q to improve the current account is

$$\eta + \eta^* > 1.$$

This is the Marshall-Lerner condition. The condition states that if the current account is initially zero, a real currency depreciation causes a current account surplus if the sum of the relative price elasticities of export and import demand exceeds 1. (If the current account is not zero initially, the condition becomes substantially more complex.) In applying the Marshall-Lerner condition, remember that its derivation assumes that disposable income is held constant when q changes.

Now that we have the Marshall-Lerner condition, we can ask whether empirical estimates of trade equations imply price elasticities consistent with this chapter's assumption that a real exchange rate depreciation improves the current account. Table 16AIII-1 presents International Monetary Fund elasticity estimates for trade in manufactured goods. The table reports export and import price elasticities measured over three successively longer time horizons, and thus allows for the possibility that export and import demands adjust gradually to relative price changes, as in our discussion of the J-curve and beachhead effects. "Impact" elasticities measure the response of trade flows to relative price changes in the first six months after the change; "short-run" elasticities apply to a one-year adjustment

Table 16AIII-1 Estimated Price Elasticities for International Trade in Manufactured Goods

Country	η Impact	η Short-run	η Long-run	η^* Impact	η^* Short-run	η^* Long-run
Austria	0.39	0.71	1.37	0.03	0.36	0.80
Belgium	0.18	0.59	1.55	—	—	0.70
Britain	—	—	0.31	0.60	0.75	0.75
Canada	0.08	0.40	0.71	0.72	0.72	0.72
Denmark	0.82	1.13	1.13	0.55	0.93	1.14
France	0.20	0.48	1.25	—	0.49	0.60
Germany	—	—	1.41	0.57	0.77	0.77
Italy	—	0.56	0.64	0.94	0.94	0.94
Japan	0.59	1.01	1.61	0.16	0.72	0.97
Netherlands	0.24	0.49	0.89	0.71	1.22	1.22
Norway	0.40	0.74	1.49	—	0.01	0.71
Sweden	0.27	0.73	1.59	—	—	0.94
Switzerland	0.28	0.42	0.73	0.25	0.25	0.25
United States	0.18	0.48	1.67	—	1.06	1.06

Note: Estimates are taken from Jacques R. Artus and Malcolm D. Knight, *Issues in the Assessment of the Exchange Rates of Industrial Countries,* Occasional Paper 29. Washington, D.C.: International Monetary Fund, July 1984, Table 4. Unavailable estimates are indicated by dashes.

period; and "long-run" elasticities measure the response of trade flows to the price changes over a hypothetical infinite adjustment period.

For most countries, the impact elasticities are so small that the sum of the impact export and import elasticities is less than 1. Since the impact elasticities usually fail to satisfy the Marshall-Lerner condition, the estimates support the existence of an initial J-curve effect that causes the real current account to deteriorate immediately following a real depreciation.

It is also true, however, that most countries represented in the table satisfy the Marshall-Lerner condition in the short run and that virtually all do so in the long run. The evidence is therefore consistent with the assumption made in the chapter: Except over short time periods, a real depreciation is likely to improve the current account while a real appreciation is likely to worsen it.

CHAPTER 17

Fixed Exchange Rates and Foreign Exchange Intervention

I n the past several chapters we have developed a model that helps us understand how a country's exchange rate and national income are determined by the interaction of asset and output markets. Using that model, we saw how monetary and fiscal policies can be used to maintain full employment and a stable price level.

To keep our discussion simple, we assumed that exchange rates are *completely* flexible, that is, that national monetary authorities themselves do not trade in the foreign exchange market to influence exchange rates. In reality, however, the assumption of complete exchange rate flexibility is rarely accurate. As we mentioned earlier, the world economy operated under a system of *fixed* dollar exchange rates between the end of World War II and 1973, with central banks routinely trading foreign exchange to hold their exchange rates at internationally agreed levels. Industrialized countries now operate under a hybrid system of **managed floating exchange rates**—a system in which governments may attempt to moderate exchange rate movements without keeping exchange rates rigidly fixed. A number of developing countries have retained some form of government exchange rate fixing, for reasons that we discuss in Chapter 22.

In this chapter we study how central banks intervene in the foreign exchange market to fix exchange rates and how macroeconomic policies work when exchange rates are fixed. The chapter will help us understand the role of central bank foreign exchange intervention in the determination of exchange rates under a system of managed floating.

Why Study Fixed Exchange Rates?

A discussion of fixed exchange rates may seem outdated in an era when newspaper headlines regularly highlight sharp changes in the exchange rates of the major industrial country currencies. Our interest in fixed exchange rates, however, is not the result of nostalgia, antiquarianism, or an unhealthy obsession with hypothetical worlds. There are four reasons why we must understand fixed exchange rates before analyzing contemporary macroeconomic policy problems:

1. *Managed floating.* As previously noted, central banks often intervene in currency markets to influence exchange rates. So while the dollar exchange rates of the industrial

481

countries' currencies are not currently fixed by governments, they are not left to fluctuate freely either. The system of floating dollar exchange rates is often referred to as a *dirty float,* to distinguish it from a *clean float* in which governments make no direct attempts to influence foreign currency values. (The model of the exchange rate developed in earlier chapters assumed a cleanly floating, or completely flexible, exchange rate.[1]) Because the present monetary system is a hybrid of the "pure" fixed and floating rate systems, an understanding of fixed exchange rates gives us insight into the effects of foreign exchange intervention when it occurs under floating rates.

2. *Regional currency arrangements.* Some countries belong to *exchange rate unions,* organizations whose members agree to fix their mutual exchange rates while allowing their currencies to fluctuate in value against the currencies of nonmember countries. Currently, for example, Denmark pegs its currency's value against the euro within the European Union's *Exchange Rate Mechanism.*

3. *Developing countries and countries in transition.* While industrial countries generally allow their currencies to float against the dollar, these economies account for less than a sixth of the world's countries. Many developing and formerly communist countries try to peg the values of their currencies, often in terms of the dollar, but sometimes in terms of a nondollar currency or some "basket" of currencies chosen by the authorities. Table 17-1 shows that about half of the world's countries engage in some sort of currency peg. Morocco pegs its currency to a basket, for example, while Barbados pegs to the U.S. dollar and Senegal pegs to the French franc. No examination of the problems of developing countries would get very far without taking into account the implications of fixed exchange rates.

4. *Lessons of the past for the future.* Fixed exchange rates were the norm in many periods, such as the decades before World War I, between the mid-1920s and 1931, and again between 1945 and 1973. Today, some economists and policymakers dissatisfied with floating exchange rates are proposing new international agreements that would resurrect some form of fixed rate system. Would this plan benefit the world economy? Who would gain or lose from such a system? To compare the merits of fixed and floating exchange rates (the topic of Chapter 19), the functioning of fixed rates must be understood.

Central Bank Intervention and the Money Supply

In Chapter 14 we defined an economy's money supply as the total amount of currency and checking deposits held by its households and firms and assumed that the central bank determined the amount of money in circulation. To understand the effects of central bank intervention in the foreign exchange market, we need to look first at how central bank financial transactions affect the money supply.[2]

---

[1]It is questionable whether a truly clean float has ever existed in reality. Most government policies affect the exchange rate, and governments rarely undertake policies without considering their exchange rate implications.

[2]As we pointed out in Chapter 12, government agencies other than central banks may intervene in the foreign exchange market, but their intervention operations, unlike those of central banks, have no significant effect on national money supplies. (In the terminology introduced below, interventions by agencies other than central banks are automatically *sterilized.*) To simplify our discussion, we continue to assume, when the assumption is not misleading, that central banks alone carry out foreign exchange intervention.

Table 17-1 | Exchange Rate Arrangements and Anchors of Monetary Policy (As of March 31, 2001)[1]

Exchange Rate Regime (Number of countries)	Monetary Policy Framework				
	Exchange rate anchor	Monetary aggregate target	Inflation targeting framework	Fund-supported or other monetary program	Other
Exchange arrangements with no separate legal tender (39)	**Another currency as legal tender** **ECCU**[2] Ecuador*　Antigua & Barbuda Kiribati　Dominica Marshall Islands　Grenada 　Rep. of　St. Kitts & Nevis Micronesia, Fed.　St. Lucia 　States of　St. Vincent & the Palau　　Grenadines Panama San Marino **CFA Franc Zone** **WAEMU**　**CAEMC** Benin*　Cameroon* Burkina Faso*　C. African Rep.* Côte d'Ivoire*　Chad* Guinea-Bissau*　Congo, Rep. of* Mali*　Equatorial Guinea Niger*　Gabon* Senegal* Togo			Benin* Burkina Faso* Cameroon* Central African 　Rep.* Chad* Congo, Rep. of* Côte d'Ivoire* Ecuador* Gabon* Guinea-Bissau* Mali* Niger* Senegal*	Euro Area[3,4] Austria Belgium Finland France Germany Greece Ireland Italy Luxembourg Netherlands Portugal Spain
Currency board arrangements (8)	Argentina* Bosnia and Herzegovina* Brunei Darussalam Bulgaria* China, P.R. Hong Kong Djibouti* Estonia* Lithuania*			Argentina* Bosnia and 　Herzegovina* Bulgaria* Djibouti* Estonia* Lithuania*	
Other conventional fixed peg arrangements (including de facto peg arrangements under managed floating) (44)	**Against a single currency (31)** Aruba　Lesotho* Bahamas, The[5]　Macedonia, FYR*[6] Bahrain[6,7]　Malaysia Barbados　Maldives[6] Belize　Namibia Bhutan　Nepal Cape Verde　Netherlands Antilles China, P.R.　Oman 　Mainland*[6]　Qatar[6,7] Comoros[8]　Saudi Arabia[6,7] Congo, Dem.　Swaziland 　Rep. of　Syrian Arab El Salvador[13]　　Republic[5] Eritrea　Trinidad & Iran[5,6]　　Tobago*[6] Iraq　Turkmenistan[6] Jordan*[6]　United Arab Lebanon[6]　　Emirates[6,7] **Against a composite (13)** Bangladesh　Myanmar[5] Botswana[5]　Samoa Fiji　Seychelles Kuwait　Solomon Islands Latvia*　Tonga Malta　Vanuatu Morocco	China, P.R.; Mainland*[6]		Jordan*[6] Latvia* Lesotho* Macedonia, 　FYR*[6] Trinidad & 　Tobago*[6]	

**ECCU: Eastern Caribbean Currency Union; WAEMU: West African Economic and Monetary Union; CAEMC: Central African Economic and Monetary Community

continued

Table 17-1 | Continued

Exchange Rate Regime (Number of countries)	Monetary Policy Framework				
	Exchange rate anchor	Monetary aggregate target	Inflation targeting framework	Fund-supported or other monetary program	Other
Pegged exchange rates within horizontal bands (6)[9]	**Within a cooperative arrangement** **ERM II (1)** Denmark **Other band arrangements (5)** Cyprus Egypt[5] Libyan A.J. Suriname[5] Vietnam[6]				
Crawling pegs (4)[6]	Bolivia* Costa Rica Nicaragua* Zimbabwe*			Bolivia* Nicaragua* Zimbabwe*	
Exchange rates within crawling bands (5)[6, 10]	Israel* Honduras* Hungary Uruguay* Venezuela, Rep. Bolivariana		Israel*	Honduras* Uruguay*	
Managed floating with no preannounced path for exchange rate (33)		Jamaica*[6] Slovenia Tunisia	Czech Republic Norway	Cambodia[5] Croatia Ethiopia Jamaica*[6] Kazakhstan Kenya Kyrgyz Republic Mauritania Nigeria Pakistan Romania Russian Federation Rwanda Sri Lanka Sudan Ukraine Yugoslavia, Fed. Rep. of	Algeria[3] Azerbaijan Belarus[3, 5] Burundi[3] Dominican Rep.[3, 5] Guatemala[3] India[3] Lao PDR[3, 5] Paraguay[3] Singapore Slovak Republic[3] Uzbekistan[3, 5]
Independently floating (47)		Gambia, The* Ghana* Guinea* Guyana* Mauritius[6] Malawi* Mexico Mongolia* Peru* Philippines* São Tomé and Príncipe* Sierra Leone* Turkey* Yemen*	Australia Brazil[12] Canada Chile[5] Colombia* Iceland Korea New Zealand Poland South Africa Sweden Thailand* United Kingdom	Albania Angola Armenia Colombia* Gambia, The* Georgia Ghana* Guinea* Guyana* Haiti Indonesia Madagascar Malawi* Moldova Mongolia*	Afghanistan[5, 11] Japan[3] Liberia[3] Somalia[5, 11] Switzerland[3] United States[3]

continued

Table 17-1 | Continued

Exchange Rate Regime (Number of countries)	Monetary Policy Framework				
	Exchange rate anchor	Monetary aggregate target	Inflation targeting framework	Fund-supported or other monetary program	Other

				Mozambique
				Papua New
				  Guinea
				Peru*
				Philippines*
				São Tomé and
				  Príncipe*
				Sierra Leone*
				Tajikistan
				Tanzania
				Thailand*
				Turkey*
				Uganda
				Yemen*
				Zambia	

Source: International Monetary Fund, *International Financial Statistics,* August 2001.

Exchange Arrangements with No Separate Legal Tender: The currency of another country circulates as the sole legal tender or the member belongs to a monetary or currency union in which the same legal tender is shared by the members of the union.

Currency Board Arrangements: A monetary regime based on an explicit legislative commitment to exchange domestic currency for a specified foreign currency at a fixed exchange rate, combined with restrictions on the issuing authority to ensure the fulfillment of its legal obligation.

Other Conventional Fixed Peg Arrangements: The country pegs its currency (formally or de facto) at a fixed rate to a major currency or a basket of currencies where the exchange rate fluctuates within a narrow margin of less than ± 1 percent around a central rate.

Pegged Exchange Rates Within Horizontal Bands: The value of the currency is maintained within margins of fluctuation around a formal or de facto fixed peg that are wider than at least ± 1 percent around a central rate.

Crawling Pegs: The currency is adjusted periodically in small amounts at a fixed, preannounced rate or in response to changes in selective quantitative indicators.

Exchange Rates Within Crawling Bands: The currency is maintained within certain fluctuation margins around a central rate that is adjusted periodically at a fixed preannounced rate or in response to changes in selective quantitative indicators.

Managed Floating with No Preannounced Path for the Exchange Rate: The monetary authority influences the movements of the exchange rate through active intervention in the foreign exchange market without specifying, or precommitting to, a preannounced path for the exchange rate.

Independent Floating: The exchange rate is market determined, with any foreign exchange intervention aimed at moderating the rate of change and preventing undue fluctuations in the exchange rate, rather than at establishing a level for it.

Note: "Country" in this publication does not always refer to a territorial entity that is a state as understood by international law and practice; the term also covers the euro area and some nonsovereign territorial entities for which statistical data are provided internationally on a separate basis.

[1] A country with * indicates that the country adopts more than one nominal anchor in conducting monetary policy. It should be noted, however, that it would not be possible, for practical reasons, to infer from this table which nominal anchor plays the principal role in conducting monetary policy.

[2] These countries have a currency board arrangement.

[3] The country has no explicitly stated nominal anchor, but rather monitors various indicators in conducting monetary policy.

[4] Until they are withdrawn in the first half of 2002, national currencies will retain their status as legal tender within their home territories.

[5] Member maintained exchange arrangements involving more than one market. The arrangement shown is that maintained in the major market.

[6] The indicated country has a de facto arrangement under a formally announced policy of managed or independent floating. In the case of Jordan, it indicates that the country has a de jure peg to the SDR but a de facto peg to the U.S. dollar. In the case of Mauritius, the authorities have a de facto policy of independent floating, with only infrequent intervention by the central bank.

[7] Exchange rates are determined on the basis of a fixed relationship to the SDR, within margins of up to $\pm 7.25\%$. However, because of the maintenance of a relatively stable relationship with the U.S. dollar, these margins are not always observed.

[8] Comoros has the same arrangement with the French Treasury as do the CFA Franc Zone countries.

[9] The band width for these countries is: Cyprus ($\pm 2.25\%$), Denmark ($\pm 2.25\%$), Egypt ($\pm 1\%$), Libya ($\pm 77.5\%$), Suriname ($\pm 9.1\%$), and Vietnam (0.1% daily movement, one sided).

[10] The band for these countries is: Honduras ($\pm 7\%$), Hungary ($\pm 2.25\%$), Israel ($\pm 20\%$), Uruguay ($\pm 3\%$), and República Bolivariana de Venezuela ($\pm 7.5\%$).

[11] There is no relevant information available for the country.

[12] Brazil maintains a Fund-supported program.

[13] For El Salvador, the U.S. dollar is also legal tender; all financial system accounts are denominated in U.S. dollars.

The Central Bank Balance Sheet and the Money Supply

The main tool we use in studying central bank transactions in asset markets is the **central bank balance sheet**, which records the assets held by the central bank and its liabilities. Like any other balance sheet, the central bank balance sheet is organized according to the principles of double-entry bookkeeping. Any acquisition of an asset by the central bank results in a positive change on the assets side of the balance sheet, while any increase in the bank's liabilities results in a positive change on the balance sheet's liabilities side.

A balance sheet for the central bank of the imaginary country of Pecunia is shown below.

Central Bank Balance Sheet

Assets		Liabilities	
Foreign assets	$1000	Deposits held by private banks	$500
Domestic assets	$1500	Currency in circulation	$2000

The assets side of the Bank of Pecunia's balance sheet lists two types of assets, *foreign assets* and *domestic assets.* Foreign assets consist mainly of foreign currency bonds owned by the central bank. These foreign assets make up the central bank's official international reserves, and their level changes when the central bank intervenes in the foreign exchange market by buying or selling foreign exchange. For historical reasons discussed later in this chapter, a central bank's international reserves also include any gold that it owns. The defining characteristic of international reserves is that they be either claims on foreigners or a universally acceptable means of making international payments (for example, gold). In the present example, the central bank holds $1000 in foreign assets.

Domestic assets are central bank holdings of claims to future payments by its own citizens and domestic institutions. These claims usually take the form of domestic government bonds and loans to domestic private banks. The Bank of Pecunia owns $1500 in domestic assets. Its total assets therefore equal $2500, the sum of foreign and domestic asset holdings.

The liabilities side of the balance sheet lists as liabilities the deposits of private banks and currency in circulation, both notes and coin. (Nonbank firms and households generally cannot deposit money at the central bank, while banks are generally required by law to hold central bank deposits as partial backing for their own liabilities.) Private bank deposits are liabilities of the central bank because the money may be withdrawn whenever private banks need it. Currency in circulation is considered a central bank liability mainly for historical reasons: At one time, central banks were obliged to give a certain amount of gold or silver to anyone wishing to exchange domestic currency for one of those precious metals. The balance sheet above shows that Pecunia's private banks have deposited $500 at the central bank. Currency in circulation equals $2000, so the central bank's total liabilities amount to $2500.

The central bank's total assets equal its total liabilities plus its net worth, which we have assumed in the present example to be zero. Because changes in central bank net worth are not important to our analysis we will also ignore those.[3]

---

[3]There are several ways in which a central bank's net worth could change. For example, the government might allow its central bank to keep a fraction of the interest earnings on its assets, and this interest flow would raise the bank's net worth if reinvested. Such changes in net worth tend to be small enough empirically that they can usually be ignored for purposes of macroeconomic analysis.

The additional assumption that net worth is constant means that the changes in central bank assets we will consider *automatically* cause equal changes in central bank liabilities. When the central bank purchases an asset, for example, it can pay for it in one of two ways. A cash payment raises the supply of currency in circulation by the amount of the bank's asset purchase. A payment by check promises the check's owner a central bank deposit equal in value to the asset's price. When the recipient of the check deposits it in her account at a private bank, the private bank's claims on the central bank (and thus the central bank's liabilities to private banks) rise by the same amount. In either case, the central bank's purchase of assets automatically causes an equal increase in its liabilities. Similarly, asset sales by the central bank involve either the withdrawal of currency from circulation or the reduction of private banks' claims on the central bank, and thus a fall in central bank liabilities to the private sector.

An understanding of the central bank balance sheet is important because changes in the central bank's assets cause changes in the domestic money supply. Our discussion of the equality between changes in central bank assets and liabilities illustrates the mechanism at work.

When the central bank buys an asset from the public, for example, its payment—whether cash or check—directly enters the money supply. The increase in central bank liabilities associated with the asset purchase thus causes the money supply to expand. The money supply shrinks when the central bank sells an asset to the public because the cash or check the central bank receives in payment goes out of circulation, reducing the central bank's liabilities to the public. Changes in the level of central bank asset holdings cause the money supply to change in the same direction because they require equal changes in the central bank's liabilities.

The process we have described may be familiar to you from studying central bank open-market operations in earlier courses. By definition, open-market operations involve the purchase or sale of domestic assets, but official transactions in foreign assets have the same direct effect on the money supply. You will also recall that when the central bank buys assets, for example, the accompanying increase in the money supply is generally *larger* than the initial asset purchase because of multiple deposit creation within the private banking system. This *money multiplier* effect, which magnifies the impact of central bank transactions on the money supply, reinforces our main conclusion: *Any central bank purchase of assets automatically results in an increase in the domestic money supply, while any central bank sale of assets automatically causes the money supply to decline.*[4]

Foreign Exchange Intervention and the Money Supply

To see in greater detail how foreign exchange intervention affects the money supply, let's look at an example. Suppose the Bank of Pecunia goes to the foreign exchange market and sells $100 worth of foreign bonds for Pecunian money. The sale reduces official holdings of foreign assets from $1000 to $900, causing the assets side of the central bank balance sheet to shrink from $2500 to $2400.

---

[4]For a detailed description of multiple deposit creation and the money multiplier, see Frederic S. Mishkin, *The Economics of Money, Banking and Financial Markets,* 5th ed., Chapter 16 (Reading, MA: Addison-Wesley, 1998).

The payment the Bank of Pecunia receives for these foreign assets automatically reduces its liabilities by $100 as well. If the Bank of Pecunia is paid with domestic currency, the currency goes into its vault and out of circulation. Currency in circulation therefore falls by $100. As a result of the foreign asset sale, the central bank's balance sheet changes as follows:

Central Bank Balance Sheet after $100 Foreign Asset Sale (Buyer Pays with Currency)

Assets		Liabilities	
Foreign assets	$900	Deposits held by private banks	$500
Domestic assets	$1500	Currency in circulation	$1900

After the sale, assets still equal liabilities, but both have declined by $100, equal to the amount of currency the Bank of Pecunia has taken out of circulation through its intervention in the foreign exchange market. The change in the central bank's balance sheet implies a decline in the Pecunian money supply.

What happens if the buyer of the foreign assets pays the Bank of Pecunia with a $100 check drawn on an account at Pecuniacorp, a private domestic bank? The Bank of Pecunia debits $100 from Pecuniacorp's central bank account and Pecuniacorp debits $100 from the buyer's checking account. Private bank deposits with the central bank fall by $100, and the Bank of Pecunia's balance sheet becomes as shown below.

Central Bank Balance Sheet after $100 Foreign Asset Sale (Buyer Pays with a Check)

Assets		Liabilities	
Foreign assets	$900	Deposits held by private banks	$400
Domestic assets	$1500	Currency in circulation	$2000

Once again, the Bank of Pecunia's liabilities fall by $100 and the Pecunian money supply shrinks.

A $100 *purchase* of foreign assets by the Bank of Pecunia would cause its liabilities to increase by $100. If the central bank paid for its purchase in cash, currency in circulation would rise by $100. If it paid by writing a check on itself, private bank deposits at the Bank of Pecunia would ultimately rise by $100. In either case, there would be a rise in the domestic money supply.

Sterilization

Central banks sometimes carry out equal foreign and domestic asset transactions in opposite directions to nullify the impact of their foreign exchange operations on the domestic money supply. This type of policy is called **sterilized foreign exchange intervention**. We can understand how sterilized foreign exchange intervention works by considering the following example.

Suppose once again that the Bank of Pecunia sells $100 of its foreign assets and receives as payment a $100 check on the private bank Pecuniacorp. This transaction causes the central bank's foreign assets and its liabilities to decline simultaneously by $100, and there is therefore a fall in the domestic money supply. If the central bank wishes to negate the effect of its foreign asset sale on the money supply, it can *buy* $100 of domestic assets, such as government bonds. This second action increases the Bank of Pecunia's domestic assets *and* its liabilities by $100 and so completely offsets the money supply effect of the $100 sale of foreign assets. If the central bank buys the government bonds with a check, for example, the two transactions (a $100 sale of foreign assets and a $100 purchase of domestic assets) have the following net effect on its balance sheet.

Central Bank Balance Sheet before Sterilized $100 Foreign Asset Sale

Assets		Liabilities	
Foreign assets	$1000	Deposits held by private banks	$500
Domestic assets	$1500	Currency in circulation	$2000

Central Bank Balance Sheet after Sterilized $100 Foreign Asset Sale

Assets		Liabilities	
Foreign assets	$900	Deposits held by private banks	$500
Domestic assets	$1600	Currency in circulation	$2000

The $100 decrease in the central bank's foreign assets is matched with a $100 increase in domestic assets, and the liabilities side of the balance sheet does not change. The sterilized foreign exchange sale therefore has no effect on the money supply.

Table 17-2 summarizes and compares the effects of sterilized and nonsterilized foreign exchange interventions.

The Balance of Payments and the Money Supply

In our discussion of balance of payments accounting in Chapter 12, we defined a country's balance of payments (or official settlements balance) as net purchases of foreign assets by the home central bank less net purchases of domestic assets by foreign central banks. Looked at differently, the balance of payments is the sum of the current account and the nonreserve component of the capital account, that is, the international payments gap that central banks must finance through their reserve transactions. A home balance of payments deficit, for example, means the country's net foreign reserve liabilities are increasing: Some combination of reserve sales by the home central bank and reserve purchases by foreign central banks is covering a home current account deficit not fully matched by net nonreserve capital inflows, or a home current account surplus that falls short of net nonreserve capital outflows.

What we have learned in this section illustrates the important connection between the balance of payments and the growth of money supplies at home and abroad. *If central banks*

Table 17-2 | Effects of a $100 Foreign Exchange Intervention: Summary

Domestic Central Bank's Action	Effect on Domestic Money Supply	Effect on Central Bank Domestic Assets	Effect on Central Bank Foreign Assets
Nonsterilized foreign exchange purchase	+$100	0	+$100
Sterilized foreign exchange purchase	0	−$100	+$100
Nonsterilized foreign exchange sale	−$100	0	−$100
Sterilized foreign exchange sale	0	+$100	−$100

are not sterilizing and the home country has a balance of payments surplus, for example, any associated increase in the home central bank's foreign assets implies an increased home money supply. Similarly, any associated decrease in a foreign central bank's claims on the home country implies a decreased foreign money supply.

The extent to which a measured balance of payments disparity will affect home and foreign money supplies is, however, quite uncertain in practice. For one thing, we have to know how the burden of balance of payments adjustment is divided among central banks, that is, how much financing of the payments gap is done through home official intervention and how much through foreign. This division depends on various factors, such as the macroeconomic goals of the central banks and institutional arrangements governing intervention (discussed later in this chapter). Second, central banks may be sterilizing to counter the monetary effects of reserve changes. Finally, as we noted in Chapter 12 (p. 316), some central bank transactions indirectly help to finance a foreign country's balance of payments deficit, but they do not show up in the latter's published balance of payments figures. Such transactions may nonetheless affect the monetary liabilities of the bank that undertakes them.

How the Central Bank Fixes the Exchange Rate

Having seen how central bank foreign exchange transactions affect the money supply, we can now look at how a central bank fixes the domestic currency's exchange rate through foreign exchange intervention.

To hold the exchange rate constant, a central bank must always be willing to trade currencies at the fixed exchange rate with the private actors in the foreign exchange market. For example, to fix the yen/dollar rate at ¥120 per dollar, the Bank of Japan must be willing to buy yen with its dollar reserves, and in any amount the market desires, at a rate of ¥120 per dollar. The bank must also be willing to buy any amount of dollar assets the market wants to sell for yen at that exchange rate. If the Bank of Japan did not remove such excess supplies or demands for yen by intervening in the market, the exchange rate would have to change to restore equilibrium.

The central bank can succeed in holding the exchange rate fixed only if its financial transactions ensure that asset markets remain in equilibrium when the exchange rate is at its fixed level. The process through which asset market equilibrium is maintained is illustrated by the model of simultaneous foreign exchange and money market equilibrium used in previous chapters.

Foreign Exchange Market Equilibrium under a Fixed Exchange Rate

To begin, we consider how equilibrium in the foreign exchange market can be maintained when the central bank fixes the exchange rate permanently at the level E^0. The foreign exchange market is in equilibrium when the interest parity condition holds, that is, when the domestic interest rate, R, equals the foreign interest rate, R^*, plus $(E^e - E)/E$, the expected rate of depreciation of the domestic currency against foreign currency. When the exchange rate is fixed at E^0, however, and market participants expect it to remain fixed, the expected rate of domestic currency depreciation is zero. The interest parity condition therefore implies that E^0 is today's equilibrium exchange rate only if

$$R = R^*.$$

Because no exchange rate change is expected by participants in the foreign exchange market, they are content to hold the available supplies of domestic and foreign currency deposits only if these offer the same interest rate.[5]

To ensure equilibrium in the foreign exchange market when the exchange rate is fixed permanently at E^0, the central bank must therefore hold R equal to R^*. Because the domestic interest rate is determined by the interaction of real money demand and the real money supply, we must look at the money market to complete our analysis of exchange rate fixing.

Money Market Equilibrium under a Fixed Exchange Rate

To hold the domestic interest rate at R^*, the central bank's foreign exchange intervention must adjust the money supply so that R^* equates aggregate real domestic money demand and the real money supply:

$$M^s/P = L(R^*, Y).$$

Given P and Y, the above equilibrium condition tells what the money supply must be if a permanently fixed exchange rate is consistent with asset market equilibrium at a foreign interest rate of R^*.

---

[5]Even when an exchange rate is currently fixed at some level, market participants may expect the central bank to change it. In such situations the home interest rate must equal the foreign interest rate plus the expected depreciation rate of the domestic currency (as usual) for the foreign exchange market to be in equilibrium. We examine this type of situation later in this chapter, but for now we assume that no one expects the central bank to alter the exchange rate.

When the central bank intervenes to hold the exchange rate fixed, it must *automatically* adjust the domestic money supply so that money market equilibrium is maintained with $R = R^*$. Let's look at an example to see how this process works. Suppose the central bank has been fixing E at E^0 and that asset markets initially are in equilibrium. Suddenly output rises. A necessary condition for holding the exchange rate permanently fixed at E^0 is that the central bank restore current asset market equilibrium at that rate, *given* that people expect E^0 to prevail in the future. So we frame our question as: What monetary measures keep the current exchange rate constant given unchanged expectations about the future rate?

A rise in output raises the demand for domestic money, and this increase in money demand normally would push the domestic interest rate upward. To prevent the appreciation of the home currency that would occur (given that people expect an exchange rate of E^0 in the future), the central bank must intervene in the foreign exchange market by buying foreign assets. This foreign asset purchase eliminates the excess demand for domestic money because the central bank issues money to pay for the foreign assets it buys. The bank automatically increases the money supply in this way until asset markets again clear with $E = E^0$ and $R = R^*$.

If the central bank does *not* purchase foreign assets when output increases but instead holds the money stock constant, can it still keep the exchange rate fixed at E^0? The answer is no. If the central bank did not satisfy the excess demand for money caused by a rise in output, the domestic interest rate would begin to rise above the foreign rate, R^*, to balance the home money market. Traders in the foreign exchange market, perceiving that domestic currency deposits were offering a higher rate of return (given expectations), would begin to bid up the price of domestic currency in terms of foreign currency. In the absence of central bank intervention, the exchange rate thus would fall below E^0. To prevent this appreciation, the bank must sell domestic currency and buy foreign assets, thereby increasing the money supply and preventing any excess money demand from pushing the home interest rate above R^*.

A Diagrammatic Analysis

The preceding mechanism of exchange rate fixing can be pictured using a diagrammatic tool developed earlier. Figure 17-1 shows the simultaneous equilibrium of the foreign exchange and domestic money markets when the exchange rate is fixed at E^0 and is expected to remain fixed at E^0 in the future.

Money market equilibrium is initially at point 1 in the lower part of the figure. The diagram shows that for a given price level, P, and a given national income level, Y^1, the money supply must equal M^1 when the domestic interest rate equals the foreign rate, R^*. The upper part of the figure shows the equilibrium of the foreign exchange market at point 1'. If the expected future exchange rate is E^0, the interest parity condition holds when $R = R^*$ only if today's exchange rate also equals E^0.

To see how the central bank must react to macroeconomic changes to hold the exchange rate permanently at E^0, let's look again at the example of an increase in income. A rise in income (from Y^1 to Y^2) raises the demand for real money holdings at every interest rate, thereby shifting the aggregate money demand function in Figure 17-1 downward. As noted above, a necessary condition for maintaining the fixed rate is to restore *current* asset market equilibrium given that E^0 is still the expected future exchange rate. So we can assume that the downward sloping curve in the figure's top panel doesn't move.

Figure 17-1 | Asset Market Equilibrium with a Fixed Exchange Rate, E^0

To hold the exchange rate fixed at E^0 when output rises from Y^1 to Y^2, the central bank must purchase foreign assets and thereby raise the money supply from M^1 to M^2.

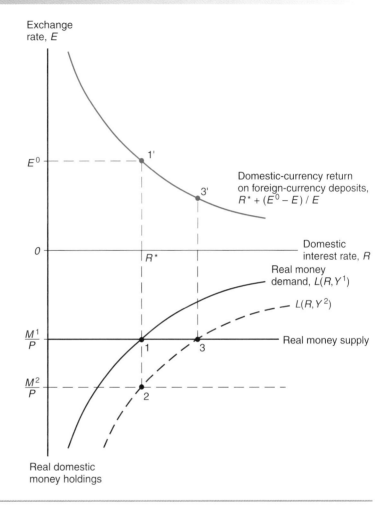

If the central bank were to take no action, the new money market equilibrium would be at point 3. Because the domestic interest rate is above R^* at point 3, the currency would have to appreciate to bring the foreign exchange market to equilibrium at point 3′.

The central bank cannot allow this appreciation of the domestic currency to occur if it is fixing the exchange rate, so it will buy foreign assets. As we have seen, the increase in the central bank's foreign assets is accompanied by an expansion of the domestic money supply. The central bank will continue to purchase foreign assets until the domestic money supply has expanded to M^2. At the resulting money market equilibrium (point 2 in the figure), the domestic interest rate again equals R^*. Given this domestic interest rate, the foreign exchange market equilibrium remains at point 1′ with the equilibrium exchange rate still equal to E^0.

Stabilization Policies with a Fixed Exchange Rate

Having seen how the central bank uses foreign exchange intervention to fix the exchange rate, we can now analyze the effects of various macroeconomic policies. In this section we consider three possible policies: monetary policy, fiscal policy, and an abrupt change in the exchange rate's fixed level, E^0.

The stabilization policies we studied in the last chapter have surprisingly different effects when the central bank fixes the exchange rate rather than allowing the foreign exchange market to determine it. By fixing the exchange rate, the central bank gives up its ability to influence the economy through monetary policy. Fiscal policy, however, becomes a more potent tool for affecting output and employment.

As in the last chapter, we use the *DD-AA* model to describe the economy's short-run equilibrium. You will recall that the *DD* schedule shows combinations of the exchange rate and output for which the output market is in equilibrium, the *AA* schedule shows combinations of the exchange rate and output for which the asset markets are in equilibrium, and the short-run equilibrium of the economy as a whole is at the intersection of *DD* and *AA*. To apply the model to the case of a permanently fixed exchange rate, we add the assumption that the expected future exchange rate, E^e, equals the rate E^0 at which the central bank is pegging.

Monetary Policy

Figure 17-2 shows the economy's short-run equilibrium as point 1 when the central bank fixes the exchange rate at the level E^0. Output equals Y^1 at point 1, and, as in the last section, the money supply is at the level where a domestic interest rate equal to the foreign rate (R^*) clears the domestic money market. Suppose now that, hoping to increase output, the central bank decides to increase the money supply through a purchase of domestic assets.

Under a floating exchange rate, the increase in the central bank's domestic assets would push the original asset market equilibrium curve AA^1 rightward to AA^2 and would therefore result in a new equilibrium at point 2 and a currency depreciation. To prevent this depreciation and hold the rate at E^0, the central bank sells foreign assets for domestic money in the foreign exchange market. The money the bank receives goes out of circulation, and the asset market equilibrium curve shifts back toward its initial position as the home money supply falls. Only when the money supply has returned to its original level, so that the asset market schedule is again AA^1, is the exchange rate no longer under pressure. The attempt to increase the money supply under a fixed exchange rate thus leaves the economy at its initial equilibrium (point 1). *Under a fixed exchange rate, central bank monetary policy tools are powerless to affect the economy's money supply or its output.*

This result is very different from our finding in Chapter 16 that a central bank can use monetary policy to raise the money supply and output when the exchange rate floats, so it is instructive to ask why the difference arises. By purchasing domestic assets under a floating rate, the central bank causes an initial excess supply of domestic money that simultaneously pushes the domestic interest rate downward and weakens the currency. Under a fixed exchange rate, however, the central bank will resist any tendency for the currency to depreciate by selling foreign assets for domestic money and so removing the initial excess supply of money its policy move has caused. Because any increase in the domestic money supply, no matter how

Figure 17-2 | Monetary Expansion Is Ineffective Under a Fixed Exchange Rate

Initial equilibrium is shown at point 1, where the output and asset markets simultaneously clear at a fixed exchange rate of E^0 and an output level of Y^1. Hoping to increase output to Y^2, the central bank decides to increase the money supply by buying domestic assets and shifting AA^1 to AA^2. Because the central bank must maintain E^0, however, it has to sell foreign assets for domestic currency, an action that decreases the money supply immediately and returns AA^2 back to AA^1. The economy's equilibrium therefore remains at point 1, with output unchanged at Y^1.

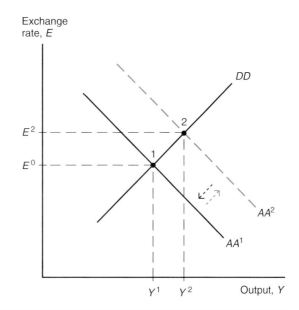

small, will cause the domestic currency to depreciate, the central bank must continue selling foreign assets until the money supply has returned to its original level. In the end, the increase in the central bank's domestic assets is exactly offset by an equal *decrease* in the bank's official international reserves. Similarly, an attempt to decrease the money supply through a sale of domestic assets would cause an equal *increase* in reserves that would keep the money supply from changing in the end. Under fixed rates, monetary policy can affect international reserves but nothing else.

By fixing the exchange rate, then, the central bank loses its ability to use monetary policy for the purpose of macroeconomic stabilization. However, the government's second key stabilization tool, fiscal policy, is more effective under a fixed rate than under a floating rate.

Fiscal Policy

Figure 17-3 illustrates the effects of expansionary fiscal policy when the economy's initial equilibrium is at point 1. As we saw in Chapter 16, fiscal expansion shifts the output market equilibrium schedule to the right. DD^1 therefore shifts to DD^2 in the figure. If the central bank refrained from intervening in the foreign exchange market, output would rise to Y^2 and the exchange rate would fall to E^2 (a currency appreciation) as a result of a rise in the home interest rate.

How does the central bank intervention hold the exchange rate fixed after the fiscal expansion? The process is the one we illustrated in Figure 17-1. Initially, there is an excess demand for money because the rise in output raises money demand. To prevent the excess

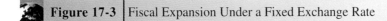

Figure 17-3 | Fiscal Expansion Under a Fixed Exchange Rate

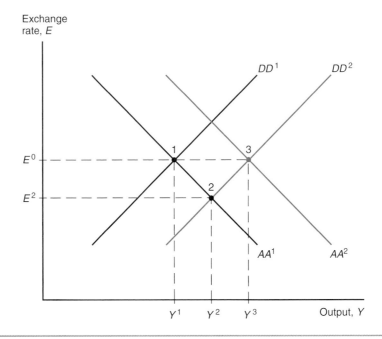

Fiscal expansion (shown by the shift from DD^1 to DD^2) and the intervention that accompanies it (the shift from AA^1 to AA^2) move the economy from point 1 to point 3.

money demand from pushing up the home interest rate and appreciating the currency, the central bank must buy foreign assets with money, thereby increasing the money supply. In terms of Figure 17-3, intervention holds the exchange rate at E^0 by shifting AA^1 rightward to AA^2. At the new equilibrium (point 3), output is higher than originally, the exchange rate is unchanged, and official international reserves (and the money supply) are higher.

Unlike monetary policy, fiscal policy can be used to affect output under a fixed exchange rate. Indeed, it is even more effective than under a floating rate! Under a floating rate, fiscal expansion is accompanied by an appreciation of the domestic currency that makes domestic goods and services more expensive and so tends to counteract the policy's positive direct effect on aggregate demand. To prevent this appreciation, a central bank that is fixing the exchange rate is forced to expand the money supply through foreign exchange purchases. The additional expansionary effect of this involuntary increase in the money supply explains why fiscal policy is more potent than under a floating rate.

Changes in the Exchange Rate

A country that is fixing its exchange rate sometimes decides on a sudden change in the foreign currency value of the domestic currency. A **devaluation** occurs when the central bank raises the domestic currency price of foreign currency, E, and a **revaluation** occurs when the central bank lowers E. All the central bank has to do to devalue or revalue is announce its willingness to trade domestic against foreign currency, in unlimited amounts, at the new exchange rate.[6]

Figure 17-4 shows how a devaluation affects the economy. A rise in the level of the fixed exchange rate, from E^0 to E^1, makes domestic goods and services cheaper relative to foreign goods and services (given that P and $P*$ are fixed in the short run). Output therefore moves to the higher level Y^2 shown by point 2 on the DD schedule. Point 2, however, does not lie on the initial asset market equilibrium schedule AA^1: At point 2, there is initially an excess demand for money due to the rise in transactions accompanying the output increase. This excess money demand would push the home interest rate above the world interest rate if the central bank did not intervene in the foreign exchange market. To maintain the exchange rate at its new fixed level, E^1, the central bank must therefore buy foreign assets and expand the money supply until the asset market curve reaches AA^2 and passes through point 2. Devaluation therefore causes a rise in output, a rise in official reserves, and an expansion of the money supply. A private capital inflow matches the central bank's reserve gain (an official outflow) in the balance of payments accounts.[7]

The effects of devaluation illustrate the three main reasons why governments sometimes choose to devalue their currencies. First, devaluation allows the government to fight domestic unemployment despite the lack of effective monetary policy. If government spending and budget deficits are politically unpopular, for example, or if the legislative process is slow, a government may opt for devaluation as the most convenient way of boosting aggregate demand. A second reason for devaluing is the resulting improvement in the current account, a development the government may believe to be desirable. The third motive behind devaluations is their effect on the central bank's foreign reserves. If the central bank is running low on reserves, a sudden, one-time devaluation can be used to draw in more.[8]

---

[6] We observe a subtle distinction between the terms *devaluation* and *depreciation* (and between *revaluation* and *appreciation*). Depreciation (appreciation) is a rise in E (a fall in E) when the exchange rate floats, while devaluation (revaluation) is a rise in E (a fall in E) when the exchange rate is fixed. Depreciation (appreciation) thus involves the active voice (as in "the currency appreciated"), while devaluation (revaluation) involves the passive voice (as in "the currency was devalued"). Put another way, devaluation (revaluation) reflects a deliberate government decision while depreciation (appreciation) is an outcome of government actions and market forces acting together.

[7] After the home currency is devalued, market participants expect that the new higher exchange rate, rather than the old rate, will prevail in the future. The change in expectations alone shifts AA^1 to the right, but without central bank intervention this by itself is insufficient to move AA^1 all the way to AA^2. At point 2, as at point 1, $R = R*$ if the foreign exchange market clears. Because output is higher at point 2 than at point 1, however, real money demand is also higher at the former point. With P fixed, an expansion of the money supply is therefore necessary to make point 2 a position of money market equilibrium, that is, a point on the new AA schedule. Central bank purchases of foreign assets are therefore a necessary part of the economy's shift to its new fixed exchange rate equilibrium.

[8] Because an unexpected devaluation lowers the foreign currency value of the government's domestic currency liabilities to the private sector, the initial reserve gain by the central bank is financed essentially by a surprise tax on holders of government bonds and money.

Figure 17-4 | Effect of a Currency Devaluation

When a currency is devalued from E^0 to E^1, the economy's equilibrium moves from point I to point 2 as both output and the money supply expand.

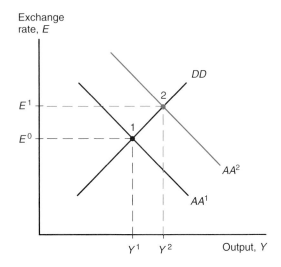

Adjustment to Fiscal Policy and Exchange Rate Changes

If fiscal and exchange rate changes occur when there is full employment and the policy changes are maintained indefinitely, they will ultimately cause the domestic price level to move in such a way that full employment is restored. To understand this dynamic process, we discuss the economy's adjustment to fiscal expansion and devaluation in turn.

If the economy is initially at full employment, fiscal expansion raises output, and this rise in output above its full-employment level causes the domestic price level, P, to begin rising. As P rises home output becomes more expensive, so aggregate demand gradually falls, returning output to the initial, full-employment level. Once this point is reached, the upward pressure on the price level comes to an end. There is no real appreciation in the short run, as there is with a floating exchange rate, but regardless of whether the exchange rate is floating or fixed, the real exchange rate appreciates *in the long run* by the same amount.[9] In the present case real appreciation (a fall in EP^*/P) takes the form of a rise in P rather than a fall in E.

At first glance, the long-run price level increase caused by a fiscal expansion under fixed rates seems inconsistent with the conclusion of Chapter 14 that for a given output level and interest rate the price level and the money supply move proportionally in the long run. There is no inconsistency because fiscal expansion *does* cause a money supply increase by forcing the central bank to intervene in the foreign exchange market. To fix the rate throughout the adjustment process, the central bank ultimately must increase the money supply through intervention in proportion to the long-run increase in P.

---

[9] To see this, observe that the long-run equilibrium real exchange rate, EP^*/P, must in either case satisfy the same equation, $Y^f = D(EP^*/P, Y^f - T, I, G)$, where Y^f, as in Chapter 16, is the full-employment output level.

The adjustment to a devaluation is similar. In fact, since a devaluation does not change long-run demand or supply conditions in the output market, the increase in the long-run price level caused by a devaluation is proportional to the increase in the exchange rate. A devaluation under a fixed rate has the same long-run effect as a proportional increase in the money supply under a floating rate. Like the latter policy, devaluation is neutral in the long run, in the sense that its only effect on the economy's long-run equilibrium is a proportional rise in all nominal prices and in the domestic money supply.

CASE STUDY

Fixing the Exchange Rate to Escape from a Liquidity Trap

During the lengthy Great Depression of the 1930s, the nominal interest rate hit zero in the United States and the country found itself caught in what economists call a *liquidity trap.* Recall from Chapter 13 that money is the most *liquid* of assets, unique in the ease with which it can be exchanged for goods. A liquidity trap is a trap because once an economy's nominal interest rate falls to zero, the central bank cannot reduce it further by increasing the money supply (that is, by increasing the economy's liquidity). Why? At negative nominal interest rates, people would find money strictly preferable to bonds and bonds therefore would be in excess supply. While a zero interest rate may please borrowers, who can borrow for free, it therefore worries makers of macroeconomic policy, who are trapped in a situation where they may no longer be able to steer the economy through conventional monetary expansion. As this Case Study shows, however, a government can escape from a liquidity trap by fixing its currency's exchange rate at a sufficiently depreciated level.

Economists thought liquidity traps were a thing of the past until Japan apparently fell into one in the late 1990s. Despite a progressive lowering of interest rates by the country's central bank, the Bank of Japan, the country's economy has stagnated for over a decade. By 1999 the country's short-term interest rates had effectively reached zero. In November 2001, for example, the Bank of Japan reported that the overnight interest rate was only 0.004 percent.

The dilemma a central bank faces when the economy is in a liquidity trap slowdown can be seen by considering the interest parity condition when the domestic interest rate $R = 0$,

$$R = 0 = R^* + (E^e - E)/E$$

Assume for the moment that the expected future exchange rate, E^e, is fixed. Suppose the central bank raises the domestic money supply so as to depreciate the currency temporarily (that is, to raise E currently but return the rate to E^e later). The interest parity condition shows that E cannot rise once $R = 0$, because the interest rate would have to become *negative.* Instead, despite the increase in the money supply, the exchange rate remains steady at the level

$$E = \frac{E^e}{1 - R^*}.$$

The currency cannot depreciate further.

How is this possible? Our usual argument that a temporary increase in the money supply reduces the interest rate (and depreciates the currency) rests on the assumption that people will add money to their portfolios only if bonds become less attractive to hold. At an interest rate of $R = 0$, however, people may be indifferent about trades of bonds and money—both yield a nominal rate of return rate equal to zero. Thus, an open-market purchase of bonds for money, say, will not disturb the markets: people will be happy to accept the additional money in exchange for their bonds with no change in the interest rate and, thus, no change in the exchange rate. In contrast to the case we examined in Chapter 16, an increase in the money supply will have no effect on the economy! A central bank that progressively *reduces* the money supply by selling bonds will eventually succeed in pushing the interest rate up—the economy cannot function without some money—but that possibility is not helpful, of course, when the economy is in a slump.

Figure 17-5 shows how the *AA-DD* diagram can be modified to depict the liquidity trap region of potential equilibrium positions. The *DD* schedule is the same, but the AA^1 schedule now has a flat segment at levels of output so low that the money market clears at an interest rate R equal to zero. The flat segment of *AA* shows that the currency cannot depreciate beyond the level $E^e/(1 - R^*)$. At the equilibrium point 1 in the diagram, output is trapped at a level Y^1 that is below the full-employment level Y^f.

Let's consider next how an open-market expansion of the money supply works in this strange zero-interest world. That action shifts *AA to the right:* at an unchanged exchange rate, an increase in output Y raises money demand, leaving people content to hold more money at the unchanged interest rate R. Notice how the horizontal stretch of *AA* becomes longer as a result. With more money in circulation, real output and money demand can rise further than before until nominal interest rates are driven to positive levels by increased money demand (resulting in currency appreciation along the downward-sloping segment of *AA*). The suprising result is that the equilibrium simply remains at point 1. Monetary expansion has no effect on output or the exchange rate. This is the sense in which the economy is "trapped."

Our earlier assumption that the expected future exchange rate is fixed at E^e is a key ingredient in this liquidity trap story. Suppose the central bank can credibly promise to raise the money supply *permanently,* so that E^e rises at the same time as the current money supply. In that case the *AA* schedule will shift up as well as to the right, so that output will expand and the currency will depreciate. Observers of Japan have argued, however, that its officials are so fearful of depreciation and inflation (as were many central bankers during the early 1930s) that markets will not believe their promises to depreciate the currency permanently. Instead they will suspect an intention to restore an appreciated exchange rate later on, and treat any monetary expansion as temporary.[10]

A more sure-fire way of jump-starting the Japanese economy has been suggested by Lars E. O. Svensson of Princeton University, who recommends pegging the exchange rate at a depreciated level so as to manage market expectations more directly. A simplified form of Svensson's

---

[10]This argument is made by Paul R. Krugman, "It's Baaack: Japan's Slump and the Return of the Liquidity Trap," *Brookings Papers on Economic Activity* 2:1998, pp. 137–205. See also Ronald McKinnon and Kenichi Ohno, "The Foreign Exchange Origins of Japan's Economic Slump and Low Interest Liquidity Trap," *World Economy* 24 (March 2001), pp. 279–315.

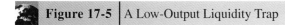

Figure 17-5 A Low-Output Liquidity Trap

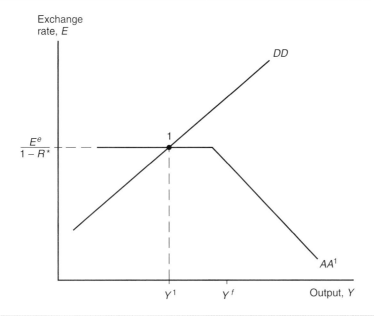

At point 1, output is below its full-employment level. Because exchange rate expectations E^e are fixed, however, a monetary expansion will merely shift AA^1 to the right, leaving the initial equilibrium point the same. The horizontal part of AA^1 gives rise to the liquidity trap.

approach is illustrated in Figure 17-6.[11] In the figure, a permanent peg of the exchange rate at the higher level E^0 shifts AA^1 upward to AA^2 and moves the economy's equilibrium immediately to point 2, where full employment is restored. Notice that in the figure, point 2 is on the downward-sloping portion of the new AA schedule, so the nominal interest rate R actually rises. But output rises too as the currency depreciation shifts world demand toward Japanese products, so the policy has an expansionary effect nonetheless.[12]

Will Japan actually adopt such a plan? The alternative is a long period of deflation that brings about an equivalent real currency depreciation. Because Japan's problems appear to be as much political as economic, it is hard to predict how and when the country will escape from its current liquidity trap.

---

[11] For a more detailed account see Svensson's article, "How Japan Can Recover," *Financial Times,* September 25, 2001.

[12] A devaluation would generally be accompanied by a change in the nominal money supply, which becomes endogenous once the exchange rate is fixed. Because the policy in Figure 17-6 simultaneously raises the nominal interest rate and output, we cannot tell whether the money supply rises or falls. In the former case, the vertical stretch of AA lengthens; in the latter case it shrinks.

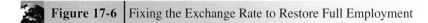

Figure 17-6 | Fixing the Exchange Rate to Restore Full Employment

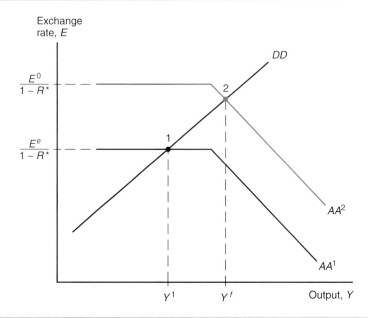

By pegging the exchange rate at E^0, the government alters exchange rate expectations and shifts AA^1 to AA^2. As a result, the economy exits the liquidity trap and returns to full employment.

Balance of Payments Crises and Capital Flight

Until now we have assumed that participants in the foreign exchange market believe that a fixed exchange rate will be maintained at its current level forever. In many practical situations, however, the central bank may find it undesirable or infeasible to maintain the current fixed exchange rate. The central bank may be running short on foreign reserves, for example, or it may face high domestic unemployment. Because market participants know the central bank may respond to such situations by devaluing the currency, it would be unreasonable for them to expect the current exchange rate to be maintained forever.

The market's belief in an impending change in the exchange rate gives rise to a **balance of payments crisis**, a sharp change in official foreign reserves sparked by a change in expectations about the future exchange rate. In this section we use our model of asset market equilibrium to examine how balance of payments crises can occur under fixed exchange rates.

Figure 17-7 shows the asset markets in equilibrium at points 1 (the money market) and 1' (the foreign exchange market) with the exchange rate fixed at E^0 and expected to remain there indefinitely. M^1 is the money supply consistent with this initial equilibrium. Suppose a sudden deterioration in the current account, for example, leads the foreign exchange market to expect the government to devalue in the future and adopt a new fixed exchange rate, E^1, that is higher than the current rate, E^0. The figure's upper part shows this

Figure 17-7 Capital Flight, the Money Supply, and the Interest Rate

To hold the exchange rate fixed at E^0 after the market decides it will be devalued to E^1, the central bank must use its reserves to finance a private capital outflow that shrinks the money supply and raises the home interest rate.

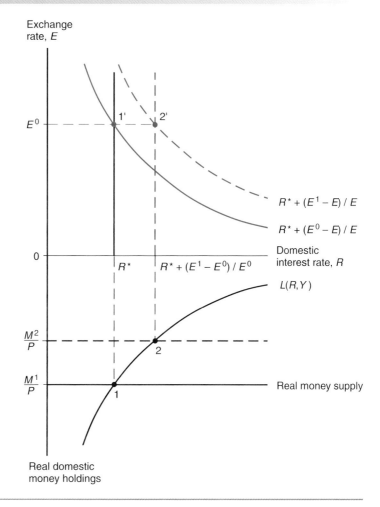

change in expectations as a rightward shift in the curve that measures the expected domestic currency return on foreign currency deposits. Since the current exchange rate still is E^0, equilibrium in the foreign exchange market (point 2′) requires a rise in the domestic interest rate to $R^* + (E^1 - E^0)/E^0$, which now equals the expected domestic currency return on foreign currency assets.

Initially, however, the domestic interest rate remains at R^*, which is below the new expected return on foreign assets. This differential causes an excess demand for foreign currency assets in the foreign exchange market; to continue holding the exchange rate at E^0 the central bank must sell foreign reserves and thus shrink the domestic money supply. The bank's intervention comes to an end once the money supply has fallen to M^2, so that the money market is in equilibrium at the interest rate $R^* + (E^1 - E^0)/E^0$ that clears the foreign exchange market (point 2). *The expectation of a future devaluation causes a balance of* *payments crisis marked by a sharp fall in reserves and a rise in the home interest rate above the world interest rate. Similarly, an expected revaluation causes an abrupt rise in foreign reserves together with a fall in the home interest rate below the world rate.*

The reserve loss accompanying a devaluation scare is often labeled **capital flight** because the associated debit in the balance of payments accounts is a private capital out-flow. Residents flee the domestic currency by selling it to the central bank for foreign exchange; they then invest the proceeds abroad. Capital flight is of particular concern to the government when fears of devaluation arise because the central bank's reserves are low to begin with. By pushing reserves even lower, capital flight may force the central bank to devalue sooner and by a larger amount than planned.[13]

What causes currency crises? Often a government is following policies that are not con-sistent with maintaining a fixed exchange rate over the longer term. Once market expecta-tions take those policies into account, the country's interest rates inevitably are forced up. For example, a country's central bank may be buying bonds from the domestic government to allow the government to run continuing fiscal deficits. Since these central bank purchases of domestic assets cause ongoing losses of central bank foreign exchange reserves, reserves will be falling toward a point where the central bank may find itself without the means to support the exchange rate. As the possibility of a collapse rises over time, so will domestic interest rates, until the central bank indeed runs out of foreign reserves and the fixed exchange rate is abandoned. (Appendix III to this chapter presents a detailed model of this type, and shows that the collapse of the currency peg can be caused by a sharp *speculative attack* in which currency traders suddenly acquire all of the central bank's remaining foreign reserves.) The only way for the central bank to avoid this fate is to stop bankrolling the government deficit, hopefully forcing the government to live within its means.

In the last example, exhaustion of foreign reserves and an end of the fixed exchange rate are inevitable, given macroeconomic policies. The capital outflows that accompany a cur-rency crisis only hasten an inevitable collapse that would have occurred anyway, albeit in slower motion, even if private capital flows could be banned. Not all crises are of this kind, however. An economy can be vulnerable to currency speculation without being in such bad shape that a collapse of its fixed exchange rate regime is inevitable. Currency crises that occur in such circumstances often are called **self-fulfilling currency crises**, although it is important to keep in mind that the government may ultimately be responsible for such crises by creating or tolerating domestic economic weaknesses that invite specu-lators to attack the currency.

As an example, consider an economy in which domestic commercial banks' liabilities are mainly short-term deposits, and in which many of the banks' loans to businesses are likely to go unpaid in the event of a recession. If speculators suspect there will be a deval-uation, interest rates will climb, raising banks' borrowing costs sharply while at the same time reducing the value of bank assets. To prevent domestic financial collapse, the central bank may well lend money to banks, losing foreign reserves in the process and possibly losing its ability to go on pegging the exchange rate. In this case, it is the emergence of

---

[13]If aggregate demand depends on the real interest rate (as in the *IS-LM* model), capital flight reduces output by shrinking the money supply and raising the real interest rate. This possibly contractionary effect of capital flight is another reason why policymakers hope to avoid it.

devaluation expectations among currency traders that pushes the economy into crisis and forces the exchange rate to be changed.

For the rest of this chapter we continue to assume that no exchange rate changes are expected by the market when exchange rates are fixed. But we draw on the preceding analysis repeatedly in later chapters when we discuss various countries' experiences with fixed exchange rates.

Managed Floating and Sterilized Intervention

In previous sections we argued that a central bank gives up its ability to influence output through monetary policy when it maintains a fixed exchange rate. Under managed floating, however, monetary policy is influenced by exchange rate changes without being completely subordinate to the requirements of a fixed rate. Instead, the central bank faces a trade-off between domestic objectives such as employment or the inflation rate and exchange rate stability. Suppose the central bank tries to expand the money supply to fight domestic unemployment, for example, but at the same time carries out foreign asset sales to restrain the resulting depreciation of the home currency. The foreign exchange intervention will tend to *reduce* the money supply, hindering but not necessarily nullifying the central bank's attempt to reduce unemployment.

Discussions of foreign exchange intervention in policy forums and newspapers often appear to ignore the intimate link between intervention and the money supply that we explored in detail above. In reality, however, these discussions often assume that foreign exchange intervention is being *sterilized,* so that opposite domestic asset transactions prevent it from affecting the money supply. Empirical studies of central bank behavior confirm this assumption and consistently show central banks to have practiced sterilized intervention throughout the twentieth century and earlier.[14]

In spite of widespread sterilized intervention, there is considerable disagreement among economists about its effects. In this section we study the role of sterilized intervention in exchange rate management.

Perfect Asset Substitutability and the Ineffectiveness of Sterilized Intervention

When a central bank carries out a sterilized foreign exchange intervention, its transactions leave the domestic money supply unchanged. A rationale for such a policy is difficult to find using the model of exchange rate determination previously developed, for the model predicts

---

[14]Three empirical studies are Leroy O. Laney and Thomas D. Willett, "The International Liquidity Explosion and Worldwide Inflation: The Evidence from Sterilization Coefficient Estimates," *Journal of International Money and Finance* 1 (August 1982), pp. 141–152; Robert E. Cumby and Maurice Obstfeld, "Capital Mobility and the Scope for Sterilization: Mexico in the 1970s," in Pedro Aspe Armella, Rudiger Dornbusch, and Maurice Obstfeld, eds., *Financial Policies and the World Capital Market: The Problem of Latin American Countries* (Chicago: University of Chicago Press, 1983), pp. 245–269; and Cristina Mastropasqua, Stefano Micossi, and Roberto Rinaldi, "Interventions, Sterilization, and Monetary Policy in European Monetary System Countries, 1979–87," in Francesco Giavazzi, Stefano Micossi, and Marcus Miller, eds., *The European Monetary System* (Cambridge, U.K.: Cambridge University Press, 1988), pp. 252–287.

MEXICO'S 1994 BALANCE OF PAYMENTS CRISIS

The events leading to the Mexican peso's December 1994 devaluation provide a vivid example of how a balance of payments crisis starts and develops. As part of a wide-ranging economic stabilization program initiated in 1987, Mexico began to limit the peso's movements against the United States' dollar. The basic motivation for exchange rate stabilization was to limit the inflation bias in Mexico's monetary policy, which had driven the country's inflation rate to very high levels in previous years.

The initial successes of the stabilization program earned Mexican leaders worldwide acclaim. But in March 1994 a slowdown in economic growth, followed by the shocking assassination of the ruling political party's presidential candidate, raised investor fears that the government might sharply devalue, contrary to its pledges. The figure below shows how peso interest rates jumped upward while foreign reserves declined dramatically, just as predicted in our discussion of Figure 17-7. After a second political assassination in November and the inauguration of a new president on December 1, devaluation rumors intensified, sparking a further interest rate jump and the nearly complete exhaustion of the country's foreign reserves. On December 20 Mexico's government finally devalued the peso.

Mexican Foreign Reserves and Interest Rates, January–December 1994

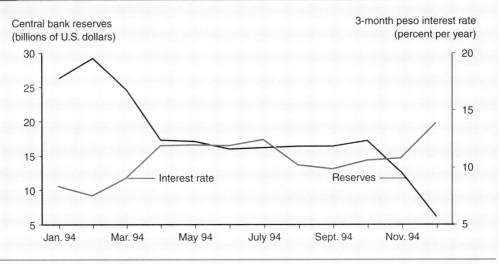

As devaluation fears intensified during 1994, Mexico's reserves fell and its interest rates rose. The interest rate shown is that on a three-month *cetes,* the Mexican government's peso-denominated debt.

Source: Jeffrey Sachs, Aaron Tornell, and Andrés Velasco, "The Collapse of the Mexican Peso: What Have We Learned?" *Economic Policy* 22 (April 1996), pp. 13–63.

that without an accompanying change in the money supply, the central bank's intervention will not affect the domestic interest rate and therefore will not affect the exchange rate.

Our model also predicts that sterilization will be fruitless under a fixed exchange rate. The example of a fiscal expansion illustrates why a central bank might wish to sterilize under a fixed rate and why our model says the policy will fail. Recall that to hold the exchange rate constant when fiscal policy becomes more expansive, the central bank must buy foreign assets and expand the home money supply. The policy raises output but also causes inflation, which the central bank may try to avoid by sterilizing the increase in the money supply that its fiscal policy has induced. But as quickly as the central bank sells domestic assets to reduce the money supply, it will have to *buy* more foreign assets to keep the exchange rate fixed. The ineffectiveness of monetary policy under a fixed exchange rate implies that sterilization is a self-defeating policy.

The key feature of our model that leads to these results is the assumption that the foreign exchange market is in equilibrium only when the expected returns on domestic and foreign currency bonds are the same.[15] This assumption is often called **perfect asset substitutability**. Two assets are perfect substitutes when, as our model assumed, investors don't care how their portfolios are divided between them provided both yield the same expected rate of return. With perfect asset substitutability in the foreign exchange market, the exchange rate is therefore determined so that the interest parity condition holds. When this is the case there is nothing a central bank can do through foreign exchange intervention that it could not do as well through purely domestic open-market operations.

In contrast to perfect asset substitutability, **imperfect asset substitutability** exists when it is possible for assets' expected returns to differ in equilibrium. As we saw in Chapter 13, the main factor that may lead to imperfect asset substitutability in the foreign exchange market is *risk*. If bonds denominated in different currencies have different degrees of risk, investors may be willing to earn lower expected returns on bonds that are less risky. Correspondingly, they will hold a very risky asset only if the expected return it offers is relatively high.

In a world of perfect asset substitutability, participants in the foreign exchange market care only about expected rates of return; since these rates are determined by monetary policy, actions such as sterilized intervention that do not affect the money supply also do not affect the exchange rate. Under imperfect asset substitutability both risk *and* return matter, so central bank actions that alter the riskiness of domestic currency assets can move the exchange rate even when the money supply does not change. To understand how sterilized intervention can alter the riskiness of domestic currency assets, however, we must modify our model of equilibrium in the foreign exchange market.

Foreign Exchange Market Equilibrium under Imperfect Asset Substitutability

When domestic and foreign currency bonds are perfect substitutes, the foreign exchange market is in equilibrium only if the interest parity condition holds:

$$R = R^* + (E^e - E)/E. \qquad (17\text{-}1)$$

When domestic and foreign currency bonds are *imperfect* substitutes, the condition above does not hold in general. Instead, equilibrium in the foreign exchange market requires that

---

[15] We are assuming that all interest-bearing (nonmoney) assets denominated in *the same* currency, whether illiquid time deposits or government bonds, are perfect substitutes in portfolios. The single term "bonds" will generally be used to refer to all these assets.

the domestic interest rate equal the expected domestic currency return on foreign bonds *plus* a **risk premium**, ρ, that reflects the difference between the riskiness of domestic and foreign bonds:

$$R = R^* + (E^e - E)/E + \rho. \tag{17-2}$$

Appendix I to this chapter develops a detailed model of foreign exchange market equilibrium with imperfect asset substitutability. The main conclusion of that model is that the risk premium on domestic assets rises when the stock of domestic government bonds available to be held by the public rises and falls when the central bank's domestic assets rise. It is not hard to grasp the economic reasoning behind this result. Private investors become more vulnerable to unexpected changes in the home currency's exchange rate as the stock of domestic government bonds they hold rises. Investors will be unwilling to assume the increased risk of holding more domestic government debt, however, unless they are compensated by a higher expected rate of return on domestic currency assets. An increased stock of domestic government debt will therefore raise the difference between the expected returns on domestic and foreign currency bonds. Similarly, when the central bank buys domestic assets the market need no longer hold them; private vulnerability to home currency exchange rate risk is thus lower, and the risk premium on home currency assets falls.

This alternative model of foreign market equilibrium implies that the risk premium depends positively on the stock of domestic government debt, denoted by *B,* less the domestic assets of the central bank, denoted by *A:*

$$\rho = \rho(B - A). \tag{17-3}$$

The risk premium on domestic bonds therefore rises when $B - A$ rises. This relation between the risk premium and the central bank's domestic asset holdings allows the bank to affect the exchange rate through sterilized foreign exchange intervention. It also implies that official operations in domestic and foreign assets may differ in their asset market impacts.[16]

The Effects of Sterilized Intervention with Imperfect Asset Substitutability

Figure 17-8 modifies our earlier picture of asset market equilibrium by adding imperfect asset substitutability to illustrate how sterilized intervention can affect the exchange rate. The lower part of the figure, which shows the money market in equilibrium at point 1, does not change. The upper part of the figure is also much the same as before, except that the downward-sloping schedule now shows how the *sum* of the expected domestic currency return on foreign assets *and* the risk premium depends on the exchange rate. (The curve continues to slope downward because the risk premium itself is assumed not to depend on the exchange rate.) Equilibrium in the foreign exchange market is at point 1′, which corresponds to a domestic government debt of *B* and central bank domestic asset holdings of A^1. At that point, the domestic interest rate equals the risk-adjusted domestic currency return on foreign deposits (as in equation (17-2)).

---

[16]The stock of central bank domestic assets is often called domestic *credit.*

Figure 17-8 | Effect of a Sterilized Central Bank Purchase of Foreign Assets under Imperfect Asset Substitutability

A sterilized purchase of foreign assets leaves the money supply unchanged but raises the risk-adjusted return that domestic currency deposits must offer in equilibrium. As a result, the return curve in the upper panel shifts up and to the right. Other things equal, this depreciates the domestic currency from E^1 to E^2.

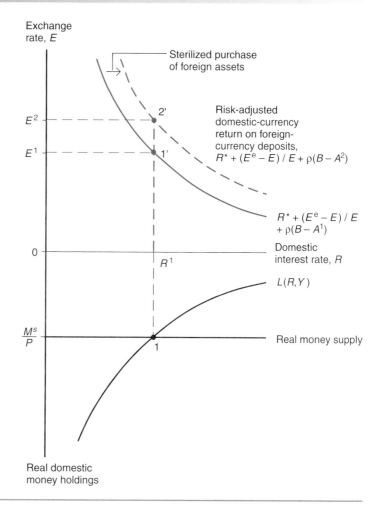

Let's use the diagram to examine the effects of a sterilized purchase of foreign assets by the central bank. By matching its purchase of foreign assets with a sale of domestic assets, the central bank holds the money supply constant at M^s and avoids any change in the lower part of Figure 17-8. As a result of the domestic asset sale, however, the central bank's domestic assets are lower (they fall to A^2) and the stock of domestic assets that the market must hold, $B - A^2$, is therefore higher than the initial stock $B - A^1$. This increase pushes the risk premium ρ upward and shifts to the right the negatively sloped schedule in the upper part of the figure. The foreign exchange market now settles at point 2', and the domestic currency depreciates to E^2.

With imperfect asset substitutability, even sterilized purchases of foreign exchange cause the home currency to depreciate. Similarly, sterilized sales of foreign exchange cause the home currency to appreciate. A slight modification of our analysis shows that the central bank can also use sterilized intervention to hold the exchange rate fixed as it varies the money supply to achieve domestic objectives such as full employment. In effect, the exchange rate and monetary policy can be managed independently of each other in the short run when sterilized intervention is effective.

Evidence on the Effects of Sterilized Intervention

In the early 1980s European countries called on the United States to intervene systematically in the foreign exchange market and resist sharp movements in the dollar's exchange rate against other currencies. Leaders of the seven largest industrial economies discussed intervention at an economic summit meeting held at Versailles in June 1982.[17] As a result of the discussion, government economists in the summit countries were asked to prepare a study of the effects of alternative intervention practices.

The conclusions of the study were published in 1983 as the "Report of the Working Group on Exchange Market Intervention." The report asked in particular if sterilized intervention might allow central banks to manage exchange rates without corresponding adjustments in domestic monetary policies. Little evidence was found to support the idea that sterilized intervention had been a major independent factor influencing exchange rates.

This conclusion agrees with the one reached by most academic studies of sterilized intervention.[18] As we discuss at length in Chapter 21, however, there is also considerable evidence against the view that bonds denominated in different currencies are perfect substitutes. Some economists conclude from these conflicting results that while risk premiums are important, they do not depend on central bank asset transactions in the simple way our model assumes.[19] Others contend that the tests that have been used to detect the effects of sterilized intervention are flawed.[20] Given the meager evidence that sterilized intervention has a reliable effect on exchange rates, however, a skeptical attitude is probably in order.

The Signaling Effect of Intervention

A phenomenon sometimes referred to as the **signaling effect of foreign exchange intervention** is an important complicating factor in econometric efforts to study the effects of sterilization. Our discussion of sterilized intervention has assumed that it does not change the market's exchange rate expectations. If market participants are unsure about the future direction of macroeconomic policies, however, sterilized intervention may give an indication of where the central bank expects (or desires) the exchange rate to move. This signal,

---

[17] The countries represented were Britain, Canada, France, Germany, Italy, Japan, and the United States.

[18] An article by Kenneth Rogoff analyzes Canadian data and surveys results for other countries. See Rogoff, "On the Effects of Sterilized Intervention: An Analysis of Weekly Data," *Journal of Monetary Economics* 14 (September 1984), pp. 133–150. The findings of the Federal Reserve participants in the Versailles project are summarized in the piece by Henderson and Sampson in Further Reading.

[19] For this view, see Robert J. Hodrick and Sanjay Srivastava, "An Investigation of Risk and Return in Forward Foreign Exchange," *Journal of International Money and Finance* 3 (April 1984), pp. 5–29.

[20] See, for example, Richard N. Cooper, "Comment," *Brookings Papers on Economic Activity* 2:1985, pp. 451–456.

in turn, can alter the market's view of the future and cause an immediate exchange rate change even when bonds denominated in different currencies are perfect substitutes.

The signaling effect is most important when the government is unhappy with the exchange rate's level and declares in public that it will alter monetary or fiscal policies to bring about a change. By simultaneously intervening on a sterilized basis, the central bank sometimes lends credibility to this announcement. A sterilized purchase of foreign assets, for example, may convince the market that the central bank intends to bring about a home currency depreciation because the bank will lose money if an appreciation occurs instead. Even central banks must watch their budgets!

A government may be tempted to exploit the signaling effect for temporary benefits, however, even when it has no intention of changing monetary or fiscal policy to bring about a different long-run exchange rate. The result of crying "Wolf!" too often is the same in the foreign exchange market as elsewhere. If governments do not follow up on their exchange market signals with concrete policy moves, the signals soon become ineffective. Thus, intervention signaling cannot be viewed as a policy weapon to be wielded independently of monetary and fiscal policy.[21]

Reserve Currencies in the World Monetary System

Until now, we have studied a single country that fixes its exchange rate in terms of a hypothetical single foreign currency by trading domestic for foreign assets when necessary. In the real world there are many currencies, and it is possible for a country to fix the exchange rates of its domestic currency against some foreign currencies while allowing them to float against others. This has been the case in the European Exchange Rate Mechanism, whose members have held their mutual exchange rates fixed while allowing their currencies' dollar prices to fluctuate.

This section and the next adopt a global perspective and study the macroeconomic behavior of the world economy under two possible systems for fixing the exchange rates of *all* currencies against each other.

The first such fixed-rate system is very much like the one we have been studying. In it, one currency is singled out as a **reserve currency**, the currency central banks hold in their international reserves, and each nation's central bank fixes its currency's exchange rate against the reserve currency by standing ready to trade domestic money for reserve assets at that rate. Between the end of World War II and 1973, the U.S. dollar was the main reserve currency and almost every country pegged the dollar exchange rate of its currency.

The second fixed-rate system (studied in the next section) is a **gold standard**. Under a gold standard, central banks peg the prices of their currencies in terms of gold, and hold

---

[21] For discussion of the role played by the signaling effect in more recent exchange rate experience, see Owen F. Humpage, "Intervention and the Dollar's Decline," *Federal Reserve Bank of Cleveland Economic Review* 24 (Quarter 2, 1988), pp. 2–16; Maurice Obstfeld, "The Effectiveness of Foreign-Exchange Intervention: Recent Experience, 1985–1988," in William H. Branson, Jacob A. Frenkel, and Morris Goldstein, eds., *International Policy Coordination and Exchange Rate Fluctuations* (Chicago: University of Chicago Press, 1990), pp. 197–237; and Kathryn M. Dominguez and Jeffrey A. Frankel, *Does Foreign Exchange Intervention Work?* (Washington, D.C.: Institute for International Economics, 1993).

gold as official international reserves. The heyday of the international gold standard was between 1870 and 1914, although many countries attempted unsuccessfully to restore a permanent gold standard after the end of World War I in 1918.

Both reserve currency standards and the gold standard result in fixed exchange rates between *all* pairs of currencies in the world. But the two systems have very different implications about how countries share the burden of balance of payments financing and about the growth and control of national money supplies.

The Mechanics of a Reserve Currency Standard

The workings of a reserve currency system are illustrated by the system based on the U.S. dollar set up at the end of World War II. Under that system, every central bank fixed the dollar exchange rate of its currency through foreign exchange market trades of domestic currency for dollar assets. The frequent need to intervene meant that each central bank had to have on hand sufficient dollar reserves to meet any excess supply of its currency that might arise. Central banks therefore held a large portion of their international reserves in the form of U.S. Treasury bills and short-term dollar deposits, which pay interest and can be turned into cash at relatively low cost.

Because each currency's dollar price was fixed by its central bank, the exchange rate between any two currencies was automatically fixed as well through arbitrage in the foreign exchange market. How did this process work? Let's suppose the French franc price of dollars was fixed at FFr 5 per dollar while the deutsche mark price of dollars was fixed at DM 4 per dollar. The exchange rate between the franc and the DM had to remain constant at DM 0.80 per franc = (DM 4 per dollar) ÷ (FFr 5 per dollar), even though no central bank was directly trading francs for DM to hold the relative price of those two currencies fixed. At a DM/FFr rate of DM 0.85 per franc, for example, you could have made a sure profit of $6.25 by selling $100 to the former French central bank, the Bank of France, for ($100) × (FFr 5 per dollar) = FFr 500, selling your FFr 500 in the foreign exchange market for (FFr 500) × (DM 0.85 per franc) = DM 425, and then selling the DM to the German Bundesbank (Germany's central bank until 1999) for (DM 425) ÷ (DM 4 per dollar) = $106.25. With everyone trying to exploit this profit opportunity by selling francs for DM in the foreign exchange market, however, the DM would have appreciated against the franc until the DM/FFr rate reached DM 0.80 per franc. Similarly, at a rate of DM 0.75 per franc, pressure in the foreign exchange market would have forced the DM to depreciate against the franc until the rate of DM 0.80 per franc was reached.

Even though each central bank tied its currency's exchange rate only to the dollar, market forces automatically held all other exchange rates—called cross rates—constant at the values implied by the dollar rates. Thus the post-World War II exchange rate system was one in which exchange rates between any two currencies were fixed.[22]

The Asymmetric Position of the Reserve Center

In a reserve currency system the country whose currency is held as reserves occupies a special position because it never has to intervene in the foreign exchange market. The reason is

---

[22]The rules of the postwar system actually allowed currencies' dollar values to move as much as 1 percent above or below the "official" values. This meant cross rates could fluctuate by as much as 4 percent.

that if there are N countries with N currencies in the world, there are only $N - 1$ exchange rates against the reserve currency. If the $N - 1$ nonreserve currency countries fix their exchange rates against the reserve currency, there is no exchange rate left for the reserve center to fix. Thus the center country need never intervene and bears none of the burden of financing its balance of payments.

This set of arrangements puts the reserve-issuing country in a privileged position because it can use its monetary policy for macroeconomic stabilization even though it has fixed exchange rates. We saw earlier in this chapter that when a country must intervene to hold its exchange rate constant, an attempt to expand its money supply is bound to be frustrated by losses of international reserves. But because the reserve center is the one country in the system that can enjoy fixed exchange rates without the need to intervene, it is still able to use monetary policy for stabilization purposes.

What would be the effect of a purchase of domestic assets by the central bank of the reserve currency country? The resulting expansion in its money supply would momentarily push its interest rate below those prevailing abroad, and thereby cause an excess demand for foreign currencies in the foreign exchange market. To prevent their currencies from appreciating against the reserve currency, all other central banks in the system would be forced to buy reserve assets with their own currencies, expanding their money supplies and pushing their interest rates down to the level established by the reserve center. Output throughout the world, as well as at home, would expand after a purchase of domestic assets by the reserve country.

Our account of monetary policy under a reserve currency system points to a basic asymmetry. The reserve country has the power to affect its own economy, as well as foreign economies, by using monetary policy. Other central banks are forced to relinquish monetary policy as a stabilization tool, and instead must passively "import" the monetary policy of the reserve center because of their commitment to peg their currencies to the reserve currency.

This inherent asymmetry of a reserve system places immense economic power in the hands of the reserve country and is therefore likely to lead eventually to policy disputes within the system. Such problems helped cause the breakdown of the postwar "dollar standard" in 1973, a topic we discuss in detail in Chapter 18.

The Gold Standard

An international gold standard avoids the asymmetry inherent in a reserve currency standard by avoiding the "Nth currency" problem. Under a gold standard, each country fixes the price of its currency in terms of gold by standing ready to trade domestic currency for gold whenever necessary to defend the official price. Because there are N currencies and N prices of gold in terms of those currencies, no single country occupies a privileged position within the system: Each is responsible for pegging its currency's price in terms of the official international reserve asset, gold.

The Mechanics of a Gold Standard

Because countries tie their currencies to gold under a gold standard, official international reserves take the form of gold. Gold standard rules also require each country to allow unhindered imports and exports of gold across its borders. Under these arrangements, a gold standard, like a reserve currency system, results in fixed exchange rates between all currencies. For example, if the dollar price of gold is pegged at $35 per ounce by the Federal Reserve while the pound price of gold is pegged at £14.58 per ounce by Britain's central bank, the Bank of England, the dollar/pound exchange rate must be constant at ($35 per ounce) ÷ (£14.58 per ounce) = $2.40 per pound. The same arbitrage process that holds cross exchange rates fixed under a reserve currency system keeps exchange rates fixed under a gold standard as well.[23]

Symmetric Monetary Adjustment under a Gold Standard

Because of the inherent symmetry of a gold standard, no country in the system occupies a privileged position by being relieved of the commitment to intervene. By considering the international effects of a purchase of domestic assets by one central bank, we can see in more detail how monetary policy works under a gold standard.

Suppose the Bank of England decides to increase its money supply through a purchase of domestic assets. The initial increase in Britain's money supply will put downward pressure on British interest rates and make foreign currency assets more attractive than British assets. Holders of pound deposits will attempt to sell them for foreign deposits, but no *private* buyers will come forward. Under floating exchange rates, the pound would depreciate against foreign currencies until interest parity had been reestablished. This depreciation cannot occur when all currencies are tied to gold, however. What happens? Because central banks are obliged to trade their currencies for gold at fixed rates, unhappy holders of pounds can sell these to the Bank of England for gold, sell the gold to other central banks for their currencies, and use these currencies to purchase deposits that offer interest rates higher than the interest rate on pounds. Britain therefore experiences a private capital outflow and foreign countries experience an inflow.

This process reestablishes equilibrium in the foreign exchange market. The Bank of England loses foreign reserves since it is forced to buy pounds and sell gold to keep the pound price of gold fixed. Foreign central banks gain reserves as they *buy* gold with their currencies. Countries share equally in the burden of balance of payments adjustment. Because official foreign reserves are declining in Britain and increasing abroad, the British money supply is falling, pushing the British interest rate back up, and foreign money supplies are rising, pushing foreign interest rates down. Once interest rates have again become equal across countries, asset markets are in equilibrium and there is no further tendency for the Bank of England to lose gold or for foreign central banks to gain it.

Our example illustrates the symmetric nature of international monetary adjustment under a gold standard. Whenever a country is losing reserves and seeing its money supply shrink as a consequence, foreign countries are gaining reserves and seeing their money supplies expand. In contrast, monetary adjustment under a reserve currency standard is highly asymmetric. Countries can gain or lose reserves without inducing any change in the money

---

[23]In practice, the costs of shipping gold and insuring it in transit determined narrow "gold points" within which currency exchange rates could fluctuate.

supply of the reserve currency country, and only the latter country has the ability to influ-ence domestic and world monetary conditions.[24]

Benefits and Drawbacks of the Gold Standard

Advocates of the gold standard argue that it has another desirable property besides symmetry. Because central banks throughout the world are obliged to fix the money price of gold, they cannot allow their money supplies to grow more rapidly than real money demand, since such rapid monetary growth eventually raises the money prices of all goods and services, including gold. A gold standard therefore places automatic limits on the extent to which central banks can cause increases in national price levels through expansionary monetary policies. These limits make the real values of national monies more stable and predictable, thereby enhancing the transaction economies arising from the use of money (see Chapter 14). No such limits to money creation exist under a reserve currency system; the reserve currency country faces no automatic barrier to unlimited money creation.

Offsetting this benefit of a gold standard are some drawbacks:

1. The gold standard places undesirable constraints on the use of monetary policy to fight unemployment. In a worldwide recession, it might be desirable for all countries to expand their money supplies jointly even if this were to raise the price of gold in terms of national currencies.

2. Tying currency values to gold ensures a stable overall price level only if the *relative* price of gold and other goods and services is stable. For example, suppose the dollar price of gold is $35 per ounce while the price of gold in terms of a typical output basket is one-third of a basket per ounce. This implies a price level of $105 per output basket. Now suppose that there is a major gold discovery in South America and the relative price of gold in terms of output falls to one-fourth of a basket per ounce. With the dollar price of gold unchanged at $35 per ounce, the price level would have to rise from $105 to $140 per basket. In fact, studies of the gold standard era do reveal surprisingly large price level fluctuations arising from such changes in gold's relative price.[25]

3. An international payments system based on gold is problematic because central banks cannot increase their holdings of international reserves as their economies grow unless there are continual new gold discoveries. Every central bank would need to hold some gold reserves to fix its currency's gold price and serve as a buffer against unfore-seen economic mishaps. Central banks might thereby bring about world unemployment as they attempted to compete for reserves by selling domestic assets and thus shrinking their money supplies.

---

[24]Originally, gold coins were a substantial part of the currency supply in gold standard countries. A country's gold losses to foreigners therefore did not have to take the form of a fall in central bank gold holdings: Private citizens could melt gold coins into ingots and ship them abroad, where they were either reminted as foreign gold coins or sold to the foreign central bank for paper currency. In terms of our earlier analysis of the central bank balance sheet, circulating gold coins is considered to make up a component of the monetary base that is not a central bank liability. Either form of gold export would thus result in a fall in the domestic money supply and an increase in foreign money supplies.

[25]See, for example, Richard N. Cooper, "The Gold Standard: Historical Facts and Future Prospects," *Brookings Papers on Economic Activity* 1:1982, pp. 1–45.

4. The gold standard could give countries with potentially large gold production, such as Russia and South Africa, considerable ability to influence macroeconomic conditions throughout the world through market sales of gold.

Because of these drawbacks, few economists favor a return to the gold standard today. As early as 1923, the British economist John Maynard Keynes characterized gold as a "barbarous relic" of an earlier international monetary system.[26] After coming to office in 1981, President Reagan set up a special commission under the direction of monetary scholar Anna Jacobson Schwartz to study whether the United States should return to the gold standard. The commission recommended against a return to gold. While most central banks continue to hold gold as part of their international reserves, the price of gold now plays no special role in influencing countries' monetary policies.

The Bimetallic Standard

Up until the early 1870s, many countries adhered to a **bimetallic standard** in which the currency was based on both silver and gold. The United States was bimetallic from 1837 until the Civil War, although the major bimetallic power of the day was France, which abandoned bimetallism for gold in 1873.

In a bimetallic system, a country's mint will coin specified amounts of gold *or* silver into the national currency unit (typically for a fee). In the United States before the Civil War, for example, 371.25 grains of silver (a grain being $1/480^{th}$ of an ounce) or 23.22 grains of gold could be turned into a silver or, respectively, gold dollar. That mint parity made gold worth $371.25/23.22 = 16$ times as much as silver.

The mint parity could differ from the market relative price of the two metals, however, and when it did, one or the other might go out of circulation. For example, if the price of gold in terms of silver were to rise to 20:1, a depreciation of silver relative to the mint parity of 16:1, no one would want to turn gold into gold dollar coins at the mint. More dollars could be obtained by instead using the gold to buy silver in the market, and then having the silver coined into dollars. As a result, gold would tend to go out of monetary circulation when its relative market price rose above the mint relative price, and silver coin would tend to disappear in the opposite case.

The advantage of bimetallism was that it might reduce the price-level instability resulting from use of one of the metals alone. Were gold to become scarce and expensive, cheaper and relatively abundant silver would become the predominant form of money, thereby mitigating the deflation that a pure gold standard would imply. Notwithstanding this advantage, by the late nineteenth century most of the world had followed Britain, the leading industrial power of the day, onto a pure gold standard.

The Gold Exchange Standard

Halfway between the gold standard and a pure reserve currency standard is the **gold exchange standard**. Under a gold exchange standard central banks' reserves consist of gold

---

[26] See Keynes, "Alternative Aims in Monetary Policy," reprinted in his *Essays in Persuasion* (New York: W. W. Norton & Company, 1963). For a dissenting view on the gold standard, see Robert A. Mundell, "International Monetary Reform: The Optimal Mix in Big Countries," in James Tobin, ed., *Macroeconomics, Prices and Quantities* (Washington, D.C.: Brookings Institution, 1983), pp. 285–293.

and currencies whose prices in terms of gold are fixed, and each central bank fixes its exchange rate to a currency with a fixed gold price. A gold exchange standard can operate like a gold standard in restraining excessive monetary growth throughout the world, but it allows more flexibility in the growth of international reserves, which can consist of assets besides gold. A gold exchange standard is, however, subject to the other limitations of a gold standard listed above.

The post-World War II reserve currency system centered on the dollar was, in fact, originally set up as a gold exchange standard. While foreign central banks did the job of pegging exchange rates, the U.S. Federal Reserve was responsible for holding the dollar price of gold at $35 an ounce. By the mid-1960s, the system operated in practice more like a pure reserve currency system than a gold standard. For reasons examined in the next chapter, President Nixon unilaterally severed the dollar's link to gold in August 1971, shortly before the system of fixed dollar exchange rates was abandoned.

Summary

1. There is a direct link between central bank intervention in the foreign exchange market and the domestic money supply. When a country's central bank purchases foreign assets, the country's money supply automatically increases. Similarly, a central bank sale of foreign assets automatically lowers the money supply. The *central bank balance sheet* shows how foreign exchange intervention affects the money supply because the central bank's liabilities, which rise or fall when its assets rise or fall, are the base of the domestic money supply process. The central bank can negate the money supply effect of intervention through *sterilization.* With no sterilization, there is a link between the balance of payments and national money supplies that depends on how central banks share the burden of financing payments gaps.

2. A central bank can fix the exchange rate of its currency against foreign currency if it is willing to trade unlimited amounts of domestic money against foreign assets at that rate. To fix the exchange rate, the central bank must intervene in the foreign exchange market whenever this is necessary to prevent the emergence of an excess demand or supply of domestic currency assets. In effect, the central bank adjusts its foreign assets—and so, the domestic money supply—to ensure that asset markets are always in equilibrium under the fixed exchange rate.

3. A commitment to fix the exchange rate forces the central bank to sacrifice its ability to use monetary policy for stabilization. A purchase of domestic assets by the central bank causes an equal fall in its official international reserves, leaving the money supply and output unchanged. Similarly, a sale of domestic assets by the bank causes foreign reserves to rise by the same amount but has no other effects.

4. Fiscal policy, unlike monetary policy, has a more powerful effect on output under fixed exchange rates than under floating rates. Under a fixed exchange rate, fiscal expansion does not, in the short run, cause a real appreciation that "crowds out" aggregate demand. Instead, it forces central bank purchases of foreign assets and an expansion of the money supply. *Devaluation* also raises aggregate demand and the money supply in the short run. (*Revaluation* has opposite effects.) In the long run,

fiscal expansion causes a real appreciation, an increase in the money supply, and a rise in the home price level, while devaluation causes the long-run levels of the money supply and prices to rise in proportion to the exchange rate change.

5. *Balance of payments crises* occur when market participants expect the central bank to change the exchange rate from its current level. If the market decides a devaluation is coming, for example, the domestic interest rate rises above the world interest rate and foreign reserves drop sharply as private capital flows abroad. *Self-fulfilling currency crises* can occur when an economy is vulnerable to speculation. In other circumstances an exchange rate collapse may be the inevitable result of inconsistent government policies.

6. A system of *managed floating* allows the central bank to retain some ability to control the domestic money supply, but at the cost of greater exchange rate instability. If domestic and foreign bonds are *imperfect substitutes,* however, the central bank may be able to control both the money supply and the exchange rate through sterilized foreign exchange intervention. Empirical evidence provides little support for the idea that sterilized intervention has a significant direct effect on exchange rates. Even when domestic and foreign bonds are *perfect substitutes,* so that there is no *risk premium,* sterilized intervention may operate indirectly through a *signaling effect* that changes market views of future policies.

7. A world system of fixed exchange rates in which countries peg the prices of their currencies in terms of a *reserve currency* involves a striking asymmetry. The reserve currency country, which does not have to fix any exchange rate, can influence economic activity both at home and abroad through its monetary policy. In contrast, all other countries are unable to influence their output or foreign output through monetary policy. This policy asymmetry reflects the fact that the reserve center bears none of the burden of financing its balance of payments.

8. A *gold standard,* in which all countries fix their currencies' prices in terms of gold, avoids the asymmetry inherent in a reserve currency standard and also places constraints on the growth of countries' money supplies. (A related arrangement was the *bimetallic standard* based on both silver and gold.) But the gold standard has serious drawbacks that make it impractical as a way of organizing today's international monetary system. Even the dollar-based *gold exchange standard* set up after World War II ultimately proved unworkable.

Key Terms

Problems

1. Show how an expansion in the central bank's domestic assets ultimately affects its balance sheet under a fixed exchange rate. How are the central bank's transactions in the foreign exchange market reflected in the balance of payments accounts?

2. Do the exercises in the previous question for an increase in government spending.

3. Describe the effects of an unexpected devaluation on the central bank's balance sheet and on the balance of payments accounts.

4. Explain why a devaluation improves the current account in this chapter's model. (Hint: Consider the *XX* curve developed in the last chapter.)

5. The following paragraphs appeared in the *New York Times* on September 22, 1986 (see "Europeans May Prop the Dollar," p. Dl):

   > To keep the dollar from falling against the West German mark, the European central banks would have to sell marks and buy dollars, a procedure known as intervention. But the pool of currencies in the marketplace is vastly larger than all the governments' holdings.
   >
   > Billions of dollars worth of currencies are traded each day. Without support from the United States and Japan, it is unlikely that market intervention from even the two most economically influential members of the European Community—Britain and West Germany—would have much impact on the markets. However, just the stated intention of the Community's central banks to intervene could disrupt the market with its psychological effect.
   >
   > Economists say that intervention works only when markets turn unusually erratic, as they have done upon reports of the assassination of a President, or when intervention is used to push the markets along in a direction where they are already headed anyway.

   a. Do you agree with the statement in the article that Germany had little ability to influence the exchange rate of the DM?

   b. Do you agree with the last paragraph's evaluation of the efficacy of intervention?

   c. Describe how "just the stated intention" to intervene could have a "psychological effect" on the foreign exchange market.

   d. Try your hand at rewriting the above paragraphs in more precise language so that they reflect what you learned in this chapter.

6. Can you think of reasons why a government might willingly sacrifice some of its ability to use monetary policy so that it can have more stable exchange rates?

7. How does fiscal expansion affect a country's current account under a fixed exchange rate?

8. Explain why temporary and permanent fiscal expansions do not have different effects under fixed exchange rates, as they do under floating.

9. Devaluation is often used by countries to improve their current accounts. Since the current account equals national saving less domestic investment, however (see Chapter 12), this improvement can occur only if investment falls, saving rises, or both. How might devaluation affect national saving and domestic investment?

10. Using the *DD-AA* model, analyze the output and balance of payments effects of an import tariff under fixed exchange rates. What would happen if all countries in the

world simultaneously tried to improve employment and the balance of payments by imposing tariffs?

11. When a central bank devalues after a balance of payments crisis, it usually gains foreign reserves. Can this capital inflow be explained using our model? What would happen if the market believed *another* devaluation was to occur in the near future?

12. Suppose that under the postwar "dollar standard" system foreign central banks had held dollar reserves in the form of green dollar bills hidden in their vaults rather than U.S. Treasury bills. Would the international monetary adjustment mechanism have been symmetric or asymmetric? (Hint: Think about what happens to the U.S. and Japanese money supplies, for example, when the Bank of Japan sells yen for dollar bills that it then keeps.)

13. "When domestic and foreign bonds are perfect substitutes, a central bank should be indifferent about using domestic or foreign assets to implement monetary policy." Discuss.

14. United States foreign exchange intervention is sometimes done by an Exchange Stabilization Fund or ESF (a branch of the Treasury Department) that manages a portfolio of U.S. government and foreign currency bonds. An ESF intervention to support the yen, for example, would take the form of a portfolio shift out of dollar and into yen assets. Show that ESF interventions are automatically sterilized and thus do not alter money supplies. How do ESF operations affect the foreign exchange risk premium?

15. Use a diagram like Figure 17-8 to explain how a central bank can alter the domestic interest rate, while holding the exchange rate fixed, under imperfect asset substitutability.

Further Reading

William H. Branson. "Causes of Appreciation and Volatility of the Dollar," in *The U.S. Dollar—Recent Developments, Outlook, and Policy Options.* Kansas City: Federal Reserve Bank of Kansas City, 1985, pp. 33–52. Develops and applies a model of exchange rate determination with imperfect asset substitutability.

Hali J. Edison. *The Effectiveness of Central-Bank Intervention: Survey of the Literature after 1982.* Princeton Special Papers in International Economics 18. International Finance Section, Department of Economics, Princeton University, July 1993. Reviews theory and evidence on sterilized foreign exchange intervention.

Milton Friedman. "Bimetallism Revisited." *Journal of Economic Perspectives* 4 (Fall 1990), pp. 85–104. Fascinating reconsideration of economists' assessments of the dual silver-gold standard.

Dale W. Henderson and Stephanie Sampson. "Intervention in Foreign Exchange Markets: A Summary of Ten Staff Studies." *Federal Reserve Bulletin* 69 (November 1983), pp. 830–836. Presents the major findings of the Federal Reserve intervention study that followed the June 1982 Versailles economic summit meeting.

Owen F. Humpage. "Institutional Aspects of U.S. Intervention." *Federal Reserve Bank of Cleveland Economic Review* 30 (Quarter 1, 1994), pp. 2–19. How the U.S. Treasury and Federal Reserve coordinate foreign exchange intervention.

Olivier Jeanne. *Currency Crises: A Perspective on Recent Theoretical Developments.* Princeton Special Papers in International Economics 20. International Finance Section, Department of Economics, Princeton University, March 2000. Recent thinking on speculative crises and attacks.

Ronald I. McKinnon. *A New Tripartite Monetary Agreement or a Limping Dollar Standard?* Princeton Essays in International Finance 106. International Finance Section, Department of Economics, Princeton University, October 1974. Critical analysis of intervention arrangements under the post-World War II fixed exchange rate system.

Robert A. Mundell. "Capital Mobility and Stabilization Policy Under Fixed and Flexible Exchange Rates." *Canadian Journal of Economics and Political Science* 29 (November 1963), pp. 475–485. Reprinted as Chapter 18 in Mundell's *International Economics.* New York: Macmillan, 1968. Classic account of the effects of monetary and fiscal policies under alternative exchange rate regimes.

Michael Mussa. "The Exchange Rate, the Balance of Payments and Monetary and Fiscal Policy Under a Regime of Controlled Floating," in Jan Herin, Assar Lindbeck, and Johan Myhrman, eds. *Flexible Exchange Rates and Stabilization Policy.* Boulder, CO: Westview Press, 1977, pp. 97–116. An exposition of the monetary approaches to the balance of payments and the exchange rate.

Michael Mussa. *The Role of Official Intervention.* Occasional Paper 6. New York: Group of Thirty, 1981. Discusses the theory and practice of central bank foreign exchange intervention under a dirty float.

Maurice Obstfeld. "Models of Currency Crises with Self-Fulfilling Features." *European Economic Review* 40 (April 1996), pp. 1037–1048. More on the nature of balance-of-payments crises.

Lucio Sarno and Mark P. Taylor. "Official Intervention in the Foreign Exchange Market: Is It Effective and, If So, How Does It Work?" *Journal of Economic Literature* 39 (September 2001). An updated survey on foreign exchange intervention.

APPENDIX I TO CHAPTER 17

Equilibrium in the Foreign Exchange Market with Imperfect Asset Substitutability

This appendix develops a model of the foreign exchange market in which risk factors may make domestic currency and foreign currency assets imperfect substitutes. The model gives rise to a risk premium that can separate the expected rates of return on domestic and foreign assets.[27]

Demand

Because individuals dislike risky situations in which their wealth may vary greatly from day to day, they decide how to allocate wealth among different assets by looking at the riskiness of the resulting portfolio as well as at the expected return it offers. Someone who puts her wealth entirely into British pounds, for example, may expect a high return but can be wiped out if the pound unexpectedly depreciates. A more sensible strategy is to invest in several currencies, even if some have lower expected returns than the pound, and thus reduce the impact on wealth of bad luck with any one currency. By spreading risk in this way among several currencies, an individual can reduce the variability of her wealth.

Considerations of risk make it reasonable to assume that an individual's demand for interest-bearing domestic currency assets increases when the interest they offer (R) rises relative to the domestic currency return on foreign currency assets $[R^* + (E^e - E)/E]$. Put another way, an individual will be willing to increase the riskiness of her portfolio by investing more heavily in domestic currency assets only if she is compensated by an increase in the relative expected return on those assets.

We summarize this assumption by writing individual i's demand for domestic currency bonds, B_i^d, as an increasing function of the rate-of-return difference between domestic and foreign bonds,

$$B_i^d = B_i^d[R - R^* - (E^e - E)/E].$$

Of course, B_i^d also depends on other factors specific to individual i, such as her wealth and income. The demand for domestic currency bonds can be negative or positive, and in the former case individual i is a net borrower in the home currency, that is, a *supplier* of domestic currency bonds.

---

[27]The Mathematical Postscript to Chapter 21 develops a microeconomic model of individual demand for risky assets.

To find the *aggregate* private demand for domestic currency bonds, we need only add up individual demands B_i^d for all individuals i in the world. This summation gives the aggregate demand for domestic currency bonds, B^d, which is also an increasing function of the expected rate of return difference in favor of domestic currency assets. Therefore,

$$\text{Demand} = B^d[R - R^* - (E^e - E)/E]$$
$$= \text{sum for all } i \text{ of } B_i^d[R - R^* - (E^e - E)/E].$$

Since some private individuals may be borrowing, and therefore supplying bonds, B^d should be interpreted as the private sector's *net* demand for domestic currency bonds.

Supply

Since we are interpreting B^d as the private sector's *net* demand for domestic currency bonds, the appropriate supply variable to define market equilibrium is the net supply of domestic currency bonds to the private sector, that is, the supply of bonds that are not the liability of any private individual. Net supply therefore equals the value of domestic currency *government* bonds held by the public, B, less the value of domestic currency assets held by the central bank, A:

$$\text{Supply} = B - A.$$

A must be subtracted from B to find the net supply of bonds because purchases of bonds by the central bank reduce the supply available to private investors. (More generally, we would also subtract from B domestic currency assets held by foreign central banks.)

Equilibrium

The risk premium, ρ, is determined by the interaction of supply and demand. The risk premium is defined as

$$\rho = R - R^* - (E^e - E)/E,$$

that is, as the expected return difference between domestic and foreign bonds. We can therefore write the private sector's net demand for domestic currency bonds as an increasing function of ρ. Figure 17AI-1 shows this relationship by drawing the demand curve for domestic currency bonds with a positive slope.

The bond supply curve is vertical at $B - A^1$ because the net supply of bonds to the market is determined by decisions of the government and central bank and is independent of the risk premium. Equilibrium occurs at point 1 (at a risk premium of ρ^1), where the private sector's net demand for domestic currency bonds equals the net supply. Notice that for given values of R, R^*, and E, the equilibrium shown in the diagram can also be viewed as determining the exchange rate, since $E = E^e/(1 + R - R^* - \rho)$.

Figure 17AI-1 shows the effect of a central bank sale of domestic assets that lowers its domestic asset holdings to $A^2 < A^1$. This sale raises the net supply of domestic currency bonds to $B - A^2$ and shifts the supply curve to the right. The new equilibrium occurs at

Figure 17AI-1 | The Domestic Bond Supply and the Foreign Exchange Risk Premium Under Imperfect Asset Substitutability

An increase in the supply of domestic currency bonds that the private sector must hold raises the risk premium on domestic currency assets.

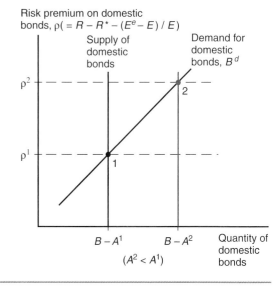

point 2, at a risk premium of $\rho^2 > \rho^1$. Similarly, an increase in the domestic currency government debt, B, would raise the risk premium.

The model therefore establishes that the risk premium is an increasing function of $B - A$, as we assumed in the discussion of sterilized intervention that led to equation (17-3).

APPENDIX II TO CHAPTER 17

The Monetary Approach to the Balance of Payments

The close link discussed above between a country's balance of payments and its money supply suggests that fluctuations in central bank reserves can be thought of as the result of changes in the money market. This method of analyzing the balance of payments is called the *monetary approach to the balance of payments.* The monetary approach was developed in the 1950s and 1960s by the International Monetary Fund's research department under Jacques J. Polak, and by Harry G. Johnson, Robert A. Mundell, and their students at the University of Chicago.[28]

The monetary approach can be illustrated through a simple model linking the balance of payments to developments in the money market. To begin, recall that the money market is in equilibrium when the real money supply equals real money demand, that is, when

$$M^s/P = L(R, Y). \tag{17AII-1}$$

Now let F^* denote the central bank's foreign assets (measured in domestic currency) and A its domestic assets (domestic credit). If μ is the *money multiplier* that defines the relation between total central bank assets ($F^* + A$) and the money supply, then

$$M^s = \mu(F^* + A). \tag{17AII-2}$$

The change in central bank foreign assets over any time period, ΔF^*, equals the balance of payments (for a nonreserve currency country). By combining (17AII-1) and (17AII-2), we can express the central bank's foreign assets as

$$F^* = (1/\mu)PL(R, Y) - A.$$

If we assume that μ is a constant, the balance of payments surplus is

$$\Delta F^* = (1/\mu)\Delta[PL(R, Y)] - \Delta A. \tag{17AII-3}$$

The last equation summarizes the monetary approach. The first term on its right-hand side reflects changes in nominal money demand and tells us that, all else equal, an increase in money demand will bring about a balance of payments surplus and an accompanying increase in the money supply that maintains money market equilibrium. The second term in

---

[28]Many original articles using the monetary approach are collected in Jacob A. Frenkel and Harry G. Johnson, eds., *The Monetary Approach to the Balance of Payments* (London: George Allen and Unwin, 1976), and International Monetary Fund, *The Monetary Approach to the Balance of Payments* (Washington, D.C.: International Monetary Fund, 1977).

the balance of payments equation reflects supply factors in the money market. An increase in domestic credit raises money supply relative to money demand, all else equal: so the balance of payments must go into deficit to reduce the money supply and restore money market equilibrium.

Because the balance of payments equals the sum of the current and (nonreserve) capital account surpluses (see Chapter 12), much of the economics literature that appeared before the monetary approach was developed explained balance of payments movements as the result of current or capital account changes. An important contribution of the monetary approach was to stress that in many situations, balance of payments problems result directly from imbalances in the money market and a policy solution that relies on monetary policy is therefore most appropriate. A large balance of payments deficit may be the result of excessive domestic credit creation, for example. Even though this balance of payments deficit will generally involve deficits in both the current and private capital accounts, it would be misleading to view it as fundamentally due to an exogenous fall in relative world demand for domestic goods or assets.

There are many realistic cases, however, in which a balance of payments analysis based on the monetary approach is roundabout and possibly misleading as a guide to policy. Suppose, for example, that a temporary fall in foreign demand for domestic products does occur. This change will cause a fall in the current account and in the balance of payments, but these effects can be counteracted (when rigid capital account restrictions are not in place) by a temporarily expansionary fiscal policy.

Because output and thus money demand fall, the monetary approach also predicts that a balance of payments deficit will result from a fall in export demand. It would be wrong, however, for policymakers to conclude that because the balance of payments deficit is associated with a fall in money demand, a contraction of domestic credit is the best response. If the central bank were to restrict domestic credit to improve the balance of payments, unemployment would remain high and might even rise.

While the monetary approach is an extremely useful analytical tool, it must be applied with caution in seeking solutions to macroeconomic problems. It is most useful for formulating solutions to policy problems that are a direct result of shifts in domestic money demand or supply.

APPENDIX III TO CHAPTER 17

The Timing of Balance of Payments Crises

In the text we modeled a balance of payments crisis as a sudden loss of confidence in the central bank's promise to hold the exchange rate fixed in the future. As previously noted, a currency crisis often is not the result of arbitrary shifts in market sentiment, as exasperated policymakers embroiled in crises often contend. Instead, an exchange rate collapse can be the inevitable result of government policies inconsistent with maintaining a fixed exchange rate permanently. In such cases, simple economic theory may allow us to predict the date of a crisis through a careful analysis of the government policies and the market's rational response to them.[29]

It is easiest to make the main points using the assumptions and notation of the monetary approach to the balance of payments (as developed in Appendix II to this chapter) and the monetary approach to the exchange rate (Chapter 15). To simplify we will assume that output prices are perfectly flexible and output is constant at its full-employment level. We will also assume that market participants have perfect foresight concerning the future, an assumption that rules out arbitrary shifts in expectations.

The precise timing of a payments crisis cannot be determined independently of government policies. In particular, we have to describe not only how the government is behaving today, but also how it plans to react to future events in the economy. Two assumptions about official behavior are made: (1) The central bank is allowing the stock of domestic credit, A, to expand steadily, and will do so forever. (2) The central bank is currently fixing the exchange rate at the level E^0, but it will allow the exchange rate to float freely forever if its foreign reserves, F^*, ever fall to zero. Furthermore, the authorities will defend E^0 to the bitter end by selling foreign reserves at that price as long as they have any to sell.

These assumptions are not very realistic, but other more complicated stories would lead to similar conclusions. You can think of assumption 1 as reflecting the government's need to finance its budget deficit by borrowing money *directly* from the central bank. Such a policy course would increase A over time by increasing the central bank's claims on government—which do count as domestic assets. You can think of assumption 2 as reflecting a limit on the central bank's ability to borrow foreign reserves to defend its currency from speculative attack. Once the central bank has used up its reserves and foreign currency credit lines, it has no choice but to give up the game and withdraw from the foreign exchange market.

The problem with the central bank's policies is that they are inconsistent with maintaining a fixed exchange rate indefinitely. The monetary approach suggests that foreign reserves will fall steadily as domestic assets continually rise. Eventually, therefore, reserves will have to

---

[29]Alternative models of balance of payments crises are developed in Paul Krugman, "A Model of Balance-of-Payments Crises," *Journal of Money, Credit and Banking* 11 (August 1979), pp. 311–325; Robert P. Flood and Peter M. Garber, "Collapsing Exchange Rate Regimes: Some Linear Examples," *Journal of International Economics* 17 (August 1984), pp. 1–14; and Maurice Obstfeld, "Rational and Self-Fulfilling Balance-of-Payments Crises," *American Economic Review* 76 (March 1986), pp. 72–81. See also the paper by Obstfeld in Further Reading.

run out and the fixed exchange rate E^0 will have to be abandoned. In fact, speculators will force the issue by mounting a speculative attack and buying all of the central bank's reserves while reserves are still at a positive level.

We can describe the timing of this crisis with the help of a definition and a diagram. The *shadow* floating exchange rate at time t, denoted E_t^S, is the exchange rate that would prevail at time t if the central bank held no foreign reserves, allowed the currency to float, but continued to allow domestic credit to grow over time. We know from the monetary approach to the exchange rate that the result would be a situation of *ongoing inflation* in which E_t^S trended upward over time in proportion to the domestic credit growth rate. The upper panel of Figure 17AIII-1 shows this upward trend in the shadow floating rate, together with the level E^0 at which the exchange rate is initially pegged. The time T indicated on the horizontal axis is defined as the date on which the shadow exchange rate reaches E^0.

The lower panel of the figure shows how reserves behave over time when domestic credit is steadily growing. (An increase in reserves is a move down from the origin along the vertical axis.) We have shown the path of reserves as a kinked curve that falls gradually until time T, at which time reserves drop in a single stroke to zero. This precipitous reserve loss (of size F_T^*) is the speculative attack that forces the end of the fixed exchange rate, and we now argue that such an attack must occur precisely at time T if assets markets are to clear at each moment.

We are assuming that output Y is fixed, so equation (17AII-3) tells us that reserves will fall over time at the same rate that domestic credit grows as long as the domestic interest rate R doesn't change. What do we know about the behavior of the interest rate? We know that while the exchange rate is convincingly fixed, R will equal the foreign interest rate R^* because no depreciation is expected. Thus, reserves fall gradually over time, as shown in Figure 17AIII-1, as long as the exchange rate remains fixed at E^0.

Imagine now that reserves first hit zero at a time like T', which is *later* than time T. Our shadow exchange rate E^S is defined as the equilibrium floating rate that prevails when foreign reserves are zero, so if reserves first hit zero at time T', the authorities abandon E^0 forever and the exchange rate jumps immediately to the higher level $E_{T'}^S$. There is something wrong with this "equilibrium," however: Each market participant knows that the home currency will depreciate very sharply at time T' and will try to profit by buying foreign reserves from the central bank, at the lower price E^0, just an instant *before* T'. Thus the central bank will lose all of its reserves before T', contrary to our assumption that reserves first hit zero *at* T'. So we have not really been looking at an equilibrium after all.

Do we get to an equilibrium by assuming instead that speculators buy out the official reserve stock at a time like T'' that is *earlier* than time T? Again the answer is no, as you can see by considering the choices facing an individual asset holder. He knows that if central bank reserves reach zero at time T'', the currency will appreciate from E^0 to $E_{T''}^S$ as the central bank leaves the foreign exchange market. It therefore will behoove him not to join any speculative attack that pushes reserves to zero at time T''; in fact, he would prefer to *sell* as much foreign currency as possible to the central bank just before time T'' and then buy it back at the lower market-determined price that would prevail after a crisis. Since every market participant would find it in his or her interest to act in this way, however, a speculative attack simply can't occur before time T. No speculator would want to buy central bank reserves at the price E^0, knowing that an immediate discrete capital loss was at hand.

Only if foreign reserves hit zero precisely at time T are asset markets continually in equilibrium. As noted above, time T is defined by the condition

Figure 17AIII-1 | How the Timing of a Balance of Payments Crisis Is Determined

The market stages a speculative attack and buys the
remaining foreign reserve
stock F_T^* at time T, when the
shadow floating exchange
rate E_T^s just equals the pre-
collapse fixed exchange
rate E^0.

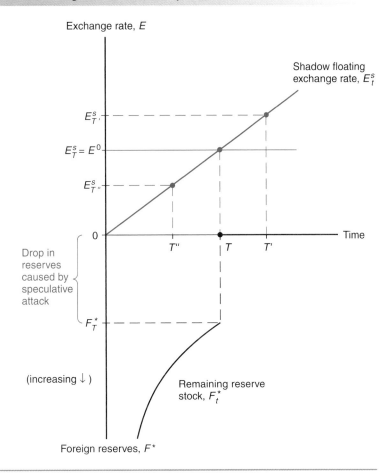

$$E_T^S = E^0,$$

which states that if reserves suddenly drop to zero at time T, the exchange rate remains
initially at its pegged level, and only subsequently floats upward.

The absence of any foreseen initial jump in the exchange rate, either upward or downward,
removes the opportunities for arbitrage (described above) that prevent speculative attacks at
times like T' or T''. In addition, the money market remains in equilibrium at time T, even
though the exchange rate doesn't jump, because two factors offset each other exactly. As
reserves drop sharply to zero, the money supply falls (see equation (17AII-2)). We also know
that at the moment the fixed exchange rate is abandoned, people will expect the currency to
begin depreciating over time. The domestic interest rate R will therefore move upward to
maintain interest parity, and this change reduces real money demand in line with the fall in the
real money supply.

We have therefore tied down the exact date on which a balance of payments crisis forces the authorities off the fixed exchange rate. Note once again that in our example, a crisis must occur at *some* point because profligate monetary policies make one inevitable. The fact that a crisis occurs while the central bank's foreign reserves are still positive might suggest to superficial observers that ill-founded market sentiment is leading to a premature panic. This is not the case here. The speculative attack we have analyzed is the only outcome that does not confront market participants with arbitrage opportunities.[30] There are alternative self-fulfilling crisis models, however, in which attacks can occur even when the exchange rate could have been sustained indefinitely in the absence of an attack.

---

[30] Our finding that reserves fall to zero in a single attack comes from our assumptions that the market can foresee perfectly the future course of events and that trading takes place continuously. If we were to allow instead some discrete uncertainty—for example, about the rate of domestic credit growth—the domestic interest rate would rise as a collapse became more probable, causing a series of "speculative" money-demand reductions prior to the final depletion of foreign reserves. Each of these preliminary attacks would be similar to the type of crisis described in the chapter.

PART 4   International Macroeconomic Policy

CHAPTER 18

The International Monetary System, 1870–1973

In the previous two chapters we saw how a single country can use monetary, fiscal, and exchange rate policy to change the levels of employment and production within its borders. Although the analysis usually assumed that macroeconomic conditions in the rest of the world were not affected by the actions of the country we were studying, this assumption is not, in general, a valid one: Any change in the home country's real exchange rate automatically implies an opposite change in foreign real exchange rates, and any shift in overall domestic spending is likely to change domestic demand for foreign goods. Unless the home country is insignificantly small, developments within its borders affect macroeconomic conditions abroad and therefore complicate the task of foreign policymakers.

The inherent interdependence of open national economies has sometimes made it more difficult for governments to achieve such policy goals as full employment and price level stability. The channels of interdependence depend, in turn, on the monetary and exchange rate arrangements that countries adopt—a set of institutions called the *international monetary system*. This chapter examines how the international monetary system influenced macroeconomic policy-making and performance during three periods: the gold standard era (1870–1914), the interwar period (1918–1939), and the post-World War II years during which exchange rates were fixed under the Bretton Woods agreement (1946–1973).

In an open economy, macroeconomic policy has two basic goals, internal balance (full employment with price stability) and external balance (avoiding excessive imbalances in international payments). Because a country cannot alter its international payments position without automatically causing an opposite change of equal magnitude in the payments position of the rest of the world, one country's pursuit of its macroeconomic goals inevitably influences how well other countries attain their goals. The goal of external balance therefore offers a clear illustration of how policy actions taken abroad may change an economy's position relative to the position its government prefers.

Throughout the period 1870–1973, with its various international currency arrangements, how did countries try to attain internal and external balance, and how successful were they? Did policymakers worry about the foreign repercussions of their actions, or did each adopt nationalistic measures that were self-defeating for the world economy as a whole? The answers to these questions depend on the international monetary system in effect at the time. ●

Macroeconomic Policy Goals in an Open Economy

In open economies, policymakers are motivated by the goals of internal and external balance. Simply defined, **internal balance** requires the full employment of a country's resources and domestic price level stability. **External balance** is attained when a country's current account is neither so deeply in deficit that the country may be unable to repay its foreign debts in the future nor so strongly in surplus that foreigners are put in that position.

In practice, neither of these definitions captures the full range of potential policy concerns. Along with full employment and stability of the overall price level, for example, policymakers may have a particular domestic distribution of income as an additional internal target. Depending on exchange rate arrangements, policymakers may worry about swings in balance of payments accounts other than the current account. To make matters even more complicated, the line between external and internal goals can be fuzzy. How should one classify an employment target for export industries, for example, when export growth influences the economy's ability to repay its foreign debts?

The simple definitions of internal and external balance given above, however, capture the goals that most policymakers share regardless of the particular economic environment. We therefore organize our analysis around these definitions and discuss possible additional aspects of internal or external balance when they are relevant.

Internal Balance: Full Employment and Price-Level Stability

When a country's productive resources are fully employed and its price level is stable, the country is in internal balance. The waste and hardship that occur when resources are underemployed is clear. If a country's economy is "overheated" and resources are *over*employed, however, waste of a different (though probably less harmful) kind occurs. For example, workers on overtime might prefer to be working less and enjoying leisure, but their contracts require them to put in longer hours during periods of high demand. Machines that are being worked more intensely than usual will tend to suffer more frequent breakdowns and to depreciate more quickly.

Under- and overemployment also lead to general price level movements that reduce the economy's efficiency by making the real value of the monetary unit less certain and thus a less useful guide for economic decisions. Since domestic wages and prices rise when the demands for labor and output exceed full-employment levels, and fall in the opposite case, the government must prevent substantial movements in aggregate demand relative to its full-employment level to maintain a stable, predictable price level.

Inflation or deflation can occur even under conditions of full employment, of course, if the expectations of workers and firms about future monetary policy lead to an upward or downward wage-price spiral. Such a spiral can continue, however, only if the central bank fulfills expectations through continuing injections or withdrawals of money (Chapter 14).

One particularly disruptive effect of an unstable price level is its effect on the real value of loan contracts. Because loans tend to be denominated in the monetary unit, unexpected price level changes cause income to be redistributed between creditors and debtors. A sudden increase in the U.S. price level, for example, makes those with dollar debts better off, since the money they owe to lenders is now worth less in terms of goods and services. At the same time, the price-level increase makes creditors worse off. Because such accidental income redistribution can cause considerable distress to those who are hurt, governments have another reason to maintain price-level stability.[1]

Theoretically, a perfectly predictable trend of rising or falling prices would not be too costly, since everyone would be able to calculate easily the real value of money at any point in the future. But in the real world, there appears to be no such thing as a predictable inflation rate. Indeed, experience shows that the unpredictability of the general price level is magnified tremendously in periods of rapid price-level change. The costs of inflation have been most apparent in the postwar period in countries like Argentina, Brazil, and Russia, where astronomical price-level increases caused the domestic currencies practically to stop functioning as units of account. (Argentina and Brazil had currency reforms as a result of the public's flight from domestic money.)

To avoid price-level instability, therefore, the government must prevent large fluctuations in output, which are also undesirable in themselves. In addition, it must avoid ongoing inflation and deflation by ensuring that the domestic money supply does not grow too quickly or too slowly.

External Balance: The Optimal Level of the Current Account

The notion of external balance is more difficult to define than internal balance because there are no natural benchmarks like "full employment" or "stable prices" to apply to an economy's external transactions. Whether an economy's trade with the outside world poses macroeconomic problems depends on several factors, including the economy's particular circumstances, conditions in the outside world, and the institutional arrangements governing its economic relations with foreign countries. A country that is committed to fix its exchange rate against a foreign currency, for example, may well adopt a different definition of external balance than one whose currency floats.

International economics textbooks often identify external balance with balance in a country's current account. While this definition is appropriate in some circumstances, it is not helpful as a general rule. Recall from Chapter 12 that a country with a current account deficit is borrowing resources from the rest of the world that it will have to pay back in the future. This situation is not necessarily undesirable. For example, the country's opportunities for investing the borrowed resources may be attractive relative to the opportunities available in the rest of the world. In this case, paying back loans from foreigners poses no problem because a profitable investment will generate a return high enough to cover the interest and principal on those loans. Similarly, a current account surplus may pose no problem if domestic savings are being invested more profitably abroad than they would be at home.

---

[1]The situation is somewhat different when the government itself is a major debtor in domestic currency. In such cases, a surprise inflation that reduces the real value of government debt may be a convenient way of taxing the public. This method of taxation has been quite common in developing countries (see Chapter 22), but elsewhere it has generally been applied with reluctance and in extreme situations (for example, during wars). A policy of trying to surprise the public with inflation undermines the government's credibility and, through the Fisher effect, worsens the terms on which the government can borrow in the future.

More generally, we may think of current account imbalances as providing another example of how countries gain from trade. The trade involved is what we have called *intertemporal trade,* that is, the trade of consumption over time (Chapter 7). Just as countries with differing abilities to produce goods at a single point in time gain from concentrating their production on what they do best and trading, countries can gain from concentrating the world's investment in those economies best able to turn current output into future output. Countries with weak investment opportunities should invest little at home and channel their savings into more productive investment activity abroad. Put another way, countries where investment is relatively unproductive should be net exporters of currently available output (and thus have current account surpluses), while countries where investment is relatively productive should be net importers of current output (and have current account deficits). To pay off their foreign debts when the investments mature, the latter countries export output to the former countries and thereby complete the exchange of present output for future output.

Other considerations may also justify an unbalanced current account. A country where output drops temporarily (for example, because of an unusually bad crop failure) may wish to borrow from foreigners to avoid the sharp temporary fall in its consumption that would otherwise occur. In the absence of this borrowing, the price of present output in terms of future output would be higher in the low-output country than abroad, so the intertemporal trade that eliminates this price difference leads to mutual gains.

Insisting that all countries be in current account equilibrium makes no allowance for these important gains from trade over time. Thus, no realistic policymaker would want to adopt a balanced current account as a policy target appropriate in all circumstances.

At a given point, however, policymakers generally adopt *some* current account target as an objective, and this target defines their external balance goal. While the target level of the current account is generally not zero, governments usually try to avoid extremely large external surpluses or deficits unless they have clear evidence that large imbalances are justified by potential intertemporal trade gains. (After the sharp rise in oil prices in the early 1970s, for example, Norway's government allowed extensive foreign borrowing to fund the development of the country's North Sea oil reserves.) Governments are cautious because the exact current account balance that maximizes the gains from intertemporal trade is difficult if not impossible to figure out. In addition, this optimal current account balance can change unpredictably over time as conditions in the economy change. Current account balances that are very wide of the mark can, however, cause serious problems.

Problems with Excessive Current Account Deficits.   Why do governments prefer to avoid current account deficits that are too large? As noted, a current account deficit (which means that the economy is borrowing from abroad) may pose no problem if the borrowed funds are channeled into productive domestic investment projects that pay for themselves with the revenue they generate in the future. Sometimes, however, large current account deficits represent temporarily high consumption resulting from misguided government policies or some other malfunction in the economy. At other times, the investment projects that draw on foreign funds may be badly planned and based on overoptimistic expectations about future profitability. In such cases, the government might wish to reduce the current account deficit immediately rather than face problems in repaying debts to foreigners later. In particular, a large current account deficit caused by an expansionary fiscal policy that does not simultaneously make domestic investment opportunities more profitable may signal a need for the government to restore external balance by changing its economic course.

At times the external target is imposed from abroad rather than chosen by the domestic government. When countries begin to have trouble meeting their payments on past foreign loans, foreign creditors become reluctant to lend them new funds and may even demand immediate repayment of the earlier loans. After 1982, many developing economies (particularly those in Latin America) faced this problem of a limited ability to borrow abroad. In such cases, the home government may have to take severe action to reduce the country's desired borrowing from foreigners to feasible levels. A large current account deficit can undermine foreign investors' confidence and contribute to a lending crisis.

Problems with Excessive Current Account Surpluses. An excessive current account surplus poses problems that are different from those posed by deficits. A surplus in the current account implies that a country is accumulating assets located abroad. Why are growing domestic claims to foreign wealth ever a problem? One potential reason stems from the fact that, for a given level of national saving, an increased current account surplus implies lower investment in domestic plant and equipment. (This follows from the national income identity, $S = CA + I$, which says that total domestic saving, S, is divided between foreign asset accumulation, CA, and domestic investment, I.) Several factors might lead policymakers to prefer that domestic saving be devoted to higher levels of domestic investment and lower levels of foreign investment. First, the returns on domestic capital may be easier to tax than those on assets abroad. Second, an addition to the home capital stock may reduce domestic unemployment and therefore lead to higher national income than an equal addition to foreign assets. Finally, domestic investment by one firm may have beneficial technological spillover effects on other domestic producers that the investing firm does not capture.

If a large home current account surplus reflects excessive external borrowing by foreigners, the home country may in the future find itself unable to collect the money it is owed. Put another way, the home country may lose part of its foreign wealth if foreigners find they have borrowed more than they can repay. In contrast, nonrepayment of a loan between domestic residents leads to a redistribution of national wealth within the home country but causes no change in the level of national wealth.

Excessive current account surpluses may also be inconvenient for political reasons. Countries with large surpluses can become targets for discriminatory protectionist measures by trading partners with external deficits. To avoid such damaging restrictions, surplus countries may try to keep their surpluses from becoming too large.

Although high surpluses, like deficits, can pose problems, governments whose economies are in deficit usually face much more intense pressures to restore external balance. This difference reflects a basic asymmetry. A borrowing country is dependent on its creditors, who may withdraw their credit at any time. In contrast, a lending country faces no such market-imposed limit on its surplus. Its government often can postpone external adjustment, if it chooses, for an indefinite period, even though the surplus may be detrimental to national welfare.

To summarize, the goal of external balance is a level of the current account that allows the most important gains from trade over time to be realized without risking the problems discussed above. Because governments do not know this current account level exactly, they usually try to avoid large deficits or surpluses unless there is clear evidence of large gains from intertemporal trade.

International Macroeconomic Policy under the Gold Standard, 1870–1914

The gold standard period between 1870 and 1914 was based on ideas about international macroeconomic policy very different from those that have formed the basis of international monetary arrangements in the second half of the twentieth century. Nevertheless, the period warrants attention because subsequent attempts to reform the international monetary system on the basis of fixed exchange rates can be viewed as attempts to build on the strengths of the gold standard while avoiding its weaknesses. (Some of these strengths and weaknesses were discussed in Chapter 17.) This section looks at how the gold standard functioned in practice before World War I and examines how well it enabled countries to attain goals of internal and external balance.

Origins of the Gold Standard

The gold standard had its origin in the use of gold coins as a medium of exchange, unit of account, and store of value. While gold has been used in this way since ancient times, the gold standard as a legal institution dates from 1819, when the British Parliament passed the Resumption Act. This law derived its name from its requirement that the Bank of England *resume* its practice—discontinued four years after the outbreak of the Napoleonic Wars (1793–1815)—of exchanging currency notes for gold on demand at a fixed rate. The Resumption Act marks the first adoption of a true gold standard because it simultaneously repealed long-standing restrictions on the export of gold coins and bullion from Britain.

Later in the nineteenth century, Germany, Japan, and other countries also adopted the gold standard. At the time, Britain was the world's leading economic power, and other nations hoped to achieve similar economic success by imitating British institutions. The United States effectively joined the gold standard in 1879 when it pegged to gold the paper "greenbacks" issued during the Civil War. The U.S. Gold Standard Act of 1900 institution-alized the dollar-gold link. Given Britain's preeminence in international trade and the advanced development of its financial institutions, London naturally became the center of the international monetary system built on the gold standard.

External Balance under the Gold Standard

Under the gold standard, the primary responsibility of a central bank was to preserve the official parity between its currency and gold; to maintain this price, the central bank needed an adequate stock of gold reserves. Policymakers therefore viewed external balance not in terms of a current account target but as a situation in which the central bank was neither gaining gold from abroad nor (more important) losing gold to foreigners at too rapid a rate.

In the modern terminology of Chapter 12, central banks tried to avoid sharp fluctuations in the *balance of payments* (or official settlements balance), the sum of the current account balance, the capital account balance, and the nonreserve component of the financial account balance. Because international reserves took the form of gold during this period, the surplus or deficit in the balance of payments had to be financed by gold shipments between central banks.[2] To avoid large gold movements, central banks adopted policies that pushed the non-reserve component of the financial account surplus (or deficit) into line with the total current plus capital account deficit (or surplus). A country is said to be in **balance of payments equilibrium** when the sum of its current, capital, and nonreserve financial accounts equals zero, so that the current plus capital account balance is financed entirely by international lending without reserve movements.

Many governments took a laissez-faire attitude toward the current account. Britain's current account surplus between 1870 and World War I averaged 5.2 percent of its GNP, a figure that is remarkably high by post-1945 standards. (Today, a current account/GNP ratio half that size would be considered sizable.) Several borrowing countries, however, did experience difficulty at one time or another in paying their foreign debts. Perhaps because Britain was the world's leading exporter of international economic theory as well as of capital during these years, the economic writing of the gold standard era places little emphasis on problems of current account adjustment.[3]

The Price-Specie-Flow Mechanism

The gold standard contains some powerful automatic mechanisms that contribute to the simultaneous achievement of balance of payments equilibrium by all countries. The most important of these, the **price-specie-flow mechanism**, was recognized by the eighteenth century (when precious metals were referred to as "specie"). David Hume, the Scottish philosopher, in 1752 described the price-specie-flow mechanism as follows:

> Suppose four-fifths of all the money in Great Britain to be annihilated in one night, and the nation reduced to the same condition, with regard to specie, as in the reigns of the Harrys and the Edwards, what would be the consequence? Must not the price of all labour and commodities sink in proportion, and everything be sold as cheap as they were in those ages? What nation could then dispute with us in any foreign market, or pretend to navigate or to sell manufactures at the same price, which to us would afford sufficient profit? In how little time, therefore, must this bring back the money which we had lost, and raise us to the level of all the neighbouring nations? Where, after we have arrived, we immediately lose the advantage of the cheapness of labour and commodities; and the farther flowing in of money is stopped by our fulness and repletion.
>
> Again, suppose that all the money in Great Britain were multiplied fivefold in a night, must not the contrary effect follow? Must not all labour and commodities rise to such an exorbitant height, that no neighbouring nations could afford to buy from us; while their commodities, on the other hand, became comparatively so cheap, that, in spite of all the laws which could be formed, they would run in upon us, and our money

---

[2] In reality, central banks had begun to hold foreign currencies in their reserves even before 1914. (The pound sterling was the leading reserve currency.) It is still true, however, that the balance of payments was financed mainly by gold shipments during this period.

[3] While the economic consequences of the current account were often ignored (at least by surplus countries), governments sometimes restricted international lending by their residents to put political pressure on foreign governments. The political dimensions of international capital flows before World War I are examined in a famous study by Herbert Feis, *Europe, the World's Banker* (New Haven: Yale University Press, 1930).

flow out; till we fall to a level with foreigners, and lose that great superiority of riches which had laid us under such disadvantages?[4]

It is easy to translate Hume's description of the price-specie-flow mechanism into more modern terms. Suppose that Britain's current plus capital account surplus is greater than its nonreserve financial account deficit. Because foreigners' net imports from Britain are not being financed entirely by British loans, the balance must be matched by flows of international reserves—that is, of gold—into Britain. These gold flows automatically reduce foreign money supplies and swell Britain's money supply, pushing foreign prices downward and British prices upward. (Notice that Hume fully understood the lesson of Chapter 14 (p. 374), that price levels and money supplies move proportionally in the long run.[5])

The simultaneous rise in British prices and fall in foreign prices—a real appreciation of the pound, given the fixed exchange rate—reduces foreign demand for British goods and services and at the same time increases British demand for foreign goods and services. These demand shifts work in the direction of reducing Britain's current account surplus and reducing the foreign current account deficit. Eventually, therefore, reserve movements stop and both countries reach balance of payments equilibrium. The same process also works in reverse, eliminating an initial situation of foreign surplus and British deficit.

The Gold Standard "Rules of the Game": Myth and Reality

The price-specie-flow mechanism could operate automatically under the gold standard to bring countries' current and capital accounts into line and eliminate international gold movements. But the reactions of central banks to gold flows across their borders furnished another potential mechanism to help restore balance of payments equilibrium. Central banks that were persistently losing gold faced the risk of becoming unable to meet their obligation to redeem currency notes. They were therefore motivated to contract their domestic asset holdings when gold was being lost, pushing domestic interest rates upward and attracting inflows of capital from abroad. Central banks gaining gold had much weaker incentives to eliminate their own imports of the metal. The main incentive was the greater profitability of interest-bearing domestic assets compared with "barren" gold. A central bank that was accumulating gold might be tempted to purchase domestic assets, thereby increasing capital outflows and driving gold abroad.

These domestic credit measures, if undertaken by central banks, reinforced the price-specie-flow mechanism in pushing all countries toward balance of payments equilibrium. After World War I, the practices of selling domestic assets in the face of a deficit and buying domestic assets in the face of a surplus came to be known as the gold standard "rules of the

---

[4] Hume, "Of the Balance of Trade," reprinted (in abridged form) in Barry Eichengreen, and Marc Flandreau, eds., *The Gold Standard in Theory and History* (London: Routledge, 1997), pp. 33–43.

[5] As mentioned in footnote 24 on p. 515, there are several ways in which the reduction in foreign money supplies, and the corresponding increase in Britain's money supply, might have occurred in Hume's day. Foreign residents could have melted gold coins into bars and used them to pay for imports. The British recipients of the gold bars could have then sold them to the Bank of England for British coins or paper currency. Alternatively, the foreign residents could have sold paper money to their central banks in return for gold and shipped this gold to Britain. Since gold coins were then part of the money supply, both transactions would have affected money supplies in the same way.

HUME VERSUS THE MERCANTILISTS

David Hume's forceful account of the price-specie-flow mechanism is another example of the skillful use of economic theory to mold economic policy. An influential school of economic thinkers called *mercantilists* held that without severe restrictions on international trade and payments, Britain might find itself impoverished and without an adequate supply of circulating monetary gold as a result of balance of payments deficits. Hume refuted their arguments by demonstrating that the balance of payments would automatically regulate itself to ensure an adequate supply of money in every country.

Mercantilism, which originated in the seventeenth century, held that silver and gold were the mainstays of national wealth and essential to vigorous commerce. Mercantilists therefore viewed specie outflows with alarm and had as a main policy goal a continuing surplus in the balance of payments (that is, a continuing inflow of precious metals). As the mercantilist writer Thomas Mun put it around 1630: "The ordinary means therefore to increase our wealth and treasure is by foreign trade, wherein we must ever observe this rule: to sell more to strangers yearly than we consume of theirs in value."

Hume's reasoning showed that a perpetual surplus is impossible: Since specie inflows drive up domestic prices and restore equilibrium in the balance of payments, any surplus eventually eliminates itself. Similarly, a shortage of currency leads to low domestic prices and a foreign payments surplus that eventually brings into the country as much money as needed. Government interference with international transactions, Hume argued, would harm the economy without bringing about the ongoing increase in "wealth and treasure" that the mercantilists favored.

Hume pointed out that the mercantilists overemphasized a single and relatively minor component of national wealth, precious metals, while ignoring the nation's main source of wealth, its productive capacity. In making this observation Hume was putting forward a very modern view. Well into the twentieth century, however, policymakers concerned with external balance often focused on international gold flows at the expense of broader indicators of changes in national wealth. Since the mercantilists were discredited by the attacks of Hume and like-minded thinkers, this relative neglect of the current account and its relation to domestic investment and productivity is puzzling. Perhaps mercantilistic instincts survived in the hearts of central bankers.

game"—a phrase reportedly coined by Keynes. Because such measures speeded the movement of all countries toward their external balance goals, they increased the efficiency of the automatic adjustment processes inherent in the gold standard.

Later research has shown that the supposed "rules of the game" of the gold standard were frequently violated before 1914. As noted, the incentives to obey the rules applied with greater force to deficit than to surplus countries, so in practice it was the deficit countries that bore the burden of bringing the payments balances of *all* countries into equilibrium. By not always taking actions to reduce gold inflows, the surplus countries worsened a problem of international policy coordination inherent in the system: Deficit countries competing for a limited supply of gold reserves might adopt overcontractionary monetary policies that harmed employment while doing little to improve their reserve positions.

In fact, countries often reversed the rules and *sterilized* gold flows, that is, sold domestic assets when foreign reserves were rising and bought domestic assets as foreign reserves fell. Government interference with private gold exports also undermined the system. The picture of smooth and automatic balance of payments adjustment before World War I therefore did not always match reality. Governments sometimes ignored both the "rules of the game" and the effects of their actions on other countries.[6]

Internal Balance under the Gold Standard

By fixing the prices of currencies in terms of gold, the gold standard aimed to limit monetary growth in the world economy and thus to ensure stability in world price levels. While price levels within gold standard countries did not rise as much between 1870 and 1914 as over the period after World War II, national price levels moved unpredictably over shorter horizons as periods of inflation and deflation followed each other. The gold standard's mixed record on price stability reflected a problem discussed in the last chapter, change in the relative prices of gold and other commodities.

In addition, the gold standard does not seem to have done much to ensure full employment. The U.S. unemployment rate, for example, averaged 6.8 percent between 1890 and 1913, but it averaged under 5.7 percent between 1946 and 1992.[7]

A fundamental cause of short-term internal instability under the pre-1914 gold standard was the subordination of economic policy to external objectives. Before World War I, governments had not assumed responsibility for maintaining internal balance as fully as they did after World War II. In the United States, the resulting economic distress led to political opposition to the gold standard, as the Case Study below explains. The importance of internal policy objectives increased after World War I as a result of the worldwide economic instability of the interwar years, 1918–1939. And the unpalatable internal consequences of attempts to restore the gold standard after 1918 helped mold the thinking of the architects of the fixed exchange rate system adopted after 1945. To understand how the post-World War II international monetary system tried to reconcile the goals of internal and external balance, we therefore must examine the economic events of the period between the two world wars.

CASE STUDY

The Political Economy of Exchange Rate Regimes: Conflict over America's Monetary Standard During the 1890s

As we learned in Chapter 17, the United States had a bimetallic monetary standard until the Civil War, with both silver and gold in circulation. Once war broke out the country moved to a paper currency (called the "greenback") and a floating exchange rate, but in 1879 a pure gold

---

[6] An influential modern study of central bank practices under the gold standard is Arthur I. Bloomfield, *Monetary Policy Under the International Gold Standard: 1880–1914* (New York: Federal Reserve Bank of New York, 1959).

[7] Data on price levels are given by Cooper (cited on p. 515 in Chapter 17) and data for U.S. unemployment are adapted from the same source. Caution should be used in comparing gold standard and post-World War II unemployment data because the methods used to assemble the earlier data were much cruder. A critical study of pre-1930 U.S. unemployment data is Christina D. Romer, "Spurious Volatility in Historical Unemployment Data," *Journal of Political Economy* 94 (February 1986), pp. 1–37.

standard (and a fixed exchange rate against other gold-standard currencies such as the British pound sterling) was adopted.

World gold supplies had increased sharply after the 1849 discoveries in California, but the 1879 return of the dollar to gold at the pre-Civil War parity required deflation in the United States. Furthermore, a global shortage of gold generated continuing downward pressure on price levels long after the American restoration of gold. By 1896, the U.S. price level was about 40 percent below its 1869 level. Economic distress was widespread and became especially severe after a banking panic in 1893. Farmers, who saw the prices of agricultural products plummet more quickly even than the general price level, were especially hard hit.

In the 1890s, a broad Populist coalition of U.S. farmers, miners, and others pressed for revival of the bimetallic silver-gold system that had prevailed before the Civil War. They desired a return to the old 16:1 relative mint parity for gold and silver, but by the early 1890s, the market price of gold in terms of silver had risen to around 30. The Populists foresaw that the monetization of silver at 16:1 would lead to an increase in the silver money stock, and possibly a reversal of deflation, as people used gold dollars to buy silver cheaply on the market and then took it in to the mint for coining. These developments would have had several advantages from the standpoint of farmers and their allies, such as undoing the adverse terms of trade trends of the previous decades and reducing the real values of farmers' mortgage debts. Western silver mine owners, in particular, were wildly enthusiastic. On the other side, eastern financiers viewed "sound money"—that is, gold and gold alone—as essential for achieving more complete American integration into world markets.

The silver movement reached its high tide in 1896 when the Democratic Party nominated William Jennings Bryan to run for president after a stemwinding convention speech in which he famously proclaimed, "Thou shalt not crucify mankind upon a cross of gold." But by 1896 new gold discoveries in South Africa, Alaska, and elsewhere were starting to reverse previous deflationary trends across the world, defusing silver as a political issue. Bryan lost the elections of 1896 and 1900 to Republican William McKinley, and in March 1900 Congress passed the Gold Standard Act, which definitively placed the dollar on an exclusive basis of gold.

Modern readers of L. Frank Baum's classic 1900 children's book, *The Wonderful Wizard of Oz,* usually don't realize that the story of Dorothy, Toto, and their friends is an allegorical rendition of the U.S. political struggle over gold. The yellow brick road represents the false promise of gold, the name "Oz" is a reference to an ounce (oz.) of gold, and Dorothy's silver slippers—changed to ruby slippers in the well-known Hollywood color film version—offer the true way home to the heavily indebted farming state of Kansas.[8]

Although farming debt is often mentioned as a prime factor in the 1890s silver agitation, Harvard political scientist Jeffry Frieden shows that a much more relevant factor was the desire of farming and mining interest to raise the prices of their products relative to nontraded goods.[9] Manufacturers, who competed with imports, had been able to obtain tariff protection as a counterweight to deflation. As a group they therefore had little interest in changing the currency standard. Because the United States was nearly exclusively an exporter of primary products, import

---

[8] An informative and amusing account is Hugh Rockoff, "The 'Wizard of Oz' as a Monetary Allegory," *Journal of Political Economy* 98 (August 1990), pp. 739–760.

[9] See "Monetary Populism in Nineteenth-Century America: An Open Economy Interpretation," *Journal of Economic History* 57 (June 1997), pp. 367–395.

tariffs would have been ineffective in helping farmers and miners. A depreciation of the U.S. dollar, however, promised to raise the dollar prices of primary products relative to the prices of nontradables. Through a careful statistical analysis of Congressional voting on bills related to the monetary system, Frieden shows that legislative support for silver was unrelated to debt levels but was indeed highly correlated with state employment in agriculture and mining.

The Interwar Years, 1918–1939

Governments effectively suspended the gold standard during World War I and financed part of their massive military expenditures by printing money. Further, labor forces and productive capacity had been reduced sharply through war losses. As a result, price levels were higher everywhere at the war's conclusion in 1918.

Several countries experienced runaway inflation as their governments attempted to aid the reconstruction process through public expenditures. These governments financed their purchases simply by printing the money they needed, as they sometimes had during the war. The result was a sharp rise in money supplies and price levels.

The German Hyperinflation

The most celebrated episode of interwar inflation is the German hyperinflation, during which Germany's price index rose from a level of 262 in January 1919 to a level of 126,160,000,000,000 in December 1923—a factor of 481.5 billion!

The Versailles Treaty ending World War I saddled Germany with a huge burden of reparations payments to the Allies. Rather than raising taxes to meet these payments, the German government ran its printing presses. The inflation accelerated most dramatically in January 1923 when France, citing lagging German compliance with the Versailles terms, sent its troops into Germany's industrial heartland, the Ruhr. German workers went on strike to protest the French occupation, and the German government supported their action by issuing even more money to pay them. Within the year, the price level rose by a factor of 452,998,200. Under these conditions, people were unwilling to hold the German currency, which became all but useless.

The hyperinflation was ended toward the end of 1923 as Germany instituted a currency reform, obtained some relief from its reparations burdens, and moved toward a balanced government budget.

The Fleeting Return to Gold

The United States returned to gold in 1919. By the early 1920s, other countries yearned increasingly for the comparative financial stability of the gold standard era. In 1922, at a conference in Genoa, Italy, a group of countries including Britain, France, Italy, and Japan agreed on a program calling for a general return to the gold standard and cooperation among central banks in attaining external and internal objectives. Realizing that gold supplies might be inadequate to meet central banks' demands for international reserves (a problem of the gold standard noted in Chapter 17), the Genoa Conference sanctioned a partial gold *exchange* standard in which smaller countries could hold as reserves the currencies of several large countries whose own international reserves would consist entirely of gold.

In 1925 Britain returned to the gold standard by pegging the pound to gold at the prewar price. Chancellor of the Exchequer Winston Churchill, a champion of the return to the old parity, argued that any deviation from the prewar price would undermine world confidence in the stability of Britain's financial institutions, which had played the leading role in international finance during the gold standard era. Though Britain's price level had been falling since the war, in 1925 it was still higher than in the days of the prewar gold standard. To return the pound price of gold to its prewar level, the Bank of England was therefore forced to follow contractionary monetary policies that contributed to severe unemployment.

British stagnation in the 1920s accelerated London's decline as the world's leading financial center. Britain's economic weakening proved problematic for the stability of the restored gold standard. In line with the recommendations of the Genoa Conference, many countries held international reserves in the form of pound deposits in London. Britain's gold reserves were limited, however, and the country's persistent stagnation did little to inspire confidence in its ability to meet its foreign obligations. The onset of the Great Depression in 1929 was shortly followed by bank failures throughout the world. Britain was forced off gold in 1931 when foreign holders of pounds (including several central banks) lost confidence in Britain's commitment to maintain its currency's value and began converting their pound holdings to gold.

International Economic Disintegration

As the depression continued, many countries renounced their gold standard obligations and allowed their currencies to float in the foreign exchange market. The United States left the gold standard in 1933 but returned to it in 1934, having raised the dollar price of gold from $20.67 to $35 per ounce. Countries that clung to the gold standard without devaluing their currencies suffered most during the Great Depression. Indeed, recent research places much of the blame for the depression's worldwide propagation on the gold standard itself (see the Case Study that follows).

Major economic harm was done by restrictions on international trade and payments, which proliferated as countries attempted to discourage imports and keep aggregate demand bottled up at home. The Smoot-Hawley tariff imposed by the United States in 1930 had a damaging effect on employment abroad. The foreign response involved retaliatory trade restrictions and preferential trading agreements among groups of countries. A measure that raises domestic welfare is called a *beggar-thy-neighbor policy* when it benefits the home country only because it worsens economic conditions abroad (Chapter 11). During the worldwide depression, tariffs and other beggar-thy-neighbor policies inevitably provoked foreign retaliation and often left all countries worse off in the end.

Uncertainty about government policies led to sharp reserve movements for countries with pegged exchange rates and sharp exchange rate movements for those with floating rates. Prohibitions on private capital account transactions were used by many countries to limit these effects of foreign exchange market developments. Some governments also used administrative methods or multiple exchange rates to allocate scarce foreign exchange reserves among competing uses. Trade barriers and deflation in the industrial economies of America and Europe led to widespread repudiations of international debts, particularly by Latin American countries, whose export markets were disappearing. In short, the world economy disintegrated into increasingly autarkic (that is, self-sufficient) national units in the early 1930s.

In the face of the Great Depression, many countries had resolved the choice between external and internal balance by curtailing their trading links with the rest of the world and eliminating, by government decree, the possibility of any significant external imbalance. But this path, by reducing the gains from trade, imposed high costs on the world economy and contributed to the slow recovery from depression, which in many countries was still incomplete in 1939. All countries would have been better off in a world with freer international trade, provided international cooperation had helped each country preserve its external balance and financial stability without sacrificing internal policy goals. It was this realization that inspired the blueprint for the postwar international monetary system, the **Bretton Woods agreement**.

CASE STUDY

The International Gold Standard and the Great Depression

One of the most striking features of the decade-long Great Depression that started in 1929 was its global nature. Rather than being confined to the United States and its main trading partners, the downturn spread rapidly and forcefully to Europe, Latin America, and elsewhere. What explains the Great Depression's nearly universal scope? Recent scholarship shows that the international gold standard played a central role in starting, deepening, and spreading the twentieth century's greatest economic crisis.[10]

In 1929 most market economies were once again on the gold standard. At the time, however, the United States, attempting to slow its overheated economy through monetary contraction, and France, having just ended an inflationary period and returned to gold, faced large capital inflows. Through the resulting balance-of-payments surpluses, both countries were absorbing the world's monetary gold at a startling rate. (By 1932 the two countries alone held more than 70 percent of it!) Other countries on the gold standard had no choice but to engage in domestic asset sales if they wished to conserve their dwindling gold stocks. The resulting worldwide monetary contraction, combined with the shock waves from the October 1929 New York stock market crash, sent the world into deep recession.

Waves of bank failures around the world only accelerated the world's downward economic spiral. The gold standard again was a key culprit. Many countries desired to safeguard their gold reserves in order to be able to remain on the gold standard. This desire often discouraged them from providing banks with the liquidity that might have allowed the banks to stay in business.

---

[10] Important contributions to this research include Ehsan U. Choudhri and Levis A. Kochin, "The Exchange Rate and the International Transmission of Business Cycle Disturbances: Some Evidence from the Great Depression," *Journal of Money, Credit, and Banking* 12 (1980), pp. 565–574, Peter Temin, *Lessons from the Great Depression* (Cambridge, MA: MIT Press, 1989), and Barry Eichengreen, *Golden Fetters: The Gold Standard and the Great Depression, 1919–1939* (New York: Oxford University Press, 1992). A concise and lucid summary is Ben S. Bernanke, "The World on a Cross of Gold: A Review of 'Golden Fetters: The Gold Standard and the Great Depression, 1919–1939,'" *Journal of Monetary Economics* 31 (April 1993), pp. 251–267.

After all, any cash provided to banks by their home governments would have increased potential private claims to the government's precious gold holdings.[11]

Perhaps the clearest evidence of the gold standard's role is the contrasting behavior of output and the price level in countries that left the gold standard relatively early, such as the United Kingdom, and those that stubbornly hung on. Figure 18-1 plots 1935 industrial production levels relative to their 1929 values against 1935 wholesale price indexes relative to their 1929 values for a number of countries. Countries that abandoned the gold standard freed themselves to adopt more expansionary monetary policies that limited (or prevented) both domestic deflation and output contraction. Thus, Figure 18-1 shows a strong positive relationship between price-level and output changes over 1929–1935. The countries with the biggest deflations and output contractions include France, Switzerland, Belgium, the Netherlands, and Poland, all of which stayed on the gold standard until 1936.

The Bretton Woods System and the International Monetary Fund

In July 1944 representatives of 44 countries meeting in Bretton Woods, New Hampshire, drafted and signed the Articles of Agreement of the **International Monetary Fund (IMF)**. Even as the war continued, statesmen in the Allied countries were looking ahead to the economic needs of the postwar world. Remembering the disastrous economic events of the interwar period, they hoped to design an international monetary system that would foster full employment and price stability while allowing individual countries to attain external balance without imposing restrictions on international trade.[12]

The system set up by the Bretton Woods agreement called for fixed exchange rates against the U.S. dollar and an unvarying dollar price of gold—$35 an ounce. Member countries held their official international reserves largely in the form of gold or dollar assets and had the right to sell dollars to the Federal Reserve for gold at the official price. The system was thus a gold exchange standard, with the dollar as its principal reserve currency. In the terminology of Chapter 17, the dollar was the "Nth currency" in terms of which the $N - 1$ exchange rates of the system were defined. The United States itself intervened only rarely in the foreign exchange market. Usually, the $N - 1$ foreign central banks

---

[11]Chang-Tai Hsieh and Christina D. Romer argue that the fear of being forced off gold cannot explain the U.S. Federal Reserve's unwillingness to expand the money supply in the early 1930s. See "Was the Federal Reserve Fettered? Devaluation Expectations in the 1932 Monetary Expansion," Working Paper 8113, National Bureau of Economic Research, February 2001.

[12]The same conference set up a second institution, the World Bank, whose goals were to help the belligerents rebuild their shattered economies and to help the former colonial territories develop and modernize theirs. Only in 1947 was the General Agreement on Tariffs and Trade (GATT) inaugurated as a forum for the multilateral reduction of trade barriers. The GATT was meant as a prelude to the creation of an International Trade Organization (ITO), whose goals in the trade area would parallel those of the IMF in the financial area. Unfortunately, the ITO was doomed by the failures of Congress and Parliament to ratify its charter. Only much later, in the 1990s, did the GATT become the current World Trade Organization (WTO).

Figure 18-1 | Industrial Production and Wholesale Price Index Changes, 1929–1935

Countries such as Australia and the United Kingdom that left the gold standard early and adopted counter-deflationary monetary policies experienced milder declines in output during the Great Depression. Countries such as France and Switzerland that stuck with the gold standard longer had greater declines in price levels and output.

Source: Ben Bernanke and Kevin Carey, "Nominal Wage Stickiness and Aggregate Supply in the Great Depression," *Quarterly Journal of Economics* 111 (August 1996), pp. 853–883.

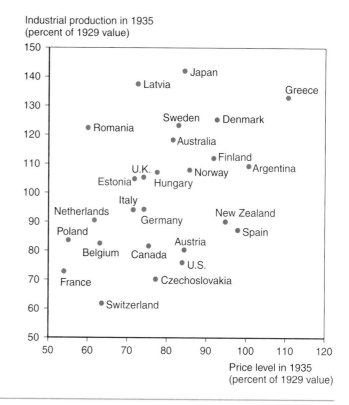

intervened when necessary to fix the system's $N - 1$ exchange rates, while the United States was responsible in theory for fixing the dollar price of gold.

Goals and Structure of the IMF

The IMF Articles of Agreement were heavily influenced by the interwar experience of financial and price level instability, unemployment, and international economic disintegration. The articles tried to avoid a repetition of those events through a mixture of discipline and flexibility.

The major discipline on monetary management was the requirement that exchange rates be fixed to the dollar, which, in turn, was tied to gold. If a central bank other than the Federal Reserve pursued excessive monetary expansion, it would lose international reserves and eventually become unable to maintain the fixed dollar exchange rate of its currency. Since high U.S. monetary growth would lead to dollar accumulation by foreign central banks, the Fed itself was constrained in its monetary policies by its obligation to redeem those dollars for gold. The official gold price of $35 an ounce served as a further brake on American monetary policy, since that price would be pushed upward if too many dollars were created. Fixed exchange rates were viewed as more than a device for imposing monetary discipline on the system, however. Rightly or wrongly, the interwar experience had convinced the Fund's architects that floating exchange rates were a cause of speculative instability and were harmful to international trade.

The interwar experience had shown also that national governments would not be willing to maintain both free trade and fixed exchange rates at the price of long-term domestic unemployment. After the experience of the Great Depression, governments were widely viewed as responsible for maintaining full employment. The IMF agreement therefore tried to incorporate sufficient flexibility to allow countries to attain external balance in an orderly fashion without sacrificing internal objectives or fixed exchange rates.

Two major features of the IMF Articles of Agreement helped promote this flexibility in external adjustment:

1. *IMF lending facilities.* The IMF stood ready to lend foreign currencies to members to tide them over periods during which their current accounts were in deficit but a tightening of monetary or fiscal policy would have an adverse effect on domestic employment. A pool of gold and currencies contributed by members provided the IMF with the resources to be used in these lending operations.

How did IMF lending work? On joining the Fund, a new member was assigned a *quota,* which determined both its contribution to the reserve pool and its right to draw on IMF resources. Each member contributed to the Fund an amount of gold equal in value to one-fourth of its quota. The remaining three-fourths of its quota took the form of a contribution of its own national currency. A member was entitled to use its own currency to purchase temporarily from the Fund gold or foreign currencies equal in value to its gold subscription. Further gold or foreign currencies (up to a limit) could be borrowed from the Fund, but only under increasingly stringent Fund supervision of the borrower's macroeconomic policies. **IMF conditionality** is the name for this surveillance over the policies of member countries who are heavy borrowers of Fund resources.

2. *Adjustable parities.* Although each country's exchange rate was fixed, it could be changed—devalued or revalued against the dollar—if the IMF agreed that the country's balance of payments was in a situation of "fundamental disequilibrium." The term *fundamental disequilibrium* was not defined in the Articles of Agreement, but the clause was meant to cover countries that suffered permanent adverse international shifts in the demand for their products. Without a devaluation, such a country would experience higher unemployment and a higher current account deficit until the domestic price level fell enough to restore internal and external balance. A devaluation, on the other hand, could simultaneously improve employment and the current account, thus sidestepping a long and painful adjustment process during which international reserves might in any case run out. Remembering Britain's experience with an overvalued currency after 1925, the IMF's founders built in the flexibility of (hopefully infrequent) exchange rate changes. This flexibility was not available, however, to the "Nth currency" of the Bretton Woods system, the U.S. dollar.

Convertibility

Just as the general acceptability of national currency eliminates the costs of barter within a single economy, the use of national currencies in international trade makes the world economy function more efficiently. To promote efficient multilateral trade, the IMF Articles of

Agreement urged members to make their national currencies convertible as soon as possible. A **convertible currency** is one that may be freely exchanged for foreign currencies. The U.S. and Canadian dollars became convertible in 1945. This meant, for example, that a Canadian resident who acquired U.S. dollars could use them to make purchases in the United States, could sell them in the foreign exchange market for Canadian dollars, or could sell them to the Bank of Canada, which then had the right to sell them to the Federal Reserve (at the fixed dollar/gold exchange rate) in return for gold. General *in*convertibility would make international trade extremely difficult. A French citizen might be unwilling to sell goods to a German in return for inconvertible marks because these marks would then be usable only subject to restrictions imposed by the German government. With no market in inconvertible francs, the German would be unable to obtain French currency to pay for the French goods. The only way of trading would therefore be through barter, the direct exchange of goods for goods.

The IMF articles called for convertibility on *current* account transactions only: Countries were explicitly allowed to restrict financial account transactions provided they permitted the free use of their currencies for transactions entering the current account. The experience of 1918–1939 had led policymakers to view private capital movements as a factor leading to economic instability, and they feared that speculative movements of "hot money" across national borders might sabotage their goal of free trade based on fixed exchange rates. By insisting on convertibility for current account transactions only, the designers of the Bretton Woods system hoped to facilitate free trade while avoiding the possibility that private capital flows might tighten the external constraints faced by policymakers.[13] Most countries in Europe did not restore convertibility until the end of 1958, with Japan following in 1964.

The early convertibility of the U.S. dollar, together with its special position in the Bretton Woods system, made it the postwar world's key currency. Because dollars were freely convertible, much international trade tended to be invoiced in dollars and importers and exporters held dollar balances for transactions. In effect, the dollar became an international money—a universal medium of exchange, unit of account, and store of value. Also contributing to the dollar's dominance was the strength of the American economy relative to the devastated economies of Europe and Japan: Dollars were attractive because they could be used to purchase badly needed goods and services that only the United States was in a position to supply. Central banks naturally found it advantageous to hold their international reserves in the form of interest-bearing dollar assets.

Internal and External Balance under the Bretton Woods System

How did the international monetary system created at Bretton Woods allow its members to reconcile their external commitments with the internal goals of full employment and price stability? As the world economy evolved in the years after World War II, the meaning of "external balance" changed and conflicts between internal and external goals increasingly threatened the fixed exchange rate system. The special external balance problem of the

---

[13] It was believed that official capital flows such as reserve movements and World Bank lending would allow countries to reap most gains from intertemporal trade.

United States, the issuer of the principal reserve currency, was a major concern that led to proposals to reform the system.

The Changing Meaning of External Balance

In the first decade of the Bretton Woods system, many countries ran current account deficits as they reconstructed their war-torn economies. Since the main external problem of these countries, taken as a group, was to acquire enough dollars to finance necessary purchases from the United States, these years are often called the period of "dollar shortage." The United States helped limit the severity of this shortage through the Marshall Plan, a program of dollar grants from the United States to European countries initiated in 1948.

Individually, each country's overall current account deficit was limited by the difficulty of borrowing any foreign currencies in an environment of heavily restricted financial account transactions. With virtually no private capital movements, current account imbalances had to be financed almost entirely through official reserve transactions and government loans. (The overall current plus capital account deficit equals the sum of the private and official financial account surpluses.) Without access to foreign credit, countries could therefore run current account deficits only if their central banks were willing to reduce their foreign exchange reserves. Central banks were unwilling to let reserves fall to low levels, in part because their ability to fix the exchange rate would be endangered.

The restoration of convertibility in 1958 gradually began to change the nature of policy-makers' external constraints. As foreign exchange trading expanded, financial markets in different countries became more tightly integrated—an important step toward the creation of today's worldwide foreign exchange market. With growing opportunities to move funds across borders, national interest rates became more closely linked and the speed with which policy changes might cause a country to lose or gain international reserves increased. After 1958, and increasingly over the next 15 years, central banks had to be attentive to foreign financial conditions or take the risk that sudden reserve losses might leave them without the resources needed to peg exchange rates. Faced with a sudden rise in foreign interest rates, for example, a central bank would be forced to sell domestic assets and raise the domestic interest rate to hold its international reserves steady.

The restoration of convertibility did not result in immediate and complete international financial integration, as assumed in the model of fixed exchange rates set out in Chapter 17. On the contrary, most countries continued to maintain restrictions on financial account transactions, as noted above. But the opportunities for *disguised* capital flows increased dramatically. For example, importers within a country could effectively purchase foreign assets by accelerating payments to foreign suppliers relative to actual shipments of goods: they could effectively borrow from foreign suppliers by delaying payments. These trade practices—known, respectively, as "leads" and "lags"—provided two of many ways through which official barriers to private capital movements could be evaded. Even though the condition of international interest rate equality assumed in the last chapter did not hold exactly, the links among countries' interest rates tightened as the Bretton Woods system matured.

Speculative Capital Flows and Crises

Current account deficits and surpluses took on added significance under the new conditions of increased private capital mobility. A country with a large and persistent current account deficit might be suspected of being in "fundamental disequilibrium" under the IMF Articles of Agreement, and thus ripe for a currency devaluation. Suspicion of an impending devaluation could, in turn, spark a balance of payments crisis (see Chapter 17).

Anyone holding pound deposits during a devaluation of the pound, for example, would suffer a loss, since the foreign currency value of pound assets would decrease suddenly by the amount of the exchange rate change. If Britain had a current account deficit, therefore, holders of pounds would become nervous and shift their wealth into other currencies. To hold the pound's exchange rate against the dollar pegged, the Bank of England would have to buy pounds and supply the foreign assets that market participants wished to hold. This loss of foreign reserves, if large enough, might force a devaluation by leaving the Bank of England without enough reserves to prop up the exchange rate.

Similarly, countries with large current account surpluses might be viewed by the market as candidates for revaluation. In this case their central banks would find themselves swamped with official reserves, the result of selling the home currency in the foreign exchange market to keep it from appreciating. A country in this position would face the problem of having its money supply grow uncontrollably, a development that could push the price level up and upset internal balance.

Balance of payments crises became increasingly frequent and violent throughout the 1960s and early 1970s. A record British trade balance deficit in early 1964 led to a period of intermittent speculation against the pound that complicated British policy-making until November 1967, when the pound was finally devalued. France devalued its franc and Germany revalued its deutschemark in 1969 after similar speculative attacks. These crises became so massive by the early 1970s that they eventually brought down the Bretton Woods structure of fixed exchange rates. The events leading up to the system's collapse are covered later in this chapter.

The possibility of a balance of payments crisis therefore lent increased importance to the external goal of a current account target. Even current account imbalances justified by differing international investment opportunities or caused by purely temporary factors might fuel market suspicions of an impending parity change. In this environment, policymakers had additional incentives to avoid sharp current account changes.

Analyzing Policy Options under the Bretton Woods System

To describe the problem an individual country (other than the United States) faced in pursuing internal and external balance under the Bretton Woods system of fixed exchange rates, let's return to the framework used in Chapter 17. Assume that domestic (R) and foreign (R^*) interest rates are always equal,

$$R = R^*.$$

As noted above, this equality does not fit the Bretton Woods facts exactly (particularly just after 1958), but it leads to a fairly accurate picture of the external constraints policymakers then faced in using their macroeconomic tools. The framework will show how a country's position with respect to its internal and external goals depends on the level of its fixed exchange rate, E, and its fiscal policy. Throughout, E is the domestic currency price of the dollar. The analysis applies to the short run because the home and foreign price levels (P and P^*, respectively) are assumed to be fixed.[14]

Maintaining Internal Balance

First consider internal balance. If both P^* and E are permanently fixed, domestic inflation depends primarily on the amount of aggregate demand pressure in the economy, not on expectations of future inflation. Internal balance therefore requires only full employment, that is, that aggregate demand equal the full-employment level of output, Y^{f}.[15]

Recall that aggregate demand for domestic output is the sum of consumption, C, investment, I, government purchases, G, and the current account, CA. Consumption is an increasing function of disposable income, $Y - T$, where T denotes net taxes. The current account surplus is a decreasing function of disposable income and an increasing function of the real exchange rate, EP^*/P (Chapter 16). Finally, investment is assumed constant. The condition of internal balance is therefore

$$Y^{f} = C(Y^{f} - T) + I + G + CA(EP^*/P, Y^{f} - T). \qquad (18\text{-}1)$$

Equation (18-1) shows the policy tools that affect aggregate demand and therefore affect output in the short run. Fiscal expansion (a rise in G or a fall in T) stimulates aggregate demand and causes output to rise. Similarly, a devaluation of the currency (a rise in E) makes domestic goods and services cheaper relative to those sold abroad and also increases demand and output. The policymaker can hold output steady at its full employment level, Y^{f}, through fiscal policy or exchange rate changes.

Notice that monetary policy is not a policy tool under fixed exchange rates. This is because, as shown in Chapter 17, an attempt by the central bank to alter the money supply by buying or selling domestic assets will cause an offsetting change in foreign reserves, leaving the domestic money supply unchanged. Domestic asset transactions by the central bank can be used to alter the level of foreign reserves but not to affect the state of employment and output.

The *II* schedule in Figure 18-2 shows combinations of exchange rates and fiscal policy that hold output constant at Y^{f} and thus maintain internal balance. The schedule is downward-sloping because currency devaluation (a rise in E) and fiscal expansion (a rise in G or a fall in T) both tend to raise output. To hold output constant, a revaluation of the currency (which reduces aggregate demand) must therefore be matched by fiscal expansion (which increases aggregate demand). Schedule *II* shows precisely how the fiscal stance must change as E changes to maintain full employment. To the right of *II* fiscal policy is more expansionary than needed for full employment, so the economy's productive factors are overemployed. To the left of *II* fiscal policy is too restrictive, and there is unemployment.

---

[14]By assumption there is no ongoing balance of payments crisis, that is, no expectation of a future exchange rate change. The point of this assumption is to highlight the difficult choices policymakers faced, even under favorable conditions.

[15]If P^* is unstable because of foreign inflation, for example, full employment alone will not guarantee price stability under a fixed exchange rate. This complex problem is considered below when worldwide inflation under fixed exchange rates is examined.

Figure 18-2 | Internal Balance (*II*), External Balance (*XX*), and the "Four Zones of Economic Discomfort"

The diagram shows what different levels of the exchange rate and fiscal ease imply for employment and the current account. Along *II,* output is at its full-employment level, Y^f. Along *XX,* the current account is at its target level, *X.*

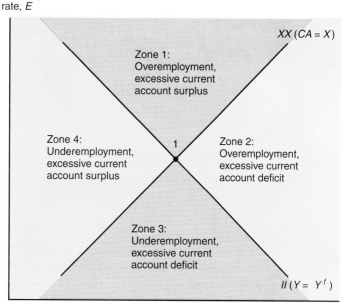

Maintaining External Balance

We have seen how fiscal policy or exchange rate changes can be used to influence output and thus help the government achieve its internal goal of full employment. How do these policy tools affect the economy's external balance? To answer this question, assume the government has a target value, *X,* for the current account surplus. The goal of external balance requires the government to manage fiscal policy and the exchange rate so that the equation

$$CA(EP^*/P, Y - T) = X \qquad (18\text{-}2)$$

is satisfied.

Given *P* and *P**, a rise in *E* makes domestic goods cheaper and improves the current account. Fiscal expansion, however, has the opposite effect on the current account. A fall in *T* raises output, *Y;* the resulting increase in disposable income raises home spending on foreign goods and worsens the current account. Similarly, a rise in *G* causes *CA* to fall by increasing *Y.*

To maintain its current account at *X* as it devalues the currency (that is, as it raises *E*), the government must expand its purchases or lower taxes. Figure 18-2 therefore shows that the

XX schedule, along which external balance holds, is positively sloped. The *XX* schedule shows how much fiscal expansion is needed to hold the current account surplus at *X* as the currency is devalued by a given amount.[16] Since a rise in *E* raises net exports, the current account is in surplus, relative to its target level *X*, above *XX*. Similarly, below *XX* the current account is in deficit relative to its target level.[17]

Expenditure-Changing and Expenditure-Switching Policies

The *II* and *XX* schedules divide the diagram into four regions, sometimes called the "four zones of economic discomfort." Each of these zones represents the effects of different policy settings. In zone 1 the level of employment is too high and the current account surplus too great; in zone 2 the level of employment is too high but the current account deficit is too great; in zone 3 there is underemployment and an excessive deficit; and in zone 4 underemployment is coupled with a current account surplus greater than the target level. Used together, fiscal and exchange rate policy can place the economy at the intersection of *II* and *XX* (point 1), the point at which both internal and external balance hold. Point 1 shows the policy setting that places the economy in the position that the policymaker would prefer.

If the economy is initially away from point 1, appropriate adjustments in fiscal policy and the exchange rate are needed to bring about internal and external balance. The change in fiscal policy that moves the economy to point 1 is called an **expenditure-changing policy** because it alters the *level* of the economy's total demand for goods and services. The accompanying exchange rate adjustment is called an **expenditure-switching policy** because it changes the *direction* of demand, shifting it between domestic output and imports. In general, both expenditure changing and expenditure switching are needed to reach internal and external balance.

Under the Bretton Woods rules, exchange rate changes (expenditure-switching policy) were supposed to be infrequent. This left fiscal policy as the main tool for moving the economy toward internal and external balance. But as Figure 18-2 shows, one instrument, fiscal policy, is generally insufficient to attain the two goals of internal and external balance. Only if the economy had been displaced horizontally from point 1 would fiscal policy be able to do the job alone. In addition, fiscal policy is an unwieldy tool, since it often cannot be implemented without legislative approval. Another drawback is that a

---

[16] Can you see how to derive the *XX* schedule in Figure 18-2 from the different (but related) *XX* schedule shown in Figure 16-17 on p. 463? (Hint: Use the latter diagram to analyze the effects of fiscal expansion.)

[17] Since the central bank does not affect the economy when it raises its foreign reserves by an open-market sale of domestic assets, no separate reserve constraint is shown in Figure 18-2. In effect, the bank can borrow reserves freely from abroad by selling domestic assets to the public. (During a devaluation scare this tactic would not work because no one would want to sell the bank foreign assets for domestic money.) Our analysis, however, assumes perfect asset substitutability between domestic and foreign bonds (see Chapter 17). Under imperfect asset substitutability, central bank domestic asset sales to attract foreign reserves would drive up the domestic interest rate relative to the foreign rate. Thus, while imperfect asset substitutability would give the central bank an additional policy tool (monetary policy), it would also make the bank responsible for an additional policy target (the domestic interest rate). If the government is concerned about the domestic interest rate because it affects investment, for example, the additional policy tool would not necessarily increase the set of attractive policy options. Imperfect substitutability was exploited by central banks under Bretton Woods, but it did not get countries out of the policy dilemmas illustrated in the text.

Figure 18-3 | Policies to Bring About Internal and External Balance

Unless the currency is devalued and the degree of fiscal ease increased, internal and external balance (point 1) cannot be reached. Acting alone, fiscal policy can attain *either* internal balance (point 3) or external balance (point 4), but only at the cost of increasing the economy's distance from the goal that is sacrificed.

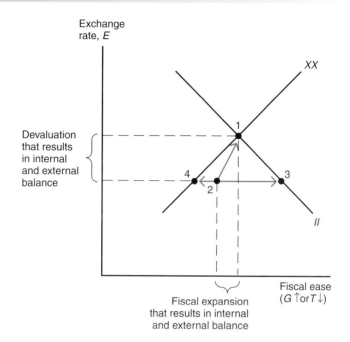

fiscal expansion, for example, might have to be reversed after some time if it leads to chronic government budget deficits.

As a result of the exchange rate's inflexibility, policymakers sometimes found themselves in dilemma situations. With the fiscal policy and exchange rate indicated by point 2 in Figure 18-3, there is underemployment and an excessive current account deficit. Only the combination of devaluation and fiscal expansion indicated in the figure moves the economy to internal and external balance (point 1). Expansionary fiscal policy, acting alone, can eliminate the unemployment by moving the economy to point 3, but the cost of reduced unemployment is a larger external deficit. While contractionary fiscal policy alone can bring about external balance (point 4), output falls as a result and the economy moves farther from internal balance. It is no wonder that policy dilemmas such as the one at point 2 gave rise to suspicions that the currency was about to be devalued. Devaluation improves the current account and aggregate demand by raising the real exchange rate EP^*/P in one stroke; the alternative is a long and politically unpalatable period of unemployment to bring about an equal rise in the real exchange rate through a fall in P.[18]

In practice, countries did sometimes use changes in their exchange rates to move closer to internal and external balance, although the changes were typically accompanied by

---

[18] As an exercise to test understanding, show that a fall in P, all else equal, lowers both II and XX, moving point 1 vertically downward.

balance of payments crises. Many countries also tightened controls on capital account transactions to sever the links between domestic and foreign interest rates and make monetary policy more effective. In this they were only partly successful, as the events leading to the breakdown of the system were to prove.

The External Balance Problem of the United States

The external balance problem of the United States was different from the one faced by other countries in the Bretton Woods system. As the issuer of the Nth currency, the United States was not responsible for pegging dollar exchange rates. Its main responsibility was to hold the dollar price of gold at $35 an ounce and, in particular, to guarantee that foreign central banks could convert their dollar holdings into gold at that price. For this purpose it had to hold sufficient gold reserves.

Because the United States was required to trade gold for dollars with foreign central banks, the possibility that other countries might convert their dollar reserves into gold was a potential external constraint on U.S. macroeconomic policy. In practice, however, foreign central banks were willing to hold on to the dollars they accumulated, since these paid interest and represented an international money *par excellence*. And the logic of the gold exchange standard dictated that foreign central banks should continue to accumulate dollars. World gold supplies were not growing quickly enough to keep up with world economic growth, so the only way central banks could maintain adequate international reserve levels (barring deflation) was by accumulating dollar assets. Official gold conversions did occur on occasion, and these depleted the American gold stock and caused concern. But as long as most central banks were willing to add dollars to their reserves and forgo the right of redeeming those dollars for American gold, the U.S. external constraint appeared looser than that faced by other countries in the system.[19]

In an influential book that appeared in 1960, the economist Robert Triffin of Yale University called attention to a fundamental long-run problem of the Bretton Woods system, the **confidence problem**.[20] At the time Triffin wrote his book, the U.S. gold stock exceeded its dollar liabilities to foreign central banks. But Triffin realized that as central banks' international reserve needs grew over time, their holdings of dollars would necessarily grow until they exceeded the U.S. gold stock. Since the United States had promised to redeem these dollars at $35 an ounce, it would no longer have the ability to meet its obligations should all dollar holders simultaneously try to convert their dollars into gold. This would lead to a confidence problem: Central banks, knowing that their dollars were no longer "as good as gold," might become unwilling to accumulate more dollars and might even bring down the system by attempting to cash in the dollars they already held. There was a historical precedent for Triffin's prediction. Recall that in 1931, official holders of

---

[19]France, in particular, was *not* willing to continue accumulating dollars. President Charles de Gaulle, criticizing the Bretton Woods system for the "exorbitant privilege" it allowed the United States to enjoy, converted a large portion of France's dollar holdings into gold in 1965. But de Gaulle's aggressive action, part of his broader campaign against the alleged "Anglo-Saxon" dominance of the Western alliance, was atypical of the behavior of most countries.

[20]See Triffin, *Gold and the Dollar Crisis* (New Haven: Yale University Press, 1960).

pounds, aware of how meager Britain's gold holdings were, helped bring down the gold standard system by suddenly attempting to redeem their pounds for gold.

One possible solution at the time was an increase in the official price of gold in terms of the dollar and all other currencies. But such an increase would have been inflationary and would have had the politically unattractive consequence of enriching the main gold-producing countries. Further, an increase in gold's price would have caused central banks to expect further decreases in the gold value of their dollar reserve holdings in the future, thus possibly worsening the confidence problem rather than solving it!

Triffin himself proposed a plan in which the IMF issued its own currency, which central banks would hold as international reserves in place of dollars. According to this plan, the IMF would ensure adequate growth of the supply of international reserves in much the same way a central bank ensures adequate growth of the domestic money supply. In effect, Triffin's plan would have transformed the IMF into a world central bank.[21]

In 1967 IMF members agreed to the creation of the **Special Drawing Right (SDR)**, an artificial reserve asset similar to the IMF currency Triffin had envisioned. SDRs are used in transactions between central banks, but their creation had relatively little impact on the functioning of the international monetary system. Their impact was limited partly because by the late 1960s, the system of fixed exchange rates was beginning to show strains that would soon lead to its collapse. These strains were closely related to the special position of the United States.

CASE STUDY

The Decline and Fall of the Bretton Woods System

The system of fixed parities made it difficult for countries to attain simultaneous internal and external balance without discrete exchange rate adjustments. As it became easier to transfer funds across borders, however, the very possibility that exchange rates *might* be changed set off speculative capital movements that made the task facing policymakers even harder. The story of the Bretton Woods system's breakdown is the story of countries' unsuccessful attempts to reconcile internal and external balance under its rules.

The Calm Before the Storm: 1958–1965

In 1958, the same year currency convertibility was restored in Europe, the U.S. current account surplus fell sharply. In 1959 it moved into deficit. Although the current account improved in 1960 as the U.S. economy entered a recession, foreign central banks converted nearly $2 billion of their dollar holdings into gold in that year, after having converted around $3 billion in 1958 and 1959. The year 1960 marked the end of the period of "dollar shortage" and the beginning of a period dominated by fears that the United States might devalue the dollar relative to gold.

---

[21] Triffin's plan was similar to one Keynes had advanced while the IMF was first being designed in the early 1940s. Keynes's blueprint was not adopted, however.

On the whole, the period from 1961 to 1965 was a calm one for the United States, although some other countries, most notably Britain, faced external problems. The U.S. current account surplus widened and the threat of large-scale conversions of dollars into gold by foreign central banks receded. Continuing private capital outflows from the United States, which augmented the dollar component of foreign official reserves, were, however, a source of concern to the Kennedy and Johnson administrations. Starting in 1963, therefore, the United States moved to discourage capital outflows by taxes on purchases of foreign assets by Americans and other measures.

Early in this period, Germany faced a dilemma between internal and external balance that was to recur more dramatically toward the end of the decade. In 1960 Germany experienced an employment boom coupled with large inflows of international reserves. In terms of Figure 18-2, the German authorities found themselves in zone 1. Attempts to restrain the boom through contractionary monetary policy only succeeded in increasing the Bundesbank's international reserves more quickly as the central bank was forced to sell DM for dollars to keep the DM from appreciating. A small revaluation of the DM (by 5 percent) in March 1961 moved the economy closer to internal and external balance as output growth slowed and the current account surplus declined. Although the system successfully avoided a major crisis in this case, this was in part due to the foreign exchange market's perception that the DM revaluation reflected German macroeconomic problems rather than American problems. That perception was to change over the next decade.

The Vietnam Military Buildup and the Great Society: 1965–1968

Many economists view the U.S. macroeconomic policy package of 1965–1968 as a major blunder that helped unravel the system of fixed exchange rates. In 1965, government military purchases began rising as President Lyndon B. Johnson widened America's involvement in the Vietnam conflict. At the same time, other categories of government spending also rose dramatically as the president's "Great Society" programs (which included funds for public education and urban redevelopment) expanded. Figure 18-4a shows how the growth rate of nominal government purchases began to rise, slowly in 1965 and then quite sharply the next year. These increases in government expenditures were not matched by a prompt increase in taxes: 1966 was an election year, and President Johnson was reluctant to invite close congressional scrutiny of his spending by asking for a tax increase.

The result was a substantial fiscal expansion that helped set U.S. prices rising and caused a sharp fall in the U.S. current account surplus (Figures 18-4b and 18-4c). Although monetary policy (as measured by the growth rate of the money supply) initially turned contractionary as output expanded, the negative effect of the resulting high interest rates on the construction industry led the Federal Reserve to choose a much more expansionary monetary course in 1967 and 1968 (Figure 18-4d). As Figure 18-4b shows, this further push to the domestic price level left the United States with an inflation rate near 6 percent per year by the end of the decade.

From the Gold Crisis to the Collapse: 1968–1973

Early signals of future problems came from the London gold market. In late 1967 and early 1968 private speculators began buying gold in anticipation of a rise in its dollar price. It was thought at the time that the speculation had been triggered by the British pound's devaluation in November 1967, but the sharp U.S. monetary expansion over 1967 and rising U.S. inflation probably influenced speculative sentiments as well. After massive gold sales by the Federal Reserve and European central banks, the Bank of England closed the gold market on March 15, 1968. Two days

Figure 18-4 | U.S. Macroeconomic Data, 1964–1972

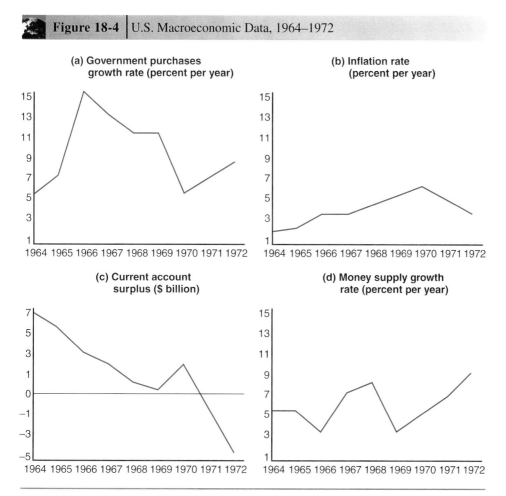

(a) Government purchases growth rate (percent per year)

(b) Inflation rate (percent per year)

(c) Current account surplus ($ billion)

(d) Money supply growth rate (percent per year)

Source: *Economic Report of the President,* 1985. Money supply growth rate is the December to December percentage increase in MI. Inflation rate is the percentage increase in each year's average consumer price index over the average consumer price index for the previous year.

later the central banks announced the creation of a *two-tier* gold market, with one tier private and the other official. Private gold traders would continue to trade on the London gold market, but the gold price set there would be allowed to fluctuate. In contrast, central banks would continue to transact with each other in the official tier at the official gold price of $35 an ounce.

The creation of the two-tier market was a turning point for the Bretton Woods system. A prime goal of the gold exchange standard created at Bretton Woods was to prevent inflation by tying down gold's dollar price. By severing the link between the supply of dollars and a fixed *market* price of gold, the central banks had jettisoned the system's built-in safeguard against inflation. The new arrangements did not eliminate the external constraint on the United States altogether, because foreign central banks retained the right to purchase gold for dollars from the

Federal Reserve. But the *official* price of gold had been reduced to a fictitious device for squaring accounts among central banks; it no longer placed an automatic constraint on worldwide monetary growth.

As Figure 18-4b shows, U.S. inflation rose in 1970 despite the onset of a recession. By then, inflationary expectations had become entrenched in the economy and were affecting wage settlements even in the face of the slowdown. Falling aggregate demand did, however, contribute to an improvement in the U.S. current account in 1970.

The improvement in the U.S. current account proved transitory. Adverse balance of payments figures released in early 1971 helped set off massive private purchases of DM in the foreign exchange market, motivated by expectations that the DM would be revalued against the dollar. On a single day, May 4, 1971, the Bundesbank had to buy $1 billion to hold its dollar exchange rate fixed in the face of the great demand for its currency. On the morning of May 5, the Bundesbank purchased $1 billion during the first hour of foreign exchange trading alone! At that point the Bundesbank gave up and allowed its currency to float, rather than see the German money supply balloon even further as a result of Bundesbank dollar purchases.

As the weeks passed, the markets became increasingly convinced that the dollar would have to be devalued against all the major European currencies. U.S. unemployment was still high in 1971 and the U.S. price level had risen substantially over the previous years. To restore full employment and a balanced current account, the United States somehow had to bring about a real depreciation of the dollar.

That real depreciation could be brought about in two ways. The first option was a fall in the U.S. price level in response to domestic unemployment, coupled with a rise in foreign price levels in response to continuing purchases of dollars by foreign central banks. The second option was a fall in the dollar's nominal value in terms of foreign currencies. The first route—unemployment in the United States and inflation abroad—seemed a painful one for policymakers to follow. The markets rightly guessed that a change in the dollar's value was inevitable. Their realization led to renewed sales of dollars in the foreign exchange market that reached a climax in August 1971.

Devaluation was no easy matter for the United States, however. Any other country could change its exchange rates against all currencies simply by fixing its *dollar* rate at a new level. But as the *N*th currency, the dollar could be devalued only if foreign governments agreed to peg their currencies against the dollar at new rates. In effect, all countries had to agree simultaneously to *revalue* their currencies against the dollar. Dollar devaluation could therefore be accomplished only through extensive multilateral negotiations. And some foreign countries were not anxious to revalue because revaluation would make their goods more expensive relative to U.S. goods and would therefore hurt their export- and import-competing industries.

President Richard M. Nixon forced the issue on August 15, 1971. First, he ended U.S. gold losses by announcing the United States would no longer automatically sell gold to foreign central banks for dollars. This action effectively cut the remaining link between the dollar and gold. Second, the president announced a 10 percent tax on all imports to the United States, to remain effective until America's trading partners agreed to revalue their currencies against the dollar.

An international agreement on exchange rate realignment was reached in December 1971 at the Smithsonian Institution in Washington, D.C. On average, the dollar was devalued against foreign currencies by about 8 percent, and the 10 percent import surcharge that the United States had imposed to force the realignment was removed. The official gold price was raised to $38 an ounce, but the move had no economic significance because the United States did not agree to resume sales of gold to foreign central banks. The Smithsonian agreement made clear that the last remnant of the gold standard had been abandoned.

The Smithsonian realignment, although hailed at the time by President Nixon as "the most significant monetary agreement in the history of the world," was in shambles less than 15 months later. Early in February 1973, another massive speculative attack on the dollar started and the foreign exchange market was closed while the United States and its main trading partners negotiated on dollar support measures. A further 10 percent devaluation of the dollar was announced on February 12, but speculation against the dollar resumed as soon as governments allowed the foreign exchange market to reopen. After European central banks purchased $3.6 billion on March 1 to prevent their currencies from appreciating, the foreign exchange market was closed down once again.

When the foreign exchange market reopened on March 19, the currencies of Japan and most European countries were floating against the dollar.[22] The floating of the industrialized countries' dollar exchange rates was viewed at the time as a temporary response to unmanageable speculative capital movements. But the interim arrangements adopted in March 1973 turned out to be permanent and marked the end of fixed exchange rates and the beginning of a turbulent new period in international monetary relations.

Worldwide Inflation and the Transition to Floating Rates

The acceleration of American inflation in the late 1960s, shown in Figure 18-4b, was a worldwide phenomenon. Table 18-1 shows that by the end of the 1960s, inflation had also speeded up in European economies. The theory in Chapter 17 predicts that when the reserve currency country speeds up its monetary growth, as the United States did in the second half of the 1960s, one effect is an automatic increase in monetary growth rates and inflation abroad as foreign central banks purchase the reserve currency to maintain their exchange rates and expand their money supplies in the process. One interpretation of the Bretton Woods system's collapse is that foreign countries were forced to *import* U.S. inflation through the mechanism described in Chapter 17: To stabilize their price levels and regain internal balance, they had to abandon fixed exchange rates and allow their currencies to float. How much blame for the system's breakdown can be placed on U.S. macroeconomic policies?

To understand how inflation can be imported from abroad unless exchange rates are adjusted, look again at the graphical picture of internal and external balance shown in Figure 18-2. Suppose the home country is faced with foreign inflation. Above, the foreign price level, P^*, was assumed to be given; now, however, P^* rises as a result of inflation abroad. Figure 18-5 shows the effect on the home economy.

---

[22] Many developing countries continued to peg to the dollar, and a number of European countries were continuing to peg their mutual exchange rates as part of an informal arrangement called the "snake." As we see in Chapter 20, the snake evolved into the European Monetary System, and ultimately led to Europe's single currency, the euro.

Table 18-1	Inflation Rates in European Countries, 1966–1972 (percent per year)						
Country	1966	1967	1968	1969	1970	1971	1972
Britain	3.6	2.6	4.6	5.2	6.5	9.7	6.9
France	2.8	2.8	4.4	6.5	5.3	5.5	6.2
Germany	3.4	1.4	2.9	1.9	3.4	5.3	5.5
Italy	2.1	2.1	1.2	2.8	5.1	5.2	5.3

Source: Organization for Economic Cooperation and Development. *Main Economic Indicators: Historical Statistics, 1964–1983.* Paris: OECD, 1984. Figures are percentage increases in each year's average consumer price index over that of the previous year.

You can see how the two schedules shift by asking what would happen if the nominal exchange rate were to fall in proportion to the rise in P^*. In this case, the real exchange rate EP^*/P would be unaffected (given P), and the economy would remain in internal balance or in external balance if either of these conditions originally held. Figure 18-5 therefore shows that for a given initial exchange rate, a rise in P^* shifts both II^1 and XX^1 downward by the same distance (equal to the proportional increase in P^* times the initial exchange rate). The intersection of the new schedules II^2 and XX^2 (point 2) lies directly below point 1.

If the economy is at point 1, a rise in P^*, *given* the fixed exchange rate and the domestic price level, therefore strands the economy in zone 1 with overemployment and an undesirably high surplus in its current account. The factor that causes this outcome is a real currency depreciation that shifts world demand toward the home country (EP^*/P rises because P^* rises).

If nothing is done by the government, overemployment puts upward pressure on the domestic price level, and this pressure gradually shifts the two schedules back to their original positions. The schedules stop shifting once P has risen in proportion to P^*. At this stage the real exchange rate, employment, and the current account are at their initial levels, so point 1 is once again a position of internal and external balance.

The way to avoid the imported inflation is to revalue the currency (that is, lower E) and move to point 2. A revaluation restores internal and external balance immediately, without domestic inflation, by using the nominal exchange rate to offset the effect of the rise in P^* on the real exchange rate. Only an expenditure-switching policy is needed to respond to a pure increase in foreign prices.

The rise in domestic prices that occurs when no revaluation takes place requires a rise in the domestic money supply, since prices and the money supply move proportionally in the long run. The mechanism that brings this rise about is foreign exchange intervention by the home central bank. As domestic output and prices rise after the rise in P^*, the real money supply shrinks and the demand for real money holdings increases. To prevent the resulting upward pressure on the home interest rate from appreciating the currency, the central bank must purchase international reserves and expand the home money supply. In this way, inflationary policies pursued by the reserve center spill over into foreign countries' money supplies.

The close association between U.S. and foreign inflation evident in Figure 18-4 and Table 18-1 suggests that some European inflation was imported from the United States. But the timing of the inflationary surges in different countries suggests that factors peculiar to

Figure 18-5 | Effect on Internal and External Balance of a Rise
in the Foreign Price Level, P^*

After P^* rises, point 1 is in
zone 1 (overemployment and
an excessive surplus). Revaluation (a fall in E) restores balance immediately by moving
the policy setting to point 2.

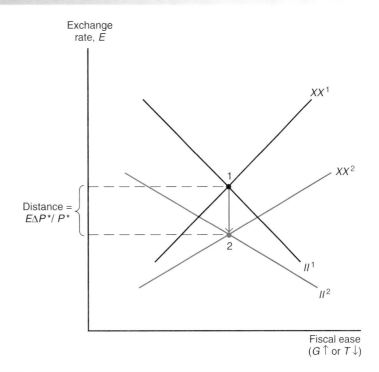

individual economies also played a role. In Britain, for example, inflation speeds up markedly in 1968, the year following the pound's devaluation. Since (as seen in the last chapter) devaluation is neutral in the long run, it must raise the long-run domestic price level proportionally. The devaluation is probably part of the explanation for the rise in British inflation. Strikes in France in 1968 led to large wage increases, a French-German currency crisis, and a devaluation of the franc in 1969. These events partly explain the sharp increase in French inflation in 1968–1969. The role of imported inflation was greatest in Germany, where the painful earlier experience with hyperinflation had made policymakers determined to resist price level increases.

Evidence on money supplies confirms that European and Japanese monetary growth accelerated in the late 1960s, as our theory predicts. Table 18-2 shows the evolution of the international reserves and money supply of West Germany over the years 1968–1972. The table shows how monetary growth rose dramatically after 1969 as the Bundesbank's international reserves expanded.[23] This evidence is consistent with the view that American

---

[23]The behavior of reserves in 1968 and 1969—a large increase followed by a large decrease—reflects speculation on a DM revaluation against the franc during the French-German currency crisis of those years.

Table 18-2	Changes in Germany's Money Supply and International Reserves, 1968–1972 (percent per year)				
Growth rate of	**1968**	**1969**	**1970**	**1971**	**1972**
Money supply	6.4	−6.3	8.9	12.3	14.7
Official international reserves	37.8	−43.6	215.7	36.1	35.8

Source: Organization for Economic Cooperation and Development. *Main Economic Indicators: Historical Statistics, 1964–1983.* Paris: OECD, 1984. Figures are percentage increases in each year's end-of-year money supply or international reserves over the level at the end of the previous year. Official reserves are measured net of gold holdings.

inflation was imported into Germany through the Bundesbank's purchases of dollars in the foreign exchange market.

The acceleration of German money growth probably cannot be explained entirely as a direct consequence of the acceleration in U.S. monetary growth, however. A comparison of Figure 18-4 and Table 18-2 shows that German monetary growth accelerated by much more than U.S. monetary growth after 1969. This difference suggests that much of the growth in Germany's international reserves reflected speculation on a possible dollar devaluation in the early 1970s and the resulting shift by market participants away from dollar assets and into deutsche mark assets.

U.S. monetary policy certainly contributed to inflation abroad by its direct effect on prices and money supplies. It helped wreck the fixed rate system by confronting foreign policymakers with a choice between fixed rates and imported inflation. But the U.S. fiscal policy that helped make a dollar devaluation necessary also contributed to foreign inflation by giving further encouragement to speculative capital flows out of dollars. U.S. fiscal policy in the later 1960s must be viewed as an additional cause of the Bretton Woods system's demise.

Thus, the collapse of the Bretton Woods system was due, in part, to the lopsided macroeconomic power of the United States. But it was also due to the fact that the key expenditure-switching tool needed for internal and external balance—discrete exchange rate adjustment—inspired speculative attacks that made both internal and external balance progressively more difficult to achieve. The architects of the Bretton Woods system had hoped its most powerful member would see beyond purely domestic goals and adopt policies geared to the welfare of the world economy as a whole. When the United States proved unwilling to shoulder this responsibility after the mid-1960s, the fixed exchange rate system came apart.

Summary

1. In an open economy, policymakers try to maintain *internal balance* (full employment and a stable price level) and *external balance* (a current account level that is neither

so negative that the country may be unable to repay its foreign debts nor so positive that foreigners are put in that position). The definition of external balance depends on a number of factors, including the exchange rate regime and world economic conditions. Because each country's macroeconomic policies have repercussions abroad, a country's ability to reach internal and external balance depends on the policies other countries adopt.

2. The gold standard system contains a powerful automatic mechanism for assuring external balance, the *price-specie-flow mechanism.* The flows of gold accompanying deficits and surpluses cause price changes that reduce current account imbalances and therefore tend to return all countries to external balance. The system's performance in maintaining internal balance was mixed, however. With the eruption of World War I in 1914, the gold standard was suspended.

3. Attempts to return to the prewar gold standard after 1918 were unsuccessful. As the world economy moved into general depression after 1929, the restored gold standard fell apart and international economic integration weakened. In the turbulent economic conditions of the period, governments made internal balance their main concern and tried to avoid the external balance problem by partially shutting their economies off from the rest of the world. The result was a world economy in which all countries' situations could have been bettered through international cooperation.

4. The architects of the *International Monetary Fund (IMF)* hoped to design a fixed exchange rate system that would encourage growth in international trade while making the requirements of external balance sufficiently flexible that they could be met without sacrificing internal balance. To this end, the IMF charter provided financing facilities for deficit countries and allowed exchange rate adjustments in conditions of "fundamental disequilibrium." All countries pegged their currencies to the dollar. The United States pegged to gold and agreed to exchange gold for dollars with foreign central banks at a price of $35 an ounce.

5. After *currency convertibility* was restored in Europe in 1958, countries' financial markets became more closely integrated, monetary policy became less effective (except for the United States), and movements in international reserves became more volatile. These changes revealed a key weakness in the system. To reach internal and external balance at the same time, *expenditure-switching* as well as *expenditure-changing* policies were needed. But the possibility of expenditure-switching policies (exchange rate changes) could give rise to speculative capital flows that undermined fixed exchange rates. As the main reserve currency country, the United States faced a unique external balance problem: the *confidence problem* that would arise as foreign official dollar holdings inevitably grew to exceed U.S. gold holdings.

6. U.S macroeconomic policies in the late 1960s helped cause the breakdown of the Bretton Woods system by early 1973. Overexpansionary U.S. fiscal policy contributed to the need for a devaluation of the dollar in the early 1970s, and fears that this would occur touched off speculative capital flows out of dollars that caused foreign money supplies to balloon. Higher U.S. money growth fueled inflation at home and abroad, making foreign governments increasingly reluctant to continue importing U.S. inflation through fixed exchange rates. A series of international crises beginning in the spring of 1971 led in stages to the abandonment of both the dollar's link to gold and fixed dollar exchange rates for the industrialized countries.

Key Terms

Problems

1. If you were in charge of macroeconomic policies in a small open economy, what qualitative effect would each of the following events have on your target for external balance?
   a. Large deposits of uranium are discovered in the interior of your country.
   b. The world price of your main export good, copper, rises permanently.
   c. The world price of copper rises temporarily.
   d. There is a temporary rise in the world price of oil.

2. Under a gold standard of the kind analyzed by Hume, describe how balance of payments equilibrium between two countries, A and B, would be restored after a transfer of income from B to A.

3. In spite of the flaws of the pre-1914 gold standard, exchange rate changes were rare. In contrast, such changes became quite frequent in the interwar period. Can you think of reasons for this contrast?

4. Under a gold standard, countries may adopt excessively contractionary monetary policies as all scramble in vain for a larger share of the limited supply of world gold reserves. Can the same problem arise under a reserve currency standard when bonds denominated in different currencies are all perfect substitutes?

5. A central bank that adopts a fixed exchange rate may sacrifice its autonomy in setting domestic monetary policy. It is sometimes argued that when this is the case, the central bank also gives up the ability to use monetary policy to combat the wage-price spiral. The argument goes like this: "Suppose workers demand higher wages and employers give in, but that the employers then raise output prices to cover their higher costs. Now the price level is higher and real balances are momentarily lower, so to prevent an interest rate rise that would appreciate the currency, the central bank must buy foreign exchange and expand the money supply. This action accommodates the initial wage demands with monetary growth and the economy moves permanently to a higher level of wages and prices. With a fixed exchange rate there is thus no way of keeping wages and prices down." What is wrong with this argument?

6. Economists have long debated whether the growth of dollar reserve holdings in the Bretton Woods years was "demand-determined" (that is, determined by central banks' desire to add to their international reserves) or "supply-determined" (that is, determined by the speed of U.S. monetary growth). What would your answer be? What are the consequences for analyzing the relationship between growth in the world stock of international reserves and worldwide inflation?

7. Suppose the central bank of a small country is faced by a rise in the world interest rate, R^*. What is the effect on its foreign reserve holdings? On its money supply? Can it offset either of these effects through domestic open-market operations?

8. How might restrictions on private financial account transactions alter the problem of attaining internal and external balance with a fixed exchange rate? What costs might such restrictions involve?

Further Reading

Michael D. Bordo and Barry Eichengreen, eds. *A Retrospective on the Bretton Woods System.* Chicago: University of Chicago Press, 1993. A collection of essays reevaluating the Bretton Woods experience.

W. Max Corden. "The Geometric Representation of Policies to Attain Internal and External Balance," in Richard N. Cooper, ed. *International Finance.* Harmondsworth, U.K.: Penguin Books, 1969, pp. 256–290. A classic diagrammatic analysis of expenditure-switching and expenditure-changing macroeconomic policies.

Barry Eichengreen and Marc Flandreau, eds. *The Gold Standard in Theory and History.* Second edition. London: Routledge, 1997. A valuable collection of readings on the performance of the gold standard in different historical periods.

Richard N. Gardner. *Sterling-Dollar Diplomacy in Current Perspective.* New York: Columbia University Press, 1980. Readable account of the negotiations that established the IMF, World Bank, and GATT.

Harold James. *The End of Globalization: Lessons from the Great Depression.* Cambridge, MA: Harvard University Press, 2001. Political and economic analysis of international economic disintegration between 1914 and 1939.

Charles P. Kindleberger. *The World in Depression 1929–1939.* Revised edition. Berkeley and Los Angeles: University of California Press, 1986. A leading international economist examines the causes and effects of the Great Depression.

Lawrence B. Krause and Walter S. Salant, eds. *Worldwide Inflation: Theory and Recent Experience.* Washington, D.C.: Brookings Institution, 1977. A collection of analytical studies on global inflationary experience in the 1960s and early 1970s.

Ronald I. McKinnon. "The Rules of the Game: International Money in Historical Perspective." *Journal of Economic Literature* 31 (March 1993), pp. 1–44. An illuminating overview of the mechanics and implicit rules of alternative international monetary arrangements.

Ragnar Nurkse. *International Currency Experience: Lessons of the Inter-War Period.* Geneva: League of Nations, 1944. Classic critique of the nationalistic macroeconomic policies many countries adopted between the world wars.

Maurice Obstfeld. "International Finance," in *The New Palgrave Dictionary of Money & Finance.* Vol. 2. New York: Stockton Press, 1992, pp. 457–466. Discusses changing conceptions of internal and external balance.

Robert Solomon. *The International Monetary System, 1945–1981.* New York: Harper & Row, 1982. Chapters 1–14 chronicle international monetary relations between World War II and the early 1970s. The author was chief of the Federal Reserve's international finance division during the period leading up to the breakdown of fixed exchange rates.

CHAPTER 19

Macroeconomic Policy and Coordination under Floating Exchange Rates

A s the Bretton Woods system of fixed exchange rates began to show signs of strain in the late 1960s, many economists recommended that countries allow currency values to be determined freely in the foreign exchange market. When the governments of the industrialized countries adopted floating exchange rates early in 1973, they viewed their step as a temporary emergency measure and were not consciously following the advice of the economists then advocating a permanent floating-rate system. So far, however, it has proved impossible to put the fixed-rate system back together again: The dollar exchange rates of the industrialized countries have continued to float since 1973.

The advocates of floating saw it as a way out of the conflicts between internal and external balance that often arose under the rigid Bretton Woods exchange rates. By the mid-1980s, however, economists and policymakers had become more skeptical about the benefits of an international monetary system based on floating rates. Some critics describe the post-1973 currency arrangements as an international monetary "nonsystem," a free-for-all in which national macroeconomic policies are frequently at odds. Many observers now think that the current exchange rate system is badly in need of reform.

Why has the performance of floating rates been so disappointing, and what direction should reform of the current system take? In this chapter our models of fixed and floating exchange rates are applied to examine the recent performance of floating rates and to compare the macroeconomic policy problems of different exchange rate regimes. ●

The Case for Floating Exchange Rates

As international currency crises of increasing scope and frequency erupted in the late 1960s, most economists began advocating greater flexibility of exchange rates. Many argued that a system of floating exchange rates (one in which central banks did not intervene in the foreign exchange market to fix rates) would not only automatically ensure exchange rate flexibility but would also produce several other benefits for the world economy. The case for floating exchange rates rested on three major claims:

    1. *Monetary policy autonomy.* If central banks were no longer obliged to intervene in currency markets to fix exchange rates, governments would be able to use monetary policy to reach internal and external balance. Furthermore, no country would be forced to import inflation (or deflation) from abroad.

2. *Symmetry.* Under a system of floating rates the inherent asymmetries of Bretton Woods would disappear and the United States would no longer be able to set world monetary conditions all by itself. At the same time, the United States would have the same opportunity as other countries to influence its exchange rate against foreign currencies.

3. *Exchange rates as automatic stabilizers.* Even in the absence of an active monetary policy, the swift adjustment of market-determined exchange rates would help countries maintain internal and external balance in the face of changes in aggregate demand. The long and agonizing periods of speculation preceding exchange rate realignments under the Bretton Woods rules would not occur under floating.

Monetary Policy Autonomy

Under the Bretton Woods fixed-rate system, countries other than the United States had little scope to use monetary policy to attain internal and external balance. Monetary policy was weakened by the mechanism of offsetting capital flows (discussed in Chapter 17). A central bank purchase of domestic assets, for example, would put temporary downward pressure on the domestic interest rate and cause the domestic currency to weaken in the foreign exchange market. The exchange rate then had to be propped up through central bank sales of official foreign reserves. Pressure on the interest and exchange rates disappeared, however, only when official reserve losses had driven the domestic money supply back down to its original level. Thus, in the closing years of fixed exchange rates, central banks imposed increasingly stringent restrictions on international payments to keep control over their money supplies. These restrictions were only partially successful in strengthening monetary policy, and they had the damaging side effect of distorting international trade.

Advocates of floating rates pointed out that removal of the obligation to peg currency values would restore monetary control to central banks. If, for example, the central bank faced unemployment and wished to expand its money supply in response, there would no longer be any legal barrier to the currency depreciation this would cause. As in the analysis of Chapter 16, the currency depreciation would reduce unemployment by lowering the relative price of domestic products and increasing world demand for them. Similarly, the central bank of an overheated economy could cool down activity by contracting the money supply without worrying that undesired reserve inflows would undermine its stabilization effort. Enhanced control over monetary policy would allow countries to dismantle their distorting barriers to international payments.

Advocates of floating also argued that floating rates would allow each country to choose its own desired long-run inflation rate rather than passively importing the inflation rate established abroad. We saw in the last chapter that a country faced with a rise in the foreign price level will be thrown out of balance and ultimately will import the foreign inflation if it holds its exchange rate fixed: By the end of the 1960s many countries felt that they were importing inflation from the United States. By revaluing its currency—that is, by lowering the domestic currency price of foreign currency—a country can insulate itself completely from an inflationary increase in foreign prices, and so remain in internal and external balance. One of the most telling arguments in favor of floating rates was their ability, in theory, to bring about automatically exchange rate changes that insulate economies from ongoing foreign inflation.

The mechanism behind this insulation is purchasing power parity (Chapter 15). Recall that when all changes in the world economy are monetary, PPP holds true in the long run: Exchange rates eventually move to offset exactly national differences in inflation. If U.S. monetary growth leads to a long-run doubling of the U.S. price level, while Germany's price level remains constant, PPP predicts that the long-run DM price of the dollar will be halved. This nominal exchange rate change leaves the *real* exchange rate between the dollar and DM unchanged and thus maintains Germany's internal and external balance. In other words, the long-run exchange rate change predicted by PPP is exactly the change that insulates Germany from U.S. inflation.

A money-induced increase in U.S. prices also causes an *immediate* appreciation of foreign currencies against the dollar when the exchange rate floats. In the short run, the size of this appreciation can differ from what PPP predicts, but the foreign exchange speculators who might have mounted an attack on fixed dollar exchange rates speed the adjustment of floating rates. Since they know foreign currencies will appreciate according to PPP in the long run, they act on their expectations and push exchange rates in the direction of their long-run levels.

Countries operating under the Bretton Woods rules were forced to choose between matching U.S. inflation to hold their dollar exchange rates fixed or deliberately revaluing their currencies in proportion to the rise in U.S. prices. Under floating, however, the foreign exchange market automatically brings about the exchange rate changes that shield countries from U.S. inflation. Since this outcome does not require any government policy decisions, the revaluation crises that occurred under fixed exchange rates are avoided.[1]

Symmetry

The second argument put forward by the advocates of floating was that abandonment of the Bretton Woods system would remove the asymmetries that caused so much international disagreement in the 1960s and early 1970s. There were two main asymmetries, both the result of the dollar's central role in the international monetary system. First, because central banks pegged their currencies to the dollar and accumulated dollars as international reserves, the U.S. Federal Reserve played the leading role in determining the world money supply and central banks abroad had little scope to determine their own domestic money supplies. Second, any foreign country could devalue its currency against the dollar in conditions of "fundamental disequilibrium," but the system's rules did not give the United States the option of devaluing against foreign currencies. Thus, when the dollar was at last devalued in December 1971, it was only after a long and economically disruptive period of multilateral negotiation.

A system of floating exchange rates, its proponents argued, would do away with these asymmetries. Since countries would no longer peg dollar exchange rates or need to hold dollar reserves for this purpose, each would be in a position to guide monetary conditions at home. For the same reason, the United States would not face any special obstacle to altering its exchange rate through monetary or fiscal policies. All countries' exchange rates

---

[1] Countries can also avoid importing undesired *deflation* by floating, since the analysis above goes through, in reverse, for a fall in the foreign price level.

would be determined symmetrically by the foreign exchange market, not by government decisions.[2]

Exchange Rates as Automatic Stabilizers

The third argument in favor of floating rates concerned their ability, theoretically, to promote swift and relatively painless adjustment to certain types of economic changes. One such change, previously discussed, is foreign inflation. Figure 19-1, which uses the DD-AA model presented in Chapter 16, examines another type of change by comparing the economy's response under a fixed and a floating exchange rate to a temporary fall in foreign demand for its exports.

A fall in demand for the home country's exports reduces aggregate demand for every level of the exchange rate, E, and so shifts the DD schedule leftward from DD^1 to DD^2. (Recall that the DD schedule shows exchange rate and output pairs for which aggregate demand equals aggregate output.) Figure 19-1a shows how this shift affects the economy's equilibrium when the exchange rate floats. Because the demand shift is assumed to be temporary, it does not change the long-run expected exchange rate and so does not move the asset market equilibrium schedule AA^1. (Recall that the AA schedule shows exchange rate and output pairs at which the foreign exchange market and the domestic money market are in equilibrium.) The economy's short-run equilibrium is therefore at point 2; compared with the initial equilibrium at point 1, the currency depreciates (E rises) and output falls. Why does the exchange rate rise from E^1 to E^2? As demand and output fall, reducing the transactions demand for money, the home interest rate must also decline to keep the money market in equilibrium. This fall in the home interest rate causes the domestic currency to depreciate in the foreign exchange market, and the exchange rate therefore rises from E^1 to E^2.

The effect of the same export demand disturbance under a fixed exchange rate is shown in Figure 19-1b. Since the central bank must prevent the currency depreciation that occurs under a floating rate, it buys domestic money with foreign currency, an action that contracts the money supply and shifts AA^1 left to AA^2. The new short-run equilibrium of the economy under a fixed exchange rate is at point 3, where output equals Y^3.

Figure 19-1 shows that output actually falls more under a fixed rate than under a floating rate, dropping all the way to Y^3 rather than Y^2. In other words, the movement of the floating exchange rate stabilizes the economy by reducing the shock's effect on employment relative to its effect under a fixed rate. Currency depreciation in the floating rate case makes domestic goods and services cheaper when the demand for them falls, partially offsetting the initial reduction in demand. In addition to reducing the departure from internal balance caused by the fall in export demand, the depreciation reduces the current account deficit that occurs under fixed rates by making domestic products more competitive in international markets.

We have considered the case of a transitory fall in export demand, but even stronger conclusions can be drawn when there is a *permanent* fall in export demand. In this case, the

---

[2]The symmetry argument is not an argument against fixed-rate systems in general, but an argument against the specific type of fixed-exchange rate system that broke down in the early 1970s. As we saw in Chapter 17, a fixed-rate system based on a gold standard can be completely symmetric. The creation of an artificial reserve asset, the SDR, in the late 1960s was an attempt to attain the symmetry of a gold standard without the other drawbacks of that system.

Figure 19-1 | Effects of a Fall in Export Demand

The response to a fall in export demand (seen in the shift from DD^1 to DD^2) differs under floating and fixed exchange rates. (a) With a floating rate, output falls only to Y^2 as the currency's depreciation (from E^1 to E^2) shifts demand back toward domestic goods. (b) With the exchanged rate fixed at E^1, output falls all the way to Y^3 as the central bank reduces the money supply (reflected in the shift from AA^1 to AA^2).

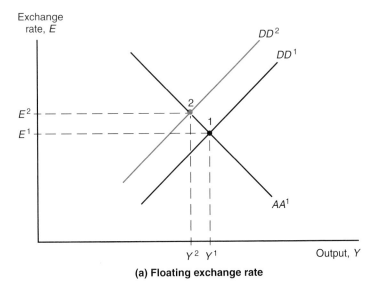

(a) Floating exchange rate

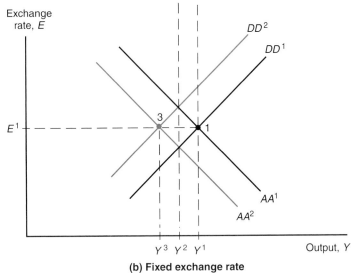

(b) Fixed exchange rate

expected exchange rate E^e also rises and AA shifts upward as a result. A permanent shock causes a greater depreciation than a temporary one, and the movement of the exchange rate therefore cushions domestic output more when the shock is permanent.

Under the Bretton Woods system, a fall in export demand such as the one shown in Figure 19-1b would, if permanent, have led to a situation of "fundamental disequilibrium" calling for a devaluation of the currency or a long period of domestic unemployment as export prices fell. Uncertainty about the government's intentions would have encouraged speculative capital outflows, further worsening the situation by depleting central bank reserves and contracting the domestic money supply at a time of unemployment. Advocates of floating rates pointed out that the foreign exchange market would automatically bring about the required *real* currency depreciation through a movement in the nominal exchange rate. This exchange rate change would reduce or eliminate the need to push the price level down through unemployment, and because it would occur immediately there would be no risk of speculative disruption, as there would be under a fixed rate.

The Case Against Floating Exchange Rates

The experience with floating exchange rates between the world wars had left many doubts about how they would function in practice if the Bretton Woods rules were scrapped. Some economists were skeptical of the claims advanced by the advocates of floating and predicted instead that floating rates would have adverse consequences for the world economy. The case against floating rates rested on five main arguments:

1. *Discipline.* Central banks freed from the obligation to fix their exchange rates might embark on inflationary policies. In other words, the "discipline" imposed on individual countries by a fixed rate would be lost.

2. *Destabilizing speculation and money market disturbances.* Speculation on changes in exchange rates could lead to instability in foreign exchange markets, and this instability, in turn, might have negative effects on countries' internal and external balances. Further, disturbances to the home money market could be more disruptive under floating than under a fixed rate.

3. *Injury to international trade and investment.* Floating rates would make relative international prices more unpredictable and thus injure international trade and investment.

4. *Uncoordinated economic policies.* If the Bretton Woods rules on exchange rate adjustment were abandoned, the door would be opened to competitive currency practices harmful to the world economy. As happened during the interwar years, countries might adopt policies without considering their possible beggar-thy-neighbor aspects. All countries would suffer as a result.

5. *The illusion of greater autonomy.* Floating exchange rates would not really give countries more policy autonomy. Changes in exchange rates would have such pervasive macroeconomic effects that central banks would feel compelled to intervene heavily in foreign exchange markets even without a formal commitment to peg. Thus, floating would increase the uncertainty in the economy without really giving macroeconomic policy greater freedom.

Discipline

Proponents of floating rates argue they give governments more freedom in the use of monetary policy. Some critics of floating rates believed that floating rates would lead to license rather than liberty: Freed of the need to worry about losses of foreign reserves, governments might embark on overexpansionary fiscal or monetary policies, falling into the inflation bias trap discussed in Chapter 16 (p. 455). Factors ranging from political objectives (such as stimulating the economy in time to win an election) to simple incompetence might set off an inflationary spiral. In the minds of those who made the discipline argument, the German hyperinflation of the 1920s epitomized the kind of monetary instability that floating rates might allow.

The pro-floaters' response to the discipline criticism was that a floating exchange rate would bottle up inflationary disturbances within the country whose government was misbehaving; it would then be up to its voters, if they wished, to elect a government with better policies. The Bretton Woods arrangements ended up imposing relatively little discipline on the United States, which certainly contributed to the acceleration of worldwide inflation in the late 1960s. Unless a sacrosanct link between currencies and a commodity such as gold were at the center of a system of fixed rates, the system would remain susceptible to human tampering. As discussed in Chapter 17, however, commodity-based monetary standards suffer from difficulties that make them undesirable in practice.

Destabilizing Speculation and Money Market Disturbances

An additional concern arising out of the experience of the interwar period was the possibility that speculation in currency markets might fuel wide gyrations in exchange rates. If foreign exchange traders saw that a currency was depreciating, it was argued, they might sell the currency in the expectation of future depreciation regardless of the currency's longer-term prospects; and as more traders jumped on the bandwagon by selling the currency the expectations of depreciation would be realized. Such **destabilizing speculation** would tend to accentuate the fluctuations around the exchange rate's long-run value that would occur normally as a result of unexpected economic disturbances. Aside from interfering with international trade, destabilizing sales of a weak currency might encourage expectations of future inflation and set off a domestic wage-price spiral that would encourage further depreciation. Countries could be caught in a "vicious circle" of depreciation and inflation that might be difficult to escape.

Advocates of floating rates questioned whether destabilizing speculators could stay in business. Anyone who persisted in selling a currency after it had depreciated below its long-run value or in buying a currency after it had appreciated above its long-run value was bound to lose money over the long term. Destabilizing speculators would thus be driven from the market, the pro-floaters argued, and the field would be left to speculators who had avoided long-term losses by speeding the adjustment of exchange rates *toward* their long-run values.

Proponents of floating also pointed out that capital flows could behave in a destabilizing manner under fixed rates. An unexpected central bank reserve loss might set up expectations of a devaluation and spark a reserve hemorrhage as speculators dumped domestic currency assets. Such capital flight might actually force an unnecessary devaluation if government measures to restore confidence proved insufficient.

A more telling argument against floating rates is that they make the economy more vulnerable to shocks coming from the domestic money market. Figure 19-2 uses the *DD-AA* model to illustrate this point. The figure shows the effect on the economy of a rise in real domestic money demand (that is, a rise in the real balances people desire to hold at each level of the interest rate and income) under a floating exchange rate. Because a lower level of income is now needed (given E) for people to be content to hold the available real money supply, AA^1 shifts leftward to AA^2: Income falls from Y^1 to Y^2 as the currency appreciates from E^1 to E^2. The rise in money demand works exactly like a fall in the money supply, and if it is permanent it will lead eventually to a fall in the home price level.

Figure 19-2 | A Rise in Money Demand under a Floating Exchange Rate

A rise in money demand (the shift from AA^1 to AA^2) works exactly like a fall in the money supply, causing the currency to appreciate to E^2 and output to fall to Y^2. Under a fixed exchange rate the central bank would prevent AA^1 from shifting by purchasing foreign exchange and thus automatically expanding the money supply to meet the rise in money demand.

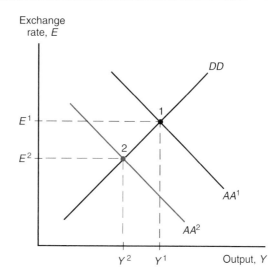

Under a fixed exchange rate, however, the change in money demand does not affect the economy at all. To prevent the home currency from appreciating, the central bank buys foreign reserves with domestic money until the real money supply rises by an amount equal to the rise in real money demand. This intervention has the effect of keeping AA^1 in its original position, preventing any change in output or the price level.

A fixed exchange rate therefore automatically prevents instability in the domestic money market from affecting the economy. This is a powerful argument in favor of fixed rates *if* most of the shocks that buffet the economy come from the home money market (that is, if they result from shifts in AA). But as we saw in the previous section, fixing the exchange rate will worsen macroeconomic performance on average if output market shocks (that is, shocks involving shifts in DD) predominate.

Injury to International Trade and Investment

Critics of floating also charged that the inherent variability of floating exchange rates would injure international trade and investment. Fluctuating currencies make importers more uncertain about the prices they will have to pay for goods in the future and make exporters more uncertain about the prices they will receive. This uncertainty, it was claimed, would make it costlier to engage in international trade, and as a result trade volumes—and with them the gains countries realize through trade—would shrink. Similarly, greater uncertainty about the payoffs on investments might interfere with productive international capital flows.

Supporters of floating countered that international traders could avoid exchange rate risk through transactions in the forward exchange market (see Chapter 13), which would grow in scope and efficiency in a floating-rate world. The skeptics replied that forward exchange markets would be expensive to use and that it was doubtful that forward transactions could be used to cover all exchange-rate risks.

At a more general level, opponents of floating rates feared that the usefulness of each country's money as a guide to rational planning and calculation would be reduced. A currency becomes less useful as a unit of account if its purchasing power over imports becomes less predictable.

Uncoordinated Economic Policies

Some defenders of the Bretton Woods system thought that its rules had helped promote orderly international trade by outlawing the competitive currency depreciations that occurred during the Great Depression. With countries once again free to alter their exchange rates at will, they argued, history might repeat itself. Countries might again follow self-serving macroeconomic policies that hurt all countries and, in the end, helped none.

In rebuttal, the pro-floaters replied that the Bretton Woods rules for exchange rate adjustment were cumbersome. In addition, the rules were inequitable because, in practice, it was deficit countries that came under pressure to adopt restrictive macroeconomic policies or devalue. The fixed-rate system had "solved" the problem of international cooperation on monetary policy only by giving the United States a dominant position that it ultimately abused.

The Illusion of Greater Autonomy

A final line of criticism held that the policy autonomy promised by the advocates of floating rates was, in part, illusory. True, a floating rate could in theory shut out foreign inflation over the long haul and allow central banks to set their money supplies as they pleased. But, it was argued, the exchange rate is such an important macroeconomic variable that policymakers would find themselves unable to take domestic monetary policy measures without considering their effects on the exchange rate.

Particularly important to this view was the role of the exchange rate in the domestic inflation process. A currency depreciation that raised import prices might induce workers to demand higher wages to maintain their customary standard of living. Higher wage settlements would then feed into final goods prices, fueling price level inflation and further wage hikes. In addition, currency depreciation would immediately raise the prices of imported goods used in the production of domestic output. Therefore, floating rates could be expected to quicken the pace at which the price level responded to increases in the money supply. While floating rates implied greater central bank control over the nominal money supply, M^s, they did not necessarily imply correspondingly greater control over the policy instrument that affects employment and other real economic variables, the *real* money supply, M^s/P. The response of domestic prices to exchange rate changes would be particularly rapid in economies where imports make up a large share of the domestic consumption basket: In such countries, currency changes have significant effects on the purchasing power of workers' wages.

The skeptics also maintained that the insulating properties of a floating rate are very limited. They conceded that the exchange rate would adjust *eventually* to offset foreign price inflation due to excessive monetary growth. In a world of sticky prices, however, countries are nonetheless buffeted by foreign monetary developments, which affect real interest rates and real exchange rates in the short run. Further, there is no reason, even in theory, why one country's fiscal policies cannot have repercussions abroad.

Critics of floating thus argued that its potential benefits had been oversold relative to its costs. Macroeconomic policymakers would continue to labor under the constraint of avoiding excessive exchange rate fluctuations. But by abandoning fixed rates, they would have forgone the benefits for world trade and investment of predictable currency values.

CASE STUDY

Exchange Rate Experience Between the Oil Shocks, 1973–1980

Which group was right, the advocates of floating rates or the critics? In this Case Study and the next we survey the experience with floating exchange rates since 1973 in an attempt to answer this question. To avoid future disappointment, however, it is best to state up front that, as is often the case in economics, the data do not lead to a clear verdict. Although a number of predictions made by the critics of floating were borne out by subsequent events, it is also unclear whether a regime of fixed exchange rates would have survived the series of economic storms that has shaken the world economy since 1973.

The First Oil Shock and Its Effects, 1973–1975

As the industrialized countries' exchange rates were allowed to float in March 1973, an official group representing all IMF members was preparing plans to restore world monetary order. Formed in the fall of 1972, this group, called the Committee of Twenty, had been assigned the job of designing a new system of fixed exchange rates free of the asymmetries of Bretton Woods. By the time the committee issued its final "Outline of Reform" in July 1974, however, an upheaval in the world petroleum market had made an early return to fixed exchange rates unthinkable.

Energy Prices and the 1974–1975 Recession.   In October 1973 war broke out between Israel and the Arab countries. To protest support of Israel by the United States and the Netherlands, Arab members of the Organization of Petroleum Exporting Countries (OPEC), an international cartel including most large oil producers, imposed an embargo on oil shipments to those two countries. Fearing more general disruptions in oil shipments, buyers bid up market oil prices as they tried to build precautionary inventories. Encouraged by these developments in the oil market, OPEC countries began raising the price they charged to their main customers, the large oil companies. By March 1974 the oil price had quadrupled from its prewar price of $3 per barrel to $12 per barrel.

The massive increase in the price of oil raised the energy prices paid by consumers and the operating costs of energy-using firms and also fed into the prices of nonenergy petroleum products, such as plastics. To understand the impact of these price increases, think of them as a large tax on oil importers imposed by the oil producers of OPEC. The oil shock had the same macroeconomic effect as a simultaneous increase in consumer and business taxes: Consumption and investment slowed down everywhere, and the world economy was thrown into recession. The current account balances of oil-importing countries worsened.

The Acceleration of Inflation.   The model we developed in Chapters 13 through 17 predicts that inflation tends to rise in booms and fall in recessions. As the world went into deep recession in 1974, however, inflation accelerated in most countries. Table 19-1 shows how inflation in the seven largest industrial countries spurted upward in that year. In a number of these countries inflation rates came close to doubling even though unemployment was rising.

What happened? An important contributing factor was the oil shock itself: By directly raising the prices of petroleum products and the costs of energy-using industries, the increase in the oil price caused price levels to jump upward. Further, the worldwide inflationary pressures that had built up since the end of the 1960s had become entrenched in the wage-setting process and were continuing to contribute to inflation in spite of the deteriorating employment picture. The same inflationary expectations that were driving new wage contracts were also putting additional upward pressure on commodity prices as speculators built up stocks of commodities whose prices they expected to rise.

Finally, the oil crisis, as luck would have it, was not the only supply shock troubling the world economy at the time. From 1972 on, a coincidence of adverse supply disturbances pushed farm prices upward and thus contributed to the general inflation. These supply disturbances included poor harvests in the United States and the Soviet Union; shortages of sugar and cocoa; and the mysterious disappearance of the Peruvian anchovies from their customary feeding grounds. Although you may think anchovies are important only to consumers of pizza and Caesar salad, they are also important to farmers since they are used in the fish meal that is fed to livestock. The precipitous drop in the anchovy catch led to sharp increases in the prices of competing feed grains (mainly corn and soybeans).

Stagflation.   To describe the unusual macroeconomic conditions of 1974–1975, economists coined a new word that has since become commonplace: **stagflation**, a combination of stagnating output and high inflation. Stagflation was the result of two factors:

1. Increases in commodity prices that directly raised inflation while at the same time depressing aggregate demand and supply.

Table 19-1 | Inflation Rates in Major Industrialized Countries, 1973–1980 (percent per year)

Country	1973	1974	1975	1976	1977	1978	1979	1980
United States	6.2	11.1	9.1	5.7	6.5	7.6	11.3	13.5
Britain	9.2	16.0	24.2	16.5	15.8	8.3	13.4	18.0
Canada	7.6	10.9	10.8	7.5	8.0	8.9	9.2	10.2
France	7.3	13.7	11.8	9.6	9.4	9.1	10.8	13.6
Germany	6.9	7.0	6.0	4.5	3.7	2.7	4.1	5.5
Italy	10.8	19.1	17.0	16.8	17.0	12.1	14.8	21.2
Japan	11.7	24.5	11.8	9.3	8.1	3.8	3.6	8.0

Source: Organization for Economic Cooperation and Development. *Economic Outlook: Historical Statistics, 1960–1986.* Paris: OECD, 1987. Figures are percentage increases in each year's average consumer price index over the average consumer price index for the previous year.

2. Expectations of future inflation that fed into wages and other prices in spite of recession and rising unemployment.

Even before the oil shock hit, the move to floating rates had allowed the industrialized countries to adopt more restrictive monetary and fiscal policies aimed at restraining the accelerating inflation. These initially restrictive policies helped deepen the 1974–1975 slump.

Regaining Internal and External Balance. The commodity shocks left most oil-importing countries further from both internal and external balance than they were when floating began in 1973. Countries were in no position to give up the expenditure-switching advantages of exchange rate flexibility and burden monetary policy with the job of defending a fixed rate. No commitment to fixed rates would have been credible in a period when countries were experiencing such different inflation rates and suffering shocks that permanently altered production costs. The speculative attacks that had brought the fixed-rate system down would have quickly undermined any attempt to fix parities anew.

How did countries use their policy tools to regain internal and external balance? As the recession deepened over 1974 and early 1975, most governments shifted to expansionary fiscal and monetary policies. In the seven largest industrial countries, monetary growth rates rose between 1974 and 1975 as central banks reacted to rising unemployment. As a result of these policy actions, a strong output recovery was underway in most industrialized countries by the second half of 1975. At the same time inflation was falling (see Table 19-1). Unfortunately, however, the unemployment rates of industrialized countries failed to return to pre-recession levels even as output recovered.

The 1974 current account deficit of the industrial countries, taken as a group, turned to a surplus in 1975 as spending fell, and was near zero in 1976. The OPEC countries, which could not raise spending quickly enough to match their increased income, were running a substantial current account surplus in 1975 and 1976, but this was matched by the deficit of the oil-importing developing countries. Because the non-oil-developing countries did not cut their spending as sharply as industrial countries, GNP growth in developing countries as a group did not become negative in 1975, as it did in many developed countries. The developing countries financed their oil deficits in part by borrowing funds that the OPEC countries had deposited in the industrial countries' financial centers.

Most economists and policymakers viewed the international adjustment to the first oil shock as a success for floating exchange rates. Freed of the need to defend a fixed exchange rate, each government had chosen the monetary and fiscal response that best suited its goals. The United States and Germany had even been able to relax the capital controls they had set up before 1974. This relaxation eased the adjustment problem of the developing countries, which were able to borrow more easily from developed country financial markets to maintain their own spending and economic growth. In turn, the relative strength of the developing world's demand for industrial country exports helped mitigate the severity of the 1974–1975 recession.

Revising the IMF's Charter, 1975–1976

Because floating rates had seemed to function well in conditions of adversity, the governments of the industrialized countries acknowledged late in 1975 that they were prepared to live with floating exchange rates for the indefinite future. Meeting at the Château de Rambouillet, near Paris, in the first of a series of annual economic summit meetings, leaders of the main industrial countries called on the IMF to revise its Articles of Agreement to take account of the reality of floating exchange rates. The participating governments committed themselves to countering "erratic fluctuations" in exchange rates but made no provision for a return to fixed parities.

In response to the Rambouillet decisions, the IMF's directors met at Kingston, Jamaica, in January 1976 to approve a revision of the fourth IMF Articles of Agreement, which covered exchange rate arrangements. The new Article IV implicitly endorsed floating rates by freeing each member country to choose any exchange rate system it preferred. Governments were urged to follow macroeconomic policies that would promote price stability and growth, and they were to avoid "manipulating exchange rates . . . to gain an unfair competitive advantage over other members." But more detailed restrictions were not placed on IMF members' policies.

The amended Article IV called on the IMF to monitor members' exchange rate policies to ensure compliance with the new guidelines. Although this "surveillance" of exchange rate policies went beyond IMF conditionality in that it applied even to countries not borrowing from the Fund, no mechanism was created to give the Fund clout in influencing nonborrowers' policies. In practice, therefore, the new article did no more than sanction what had already existed for nearly three years: a scheme of decentralized policy-making in which each country pursued what it perceived as its own interest.

The Weak Dollar, 1976–1979

As the recovery from the 1974–1975 recession slowed in late 1976 and unemployment remained persistently high, the United States urged the two other industrial giants, Germany and Japan, to join it in adopting expansionary policies that would pull the world economy out of its doldrums. Only at the Bonn economic summit of July 1978 did Germany and Japan, less fearful of inflation than they had been two years earlier, agree to join the United States as "locomotives" of world economic growth. Until then, the United States had been attempting to go it alone, and its policies, while causing a sharp drop in the U.S. unemployment rate (to 6.0 percent in 1978 from a recession high of 8.3 percent in 1975), had reignited inflation and pushed the U.S. current account into deficit. In contrast, inflation in Germany and Japan had reached relatively low levels by 1978 (see Table 19-1).

The result of this policy imbalance—vigorous expansion in the United States unmatched by expansion abroad—was a steep depreciation of the dollar starting in 1976. The depreciation of the dollar in these years is evident in Figure 19-3, which shows both **nominal and real effective exchange rate indexes** of the dollar. These indexes measure, respectively, the price of a dollar in terms of a basket of foreign currencies and the price of U.S. output in terms of a basket of foreign outputs. Thus, a rise in either index is a (nominal or real) dollar appreciation, while a fall is a depreciation.

International investors had little confidence in the dollar's future value in view of the widening gap between U.S. and foreign inflation rates. In addition, the weakening dollar helped fuel U.S. inflation by raising import prices and the inflation expectations of wage setters. To restore confidence in the dollar, President Carter appointed a new Federal Reserve Board chairman with broad experience in international financial affairs, Paul A. Volcker. The dollar remained weak in the foreign exchange market until October 1979, when Volcker announced a tightening of U.S. monetary policy and the adoption by the Fed of more stringent procedures for controlling money supply growth.

The sharp U.S. monetary turnaround of 1979 illustrated the truth of one point made by the critics of floating exchange rates. Governments could not be indifferent to the behavior of

Figure 19-3 | Nominal and Real Effective Dollar Exchange Rate Indexes, 1975–2000

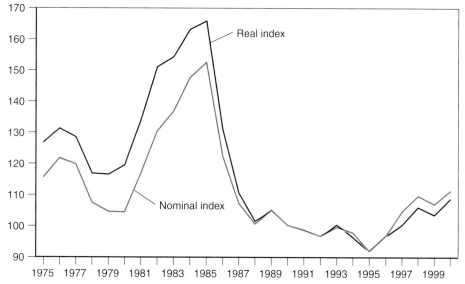

The indexes are measures of the nominal and real value of the U.S. dollar in terms of a basket of 15 industrial-country currencies. An increase in the indexes is a dollar appreciation, a decrease a dollar depreciation. For both indexes, the 1990 value is 100.

Source: International Monetary Fund, *International Financial Statistics.*

exchange rates and inevitably surrendered some of their policy autonomy in other areas to prevent exchange rate movements they viewed as harmful to their economies.

The Second Oil Shock, 1979–1980

The fall of the Shah of Iran in 1979 sparked a second round of oil price increases by disrupting oil exports from that country. Oil prices rose from around $13 per barrel in 1978 to nearly $32 per barrel in 1980. As they had after the 1973–1974 episode, oil-importing economies faced stagflation. Table 19-1 shows that inflation accelerated sharply in all the industrialized economies between 1978 and 1980. Output growth generally slowed and unemployment generally rose, but the effects were neither as uniform nor as dramatic as those of the first oil shock. Oil-importing developing countries, like the developed countries, experienced higher inflation coupled with slower growth.

In 1975 macroeconomic policymakers in the industrial countries had responded to the first oil shock with expansionary monetary and fiscal policies. They responded very differently to the second oil shock. Over 1979 and 1980, monetary growth was actually *restricted* in most major industrial countries in an attempt to offset the rise in inflation accompanying the oil price increase. After struggling to reduce the higher inflation of the early 1970s, central banks were now worried that the 1978–1980 upswing in inflation might be hard to reverse later if it were allowed to be built into inflationary expectations and the wage-setting process.

The fight against inflation had a high price in terms of employment and output. Unemployment appeared to take a ratchet step upward by 1982 (see Table 19-2), and restrictive macroeconomic policies blocked a decisive output recovery. In fact, the recovery from the oil shock barely had time to start up before the world economy, in 1981, plunged into the deepest recession since the Great Depression of the 1930s.

Macroeconomic Interdependence under a Floating Rate

Up until now, our modeling of the open economy has focused on the relatively simple case of a small country that cannot affect foreign output, price levels, or interest rates through its own monetary and fiscal policies. That description obviously does not fit the United States, however, with a national output level equal to about a fifth of the world's total product. To discuss macroeconomic interactions between the United States and the rest of the world, we therefore must think about the transmission of policies between countries linked by a floating exchange rate. We will offer a brief and intuitive discussion rather than a formal model, and restrict ourselves to the short run in which we can assume that nominal output prices are fixed.

Imagine a world economy made up of two large countries, Home and Foreign. Our goal is to evaluate how Home's macroeconomic policies affect Foreign. The main complication is that neither country can be thought of any longer as facing a fixed external interest rate or a fixed level of foreign export demand. To simplify, we consider only the case of *permanent* shifts in monetary and fiscal policy.

Let's look first at a permanent monetary expansion by Home. We know that in the small-country case (Chapter 16), Home's currency would depreciate and its output would rise. The same happens when Home's economy is large, but now, the rest of the world is affected too. Because Home is experiencing a real currency depreciation, Foreign must be experiencing a real currency *appreciation,* which makes Foreign goods relatively expensive and thus has a depressing effect on Foreign output. The increase in Home output, however, works in the opposite direction, since Home spends some of its extra income on Foreign goods and, on that account, aggregate demand for Foreign output rises. Home's monetary expansion therefore has two opposing effects on Foreign output, with the net result depending on which effect is the stronger. Foreign output may rise or fall.[3]

Next let's think about a permanent expansionary fiscal policy in Home. In the small-country case of Chapter 16, a permanent fiscal expansion caused a real currency appreciation and a current account deterioration that fully nullified any positive effect on aggregate demand. In effect, the expansionary impact of the Home fiscal ease leaked entirely abroad (because the counterpart of Home's lower current account balance must be a higher current account balance abroad). In the large-country case, Foreign output still rises, since Foreign's

---

[3]The Foreign money-market equilibrium condition is $M^*/P^* = L(R^*, Y^*)$. Because M^* is not changing and P^* is sticky and therefore fixed in the short run, Foreign output can rise only if the Foreign nominal interest rate rises too, and can fall only if the Foreign nominal interest rate falls. Home's nominal interest rate always falls.

Table 19-2 | Unemployment Rates in Major Industrialized Countries, 1978–2000 (percent of civilian labor force)

Year	United States	Britain	Canada	France	Germany	Italy	Japan
1978	6.1	5.7	8.4	4.7	3.0	5.3	2.2
1979	5.8	4.7	7.5	5.3	2.7	5.8	2.1
1980	7.2	6.2	7.5	5.8	2.6	5.6	2.0
1981	7.6	9.7	7.6	7.0	4.0	6.2	2.2
1982	9.7	11.1	11.0	7.7	5.7	6.8	2.4
1983	9.6	11.1	11.9	8.1	6.9	7.7	2.7
1984	7.5	11.1	11.3	9.7	7.1	8.1	2.7
1985	7.2	11.5	10.5	10.1	7.2	8.4	2.6
1986	7.0	11.5	9.6	10.2	6.5	9.2	2.8
1987	6.2	10.6	8.8	10.4	6.3	9.9	2.8
1988	5.5	8.7	7.8	9.8	6.2	10.0	2.5
1989	5.3	7.3	7.5	9.3	5.6	10.0	2.3
1990	5.6	7.1	8.1	9.0	4.8	9.1	2.1
1991	6.8	8.8	10.4	9.5	4.2	8.8	2.1
1992	7.5	10.1	11.3	10.4	4.5	9.0	2.2
1993	6.9	10.5	11.2	11.7	7.9	10.3	2.5
1994	6.1	9.6	10.4	12.3	8.4	11.4	2.9
1995	5.6	8.8	9.5	11.7	8.2	11.9	3.1
1996	5.4	8.2	9.7	12.4	8.9	12.0	3.4
1997	4.9	7.0	9.1	12.3	9.9	11.7	3.4
1998	4.5	6.3	8.3	11.8	9.3	11.8	4.1
1999	4.2	6.1	7.6	11.2	8.6	11.3	4.7
2000	4.0	5.5	6.8	9.5	7.9	10.5	4.7

Source: Organization for Economic Cooperation and Development. *OECD Economic Outlook* 62 (December 1997, June 2001), Annex Table 22. Data for Germany do not include the former East Germany.

exports become relatively cheaper when Home's currency appreciates. In addition, now some of Foreign's increased spending increases Home exports, so Home's output actually does increase along with Foreign's.[4]

We summarize our discussion of macroeconomic interdependence between large countries as follows:

1. *Effect of a permanent monetary expansion by Home.* Home output rises, Home's currency depreciates, and Foreign output may rise or fall.
2. *Effect of a permanent fiscal expansion by Home.* Home output rises, Home's currency appreciates, Foreign output rises.

---

[4]By considering the Home money-market equilibrium condition (in analogy to the previous footnote), you will see that Home's nominal interest rate must rise. A parallel argument shows that Foreign's interest rate rises at the same time.

CASE STUDY

Disinflation, Growth, Crisis, and Recession, 1980–2002

The years after 1980 brought a number of dramatic changes in the world economy. On the positive side, inflation rates throughout the industrialized world fell to levels even below those of the Bretton Woods years (see Table 19-3). At long last, price stability seemed to have been restored. But the negative events of the period were so severe that they threatened the relatively open world trading and financial system that had been built up so laboriously after World War II. Many economists and policymakers began to see floating exchange rates as a major cause of the world economy's problems and urged a return to more limited exchange rate flexibility.

Disinflation and the 1981–1983 Recession

In October 1979, Federal Reserve Chairman Volcker announced an abrupt change in U.S. monetary policy aimed at fighting domestic inflation and stemming the dollar's fall. Volcker's monetary slowdown convinced the foreign exchange market that the Fed chairman would make good his promise to wring inflation out of the American economy. With the November 1980 election of President Reagan, who had campaigned on an anti-inflation platform, the dollar's value soared. Between the end of 1979 and the end of 1981, the dollar appreciated against the DM by 23.2 percent. U.S. interest rates also rose sharply late in 1979; by 1981, short-term interest rates in the United States were nearly double their 1978 levels.

By pushing up the U.S. interest rate and causing investors to expect a stronger dollar in the future, the U.S. action led to an immediate appreciation of the dollar. This appreciation made U.S. goods more expensive relative to foreign goods, thereby reducing U.S. output.

The dollar's appreciation was not welcomed abroad, however, even though it could, in theory, have lent foreign economies some positive stimulus in a period of slow growth. The reason was that a stronger dollar hindered foreign countries in their own fights against inflation, both by raising the import prices they faced and by encouraging higher wage demands by their workers. A stronger dollar had the opposite effect in the United States, hastening the decline of inflation there. The tight U.S. monetary policy therefore had a beggar-thy-neighbor effect on foreign economies, in that it lowered American inflation in part by exporting inflation to foreign economies.

Foreign central banks responded by intervening in the foreign exchange market to slow the dollar's rise. Through the process of selling dollar reserves and buying their own currencies, some central banks reduced their monetary growth rates for 1980 and 1981, driving interest rates upward.

Synchronized monetary contraction in the United States and abroad, following fast on the heels of the second oil shock, threw the world economy into a deep recession, the most severe since the Great Depression of the 1930s. Table 19-2 shows how unemployment moved in the major industrial countries. In 1982 and 1983 unemployment throughout the world rose to levels unprecedented in the post-World War II period. You can appreciate the severity of the unemployment rates shown in the table by comparing them with the average unemployment rate for the same seven countries over the years 1963–1972 (3.2 percent). As Table 19-3 shows, however,

Table 19-3 | Inflation Rates in Major Industrialized Countries 1981–2000, and 1961–1971 Average (percent per year)

	United States	Britain	Canada	France	Germany	Italy	Japan
1981	10.4	11.9	12.5	13.4	6.3	19.5	4.9
1982	6.1	8.6	10.8	11.8	5.3	16.5	2.7
1983	3.2	4.6	5.8	9.6	3.3	15.0	1.9
1984	4.3	5.0	4.3	7.4	2.4	10.6	2.2
1985	3.5	6.1	4.0	5.8	2.2	8.6	2.0
1986	1.9	3.4	4.2	2.7	−0.1	6.1	0.6
1987	3.7	4.1	4.4	3.1	0.2	4.6	0.1
1988	4.1	4.9	4.0	2.7	1.3	5.0	0.7
1989	4.8	7.8	5.0	3.6	2.8	6.6	2.3
1990	5.4	9.5	4.8	3.4	2.7	6.1	3.1
1991	4.2	5.9	5.6	3.2	3.5	6.4	3.3
1992	3.0	1.7	1.5	2.4	4.0	5.1	1.7
1993	3.0	1.3	1.9	2.1	4.1	4.2	1.3
1994	2.5	0.7	0.2	1.7	3.0	3.9	0.7
1995	2.8	3.4	2.1	1.7	1.8	5.2	−0.1
1996	2.9	2.5	1.6	2.0	1.5	4.0	0.1
1997	2.4	3.1	1.6	1.2	1.8	2.1	1.8
1998	1.6	3.4	1.0	1.5	1.0	2.0	0.7
1999	2.1	1.6	1.8	1.2	0.6	1.6	−0.3
2000	3.4	2.9	2.6	3.3	2.0	2.6	−0.7
1961-71 average	3.1	4.6	2.9	4.3	3.0	4.2	5.9

Source: Organization for Economic Cooperation and Development. *Main Economic Indicators,* various issues. Figures are percentage increases in each year's average consumer price index over the average consumer price index for the previous year.

monetary contraction and the recession it brought quickly led to a dramatic drop in the inflation rates of industrialized countries.

Fiscal Policies, the Current Account, and the Resurgence of Protectionism

During his election campaign, President Reagan had promised to lower taxes and balance the federal budget. He made good on the first of these promises in 1981 when Congress approved legislation lowering personal taxes and providing fiscal investment incentives to businesses. At the same time, the Reagan administration pushed for an acceleration of defense spending, accompanied by cuts in government spending on domestic programs. The net result of these and subsequent congressional actions was a ballooning U.S. government budget deficit and a sharp fiscal stimulus to the economy.

An analysis of U.S. fiscal moves is complicated because the fiscal policy mandated in 1981 was a phased one that began only in 1982, and whose expansionary impact was probably not felt fully until 1983. The *anticipation* of future fiscal expansion in 1981 would simply have appreciated the dollar, thereby deepening the early stages of the 1981–1983 recession in the United States. Only by late 1982 or 1983 can we draw on the last section's discussion to conclude that U.S. fiscal expansion stimulated output both at home and abroad.

All along, however, the U.S. fiscal stance encouraged continuing dollar appreciation (see Figure 19-3), as did the contractionary fiscal policies pursued at the time by Germany and Japan. By February 1985 the dollar's cumulative appreciation against the DM since the end of 1979 was 47.9 percent. The recession reached its low point in the United States in December 1982, and output began to recover both there and abroad as the U.S. fiscal stimulus was transmitted to foreign countries through the dollar's steady appreciation. Also contributing to the recovery was a looser Federal Reserve monetary policy.

Foreign central banks remained fearful of encouraging inflation through expansionary policies of their own. As easier U.S. money brought dollar interest rates down in the second half of 1982, however, some foreign central banks began to feel they could ease their monetary policies without causing their currencies to depreciate too sharply. By early 1984 U.S. unemployment had fallen and U.S. output was growing rapidly. Unemployment remained high in other industrialized countries, however, and the growth of output abroad was slow by historical standards.

While the U.S. fiscal expansion contributed to world recovery, growing federal budget deficits raised serious worries about the future stability of the world economy. Increasing government deficits were not met with offsetting increases in private saving or decreases in investment, so the American current account balance deteriorated sharply. By 1987 the United States had become a net debtor to foreign countries and its current account deficit was at the postwar record level of 3.6 percent of GNP. Some analysts worried that foreign creditors would lose confidence in the future value of the dollar assets they were accumulating and sell them, causing a sudden, precipitous dollar depreciation.

Equally worrisome was the strong dollar's impact on the distribution of income within the United States. The dollar's appreciation had reduced U.S. inflation and allowed consumers to purchase imports more cheaply, but those hurt by the terms of trade change were better organized and more vocal than those who had benefited. Persistently poor economic performance in the 1980s had led to increased pressures on governments to protect industries in the exporting and import-competing sectors. As the U.S. recovery slowed late in 1984, protectionist pressures snowballed.

The Reagan administration had, from the start, adopted a policy of "benign neglect" toward the foreign exchange market, refusing to intervene except in unusual circumstances (for example, after a would-be assassin shot President Reagan). By 1985, however, the link between the strong dollar and the gathering protectionist storm became impossible to ignore.

From the Plaza to the Louvre and Beyond:
Trying to Manage Exchange Rates

Fearing a disaster for the international trading system, economic officials of the Group of Five (G-5) countries—the United States, Britain, France, Germany, and Japan—announced at New York's Plaza Hotel on September 22, 1985, that they would jointly intervene in the foreign exchange market to bring about a dollar depreciation. The dollar dropped sharply the next day and continued to decline through 1986 and early 1987 as the United States maintained its loose monetary policy and pushed dollar interest rates down relative to foreign currency rates. (See Figure 19-3.)

The G-5 Plaza announcement represented a sharp change in the policy of the Reagan administration, a reversal of its opposition to foreign exchange intervention. The Plaza communiqué indicated growing dissatisfaction in government circles with the performance of floating exchange rates and marked the start of a period in which countries including the United States readily intervened, sometimes massively and in a cooperative fashion, to influence exchange rates.

By the end of 1986, the dollar's exchange rate had become a focus of disagreement among governments. The United States still had a large current account deficit. Faced with foreign reluctance to adopt expenditure-changing policies, American leaders pushed to restore external balance through the expenditure-switching policy of further dollar depreciation. Leaders of other industrial countries, however, felt the appreciation of their currencies had gone far enough. Their own tradables industries were finding it difficult to meet foreign competition, and so the expenditure change of a U.S. fiscal and monetary contraction appeared preferable to them.

A renewed effort to cooperate on exchange rates followed a meeting at the Louvre in Paris on February 22, 1987. Finance ministers and central bank governors from the G-5 countries plus Canada issued a statement pledging to stabilize nominal exchange rates around the levels then prevailing, which the officials viewed as "broadly consistent with underlying economic fundamentals," including the requirement of generalized external balance. The Louvre accord was far more, however, than a mere verbal pronouncement on exchange rates. In an unpublished agreement, governments set up target zones for exchange rates and agreed to defend them by intervening in the foreign exchange market. While these target zones were not made public, observers believe the Louvre accord called for bands of plus or minus 5 percent around the rates of DM 1.8250 per dollar and ¥153.50 per dollar. (In contrast, exchange rates in the weeks after the Plaza announcement were in the neighborhood of DM 2.750 per dollar and ¥250 per dollar.)

After adjusting the range for the yen/dollar rate in April 1987, the industrial countries succeeded in maintaining their new exchange rate bands for several months. The U.S. external deficit remained high, however, and the dollar stayed under heavy selling pressure; the bands thus could be maintained only with the help of slow U.S. money supply growth and a steadily rising interest difference favoring dollar assets. Market participants wondered whether the U.S. economy would be thrown into recession to enforce nominal exchange rate targets that seemed increasingly inconsistent with current account equilibrium, given output prices in the United States and abroad.

In October 1987 the brief period of exchange stability ended abruptly when the U.S. stock market dropped and then crashed following American criticism of a German interest rate hike. Major stock markets around the world followed Wall Street's dizzying plunge. In the United States, a more general economic crisis was turned aside by the new Federal Reserve chairman, Alan Greenspan, who announced the Fed's readiness to provide liquidity to a troubled financial system. Governors of foreign central banks acted similarly and interest rates throughout the world declined. In the process, however, U.S. authorities allowed the dollar to depreciate far beyond its Louvre limits.

New exchange rate zones were subsequently established, but these apparently have been changed on several occasions, never with on-the-record public acknowledgment. By the early 1990s, any pretense of zones had been abandoned. Figure 19-4 gives an overview of exchange rate movements after the Louvre accord. Skeptics argue that the implicit zones for exchange

Figure 19-4 | Exchange Rate Changes Since the Louvre Accord

$/¥ and $/DM exchange rates
(percent changes relative to rate at end of February 1987)

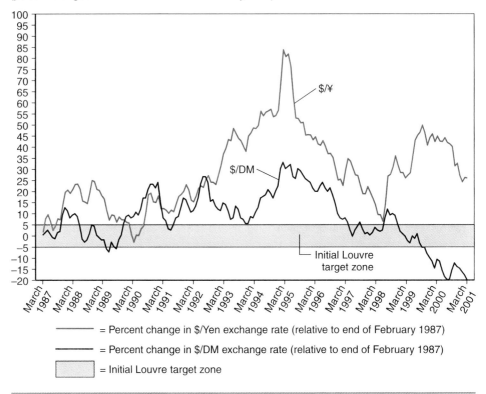

——— = Percent change in $/Yen exchange rate (relative to end of February 1987)

——— = Percent change in $/DM exchange rate (relative to end of February 1987)

▢ = Initial Louvre target zone

The dollar prices of the German and Japanese currencies took wide swings after the February 1987 Louvre meeting despite an initial international agreement to keep those exchange rates within bands 10 percent wide.

Source: International Monetary Fund, *International Financial Statistics.*

rates had no real force and that the authorities' reluctance to announce the zones, rather than keeping the market guessing, served mainly to cover repeated official failures to stand up to market pressures. Supporters argue that exchange rates would have moved even more than they did had zones not been adopted. What seems clear is that official attempts to influence exchange rates have been successful only when backed up by changes in monetary or fiscal policy rather than the milder expedient of sterilized intervention (which at times has been heavy). Authorities have thus faced genuine and sometimes painful trade-offs between internal balance and exchange stability, as the United States did in October 1987, and none of them has shown that in a crunch, exchange stability is the more important of these two goals.

Global Slump Once Again, Recovery, Crisis, and Slowdown

Toward the end of the 1980s inflationary pressures reappeared in the main industrial countries (see Table 19-3). Inflation was the result of national developments rather than a global shock, and it emerged with different timing and force in each country.

In the United States, rapid monetary growth in 1985 and 1986 helped push inflation upward by 1987 and 1988. The Federal Reserve responded with exceptionally tight monetary policy, which tilted the U.S. economy into a prolonged economic downturn by the summer of 1990. The U.S. economic rebound, starting in 1992, set the stage for a prolonged American expansion characterized by low inflation, a booming stock market, and low unemployment rates unmatched since before the first oil shock in the early 1970s.

The reunification of West and East Germany on July 1, 1990, following the collapse of the former Soviet Union's empire in eastern Europe, set off inflationary pressures in Germany. At the same time, other European countries were pegging their exchange rates to Germany's former currency, the DM, within the European Union's fixed exchange rate mechanism, the European Monetary System (EMS). Germany's contractionary monetary response to its internal inflation pressures led to slower growth in its EMS partners, many of whom were not afflicted by rising inflation as Germany was. The resulting asymmetric pressures within the EMS led to a massive speculative attack on the EMS fixed parities, as we shall see in Chapter 20.

Japanese inflation rose in 1989, in part the result of a relatively loose monetary policy from 1986 to 1988. Two very visible symptoms of these pressures were skyrocketing prices for Japanese real estate and stocks. The Bank of Japan's strategy of puncturing these asset price bubbles through restrictive monetary policy and high interest rates succeeded well, and Tokyo's Nikkei stock price index lost more than half its value between 1990 and 1992. Unfortunately, the sharp fall in asset prices threw Japan's banking system into crisis and the economy into recession by early 1992. Even by 2001 the banking crisis was still unresolved.

Japan's growth picked up in 1996, but its government, worried by a growing public debt, raised taxes. The economy slowed in 1997, the deep and widespread problems of Japanese financial institutions became more apparent, and the yen fell sharply, dropping staggeringly from ¥80 per dollar early in 1995 to around ¥145 per dollar in the summer of 1998, before recovering somewhat later that year. By 1998, however, the Japanese economy seemed to be in free fall, with shrinking GDP, declining prices, and its highest unemployment level in more than four decades.

The problems of the Japanese economy spilled over to the developing countries in East Asia, with which it trades heavily. As we shall see in Chapter 22, many of these economies had experienced spectacularly rapid rates of GDP growth for many years through 1997. Many of them also held their exchange rates fixed, or in target ranges, against the U.S. dollar. Japan's slowdown in 1997 therefore weakened the East Asian economies directly, but also through an exchange-rate channel. Being tied to the dollar, East Asian currencies tended to appreciate against the yen as the yen slid against the dollar. The East Asian economies, feeling the direct effect of Japan's slower growth on the demand for their imports, simultaneously found their exports priced out of foreign markets.

The eventual result was a cascading series of speculative attacks on East Asian currencies, beginning with Thailand's baht in the spring of 1997 and moving on to Malaysia, Indonesia, and Korea. These economies fell into deep recessions, as we shall discuss in detail in Chapter 22, pulled down by Japan but also pulling Japan down in a vicious circle. Other economies in the region, including Singapore, Hong Kong, and China, also experienced slower growth in 1998, as did Latin America. Russia defaulted on its internal and external debts, setting off global investor jitters and domestic financial chaos. The fear of a worldwide depression prompted a series of interest rate cuts by the Federal Reserve late in 1998, as well as an unprecedented coordinated interest-rate cut by the eleven European countries preparing to give up their national currencies in 1999 in favor of the euro.

These measures helped to avert a global economic meltdown. By the end of 1999 the worst of the financial crisis seemed to be past. In the spring of 2001, however, the U.S. economy went into a mild recession as a ten-year spell of uninterrupted growth came to an end. For much of the previous decade America had been the world's main engine of economic growth. With Japan's problems only intensifying and Europe's economies slowing as well, capital flows to the developing world paused. In the first half of 2002 world economic growth was still on hold.

What Has Been Learned Since 1973?

The first two sections of this chapter outlined the main elements of the cases for and against floating exchange rates. Having examined the events of the recent floating-rate period, we now compare experience with the predictions made before 1973 by the proponents and opponents of floating and ask whether recent history supports a definitive judgment about reforming the current exchange rate system.

Monetary Policy Autonomy

There is no question that floating gave central banks the ability to control their money supplies and to choose their preferred rates of trend inflation. A comparison of Tables 19-1 and 19-3 (which show inflation rates over the floating-rate period) with Table 18-1 and Figure 18-3 (which apply to the fixed-rate period) shows that floating rates allowed a much larger international divergence in inflation rates. Did exchange depreciation offset inflation differentials between countries over the floating-rate period? Figure 19-5 compares domestic currency depreciation against the dollar with the difference between domestic and U.S. inflation for the six largest industrial market economies outside the United States. The PPP theory predicts that the points in the figure should lie along the 45-degree line, indicating proportional exchange rate and relative price level changes, but this is not exactly the case. While Figure 19-5 therefore confirms the lesson of Chapter 15 that PPP has not held closely, it does show that on balance, high-inflation countries have tended to have weaker currencies than their low-inflation neighbors. Furthermore, most of the difference in depreciation rates is due to inflation differences, making PPP a major factor behind long-run nominal exchange-rate variability.

While the inflation insulation part of the policy autonomy argument is broadly supported as a *long-run* proposition, economic analysis and experience both show that in the short run, the effects of monetary as well as fiscal changes are transmitted across national borders under floating rates. The two-country macroeconomic model developed earlier, for example, shows that monetary policy affects output in the short run both at home and abroad as long as it

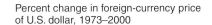

Figure 19-5 | Exchange Rate Trends and Inflation Differentials, 1973–2000

Over the floating-rate period as a whole, higher inflation has been associated with greater currency depreciation. The exact relationship predicted by relative PPP, however, has not held for most countries. The inflation difference on the horizontal axis is calculated as $(\pi - \pi_{US}) \div (1 + \pi_{US}/100)$ using the exact relative PPP relation given in footnote 1 on p. 391.

Source: *International Financial Statistics Yearbook, 2001.*

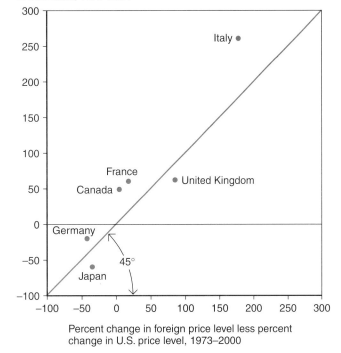

alters the real exchange rate. The critics of floating were therefore right in claiming that floating rates would not insulate countries completely from foreign policy shocks.

Experience has also given dramatic support to the skeptics who argued that no central bank can be indifferent to its currency's value in the foreign exchange market. After 1973 central banks intervened repeatedly in the foreign exchange market to alter currency values, and even the Reagan administration's laissez-faire policy on exchange rates was abandoned when the G-5 Plaza initiative of September 1985 was launched. The post-1973 floating of exchange rates is often characterized as a "dirty float" rather than a "clean float" because central banks intervened on a discretionary basis and continued to hold foreign exchange reserves (Chapter 17). Advocates of floating had argued that central banks would not need to hold foreign reserves, but between 1972 and December 1999, the international reserves of the industrial countries rose in value from $113 billion to $755 billion.

Why did central banks continue to intervene even in the absence of any formal obligation to do so? As we saw in the example of a change in domestic money demand, intervention to fix the exchange rate can stabilize output and the price level when certain disturbances occur, and central banks sometimes felt that exchange rate movements were due to such factors. But even in the presence of output market disturbances, central banks wanted to slow exchange rate movements to prevent sharp changes in the international competitiveness of their tradable goods sectors. Such changes, if reversed later, might generate excessive sectoral employment fluctuations, and they might also lead to pressures for protection. Finally, central banks worried that even temporary exchange rate shifts might have medium-term inflationary effects that would be hard to wring out of the economy.

Those skeptical of the autonomy argument had also predicted that while floating would allow central banks to control nominal money supplies, their ability to affect output would still be limited by the price level's tendency to respond more quickly to monetary changes under a floating rate. This prediction was partially borne out by experience. Monetary changes clearly had a much greater short-run effect on the *real* exchange rate under a floating nominal exchange rate than under a fixed one, increasing the immediate influence of money on output in some countries. In many cases, however, this influence turned out to be short-lived. The quick response of the exchange rate to money supply changes affected import prices and wage settlements, shortening the time span over which money could alter real economic activity without changing nominal output prices. The link between exchange depreciation and inflation was illustrated by the U.S. experience of 1976–1979 and by the rapid inflation that resulted from attempts by Britain, France, and Italy, at various times, to spur output growth through monetary expansion. The U.S. disinflation after 1979 illustrated that a floating rate could also speed the translation of monetary contraction into lower inflation.

Symmetry

Because central banks continued to hold dollar reserves and intervene, the international monetary system did not become symmetric after 1973. The DM and the yen gained importance as international reserve currencies (and the British pound declined), but the dollar remained the primary component of most central banks' official reserves.

Economist Ronald McKinnon of Stanford University has argued that the current floating-rate system is similar in some ways to the asymmetric reserve currency system underlying the Bretton Woods arrangements.[5] He suggests that changes in the world money supply would have been dampened under a more symmetric monetary adjustment mechanism. Intervention outside the United States to slow the dollar's rise after 1979, for example, led to monetary contraction abroad with no symmetric increase in the U.S. money supply. The resulting world monetary crunch was harsher because of this asymmetry, which therefore helped deepen the recession that followed.

The Exchange Rate as an Automatic Stabilizer

The world economy has undergone major structural changes since 1973. Because these shifts changed relative national output prices (Figure 19-5), it is doubtful that any pattern of fixed exchange rates would have been viable without some significant parity changes. The industrial economies certainly wouldn't have weathered the two oil shocks as well as they did while defending fixed exchange rates. In the absence of capital controls, speculative attacks similar to those that brought down the Bretton Woods system would have occurred periodically, as recent experience has shown. Under floating, however, many countries were able to relax the capital controls put in place earlier. The progressive loosening of con-

---

[5] Ronald I. McKinnon, *An International Standard for Monetary Stabilization*, Policy Analyses in International Economics 8 (Washington, D.C.: Institute for International Economics, 1984).

trols spurred the rapid growth of a global financial industry and allowed countries to realize greater gains from intertemporal trade.

The effects of the U.S. fiscal expansion after 1981 illustrate the stabilizing properties of a floating exchange rate. As the dollar appreciated, U.S. inflation was slowed, American consumers enjoyed an improvement in their terms of trade, and economic recovery was spread abroad.

The dollar's appreciation after 1981 also illustrates a problem with the view that floating rates can cushion the economy from real disturbances such as shifts in aggregate demand. Even though *overall* output and the price level may be cushioned, some sectors of the economy may be hurt. For example, while the dollar's appreciation helped transmit U.S. fiscal expansion abroad in the 1980s, it worsened the plight of American agriculture, which did not benefit directly from the higher government demand. Real exchange rate changes can do damage by causing excessive adjustment problems in some sectors and by generating calls for increased protection.

Permanent changes in goods market conditions require eventual adjustment in real exchange rates that can be speeded by a floating-rate system. Foreign exchange intervention to peg nominal exchange rates cannot prevent this eventual adjustment because money is neutral in the long run and thus is powerless to alter relative prices permanently. The events of the 1980s show, however, that if it is costly for factors of production to move between sectors of the economy, there is a case for pegging rates in the face of temporary output market shocks. Unfortunately, this lesson leaves policymakers with the difficult task of determining which disturbances are temporary and which are permanent.

An indictment of floating exchange rates is sometimes based on the poor economic growth performance of industrial countries in the 1970s and 1980s compared with the 1950s and 1960s. As noted above, unemployment rates in industrial countries rose sharply after the 1960s; in addition, labor productivity and real GNP growth rates dropped. These adverse developments followed the adoption of floating dollar exchange rates, but this coincidence does not prove that floating rates were their cause. Although economists have not yet fully explained the growth slowdown or the rise in unemployment rates, the likely culprits are structural changes that had little to do with floating rates. Examples include the oil price shocks, restrictive labor market practices, and worker displacement caused by the emergence of several developing countries as major exporters of manufactured goods. Much of the international trade of the European Monetary System has taken place at fixed exchange rates, yet the record of EMS countries in generating jobs and keeping down unemployment has not been superior to that of the United States or Japan.

Discipline

Did countries abuse the autonomy afforded by floating rates? Inflation rates did accelerate after 1973 and remained high through the second oil shock. But the concerted disinflation in industrial countries after 1979 proved that central banks could resist the temptations of inflation under floating rates. On several occasions, voters in industrial countries showed that they viewed a weak currency as a sign of economic mismanagement. For this reason, currency depreciation sometimes brought sharp changes in monetary policies, as in the United States in 1979.

The system placed fewer obvious restraints on unbalanced fiscal policies, for example, the high U.S. government budget deficits of the 1980s. While some observers felt that fixed rates would have forced a more moderate American fiscal stance, their arguments were not compelling. In the late 1960s, fixed rates had failed to restrain the Johnson administration's fiscal expansion, a policy move that contributed to the collapse of the Bretton Woods system, nor did the EMS restrain Germany in the early 1990s.

Destabilizing Speculation

Floating exchange rates have exhibited much more day-to-day volatility than the early advocates of floating would have predicted, but as we saw in Chapter 13, exchange rates are asset prices, and so considerable volatility is to be expected. The asset price nature of exchange rates was not well understood by economists before the 1970s.

Even with the benefit of hindsight, however, short-term exchange rate movements can be quite difficult to relate to actual news about economic events that affect currency values. Part of the difficulty is that government officials often try to influence exchange rates by hinting at intended policy changes, thus making expectations about future macroeconomic policies volatile. The question of whether exchange rate volatility has been "excessive" relative to the theoretical determinants of exchange rates is a controversial one and provides an active research area for academic economists (Chapter 21).

Over the longer term, however, exchange rates have roughly reflected fundamental changes in monetary and fiscal policies, and their broad movements do not appear to be the result of destabilizing speculation. The decline of the dollar in the late 1970s (Figure 19-3) coincides with loose U.S. monetary policies, while its steep ascent between 1980 and 1985 occurred as the United States embarked on disinflation and a fiscal expansion of a size unprecedented in peacetime. While most economists agree that the direction of these exchange rate swings was appropriate, there is continuing debate about their magnitude. Some feel the foreign exchange market overreacted to government actions and that more systematic foreign exchange intervention would have been beneficial.

The experience with floating rates has not supported the idea that arbitrary exchange rate movements can lead to "vicious circles" of inflation and depreciation. Britain, Italy, and, to a lesser extent, France experienced inflationary spirals similar to those predicted by the vicious circle theory. But the currency depreciation that accompanied these spirals was not the arbitrary result of destabilizing exchange rate speculation. As Figure 14-10 (page 376) shows, industrial countries with poor inflation performances under floating exchange rates have also tended to have relatively rapid rates of monetary growth.

International Trade and Investment

Critics of floating had predicted that international trade and investment would suffer as a result of increased uncertainty. The prediction was certainly wrong with regard to investment, for international financial intermediation expanded strongly after 1973 as countries lowered barriers to capital movement (see Chapter 21).

There is controversy about the effects of floating rates on international trade. The use of forward markets and other derivatives expanded dramatically, just as advocates of floating had foreseen, and innovative financial instruments were developed to help traders avoid exchange rate risk. But some economists contend that the costs of avoiding exchange rate risk have had an effect similar to increased international transport costs in reducing the available gains from trade. They argue that as a result of these costs, international trade has grown more slowly than it would have under a hypothetical fixed exchange rate regime.

A very crude but direct measure of the extent of a country's international trade is the average of its imports and exports of goods and services, divided by its output. For most countries, the extent of trade shows a rising trend over the whole postwar period, with no marked slowdown in trend after the move to floating. Furthermore, to compare world trade growth before and after the early 1970s is to stack the deck against floating rates, because while the 1950s and 1960s were periods of dramatic trade liberalization, the 1970s and 1980s were marked by a surge in nontariff barriers to trade.[6]

Evaluation of the effects of floating rates on world trade is complicated further by the activities of multinational firms, many of which vastly expanded their international production operations in the years after 1973. Facing a more turbulent economic environment, multinationals may have spread their activities over more countries in the hope of reducing their dependence on any individual government's economic policies. Because trade and capital movements can substitute for each other, however, the displacement of some trade by multinational firms' overseas production does not necessarily imply that welfare-improving trade gains have been lost.[7]

International trade has recently been threatened by the resurgence of protectionism, a symptom of slower economic growth and wide swings in real exchange rates, which have been labeled *misalignments*. (The dollar's misalignment of the mid-1980s, prominently visible in Figure 19-3, is a leading example.) It is possible, however, that similar pressures to limit trade would have emerged under fixed exchange rates. Misalignments have had an especially severe impact on those who lose jobs as a result and have few other financial resources.

Policy Coordination

Floating exchange rates themselves have not promoted international policy coordination. On several occasions, for example, during the disinflation of the early 1980s, industrial countries as a group could have attained their macroeconomic goals more effectively by negotiating a joint approach to common objectives. The appendix to this chapter presents a formal model that illustrates how all countries can gain through international policy coordination.

While beggar-thy-neighbor policies sometimes have been a problem, critics of floating have not made a strong case that the problem would disappear under an alternative currency regime. Under fixed rates, for example, countries can always devalue their currencies unilaterally to attain nationalistic goals. The results of the informal target zone arrangements set up by the Louvre accord illustrate the wide gap between agreeing on exchange rates and true policy coordination.

---

[6] There is a large econometric literature that studies how exchange rate volatility affects trade growth, and some authors reach conclusions different from those in the preceding paragraph. Unfortunately, various researchers differ in terms of their measures of trade volume, definitions of exchange rate volatility, and choices of estimation period, so it is difficult to draw unambiguous conclusions from this body of work. We will discuss this topic in greater detail in the next chapter.

[7] A study documenting the growth of U.S. multinationals' foreign exporting activities is Robert E. Lipsey and Irving B. Kravis, "The Competitiveness and Comparative Advantage of U.S. Multinationals, 1957–1984," *Banca Nazionale del Lavoro Quarterly Review* (June 1987), pp. 147–165.

Governments, like people, often are motivated by their own interest rather than that of the community. Legal penalties discourage antisocial actions by individuals, but it is a more difficult matter to design sanctions that bind sovereign governments. It seems doubtful that an exchange rate system alone can restrain a government from following its own perceived interest when it formulates macroeconomic policies.

Are Fixed Exchange Rates Even an Option for Most Countries?

The post-Bretton Woods experience suggests another hypothesis: durable fixed exchange rate arrangements may not even be *possible*. In a financially integrated world in which funds can move instantly between national financial markets, fixed exchange rates cannot be credibly maintained over the long run unless countries are willing to maintain strict controls over capital movements (as China does), or, at the other extreme, move to a shared single currency with their monetary partners (as in Europe). Short of these measures, the argument goes, attempts to fix exchange rates will necessarily lack credibility and be relatively short-lived. Under such conditions, fixed rates will not deliver the benefits promised by their proponents.[8]

This pessimistic view of fixed exchange rates is based on the theory that speculative currency crises can, at least in part, be self-fulfilling events (recall Chapter 17). According to that view, even a country following prudent monetary and fiscal policies is not safe from speculative attacks on its fixed exchange rate. Once the country encounters an economic reversal, as it eventually must, currency speculators will pounce, forcing domestic interest rates sky-high and inflicting enough economic pain that the government will choose to abandon its exchange-rate target.

At the turn of the twenty-first century, speculative attacks on fixed exchange rate arrangements—in Europe, East Asia, and elsewhere—were occurring with seemingly increasing frequency. The number and circumstances of those crises lent increasing plausibility to the argument that it is impossible to peg currency values for long while maintaining open capital markets and national policy sovereignty.

Directions for Reform

The experience with floating exchange rates since 1973 shows that neither side in the debate over floating was entirely right in its predictions. The floating-rate system has not been free of serious problems, but neither has it been the fiasco its opponents predicted it would be.

---

[8]For an early statement of the hypothesis that fixed exchange rates combined with mobile capital can be unstable, see Maurice Obstfeld, "Floating Exchange Rates: Experience and Prospects," *Brookings Papers on Economic Activity* 2:1985, pp. 369–450. For more recent discussions see Barry Eichengreen, *International Monetary Arrangements for the 21st Century* (Washington, D.C.: Brookings Institution, 1994); Lars E. O. Svensson, "Fixed Exchange Rates as a Means to Price Stability: What Have We Learned?" *European Economic Review* 38 (May 1994), pp. 447–468; and Maurice Obstfeld and Kenneth Rogoff, "The Mirage of Fixed Exchange Rates," *Journal of Economic Perspectives* 9 (Fall 1995), pp. 73–96.

An important lesson of this chapter and the previous one is that no exchange rate system works well when countries "go it alone" and follow narrowly perceived self-interest. The Bretton Woods system functioned reasonably well until the United States unilaterally adopted overexpansionary policies under President Lyndon B. Johnson. The EMS experience surveyed in the next chapter provides another example. Similarly, the worst problems of the floating-rate system occurred when countries failed to take coordinated action on common macroeconomic problems. Globally balanced and stable policies are a prerequisite for the successful performance of any international monetary system.

Current proposals to reform the international monetary system run the gamut from a more elaborate system of target zones for the dollar to the resurrection of fixed rates to the introduction of a single world currency. Because countries seem unwilling to give up the autonomy floating dollar rates have given them, it is unlikely that any of these changes is in the cards.[9] Since the Plaza announcement of September 1985, however, the United States has tended to show a greater awareness of its interdependence with other industrial economies. Although this development has not prevented serious international disagreement over policies, it certainly is a positive step toward improving the existing system.

With greater policy cooperation among the main players, there is no reason why floating exchange rates should not function tolerably well in the future. International policy cooperation is not unprecedented, as the GATT rounds of tariff reduction and the founding of the IMF, World Bank, and WTO indicate. Events of the last few years suggest, however, that cooperation should be sought as an end in itself and not as the indirect result of exchange rate rules that eventually are discredited through repeated amendment or violation.

Summary

1. The weaknesses of the Bretton Woods system led many economists to advocate floating exchange rates before 1973. They made three main arguments in favor of floating. First, they argued that floating rates would give national macroeconomic policymakers greater autonomy in managing their economies. Second, they predicted that floating rates would remove the asymmetries of the Bretton Woods arrangements. Third, they pointed out that floating exchange rates would quickly eliminate the "fundamental disequilibriums" that had led to parity changes and speculative attacks under fixed rates.

2. Critics of floating rates advanced several counterarguments. Some feared that floating would encourage monetary and fiscal excesses and beggar-thy-neighbor policies. Other lines of criticism asserted that floating rates would be subject to *destabilizing speculation* and that uncertainty over exchange rates would retard international trade and investment. Finally, a number of economists questioned whether countries would

---

[9] An extended target zone proposal is outlined in John Williamson and Marcus H. Miller, *Targets and Indicators: A Blueprint for the International Coordination of Macroeconomic Policies,* Policy Analyses in International Economics 22 (Washington, D.C.: Institute for International Economics, 1987). McKinnon, op. cit., presents a program for reestablishing fixed rates for the currencies of the main industrial country groups. The case for a single currency for the industrialized democracies is made by Richard N. Cooper, "A Monetary System for the Future," *Foreign Affairs* 63 (1984), pp. 166–184.

be willing in practice to disregard the exchange rate in formulating their monetary and fiscal policies. The exchange rate, they felt, was an important enough price that it would become a target of macroeconomic policy in its own right.

3. Between 1973 and 1980 floating rates seemed on the whole to function well. In particular, it is unlikely that the industrial countries could have maintained fixed exchange rates in the face of the *stagflation* caused by two oil shocks. The dollar suffered a sharp depreciation after 1976, however, as the United States adopted macroeconomic policies more expansionary than those of other industrial countries.

4. A sharp turn toward slower monetary growth in the United States, coupled with a rising U.S. government budget deficit, contributed to massive dollar appreciation between 1980 and early 1985. Other industrial economies pursued disinflation along with the United States, and the resulting worldwide monetary slowdown, coming soon after the second oil shock, led to the deepest recession since the 1930s. As the recovery from the recession slowed in late 1984 and the U.S. current account began to register record deficits, political pressure for wide-ranging trade restrictions gathered momentum in Washington. The drive for protection was slowed (but not defeated) by the September 1985 decision of the Group of Five countries to take concerted action to bring down the dollar. An experiment with vaguely defined exchange rate target zones, initiated by the Louvre accord of February 1987, had mixed success in promoting more stable currency values. Exchange rate stability was downplayed as a prime policy goal in the 1990s. Instead, governments aimed to restrain domestic inflation while maintaining economic growth.

5. The experience of floating does not fully support either the early advocates of that exchange rate system or its critics. One unambiguous lesson of experience, however, is that no exchange rate system functions well when international economic cooperation breaks down. Severe limits on exchange rate flexibility are unlikely to be reinstated in the near future. But increased consultation among policymakers in the industrial countries should improve the performance of floating rates.

Key Terms

destabilizing speculation, p. 574   stagflation, p. 578
nominal and real effective exchange
    rate indexes, p. 580

Problems

1. Use the *DD-AA* model to examine the effects of a one-time rise in the foreign price level, P^*. If the expected future exchange rate E^e rises immediately in proportion to P^* (in line with PPP), show that the exchange rate will also appreciate immediately in proportion to the rise in P^*. If the economy is initially in internal and external balance, will its position be disturbed by such a rise in P^*?

2. Analyze a transitory increase in the foreign interest rate, R^*. Under which type of exchange rate is there a smaller effect on output—fixed or floating?

3. Suppose now that R^* rises permanently. What happens to the economy, and how does your answer depend on whether the change reflects a rise in the foreign real interest rate or in foreign inflation expectations (the Fisher effect)?

4. If the foreign *inflation rate* rises permanently, would you expect a floating exchange rate to insulate the domestic economy in the short run? What would happen in the long run? In answering the latter question, pay attention to the long-run relationship between domestic and foreign nominal interest rates.

5. Imagine that domestic and foreign currency bonds are imperfect substitutes and that investors suddenly shift their demand toward foreign currency bonds, raising the risk premium on domestic assets (Chapter 17). Which exchange rate regime minimizes the effect on output—fixed or floating?

6. How would you analyze the use of monetary and fiscal policy to maintain internal and external balance under a floating exchange rate?

7. The chapter described how the United States tried after 1985 to reduce its current account deficit by accelerating monetary growth and depreciating the dollar. Assume that the United States was in internal balance but external balance called for an expenditure-reducing policy (a cut in the government budget deficit) as well as the expenditure switching caused by currency depreciation. How would you expect the use of monetary expansion alone to affect the U.S. economy in the short and long runs?

8. After 1985 the United States asked Germany and Japan to adopt fiscal and monetary expansion as ways of increasing foreign demand for U.S. output and reducing the American current account deficit. Would fiscal expansion by Germany and Japan have accomplished these goals? What about monetary expansion? Would your answer change if you thought different German and Japanese policies might facilitate different U.S. policies?

9. A high volume of foreign exchange intervention occurred in 1987 in connection with the Louvre accord. What data might allow you to tell whether a large portion of this intervention was sterilized? Try to find the relevant data for Germany and Japan in back issues of the IMF's *International Financial Statistics*.

10. Suppose the U.S. and Japanese governments both want to depreciate their currencies to help their tradables industries but fear the resulting inflation. The two policy choices available to them are (1) expansionary monetary policy and (2) no change in monetary policy. Develop an analysis like the one in the appendix to show the consequences of different policy choices. Can Japan and the United States do better by cooperating than by acting individually?

Further Reading

Ralph C. Bryant. *International Coordination of National Stabilization Policies.* Washington, D.C.: Brookings Institution, 1995. Examines the interaction among national economic policies and the scope for international coordination.

Richard H. Clarida. *G-3 Exchange Rate Relationships: A Review of the Record and Proposals for Change.* Princeton Essays in International Economics 219. International Economics Section, Department of Economics, Princeton University, September 2000. Critical review of various target zone proposals.

Martin S. Feldstein. "Distinguished Lecture on Economics in Government: Thinking About International Economic Coordination." *Journal of Economic Perspectives* 2 (Spring 1988), pp. 3–13. The case *against* international macroeconomic policy coordination.

Milton Friedman. "The Case for Flexible Exchange Rates," in *Essays in Positive Economics.* Chicago: University of Chicago Press, 1953, pp. 157–203. A classic exposition of the merits of floating exchange rates.

Morris Goldstein. *The Exchange Rate System and the IMF: A Modest Agenda.* Policy Analyses in International Economics 39. Washington, D.C.: Institute for International Economics, 1995. An analysis of the roles of international coordination and the IMF in the present exchange-rate system.

Harry G. Johnson. "The Case for Flexible Exchange Rates, 1969." *Federal Reserve Bank of St. Louis Review* 51 (June 1969), pp. 12–24. An influential statement of the case for replacing the Bretton Woods system by floating rates.

Charles P. Kindleberger, "The Case for Fixed Exchange Rates, 1969," in *The International Adjustment Mechanism,* Conference Series 2. Boston: Federal Reserve Bank of Boston, 1970, pp. 93–108. Prescient analysis of problems with a floating-rate system.

Michael Mussa. "Macroeconomic Interdependence and the Exchange Rate Regime," in Rudiger Dornbusch and Jacob A. Frenkel, eds. *International Economic Policy.* Baltimore: Johns Hopkins University Press, 1979, pp. 160–204. Analyzes macroeconomic policy interactions under fixed and floating exchange rates.

Maurice Obstfeld. "International Currency Experience: New Lessons and Lessons Relearned." *Brookings Papers on Economic Activity* 1:1995, pp. 119–220. A broad overview of exchange rates and policy-making since the onset of floating rates.

Robert Solomon. *The International Monetary System, 1945–1981.* New York: Harper & Row, 1982. Chapters 15–19 cover the early years of floating exchange rates.

Robert Solomon. *Money on the Move: The Revolution in International Finance since 1980.* Princeton, NJ: Princeton University Press, 1999. Wide-ranging review of international financial developments after 1980.

John Williamson. *The Exchange Rate System,* 2nd edition. Policy Analyses in International Economics 5. Washington, D.C.: Institute for International Economics, 1985. An indictment of floating exchange rates and a case for target zones.

APPENDIX TO CHAPTER 19

International Policy Coordination Failures

This appendix illustrates the importance of macroeconomic policy coordination by showing how all countries can suffer as a result of self-centered policy decisions. The phenomenon is another example of the Prisoner's Dilemma of game theory (Chapter 9). Governments can achieve macroeconomic outcomes that are better for all if they choose policies cooperatively.

These points are made using an example based on the disinflation of the early 1980s. Recall that contractionary monetary policies in the industrial countries helped throw the world economy into a deep recession in 1981. Countries hoped to reduce inflation by slowing monetary growth, but the situation was complicated by the influence of exchange rates on the price level. A government that adopts a less restrictive monetary policy than its neighbors is likely to face a currency depreciation that partially frustrates its attempts to disinflate.

Many observers feel that in their individual attempts to resist currency depreciation, the industrial countries as a group adopted overly tight monetary policies that deepened the recession. All governments would have been happier if everyone had adopted looser monetary policies, but given the policies that other governments did adopt, it was not in the interest of any individual government to change course.

The argument above can be made more precise with a simple model. There are two countries, Home and Foreign, and each country has two policy options, a very restrictive monetary policy and a somewhat restrictive monetary policy. Figure 19A-1, which is similar to a diagram we used to analyze trade policies, shows the results in Home and Foreign of different policy choices by the two countries. Each row corresponds to a particular monetary policy decision by Home and each column to a decision by Foreign. The boxes contain entries giving changes in annual inflation rates ($\Delta\pi$ and $\Delta\pi^*$) and unemployment rates (ΔU and ΔU^*). Within each box, lower-left entries are Home outcomes and upper-right entries are Foreign outcomes.

The hypothetical entries in Figure 19A-1 can be understood in terms of this chapter's two-country model. Under somewhat restrictive policies, for example, inflation rates fall by 1 percent and unemployment rates rise by 1 percent in both countries. If Home suddenly shifts to a very restrictive policy while Foreign stands pat, Home's currency appreciates, its inflation drops further, and its unemployment rises. Home's additional monetary contraction, however, has two effects on Foreign. Foreign's unemployment rate falls, but because Home's currency appreciation is a currency *de*preciation for Foreign, Foreign inflation goes back up to its pre-disinflation level. In Foreign, the deflationary effects of higher unemployment are offset by the inflationary impact of a depreciating currency on import prices and wage demands. Home's sharper monetary crunch therefore has a beggar-thy-neighbor effect on Foreign, which is forced to "import" some inflation from Home.

To translate the outcomes in Figure 19A-1 into policy payoffs, we assume each government wishes to get the biggest reduction in inflation at the lowest cost in terms of unemployment. That is, each government wishes to maximize $-\Delta\pi/\Delta U$, the inflation reduction

Figure 19A-1 | Hypothetical Effects of Different Monetary Policy Combinations on Inflation and Unemployment

Monetary policy choices in one country affect the outcomes of monetary policy choices made abroad.

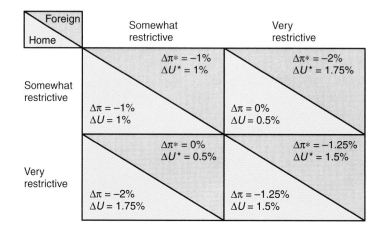

per point of increased unemployment. The numbers in Figure 19A-1 lead to the payoff matrix shown as Figure 19A-2.

How do Home and Foreign behave faced with the payoffs in this matrix? Assume each government "goes it alone" and picks the policy that maximizes its own payoff given the other player's policy choice. If Foreign adopts a somewhat restrictive policy, Home does better with a very restrictive policy (payoff = $\frac{5}{7}$) than with a somewhat restrictive one (payoff = 1). If Foreign is very restrictive, Home still does better by being very restrictive (payoff = $\frac{5}{6}$) than by being somewhat restrictive (payoff = 0). So no matter what Foreign does, Home's government will always choose a very restrictive monetary policy.

Foreign finds itself in a symmetric position. It, too, is better off with a very restrictive policy regardless of what Home does. The result is that both countries will choose very restrictive monetary policies, and each will get a payoff of $\frac{5}{6}$.

Notice, however, that *both* countries are actually better off if they simultaneously adopt the somewhat restrictive policies. The resulting payoff for each is 1, which is greater than $\frac{5}{6}$. Under this last policy configuration, inflation falls less in the two countries, but the rise in unemployment is far less than under very restrictive policies.

Since both countries are better off with somewhat restrictive policies, why aren't these adopted? The answer is at the root of the problem of policy coordination. Our analysis assumed that each country "goes it alone" by maximizing its own payoff. Under this assumption, a situation where both countries were somewhat restrictive would not be stable: Each country would want to reduce its monetary growth further and use its exchange rate to hasten disinflation at its neighbor's expense.

For the superior outcome in the upper-left corner of the matrix to occur, Home and Foreign must reach an explicit agreement, that is, they must *coordinate* their policy choices. Both countries must agree to forgo the beggar-thy-neighbor gains offered by very restrictive policies, and each country must abide by this agreement in spite of the incentive to cheat.

Figure 19A-2 | Payoff Matrix for Different Monetary Policy Moves

Each entry equals the reduction in inflation per unit rise in the unemployment rate (calculated as $-\Delta\pi/\Delta U$). If each country "goes it alone," they both choose very restrictive policies. Somewhat restrictive policies, if adopted by both countries, lead to an outcome better for both.

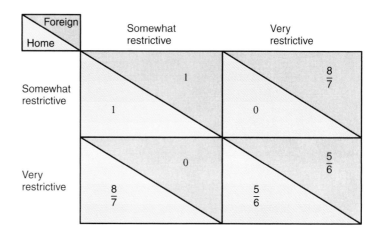

If Home and Foreign can cooperate, both end up with a preferred mix of inflation and unemployment.

The reality of policy coordination is more complex than in this simple example because the choices and outcomes are more numerous and more uncertain. These added complexities make policymakers less willing to commit themselves to cooperative agreements and less certain that their counterparts abroad will live up to the agreed terms.

CHAPTER 20

Optimum Currency Areas and the European Experience

On January 1, 1999, eleven member countries of the European Union (EU) adopted a common currency, the euro. Two years later they were joined by Greece. Europe's bold experiment in Economic and Monetary Union (EMU), which many had viewed as a visionary fantasy only a few years earlier, created a currency area with more than 300 million consumers—roughly 10 percent more populous than the United States. If the countries of eastern Europe enter the EU, the euro zone may eventually comprise more than twenty-five countries and stretch from the Arctic Ocean in the north to the Mediterranean Sea in the south, and from the Atlantic Ocean in the west to the Black Sea in the east. Figure 20-1 shows the extent of the euro zone as of 2001.

The birth of the euro resulted in fixed exchange rates between all EMU member countries. In deciding to share a single currency, however, EMU countries sacrificed even more sovereignty over their monetary policies than a fixed exchange rate regime normally requires. They agreed to give up national currencies entirely and to hand over control of their monetary policies to a shared European System of Central Banks (ESCB).

The European experience raises a host of important questions. How and why did Europe set up its single currency? Will the euro be good for the economies of its members? How will the euro affect countries outside of EMU, notably the United States? And what lessons does the European experience carry for other potential currency blocs, such as the Mercosur trading group in South America?

This chapter focuses on Europe's experience of monetary unification to illustrate the economic benefits and costs of fixed exchange rate agreements and more comprehensive currency unification schemes. As we see in Europe's experience, the effects of joining a fixed exchange rate agreement are complex and depend crucially on microeconomic *and* macroeconomic factors. Our discussion of Europe will throw light not only on the forces promoting greater unification of national economies but also on the forces that make a country think twice before giving up completely its control over domestic monetary policy.

How the European Single Currency Evolved

The Bretton Woods system (which fell apart in 1973) fixed every member country's exchange rate against the U.S. dollar and as a result also fixed the exchange rate between

Figure 20-1 | Members of the Euro Zone as of January 1, 2001

The shaded countries on the map are the twelve members of EMU. They are: Austria, Belgium, Finland, France, Germany, Greece, Ireland, Italy, Luxembourg, the Netherlands, Portugal, and Spain.

every pair of nondollar currencies. Earlier chapters described the reasons for the Bretton Woods system's breakdown and how countries hoped to free their monetary policies by changing from fixed dollar exchange rates to floating rates. While allowing their currencies to float against the dollar, however, EU countries have tried progressively to narrow the extent to which they let their currencies fluctuate against each other. These efforts culminated in the birth of the euro on January 1, 1999.

What factors made European leaders averse to fluctuations in the mutual exchange rates of their currencies? How did the quest for exchange rate stability within Europe lead to the birth of the single European currency? To understand how the euro evolved, we must start in the late 1960s, when currency crises were disrupting exchange rate relationships within Europe.

European Currency Reform Initiatives, 1969–1978

European leaders meeting at The Hague in December 1969 initiated the drive toward European monetary unification. They appointed Pierre Werner, prime minister and finance minister of Luxembourg, to head a committee that would outline concrete steps for eliminating intra-European exchange rate movements, centralizing EU monetary policy decisions, and lowering remaining trade barriers within Europe. The Werner report, adopted by the EU in March 1971, proposed a three-phase program that, when completed, would result in locked EU exchange rates and the integration of the individual national central banks into a federated European system of banks.

Table 20-1	A Brief Glossary of Euronyms
ECB	European Central Bank
ESCB	European System of Central Banks
EMS	European Monetary System
EMU	Economic and Monetary Union
ERM	Exchange Rate Mechanism
SGP	Stability and Growth Pact

What prompted the EU countries to seek closer coordination of monetary policies and greater exchange rate stability in the late 1960s? Two main motives inspired these moves and have remained major reasons for the adoption of the euro:

1. *To enhance Europe's role in the world monetary system.* The currency crises of 1969 were accompanied by declining European confidence in the readiness of the United States to place its international monetary responsibilities ahead of its national interests (Chapter 18). By speaking with a single voice on monetary issues, EU countries hoped to defend more effectively their economic interests in the face of an increasingly self-absorbed United States.

2. *To turn the European Union into a truly unified market.* Even though the 1957 Treaty of Rome founding the EU had established a customs union, significant official barriers to the movements of goods and factors within Europe remained. A consistent goal of EU members has been to eliminate all such barriers and transform the EU into a huge unified market on the model of the United States. European officials believed, however, that exchange rate uncertainty, like official trade barriers, was a major factor reducing trade within Europe. They also feared that if exchange rate swings caused large changes in intra-European relative prices, political forces hostile to free trade within Europe would be strengthened. In their view, a truly unified European market therefore could never be achieved unless mutual European exchange rates were fixed.[1]

The key to understanding how Europe has come so far in both market and monetary unification lies in the continent's war-torn history. After 1945, many European leaders agreed that economic cooperation and integration among the former belligerents would be the best guarantee against a repetition of the twentieth century's two devastating wars. The

---

[1]A very important administrative reason Europeans have sought to avoid big movements in European cross exchange rates is related to the Common Agricultural Policy (CAP), the EU's system of agricultural price supports. Prior to the euro, agricultural prices were quoted in terms of the European Currency Unit (ECU), a basket of EU currencies. Exchange rate realignments within Europe would abruptly alter the real domestic value of the supported prices, provoking protests from farmers in the revaluing countries. The book by Giavazzi and Giovannini in Further Reading describes the contorted policies the EU used to adopt to minimize such internal redistributions after realignments. While the annoyance of administering the CAP under exchange rate realignments was undoubtedly crucial in starting Europeans on the road to currency unification, the two motives cited in the text are more important in explaining how Europe ultimately came to embrace a common currency.

result was a gradual ceding of national economic policy powers to centralized European Union governing bodies, such as the European Commission in Brussels, Belgium (the EU's executive body), and the European System of Central Banks (ESCB), headquartered in Frankfurt, Germany. Europeans' willingness to give up national policy sovereignty thus reflects the fervent desire of a majority of Europeans to maintain peace by aligning countries' economic interests. Many in Europe still hope that the substantial economic unification the EU has achieved will eventually lead to some form of political unification.

The European Monetary System, 1979–1998

The Werner committee's vision of a centralized European monetary policy was ahead of its time. Faced with the economic turbulence surrounding the 1971–1973 dollar crises, most European leaders did not want to give up completely the ability to direct domestic monetary policy toward domestic goals. Instead, Germany, the Netherlands, Belgium, and Luxembourg—joined for periods by other European countries—participated in an informal joint float against the dollar known as the "snake." French, Italian, and British participation in the snake arrangements of the 1970s was brief and sporadic; nonetheless, the snake served as a prologue to the more comprehensive **European Monetary System (EMS)**.

The eight original participants in the EMS's exchange rate mechanism—France, Germany, Italy, Belgium, Denmark, Ireland, Luxembourg, and the Netherlands—began operating a formal network of mutually pegged exchange rates in March 1979. A complex set of EMS intervention arrangements worked to restrict the exchange rates of participating currencies within specified fluctuation margins.[2]

When the EMS was founded on the initiative of France and Germany, skeptics predicted that the system would do no better than its predecessor the snake: Speculative attacks would soon shatter its parities, forcing France, Italy, and some of the smaller countries out. The prospects for a successful fixed-rate area Europe seemed bleak indeed in early 1979, when recent yearly inflation rates ranged from Germany's 2.7 percent to Italy's 12.1 percent (see Table 19-1). Through a mixture of policy cooperation and realignment, however, the EMS fixed exchange rate club survived and even grew, adding Spain to its ranks in 1989, Britain in 1990, and Portugal early in 1992. Only in September 1992 did this growth suffer a sudden setback when Britain and Italy left the EMS exchange rate mechanism at the start of a protracted European currency crisis that forced the remaining members in August 1993 to retreat to very wide exchange rate margins.

The EMS's operation was aided by several safety valves that initially helped reduce the frequency of such crises. Most exchange rates "fixed" by the EMS until August 1993 actually could fluctuate up or down by as much as 2.25 percent relative to an assigned par value. Spain's peseta and Portugal's escudo had bands of $\pm$ 6 percent, as did the British pound until its float against EMS currencies was renewed in September 1992. The Italian lira likewise had a 6 percent band until January 1990, when Italy adopted the standard $\pm$ 2.25 percent band. Inflationary instability was common in Italy during the 1970s, and the country's special exchange rate band was meant to give it a greater latitude than other

---

[2]As a technical matter, all EU members were members of the EMS, but only those EMS members who enforced the fluctuation margins belonged to the EMS *exchange rate mechanism (ERM)*.

exchange rate mechanism members to choose monetary policies. Similarly, the later entrants, Spain, Portugal, and Britain, desired greater room for maneuver during their initiation periods and therefore also chose to start out with wide bands. In August 1993 all EMS bands (other than that between the DM and Dutch guilder) were widened to $\pm$ 15 percent under the pressure of speculative attacks.

As another crucial safety valve, the EMS developed generous provisions for the extension of credit from strong- to weak-currency members. If the French franc depreciated too far against the DM, for example, Germany's central bank, the Bundesbank, was expected to lend the Bank of France DM that could be sold for francs in the foreign exchange market.

Finally, during the system's initial years of operation several members (notably France and Italy) reduced the possibility of speculative attack by maintaining *exchange controls* that directly limited domestic residents' sales of home for foreign currencies. All French, Italian, Danish, and Belgian controls were dismantled in a series of stages completed in 1990. The remaining restrictions on payments within the EU were scrapped by 1995.

The EMS went through periodic currency realignments. In all, 11 realignments occurred between the start of the EMS in March 1979 and January 1987. Exchange controls played the important role of shielding members' reserves from speculators during these adjustments.

Starting in 1987, a phased removal of exchange controls by EMS countries increased the possibility of speculative attacks and thus reduced governments' willingness openly to consider devaluing or revaluing. At the same time the countries that dismantled controls sharply reduced their power to reach national employment or inflation goals through domestic monetary policy (recall the monetary policy ineffectiveness result of Chapter 17). Freedom of payments and capital movements within the EU has always been a key element of EU countries' plan to turn Europe into a unified single market. By agreeing to remove exchange controls, EU governments were saying that it was less important to use monetary and exchange rate policy for domestic purposes than to speed up progress toward a single European market.

For a period of five and a half years after January 1987, no adverse economic event was able to shake the EMS's commitment to its fixed exchange rates. This state of affairs came to an end in 1992, however, as economic shocks caused by the reunification of eastern and western Germany in 1990 led to asymmetrical macroeconomic pressures in Germany and in its major EMS partners.

German reunification was accompanied by a massive domestic fiscal expansion as the Bonn government borrowed to rebuild east Germany and transfer income to its relatively poor citizens. At the same time, reunification raised the economic aspirations of east Germans, who consumed more and demanded higher wages. The result of these changes was a boom in Germany and higher inflation, which Germany's central bank, the Bundesbank, resisted through sharply higher interest rates.

Other EMS countries such as France, Italy, and the United Kingdom, however, were not simultaneously booming. By matching the high German interest rates to hold their currencies fixed against Germany's, they were unwillingly pushing their own economies into deep recession. Germany refused to heed its partners' calls for lower interest rates, fearing domestic inflation. At the same time, other EMS countries feared that by devaluing their currencies to stimulate their own economies, they would slow progress toward the common EU currency and lose the policy credibility they had built up by avoiding exchange rate realignments for 5 years. The policy conflict between Germany and its partners led to a series of fierce speculative attacks on the EMS exchange parities starting in September

1992. By August 1993, as previously noted, the EMS was forced to retreat to very wide (±15 percent) bands, which it kept in force until the introduction of the euro in 1999.[3]

German Monetary Dominance and the Credibility Theory of the EMS

Earlier we identified two main reasons why the European Union sought to fix internal exchange rates: a desire to defend Europe's economic interests more effectively on the world stage and the ambition to achieve greater internal economic unity.

Europe's experience of high inflation in the 1970s suggests an additional purpose that the EMS came to fulfill. By fixing their exchange rates against the DM, the other EMS countries in effect imported the German Bundesbank's credibility as an inflation fighter and thus discouraged the development of inflationary pressures at home—pressures they might otherwise have been tempted to accommodate through monetary expansion. This view, the **credibility theory of the EMS**, is a variant of the "discipline" argument against floating exchange rates (Chapter 19): The political costs of violating an international exchange rate agreement can restrain governments from depreciating their currencies to gain the short-term advantage of an economic boom at the long-term cost of higher inflation.

To evaluate the credibility theory, we need first to understand how the German Bundesbank gained its low-inflation reputation. Germany's experiences with hyperinflation in the 1920s and again after World War II left its electorate with a deeply rooted fear of inflation. For this reason, the law establishing the Bundesbank singled out the defense of the DM's real value as the central bank's primary goal. Consistent with this goal, the bank's governing council has powers and membership rules that make it unusually independent of pressures from the politicians who run the rest of the German government.[4]

The way EMS intervention practices evolved after the mid-1980s supports the view that Germany's EMS partners sought to import its anti-inflation credibility. Increasingly, EMS countries other than Germany came to hold DM in their reserves and to use these as an intervention medium when their exchange rates got too far from the official DM parity. (Germany also carried out some interventions in EMS currencies, especially during turbulent periods, but it instantly sterilized any effects that these interventions might have had on Germany's money supply.) The result was a system that functioned very much in the asymmetric way the Bretton Woods system did under U.S. dominance. In practice, the EMS's Nth currency problem (Chapter 17) was solved by having Germany set the system's monetary policy while the other countries pegged their currencies' DM exchange rates.

Policymakers in inflation-prone EMS countries, such as Italy, clearly gained credibility by placing monetary policy decisions in the hands of the German central bank. Devaluation

---

[3]Despite the adoption of wider bands in August 1993, both Portugal and Spain subsequently devalued their currencies within the EMS. Ireland's punt was revalued by a small amount in March 1998.

[4]Two interesting studies show that central bank independence appears to be associated with lower inflation. See Vittorio Grilli, Donato Masciandaro, and Guido Tabellini, "Political and Monetary Institutions and Public Financial Policies in the Industrial Countries," *Economic Policy* 13 (October 1991), pp. 341–392; and Albeno Alesina and Lawrence H. Summers, "Central Bank Independence and Macroeconomic Performance: Some Comparative Evidence," *Journal of Money, Credit and Banking* 25 (May 1993), pp. 151–162. Empirical studies such as these have helped to promote central bank independence around the world. For a critical view of this literature, see Adam Posen, "Declarations Are Not Enough: Financial Sector Sources of Central Bank Independence," *NBER Macroeconomics Annual* 10 (1995), pp. 253–274.

was still possible, but only subject to EMS restrictions. Because politicians also feared they would look incompetent to voters if they devalued, a government's decision to peg to the DM reduced both its willingness and ability to create domestic inflation.[5]

Added support for the credibility theory comes from the behavior of inflation rates relative to Germany's, shown in Figure 20-2 for six of the other original EMS members.[6] As the figure shows, annual inflation rates gradually converged toward the low German levels. Even France managed to bring its inflation rate below Germany's by the early 1990s, something most observers would have thought impossible a decade earlier.[7]

The EU "1992" Initiative

The EU countries have tried to achieve greater internal economic unity not only by fixing mutual exchange rates, but also through direct measures to encourage the free flow of goods, services, and factors of production. Later in this chapter you will learn that the extent of product and factor market integration within Europe helps to determine how fixed exchange rates affect Europe's macroeconomic stability. Europe's efforts to raise *microeconomic* efficiency through direct market liberalization have also increased its preference for mutually fixed exchange rates on *macroeconomic* grounds. The most recent phase of EU market liberalization, an ambitious plan known as the "1992" initiative because all of its goals were supposed to have been met by January 1, 1993, therefore is an important consideration in our discussion of European exchange rate policy.

The process of market unification that began when the original EU members formed their customs union in 1957 was still incomplete 30 years later. In a number of industries, such as automobiles and telecommunications, trade within Europe was discouraged by government-imposed standards and registration requirements; often government licensing or purchasing practices gave domestic producers virtual monopoly positions in domestic markets. Differing national tax structures and health and safety regulations also inhibited trade. For example, countries with high value-added taxes had to post customs officials at EU frontiers to prevent their citizens from shopping in neighboring low-tax countries. Similarly, customs checks were needed to enforce national product standards. Significant barriers to factor movements within Europe also remained.[8]

In June 1985 the EU's executive body, the European Commission, issued a White Paper containing 300 proposals for "Completing the Internal Market" by the end of 1992, that is, for removing all remaining internal barriers to trade, capital movements, and labor migra-

---

[5] The general theory that an inflation-prone country gains from vesting its monetary policy decisions with a "conservative" central bank is developed in an influential paper by Kenneth Rogoff. See "The Optimal Degree of Commitment to an Intermediate Monetary Target," *Quarterly Journal of Economics* 100 (November 1985), pp. 1169–1189. For application to the EMS, see Francesco Giavazzi and Marco Pagano, "The Advantage of Tying One's Hands: EMS Discipline and Central Bank Credibility," *European Economic Review* 32 (June 1988), pp. 1055–1082.

[6] Figure 20-2 does not include the tiny country of Luxembourg because before 1999 that country had a currency union with Belgium and an inflation rate very close to Belgium's.

[7] Those skeptical of the credibility theory of EMS inflation convergence point out that the United States, Britain, and Japan also reduced inflation to low levels over the 1980s, but did so without fixing their exchange rates. After the euro was introduced in 1999 there was some widening of inflation differences, as we discuss below.

[8] An excellent discussion of the microeconomic objectives of 1992 is in Harry Flam, "Product Markets and 1992: Full Integration, Large Gains?" *Journal of Economic Perspectives* 6 (Fall 1992), pp. 7–30.

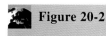 **Figure 20-2** | Inflation Convergence Within Six Original
EMS Members, 1978–2000

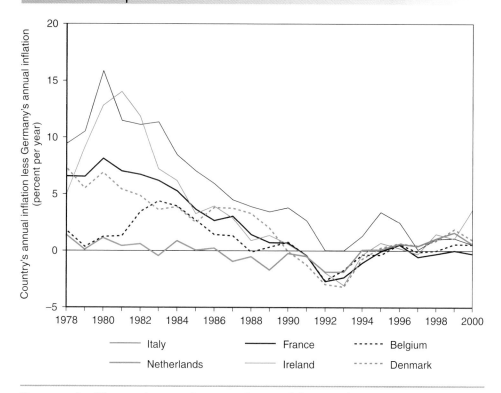

Shown are the differences between domestic inflation and German inflation for six of the original
EMS members, Belgium, Denmark, France, Ireland, Italy, and the Netherlands. As of 1997 all national
inflation rates were very close to the German levels.

Source: CPI inflation rates from IMF, *International Financial Statistics.*

tion. In the Single European Act of 1986 (which amended the founding Treaty of Rome),
EU members took the crucial political steps to translate the White Paper's 1992 into reality. Most important, they dropped the Treaty of Rome's requirement of unanimous consent
for measures related to market completion, so that one or two self-interested EU members
could not block trade liberalization measures as in the past. The Single European Act thus
gave the European Union the procedural tools needed to attain its ambitious goal, namely,
that "the internal market shall comprise an area without internal frontiers in which the free
movement of goods, persons, services and capital is ensured."

By now most of 1992's market integration measures have been implemented. National
economic barriers within EU Europe generally are lower than in the mid-1980s, but 1992
has been more effective in some areas than in others. Financial capital, for example, can
move quite freely, not only within the European Union, but between the European Union
and outside jurisdictions.

Progress has been slower, however, in lowering barriers to the free movement of *people* within the European Union. EU workers are legally free to seek jobs or reside anywhere in the Union, but labor mobility remains limited. Several EU members feared illegal immigration from outside the European Union, however, and as a result the original goal to abolish passport checks at EU members' common borders by January 1, 1993, was not fully met.

European Economic and Monetary Union

Countries can link their currencies together in many ways. We can imagine that the different modes of linkage form a spectrum, with the arrangements at one end requiring little sacrifice of monetary policy independence while those at the other end require independence to be given up entirely.

The early EMS, characterized by frequent currency realignments and widespread government control over capital movements, left significant scope for national monetary policies. In 1989 a committee headed by Jacques Delors, president of the European Commission, recommended a three-stage transition to a goal at the other extreme end of the policy spectrum just described. That goal is an **economic and monetary union (EMU)**, a European Union in which national currencies are replaced by a single EU currency managed by a sole central bank that operates on behalf of all EU members.

In stage 1 of the Delors plan all EU members were to join the EMS exchange rate mechanism (ERM). In stage 2 exchange rate margins were to be narrowed and certain macroeconomic policy decisions placed under more centralized EU control. Finally, stage 3 of the Delors plan involved the replacement of national currencies by a single European currency and the vesting of all monetary policy decisions in a European System of Central Banks, similar in structure to the U.S. Federal Reserve System and headed by a European Central Bank.

On December 10, 1991, the leaders of the EU countries met at the ancient Dutch city of Maastricht and agreed to propose for national ratification far-reaching amendments to the Treaty of Rome. These amendments were meant to place the EU squarely on the road to EMU. Included in the 250-page **Maastricht Treaty** were provisions calling for a start to stage 2 of the Delors plan on January 1, 1994, and a start to stage 3 no later than January 1, 1999. In addition to its *monetary policy* provisions, the Maastricht Treaty included steps toward harmonizing social policy within the European Union (such as workplace safety, consumer protection, and immigration rules) and toward centralizing foreign and defense policy decisions that each EU member currently makes on its own. By 1993, all twelve countries then belonging to the EU had ratified the Maastricht Treaty. On joining the EU in 1995, Austria, Finland, and Sweden accepted the Treaty's provisions (as well as the rest of the EU's laws).[9]

Why did the EU countries move away from the EMS and toward the much more ambitious goal of a single shared currency? They did so for four reasons:

1. They believed a single EU currency would produce a greater degree of European market integration than fixed exchange rates by removing the threat of EMS currency realignments and eliminating the costs to traders of converting one EMS currency into

---

[9]Denmark and the United Kingdom, however, ratified the Maastricht Treaty subject to special exceptions allowing them to "opt out" of the Treaty's monetary provisions and retain their national currencies.

another. The single currency was viewed as a necessary complement to the 1992 plan for unifying EU markets into a single continent-wide market.

2. Some EU leaders thought Germany's management of EMS monetary policy had placed a one-sided emphasis on German macroeconomic goals at the expense of its EMS partners' interests. The European Central Bank that would replace the German Bundesbank under EMU would have to be more considerate of other countries' problems, and it would automatically give those countries the same opportunity as Germany to participate in system-wide monetary policy decisions.

3. Given the move to complete freedom of capital movements within the EU, there seemed to be little to gain, and much to lose, from keeping national currencies with fixed (but adjustable) parities rather than irrevocably locking parities through a single currency. Any system of fixed exchange rates among distinct national currencies would be subject to ferocious speculative attacks, as in 1992–1993. If Europeans wished to combine permanently fixed exchange rates with freedom of capital movements, a single currency was the best solution.

4. As previously noted, all of the EU countries' leaders hoped the Maastricht Treaty's provisions would guarantee the *political* stability of Europe. Beyond its purely economic functions, the single EU currency was intended as a potent symbol of Europe's desire to place cooperation ahead of the national rivalries that often had led to war in the past. Under this scenario, the new currency would align the economic interests of individual European nations to create an overwhelming political constituency for peace on the continent.

The Maastricht Treaty's critics denied that EMU would have these positive effects and opposed the treaty's provisions for vesting stronger governmental powers with the European Union. To these critics, EMU was symptomatic of a tendency for the European Union's central institutions to ignore local needs, meddle in local affairs, and downgrade prized symbols of national identity (including, of course, national currencies).

The Euro and Economic Policy in the Euro Zone

The Maastricht Treaty's limited initiatives in the areas of social and political integration have not had much effect, but its more detailed blueprint for EMU came to fruition on schedule when the euro was introduced in eleven EU countries at the start of 1999. Interestingly, the Maastricht Treaty does not contain the name "euro" but refers to the single currency as the ECU (or European Currency Unit). European leaders picked the name "euro" only in December 1995 (see the box on p. 616–617). Figure 20-3, reproduced from the *Financial Times,* shows the euro's behavior against other major currencies since its launch.

How were the initial members of EMU chosen, how will new members be admitted, and what is the structure of the complex of financial and political institutions that govern economic policy in the euro zone? This section provides an overview.

The Maastricht Convergence Criteria and the Stability and Growth Pact

The Maastricht Treaty specifies that EU member countries must satisfy several macroeconomic convergence criteria before they can be admitted to EMU. Among these criteria are:

Figure 20-3 | Behavior of the Euro's Exchange Rates against Major Currencies

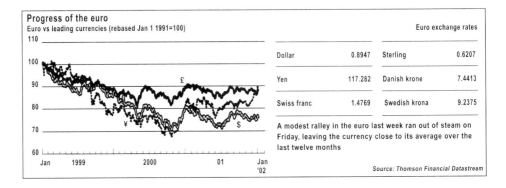

Progress of the euro
Euro vs leading currencies (rebased Jan 1 1991=100)

	Euro exchange rates		
Dollar	0.8947	Sterling	0.6207
Yen	117.282	Danish krone	7.4413
Swiss franc	1.4769	Swedish krona	9.2375

A modest rally in the euro last week ran out of steam on Friday, leaving the currency close to its average over the last twelve months

Source: Thomson Financial Datastream

Every Monday the *Financial Times* summarizes the recent behavior of the euro in the foreign exchange market. After its introduction, the euro depreciated against the dollar.

Source: *Financial Times,* February 22, 1999, p. 1. Courtesy of Financial Times Graphics.

1. The country's inflation rate in the year before admission must be no more than 1.5 percent above the average of the three EU member states with lowest inflation.
2. The country must have maintained a stable exchange rate within the ERM without devaluing on its own initiative.
3. The country must have a public-sector deficit no higher than 3 percent of its GDP (except in exceptional and temporary circumstances).
4. The country must have a public debt that is below or approaching a reference level of 60 percent of its GDP.

The Treaty provides for the ongoing monitoring of criteria 3 and 4 above by the European Commission even after admission to EMU, and for the levying of penalties on countries that violate these fiscal rules and do not correct situations of "excessive" deficits and debt. The surveillance and sanctions over high deficits and debts place national governments under constraints in the exercise of their national fiscal powers. For example, a highly indebted EMU country facing a national recession might be unable to use expansionary fiscal policy for fear of breaching the Maastricht limits—a possibly costly loss of policy autonomy, given the absence of a national monetary policy!

In addition, a supplementary **Stability and Growth Pact (SGP)** negotiated by European leaders in 1997 tightens the fiscal straitjacket further. The SGP sets out "the medium-term budgetary objective of positions close to balance or in surplus." It also sets out a timetable for the imposition of financial penalties on countries that fail to correct situations of "excessive" deficits and debt promptly enough. Only time will tell if the SGP will be strictly enforced in practice.

What explains the macroeconomic convergence criteria, the fear of high public debts, and the SGP? Before they would sign the Maastricht Treaty, low-inflation countries such as Germany wanted assurance that their EMU partners had learned to prefer an environment of low inflation and fiscal restraint. They feared that otherwise, the euro might be a weak currency, falling prey to the types of policies that have fueled French, Italian, Portuguese, Spanish, and United Kingdom inflation at various points since the early 1970s. The architects of the Maastricht Treaty also feared that high public deficits and debts would lead to pressures on the new European Central Bank to purchase government debt directly, thereby fueling money-supply growth and inflation.[10]

As EMU came closer in 1997, German public opinion remained opposed to the euro because of widespread skepticism that the new currency would be as strong as the DM had been. The German government demanded the SGP as a way of convincing domestic voters that the new eurosystem would indeed produce low inflation.

By May 1998, it was clear that eleven EU countries had satisfied the convergence criteria on the basis of 1997 data and would be founder members of EMU: Austria, Belgium, Finland, France, Germany, Ireland, Italy, Luxembourg, the Netherlands, Portugal, and Spain. Britain and Denmark exercised their privileges to stand apart from monetary union. Sweden failed to satisfy the exchange-rate criterion (criterion 2 above), having not previously been a member of the ERM. Greece failed to qualify on any of the criteria in 1998, although it ultimately passed all of its tests and entered EMU on January 1, 2001.

The European System of Central Banks

The European System of Central Banks, which conducts monetary policy for the euro zone, consists of the European Central Bank in Frankfurt plus the twelve national central banks, which now play a role analogous to the regional Federal Reserve banks in the United States. Decisions of the ESCB are made by votes of the governing council of the ECB, consisting of a six-member ECB executive board (including the president of the ECB, currently Willem F. Duisenberg of the Netherlands) and the heads of the national central banks. In this way, the central ECB management consisting of the executive board interacts with national central bank representatives to set monetary policy for the entire euro area. (Strictly speaking, *all* EU national central banks, whether in the euro zone or out, are part of the ESCB, and their heads sit on an ECB "general council." The ECB general council, however, in contrast to its *governing* council, has few powers and does not make the decisions on euro zone interest rates.)

The authors of the Maastricht Treaty hoped to create an independent central bank free of the political influences that might lead to inflation. The Treaty gives the ESCB an overriding mandate to pursue price stability and includes many provisions intended to insulate monetary policy decisions from political influence. In addition, unlike any other central bank in the world, the ESCB operates above and beyond the reach of any single national government. In the United States, for example, the Congress could easily pass laws reducing the independence of the Federal Reserve. The ESCB is required to brief the European Parliament regularly on its activities, but the European Parliament has no power to alter the ESCB's statute. That would require an amendment to the Maastricht Treaty, approved by legislatures or voters in every member country of the EU. Critics of the Treaty argue that it goes too far in shielding the ESCB from normal democratic processes. The special position

---

[10]For an excellent discussion of the negotiations behind the Treaty and the convergence criteria, see the book by Kenen in Further Reading. On the push to fulfill the criteria in 1997, see Maurice Obstfeld, "Europe's Gamble," *Brookings Papers on Economic Activity* 2:1997, pp. 241–317.

DESIGNING AND NAMING A NEW CURRENCY

Among the least of the obstacles to achieving the comprehensive monetary union envisaged in the Maastricht Treaty are the choices of a look and a name for the new single European currency. Nonetheless, agreement was hard to reach.

Some European leaders wanted to retain a national symbol on the euro bills their national central banks issued, although the national bills would circulate throughout Europe in the same way that U.S. dollars bills bearing the imprint of the Federal Reserve Bank of Chicago, for example, may turn up in New Yorker's wallets. The British, in particular, insisted that their monarch appear on their banknotes, regardless of what the rest of Europe did. In the end, a compromise was reached. Euro notes do not carry national symbols. Euro coins, however, do have a "European," side and a "national" side upon which national symbols of the issuing country may appear.

A generic euro note superimposes the EU flag (a circle of 12 yellow stars on a field of dark blue) upon an imaginary European architectural masterpiece. The European Union gave a full description of the notes and the rationale for their design (see the EU website, http://europa.eu.int/euro/html):

There are 7 euro notes. In different colours and sizes they are denominated in 500, 200, 100, 50, 20, 10 and 5 euros. The designs are symbolic for Europe's architectural heritage. They do not represent any existing monuments. Windows and gateways dominate the front side of each banknote as symbols of the spirit of openness and cooperation in the EU. The reverse side of each banknote features a bridge from a particular age, a metaphor for communication among the people of Europe and between Europe and the rest of the world. Final designs were announced in December 1996 at the Dublin European Council. All notes will carry advanced security features.

There were even more exotic proposals in the air, however, before the current design was chosen. Among the ideas floated: notes carrying Michelangelo's *David* or the Phoenician princess Europa who, in Greek mythology, was carried off to Crete

of the ESCB risks alienating the public, these critics charge, by removing any mechanism that might make the ESCB accountable to electorates for its actions.

Notwithstanding its high degree of statutory independence, the ESCB is dependent on politicians in at least two respects. First, the ESCB's members are political appointments (albeit with fixed, nonrenewable terms). Second, the Maastricht Treaty leaves *exchange rate* policy for the euro zone ultimately in the hands of the political authorities. This assignment of powers is puzzling, since choices over exchange rates determine those over monetary policy and the ESCB therefore can have no true monetary independence if it lacks the sole authority to choose exchange rates for the euro. Even in the months before the euro's birth, the French and German finance ministers were suggesting possible target zones involving the euro, the dollar, and the yen. It remains to be seen whether EMU politicians and the ESCB will clash head-on over the exchange rate of the euro. Existing EU law seems to give the ESCB the right to reject politicians' exchange rate objectives if these threaten price stability.

The Revised Exchange Rate Mechanism

For EU countries that are not yet members of EMU, a revised exchange rate mechanism—referred to as ERM 2—defines broad exchange rate zones against the euro and specifies reciprocal intervention arrangements to support these target zones. ERM 2 was viewed as necessary to discourage competitive devaluations against the euro by EU members outside

by the god Zeus (who took the form of a bull for the occasion).

The EU states regarding euro coins:

There are 8 euro coins denominated in 2 and 1 euros, then 50, 20, 10, 5, 2 and 1 cents. Every euro coin will carry a common European face. On the obverse, each Member State will decorate the coins with their own motifs. *No matter which motif is on the coins they can be used anywhere inside the 11 Member States. For example, a French citizen will be able to buy a hot dog in Berlin using a euro coin carrying the imprint of the King of Spain.* The common European face of the coins represents a map of the European Union against a background of transverse lines to which are attached the stars of the European flag. The 1, 2, and 5 cent coins put emphasis on Europe's place in the world while the 10, 20, and 50 present the Union as a gathering of nations. The 1 and 2 euro coins depict Europe without frontiers. Final designs were agreed at the European Council meeting in Amsterdam in June 1997.

The new currency's name was another problem until "euro" was chosen in December 1995. The Maastricht Treaty, as previously noted, refers to the single currency as the ECU, but most European leaders thought it would be misleading and politically awkward to adopt the name of a preexisting currency basket—and one that has depreciated sharply against the DM at that. A further problem was German chancellor Kohl's reported objection that in German "ein ECU" sounds like "eine Kuh," German for "a cow."* Other proposed names included the franken and the shilling.

For some, christening the new currency "euro" was a reluctant compromise. Britain's prime minister complained that the name euro didn't send the blood coursing through his veins (unlike pound, presumably). The Greeks noted that euro sounds like their word for urine.† Nonetheless, euro it is.

---

* See "What Fits in Europe's Wallet?" *New York Times,* July 11, 1995. p. C1.

† "Europeans Agree on New Currency," *New York Times,* December 16, 1995, p. 1.

---

the euro zone and to give would-be EMU entrants a way of satisfying the Maastricht Treaty's exchange rate stability convergence criterion. Under ERM 2 rules, either the ECB or the national central bank of an EU member with its own currency can suspend euro intervention operations if they result in money supply changes that threaten to destabilize the domestic price level. ERM 2 is as asymmetric as the old ERM, with peripheral countries pegging to the euro and adjusting passively to ECB decisions on interest rates.

The Theory of Optimum Currency Areas

There is little doubt that the European monetary integration process has helped advance the *political* goals of its founders by giving the European Union a stronger position in international affairs. The survival and future development of the European monetary experiment depend more heavily, however, on its ability to help countries reach their *economic* goals. Here the picture is less clear because a country's decision to fix its exchange rate can in principle lead to economic sacrifices as well as to benefits.

We saw in Chapter 19 that by changing its exchange rate, a country may succeed in cushioning the disruptive impact of various economic shocks. On the other hand, exchange rate flexibility can have potentially harmful effects, such as making relative prices less predictable or undermining the government's resolve to keep inflation in check. To weigh the economic costs of joining a group of countries with mutually fixed exchange rates against the advantages, we need a framework for thinking systematically about the stabilization powers a country sacrifices and the gains in efficiency and credibility it may reap.

In this section we show that a country's costs and benefits from joining a fixed-exchange rate area such as the EMS depend on how well-integrated its economy is with those of its potential partners. The analysis leading to this conclusion, which is known as the theory of **optimum currency areas**, predicts that fixed exchange rates are most appropriate for areas closely integrated through international trade and factor movements.[11]

Economic Integration and the Benefits of a Fixed Exchange Rate Area: The *GG* Schedule

Consider how an individual country, for example, Norway, might approach the decision of whether to join an area of fixed exchange rates, for example, the euro zone. Our goal is to develop a simple diagram that clarifies Norway's choice.

We begin by deriving the first of two elements in the diagram, a schedule called *GG* that shows how the potential gain to Norway from joining the euro zone depends on Norway's trading links with that region. Let us assume Norway is considering pegging its currency, the krone, to the euro.

A major economic benefit of fixed exchange rates is that they simplify economic calculations and provide a more predictable basis for decisions that involve international transactions than do floating rates. Imagine the time and resources American consumers and businesses would waste every day if each of the 50 United States had its own currency that fluctuated in value against the currencies of all the other states! Norway faces a similar disadvantage in its trade with the euro zone when it allows its krone to float against the euro. The **monetary efficiency gain** from joining the fixed exchange rate system equals the joiner's saving from avoiding the uncertainty, confusion, and calculation and transaction costs that arise when exchange rates float.[12]

In practice, it may be hard to attach a precise number to the total monetary efficiency gain Norway would enjoy as a result of pegging to the euro. We can be sure, however, that this gain will be higher if Norway trades a lot with euro zone countries. For example, if Norway's trade with the euro zone amounts to 60 percent of its GNP while its trade with the United States amounts to only 5 percent of GNP, then, other things equal, a fixed krone/euro exchange rate clearly yields a greater monetary efficiency gain to Norway traders than a fixed krone/dollar rate. Similarly, the efficiency gain from a fixed krone/euro rate is greater when trade between Norway and the euro zone is extensive than when it is small.

The monetary efficiency gain from pegging the krone to the euro will also be higher if factors of production can migrate freely between Norway and the euro area. Norwegians who invest in euro zone countries benefit when the returns on their investments are more

---

[11] The original reference is Robert A. Mundell's classic, "The Theory of Optimum Currency Areas," *American Economic Review* 51 (September 1961), pp. 717–725. Subsequent contributions are summarized in the book by Tower and Willett listed in Further Reading.

[12] To illustrate just one component of the monetary efficiency gain, potential savings of commissions paid to brokers and banks on foreign exchange transactions, Charles R. Bean of the London School of Economics estimated that in 1992 a "round-trip" through all the European Union currencies would result in the loss of fully *half* the original sum. See the paper by Bean in this chapter's Further Reading.

Figure 20-4 | The *GG* Schedule

The upward sloping *GG* schedule shows that a country's monetary efficiency gain from joining a fixed exchange rate area rises as the country's economic integration with the area rises.

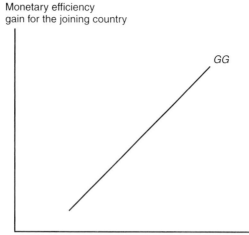

Monetary efficiency gain for the joining country

GG

Degree of economic integration between the joining country and the exchange rate area

predictable. Similarly, Norwegians who work in euro zone countries may benefit if a fixed exchange rate makes their wages more stable relative to Norway's cost of living.

Our conclusion is that *a high degree of economic integration between a country and a fixed exchange rate area magnifies the monetary efficiency gain the country reaps when it fixes its exchange rate against the area's currencies.* The more extensive are cross-border trade and factor movements, the greater is the gain from a fixed cross-border exchange rate.

The upward-sloping curve *GG* in Figure 20-4 shows the relation between a country's degree of economic integration with a fixed exchange rate area and the monetary efficiency gain to the country from joining the area. The figure's horizontal axis measures the extent to which Norway (the joining country in our example) is economically integrated into euro zone product and factor markets. The vertical axis measures the monetary efficiency gain to Norway from pegging to the euro. *GG*'s positive slope reflects the conclusion that the monetary efficiency gain a country gets by joining a fixed exchange rate area rises as its economic integration with the area increases.

In our example we have implicitly assumed that the larger exchange rate area, the euro zone, has a stable and predictable price level. If it does not, the greater variability in Norway's price level that would follow a decision to join the exchange rate area would likely offset any monetary efficiency gain a fixed exchange rate might provide. A different problem arises if Norway's commitment to fix the krone's exchange rate is not fully believed by economic actors. In this situation, some exchange rate uncertainty would remain and Norway would therefore enjoy a smaller monetary efficiency gain. If the euro zone's price level is stable and Norway's exchange rate commitment is firm, however, the main conclusion follows: When Norway pegs to the euro, it gains from the stability of its currency against the euro, and this efficiency gain is greater the more closely tied are Norway's markets with euro zone markets.

Earlier in this chapter we learned that a country may wish to peg its exchange rate to an area of price stability to import the anti-inflationary resolve of the area's monetary authorities. When the economy of the pegging country is well integrated with that of the low-inflation area, however, low domestic inflation is easier to achieve. The reason is that close economic integration leads to international price convergence and therefore lessens the scope for independent variation in the pegging country's price level. This argument provides another reason why high economic integration with a fixed exchange rate area enhances a country's gain from membership.

Economic Integration and the Costs of a Fixed Exchange Rate Area: The *LL* Schedule

Membership in an exchange rate area may involve costs as well as benefits, even when the area has low inflation. These costs arise because a country that joins an exchange rate area gives up its ability to use the exchange rate and monetary policy for the purpose of stabilizing output and employment. This **economic stability loss** from joining, like the country's monetary efficiency gain, is related to the country's economic integration with its exchange rate partners. We can derive a second schedule, the *LL* schedule, that shows the relationship graphically.

In Chapter 19's discussion of the relative merits of fixed and floating exchange rates, we concluded that when the economy is disturbed by a change in the output market (that is, by a shift in the *DD* schedule), a floating exchange rate has an advantage over a fixed rate: It automatically cushions the economy's output and employment by allowing an immediate change in the relative price of domestic and foreign goods. Furthermore, you will recall from Chapter 17 that when the exchange rate is fixed, purposeful stabilization is more difficult because monetary policy has no power at all to affect domestic output. Given these two conclusions, we would expect changes in the *DD* schedule to have more severe effects on an economy in which the monetary authority is required to fix the exchange rate against a group of foreign currencies. The *extra* instability caused by the fixed exchange rate is the economic stability loss.[13]

To derive the *LL* schedule we must understand how the extent of Norway's economic integration with the euro zone will affect the size of this loss in economic stability. Imagine that Norway is pegging to the euro and there is a fall in the aggregate demand for Norway's output—leftward shift of Norway's *DD* schedule. If the *DD* schedules of the other euro

---

[13] You might think that when Norway unilaterally fixes its exchange rate against the euro, but leaves the krone free to float against non-euro currencies, it is able to keep at least some monetary independence. Perhaps surprisingly, this intuition is *wrong*. The reason is that any independent money supply change in Norway would put pressure on krone interest rates and thus on the krone/euro exchange rate. So by pegging the krone even to a single foreign currency, Norway completely surrenders its domestic monetary control. This result has, however, a positive side for Norway. After Norway unilaterally pegs the krone to the euro, domestic money market disturbances (shifts in the *AA* schedule) will no longer affect domestic output, despite the continuing float against non-euro currencies. Why? Because Norway's interest rate must equal the euro interest rate, any pure shifts in *AA* will (as in Chapter 19) result in immediate reserve inflows or outflows that leave Norway's interest rate unchanged. Thus, a krone/euro peg alone is enough to provide automatic stability in the face of any monetary shocks that shift the *AA* schedule. This is why the discussion in the text can focus on shifts in the *DD* schedule.

zone countries happen simultaneously to shift to the left, the euro will simply depreciate against outside currencies, providing the automatic stabilization we studied in the last chapter. Norway has a serious problem only when it *alone* faces a fall in demand—for example, if the world demand for oil, one of Norway's main exports, drops.

How will Norway adjust to this shock? Since nothing has happened to budge the euro, to which Norway is pegged, its krone will remain stable against *all* foreign currencies. Full employment will be restored only after a period of costly slump during which the prices of Norwegian goods and the wages of Norwegian workers fall.

How does the severity of this slump depend on the level of economic integration between the Norwegian economy and those of the EMU countries? The answer is that greater integration implies a shallower slump, and therefore a less costly adjustment to the adverse shift in *DD.* There are two reasons for this reduction in the cost of adjustment. First, if Norway has close trading links with the euro zone, a small reduction in its prices will lead to an increase in euro zone demand for Norwegian goods that is large relative to Norway's output. Thus, full employment can be restored fairly quickly. Second, if Norway's labor and capital markets are closely meshed with those of its euro zone neighbors, unemployed workers can easily move abroad to find work and domestic capital can be shifted to more profitable uses in other countries. The ability of factors to migrate abroad thus reduces the severity of unemployment in Norway and the fall in the rate of return available to investors.[14]

Notice that our conclusions also apply to a situation in which Norway experiences an *increase* in demand for its output (a rightward shift of *DD*). If Norway is tightly integrated with euro zone economies, a small increase in Norway's price level, combined with some movement of foreign capital and labor into Norway, quickly eliminates the excess demand for Norwegian products.[15]

Notice that closer trade links between Norway and countries *outside* the euro zone will also aid the country's adjustment to Norwegian *DD* shifts that are not simultaneously experienced by the euro zone. However, greater trade integration with countries outside the euro zone is a two-edged sword, with negative as well as positive implications for macroeconomic stability. The reason is that when Norway pegs the krone to the euro, euro zone disturbances that change the euro's exchange rate will have more powerful effects on Norway's economy as its trading links with non-euro countries are more extensive. The effects would

---

[14]Installed plant and equipment typically is costly to transport abroad or to adapt to new uses. Owners of such relatively immobile Norwegian capital therefore will always earn low returns on it after an adverse shift in the demand for Norwegian products. If Norway's capital market is integrated with those of its EMU neighbors, however, Norwegians will invest some of their wealth in other countries, while at the same time part of Norway's capital stock will be owned by foreigners. As a result of this process of international wealth *diversification* (see Chapter 21), unexpected changes in the return to Norway's capital will automatically be shared among investors throughout the fixed exchange rate area. Thus, even owners of capital that cannot be moved can avoid more of the economic stability loss due to fixed exchange rates when Norway's economy is open to capital flows.

When international labor mobility is low or nonexistent, higher international capital mobility may *not* reduce the economic stability loss from fixed exchange rates, as we discuss evaluating the European experience in the Case Study on pp. 625–630.

[15]The preceding reasoning applies to other economic disturbances that fall unequally on Norway's output market and those of its exchange rate partners. A problem at the end of this chapter asks you to think through the effects of an increase in demand for EMU exports that leaves Norway's export demand schedule unchanged.

be analogous to an increase in the size of movements in Norway's *DD* curve and would raise Norway's economic stability loss from pegging to the euro. In any case, these arguments do not change our earlier conclusion that Norway's stability loss from fixing the krone/euro exchange rate falls as the extent of its economic integration with the euro zone rises.

An additional consideration that we have not yet discussed strengthens the argument that the economic stability loss to Norway from pegging to the euro is lower when Norway and the euro zone engage in a large volume of trade. Since imports from the euro zone make up a large fraction of Norwegian workers' consumption in this case, changes in the krone/euro exchange rate may quickly affect nominal Norwegian wages, reducing any impact on employment. A depreciation of the krone against the euro, for example, causes a sharp fall in Norwegians' living standards when imports from the euro zone are substantial; workers are likely to demand higher nominal wages from their employers to compensate them for the loss. In this situation the additional macroeconomic stability Norway gets from a floating exchange rate is small, so the country has little to lose by fixing the krone/euro exchange rate.

We conclude that *a high degree of economic integration between a country and the fixed exchange rate area that it joins reduces the resulting economic stability loss due to output market disturbances.*

The *LL* schedule shown in Figure 20-5 summarizes this conclusion. The figure's horizontal axis measures the joining country's economic integration with the fixed exchange rate area, the vertical axis the country's economic stability loss. As we have seen, *LL* has a negative slope because the economic stability loss from pegging to the area's currencies falls as the degree of economic interdependence rises.

The Decision to Join a Currency Area: Putting the *GG* and *LL* Schedules Together

Figure 20-6 combines the *GG* and *LL* schedules to show how Norway should decide whether to fix the krone's exchange rate against the euro. The figure implies that Norway should do so if the degree of economic integration between Norwegian markets and those of the euro zone is at least equal to θ_1, the integration level determined by the intersection of *GG* and *LL* at point 1.

Let's see why Norway should peg to the euro if its degree of economic integration with euro zone markets is at least θ_1. Figure 20-6 shows that for levels of economic integration below θ_1 the *GG* schedule lies below the *LL* schedule. Thus, the loss Norway would suffer from greater output and employment instability after joining exceeds the monetary efficiency gain, and the country would do better to stay out.

When the degree of integration is θ_1 or higher, however, the monetary efficiency gain measured by *GG* is greater than the stability sacrifice measured by *LL*, and pegging the krone's exchange rate against the euro results in a net gain for Norway. Thus the intersection of *GG* and *LL* determines the minimum integration level (here, θ_1) at which Norway will desire to peg its currency to the euro.

The *GG-LL* framework has important implications about how changes in a country's economic environment affect its willingness to peg its currency to an outside currency area. Consider, for example, an increase in the size and frequency of sudden shifts in the demand for the country's exports. As shown in Figure 20-7, such a change pushes LL^1 upward to LL^2: At any level of economic integration with the currency area, the extra

Figure 20-5 | The *LL* Schedule

The downward sloping *LL* schedule shows that a country's economic stability loss from joining a fixed exchange rate area falls as the country's economic integration with the area rises.

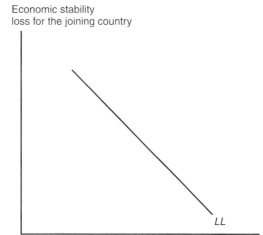

Economic stability loss for the joining country

LL

Degree of economic integration between the joining country and the exchange rate area

Figure 20-6 | Deciding When to Peg the Exchange Rate

The intersection of *GG* and *LL* at point I determines a critical level of economic integration θ_1 between a fixed exchange rate area and a country considering whether to join. At any level of integration above θ_1, the decision to join yields positive net economic benefits to the joining country.

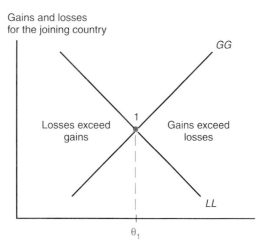

Gains and losses for the joining country

GG

Losses exceed gains

1

Gains exceed losses

LL

θ_1

Degree of economic integration between the joining country and the exchange rate area

Figure 20-7 | An Increase in Output Market Variability

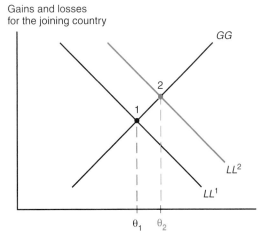

A rise in the size and frequency of country-specific disturbances to the joining country's product markets shifts the *LL* schedule upward from LL^1 to LL^2 because for a given level of economic integration with the fixed exchange rate area the country's economic stability loss from pegging its exchange rate rises. The shift in *LL* raises the critical level of economic integration at which the exchange rate area is joined to θ_2.

Gains and losses for the joining country

Degree of economic integration between the joining country and the exchange rate area

output and unemployment instability the country suffers by fixing its exchange rate is now greater. As a result, the level of economic integration at which it becomes worthwhile to join the currency area rises to θ_2 (determined by the intersection of *GG* and LL^2 at point 2). Other things equal, increased variability in their product markets makes countries less willing to enter fixed exchange rate areas—a prediction that helps explain why the oil price shocks after 1973 made countries unwilling to revive the Bretton Woods system of fixed exchange rates (Chapter 19).

What Is an Optimum Currency Area?

The *GG-LL* model we have developed suggests a theory of the optimum currency area. *Optimum currency areas* are groups of regions with economies closely linked by trade in goods and services and by factor mobility. This result follows from our finding that a fixed exchange rate area will best serve the economic interests of each of its members if the degree of output and factor trade among the included economies is high.

This perspective helps us understand, for example, why it may make sense for the United States, Japan, and Europe to allow their mutual exchange rates to float. Even though these regions trade with each other, the extent of that trade is modest compared with regional GNPs and interregional labor mobility is low. In 1997, for example, U.S. merchandise trade with Western Europe (measured as the average of imports and exports) amounted to only about 2 percent of U.S. GNP; U.S. merchandise trade with Japan was even smaller.

The more interesting question, and the critical one for judging the economic success of EMU, is whether Europe itself makes up an optimum currency area. We take up this topic next.

CASE STUDY

Is Europe an Optimum Currency Area?

The theory of optimum currency areas gives us a useful framework for thinking about the considerations that determine whether a group of countries will gain or lose by fixing their mutual exchange rates. A nation's gains and losses from pegging its currency to an exchange rate area are hard to measure numerically, but by combining our theory with information on actual economic performance we can evaluate the claim that Europe, most of which is likely to adopt or peg to the euro, is an optimum currency area.

The Extent of Intra-European Trade

Our earlier discussion suggested that a country is more likely to benefit from joining a currency area if the area's economy is closely integrated with its own. The overall degree of economic integration can be judged by looking at the integration of product markets, that is, the extent of trade between the joining country and the currency area, and at the integration of factor markets, that is, the ease with which labor and capital can migrate between the joining country and the currency area.

Most EU members export from 10 to 20 percent of their output to other EU members. These numbers are larger than those for EU-U.S. trade, which is only around 2 percent of U.S. GNP and an even smaller percentage of EU GNP, but much smaller than the amount of trade between regions of the United States. If we take trade relative to GNP as a measure of economic integration, the *GG-LL* model of the last section suggests that a joint float of Europe's currencies against the rest of the world is a better strategy for EU members than a fixed dollar/euro exchange rate would be. The extent of intra-European trade is not large enough, however, to give us an overwhelming reason for believing the European Union itself is an optimum currency area.

To some degree intra-EU trade may have been artificially limited by trade restrictions that the 1992 reforms largely removed. Now, however, years after 1992, intra-EU trade is only slightly above its prior (1989) peak (see Figure 20-8). Furthermore, deviations from the law of one price remain. For some goods (such as consumer electronics) there has been considerable price convergence across EU countries, but for other product types, similar items still sell for widely different prices in different European locations. The auto market provides a glaring example. In 1998, prices for the BMW 520i varied by as much as 29.5 percent between the United Kingdom and the Netherlands. Prices for the Ford Fiesta varied as much as 43.5 percent between the United Kingdom and Portugal![16]

One hypothesis about the persistence of such price differentials conjectures a gradual impact of the 1992 reforms. Another—one favored by enthusiasts of the euro—is that multiple currencies have made big price discrepancies possible. It remains to be seen whether the euro, by

---

[16] See "What's £9.99 in Euros, Then?" *Financial Times,* April 21, 1998, p. 27. An important factor in explaining big intra-EU price differences in the auto industry is that dealers discriminate among buyers based on nationality. For example, the preceding article reported that the European Commission had fined Volkswagen for prohibiting its dealers in Italy from selling cars to buyers in Austria and Germany.

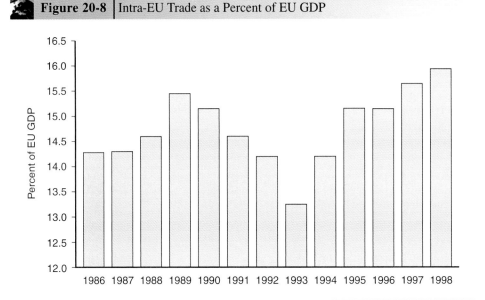

Figure 20-8 | Intra-EU Trade as a Percent of EU GDP

Trade of EU countries with other EU countries has shown no trend since the late 1980s and has remained between 10 and 20 percent of GDP on average. In constructing the figure, the extent of an EU country's trade with EU members is defined as the average of its imports from and exports to other EU countries. The numbers shown are calculated from total intra-EU trade (for all EU members) divided by the total GDP of the EU.

Source: *Eurostat Yearbook,* 1997, 2000.

making price comparisons more transparent, will foster greater integration in EMU product markets. Even if a marked tendency toward price convergence does set in, however, its cause may be a factor unrelated to the 1992 measures or the euro: internet marketing.

On balance, it seems doubtful that the 1992 measures have yet pushed Europe dramatically closer to being an optimum currency area. It may happen, however, that the single currency itself fosters greater trade among members of the euro zone. The box on p. 628 discusses some new evidence on that prospect.

How Mobile Is Europe's Labor Force?

Earlier we mentioned that the European Union did not succeed in removing internal passport checks by the original deadline of January 1, 1993. The main barriers to labor mobility within Europe are probably not due to border controls, however. Differences in language and culture discourage labor movements between European countries to a greater extent than is true, for example, between regions of the United States. In one econometric study comparing unemployment patterns in U.S. regions with those in EU countries, Barry Eichengreen of the Uni-

Table 20-2	People Changing Region of Residence in 1986 (percent of total population)				
Britain	France	Germany	Italy	Japan	United States
1.1	1.3	1.1	0.6	2.6	3.0

Source: Organization for Economic Cooperation and Development. *OECD Employment Outlook.* Paris: OECD, July 1990, Table 3.3.

versity of California, Berkeley, found that differences in regional unemployment rates are smaller and less persistent in the United States than are differences between national unemployment rates in the European Union.[17]

Even *within* European countries labor mobility appears limited, partly because of government regulations. For example, the requirement in some countries that workers establish residence before receiving unemployment benefits makes it harder for unemployed workers to seek jobs in regions that are far from their current homes. Table 20-2 presents evidence on the frequency of regional labor movement in the largest EU countries, as compared with Japan and the United States. Although these data must be interpreted with caution because the definition of "region" differs from country to country, they do suggest that in a typical year Japanese and Americans were significantly more footloose than Europeans.[18]

Other Considerations

While the *GG-LL* model is useful for organizing our thinking about optimum currency areas, it is not the whole story. At least two other elements affect our evaluation of the euro currency area's past and prospective performance.

Similarity of Economic Structure. The *GG-LL* model tells us that extensive trade with the rest of the euro zone makes it easier for a member to adjust to output market disturbances that affect it and its currency partners differently. But it does not tell us what factors will reduce the frequency and size of member-specific product market shocks.

A key element in minimizing such disturbances is similarity in economic structure, especially in the types of products produced. Euro zone countries are not entirely dissimilar in manufacturing structure, as evidenced by the very high volume of *intraindustry trade*—trade in similar products—within Europe (see Chapter 6). There are also important differences, however: The countries of northern Europe are better endowed with capital and skilled labor than the countries

---

[17] See Eichengreen, "One Money for Europe? Lessons of the U.S. Currency Union," *Economic Policy* 10 (April 1990), pp. 118–166. Further study of the U.S. labor market has shown that regional unemployment is eliminated almost entirely by worker migration rather than by changes in regional real wages. This pattern of labor market adjustment is unlikely to be possible in Europe in the near future. See Olivier Jean Blanchard and Lawrence F. Katz, "Regional Evolutions," *Brookings Papers on Economic Activity* 1:1992, pp. 1–75.

[18] For a more detailed discussion of the evidence, see Maurice Obstfeld and Giovanni Peri, "Regional Non-Adjustment and Fiscal Policy," *Economic Policy* 26 (April 1998), pp. 205–259.

HOW MUCH TRADE DO CURRENCY UNIONS CREATE?

Econometric studies seeking to estimate the effects of exchange rate volatility on trade have generally proven inconclusive. EMU is much more, however, than a fixed exchange rate system. It is a true *currency union* in which all members share a single money issued by a single central bank. Thus, it is not clear at all that the sole effect of EMU on international trade is that of reduced exchange rate volatility. In addition, the possibilities of devaluation, revaluation, and exchange controls are eliminated forever; foreign exchange transaction costs are eliminated; there is a union-wide low-cost system for making payments in the different countries; and price comparisons in different countries are absolutely transparent. In principle, therefore, currency unions such as EMU might have large positive effects on trade among members even if the effects of reduced exchange-rate volatility alone are much weaker.

Andrew Rose of the University of California, Berkeley, set out to test this hypothesis, using 1970–1990 data on 186 countries, dependencies, territories, and colonies. One main innovation in his approach was to study the average effects of currency union not only across time but across different countries. The other was to correct his estimates for determinants of trade other than currency union—including incomes, distance between trading partners, membership in free-trade arrangements, and so on.*

The findings were unexpectedly favorable to the hypothesis that currency unions promote trade. Rose found that on average, two countries that are members of the same currency union trade *three*

times as much with each other as countries that do not share a currency. This is a remarkably big trade-creating effect. Rose also finds significant trade-creating effects of reduced exchange-rate volatility even when it occurs without currency union, but those effects are much smaller than those of currency union.

Rose's results have not gone unchallenged. For example, it could be that countries that have substantial mutual trade for reasons unrelated to monetary arrangements are more likely to form currency unions. In Rose's pre-EMU sample, moreover, there are very few examples of currency union—slightly less than 1 percent of his total observations. And most of these cases involve tiny countries. Thus, it is not clear that the findings can accurately predict the effects of currency union on the members of EMU, most of whom are fairly large. One relevant case study that is available concerns the dissolution of the more than half-century old Anglo-Irish currency link in 1979, when Ireland joined the EMS and therefore had to decouple its currency from Britain's pound sterling. (Recall Britain remained outside the EMS until its brief and ill-fated membership in the early 1990s.) Trade between Ireland and Britain has not suffered greatly.†

Rose anticipates some of these criticisms in his paper and tries to meet them. In any case, as he points out, even if the euro were to raise trade within the euro zone by 50 percent (rather than by the 200 percent his estimates imply), the positive effect on people's welfare could be immense.‡ Time will tell if the implications of Rose's study are borne out in Europe.

---

* Andrew K. Rose, "One Money, One Market: The Effect of Common Currencies on Trade," *Economic Policy* 30 (April 2000), pp. 8–45.

† See Rodney Thom and Brendan Walsh, "The Effect of a Common Currency on Trade: Ireland before and after the Sterling Link," *European Economic Review* 46 (June 2002).

‡ Indeed, a later sudy by Rose and Eric van Wincoop of the University of Virginia suggests that the true effect of the euro will be closer to a 50 percent increase in intra-European trade. See "National Money as a Barrier to International Trade: The Real Case for Currency Union," *American Economic Review* 91 (May 2001), pp. 386–390. This estimated trade-creating effect is smaller than the one Rose found in his original work because Rose and van Wincoop use a more sophisticated model of international trade patterns.

in Europe's South, and EU products that make intensive use of low-skill labor thus are likely to come from Portugal, Spain, Greece, or southern Italy. It is not yet clear whether completion of the single European market will remove these differences by redistributing capital and labor across Europe or increase them by encouraging regional specialization to exploit economies of scale in production.

The first years of the euro were characterized by quite different growth performance among the EMU members. The European Central Bank's monetary policy stance probably was not appropriate for all. One result was some divergence in inflation rates. Figure 20-9 shows the difference between the twelve-month inflation rates in Ireland and the Netherlands and the average of the three lowest national inflation rates in the euro zone. Both Ireland and the Netherlands had more rapid growth than the euro zone average, and as a result, the ECB's policies led to higher inflation there. Indeed, both countries breached the inflation convergence criterion (criterion 1 on p. 614) that had qualified them for admission to EMU!

Fiscal Federalism.   Another consideration in evaluating the euro zone is the European Union's ability to transfer economic resources from members with healthy economies to those suffering economic setbacks. In the United States, for example, states faring poorly relative to the rest of the nation automatically receive support from Washington in the form of welfare benefits and other federal transfer payments that ultimately come out of the taxes other states pay. Such **fiscal federalism** can help offset the economic stability loss due to fixed exchange rates, as it does in the United States. Unfortunately, its limited taxation powers allow the European Union to practice fiscal federalism only on a very small scale.

Summing Up

How should we judge Europe in light of the theory of optimum currency areas? On balance, there is little evidence that Europe's product and factor markets are sufficiently unified yet to make it an optimum currency area. Trade with EU partners typically is still less than a quarter of each member's GNP, and while capital moves with little interference, labor mobility is nowhere near the high level countries would need to adjust smoothly to product market disturbances through labor migration. There *is* evidence that national financial markets have become better integrated with each other as a result of the euro.

The "1992" drive toward economic liberalization may have moved the European Union closer to being an optimum currency area in some respects, but it has done very little to promote labor mobility within Europe. Because labor income makes up around two-thirds of GNP in the European Union and the hardships of unemployment are so severe, the low labor mobility between and within EU countries implies that the economic stability loss from euro zone membership could be high. Evidence such losses may turn out to be costly indeed is provided by the persistently high unemployment rates in some euro zone countries (see Table 19-2).

The European Union's current combination of rapid capital migration with limited labor migration may actually *raise* the cost of adjusting to product market shocks without exchange rate changes. If the Netherlands suffers an unfavorable shift in output demand, for example, Dutch capital can flee abroad, leaving even more unemployed Dutch workers behind than if government regulations were to bottle the capital up within national borders. Severe and persistent regional depressions could result, worsened by the likelihood that the relatively few workers who did successfully emigrate would be precisely those who are most skilled, reliable,

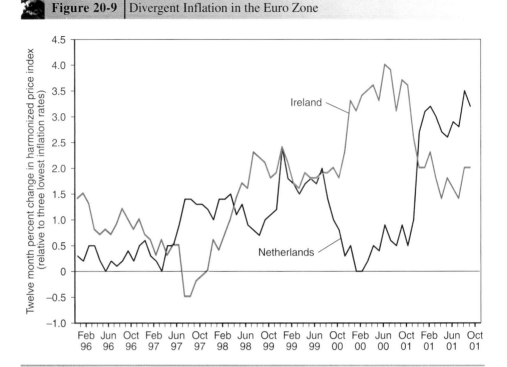

Figure 20-9 | Divergent Inflation in the Euro Zone

In 1997 Ireland and the Netherlands both had inflation rates no more than 1.5 percent above the average of the three lowest EU inflation rates. Subsequently, however, both countries violated that norm, which is one of the Maastricht Treaty's tests for admission to the euro club.

and enterprising. Given that labor remains relatively immobile within Europe, the European Union's success in liberalizing its capital flows may have worked perversely to worsen the economic stability loss due to the process of monetary unification. This possibility is another example of the *theory of the second best* (Chapter 9), which implies that liberalization of one market (the capital market) can reduce the efficiency of EU economies if another market (the labor market) continues to function poorly.

The Future of EMU

Europe's single currency experiment is the boldest attempt ever to reap the efficiency gains from using a single currency over a large and diverse group of sovereign states. If EMU succeeds, it will promote European political as well as economic integration, fostering peace and prosperity in a region that could someday include eastern Europe. If EMU fails, however, its driving force, the goal of European political unification, will be set back.

What problems will EMU face in the coming years? There are several, some of which we have already discussed:

1. Europe is not an optimum currency area. Therefore, asymmetric economic developments within different countries of the euro zone—developments that might well call for different national interest rates under a regime of individual national currencies—will be hard to handle through monetary policy. Even as the euro's launch was being prepared at the end of 1998, for example, Germany's economy was experiencing negative growth rates while those of Spain, Portugal, and Ireland were growing at healthy rates. Since the national governments within the EU until recently have been accustomed to having full sovereignty over national economic policies, such macroeconomic asymmetries are likely to lead to political pressures on the ECB much stronger than the ones that typically emerge in long-standing political unions such as the United States.

2. A related potential problem is that the single currency project has taken economic union to a level far beyond what the EU has been able (or willing) to do in the area of political union. European economic unification has a centralized power (the ECB) and a tangible expression in the euro; the political counterparts are much weaker. Many Europeans hope that economic union will lead to closer political union, but it is also possible that quarrels over economic policies will sabotage that aim. Furthermore, the lack of a strong EU political center may limit the ECB's political legitimacy in the eyes of the European public. There is a danger that voters throughout Europe will come to view the ECB as a distant and politically unaccountable group of technocrats unresponsive to people's needs. The Bundesbank became a venerated and powerful institution within Germany because of its track record in delivering price stability and its constant efforts to remind the German public about the dangers of inflation. The ECB began its life with no track record at all—and facing a European public less scarred than the Germans by an inflationary past.

3. In most of the larger EU countries, labor markets remain highly unionized and subject to high government employment taxes and other regulations that impede labor mobility between industries and regions. The result has been persistently high levels of unemployment. Unless labor markets become much more flexible, as in the United States currency union, individual euro zone countries will have a difficult time adjusting to economic shocks. Advocates of the euro have argued that the single currency, by removing the possibility of intra-EMU currency realignments, will impose discipline on workers' wage demands and speed the reallocation of labor within national economies. It is equally plausible, however, that workers in different euro zone countries will press for wage harmonization to reduce the very high incentive of capital to migrate to the EMU countries with lowest wages.

4. Constraints on national fiscal policy due to the Stability and Growth Pact (SGP) are likely to be especially painful due to the absence of substantial fiscal federalism within the EU. It remains to be seen if the SGP will be strictly enforced, and if the EU will develop more elaborate institutions for carrying out fiscal transfers from country to country within the euro zone. In the run-up to 1998, EU countries made heroic efforts to squeeze their government budget deficits within the 3 percent of GDP limit set by the Maastricht Treaty. Some euro zone countries may still run afoul of the SGP, however, because their apparent fiscal cuts in many cases involved one-time measures or "creative accounting." All of these countries must carry out further fiscal restructuring, in any event, to avoid huge government deficits in the future. Unfortunately the SGP, unless it is loosely enforced, may require the most severe restructuring during recessions, when the contractionary effects would be most damaging.

5. The EU is considering a large-scale expansion of its membership into eastern Europe and the Mediterranean. That plan raises numerous far-reaching challenges for the EU, but some of them have obvious implications for the EMU project. For example, the ESCB's governing council, where every euro-zone member country has a representative and a vote, would become very unwieldy with twice as many national governors present. Agreement must be reached on some scheme of rotating representation, yet it is hard to imagine Germany, for example, ceding its seat, even temporarily, to tiny countries like Latvia and Cyprus. As more countries enter the euro zone the possibility of asymmetric economic shocks will rise, so countries may become less rather than more willing to delegate their votes to regional representatives.

Thus, EMU faces significant challenges in the years ahead. The experience of the United States shows that a large monetary union comprising diverse economic regions can work quite well. For EMU to achieve comparable economic success, however, it will have to make progress in creating a flexible EU-wide labor market, in reforming its fiscal systems, and in deepening its political union. European unification itself will be imperiled unless EMU and its defining institution, the ECB, succeed in delivering prosperity as well as price stability.

Summary

1. European Union countries have had two main reasons for favoring mutually fixed exchange rates: They believe monetary cooperation will give them a heavier weight in international economic negotiations, and they view fixed exchange rates as a complement to EU initiatives aimed at building a common European market.

2. The *European Monetary System* of fixed intra-EU exchange rates was inaugurated in March 1979 and originally included Belgium, Denmark, France, Germany, Ireland, Italy, Luxembourg, and the Netherlands. Austria, Britain, Portugal, and Spain joined much later. Capital controls and frequent realignments were essential ingredients in maintaining the system until the mid-1980s, but since then controls have been abolished as part of the European Union's wider "1992" program of market unification. During the currency crisis that broke out in September 1992, Britain and Italy allowed their currencies to float. In August 1993 most EMS currency bands were widened to ± 15 percent in the face of continuing speculative attacks.

3. In practice all EMS currencies were pegged to the DM. As a result Germany was able to set monetary policy for the EMS, just as the United States did in the Bretton Woods system. The *credibility theory of the EMS* holds that participating governments profited from the German Bundesbank's reputation as an inflation fighter when they pegged their currencies to the DM. In fact, inflation rates in EMS countries ultimately tended to converge around Germany's generally low inflation rate. Critics of Germany charge, however, that on occasion it abused its dominant position by neglecting the effects its policies had on other EMS countries.

4. On January 1, 1999, eleven EU countries initiated an *economic and monetary union (EMU)* by adopting a common currency, the euro, issued by a European System of Central Banks (ESCB). (The initial eleven members were joined by Greece two years later.) The ESCB consists of EU members' national central banks and a European Central Bank, headquartered in Frankfurt, whose governing council runs monetary policy in EMU. The transition process from the EMS fixed exchange rate system to EMU was spelled out in the *Maastricht Treaty,* signed by European leaders in December 1991.

5. The Maastricht Treaty specified a set of macroeconomic convergence criteria that EU countries would need to satisfy to qualify for admission to EMU. A major purpose of the convergence criteria was to reassure voters in low-inflation countries such as Germany that the new, jointly managed European currency would be as resistant to inflation as the DM had been. A *Stability and Growth Pact (SPG),* devised by EU leaders in 1997 at Germany's insistence, may restrict the flexibility of EMU members to carry out fiscal policy at the national level. The SPG and EMU together could therefore deprive individual countries in the euro zone of national fiscal as well as monetary policy.

6. The theory of *optimum currency areas* implies that countries will wish to join fixed exchange rate areas closely linked to their own economies through trade and factor mobility. A country's decision to join an exchange rate area is determined by the difference between the *monetary efficiency gain* from joining and the *economic stability loss* from joining. The *GG-LL* diagram relates both of these factors to the degree of economic integration between the joining country and the larger fixed exchange rate zone. Only when economic integration passes a critical level is it beneficial to join.

7. The European Union does not appear to satisfy all of the criteria for an optimum currency area. Although 1992 removed many barriers to market integration within the European Union, intra-EU trade still is not very extensive. In addition, labor mobility between and even within EU countries appears more limited than within other large currency areas, such as the United States. Finally, the level of *fiscal federalism* in the European Union is too small to cushion member countries from adverse economic events.

Key Terms

credibility theory of the EMS, p. 609
economic and monetary union (EMU), p. 612
economic stability loss, p. 620
European Monetary System (EMS), p. 607
fiscal federalism, p. 629

Maastricht Treaty, p. 612
monetary efficiency gain, p. 618
optimum currency areas, p. 618
Stability and Growth Pact (SGP), p. 614

Problems

1. Why might EMS provisions for the extension of central bank credits from strong- to weak-currency members have increased the stability of EMS exchange rates?

2. In the EMS before September 1992 the lira/DM exchange rate could fluctuate by up to 2.25 percent up *or* down. Assume that the lira/DM central parity and band were set in this way and could not be changed. What would have been the maximum possible

difference between the interest rates on *one-year* lira and DM deposits? What would have been the maximum possible difference between the interest rates on *six-month* lira and DM deposits? On three-month deposits? Do the answers surprise you? Give an intuitive explanation.

3. Continue with the last question. Imagine that in Italy the interest rate on five-year government bonds was 11 percent per annum; in Germany the rate on five-year government bonds was 8 percent per annum. What would have been the implications for the credibility of the current lira/DM exchange parity?

4. Do your answers to the last two questions require an assumption that interest rates and expected exchange rate changes are linked by interest parity? Why or why not?

5. Norway pegs to the euro, but soon after, EMU benefits from a favorable shift in the world demand for non-Norwegian EMU exports. What happens to the exchange rate of the Norwegian krone against non-euro currencies? How is Norway affected? How does the size of this effect depend on the volume of trade between Norway and the euro zone economies?

6. Use the *GG-LL* diagram to show how an increase in the size and frequency of unexpected shifts in a country's money demand function affects the level of economic integration with a currency area at which the country will wish to join.

7. During the speculative pressure on the EMS exchange rate mechanism (ERM) shortly before Britain allowed the pound to float in September 1992, the *Economist,* a London weekly news magazine, opined as follows:

> The [British] government's critics want lower interest rates, and think this would be possible if Britain devalued sterling, leaving the ERM if necessary. They are wrong. Quitting the ERM would soon lead to higher, not lower, interest rates, as British economic management lost the degree of credibility already won through ERM membership. Two years ago British government bonds yielded three percentage points more than German ones. Today the gap is half a point, reflecting investors' belief that British inflation is on its way down—permanently. (See "Crisis? What Crisis?" *Economist,* August 29, 1992, p. 51.)

   a. Why might the British government's critics have thought it possible to lower interest rates after taking sterling out of the ERM? (Britain was in a deep recession at the time the article appeared.)

   b. Why did the *Economist* think the opposite would occur soon after Britain exited the ERM?

   c. In what way might ERM membership have gained credibility for British policymakers? (Britain entered the ERM in October 1990.)

   d. Why would a high level of British nominal interest rates relative to German rates have suggested an expectation of high future British inflation? Can you think of other explanations?

   e. Suggest two reasons why British interest rates might have been somewhat higher than German rates at the time of writing, despite the alleged "belief that British inflation is on its way down—permanently."

8. Imagine that the EMS became a monetary union with a single currency but that it created no European Central Bank to manage this currency. Instead, imagine that the task was left to the various national central banks, each of which was allowed to issue

as much of the European currency as it liked and to conduct open-market operations. What problems can you foresee arising from such a scheme?

9. Why would the failure to create a unified EU labor market be particularly harmful to the prospects for a smoothly functioning EMU?

Further Reading

Tamim Bayoumi. "A Formal Model of Optimum Currency Areas." *International Monetary Fund Staff Papers* 41 (December 1994), pp. 537–554. Provides a new model and welfare analysis of optimum currency areas.

Charles R. Bean. "Economic and Monetary Union in Europe." *Journal of Economic Perspectives* 6 (Fall 1992), pp. 31–52. Overview of the debate over European monetary unification, written just before the currency crisis in the autumn of 1992.

W. Max Corden. *Monetary Integration.* Princeton Essays in International Finance 32. International Finance Section, Department of Economics, Princeton University, April 1972. Classic analysis of monetary unification.

Barry Eichengreen and Charles Wyplosz. "The Stability Pact: More Than a Minor Nuisance?" *Economic Policy* 26 (April 1998), pp. 65–113. A thorough critique and analysis of the Stability and Growth Pact.

Martin Feldstein. "The Political Economy of the European Economic and Monetary Union: Political Sources of an Economic Liability." *Journal of Economic Perspectives* 11 (Fall 1997), pp. 23–42. A leading American economist makes the case against EMU.

Francesco Giavazzi and Alberto Giovannini. *Limiting Exchange Rate Flexibility: The European Monetary System.* Cambridge, MA: MIT Press, 1989. A comprehensive and fascinating account of EMS institutions and experience.

Peter B. Kenen. *Economic and Monetary Union in Europe.* Cambridge, U.K.: Cambridge University Press, 1995. A thorough economic analysis of the Maastricht Treaty's vision of EMU and of practical difficulties in the transition to EMU.

Jay H. Levin. *A Guide to the Euro.* Boston: Houghton Mifflin, 2000. Concise but thorough survey of European monetary unification.

Swedish Economic Policy Review 4 (Spring 1997, Autumn 1997). Two issues of this journal are entirely devoted to analyses of various aspects of EMU. The papers provided background for Sweden's decision not to seek EMU entry with the first round of participants.

Edward Tower and Thomas D. Willett. *The Theory of Optimal Currency Areas and Exchange Rate Flexibility.* Princeton Special Papers in International Economics 11. International Finance Section, Department of Economics, Princeton University, May 1976. Surveys the theory of optimum currency areas.

CHAPTER 21

The Global Capital
Market: Performance
and Policy Problems

I f a financier named Rip van Winkle had gone to sleep in the early 1960s and awakened three decades later, he would have been shocked by changes in both the nature and the scale of international financial activity. In the early 1960s, for example, most banking business was purely domestic, involving the currency and customers of the bank's home country. Two decades later many banks were deriving a large share of their profits from international activities. To his surprise, Rip would have found that he could locate branches of Citibank in São Paulo, Brazil, and branches of Britain's National Westminster Bank in New York. He would also have discovered that by the early 1980s, it had become routine for a branch of an American bank located in London to accept a deposit denominated in Japanese yen from a Swedish corporation, or to lend Swiss francs to a Dutch manufacturer.

The market in which residents of different countries trade assets is called the **international capital market**. The international capital market is not really a single market; it is a group of closely interconnected markets in which asset exchanges with some international dimension take place. International currency trades take place in the foreign exchange market, which is an important part of the international capital market. The main actors in the international capital market are the same as those in the foreign exchange market (Chapter 13): commercial banks, large corporations, nonbank financial institutions, central banks, and other government agencies. And, like the foreign exchange market, the international capital market's activities take place in a network of world financial centers linked by sophisticated communications systems. The assets traded in the international capital market, however, include different countries' stocks and bonds in addition to bank deposits denominated in their currencies.

This chapter discusses three main questions about the international capital market. First, how has this well-oiled global financial network enhanced countries' gains from international trade? Second, what caused the rapid growth in international financial activity that has occurred since the early 1960s? And third, how can policymakers minimize problems raised by a worldwide capital market without sharply reducing the benefits it provides?

The International Capital Market and the Gains from Trade

In earlier chapters, the discussion of gains from international trade concentrated on exchanges involving goods and services. By providing a worldwide payments system that lowers transaction costs, banks active in the international capital market enlarge the trade gains that result from such exchanges. But most deals that take place in the international capital market result in exchanges of assets between residents of different countries, for example, the exchange of a share of IBM stock for some British government bonds. Although such asset trades are sometimes derided as unproductive "speculation," they do, in fact, lead to gains from trade that can make consumers everywhere better off.

Three Types of Gain from Trade

All transactions between the residents of different countries fall into one of three categories: trades of goods or services for goods or services, trades of goods or services for assets, and trades of assets for assets. At any moment, a country is generally carrying out trades in each of these categories. Figure 21-1 (which assumes that there are two countries, Home and Foreign) illustrates the three types of international transaction, each of which involves a different set of possible gains from trade.

So far in this book we have discussed two types of trade gain. Chapters 2 through 6 showed that countries can gain by concentrating on the production activities in which they are most efficient and using some of their output to pay for imports of other products from abroad. This type of trade gain involves the exchange of goods or services for other goods or services. The top horizontal arrow in Figure 21-1 shows exchanges of goods and services between Home and Foreign.

A second set of trade gains results from *intertemporal* trade, which is the exchange of goods and services for claims to future goods and services, that is, for assets (Chapters 7 and 18). When a developing country borrows abroad (that is, sells a bond to foreigners) so that it can import materials for a domestic investment project, it is engaging in intertemporal trade. The borrowing country gains from this trade because it can carry out a project that it could not easily finance out of its domestic savings alone; the lending country gains because it gets an asset that yields a higher return than is available at home. The diagonal arrows in Figure 21-1 indicate trades of goods and services for assets. If Home has a current account deficit with Foreign, for example, it is a net exporter of assets to Foreign and a net importer of goods and services from Foreign.

The bottom horizontal arrow in Figure 21-1 represents the last category of international transaction, trades of assets for assets, such as the exchange of real estate located in France for U.S. Treasury bonds. In Table 12-2, which shows the year 2000 U.S. balance of payments accounts, you will see under the financial account both a $553.3 billion purchase of foreign assets by U.S. residents (a financial outflow) and a $952.4 billion purchase of U.S. assets by foreign residents (a financial inflow). So while the United States could have financed its $435.4 billion current account deficit for 2000 simply by selling to foreigners $435.4 billion worth of assets, U.S. and foreign residents also engaged in a considerable volume of pure asset swapping. Such a large volume of trade in assets between countries occurs because international asset trades, like trades involving goods and services, can yield benefits to all the countries involved.

Figure 21-1 | The Three Types of International Transaction

Residents of different countries can trade goods and services for other goods and services, goods and services for assets (that is, for future goods and services), and assets for other assets. All three types of exchange lead to gains from trade.

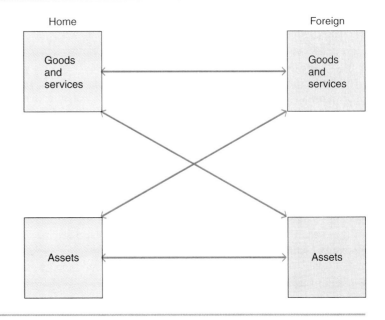

Risk Aversion

When individuals select assets, an important factor in their decisions is the riskiness of each asset's return (Chapter 13). Other things equal, people dislike risk. Economists call this property of peoples' preferences **risk aversion**. Chapter 17 showed that risk-averse investors in foreign currency assets base their demand for a particular asset on its riskiness (as measured by a risk premium) in addition to its expected return.

An example will make the meaning of risk aversion clearer. Suppose you are offered a gamble in which you win $1000 half the time but lose $1000 half the time. Since you are as likely to win as to lose the $1000, the average payoff on this gamble—its *expected value*— is $(\frac{1}{2}) \times (\$1000) + (\frac{1}{2}) \times (-\$1000) = 0$. If you are risk averse, you will not take the gamble because, for you, the possibility of losing $1000 outweighs the possibility that you will win, even though both outcomes are equally likely. Although some people (called risk lovers) enjoy taking risks and would take the gamble, there is much evidence that risk-averse behavior is the norm. For example, risk aversion helps explain the profitability of insurance companies, which sell policies that allow people to protect themselves or their families from the financial risks of theft, illness, and other mishaps.

If people are risk averse, they value a collection (or portfolio) of assets not only on the basis of its expected return but also on the basis of the riskiness of that return. Under risk aversion, for example, people may be willing to hold bonds denominated in several different currencies, even if the interest rates they offer are not linked by the interest parity condition, if the resulting portfolio of assets offers a desirable combination of return and risk.

In general, a portfolio whose return fluctuates wildly from year to year is less desirable than one that offers the same average return with only mild year-to-year fluctuations. This observation is basic to understanding why countries exchange assets.

Portfolio Diversification as a Motive for International Asset Trade

International trade in assets can make both parties to the trade better off by allowing them to reduce the riskiness of the return on their wealth. Trade accomplishes this reduction in risk by allowing both parties to diversify their portfolios—to divide their wealth among a wider spectrum of assets and thus reduce the amount of money they have riding on each individual asset. The late economist James Tobin of Yale University, an originator of the theory of portfolio choice with risk aversion, once described the idea of **portfolio diversification** as: "Don't put all your eggs in one basket." When an economy is opened to the international capital market, it can reduce the riskiness of its wealth by placing some of its "eggs" in additional foreign "baskets." This reduction in risk is the basic motive for asset trade.

A simple two-country example illustrates how countries are made better off by trade in assets. Imagine that there are two countries, Home and Foreign, and that residents of each own only one asset, domestic land yielding an annual harvest of kiwi fruit.

The yield of the land is uncertain, however. Half the time, Home's land yields a harvest of 100 tons of kiwi fruit at the same time as Foreign's land yields a harvest of 50 tons. The other half the time the outcomes are reversed: The Foreign harvest is 100 tons, but the Home harvest is only 50. On average, then, each country has a harvest of $(\frac{1}{2}) \times (100) + (\frac{1}{2}) \times (50) = 75$ tons of kiwi fruit, but its inhabitants never know whether the next year will bring feast or famine.

Now suppose the two countries can trade shares in the ownership of their respective assets. A Home owner of a 10 percent share in Foreign land, for example, receives 10 percent of the annual Foreign kiwi fruit harvest, and a Foreign owner of a 10 percent share in Home land is similarly entitled to 10 percent of the Home harvest. What happens if international trade in these two assets is allowed? Home residents will buy a 50 percent share of Foreign land, and they will pay for it by giving Foreign residents a 50 percent share in Home land.

To understand why this is the outcome, think about the returns to the Home and Foreign portfolios when both are equally divided between titles to Home and Foreign land. When times are good in Home (and therefore bad in Foreign), each country earns the same return on its portfolio: half of the Home harvest (100 tons of kiwi fruit) plus half of the Foreign harvest (50 tons of kiwi fruit), or 75 tons of fruit. In the opposite case—bad times in Home, good times in Foreign—each country *still* earns 75 tons of fruit. If the countries hold portfolios equally divided between the two assets, therefore, each country earns a *certain* return of 75 tons of fruit—the same as the average harvest each faced before international asset trade was allowed.

Since the two available assets—Home and Foreign land—have the same return on average, any portfolio consisting of those assets yields an expected (or average) return of 75 tons of fruit. Since people everywhere are risk averse, however, all prefer to hold the 50-50 portfolio described above, which gives a sure return of 75 tons of fruit every year. After trade is opened, therefore, residents of the two counties will swap titles to land until the 50-50 outcome is reached. Because this trade eliminates the risk faced by both countries without changing average returns, both countries are clearly better off as a result of asset trade.

The above example is oversimplified because countries can never really eliminate *all* risk through international asset trade. (Unlike the model's world, the real world is a risky place even in the aggregate!) The example does demonstrate that countries can nonetheless *reduce* the riskiness of their wealth by diversifying their asset portfolios internationally. A major function of the international capital market is to make this diversification possible.[1]

The Menu of International Assets: Debt Versus Equity

International asset trades can be exchanges of many different types of assets. Among the many assets traded in the international capital market are bonds and deposits denominated in different currencies, shares of stock, and more complicated financial instruments such as stock or currency options. A purchase of foreign real estate and the direct acquisition of a factory in another country are other ways of diversifying abroad.

In thinking about asset trades it is frequently useful to make a distinction between **debt instruments** and **equity instruments**. Bonds and bank deposits are debt instruments, since they specify that the issuer of the instrument must repay a fixed value (the sum of principal plus interest) regardless of economic circumstances. In contrast, a share of stock is an equity instrument: It is a claim to a firm's profits, rather than to a fixed payment, and its payoff will vary according to circumstance. Similarly, the kiwi fruit shares traded in our example are equity instruments. By choosing how to divide their portfolios between debt and equity instruments, individuals and nations can arrange to stay close to desired consumption and investment levels despite the different eventualities that could occur.

The dividing line between debt and equity is not a neat one in practice. Even if an instrument's money payout is the same in different states of the world, its *real* payout in a particular state will depend on national price levels and exchange rates. In addition, the payments that a given instrument promises to make may not occur in cases of bankruptcy, government seizure of foreign-owned assets, and so on. Assets like low-grade corporate bonds, which superficially appear to be debt, may in reality be like equity in offering payoffs that depend on the doubtful financial fortunes of the issuer. The same has turned out to be true of the debt of many developing countries, as we will see in Chapter 22.

International Banking and the International Capital Market

The Home-Foreign kiwi fruit example above portrayed an imaginary world with only two assets. Since the number of assets available in the real world is enormous, specialized institutions have sprung up to bring together buyers and sellers of assets located in different countries.

---

[1]The Mathematical Postscript to this chapter develops a detailed model of international portfolio diversification. You may have noticed that in our example, countries could reduce risk through transactions other than the asset swap we have described. The high-output country could run a current account surplus and lend to the low-output country, for example, thereby partially evening out the cross-country consumption difference in every state of the world economy. The economic functions of intertemporal trades and of pure asset swaps thus can overlap. To some extent, trade over time can substitute for trade across states of nature, and vice versa, simply because different economic states of the world occur at different points in time. But, in general, the two types of trade are not perfect substitutes for each other.

The Structure of the International Capital Market

As we noted above, the main actors in the international capital market include commercial banks, corporations, nonbank financial institutions (such as insurance companies and pension funds), central banks, and other government agencies.

1. *Commercial banks.* Commercial banks are at the center of the international capital market, not only because they run the international payments mechanism but because of the broad range of financial activities they undertake. Bank liabilities consist chiefly of deposits of various maturities, while their assets consist largely of loans (to corporations and governments), deposits at other banks (interbank deposits), and bonds. Multinational banks are also heavily involved in other types of asset transaction. For example, banks may *underwrite* issues of corporate stocks and bonds by agreeing, for a fee, to find buyers for those securities at a guaranteed price. One of the key facts about international banking is that banks are often free to pursue activities abroad that they would not be allowed to pursue in their home countries. This type of regulatory asymmetry has spurred the growth of international banking over the last 40 years.

2. *Corporations.* Corporations—particularly those with multinational operations—routinely finance their investments by drawing on foreign sources of funds. To obtain these funds, corporations may sell shares of stock, which give owners an equity claim to the corporation's assets, or they may use debt finance. Debt finance often takes the form of borrowing from and through international banks or other institutional lenders; when longer-term borrowing is desired, firms may sell corporate debt instruments in the international capital market. Corporations frequently denominate their bonds in the currency of the financial center in which the bonds are being offered for sale. Increasingly, however, corporations have been pursuing novel denomination strategies that make their bonds attractive to a wider spectrum of potential buyers.

3. *Nonbank financial institutions.* Nonbank institutions such as insurance companies, pension funds, and mutual funds have become important players in the international capital market as they have moved into foreign assets to diversify their portfolios. Of particular importance are *investment banks* such as First Boston Corporation, Goldman Sachs, and Lazard Frères, which are not banks at all but specialize in underwriting sales of stocks and bonds by corporations and (in some cases) governments. In 1933 U.S. commercial banks were barred from investment banking activity within the United States (and from most other domestic transactions involving corporate stocks and bonds), although the U.S. government is in the process of easing some of these barriers. But U.S. commercial banks have long been allowed to participate in investment banking activities overseas, and such banks as Citicorp, Morgan Guaranty, and Bankers Trust have competed vigorously with the more specialized investment banks. Figure 21-2 shows how an international consortium of underwriters announced a tobacco company's issue of euro-denominated bonds.

4. *Central banks and other government agencies.* Central banks are routinely involved in the international financial markets through foreign exchange intervention. In addition, other government agencies frequently borrow abroad. Developing country governments and state-owned enterprises have borrowed substantially from foreign commercial banks. Even the governments of some Eastern European countries such as

Figure 21-2 | Borrowing in the International Capital Market

This announcement appears as a matter of record only.

BRITISH AMERICAN TOBACCO

B.A.T. International Finance p.l.c.

€1.7 billion
4.875% Eurobonds due 2009

Guaranteed by British American Tobacco p.l.c.

Issued under US$3,000,000,000
Euro Medium Term Note Programme

Sole Bookrunner and Joint Lead Manager

Dresdner Kleinwort Benson

Joint Lead Managers

Banque Nationale de Paris   **HSBC Markets**

Senior Co-Lead Manager

SG Investment Banking

Co-Lead Managers

ABN AMRO   **Banco Central Hispano**

Morgan Stanley Dean Witter   **Salomon Smith Barney International**

Sumitomo Finance International plc

February 1999

In 1999 a consortium of international underwriters helped a tobacco company issue euro-denominated bonds.

Source: *Financial Times*, March 3, 1999. Used with permission of Dresdner Kleinwort Benson.

Poland and Hungary, which once had communist regimes, are heavily indebted to Western capitalist bankers.

Growth of the International Capital Market

On any measure, the scale of transactions in the international capital market has grown more quickly than world GDP since the early 1970s. One major factor in this development is that countries, starting with countries in the industrial world, have progressively dismantled barriers to private capital flows across their borders.

An important reason for that development is related to exchange rate systems. We saw in Chapter 17 that a country that fixes its currency's exchange rate while allowing international capital movements gives up control over domestic monetary policy. This sacrifice shows the impossibility of a country's having more than two items from the following list:

1. Fixed exchange rate.
2. Monetary policy oriented toward domestic goals.
3. Freedom of international capital movements.

The result is a "trilemma" for policy regimes—*tri*lemma rather than *di*lemma because the available options are three: 1 and 2, 1 and 3, or 2 and 3. Under the gold standard (Chapter 18), for example, countries gave up monetary policy in favor of fixed exchange rates and freedom of international payments, opting for a monetary system based on 1 and 3 from the preceding list.

When industrialized countries gave up fixed exchange rates at the end of the Bretton Woods period, they chose a system that allowed them to combine international capital mobility with a domestically oriented monetary policy. As a result, they had leeway to allow greater freedom of international asset trade. The countries of the European economic and monetary union have followed a different route with respect to their mutual exchange rates. By vesting monetary policy in a common central bank, they have given up 2 above while embracing 1 and 3. However, the euro floats against foreign currencies and the euro zone as a unit orients its monetary policy toward internal macroeconomic goals while permitting freedom of cross-border payments.

Offshore Banking and Offshore Currency Trading

One of the most pervasive features of the commercial banking industry in the 1990s is that banking activities have become globalized as banks have branched out from their home countries into foreign financial centers. In 1960 only eight American banks had branches in foreign countries, but now hundreds have such branches. Similarly, the number of foreign bank offices in the United States has risen steadily.

The term **offshore banking** is used to describe the business that banks' foreign offices conduct outside of their home countries. Banks may conduct foreign business through any of three types of institution:

1. An *agency* office located abroad, which arranges loans and transfers funds but does not accept deposits.
2. A *subsidiary* bank located abroad. A subsidiary of a foreign bank differs from a local bank only in that a foreign bank is the controlling owner. Subsidiaries are subject to

the same regulations as local banks but are not subject to the regulations of the parent bank's country.

3. A foreign *branch,* which is simply an office of the home bank in another country. Branches carry out the same business as local banks and are usually subject to local *and* home banking regulations. Often, however, branches can take advantage of cross-border regulatory differences.

The growth of **offshore currency trading** has gone hand in hand with that of offshore banking. An offshore deposit is simply a bank deposit denominated in a currency other than that of the country in which the bank resides—for example, yen deposits in a London bank or dollar deposits in Zurich. Many of the deposits traded in the foreign exchange market are offshore deposits. Offshore currency deposits are usually referred to as **Eurocurrencies**, something of a misnomer since much Eurocurrency trading occurs in such non-European centers as Singapore and Hong Kong. Dollar deposits located outside the United States are called **Eurodollars**. Banks that accept deposits denominated in Eurocurrencies (including Eurodollars) are called **Eurobanks**. The advent of the new European currency, the euro, has made this terminology even more confusing!

One motivation for the rapid growth of offshore banking and currency trading has been the growth of international trade and the increasingly multinational nature of corporate activity. American firms engaged in international trade, for example, require overseas financial services, and American banks have naturally expanded their domestic business with these firms into foreign areas. By offering more rapid clearing of payments and the flexibility and trust established in previous dealings, American banks compete with the foreign banks that could also serve American customers. Eurocurrency trading is another natural outgrowth of expanding world trade in goods and services. British importers of American goods frequently need to hold dollar deposits, for example, and it is natural for banks based in London to woo their business.

World trade growth alone, however, cannot explain the growth of international banking since the 1960s. Several other factors have driven the rapid expansion of international banking beyond what would be required by the growth of world trade. One factor is the banks' desire to escape domestic government regulations on financial activity (and sometimes taxes) by shifting some of their operations abroad and into foreign currencies. A second factor is in part political: the desire by some depositors to hold currencies outside the jurisdictions of the countries that issue them. In recent years, the tendency for countries to open their financial markets to foreigners has allowed international banks to compete globally for new business.

The Growth of Eurocurrency Trading

The growth of Eurocurrency trading illustrates the importance of all these factors in the internationalization of banking.

Eurodollars were born in the late 1950s, a response to the needs generated by a growing volume of international trade. European firms involved in trade frequently wished to hold dollar balances or to borrow dollars. In many cases, banks located in the United States could have served these needs, but Europeans often found it cheaper and more convenient to deal with local banks familiar with their circumstances. As currencies other than the dollar became increasingly convertible after the late 1950s, offshore markets for them sprang up also.

While the convenience of dealing with local banks was a key factor inspiring the invention of Eurodollars, the growth of Eurodollar trading was encouraged at an early stage by both of the two other factors we have mentioned: official regulations and political concerns.

In 1957, at the height of a balance of payments crisis, the British government prohibited British banks from lending pounds to finance non-British trade. This lending had been a highly profitable business, and to avoid losing it British banks began financing the same trade by attracting dollar deposits and lending dollars instead of pounds. Because stringent financial regulations prevented the British banks' nonsterling transactions from affecting Britain's domestic asset markets, the government was willing to take a laissez-faire attitude toward foreign currency activities. As a result, London became—and has remained—the leading center of Eurocurrency trading.

The political factor stimulating the Eurodollar market's early growth was a surprising one—the Cold War between the United States and the U.S.S.R. During the 1950s the Soviet Union acquired dollars (largely through sales of gold and other raw materials) so that it could purchase goods such as grains from the West. The Soviets feared the United States might confiscate dollars placed in American banks if the Cold War were to heat up. So instead, Soviet dollars were placed in European banks, which had the advantage of residing outside America's jurisdiction. Indeed, the folklore of international banking has it that the term *Eurobank* originated as the telex code of a Soviet-controlled Paris bank.

The Eurodollar system mushroomed in the 1960s as a result of new U.S. restrictions on capital outflows and U.S. banking regulations. As America's balance of payments weakened in the 1960s, the Kennedy and Johnson administrations imposed a series of measures to discourage American lending abroad. The first of these was the Interest Equalization Tax of 1963, which discouraged Americans from buying foreign assets by taxing those assets' returns. Next, in 1965, came "voluntary" guidelines on the amounts U.S. commercial banks could lend abroad, followed three years later by a set of wide-ranging mandatory controls. All these measures increased the demand for Eurodollar loans by making it harder for would-be dollar borrowers located abroad to obtain the funds they wanted in the United States.

Federal Reserve regulations on U.S. banks also encouraged the creation of Eurodollars—and new Eurobanks—in the 1960s. The Fed's Regulation Q (which was phased out after 1980) placed a ceiling on the interest rates U.S. banks could pay on time deposits. When U.S. monetary policy was tightened at the end of the 1960s to combat rising inflationary pressures (see Chapter 18), market interest rates were driven above the Regulation Q ceiling and American banks found it impossible to attract time deposits for relending. The banks got around the problem by borrowing funds from their European branches, which faced no restriction on the interest they could pay on Eurodollar deposits and were able to attract deposits from investors who might have placed their funds with U.S. banks in the absence of Regulation Q. Many American banks that had previously not had foreign branches established them in the late 1960s so that they could end-run Regulation Q.

With the move to floating exchange rates in 1973, the United States and other countries began to dismantle controls on capital flows across their borders, removing an important impetus to the growth of Eurocurrency markets in earlier years. But at that point, the political factor once again came into play in a big way. Arab members of OPEC accumulated vast wealth as a result of the oil shocks of 1973–1974 and 1979–1980 but were reluctant to place most of their money in American banks for fear of possible confiscation. Instead, these countries placed funds with Eurobanks. (In 1979 Iranian assets in U.S. banks and their European branches were frozen by President Carter in response to the taking of hostages at the American embassy in Teheran. A similar fate befell Iraq's U.S. assets after that country invaded neighboring Kuwait in 1990, and the assets of suspected terrorist organizations after the September 11, 2001 attacks on New York's World Trade Center and the Pentagon.)

The history of Eurocurrencies shows how the growth of world trade, financial regulations, and political considerations all helped form the present system. The major factor behind the continuing profitability of Eurocurrency trading is, however, regulatory: In formulating bank regulations, governments in the main Eurocurrency centers discriminate between deposits denominated in the home currency and those denominated in others and between transactions with domestic customers and those with foreign customers. Domestic currency deposits are heavily regulated as a way of maintaining control over the domestic money supply, while banks are given much more freedom in their dealings in foreign currencies. Domestic currency deposits held by foreign customers may receive special treatment, however, if regulators feel they can insulate the domestic financial system from shifts in foreigners' asset demands.

The example of U.S. *reserve requirements* shows how regulatory asymmetries can operate to enhance the profitability of Eurocurrency trading. Every time a U.S. bank operating onshore accepts a deposit, it must place some fraction of that deposit in a non-interest-bearing account at the Fed as part of its required reserves.[2] The British government imposes reserve requirements on *pound sterling* deposits within its borders, but it does not impose reserve requirements on *dollar* deposits within its borders. Nor are the London branches of U.S. banks subject to U.S. reserve requirements on dollar deposits, provided those deposits are payable only outside the United States. A London Eurobank therefore has a competitive advantage over a bank in New York in attracting dollar deposits: It can pay more interest to its depositors than the New York bank while still covering its operating costs. The Eurobank's competitive advantage comes from its ability to avoid a "tax" (the reserve requirement) that the Fed imposes on domestic banks' dollar deposits.

Freedom from reserve requirements is probably the most important regulatory factor that makes Eurocurrency trading attractive to banks and their customers, but there are others. For example, Eurodollar deposits are available in shorter maturities than the corresponding time deposits banks are allowed to issue in the United States. Regulatory asymmetries like these explain why those financial centers whose governments impose the fewest restrictions on foreign currency banking have become the main Eurocurrency centers. London is the leader in this respect, but it has been followed by Luxembourg, Bahrain, Hong Kong, and other countries that have competed for international banking business by lowering restrictions and taxes on foreign bank operations within their borders.

Neither the United States nor Germany has attracted a significant share of the world's Eurocurrency business because both countries apply fairly uniform regulations to all domestic deposits, regardless of their currency of denomination. Recently, however, the U.S. government has tried to help the American banking industry get more of the action. In 1981, the Fed allowed resident banks to set up **international banking facilities (IBFs)** in the United States for the purpose of accepting time deposits and making loans to foreign customers. IBFs are not subject to reserve requirements or interest rate ceilings, and they are exempt from state and local taxes. But an IBF is prohibited from accepting deposits from or

---

[2] Alternatively, the bank could add the same amount to its holdings of vault cash, which also pay no interest. The discussion assumes the bank holds reserves at the Fed.

lending money to U.S. residents (other than the establishing bank or another IBF). Before 1981, much of the business currently carried out by IBFs was done less efficiently through "shell" branch offices located in the Caribbean.

Technically speaking, a dollar deposit in an IBF is not a Eurodollar because the IBF resides physically within the United States. U.S. regulators have imposed rules, however, that fence off IBFs from onshore banks as effectively as if the IBF were overseas. IBFs provide an excellent example of how countries have lured lucrative international banking business to their shores while trying to insulate domestic financial systems from the banks' international activities. Similar international banking enclaves in other countries include the Offshore Banking Units of Bahrain, the Asian Currency Units of Singapore, and the Tokyo Offshore Market.

Regulating International Banking

Many observers believe the largely unregulated nature of global banking activity leaves the world financial system vulnerable to bank failure on a massive scale. Is this a real threat? If so, what measures have governments taken to reduce it?

The Problem of Bank Failure

A bank fails when it is unable to meet its obligations to its depositors. Banks use depositors' funds to make loans and to purchase other assets, but some of a bank's borrowers may find themselves unable to repay their loans, or the bank's assets may decline in value for some other reason. In these circumstances the bank could find itself unable to pay off its deposits.

A peculiar feature of banking is that a bank's financial health depends on the confidence of depositors in the value of its assets. If depositors come to believe many of the bank's assets have declined in value, each has an incentive to withdraw his or her funds and place them in another bank. A bank faced with the wholesale loss of deposits is likely to close its doors, however, even if the asset side of its balance sheet is fundamentally sound. The reason is that many bank assets are illiquid and cannot be sold quickly to meet deposit obligations without substantial loss to the bank. If an atmosphere of financial panic develops, therefore, bank failure may not be limited to banks that have mismanaged their assets. It is in the interest of each depositor to withdraw his or her money from a bank if all other depositors are doing the same, even when the bank's assets are sound.

Bank failures obviously inflict serious financial harm on individual depositors who lose their money. But beyond these individual losses, bank failure can harm the economy's macroeconomic stability. One bank's problems may easily spread to sounder banks if they are suspected of having lent to the bank that is in trouble. Such a general loss of confidence in banks undermines the payments system on which the economy runs. And a rash of bank failures can bring a drastic reduction in the banking system's ability to finance investment and consumer-durable expenditure, thus reducing aggregate demand and throwing the economy into a slump. There is evidence that the string of U.S. bank closings in the early 1930s helped start and worsen the Great Depression.[3]

---

[3]For an evaluation, see Ben S. Bernanke, "Nonmonetary Effects of the Financial Crisis in the Propagation of the Great Depression," *American Economic Review* 73 (June 1983), pp. 257–276.

Because the potential consequences of a banking collapse are so harmful, governments attempt to prevent bank failures through extensive regulation of their domestic banking systems. Well-managed banks themselves take precautions against failure even in the absence of regulation, but because the costs of failure extend far beyond the bank's owners, some banks might be led by their own self-interest to shoulder a level of risk greater than what is socially optimal. In addition, even banks with cautious investment strategies may fail if rumors of financial trouble begin circulating. Many of the precautionary bank regulation measures taken by governments today are a direct result of their countries' experiences during the Great Depression.

In the United States an extensive "safety net" has been set up to reduce the risk of bank failure; other industrialized countries have taken similar precautions. The main U.S. safeguards are:

1. *Deposit insurance.* The Federal Deposit Insurance Corporation (FDIC) insures bank depositors against losses up to $100,000. Banks are required to make contributions to the FDIC to cover the cost of this insurance. FDIC insurance discourages "runs" on banks because small depositors, knowing their losses will be made good by the government, no longer have an incentive to withdraw their money just because others are doing so. Since 1989, the FDIC has also provided insurance for deposits with savings and loan (S&L) associations.[4]

2. *Reserve requirements.* Reserve requirements are central to monetary policy as a main channel through which the central bank influences the relation between the monetary base and monetary aggregates. At the same time, reserve requirements force the bank to hold a portion of its assets in a liquid form easily mobilized to meet sudden deposit outflows.

3. *Capital requirements and asset restrictions.* The difference between a bank's assets and its liabilities, equal to the bank's net worth, is also called its *bank capital.* Bank capital is the equity that the bank's shareholders acquire when they buy the bank's stock, and since it equals the portion of the bank's assets that is *not* owed to depositors it gives the bank an extra margin of safety in case some of its other assets go bad. U.S. bank regulators set minimum required levels of bank capital to reduce the system's vulnerability to failure. Other rules prevent banks from holding assets that are "too risky," such as common stocks, whose prices tend to be volatile. Banks also face rules against lending too large a fraction of their assets to a single private customer or to a single foreign government borrower.

4. *Bank examination.* The Fed, the FDIC, and the Office of the Comptroller of the Currency all have the right to examine a bank's books to ensure compliance with bank capital standards and other regulations. Banks may be forced to sell assets that the examiner deems too risky or to adjust their balance sheets by writing off loans the examiner thinks will not be repaid.

---

[4]Holders of deposits over $100,000 still have an incentive to run if they scent trouble, of course. When rumors began circulating in May 1984 that the Continental Illinois National Bank had made a large number of bad loans, the bank began rapidly to lose its large, uninsured deposits. As part of its rescue effort, the FDIC extended its insurance coverage to all of Continental Illinois's deposits, regardless of size. This and later episodes have convinced people that the FDIC is following a "too-big-to-fail" policy of fully protecting all depositors at the largest banks. Officially, however, FDIC insurance still applies automatically only up to the $100,000 limit.

5. *Lender of last resort facilities.* U.S. banks can borrow from the Fed's discount window. While discounting is a tool of monetary management, the Fed can also use discounting to prevent bank panics. Since the Fed has the ability to create currency, it can lend to banks facing massive deposit outflows as much as they need to satisfy their depositors' claims. When the Fed acts in this way, it is acting as a **lender of last resort (LLR)** to the bank. When depositors know the Fed is standing by as the LLR, they have more confidence in the bank's ability to withstand a panic and are therefore less likely to run if financial trouble looms. The administration of LLR facilities is complex, however. If banks think the central bank will *always* bail them out, they will take excessive risks. So the central bank must make access to its LLR services conditional on sound management. To decide when banks in trouble have not brought it on themselves through unwise risk taking, the LLR must be involved in the bank examination process.

The banking safeguards listed above are interdependent: Laxity in one area may cause other safeguards to backfire. Deposit insurance alone, for example, may encourage bankers to make risky loans because depositors no longer have any reason to withdraw their funds even from carelessly managed banks. The recent U.S. S&L crisis is a case in point. In the early 1980s, the U.S. deregulated the S&Ls. Before deregulation, S&Ls had largely been restricted to home mortgage lending; after, they were allowed to make much riskier loans, for example, loans on commercial real estate. At the same time this deregulation was occurring, bank examination was inadequate for the new situation and depositors, lulled by government-provided insurance, had no reason to be vigilant about the possibility that S&L managers might finance foolish ventures. The result was a wave of S&L failures that left taxpayers holding the bill for the insured deposits.

The U.S. commercial bank safety net worked reasonably well until the late 1980s, but as a result of deregulation, the 1990–1991 recession, and a sharp fall in commercial property values, bank closings rose dramatically and the FDIC insurance fund was depleted. Like the United States, other countries that deregulated domestic banking in the 1980s—including Japan, the Scandinavian countries, the United Kingdom, and Switzerland—faced serious problems a decade later. Many have overhauled their systems of banking safeguards as a result.

Difficulties in Regulating International Banking

Banking regulations of the type used in the United States and other countries become even less effective in an international environment where banks can shift their business among different regulatory jurisdictions. A good way of seeing why an international banking system is harder to regulate than a national one is to look at how the effectiveness of the U.S. safeguards just described is reduced as a result of offshore banking activities.

1. Deposit insurance is essentially absent in international banking. National deposit insurance systems may protect domestic and foreign depositors alike, but the amount of insurance available is invariably too small to cover the size of deposit usual in international banking. In particular, interbank deposits are unprotected.

2. The absence of reserve requirements has been a major factor in the growth of Eurocurrency trading. While Eurobanks derive a competitive advantage from escaping the required reserve tax, there is a social cost in terms of the reduced stability of the banking system. No country can solve the problem single-handedly by imposing reserve requirements on its own banks' overseas branches. Concerted international action is blocked, however, by the political and technical difficulty of agreeing on an internationally uniform set of regulations and by the reluctance of some countries to drive banking business away by tightening regulations.

3. and **4.** Bank examination to enforce capital requirements and asset restrictions becomes more difficult in an international setting. National bank regulators usually monitor the balance sheets of domestic banks and their foreign branches on a consolidated basis. But they are less strict in keeping track of banks' foreign subsidiaries and affiliates, which are more tenuously tied to the parent bank but whose financial fortunes may affect the parent's solvency. Banks have often been able to take advantage of this laxity by shifting risky business that home regulators might question to regulatory jurisdictions where fewer questions are asked. Further, it is often unclear which group of regulators has responsibility for monitoring a given bank's assets. Suppose the London subsidiary of an Italian bank deals primarily in Eurodollars. Should the subsidiary's assets be the concern of British, Italian, or American regulators?

5. There is uncertainty over which central bank, if any, is responsible for providing LLR assistance in international banking. The problem is similar to the one that arises in allocating responsibility for bank supervision. Let's return to the example of the London subsidiary of an Italian bank. Should the Fed bear responsibility for saving the subsidiary from a sudden drain of dollar deposits? Should the Bank of England step in? Or should the Banca d'Italia bear the ultimate responsibility? When central banks provide LLR assistance they increase their domestic money supplies and may compromise domestic macroeconomic objectives. In an international setting, a central bank may also be providing resources to a bank located abroad whose behavior it is not equipped to monitor. Central banks are therefore reluctant to extend the coverage of their LLR responsibilities. The problems surrounding the 1982 failure of Italy's Banco Ambrosiano, discussed in the box on page 651, illustrate how international banking can lead to gaps in LLR coverage.

International Regulatory Cooperation

The internationalization of banking has weakened national safeguards against banking collapse, but at the same time it has made the need for effective safeguards more urgent. Offshore banking involves a tremendous volume of interbank deposits—roughly 80 percent of all Eurocurrency deposits, for example, are owned by private banks. A high level of interbank depositing implies that problems affecting a single bank could be highly contagious and could spread quickly to banks with which it is thought to do business. Through this ripple effect, a localized disturbance could, conceivably, set off a banking panic on a global scale.

This nightmarish scenario has haunted central bankers and other government officials since offshore banking began to grow rapidly in the 1960s. Little was done, however, until 1974. In that year a number of banks failed as a result of foreign exchange losses, among them the Franklin National Bank in the United States and Germany's Bankhaus I. D. Herstatt. The failures sent tremors through the international financial markets, and the volume of international lending dropped sharply.

In response to the 1974 banking crises, central bank heads from 11 industrialized countries set up a group called the **Basel Committee** whose job was to achieve "a better coor-

THE BANCO AMBROSIANO COLLAPSE

The collapse of Italy's most important private bank in June 1982 is a vivid illustration of how the intricate cross-border links between financial institutions can frustrate bank supervisors and cause financial crises. The Banco Ambrosiano failure is notorious, however, because of the bank president's close connections with a subversive political group and with the Vatican. Robert Calvi, the president of Banco Ambrosiano, stood at the center of a vast international financial network spanning Europe, the Caribbean, and South America. In 1981 Calvi was convicted of violating Italian foreign exchange regulations. At the same time, government investigators obtained the membership roster of a secret lodge of right-wing freemasons known as Propaganda-2 (or P-2). P-2 numbered Calvi and many other influential Italians among its members, including two cabinet ministers. The government of Prime Minister Arnaldo Forlani was forced to resign, and P-2 was outlawed.

Because Banco Ambrosiano had become the object of such close scrutiny by the government and the press, it soon became known that some of the bank's loans were weak. This revelation led to a deposit run. Italy's central bank, the Banca d'Italia, set up a consortium of Italy's major banks that took over many of Banco Ambrosiano's assets and liabilities and established a new bank, Nuovo Banco Ambrosiano.

The Banca d'Italia exercised its LLR function by ensuring that Nuovo Banco Ambrosiano repaid domestic and foreign residents who had placed deposits with Banco Ambrosiano itself. The central bank did not, however, guarantee the liabilities of Banco Ambrosiano's foreign subsidiaries. Banco Ambrosiano and its subsidiaries allegedly had extensive financial connections with the Catholic Church's Institute for Religious Works (sometimes called the "Vatican bank"). As a result of the many claims raised by Banco Ambrosiano's failure, the Vatican bank's finances came under investigation.

Calvi himself never saw the ramifications of his bank's collapse. In mid-June 1982 he disappeared from Italy. Shortly afterward he was found dead, hanging from Blackfriars Bridge in London, his pockets stuffed with rocks. It has not yet been determined whether he died by suicide or murder.*

---

*For a lively account of the Banco Ambrosiano scandal and its background, see Rupert Cornwell, "God's Banker" (New York: Dodd, Mead & Company, 1984). The 1991 film *The Godfather, Part III* derived part of its plot from the Ambrosiano affair.

---

dination of the surveillance exercised by national authorities over the international banking system. . . ." (The group was named after Basel, Switzerland, the home of the central bankers' meeting place, the Bank for International Settlements.) The Basel Committee remains the major forum for cooperation among bank regulators from different countries.

In 1975 the Committee reached an agreement, called the Concordat, which allocated responsibility for supervising multinational banking establishments between parent and host countries. (A revised Concordat was issued in 1983.) In addition, the Concordat called for the sharing of information about banks by parent and host regulators and for "the granting of permission for inspections by or on behalf of parent authorities on the territory of the host authority."[5] In further work the Basel Committee has located loopholes in the supervision of

---

[5] The Concordat was summarized in these terms by W. P. Cooke of the Bank of England, then chairman of the Basel Committee, in "Developments in Co-operation among Banking Supervisory Authorities," *Bank of England Quarterly Bulletin* 21 (June 1981), pp. 238–244.

multinational banks and brought these to the attention of national authorities. The Committee has recommended, for example, that regulatory agencies monitor the assets of banks' foreign subsidiaries as well as their branches. Much of the group's work has been devoted to developing better data on the balance sheets of multinational banks, a prerequisite to more effective supervision.

A big step toward reconciling countries' supervisory practices was taken in January 1988 when the Basel Committee agreed to a set of common standards for assessing bank capital adequacy. These standards require international banks to hold capital equal to at least 8 percent of their risk-weighted assets plus off-balance-sheet commitments. It has proven difficult to implement the Basel capital adequacy standards in a uniform manner in different countries. National regulators have tended to interpret the standards loosely to favor domestic banks, in the process diluting the rules' effectiveness. For example, Japanese regulators have allowed domestic banks to value stock shares that they hold as capital at their purchase prices rather than at their lower market values. Japanese banks would otherwise have been obliged to reduce the sizes of their loan portfolios. The Basel Committee has been working to reduce such problems and a new capital accord is in the works.

A major change in international financial relations in the 1990s has been the rapidly growing importance of new **emerging markets** as sources and destinations for private capital flows. Emerging markets are the capital markets of poorer, developing countries that have liberalized their financial systems to allow private asset trade with foreigners. Countries such as Brazil, Mexico, Indonesia, and Thailand were all major recipients of private capital inflows from the industrial world in the early and mid-1990s.

Emerging market financial institutions have, however, generally proven to be weaker than those in industrialized countries. This vulnerability contributed to the severe emerging markets financial crisis of 1997–1999 (Chapter 22). Among other problems, developing countries tend to lack experience in bank regulation, have looser prudential and accounting standards than developed countries, and have been more prone to offer domestic banks implicit guarantees that they will be bailed out if they get into trouble.

Thus, the need to extend internationally accepted "best practice" regulatory standards to emerging market countries is now seen as urgent. In September 1997 the Basel Committee issued its *Core Principles for Effective Banking Supervision,* worked out in cooperation with representatives from many developing countries. That document sets out 25 principles deemed to describe the minimum necessary requirements for effective bank supervision, covering licensing of banks, supervision methods, reporting requirements for banks, and cross-border banking. The Basel Committee and the IMF are monitoring the implementation of these standards around the world.

While the work of the Basel Committee has improved the supervision of multinational banks, little has been done to clarify the division of LLR responsibilities among countries. Following the 1974 bank failures, central bankers discussed the provision of international LLR facilities but declined to announce any definite agreement. There is speculation that such an agreement exists but that central bankers have kept it secret to avoid suggesting an automatic bailout for banks that take unwise risks and get into trouble.

The international activities of nonbank financial institutions are another potential trouble spot. International cooperation in bank supervision has come a long way since the early 1970s, and regulators are now starting to grapple with the problems raised by nonbank financial firms. Their task is an important one. The failure of a major securities house, for example, like the failure of a bank, could seriously disrupt national payments and credit networks. Increasing **securitization** (in which bank assets are repackaged in readily marketable forms) and trade in options and other "derivative" securities has made it harder for regulators to get an accurate picture of global financial flows by examining bank balance sheets alone. As a result, the need for authorities to collect and pool data on internationally active nonbanks has become acute. The near-collapse of the global investment fund Long Term Capital Management in September 1998 is an example of the nightmare that haunts global regulators' sleep (see the Case Study below).

CASE STUDY

The Day the World Almost Ended

Formed in 1994, Long Term Capital Management (LTCM) was a well-known and successful investment fund numbering two winners of the economics Nobel Prize among its partners. Readers of the financial press therefore were shocked to learn on September 23, 1998, that LTCM was at the brink of failure and had been taken over by a consortium of major financial institutions. The reasons LTCM ran into problems, and the fears that led the Federal Reserve Bank of New York to organize its takeover, illustrate how the activities of unregulated nonbank financial institutions can make the entire international financial system more fragile, and even vulnerable to collapse.

Long Term Capital Management specialized in trades involving similar securities that differ slightly in yields due to their liquidity or risk characteristics. In a typical trade, LTCM would obtain money by promising to repay with newly issued 30-year United States Treasury bonds. The fund then would invest those funds in *previously issued* 30-year Treasury bonds, which have a smaller market than the newly issued ones, are harder to sell (less liquid), and therefore must offer a slightly higher yield. Long Term Capital Management would make this trade when the liquidity yield spread between the old and new bonds was unusually high; but since even unusually high spreads generally amount to only a small fraction of a percentage point, the trade would have to be very, very large to generate much profit. Where did the necessary money come from?

The LTCM reputation for financial wizardry and its initially favorable track record gave it access to many big lenders willing to provide huge sums for such trades. Given the resources available to it and a desire to diversify, LTCM traded across countries and currencies. The firm amassed a huge global portfolio of assets and liabilities, the difference between the two representing capital invested by the firm's partners and customers. LTCM's capital at the start of 1998 was $4.8 billion; but at the same time, it was involved in financial contracts totaling almost $1.3 *trillion*, roughly 15 percent of a year's United States GNP! (Such magnitudes are not uncommon for major financial institutions.) Although its massive positions generated high profits when things went right for LTCM, the possibility of correspondingly huge losses was also there, provided that enough of LTCM's assets fell in value while the assets they had promised to deliver rose. An analysis of historical data by LTCM suggested that such an event was extremely improbable.

In August and September 1998, however, the extremely improbable event happened. A debt default by Russia in August (to be discussed in Chapter 22) sparked what the International

Monetary Fund has called "a period of turmoil in mature markets that is virtually without precedent in the absence of a major inflationary or economic shock."[6] The assets of LTCM plummeted in value and the value of its liabilities soared as frightened financial market participants around the world scrambled for safety and liquidity. Since LTCM now appeared very risky, its funding sources dried up and it had to dig into its capital to repay loans and provide additional collateral to its creditors.

With LTCM's capital down to a "paltry" $600 million, the Federal Reserve Bank of New York organized a rescue. Fourteen major American and European financial institutions, most of them creditors, agreed to provide the firm with $3.6 billion in new capital in return for a claim to 90 percent of LTCM's profits *and* control over all its important decisions. Most of the institutions participating in the consortium would have made large immediate losses if LTCM had failed, as it certainly would have in the absence of a coordinated rescue effort. Even the news that LTCM had been saved from disaster, however, was enough to spook markets further. Only much later did a semblance of calm return to world asset markets.

Why did the New York Fed step in to organize a rescue for LTCM, rather than simply letting the troubled fund fail? The Fed feared that an LTCM failure could provoke financial panic on a global scale, leading to a cascade of bank failures around the world at a time when Asia and Latin America were already facing a steep economic slowdown. If LTCM had failed, financial panic could have arisen through several channels. Banks that had lent money to LTCM could have become targets for bank runs. Moreover, a rapid move by LTCM to sell its relatively illiquid investments (to meet creditors' demands for repayment) would have driven their prices down steeply, pushing global interest rates up and calling into question the solvency of the many other financial institutions with portfolios similar to LTCM's. In contrast, the strategy adopted by the Fed gave LTCM time to unwind its positions gradually without creating a selling panic.

Was the Fed's action necessary or advisable? Critics claim that international investors will take excessive risks if they believe that the government will always save them from the results of their own imprudence. The possibility that you will take less care to prevent an accident if you are insured against it is called **moral hazard**. (Domestic bank supervision is necessary to limit the moral hazard resulting from deposit insurance and access to the lender of last resort, which otherwise would lead banks to make excessively risky loans.)

The Fed's reply to its critics is that it did not use its LLR abilities to bail out LTCM. No public funds were injected into the ailing fund. Instead, major creditors were "bailed in" by being asked to put more of their money at risk to keep LTCM afloat. The additional risks they were forced to take—as well as the costs to the LTCM partners, who lost their wealth and their control over the fund—should be adequate deterrents to moral hazard, in the Fed's view. Nonetheless, in the wake of the incident there were numerous calls for the official regulation of large global funds such as LTCM.

Not surprisingly, the debate rages on because the tradeoff between financial stability and moral hazard is inevitable. Any action by government to reduce the systemic risk inherent in financial markets will also reduce the risks that private operators perceive, and thereby encourage excessive gambling. In the LTCM case, the Fed clearly judged that the risk of a global financial meltdown was too serious to allow.

---

[6] See *World Economic Outlook and International Capital Markets: Interim Assessment.* Washington, D.C.: International Monetary Fund, December 1998, p. 36.

How Well Has the International Capital Market Performed?

The present structure of the international capital market involves risks of financial instability that can be reduced only through the close cooperation of bank supervisors in many countries. But the same profit motive that leads multinational financial institutions to innovate their way around national regulations can also provide important gains for consumers. As we have seen, the international capital market allows residents of different countries to diversify their portfolios by trading risky assets. Further, by ensuring a rapid international flow of information about investment opportunities around the world, the market can help allocate the world's savings to their most productive uses. How well has the international capital market performed in these respects?

The Extent of International Portfolio Diversification

Since accurate data on the overall portfolio positions of a country's residents are often impossible to assemble, it is not feasible to gauge the extent of international portfolio diversification by direct observation. Nonetheless, some U.S. data can be used to get a rough idea about changes in international diversification in recent years.

In 1970 the foreign assets held by U.S. residents were equal in value to 6.2 percent of the U.S. capital stock. Foreign claims on the United States amounted to 4.0 percent of its capital stock (including residential housing). By 1999, U.S.-owned assets abroad equaled about 30 percent of U.S. capital, while foreign assets in the United States had risen to about 36 percent of U.S. capital.

These percentages seem too small; with full international portfolio diversification, we would expect them to reflect the size of the U.S. economy relative to that of the rest of the world. Thus, in a fully diversified world economy, something like 80 percent of the U.S. capital stock would be owned by foreigners, while U.S. residents' claims on foreigners would equal around 80 percent of the value of the U.S. capital stock. What makes the apparently low extent of international portfolio diversification even more puzzling is the presumption most economists would make that the potential gains from diversification are large. An influential study by the French financial economist Bruno Solnik, for example, estimated that a U.S. investor holding only American stocks could more than halve the riskiness of her portfolio by further diversification into stocks from European countries.[7]

The data do show, however, that diversification has increased substantially as a result of the growth of the international capital market since 1970. Further, international asset holdings are large in absolute terms. At the end of 1999, for example, U.S. claims on foreigners were $7.21 trillion, equal to about 76 percent of the U.S. GNP in that year, while foreign claims on the United States were $8.61 trillion, or about 93 percent of U.S. GNP. Stock exchanges around the world are establishing closer communication links, and companies are showing an increasing readiness to sell shares on foreign exchanges. Japan (as noted previously) began a gradual but continuing opening of its financial markets in

---

[7]See Solnik, "Why Not Diversify Internationally Rather than Domestically?" *Financial Analysts Journal* (July–August 1974), pp. 48–54.

the late 1970s; Britain removed restrictions barring its public from international asset trade in 1979; and the European Union embarked in the late 1980s on a broad program of market unification meant to integrate its financial markets more fully into the global capital market.

The seemingly low extent of international portfolio diversification attained so far is not a strong indictment of the world capital market. The market has certainly contributed to a rise in diversification since the early 1970s, despite some remaining impediments to international capital movement. Further, there is no foolproof measure of the socially optimal extent of diversification; in particular, the existence of nontraded products can cut down significantly the gains from international asset trade. What seems certain is that asset trade will continue to expand as barriers to the international flow of capital are progressively dismantled.

The Extent of Intertemporal Trade

An alternative way of evaluating the performance of the world capital market has been suggested by the economists Martin Feldstein and Charles Horioka. Feldstein and Horioka pointed out that a smoothly working international capital market allows countries' domestic investment rates to diverge widely from their saving rates. In such an idealized world, saving seeks out its most productive uses worldwide, regardless of their location; at the same time, domestic investment is not limited by national saving because a global pool of funds is available to finance it.

For many countries, however, differences between national saving and domestic investment rates (that is, current account balances) have not been large since World War II: countries with high saving rates over long periods also have high investment rates, as Figure 21-3 illustrates. Feldstein and Horioka concluded from this evidence that cross-border capital mobility is low, in the sense that most of any sustained increase in national saving will lead to increased capital accumulation at home. The world capital market, according to this view, does not do a good job of helping countries reap the long-run gains from intertemporal trade.[8]

The main problem with the Feldstein-Horioka argument is that it is impossible to gauge whether the extent of intertemporal trade is deficient without knowing if there are unexploited trade gains, and knowing this requires more knowledge about actual economies than we generally have. For example, a country's saving and investment may usually move together simply because the factors that generate a high saving rate (such as rapid economic growth) also generate a high investment rate. In such cases, the country's gain from intertemporal trade may simply be small. An alternative explanation of high saving-investment correlations is that governments have tried to manage macroeconomic policy to avoid large current account imbalances. In any case, events appear to be overtaking this particular debate. For industrialized countries, the empirical regularity noted by Feldstein and Horioka seems to have weakened recently in the face of the historically high external imbalances of the United States, Germany, and Japan.

---

[8] See Martin Feldstein and Charles Horioka, "Domestic Savings and International Capital Flows," *Economic Journal* 90 (June 1980), pp. 314–329.

Figure 21-3 | Saving and Investment Rates for 25 Countries, 1990–1997 Averages

OECD countries' saving and investment ratios to GNP tend to be positively related.

Source: OECD, *National Income Accounts.*

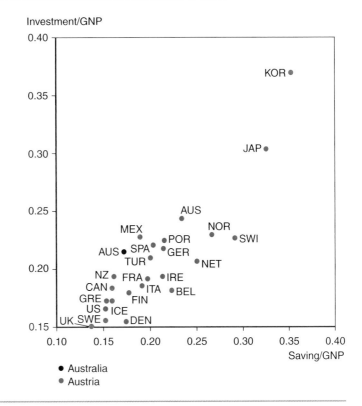

Onshore-Offshore Interest Differentials

A quite different barometer of the international capital market's performance is the relationship between onshore and offshore interest rates on similar assets denominated in the same currency. If the world capital market is doing its job of communicating information about global investment opportunities, these interest rates should move closely together and not differ too greatly. Large interest rate differences would be strong evidence of unrealized gains from trade.

Figure 21-4 shows data since 1982 on the interest rate difference between two comparable dollar bank liabilities, three-month Eurodollar deposits and certificates of deposit issued in the United States. These data provide no indication of any remaining large unexploited gains.

Studies of Germany and the Netherlands, countries with long-standing open capital markets, also show an approximate equality between onshore and offshore interest rates. The same equality has held for Japan since it completed a major step in its program of phased capital account liberalization in December 1980. France and Italy maintained capital controls until the late 1980s, but onshore and offshore rates, which had tended to move

Figure 21-4 | Comparing Eurodollar and Onshore United States Interest Rates

The difference between the Eurodollar interest rate and the domestic U.S. certificate of deposit rate has approached zero as international capital mobility has grown.

Source: Datastream and *International Financial Statistics*, monthly data.

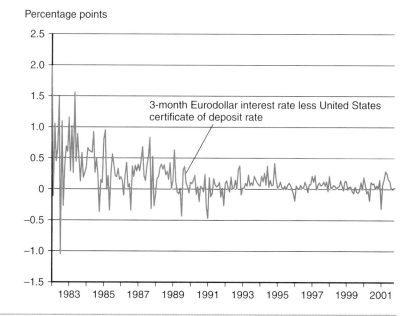

in tandem even before, converged quickly after those countries began dismantling the restrictions.[9]

The Efficiency of the Foreign Exchange Market

The foreign exchange market is a central component of the international capital market, and the exchange rates it sets help determine the profitability of international transactions of all types. Exchange rates therefore communicate important economic signals to households and firms engaged in international trade and investment. If these signals do not reflect all available information about market opportunities, a misallocation of resources will result. Studies of the foreign exchange market's use of available information are therefore potentially important in judging whether the international capital market is sending the right signals to markets.

[9] On the European countries, see Francesco Giavazzi and Marco Pagano, "Capital Controls and the European Monetary System" in *Capital Controls and Foreign Exchange Legislation*, Occasional Paper 1. Milan, Italy: Euromobiliare, June 1985, pp. 19–38. The Japanese case is investigated by Takatoshi Ito, "Capital Controls and Covered Interest Parity," *Economic Studies Quarterly* 37 (September 1986), pp. 223–241. A detailed study on the United States is in Lawrence L. Kreicher, "Eurodollar Arbitrage," *Federal Reserve Bank of New York Quarterly Review* 7 (1982), pp. 10–21. An examination of Germany between 1970 and 1974, when capital controls were in effect, found large differences between onshore and offshore DM interest rates. See Michael P. Dooley and Peter Isard, "Capital Controls, Political Risk, and Deviations from Interest-Rate Parity," *Journal of Political Economy* 88 (April 1980), pp. 370–384. An overview is contained in the paper by Obstfeld in Further Reading.

Studies Based on Interest Parity.   The interest parity condition that was the basis of the discussion of exchange rate determination in Chapter 13 has also been used to study whether market exchange rates incorporate all available information. Recall that interest parity holds when the interest difference between deposits denominated in different currencies is the market's forecast of the percentage by which the exchange rate between those two currencies will change. More formally, if R_t is the date-t interest rate on home currency deposits, R_t^* the interest rate on foreign currency deposits, E_t the exchange rate (defined as the home-currency price of foreign currency), and E_{t+1}^e the exchange rate market participants expect when the deposits paying interest R_t and R_t^* mature, the interest parity condition is

$$R_t - R_t^* = (E_{t+1}^e - E_t)/E_t. \tag{21-1}$$

Equation (21-1) implies a simple way to test whether the foreign exchange market is doing a good job of using current information to forecast exchange rates. Since the interest difference, $R_t - R_t^*$, is the market's forecast, a comparison of this *predicted* exchange rate change with the *actual* exchange rate change that subsequently occurs indicates the market's skill in forecasting.[10]

Statistical studies of the relationship between interest rate differences and later depreciation rates show that the interest difference has been a very bad predictor, in the sense that it has failed to catch any of the large swings in exchange rates. Even worse, the interest difference has, on average, failed to predict correctly the *direction* in which the spot exchange rate would change. If the interest rate difference were a poor but unbiased predictor, we could argue that the market is setting the exchange rate according to interest parity and doing the best job possible in a rapidly changing world where prediction is inherently difficult. The finding of bias, however, seems at odds with this interpretation of the data.

The interest parity condition also furnishes a test of a second implication of the hypothesis that the market uses all available information in setting exchange rates. Suppose that E_{t+1} is the actual future exchange rate people are trying to guess; then the forecast error they make in predicting future depreciation, u_{t+1}, can be expressed as actual minus expected depreciation:

$$u_{t+1} = (E_{t+1} - E_t)/E_t - (E_{t+1}^e - E_t)/E_t. \tag{21-2}$$

If the market is making use of all available information, its forecast error, u_{t+1}, should be statistically unrelated to data known to the market on date t, when expectations were formed. In other words, there should be no opportunity for the market to exploit known data to reduce its later forecast errors.

---

[10]Most studies of exchange market efficiency study how the forward exchange rate premium does as a predictor of subsequent spot exchange rate change. That procedure is equivalent to the one we are following if the covered interest parity condition holds, so that the interest difference $R_t - R_t^*$ equals the forward premium (see the appendix to Chapter 13). As noted in Chapter 13, there is strong evidence that covered interest parity holds when the interest rates being compared apply to deposits in the same financial center—for example, London Eurocurrency rates.

Under interest parity, this hypothesis can be tested by writing u_{t+1} as actual currency depreciation less the international interest difference:

$$u_{t+1} = (E_{t+1} - E_t)/E_t - (R_t - R_t^*). \tag{21-3}$$

Statistical methods can be used to examine whether u_{t+1} is predictable, on average, through use of past information. A number of researchers have found that forecast errors, when defined as above, *can* be predicted. For example, past forecast errors, which are widely known, are useful in predicting future errors.[11]

The Role of Risk Premiums.   One explanation of the research results described above is that the foreign exchange market simply ignores easily available information in setting exchange rates. Such a finding would throw doubt on the international capital market's ability to communicate appropriate price signals. Before jumping to this conclusion, however, recall that when people are risk averse, the interest parity condition may *not* be a complete account of how exchange rates are determined. If, instead, bonds denominated in different currencies are *imperfect* substitutes for investors, the international interest rate difference equals expected currency depreciation *plus* a risk premium, ρ_t:

$$R_t - R_t^* = (E_{t+1}^e - E_t)/E_t + \rho_t \tag{21-4}$$

(see Chapter 17). In this case, the interest difference is not necessarily the market's forecast of future depreciation. Thus, under imperfect asset substitutability, the empirical results just discussed cannot be used to draw inferences about the foreign exchange market's efficiency in processing information.

Because people's expectations are inherently unobservable, there is no simple way to decide between equation (21-4) and the interest parity condition, which is the special case that occurs when ρ_t is always zero. Several econometric studies have attempted to explain departures from interest parity on the basis of particular theories of the risk premium, but none has been entirely successful.[12]

The mixed empirical record leaves the following two possibilities: Either risk premiums are important in exchange rate determination, or the foreign exchange market has been ignoring the opportunity to profit from easily available information. The second alternative seems unlikely in light of foreign exchange traders' powerful incentives to make profits. The first alternative, however, awaits solid statistical confirmation. It is certainly not supported by the evidence reviewed in Chapter 17, which suggests that sterilized foreign exchange intervention has not been an effective tool for exchange rate management. More sophisti-

---

[11] For further discussion, see Robert E. Cumby and Maurice Obstfeld, "International Interest Rate and Price Level Linkages Under Flexible Exchange Rates: A Review of Recent Evidence," in John F. O. Bilson and Richard C. Marston, eds., *Exchange Rate Theory and Practice* (Chicago: University of Chicago Press, 1984), pp. 121–151; and Lars Peter Hansen and Robert J. Hodrick, "Forward Exchange Rates as Optimal Predictors of Future Spot Rates: An Econometric Analysis," *Journal of Political Economy* 88 (October 1980), pp. 829–853.

[12] For recent surveys see Charles Engel, "The Forward Discount Anomaly and the Risk Premium: A Survey of Recent Evidence," *Journal of Empirical Finance,* 3(1996), pp. 123–192; and Karen Lewis, "Puzzles in International Finance," in Gene M. Grossman and Kenneth Rogoff, *Handbook of International Economics,* vol. 3 (Amsterdam: North-Holland, 1996).

cated theories show, however, that sterilized intervention may be powerless even under imperfect asset substitutability. Thus, a finding that sterilized intervention is ineffective does not necessarily imply that risk premiums are absent.

Tests for Excessive Volatility. One of the most worrisome findings is that statistical forecasting models of exchange rates based on standard "fundamental" variables like money supplies, government deficits, and output perform badly—even when *actual* (rather than predicted) values of future fundamentals are used to form exchange rate forecasts! Indeed, in a famous study, Richard A. Meese of the University of California, Berkeley, and Kenneth Rogoff of Harvard University showed that a naive "random walk" model, which simply takes today's exchange rate as the best guess of tomorrow's, does better. Some have viewed this finding as evidence that exchange rates have a life of their own, unrelated to the macroeconomic determinants we have emphasized in our models. More recent research has confirmed, however, that while the random walk outperforms more sophisticated models for forecasts up to a year away, the models seem to do better at horizons longer than a year and have explanatory power for long-run exchange rate movements.[13]

An additional line of research on the foreign exchange market examines whether exchange rates have been excessively volatile, perhaps because the foreign exchange market "overreacts" to events. A finding of excessive volatility would prove that the foreign exchange market is sending confusing signals to traders and investors who base their decisions on exchange rates. But how volatile must an exchange rate be before its volatility becomes excessive? As we saw in Chapter 13, exchange rates *should* be volatile, because to send the correct price signals they must move swiftly in response to economic news. Exchange rates are generally less volatile than stock prices. It is still possible, though, that exchange rates are substantially more volatile than the underlying factors that move them— such as money supplies, national outputs, and fiscal variables. Attempts to compare exchange rates' volatility with those of their underlying determinants have, however, produced inconclusive results.[14] A basic problem underlying tests for excessive volatility is the impossibility of quantifying exactly all the variables that convey relevant news about the economic future. For example, how does one attach a number to a political assassination attempt or a major bank failure?

The Bottom Line. The ambiguous evidence on the foreign exchange market's performance warrants an open-minded view. Such a view is particularly advisable because the statistical methods that have been used to study exchange rates are very imperfect. A judgment that the market is doing its job well would support a laissez-faire attitude by governments

---

[13]The original Meese-Rogoff study is "Empirical Exchange Rate Models of the Seventies: Do They Fit out of Sample?" *Journal of International Economics* 14 (February 1983), pp. 3–24. On longer-run forecasts, see Menzie D. Chinn and Richard A. Meese, "Banking on Currency Forecasts: How Predictable Is Change in Money?" *Journal of International Economics* 38 (February 1995), pp. 161–178; and Nelson C. Mark, "Exchange Rates and Fundamentals: Evidence on Long-Horizon Predictability," *American Economic Review* 85 (March 1995), pp. 201–218.

[14]See, for example, Richard A. Meese, "Testing for Bubbles in Exchange Markets: A Case of Sparkling Rates?" *Journal of Political Economy* 94 (April 1986), pp. 345–373; and Kenneth D. West, "A Standard Monetary Model and the Variability of the Deutschemark-Dollar Exchange Rate," *Journal of International Economics* 23 (August 1987), pp. 57–76.

and a continuation of the present trend toward increased cross-border financial integration in the industrial world. A judgment of market failure, on the other hand, might imply a need for increased foreign exchange intervention by central banks and a reversal of the trend toward capital account liberalization. The stakes are high, and more research and experience are needed before a firm conclusion can be reached.

Summary

1. When people are *risk averse*, countries can gain through the exchange of risky assets. The gains from trade take the form of a reduction in the riskiness of each country's consumption. International *portfolio diversification* can be carried out through the exchange of *debt instruments* or *equity instruments*.

2. The *international capital market* is the market in which residents of different countries trade assets. One of its important components is the foreign exchange market. Banks are at the center of the international capital market, and many operate offshore, that is, outside the countries where their head offices are based.

3. Regulatory and political factors have encouraged *offshore banking*. The same factors have encouraged *offshore currency trading*, that is, trade in bank deposits denominated in currencies of countries other than the one in which the bank is located. Such *Eurocurrency* trading has received a major stimulus from the absence of reserve requirements on deposits in *Eurobanks*.

4. Creation of a Eurocurrency deposit does not occur because that currency leaves its country of origin; all that is required is that a Eurobank accept a deposit liability denominated in the currency. Eurocurrencies therefore pose no threat for central banks' control over their domestic monetary bases. Fears that *Eurodollars,* for example, will some day come "flooding in" to the United States are misplaced. Eurocurrency creation can add significantly to the broader monetary aggregates, however, and may complicate central bank monetary management by shifting money multipliers unpredictably.

5. Offshore banking is largely unprotected by the safeguards national governments have imposed to prevent domestic bank failures. In addition, the opportunity banks have to shift operations offshore has undermined the effectiveness of national bank supervision. Since 1974, the *Basel Committee* of industrial country bank supervisors has worked to enhance regulatory cooperation in the international area. That group's 1975 Concordat allocated national responsibility for monitoring banking institutions and provided for information exchange. There is still uncertainty, however, about a central bank's obligations as an international *lender of last resort*. That uncertainty may reflect an attempt by international authorities to reduce *moral hazard*. The trend toward *securitization* has increased the need for international cooperation in monitoring and regulating nonbank financial institutions. So has the rise of *emerging markets*.

6. The international capital market has contributed to an increase in international portfolio diversification since 1970, but the extent of diversification still appears small compared with what economic theory would predict. Similarly, some observers have claimed that the extent of intertemporal trade, as measured by countries' current account balances, has been too small. Such claims are hard to evaluate without more

detailed information about the functioning of the world economy than is yet available. Less ambiguous evidence comes from international interest rate comparisons, and this evidence points to a well-functioning market. Rates of return on similar deposits issued in the major financial centers are quite close.

7. The foreign exchange market's record in communicating appropriate price signals to international traders and investors is mixed. Tests based on the interest parity condition seem to suggest that the market ignores readily available information in setting exchange rates, but since the interest parity theory ignores risk aversion and the resulting risk premiums, it may be an oversimplification of reality. Attempts to model risk factors empirically have not, however, been very successful. Tests of excessive exchange rate volatility also yield a mixed verdict on the foreign exchange market's performance.

Key Terms

Basel Committee, p. 650

debt instrument, p. 640

emerging markets, p. 652

equity instrument, p. 640

Eurobank, p. 644

Eurocurrencies, p. 644

Eurodollar, p. 644

international banking
   facilities (IBFs), p. 646

international capital market, p. 636

lender of last resort (LLR), p. 649

moral hazard, p. 654

offshore banking, p. 643

offshore currency trading, p. 644

portfolio diversification, p. 639

risk aversion, p. 638

securitization, p. 653

Problems

1. Which portfolio is better diversified, one that contains stock in a dental supply company and a candy company or one that contains stock in a dental supply company and a dairy product company?

2. Imagine a world of two countries in which the only causes of fluctuations in stock prices are unexpected shifts in monetary policies. Under which exchange rate regime would you expect the gains from international asset trade to be greater, fixed or floating?

3. The text points out that covered interest parity holds quite closely for deposits of differing currency denomination issued in a single financial center. Why might covered interest parity fail to hold when deposits issued in *different* financial centers are compared?

4. When a U.S. bank accepts a deposit from one of its foreign branches, or from its own IBF, that deposit is subject to Fed reserve requirements. Similarly, reserve requirements are imposed on any loan from a U.S. bank's foreign branch to a U.S. resident, or on any asset purchase by the branch bank from its U.S. parent. What do you think is the rationale for these regulations?

5. The Swiss economist Alexander Swoboda has argued that the Eurodollar market's early growth was fueled by the desire of banks outside the United States to appropriate some of the revenue the United States was collecting as issuer of the principal

reserve currency. (This argument is made in *The Euro-Dollar Market: An Interpretation,* Princeton Essays in International Finance 64. International Finance Section, Department of Economics, Princeton University, February 1968.) Do you agree with Swoboda's interpretation?

6. After the developing country debt crisis began in 1982 (see the next chapter), U.S. bank regulators imposed tighter supervisory restrictions on the lending policies of American banks and their subsidiaries. Over the 1980s, the share of U.S. banks in London banking activity declined. Can you suggest a connection between these two developments?

7. Why might growing securitization make it harder for bank supervisors to keep track of risks to the financial system?

Further Reading

Ralph C. Bryant. *International Financial Intermediation.* Washington, D.C.: Brookings Institution, 1987. A review of the growth and regulation of the international capital market, with emphasis on the interdependence of different governments' regulatory decisions.

Kenneth A. Froot and Richard H. Thaler. "Anomalies: Foreign Exchange." *Journal of Economic Perspectives* 4 (Summer 1990), pp. 179–192. Clear, nontechnical discussion of the foreign exchange market's efficiency.

Morris Goldstein. *The Case for an International Banking Standard.* Washington, D.C.: Institute for International Economics, 1997. A proposal to reduce financial fragility in international banking.

Jack Guttentag and Richard Herring. *The Lender-of-Last-Resort Function in an International Context.* Princeton Essays in International Finance 151. International Finance Section, Department of Economics, Princeton University, May 1983. A study of the need for and the feasibility of an international lender of last resort.

Richard M. Levich. "Is the Foreign Exchange Market Efficient?" *Oxford Review of Economic Policy* 5 (1989), pp. 40–60. Valuable survey of research on the efficiency of the foreign exchange market.

Haim Levy and Marshall Sarnat. "International Portfolio Diversification," in Richard J. Herring, ed. *Managing Foreign Exchange Risk.* Cambridge, U.K.: Cambridge University Press, 1983, pp. 115–142. A nice exposition of the logic of international asset diversification.

Warren D. McClam. "Financial Fragility and Instability: Monetary Authorities as Borrowers and Lenders of Last Resort," in Charles P. Kindleberger and Jean-Pierre Laffargue, eds. *Financial Crises: Theory, History, and Policy.* Cambridge, U.K.: Cambridge University Press, 1982, pp. 256–291. Historical overview of instability in the international capital market.

Maurice Obstfeld. "The Global Capital Market: Benefactor or Menace?" *Journal of Economic Perspectives* 12 (Fall 1998), pp. 9–30. Overview of the functions, operation, and implications for national sovereignty of the international capital market.

Maurice Obstfeld and Alan M. Taylor, "The Great Depression as a Watershed: International Capital Mobility Over the Long Run," in Michael D. Bordo, Claudia Goldin, and Eugene N. White, eds. *The Defining Moment: The Great Depression and the American Economy in the Twentieth Century.* Chicago: University of Chicago Press, 1998, pp. 353–402. Discusses linkages between capital mobility, the exchange rate system, and monetary policy.

CHAPTER 22

Developing Countries: Growth, Crisis, and Reform

U ntil now, we have studied macroeconomic interactions between industrialized market economies like those of the United States and western Europe. Richly endowed with capital and skilled labor, these politically stable countries generate high levels of GNP for their residents. And their markets, compared to those of some poorer countries, have long been relatively free of direct government control.

Several times since the early 1980s, however, the macroeconomic problems of the world's developing countries have been at the forefront of concerns about the stability of the entire international economy. Over a period of more than four decades following World War II, trade between developing and industrializing nations expanded, as did developing country borrowing from richer lands. In turn, the more extensive links between the two groups of economies made each group more dependent than before on the economic health of the other. Events in developing countries therefore have a significant impact on welfare and policies in more advanced economies. That interdependence was brought home again recently as numerous developing countries suffered financial crises starting in 1997 and world economic growth slowed.

This chapter studies the macroeconomic problems of developing countries and the repercussions of those problems on the developed world. Although the insights from international macroeconomics gained in previous chapters also apply to developing countries, the distinctive problems those countries have faced in their quest to catch up to the rich economies warrant separate discussion. In addition, the lower income levels of developing areas make macroeconomic slumps there even more painful than in developed economies, with consequences that can threaten political and social cohesion. ●

Income, Wealth, and Growth in the World Economy

Poverty is the basic problem of developing countries and escaping from poverty is their overriding economic and political challenge. Compared with industrialized economies, most developing countries are poor in the factors of production essential to modern industry: capital and skilled labor. The relative scarcity of these factors contributes to low levels of per-capita income and often prevents developing countries from realizing economies of scale from which many richer nations benefit. Political instability, insecure property rights, and misguided economic policies frequently have discouraged investment in capital and skills, while also reducing economic efficiency in other ways.

The Gap between Rich and Poor

The world's economies can be divided into four main categories according to their annual per-capita income levels: low-income economies (including India, Pakistan, and their neighbors, along with much of sub-Saharan Africa); lower middle-income economies (including mainland China, the smaller Latin American and Caribbean countries, many former Soviet bloc countries, and most of the remaining African countries); upper middle-income economies (including the largest Latin American countries, Saudi Arabia, Malaysia, Turkey, South Africa, Poland, Hungary, and the Czech and Slovak Republics); and high-income economies (including the rich industrial market economies and a handful of exceptionally fortunate "developing" countries such as Israel, oil-rich Kuwait, and Singapore). The first three categories consist mainly of countries at a backward stage of development relative to industrial economies. Table 22-1 shows 1999 average per-capita annual income levels (measured in dollars) for these country groups, together with another indicator of economic well-being, average life expectancy at birth.

Table 22-1 illustrates the sharp disparities in international income levels close to the end of the twentieth century. Average per-capita GNP in the richest economies is 63 times that of the average in the poorest developing countries! Even the upper middle-income countries enjoy only about one-fifth of the per-capita GNP of the industrial group. The life expectancy figures generally reflect international differences in income levels. Average life spans fall as relative poverty increases.[1]

Has the World Income Gap Narrowed over Time?

Explaining the income differences between countries is one of the oldest goals of economics. It is no accident that Adam Smith's classic 1776 book was entitled the *Wealth of Nations*! Since at least the days of the mercantilists, economists have sought not only to explain why countries' incomes differ at a given point in time, but also to solve the more challenging puzzle of why some countries become rich while others stagnate. Debate over the best policies for promoting economic growth has been fierce, as we shall see in this chapter.

Both the depth of the economic growth puzzle and the payoff to finding growth-friendly policies are illustrated in Table 22-2, which shows per-capita output *growth rates* for several country groups between 1960 and 1992. (These real output data have been corrected to account for departures from puchasing power parity.) Over that period, the United States grew at roughly the 2 percent rate that many economists would argue is the long-run max-

---

[1]Chapter 15 showed that an international comparison of *dollar* incomes portrays relative welfare levels inaccurately because countries' price levels measured in a common currency (here, U.S. dollars) generally differ. A detailed description of how the numbers in Table 22-1 were constructed is given in their source, the World Bank's *World Development Report 2000/2001*. The World Bank report also supplies national income numbers that have been adjusted to take account of deviations from purchasing power parity (PPP). Those numbers greatly reduce, without eliminating, the disparities in Table 22-1. In PPP-adjusted 1999 dollars, the average per-capita incomes of the four country groups in the table were $1,730, $3,960, $8,320, and $24,430, respectively. On that measure, the ratio of the highest to the lowest group's average income is "only" about 14 to one.

Table 22-1	Indicators of Economic Welfare in Four Groups of Countries, 1999

Income group	GNP per capita (U.S. dollars)	Life expectancy (years)*
Low-income	410	60.0
Lower middle-income	1,200	69.5
Upper middle-income	4,900	70.5
High-income	25,730	78.0

*Simple average of male and female life expectancies.

Source: World Bank, *World Development Report 2000/2001.*

imum for a mature economy. Canada, which was 27 percent poorer than its southern neighbor in 1960, has grown at a higher rate since then, so that by 1992 it was only 9 percent behind—thereby having closed the earlier income gap by two-thirds.

Canada's catching-up process illustrates a more general phenomenon: the tendency for gaps between *industrial* countries' living standards to disappear over the postwar era. The theory behind this observed **convergence** in per-capita incomes is deceptively simple. If trade is free, if capital can move to countries offering the highest returns, and if knowledge itself moves across political borders so that countries always have access to cutting-edge production technologies, then there is no reason for international income differences to persist for long.

Despite the appeal of that simple theory, no clear tendency for per-capita incomes to converge characterizes the world as a whole, as the rest of Table 22-2 shows. There we see vast discrepancies in long-term growth rates among different regional country groupings, but no general tendency for poorer countries to grow faster. Countries in Africa, although mostly at the bottom of the world income scale, have grown at rates far below those of the main industrial countries.[2] Growth has also been relatively slow in Latin America, where only a few countries have matched the growth rate of Canada, despite much lower income levels.

In contrast, East Asian countries *have* tended to grow at rates far above those of the industrialized world, as the convergence theory would predict. South Korea, with an income level close to Ghana's in 1960, has grown at almost 7 percent per year since then and in 1997 was classified as a high-income developing country by the World Bank. Singapore's 6.6 percent annual average growth rate likewise propelled it to high-income status.

A country that can muster even a 3-percent annual growth rate will see its real per-capita income double every generation. But at the growth rates seen until recently in East Asian countries such as Hong Kong, Singapore, South Korea, and Taiwan, per-capita real income increases *fivefold* every generation! As detailed later in this chapter, rapid growth came to a halt in East Asia in the late 1990s as a severe financial crisis erupted.

What explains the sharply divergent long-run growth patterns in Table 22-2? The answer lies in the economic and political features of developing countries and the ways these have

---

[2]There naturally are exceptions to any such generalization. Botswana in southern Africa enjoyed an average per-capita growth rate well above 5 percent per year during the three decades after 1960. As a result it is now classified as upper middle-income by the World Bank.

Table 22-2	Output Per Capita in Selected Countries, 1960–1992 (in 1985 U.S. dollars)		

Country	1960	1992	1960–1992 Annual growth rate (percent per year)
North America			
Canada	7,240	16,371	2.6
United States	9,908	17,986	1.9
Africa			
Ghana	886	956	0.2
Kenya	646	915	1.1
Nigeria	560	978	1.8
Senegal	1,062	1,145	0.3
Latin America			
Argentina	4,481	4,708	0.2
Brazil	1,780	3,886	2.5
Chile	2,897	4,886	1.6
Mexico	2,825	6,250	2.5
East Asia			
Hong Kong	2,231	16,461	6.4
Malaysia	1,409	5,729	4.5
Singapore	1,626	12,633	6.6
South Korea	898	6,665	6.9
Thailand	940	3,924	4.6
Taiwan	1,255	8,067	6.4

Note: Data for Argentina, Senegal, Taiwan, and Korea only through 1990. Their growth rates are for 1960–1990 only. Data are taken from the Penn World Table, Mark 5.6, and use PPP exchange rates to compare national incomes. For a description see Robert Summers and Alan Heston, "The Penn World Table (Mark 5): An Expanded Set of International Comparisons, 1950–1988," *Quarterly Journal of Economics* 106 (May 1991), pp. 327–368.

changed over time in response to both world events and internal pressures. The structural features of developing countries have also helped to determine their success in pursuing key macroeconomic goals other than rapid growth, such as low inflation, low unemployment, and financial-sector stability.

Structural Features of Developing Countries

Developing countries differ widely among themselves these days, and no single list of "typical" features would accurately describe all developing countries. In the early 1960s, these countries were much more similar to each other in their approaches to trade policy, macroeconomic policy, and other government interventions in the economy. Then things began to change. East Asian countries abandoned import-substituting industrialization, embracing an export-oriented development strategy instead. Later on, countries in Latin America also reduced trade barriers, while simultaneously attempting to rein in government's role in the economy, to reduce chronically high inflation, and, in many cases, to open capital accounts to private transactions.

While many developing countries therefore have reformed their economies to come closer to the structures of the successful industrial economies, the process remains incomplete and most developing countries tend to be characterized by at least some of the following features:

1. There is a history of extensive direct government control of the economy, including restrictions on international trade, government ownership or control of large industrial firms, direct government control over internal financial transactions, and a high level of government consumption as a share of GNP. Developing countries differ widely among themselves in the extent to which the role of government in the economy has been reduced in these various areas over the past decade or so.

2. There is a history of high inflation. In many countries the government was unable to pay for its heavy expenditures and the losses of state-owned enterprises through taxes alone. Tax evasion was rampant, and much economic activity was driven underground, so it proved easiest simply to print money. **Seigniorage** is the name economists give to the real resources a government earns when it prints money that it spends on goods and services. When their governments were expanding money supplies continually to extract high levels of seigniorage, developing countries experienced inflation and even hyperinflation. (See, for example, the box on inflation and money-supply growth in Latin America in Chapter 14, p. 377.)

3. Where domestic financial markets have been liberalized, weak credit institutions often abound. Banks frequently lend funds they have borrowed to finance poor or very risky projects. Loans may be made on the basis of personal connections rather than prospective returns, and government safeguards against financial fragility, such as bank supervision (Chapter 21), tend to be ineffective due to incompetence, inexperience, and outright fraud. While public trade in stock shares has developed in many emerging markets, it is usually harder than in developing countries for shareholders to find out how a firm's money is being spent or to control firm managers. The legal framework for resolving asset ownership in cases of bankruptcy typically is also weak. Compared to the industrial countries, developing countries' financial markets therefore do a worse job of directing savings toward their most efficient investment uses. As a result they are even more prone to crisis.

4. Exchange rates tend to be pegged, or at least managed heavily, by the government. Government measures to limit exchange rate flexibility reflect both a desire to keep inflation under control and the fear that floating exchange rates would be subject to huge volatility in the relatively thin markets for developing country currencies. There is a history of allocating foreign exchange through government decree rather than through the market, a practice (called *exchange control*) that some developing countries still maintain. Most developing countries have, in particular, tried to control capital movements by limiting foreign exchange transactions connected with trade in assets. A number have, however, opened their capital accounts.

5. Natural resources or agricultural commodities make up an important share of exports for many developing countries—for example, Russian petroleum, Malaysian timber, South African gold, and Colombian coffee (and cocaine).

6. Attempts to circumvent government controls, taxes, and regulation have helped to make corrupt practices such as bribery and extortion a way of life in many if not most developing countries. The development of underground economic activity has in some instances aided economic efficiency by restoring a degree of market-based resource allocation, but on balance it is clear from the data that corruption and poverty go hand in hand.

For a large sample of developing and industrial countries, Figure 22-1 shows the strong positive relationship between annual real per-capita GDP and an inverse index of corruption—ranging from 1 (most corrupt) to 10 (cleanest)—published by the organization Transparency International.[3] Several factors underlie this strong positive relationship. Government regulations that promote corruption also harm economic prosperity. Statistical studies have found that corruption itself tends to have a net negative economic efficiency and growth.[4] Finally, poorer countries lack the resources to police corruption effectively, and poverty itself breeds a greater willingness to go around the rules.

Many of the broad features that still characterize developing countries today took shape in the 1930s and can be traced to the Great Depression (Chapter 18). Most developing countries experimented with direct controls over trade and payments to conserve foreign exchange reserves and safeguard domestic employment. Faced with a massive breakdown of the world market system, industrial and developing countries alike allowed their governments to assume increasingly direct roles in employment and production. Often, governments reorganized labor markets, established stricter control over financial markets, controlled prices, and nationalized key industries. The trend toward government control of the economy proved much more persistent in developing countries, however, where political institutions allowed those with vested financial interests in the status quo to perpetuate it.

Cut off from traditional suppliers of manufactures during World War II, developing countries encouraged new manufacturing industries of their own. Political pressure to pro-

---

[3] According to Transparency International's 2000 rankings, the cleanest country in the world was Finland (scoring a nearly perfect 9.9) and the most corrupt was Nigeria (scoring a dismal 1.0). The score for the United States was 7.6. For detailed data and a general overview of the economics of corruption, see Vito Tanzi, "Corruption around the World," *International Monetary Fund Staff Papers* 45 (December 1998), pp. 559–594.

[4] There is, of course, abundant anecdotal evidence on the economic inefficiencies associated with corruption. Consider the following recent description of doing business in Brazil, which had a 2000 Transparency International ranking of 4.0 and was considered by the World Bank to be an upper middle-income developing country in that year:

> Corruption goes well beyond shaking down street sellers. Almost every conceivable economic activity is subject to some form of official extortion.
>
> Big Brazilian companies generally agree to pay bribes, but multinationals usually refuse and prefer to pay fines. The money—paid at municipal, state and federal levels—is shared out between bureaucrats and their political godfathers. They make sure that it is impossible to comply fully with all of Brazil's tangle of laws, regulations, decrees and directives.
>
> The bribes and fines make up part of the Brazil Cost, shorthand for the multitude of expenses that inflate the cost of conducting business in Brazil.

See "Death, Decay in São Paulo May Stir Reformist Zeal," *Financial Times,* March 20/21 1999, p. 4.

Figure 22-1 | Corruption and Per Capita Income

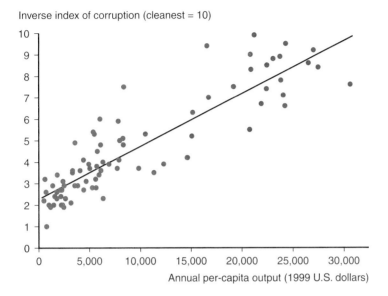

Corruption tends to rise as real per-capita income falls.

Note: The figure plots 2000 values of an (inverse) index of corruption and 1999 values of PPP-adjusted real per-capita output, measured in 1999 United States dollars (the amount a dollar could buy in the U.S. in 1999). The straight line represents a statistician's best guess at a country's corruption level based on its real per-capita output.

Source: Transparency International (for corruption data); *World Development Report 2000/2001* for output data.

tect these industries was one factor behind the popularity of import-substituting industrialization in the first postwar decades. In addition, former colonial areas liberated after the war believed they could attain the income levels of their former rulers only through rapid, government-directed industrialization and urbanization. Finally, developing country leaders feared that their efforts to escape poverty would be doomed if they continued to specialize in primary commodity exports such as coffee, copper, and wheat. In the 1950s, some influential economists argued that developing countries would suffer continually declining terms of trade unless they used commercial policy to move resources out of primary exports and into import substitutes.

Developing Country Borrowing and Debt

One further feature of developing countries is crucial to understanding their macroeconomic problems: They rely heavily on capital inflows from abroad to finance domestic investment. Before World War I and in the period up to the Great Depression, developing countries (including the United States for much of the nineteenth century) received large capital inflows from richer lands. In the decades after World War II, developing economies again tapped the savings of richer countries and built up a substantial debt to the rest of the world (around $2.1 trillion at the end of 1996). That debt was at the center of several international lending crises that preoccupied economic policymakers throughout the world in the last two decades of the twentieth century.

The Economics of Capital Inflows to Developing Countries

Many developing countries have received extensive capital inflows from abroad and now carry substantial debts to foreigners. Table 22-3 shows the recent pattern of borrowing by non-oil developing countries. The sums are substantial once we remember how small the economy of the developing world is relative to that of the industrial world. What factors lie behind capital inflows to the developing world?

Recall the identity (analyzed in Chapter 12) that links national saving, S, domestic investment, I, and the current account balance, $CA: S - I = CA$. If national saving falls short of domestic investment, the difference equals the current account deficit. Because of poverty and poor financial institutions, national saving often is low in developing countries. Because these same countries are relatively poor in capital, however, the opportunities for profitably introducing or expanding plant and equipment can be abundant. Such opportunities justify a high level of investment. By running a deficit in its current account, a country can obtain resources from abroad to invest even if its domestic saving level is low. A deficit in the current account implies, however, that the country is borrowing abroad. In return for being able to import more foreign goods today than its current exports can pay for, the country must promise to repay in the future, either the interest and principal on loans or the dividends on shares in firms sold to foreigners.

Thus, much developing country borrowing could potentially be explained by the incentives for *intertemporal trade* examined in Chapter 7. Low-income countries generate too little saving of their own to take advantage of all their profitable investment opportunities, so they must borrow abroad. In capital-rich countries, on the other hand, the most productive investment opportunities have been exploited already but saving levels are relatively high. Savers in developed countries can earn higher rates of return, however, by lending to finance investments in the developing world.

Notice that when developing countries borrow to undertake productive investments that they would not otherwise carry out, both they and lenders reap gains from trade. Borrowers gain because they can build up their capital stocks despite limited national savings. Lenders simultaneously gain by earning higher returns to their savings than they could earn at home.

While the reasoning above provides a rationale for developing country external deficits and debt, it does not imply that all loans from developed to developing countries are justified. Loans that finance unprofitable investments—for example, huge shopping malls that are never occupied—or imports of consumption goods may result in debts that borrowers cannot repay. In addition, faulty government policies that artificially depress national saving rates may lead to excessive foreign borrowing.

The Problem of Default

Potential gains from international borrowing and lending will not be realized unless lenders are confident they will be repaid. A loan is said to be in **default** when the borrower fails to repay on schedule according to the loan contract, without the agreement of the lender. Both social and political instability in developing countries, as well as the frequent weak-

Table 22-3 Current Account Balances of Major Oil Exporters, Other Developing Countries, and Industrial Countries, 1973–2000 (billions of dollars)

Year	Major oil exporters	Other developing countries	Industrial countries
1973	9.86	−8.51	n.a.
1974	71.90	−23.86	−41.56
1975	43.75	−38.10	−9.27
1976	40.12	−26.28	−27.08
1977	23.91	−20.33	−32.84
1978	4.57	−31.29	4.91
1979	60.74	−37.42	−38.26
1980	99.98	−54.36	−78.03
1981	49.70	−82.90	−42.58
1982	−8.47	−69.60	−34.33
1983	−17.09	−41.97	−26.64
1984	−8.80	−31.91	−51.85
1985	−1.95	−37.16	−55.74
1986	−31.54	−41.27	−13.77
1987	−11.98	−25.73	−43.14
1988	−21.46	−34.69	−30.75
1989	1.87	−40.67	−56.12
1990	17.65	−42.44	−86.33
1991	−59.92	−38.09	−23.75
1992	−24.69	−54.21	−17.50
1993	−25.22	−96.10	61.75
1994	−6.90	−82.67	32.72
1995	1.16	−96.57	51.35
1996	31.23	−103.11	33.51
1997	19.85	−82.44	71.79
1998	−29.60	−57.20	35.80
1999	19.00	−29.50	−121.10
2000	97.90	−37.70	−248.40

Source: International Monetary Fund. Global current accounts may not sum to zero because of errors, omissions, and the exclusion of some countries (for example, members of the former Soviet bloc.)

ness of their public finances and financial institutions, make it much more risky to lend to developing than to industrial countries. And indeed, the history of capital flows to developing countries is strewn with the wreckage of financial crises and defaulted loan contracts:

    1. In the early nineteenth century, a number of American states defaulted on European loans they had taken out to finance the building of canals.

    2. Latin American countries ran into repayment problems throughout the nineteenth century, notably Argentina, which sparked a global financial crisis in 1890 (the Baring Crisis) when it proved unable to meet its obligations.

3. In 1917, the new communist government of Russia repudiated the foreign debts incurred by previous rulers. The communists closed the Soviet economy to the rest of the world, embarking on a program of centrally planned economic development, often ruthlessly enforced.

4. During the Great Depression of the 1930s world economic activity collapsed and developing countries found themselves shut out of industrial country export markets by a wall of protection (recall Chapter 18). Nearly every developing country defaulted on its external debts as a result, and private capital flows to developing countries dried up for four decades. Even some industrial countries, such as Nazi Germany, defaulted on foreign obligations.

Sharp contractions in a country's output and employment invariably result from a crisis in which the country suddenly loses access to all foreign sources of funds. At a very basic level, the necessity for such contractions can be seen from the current account identity, $S - I = CA$. Imagine that a country is running a current account deficit (and thus borrowing from abroad) 5 percent of its initial GNP when suddenly foreign lenders become fearful of default and cut off all new loans. Since their action forces the current account balance to be at least zero ($CA \geq 0$), the identity $S - I = CA$ tells us that through some combination of a fall in investment or a rise in saving, $S - I$ must immediately rise by at least 5 percent. The required sharp fall in aggregate demand necessarily depresses the country's output dramatically. Even if the country was not on the verge of default initially—imagine that foreign lenders were originally seized by a sudden irrational panic—the harsh contraction in output that the country suffers will make default a real possibility.

Indeed, matters are likely to be far worse for the country even than the preceding example suggests. Foreign lenders will not only withhold new loans if they fear default, they will naturally try to get as much money as possible out of the country by demanding the *full* repayment on any loans for which principal can be demanded on short notice (for example, liquid short-term bank deposits). When the developing country repays the principal on debt, it is increasing its net foreign wealth (a capital outflow), and these repayments enter the capital account balance with negative signs. To generate the mirror-image positive current account item (see Chapter 12), the country must somehow raise its net exports. Thus, in a lending crisis, the country will not only have to run a current account of zero, it will actually be called upon to run a *surplus* ($CA > 0$). The bigger the country's *short-term* foreign debt—debt whose principal can be demanded by creditors—the larger the rise in saving or compression of investment that will be needed to avoid a default on foreign debts.

You already may have noticed that developing country default crises are driven by a self-fulfilling mechanism analogous to the ones behind self-fulfilling balance of payments crises (Chapter 17) and bank runs (Chapter 21). Indeed, the underlying logic is the same. Furthermore, default crises in developing countries are likely to be accompanied by balance of payments crises (when the exchange rate is pegged) *and* bank runs. A balance of payments crisis results because the country's official foreign exchange reserves may be the only ready means it has to pay off foreign short-term debts. By running down its official reserves (a capital inflow), the government can cushion aggregate demand by reducing the size of the current account surplus needed to meet creditors' demands for repayment.[5] But the loss of its

---

[5]Make certain you see why this is so. If necessary, review the open-economy accounting concepts from Chapter 12.

reserves leaves the government unable to peg the exchange rate any longer. At the same time the banks get in trouble as domestic and foreign depositors, fearing currency depreciation and the consequences of default, withdraw funds and purchase foreign reserves, hoping to repay foreign-currency debts or to send wealth safely abroad. Since the banks are often weak to begin with, the large-scale withdrawals quickly push them to the brink of failure.

Each of these crisis "triplets" reinforces the others, so that a developing country's financial crisis is likely to be severe, to have widespread negative effects on the economy, and to snowball very quickly. The immediate origin of such a pervasive economic collapse can be in the capital account, in the foreign exchange market, or in the banking system, depending on the situation of the particular country.

Default crises were rare in the first three decades after World War II. Debt issue by developing countries was limited and the lenders typically were governments or official international agencies such as the International Monetary Fund (IMF) and World Bank. As the free flow of private global capital expanded after the early 1970s, however, major default crises occurred repeatedly, as we shall see, leading many to question the stability of the world capital market.[6]

Alternative Forms of Capital Inflow

When a developing country has a current account deficit, it is selling assets to foreigners to finance the difference between its spending and its income. While we have lumped these asset sales together under the catch-all term *borrowing,* the capital inflows that finance developing countries' deficits (and indeed, any country's deficit) can take several forms. Different types of capital inflow have predominated in different historical periods. Because different obligations to foreign lenders result, an understanding of the macroeconomic scene in developing countries requires a careful analysis of the five major channels through which they have financed their external deficits.

    1. *Bond finance.* Developing countries have sometimes sold bonds to private foreign citizens to finance their deficits. Bond finance was dominant in the period up to 1914 and in the interwar years (1918–1939). It regained popularity after 1990 as many developing countries tried to liberalize and modernize their financial markets.

    2. *Bank finance.* Between the early 1970s and late 1980s, developing countries borrowed extensively from commercial banks in the developing economies. In 1970, roughly a quarter of developing country external finance was provided by banks. In 1981 banks provided an amount of finance roughly equal to the non-oil developing countries' aggregate current account deficit for that year. Banks still lend directly to developing countries, but in the 1990s the importance of bank lending has shrunk.

    3. *Official lending.* Developing countries sometimes borrow from official foreign agencies such as the World Bank or Inter-American Development Bank. Such loans can

---

[6]On the history of default through the mid-1980s, see Peter H. Lindert and Peter J. Morton, "How Sovereign Debt Has Worked," in Jeffrey D. Sachs, ed., *Developing Country Debt and Economic Performance,* vol. 1 (Chicago: University of Chicago Press, 1989). A good overview of private capital inflows to developing countries over the same period is given by Eliana A. Cardoso and Rudiger Dornbusch, "Foreign Private Capital Inflows," in Hollis Chenery and T. N. Srinivasan, eds., *Handbook of Development Economics,* vol. 2 (Amsterdam: Elsevier Science Publishers, 1989).

be made on a "concessional" basis, that is, at interest rates below market levels, or on a market basis that allows the lender to earn the market rate of return. Official lending flows to developing nations have shrunk relative to total flows over the post-World War II period, although they remain dominant for some countries, for example, most of those in sub-Saharan Africa.

   4. *Direct foreign investment.* In direct foreign investment, a firm largely owned by foreign residents acquires or expands a subsidiary firm or factory located domestically (Chapter 7). A loan from IBM to its assembly plant in Mexico, for example, would be a direct investment by the United States in Mexico. The transaction would enter Mexico's balance of payments accounts as a capital inflow (and the U.S. balance of payments accounts as an equal capital outflow). Since World War II, direct investment has been a consistently important source of developing country capital.

   5. *Portfolio investment in ownership of firms.* Since the early 1990s investors in developed countries have shown an increased appetite for purchasing shares of stock in developing countries' firms. The trend has been reinforced by many developing countries' efforts at **privatization**—that is, selling to private owners large state-owned enterprises in key areas such as electricity, telecommunications, and petroleum. (Figure 22-2 shows how the African nation of Senegal advertised in 1999 to find private shareholders for a large state-owned producer of food products.) In the United States, numerous investment companies offer mutual funds specializing in emerging market shares.

The five types of finance just described can be classified into two categories: *debt* and *equity* finance (Chapter 21). Bond, bank, and official finance are all forms of debt finance. The debtor must repay the face value of the loan, plus interest, regardless of its own economic circumstances. Direct investment and portfolio purchases of stock shares are, on the other hand, forms of equity finance. Foreign owners of a direct investment, for example, have a claim to a share of its net return, not a claim to a fixed stream of money payments. Adverse economic events in the host country thus result in an automatic fall in the earnings of direct investments and in the dividends paid to foreigners.

The distinction between debt and equity finance is useful in analyzing how developing country payments to foreigners adjust to unforeseen events such as recessions or terms of trade changes. When a country's liabilities are in the form of debt, its scheduled payments to creditors do not fall if its real income falls. It may then become very painful for the country to continue honoring its foreign obligations—painful enough to cause the country to default. Life often is easier, however, with equity finance. In the case of equity, a fall in domestic income automatically reduces the earnings of foreign shareholders without violating any loan agreement. By acquiring equity, foreigners have effectively agreed to share in both the bad and the good times of the economy. Equity rather than debt financing of its investments therefore leaves a developing country much less vulnerable to the risk of a foreign lending crisis.

Latin America: From Crisis to Uneven Reform

Despite enormous natural resources, much of Latin America's population remains mired in poverty and the region has been battered repeatedly by financial crises. The Case Study of Argentina (pp. 681–683) shows how that country, despite its riches at the start of the

Figure 22-2 | Privatization in Africa

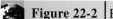

Privatisation Announcement

Republic of Senegal

The Government of Senegal, as part of its program to liberalise the economy through the implementation of market based reforms, announces its intention to privatise SONACOS (Société Nationale de Commercialisation des Oléagineux du Sénégal).

SONACOS, the leading agro-industrial company in Senegal, is active in three main areas: refining and exporting of peanut oil and related by-products, importing, refining and marketing of vegetable oil and manufacturing of consumer products (soap, mustard, vinegar, margarine, etc.). A summary of the company's strengths follows:

- leading supplier of peanut oil to Europe
- estimated 90% market share of the edible oil market in Senegal
- large industrial base in Senegal (5 factories including 2 port facilities)
- turnover of FCFA 98 billion (USD 176 million) expected for 1998

The Government is seeking to sell a minimum of 51% of the share capital to a strategic investor with the industrial know how and financial strength to realise SONACOS's full potential. Tender documents will be available after March 15, 1999 at a cost of FCFA 250,000.

For further information, interested investors are invited to contact the Ministry of the Economy and Finance with copy to the adviser to the Government, HSBC Equator Bank, at the addresses mentioned below.

Ministère de l'Economie et des Finances, Cellule de Gestion et de Contrôle du Portefeuille de l'Etat: Mr. Serigne Ahmadou CAMARA 11, rue Malan - Immeuble Electra II - 3e étage Dakar, Senegal phone: (221) 823 34 28 facsimile: (221) 822 56 31

HSBC Equator Bank plc: Mr. James N. SHEFFIELD 66 Warwick Square SW1V 2AL London, UK phone: (44) 171 821-8797 facsimile: (44) 171 821-6221

HSBC Equator Bank plc

Member HSBC Group
Regulated by the SFA

In 1999, the government of Senegal advertised for a large private investor willing to buy a majority stake in a state-owned manufacturer of vegetable oil products.

Source: *Financial Times,* March 4, 1999, p. 14.

twentieth century, has failed repeatedly to restore sustained economic growth. Argentina's problems have persisted despite its having made serious (albeit incomplete) attempts at economic reform. Many of its neighbors have also sought to avoid the policy mistakes of the past, with varying results. While a difficult road lies ahead for several countries in the region, some have made substantial progress toward economic stability and sustainably growing living standards. This section summarizes Latin America's progress through the start of the 1997 developing country economic crisis. The experience holds important lessons for countries in other regions.

Inflation and the 1980s Debt Crisis in Latin America

The true costs of the inward-oriented import-substituting approach did not become evident in Latin America until the 1970s. In the prosperous world economic environment of the 1950s and 1960s, many countries in the region were able to attain healthy (if not spectacular) growth rates by exploiting the initially high returns from moving resources into industrial uses from inefficient agricultural activities. This easy source of gain disappeared over time. As national planners were called on to make increasingly complex investment decisions that would have been better left to market forces, inefficiency proliferated. Sheltered behind protectionist walls, domestic industries exercised market power at customers' expense. At the same time, the revenues available to those able to exploit captive domestic markets inspired lobbying for import licenses and exemptions, as well as corruption. Inequality in the import-substituting economies and poverty at the lowest income levels grew over time.

The oil shocks in the early 1970s and the productivity slowdown in the industrial countries, coupled with the demise of the Bretton Woods system of fixed exchange rates (Chapter 18), began a period of inferior macroeconomic performance in many Latin American economies. Governments expanded their expenditures to meet demands for greater social equality. At the same time, increased government demand attempted to offset the effects of more expensive oil. On a scale unseen for many decades, governments borrowed abroad to support their fiscal expansions. They also printed money at increasing rates in efforts to raise seigniorage. The result of such policies was an explosion of inflation and external debt. Often, the resulting economic dislocation helped military dictatorships come to power.

Unsuccessful Assaults on Inflation: The _Tablitas_ of the 1970s.   In 1978 Argentina, Chile, and Uruguay all turned to a new exchange rate–based strategy in the hope of taming inflation. In Spanish the approach was called the _tablita:_ a preannounced schedule (or "little table") of declining rates of domestic currency depreciation against the U.S. dollar. The _tablita_ was a type of exchange rate regime known as a **crawling peg**. Earlier uses of crawling pegs by Latin American countries had been aimed at preventing domestic inflation from making domestic goods too expensive relative to foreign goods, that is, at avoiding real appreciation of the currency. The _tablita_ strategy was different: a declining rate of currency depreciation against the dollar, by reducing the rate of increase in the prices of internationally tradable goods, would force overall inflation down.[7] All three "Southern Cone" countries simultaneously undertook trade reforms, allowed more freedom to banks and other financial institutions, and opened up their economies to private capital flows.

---

[7]The basic philosophy motivating the _tablitas_ thus was similar to that underlying the "credibility theory" of the European Monetary System of pegged exchange rates (Chapter 20).

THE SIMPLE ALGEBRA OF MORAL HAZARD

The moral hazard that results from a combination of perceived government guarantees and weak regulation of the guaranteed institution has helped fuel excessively speculative investment in many economies. To see how it works, imagine that there is a potential investment—say, a large real estate development—that will cost $70 million up front. If all goes well, the project will yield a return of $100 million; but there is only a one-third chance of this, and a two-thirds chance that the investment will yield only $25 million. The expected payoff, then, is only (1/3 × $100 million) + (2/3 × $25 million) = $50 million, which is far below the $70 million up-front cost. Ordinarily, this investment simply would never be made.

Government bailout guarantees change the result, however. Suppose that a real estate developer is able to *borrow* the entire $70 million, because he can convince lenders that the government will protect them if his project fails and he cannot repay. Then from his point of view, he has a one-third chance of making $30 million (= $100 million − $70 million). Otherwise he simply walks away from the project. It's heads he wins, tails the taxpayers lose.

The preceding example may seem extreme, but this kind of logic has led to financial disasters in many countries, including the United States. In the 1980s the U.S. savings and loan industry was granted what amounted to privilege without responsibility: government guarantees on deposits, without close regulation of risk-taking. The eventual bill to U.S. taxpayers was $150 billion. Similar mishandling of the financial sector led to large bank losses in the 1990s in industrial countries as diverse as Sweden and Japan. In developing countries, the fallout from the resulting financial crises has usually been much more devastating than in the developed world.

Inflation did not fall into line with the *tablitas'* declining depreciation rates, however. In Chile, for example, inflation was still running at 2.5 percent *per month* when the country's rulers decided to fix its exchange rate against the dollar in June 1979. With domestic inflation way above that in the U.S. and their currencies depreciating by far less than the inflation difference, Southern Cone countries experienced massive real currency appreciations and current account deficits during their *tablita* experiments.[8] (Data from Argentina and Chile are shown in panels (a) and (b) of Figure 22-3, in which a move up along the left-hand axis is a rise in the current account *deficit* and a move up along the right-hand axis is a real *appreciation* of domestic currency against the U.S. dollar.)

Private capital inflows into these countries far exceeded their current account deficits because central banks were accumulating foreign reserves. Private foreign funds often flowed into newly liberalized but inadequately regulated financial institutions, which were prone to use the money to extend risky domestic loans. In the cases of Argentina and Uruguay, capital inflows also financed government deficits that remained largely as they

---

[8]The real appreciation pattern is quite common in exchange rate–based stabilization plans, and there are several potential causes. First, persistent inflation based on slowly adjusting expectations or lagged indexation provisions in contracts can cause real appreciation. Second, lack of credibility of the exchange rate announcement can cause price setters to engineer relatively high inflation in the expectation of an unplanned devaluation. Finally, productivity shifts resulting from inflation reduction or accompanying reforms might lead to real appreciation, as in Chapter 15's discussion of the Balassa-Samuelson effect. The last reason for real appreciation is benign, whereas the first two usually spell trouble for a government trying to quell inflation.

Figure 22-3 | Current Account Deficits and Real Currency Appreciation in Four Stabilizing Economies, 1976–1997

Current account
(percent of GDP)

Real exchange rate
(Index, 1990 = 100)

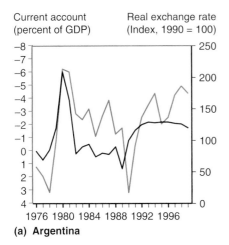

(a) Argentina

Current account
(percent of GDP)

Real exchange rate
(Index, 1990 = 100)

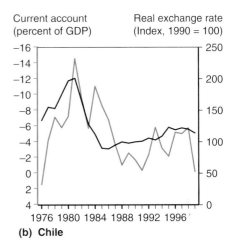

(b) Chile

Current account
(percent of GDP)

Real exchange rate
(Index, 1990 = 100)

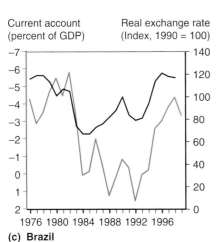

(c) Brazil

Current account
(percent of GDP)

Real exchange rate
(Index, 1990 = 100)

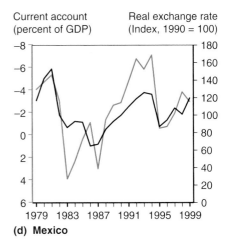

(d) Mexico

———— Current account
———— Real exchange rate

Countries attempting to stabilize inflation by pegging their nominal exchange rates have experienced sharp real exchange rate swings associated with sharp movements in current account balances.

Source: International Monetary Fund, *International Financial Statistics,* and World Bank, World Development Indicators. The left-hand vertical axis shows the current account deficit, the right-hand vertical axis the real exchange rate defined as P/EP_{US}, where P is the domestic price level and E the price of the U.S. dollar in domestic currency terms (making an upward movement in the real exchange rate index a real appreciation of the domestic currency against the dollar).

had been before the introduction of the *tablitas*. In one of the speculative attack models discussed in Chapter 17, a country that pegs its exchange rate while running a large government deficit will eventually run out of foreign reserves and suffer a speculative attack on its currency. These tendencies were present in the Southern Cone experiences, but were initially masked by the huge reserve inflows that accompanied the starting phases of the *tablita* programs.

Over the course of 1981–1982, with interest rates at historic highs in the industrial world, the appreciated currencies and large current account deficits in Latin America's Southern Cone became impossible to sustain. All three stabilization programs were abandoned in the midst of speculative attacks on exchange rates and runs on the countries' fragile financial institutions.

An analysis of the countries' financial fragility carries lessons about the importance of banking in developing countries that will recur throughout this chapter. Chile offers a particularly vivid example. Prior to the 1981–1982 crisis, Chile's financial institutions borrowed extensively abroad and lent the proceeds recklessly in the belief that they would be fully bailed out by the government if their loans went sour. Government guarantees, combined with the weak bank regulation then prevailing, led to an extreme form of the *moral hazard* problem we discussed in the last chapter. The box on p. 679 presents a concrete example of how moral hazard of the type Chile fostered leads borrowers to undertake imprudent investments. The country's shaky banks quickly became insolvent when trouble arrived in the early 1980s. The resulting official bailouts increased the fiscal burden on Chile's government enormously, and magnified the country's crisis.[9]

Chronic inflation returned to the Southern Cone with renewed force after the *tablita* programs fell apart. But the magnitude of the accompanying collapse reflected more than purely domestic problems. The year 1982 marked the beginning of a much broader developing country debt crisis that was to slow lending to Latin America for the rest of the decade.

CASE STUDY

Argentina's Economic Stagnation

Despite being one of the world's richest countries at the start of the twentieth century, Argentina has become progressively poorer relative to the industrial countries with which it compared so favorably in 1900. A low point came in the early 1990s when the World Bank demoted Argentina to the status of a lower middle-income developing country. The table below tells the story, one that continues to fascinate economists and economic historians:

---

[9] A classic account of these events is given by Carlos F. Díaz Alejandro, "Good-bye Financial Repression, Hello Financial Crash," *Journal of Development Economics* 19 (September-October 1985), pp. 1–24. Chile's finance minister had announced in 1975 that: "All financial operations of the banking system as well as of the Savings and Loan Associations are guaranteed by the Central Bank, which has been financing the Savings and Loan deficits and shall continue to do so whenever this should be required." Such clearly-stated unconditional public guarantees, coupled with a failure to stop excessive risk taking, always lead to problems.

Output per Capita Since 1900: Argentina Compared
with Industrial Countries (1980 dollars)

Country	1900	1913	1929	1950	1973	1987
Argentina	1,284	1,770	2,036	2,324	3,713	3,302
Australia	2,923	3,390	3,146	4,389	7,696	9,533
Canada	1,808	2,773	3,286	4,822	9,350	12,702
OECD	1,817	2,224	2,727	3,553	7,852	10,205

Source: Angus Maddison, *The World Economy in the 20th Century.* Paris: OECD, 1989.

In 1987, Argentina's output had grown by only 157 percent since 1900—it had not even tripled. In contrast, Canada's income had risen by 603 percent and that of the OECD as a whole by 462 percent. By 1987 Australia's output had increased a mere 226 percent over its 1900 level, but Australia started out being more than twice as rich as Argentina! Argentina's dismal growth performance left it only about a third as well-off as Australia near the twentieth century's end.

What explains Argentina's regress from riches to rags? As usual, the answer is complex, but the country's inward orientation and macroeconomic instability appear to be major culprits.

Inward orientation during the interwar period (1918–1939) was to some degree imposed by foreigners. Prior to 1914, Argentina saved little and depended on capital inflows, mainly from Britain, to finance investment and growth. Alan M. Taylor of the University of California, Davis, argues that World War I, by ending Britain's role as the world's main lender, deprived Argentina of its customary source of savings. Slower capital accumulation inevitably translated into slower growth of output. The worldwide depression of the 1930s, bringing a breakdown of capital movements and trade, only cemented Argentina's economic isolation.[10]

Argentina's economy became even less open after Juan Perón (husband of the famous Evita) came to power in 1946. Seeking the support of urban workers, Perón went beyond the policies of the 1930s in favoring import substitutes over traditional agricultural exports such as wheat and beef. Expansionary fiscal measures aimed at supporting private consumption discouraged investment and led to balance-of-payments and inflation pressures.

In the end, it is questionable whether Argentine import substitution policies even succeeded in their avowed goal of promoting industrialization. Carlos Díaz Alejandro, one of the great economic historians of Latin America, pointed out that Argentina's manufacturing output grew by 5.6 percent annually between 1900 and 1929, but by only 3.7 percent per year during the 1929–1965 period of import-substituting industrialization.[11]

The political movement Perón founded remains powerful in Argentina to the present day, and its influence has made it difficult for successive Argentine governments to dismantle trade barriers, make labor markets more flexible, reduce government involvement in industry, or impose

---

[10] See Taylor, "External Dependence, Demographic Burdens, and Argentine Economic Decline after the *Belle Époque*," *Journal of Economic History* 52 (December 1992), pp. 907–936.

[11] Carlos F. Díaz Alejandro, *Essays on the Economic History of the Argentine Republic* (New Haven: Yale University Press, 1970), p. 138.

control over public spending and inflation. Macroeconomic instability and slow growth have been the result. Only after the country experienced true hyperinflation at the end of the 1980s was a reform-minded government able, starting in 1991, to remove long-standing barriers to economic growth (see the discussion on pp. 684–685). Argentina's economy initially responded well to the reforms started in 1991, growing at an average annual rate of 6 percent (until a developing country recession hit late in 1997) and moving back into the ranks of upper middle-income developing countries. Afterward growth slowed dramatically, as we will see, and by 2002 the economy was once again in crisis.

The Debt Crisis of the 1980s.   In 1981–1983 the world economy suffered a steep recession. Just as the Great Depression made it hard for developing countries to make payments on their foreign loans—quickly causing an almost universal default—the great recession of the early 1980s also sparked a crisis over developing country debt.

Chapter 19 described how the U.S. Federal Reserve in 1979 adopted a tough anti-inflation policy that helped push the world economy into recession by 1981. The fall in industrial countries' aggregate demand had a direct negative impact on the developing countries, of course, but three other mechanisms were even more important. Because the developing world had extensive dollar-denominated debts, there was an immediate and spectacular rise in the interest burden debtor countries had to pay. The problem was exacerbated by the dollar's sharp appreciation in the foreign exchange market, which raised the real value of the dollar debt burden substantially. Finally, primary commodity prices collapsed, depressing the terms of trade of many poor economies.

The crisis began in August 1982 when Mexico announced that its central bank had run out of foreign reserves and that it could no longer meet payments on its $80 billion in foreign debt. Seeing potential similarities between Mexico and other large Latin American debtors such as Argentina, Brazil, and Chile, banks in the industrial countries—the largest private lenders to Latin America—scrambled to reduce their risks by cutting off new credits and demanding repayment on earlier loans.

The result was a widespread inability of developing countries to meet prior debt obligations, and a rapid move to the edge of a generalized default. Latin America was perhaps hardest hit, but so were Soviet bloc countries like Poland that had borrowed from the European banks. African countries, most of whose debts were to official agencies such as the IMF and World Bank, also became overdue on their debts. Most countries in East Asia were able to maintain economic growth and avoid rescheduling their debt (that is, stretching out repayments by promising to pay additional interest in the future). Nonetheless, by the end of 1986 more than 40 countries had encountered severe external financing problems. Growth had slowed sharply (or gone into reverse) in much of the developing world.

Initially industrial countries, with heavy involvement by the International Monetary Fund, attempted to persuade the large banks to continue lending, arguing that a coordinated lending response was the best assurance that earlier debts would be repaid. Policymakers in the industrialized countries feared that banking giants like Citicorp and Bank of America, which had significant loans in Latin America, would fail in the event of a generalized default, dragging down the world financial system with them. But the crisis didn't end until 1989 when the United States, fearing political instability to its south, insisted that

American banks give some form of debt relief to indebted developing countries. In 1990 banks agreed to reduce Mexico's debt by 12 percent, and within a year debt reduction agreements had also been negotiated by the Philippines, Costa Rica, Venezuela, Uruguay, and Niger. When Argentina and Brazil reached preliminary agreements with their creditors in 1992, it looked as if the debt crisis had finally been resolved.

Reforms, Capital Inflows, and the Return of Crisis

The early 1990s saw a renewal of private capital flows into developing countries, including some of the highly indebted Latin American countries at the center of the previous decade's debt crisis. As Table 22-3 shows, the foreign borrowing of non-oil developing countries as a group expanded sharply after 1992.

Low interest rates in the U.S. in the early 1990s certainly provided an initial impetus to these renewed capital flows. Perhaps more important, however, were serious efforts in the recipient economies to stabilize inflation, a move requiring that governments limit their roles in the economy and reduce tax evasion. At the same time, governments sought to lower trade barriers, to deregulate labor and product markets, and to improve the efficiency of financial markets. Widespread privatization has served both the microeconomic goals of fostering efficiency and competition, and the macroeconomic goals of eliminating the government's need to cover the losses of sheltered and mismanaged state-owned firms.

What finally pushed countries to undertake serious reform, despite the vested political interests favoring the status quo? One factor was the 1980s debt crisis itself, which resulted in what many commentators have called a "lost decade" of Latin American growth. Many of the relatively young policymakers who came to power in Latin America as the debt crisis ended were well-trained economists who believed that misguided economic policies and institutions had brought on the crisis and worsened its effects. Another factor was the example of East Asia, which had survived the 1980s debt crisis largely unscathed. Despite having been poorer than Latin America as recently as 1960, East Asia now was richer.

Recent economic reforms have taken different shapes in different Latin American countries, and some have made little progress. Here we contrast the macroeconomic aspects of the approaches taken in four large countries that have made wide-ranging (though not equally successful) reform attempts.

Argentina. As we have seen, Argentina tried unsuccessfully to stabilize inflation in the 1970s through a crawling peg. An Achilles' heel of its failed policy was a failure to permanently reduce the government budget deficit. Over the course of the 1980s, Argentina governments implemented successive inflation stabilization plans involving currency reforms, price controls, and other measures. The fundamental problem of government deficits was not decisively repaired and the new programs, typically after a short initial period of promise, failed. Pervasive economic instability spilled over to affect domestic financial institutions, which suffered runs and collapse. Argentina slipped into hyperinflation. In July 1989 alone, the month the Perónist president Carlos Menem was inaugurated after street rioting and the virtual breakdown of Argentina's payments system, the price level increased by 197 percent!

Argentina finally turned to radical institutional reform in a bid to end its sad history of inflation. In January 1991, President Menem appointed Domingo Cavallo, a Harvard-trained economist, as his economy minister. Under his leadership, import tariffs were slashed, government expenditures were cut, major state companies including the national airline were privatized, and tax reforms led to increased government revenues.

The most daring component of Cavallo's program, however, was the new Convertibility Law of April 1991 making Argentina's currency, then the austral, fully convertible into U.S. dollars at a *fixed* rate of 10,000 australs per dollar, changeable only by an act of the Argentine congress. At the start of the following year the currency was reformed, with one new Argentine peso replacing every 10,000 australs and thus trading at the very convenient fixed exchange rate of exactly one peso per dollar.

The Convertibility Law also required that the monetary base be backed entirely by gold or foreign currency, so in one stroke it sharply curtailed the central bank's ability to finance government deficits through continuing money creation. Argentina's Convertibility Law represented an extreme version of the exchange rate–based approach to reducing inflation that had been tried many times in the past.

This time the approach worked. Backed as it was by genuine economic and political reforms, the Cavallo plan had a dramatic effect on inflation, which has remained very low after dropping from 800 percent in 1990 to well under 5 percent by 1995. Continuing inflation in the first years of the convertibility plan, despite a fixed exchange rate, implied a steep real appreciation of the peso. From 1990 to 1995 the currency appreciated in real terms by about 30 percent. (See panel (a) of Figure 22-3.)

The peso's real appreciation led to unemployment and a growing current account deficit. After a Mexican financial crisis erupted at the turn of 1994–1995, speculators attacked Argentina's currency and domestic interest rates rose sharply. Unexpectedly higher borrowing costs placed Argentina's banks under severe pressure. The central bank could do little to help because the Convertibility Law made it hard to print pesos and lend them to the banking system as a lender of last resort. Instead, the government arranged for credits from official foreign agencies such as the World Bank. Nonetheless, output slumped and unemployment jumped; in 1996 Menem fired Cavallo.

Scarred by hyperinflation, Argentines continued to support their new monetary system despite Cavallo's departure. The peso's real appreciation process ended and Argentina's government strengthened the banking system to reduce the weaknesses that had been revealed in the 1995 crisis. By 1997 the economy was growing rapidly once again, although growth slowed subsequently in the developing country crisis. Growth turned negative subsequently and as the world economy slipped into recession in 2001, Argentina's foreign credit dried up. The country defaulted on its debts in December 2001 and abandoned the peso-dollar peg in January 2002.

Brazil. Like Argentina, Brazil suffered runaway inflation in the 1980s, as well as multiple failed attempts at stabilization accompanied by currency reforms. The country took longer to get inflation under control, however, and approached its disinflation less systematically than the Argentines did.[12]

In 1994 the Brazilian government introduced a new currency, the real (pronounced ray-AL), pegged to the dollar. At the cost of widespread bank failures, Brazil defended the new exchange rate with high interest rates in 1995, then shifted to a fixed upwardly crawling

---

[12]For an account, see Rudiger Dornbusch, "Brazil's Incomplete Stabilization and Reform," *Brookings Papers on Economic Activity* 1:1997, pp. 367–404.

peg in the face of substantial real appreciation (see panel (c) of Figure 22-3). Inflation dropped from an annual rate of 2,669 percent (1994) to under 10 percent in 1997.

Economic growth remained unimpressive, however. Although Brazil's government undertook a reduction in import barriers, privatization, and fiscal reforms, the country's overall progress on economic reform was much slower than in the case of Argentina and the government fiscal deficit remained worryingly high. A good part of the problem was the very high interest rate the government had to pay on its debt, a rate that reflected skepticism in markets that the limited upward crawl of the real against the dollar could be maintained. The skepticism proved warranted in 1999, as we see later in this chapter.

Chile.   Having learned the lessons of its deep unemployment and financial collapse at the start of the 1980s, Chile implemented more consistent reforms later in the decade. Very importantly, the country instituted a tough regulatory environment for domestic financial institutions and removed its explicit bailout guarantee. A crawling peg type of exchange rate regime was used to bring inflation down gradually, but the system was operated flexibly to avoid the extreme real appreciation that had emerged in the late 1980s. (See Figure 22-3, panel (b).) The Chilean central bank was made independent of the fiscal authorities in 1990 (the same year a democratic government replaced the former military regime). That action further solidified the commitment not to monetize government deficits.[13]

Another new policy required all capital inflows (other than equity purchases) to be accompanied by a 1-year, non-interest-bearing deposit equal to as much as 30 percent of the transaction. Because the duration of the deposit requirement was limited, the penalty fell disproportionately on short-term inflows, those most prone to be withdrawn by foreign investors in a crisis. One motivation for the implied capital inflow tax was to limit real currency appreciation; the other was to reduce the risk that a sudden withdrawal of foreign short-term funds would provoke a financial crisis. There is considerable controversy among economists as to whether the Chilean capital inflow barriers succeeded in their aims, although it is doubtful that they did much harm.[14]

Chile's policies have paid off handsomely. Between 1991 and 1997 the country enjoyed GDP growth rates averaging better than 8 percent per year. At the same time, inflation dropped from 26 percent per year in 1990 to only 6 percent in 1997. Chile has been rated not only as being the least corrupt country in Latin America, but as being cleaner than several European Union members.

Mexico.   Mexico introduced a broad stabilization and reform program in 1987, combining an aggressive reduction in public-sector deficits and debt with exchange rate targeting and wage-price guidelines negotiated with representatives of industry and labor unions.[15]

---

[13]For an overview of aspects of the Chilean approach to economic reform, see Barry P. Bosworth, Rudiger Dornbusch, and Raúl Labán, eds., *The Chilean Economy: Policy Lessons and Challenges* (Washington, D.C.: Brookings Institution, 1994).

[14]For a discussion, see Chapter 5 of the book by Kenen listed in this chapter's Further Reading.

[15]The ideas underlying the Mexican approach are explained by one of its architects, Pedro Aspe Armella, an economist trained at the Massachusetts Institute of Technology who was Mexico's finance minister from 1988–1994. See his book, *Economic Transformation the Mexican Way* (Cambridge, MA: MIT Press, 1993). See also Nora Lustig, *Mexico: The Remaking of an Economy* (Washington, D.C.: Brookings Institution, 1992).

That same year the country made a significant commitment to free trade by joining the GATT. (Mexico subsequently joined the Organization for Economic Cooperation and Development and, in 1994, joined the North American Free Trade Area.)

Mexico fixed its peso's exchange rate against the U.S. dollar at the end of 1987, moved to a crawling peg at the start of 1989, and to a crawling band at the end of 1991. The government kept a level ceiling on the peso's possible appreciation but, *tablita*-style, announced each year after 1991 a gradually rising limit on the currency's allowable depreciation. Thus, the range of allowable exchange rate fluctuation was allowed to increase over time.

Despite this potential flexibility, the Mexican authorities held the exchange rate near its appreciation ceiling. The peso therefore appreciated sharply in real terms, and a large current account deficit emerged; see Figure 22-3, panel (d). Over 1994 the country's foreign exchange reserves fell to very low levels. Civil strife, a looming presidential transition, and devaluation fears contributed to this (recall the box on Mexico's 1994 balance-of-payments crisis in Chapter 17, p. 506). Another important factor behind the foreign reserve leakage, however, was a continuing extension of government credits to banks experiencing loan losses. Mexico had rapidly privatized its banks without adequate regulatory safeguards, and it had also opened its capital account, giving the banks free access to foreign funds. As in Chile a dozen years earlier, moral hazard was rampant.

Hoping to spur growth and reduce a current account deficit that by then was nearly 8 percent of GNP, the new Mexican government devalued the peso 15 percent beyond the depreciation limit promised a year before. The devalued currency peg was immediately attacked by speculators and the government retreated to a float. Foreign investors panicked, pushing the peso down precipitously, and soon Mexico found itself unable to borrow except at penalty interest rates. As in 1982 default loomed again. The country avoided disaster only with the help of a $50 billion emergency loan orchestrated by the U.S. Treasury and the IMF.

Inflation, which had dropped from 159 percent in 1987 to only 7 percent in 1994, soared as the peso depreciated. Mexico's national output shrank by more than 6 percent in 1995. Unemployment more than doubled amid sharp fiscal cutbacks, sky-high interest rates, and a generalized banking crisis. But the contraction lasted only a year. By 1996 inflation was falling and the economy was recovering as the peso continued to float. Mexico regained access to private capital markets and repaid the U.S. Treasury ahead of schedule.

East Asia: Success and Crisis

Until 1997 the countries of East Asia were the envy of the developing world. Their rapid growth rates were bringing them far up the development scale, putting several in striking distance of advanced-country status. Then they were overwhelmed by a disastrous financial crisis. The speed with which East Asia's economic success turned into economic chaos came as a rude shock to most observers. East Asia's setback sparked a broader crisis that engulfed developing countries as distant as Russia and Brazil. In this section we review the East Asian experience and the global repercussions of the region's crisis. The lessons, as we see, reinforce those from Latin America.

The East Asian Economic Miracle

As we saw in Table 22-2, South Korea was a desperately poor nation in the 1960s, with little industry and apparently with few economic prospects. In 1963, however, the country launched a series of economic reforms, shifting from an inward-looking, import-substitution development strategy to one that emphasized exports. And the country began a remarkable economic ascent. Over the next 33 years South Korea increased its per-capita GDP by a factor of 8—roughly the same increase that the United States has achieved over the past century.

What was even more remarkable was that South Korea was not alone. Its economic rise was paralleled by that of a number of other East Asian economies. In the first wave were Hong Kong, Taiwan, and Singapore, all of which began growing rapidly in the 1960s. In the course of the 1970s and 1980s the club of rapidly growing Asian economies expanded to include Malaysia, Thailand, Indonesia, and—awesomely—China, the world's most populous nation. For the first time since the rise of Japan as an industrial power in the late nineteenth century, a substantial part of the world appeared to be making the transition from Third World to First.

There remains considerable dispute about the reasons for this economic "miracle," as we discussed in Chapter 10. In the early 1990s it was fashionable among some commentators to ascribe Asia's growth to a common Asian system of industrial policy and business-government cooperation. However, even a cursory look at the economies involved makes the claim of a common system dubious. The high-growth economies did include regimes like South Korea's, where the government took an active role in the allocation of capital between industries; but it also included regimes like those of Hong Kong and Taiwan, where such industrial policy was largely absent. Some economies, like those of Taiwan and Singapore, relied heavily on the establishment of local subsidiaries of multinational firms. Others, like South Korea and Hong Kong, relied mainly on domestic entrepreneurs.

What the high-growth economies did have in common were high rates of saving and investment; rapidly improving educational levels among the work force; and if not free trade, at least a high degree of openness to and integration with world markets.

Perhaps surprisingly, before 1990 most rapidly growing Asian economies financed the bulk of their high investment rates out of domestic savings. In the 1990s, however, the growing popularity of "emerging markets" among lenders and investors in the advanced world led to substantial capital inflows to developing Asia; as Table 22-4 shows, as a counterpart to these inflows several of the Asian countries began running large current account deficits as a share of GDP. A few economists worried that these deficits might pose the risk of a crisis similar to that which hit Mexico in late 1994, but most observers regarded large capital flows to such rapidly growing and macroeconomically stable economies as justified by the expected profitability of investment opportunities.

Table 22-4 | East Asian CA/GDP

Country	1990	1991	1992	1993	1994	1995	1996	1997
Indonesia	−2.6	−3.3	−2.0	−1.3	−1.6	−3.2	−3.4	−2.3
South Korea	−0.8	−2.8	−1.3	0.3	−1.0	−1.7	−4.4	−1.7
Malaysia	−2.0	−8.5	−3.7	−4.5	−6.1	−9.7	−4.4	−5.9
Philippines	−6.1	−2.3	−1.9	−5.5	−4.6	−2.7	−4.8	−5.3
Thailand	−8.5	−7.7	−5.7	−5.1	−5.6	−8.1	−8.1	−2.0

Source: World Bank, World Development Indicators.

WHAT DID ASIA DO RIGHT?

The growth of Asian economies between the 1960s and the 1990s demonstrated that it is possible for a country to move rapidly up the development ladder. But what are the ingredients for such success?

One way to answer this question may be to look at the distinctive attributes of what the World Bank, in its 1993 study entitled *The East Asian Miracle*, dubs the HPAEs, for high-performing Asian economies.

One important ingredient was a high saving rate: in 1990 HPAEs saved 34 percent of GDP, compared with only half that in Latin America, slightly more in South Asia.

Another important ingredient was a strong emphasis on education. Even in 1965, when the HPAEs were still quite poor, they had high enrollment rates in basic education: essentially all children received basic schooling in Hong Kong, Singapore, and South Korea, and even desperately poor Indonesia had a 70 percent enrollment rate. By 1987, rates of enrollment in secondary school in Asia were well above those in Latin American nations such as Brazil.

Finally, two other characteristics of the HPAEs were a relatively stable macroeconomic environment, free from high inflation or major economic slumps, and a high share of trade in GDP. The accompanying table shows annual average inflation rates from 1961 to 1991 and 1988 trade shares (exports plus imports as a share of GDP) for selected Asian countries, comparing them with other developing areas. The contrast in stability and openness with Latin America is particularly clear.

These contrasts played an important role in the "conversion" of many leaders in Latin America and elsewhere to the idea of economic reform, both in terms of a commitment to price stability and opening markets to the world.

Country	Inflation rate, 1961–1991	Trade share, 1988 (ratio)
Hong Kong	8.8	2.82
Indonesia	12.4	0.42
South Korea	12.2	0.66
Malaysia	3.4	1.09
Singapore	3.6	3.47
Taiwan	6.2	0.90
Thailand	5.6	0.35
South Asia	8.0	0.19
Latin America	192.1	0.23

Asian Weaknesses

As it turned out, in 1997 Asian economies did indeed experience a severe financial crisis. And with the benefit of hindsight, several weaknesses in their economic structures—some shared by Latin American countries that had gone through crises—became apparent. Three issues in particular stood out:

Productivity. Although the rapid growth of Asian economies was not in any sense an illusion, even before the crisis a number of studies had suggested that some limits to expansion were appearing. The most surprising result of several studies was that the bulk of

Asian output growth could be explained simply by the rapid growth of production *inputs*—capital and labor—and that there had been relatively little increase in productivity, that is, in output per unit of input. Thus in South Korea, for example, the convergence toward advanced-country output per capita appeared to be mainly due to a rapid shift of workers from agriculture to industry, a rise in educational levels, and a massive increase in the capital-labor ratio within the nonagricultural sector. Evidence for a narrowing of the technologic gap with the West was unexpectedly hard to find. The implication of these studies' conclusions was that continuing high rates of capital accumulation would eventually produce diminishing returns, and, possibly, that the large capital inflows taking place were not justified by future profitability after all.

Banking regulation. Of more immediate relevance to the crisis was the poor state of banking regulation in most Asian economies. Domestic depositors and foreign investors regarded Asian banks as safe, not only because of the strength of the economies, but because they believed that governments would stand behind the banks in case of any difficulties. But banks and other financial institutions were not subject to effective government supervision over the kinds of risks they were undertaking. As the experience in Latin America should have made clear, moral hazard was present in spades. Despite this, several of the East Asian countries had eased private access to capital inflows in the 1990s, and foreign money was readily available both to East Asian banks and directly to East Asian corporate borrowers.

In several Asian countries, close ties between business interests and government officials appear to have helped foster considerable moral hazard in lending. In Thailand so-called "finance companies," often run by relatives of government officials, lent money to highly speculative real estate ventures; in Indonesia lenders were far too eager to finance ventures by members of the president's family. These factors help to explain how, despite high saving rates, East Asian countries were led to invest so much that their current accounts were in deficit prior to the crisis.

Some analysts have suggested that excessive lending, driven by moral hazard, helped create an unsustainable boom in Asian economies, especially in real estate, that temporarily concealed the poor quality of many of the investments; and that the inevitable end of this boom caused a downward spiral of declining prices and failing banks. However, while moral hazard was certainly a factor in the runup to crisis, its importance remains a subject of considerable dispute.

Legal framework. One important weakness of Asian economies only became apparent after they stumbled: the lack of a good legal framework for dealing with companies in trouble. In the United States, there is a well-established procedure for bankruptcy—that is, for dealing with a company that cannot pay its debts. In such a procedure, the courts take possession of the firm on behalf of the creditors, then seek to find a way to satisfy their claims as well as possible. Often this means keeping the company in existence and converting the debts it cannot pay into ownership shares. In Asian economies, however, bankruptcy law was weak, in part because the astonishing growth of the economies had made corporate failures a rare event. When times did turn bad, a destructive impasse developed. Troubled companies would simply stop paying their debts. They then could not operate effectively because nobody would lend to them until the outstanding debts were repaid. Yet the creditors lacked any way to seize the limping enterprises from their original owners.

Of course, every economy has weaknesses, but the performance of the East Asian economies had been so spectacular that few paid much attention to theirs. Even those who were aware that the "miracle" economies had problems could hardly have anticipated the catastrophe that overtook them in 1997.

The Asian Financial Crisis

The Asian financial crisis is generally considered to have started on July 2, 1997, with the devaluation of the Thai baht. Thailand had been showing signs of financial strain for more than a year. During 1996 it became apparent that far too many office towers had been built; first the nation's real estate market, then its stock market, went into decline. In the first half of 1997 speculation about a possible devaluation of the baht led to an accelerating loss of foreign exchange reserves, and on July 2 the country attempted a controlled 15 percent devaluation. As in the case of Mexico in 1994, however, the attempted moderate devaluation spun out of control, sparking massive speculation and a far deeper plunge.

Thailand itself is a small economy. However, the sharp drop in the Thai currency was followed by speculation against the currencies first of its immediate neighbor Malaysia, then of Indonesia, and eventually of the much larger and more developed economy of South Korea. All of these economies seemed to speculators to share with Thailand the weaknesses previously listed; all were feeling the effects in 1997 of renewed economic slowdown in their largest industrial neighbor, Japan. In each case governments were faced with awkward dilemmas, stemming partly from the dependence of their economies on trade, partly from the fact that domestic banks and companies had large debts denominated in dollars. If the countries simply allowed their currencies to drop, rising import prices would threaten to produce dangerous inflation, and the sudden increase in the domestic-currency value of debts might push many potentially viable banks and companies into bankruptcy. On the other hand, to defend the currencies would require at least temporary high interest rates to persuade investors to keep their money in the country, and these high interest rates would themselves produce an economic slump and cause banks to fail.

All of the afflicted countries except Malaysia turned to the IMF for assistance, and received loans in return for implementation of economic plans that were supposed to contain the damage: higher interest rates to limit the exchange rate depreciation, efforts to avoid large budget deficits, and "structural" reforms that were supposed to deal with the weaknesses that had brought on the crisis in the first place. Despite the IMF's aid, however, the result of the currency crises was a sharp economic downturn. As Table 22-5 indicates, all of the troubled countries went from growth rates in excess of 6 percent in 1996 to a severe contraction in 1998, with many observers expecting further decline in 1999.

Worst of all was the case of Indonesia, where economic crisis and political instability reinforced each other in a deadly spiral, all made much worse by a collapse of confidence by domestic residents in the nation's banks. By the summer of 1998 the Indonesian rupiah had lost 85 percent of its original value, and few if any major companies were solvent. The Indonesian population was faced with mass unemployment, and in some cases with inability to afford even basic foodstuffs. Ethnic violence broke out.

As a consequence of the collapse of confidence, the troubled Asian economies were also forced into a dramatic reversal of their current account positions: as Table 22-5 shows, they moved from large deficits in 1996 to huge surpluses only 2 years later. Most of this reversal

Table 22-5 Growth and the Current Account, Five Asian Crisis Countries						
Variable	1996	1997	1998	1999	2000	2001
Real output growth (percent per year)	7.0	4.5	–8.1	6.9	7.0	1.6
Current account (percent of output)	–5.1	–2.7	10.5	7.6	5.1	3.9

The countries are those listed in Table 22-4.

Source: Institute for International Finance.

came not through increased exports but through a huge drop in imports, as the economies contracted.

Currencies stabilized throughout crisis-stricken Asia and interest rates decreased, but the direct spillover from the region's slump caused slowdowns or recessions in several neighboring countries, including Hong Kong, Singapore, and New Zealand. Japan and even parts of Europe and Latin America were feeling the effects. Most governments continued to take IMF-prescribed medicine, but in September 1998 Malaysia—which had never accepted an IMF program—broke ranks and imposed extensive controls on capital movements, hoping that the controls would allow it to ease monetary and fiscal policy without sending its currency into a tailspin.

Fortunately, the downturn in East Asia was "V-shaped": after the sharp output contraction in 1998, growth returned in 1999 (see Table 22-5) as depreciated currencies spurred higher exports. Not all of the region's economies fared equally well, and controversy remains over the effectiveness of Malaysia's experiment with capital controls. As the United States economy entered recession early in 2001, however, Asia's growth slowed sharply.

Crises in Other Developing Regions

Asia's woes sparked a general flight by investors from emerging markets, putting severe pressure on the economic policies of distant developing nations. Two countries, Russia and Brazil, were affected soon after. A third, Argentina, held on to its fixed exchange rate for three agonizing years before yielding to market pressure and devaluing in January 2002.

Russia's Crisis.   Starting in 1989, the countries of the Soviet bloc, and ultimately the Soviet Union itself, shook off communist rule and embarked on transitions from centrally planned economic allocation to the market.

These transitions were uniformly traumatic, involving rapid inflation, steep output declines, and a phenomenon that had been largely unknown in planned economies—unemployment. Such traumatic beginnings were inevitable. In most of the formerly communist countries nearly the entire economy had to be privatized. Financial markets and banking practices were largely unknown, there was no legal framework for private economic relations or corporate governance, and initial property rights were ambiguous. States lacked the modern fiscal machinery through which industrial countries design and collect taxes, and given the cautious attitude of foreign investors and the absence of domestic capital markets, the monetary printing press was the only way to finance needed social expenditures.

Table 22-6	Real Output Growth and Inflation: Russia and Poland, 1991–2000 (percent per year)									
	1991	1992	1993	1994	1995	1996	1997	1998	1999	2000
Real Output Growth										
Russia	−5.4	−19.4	−10.4	−11.6	−4.2	−3.4	0.9	−4.9	3.2	7.5
Poland	−7.0	2.6	4.3	5.2	6.8	6.0	6.8	4.8	4.1	4.1
Inflation Rate										
Russia	92.7	1,353.0	875.0	307.0	197.0	47.6	14.7	27.7	85.7	20.8
Poland	70.3	43.0	35.3	32.2	27.9	19.9	14.9	11.8	7.3	10.1

Source: IMF, *World Economic Outlook,* various issues.

By the end of the 1990s, a handful of East European economies including Poland, Hungary, and the Czech Republic had made successful transitions to the capitalist order.[16] Not surprisingly each of these countries was geographically close to the EU and had a recent tradition (prior to Soviet occupation in the late 1940s) of industrial capitalism, including a body of contract and property law. Many of the other successor states that emerged from the wreckage of the Soviet Union were still faring quite badly even as the twentieth century ended. The largest was Russia, which retained much of the nuclear weaponry left by the Soviet Union. Table 22-6 compares Russia's output and inflation performance with that of one of the most successful countries in the region, Poland.

Over the course of the 1990s, Russia's weak government was unable to collect taxes or even to enforce basic laws; the country was riddled with corruption and organized crime. It is no wonder that measured output shrank steadily and that inflation was hard to control, so that at the end of the 1990s most Russians were substantially worse off than under the old Soviet regime. In 1997 the government managed to stabilize the ruble and reduce inflation with the help of IMF credits, and the economy even managed to eke out a (barely) positive GDP growth rate that year. However, the government had slowed inflation by substituting borrowing for seigniorage; neither the government's attempts to collect taxes or reduce spending were very successful, and the state debt therefore had ballooned. When, in addition, the prices of oil and other key Russian commodity exports were depressed by the crisis in Asia, investors began to fear in the spring of 1998 that the ruble, like many of the Asian currencies the year before, was in for a steep devaluation. Interest rates on government borrowing rose, inflating Russia's fiscal deficit.

Despite Russia's failure to abide by earlier IMF stabilization programs, the Fund nonetheless entered into a new agreement with its government and provided billions to back up the ruble's exchange rate. The IMF feared that a Russian collapse could lead to renewed turbulence in the developing world, as well as posing a nuclear threat if Russia decided to

---

[16]These three countries were admitted to the North Atlantic Treaty Organization (NATO) in 1999, and were on the short list for admission into the European Union (EU) early in the twenty-first century.

sell off its arsenal. In mid-August, however, the Russian government abandoned its exchange rate target; at the same time as it devalued, it defaulted on its debts and froze international payments. The government resumed printing money to pay its bills and within a month the ruble had lost half its value. As Table 22-6 shows, inflation took off and output slumped. Despite Russia's rather small direct relevance to the wealth of international investors, its actions set off panic in the world capital market as investors tried to increase their liquidity by selling emerging market securities. In response the U.S. Federal Reserve lowered dollar interest rates sharply, possibly (we will never know for sure!) averting a worldwide financial collapse. Output recovered partially in 1999 and growth was rapid in 2000, helped by higher world oil prices and low Russian output prices following the ruble's sharp depreciation.

Brazil's 1999 Crisis.   Brazil was particularly badly hit by the sell-off following the Russian crisis. Like Russia, Brazil had a public debt problem. Continuing speculation against the real had raised domestic interest rates and swollen government deficits. In the fall of 1998 speculative pressure intensified and Brazil's foreign exchange reserves began bleeding away very quickly.

Concerned that a Brazilian crisis would destabilize world capital markets even further and threaten the hard-won stability of neighboring countries such as Argentina, Chile, and Mexico, the IMF helped put together a stabilization fund of over $40 billion to help Brazil defend the real. Effectively doubling Brazil's foreign exchange reserves, the loan facility was meant to calm investors' fears while Brazil's government put its fiscal house in order.

The plan failed: in January 1999 Brazil devalued the real by 8 percent, then allowed it to float. Very quickly the real lost 40 percent of its value against the dollar. Recession followed as the government struggled to prevent the real from going into a free fall. But the recession proved short lived, inflation did not take off, and (because Brazil's financial institutions, unlike East Asia's, had avoided heavy borrowing in dollars), financial-sector collapse was avoided.

Argentina's 2001–2002 Crisis.   Immediate fears that Brazil's devaluation would lead to crises in its big regional neighbors, notably Argentina, proved unfounded, although Argentina, Chile, and Mexico all experienced slower growth. While the flexible exchange rate arrangements of Chile and Mexico proved adaptable to global economic changes, however, Argentina's rigid peg of its peso to the dollar proved increasingly painful as the dollar itself appreciated in the foreign exchange market. As panel (a) of Figure 22-3 shows, the peso's real exchange rate remained high despite high domestic unemployment, and the country's current account deficit remained high. A new government took over in 1999, but the slowdown in U.S. growth starting in 2000, coupled with worsening fiscal deficits, spooked foreigners who otherwise might have continued investing in the country. In 2001 Argentina's foreign borrowing rates skyrocketed. Even the increasingly desperate efforts of Convertibility Law architect Domingo Cavallo, recalled from private life to turn the economy around, proved insufficient. Late in 2001 the government restricted residents' withdrawals from banks in order to stem the run on the peso, and then the government stopped payment on its foreign debts. Following this default, the government in January 2002 established a dual exchange rate system, with controls on capital outflow and separate exchange rates for current account and financial transactions. The current account exchange rate was devalued to a fixed level of 1.40 pesos per U.S. dollar, while the floating financial rate headed quickly to 2 pesos per dollar, double the rate that had prevailed for the previous decade. A month later a single floating-rate system for the peso was established. Later in 2002, residents' access to their bank accounts was blocked and the exchange rate touched 4 pesos per dollar. As had happened so often in the past, Argentina again faced political and economic chaos.

CASE STUDY

Can Currency Boards Make Fixed Exchange Rates Credible?

Argentina's 1991 monetary law requiring 100 percent foreign exchange backing for the monetary base made it an example of a **currency board**, in which the monetary base is backed entirely by foreign currency and the central bank therefore holds no domestic assets (Chapter 17). A major advantage of the currency board system, aside from the constraint it places on fiscal policy, is that the central bank can never run out of foreign exchange reserves in the face of a speculative attack on the exchange rate.[17]

Developing countries are often advised by observers to adopt currency board systems. How do currency boards work, and can they be relied on to insulate economies from speculative pressures?

In a currency board regime, a note-issuing authority announces an exchange rate against some foreign currency and, at that rate, simply carries out any trades of domestic currency notes against the foreign currency that the public initiates. The currency board is prohibited by law from acquiring any *domestic* assets, so all the currency it issues automatically is fully backed by foreign reserves. In most cases the note-issuing authority is not even a central bank: its primary role could be performed as well by a vending machine.

Currency boards originally arose in the colonial territories of European powers. By adopting a currency board system, the colony effectively let its imperial ruler run its monetary policy, at the same time handing the ruling country all seigniorage coming from the colony's demand for money. Hong Kong has a currency board that originated this way, although the British crown colony (as it was before reverting to China on July 1, 1997) switched from being a pound sterling currency board to being a U.S. dollar currency board after the Bretton Woods system fell apart.

More recently, the automatic, "vending machine" character of currency boards has been seen as a way to import anti-inflation credibility from the country to which the domestic currency is pegged. Thus Argentina, with its experience of hyperinflation, mandated a currency board rule in its 1991 Convertibility Law in an attempt to convince a skeptical world that it would not even have the option of inflationary policies in the future. Similarly, Estonia and Latvia, with no recent track record of monetary policy after decades of Soviet rule, hoped to establish low-inflation reputations by setting up currency boards after they gained independence.

---

[17]Strictly speaking, Argentina's version of a currency board involved a slight fudge. A limited fraction of the monetary base could be held in the form of U.S. dollar–denominated Argentine government debt. This provision was analogous to the "fiduciary issue" of domestic credit that central banks were entitled to extend under the pre-1914 gold standard.

While a currency board has the advantage of moving monetary policy farther away from the hands of politicians who might abuse it, it also has disadvantages, even compared to the alternative of a conventional fixed exchange rate. Since the currency board may not acquire domestic assets, it cannot lend currency freely to domestic banks in times of financial panic (a problem Argentina encountered, as we have seen). There are other ways for the government to backstop bank deposits, for example, deposit insurance, which amounts to a government guarantee to use its taxation power, if necessary, to pay depositors. But the flexibility to print currency when the public is demanding it from banks gives the government's deposit guarantee extra clout.

Another drawback compared to a conventional fixed exchange rate is in the area of stabilization policies. For a country that is completely open to international capital movements monetary policy is ineffective anyway under a fixed rate, so the sacrifice of open-market operations in domestic assets is costless (recall Chapter 17). This is not true, however, for the many developing countries that maintain some effective capital account restrictions—for them, monetary policy can have effects, even with a fixed exchange rate, because domestic interest rates are not tightly linked to world rates. As we saw in Chapter 17, moreover, a devaluation that *surprises* market participants can help to reduce unemployment, even when capital is fully mobile. The devaluation option becomes a problem, though, when people *expect* it to be used. In that case, expectations of devaluation, by themselves, raise real interest rates and slow the economy. By foreswearing the devaluation option, countries that adopt currency boards hope to have a long-term stabilizing effect on expectations that outweighs the occasional inconvenience of being unable to surprise the markets.

In the wake of Mexico's 1994–1995 crisis, several critics of the country's policies suggested it would do well to turn to a currency board. The subsequent crisis that started in Asia generated calls for currency boards in Indonesia, Brazil, and even Russia. Can a currency board really enhance the credibility of fixed exchange rates and low-inflation policies?

Since a currency board typically may not acquire government debt, some argue that it can discourage fiscal deficits, thus reducing a major cause of inflation and devaluation (although Argentina's experience in this area provides a counter-example). The high level of foreign reserves relative to the monetary base also enhances credibility. Other factors, however, including the banking sector's increased vulnerability, can put the government under pressure to abandon the currency board link altogether. If markets anticipate the possibility of devaluation, some of the potential benefits of a currency board will be lost, as Argentina's experience shows. For just that reason, some Argentine policymakers suggested that their country adopt a policy of **dollarization**, under which it would forgo having a domestic currency altogether and simply use the U.S. dollar instead. The only loss, they argued, would have been the transfer of some seigniorage to the United States. But the possibility of devaluation would have been banished, leading to a fall in domestic interest rates.

For a country with a legacy of high inflation, the most solemn commitment to maintain a currency will fail to bring automatic immunity from speculation. Even Hong Kong's long-standing link to the dollar was fiercely attacked by speculators during the Asian crisis, leading to very high interest rates and a deep recession. Currency boards can bring credibility only if countries also have the political will to repair the economic weaknesses—such as rigid labor markets, fragile banking systems, and shaky public finances—that could make them vulnerable to speculative attack. On this criterion, Indonesia and Brazil probably do not qualify and Russia certainly does not. With its lack of wage flexibility and unstable public finances, Argentina ultimately failed the test. Developing countries that are too unstable to manage flexible exchange rates successfully are best advised to dispense with a national currency altogether and adopt a widely used and stable foreign money.[18] Even then, they will remain vulnerable to credit crises if foreign lenders fear the possibility of default.

Lessons of Developing Country Crises

The emerging market crisis that started with Thailand's 1997 devaluation produced what might be called an orgy of finger-pointing. Some Westerners blamed the crisis on the policies of the Asians themselves, especially the "crony capitalism" under which businessmen and politicians had excessively cozy relationships. Some Asian leaders, in turn, blamed the crisis on the machinations of Western financiers; even Hong Kong, normally a bastion of free-market sentiment, began intervening to block what it described as a conspiracy by speculators to drive down its stock market and undermine its currency. And almost everyone criticized the IMF, although some said it was wrong to tell countries to try to limit the depreciation of their currencies, others that it was wrong to allow the currencies to depreciate at all.

Nonetheless some very clear lessons emerge from a careful study of the recent crisis and earlier developing country crises in Latin America and elsewhere.

1. *Choosing the right exchange rate regime.* It is perilous for a developing country to fix its exchange rate unless it has the means and commitment to do so, come what may. East Asian countries found that confidence in official exchange rate targets encouraged borrowing in foreign currencies. When devaluation occurred nonetheless, much of the financial sector and many corporations became insolvent. The developing countries that have successfully stabilized inflation have adopted more flexible exchange rate systems or moved to greater flexibility quickly after an initial period of pegging aimed at reducing inflation expectations. When they have not done this, they have tended to experience real appreciations and current account deficits that leave them vulnerable to speculative attack. Even in Argentina, where the public's fear of returning to the hyperinflationary past instilled a widely shared determination to prevent inflation, a fixed exchange rate proved untenable over the long term. Mexico's experience since 1995 shows that larger developing countries can manage quite well with a floating exchange rate, and it is hard to believe that, if Mexico had been fixing, it would have survived 1998 without a currency crisis.

2. *The central importance of banking.* A large part of what made the Asian crisis so devastating was that it was not purely a currency crisis, but rather a currency crisis

---

[18]For a clear overview of the theory and practice of currency boards, see Owen F. Humpage and Jean M. McIntire, "An Introduction to Currency Boards," *Federal Reserve Bank of Cleveland Economic Review* 31 (Quarter 2, 1995), pp. 2–11. See also Tomás J. T. Baliño, Charles Enoch, et al., *Currency Board Arrangements: Issues and Experiences,* Occasional Paper 151 (Washington, D.C.: International Monetary Fund, August 1997). For a skeptical view of even the case for dollarization, see Sebastian Edwards, "The False Promise of Dollarisation," *Financial Times,* May 11, 2001, p. 17.

inextricably mixed with a banking and financial crisis. In the most immediate sense, governments were faced with the conflict between restricting the money supply to support the currency and the need to print large quantities of money to deal with bank runs. More broadly, the collapse of many banks disrupted the economy by cutting off channels of credit, making it difficult for even profitable companies to continue business. This should not have come as a surprise in Asia. Similar effects of banking fragility played roles in the crises of the Southern Cone economies in the 1980s and of Mexico in 1994–1995, and even in those of industrial countries like Sweden during the 1992 attacks on the EMS (Chapter 20). Unfortunately, Asia's spectacular economic performance prior to its crisis blinded people to its financial vulnerabilities. In the future, wise governments will devote a great deal of attention to shoring up their banking systems to minimize moral hazard, in the hope of becoming less vulnerable to financial catastrophes.

3. *The proper sequence of reform measures.* Economic reformers in developing countries have learned the hard way that the order in which liberalization measures are taken really does matter. That truth also follows from basic economic theory: the principle of the *second best* tells us (recall Chapter 9) that when an economy suffers from multiple distortions, the removal of only a few may make matters worse, not better. Developing countries generally suffer from many, many distortions, so the point is especially important for them. Consider the sequencing of capital account liberalization and financial sector reform, for example. It is clearly a mistake to open up the capital account before sound safeguards and supervision are in place for domestic financial institutions. Otherwise, the ability to borrow abroad will simply encourage reckless lending by domestic banks. When the economy slows down, foreign capital will flee, leaving domestic banks insolvent. Thus, developing countries should delay opening the capital account until the domestic financial system is strong enough to withstand the sometimes violent ebb and flow of world capital. Economists also argue that trade liberalization should precede capital account liberalization. Capital account liberalization may cause real exchange rate volatility and impede the movement of factors of production from nontraded into traded goods industries.

4. *The importance of contagion.* A final lesson of developing country experience is the vulnerability of even seemingly healthy economies to crises of confidence generated by events elsewhere in the world—a domino effect that has come to be known as **contagion**. Contagion was at work when the crisis in Thailand, a small economy in Southeast Asia, provoked another crisis in South Korea, a much larger economy some 7,000 miles away. An even more spectacular example emerged in August 1998, when a plunge in the Russian ruble sparked massive speculation against Brazil's real. The problem of contagion, and the concern that even the most careful economic management may not offer full immunity, has become central to the discussion of possible reforms of the international financial system, to which we now turn.

Reforming the World's Financial "Architecture"

Economic difficulties lead, inevitably, to proposals for economic reforms. The Asian economic crisis and its repercussions suggested to many people that the international monetary system, or at least the part of it that applied to developing countries, was in need of an overhaul. Proposals for such an overhaul have come to be grouped under the impressive if vague title of plans for a new financial "architecture."

Why did the Asian crisis convince nearly everyone of an urgent need for rethinking international monetary relations, when earlier crises of the 1990s did not? One reason was that the Asian countries' problems seemed to stem primarily from their connections with the world capital market. The crisis clearly demonstrated that a country can be vulnerable to a currency crisis even if its position looks healthy by normal measures. None of the troubled Asian economies had serious budget deficits, excessive rates of monetary expansion, worrisome levels of inflation, or any of the other indicators that have traditionally signaled vulnerability to speculative attack. If there were severe weaknesses in the economies—a proposition that is the subject of dispute, since some economists argue that they would have been quite healthy had it not been for the speculative attacks—they involved issues like the strength of the banking system that might have remained dormant in the absence of sharp currency depreciations.

The second reason for rethinking international finance was the apparent strength of contagion through the international capital markets. The speed and force with which market disturbances could be spread between distant economies suggested that preventive measures taken by individual economies might not suffice. Just as a concern about economic interdependence had inspired the Bretton Woods blueprint for the world economy in 1944, world policymakers again put the reform of the international system on their agendas. It is unclear which, if any, plans have a serious chance of being adopted, but we can at least look at some of the main issues involved.

Capital Mobility and the Trilemma of the Exchange Rate Regime

One effect of the Asian crisis has been to dispel any illusions we may have had about the availability of easy answers to the problems of international macroeconomics and finance. The crisis and its spread made it all too clear that some well-known policy trade-offs for open economies remain as stark as ever—and perhaps have become even more difficult to manage.

Chapter 21 spelled out the basic macroeconomic policy *trilemma* for open economies. Of three goals that most countries share—*independence in monetary policy, stability in the exchange rate,* and the *free movement of capital*—only two can be reached simultaneously. Figure 22-4 shows these three objectives schematically as the vertices of a triangle. Exchange rate stability is more important for the typical developing country than for the typical developed country. Developing countries have less ability to influence their terms of trade than developed countries do, and exchange rate stability can be more important for keeping inflation expectations in check in developing countries.

The dilemmas facing would-be reformers of the world's financial architecture can then be summarized as follows: Because of the threat of the kind of currency crises that hit Mexico in 1994–1995 and Asia in 1997, it seems to be hard if not impossible to achieve all three objectives at the same time. To achieve one, that is, one must give up one of the others. Schematically, one must choose one of the sides of the triangle.

Until the late 1970s most developing countries maintained exchange controls and limited private capital movements in particular, as we have seen. (Some major developing countries, notably China and India, still retain such controls.) While there was considerable evasion of the controls, they did slow up the movement of capital. As a result, countries could peg their exchange rates for extended periods—producing exchange rate stability—yet

Figure 22-4 | The Policy Trilemma for Open Economies

The vertices of the triangle show three goals that policymakers in open economies would like to achieve. Unfortunately, at most two can coexist: one of the triangle's three sides must be chosen. Each of the three policy regime labels (floating exchange rates, currency board, capital controls) is consistent with the two goals that it lies between in the diagram.

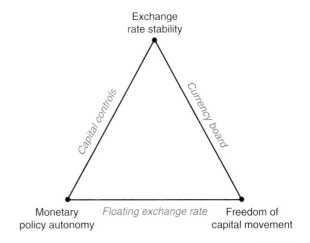

devalue their currencies on occasion, offering considerable monetary autonomy. This "adjustable peg" system is shown along one of the sides of the triangle in Figure 22-4. The main problem with it was that it imposed onerous restrictions on international transactions, reducing efficiency and contributing to corruption.

In the last two decades of the twentieth century capital became substantially more mobile, largely because controls were lifted, but also because of improved communications technology. This new capital mobility made adjustable peg regimes extremely vulnerable to speculation, since capital would flee a currency on the slightest hint that it might be devalued. (The same phenomenon occurred among developed countries in the 1960s, as we saw in Chapter 18.) The result has been to drive developing countries toward one of the other sides of the triangle: either rigidly fixed exchange rates and a renunciation of monetary autonomy, like the currency board system described on pp. 695–697, or toward flexibly managed (and even floating) exchange rates. But despite the lesson of experience that intermediate positions are dangerous, developing countries have been uncomfortable with both extremes. While a major economy like the United States can accept a widely fluctuating exchange rate, a smaller economy often finds the costs of such volatility hard to sustain. Meanwhile, as we have seen, a rigid system like a currency board can deprive a country of much-needed flexibility, especially when dealing with financial crises where the central bank must act as lender of last resort.

Some respected economists, including Columbia University's Jagdish Bhagwati and Harvard University's Dani Rodrik, have argued that developing countries should keep or reinstate restrictions on capital mobility to be able to exercise monetary autonomy while enjoying stable exchange rates.[19] In the face of the crisis, China and India, for example,

---

[19]See Jagdish N. Bhagwati, "The Capital Myth," *Foreign Affairs* 77 (May–June, 1998); and Dani Rodrik, "Who Needs Capital-Account Convertibility?" in Stanley Fischer et al., *Should the IMF Pursue Capital-Account Convertibility?* Princeton Essays in International Finance 207 (May 1998).

have put plans to liberalize their capital accounts on hold; some countries that had liberalized capital movements considered the possibility of reimposing restrictions (as Malaysia actually did). However, most policymakers, both in the developing world and in the West, continued to regard capital controls as either impossible to enforce or too disruptive of normal business relationships (as well as a potent source of corruption). Thus most discussion of financial architecture focused instead on meliorative measures—on ways to make the remaining choices less painful.

"Prophylactic" Measures

Since the risk of financial crisis is what makes the choices surrounding the choice of exchange rate regime so difficult, some recent proposals focus on ways to reduce that risk. Typical proposals include calls for the following:

More "transparency." At least part of what went wrong in Asia was that foreign banks and other investors lent money to Asian enterprises without any clear idea of what the risks were, and then pulled their money out equally blindly when it became clear that those risks were larger than they imagined. There have therefore been many proposals for greater "transparency"—that is, better provision of financial information, in the same way that corporations in the United States are required to provide accurate public reports of their financial positions. The hope is that increased transparency will reduce both the tendency of too much money to rush into a country when things are going well, and the rush for the exits when the truth turns out to be less favorable than the image.

Stronger banking systems. As we have seen, one factor that made the Asian crisis so severe was the way that currency crisis interacted with bank runs. It is at least possible that these interactions would be milder if banks themselves were stronger. So there have also been many proposals for strengthening banks, both through closer regulation of the risks they take and through increased capital requirements, which ensure that substantial amounts of the owners' own money is at risk.

Enhanced credit lines. Some reformers also want to establish special credit lines that nations can draw on in the event of a currency crisis, in effect adding to their foreign exchange reserves. The idea would be that the mere existence of these credit lines would usually make them unnecessary: as long as speculators knew that countries had enough credit to meet even a large outflow of funds, they would not hope or fear that their own actions would produce a sudden devaluation. Such credit lines could be provided by private banks, or by public bodies such as the IMF.

Increased equity capital inflows relative to debt inflows. If developing countries financed a greater proportion of their private foreign capital inflows through equity portfolio investment or direct foreign investment rather than through debt issuance, the probability of default would be much lower. The country's payments to foreigners would then be more closely linked to its economic fortunes, falling automatically when times were hard.

How effective these various measures might be remains a matter of dispute. Cynics suggest that there was plenty of negative information about Asian economies before the crisis, if investors had only been willing to see it, and that the size of the capital flight that actually took place would have swamped any bank capital and any credit line. Nonetheless, it seems likely at the time of writing that some of these measures will be put into effect.

Coping with Crisis

Even with the proposed prophylactic measures, crises would still surely happen. Thus there have also been proposals for modifying the way the world responds to such crises.

Many of these proposals relate to the role and policies of the IMF. Here opinion is bitterly divided. Some conservative critics believe that the IMF should simply be abolished, arguing that its very existence encourages irresponsible lending by making lenders believe that they will always be saved from the consequences of their actions—a version of the moral hazard argument previously described. Other critics argue that the IMF is necessary, but that it has misconstrued its role—for example, by trying to insist on structural reform when it should restrict itself to narrowly financial issues. Finally, defenders of the IMF—and also some of its critics—argue that the agency is simply underfunded for its task, that in a world of high capital mobility it needs the ability to provide much larger loans much more quickly than it presently can.

Another set of proposals is based on the proposition that sometimes a country simply cannot pay its debts, and therefore needs the equivalent of bankruptcy proceedings for a company. Proposals for an international "Chapter 11" mechanism (named after the relevant clause in U.S. bankruptcy law) envision a formal procedure whereby a country can seek international legal authorization to temporarily stop paying its debts, and then negotiate a settlement that gives it more time to repay, or in extreme circumstances actually writes off part of its obligations. As we noted in our discussion of the Latin American debt crisis of the 1980s, limited debt writeoffs did bring that crisis to an end. Proponents of an international Chapter 11 argue that such procedures should become, if not routine, at least regularized. Critics argue that such a procedure will be either ineffective or counterproductive (because it would encourage countries to borrow too much, in the knowledge that they can easily repudiate their debts—moral hazard once again).

A Confused Future

If this brief discussion seems to suggest a high degree of confusion about the future financial "architecture," you have the right idea. At this point the one really clear thing is that while large advanced countries may be comfortable with floating exchange rates and international capital mobility, developing countries do not seem to have any entirely satisfactory alternatives. A good guess is that the next few years will see considerable experimentation, with many different schemes for global reform, and with developing individual countries trying a variety of approaches—floating exchange rates (as in Mexico and Brazil), capital controls (as in China and Malaysia), currency boards (as in Estonia and Hong Kong), and perhaps even abolition of national currencies and adoption of the dollar or euro for domestic transactions. Whether or when a coherent architecture will emerge from this free-for-all is anyone's guess.

Summary

1. There are vast differences in per-capita income and in well-being between countries at different stages of economic development. Furthermore, developing countries have not shown a uniform tendency of *convergence* to the income levels of industrial

countries. Some developing countries, however, notably several in East Asia, have seen dramatic increases in living standards since the 1960s. Explaining why some countries remain poor and which policies can promote economic growth remains one of the most important challenges in economics.

2. Developing countries form a heterogeneous group, especially since many have embarked on wide-ranging economic reform in recent years. Most have at least some of the following features: heavy government involvement in the economy, including a large share of public spending in GNP; a track record of high inflation, usually reflecting government attempts to extract *seigniorage* from the economy in the face of ineffective tax collection; weak credit institutions and undeveloped capital markets; pegged exchange rates and exchange or capital controls, including *crawling peg* exchange rate regimes aimed at either controlling inflation or preventing real appreciation; a heavy reliance on primary commodity exports. Corruption seems to increase as a country's relative poverty rises. Many of the preceding developing country features date from the Great Depression of the 1930s, when industrialized countries turned inward and world markets collapsed.

3. Because many developing economies offer potentially rich opportunities for investment, it is natural that they have current account deficits and borrow from richer countries. In principle, developing country borrowing can lead to gains from trade that make both borrowers and lenders better off. In practice, however, borrowing by developing countries has sometimes led to *default* crises that generally interact with currency and banking crises. Like currency and banking crises, default crises can contain a self-fulfilling element, even though their occurrence depends on fundamental weaknesses in the borrowing country.

4. In the 1970s, as the Bretton Woods system collapsed, countries in Latin America entered an era of distinctly inferior macroeconomic performance with respect to growth and inflation. In the 1970s countries in Latin America's Southern Cone made unsuccessful attempts at exchange rate–based inflation reduction, which invariably produced massive real appreciation and currency collapse. Uncontrolled external borrowing led in the 1980s to a generalized developing country debt crisis, with its greatest impact in Latin America and in Africa. Starting with Chile in the mid-1980s, some large Latin American countries started to undertake more thorough economic reform, including not just disinflation but also control of the government budget, vigorous *privatization,* deregulation, and trade policy reform. Argentina adopted a *currency board* in 1991. Not all the Latin American reformers succeeded equally in strengthening their banks, and failures were evident in Mexico and Argentina in the mid-1990s.

5. Despite their astoundingly good records of high output growth and low inflation and budget deficits, several key developing countries in East Asia were hit by severe panics and devastating currency depreciation in 1997. In retrospect, the affected countries had several vulnerabilities, most related to widespread moral hazard in domestic banking and finance. The effects of the crisis spilled over to countries as distant as Russia and Brazil, illustrating the element of *contagion* in modern-day international financial crises. This factor, plus the fact that the East Asian countries had few apparent problems before their crises struck, has given rise to demands for rethinking the international financial "architecture."

6. Proposals to reform the international architecture can be grouped as preventive measures or as ex-post measures, with the latter applied once safeguards have failed to

stop a crisis. Among preventive measures are greater transparency concerning countries' policies and financial positions; enhanced regulation of domestic banking; and more extensive credit lines, either from private sources or from the IMF. Ex-post measures that have been suggested include more extensive lending by the IMF and a kind of "Chapter 11" bankruptcy proceeding for the orderly resolution of creditor claims on developing countries that cannot pay in full. Some observers suggest more extensive use of capital controls, both to prevent and manage crises. In the years to come, developing countries will no doubt experiment with capital controls, *dollarization,* floating exchange rates, and other regimes. The architecture that will ultimately emerge is not at all clear.

Key Terms

contagion, p. 698
convergence, p. 667
crawling peg, p. 678
currency board, p. 695

default, p. 672
dollarization, p. 696
privatization, p. 676
seigniorage, p. 669

Problems

1. Can a government always collect more seigniorage simply by letting the money supply grow faster? Explain your answer.

2. Assume that a country's inflation rate was 100 percent per year in both 1980 and 1990 but that inflation was falling in the first year and rising in the second. Other things equal, in which year was seigniorage revenue greater? (Assume that asset holders correctly anticipated the path of inflation.)

3. In the early 1980s, Brazil's government, through an average inflation rate of 147 percent per year, got only 1.0 percent of output as seigniorage, while Sierra Leone's government got 2.4 percent through an inflation rate less than a third as high. Can you think of differences in financial structure that might partially explain this contrast? (Hint: In Sierra Leone the ratio of currency to nominal output averaged 7.7 percent; in Brazil it averaged only 1.4 percent.)

4. Suppose an economy open to international capital movements has a crawling peg exchange rate under which its currency is continuously devalued at a rate of 10 percent per year. How would the domestic nominal interest rate be related to the foreign nominal interest rate? What if the crawling peg is not fully credible?

5. The external debt buildup of some developing countries (such as Argentina) in the 1970s was in part due to (legal or illegal) capital flight in the face of expected currency devaluation. (Governments and central banks borrowed foreign currencies to prop up their exchange rates, and these funds found their way into private hands and into bank accounts in New York and elsewhere.) Since capital flight leaves a government with a large debt but creates an offsetting foreign asset for citizens who take money abroad, the consolidated net debt of the country as a whole does not change. Does this mean that countries whose external government debt is largely the result of capital flight face no debt problem?

6. Much developing country borrowing during the 1970s was carried out by state-owned companies. In some of these countries there have been moves to privatize the

economy by selling state companies to private owners. Would the countries have borrowed more or less if their economies had been privatized earlier?

7. How might a developing country's decision to reduce trade restrictions such as import tariffs affect its ability to borrow in the world capital market?

8. Given output, a country can improve its current account by either cutting investment or cutting consumption (private or government). After the debt crisis of the 1980s began, many developing countries achieved improvements in their current accounts by cutting investment. Is this a sensible strategy?

9. During the 1980s debt crises, economist Peter B. Kenen of Princeton University suggested the creation of a government-sponsored International Debt Discount Corporation (IDDC) that would issue its own long-term bonds to banks in exchange for their loans to developing countries. How might an IDCC have facilitated debt relief for developing countries? What problems can you see in operating such a facility? (For a symposium on these and related questions, see the Winter 1990 issue of the *Journal of Economic Perspectives.*)

10. Why would Argentina have to give the United States seigniorage if it gave up its peso and dollarized its economy completely? How would you measure the size of Argentina's sacrifice of seigniorage? (To do this exercise, think through the actual steps Argentina would have to take to dollarize its economy. You may assume that the Argentine central bank's assets consist 100 percent of interest-bearing U.S. Treasury bonds.)

Further Reading

Bela Balassa. "Adjustment Policies in Developing Countries: A Reassessment." *World Development* 12 (September 1984), pp. 955–972. A review of trade and macroeconomic policies in developing countries after 1973.

Guillermo A. Calvo and Carmen M. Reinhart. "Fear of Floating." *Quarterly Journal of Economics* 117 (May 2002). The authors argue that developing countries with "floating" exchange rates actually manage those rates heavily.

Paul Collier and Jan Willem Gunning. "Explaining African Economic Performance." *Journal of Economic Literature* 37 (March 1999), pp. 69–111. Surveys the causes of Africa's generally poor record of economic growth and stability.

Susan M. Collins. "Multiple Exchange Rates, Capital Controls, and Commercial Policy," in Rudiger Dornbusch and F. Leslie C. H. Helmers, eds. *The Open Economy: Tools for Policymakers in Developing Countries.* New York: Oxford University Press (for the World Bank), 1988. Describes how developing country governments have regulated trade and capital flows to achieve policy goals.

Sebastian Edwards. *Crisis and Reform in Latin America: From Despair to Hope.* Oxford, U.K.: Oxford University Press, 1995. A comprehensive account of the background and progress of recent economic reform efforts in Latin America.

Stanley Fischer. "Exchange Rate Regimes: Is the Bipolar View Correct?" *Journal of Economic Perspectives* 15 (Spring 2001), pp. 3–24. Assesses countries' choices of increasingly extreme exchange-rate regimes.

Albert Fishlow. "Lessons from the Past: Capital Markets During the 19th Century and the Interwar Period." *International Organization* 39 (Summer 1985), pp. 383–439. Historical review of international borrowing experience, including comparisons with the post-1982 debt crisis.

Peter B. Kenen. *The International Financial Architecture: What's New? What's Missing?* Washington, D.C.: Institute for International Economics, 2001. Reviews recent crises and the consequent proposals to reform the global financial system.

Charles P. Kindleberger. *Manias, Panics, and Crashes: A History of Financial Crises.* 3d ed. New York: John Wiley & Sons, 1996. A historical review of international financial crises from the seventeenth century to the present day.

David S. Landes. *The Wealth and Poverty of Nations.* New York: Norton, 1999. Broad-ranging overview of the global development experience.

Ronald I. McKinnon. *The Order of Economic Liberalization: Financial Control in the Transition to a Market Economy.* 2d ed. Baltimore: Johns Hopkins University Press, 1993. Essays on the proper sequencing of economic reforms.

Dani Rodrik. "Getting Interventions Right: How South Korea and Taiwan Grew Rich." *Economic Policy* 20 (April 1995), pp. 53–107. Skeptical view of the role of trade reform in East Asian growth.

Mathematical
Postscripts

POSTSCRIPT TO CHAPTER 3

The Specific Factors Model

In this postscript we set out a formal mathematical treatment for the specific factors model of production explained in Chapter 3. The mathematical treatment is useful in deepening understanding of the model itself, and it also provides an opportunity to develop concepts and techniques that apply to subsequent models. In particular it is a good place to introduce an extremely useful tool of analysis, the so-called hat algebra.

Factor Prices, Costs, and Factor Demands

The specific factors model has two sectors: manufactures and food. In each sector, two factors of production are employed; capital and labor in manufactures, land and labor in food. Before turning to the full model, let us examine in general how costs and the demand for factors of production are related to the prices of factors when producers employ two factors.

Consider the production of some good that requires capital and labor as factors of production. Provided the good is produced with constant returns to scale, the technology of production may be summarized in terms of the *unit isoquant* (*II* in Figure 3P-1), a curve showing all the combinations of capital and labor that can be used to produce one unit of the good. Curve *II* shows that there is a trade-off between the quantity of capital used per unit of output, a_K, and the quantity of labor per unit of output, a_L. The curvature of the unit isoquant reflects the assumption that it becomes increasingly difficult to substitute capital for labor as the capital-labor ratio increases, and conversely.

In a competitive market economy, producers will choose the capital-labor ratio in production that minimizes their cost. Such a cost-minimizing production choice is shown in Figure 3P-1 as point *E*. It is the point at which the unit isoquant *II* is tangent to a line whose slope is equal to minus the ratio of the price of labor, *w*, to the price of capital, *r*.

The actual cost of production is equal to the sum of the cost of capital and labor inputs,

$$C = a_K r + a_L w, \tag{3P-1}$$

where the input coefficients, a_K and a_L, have been chosen to minimize *C*.

Because the capital-labor ratio has been chosen to minimize costs, it follows that a change in that ratio cannot reduce costs. Costs cannot be reduced by increasing a_K while reducing a_L, nor conversely. It follows that an infinitesimal change in the capital-labor ratio from the cost-minimizing choice must have no effect on cost. Let da_K, da_L be small changes from the optimal input choices. Then

$$r\,da_K + w\,da_L = 0 \tag{3P-2}$$

for any movement along the unit isoquant.

Consider next what happens if the factor prices *r* and *w* change. This alteration will have two effects: It will change the choice of a_K and a_L, and it will change the cost of production.

Figure 3P-1 | Efficient Production

The cost-minimizing capital-labor ratio depends on factor prices.

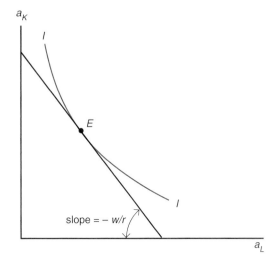

First, consider the effect on the relative quantities of capital and labor used to produce one unit of output. The cost-minimizing labor-capital ratio depends on the ratio of the price of labor to that of capital:

$$\frac{a_K}{a_L} = \Phi\left(\frac{w}{r}\right). \tag{3P-3}$$

The cost of production will also change. For small changes in factor prices dr and dw, the change in production cost is

$$dC = a_K dr + a_L dw + r da_K + w da_L. \tag{3P-4}$$

From equation (3P-2), however, we already know that the last two terms of equation (3P-4) sum to zero. Hence the effect of factor prices on cost may be written

$$dC = a_K dr + a_L dw. \tag{3P-4'}$$

It turns out to be very convenient to derive a somewhat different equation from equation (3P-4'). Dividing and multiplying some of the elements of the equation, a new equation can be derived that looks as follows:

$$\frac{dC}{C} = \left(\frac{a_K r}{C}\right)\left(\frac{dr}{r}\right) + \left(\frac{a_L w}{C}\right)\left(\frac{dw}{w}\right). \tag{3P-5}$$

The term dC/C may be interpreted as the *percentage change* in C, and may conveniently be designated as $\hat{C}$; similarly, let $dr/r = \hat{r}$ and $dw/w = \hat{w}$. The term $a_K r/C$ may be interpreted as the *share of capital in total production costs;* it may be conveniently designated θ_K. Thus equation (3P-5) can be compactly written

$$\hat{C} = \theta_K \hat{r} + \theta_L \hat{w}, \tag{3P-5'}$$

where

$$\theta_K + \theta_L = 1.$$

This is an example of "hat algebra," an extremely useful way to express mathematical relationships in international economics.

The relationship between factor prices and the capital-labor ratio can also be expressed in hat algebra. A rise in the price of labor relative to the price of capital lowers the ratio of labor to capital; this statement may be written

$$\hat{a}_L - \hat{a}_K = -\sigma(\hat{w} - \hat{r}), \tag{3P-6}$$

where σ is the percentage change in the labor-capital ratio that results from a 1 percent change in the ratio of factor prices, and is known as the *elasticity of substitution.*

Factor Price Determination in the Specific Factors Model

The specific factors model has two sectors, each of which is like that just described. Manufactures are produced using capital (the specific factor) and labor:

$$Q_M = Q_M(K, L_M). \tag{3P-7}$$

Food is produced using the specific factor land and labor:

$$Q_F = Q_F(T, L_F). \tag{3P-8}$$

The supplies of capital and land to each sector are simply whatever they are. Labor, however, can be allocated to either sector:

$$L_M + L_F = \bar{L}, \tag{3P-9}$$

where $\bar{L}$ is the economy's total supply of labor.

In a perfectly competitive economy, the price of each good must just equal its cost of production. In manufactures, then,

$$P_M = a_{KM} r_K + a_{LM} w, \tag{3P-10}$$

where r_K is the price of capital, w the wage rate of labor, and a_{KM} and a_{LM} the unit input coefficients. Using the notation introduced in equation (3P-6), it follows that

$$\hat{P}_M = \theta_{KM} \hat{r}_K + \theta_{LM} \hat{w}, \tag{3P-11}$$

or

$$\hat{r}_K = \left(\frac{1}{\theta_{KM}}\right)(\hat{P}_M - \theta_{LM}\hat{w}) = \hat{P}_M + \left(\frac{\theta_{LM}}{\theta_{KM}}\right)(\hat{P}_M - \hat{w}). \qquad \text{(3P-12)}$$

Similarly, with parallel notation, in the food sector

$$\hat{r}_T = \left(\frac{1}{\theta_{TF}}\right)(\hat{P}_F - \theta_{LF}\hat{w}) = \hat{P}_F + \left(\frac{\theta_{LF}}{\theta_{TF}}\right)(\hat{P}_F - \hat{w}). \qquad \text{(3P-13)}$$

Equations (3P-12) and (3P-13) allow derivation of the change in the prices of capital and land, given the changes in the prices of manufactures, food, and labor. The next step is to derive the change in the wage rate, which we do by examining the demand and supply for labor.

Notice first that

$$K = a_{KM}Q_M \qquad \text{(3P-14)}$$

and

$$L_M = a_{LM}Q_M. \qquad \text{(3P-15)}$$

If follows that

$$L_M = \left(\frac{a_{LM}}{a_{KM}}\right)K. \qquad \text{(3P-16)}$$

Because the supply of the specific factor capital is fixed, employment of labor in the production of manufactures can change only through changes in the capital-labor ratio. Using the hat notation, the following can be derived:

$$\hat{L}_M = \hat{a}_{LM} - \hat{a}_{KM} = -\sigma(\hat{w} - \hat{r}_K). \qquad \text{(3P-17)}$$

From equation (3P-12), it can be shown that

$$\hat{r}_K - \hat{w} = \left(\frac{1}{\theta_{KM}}\right)(\hat{P}_M - \hat{w}). \qquad \text{(3P-18)}$$

Hence,

$$\hat{L}_M = \sigma_M\left(\frac{1}{\theta_{KM}}\right)(\hat{P}_M - \hat{w}), \qquad \text{(3P-19)}$$

where σ_M is the elasticity of substitution in manufactures and, by analogy,

$$\hat{L}_F = \sigma_F\left(\frac{1}{\theta_{TF}}\right)(\hat{P}_F - \hat{w}). \qquad \text{(3P-20)}$$

Now turn to the full-employment condition for labor, equation (3P-9). If total employment is to remain unchanged, an increase in one sector's employment must be offset by a decline in the other sector:

$$dL_M + dL_F = 0. \tag{3P-21}$$

As before, this expression can be transformed into one that uses the hat algebra:

$$\left(\frac{dL_M}{L_M}\right)\left(\frac{L_M}{L}\right) + \left(\frac{dL_F}{L_F}\right)\left(\frac{L_F}{L}\right) = 0 \tag{3P-22}$$

or

$$\alpha_M \hat{L}_M + \alpha_F \hat{L}_F = 0, \tag{3P-22'}$$

where $\alpha_M = L_M/L$ is the share of the labor employed in manufactures in the economy's total labor supply.

The last step is to substitute the labor-demand equations (3P-19) and (3P-20) into equation (3P-22'):

$$(\alpha_M \sigma_M/\theta_{KM})\hat{P}_M + (\alpha_F \sigma_F/\theta_{TF})\hat{P}_F = [(\alpha_M \sigma_M/\theta_{KM}) + (\alpha_F \sigma_F/\theta_{TF})]\hat{w} \tag{3P-23}$$

or

$$\hat{w} = \frac{[(\alpha_M \sigma_M/\theta_{KM})\hat{P}_M + (\alpha_F \sigma_F/\theta_{TF})\hat{P}_F]}{[(\alpha_M \sigma_M/\theta_{KM}) + (\alpha_F \sigma_F/\theta_{TF})]} \tag{3P-23'}$$

That is, the rise in the wage rate is a weighted average of the increases in the prices of manufactures and food.

Effects of a Change in Relative Prices

Suppose the price of manufactures rises relative to that of food; that is, $\hat{P}_M > \hat{P}_F$. Then, because the change in the wage rate is a weighted average of the change in the two goods prices,

$$\hat{P}_M > \hat{w} > \hat{P}_F.$$

The effect on the allocation of labor is apparent from equations (3P-19) and (3P-20): Because $\hat{P}_M > \hat{w}$, $\hat{L}_M > 0$; since $\hat{P}_F < \hat{w}$, $\hat{L}_F < 0$. Employment in manufactures rises and employment in food falls.

The effects on the prices of capital and land may be seen from equations (3P-12) and (3P-13). Again, because $\hat{P}_M > \hat{w}$, $\hat{r}_K$ must rise by *more* than P_M, while conversely r_T rises by less than P_F. Thus the overall description of the relation of goods price and factor price changes is

$$\hat{r}_K > \hat{P}_M > \hat{w} > \hat{P}_F > \hat{r}_T. \tag{3P-24}$$

Because the price of capital rises in terms of both goods, someone who derived his or her income entirely from capital would be unambiguously better off. Because the price of land falls relative to both goods, someone deriving his or her income entirely from land would be unambiguously worse off. Someone deriving income from labor would find that the purchase power of that income had risen in terms of food and fallen in terms of manufactures.

POSTSCRIPT TO CHAPTER 4

The Factor Proportions Model

The factor proportions model with flexible coefficients is very similar to the specific factors model: It has two sectors, each of which uses two factors of production. The only difference is that these are the *same* factors of production, so that both labor and the other factor (land in this example) can be allocated across sectors.

The Basic Equations in the Factor Proportions Model

Suppose a country produces two goods, X and Y, using two factors of production, land and labor. Assume that X is land intensive. The price of each good must equal its production cost:

$$P_X = a_{TX}r + a_{LX}w, \tag{4P-1}$$

$$P_Y = a_{TY}r + a_{LY}w, \tag{4P-2}$$

where a_{TX}, a_{LX}, a_{TY}, a_{LY} are the cost-minimizing input choices given the price of land, r and labor, w.

Also, the economy's factors of production must be fully employed:

$$a_{TX}Q_X + a_{TY}Q_Y = T, \tag{4P-3}$$

$$a_{LX}Q_X + a_{LY}Q_Y = L, \tag{4P-4}$$

where T, L, are the total supplies of land and labor.

The factor price equations (4P-1) and (4P-2) imply equations for the rate of change for factor prices, just as in the specific factors model:

$$\hat{P}_X = \theta_{TX}\hat{r} + \theta_{LX}\hat{w}, \tag{4P-5}$$

$$\hat{P}_Y = \theta_{TY}\hat{r} + \theta_{LY}\hat{w}, \tag{4P-6}$$

where θ_{TX} is the share of land in production cost of X, etc., $\theta_{TX} > \theta_{TY}$ and $\theta_{LX} < \theta_{LY}$ because X is more land intensive than Y.

The quantity equations (4P-3) and (4P-4) must be treated more carefully. The unit inputs a_{TX}, etc. can change if factor prices change. If goods prices are held constant, however, then factor prices will not change. Thus for *given* prices of X and Y, it is also possible to write hat equations in terms of factor supplies and outputs:

$$\alpha_{TX}\hat{Q}_X + \alpha_{TY}\hat{Q}_Y = \hat{T}, \tag{4P-7}$$

$$\alpha_{LX}\hat{Q}_X + \alpha_{LY}\hat{Q}_Y = \hat{L}, \tag{4P-8}$$

where α_{TX} is the share of the economy's land supply that is used in production of X, etc. $\alpha_{TX} > \alpha_{LX}$ and $\alpha_{TY} < \alpha_{LY}$ because of the greater land intensity of X production.

Goods Prices and Factor Prices

The factor price equations (4P-5) and (4P-6) may be solved together to express factor prices as the outcome of goods prices (these solutions make use of the fact that $\theta_{LX} = 1 - \theta_{TX}$ and $\theta_{LY} = 1 - \theta_{TY}$):

$$\hat{r} = \left(\frac{1}{D}\right)[(1 - \theta_{TY})\hat{P}_X - \theta_{LX}\hat{P}_Y], \tag{4P-9}$$

$$\hat{w} = \left(\frac{1}{D}\right)[\theta_{TX}\hat{P}_Y - \theta_{TY}\hat{P}_X], \tag{4P-10}$$

where $D = \theta_{TX} - \theta_{TY}$ (implying that $D > 0$). These may be arranged in the form

$$\hat{r} = \hat{P}_X + \left(\frac{\theta_{LX}}{D}\right)(\hat{P}_X - \hat{P}_Y), \tag{4P-9'}$$

$$\hat{w} = \hat{P}_Y + \left(\frac{\theta_{TY}}{D}\right)(\hat{P}_X - \hat{P}_Y). \tag{4P-10'}$$

Suppose that the price of X rises relative to the price of Y, so that $\hat{P}_X > \hat{P}_Y$. Then it follows that

$$\hat{r} > \hat{P}_X > \hat{P}_Y > \hat{w}. \tag{4P-11}$$

That is, the real price of land rises in terms of both goods, while the real price of labor falls in terms of both goods. In particular, if the price of X were to rise with no change in the price of Y, the wage rate would actually fall.

Factor Supplies and Outputs

As long as goods prices may be taken as given, equations (4P-7) and (4P-8) can be solved, using the fact that $\alpha_{TY} = 1 - \alpha_{TX}$ and $\alpha_{LY} = 1 - \alpha_{LX}$, to express the change in output of each good as the outcome of changes in factor supplies:

$$\hat{Q}_X = \left(\frac{1}{\Delta}\right)[\alpha_{LY}\hat{T} - \alpha_{TY}\hat{L}], \tag{4P-12}$$

$$\hat{Q}_Y = \left(\frac{1}{\Delta}\right)[-\alpha_{LX}\hat{T} + \alpha_{TX}\hat{L}], \tag{4P-13}$$

where $\Delta = \alpha_{TX} - \alpha_{LX}$, $\Delta > 0$.
  These equations may be rewritten

$$\hat{Q}_X = \hat{T} + \left(\frac{\alpha_{TY}}{\Delta}\right)(\hat{T} - \hat{L}), \tag{4P-12'}$$

$$\hat{Q}_Y = \hat{L} - \left(\frac{\alpha_{LX}}{\Delta}\right)(\hat{T} - \hat{L}). \tag{4P-13'}$$

Suppose that P_X and P_Y remain constant, while the supply of land rises relative to the supply of labor—$\hat{T} > \hat{L}$. Then it is immediately apparent that

$$\hat{Q}_X > \hat{T} > \hat{L} > \hat{Q}_Y. \tag{4P-14}$$

In particular, if T rises with L remaining constant, output of X will rise more than in proportion while output of Y will actually fall.

POSTSCRIPT TO CHAPTER 5

The Trading World Economy

Supply, Demand, and Equilibrium

World Equilibrium

Although for graphical purposes it is easiest to express world equilibrium as an equality between relative supply and relative demand, for a mathematical treatment it is preferable to use an alternative formulation. This approach is to focus on the conditions of equality between supply and demand of either one of the two goods, cloth and food. It does not matter which good is chosen because equilibrium in the cloth market implies equilibrium in the food market and vice versa.

To see this condition, let Q_C, Q_C^* be the output of cloth in Home and Foreign, respectively, D_C, D_C^* the quantity demanded in each country, and corresponding variables with an F subscript refer to the food market. Also, let p be the price of cloth relative to that of food.

In all cases world expenditure will be equal to world income. World income is the sum of income earned from sales of cloth and sales of food; world expenditure is the sum of purchases of cloth and food. Thus the equality of income and expenditure may be written

$$p(Q_C + Q_C^*) + Q_F + Q_F^* = p(D_C + D_C^*) + D_F + D_F^*. \qquad \text{(5P-1)}$$

Now suppose that the world market for cloth is in equilibrium; that is,

$$Q_C + Q_C^* = D_C + D_C^*. \qquad \text{(5P-2)}$$

Then from equation (5P-1) it follows that

$$Q_F + Q_F^* = D_F + D_F^*. \qquad \text{(5P-3)}$$

That is, the market for food must be in equilibrium as well. Clearly the converse is also true: If the market for food is in equilibrium, so too is the market for cloth.

It is therefore sufficient to focus on the market for cloth to determine the equilibrium relative price.

Production and Income

Each country has a production possibility frontier along which it can trade off between producing cloth and food. The economy chooses the point on that frontier which maximizes the value of output at the given relative price of cloth. This value may be written

$$V = pQ_C + Q_F. \qquad \text{(5P-4)}$$

As in the cost-minimization cases described in earlier postscripts, the fact that the output mix chosen maximizes value implies that a small shift in production along the production possibility frontier away from the optimal mix has no effect on the value of output:

$$pdQ_C + dQ_F = 0. \tag{5P-5}$$

A change in the relative price of cloth will lead to both a change in the output mix and a change in the value of output. The change in the value of output is

$$dV = Q_C dp + pdQ_C + dQ_F; \tag{5P-6}$$

however, because the last two terms are, by equation (5P-5), equal to zero, this expression reduces to

$$dV = Q_C dp. \tag{5P-6'}$$

Similarly, in Foreign,

$$dV^* = Q_C^* dp. \tag{5P-7}$$

Income, Prices, and Utility

Each country is treated as if it were one individual. The tastes of the country can be represented by a utility function depending on consumption of cloth and food:

$$U = U(D_C, D_F). \tag{5P-8}$$

Suppose a country has an income I in terms of food. Its total expenditure must be equal to this income, so that

$$pD_C + D_F = I. \tag{5P-9}$$

Consumers will maximize utility given their income and the prices they face. Let MU_C, MU_F be the marginal utility that consumers derive from cloth and food; then the change in utility that results from any change in consumption is

$$dU = MU_C dD_C + MU_F dD_F. \tag{5P-10}$$

Because consumers are maximizing utility given income and prices, there cannot be any affordable change in consumption that makes them better off. This condition implies that at the optimum,

$$\frac{MU_C}{MU_F} = p. \tag{5P-11}$$

Now consider the effect on utility of changing income and prices. Differentiating equation (5P-9) yields

$$pdD_C + dD_F = dI - D_C dp. \tag{5P-12}$$

But from equations (5P-10) and (5P-11),

$$dU = MU_F[pdD_C + dD_F].$$ (5P-13)

Thus

$$dU = MU_F[dI - D_C dp].$$ (5P-14)

It is convenient to introduce now a new definition: The change in utility divided by the marginal utility of food, which is the commodity in which income is measured, may be defined as the change in *real income*, and indicated by the symbol *dy:*

$$dy = \frac{dU}{MU_F} = dI - D_C dp.$$ (5P-15)

For the economy as a whole, income equals the value of output: $I = V$. Thus the effect of a change in the relative price of cloth on the economy's real income is

$$dy = [Q_C - D_C]dp.$$ (5P-16)

The quantity $Q_C - D_C$ is the economy's exports of cloth. A rise in the relative price of cloth, then, will benefit an economy that exports cloth; it is an improvement in that economy's terms of trade. It is instructive to restate this idea in a slightly different way:

$$dy = [p(Q_C - D_C)]\left(\frac{dp}{p}\right).$$ (5P-17)

The term in brackets is the value of exports; the term in parentheses is the percentage change in the terms of trade. The expression therefore says that the real income gain from a given percentage in terms of trade change is equal to the percentage change in the terms of trade multiplied by the initial value of exports. If a country is initially exporting $100 billion and its terms of trade improve by 10 percent, the gain is equivalent to a gain in national income of $10 billion.

Supply, Demand, and the Stability of Equilibrium

In the market for cloth, a change in the relative price will induce changes in both supply and demand.

On the supply side, a rise in p will lead both Home and Foreign to produce more cloth. We will denote this supply response as s, s^* in Home and Foreign, respectively, so that

$$dQ_C = s\, dp,$$ (5P-18)

$$dQ_C^* = s^*\, dp.$$ (5P-19)

The demand side is more complex. A change in p will lead to both *income* and *substitution* effects. These effects are illustrated in Figure 5P-1. The figure shows an economy that

Figure 5P-1 | Consumption Effects of a Price Change

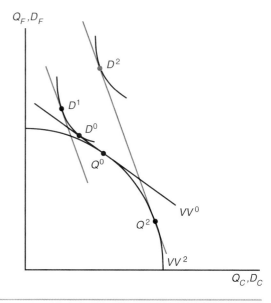

A change in relative prices produces
both income and substitution effects.

initially faces a relative price indicated by the slope of the line VV^0. Given this relative
price, the economy produces at point Q^0 and consumes at point D^0. Now suppose the relative price of cloth rises to the level indicated by the slope of VV^2. If there were no increase
in utility, consumption would shift to D^1, which would involve an unambiguous fall in consumption of cloth. There is also, however, a change in the economy's real income; in this
case, because the economy is initially a net exporter of cloth, real income rises. This change
leads to consumption at D^2 rather than D^1, and this income effect tends to raise consumption
of cloth. Analyzing the effect of change in p on demand requires taking account of both the
substitution effect, which is the change in consumption that would take place if real income
were held constant, and the income effect, which is the additional change in consumption
that is the consequence of the fact that real income changes.

Let the substitution effect be denoted by $-e\ dp$; it is always negative. Also, let the
income effect be denoted by $n\ dy$; as long as cloth is a normal good, for which demand rises
with real income, it is positive if the country is a net exporter of cloth, negative if it is a net
importer.[1] Then the total effect of a change in p on Home's demand for cloth is

$$dD_C = -e\ dp + n\ dy$$
$$= [-e + n(Q_C - D_C)]dp. \tag{5P-20}$$

---

[1]If food is also a normal good, n must be less than $1/p$. To see this effect, notice that if I were to rise by dI without
any change in p, spending on cloth would rise by $np\ dI$. Unless $n < 1/p$, then, more than 100 percent of the
increase in income would be spent on cloth.

The effect on Foreign's demand similarly is

$$dD_C^* = [-e^* + n^*(Q_C^* - D_C^*)]dp. \tag{5P-21}$$

Because $Q_C^* - D_C^*$ is negative, the income effect in Foreign is negative.

The demand and supply effect can now be put together to get the overall effect of a change in p on the market for cloth. The *excess supply* of cloth is the difference between desired world production and consumption:

$$ES_C = Q_C + Q_C^* - D_C - D_C^*. \tag{5P-22}$$

The effect of a change in p on world excess supply is

$$dES_C = [s + s^* + e + e^* - n(Q_C - D_C) - n^*(Q_C^* - D_C^*)]dp. \tag{5P-23}$$

If the market is initially in equilibrium, however, Home's exports equal Foreign's imports, so that $Q_C^* - D_C^* = -(Q_C - D_C)$; the effect of p on excess supply may therefore be written

$$dES_C = [s + s^* + e + e^* - (n - n^*)(Q_C - D_C)]dp. \tag{5P-23'}$$

Suppose the relative price of cloth were initially a little higher than its equilibrium level. If the result were an excess supply of cloth, market forces would push the relative price of cloth down and thus lead to restoration of equilibrium. On the other hand, if an excessively high relative price of cloth leads to an excess *demand* for cloth, the price will rise further, leading the economy away from equilibrium. Thus equilibrium will be *stable* only if a small increase in the relative price of cloth leads to an excess supply of cloth; that is, if

$$\frac{dES_C}{dp} > 0. \tag{5P-24}$$

Inspection of equation (5P-23') reveals the factors determining whether or not equilibrium is stable. Both supply effects and substitution effects in demand work toward stability. The only possible source of instability lies in income effects. The net income effect is of ambiguous sign: It depends on whether $n > n^*$; that is, on whether Home has a higher marginal propensity to consume cloth when its real income increases than Foreign does. If $n > n^*$, the income effect works against stability, while if $n < n^*$, it reinforces the other reasons for stability.

In what follows it will be assumed that equation (5P-24) holds, so that the equilibrium of the world economy is in fact stable.

Effects of Changes in Supply and Demand

The Method of Comparative Statics

To evaluate the effects of changes in the world economy, a method known as *comparative statics* is applied. In each of the cases considered in the text, the world economy is subjected to some change, which will lead to a change in the world relative price of cloth. The first step in the method of comparative statics is to calculate the effect of the change in the world economy on the excess supply of cloth *at the original p*. This change is denoted by $dES|_p$. Then the change in the relative price needed to restore equilibrium is calculated by

$$dp = \frac{-dES|_p}{(dES/dp)}, \tag{5P-25}$$

where dES/dp reflects the supply, income, and substitution effects described earlier.

The effects of a given change on national welfare can be calculated in two stages. First there is whatever direct effect the change has on real income, which we can denote by $dy|_p$; then there is the indirect effect of the resulting change in the terms of trade, which can be calculated using equation (5P-16). Thus the total effect on welfare is

$$dy = dy|_p + (Q_C - D_C)dp. \tag{5P-26}$$

Economic Growth

Consider the effect of growth in the Home economy. As pointed out in the text, by growth we mean an outward shift in the production possibility frontier. This change will lead to changes in both cloth and food output at the initial relative price p; let dQ_C, dQ_F be these changes in output. If growth is strongly biased, one or the other of these changes may be negative, but because production possibilities have expanded, the value of output at the initial p must rise:

$$dV = p \, dQ_C + dQ_F = dy|_p > 0. \tag{5P-27}$$

At the initial p the supply of cloth will rise by the amount dQ_C. The demand for cloth will also rise, by an amount $n \, dy|_p$. The net effect on world excess supply of cloth will therefore be

$$dES|_p = dQ_C - n(p \, dQ_C + dQ_F). \tag{5P-28}$$

This expression can have either sign. Suppose first that growth is biased toward cloth, so that while $dQ_C > 0$, $dQ_F \leq 0$. Then demand for cloth will rise by

$$dD_C = n(p \, dQ_C + dQ_F) \leq np \, dQ_C > dQ_C.$$

(See footnote 1.)

Thus the overall effect on excess supply will be

$$dES|_p = dQ_C - dD_C > 0.$$

As a result, $dp = -dES|_p/(dES/dp) < 0$: Home's terms of trade worsen.

On the other hand, suppose that growth is strongly biased toward food, so that $dQ_C \leq 0$, $dQ_F > 0$. Then the effect on the supply of cloth at the initial p is negative, but the effect on the demand for cloth remains positive. It follows that

$$dES\big|_p = dQ_C - dD_C < 0,$$

so that $dp > 0$. Home's terms of trade improve.

Growth that is less strongly biased can move p either way, depending on the strength of the bias compared with the way Home divides its income at the margin.

Turning next to the welfare effects, the effect on Foreign depends only on the terms of trade. The effect on Home, however, depends on the combination of the initial income change and the subsequent change in the terms of trade, as shown in equation (5P-26). If growth turns the terms of trade against Home, this condition will oppose the immediate favorable effect of growth.

But can growth worsen the terms of trade sufficiently to make the growing country actually worse off? To see that it can, consider first the case of a country that experiences a biased shift in its production possibilities that raises Q_C and lowers Q_F while leaving the value of its output unchanged at initial relative prices. (This change would not necessarily be considered growth, because it violates the assumption of equation (5P-27), but it is a useful reference point.) Then there would be no change in demand at the initial p, while the supply of cloth rises; hence p must fall. The change in real income is $dI\big|_p - (Q_C - D_C)dp$; by construction, however, this is a case in which $dI\big|_p = 0$, so dy is certainly negative.

Now this country did not grow, in the usual sense, because the value of output at initial prices did not rise. By allowing the output of either good to rise slightly more, however, we would have a case in which the definition of growth is satisfied. If the extra growth is sufficiently small, however, it will not outweigh the welfare loss from the fall in p. Therefore, sufficiently biased growth can leave the growing country worse off.

The Transfer Problem

Suppose Home makes a transfer of some of its income to Foreign, say as foreign aid. Let the amount of the transfer, measured in terms of food, be da. What effect does this alteration have?

At unchanged relative prices there is no effect on supply. The only effect is on demand. Home's income is reduced by da, while Foreign's is raised by the same amount. This adjustment leads to a decline in D_C by $-n\, da$, while D_C^* rises by n^*da. Thus

$$dES\big|_p = (n - n^*)da \tag{5P-29}$$

and the change in the terms of trade is

$$dp = -da\,\frac{(n - n^*)}{(dES/dp)}. \tag{5P-30}$$

Home's terms of trade will worsen if $n > n^*$, which is widely regarded as the normal case; they will, however, improve if $n^* > n$.

The effect on Home's real income combines a direct negative effect from the transfer and an indirect terms of trade effect that can go either way. Is it possible for a favorable terms of trade effect to outweigh the income loss? In this model it is not.

To see the reason, notice that

$$dy = dy\big|_p + (Q_C - D_C)dp$$

$$= -da + (Q_C - D_C)dp$$

$$= -da\left\{1 + \frac{(n - n^*)(Q_C - D_C)}{s + s^* + e + e^* -(n - n^*)(Q_C - D_C)}\right\}$$

$$= -da\frac{(s + s^* + e + e^*)}{[s + s^* + e + e^* -(n - n^*)(Q_C - D_C)]} < 0. \qquad (5P\text{-}31)$$

Similar algebra will reveal correspondingly that a transfer cannot make the recipient worse off.

An intuitive explanation of this result is the following. Suppose p were to rise sufficiently to leave Home as well off as it would be if it made no transfer and to leave Foreign no better off as a result of the transfer. Then there would be no income effects on demand in the world economy. But the rise in price would produce both increased output of cloth and substitution in demand away from cloth, leading to an excess supply that would drive down the price. This result demonstrates that a p sufficiently high to reverse the direct welfare effects of a transfer is above the equilibrium p.

In the text we mention that recent work shows how perverse effects of a transfer are nonetheless possible. This work depends on relaxing the assumptions of this model, either by breaking the assumption that each country may be treated as if it were one individual or by introducing more than two countries.

A Tariff

Suppose Home places a tariff on imports, imposing a tax equal to the fraction t of the price. Then for a given world relative price of cloth p, Home consumers and producers will face an internal relative price $\bar{p} = p/(1 + t)$. If the tariff is sufficiently small, the internal relative price will be approximately equal to

$$\bar{p} = p - pt. \qquad (5P\text{-}32)$$

In addition to affecting p, a tariff will raise revenue, which will be assumed to be redistributed to the rest of the economy.

At the initial terms of trade, a tariff will influence the excess supply of cloth in two ways. First, the fall in relative price of cloth inside Home will lower production of cloth and induce consumers to substitute away from food toward cloth. Second, the tariff may affect Home's real income, with resulting income effects on demand. If Home starts with no tariff and imposes a small tariff, however, the problem may be simplified, because the tariff will have a negligible effect on real income. To see this relation, recall that

$$dy = p\,dD_C + dD_F.$$

The value of output and the value of consumption must always be equal at world prices, so that

$$p\,dD_C + dD_F = p\,dQ_C + dQ_F$$

at the initial terms of trade. But because the economy was maximizing the value of output before the tariff was imposed,

$$p\,dQ_C + dQ_F = 0.$$

Because there is no income effect, only the substitution effect is left. The fall in the internal relative price $\bar{p}$ induces a decline in production and a rise in consumption:

$$dQ_C = -sp\,dt, \tag{5P-33}$$

$$dD_C = ep\,dt, \tag{5P-34}$$

where dt is the tariff increase. Hence

$$dES\big|_p = -(s + e)p\,dt < 0, \tag{5P-35}$$

implying

$$dp = \frac{-dES\big|_p}{(dES/dp)}$$

$$= \frac{p\,dt(s + e)}{[s + s^* + e + e^* - (n - n^*)(Q_C - D_C)]} > 0. \tag{5P-36}$$

This expression shows that a tariff unambiguously improves the terms of trade of the country that imposes it.

Can a tariff actually improve the terms of trade so much that the internal relative price of the imported goods falls and the internal price of the exported good rises? The change in $\bar{p}$ is

$$d\bar{p} = dp - p\,dt, \tag{5P-37}$$

so that this paradoxical result will occur if $dp > p\,dt$.

By inspecting equation (5P-36) it can be seen that this result, the famous Metzler paradox, is indeed possible. If $s^* + e^* - (n - n^*)(Q_C - D_C) < 0$, there will be a Metzler paradox; this need not imply instability, because the extra terms s and e help give the denominator a positive sign.

POSTSCRIPT TO CHAPTER 6

The Monopolistic Competition Model

We want to consider the effects of changes in the size of the market on equilibrium in a monopolistically competitive industry. Each firm has the total cost relationship

$$C = F + cX, \qquad \text{(6P-1)}$$

where c is marginal cost, F a fixed cost, and X the firm's output. This implies an average cost curve of the form

$$AC = C/X = F/X + c. \qquad \text{(6P-2)}$$

Also, each firm faces a demand curve of the form

$$X = S[1/n - b(P - \overline{P})], \qquad \text{(6P-3)}$$

where S is total industry sales (taken as given), n is the number of firms, and $\overline{P}$ is the average price charged by other firms (which each firm is assumed to take as given).

Each firm chooses its price to maximize profits. Profits of a typical firm are

$$\pi = PX - C = PS[1/n - b(P - \overline{P})] - F - cS[1/n - b(P - \overline{P})]. \qquad \text{(6P-4)}$$

To maximize profits, a firm sets the derivative $d\pi/dP = 0$. This implies

$$X - SbP + Sbc = 0. \qquad \text{(6P-5)}$$

Since all firms are symmetric, however, in equilibrium $P = \overline{P}$ and $X = S/n$. Thus (6P-5) implies

$$P = 1/bn + c, \qquad \text{(6P-6)}$$

which is the relationship derived in the text.

Since $X = S/n$, average cost is a function of S and n,

$$AC = Fn/S + c. \qquad \text{(6P-7)}$$

In zero-profit equilibrium, however, the price charged by a typical firm must also equal its average cost. So we must have

$$1/bn + c = Fn/S + c, \qquad \text{(6P-8)}$$

which in turn implies

$$n = \sqrt{S/bF}. \qquad \text{(6P-9)}$$

This shows that an increase in the size of the market, S, will lead to an increase in the number of firms, n, but not in proportion—for example, a doubling of the size of the market will increase the number of firms by a factor of approximately 1.4.

The price charged by the representative firm is

$$P = 1/bn + c = c + \sqrt{F/Sb}, \tag{6P-10}$$

which shows that an increase in the size of the market leads to lower prices.

Finally, notice that the sales per firm, X, equal

$$X = S/n = \sqrt{SbF}. \tag{6P-11}$$

This shows that the scale of each individual firm also increases with the size of the market.

POSTSCRIPT TO CHAPTER 21

Risk Aversion and International Portfolio Diversification

This postscript develops a model of international portfolio diversification by risk-averse investors. The model shows that investors generally care about the risk as well as the return of their portfolios. In particular, people may hold assets whose expected returns are lower than those of other assets if this strategy reduces the overall riskiness of their wealth.

A representative investor can divide her real wealth, W, between a Home asset and a Foreign asset. Two possible states of nature can occur in the future, and it is impossible to predict in advance which one it will be. In state 1, which occurs with probability q, a unit of wealth invested in the Home asset pays out H_1 units of output and a unit of wealth invested in the Foreign asset pays out F_1 units of output. In state 2, which occurs with probability $1 - q$, the payoffs to unit investments in the Home and Foreign assets are H_2 and F_2, respectively.

Let α be the share of wealth invested in the Home asset and $1 - \alpha$ the share invested in the Foreign asset. Then if state 1 occurs, the investor will be able to consume the weighted average of her two assets' values,

$$C_1 = [\alpha H_1 + (1 - \alpha)F_1] \times W. \tag{21P-1}$$

Similarly, consumption in state 2 is

$$C_2 = [\alpha H_2 + (1 - \alpha)F_2] \times W. \tag{21P-2}$$

In any state, the investor derives utility $U(C)$ from a consumption level of C. Since the investor does not know beforehand which state will occur, she makes the portfolio decision to maximize the average or *expected* utility from future consumption,

$$qU(C_1) + (1 - q)U(C_2).$$

An Analytical Derivation of the Optimal Portfolio

After the state 1 and 2 consumption levels given by (21P-1) and (21P-2) are substituted into the expected utility function above, the investor's decision problem can be expressed as follows: Choose the portfolio share α to maximize expected utility,

$$qU\{[\alpha H_1 + (1 - \alpha)F_1] \times W\} + (1 - q)U\{[\alpha H_2 + (1 - \alpha)F_2] \times W\}.$$

This problem is solved (as usual) by differentiating the expected utility above with respect to α and setting the resulting derivative equal to 0.

Let $U'(C)$ be the derivative of the utility function $U(C)$ with respect to C; that is, $U'(C)$ is the *marginal utility* of consumption. Then α maximizes expected utility if

$$\frac{H_1 - F_1}{H_2 - F_2} = -\frac{(1 - q)U'\{[\alpha H_2 + (1 - \alpha)F_2] \times W\}}{qU'\{[\alpha H_1 + (1 - \alpha)F_1] \times W\}}. \quad \text{(21P-3)}$$

This equation can be solved for α, the optimal portfolio share.

For a risk-averse investor, the marginal utility of consumption, $U'(C)$, falls as consumption rises. Declining marginal utility explains why someone who is risk averse will not take a gamble with an expected payoff of zero: The extra consumption made possible by a win yields less utility than the utility sacrificed if the gamble is lost. If the marginal utility of consumption does not change as consumption changes, we say the investor is *risk neutral* rather than risk averse. A risk neutral investor is willing to take gambles with a zero expected payoff.

If the investor is risk neutral, however, so that $U'(C)$ is constant for all C, equation (21P-3) becomes

$$qH_1 + (1 - q)H_2 = qF_1 + (1 - q)F_2,$$

which states that *the expected rates of return on Home and Foreign assets are equal.* This result is the basis for the assertion in Chapter 13 that all assets must yield the same expected return in equilibrium when considerations of risk (and liquidity) are ignored. Thus, the interest parity condition of Chapter 13 is valid under risk-neutral behavior, but not, in general, under risk aversion.

For the analysis above to make sense, neither of the assets can yield a higher return than the other in *both* states of nature. If one asset did dominate the other in this way, the left-hand side of equation (21P-3) would be positive while its right-hand side would be negative (because the marginal utility of consumption is usually assumed to be positive). Thus, (21P-3) would have no solution. Intuitively, no one would want to hold a particular asset if another asset that *always* did better were available. Indeed, if anyone did, other investors would be able to make riskless arbitrage profits by issuing the low-return asset and using the proceeds to purchase the high-return asset.

To be definite, we therefore assume that $H_1 > F_1$ and $H_2 < F_2$, so that the Home asset does better in state 1 but does worse in state 2. This assumption is now used to develop a diagrammatic analysis that helps illustrate additional implications of the model.

A Diagrammatic Derivation of the Optimal Portfolio

Figure 21P-1 shows indifference curves for the expected utility function described by $qU(C_1) + (1 - q)U(C_2)$. The points in the diagram should be thought of as contingency plans showing the level of consumption that will occur in each state of nature. The preferences represented apply to these contingent consumption plans rather than to consumption of different goods in a single state of nature. As with standard indifference curves, however, each curve in the figure represents a set of contingency plans for consumption with which the investor is equally satisfied.

To compensate the investor for a reduction of consumption in state 1 (C_1), consumption in state 2 (C_2) must rise. The indifference curves therefore slope downward. Each curve becomes flatter, however, as C_1 falls and C_2 rises. This property of the curves reflects the property of $U(C)$ that the marginal utility of consumption declines when C rises. As C_1

Figure 21P-1 | Indifference Curves and Budget Line for the Portfolio-Selection Problem

The indifference curves are sets of state-contingent consumption plans with which the individual is equally happy. The budget line describes the trade-off between state 1 and state 2 consumption that results from portfolio shifts between Home and Foreign assets.

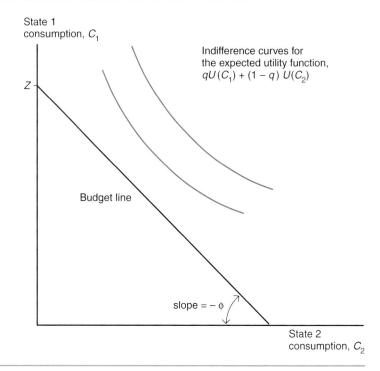

falls, the investor can be kept on her original indifference curve only by successively greater increments in C_2: Additions to C_2 are becoming less enjoyable at the same time as subtractions from C_1 are becoming more painful.

Equations (21P-1) and (21P-2) imply that by choosing the portfolio division given by α, the investor also chooses her consumption levels in the two states of nature. Thus, the problem of choosing an optimal portfolio is equivalent to one of optimally choosing the contingent consumption levels C_1 and C_2. Accordingly, the indifference curves in Figure 21P-1 can be used to determine the optimal portfolio for the investor. All that is needed to complete the analysis is a budget line showing the trade-off between state 1 consumption and state 2 consumption that the market makes available.

This trade-off is given by equations (21P-1) and (21P-2). If equation (21P-2) is solved for α, the result is

$$\alpha = \frac{F_2 W - C_2}{F_2 W - H_2 W}.$$

After substitution of this expression for α in (21P-1), the latter equation becomes

$$C_1 + \phi C_2 = Z, \tag{21P-4}$$

Figure 21P-2 | Solving the International Investor's Problem

To maximize expected utility, the investor makes the state-contingent consumption choices shown at point 1, where the budget line is tangent to the highest attainable indifference curve, II_1. The optimal portfolio share, α, can be calculated as $(F_2W - C_2^1) \div (F_2W - H_2W)$.

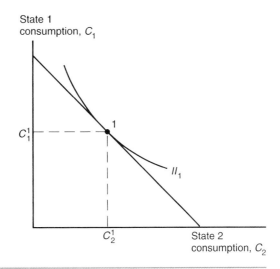

where $\phi = (H_1 - F_1)/(F_2 - H_2)$ and $Z = W \times (H_1F_2 - H_2F_1)/(F_2 - H_2)$. Notice that because $H_1 > F_1$ and $H_2 < F_2$, both ϕ and Z are positive. Thus, equation (21P-4) looks like the budget line that appears in the usual analysis of consumer choice, with ϕ playing the role of a relative price and Z the role of income measured in terms of state 1 consumption. This budget line is graphed in Figure 21P-1 as a straight line with slope $-\phi$ intersecting the vertical axis at Z.

To interpret ϕ as the market trade-off between state 2 and state 1 consumption (that is, as the price of state 2 consumption in terms of state 1 consumption), suppose the investor shifts one unit of her wealth from the Home to the Foreign asset. Since the Home asset has the higher payoff in state 1, her net loss of state 1 consumption is H_1 *less* the Foreign asset's state 1 payoff, F_1. Similarly, her net gain in state 2 consumption is $F_2 - H_2$. To obtain additional state 2 consumption of $F_2 - H_2$, the investor therefore must sacrifice $H_1 - F_1$ in state 1. The price of a single unit of C_2 in terms of C_1 is therefore $H_1 - F_1$ divided by $F_2 - H_2$, which equals ϕ, the absolute value of the slope of budget line (21P-4).

Figure 21P-2 shows how the choices of C_1 and C_2—and, by implication, the choice of the portfolio share α—are determined. As usual, the investor picks the consumption levels given by point 1, where the budget line just touches the highest attainable indifference curve, II_1. Given the optimal choices of C_1 and C_2, α can be calculated using equation (21P-1) or (21P-2). As we move downward and to the right along the budget constraint, the Home asset's portfolio share, α, falls. (Why?)

For some values of C_1 and C_2, α may be negative or greater than 1. These possibilities raise no conceptual problems. A negative α, for example, means that the investor has "gone short" in the Home asset, that is, issued some positive quantity of state-contingent claims that promise to pay their holders H_1 units of output in state 1 and H_2 units in state 2. The proceeds of this borrowing are used to increase the Foreign asset's portfolio share, $1 - \alpha$, above 1.

Figure 21P-3 | Nondiversified Portfolios

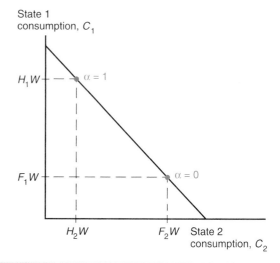

When $\alpha = 1$, the investor holds all her wealth in the Home asset. When $\alpha = 0$ she holds all her wealth in the Foreign asset. Moves along the budget constraint upward and to the left from $\alpha = 1$ correspond to short sales of the Foreign asset, which raise α above 1. Moves downward and to the right from $\alpha = 0$ correspond to short sales of the Home asset, which push α below 0.

Figure 21P-3 shows the points on the investor's budget constraint at which $\alpha = 1$ (so that $C_1 = H_1W$, $C_2 = H_2W$) and $\alpha = 0$ (so that $C_1 = F_1W$, $C_2 = F_2W$). Starting from $\alpha = 1$, the investor can move upward and to the left along the constraint by going short in the Foreign asset (thereby making α greater than 1 and $1 - \alpha$ negative). She can move downward and to the right from $\alpha = 0$ by going short in the Home asset.

The Effects of Changing Rates of Return

The diagram we have developed can be used to illustrate the effect of changes in rates of return under risk aversion. Suppose, for example, the Home asset's state 1 payoff rises while all other payoffs and the investor's wealth, W, stay the same. The rise in H_1 raises ϕ, the relative price of state 2 consumption, and therefore steepens the budget line shown in Figure 21P-3.

We need more information, however, to describe completely how the position of the budget line in Figure 21P-3 changes when H_1 rises. The following reasoning fills the gap. Consider the portfolio allocation $\alpha = 0$ in Figure 21P-3, under which all wealth is invested in the Foreign asset. The contingent consumption levels that result from this investment strategy, $C_1 = F_1W$, $C_2 = F_2W$, do not change as a result of a rise in H_1, because the portfolio we are considering does not involve the Home asset. Since the consumption pair associated with $\alpha = 0$ does not change when H_1 rises, we see that $C_1 = F_1W$, $C_2 = F_2W$ is a point on the new budget constraint: After a rise in H_1, it is still feasible for the investor to put all of her wealth into the Foreign asset. It follows that the effect of a rise in H_1 is to make the budget constraint in Figure 21P-3 pivot clockwise around the point $\alpha = 0$.

Figure 21P-4 | Effects of a Rise in H_1 on Consumption

A rise in H_1 causes the budget line to pivot clockwise around $\alpha = 0$, and the investor's optimum shifts to point 2. State 1 consumption always rises; in the case shown, state 2 consumption falls.

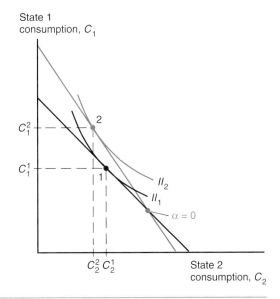

The effect on the investor of a rise in H_1 is shown in Figure 21P-4, which assumes that initially $\alpha > 0$ (that is, the investor initially owns a positive amount of the Home asset).[1] As usual, both a "substitution" and an "income" effect influence the shift of the investor's contingent consumption plan from point 1 to point 2. The substitution effect is a tendency to demand more C_1, whose relative price has fallen, and less C_2, whose relative price has risen. The income effect of the rise in H_1, however, pushes the entire budget line outward and tends to raise consumption in *both* states (as long as $\alpha > 0$ initially). Because the investor will be richer in state 1, she can afford to shift some of her wealth toward the Foreign asset (which has the higher payoff in state 2) and thereby even out her consumption in the two states of nature. Risk aversion explains the investor's desire to avoid large consumption fluctuations across states. As Figure 21P-4 suggests, C_1 definitely rises while C_2 may rise or fall. (In the case illustrated, the substitution effect is stronger than the income effect and C_2 falls.)

Corresponding to this ambiguity is an ambiguity concerning the effect of the rise in H_1 on the portfolio share, α. Figure 21P-5 illustrates the two possibilities. The key to understanding this figure is the observation that if the investor does *not* change α in response to the rise in H_1, her consumption choices are given by point 1′, which lies on the new budget constraint vertically above the initial consumption point 1. Why is this the case? Equation (21P-2) implies that $C_2^1 = [\alpha H_2 + (1 - \alpha)F_2] \times W$ doesn't change if α doesn't change; the new, higher value of state 1 consumption corresponding to the original portfolio choice is

---

[1] The case in which $\alpha < 0$ initially is left as an exercise.

Figure 21P-5 | Effects of a Rise in H_1 on Portfolio Shares

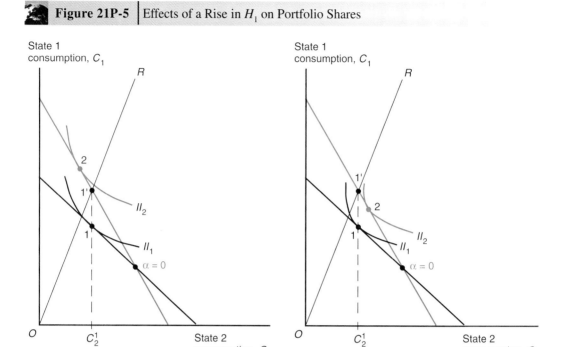

Panel (a): If the investor is not too risk averse, she shifts her portfolio toward the Home asset, picking a C_1/C_2 ratio greater than the one indicated by the slope of *OR*. Panel (b): A very risk-averse investor might increase state 2 consumption by shifting her portfolio toward the Foreign asset.

then given by the point on the new budget constraint directly above C_2^1. In both panels of Figure 21P-5, the slope of the ray *OR* connecting the origin and point 1′ shows the ratio C_1/C_2 implied by the initial portfolio composition after the rise in H_1.

It is now clear, however, that to shift to a lower value of C_2 the investor must raise α above its initial value, that is, shift the portfolio toward the Home asset. To raise C_2 she must lower α that is, shift toward the Foreign asset. Figure 21P-5a shows again the case in which the substitution effect outweighs the income effect. In that case, C_2 falls as the investor shifts her portfolio toward the Home asset, whose expected rate of return has risen relative to that on the Foreign asset. This case corresponds to those we studied in the text, in which the portfolio share of an asset rises as its relative expected rate of return rises.

Figure 21P-5b shows the opposite case, in which C_2 rises and α falls, implying a portfolio shift toward the Foreign asset. You can see that the factor giving rise to this possibility is the sharper curvature of the indifference curves *II* in Figure 21P-5b. This curvature is precisely what economists mean by the term *risk aversion*. An investor who becomes more risk averse regards consumptions in different states of nature as poorer substitutes, and thus requires a larger increase in state 1 consumption to compensate her for a fall in state 2 consumption (and vice versa). Note that the paradoxical case shown in Figure 21P-5b, in which a rise in an asset's expected rate of return can cause investors to demand *less* of it, is unlikely in the real world. For example, an increase in the interest rate a currency offers, other things equal, raises the expected rate of return on deposits of that currency in all states of nature, not just in one. The portfolio substitution effect in favor of the currency therefore is much stronger.

The results we have found are quite different from those that would occur if the investor were risk neutral. A risk-neutral investor would shift all of her wealth into the asset with the higher expected return, paying no attention to the riskiness of this move.[2] The greater the degree of risk aversion, however, the greater the concern with the riskiness of the overall portfolio of assets.

---

[2] In fact, a risk-neutral investor would always like to take the maximum possible short position in the low-return asset and, correspondingly, the maximum possible long position in the high-return asset. It is this behavior that gives rise to the interest parity condition.

INDEX

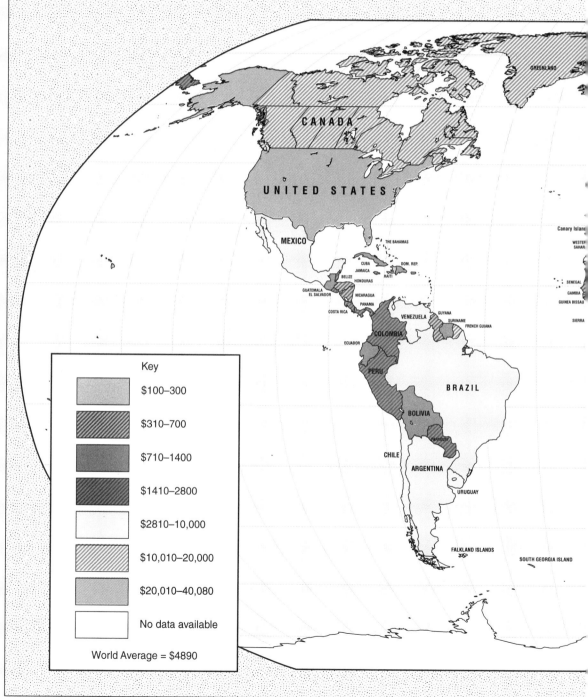

Gross National Product per Capita (in 1998 d

Key

	$100–300
	$310–700
	$710–1400
	$1410–2800
	$2810–10,000
	$10,010–20,000
	$20,010–40,080
	No data available

World Average = $4890